There's a unique place in the world ...
Where Sun, Sea and
Freedom Meet.
Provincetown

Olivia

CRUISES & RESORTS

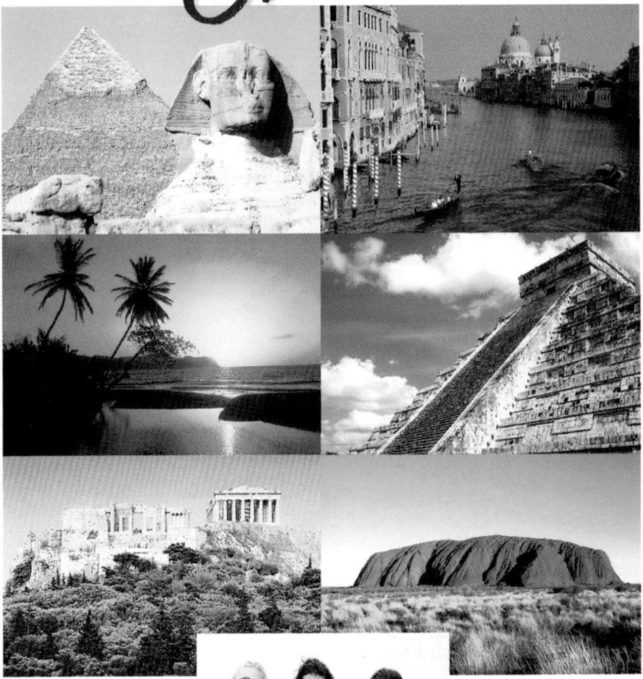

CST#1009281-40CST#1009273-40

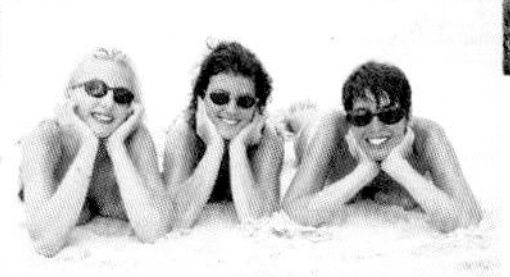

VACATIONS
for Women

4400 Market Street
Oakland, CA 94608
Phone: 510.655.0364
Fax: 510.655.4334
Email: info@oliviatravel.com

2000 Vacations

- Australia/New Zealand Tour – March
- Mexican Caribbean Cruise – April
- Rome to Venice Windstar Cruise – June
- Greece/Israel/Egypt Cruise – July
- Mexico Resort – October
- Eastern Caribbean Thanksgiving Cruise – November

2001 Vacations

- Four Night Caribbean Valentine's Cruise – February

FOR OUR **FREE** CATALOG

800-631-6277

or www.oliviatravel.com

Visit our web site to win a FREE cruise!

AA® American Airlines the official airline of Olivia Cruises & Resorts.

IGLTA

Our largest Dinah Shore Weekend
Six huge parties, including our famous pool parties, comedy night, & more
Palm Springs, California
March 23rd - 26th 2000

At The Luxurious
Wyndham Hotel 760-322-6000
Doral Resort 888-funinps
Rooms start at $149 & $159
Mention The Dinah 2000

Call direct @ 415.648-2464
e-mail: info@clubskirts.com info@girlbar.com
IGLTA & TAG member
Travel agents, call our hotline to receive your travel agent code #

VINCE GABRIELLY
www.ravengallery.com
PHOTOGRAPHY

Specializing In:

- Vacation & cruise planning anywhere in the world
- Domestic & international planning
- All-inclusive gay parties & vacations
- Group & independent travel
- Convention planning
- Corporate travel

Visit us at
www.damron.com
for luxury golf cruises and Swords & Sabres Week.

Letter from the Deputy Editor

Photo: J.W. Diehl

Erika O'Connor, *deputy editor (L)* *and* **Gina Gatta**, *editor-in-chief*

I continue to be amazed by the ever-increasing number of women-oriented and women-owned events and adventures there are to enjoy on the eve of the 21st Century. It has been a challenge and a real pleasure for me to find them and bring them to you.

With the thousands of listings in the **Women's Traveller**, *I hope that we can inspire the wanderer in you, and that you will use the book as a starting point to create your own adventures. Whether as a day-trip to a nearby town, a white-water rafting excursion, a night-on-the-town, or a tour across the country, the information here should spark your curiosity and motivate you to visit places you've never been.*

All of us at Damron want you to see and celebrate for yourself the diversity of our community. And each of us has worked hard to make sure that our book acts as your faithful guide. But there is one person I'd like to single out and thank for her invaluable assistance: Rebecca Davenport. Not only did Rebecca edit half the book but she single-handedly researched and revitalized many of our listings.

Finally, I can't stress enough how important your feedback is. You, the correspondent in the field, contribute immensely to the content of the Women's Traveller.

Keep in touch. Send in any information you'd like to share with other readers, and remember that your participation will help keep the Damron Women's Traveller the nation's best-selling women's travel guide.

the Damron Women's Traveller®

is produced by:

Publisher	**Damron Company**
President & Editor-in-Chief	**Gina M. Gatta**
Managing Editor	**Ian Philips**
Deputy Editor	**Erika O'Connor**
Editor	**Rebecca Davenport**
Assistant Editor	**Roberta Arnold**
Director of Sales	**Robert Goins**
Art Director	**Kathleen Pratt**
Graphic Designer	**Mark Guillory**
Cover Photo	**Rebecca McBride**
Cover Design	**Beth Rabena Carr**

How to Contact Us

Mail:	PO Box 422458, San Francisco, CA 94142-2458
Email:	damron@damron.com
Web:	http://www.damron.com
Fax:	(415) 703-9049
Phone:	(415) 255-0404

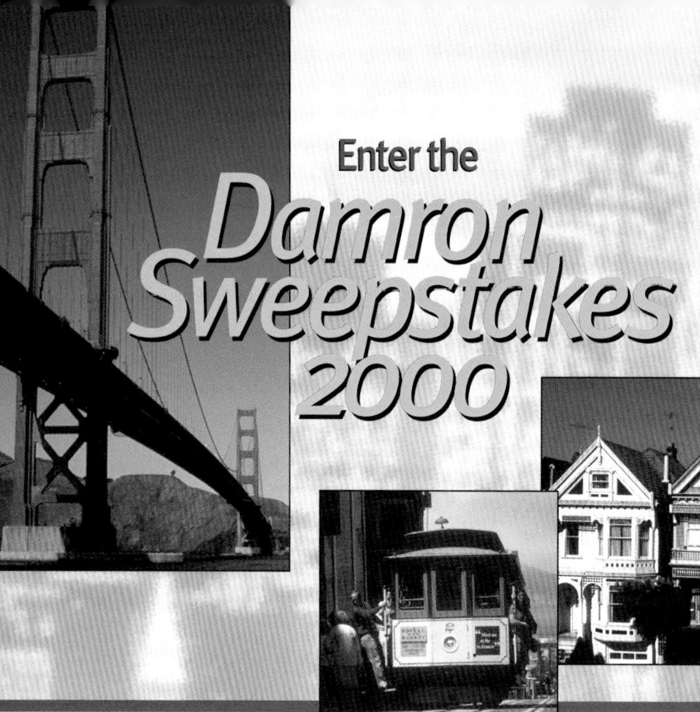

Sweepstakes Rules

Responsibility: Damron Company assumes no responsibility for any delay, loss or accident caused by fault or negligence of any hotel, transportation company or local operator rendering any part of tour services, nor for any damage or inconvenience caused by late air travel. Damron Company shall not be responsible for any expense caused by loss or damage of personal items including but not limited to luggage and its contents.

Deadline: Entries must be received by June 15, 2000.

Prize: 4 nights lodging in a Joie de Vivre hotel, San Francisco, CA. Airfare and/or transportation not included.

Drawing: Prize winner will be determined by random drawing on June 20, 2000 from all entries received. Prize winners will be notified by mail and/or phone.

Eligibility: Open to anyone over 18 years of age, except employees of Damron Company, their affiliates and agencies or employees and agents for the resorts participating in these sweepstakes. Void where prohibited or restricted by law. All federal, state and local laws apply.

No purchase necessary. One entry per person. Complete entry form and mail to the Damron Company at address shown.

Traveller Codes

Most of the codes used in this book are self-explanatory. Here are the few, however, which aren't.

▲—This symbol marks an advertiser. Please look for their display ad near this listing, and be sure to tell them you saw their ad in the *Damron Women's Traveller.*

Popular—So we've heard from the business and/or a reader.

Mostly Women—80-90% lesbian crowd.

Mostly Gay Men—Women welcome.

Lesbians/Gay Men—60%(L)/40%(G) to a 40%(L)/60%(G) mix.

LGBT—Lesbian, Gay, Bisexual, and Transgendered.

Gay-Friendly—LGBT folk are definitely welcome but are rarely the ones hosting the party.

Neighborhood Bar—Regulars and a local flavor, often has a pool table.

Dancing/DJ—Usually has a DJ at least Fri and Sat nights.

Transgender-Friendly—Transsexuals, cross-dressers, and other transgendered people welcome.

Live Shows—From a piano bar to drag queens and dancers.

Multi-Racial—A good mix of women of color and their friends.

Beer/Wine—Beer and/or wine. No hard liquor.

Smokefree—No smoking anywhere inside premises.

Private Club—Found mainly in the US South where it's the only way to keep a liquor license. Call the bar before you go out and tell them you're visiting. They will advise you of their policy regarding membership. Usually have set-ups so you can BYOB.

Wheelchair Access—Includes restrooms.

IGLTA—Member of International Gay and Lesbian Travel Association (please support our industry).

National Resources

LGBT INFOLINES

Gay/Lesbian National Hotline	[888] 843-4564

AIDS/HIV

National AIDS/HIV Hotlines	[800] 342-2437
	TTY: [800] 243-7889
	en español: [800] 344-7432
Sexual Health Information Line (Canada)	[613] 563-2437

HATE CRIMES

National Hate Crimes Hotline	[800] 347-4283

LEGAL RIGHTS

Lambda Legal Defense Fund (New York City, NY)	[212] 995-8585
National Gay/Lesbian Task Force (Washington, DC)	[202] 332-6483 *TTY:* [202] 332-6219

YOUTH SERVICES

Hetrick-Martin Institute (New York City, NY)	*voice/TTY:* [212] 674-2400
LYRIC – Lavendar Youth Recreation/ Information Center (San Francisco, CA)	[800] 246-7743 [415] 863-3636

CHEMICAL DEPENDENCY

Pride Institute	[800] 547-7433

GAY TRAVEL

International Gay/Lesbian Travel Association (IGLTA)	[800] 448-8550
National Association of Lesbian/ Gay Community Centers (New York City, NY)	[212] 620-7310
Damron Travel Agency	[888] 907-9771
Damron Website & Database	http://www.damron.com

Table of Contents

United States

Alabama	32
Alaska	34
Arizona	37
Arkansas	45
California	49
Colorado	142
Connecticut	148
Delaware	153
District of Columbia	156
Florida	164
Georgia	200
Hawaii	211
Idaho	225
Illinois	227
Indiana	240
Iowa	244
Kansas	247
Kentucky	249
Louisiana	253
Maine	263
Maryland	270
Massachusetts	273
Michigan	305
Minnesota	312
Mississippi	318
Missouri	318
Montana	325
Nebraska	328
Nevada	329
New Hampshire	332
New Jersey	335
New Mexico	339
New York	348
North Carolina	370
North Dakota	379
Ohio	379

Table of Contents

Oklahoma	392
Oregon	396
Pennsylvania	405
Rhode Island	418
South Carolina	420
South Dakota	423
Tennessee	423
Texas	429
Utah	450
Vermont	452
Virginia	455
Washington	459
West Virginia	470
Wisconsin	472
Wyoming	480

International

Canada	483
Caribbean	514
Mexico	522
Costa Rica	534
Austria • Vienna	536
England • London	539
France • Paris	548
Germany • Berlin	557
Italy • Rome	563
The Netherlands • Amsterdam	565
Spain • Barcelona & Madrid	571

Calendar of Tours & Events

Camping & RV Spots	580
2000 Tours & Tour Operators	585
2000 Calendars of Events	601
Mail Order	627
Update Form	631

ALABAMA

Statewide

INFO LINES & SERVICES

Alabama Bureau of Tourism & Travel 334/242-4169, 800/252-2262

Atmore

ACCOMMODATIONS

Royal Oaks B&B 5415 Hwy 21 N **334/368-8722, 800/308-8762** • gay/straight • full brkfst • swimming • $65-75

Birmingham

INFO LINES & SERVICES

Birmingham Gay & Lesbian Info Line 205 32nd St S #201 **205/326-8600** • 7pm-10pm Mon-Fri

ACCOMMODATIONS

The Tutwiler 2021 Park Pl N (at 21st St N) **205/322-2100** • gay-friendly • also restaurant & lounge • wheelchair access • $104-188

BARS

Joe 731 29th St S **205/252-3737** • clsd Sun-Mon • lounge more gay Th-Sat • restaurant opens 11am • outdoor porch seating • jazz pianist Fri-Sat

Misconceptions Tavern 600 32nd St S (at 6th Ave S) **205/322-1210** • noon-3am • mostly gay men • videos • patio

Tool Box 5120 5th Ave S (at 51st) **205/595-5120** • 2pm-close, till 2am Sat • mostly gay men • more women Wed for country/western • neighborhood bar • dancing/DJ • patio • wheelchair access

NIGHTCLUBS

22nd Street Jazz Cafe 710 22nd St S (at 7th Ave S) **205/252-0407** • open from 5pm, clsd Sun-Tue • gay-friendly • call for events • alternative night Wed • food served

Bill's Club 208 N 23rd St (btwn 2nd & 3rd) **205/254-8634** • 5pm-close, from 4pm Sun • mostly women • dancing/DJ • live shows • karaoke Wed • private club • wheelchair access

Club 21 117-1/2 21st St N (at 2nd Ave N) **205/322-0469** • 10pm-4am Th-Sat • gay-friendly • dancing/DJ • mostly African-American • live shows

The Club Latroy 316 20th St S (btwn 3rd & 4th Ave S) **205/322-8338** • 11pm-close Fri-Sat, noon-9pm Sun • lesbians/gay men • dancing/DJ • multi-racial clientele • live shows • 19+ • wheelchair access • cover charge (none Sun)

The Quest Club 416 24th St S (at 5th Ave S) **205/251-4313** • 24hrs • lesbians/gay men • dancing/DJ • 19+ Wed-Sun (nights only) • private club • patio • wheelchair access

Birmingham

Lesbigay Pride: June.

Annual Events: April/May - Festival of the Arts.
June - City Stages.
June - Shakespeare Renaissance Fair 334/271-5353 or 800/841-4273.

City Info: 205/458-8000, web: www.birminghamal.org.

Attractions: Alabama Jazz Hall of Fame 205/254-2731.
Civil Rights Museum 205/328-9696.
Birmingham Zoo & Botanical Gardens 205/879-0408.
Vulcan Statue on 20th atop Red Mountain.

Best View: Overlook Park.

Weather: Hot and humid in the 80°s and 90°s during the summer, mild in the 50°s to low 40°s during the winter.

Transit: ABC Taxi 205/833-6974. Birmingham Transit Authority 205/521-0101.

The Station 2025 Morris Ave (at 21st) **205/254-3750** • 10pm-6am Sat • lesbians/gay men • dancing/DJ • patio • wheelchair access

Restaurants

Anthony's 2131 7th Ave S (at 20th) **205/324-1215** • 6pm-midnight, clsd Sun-Mon • lesbians/gay men • cont'l/Italian • some veggie • full bar • wheelchair access • $6-15

Bottega Cafe & Restaurant 2240 Highland Ave (btwn 22nd & 23rd) **205/939-1000** • lunch & dinner, clsd Sun • some veggie • full bar • $17-21

Crestwood Grill 5500 Crestwood Blvd **205/595-1995** • lunch & dinner • full bar • live jazz Sat

Highlands Bar & Grill 2011 11th Ave S (20th St) **205/939-1400** • 6pm-midnight, bar from 4pm, clsd Sun-Mon • wheelchair access

John's 112 21st St N (at 1st Ave N) **205/322-6014** • 11am-10pm, clsd Sun • seafood & steak • full bar • wheelchair access

PT's Sports Grill 350 Hollywood (at Hwy 280 S) **205/879-8519** • from 11am daily • burgers & seafood • wheelchair access

Sarvac's 401 18th St S (btwn 4th & 5th) **205/251-0347** • 10:30am-3pm, clsd Sat • Southern cuisine • wheelchair access

Entertainment & Recreation

Terrific New Theater 2821 2nd Ave S **205/328-0868**

Bookstores

Lodestar Books 2020-B 11th Ave S (btwn 20th & 21st) **205/939-3356** • 11am-6pm, clsd Sun-Mon • lesbigay/feminist • wheelchair access

Retail Shops

Bad Seed 2030 11th Ave S (btwn 20th & 21st) **205/933-7333** • noon-8pm • music, videos & gifts • gay-owned/run

Publications

Alabama Forum 205/328-9228 • statewide paper

Spiritual Groups

Covenant MCC 5117 1st Ave N **205/599-3363** • 11am & 7pm Sun

Erotica

Alabama Adult Books 801 3rd Ave N (at 8th) **205/322-7323** • 24hrs

Decatur

Accommodations

Days Inn 810 6th Ave NE (at Church) **256/355-3520, 800/DAYS-INN** • gay-friendly • swimming • wheelchair access

Dothan

Nightclubs

The Vault 111 E Main St (at Foster) **334/794-0230** • 9pm-6am Th-Sun • lesbians/gay men • dancing/DJ • live shows • 19+ • wheelchair access

Gadsden

Nightclubs

Nitro 2461 E Meighan Blvd **256/492-9724** • 8pm-close Wed & Fri, till 2am Sat • lesbians/gay men • dancing/DJ • transgendered friendly • live shows

Spiritual Groups

MCC Gadsden 130 S 12th St **256/546-1143** • 11am Sun, 7pm Wed • wheelchair access

Huntsville

Bars

Vieux Carre 1204 Posey (at Larkin) **256/534-5970** • 7pm-2am • lesbians/gay men • neighborhood bar • DJ Fri-Sat • shows Sun • patio • wheelchair access

Bookstores

Rainbow's Ltd 522 Jordan Ln (at Holmes) **256/536-5900** • 11am-7pm Tue-Sat, clsd Sun-Mon • lesbigay • wheelchair access

Spiritual Groups

MCC 3015 Sparkman Dr NW (at Pulaski Pike) **256/851-6914** • 11am & 6:30pm Sun

Mobile

see also Pensacola, FL

Info Lines & Services

Pink Triangle AA Group at Cornerstone MCC **334/438-1679 (AA#)** • call for mtg times

Bars

B-Bob's 6157 Airport Blvd #201 **334/341-0102** • 5pm-close • lesbians/gay men • country/western dancing Th • DJ Th-Sun • live shows Fri • private club • also lesbigay giftshop • wheelchair access

Gabriel's Downtown 55 S Joachim St (at Government) **334/432-4900** • 5pm-close, from 3pm Sun • lesbians/gay men • videos • private club

Society Lounge 51 S Conception (at Conti) **334/433-9141** • noon-close • popular • lesbians/gay men • dancing/DJ • live shows • private club • wheelchair access

Nightclubs

On The Roxx 20 S Conception **334/432-9056** • 4pm-close, clsd Mon-Tue • mostly women • dancing/DJ • live shows • women-owned/run

Troopers 215 Conti St (nr Joachim) **334/433-7436** • 8pm-close • lesbians/gay men • dancing/DJ • live shows Th • private club • open since 1965!

Cafes

Big E's Delicatessen 274 Dauphin St (at S Jackson St) **334/694-0585** • brkfst & lunch Mon-Fri, dinner Th-Sat, clsd Sun

Spiritual Groups

Cornerstone MCC 2201 Government St (at Mohawk) **334/476-4621** • 11:30am & 7pm Sun, teen spirituality group 4th Sat

Montgomery

Nightclubs

Area 51 211 Lee St (nr Civic Ctr) **334/264-5933** • 7pm-close • lesbians/gay men • dancing/DJ • private club

The Fountain 62 Dexter Ave **334/263-3100** • 6pm-close • lesbians/gay men • dancing/DJ Fri-Sat • karaoke • live shows Sun • private club • wheelchair access

The Plex 121 Coosa St (at Madison Ave) **334/269-9672** • 8pm-close, till 2am Sat • popular • lesbians/gay men • dancing/DJ • live shows • private club

Spiritual Groups

New Hope MCC 5280 Vaughn Rd (at Unitarian Fellowship) **334/279-7894** • 5:30pm Sun

Tuscaloosa

Bars

Michael's 2201 6th St (at 22nd Ave) **205/758-9223** • 6pm-close, clsd Sun • lesbians/gay men • dancing/DJ • live shows

Spiritual Groups

MCC Living Waters 2506 Lurleen Wallace Blvd (at Unity Church) **205/330-1108** • 6:30pm Sun • wheelchair access

Alaska

Statewide

Info Lines & Services

Alaska Tourism Marketing Council **907/465-2010** • ask for vacation planner

Anchorage

Info Lines & Services

AA Gay/Lesbian **907/272-2312** • call for mtg times or check Identity Northview's calendar

Gay/Lesbian Helpline **907/258-4777** • 6pm-11pm, ask about women's events: traditionally something every Sat except summers when everyone's outdoors

IMRU2 640 W 36th Ave (at 'Q Cafe,' in back lounge) **907/566-4678** • 5:30pm-7:30pm 1st & 3rd Wed • lesbigaytrans youth support group

Women Over 50 **907/337-6779** • 7pm Mon • social support group

Women's Coffeehouse **907/258-4777** **(HELPLINE #)** • 2nd Sat (winters)

Women's Resource Center 111 W 9th St (at A St) **907/276-0528** • 8:30am-5pm, clsd wknds • one-on-one counseling & referrals • wheelchair access

Accommodations

Alaska Bear Company B&B 535 E 6th Ave (at Fairbanks) **907/277-2327** • gay-friendly • in downtown Anchorage

Aurora Winds Resort B&B 7501 Upper O'Malley **907/346-2533** • lesbians/gay men • on a hillside above Anchorage • $55-175

Cheney Lake B&B 6333 Colgate Dr (at Baxter) **907/337-4391, 888/337-4391** • gay-friendly • smokefree • lesbian-owned/run • $65-95

Gallery B&B 1229 'G' St (at 12th) **907/274-2567** • gay-friendly • $35-85

Rose-Beth's B&B 717 'O' St (at 7th) **907/337-6779** • women only (primarily over 50) • $55

Bars

Mad Myrna's 530 E 5th Ave (at Fairbanks) **907/276-9762** • 3pm-3am, noon-close Sun • lesbians/gay men • neighborhood bar • dancing/DJ • food served • live shows

Raven 618 Gambell St (at 6th Ave) **907/276-9672** • 11am-3am • lesbians/gay men • neighborhood bar • wheelchair access

Restaurants

At Last A Deli 701 W 36th Ave (at Arctic Blvd) **907/563-3354** • 7:30am-6pm, 11am-4pm Sat, clsd Sun

China Lights 12110 Business Blvd, Eagle River **907/694-8080** • 10:30am-10pm

Garcia's Business Blvd (next to Safeway), Eagle River **907/694-8600** • Mexican • $9-15

Kodiak Kafe & Dinner House 225 E 5th Ave (btwn Cordova & Barrow) **907/258-5233** • brkfst, lunch & dinner

O'Brady's Burgers & Brew 6901 E Tudor Rd (in Chugach Sq) **907/338-1080** • 11am-midnight, noon-10pm Sun • gay-friendly • some veggie • also at 800 E Dimond (in Dimond Center), 907/344-8033

Simon & Seafort's 420 'L' St (btwn 4th & 5th) **907/274-3502** • lunch & dinner • seafood & prime rib

Entertainment & Recreation

Capri 3425 E Tudor (at Dale) **907/561-0064** • often shows lesbigay & alternative films

Bookstores

Cyrano's Bookstore & Cafe 413 'D' St (btwn 1st & 5th) **907/274-2599** • 11am-7pm, from 10am summer • open later on wknds • live shows • food served • beer/wine • wheelchair access

Retail Shops

The Sports Shop 570 E Benson Blvd **907/272-7755** • women's outdoor clothing • adventure gear & equipment

Publications

Anchorage Press 907/561-7737 • alternative paper • arts & entertainment listings

Identity Northview 907/258-4777 • lesbigay • also sponsors 4th Fri potluck

Klondyke Kontact 907/345-3818 • newsmagazine published every other month

Spiritual Groups

Lamb of God MCC 2311 Pembroke (at Immanuel Presb Church) **907/258-5266** • 2pm Sun

Anchorage

Annual Events: March - Iditarod Sled Dog Race 907/376-5155.
Int'l Ice Carving Competition 907/276-5015.
June - Midnight Sun Marathon 907/343-4474.
August - Alaska State Fair 907/754-4827.
October - Quyana Alaska (native dance celebration) 907/274-3611.

City Info: 907/276-4118 or 800/478-1255, web: www.anchorage.net.

Attractions: Alaska Museum of Natural History, 907/694-0819.
Alaska Native Heritage Center 907/330-8000 or 800/315-6608.
Big Game Drive-Thru Wildlife Park (in Portage) 907/783-2025.
Portage Glacier.
Wolf Song of Alaska museum 907/346-3073.

Weather: Anchorage's climate is milder than one might think, due to its coastal location. It is cold in the winter (but rarely below 0°F), and it does warm up considerably in June, July, and August. Winter sets in around October. Expect more rain in late summer/early fall.

Transit: Ride Line (bus) 907/343-6543.

Unitarian Universalist Fellowship 3201 Turnagain St (at 32nd) **907/248-3737, 907/248-0715** • 9am & 10:30am Sun • wheelchair access

Erotica

Ace's 305 W Dimond Blvd **907/522-1987** • 24hrs

Fairbanks

Info Lines & Services

Gay/Lesbian Info Line 907/458-8288 • 8pm-10pm Tue & Th

Accommodations

Ah, Rose Marie B&B 302 Cowles St (at 3rd Ave) **907/456-2040** • gay/straight • full brkfst • gay-owned • $50-75

Billie's Backpackers Hostel 2895 Mack Rd **907/457-2034** • gay-friendly • hostel & campsites • kids ok • food served • women-owned/run • $18

Crabtree Guest House 724 College Rd **907/451-6501** • mostly gay men • shared baths • kitchens • kids ok

Fairbanks Hotel 517 3rd Ave (btwn Cushman & Lacey) **907/456-6411, 888/329-4685** • gay-friendly • recently restored to art deco style • lesbian-owned/run • $55-95

Bars

Palace Saloon 3175 College Rd (at Alaskaland) **907/451-1858, 907/456-5960** • 7pm-10pm, till 3am Fri-Sat (seasonal) • gay-friendly • dancing/DJ • live shows • gay after 11pm Fri-Sat only

Nightclubs

Club G 150 Farmers Loop Rd **907/451-7625** • 9pm-2am Th, till 3:30am Fri-Sat, clsd Sun-Wed • gay-friendly • dancing/DJ • alternative • eclectic style—from fire eaters to swing dancers • live jazz & shows midnight Fri-Sat • wheelchair access

Bookstores

Into the Woods Bookshop 3560 College Rd **907/479-7701** • 11am-midnight, till 2am Fri-Sat, 6pm-10pm Mon • new/used titles • also coffeehouse w/ wheelchair access

Spiritual Groups

Unitarian Universalist Fellowship Pikes Landing Rd (across from the 'Princess Hotel') **907/451-8838** • 9:30am & 11am Sun

Homer

Accommodations

Island Watch B&B 4241 Claudia St (at West Hill Rd) **907/235-2265** • gay-friendly • also cabins • full brkfst • kitchens • smokefree • kids/pets ok • wheelchair access • women-owned/run • $85-110/double

The Shorebird Guest House 4774 Kachemak Dr **907/235-2107** • gay/straight • cottage rental • beach access • wheelchair access

Skyline B&B 60855 Skyline Dr **907/235-3823** • gay-friendly • full brkfst • hot tub • lesbian-owned/run • $70-110

Entertainment & Recreation

Alaska Fantastic Fishing Charters 800/478-7777 • deluxe cabin cruiser for big-game fishing (halibut) • $155 (per person)

Juneau

Info Lines & Services

SEAGLA (Southeast Alaska Gay & Lesbian Alliance) PO Box 21542, 99802 **907/586-4297** • also publishes newsletter

Accommodations

Pearson's Pond Luxury Inn 4541 Sawa Cir **907/789-3772, 888/658-6328** • gay-friendly • hot tub • smokefree • $99-249

Restaurants

Inn at the Summit Waterfront Cafe 455 S Franklin St **907/586-2050** • 5pm-10pm • full bar • $15-38

Entertainment & Recreation

Women's Prerogative KTO 104.3 & 103.1 FM **907/586-1670** • 9pm Wed • women's music

Ketchikan

Accommodations

Millar Street House 1430 Millar St **907/225-1258, 800/287-1607** • gay-friendly • also kayak tours • $85

Kodiak

Spiritual Groups

St James the Fisherman Episcopal Church 421 Thorsheim **907/486-5276** • 7:30am & 10am Sun

Seward

Accommodations

Sauerdough Suites 907/224-8946 • gay-friendly • $125-210

Sitka

Accommodations

A Crescent Harbor Hideaway 709 Lincoln St **907/747-4900** • gay-friendly • restored historic waterfront home • hosts also offer educational wildlife & marine tours • $95-125

Bars

Rookie's 1617 Sawmill Creek Rd **907/747-7607** • 11am-11pm, till 2am Th-Sat • gay-friendly • also restaurant • gay-owned/run

Restaurants

The Marina Restaurant 205 Harbor Dr **907/747-8840** • 11am-10pm • seafood • gay-owned/run

Arizona

Apache Junction

Entertainment & Recreation

RVing Women Inc PO Box 1940, 85217 **888/557-8464 (55R-VING), 480/983-4678** • RV club for women only

Bisbee

Bars

St Elmo's 36 Brewery Gulch Ave **520/432-5578** • 10am-1am • gay-friendly • live bands Fri-Sat

Bullhead City

includes Laughlin, Nevada

Bars

The Lariat Saloon 1161 Hancock Rd (at 95) **520/758-8479** • lesbians/gay men • neighborhood bar • multi-racial clientele • wheelchair access

Flagstaff

Accommodations

Chalet in the Pines PO Box 25640, Munds Park, 86017 **520/286-2417** • mostly gay men • full brkfst • jacuzzi • $75-125

Hotel Monte Vista 100 N San Francisco St **520/779-6971, 800/545-3068** • gay-friendly • historic lodging circa 1927 • private/shared bath • food served • full bar • cafe • $40-120

Piñon Country Cottage 5339 Parsons Ranch Rd **520/526-4797** • mostly women • cabin • $65

Bars

Charlie's 23 N Leroux (at Aspen) **520/779-1919** • 11am-1am • gay-friendly • food served • some veggie • patio • wheelchair access • $7-14

Monte Vista Lounge 100 N San Francisco St (at Aspen) **520/779-6971** • 11am-1am, cafe from 6am • gay-friendly • live shows • some veggie

Restaurants

Cafe Olé 119 S San Francisco (at Butler) **520/774-8272** • till 8pm • plenty veggie • beer/wine

Pasto 19 E Aspen (at San Francisco) **520/779-1937** • 5pm-9pm, till 10pm Fri-Sat • Italian • beer/wine • wheelchair access • $7-15

Bookstores

Aradia Books 116 W Cottage (at Beaver) **520/779-3817** • 10:30am-5:30pm, clsd Sun • lesbian/feminist • wheelchair access • women-owned/run • also mail-order

Fort Mohave

Erotica

Karen's Adult Bookstore & Ladies Lingerie 4350 Hwy 95 #1 **520/763-5600**

Jerome

Accommodations

The Cottage Inn Jerome 520/634-0701 • gay-friendly • kids ok • pets ok • $70

Kingman

Accommodations

Kings Inn Best Western 2930 E Andy Devine **520/753-6101, 800/528-1234** • gay-friendly • swimming • non-smoking rms available • food served • bakery on premises

Mesa

Erotica

Castle Superstore 8315 E Apache Trail **480/986-6114** • 24hrs

Mohave Valley

Erotica

Eros Adult Emporium 10185 Harbor Ave **520/768-6300**

Phoenix

Can't stand another cloudy day? Sick of spending your summers in a fog bank and your winters in a snowdrift? Try Phoenix, a sun worshiper's paradise. Here the winters are warm and the summers sizzle. And each day ends with a dramatic desert sunset.

The people of Phoenix have perfected many ways to soak up the incredible sunshine. Some do it as they hike or ride horseback on the many trails along Squaw Peak (off Lincoln Drive) or Camelback Mountain. Some do it by the pool or on the golf course or tennis court. Some do it as they hover over the valley in a hot air balloon.

Some do it between galleries as they enjoy the popular Thursday night Art Walk along Main Street, Marshall Way, and 5th Avenue in Scottsdale. Others do it dashing from the car to the Scottsdale Galleria or Fashion Square. Still others get sun on the half-hour trip north to Rawhide (602/563-1880), Arizona's real live Old West town and Native American village, complete with gunfights and hayrides.*

What do lesbians do in Phoenix? Pretty much the same things, but usually in couples. Couples will feel free to enjoy themselves at **Mom's,** a women-only B&B. The single lesbian traveler searching for someone to share her journeys should try one of the friendly women's bars in town: **Desert Rose, Ain't Nobody's Bizness,** or **Incognito Lounge.** Phoenix also has a large sober women's community and its own AA club house. And many lesbians just like to get away from it all on camping, fishing, or hiking trips.

*Driving in the Arizona desert during the summer can be dangerous. Always carry a few gallons of water in your vehicle, and check all fluids in your car both before you leave and frequently during your trip.

Phoenix

see also Scottsdale & Tempe

Info Lines & Services

AA Lambda Club 2622 N 16th St **602/264-1341** • 6pm & 8pm

Arizona Office of Tourism 2702 N 3rd St #4015 **602/230-7733, 800/842-8257**

Lesbian/Gay Community Switchboard 24 W Camelback Rd (at Central Ave) **602/234-2752 (also TDD)** • 10am-10pm (volunteers permitting)

Valley One In Ten 24 W Camelback **602/264-5437** • 7pm Wed • youth group • HIV peer education

Accommodations

Arrowzona 'Private' Casitas 623/561-1200 • lesbians/gay men • condos • hot tub • IGLTA • $69-199

Larry's B&B 502 W Claremont Ave (btwn Maryland & Bethany Home) **602/249-2974** • mostly gay men • B&B-private home • full brkfst • swimming • hot tub • nudity • $60-80

Mom's B&B 5903 W Cortez (at 59th), Glendale **623/979-2869** • women only • swimming • available for outdoor weddings/commitment ceremonies • wheelchair access • women-owned/run • $75+

Windsor Cottage B&B 62 W Windsor (btwn 3rd Ave & Thomas) **602/264-6309** • lesbians/gay men • 2 English Tudor-style cottages • swimming • nudity • patio • gay-owned/run • $65-125

Bars

307 Lounge 222 E Roosevelt (at 3rd St) **602/252-0001** • 6am-1am, brunch Sun • lesbians/gay men • neighborhood bar • transgender-friendly • live shows • wheelchair access

Ain't Nobody's Bizness 3031 E Indian School #7 (at 32nd St) **602/224-9977** • 2pm-1am • mostly women • dancing/DJ • wheelchair access

Amsterdam 718 N Central Ave (btwn Roosevelt & McKinley) **602/258-6122** • 4pm-1am • lesbians/gay men • upscale piano bar

Phoenix

Where the Girls Are: Everywhere. Phoenix doesn't have one section of town where lesbians hang out, but the area between 5th Ave. & 32nd St., and Camelback & Thomas Streets does contain most of the women's bars.

Lesbigay Pride: April. 602/279-1771.

Annual Events: October - AIDS Walk 602/253-2437.

City Info: 602/254-6500. Arizona Office of Tourism 602/230-7733 or 800/842-8257, web: www.phxcenter.org; www.phoenix-center.org.

Attractions: Castles & Coasters Park on Black Canyon Fwy & Peoria 602/997-7577.
Heard Museum 602/252-8840.
Phoenix Zoo & Desert Botanical Garden in Papago Park.

Best View: South Mountain Park at sunset, watching the city lights come on.

Weather: Beautifully mild and comfortable (60°s-80°s) October through March or April. Hot (90°s-100°s) in summer. August brings the rainy season (severe monsoon storms) with flash flooding.

Transit: Yellow Cab 602/252-5252. Super Shuttle 602/244-9000. Phoenix Transit 602/253-5000.

Apollos 5749 N 7th St (south of Bethany Home) **602/277-9373** • 8am-1am, from 10am Sun • mostly gay men • neighborhood bar • karaoke • darts

Cash Inn 2140 E McDowell Rd (at 22nd St) **602/244-9943** • 4pm-1am, clsd Mon • lesbians/gay men • dancing/DJ • country/western • wheelchair access

The Crowbar 702 N Central (north of Van Buren) **602/258-8343** • 8pm-4am Fri-Sun • mostly gay men • dancing/DJ • live shows

Desert Rose 4301 N 7th Ave (at Indian School Rd) **602/265-3233** • 4pm-close, 11am-1am wknds • mostly women • live shows • country/western Fri • wheelchair access • women-owned/run

Harley's 155 155 W Camelback Rd (btwn 3rd Ave & Central Ave) **602/274-8505** • noon-1am • lesbians/gay men • dancing/DJ • also 'The Cell' in back • mostly gay men • leather

Incognito Lounge 2424 E Thomas Rd (at 24th St) **602/955-9805** • 3pm-1am, till 3am Fri-Sat, clsd Mon • lesbians/gay men • dancing/DJ • wheelchair access

JC's Fun One Lounge 5542 N 43rd Ave (at Missouri), Glendale **623/939-0528** • noon-1am, from 11am wknds • lesbians/gay men • dancing/DJ • live shows • wheelchair access

Marlys' 15615 N Cave Creek Rd (btwn Greenway Pkwy & Greenway Rd) **602/867-2463** • 3pm-1am • lesbians/gay men • neighborhood bar • live bands

Nasty Habits 3108 E McDowell Rd (at 32nd St) **602/231-9427** • noon-1am • lesbians/gay men • sports bar • karaoke

Pookie's Cafe 4540 N 7th St (at Camelback) **602/277-2121** • 11am-midnight, kitchen till 11pm, Sun brunch • lesbians/gay men • live shows • videos • wheelchair access

Roscoe's on 7th 4531 N 7th St (at Coolidge) **602/285-0833** • 3pm-1am, from 11am Sun • mostly gay men • appetizers • sports bar

Trax 1724 E McDowell (at 16th St) **602/254-0231** • 2pm-1am, till 3am Fri-Sat • mostly gay men • dancing/DJ • alternative • leather • young crowd • wheelchair access

The Waterhole 8830 N 43rd Ave (at Dunlap) **602/937-3139** • 11am-1am • lesbians/gay men • neighborhood bar

Winks 5707 N 7th St **602/265-9002** • 10am-1am • popular • lesbians/gay men • cabaret • piano bar • lunch & Sun brunch served • wheelchair access • $5-9

Nightclubs

Studio 43 4343 N 7th Ave (at Indian School Rd) **602/230-2515** • lesbians/gay men • dancing/DJ • wheelchair access

Restaurants

Alexi's 3550 N Central (in 'Valley Bank Bldg' at Osborn) **602/279-0982** • clsd Sun • full bar • patio • wheelchair access • $6-9

Katz's Deli 5144 N Central (at Camelback) **602/277-8814** • 7am-3pm, till 7pm Tue-Fri, from 8am Sun • kosher-style deli

Los Dos Molinos 8646 S Central Ave **602/243-9113** • 11am-9pm, clsd Sun-Mon • robust home cooking

Vincent Guerithault on Camelback 3930 E Camelback Rd (at 40th St) **602/224-0225** • lunch Mon-Fri • dinner nightly • Southwestern • some veggie • wheelchair access • $20 à la carte

Bookstores

▲ **Obelisk the Bookstore** 24 W Camelback #A (at Central) **602/266-2665** • 10am-10pm • lesbigay • wheelchair access

Retail Shops

Unique on Central 4700 N Central Ave #105 (at Camelback) **602/279-9691, 800/269-4840 (MAIL ORDER)** • 10am-9pm, till 6pm Sun • cards & gifts

Publications

Echo Magazine **602/266-0550** • biweekly newsmagazine

Spiritual Groups

Augustana Lutheran Church 2604 N 14th St **602/265-8400** • 10:30am Sun

Casa de Cristo Evangelical Church 1029 E Turney (at Indian School) **602/265-2831** • 10am & 6:30pm Sun, 6:30pm Wed

Community Church of Hope 4400 N Central (at Turney) **602/234-2180** • 9am & 11am Sun • independent Christian church & counseling center

Dignity/Integrity Phoenix 2601 N 14th St (at Virginia), Tempe **480/222-8664** • weekly services in Phoenix & Tempe • call for info

Gentle Shepherd MCC 7820 N 27th Ave **602/864-6404** • 9:15am Sun (traditional) • 11am Sun (contemporary)

Erotica

Adult Shoppe 111 S 24th St (at Jefferson) **602/306-1130** • 24hrs

The Barn 5021 W Indian School Rd (at 51st Ave) **602/245-3008** • 24hrs

Castle Superstore 300 E Camelback (at Central) **602/266-3348** • 24hrs • also 5501 E Washington 602/231-9837 • 8802 N Black Canyon Fwy 602/995-1641 • 8315 E Apache Trl 602/986-6114

International Bookstore 3640 E Thomas Rd (at 36th St) **602/955-2000** • 24hrs

Tuff Stuff 1714 E McDowell Rd (at 17th St) **602/254-9651** • 10am-6pm, till 4pm Sat, clsd Sun-Mon • leather shop

Scottsdale

Accommodations

Southwest Inn at Eagle Mountain 9800 N Summer Hill Blvd, Fountain Hills **480/816-3000, 800/992-8083** • gay-friendly • on 18-hole championship golf course • 1/4 mile from Scottsdale

Bars

BS West 7125 5th Ave (in pedestrian mall) **480/945-9028** • 1pm-1am • lesbians/gay men • dancing/DJ • videos • Sun BBQ • wheelchair access

Cafes

Espresso Country 1422 N Scottsdale Rd (at McDowell) **480/994-5110** • 6am-8pm, till 10pm Th-Sat, 7am-6pm Sun • bagels & sandwiches

Restaurants

AZ-88 7535 E Scottsdale Mall **480/994-5576** • 11am-midnight • upscale American • some veggie • $8-15

Malee's 7131 E Main **480/947-6042** • lunch & dinner • Thai • plenty veggie • full bar • $12-20

Erotica

Zorba's Adult Book Shop 2924 N Scottsdale Rd **480/941-9891** • 24hrs

Sedona

Accommodations

Apple Orchard Inn 656 Jordan Rd **520/282-5328, 800/663-6968** • gay-friendly • full brkfst • wheelchair access • $135-220

Cactus Cowgirls **520/203-4818** • mostly women • kitchenette • near outdoor recreation • $85-100

Huff & Puff, A Straw Bale Inn **520/567-9066** • lesbians/gay men • wheelchair access • $60-70

Iris Garden Inn 390 Jordan Rd **520/282-2552, 800/321-8988** • gay-friendly • motel • jacuzzi • smokefree • wheelchair access • $74-125

Mustang B&B 4257 Mustang Dr, Cottonwood **520/646-5929** • lesbians/gay men • full brkfst • 25 minutes from Sedona • smokefree • 1 RV hookup • movie theater • $35-65

Paradise by the Creek B&B 215 Disney Ln **520/282-7107** • mostly women • private suite • from $75

Southwest Inn at Sedona 3250 W Hwy 89-A **520/282-3344, 800/483-7422** • gay-friendly • combo b&b/small luxury hotel • Santa Fe-style architecture & furnishings • smokefree

Restaurants

Judi's 40 Soldier Pass Rd **520/282-4449** • 11:30am-9pm • some veggie • full bar • $11-21

Shugrue's West 2250 W Sedona **520/282-2943** • 11:30am-3pm & 5pm-8:30pm • some veggie • also bar • wheelchair access

Tempe

Nightclubs

Millennium 2001 3300 S Price Rd (at Mill Steakhouse & Saloon) **480/756-2445** • 3pm-1am, from 7pm wknds • lesbians/gay men • dancing/DJ • also restaurant

Restaurants

Restaurant Mexico 16 E 7th St **480/967-3280**

Bookstores

Changing Hands 414 S Mill (btwn 4th & 5th) **480/966-0203** • 10am-9pm, till 10pm Fri-Sat, noon-5pm Sun • general • lesbigay section

Erotica

Modern World 1812 E Apache **480/967-9052** • 24hrs

Tucson

Info Lines & Services

AA Gay/Lesbian 520/624-4183 • many mtgs • call for schedule

Wingspan Community Center 300 E 6th St (at 5th Ave) **520/624-1779** • lesbigay & youth info • lesbigay AA • library • call for events

Accommodations

Adobe Desert Vacation Rentals 520/578-3998 • gay-friendly • hot tub • smokefree • kids ok • patio • $550-1400 weekly

Adobe Rose Inn B&B 940 N Olsen Ave **520/318-4644, 800/328-4122** • gay-friendly • full brkfst, always veggie option • swimming • hot tub • $45-125

Adobeland Campground 12150 W Calle Seneca **520/883-6471** • women only • $3/night

Tucson

Annual Events: February - La Fiesta de los Vaqueros.

City Info: 520/624-1817.

Attractions: Arizona-Sonora Desert Museum 520/883-2702.
Arizona State Museum 520/621-6302.
Biosphere 2 800/828-2462.
Catalina State Park.
Colossal Cave.
Mission San Xavier del Bac.
Old Tucson.
Saguaro National Park.

Best View: From a ski lift heading up to the top of Mount Lemmon.

Weather: 350 days of sunshine a year. Need we say more?

Tucson

Mention Tucson's torrid weather, and you're likely to hear, "Yeah, but it's dry heat!"

Whether you believe that or know better, you can make the most of Tucson's sunshine. Leave your overcoat at home, pack your SPF 160 sun lotion and a good pair of shades, and prepare for a great time.

You'll see the rainbow everywhere, but mainly around shops on 4th Avenue, the downtown Arts District, and residences in the Armory Park Historic neighborhood. (The annual homes tour might as well be called the 'who's who of home-owning homos'!)

Downtown is where you'll find such gay-friendly establishments as **Rainbow Planet Coffee House,** the **Grill on Congress, Cafe Quebec,** and **Hydra,** purveyor of fine BDSM gear. At night, grab a beer in the **Tap Room** at **Hotel Congress** or pay a visit to the women's bar, **Ain't Nobody's Bizness.**

Just a few blocks northeast is 4th Avenue, where you'll find queer businesses standing strong between sports bars. In addition to gay-owned hair and skin care salons, real estate offices, restaurants, and retail stores, you'll find **Wingspan,** the lesbigay community center which hosts various women's groups and events, as well as **Antigone Books,** one of the best women's bookstores in the Southwest.

If you're traveling with your laptop, check out the Tucson Lesbian Community Home Page at http://www.flash.net/~cbozarth/ for the latest in what's going on about town.

West of Tucson, near the famed Desert Museum, is a women's community called **Adobe Land**. For general outdoor hilarity, Tucson's gay softball league can't be beat.

Lesbigay spirituality and healing groups abound, as do Latina, discussion, writers, and readers groups. For films, try the Loft or Catalina Theater, or The Screening Room. Tucson also hosts three film festivals, including the Lesbian & Gay Film Festival in October.

When you're done with the entertainment, and the temperature at midnight has dropped its usual 30 or 40 degrees, settle in at one of the many gay-owned or gay-friendly B&Bs in town, like women-only **Hills of Gold B&B.**

Armory Park Guesthouse 219 S 5th Ave **520/206-9252** • gay-friendly • renovated 1896 residence w/ 2 detached guest units • in the historic Armory Park neighborhood

Casa Alegre B&B Inn 316 E Speedway Blvd **520/628-1800, 800/628-5654** • gay-friendly • 1915 craftsman-style bungalow • full brkfst • hot tub • swimming • smokefree • kids ok by arrangement • patio • $70-125

Catalina Park Inn 309 E 1st St **520/792-4541, 800/792-4885** • gay-friendly • full brkfst • smokefree • kids 10+ ok • $75-115

Desert Trails B&B 12851 E Speedway Blvd **520/885-7295** • gay-friendly • adobe hacienda on 3 acres bordering Saguaro Nat'l Park • far from the maddening crowd • swimming • smoking outside only • $70-110

Dillinger House B&B 927 N 2nd Ave **520/622-4306** • gay-friendly • 2 lovely cottages • nat'l historic home & place of gangster John Dillinger's 1934 arrest • full brkfst • gay-owned/run • $60-125

Elysian Grove Market B&B 400 W Simpson **520/628-1522** • gay-friendly • renovated historic adobe building w/garden • full brkfst • smokefree • kitchen in suite • women-owned/run • $75

Gateway Villas B&B 228 N 4th Ave (at 9th St) **520/740-0767** • gay-friendly • rms & suites • swimming • some kitchens • $69-99

Hacienda del Sol Guest Ranch Resort 5601 N Hacienda del Sol Rd **520/299-1501, 800/728-6514** • gay-friendly • rms & casitas • food served • swimming • wheelchair access • $155-395

Hills of Gold B&B 3650 W Hills of Gold **520/743-4229** • women only • 1 suite (up to 4 people) • swimming • hot tub • smoking on deck only • $80

Hotel Congress 311 E Congress **520/622-8848, 800/722-8848** • gay-friendly • $29-55 • also 'Cup Cafe' • plenty veggie • also bar

Montecito House **520/795-7592** • gay-friendly • smokefree • kids ok by arrangement • lesbian-owned/run • $35-45 • $250-280 weekly

Natural B&B **520/881-4582** • lesbians/gay men • full brkfst • smokefree • non-toxic/allergenic • private/shared baths • kids ok • massage available • stay 2+ days & get free 1/2-hr massage • $65-75

Bars

Ain't Nobody's Bizness 2900 E Broadway #118 (at Tucson) **520/318-4838** • 2pm-1am • mostly women • dancing/DJ • wheelchair access

Congress Tap Room 311 E Congress (at Hotel Congress) **520/622-8848** • 11am-1am • dance club from 9pm • gay-friendly • alternative • live bands • theme nights

Hours 3455 E Grant (at Palo Verde) **520/327-3390** • 3pm-1am, from 1pm wknds, clsd Mon • popular • lesbians/gay men • neighborhood bar • dancing/DJ • country/western Th-Sun • patio • wheelchair access

IBT's (It's About Time) 616 N 4th Ave (at University) **520/882-3053** • noon-1am • lesbians/gay men • dancing/DJ • live shows • wheelchair access

Stonewall Eagle 2921 N 1st Ave (btwn Ft Lowell & Glen) **520/624-8805** • noon-1am • 'Stonewall' from 9pm • dancing/DJ • Latino/a clientele • drag shows • patio • wheelchair access

Nightclubs

The Fineline 2520 N Oracle (at Grant) **520/882-4953** • 9pm-1am Th, till 4am Fri-Sat • gay-friendly • dancing/DJ • 18+

Cafes

Cafe Quebec 121 E Broadway (at Arizona Ave) **520/798-3552** • mostly veggie • wheelchair access

The Cottage Bakery Cafe 3022 E Broadway (at Country Club) **520/325-5549** • 7am-5:30pm, 8am-4:30pm Sat, clsd Sun • low-fat baked goods • gourmet lunch menu

Rainbow Planet Coffee House 606 N 4th Ave **520/620-1770** • 7:30am-10:30pm • 9am-12:30am wknds • lesbians/gay men • plenty veggie

Restaurants

Blue Willow 2616 N Campbell (at Grant) **520/795-8736** • brkfst served all day • $5-8

Cafe Sweetwater 340 E 6th St (at 4th) **520/622-6464** • lunch & dinner • $5-15

Cafe Terra Cotta 4310 N Campbell Ave (at River) **520/577-8100** • dinner till 10:30pm • full bar • wheelchair access • $6-20

The Grill on Congress 100 E Congress (at Scott) **520/623-7621** • plenty veggie • beer/wine

Bookstores

Antigone Books 411 N 4th Ave (at 7th St) **520/792-3715** • 10am-6pm, till 9pm Fri-Sat, noon-5pm Sun • lesbigay/feminist • wheelchair access

Retail Shops

Desert Pride 300 E 6th St, Ste 1-A (at 5th Ave) **520/388-9829** • noon-7pm, clsd Mon-Tue • pride gifts • t-shirts • videos • magazines • CDs

Publications

The Observer 520/622-7176

Spiritual Groups

Cornerstone Fellowship 2902 N Geronimo (at Glen) **520/622-4626** • 10:30am Sun • 7pm Wed Bible study

Water of Life MCC 3269 N Mountain Ave **520/292-9151** • 9:15am & 11:15am Sun

Erotica

The Bookstore Southwest 5754 E Speedway Blvd **520/790-1550**

Caesar's Bookstore 2540 N Oracle Rd (btwn Glen & Grant) **520/622-9479**

Hydra 145 E Congress (at 6th) **520/791-3711** • SM gear

Wickenburg

Accommodations

Sombrero Ranch 31910 W Bralliar Rd **520/684-0222** • gay-friendly • 50 acres of peace & beauty

ARKANSAS

Statewide

Info Lines & Services

Arkansas Department of Tourism 800/628-8725

Crossett

Cafes

Pig Trail Cafe Rte 16 (east of Elkins) **501/643-3307** • 6am-9pm • popular • American/Mexican • under $5

Eureka Springs

Accommodations

11 Singleton House B&B 11 Singleton **501/253-9111, 800/833-3394** • gay-friendly • full brkfst • kids ok • restored 1890s country Victorian home • near shops • woman-owned/run • $75-110

A Cliff Cottage B&B Inn 42 Armstrong St **501/253-7409, 800/799-7409** • gay-friendly • suites & guestrooms • full brkfst • Victorian picnic lunches, gourmet dinner & dinner cruises • smokefree • massage • women-owned/run • $120-160

Arbour Glen Victorian Inn B&B 7 Lema **501/253-9010, 800/515-4536** • gay-friendly • historic Victorian home • full brkfst • jacuzzis • fireplaces • $75-125

Basin Park Hotel 12 Spring St **501/253-7837, 800/643-4972** • gay/straight • $41-160

Comfort Inn of Eureka Springs Hwy 62 E (at Jct 23 S) **501/253-5241, 800/828-0109** • gay-friendly • 3-story Victorian hotel • swimming • wheelchair access • $39-84

The Gardener's Cottage 501/253-9111, 800/833-3394 • gay-friendly • private cottage on wooded site • jacuzzi • seasonal • smokefree • kitchens • kids ok • woman-owned/run • $105-125

Golden Gate Cottage 501/253-5291 • women only • on the lake • hot tub • swimming • kitchens • women-owned/run • $45-60

Greenwood Hollow Ridge B&B 501/253-5283 • exclusively lesbigay • on 5 quiet acres • full brkfst • near outdoor recreation • shared/private baths • kitchens • pets ok • RV hookups • wheelchair access • gay-owned • $45-65

Maple Leaf Inn 6 Kings Hwy **501/253-6876, 800/372-6542** • gay/straight • restored Victorian • full brkfst • jacuzzi • kids ok • gay-owned/run • $85-110

Mark E Cook Historic Guest House 27 Paxos (at Edgewood Manor) **501/253-6555, 800/210-5683** • gay/straight • Victorian suites & cottages • jacuzzis • fireplaces • $99-139

Morningstar Retreat 501/253-5995, 800/298-5995 • gay-friendly • cabins • $75-130/double • $10/each add'l person

Palace Hotel & Bath House 135 Spring St **501/253-7474** • gay-friendly • historic bath house open to all • wheelchair access in hotel • $135-155

Pond Mountain Lodge 501/253-5877, 800/583-8043 • gay/straight • mountain-top inn on 159 acres • cabins • full brkfst • swimming • smokefree • kids ok • wheelchair access • lesbian-owned/run • $90-160

Rock Cottage Gardens 10 Eugenia St **501/253-8659, 800/624-6646** • lesbians/gay men • cottages • full brkfst • jacuzzis in room • fireplaces • gay-owned/run • $115-125

Villa Avarana 38 Prospect Ave **501/253-0667, 800/282-7262** • gay/straight • 1898 Victorian mansion w/ huge verandas • full brkfst • jacuzzi • gay-owned/run • $85-129

The Woods 50 Wall St **501/253-8281** • gay-friendly • cottages • jacuzzis • kitchens • smokefree • $110-150

Bars

Center Street Bar & Grille 10 Center St **501/253-8102** • 6pm-2am, till 10pm Sun • gay-friendly • dancing/DJ • live shows • kitchen open till 10pm Th-Mon • Mexican • plenty veggie

Chelsea's Corner Cafe 10 Mountain St **501/253-6723** • 11am-2am, clsd Sun • gay-friendly • patio • also restaurant • plenty veggie • women-owned/run • $5-8

Restaurants

Autumn Breeze Hwy 23 S **501/253-7734** • 5pm-9pm, clsd Sun • cont'l • $9-18

Cottage Inn Hwy 62 W **501/253-5282** • seasonal • lunch & dinner, clsd Mon • Mediterranean • full bar • $8-19

Ermilio's 26 White **501/253-8806** • 5pm-8:30pm, clsd Th • Italian • plenty veggie • full bar • $8-17

Jim & Brent's Bistro 173 S Main **501/253-7457** • 5pm-11pm, clsd Wed-Th

The Plaza 55 S Main **501/253-8866** • lunch & dinner • French • full bar • $9-19

Retail Shops

The Emerald Rainbow 45-1/2 Spring St **501/253-5445** • 10am-5pm, till 7pm Fri-Sat (summers) • metaphysical • some lesbigay titles

Spiritual Groups

MCC of the Living Spring 17 Elk St (at Unitarian Church) **501/253-9337** • 7pm Sun

Fayetteville

Info Lines & Services

AA Gay/Lesbian 501/443-6366 (AA#)

Community Info Line of NW Arkansas 17 1/2 N Block Ave (1/2 blk from Fayetteville Sq) **501/582-4636** • also 'Women's Library,' 3:30pm-6pm Th & noon-2pm Sat

Bars

Edna's 9 S School Ave **501/442-2845** • opens 7pm, from 4:30pm Tue, clsd Sun-Mon • lesbians/gay men • neighborhood bar • DJ Fri-Sat • private club • wheelchair access

Ron's Place 523 W Poplar **501/442-3052** • 9pm-2am Th-Sun • mostly gay men • live shows Sun

Bookstores

Hastings Bookstore 3009 N College Ave (Fiesta Sq Shopping Ctr) **501/521-0244**

Passages 200 W Dickson (at Church) **501/442-5845** • 10am-6pm, till 8pm Fri, noon-6pm Sun • new age/metaphysical

Fort Smith

Bars

The Corridor 1004 1/2 Garrison Ave (at Towson) **501/783-9988** • 5pm-1am Mon-Tue, from 1pm Wed-Fri, till midnight Sat • lesbians/gay men • neighborhood bar • dancing/DJ • live shows • 18+

Nightclubs

Burnzee's on the Hill 1217 S 'W' **501/494-7300** • 6pm-2am, clsd Mon • popular • lesbians/gay men • dancing/DJ • live shows • private club

Helena

Accommodations

Foxglove B&B 229 Beech **870/338-9391, 800/863-1926** • gay-friendly • $79-109

Hot Springs

Nightclubs

Our House Lounge & Restaurant 660 E Grand Ave **501/624-6868** • 7pm-3am, till close Sat, clsd Sun • popular • lesbians/gay men • dancing/DJ • shows monthly • wheelchair access

Huntsville

see also Eureka Springs & Fayetteville

Accommodations

Ribbon Ridge Farm RR 5 Box 2025 **501/665-4151** • lesbians/gay men • deluxe 2-rm cabin • 5-person jacuzzi • horseback riding available • $90

Little Rock

Info Lines & Services

AA Gay/Lesbian 501/224-6769 (PRIVATE HOME)

PALS (People of Alternative Lifestyles) 201 S Pulaski St **501/374-3605** • for teenagers & young adults up to 24

Bars

Backstreet 1021 Jessie Rd #Q (btwn Cantrell & Riverfront) **501/664-2744** • 5pm-5am • lesbians/gay men • dancing/DJ • live shows • private club • wheelchair access

C.O.A.D. 412 S Louisiana St **501/372-3070** • 5pm-1am, clsd Sun • mostly gay men

Discovery III 1021 Jessie Rd (btwn Cantrell & Riverfront) **501/664-4784** • 9pm-5am Sat • popular • gay-friendly • dancing/DJ • transgender-friendly • live shows • private club • wheelchair access

Silver Dollar 2710 Asher Ave (at Woodrow) **501/663-9886** • 5pm-1am, till midnight Sat, clsd Sun • mostly women • dancing/DJ • karaoke Th & Sat • live shows Fri • beer/wine • wheelchair access

Cafes

Beyond the Edge Cafe 1009 W 7th St **501/372-0660** • 10am-2pm & 5pm-10pm, clsd Sun-Mon

Little Rock

If you want a city with a pace of life all its own, a city whose history reflects the dramatic changes within the South, and a city surrounded by natural beauty, you've made the right choice to visit Little Rock.

Here you can enjoy relaxing summer days in the shade beside the slow-moving Arkansas River that winds through town. Or you can take off to the nearby lakes and national forests to camp, rock climb, or water-ski. Stay in town and you can spend your days exploring the state capital, touring the historic homes of the Quapaw Quarter district, or browsing in Little Rock's many shops. Rumor has it that Bill Clinton's boyhood home is owned by a friendly lesbian couple.

At night, you can make an evening of it with dinner, a program at the Arkansas Arts Center, and a visit to Little Rock's lesbian bar, the **Silver Dollar.** If you're in town at the right time of the month, cruise by the monthly women's coffeehouse at **Vino's Pizza**—call the **Women's Project** bookstore to find out when.

Of course, if that isn't enough excitement, you can always head out for the northwest corner of the state. We've heard there are many lesbian landowners, living alone and in groups, throughout this region. And while you're out there, be sure to visit the funky Ozark Mountain resort town of Eureka Springs. There are loads of gay-friendly B&Bs in this quaint, old-fashioned town, as well as a popular Passion Play. **Golden Gate Cottage** is a women-only B&B, **Greenwood Hollow Ridge B&B** offers exclusively lesbigay accommodations, and **Center Street Bar & Grille** is the casual place to dance.

Restaurants

Vino's Pizza 923 W 7th St (at Chester) **501/375-8466** • 11am-midnight, till 10pm Tue-Wed • beer/wine • inquire about monthly women's coffeehouse

Entertainment & Recreation

The Weekend Theatre W 7th St (at Chester) **501/374-3761** • beer & wine • plays & musicals on weekends • gay-owned

Bookstores

Women's Project 2224 Main St (at 23rd) **501/372-5113, 501/372-6853 (TDD)** • 10am-5pm Mon-Sat • educational group • lesbian support group 7pm 2nd & 4th Tue

Retail Shops

A Twisted Gift Shop 1007 West 7th St **501/376-7723** • 11am-10pm, clsd Tue • gift shop • also 7201 Asher Ave 501/568-4262

Wild Card 400 N Bowman (at Maralynn) **501/223-9071** • 10am-8pm, noon-6pm Sun • novelties & gifts

Publications

Lesbian/Gay News Telegraph **314/664-6411, 800/301-5468** • regional • some AR coverage

Spiritual Groups

MCC of the Rock 2017 Chandler, North Little Rock **501/753-7075** • 11am Sun, 7pm Wed

Unitarian Universalist Church 1818 Reservoir Rd **501/225-1503** • 10:30am Sun • wheelchair access

Little Rock

Where the Girls Are: Scattered. Popular hangouts are the Women's Project, local bookstores, and Vino's Pizza - women's coffee-house.

Lesbigay Pride: June.

Annual Events: October - State Fair.

City Info: Arkansas Dept. of Tourism 800/628-8725.
What's Going on in Little Rock 502/244-8463, web: www.little-rock.com.

Attractions: Check out Bill & Hillary's old digs at 18th & Center Sts.
Decorative Arts Museum 501/372-4000.

Best View: Quapaw Quarter (in the heart of the city).

Weather: When it comes to natural precipitation, Arkansas is far from being a dry state. Be prepared for the occasional severe thunder-storm or ice storm. Summers are hot and humid (mid 90°s). Winters can be cold (30°s) with some snow and ice. Spring and fall are the best times to come and be awed by the colorful beauty of Mother Nature.

Transit: Black & White Cab 501/374-0333.
Central Arkansas Transit 501/375-1163.

CALIFORNIA

Anaheim

INFO LINES & SERVICES

Gay/Lesbian Community Services Center 12832 Garden Grove Blvd #A (at Harbor) **714/534-0862** • 10am-10pm

SPIRITUAL GROUPS

Calvary Open Door Center 161518 Adenmore Ave (at Belmont), Bellflower **714/284-5775** • 10:15am Sun

Apple Valley

BARS

Victor Victoria's 22581 Outer Hwy 18 **760/240-8018** • 4pm-2am, clsd Mon • lesbians/gay men • dancing/DJ • patio

Arnold

ACCOMMODATIONS

Dorrington Inn 3450 Hwy 4 (at Boards Crossing), Dorrington **209/795-2164, 888/874-2164** • gay-friendly • cottages & suites • 3 hours from San Francisco, 18 miles from Bear Valley • gay-owned/run

Atascadero

EROTICA

Diamond Adult World 5915 El Camino Real (at Traffic Wy) **805/462-0404** • books • toys • videos

Bakersfield

INFO LINES & SERVICES

Friends 805/323-7311 • 6:30pm-11pm • info • support groups & community outreach

ACCOMMODATIONS

Rio Bravo Resort 11200 Lake Ming Rd **805/872-5000, 888/517-5500** • gay-friendly • wheelchair access • $80-150

BARS

Casablanca Club 1030 20th St **805/324-1384** • 7pm-2am, clsd Mon • lesbians/gay men • neighborhood bar • dancing/DJ

The Mint 1207 19th St (btwn 'M' & 'L') **805/325-4048** • 6pm-2am • gay-friendly • more gay wknds • neighborhood bar

Padre Bar 1813 'H' St (at Padre Hotel) **805/324-2594** • 10am-2am • gay-friendly

NIGHTCLUBS

Rainbow Club Wilson & Railroad (in the Kmart shopping ctr) **661/832-7711** • 7pm-2am • lesbians/gay men • dancing/DJ

SPIRITUAL GROUPS

MCC of the Harvest 2421 Alta Vista Dr **805/327-3724** • 7pm Sun

EROTICA

Deja Vu 1524 Golden State Hwy **805/322-7300**

Wildcat Books 2620 Chester Ave (at 21st) **805/324-4243**

Bell Gardens

EROTICA

▲ **Le Sex Shoppe** 6816 Eastern Ave **323/560-9473** • 24hrs

Benicia

see Vallejo

Berkeley

see East Bay

Big Bear Lake

ACCOMMODATIONS

Eagles' Nest B&B 41675 Big Bear Blvd **909/866-6465** • gay-friendly • 5 cottages • spa • $85-170

Grey Squirrel Resort 909/866-4335 • gay-friendly • 15 private rental homes • swimming • lesbian-owned • $62-400

Happy Bear Village Resort 40154 Big Bear Blvd **909/866-2415, 800/356-1811** • gay/straight • B&B • cabins • near outdoor recreation • hot tub • fireplaces • kids/pets ok • wheelchair access • $69-129

Hillcrest Lodge 40241 Big Bear Blvd **909/866-6040, 800/843-4449** • gay/straight • motel • cabins • jacuzzi suites • kitchens • fireplaces • non-smoking rms available • kids ok • wheelchair access • gay-owned/run • $35-169

Shore Acres Lodge PO Box 110410, 92315 **909/866-8200, 800/524-6600** • gay-friendly • cabins • rental homes • wheelchair access

Big Sur

ACCOMMODATIONS

Lucia Lodge Hwy 1 **831/667-2391** • gay-friendly • cabins • kids ok • seasonal • store • ocean view • $75-150 • also restaurant • American/seafood • full bar • $8-24 • IGLTA

Bishop

Accommodations

Starlite Motel 192 Short St **760/873-4912** • gay-friendly • swimming • $34

Bookstores

Spellbinder Books 124 S Main (at Line) **760/873-4511** • 9am-5:30pm, 11am-4pm Sun • women's section • wheelchair access

Buena Park

Bars

Ozz Supper Club 6231 Manchester Blvd **714/522-1542** • 6pm-2am, clsd Mon • popular • lesbians/gay men • dancing/DJ • live shows • cabaret • women's country/western dancing Wed • call for events • also restaurant • some veggie • $9-25

Capistrano Beach

Accommodations

Capistrano Seaside Inn 34862 Pacific Coast Hwy **949/496-1399, 800/252-3224** • gay-friendly • outdoor jacuzzi • ocean views

Carmel

see also Monterey

Accommodations

Happy Landing Inn 831/624-7917 • gay-friendly • Hansel & Gretel 1925 inn • full brkfst • smokefree • kids 13+ ok • wheelchair access • $90-175

Castroville

Nightclubs

Franco's Norma Jean 10639 Merritt **831/633-6129** • 8pm Sat only • mostly gay men • dancing/DJ • Latina clientele

Chico

Info Lines & Services

Stonewall Alliance Center 820 W 7th St **530/893-3338, 530/893-3336** • hotline • social 6pm-10pm Fri • Gay AA 7pm Tue

Accommodations

Inn at Shallow Creek Farm 4712 Road DD, Orland **530/865-4093, 800/865-4093** • gay-friendly • smokefree • private/shared bath • $60-85

Chula Vista

Erotica

▲ **F St Bookstore** 1141 3rd Ave (at Naples) **619/585-3314** • 24hrs

Clearlake

Accommodations

Blue Fish Cove Resort 10573 E Hwy 20, Clearlake Oaks **707/998-1769** • gay-friendly • lakeside resort cottages • fishing • kitchens • kids ok • pets ok by arrangement • boat facilities & rentals • $45-95

Edgewater Resort 6420 Soda Bay Rd (at Hohape Rd), Kelseyville **707/279-0208, 800/396-6224** • 'gay-owned, straight-friendly' • cabin • camping & RV hookups • lake access & pool • theme wknds • boat facilities • smoking outside • pets ok • $25-250

Lake Vacation Rentals 1855 S Main St, Lakeport **707/263-7188** • gay-friendly • $110-400

Sea Breeze Resort 9595 Harbor Dr, Glenhaven **707/998-3327** • gay/straight • cottages • swimming • 2 night minimum • gay-owned/run • $60-90

Restaurants

The Brentwood 6271 E Hwy 20, Lucerne **707/274-2301** • dinner only, clsd Tue-Wed • $7-14

Kathy's Inn 14677 Lake Shore Dr **707/994-9933** • lunch Wed-Fri, open from 4pm wknds, clsd Mon-Tue • full bar • wheelchair access

Cloverdale

Accommodations

Asti Ranch 25750 River Rd **707/894-5960** • women only • cottage near lake & river in wine country • wheelchair access • $500-750 weekly, $200-300 wknds

Columbia

Entertainment & Recreation

Ahwahnee Whitewater Expeditions 209/533-1401 • women-only, co-ed & charter rafting

Concord

Erotica

Pleasant Hill Adult Books & Videos 2294 Monument (at Buskirk) **925/676-2962**

Corona

Cafes

Backstreet Cafe 430 River Rd Ste E **909/737-8025** • 8:30am-5pm, 10am-3pm Sat, clsd Sun • wknd crafts & events for lesbians

Costa Mesa

Bars

Tin Lizzie Saloon 752 St Clair (at Bristol) **949/966-2029** • 11am-2am • mostly gay men • neighborhood bar • wheelchair access

Nightclubs

Lion's Den 719 W 19th St (at Pomona) **949/645-3830** • 8pm-2am • lesbians/gay men • neighborhood bar • dancing/DJ • karaoke • live shows • young crowd

Cupertino

Bars

Silver Fox 10095 Saich Wy (at Stevens Creek Blvd) **408/255-3673** • 4pm-2am • mostly gay men • neighborhood bar • live shows • wheelchair access

Davis

see also Sacramento

Info Lines & Services

DavisDykes **530/752-2452 (CENTER#)** • social group • call for events

LGBT Resource Center 105 University House, UCDavis **530/752-2452** • info • referrals • mtgs • call for hours • wheelchair access

Cafes

Cafe Roma 231 'E' St (btwn 2nd & 3rd) **530/756-1615** • 6:30am-11pm • coffee & pastries • student hangout

East Bay

includes Berkeley & Oakland, see also Concord, Fremont, Lafayette, Hayward, Pleasant Hill, San Lorenzo, Walnut Creek

Info Lines & Services

La Peña 3105 Shattuck Ave, Berkeley **510/849-2568, 510/849-2572** • 10am-5pm Mon-Fri • also cafe 6pm-10pm Wed-Sun • multicultural center • hosts meetings, dances, events • mostly Latino-American /African-American

Lesbians of Color Group 2712 Telegraph Ave (at Derby, in the Pacific Center), Berkeley **510/548-8283** • 7pm Th

Pacific Center 2712 Telegraph Ave (at Derby), Berkeley **510/548-8283** • 10am-10pm, from noon Sat, 6pm-9pm Sun • also 'Lavender Line' 510/841-6224 (also TDD) • 4pm-10pm Mon-Fri, 6pm-9pm Sat

SMAAC (Sexual Minority Alliance of Alameda County) 1738 Telegraph (nr 17th), Oakland **510/834-9578** • 2pm-10pm, clsd Sun-Mon • center for young people of color questioning their sexuality

What's Up! Events Hotline for Sistahs **510/835-6126** • for lesbians of African descent

Accommodations

Bates House B&B 399 Bellevue Ave (at Van Buren), Oakland **510/893-3881** • gay/straight • gay-owned/run • $75-105

Elmwood House 2609 College Ave, Berkeley **510/540-5123, 800/540-3050** • gay/straight • guesthouse • gay-owned/run • $60-85

Bars

Bench & Bar 120 11th St (btwn Madison & Oak), Oakland **510/444-2266** • 3pm-2am • popular • mostly gay men • dancing/DJ • professional • multi-racial clientele • live shows • Latin nights Fri & Mon • wheelchair access

Cabel's Reef 2272 Telegraph Ave (at Grand), Oakland **510/451-3777** • 1pm-2am • lesbians/gay men • women's night Wed • dancing/DJ • multi-racial

The Rainbow Spot 435 13th St (at McNally's Downtown, nr 12th St BART), Oakland **510/654-2805** • from noon Sun only • mostly women • sports bar

White Horse 6551 Telegraph Ave (at 66th), Oakland **510/652-3820** • 1pm-2am, from 3pm Mon-Tue • popular Sat night • lesbians/gay men • dancing/DJ • wheelchair access

Cafes

Cafe Sorrento 2510 Channing (at Telegraph), Berkeley **510/548-8220** • 7am-8pm, 9am-4pm Sat, clsd Sun • multi-racial • Italian • vegetarian • $5-10

Cafe Strada 2300 College Ave (at Bancroft), Berkeley **510/843-5282** • 6:30am-midnight • popular • students • great patio & bianca (white chocolate) mochas

Mimosa Cafe 462 Santa Clara (at Grand), Oakland **510/465-2948** • 11am-9pm, from 9am wknds, till 2pm Sun, clsd Mon • natural & healthy • plenty veggie • beer/wine • $7-12

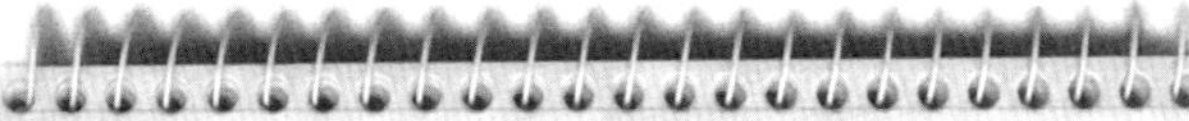

East Bay
Berkeley and Oakland

So what exactly is the East Bay? To most Northern Californians, it's simply the string of cities and counties across the Bay Bridge from San Francisco—with weather that's consistently sunnier and 10 to 20 degrees warmer than Fog City. For the *Damron Women's Traveller*, it is the more lesbian-friendly cities of Berkeley and Oakland.

Berkeley—both the campus of the University of California and the city where it's located—was immortalized in the '60s as a hotbed of student/counterculture activism. Today, most of the people taking to the streets, especially Telegraph and College Avenues, are tourists or kids from the suburbs in search of consumer thrills such as a good book, exotic cuisine, the perfect cup of java, and anything tie-dyed.

Locals and visitors alike will enjoy people-watching on Telegraph or University Avenue. Or you can just take to the hills—vast Tilden Park offers incredible views and trails to hike and bike.

As for Oakland, Gertrude Stein once said, "There is no there there." Well, Gertrude, a lot has happened since you were in Oakland!

Today Oakland is a city with an incredible diversity of races, cultures, and classes. The birthplace of the Black Panthers, this city has been especially influential in urban African-American music, fashion, and politics. Lately Oakland has also become a vital artists' enclave, as Bay Area artists flee high rent in San Francisco for spacious lofts downtown or in West Oakland.

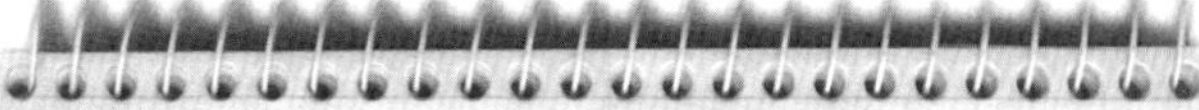

And where are all the women? Well, many are in couples or covens or both, which can make them hard to find. But if you want to start a couple or a coven of your own, stop by **Mama Bears** or one of the other women's bookstores—they're also great informal resource centers, and often host popular performances and author signings. And speaking of "hot mamas," try the popular weekend brunch at **Mama's Royale**. The Emeryville Marina Public Market off I-80 is popular with gastronomically inclined lesbians.

For info on groups and events, cruise by the **Pacific Center**, still the Bay Area's only lesbian/gay center, located in Berkeley. The center hosts meetings for lesbian moms & kids, bisexuals, transgendered women, separatists, and more. Those interested in women's spirituality should drop by **Ancient Ways**, the pagan emporium extraordinaire.

If you're the outdoors type, consider an adventure in Northern California with **Mariah Wilderness Expeditions**. Or make a day of it at one of the nearby state parks: Point Reyes is a beautiful destination with a hostel, and Point Isabel is rumored to be a good meeting place for dykes with dogs.

If you'd rather exercise indoors, make some moves on the dance floor of the **White Horse**. On Sundays, gather with the local women to watch the game at the **Rainbow Spot**, a sports bar in Oakland. For plays, performances, and events, grab a copy of the **Bay Times** and check out the calendar section. Or pick up some entertainment of your own at the East Bay **Good Vibrations** or **Passion Flower**—both are women-friendly, clean sex toy stores.

There are also lots of resources for women of color in the East Bay. Start with **La Peña Cultural Center**, an active center with many events for Latina-Americans and African-Americans. There's also **What's Up!**, an events hotline for lesbian sistahs of African descent.

Restaurants

Betty's To Go 1807 4th St (at Hearst), Berkeley **510/548-9494** • 6:30am-5pm, from 8am wknds • sandwiches • some veggie • $5

Bison Brewery 2598 Telegraph (at Parker), Berkeley **510/841-7734** • 11am-1am • live music • sandwiches • some veggie • beer/wine • wheelchair access • $5-10

Chez Panisse 1517 Shattuck Ave (at Cedar), Berkeley **510/548-5525** • nouvelle Californian • beer/wine • $38-68

La Mediterranée 2936 College Ave (at Ashby), Berkeley **510/540-7773** • 10am-10pm • beer/wine • $12-17

Mama's Royale 4012 Broadway (at 40th), Oakland **510/547-7600** • 7am-3pm, from 8am wknds • popular • mostly lesbians • come early for excellent weekend brunch • beer/wine • wheelchair access • $5-10

Bookstores

Boadecia's Books 398 Colusa Ave (1/2 mile from Solano), North Berkeley **510/559-9184** • 11am-8pm, clsd Mon • lesbigaytrans • readings • wheelchair access • lesbian-owned/run • special events

Cody's 2454 Telegraph Ave (at Haste), Berkeley **510/845-7852** • 10am-10pm • general • lesbigay section • frequent readings & lectures • wheelchair access

Easy Going 1385 Shattuck (at Rose), Berkeley **510/843-3533** • 10am-7pm, till 6pm Sat, noon-6pm Sun • travel books & accessories • also 1617 Locust, Walnut Creek 510/947-6660

Gaia Bookstore & Catalogue Co 1400 Shattuck Ave (at Rose), Berkeley **510/548-4172** • 10am-7:30pm • feminist • events • eco-spiritual/goddess

▲ **Mama Bears Women's Bookstore** 6536 Telegraph Ave (btwn Alcatraz & Ashby), Oakland **510/428-9684, 800/643-8629** • 10:30am-8pm • women's books • readings & performances • coffeebar • also 'Mama Bears News & Notes' book review • lesbian-owned/run

Shambhala Booksellers 2482 Telegraph Ave (at Dwight), Berkeley **510/848-8443** • 11am-8pm • metaphysical feminist/goddess section • wheelchair access

East Bay

Where the Girls Are: Though there's no lesbian ghetto, you'll find more of us in north Oakland (Rockridge) and north Berkeley, Lake Merritt, around Grand Lake & Piedmont, the Solano/Albany area, or at a cafe along 4th St. Berkeley.

Lesbigay Pride: June in Berkeley. 510/663-3980. September - Mardi Gras East Bay Pride 510/663-3980.

Annual Events: June - Gay Prom / Project Eden 510/247-8200. October/November - Halloween Spiral Dance 510/444-7724. Annual rite celebrating the crone.

City Info: Oakland Convention Center 510/839-9000 or 800/262-5526.

Attractions: Jack London Square, Oakland.
Emeryville Marina Public Market.
UC Berkeley.
The Claremont Hotel Restaurant, Berkeley 510/843-3000.
The Paramount Theater, Oakland 510/893-2300.

Best View: Claremont Hotel, or various locations in Berkeley and Oakland Hills.

Weather: While San Francisco is fogged in during the summers, the East Bay remains sunny and warm. Some areas even get hot (90°s-100°s). As for the winter, the temperature drops along with rain (upper 30°s-40°s in the winter). Spring is the time to come – the usually brown hills explode with the colors of green grass and wildflowers.

Transit: Yellow Cab (Berkeley) 510/848-3333. Yellow Cab (Oakland) 510/836-1234. AC Transit 510/839-2882. Bay Area Rapid Transit (subway) 415/992-2278.

Retail Shops

Ancient Ways 4075 Telegraph Ave (at 41st), Oakland **510/653-3244** • 11am-7pm • extensive occult supplies • classes • readings • woman-owned/run

Afrataaset AfraGoddess™ Home & AfraWellness™ Center 6025 Shattuck Ave (at 60th St), Berkeley **510/658-7123** • noon-dusk, clsd Sun-Mon • spiritual counseling • readings • gifts • events & workshops • 'by/for/about Afrikan Wimmin'

Publications

San Francisco Bay Times 415/626-0260 • popular • a 'must read' for Bay Area resources & personals

Spiritual Groups

Albany Unified Methodist Church 980 Stannage Ave (at Marin), Albany **510/526-7346** • 10am Sun

MCC New Life 1823 9th St (at Hearst), Berkeley **510/843-9355** • 12:30pm Sun • wheelchair access

Moon Sistahs 510/547-8386 • drumming circles & classes open to 'womyn on all spiritual paths'

Erotica

▲ **Good Vibrations** 2504 San Pablo (at Dwight Way), Berkeley **510/841-8987** • 11am-7pm, till 8pm Fri-Sat • clean, well-lighted sex toy store • also mail order • wheelchair access • (see ad in San Francisco section)

Passion Flower 4 Yosemite Ave (at Piedmont), Oakland **510/601-7750** • noon-8pm, noon-6pm Sun, clsd Mon • toys • lingerie • leather

El Cajon

Erotica

▲ **F St Bookstore** 158 E Main (at Magnolia) **619/447-0381** • 24hrs • wheelchair access

Eureka

Info Lines & Services

Northcoast Lesbian, Gay, Bisexual & Transgender Alliance ('The Center') 707/445-9760, 707/444-1061 • hours vary, clsd Mon • various services • wheelchair access

Women's Resource Center 707/725-5239, 707/442-5239 • call for hours

Accommodations

A Weaver's Inn 1440 'B' St **707/443-8119, 800/992-8119** • gay-friendly • stately Queen Anne w/ beautiful gardens • $75-125

An Elegant Victorian Mansion 1406 'C' St **707/444-3144** • gay-friendly • smokefree • $85-185

Carter House Victorians 301 'L' St **707/444-8062, 800/404-1390** • gay-friendly • enclave of 4 unique inns • full brkfst • smokefree • kids ok • wheelchair access • $154-497

Bars

Lost Coast Brewery Pub 617 4th St (btwn 'G' & 'H') **707/445-4480** • 11am-midnight • gay-friendly • food served • beer/wine • wheelchair access • women-owned/run

Nightclubs

Club Triangle (Club West) 535 5th St (at 'G' St) **707/444-2582** • 9pm-2am • gay-friendly • gay Sun • dancing/DJ • alternative • country/western • 18+ • also restaurant • wheelchair access

Restaurants

Folie Deuce 1551 'G' St, Arcata **707/822-1042** • dinner from 5:30pm, clsd Sun-Mon • bistro • $8-20

Seafood Grotto 605 Broadway (at 6th) **707/443-2075** • low prices • informal setting • also a fish market

Bookstores

Booklegger 402 2nd St (at 'E' St) **707/445-1344** • 10am-5:30pm, 11am-4pm Sun • mostly used • some lesbian titles • women-owned/run • wheelchair access

Publications

The 'L' Word PO Box 272, Bayside, 95524 • lesbian newsletter for Humboldt Co • available at 'Booklegger'

Fairfield

see Vacaville

Ferndale

Accommodations

The Gingerbread Mansion Inn 400 Berding St **707/786-4000, 800/952-4136** • popular • gay-friendly • a grand lady w/beautifully restored interior • full brkfst • afternoon tea • near outdoor recreation • smokefree • kids ok • $140-350

Fontana

Erotica

▲ **Le Sex Shoppe** 14589 Valley Blvd (at Cherry) **909/350-4717** • 24hrs

Fort Bragg

Accommodations

Annie's Jug Handle Beach B&B 32980 Gibney Ln **707/964-1415, 800/964-9957** • gay-friendly • full brkfst • smoking outside only • kids ok • $79-189

Aslan House 24600 N Hwy 1 **707/964-2788** • gay-friendly • cottages • ideal place for romance & privacy on the Mendocino Coast • partial ocean view • hot tub • kids 10+ ok • $145 + $10 extra person (4 max)

Cleone Garden Inn 24600 N Hwy 1 **707/964-2788, 800/400-2189 (CA only)** • gay-friendly • rooms & cottage suite • country garden retreat on 9 1/2 acres • hot tub • $78-160 (2 persons)

Restaurants

Purple Rose Mill Creek Dr **707/964-6507** • 5pm-9pm, clsd Mon-Tue • Mexican

Bookstores

Windsong Books & Records 324 N Main (at Redwood Ave) **707/964-2050** • 10am-5:30pm, till 4pm Sun • mostly used • large selection of women's titles

Fremont

Erotica

L'Amour Shoppe 40555 Grimmer Blvd (at Fremont) **510/659-8161** • 24hrs

Fresno

Info Lines & Services

Community Link **559/266-5465** • info • lesbigay support • also publishes 'Pink Pages'

GUS (Gay United Service) 1999 Tuolumne #625 (at Fulton) **559/268-3541** • 8am-5pm Mon-Fri • counseling & referrals

Serenity Fellowship AA 2812 N Blackstone (at Princeton) **559/221-6907** • various mtg times • women's mtg 7pm Mon at Alano Club (1350 N 11th St)

The Yosemite Chapter, Knights of Malta **559/224-2368** • lesbigay leather group

Bars

El Sombrero 3848 E Belmont Ave (btwn 8th & 9th) **559/442-1818** • 9pm-1am Wed, 6pm-1am Fri-Sun • lesbians/gay men • multi-racial clientele • live shows • women-owned/run

The Express 708 N Blackstone (at Belmont) **559/233-1791** • hours vary • lesbians/gay men • dancing/DJ • piano bar • cafe • videos • popular patio • wheelchair access

Palace 4030 E Belmont Ave (at 11th) **559/264-8283** • 3pm-2am • mostly women • neighborhood bar • dancing/DJ • wheelchair access

Red Lantern 4618 E Belmont Ave (at Maple) **559/251-5898** • 2pm-2am • mostly gay men • neighborhood bar • country/western • wheelchair access

Cafes

Java Cafe 805 E Olive (at Wishon) **559/486-8825** • 6:30am-11pm, till midnight Fri-Sat • popular • bohemian • plenty veggie • live shows • wheelchair access • $8-12

Spiritual Groups

Wesley United Methodist Church 1343 E Barstow Ave (at 4th) **559/224-1947** • 8:30am & 11am Sun • reconciling congregation

Erotica

Only For You 1460 N Van Ness Ave (at McKinley) **559/498-0284** • noon-9pm, till 10pm Th-Sat • lesbigay

Wildcat Book Store 1535 Fresno St (at 'G' St) **559/237-4525**

Garberville

Accommodations

Giant Redwoods RV & Camp **707/943-3198** • gay-friendly • campsites • RV • located off the Avenue of the Giants on the Eel River • shared baths • kids/pets ok • $19(tent)-27

Garden Grove

Bars

Frat House 8112 Garden Grove Blvd **714/897-3431** • 9am-2am • popular • lesbians/gay men • dancing/DJ • multi-racial • live shows • theme nights • piano bar • wheelchair access

Happy Hour 12081 Garden Grove Blvd (at Harbor) **714/537-9079** • 2pm-2am, from noon wknds • mostly women • dancing/DJ • wheelchair access • lesbian-owned/run for over 30 years!

Erotica

Hip Pocket 12686 Garden Grove Blvd **714/638-8595**

Glendale

Spiritual Groups

MCC Divine Redeemer 346 Riverdale Dr **818/500-7124** • 11am Sun

Grass Valley

Accommodations

Murphy's Inn 318 Neal St **530/273-6873** • gay-friendly • full brkfst • smokefree • $105-160

Restaurants

Friar Tucks 111 N Pine St (at Commercial), Nevada City **530/265-9093** • dinner from 5pm • American/fondue • full bar • wheelchair access • $15-20

Gualala

Accommodations

Breakers Inn 39300 S Hwy 1 **707/884-3200, 800/BREAKER** • gay/straight • women-owned/run • $85-235

Half Moon Bay

Accommodations

Mill Rose Inn 615 Mill St **650/726-8750, 800/900-7673** • gay-friendly • classic European elegance by the sea • full brkfst • hot tub • smokefree • kids 10+ ok • $165-285

Restaurants

Moss Beach Distillery Beach & Ocean **650/728-5595** • lunch & dinner • some veggie • $9-20

Pasta Moon 315 Main St **650/726 5125** • beer/wine • wheelchair access

San Benito House 356 Main St **650/726-3425** • dinner Th-Sun • Mediterranean • full bar • wheelchair access • $11-17

Hayward

Bars

Rainbow Room 21859 Mission Blvd (at Sunset) **510/582-8078** • noon-2am • lesbians/gay men • dancing/DJ • women-owned/run

Rumors 22554 Main St (btwn 'A' & 'B') **510/733-2334** • noon-2am, 10am-2am wknds • mostly gay men • neighborhood bar • dancing/DJ • wheelchair access

Turf Club 22517 Mission Blvd (at 'A') **510/881-9877** • 10am-2am • lesbians/gay men • dancing/DJ • live shows • patio

Erotica

L'Amour Shoppe 22553 Main St (btwn 'A' & 'B') **510/886-7777**

Healdsburg

Accommodations

Camellia Inn 211 North St **707/433-8182, 800/727-8182** • gay-friendly • full brkfst • smokefree • $75-165

Madrona Manor 707/433-4231 • gay-friendly • elegant Victorian country inn • full brkfst • swimming • smokefree • some rooms ok for kids • pets ok in 1 room • wheelchair access • $155-255

Twin Towers River Ranch 615 Bailhache (at Redwood Hwy) **707/433-4443** • gay-friendly • 1864 Victorian farmhouse located on 5 rolling acres • also vacation house • kids & pets by arrangement

Vintage Towers B&B 302 N Main St (at 3rd), Cloverdale **707/894-4535, 888/886-9377** • gay-friendly • Queen Anne mansion • full brkfst • smokefree • kids 10+ ok • $75-165

Restaurants

Chateau Souverain 400 Souverain Rd, Geyserville **707/433-8281** • lunch weekly, dinner Fri-Sun only • fine dining

Hermosa Beach

Erotica

USJ Video & Books 544 Pacific Coast Hwy (at 6th) **310/374-9207**

Huntington Beach

Erotica

Paradise Specialties 7344 Center (at Gothard) **714/898-0400**

Idyllwild

Accommodations

The Pine Cove Inn 23481 Hwy 243 **909/659-5033, 888/659-5033** • gay-friendly • full brkfst • $70-100

The Rainbow Inn 909/659-0111 • gay/straight • full brkfst • smokefree • patio • gay-owned/run

Imperial Beach

Erotica

Palm Avenue Books 1177 Palm Ave **619/575-5081** • 24hrs

Joshua Tree Nat'l Park

Accommodations

Mojave Rock Ranch Lodge 64976 Starlight **760/366-8455** • gay/straight • private 55-acre ranch & bungalow • funky & unique • $175-195 per cabin

Klamath

Accommodations

Rhodes' End B&B 115 Trobitz Rd **707/482-1654** • gay-friendly

Laguna Beach

Info Lines & Services

AA Gay/Lesbian 31872 Coast Hwy (at South Coast Medical Hospital) **949/499-7150** • 8:30pm Fri

Laguna Outreach 949/497-4237 • educational/social group for Orange County

Accommodations

Best Western Laguna Brisas Spa Hotel 1600 S Coast Hwy (at Bluebird) **949/497-7272, 800/624-4442** • gay-friendly • resort hotel • swimming • wheelchair access

By The Sea Inn 475 N Coast Hwy **949/497-6645, 800/297-0007** • gay-friendly • hot tub • swimming • kids ok • wheelchair access • $69-189

Casa Laguna B&B Inn 2510 S Coast Hwy **949/494-2996, 800/233-0449** • gay-friendly • inn & cottages overlooking the Pacific • swimming • $69-225

The Coast Inn 1401 S Coast Hwy **949/494-7588, 800/653-2697** • lesbians/gay men • resort • swimming • oceanside location • 2 bars & restaurant • $64-190

Holiday Inn Laguna Beach 696 S Coast Hwy **949/494-1001, 800/228-5691** • gay-friendly • swimming • kids ok • food served • wheelchair access • $99-179

Bars

Main St 1460 S Coast Hwy **949/494-0056** • 2pm-2am • mostly gay men • piano bar

Woody's at the Beach 1305 S Coast Hwy (at Cress) **949/376-8809** • 4pm-2am, from noon Sun • mostly gay men • also restaurant • patio

Nightclubs

Boom Boom Room 1401 S Coast Hwy (at the Coast Inn) **949/494-7588** • 10am-2am • popular • lesbians/gay men • dancing/DJ • live shows • videos • wheelchair access

Cafes

Cafe Zinc 350 Ocean Ave **949/494-6302** • 7am-4:30pm, till 5pm Sun • vegetarian • beer/wine • patio • also market • wheelchair access • $5-10

The Koffee Klatch 1440 S Coast Hwy (btwn Mountain & Pacific Coast Hwy) **949/376-6867** • 7am-11pm, till 1am Fri-Sat • brkfst, lunch & dinner • desserts

Restaurants

Cafe Zoolu 860 Glenneyre **949/494-6825** • dinner only • Californian • some veggie • wheelchair access • $10-20

The Cottage 308 N Coast Hwy **949/494-3023** • lunch & dinner • homestyle cooking • some veggie

Dizz's As Is 2794 S Coast Hwy **949/494-5250** • open 5:30pm, seating at 6pm, clsd Mon • cont'l • full bar • patio • $16-27

Drew's Caribbean Cafe 31732 Pacific Coast Hwy (at 3rd), South Laguna Beach **949/499-6311** • 5pm-9pm, till 10pm Fri-Sat, clsd Mon • beer/wine • gay-owned/run

Mark's Restaurant 858 S Coast Highway **949/494-6711** • dinner Mon-Sat • also full bar • gay-friendly

Bookstores

Different Drummer Books 1294-C S Coast Hwy **949/497-6699** • 11am-8pm, till 10pm Fri-Sat • large lesbigay section • wheelchair access • gay-owned/run

Retail Shops

▲ **Jewelry by Poncé** 1417 S Coast Hwy **949/494-1399, 800/969-RING** • 11am-7pm Wed-Sun, by appt Mon-Tue • lesbigay commitment rings & other jewelry • (see ad in mail order section)

Publications

Orange County/ Long Beach Blade 949/494-4898

Spiritual Groups

Christ Chapel of Laguna 286 St Anne's Dr **949/376-2099** • 10am Sun

Unitarian Universalist Fellowship 429 Cypress Dr **949/497-4568, 714/645-8597** • 10:30am Sun

Holly's
A Special Place For All Women
Private Cozy Cabins, Hot Tub, Pot Luck BBQ's, Wine & Cheese Welcome Friday Nights, Fireplaces, Boat Cruises, Commitment Ceremonies.
Dog Friendly!
LAKE TAHOE, CA
800-745-7041
www.hollysplace.com

Erotica

Gay Mart 168 Mountain Rd **949/497-9108** • 10am-midnight, till 1am Fri-Sat

Video Horizons 31674 Coast Hwy (at 3rd Ave) **949/499-4519**

Lake Tahoe

see also Lake Tahoe, Nevada

Accommodations

Black Bear Inn 530/544-4411, 800/431-4411 • gay/straight • hot tub • fireplaces • smokefree • gay-owned/run • $150-200

▲ **Holly's Place 530/544-7040, 800/745-7041** • women only • guesthouse • cabin • kitchens • smokefree • kids/pets ok • lesbian-owned/run • $88-198

Ridgewood Inn 1341 Emerald Bay Rd **530/541-8589** • gay-friendly • hot tub • quiet wooded setting • $40-185

Secrets Honeymooners' Inn 924 Park Ave, South Lake Tahoe **530/544-6767, 800/441-6610 EXT. 81-D** • gay-friendly • quiet, romantic adult-only inn • spas • $58-158

Sierrawood Guest House South Lake Tahoe **530/577-6073, 800/700-3802** • lesbians/gay men • hot tub • cozy, romantic chalet • gay-owned/run • $110-150

Silver Shadows Lodge 1251 Emerald Bay Rd, South Lake Tahoe **530/541-3575** • gay-friendly • motel • swimming • kids/pets ok • $35 & up

Spruce Grove 530/544-0549, 800/777-0914 • gay/straight • private cabins & cottages • near Heavenly ski resort & lake

Tradewinds Resort & Suites 944 Friday (at Cedar), South Lake Tahoe **530/544-6459, 800/628-1829** • gay-friendly • swimming • suite w/spas & fireplace available • $30-120

Nightclubs

Faces 270 Kingsbury Grade, NV **702/588-2333** • 5pm-4am, from 3pm Sun • lesbians/gay men • dancing/DJ

Cafes

Syd's Bagelry 550 North Lake Blvd, Tahoe City **530/583-2666** • 6:30am-6:30pm daily • bagel sandwiches • plenty veggie

Restaurants

Driftwood Cafe 4119 Laurel Ave (at Poplar) **530/544-6545** • 7:30am-2pm • homecooking • some veggie • $4-8

Passaretti's 1181 Emerald Bay Rd /Hwy 50 **530/541-3433** • 9am-9:30pm • Italian

Lancaster

Info Lines & Services

Antelope Valley Gay/Lesbian Alliance 661/942-2812 • call for events

Nightclubs

Back Door 1255 W Ave 'I' (at 13th St W) **661/945-2566** • 6pm-2am • lesbians/gay men • dancing/DJ

Spiritual Groups

Antelope Valley Unitarian Universalist Fellowship 43843 N Division St (at Masonic Lodge) **661/943-8225** • 11am Sun

Sunrise MCC of the High Desert 39149 8th St E **661/265-6156** • 1pm Sun

Leucadia

Accommodations

Ocean Inn 1444 N Hwy 101 **760/436-1988, 800/546-1598** • gay-friendly • mission decor in quiet neighborhood setting • $79-139

Long Beach

Info Lines & Services

AA Gay/Lesbian (Atlantic Alano Club) 441 E 1st St **562/432-7476** • hours vary

Lesbian/Gay Center & Switchboard 2017 E 4th St (at Cherry) **562/434-4455** • 9am-10pm, till 6pm Sat, 3pm-9pm Sun • also newsletter

Accommodations

Bed & Breakfast California 3924 E 14th St **800/383-3513** • reservation service

Bars

Birds of Paradise 1800 E Broadway (at Hermosa) **562/590-8773** • 10am-1am • lesbians/gay men • neighborhood bar • food served • live shows • wheelchair access

The Brit 1744 E Broadway (at Cherry) **562/432-9742** • 10am-2am • mostly gay men • neighborhood bar

The Broadway 1100 E Broadway (at Cerritos) **562/432-3646** • 10am-2am • lesbians/gay men • neighborhood bar

Club 5211 5211 N Atlantic St (at 52nd) **562/428-5545** • 10am-1am, 24hrs on wknds • lesbians/gay men • neighborhood bar • wheelchair access

Club Broadway 3348 E Broadway (at Redondo) **562/438-7700** • 11am-2am • mostly women • neighborhood bar • women-owned/run

The Crest 5935 Cherry Ave (at South) **562/423-6650** • 2pm-2am, from 6pm Tue • mostly gay men • leather

Pistons 2020 E Artesia (at Cherry) **562/422-1928** • 6pm-2am, till 4am Fri-Sat, from 3pm Sun • mostly gay men • leather • patio

Que Será 1923 E 7th St (at Cherry) **562 /599-6170** • 5pm-2am, from noon Sun • gay/straight • dancing/DJ

Ripples 5101 E Ocean (at Granada) **562/433-0357** • noon-2am • popular • mostly gay men • dancing/DJ • food served • videos • patio

Silver Fox 411 Redondo (at 4th) **562/439-6343** • noon-2am • popular happy hour • mostly gay men • karaoke Wed & Sun • videos • wheelchair access

Sweetwater Saloon 1201 E Broadway (at Orange) **562/432-7044** • 6am-2am • popular days • lesbians/gay men • neighborhood bar • wheelchair access

Nightclubs

Executive Suite 3428 E Pacific Coast Hwy (at Redondo) **562/597-3884** • from 4pm, from 5pm wknds • popular • lesbians/gay men • dancing/DJ • theme nights

Cafes

Cousin's Coffee & Tea 1708 E Broadway (at Gaviota) **562/437-3785** • 7am-midnight, from 7:30am wknds

The Underground Cafe 1512 E Broadway (at Falcon) **562/432-5211** • 11am-11pm • also gift shop • gay-owned/run

Restaurants

Cha Cha Cha 762 8th (at Pacific Ave) **562/436-3900** • lunch & dinner • Caribbean • plenty veggie • wheelchair access

Long Beach

Where the Girls Are: Schmoozing with the boys on Broadway between Atlantic and Cherry Avenues, or elsewhere between Pacific Coast Hwy. and the beach. Or at home snuggling.

Lesbigay Pride: 3rd wknd in May. 562/987-9191.

Annual Events: April - AIDS Walk. September - Pride Picnic. November - The Gatsby Show at the Sheraton, benefitting the Center.

City Info: 562/426-6773, web: www.longbeach.com

Attractions: The Queen Mary 562/435-3511.
Long Beach Downtown Marketplace, 10am-4pm Fri.
Belmont Shores area on 2nd St., south of Pacific Coast Highway – lots of restaurants & shopping, only blocks from the beach.

Best View: On the deck of the Queen Mary, docked overlooking most of Long Beach. Or Signal Hill, off 405. Take the Cherry exit.

Weather: Quite temperate: highs in the mid-80°s July through September, and cooling down at night. In the winter, January to March, highs are in the upper 60°s, and lows in the upper 40°s.

Transit: Long Beach Taxi Co-op 562/435-6111.
Long Beach Transit & Runabout (free downtown shuttle) 562/591-2301.

Egg Heaven 4358 E 4th St **562/433-9277** • 7am-2pm, till 3pm wknds • some veggie

House of Madame JoJo 2941 E Broadway (btwn Temple & Redondo) **562/439-3672** • 5pm-10pm • popular • lesbians/gay men • Mediterranean • some veggie • beer/wine • wheelchair access • $12-20

Original Park Pantry 2104 E Broadway (at Junipero) **562/434-0451** • lunch & dinner • lesbians/ gay men • int'l • some veggie • wheelchair access • $8-12

Retail Shops

Hot Stuff 2121 W Broadway (at Cherry) **562/433-0692** • 11am-7pm, till 6pm wknds • cards • gifts • novelties

Spiritual Groups

Christ Chapel 3935 E 10th St **562/438-5303** • 10am & 6pm Sun, 7pm Wed • non-denominational • wheelchair access

Dignity **562/984-8400** • call for service times & locations

First United Methodist Church 507 Pacific Ave **562/437-1289** • 10am Sun • wheelchair access

Lesbian & Gay Havurah 3801 E Willow St (at Jewish Comm Ctr) **562/426-7601 x31**

Trinity Lutheran Church 759 Linden Ave (btwn 7th & 8th) **562/437-4002** • 10am Sun • wheelchair access

Erotica

The Crypt on Broadway 1712 E Broadway (btwn Cherry & Falcon) **562/983-6560** • leather • toys

The Rubber Tree 5018 E 2nd St (at Granada) **562/434-0027** • 11am-9pm, noon-7pm Sun • gifts for lovers • women-owned

Long Beach

Though it's often overshadowed by its neighbor Los Angeles, Long Beach is a large harbor city with plenty of bars and shopping of its own...and, of course, lesbians.

According to local rumor, Long Beach is second only to San Francisco in lesbian/gay population, at approximately 45,000–though many of these gay residents are 'married,' making Long Beach a bedroom community of professional couples.

The city itself is melded from overlapping suburbs and industrial areas. The cleaner air, mild weather, and reasonable traffic make it an obvious choice for those looking for a livable refuge away from L.A. Of course the nightlife is milder as well, but nobody's complaining about the one women's bar–**Club Broadway,** perfect for casual hanging out. Though it's a mixed lesbigay club, we hear that the **Executive Suite** is popular with lesbians on weekends. For other events, check with the **Lesbian/Gay Center**.

Los Angeles

LA—Overview

Los Angeles is divided into 7 geographical areas:
LA—Overview
LA—West Hollywood
LA—Hollywood
LA—West LA & Santa Monica
LA—Silverlake
LA—Midtown
LA—Valley

Info Lines & Services

Alcoholics Together Center 1773 Griffith Park Blvd (at Hyperion) **323/663-8882, 323/936-4343 (AA#)** • call for mtg times • 12-step groups

Asian/Pacific Gays & Friends **323/980-7874** • call for events

COOL (Coalition of Older Lesbians) at 'The Village' **323/913-3722** • social/support group • rap 1pm 3rd Sat • wheelchair access

Ellas 5301 E Beverly Blvd (at La Casa/Bienestar Ctr) **323/727-7897** • social/support group for lesbian/bi Latinas & Chicanas 21+

Gay/Lesbian Youth Talk Line **323/993-7475** • 7pm-10pm, clsd Sun • referrals & support for those 23 & under • women's night Mon

GLLU (Gay/Lesbian Latinos Unidos) **213/243-9443** • social/support group • call for events

LAAPIS (Los Angeles Asian Pacific Islander Sisters) **323/969-4084** • monthly social events & on-going chat groups

Los Angeles Gay/Lesbian Community Center 1625 N Shrader **323/993-7400** • 9am-9pm, clsd Sat-Sun • wide variety of services

Sisters Stepping Out 105 S Locust St (at the 'Amassi Center') **310/419-1969** • 7pm Mon • social/support group for African-American women who love women

South Bay Lesbian/Gay Community Organization 2009 Artesia Blvd #A, Redondo Beach **310/379-2850** • support/education for Manhattan, Hermosa & Redondo Beaches, Torrance, Palos Verdes, El Segundo

ULOAH (United Lesbians of African Heritage) **323/960-5051** • empowerment group 'for all lesbian decendants of the African Diaspora'

GAY BLACK FEMALE MAGAZINE™
10 ISSUES $15 w/o t-shirt or $25 w/t-shirt
Also Available GBF Compilation of short films $19.95 (no shipping charge)
*Never Say Never (1995) *Rashida X (1996) *Train Station (1997) *Gay Black Female (1998) *If She Only Knew (1999)
gayblackfemale.com 6312 Hollywood Blvd. #23 Hollywood, CA 90028 (323) 376-2157 gbf@pacbell.net

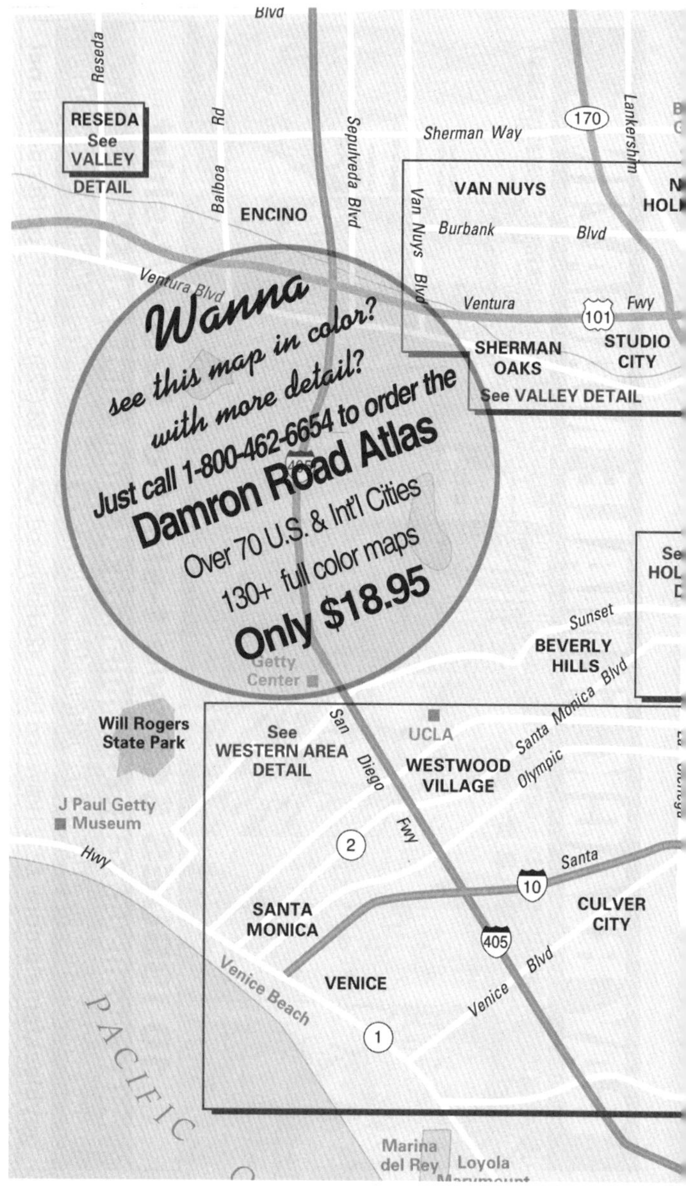

Blvd
Reseda
RESEDA
See
VALLEY
DETAIL
Balboa
Rd
ENCINO
Sepulveda Blvd
Sherman Way
170
Lankershim
VAN NUYS
Van Nuys Blvd
Burbank
Blvd
Ventura Blvd
Ventura
101
Fwy
SHERMAN
OAKS
STUDIO
CITY
See VALLEY DETAIL
Wanna
see this map in color?
with more detail?
Just call 1-800-462-6654 to order the
Damron Road Atlas
Over 70 U.S. & Int'l Cities
130+ full color maps
Only $18.95
Getty
Center
Sunset
BEVERLY
HILLS
Santa Monica Blvd
Will Rogers
State Park
See
WESTERN AREA
DETAIL
San
Diego
Fwy
UCLA
WESTWOOD
VILLAGE
Olympic
J Paul Getty
Museum
Hwy
2
Santa
10
CULVER
CITY
SANTA
MONICA
405
Blvd
Venice
Venice Beach
VENICE
1
PACIFIC
Marina
del Rey
Loyola

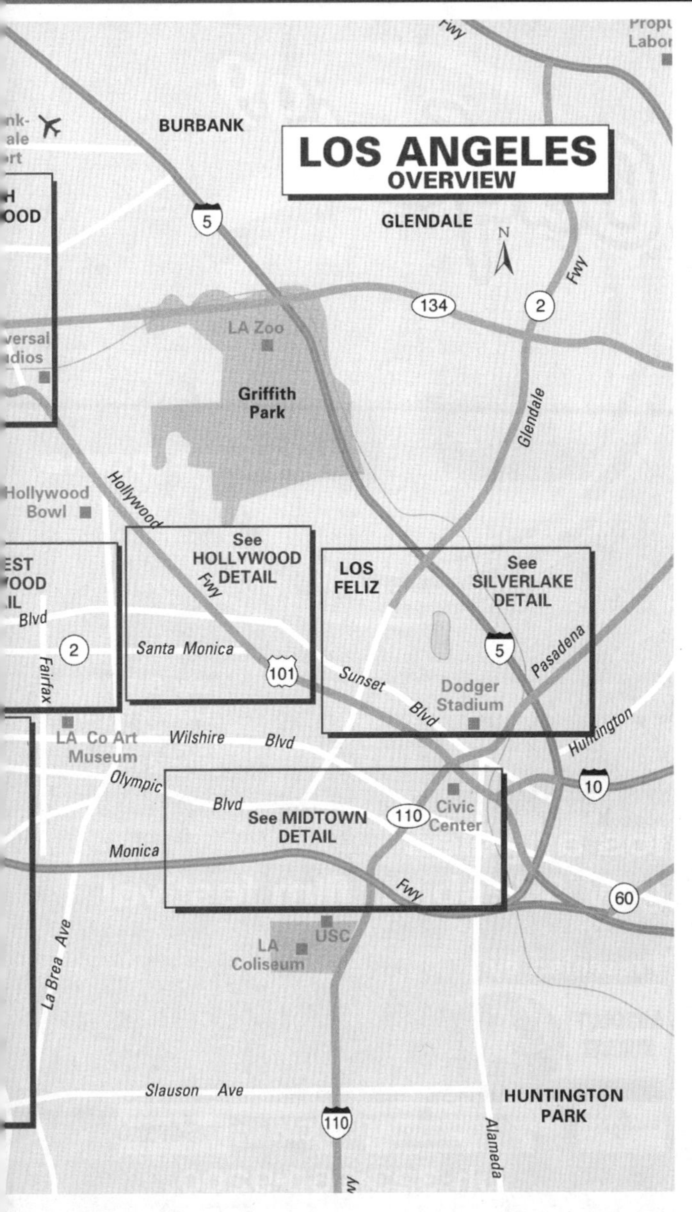

LOS ANGELES
OVERVIEW
BURBANK
GLENDALE
LA Zoo
Griffith
Park
Hollywood
Bowl
Hollywood
Fwy
See
HOLLYWOOD
DETAIL
Santa Monica
Blvd
Fairfax
LOS
FELIZ
See
SILVERLAKE
DETAIL
Pasadena
Sunset
Blvd
Dodger
Stadium
Huntington
Glendale
Fwy
LA Co Art
Museum
Wilshire
Blvd
Olympic
Blvd
See MIDTOWN
DETAIL
Civic
Center
Monica
Fwy
USC
LA
Coliseum
La Brea Ave
Slauson
Ave
HUNTINGTON
PARK
Alameda
5
134
2
101
110
10
60

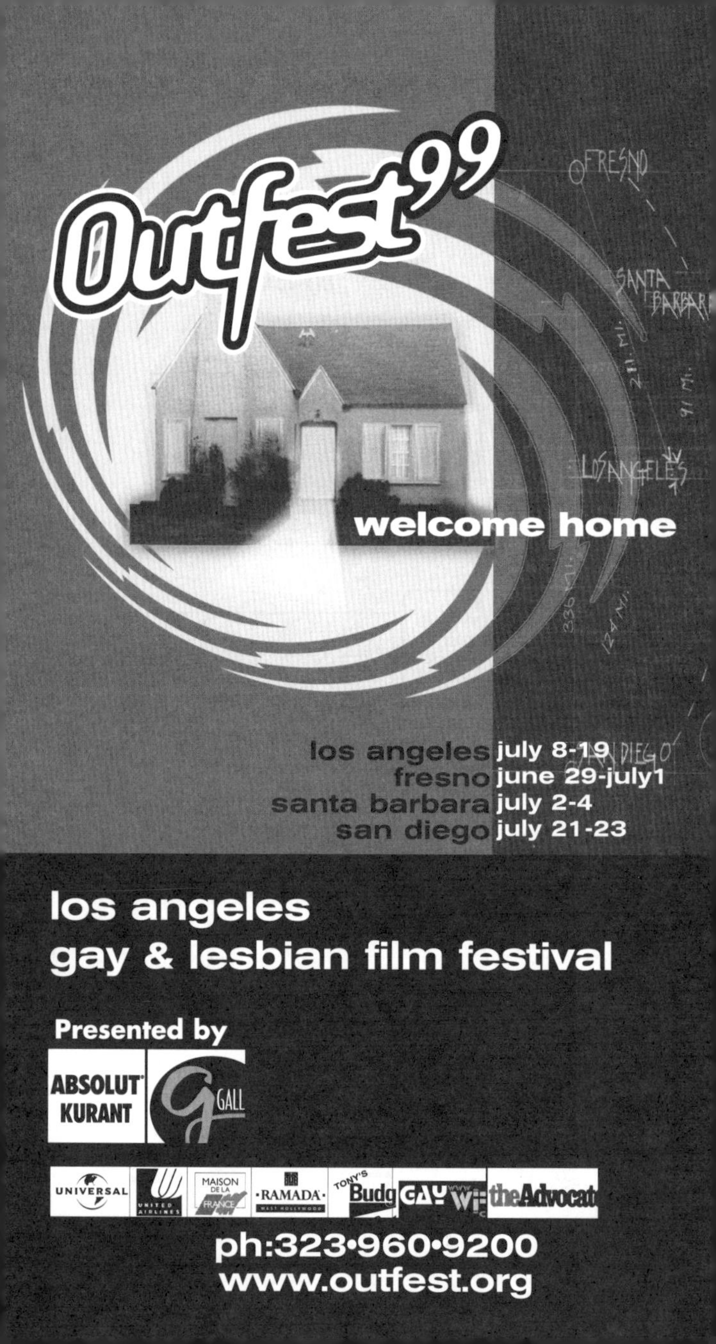
Outfest 99
FRESNO
SANTA
211 MI.
91 MI.
LOSANGELES
welcome home
los angeles july 8-19
fresno june 29-july1
santa barbara july 2-4
san diego july 21-23
los angeles
gay & lesbian film festival
Presented by
ABSOLUT KURANT
GALL
UNIVERSAL
UNITED AIRLINES
MAISON DE LA FRANCE
RAMADA
WEST HOLLYWOOD
theAdvocate
ph:323•960•9200
www.outfest.org

Where the Girls Are: Hip dykes hang out in West Hollywood, with the boys along Santa Monica Blvd, or cruising funky Venice Beach and Santa Monica. The S&M ('Stand & Model') glamourdykes pose in chichi clubs and posh eateries in West LA and Beverly Hills. There's a scattered community of women in Silverlake. And more suburban lesbians frequent the gay bars in Studio City and North Hollywood. If you're used to makeup-free lesbians, you may be surprised that coiffed and lipsticked lesbian style is the norm in LA.

Entertainment: Gay Men's Chorus 323/650-0756, web: www.gmcla.org.

Lesbigay Pride: June. 323/860-0701. Christopher St. West.

Annual Events: April - AIDS Walk-a-thon 323/466-9255.
May/June - California AIDS Ride 323/874-7474 or 800/825-1000. AIDS benefit bike ride from San Francisco to L.A.
July - Outfest 323/960-9200. Los Angeles' lesbian & gay film and video festival.
August - Sunset Junction Fair 323/661-7771. Carnival, arts & information fair on Sunset Blvd. in Silverlake benefits Sunset Junction Youth Center.
September - Gay Night at Knotts Berry Farm 805/222-7788.
November - Gay Night at Disneyland 805/222-7788.

City Info: 323/689-8822 (multi-lingual) or 800/228-2452, web: www.lacvb.com.

Attractions: City Walk in Universal Studios.
Westwood Village premiere movie theaters & restaurants.
Mann's Chinese Theater on Hollywood Blvd 323/464-8186.
Melrose Ave, hip commercial district in West Hollywood.
Venice Beach.
3rd St. outdoor mall in Santa Monica.
Chinatown, near downtown.
Watts Towers in Watts, not far from LAX 213/847-4646.
Theme Parks: Disneyland, Knotts Berry Farm or Magic Mountain.
Dead Tours — tours of (in)famous deaths, violence and the supernatural 213/469-4149.

Best View: Drive up Mulholland Drive, in the hills between Hollywood and the Valley, for a panoramic view of the city, and the Hollywood sign.

Weather: Summers are hot, dry and smoggy with temperatures in the 80°s-90°s. LA's weather is at its finest — sunny, blue skies and moderate temperatures (mid 70°s) — during the months of March, April and May.

Transit: Green & White Taxi 323/870-4664.
LA Express 800/427-7483.
Super Shuttle 310/782-6600.
Metro Transit Authority 323/626-4455.

Los Angeles

There is no city that better embodies the extremes of American life than Los Angeles. Here fantasy and reality have become inseparable. The mere mention of the 'City of Angels' conjures up images of palm-lined streets, sun-drenched beaches, and wealth beyond imagination, along with smog, overcrowded freeways, searing poverty, and urban violence.

Most travelers come only for the fantasy. They want to star-gaze at Mann's Chinese Theatre in Hollywood; at movie and television studios (Fox, Universal) in Burbank; at famous restaurants (Spago, The City, Chasen's, Citrus, Ivy's, Chaya Brasserie, Morton's, etc.); and, of course, all along Rodeo Drive. (Our favorite star-gazing location is Canter's Deli after 2am.)

But if you take a moment to focus your sights past the usual tourist traps, you'll see the unique—and often tense—diversity that L.A. offers as a city on the borders of Latin America, the Pacific Rim, Suburbia USA, and the rest of the world. You'll find museums, centers, and theaters celebrating the cultures of the many peoples who live in this valley. An excellent example is West Hollywood's **June Mazer Lesbian Collection**. Other cultural epicenters include Olvera Street, Korea Town, China Town, and the historically Jewish Fairfax District. Call the L.A. Visitor's Bureau for directions and advice.

L.A.'s art scene rivals New York's, so if you're an art lover be sure to check out the galleries and museums, as well as the performance art scene (check a recent *L.A. Weekly*).

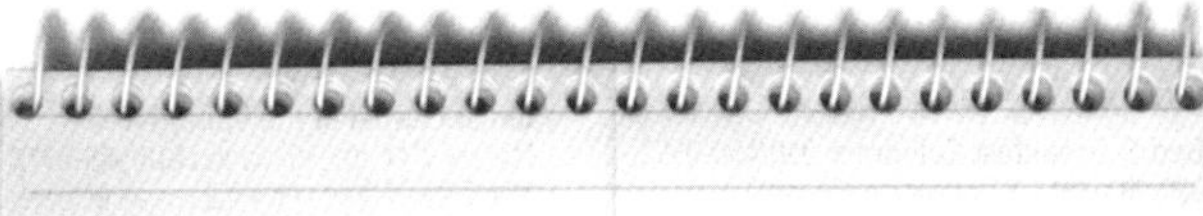

This is a car-driven city—remember the song, "Nobody Walks in L.A."? Nobody takes the bus, either, if they can avoid it. So plan on spending a day just driving; don't miss Mulholland Drive at night.

During the day, shop along trendy Melrose Avenue (that's right, avenue not place). Or check out Los Feliz (pronounced anglo-style: *Lahss Feel-iss*), the funky neighborhood to cruise between Silverlake and Hollywood. Los Feliz is home to many hip thrift shops, as well as (rumor has it) to Madonna and little Lourdes. For coffee and girls with British accents, stop by **Van Go's Ear** in Venice.

As for lesbian nightlife in L.A., there are several full-time women's bars (some of them in the Valley), and many women's nights. L.A. is where the one-nighter women's dance bar revolution began, so make sure to double-check the papers before you go out (**Female FYI**, **L.A. Girl Guide**, or the more topical **Lesbian News**). On Fridays, don't miss **Girl Bar** at the Factory, or **Hot Box** at the El Rey Theatre.

For serious girl-watching, cruise by **Michele's XXX All-Female Topless Revue** at 7969 on Tuesdays. Women strip for women at **Puss 'n' Boots** on Thursdays at Jewel's Catch One. And you can always visit that perennially popular lesbian night spot, **The Palms**.

The Village (Gay/Lesbian Center Extension) 1125 N McCadden Pl (at Santa Monica) **323/461-2633, 323/860-7302** • cafe • theaters • shops • call for events & hours

Accommodations

Bed & Breakfast California 310/498-0552, 800/383-3513 • reservation service

Entertainment & Recreation

The Celebration Theatre 7051-B Santa Monica Blvd (at La Brea) **323/957-1884** • lesbigay theater • call for more info

Gay Men's Chorus 323/650-0756

The Getty Center 1200 Getty Center Dr, Brentwood **310/440-7300** • LA's shining city on a hill & world-class museum • of course, it's still in LA so you'll need to make reservations for parking (!)

Highways 1651 18th St, Santa Monica **310/315-1459 (INFO/RESERVATION LINE), 310/453-1755 (ADMIN LINE)** • 'full-service performance center'

IMRU Gay Radio KPFK LA 90.7 FM **818/985-2711** • 10pm Sun • also 'This Way Out' 3pm Tue

Ivy Theater 1612 S Stanley Ave **323/939-4967** • lesbian theater company

ONE Institute/IGLA 310/854-0271 • int'l lesbigay archives • call for appt

Sunwolf Farms 805/245-9653 • private ranch w/customized day trips • lesbian-owned/run

Publications

4-Front Magazine 323/650-7772 • club listings

Community Yellow Pages 323/469-4454 • annual survival guide to lesbigay southern CA

The Edge 323/962-6994 • newsmagazine w/listings

Fab! 323/655-5716 • free club listings

Female FYI 323/460-7025 • monthly • LA lesbian club scene

▲ **GBF (Gay Black Female) 323/376-2157** • nat'l newsmagazine w/ some listings for LA

LA Girl Guide 818/242-3607, 800/473-3475 x224

▲ **Lesbian News 310/787-8658, 800/458-9888** • nat'l w/strong coverage of southern CA • see ad front color section

Nightlife 323/462-5400 • club listings

Odyssey Magazine 323/874-8788 • all the dish on LA's club scene

The Women's Yellow Pages 818/995-6646

Spiritual Groups

Beth Chayim Chadashim (BCC) 6000 W Pico Blvd (at Crescent Hts) **323/931-7023** • 8pm Fri

Christ Chapel of the Valley 11050 Hartsook, North Hollywood **818/985-8977** • 10am Sun, 7:30pm Fri • full gospel fellowship

Congregation Kol Ami 7350 Sunset Blvd (at Martel) **310/248-6320** • 8pm Fri

Dignity LA 126 S Ave 64 **323/344-8064** • 5:30pm Sun • Spanish Mass 3rd Sat

Holy Trinity Community Church 4209 Santa Monica Blvd (at Delmar) **323/662-9118** • 10am Sun

MCC in the Valley 5730 Cahuenga Blvd (at Burbank Blvd), North Hollywood **818/762-1133** • 10:30am Sun

MCC LA 8714 Santa Monica Blvd (at Westbourne) **310/854-9110** • 9am, 11am, 1pm (en español) & 6pm gospel service Sun • wheelchair access

St Andrew's Episcopal Church 1432 Engracia Ave (at Cabrillo), Torrance **310/328-3781** • 8am & 10am Sun

Unity Fellowship Church 5148 W Jefferson Blvd **323/936-4948, 323/938-8322** • 11:30am Sun • mostly African-American congregation • wheelchair access

West Hollywood Presbyterian Church 7350 Sunset Blvd (at Martel) **323/874-6646** • 11am Sun • wheelchair access

LA—West Hollywood

Accommodations

The Grove Guesthouse 1325 N Orange Grove Ave (at Sunset) **323/876-7778** • lesbians/gay men • 1-bdrm villa • hot tub • swimming • smokefree • kitchens • pets ok by arrangement • gay-owned/run • $150+

Holloway Motel 8465 Santa Monica Blvd (at La Cienega) **213/654-2454, 888/654-6400** • gay/straight • kitchens • centrally located • wheelchair access • IGLTA • gay-owned/run • $55-85

▲ **Le Montrose Suite Hotel** 900 Hammond St (at Sunset) **310/855-1115, 800/776-0666** • gay-friendly • hot tub • swimming • kitchens • fireplaces • smokefree • kids/pets ok • gym • also full restaurant • rooftop patio • wheelchair access • IGLTA • $240-560

Le Reve 8822 Cynthia St (at Larrabee) **310/854-1114, 800/835-7997** • gay-friendly • swimming • kids ok • wheelchair access • IGLTA

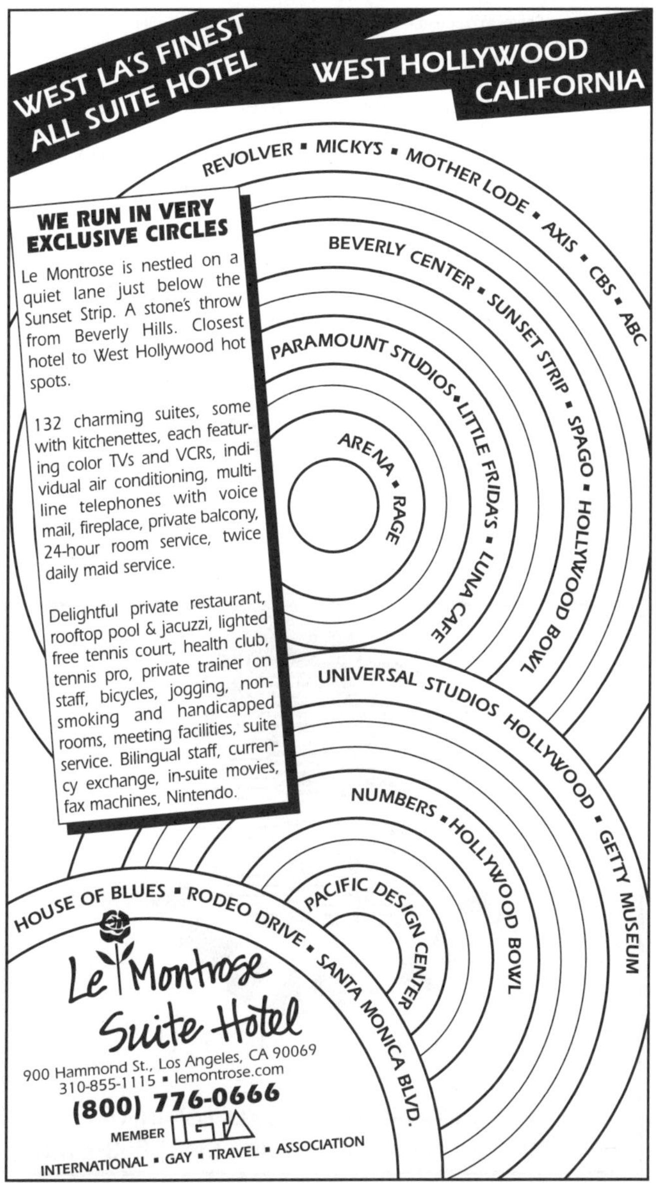
WEST LA'S FINEST
ALL SUITE HOTEL
WEST HOLLYWOOD
CALIFORNIA
REVOLVER ▪ MICKY'S ▪ MOTHER LODE ▪ AXIS ▪ CBS ▪ ABC
BEVERLY CENTER ▪ SUNSET STRIP ▪ SPAGO ▪ HOLLYWOOD BOWL
PARAMOUNT STUDIOS ▪ LITTLE FRIDA'S ▪ LUNA CAFE
ARENA ▪ RAGE
UNIVERSAL STUDIOS HOLLYWOOD ▪ GETTY MUSEUM
NUMBERS ▪ HOLLYWOOD BOWL
PACIFIC DESIGN CENTER
HOUSE OF BLUES ▪ RODEO DRIVE ▪ SANTA MONICA BLVD.
WE RUN IN VERY EXCLUSIVE CIRCLES
Le Montrose is nestled on a quiet lane just below the Sunset Strip. A stone's throw from Beverly Hills. Closest hotel to West Hollywood hot spots.
132 charming suites, some with kitchenettes, each featuring color TVs and VCRs, individual air conditioning, multi-line telephones with voice mail, fireplace, private balcony, 24-hour room service, twice daily maid service.
Delightful private restaurant, rooftop pool & jacuzzi, lighted free tennis court, health club, tennis pro, private trainer on staff, bicycles, jogging, non-smoking and handicapped rooms, meeting facilities, suite service. Bilingual staff, currency exchange, in-suite movies, fax machines, Nintendo.
Le Montrose
Suite Hotel
900 Hammond St., Los Angeles, CA 90069
310-855-1115 ▪ lemontrose.com
(800) 776-0666
MEMBER IGTA
INTERNATIONAL ▪ GAY ▪ TRAVEL ▪ ASSOCIATION

Ma Maison Sofitel 8555 Beverly Blvd (at La Cienega) **310/278-5444, 800/521-7772** • gay-friendly • swimming • food served • wheelchair access • IGLTA

The Park Sunset 8462 W Sunset Blvd (at La Cienega) **323/654-6470** • gay-friendly • swimming • sundeck • panoramic views • located in heart of Sunset Strip

Ramada West Hollywood 8585 Santa Monica Blvd (at La Cienega) **310/652-6400, 800/845-8585** • gay-friendly • modern art deco hotel & suites • swimming • kids ok • wheelchair access • IGLTA • $79-250

San Vicente Inn Resort 845 N San Vicente Blvd (at Santa Monica) **310/854-6915** • mostly gay men • swimming • hot tub • nudity • gay-owned/run • $59-199

West Hollywood Suites 1000 Westmount (at Santa Monica) **310/652-9600** • gay/lesbian • studio apts • gay-owned/run

Bars

7702 SM Club 7702 Santa Monica Blvd (at Spaulding) **323/654-3336** • 24hrs • lesbians/gay men • neighborhood bar • dancing/DJ

Comedy Store 8433 Sunset Blvd (at La Cienega) **323/656-6225** • 8pm-1am • gay-friendly • stand-up club

Improvisation 8162 Melrose Ave (at Crescent Heights) **323/651-2583** • gay-friendly • stand-up comedy • also restaurant

Mouth To Mouth at Oxygen Bar 8788 Sunset Blvd (at Holloway & Palm) **323/969-2530** • 9pm Sun • lesbians/gay men • hip sober party

The Normandie Room 8737 Santa Monica Blvd (at Westbourne) **310/659-6204** • 5pm-2am • gay-friendly • neighborhood bar • wheelchair access

▲**The Palms** 8572 Santa Monica Blvd (at La Cienega) **310/652-6188** • 2pm-2am • popular • mostly women • neighborhood bar • dancing/DJ • wheelchair access

Rage 8911 Santa Monica Blvd (at San Vicente) **310/652-7055** • noon-2am • popular • mostly gay men • dancing/DJ • live shows • videos • lunch & dinner daily • wheelchair access

Revolver 8851 Santa Monica Blvd (at San Vicente) **310/659-8851** • 4pm-2am, till 4am Fri-Sat, from 2pm Sun • mostly gay men • alternative • videos

Tempest 7323 Santa Monica Blvd (at Poinsettia) **323/850-5115** • from 8:30pm • popular • gay-friendly • dancing/DJ • live shows • theme nights • also restaurant (dinner only) • French/Italian • some veggie • patio

Viper Room 8852 Sunset Blvd (at San Vicente) **310/358-1880** • 9pm-2am • gay-friendly • dancing/DJ • live shows • cover charge

Nightclubs

7969 7969 Santa Monica Blvd (at Fairfax) **323/654-0280** • 9pm-2am • gay-friendly • dancing/DJ • transgender-friendly • also 'Michele's XXX Review' 9pm Tue • strip show/dance club for women

The Factory 652 N La Peer (at Santa Monica) **310/659-4551** • 9pm-2am Tue-Sun • mostly gay men • women's night Fri for 'Girl Bar' • dancing/DJ • alternative • live shows • videos

Girl Bar 652 N La Peer (at Santa Monica (at 'The Factory')) **877/447-5252** • popular • Fri only • women only • dancing/DJ • call hotline for events

La Femme 9041 Sunset Blvd (1 blk E of Doheny, at the Key Club) **818/750-9212** • mostly women • dancing/DJ

Cafes

Big Cup 7965 Beverly Blvd (at Fairfax) **323/653-5358** • 8am-3pm, clsd Mon

Club Cafe 8560 Santa Monica Blvd (at La Cienega, in 'Athletic Club') **310/659-6630** • 6am-8pm, 7am-8pm wknds • salads & sandwiches • $5-10

Eat-Well 8252 Santa Monica Blvd **323/656-1383** • 7am-3pm & 5:30pm-10pm, 8am-3pm Sat-Sun

Mani's Bakery 519 S Fairfax Ave **323/938-8800** • 6:30am-midnight, 7:30am-1am wknds • coffee & dessert bar • wheelchair access

Stonewall Gourmet Coffee Company 8717 Santa Monica Blvd (nr La Cienega) **310/659-8009** • 7am-midnight Sun-Wed, till 3am Th-Sat

WeHo Lounge 8861 Santa Monica Blvd (at San Vicente) **310/659-6180** • desserts & light lunch & dinner fare • also AIDS treatment center

Who's On Third Cafe 8369 W 3rd St (at Orlando) **323/651-2928** • 8am-6pm, till 3pm Sun

Restaurants

A Votre Sante 345 N La Brea (btwn Melrose &Beverly) **323/857-0412** • 10am-10pm • pastas, salads & wraps • plenty veggie & vegan • cheap • also 13016 San Vicente (at 26th) in Venice, 310/451-1813 • also 1025 Abbott Kinney in Brentwood, 310/314-1187

The Abbey 692 N Robertson (at Santa Monica) **310/289-8410** • 7am-3am • lesbians/gay men • beer/wine • patio • wheelchair access

African Restaurant Row Fairfax (btwn Olympic & Pico) • many Ethiopian, Nigerian & other African restaurants to choose from on this block

Alto Palato 755 N La Cienega Blvd (at Waring) **310/657-9271** • 6pm-11pm, lunch wknds • bargain pasta & comfortable chairs • full bar • $12-17

Baja Bud's 8575 Santa Monica Blvd (at La Cienega) **310/659-1911** • 7am-10pm, till 11pm Fri-Sat • healthy Mexican • patio

Benvenuto 8512 Santa Monica Blvd (at La Cienega) **310/659-8635** • lunch wkdys, dinner nightly • Italian • wheelchair access • $8-16

Bossa Nova 685 N Robertson Blvd (at Santa Monica) **310/657-5070** • 11am-11pm • Brazilian • patio • wheelchair access

Caffe Luna 7463 Melrose Ave (nr Vista) **323/655-9177** • 8am-3am, till 4am wknds • popular after-hours • country Italian • some veggie

Canter's Deli 419 N Fairfax (btwn Melrose & Beverly) **213/651-2030** • 24hrs • hip after-hours • Jewish/American • some veggie • wheelchair access

The Cobalt Cantina 616 N Robertson Blvd (at Melrose) **310/659-8691** • noon-11pm, 10am-10pm Sun, lunch & dinner Mon • lesbians/gay men • Cal-Mex • some veggie • full bar • patio • $10-15

Figs 7929 Santa Monica Blvd (at Fairfax) **323/654-0780** • dinner, Sun brunch • Californian • some veggie • full bar • $8-15

French Quarter Market Place 7985 Santa Monica Blvd (btwn Fairfax & Crescent Hts) **213/654-0898** • 7am-midnight, till 3am Fri-Sat • American/cont'l • some veggie

The Heights Cafe 1118 N Crescent Heights Blvd (at Santa Monica) **323/650-9688** • 9am-11pm, from 4pm Sun • lesbians/gay men • bistro • plenty veggie • beer/wine • patio

Hoy's Wok 8163 Santa Monica Blvd (at Crescent Hts) **323/656-9002** • noon-11pm, from 4pm Sun • Mandarin • plenty veggie • wheelchair access • $8-12

Il Pastaio 400 N Cannon Dr (at Wilshire), Beverly Hills **310/205-5444** • lunch & dinner • homemade pasta & great colorful risotto • $8-12

Il Piccolino Trattoria 350 N Robertson Blvd (btwn Melrose & Beverly) **310/659-2220** • 11am-11pm, Sun brunch, clsd Mon • patio

Itana Bahia 8711 Santa Monica Blvd **310/657-6306** • 6pm-11pm • great Brazilian food • live music Wed-Fri

Koo Koo Roo 8520 Santa Monica Blvd (at La Cienega Blvd) **310/657-3300** • 7am-11pm • lots of healthy chicken dishes • plenty veggie • beer/wine

L'Orangerie 903 N La Cienega Blvd (btwn Melrose & Santa Monica) **310/652-9770** • dinner, clsd Mon • haute French • patio • $28-38

La Masía 9077 Santa Monica Blvd (at Robertson) **310/273-7066** • clsd Mon-Tue • Spanish/cont'l • $14-24

Louise's Trattoria 7505 Melrose Ave **323/651-3880** • 11am-11pm, till midnight Fri-Sat • Italian • great foccacia bread • beer/wine

Lucques 8474 Melrose Ave (at La Cienega) **323/655-6277** • dinner • French • patio • full bar • $12-17

Luna Park 665 N Robertson (btwn Melrose & Santa Monica) **310/652-0611** • dinner, clsd Sun-Mon • progressive American • some veggie • cabaret • patio • wheelchair access • $10-15

Marco's Trattoria 8136 Santa Monica (at Crescent Hts) **323/650-2771** • 11am-10pm, from 3pm Sun

Marix Tex Mex 1108 N Flores (btwn La Cienega & Fairfax) **323/656-8800** • lunch & dinner, brunch wknds • lesbians/gay men • some veggie • great margaritas • $10-15

Mark's Restaurant 861 N La Cienega Blvd (at Santa Monica) **310/652-5252** • 6pm-10pm, till 11:30pm Fri-Sat, Sun brunch • full bar

North 8029 W Sunset (at Laurel Canyon, enter rear) **323/654-1313** • 6pm-2am • popular • full bar • 70s ski lodge decor

Sapora Cucina 8945 Santa Monica Blvd (at Robertson) **310/275-9518** • Italian • some veggie

Skewers 8939 Santa Monica Blvd (at Robertson) **310/271-0555** • 11am-2am • grill, salads, dips • beer/wine • under $10

Swing Cafe 8545 Santa Monica Blvd (W of La Cienega) **310/652-8838** • 8:30am-11pm, till 10pm Sun • eclectic & intimate • patio

Tacos Tacos 8948 Santa Monica Blvd (at N Robertson) **310/657-4832** • 11am-11pm, till 1am wknds • yummy • fresh • inexpensive Mexican • plenty veggie

Tango Grill 8807 Santa Monica Blvd (at San Vicente) **310/659-3663** • 11:30am-midnight • lesbians/gay men • Argentinian • some veggie • beer/wine • wheelchair access • $6-12

Tommy Tang's 7313 Melrose Ave (at Poinsettia) **323/937-5733** • noon-11pm • popular Tue nights w/'Club Glenda' • beer/wine

Trocadero 8280 Sunset Blvd (at Sweetzer) **213/656-7161** • 6pm-3am, clsd Sun-Mon • pastas & salads • full bar • patio • $6-14

Yukon Mining Co 7328 Santa Monica Blvd (at Fuller) **213/851-8833** • 24hrs • popular • champagne brunch wknds • beer/wine • $6-11

Bookstores

A Different Light 8853 Santa Monica Blvd (at San Vicente) **310/854-6601** • 10am-midnight • popular • lesbigay

Book Soup 8818 Sunset Blvd (at Larrabee) **310/659-3110** • 9am-midnight • lesbigay section

Retail Shops

Dorothy's Surrender 7985 Santa Monica Blvd #111 (at Laurel) **213/650-4111** • 10am-11:30pm • cards • magazines • gifts

Skin Graffiti Tattoo 868 Huntley Dr (at Santa Monica) **310/358-0349** • noon-7pm, till 4pm Sun, clsd Mon

Gyms & Health Clubs

Easton's Gym 8053 Beverly Blvd (at Crescent Hts) **323/651-3636** • gay-friendly

Erotica

Circus of Books 8230 Santa Monica Blvd (at La Jolla) **323/656-6533** • videos • erotica • toys

Drake's 8932 Santa Monica Blvd (at San Vicente) **310/289-8932** • gifts • toys • videos • also at 7566 Melrose Ave, 323/651-5600

Hollywood Hustler 8920 Sunset Blvd (at San Vicente) **310/860-9009** • chic erotic department store • also cafe

▲ **Pleasure Chest** 7733 Santa Monica Blvd (at Genesee) **323/650-1022** • 10am-midnight, till 1am wknds

Unicorn Bookstore 8940 Santa Monica (at Robertson) **310/652-6253** • wheelchair access

LA—Hollywood

Accommodations

Club Hotel by Doubletree Hollywood 2005 N Highland (at Franklin) **323/850-5811** • gay-friendly • swimming • exercise room • wheelchair access • $99-139

Hollywood Celebrity Hotel 1775 Orchid Ave (btwn Hollywood & Franklin) **213/850-6464, 800/222-7017** • gay-friendly • 1930s art deco hotel • kids/pets ok • non-smoking rms available • IGLTA • $55-115

Hollywood Metropolitan Hotel 5825 Sunset Blvd (btwn Bronson & Van Ness) **323/962-5800, 800/962-5800** • gay-friendly • kids ok • also restaurant • $79-145

Ramada Hotel Hollywood 1160 N Vermont Ave (at Santa Monica) **323/660-1788, 800/272-6232** • gay-friendly • $69-139

Bars

Blacklite 1159 N Western (at Santa Monica) **323/469-0211** • 6am-2am • lesbians/gay men • neighborhood bar • transgender-friendly

Faultline 4216 Melrose Ave (at Normandie) **323/660-0889** • 4pm-2am, till 4am Fri-Sat, clsd Mon • occasional women's events • patio • also Faultline Store, 323/660-2952

Spit 4216 Melrose Ave (at Vermont, at 'Faultine') **323/969-2530** • 9pm-3am 3rd Sat •gay/straight • dancing/DJ • eclectic mix of music & people

Nightclubs

Raw 1743 Cahuenga Blvd (at 'Crush Bar', btwn Hollywood Blvd & Franklin) **818/780-3249** • from 10pm Th • mostly women • dancing/DJ • theme nights

Tempo 5520 Santa Monica Blvd (at Western) **323/466-1094** • from 9pm, from 2pm Sun, till 4am wknds • mostly gay men • dancing/DJ • mostly Latino/a • live shows

Cafes

Bourgeois Pig 5931 Franklin Ave **323/962-6366** • 8am-2am, from 9am wknds

Lucy Florence 6541 Santa Monica Blvd (btwn Highland & Wilcox) **323/463-7585** • 11am-2am • spoken word nights & other events

Restaurants

360° Restaurant & Lounge 6290 Sunset Blvd (at Vine) **323/871-2995** • lunch & dinner, dinner only Sat • more gay Tue • amazing views • live jazz • wheelchair access • gay-owned/run

Hollywood Canteen 1006 N Seward St (at Santa Monica) **323/465-0961** • 11:30am-10pm, dinner only Sat, clsd Sun • popular • classic

La Poubelle 5907 Franklin Ave (at Bronson) **323/465-0807** • noon-2am, from 6pm Mon • French/Italian • some veggie • wheelchair access • $20-25

Musso & Frank Grill 6667 Hollywood Blvd **323/467-7788** • the grand-dame diner/steakhouse of Hollywood • great pancakes, potpie & Martinis!

Off Vine 6263 Leland Wy (at Vine) **323/962-1900** • lunch & dinner, Sun brunch • beer/wine

Prado 244 N Larchmont Blvd (at Beverly) **323/467-3871** • lunch & dinner, dinner only Sun • Caribbean • some veggie • wheelchair access • $20-30

Quality 8030 W 3rd St (at Laurel) **323/658-5959** • 8am-3pm • homestyle brkfst • some veggie • wheelchair access • $8-12

Rosco's House of Chicken & Waffles 1514 N Gower (at Sunset) **323/466-7453** • 9am-midnight

Retail Shops

Archaic Idiot/Mondo Video 1718 N Vermont (at Hollywood) **323/953-8896** • noon-10pm • vintage clothes • cult & lesbigay videos

Videoactive 2522 Hyperion Ave (at Griffith Park Blvd) **323/669-8544** • 10am-11pm, till midnight wknds • lesbigay section • adult videos

Gyms & Health Clubs

Gold's Gym 1016 N Cole Ave (nr Santa Monica & Vine) **323/462-7012**

Erotica

▲ **Le Sex Shoppe** 6315-1/2 Hollywood Blvd (at Vine) **323/464-9435** • 24hrs

LA—West LA & Santa Monica

Accommodations

The Georgian Hotel 1415 Ocean Ave (btwn Santa Monica & Broadway), Santa Monica **310/395-9945, 800/538-8147** • gay-friendly • food served • wheelchair access • $185-340

Rose Avenue Beach House 55 Rose Ave (at Pacific), Venice **310/396-2803** • gay-friendly • Victorian beach house • 1 blk from ocean & boardwalk • $50-90

Westwood Marquis Hotel & Gardens 930 Hilgard Ave (at Le Conte) **310/208-8765, 800/421-2317** • gay-friendly • IGLTA • $219-379

Bars

Annex 835 S La Brea (at Arbor Vitae), Inglewood **310/671-7323** • 3pm-2am • mostly men • neighborhood bar

Dolphin 1995 Artesia Blvd (at Aviation Blvd), Redondo Beach **310/318-3339** • noon-2am • lesbians/gay men • neighborhood bar • karaoke • patio • wheelchair access

El Capitan 13825 S Hawthorne Blvd (at 138th), Hawthorne **310/675-3436** • 4pm-2am, from noon Fri-Sun • lesbians/gay men • neighborhood bar • beer/wine • more women Tue

Maverick's 2692 S La Cienega (at Washington Blvd) **310/837-7443** • 11am-2am • mostly gay men • neighborhood bar • food served • karaoke • live shows • wheelchair access

Nightclubs

Hot Box 5515 Wilshire Blvd (at 'El Rey Theatre') **310/394-6541** • Fri only from 10pm • mostly women • dancing/DJ

The Pink 2810 Main St (2 blks S of Ocean) **310/392-1077** • from 10:30pm Wed-Sun • gay-friendly • dancing/DJ • alternative • theme nights (from techno to bossa nova to RB/hip hop) • cover charge

Cafes

Anastasia's Asylum 1028 Wilshire Blvd (at 9th St), Santa Monica **310/394-7113** • 8am-2am, till 1am Sun • plenty veggie • live music evenings

Van Go's Ear 796 Main St (at Brooks), Venice **310/396-1987** • 24hrs • $2-9

Restaurants

12 Washington 12 Washington Blvd (at Pacific), Venice **310/822-5566** • dinner from 6pm • cont'l • $10-30

Baja Cantina 311 Washington Blvd (at Sanborn), Venice **310/821–2252** • lunch & dinner wkdys, also brkfst wknds

Cheesecake Factory 4142 Via Marina (at Washington), Venice **310/306–3344** • 11am-11:30pm • full menu • $5-20

Drago 2628 Wilshire Blvd (btwn 26th & Princeton), Santa Monica **310/828–1585** • lunch & dinner • Sicilian Italian

Golden Bull 170 W Channel Rd (at Pacific Coast Hwy), Santa Monica **310/230–0402** • dinner only, Sun brunch • full bar

Joe's 1023 Abbot Kinney Blvd, Venice **310/399–5811** • clsd Mon • French/Californian

The Local Yolk 3414 Highlands Ave (at Rosecranz), Manhattan Beach **310/546–4407** • 6:30am-2:30pm

Siamese Princess 8048 W 3rd St **323/653–2643** • 5:30pm-11pm, clsd Mon & Th, lunch wkdys • Thai • beer/wine • $6-10

Wolfgang Puck Cafe 1323 Montana Ave (at 14th St), Santa Monica **310/393–0290** • colorful entrees à la Puck (fast food versions) • $10-13

Erotica

The Love Boutique 2924 Wilshire Blvd (W of Bundy), Santa Monica **310/453–3459** • toys

LA—Silverlake

Accommodations

The Sanborn House 1005 Sanborn Ave (nr Sunset) **323/666–3947, 800/663–7262** • gay/straight • private unit w/kitchen • gay-owned/run • $49-59

Nightclubs

Dragstrip 66 2500 Riverside Dr (at Fletcher, in 'Rudolpho's') **323/969–2596** • popular • queer dance club • call for events

Meow Mix West 4519 Santa Monica Blvd (at Virgil, in 'The Garage') **323/662–6802** • women's nightclub Fri • call for events

Rudolpho's 2500 Riverside Dr (at Fletcher) **323/669–1226** • 8pm-2am • lesbians/gay men • salsa music & dancing lessons • patio

Cafes

The Coffee Table 2930 Rowena Ave **323/644–8111** • 7am-10pm • patio • fab mosaic magic

Tsunami 4019 Sunset Blvd (btwn Sanborn & Santa Monica) **323/661–7771** • 10:30am-10pm • monthly artist parties

Restaurants

Casita Del Campo 1920 Hyperion Ave **323/662–4255** • 11am-10pm • popular • Mexican • patio • also 'The Plush Life' cabaret Sat • call 323/969–2596 for details

Cha Cha Cha 656 N Virgil (at Melrose) **323/664–7723** • 8am-10pm, till 11pm Fri-Sat • Caribbean • plenty veggie

The Cobalt Cantina 4326 Sunset Blvd (at Fountain) **323/953–9991** • 11am-11pm • lesbians/gay men • Cal-Mex • some veggie • full bar • patio • wheelchair access • $10-15

The Crest Restaurant 3725 Sunset Blvd (at Lucille) **323/660–3645** • 6am-11pm • diner/Greek • $5-10

Da Giannino 2630 Hyperion Ave (at Griffith Park Blvd) **323/664–7979** • lunch Mon-Fri, dinner nightly • patio

El Conquistador 3701 Sunset Blvd (at Lucille) **323/666–5136** • lunch & dinner • Mexican • patio • $5-10

Vida 1930 Hillhurst Ave (at Franklin, in Los Feliz) **323/660–4446** • hip with Asian accent • $12-17

Zen Restaurant 2609 Hyperion Ave (at Griffith Park) **323/665–2929, 323/665–2930** • 11:30am-2am • Japanese • some veggie • $9-12

Retail Shops

Girl Gear 4001 1/2 Sunset Blvd (at Sanborn) **323/644–1086** • noon-6pm, from 2pm wknds, clsd Mon

Gyms & Health Clubs

Body Builders 2516 Hyperion Ave (at Griffith Park Blvd) **323/668–0802** • gay-friendly

Erotica

Circus of Books 4001 Sunset Blvd (at Sanborn) **323/666–1304** • 24hrs Fri-Sat

LA—Midtown

Bars

The Red Head (Red'z) 2218 E 1st St (btwn Soto & Chicago, Boyle Hts) **323/263–2995** • 2pm-midnight, till 2am wknds • mostly women • neighborhood bar • mostly Latina

Nightclubs

Jewel's Catch One Disco 4067 W Pico Blvd (at Crenshaw) **323/734–8849** • noon-2am, till 5am Fri-Sat • lesbians/gay men • dancing/DJ • alternative • multi-racial • wheelchair access

Restaurants

Atlas 3760 Wilshire Blvd (at Western) **213/380-8400** • lunch & dinner, clsd Sun • global cuisine • some veggie • full bar • live shows • $8-19

Cassell's 3266 W 6th St (at Vermont) **323/480-8668** • 10:30am-4pm, clsd Sun • great burgers

Du-Par's 6333 W 3rd St (at the Farmer's Market) **323/933-8446** • 6am-1am • plush diner schmoozing

LA—Valley

includes San Fernando & San Gabriel Valleys

Bars

Apache Territory 11608 Ventura Blvd (at Laurel Canyon), Studio City **818/506-0404** • 3pm-2am, from noon wknds, till 4am Fri-Sat • mostly gay men • dancing/DJ • live shows

Bananas 7026 Reseda Blvd (at Hart), Reseda **818/996-2976** • 3pm-2am • popular • mostly gay men • dancing/DJ • patio • wheelchair access

Escapades 10437 Burbank Blvd (at Cahuenga), North Hollywood **818/508-7008** • 1pm-2am • popular • lesbians/gay men • neighborhood bar • live shows • wheelchair access

Gold 9 13625 Moorpark St (at Woodman), Sherman Oaks **818/986-0285** • 11am-2am • mostly gay men • neighborhood bar

Mag Lounge 5248 N Van Nuys Blvd (at Magnolia), Van Nuys **818/981-6693** • 1pm-2am • piano bar Wed-Sat • popular • mostly gay men

Oasis 11916 Ventura Blvd (at Laurel Canyon), Studio City **818/980-4811** • 3pm-2am • lesbians/gay men • neighborhood bar • piano bar • patio

Oxwood Inn 13713 Oxnard (at Woodman), Van Nuys **818/997-9666 (PAY PHONE)** • 3pm-2am, from noon Fri, 2pm-2am Sat-Sun • mostly women • neighborhood bar • one of the oldest lesbian bars in the country • women-owned/run

Plush Pony 5261 Alhambra Ave (btwn Valley & Fremont) **323/224-9488** • 4pm-2am, clsd Mon • lesbians/gay men • neighborhood bar • DJ Fri-Sat • mostly Latina • live shows

Queen Mary 12449 Ventura Blvd (at Whitsett), Studio City **818/506-5619** • 5pm-2am, clsd Mon-Tue • popular • gay-friendly • dancing/DJ • karaoke • shows wknds

Rawhide & Shooterz 10937 Burbank Blvd (at Vineland), North Hollywood **818/760-9798** • 6:30pm-2am, from 2pm wknds • popular • mostly gay men • dancing/DJ • country/western

Rumors 10622 Magnolia Blvd (at Cahuenga) **818/506-9651** • 6pm-2am, from 3pm Fri • mostly women • neighborhood bar • karaoke • women-owned/run

Silver Rail 11518 Burbank Blvd (btwn Colfax & Lankershim) **818/980-8310** • 4pm-2am, from noon wknds • lesbians/gay men • neighborhood bar

Sugar Shack 4101 Arden Dr (at Valley Blvd), El Monte **626/448-6579** • 3pm-2am • lesbians/gay men • neighborhood bar • DJ Wed & Fri • live shows • wheelchair access

Cafes

Boom Boom Room Coffeehouse 11651 Riverside Dr (E of Colfax), North Hollywood **818/753-9966** • 7am-midnight

Coffee Junction 19221 Ventura Blvd, Tarzana **818/342-3405** • 7am-7pm, til 11pm Fri-Sat, 9am-5pm Sun • live music Th-Sat • women-owned/run

Restaurants

Du-Par's 12036 Ventura Blvd, Studio City **818/766-4437** • 6am-1am • plush diner schmoozing

Du-Par's 75 W Thousand Oaks Blvd, Thousand Oaks **805/373-8785** • 6am-1am • plush diner schmoozing

Venture Inn 11938 Ventura Blvd (at Laurel Canyon), Studio City **818/769-5400** • lunch & dinner, champagne brunch Sun • popular • lesbians/gay men • full bar • $10-15

Gyms & Health Clubs

Gold's Gym 6233 N Laurel Canyon Blvd (at Oxnard), North Hollywood **818/506-4600**

Erotica

▲ **Le Sex Shoppe** 12323 Ventura Blvd (at Laurel Canyon), Studio City **818/760-9352** • 24hrs

▲ **Le Sex Shoppe** 21625 Sherman Way (at Nelson), Canoga Park **818/992-9801** • 24hrs

▲ **Le Sex Shoppe** 4539 Van Nuys Blvd (at Ventura), Sherman Oaks **818/501-9609** • 24hrs

▲ **Le Sex Shoppe** 4877 Lankershim Blvd (at Houston), North Hollywood **818/760-9529** • 24hrs

Stan's Video 7505 Foothill Blvd (at Fernglen Blvd), Tujunga **818/352-8735**

Manhattan Beach

see also LA—West LA & Santa Monica

ACCOMMODATIONS

▲ **Seaview Inn at the Beach** 3400 Highland Ave **310/545-1504** • gay-friendly • swimming • non-smoking rms available • kids ok • courtyard • $90-175

Marin County

includes Corte Madera, Mill Valley, San Rafael, Sausalito, Tiburon

INFO LINES & SERVICES

Spectrum Center for LGBT Concerns 1000 Sir Francis Drake Blvd Ste 10, San Anselmo **415/457-1115** • referrals noon-9pm Mon-Th • also variety of social/support groups • wheelchair access

ACCOMMODATIONS

Design Hotels 323 Pine St #B, Sausalito **415/332-4885, 800/337-4685** • reservation service • IGLTA

Marin Suites Hotel 45 Tamal Vista Blvd (at Lucky Dr), Corte Madera **415/924-3608** • gay-friendly • variety of apt-style rooms • IGLTA • $85-199

Tiburon Lodge 1651 Tiburon Blvd, Tiburon **415/435-3133** • gay-friendly • hotel • swimming • $154-289

BARS

Lunacee 815 W Francisco Blvd, San Rafael **415/459-6079** • 4pm-midnight, till 2am Fri-Sat • lesbians/gay men • dancing/DJ • wheelchair access

PUBLICATIONS

The Slant 415/927-3670 • monthly, lesbigay

SPIRITUAL GROUPS

Unitarian Universalist Congregation of Marin 240 Channing Wy, San Rafael **415/479-4131** • call for directions

Marina del Rey

ACCOMMODATIONS

The Mansion Inn 327 Washington Blvd, Venice **310/821-2557, 800/828-0688** • gay-friendly • European-style inn • kids ok • wheelchair access • $69-125

Mendocino

Accommodations

Agate Cove Inn 11201 N Lansing **707/937–0551, 800/527–3111** • gay-friendly • full brkfst • fireplaces • smokefree • $99-250

Bellflower 707/937–0783 • lesbians only • secluded cabin w/ kitchen • near outdoor recreation • hot tub • fireplaces • smokefree • kids/pets ok • 2-night minimum • $65

Blair House & Cottage 45118 Little Lake St (at Ford St) **707/937–1800** • gay-friendly • smokefree • $80-165

Glendeven Inn 8221 N Hwy 1, Little River **707/937–0083** • gay-friendly • charming farmhouse on the coast • full brkfst • smokefree • kids ok • $98-179

Inn at Schoolhouse Creek 7051 N Hwy 1, Little River **707/937–5525, 800/731–5525** • gay/straight • B&B w/cottages • hot tub • $80-160

MacCallum House Inn 45020 Albion St (at Lansing) **707/937–0289, 800/609–0492** • gay/straight • smokefree • wheelchair access • kids ok • $100-190

McElroy's Inn 998 Main St **707/937–1734, 707/937–3105** • gay-friendly • pleasant rms & suites • located in the village • smokefree • kids ok • $70-110

Mendocino Coastal Reservations 800/262–7801 • 9am-6pm • gay-friendly • call for available rentals

Mendocino Hotel 45080 Main St **800/548–0513** • gay-friendly • Victorian w/garden cottages • $85-275

Sallie & Eileen's Place 707/937–2028 • women only • cabins • hot tub • kitchens • fireplaces • kids/pets ok • 2 night minimum • $73-90 • $15/ additional person

Seagull Inn 44594 Albion St **707/937–5204** • gay-friendly • 9 units in the heart of historic Mendocino • smokefree • kids ok • wheelchair access • $75-145

Stanford Inn by the Sea Coast Hwy 1 & Comptche-Ukiah Rd **707/937–5615, 800/331–8884** • gay-friendly • full brkfst • hot tub • swimming • kitchens • fireplaces • smokefree • kids/pets ok • wheelchair access • $215-275

Wildflower Ridge 925/735–2079 • women only • secluded cabin in Medocino • kids ok (no male children over 8) • pets ok ($5/night for dogs) • women-owned/run • $55

Cafes

Cafe Beaujolais 961 Ukiah **707/937–5614** • dinner from 5:45pm • California country food • some veggie • wheelchair access • $20-30

Bookstores

The Book Loft 45050 Main **707/937–0890** • 10am-6pm, till 9:30pm Fri-Sat • wheelchair access

Menlo Park

see Palo Alto

Mill Valley

see Marin County

Modesto

see also Stockton

Bars

Brave Bull 701 S 9th **209/529–6712** • 7pm-2am, from 4pm Sun • mostly men • leather

Nightclubs

The Mustang Club 413 N 7th St **209/577–9694** • 4pm-2am, from 2pm Fri-Sun • open 30+ years! • lesbians/gay men • dancing/DJ • live shows • women-owned/run

Cafes

Espresso Caffe 3025 McHenry Ave (at Rumble) **209/571–3337** • 7am-11pm, till midnight Fri-Sat • $4-7

Erotica

Liberty Adult Book Store 1030 Kansas Ave **209/524–7603** • 24hrs

Monterey

Info Lines & Services

AA Gay/Lesbian 831/373–3713 (AA#)

Accommodations

Gosby House Inn 643 Lighthouse Ave (at 18th), Pacific Grove **831/375–1287, 800/527–8828** • gay-friendly • full brkfst • smokefree • kids ok • wheelchair access • $90-160

Monterey Fireside Lodge 1131 10th St **831/373–4172, 800/722–2624** • gay-friendly • hot tub • fireplaces • non-smoking rms available • kids ok • $79-250

Bars

Eddie's 2200 N Fremont (at De La Vina) **831/375–6116** • lesbians/gay men • women's night Sat • dancing/DJ • neighborhood bar

Lighthouse Bar & Grill 281 Lighthouse Ave (at Dickman), New Monterey **831/373-4488** • 5pm-2am, from 11:30am Fri, from 2pm wknds • lesbians/gay men

Restaurants

Cafe Abrego 565 Abrego St **831/375-6100** • lunch & dinner, lunch only Mon, Sun brunch • fine dining • some veggie • patio • full bar • wheelchair access • $10-22

Fisherman's Grotto 39 Fisherman's Wharf #1 **831/375-4604** • 11am-9pm • $20-40

Tarpy's Roadhouse 2999 Hwy 68 (at Canyon Dr) **831/647-1444** • lunch & dinner

Spiritual Groups

Lavender Road MCC Mariposa Hall, 801 Lighthouse Ave **831/459-8442** • 10am Sun • wheelchair access

Mountain View

Bars

Daybreak 1711 W El Camino Real (at El Monte) **650/940-9778** • 3pm-2am, from 4pm wknds • lesbians/gay men • dancing/DJ • karaoke Th & Sun • wheelchair access

Napa Valley

Accommodations

Beazley House B&B Inn 1910 First St, Napa **707/257-1649, 800/559-1649** • gay-friendly

Bed & Breakfast Inns of Napa Valley Napa **707/944-4444** • reservation service

Chateau de Vie 3250 Hwy 128, Calistoga **707/942-6446** • gay/straight • gay-owned/run • $150-225

Gaige House Inn 13540 Arnold Dr, Glen Ellen **707/935-0237, 800/935-0237** • gay-friendly • swimming • in the Wine Country

The Ink House B&B 1575 St Helena Hwy, St Helena **707/963-3890** • gay-friendly • 1884 Italianate Victorian among the vineyards • full brkfst • smokefree • kids ok • $99-195

▲ **Tara Guest House** 4009 Spring Mt Rd, St Helena **707/967-9347** • lesbians/gay men • 1-bdrm cabin • kitchen • wood stove • lesbian-owned/run

White Sulphur Springs Resort & Spa 3100 White Sulphur Springs Rd, St Helena **707/963-8588, 800/593-8873 (in CA & NV only)** • gay-friendly • secluded Napa Valley retreat • swimming • natural sulphur pool • $85-185

Restaurants

Mustard's Grill 7399 Hwy 29, St Helena **707/944-2424** • lunch & dinner

Travigne 1050 Charter Oak Ave, St Helena **707/963-4444** • 11:30am-10pm • Northern Italian • $15

Nice

Accommodations

Gingerbread Cottages B&B 4057 E Hwy 20 **707/274-0200** • gay-straight • lakefront w/private beach • swimming • $125-250

Oakland

see East Bay

Oceanside

Bars

Capri Lounge 207 N Tremont (at Mission) **760/722-7284** • 10am-2am • mostly gay men • neighborhood bar • wheelchair access

Restaurants

Greystokes 1903 S Coast Hwy (btwn Kelly & Vista Wy) **760/757-2955** • 9am-2am • lesbians/gay men • live shows • $8-14

Orange County

see also Anaheim, Costa Mesa, Garden Grove, Huntington Beach, Laguna Beach, Newport Beach

Oxnard

Erotica

▲ **Le Sex Shoppe** 2320 N Vineyard (at St Mary's Dr) **805/981-4611** • 24hrs

Palm Springs

Info Lines & Services

AA Gay/Lesbian 760/324-4880 (AA#) • call for mtg schedule

SCWU Desert Women 800/798-7298 • social/support group

Accommodations

▲ **Bee Charmer Inn** 1600 E Palm Canyon Dr (btwn Calle Marcus & Sunrise) **760/778-5883, 888/321-5699** • women only • swimming • smokefree • lesbian-owned/run • IGLTA • $95-125

▲ **Casitas Laquita** 450 E Palm Canyon Dr (at Sunrise) **760/416-9999, 877/203-3410** • women only • studios & suites • swimming • pets welcome • $95-192

Desert Palms Inn 67-580 E Palm Canyon Dr (at Gene Autry Tr), Cathedral City **760/324-3000, 800/801-8696** • mostly gay men • hot tub • swimming • huge courtyard • also restaurant • some veggie • full bar • wheelchair access • IGLTA • gay-owned/run

Desert Shadows 1533 Chaparral Rd (at Indian Canyon) **760/325-6410, 800/292-9298** • gay-friendly • naturist hotel • hot tub • swimming • nudity • kids ok • also restaurant • $100-200

Estrella Inn & Villas 415 S Belardo Rd (at Ramon) **760/320-4117, 800/237-3687** • gay-friendly • swimming • $115-350

Flamingo Resort Hotel & Spa 67221 Pierson Blvd (at Foxdale), Desert Hot Springs **760/251-1455, 800/438-4379** • gay/straight • swimming • jacuzzi • $59-99

Ingleside Inn 200 W Ramon Rd (at Palm Canyon Dr) **760/325-0046** • gay-friendly • hot tub • swimming • also restaurant • French con'tl • wheelchair access • $95-385

Mira Loma Hotel 1420 N Indian Canyon Dr (at Vista Chino) **760/320-1178** • gay/straight • swimming • kids ok • $79-129

Mountain View Villas 305/294-1525 • vacation rental • 3-day min • $99-169

Priscilla's 528 S Camino Real (at Ramon) **760/416-0168, 888/289-9555** • gay/straight • 1 & 2-bdrm apartments • swimming • $125-175/nt, $700-900/wk

Vagabond Inn 1699 S Palm Canyon (at E Palm Canyon) **760/325-7211** • gay/straight • IGLTA • gay-owned/run

Villa Mykonos 67-590 Jones Rd (at Cree), Cathedral City **760/321-2898** • lesbians/gay men • swimming • IGLTA • $150-250

The Villa Resort 67-670 Carey Rd (at Cree), Cathedral City **760/328-7211, 800/845-5265** • mostly gay men • individual bungalows • hot tub • swimming • sauna • massage • kitchens • IGLTA • $49-140

Palm Springs

Where the Girls Are: Socializing with friends at private parties - you can meet them by getting in touch with a women's social organization like the SCWU Desert Women. Vacationers will be staying on E. Palm Canyon near Sunrise Way. Women do hang out at the boys' bars too. Try the bar at The Desert Palms Inn, or just about anywhere on Perez Rd.

Lesbigay Pride: November. 760/322-8769.

Annual Events: Spring - Nabisco Dinah Shore Golf Tournament 310/281-7358 & 888/443-4624, one of the biggest gatherings of lesbians on the continent.
White Party, popular circuit party/fundraiser.

City Info: Palm Springs Visitors Bureau 760/778-8418, web: www.palm-springs.org.
Desert Gay Tourism Guild 888/200-4469.

Attractions: Palm Springs Aerial Tramway to the top of Mt. San Jacinto, on Tramway Rd.

Best View: Top of Mt. San Jacinto. Driving through the surrounding desert, you can see great views of the mountains. Be careful in the summer-always carry water in your vehicle, and be sure to check all fluids in your car before you leave and frequently during your trip.

Weather: Palm Springs is sunny and warm in the winter, with temperatures in the 70°s. Summers are scorching (100°+).

Transit: Airport Taxi 760/321-4470.
Rainbow Cab 760/327-5702.
Desert Valley Shuttle 760/251-4200 or 800/413-3999.
Sun Line Transit Agency 760/343-3451.

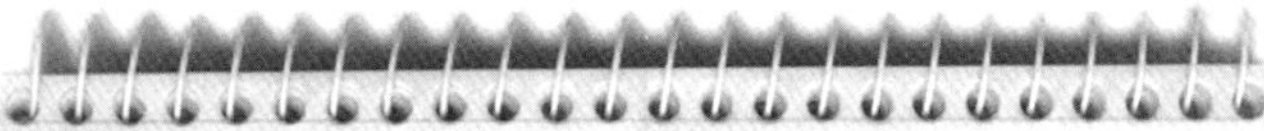

Palm Springs

Each and every spring, since 1972, the LPGA has converged upon the city of Palm Springs to present the premier event of its tournament schedule. Many women plan their vacations around the **Nabisco Dinah Shore,** and calendars are blocked out as soon as the tournament dates for the following year are released. Visitors pour into the valley to admire the beauty of springtime and to engage in the myriad of events that occur between March and May.

But did you know Palm Springs is open for business during the other nine months of the year as well? This has been a well-kept secret, but we are willing to divulge this information to expose the different faces and personalities of a truly year-round resort destination for women.

Year-round businesses that welcome women are abundant. All you have to do is stroll along Arenas Road to find food, merchandise, and entertainment. Friendly faces welcome you at the door of **Streetbar** and **Village Pride Coffee House,** and you can pick up sex supplies and pride items at **Gay Mart.** For a little danger and an amazing view, catch a ride on the Aerial Tram that goes from the desert floor to the top of Mount San Jacinto. When you come back to earth, it's time to lay back and treat yourself to some sun and outdoor fun.

Of course, you are going to need a place to rest, rejuvenate, and recharge for the next day's activities. The **Bee Charmer Inn** and **Casitas Laquita,** the two women-only establishments, provide travelers with comfortable and friendly accommodations. As you bask in the sun, soak up the warm desert air, and drift into a peaceful state of tranquility, you'll ask yourself why you didn't visit paradise sooner.

Bars

Backstreet Pub 72–695 Hwy 111 #A–7 (at El Paseo), Palm Desert **760/341–7966** • 2pm-2am • lesbians/gay men • neighborhood bar • wheelchair access • women-owned/run

Bamboo Bar & Restaurant 2743 N Indian Canyon (at Racquet Club) **760/325–1281** • from 11am • lesbians/gay men • also piano bar

Ground Zero 36–737 Cathedral Canyon Dr (at Commercial), Cathedral City **760/321–0031** • 2pm-2am • lesbians/gay men • dancing/DJ • country/western • line dance lessons Wed-Th • karaoke Mon & Fri

Hunter's 302 E Arenas Rd (at Calle Encilia) **760/323–0700** • 10am-2am • mostly gay men • dancing/DJ • videos

Streetbar 224 E Arenas Rd (at Indian) **760/320–1266** • 10am-2am • popular • lesbians/gay men • neighborhood bar • live shows • wheelchair access

Sweetwater Saloon 2420 N Palm Canyon (at Racquet Club Dr) **760/320–8878** • 11am-2am • lesbians/gay men • neighborhood bar

Tramps 440 El Cielo Rd **760/325–7072** • 7am-midnight • bar & grill (till 9pm)

Nightclubs

Amnesia 68–449 Perez Rd (at Palm Canyon), Cathedral City **760/770–6464** • 2pm-2am • lesbians/gay men • dancing/DJ • videos • also piano bar

Cafes

Village Pride Coffee House 214 E Arenas Rd (at Indian Canyon) **760/323–9120** • 8am-midnight • food served • special events

Restaurants

Bangkok 5 69–930 Hwy 111 (at Country Club Dr), Rancho Mirage **760/770–9508** • lunch & dinner • seasonal • Thai • $8-15

Billy Reed's 1800 N Palm Canyon Rd (at Vista Chino) **760/325–1946** • some veggie • full bar • also bakery • $7-13

El Gallito Mexican Restaurant 68820 Grove St (at Palm Canyon), Cathedral City **760/328–7794** • beer/wine • $3-8

Las Casuelas 368 N Palm Canyon Dr (btwn Amado & Alejo) **760/325–3213** • 10am-9:30pm • Mexican • some veggie

Maria's Italian Cuisine 67–778 Hwy 111 (at Perez), Cathedral City **760/328–4378** • 5:30pm-9:30pm dinner only, clsd Mon • plenty veggie • beer/wine • $8-15

Rainbow Cactus Cafe 212 S Indian Canyon (at Arenas) **760/325–3868** • lunch & dinner, Sun brunch only • Mexican • full bar

Red Pepper & Red Tomato 68–784 E Palm Canyon (at Hwy 111), Cathedral City **760/328–7518, 760/328–6858** • 5pm-10pm • pizza & pasta • plenty veggie • beer/wine • wheelchair access • $10-15

Robí 78–085 Avenida La Fonda (at Washington), La Quinta **760/564–0544** • dinner only, clsd Mon (seasonal April-Oct) • prix fixe • cont'l • some veggie • wheelchair access • $48

Rose Tattoo 72185 Painters Path (at 111), Palm Desert **760/341–1323** • 5pm-10pm • also piano bar

Shame on the Moon 69–950 Frank Sinatra Dr (at Hwy 111), Rancho Mirage **760/324–5515** • 5:30pm-10:30pm, clsd Mon • cont'l • plenty veggie • full bar • patio • wheelchair access • $10-20

Simba's 190 N Sunrise **760/778–7630** • lunch & dinner, clsd Mon-Tue • ribs

Triangles 68–805 Hwy 111, Cathedral City **760/321–9555** • 5:30pm-10pm, till midnight Fri-Sat, clsd Mon

Venezia Ristorante 70–065 Hwy 111, Rancho Mirage **760/328–5650** • clsd Mon • seasonal • Italian • some veggie

The Wilde Goose 67–938 Hwy 111 (at Perez), Cathedral City **760/328–5775** • from 5pm • cont'l/wild game • plenty veggie • full bar • live shows • $20-40

Entertainment & Recreation

Ruddy's 1930s General Store Museum 221 S Palm Canyon Dr **760/327–2156** • 10am-4pm Th-Sun • 'the most you can spend is 50¢'

Bookstores

Bloomsbury Books 555 S Sunrise Wy (at Ramon) **760/325–3862** • 10am-6pm, clsd Sun • lesbigay (secondhand) • wheelchair access • gay-owned/run

Retail Shops

Blink 319 E Arenas Rd **760/323–1667** • noon-10pm, clsd Tue • books, gifts & clothing for gay men & dykefags

Publications

The Bottom Line 760/323–0552 • lesbigay newsmagazine

Desert Daily Guide 760/320–3237

Spiritual Groups

Unity Church of Palm Springs 815 S Camino Real (at Riverside S) **760/325-7377** • 11am Sun, 7:30pm Tue • also bookstore & classes

Gyms & Health Clubs

Gold's Gym 40-70 Airport Center Dr (at Ramon) **760/322-4653** • gay-friendly

The Guest House 246 N Palm Canyon Dr (at Amado) **760/320-3366** • clsd Mon-Tue • reservations only • tropical day spa • also side-by-side couples treatment in candlelit room

Erotica

Black Moon Leather 68-449 Perez Rd #7 (at Cathedral Canyon), Cathedral City **760/770-2925, 800/945-3284** • 3pm-10pm, till 2am wknds • also 67-625 Hwy. 111 location (inside 'Wolfs' bar), 9pm-midnight Wed-Sun

Gay Mart 305 E Arenas Rd (at Indian Canyon) **760/320-0606**

Palo Alto

Info Lines & Services

Peninsula Women's Group 605 Cambridge Ave (at El Camino Rd, in 'Lavender Dragon'), Menlo Park **650/323-4778** • 7:30pm Wed

Bookstores

Books Inc 157 Stanford Shopping Center **650/321-0600** • 9:30am-9pm, 10am-8pm Sat, till 6pm Sun • general • lesbigay section

▲ **Lavender Dragon/ Two Sisters Bookshop** 605 Cambridge Ave (at El Camino Rd), Menlo Park **650/323-4778** • 11am-9pm, 10am-5pm Sat, from noon Sun, clsd Mon • women's • wheelchair access • women-owned/run

Stacey's Bookstore 219 University Ave (at Emerson) **650/326-0681** • 9am-9pm, till 10pm Fri-Sat, 11am-6pm Sun • general • lesbigay section

Pasadena

Bars

Boulevard 3199 E Foothill Blvd (at Sierra Madre Villa) **626/356-9304** • 3pm-2am • mostly gay men • neighborhood bar • piano bar Sun

Encounters 203 N Sierra Madre Blvd (at Foothill) **626/792-3735** • 4pm-2am, 3pm-2am wknds • lesbians/gay men • neighborhood bar • dancing/DJ • patio

Nardi's 162 N Sierra Madre Blvd (at Foothill) **626/449-3152** • 1pm-2am • lesbians/gay men • neighborhood bar • dancing/DJ • shows • wheelchair access

Restaurants

Cafe Sol 1453 N Lake Ave (at Washington) **626/797-9903** • lunch & dinner, Sun brunch, clsd Mon-Tue • California cuisine

Twin Palms 101 W Green St (at De Lacey Ave) **626/577-2567** • chic decor • reasonable prices • huge menu w/unusual combinations • $7-15

Spiritual Groups

First Congregational United Church of Christ 464 E Walnut (at Las Robles) **626/795-0696** • 10am Sun

Pescadero

Accommodations

Estancia del Mar **650/879-1500** • gay friendly • cottage rentals w/ocean views • pets welcome • $85-1475

Petaluma

Restaurants

Twisted Vine on Kentucky (in Lanmart Bldg) **707/766-8162** • lunch & dinner, clsd Sun-Mon • also wine store

Bookstores

Copperfields 140 Kentucky St (btwn Western & Washington, downtown) **707/762-0563** • 9am-9pm, till 10pm Fri-Sat, till 6pm Sun • new & used books • also great little cafe

Pismo Beach

Accommodations

The Palomar Inn 1601 Shell Beach Rd, Shell Beach **805/773-4204** • lesbians/gay men • close to nude beach • gay-owned/run • $32-63

Placerville

Accommodations

Rancho Cicada Retreat **209/245-4841** • mostly gay men • secluded riverside retreat in the Sierra foothills w/two-person tents & cabin • swimming • nudity • gay-owned/run • $100-200 (lower during wk)

Pleasant Hill

Erotica

Pleasant Hill Books 2298 Monument Blvd (at Buskirk) **925/676-2962**

Pomona

Info Lines & Services

Gay/Lesbian Community Center Hotline **909/882-4488** • 6:30pm-10pm

Bars

Alibi East 225 San Antonio Ave (at 2nd) **909/623-9422** • 10am-2am, till 4am Fri-Sat • mostly gay men • dancing/DJ • strip shows Sat

Mary's 1047 E 2nd St (at Pico) **909/622-1971** • 5pm-2am, 2pm-2am Fri-Sun • lesbians/gay men • dancing/DJ • also restaurant • wheelchair access

Nightclubs

Robbie's 390 E 2nd St (at College Plaza) **909/620-4371** • 6pm-2am Th, Sat-Sun, 8pm-2am Fri, clsd Mon-Wed • lesbians/gay men • ladies' night Th • dancing/DJ • live shows • call for events

Cafes

Café Con Libros 252-C South Main St **909/623-4492**

Erotica

Mustang Books 961 N Central, Upland **909/981-0227**

Redding

Nightclubs

Club 501 1244 California St (at Center & Division, enter rear) **530/243-7869** • 6pm-2am, from 4pm Sun • lesbians/gay men • dancing/DJ • food served

Redondo Beach

Info Lines & Services

South Bay Lesbian, Gay & Bi Community Organization 2009 Artesia Blvd #A **310/379-2850** • support/education for Manhattan, Hermosa & Redondo Beaches, Torrance, Palos Verdes, El Segundo

Accommodations

Palos Verdes Inn 1700 S Pacific Coast Hwy **310/316-4211** • gay-friendly • IGLTA • $86-96

Redwood City

Bars

Shouts 2034 Broadway (at Main St) **650/369-9651** • 3pm-2am, from noon wknds • lesbians/gay men • neighborhood bar • wheelchair access

Riverside

see also San Bernardino

Nightclubs

Menagerie 3581 University Ave (at Orange) **909/788-8000** • 4pm-2am • mostly gay men • dancing/DJ • wheelchair access • women-owned/run

VIP Club 3673 Merrill Ave (at Magnolia) **909/784-2370** • 4pm-2am • lesbians/gay men • dancing/DJ • food served • wheelchair access

Spiritual Groups

St Bride's 3645 Locust St **909/369-0992** • 11am Sun • Celtic Catholic service

Erotica

▲ **Riverside Bookstore** 3945 Market St (at University) **909/788-5194** • 24hrs

Russian River

includes Cazadero, Forestville, Guerneville & Monte Rio

Info Lines & Services

Russian River Tourist Bureau 800/253-8800

Accommodations

Applewood—An Estate Inn 13555 Hwy 116 (at Mays Canyon), Guerneville **707/869-9093, 800/555-8509** • gay-friendly • 21+ • full brkfst • swimming • smokefree • food served • wheelchair access • $135-325

Avalon 4th & Mill Sts, Guerneville **707/869-9566** • gay-friendly • swimming • $50-175

Eagle's Peak Retreat 11644 Our Peak Rd (at McPeak Rd), Forestville **707/887-9218** • mostly gay men • vacation house w/ deck & spa on 26 acres • gay-owned/run • $175

Faerie Ring Campground 16747 Armstrong Woods Rd, Guerneville **707/869-2746** • gay-friendly • on 14 acres • RV spaces • near outdoor recreation • pets ok • $20-25

▲ **Fern Falls 707/632-6108** • lesbians/gay men • main house w/deck overlooking creek • also cabin • hot tub • waterfall • smokefree • kids ok by arrangement • pets ok

Russian River

The Russian River resort area is hidden away in the redwood forests of Northern California, an hour and a half north of the San Francisco Bay Area. The warm summer days and cool starlit nights have made it a favorite secret getaway for many of San Francisco's lesbians and gays—especially when they can't stand another foggy, cold day in the City.

Life at 'The River,' as it's fondly called, is laid back. You can take a canoe ride, hike under the redwoods, or just lie back on the riverbank and soak up the sun. There's plenty of camping and RV parking, including the **Redwood Grove, The Willows** (camping), and **Fife's Resort** (camping & RV). If you're in the mood for other soothing and sensual delights, you're in luck. The River is in the heart of the famous California Wine Country. Plan a tour to the many wineries, and don't forget to designate a sober driver, so you can taste the world-class wines as you go. Or see some of the world's most beautiful coastline as you cruise the car along the Pacific Coast Highway—only fifteen minutes away!

The River becomes a lesbian garden of earthly delights several times a year. **Women's Weekend** happens in May and late September, with shuttles taking women from resort to resort as they enjoy the many entertainers, dances, and barbecues.

Russian River

Where the Girls Are: Guerneville is a small town, so you won't miss the scantily-clad, vacationing women walking toward the bars downtown or the beach.

Annual Events: May & September - Women's Weekend 707/869-9000. September - Jazz Festival.

City Info: Russian River Visitors Info 800/253-8800.

Attractions: Armstrong Redwood State Park.
Bodega Bay.
Mudbaths of Calistoga.
Wineries of Napa and Sonoma counties.

Best View: Anywhere in Armstrong Woods, the Napa Wine Country and on the ride along the coast on Highway 1.

Weather: Summer days are sunny and warm (80°s-90°s) but usually begin with a dense fog. Winter days have the same pattern but are a lot cooler and wetter. Winter nights can be very damp and chilly (low 40°s).

Transit: Bill's Taxi Service 707/869-2177.
The area is easiest to reach by car.

▲ **Fife's Resort** 16467 River Rd (at Brookside Lane), Guerneville **707/869–0656, 800/734–3371** • lesbians/gay men • cabins • campsites • also restaurant • some veggie • full bar • gym • $50-215

Golden Apple Ranch 17575 Fitzpatrick Ln (at Joy Rd), Occidental **707/874–3756** • gay-friendly • smokefree • wheelchair access • $95-185

▲ **Highlands Resort** 14000 Woodland Dr, Guerneville **707/869–0333** • lesbians/gay men • country retreat on 4 wooded acres • hot tub • swimming • nudity • pets ok • $45-125

Huckleberry Springs Country Inn 8105 Old Beedle, Monte Rio **707/865–2683, 800/822–2683** • gay-friendly • private cottages • swimming • Japanese spa • massage therapy • smokefree • full brkfst • IGLTA • women-owned/run • $155-165

Jacques' Cottage at Russian River 6471 Old Trenton Rd, Forestville **707/575–1033** • lesbians/gay men • hot tub • swimming • nudity • pets ok • $100-125

Mikki's River View Retreat 14603 River Rd, Guerneville **707/869–3040** • gay-friendly • vacation home • hot tub • deck • 2 bikes provided

▲ **Paradise Cove Resort** 14711 Armstrong Woods Rd, Guerneville **707/869–2706** • lesbians/gay men • studio units • hot tub • fireplaces • decks • $70-135

Redwood Properties 707/869–7368 • rental homes

Rio Villa Beach Resort 20292 Hwy 116 (at Bohemian Hwy), Monte Rio **707/865–1143** • gay-friendly • on the river • cabins • kids ok • $69-179

Russian River Resort/Triple 'R' Resort 16390 4th St (at Mill), Guerneville **707/869–0691, 800/417–3767** • lesbians/gay men • hot tub • swimming • also restaurant • some veggie • full bar • wheelchair access • $40-90

Schoolhouse Canyon Park 12600 River Rd (at Oddfellows Park Rd) **707/869–2311** • gay-friendly • campsites • RV • private beach • kids/pets ok • $20

Tim & Tony's Treehouse 707/887–9531, 888/887–9531 • lesbians/gay men • studio cottage • swimming • hot tub • sauna • smokefree • $95-125

Wildwood Resort Retreat Old Cazadero Rd (at River Rd), Guerneville **707/632-5321** • gay-friendly • facilities are for groups of 20 or more • swimming • smokefree • $80-100 (meals included)

The Willows 15905 River Rd (at Hwy 116), Guerneville **707/869-2824, 800/953-2828** • lesbians/gay men • old-fashioned country lodge & campground • smokefree • $69-139

Bars

Molly Brown's Saloon 14120 Old Cazadero Rd (at River Rd), Guerneville **707/869-0511** • 4pm-2am, from noon wknds, till midnight Sun-Th • lesbians/gay men • food served

McT's Bullpen 16246 1st St (at Church), Guerneville **707/869-3377** • 6am-2am • gay/straight • sports bar • patio • wheelchair access

Rainbow Cattle Co 16220 River Rd (at Armstrong Woods Rd), Guerneville **707/869-0206** • 6am-2am • mostly gay men • neighborhood bar

River Business 16225 Main St (at Armstrong Woods Rd), Guerneville **707/869-3400** • noon-2am (seasonal) • mostly gay men • neighborhood bar • wheelchair access

Nightclubs

Club Fab 16135 River Rd (at Armstrong Woods Rd), Guerneville **707/869-5708** • 9pm-2am, 4pm-close Sun, clsd Mon-Wed • mostly gay men • dancing/DJ

Cafes

Coffee Bazaar 14045 Armstrong Woods Rd (at River Rd), Guerneville **707/869-9706** • 6am-8pm • cafe • soups • salads • pastries

Restaurants

Big Bertha's Burgers 16357 Main St, Guerneville **707/869-2239** • 11am-8pm • beer/wine

Burdon's 15405 River Rd (at Orchard Rd), Guerneville **707/869-2615** • dinner Wed-Sun • lesbians/gay men • cont'l/pasta • plenty veggie • full bar • wheelchair access • $10-15

Cape Fear Cafe 25191 Main St, Duncans Mills **707/865-9246** • 9am-9pm, clsd 3pm-5pm • also Graton location: 8989 Graton Rd, 707/824-8284

Cat's Place at George's Hideaway 18100 Hwy 116 (at Old Cazadero Rd) **707/869-3634** • 4pm-9pm, till 10pm wknds, clsd Mon-Tue • homecooking • full bar

Flavors Unlimited 16450 Main St / River Rd, Guerneville **707/869-0425** • hours vary • custom-blended ice cream • women-owned/run

Mill St Grill 16390 4th St (at 'Triple 'R' Resort'), Guerneville **707/869-0691** • lesbians/gay men • some veggie • full bar • patio • wheelchair access • $5-10

River Inn Restaurant 16141 Main St, Guerneville **707/869-0481** • seasonal • local favorite • wheelchair access • $10-15

Sweet's River Grill 16251 Main St (at Armstrong Woods Rd), Guerneville **707/869-3383** • noon-9pm • popular

Bookstores

River Reader 16355 Main St (at Mill), Guerneville **707/869-2240** • 10am-6pm, extended hours during summer

Retail Shops

Up the River 16212 Main St (at Armstrong Woods Rd), Guerneville **707/869-3167** • cards • gifts • T-shirts

Spiritual Groups

MCC of the Redwood Empire 14520 Armstrong Woods Rd (at Guerneville Community Church), Guerneville **707/869-0552** • 6pm Sun

Sacramento

Info Lines & Services

Lambda Community Center 1927 'L' St **916/442-0185** • 3pm-9pm • youth groups & more

Northall Gay AA 2015 'J' St #32 **916/454-1100** • 8pm Mon, noon Wed

Accommodations

Hartley House B&B Inn 700 22nd St (at 'G' St) **916/447-7829, 800/831-5806** • gay-friendly • turn-of-the-century mansion • full brkfst • smokefree • older kids ok • conference facilities • gay-owned/run • $99-165

Verona Village River Resort 6985 Garden Hwy, Nicolaus **530/656-1320** • lesbians/gay men • RV space $15 • full bar • restaurant • store • marina

Bars

The Depot 2001 'K' St **916/441-6823** • 4pm-2am, till 4am Fri-Sat, from 2pm wknds • popular • mostly gay men • neighborhood bar • transgender-friendly • videos • wheelchair access

Joseph's 1454 Del Paso Blvd (at Arden Wy) **916/922-8899** • 11am-2am, from 9am wknds • lesbians/gay men • dancing/DJ • live shows • also restaurant • brunch wknds • Italian • some veggie • $4-12

Mirage 601 15th St (at 'F' St) **916/444-3238** • 5pm-2am • lesbians/gay men • neighborhood bar • karaoke • wheelchair access

The Townhouse 1517 21st St (at 'P' St) **916/441-5122** • 3pm-2am • lesbians/gay men • neighborhood bar • also restaurant • wheelchair access

Nightclubs

Faces 2000 'K' St (at 20th St) **916/448-7798** • 1pm-2am • lesbians/gay men • dancing/DJ • country/western • transgender-friendly • live shows • karaoke • videos • wheelchair access

Cafes

New Helvetia Roasters & Bakers 1215 19th St **916/441-1106** • 6:30am-11pm • cool coffeehouse in converted firehouse • patio

Restaurants

Ernesto's 1901 16th St (at 'S' St) **916/441-5850** • 11am-10pm, from 9am wknds • Mexican • full bar

Hamburger Mary's 1630 'J' St (at 17th) **916/441-4340** • 11am-11pm, till 1am Sat, from 10am Sun • full bar

Rick's Dessert Diner 2322 'K' St (at 23rd) **916/444-0969** • 10am-11pm Sun-Mon, till midnight Tue-Th, till 1am Fri-Sat • coffee & dessert

Bookstores

Lioness Book Store 2224 'J' St (btwn 22nd & 23rd) **916/442-4657, 800/784-3939** • 11am-7pm, noon-6pm Sat, noon-5pm Sun, clsd Mon • women's • wheelchair access • women-owned/run

The Open Book 910 21st St (btwn 'I' & 'J' Sts) **916/498-1004** • 10am-11pm, till midnight Fri-Sat • lesbigay • also coffeehouse • wheelchair access

Publications

MGW (Mom Guess What) 916/441-6397 • lesbigay newspaper • women-owned/run

Outword 916/329-9280 • lesbigay newspaper

Spiritual Groups

Integrity Northern California 916/394-1715, 916/446-2513 • 4pm 2nd Sun • lesbigay Episcopalians • call for location

Erotica

Goldie's I 201 N 12th St (at North 'B' St) **916/447-5860** • 24hrs • also 2138 Del Paso Blvd location, 916/922-0103

Goldie's Outlet 1800 Del Paso Blvd (at Oxford Blvd) **916/920-8659**

Kiss-N-Tell 4201 Sunrise Blvd (at Fair Oaks) **916/966-5477**

L'Amour Shoppe 2531 Broadway (at 26th) **916/736-3467**

Salinas

Spiritual Groups

St Paul's Episcopal Church 1071 Pajaro St (at San Miguel Ave) **831/424-7331** • 8am & 10am Sun

Erotica

L'Amour Shoppe 325 E Alisal St **831/758-9600**

San Bernardino

see also Riverside

Info Lines & Services

AA Gay/Lesbian 909/825-4700 • numerous mtgs for Inland Empire • call for times

Project Teen 909/335-2005 • 7:30pm Tue • support group for lesbigay teens

Erotica

Bearfacts Book Store 1434 E Baseline **909/885-9176** • 24hrs

San Diego

Info Lines & Services

AA Gay/Lesbian 3867 Monroe St (at Park) **619/298-8008** • 10:30am-10pm • 'Live & Let Live Alano' • also contact for 'Sober Sisters'

Lesbian/Gay Men's Community Center 3916 Normal St (at Blaine) **619/692-2077** • 9am-10pm, till 7pm Sat, clsd Sun

SAGE of California **619/282-1395** • seniors' social group • 1st Wed

Accommodations

Balboa Park Inn 3402 Park Blvd (at Upas) **619/298-0823, 800/938-8181** • gay-friendly • charming guest house in the heart of San Diego • wheelchair access • IGLTA • $80-200

Banker's Hill B&B 3315 2nd Ave (at Upas) **619/260-0673, 800/338-3748** • lesbians/gay men • swimming • IGLTA • gay-owned/run • $85-175

The Beach Place 2158 Sunset Cliffs Blvd (at Muir) **619/225-0746** • lesbians/gay men • hot tub • nudity • kids ok • pets by arrangement • 4 blks from beach • IGLTA • $50-60 (nightly) • $300-350 (weekly)

The Blom House B&B 1372 Minden Dr (nr Friars & Ulric) **619/467-0890, 800/797-2566** • gay-friendly • charming 1948 cottage-style home • magnificent view • smokefree • $75-95

Dmitri's Guesthouse 931 21st St (at Broadway) **619/238-5547** • lesbians/gay men • swimming • hot tub • smokefree • overlooks downtown • wheelchair access • $75-100

Elsbree House 5054 Narragansett Ave (at Sunset Cliffs Blvd) **619/226-4133** • gay-friendly • near beach • smokefree • $95-105 B&B • $1250/wk condo

Friendship Hotel 3942 8th Ave (btwn University & Washington Sts) **619/298-9898** • gay-friendly • kids/pets ok • $20-39

The Gallery B&B 1404 Meade Ave (at Maryland St) **619/692-0041, 888/355-6439** • mostly lesbians • 1907 home • queen suite w/fireplace • spa • $60-80

Heritage Park Inn 2470 Heritage Park Row (at Juan) **619/239-4738, 800/995-2470** • gay-friendly • full brkfst • afternoon tea • smokefree • kids ok • wheelchair access • $100-235

▲ **Hillcrest Inn Hotel** 3754 5th Ave (btwn Robinson & Pennsylvania) **619/293-7078, 800/258-2280** • lesbians/gay men • int'l hotel in the heart of Hillcrest • wheelchair access • IGLTA • $49-55

Inn Suites Hotel 2223 El Cajon Blvd (btwn Louisiana & Mississippi) **619/296-2101** • gay-friendly • swimming • kids ok • also restaurant • wheelchair access • $89-149

San Diego

Where the Girls Are: Lesbians tend to live near Normal Heights, in the northwest part of the city. But for partying, women go to the bars near I-5, or to Hillcrest to hang out with the boys.

Lesbigay Pride: July. 619/297-7683.

City Info: San Diego Visitors Bureau 619/232-3101, web: www.sandiego.com.

Attractions: Globe Theatre 619/231-1941.
San Diego Wild Animal Park 760/747-8702.
San Diego Zoo 619/234-3153.
Sea World 619/226-3915.

Best View: Cabrillo National Monument on Point Loma or from a harbor cruise.

Weather: San Diego is sunny and warm (upper 60°s-70°s) year-round, with higher humidity in the summer.

Transit: Orange Cab 619/234-6161.
San Diego Cab 619/232-6566.
Silver Cab/Co-op 619/280-5555.
Cloud Nine Shuttle 800/974-8885.
San Diego Transit System 619/233-3004.
San Diego Trolley (through downtown or to Tijuana).

Kasa Korbett 1526 Van Buren Ave (at Cleveland) **619/291-3962, 800/757-5272** • lesbians/gay men • comfortable craftsman-designed B&B in Hillcrest • wheelchair access • spa • smokefree • kids ok

Keating House 2331 2nd Ave (at Juniper) **619/239-8585, 800/995-8644** • gay-friendly • graceful Victorian on Bankers Hill • full brkfst • smokefree • kids ok • IGLTA • $75-95

Park Manor Suites 525 Spruce St (btwn 5th & 6th) **619/291-0999, 800/874-2649** • gay-friendly • 1926 hotel • kids/pets ok • IGLTA • $79-179

Villa Serena B&B 2164 Rosecrans St (btwn Udall & Voltaire) **619/224-1451, 800/309-2778** • gay-friendly • Italian villa in residential neighborhood • full brkfst • swimming • hot tub

Bars

The Arena 3040 North Park Wy **619/295-8072** • 4pm-2am • mostly gay men • leather • wheelchair access

Club Bombay 3175 India St (enter on Spruce St) **619/296-6789** • 4pm-2am, from 2pm wknds • popular • mostly women • dancing/DJ • live shows • Sun BBQ • patio • wheelchair access • women-owned/run

San Diego

San Diego is a West Coast paradise. This city sprawls from the bays and beaches of the Pacific to the foothills of the desert mountains. The days are always warm, and the nights can be refreshingly cool.

Stay at one of the city's quaint lesbian-friendly inns. During the days, follow the tourist circuit which includes the world-famous San Diego Zoo and Sea World. Call the Visitor's Center for a brochure on all the sites.

Once the sun sets, you're ready to tour the lesbian circuit. Where to begin? Check out **Club Bombay** and **The Flame**, San Diego's two lesbian dance bars. If you're a country/western gal, **Kickers** is a popular place to two-step.

In mid-August, check out the the Hillcrest Street Fair, popular with the many lesbian and gay residents of the happening Hillcrest district. (Be warned though: Because of its location between super-freeways and construction, rush-hour traffic has been known to crawl through Hillcrest.)

If you're feeling adventurous, cruise by the **Crypt** for some sex toys or a piercing, and pick up your safer sex supplies at **Condoms Plus**. If you just want to network, stop in at the **Community Center** or pick up one of the lesbigay papers at **Obelisk the Bookstore** for all the latest information about San Diego's lesbian community.

The Flame 3780 Park Blvd (at University) **619/295-4163** • 5pm-2am, from 4pm Fri • popular • mostly women • dancing/DJ • theme nights • women-owned/run

Kickers 308 University Ave (at 3rd Ave) **619/491-0400** • 7pm-2am • mostly gay men • dancing/DJ • country/western • lessons at 7pm • wheelchair access

Matador 4633 Mission Blvd (btwn Diamond & Emerald), Pacific Beach **858/483-6943** • mostly gay men • noon-2am • beach bar

No 1 Fifth Ave (no sign) 3845 5th Ave (at University) **619/299-1911** • noon-2am • mostly gay men • professional • videos • patio

Redwing Bar & Grill 4012 30th St (at Lincoln) **619/281-8700** • 10am-midnight, till 2am Fri-Sat • mostly gay men • cocktail lounge • food served • $5-10

Nightclubs

Club Montage 2028 Hancock St (at Washington Ave) **619/294-9590** • 8pm-2am, till 4am Fri-Sat • mostly gay men • dancing/DJ • live shows • videos • also restaurant • wheelchair access

Cafes

The Big Kitchen 3003 Grape St **619/234-5789** • 8am-2pm, 7am-3pm wknds • some veggie • wheelchair access • women-owned/run • $5-10

Cafe Roma UCSD Price Center #76 (at Voight), La Jolla **858/450-2141** • 7am-midnight

David's Place 3766 5th Ave (at Robinson) **619/296-4173** • 7am-midnight, till 2:30am wknds • coffeehouse for positive people & their friends • patio

Euphoria 1045 University Ave (at 10th Ave) **619/295-1769** • 6am-1am, till 3am Fri-Sat

Extraordinary Desserts 2929 5th Ave **619/294-7001** • 8:30am-11pm, till midnight Fri-Sat • the name says it all

Restaurants

Adams Avenue Grill 2201 Adams Ave (at Mississippi) **619/298-8440** • lunch, dinner & wknd brunch • bistro • plenty veggie • beer/wine • wheelchair access • gay-owned/run

Bayou Bar & Grill 329 Market St (btwn 3rd & 4th) **619/696-8747** • lunch & dinner, Sun champagne brunch • Creole/Cajun • wheelchair access • $12-16

Cafe Eleven 1440 University Ave **619/260-8023** • dinner, clsd Mon • country French • some veggie • wheelchair access • $15-20

California Cuisine 1027 University Ave (at 10th Ave) **619/543-0790** • 11am-10pm, from 5pm wknds, clsd Mon • French/Italian • some veggie • also bar • wheelchair access • women-owned/run • $15-20

City Deli 535 University Ave (at 6th Ave) **619/295-2747** • 7am-midnight, till 2am Fri-Sat • NY deli • plenty veggie

The Cottage 7702 Fay (at Klein), La Jolla **858/454-8409** • fresh-baked items

Crest Cafe 425 Robinson (btwn 4th & 5th) **619/295-2510** • 7am-midnight • some veggie • wheelchair access • $5-10

Hamburger Mary's 308 University Ave (at 3rd) **619/491-0400** • 11am-10pm, from 9am wknds • some veggie • full bar • wheelchair access • $5-10

Liaison 2202 4th Ave (at Ivy) **619/234-5540** • dinner only, clsd Mon • French country • wheelchair access • $18-24 (prix fixe)

The Mission 3795 Mission Blvd (at San Jose), Mission Beach **858/488-9060** • mostly lesbians/gay men • brkfst & lunch • gay-owned

Mixx 3671 5th Ave **619/299-6499** • mostly lesbians/gay men • dinner only • live shows • gay-owned

Vegetarian Zone 2949 5th Ave (at Quince) **619/298-7302** • 10am-9pm • deli & restaurant

Entertainment & Recreation

Aztec Bowl 4356 30th St, North Park **619/283-3135** • gay Mon night

Diversionary Theatre 4545 Park Blvd #101 (at Madison) **619/220-6830, 619/220-0097 (box office #)** • lesbigay theater

Bookstores

Blue Door Bookstore 3823 5th Ave (at University) **619/298-8610** • 9am-9:30pm, 10am-9pm Sun • large lesbigay section • wheelchair access

Groundworks Books UCSD Student Center 0323 (at Gilman Dr), La Jolla **858/452-9625** • 9am-7pm, 10am-6pm Fri-Sat, clsd Sun • alternative • lesbigay section • wheelchair access

Heather Grace Books 3341 Adams Ave (btwn Felton & 34th) **619/283-4341** • 10am-6pm, clsd Mon • lesbigay section • secondhand • wheelchair access

▲ **Obelisk the Bookstore** 1029 University Ave (at 10th) **619/297-4171** • 10am-11pm • lesbigay • wheelchair access

Retail Shops

Auntie Helen's 4028 30th St (at Lincoln) **619/584-8438** • 10am-5pm, clsd Sun-Mon • thrift shop benefits PWAs • wheelchair access

Flesh Skin Grafix 1228 Palm Ave, Imperial Beach **619/424-8983** • tattoos • piercing

Mastodon 4638 Mission Blvd (at Emerald), Pacific Beach **858/272-1188, 800/743-8743** • body piercing

Rainbow Road 141 University Ave **619/296-8222** • 10am-10pm • gay gifts

Publications

Gay/Lesbian Times 3911 Normal St **619/299-6397, 800/438-8786** • newsmagazine

Update 619/299-4104

Spiritual Groups

Dignity 4190 Front St (at First Unitarian Universalist Church in Hillcrest) **619/645-8240** • 6pm Sun

First Unitarian Universalist Church 4190 Front St **619/298-9978** • 10am (July-Aug) • 9am & 11am (Sept-June)

MCC 4333 30th St (at El Cajon Blvd) **619/280-4333** • 9am, 11am, 1:30pm (bilingual), 7pm Sun, 7pm Wed

Gyms & Health Clubs

Frog's Athletic Club 901 Hotel Circle South (at Washington), Mission Valley **858/291-3500**

Hillcrest Gym 142 University Ave (at 3rd) **619/299-7867** • lesbians/gay men

Erotica

Condoms Plus 1220 University Ave (at Vermont) **619/291-7400** • 11am-midnight, till 2am Fri-Sat, 1pm-9pm Sun • safer sex gifts for men & women

The Crypt 3841 Park Blvd (at University) **619/692-9499** • also 30th St location, 619/284-4724

▲ **F St Bookstore** 2004 University Ave (at Florida) **619/298-2644** • 24hrs

▲ **F St Bookstore** 3112 Midway Dr (at Rosecrans) **619/221-0075** • 24hrs

Video Specialties
2322 So. Escondido Blvd., Escondido (760) 745-6697
Hip Pocket Books
12686 Garden Grove Blvd., (714) 638-8595
Midnight Book & Video Center
8745 Garden Grove Blvd., (714) 534-9823
The Party House
8751 Garden Grove Blvd., (714) 534-9823
Video Preview & Rental Center
8743 Garden Grove Blvd., (714) 534-9823
Palm Avenue Books
1177 Palm Ave., Imperial Beach (619) 575-5081
Funhouse II
316 Pierview Way, Oceanside (760) 757-7832
Mr. K's
623 W. Hueneme, Oxnard (805) 488-5494
Fantasy 66
835 E. Foothills Blvd., Rialto (909) 820-6315
Video Fantasies
5327 Mission Blvd., Rubidoux (909) 782-8056
Hillcrest Books
1407 University Ave., San Diego (619) 299-7186
Midnight Books
4792 El Cajon Blvd., San Diego (619) 582-1997
Midway Books
3606 Midway Dr., San Diego (619) 222-9973
Pleasureland
836 5th Ave., San Diego (619) 237-9056
• Swingers Sections • Adult Magazines
• 25¢ Arcades • Oils, Lotions, Leather & More!
MIDNIGHT BOOK & VIDEO
California's Best!
www.goalie-usa.com

- ▲ **F St Bookstore** 4626 Albuquerque **619/581–0400** • 24hrs
- ▲ **F St Bookstore** 751 4th Ave (at F St) **619/236–0841** • 24hrs
- ▲ **F St Bookstore** 7865 Balboa Ave (at Mercury), Kearny Mesa **858/292–8083** • 24hrs
- ▲ **F St Bookstore** 7998 Miramar Rd (at Dowdy) **619/549–8014** • 24hrs
- ▲ **F St Bookstore** 4650 Border Village (at San Ysidro Blvd), San Ysidro **619/497–6042**

Gay Mart 550 University Ave (at 6th Ave) **619/543–1221** • 10am-midnight, till 10pm Sun

- ▲ **Midnight Videos** 1407 University Ave (at Richmond) **619/299–7186** • 24hrs
- ▲ **Midnight Videos** 3606 Midway Dr (at Kemper) **619/222–9973** • 24hrs
- ▲ **Midnight Videos** 4792 El Cajon Blvd (at 48th) **619/582–1997** • 24hrs
- ▲ **Midnight Videos** 836 5th Ave (btwn E & F Sts) **619/237–9056** • 24hrs

San Francisco

San Francisco is divided into 7 geographical areas:
SF—Overview
SF—Castro & Noe Valley
SF—South of Market
SF—Polk Street Area
SF—Downtown & North Beach
SF—Mission District
SF—Haight, Fillmore, Hayes Valley

SF—Overview

Info Lines & Services

AA Gay/Lesbian 415/621–1326

Bay Area American Indian Two Spirits 150 Eureka St (btwn 18th & 19th Sts, in MCC) **415/282–4176** • 6:30pm Mon • social/cultural group for lgbt Native Americans

The Bay Area Bisexual Resources Line 415/703–7977

The Exiles 3543 18th St (btwn Guerrero & Valencia, in the 'Women's Bldg') **415/487–5170** • mtgs 3rd Fri • social/educational group for all women over 21 interested in SM btwn women

FTM International 415/553–5987 • 2pm-5pm 2nd Sun • info & support for female-to-male transgendered people • newsletter • resource guide

Gay/Lesbian Outreach to Elders 1853 Market St **415/626–7000**

Gay/Lesbian Sierrans 415/281–5666 • outdoor group

Lavender Line 510/548–8283 • 10am-10pm Mon-Fri • info • referrals • rap line

LGBA (Lesbian/Gay/Bisexual Alliance) 415/338–1952 • student group at SF State

LINKS 415/703–7159 • S/M play parties & calendar • transgender-friendly

LYRIC (Lavender Youth Recreation/Information Cntr) 127 Collingwood **415/703–6150, 800/246–7743 (OUTSIDE BAY AREA)** • support & social groups • also crisis counseling for lesbigay & transgendered youth under 24 at 415/863-3636 (hotline #)

New Leaf 415/626–7000 • 9am-7pm Mon-Fri • variety of services • lesbigay AA mtgs at 15th & Market

New Village 973 Market St #650 **415/674–0900** • transgender support group • call for info

TARC (Tenderloin AIDS Resource Center) 187 Golden Gate Ave (at Leavenworth) **415/431–7476** • 9am-noon (drop-in) & 1pm-4pm (appt only)

Transgender Support Group 187 Golden Gate Ave (at TARC) **415/255–8272** • 4pm-6pm Mon-Fri

Transgender Support Groups 50 Lech Walesa (at Tom Waddell Clinic, btwn Polk & Van Ness and Grove & Hayes Sts) **415/554–2940** • 6-7:30pm Tue • support groups & counseling for MTF & FTM transsexuals • low-cost TG health clinic

What's Up! Events Hotline for Sistahs East Bay **510/835–6126** • for lesbians of African descent

Women's Building 3543 18th St (btwn Valencia & Guerrero) **415/431–1180** • 9am-5pm Mon-Fri • space for many women's organizations • social/support groups • housing & job listings • beautiful murals

Accommodations

American Property Exchange 2800 Van Ness Ave (at Lombard) **415/447–2000, 800/747–7784** • daily, weekly & monthly furnished rentals • women-owned/run

Dockside Boat & Bed 510/444–5858, 800/436–2574 • gay-friendly • private houseboats • kitchen • smokefree • kids ok • $115-300

Mi Casa Su Casa 510/268–8534, 800/215–2272 • lesbians/gay men • int'l home exchange network

Nightclubs

▲ **Club Q** 177 Townsend **415/647-8258** • 1st Fri • women only • popular dance party

MT Productions **415/337-4962** • mostly women • dance parties including 'Girl Spot' & 'Club Skirts' and weekend events

Entertainment & Recreation

Beach Blanket Babylon 678 Green St (at Powell, in 'Club Fugazi') **415/421-4222** • the USA's longest running musical revue & wigs that must be seen to be believed • also restaurant & full bar

Brava! 2180 Bryant St #208 (at 20th St) **415/641-7657** • culturally diverse performances by women • theater at 2789 24th St (formerly 'York Theater') • wheelchair access

Castro Theatre 429 Castro (btwn 17th & Market) **415/621-6120** • art house cinema • many lesbigay & cult classics • live organ evenings

Cruisin' the Castro **415/550-8110** • guided walking tour of the Castro • IGLTA

San Francisco

San Francisco may be a top tourist destination because of its cable cars, beatniks, quaint beauty, and the Haight-Ashbury district, but we know what really makes it shine: its legendary lesbian and gay community. So unless standing in long lines for a little kitsch is your thing, skip Fisherman's Wharf and the cable cars, and head for San Francisco's queerest and quirkiest neighborhoods: the Mission, the Castro, Noe Valley, or South of Market (SoMa).

Any lesbian walking along Valencia between Market Street and 24th Street can't miss all the hot women of all sizes and colors that live in this neighborhood. Valencia Street borders the upscale, predominantly gay Castro area, and the Mission, San Francisco's largest Latino neighborhood. This intersection of cultures results in a truly San Franciscan mix of punk dykes, dykes of color, lesbian-feminists, working class straights, and funky artists.

Your first stop in the Mission should be either punk dyke hangout **Red Dora's Bearded Lady Cafe & Gallery** (be sure to check out **Black & Blue Tattoo** next door) on 14th Street or the more traditional resource center, **The Women's Building**, on 18th Street. (You can't miss their stunning murals.) Along the way from 14th to 18th, pick up a famous 'San Francisco Mission-Style Burrito' (as they're advertised in New York these days) at one of the many cheap and delicious taquerias. After that, rush up to 23rd Street to **Good Vibrations** women's sex toy store before they close at 7pm.

You might have heard the legends about the Mission's one-time women's bar, Amelia's. Sadly, it's long gone. Instead, head for its hip little sister, **The Lexington Club**, a popular dyke hangout. Another must for lesbians along Valencia Street is **Osento**, the women's bathhouse. Just off Valencia on 16th is **The Roxie**, a dyke-friendly repertory cinema.

The Mission also has lots of fun queer performance at places like **Build** and **Brava!** and **Luna Sea**—check the biweekly **Bay Times** calendar. If you're into artsy or radical video, get a calendar from **Artists' Television Access** (415/824-3890).

You'll also find lots of lesbians in nearby Noe Valley, though this area tends to be a couples heaven for professional women and lesbian moms. If that's your dream, call **Bay Area Career Women** (415/495-5393) about their upcoming social events, or drop in on their TGIF social, downtown. You'll also enjoy an afternoon in one or all of the many quirky shops and cafes along upper 24th Street.

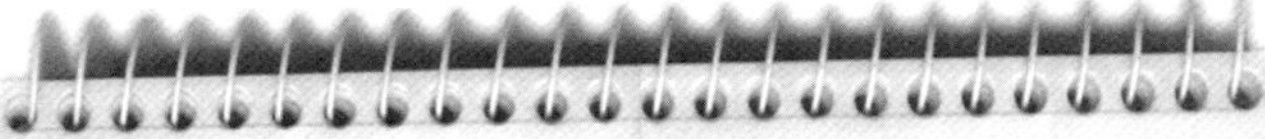

If you cruise the Castro, you'll be surprised how many sisters–ranging from executives to queer chicks–you'll see walking the streets of what was the 'Boys' Town' of the 1970s. Drop in at **A Different Light**, the lesbigay bookstore, or **The Cafe** for a game of pool or girl-watching from the balcony. The Castro also boasts three great 24-hour diners–**Bagdad Cafe**, **Sparky's**, and **Orphan Andy's**. For lesbian/gay-themed films, don't miss an evening at **The Castro Theater** .

SoMa (South of Market) also contains lots of art, poetry, and kink for the daring. And plenty of schmoozing for women of color and friends at the **CoCo Club** (8th & Minna), a small but lively women's cabaret & speakeasy, with events seven nights a week. Our favorite is a Friday evening 'In Bed with Fairy Butch'. During the day, enjoy a cup of coffee and a sandwich upstairs at the **Chat House**.

While you're still south of Market, you might also want to check out the women's S/M scene in this kinky city: **Stormy Leather** is a women-owned/run fetish store. And if you're inspired to get that piercing you've been thinking about, visit one of the queer-friendly piercing parlors in town–we like **Body Manipulations**, right between the Mission and the Castro on 16th Street at Guerrero.

You still have energy? Wanna dance? If it's Thursday night, get it going at **The Box** where the Rainbow Coalition is alive and groovin'. Single (or not) on a Saturday night? Then boogie on down to the ever-popular **G-Spot** (Girl Spot). But don't stop there. Be sure to check out the extensive listings in **Creampuff**, **Female FYI**, or the 'Jet Girl' section of **Odyssey**, to see if tonight's the night for those legendary one-night clubs like **Sugar** or **Dollhouse,** or monthly parties like **Club Q** and **Backstreet**. Call the 'Red Line' at 415/339-8310 for other women's dance parties around town.

Finally, if you're a fan of Diane Di Prima, Anne Waldman, the late Allen Ginsberg, or other beatniks, **City Lights Bookstore** in North Beach is a required pilgrimage. Afterward, have a drink or an espresso at beatnik hangout Café Vesuvius, just across Jack Kerouac Alley from City Lights.

Sound like a lot? They don't call it Mecca for nothing.

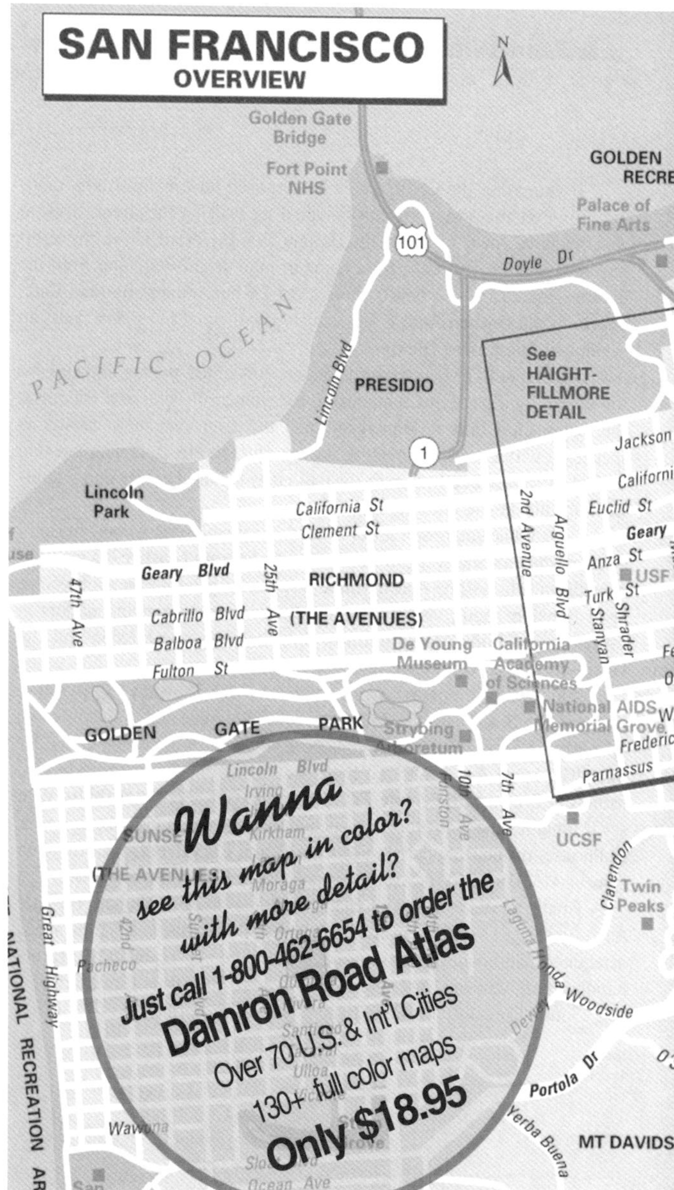
SAN FRANCISCO
OVERVIEW
Golden Gate Bridge
Fort Point NHS
GOLDEN
RECRE
Palace of Fine Arts
101
Doyle Dr
PACIFIC OCEAN
Lincoln Blvd
PRESIDIO
See HAIGHT-FILLMORE DETAIL
Jackson
1
Lincoln Park
California St
Clement St
2nd Avenue
Arguello Blvd
Euclid St
Geary
Geary Blvd
25th Ave
RICHMOND
(THE AVENUES)
47th Ave
Anza St
USF
Turk St
Stanyan
Shrader
Cabrillo Blvd
Balboa Blvd
Fulton St
De Young Museum
California Academy of Sciences
National AIDS Memorial Grove
GOLDEN
GATE
PARK
Strybing Arboretum
Frederic
Parnassus
Lincoln Blvd
10th Ave
7th Ave
UCSF
Clarendon
Twin Peaks
Great Highway
NATIONAL RECREATION AR
Woodside
Portola Dr
Yerba Buena
MT DAVIDS
Wanna see this map in color? with more detail?
Just call 1-800-462-6654 to order the
Damron Road Atlas
Over 70 U.S. & Int'l Cities
130+ full color maps
Only $18.95

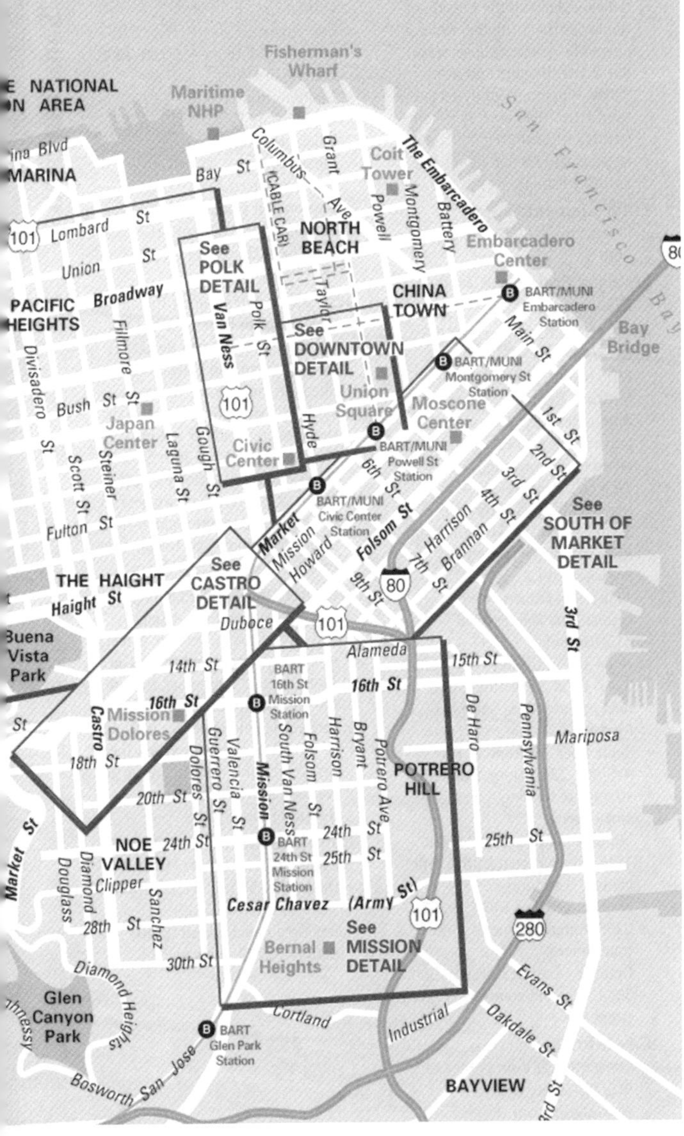
Fisherman's Wharf
Maritime NHP
E NATIONAL
N AREA
MARINA
Bay St
Columbus
(CABLE CAR)
Grant Ave
Coit Tower
The Embarcadero
Montgomery
Powell
Battery
San Francisco Bay
Lombard St
Union St
Broadway
PACIFIC HEIGHTS
See POLK DETAIL
Van Ness
Polk St
NORTH BEACH
Taylor
Embarcadero Center
CHINA TOWN
BART/MUNI Embarcadero Station
Main St
Bay Bridge
See DOWNTOWN DETAIL
BART/MUNI Montgomery St Station
Union Square
Moscone Center
Divisadero St
Fillmore St
Bush St
Japan Center
Laguna St
Gough St
Civic Center
Hyde
BART/MUNI Powell St Station
1st St
2nd St
3rd St
4th St
Scott St
Steiner
Fulton St
6th St
BART/MUNI Civic Center Station
Folsom St
Harrison
Brannan
7th St
See SOUTH OF MARKET DETAIL
Market
Mission
Howard
9th St
See CASTRO DETAIL
THE HAIGHT
Haight St
Duboce
Buena Vista Park
Alameda
14th St
BART 16th St Mission Station
16th St
15th St
3rd St
Castro
Mission Dolores
De Haro
Pennsylvania
Mariposa
18th St
Valencia St
Guerrero St
Dolores St
Mission
South Van Ness
Folsom St
Harrison
Bryant
Potrero Ave
POTRERO HILL
20th St
24th St
25th St
25th St
NOE VALLEY
BART 24th St Mission Station
Market St
Douglass
Diamond
Clipper
28th St
Sanchez
Cesar Chavez (Army St)
See MISSION DETAIL
Bernal Heights
30th St
Diamond Heights
Glen Canyon Park
Cortland
Industrial
Evans St
Oakdale St
BART Glen Park Station
San Jose
Bosworth
BAYVIEW
80
101
280

Where the Girls Are: Younger, radical dykes call the Mission or the lower Haight home, while upwardly-mobile couples stake out Bernal Heights and Noe Valley. Hip, moneyed dykes live in the Castro. The East Bay is home to lots of lesbian feminists, older lesbians and lesbian moms (see East Bay listing).

Entertainment: Theatre Rhinoceros 415/861-5079, 2926 16th St.

Lesbigay Pride: June. 415/864-3733.

Annual Events: March - AIDS Dance-a-thon 415/282-2072. AIDS benefit dance at the Moscone Center.
April - Readers/Writers Conference 415/431-0891. Annual weekend of workshops at Women's Building.
May - California AIDS Ride 800/825-1000 or 415/908-0400. AIDS benefit bike ride from San Francisco to L.A.
June - San Francisco Int'l Lesbian/Gay Film Festival 415/703-8650.
July - Up Your Alley Fair 415/861-3247. Local SM/leather street fair held in Dore Alley, South-of-Market.
September - Folsom St. Fair 415/861-3247. Huge SM/leather street fair, topping a week of kinky events.
Mr. Drummer Contest 415/252-1195. International leather title contest & vendors.
Festival of Babes 510/452 392-9255. Annual women's soccer tournament.
October - Castro St. Fair 415/467-3354. Arts and community groups street fair.

City Info: San Francisco Convention & Visitors Bureau 415/391-2000, web: www.sfvisitor.org

Attractions: Alcatraz.
Chinatown.
Coit Tower.
De Young Museum 415/750-3600.
Fisherman's Warf.
Exploratorium 415/397-5673.
Golden Gate Park.
Haight & Ashbury Sts.
Japantown.
North Beach.
Mission San Francisco de Assisi.
SF Museum of Modern Art 415/357-4035.
Twin Peaks.

Best View: After a great Italian meal in North Beach, go to the top floor of the North Beach parking garage on Vallejo near Stockton, next to the police station. If you're in the Castro or the Mission, head for Dolores Park, at Dolores and 20th St. Other good views: Golden Gate Bridge, Kirby Cove (a park area to the left just past the Golden Gate Bridge in Marin), Coit Tower, Twin Peaks.

Weather: A beautiful summer comes at the end of September and lasts through October. Much of the city is cold and fogged-in June through September, though the Castro and Mission are usually sunny. The cold in winter is damp, so bring lots of layers. When there isn't a drought, it also rains in the winter months of November through February.

Transit: Yellow Cab 415/626-2345.
Luxor Cab 415/282-4141.
Quake City Shuttle 415/255-4899.
Muni 415/673-6864.
Bay Area Rapid Transit (BART) 650/992-2278, subway

▲ **Frameline** 346 9th St **415/703-8650, 800/869-1996 (OUTSIDE CA)** • lesbigay media arts foundation • sponsors annual SF Int'l Lesbian/Gay Film Festival in June (see ad in front color section)

Luna Sea 2940 16th St Rm 216-C (btwn Capp & So Van Ness) **415/863-2989** • lesbian performance space

The Marsh 1062 Valencia (at 22nd St) **415/641-0235** • queer-positive theater

▲ **National AIDS Memorial Grove** Golden Gate Park **415/750-8345, 888/294-7683** • located in a lush, historic dell • guided tours available • wheelchair access

SF GayTours.com 415/648-7758 • SF Queer history tour • also commitment ceremonies

Theatre Rhinoceros 2926 16th St (at S Van Ness) **415/861-5079** • lesbigay theater

Victorian Home Walks 415/252-9485 • custom-tailored walking tours w/San Francisco resident • IGLTA

Publications

BAR (Bay Area Reporter) 415/861-5019 • the weekly lesbigay newspaper

Creampuff Magazine 415/554-0565 • extensive listings for clubs, arts & entertainment

Female FYI 888/460-7001 • monthly • SF lesbian club scene

Odyssey Magazine 415/621-6514 • all the dish on SF's club scene

Q San Francisco 800/999-9718 (SUBSCRIPTIONS) • glossy w/extensive arts, clubs & restaurant listings for the City

San Francisco Bay Times 415/626-0260 • popular • a 'must read' for Bay Area resources

San Francisco Frontiers 415/487-6000 • lesbigay newsmagazine

Spiritual Groups

Bay Area Pagan Assemblies 408/559-4242

Dignity San Francisco 1329 7th Ave (at Presbyterian church, btwn Irving & Judah) **415/681-2491** • 5:30pm Sun • lesbigay Roman Catholic services

Hartford Street Zen Center 57 Hartford St (btwn 17th & 18th Sts) **415/863-2507**

Q-Spirit 415/281-9377 • queer spirituality events & discussions

Reclaiming 415/929-9249 • pagan infoline & network • classes • newsletter

SF—Castro & Noe Valley

Accommodations

24 Henry 24 Henry St (btwn Sanchez & Noe) **415/864-5686, 800/900-5686** • mostly gay men • smokefree • one-bdrm apt also available • IGLTA • $60-105

Albion House Inn 135 Gough St (at Fell) **415/621-0896, 800/625-2466** • gay-friendly • full brkfst • smokefree • kids ok • also restaurant • $115-165

Beck's Motor Lodge 2222 Market St (at Sanchez) **415/621-8212** • gay-friendly • in the heart of the Castro • $95-114

▲ **Belvedere House** 598 Belvedere St (at 17th) **415/731-6654, 888/224-9527 PIN7606** • lesbians/gay men • hot tub • wall-to-wall books, art & style • $55-75

Castro Vacation Rental 72 Eureka St (at Market) **415/626-7126, 888/626-7126** • apt 3 blks from the Castro • weekly

Church Street B&B 325 Church St (at 15th) **415/565-6755** • lesbians/gay men • restored 1905 Edwardian in the Castro

The Cumberland 415/255-3086, 800/605-1357 • gay-friendly • guesthouse above the Castro • full brkfst • $100-175

Dolores Park Inn 3641 17th St (btwn Church & Dolores) **415/621-0482** • gay-friendly • Italianate Victorian mansion • hot tub • private/shared baths • kitchens • fireplaces • smokefree • kids ok • $90-200

Ethel's Garden in the Castro 415/864-6171 • women only • hot tub • kitchenette • private entrance • near everything • $85

House O' Chicks Guesthouse 415/861-9849 • women only • $75-125

Inn on Castro 321 Castro St (btwn 16th & 17th) **415/861-0321** • lesbians/gay men • B&B known for its hospitality & friendly atmosphere • full brkfst • smokefree • $90-200

Le Grenier 347 Noe St (at 16th St) **415/864-4748** • lesbians/gay men • suite • $60-90

Nancy's Bed 415/239-5692 • women only • private home • kitchen • smokefree • kids ok • $25/person

Noe's Nest B&B 3973 23rd St (at Noe) **415/821-0751** • gay-friendly • full brkfst • hot tub • fireplace • smokefree • kids ok • dogs ok (no cats) • $95-170

▲ **The Parker House** 520 Church St (at 17th) **415/621-3222, 888/520-7275** • popular • mostly gay men • Edwardian guest house w/gardens • full brkfst • $99-179 • IGLTA

▲ **Pension San Francisco** 1668 Market St (btwn Franklin & Gough) **415/864-1271, 888/864-8070** • gay-friendly • shared baths • kids ok • $50-80

Ruth's House 415/641-8898 • women only • shared bath • smokefree • small kids ok • lesbian-owned/run • $35-45

Terrace Place 415/241-0425 • lesbians/gay men • guest suite • $100-200

Travelodge Central 1707 Market St (at Valencia) **415/621-6775, 800/578-7878** • gay-friendly • smokefree rooms available • $99-169

The Willows B&B Inn 710 14th St (at Church) **415/431-4770** • mostly gay men • non-smoking rms available • $80-135

Bars

The Bar on Castro 456 Castro St **415/626-7220** • 3am-2am, from noon Sat-Sun • mostly gay men • neighborhood bar • a little bit of South Beach in SF • wheelchair access

▲ **The Cafe** 2367 Market St **415/861-3846** • 12:30pm-2am • lesbians/gay men • dancing/DJ • young crowd • deck overlooking Castro & Market • more women Fri night

Cafe du Nord 2170 Market St (at Sanchez) **415/861-5016** • 6pm-2am, from 4pm Wed-Sat • gay-friendly • live jazz • food served 6:30pm-11pm Wed-Sat • some veggie • $5-10 • theme nights

Daddy's 440 Castro St **415/621-8732** • 9am-2am, from 8am wknds • popular • mostly gay men • neighborhood bar • leather • women genuinely welcome

Harvey's 500 Castro St **415/431-4278** • 11am-2am, from 9am wknds • lesbians/gay men • neighborhood bar • live shows • also restaurant • wheelchair access • under $10

Martuni's 4 Valencia St (at Market) **415/241-0205** • 4pm-2am • mostly gay men • neighborhood bar • professional • piano bar • great martinis

The Metro 3600 16th St (at Noe) **415/703-9750** • 2:30pm-2am • mostly gay men • karaoke Tue • deck overlooking Market St • also Chinese restaurant

The Mint 1942 Market St (at Buchanan) **415/626-4726** • 11am-2am • lesbians/gay men • popular karaoke bar nights • videos • also restaurant • food served till 10pm (till 11pm wknds)

Moby Dick's 4049 18th St • mostly gay men • neighborhood bar • videos

Pilsner Inn 225 Church St (at Market) **415/621-7058** • 9am-2am • popular • mostly gay men • neighborhood bar • young crowd • great patio

Uncle Bert's Place 4086 18th St **415/431-8616** • 6am-2am • mostly gay men • neighborhood bar • heated patio

Cafes

Cafe Flore 2298 Market St **415/621-8579** • 7am-11pm • some veggie • great patio

Jumpin' Java 139 Noe St (at 14th St) **415/431-5282** • 6am-10pm, from 7am wknds

Just Desserts 248 Church St **415/626-5774** • 7am-11pm • lesbians/gay men • cafe • delicious cakes • quiet patio

Orbit Room Cafe 1900 Market St (at Laguna) **415/252-9525** • 8am-1am, till 2am Fri-Sat, till midnight Sun • food served • great view of Market St

Sweet Inspiration 2239 Market St **415/621-8664** • popular wknd nights • fabulous desserts

Restaurants

2223 Market 2223 Market St **415/431-0692** • dinner, brunch wknds • popular • contemporary American • full bar • wheelchair access • $13-16

Alfred Schilling 1695 Market St (at Valencia) **415/431-8447** • lunch & dinner • gourmet fare • also outdoor cafe & chocolatier

Anchor Oyster Bar 579 Castro St (at 19th) **415/431-3990** • lesbians/gay men • seafood • some veggie • beer/wine • women-owned/run • $10-20

Bagdad Cafe 2295 Market St **415/621-4434** • 24hrs • lesbians/gay men • diner • some veggie • $5-10

Blue 2337 Market St **415/863-2583** • 5pm-11pm • popular • mostly gay men • homecooking served w/ style • some veggie • beer/wine • $7-15

Cafe Cuvee 2073 Market St (at 14th St) **415/621-7488** • brkfst & lunch wkdys, dinner Tue-Sat, brunch wknds, clsd Mon • lesbian-owned/run

Caffe Luna Piena 558 Castro St **415/621-2566** • lunch & dinner, clsd Mon • lesbians/gay men • Californian • patio

Carta 1760 Market St (nr Gough) **415/863-3516** • lunch & dinner, Sun brunch • theme menus • gay-owned/run

China Court 599 Castro **415/626-5358** • lunch & dinner • Chinese • some veggie • beer/wine • $5-10

Chloe's Cafe 1399 Church St, Noe Valley (at 26th St) **415/648-4116** • 8am-3pm, till 4pm wknds • come early for the excellent wknd brunch

Chow 215 Church St **415/552-2469** • 11am-10pm, till midnight Th-Sat • popular • eclectic & affordable

Cove Cafe 434 Castro St **415/626-0462** • 7am-10pm • lesbians/gay men • some veggie • wheelchair access • $8-12

Dame 1815 Market St (at Octavia) **415/255-8818** • lunch & dinner, Sun brunch

Eric's Chinese Restaurant 1500 Church St, Noe Valley (at 27th St) **415/282-0919** • 11am-9pm • popular • some veggie • $7-12

Hot 'N Hunky 4039 18th St **415/621-6365** • 11am-midnight • lesbians/gay men • hamburgers • some veggie • $5-10

It's Tops 1801 Market St (at Octavia) **415/431-6395** • 8am-3pm, till 3am Wed-Sat • classic diner

Little Italy 4109 24th St **415/821-1515** • dinner only • plenty veggie • beer/wine • $15-20

M&L Market (May's) 691 14th St (at Church) **415/431-7044** • clsd Sun • great huge sandwiches

Ma Tante Sumi 4243 18th St (at Collingwood) **415/552-6663** • 5:30pm-10pm • cont'l/Japanese

Mecca 2029 Market St (at Dolores) **415/621-7000** • dinner from 6pm • popular • Mediterranean • swanky bar • valet parking • wheelchair access • $13-19

Orphan Andy's 3991 17th St **415/864-9795** • 24hrs • diner • gay-owned/run

Pasta Pomodoro 2304 Market St **415/558-8123** • open till midnight • popular • inexpensive Italian

Patio Cafe 531 Castro St **415/621-4640** • lesbians/gay men • California cuisine • enclosed patio • popular brunch • $10-20

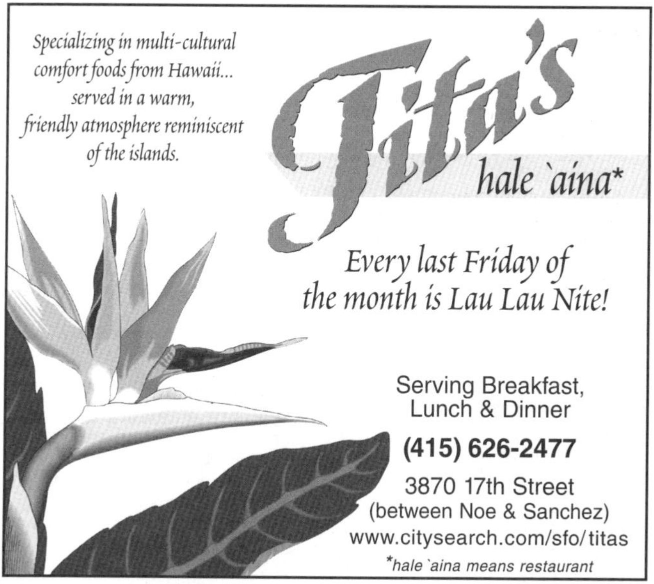
Specializing in multi-cultural comfort foods from Hawaii... served in a warm, friendly atmosphere reminiscent of the islands.
Tita's
hale `aina*
Every last Friday of the month is Lau Lau Nite!
Serving Breakfast, Lunch & Dinner
(415) 626-2477
3870 17th Street
(between Noe & Sanchez)
www.citysearch.com/sfo/titas
*hale `aina means restaurant

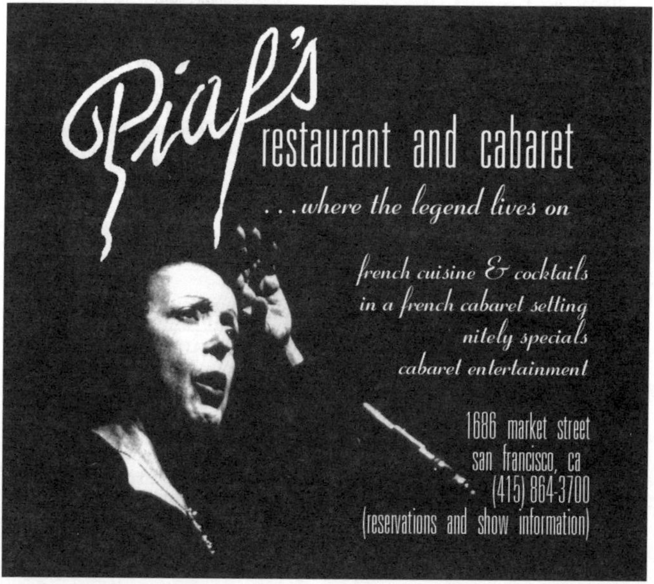
Piaf's
restaurant and cabaret
. . .where the legend lives on
french cuisine & cocktails
in a french cabaret setting
nitely specials
cabaret entertainment
1686 market street
san francisco, ca
(415) 864-3700
(reservations and show information)

▲**Piaf's** 1686 Market St (at Gough) **415/864-3700** • dinner Tue-Sun, Sun brunch, clsd Mon • French cuisine & cocktails • also cabaret

The Sausage Factory 517 Castro St **415/626-1250** • noon-1am • lesbians/gay men • pizza & pasta • some veggie • beer/wine • $8-15

Sparky's 242 Church St **415/626-8666** • 24hrs • diner • some veggie • popular late night • $8-12

Tin-Pan Asian Bistro 2251 Market St **415/565-0733** • 11am-11pm, wknd brunch • sake cocktails

▲**Tita's Hale'aine** 3870 17th St (btwn Sanchez & Noe) **415/626-2477** • 11am-10pm, from 9am Sat, till 3pm Sun, clsd Mon • popular • traditional Hawaiian • plenty veggie • wheelchair access • lesbian-owned/run • $6-10

Valentine's Cafe 1793 Church St, Noe Valley (at 30th St) **415/285-2257** • clsd Mon-Tue, call for hours • lunch, dinner, wknd brunch • plenty veggie

Welcome Home 464 Castro St **415/626-3600** • 8am-11pm • popular • lesbians/gay men • homestyle • some veggie • beer/wine • $7-12

Zuni Cafe 1658 Market St (at Haight) **415/552-2522** • clsd Mon • popular • upscale cont'l/Mediterranean • full bar • $30-40

Entertainment & Recreation

Castro Country Club 4058 18th St **415/552-6102** • 2pm-11pm, till midnight Sat, from 10am wknds • alcohol & drug-free club

Bookstores

A Different Light 489 Castro St **415/431-0891** • 10am till midnight • bookstore & queer info clearinghouse

Aardvark Books 227 Church St **415/552-6733** • 10:30am-10:30pm, from 9:30am Sun • mostly used • good lesbigay section • say hello to Ace, the bookstore cat par excellence

Get Lost 1825 Market St (at Guerrero) **415/437-0529** • 10am-7pm, till 6pm Sat, 11am-5pm Sun • travel books • lesbigay section

Retail Shops

Does Your Father Know? 548 Castro St **415/241-9865** • 9:30am-10pm, till 11pm Fri-Sat, 10am-9pm Sun • lesbigay gifts & videos

Does Your Mother Know? 4079 18th St **415/864-3160** • 9:30am-10pm • cards • T-shirts

Don't Panic 541 Castro St **415/553-8989** • 10am-9pm • campy T-shirts • gifts

Image Leather 2199 Market St (at Sanchez) **415/621-7551** • 9am-10pm, 11am-7pm Sun • custom leather clothing • accessories • toys

Just for Fun 3982 24th St, Noe Valley (at Noe) **415/285-4068** • 9am-9pm, till 8pm Sat, 10am-6pm Sun • gift shop

La Sirena Botanica 1509 Church St (at 27th St) **415/285-0612** • 11am-7pm • Afro-Caribbean religious articles

Leather Zone of San Francisco 2352 Market St **415/255-8585** • 11am-7pm, noon-6pm Sun, open later in summer • new & used fetishwear

▲ **Rolo** 2351 Market St **415/431-4545** • 10am-8pm, till 7pm Sun • designer labels • also 450 Castro location, 415/626-7171

Uncle Mame 2241 Market St **415/626-1953** • kitsch lover's wonderland

Under One Roof 549 Castro **415/252-9430** • 11am-7pm • 100% donated to AIDS relief • wheelchair access

Spiritual Groups

Congregation Sha'ar Zahav 290 Dolores (at 16th) **415/861-6932** • 8:15pm Fri • lesbian/gay synagogue

MCC of San Francisco 150 Eureka St (btwn 18th & 19th Sts) **415/863-4434** • 9am, 11am & 7pm Sun, 7pm Wed

Most Holy Redeemer Church 100 Diamond St (at 18th St) **415/863-6259** • 7:30am & 10am Sun, 5pm Sat (vigil mass) • mostly gay/lesbian Roman Catholic parish

Gyms & Health Clubs

Market Street Gym 2301 Market St **415/626-4488** • lesbians/gay men • day passes available

SF—South of Market

Accommodations

Ramada Market St 1231 Market St (btwn 8th & 9th) **415/626-8000, 800/227-4747** • gay-friendly • wheelchair access • IGLTA

Victorian Hotel 54 4th St (btwn Market & Mission) **415/986-4400, 800/227-3804** • gay-friendly • 1913 landmark hotel • private/shared baths • also restaurant • SF cuisine • full bar • $49-149

Bars

CW Saloon 917 Folsom St (at 5th St) **415/974-1585** • 4:30pm-2am • gay-friendly • neighborhood bar • theme nights

Rawhide II 280 7th St (btwn Howard & Folsom) **415/621-1197** • 4pm-2am, from noon wknds • mostly gay men • dancing/DJ • country/western • dance lessons 7:30pm-9:30pm Mon-Fri

San Francisco Eagle 398 12th St (at Harrison) **415/626-0880** • noon-2am • mostly gay men • leather • occasional women's leather events • patio

Nightclubs

1015 Folsom 1015 Folsom St (at 6th) **415/431-1200** • gay/straight • 10pm-4:30am • call for events • cover charge

Asia SF 201 9th St (at Howard) **415/255-2742** • gay/straight • 10pm-close Wed-Sat • dancing/DJ • multi-racial Asian • theme nights • go-go boys • also Cal-Asian restaurant 5pm-10pm Wed-Sun

Brown Suga 139 8th St (at Minna St, at the 'CoCo Club') **415/245-2753** • 1st Fri • mostly women • dancing/DJ • hip hop • multi-racial

Club Asia 174 King St (in 'King St Garage') **415/285-2742** • 10pm-close 2nd & 4th Fri • mostly men • dancing/DJ • multi-racial Asian • cover charge

Club Mami 201 9th St (at Howard, at 'Asia SF') **415/248-1340** • mostly women • dancing/DJ • monthly parties • multi-racial clientele • call for info

Club Universe 177 Townsend (at 3rd St) **415/974-6020, 415/289-6650** • 9:30pm-7am Sat • popular • mostly gay men • dancing/DJ • cover charge

The CoCo Club 139 8th St (btwn Mission & Howard, enter on Minna) **415/626-2337** • 8:30pm-2am, clsd Mon-Tue • mostly women • many events for women of color • live shows • very popular 'In Bed With Fairy Butch' cabaret alternate Fridays • call for events

Doll House 399 9th St (at Harrison, at 'The Stud') **415/505-8934** • Fri • mostly women • rock & roll dance club for dykes & queers • call for info on other women's clubs

Endup 401 6th St (at Harrison) **415/357-0827** • clsd Tue • mostly gay men • dancing/DJ • multi-racial • many different theme nights • popular Sun mornings

Funk & Soul Night 399 9th St (at Harrison, in 'The Stud') **415/252-7883 (Stud #)** • 9am-2am Mon • mostly gay men • dancing/DJ • mostly African-American • young crowd

Futura 174 King St (at 3rd St, in 'King St Garage') **415/665-6715** • 10pm-3am 2nd & 4th Sat • popular • mostly gay men • dancing/DJ • mostly Latino-American • live shows • cover charge

Girl Spot (G-Spot) 401 6th St (at the 'Endup') **415/337-4962 (Endup#)** • from 9pm Sat only • popular • mostly women • dancing/DJ • go-go dancers

Jaded 314 11th St (at Folsom, in the 'Transmission Theater') **650/697-0375x3** • monthly • lesbians/gay men • dancing/DJ • multi-racial • transgender-friendly

Pleasuredome 177 Townsend (at 3rd St) **415/289-6699, 415/974-6020** • Sun night dance club • mostly gay men • dancing/DJ • call hotline for details • cover charge

▲ **Red** 399 9th St (at Harrison, at 'The Stud') **415/339-8310** • 9pm-2am 3rd Fri • women only • dancing/DJ • multi-racial clientele

Soul SF 1190 Folsom St (at 8th) **415/647-8258** • 9pm-3am Sat • lesbians/gay men • dancing/DJ • multi-racial clientele

Sound Factory 525 Harrison St (1st St) **415/339-8686** • 9:30pm-4am Fri-Sat only • mostly gay men • dancing/DJ

The Stud 399 9th St (at Harrison) **415/252-7883 (info line), 415/863-6623** • 5pm-2am • popular • lesbians/gay men • dancing/DJ • theme nights • outrageous 'Trannyshack' Tue

Sugar 399 9th St (at Harrison, in 'The Stud') **415/252-7883 (Stud #)** • 9am-5am Sat • mostly gay men • dancing/DJ • great music & wall-to-wall alternababes

Cafes

Brain Wash 1122 Folsom St (at 7th St) **415/861-3663, 415/431-9274** • 7:30am-midnight, till 1am Fri-Sat • cafe & laundromat

The Chat House 139 8th St (at Minna) **415/255-8783** • brkfst & lunch menu • often cute women waiting or sitting at tables • beer/wine • women-owned/run

Restaurants

42 Degrees 235 16th St (at 3rd St) **415/777-5558** • lunch wkdys, dinner Wed-Sat • 'jazz supper club' • full bar

Boulevard 1 Mission St (at Steuart) **415/543-6084** • lunch & dinner • one of SF's finest

Caribbean Zone 55 Natoma St (btwn 1st & 2nd) **415/541-9465** • lunch & dinner, clsd Sun • some veggie • cocktails • festive decor • $7-15

Fringale 570 4th St (btwn Bryant & Brannan) **415/543-0573** • lunch & dinner, clsd Sun • Mediterranean • wheelchair access • $11-16

Hamburger Mary's 1582 Folsom St (at 12th St) **415/626-5767, 415/626-1985** • 11:30am-2am, from 10am wknds, clsd Mon • some veggie • wheelchair access • $7-15

Hawthorne Lane 22 Hawthorne St (btwn 2nd & 3rd off Howard) **415/777-9779** • dinner nightly, lunch Mon-Fri

Le Charm 315 5th St (at Folsom) **415/546-6128** • clsd Sun, dinner only Sat

Line Up 398 7th St (at Harrison) **415/861-2887** • 11am-10pm • lesbians/gay men • Mexican • some veggie • $8-15

Lulu 816 Folsom St (at 4th St) **415/495-5775** • lunch & dinner • upscale Mediterrranean • some veggie • full bar • $12-20

Manora's Thai Cuisine 1600 Folsom (at 12th) **415/861-6224** • lunch & dinner • some veggie

Wa-Ha-Ka! 1489 Folsom (at 11th St) **415/861-1410** • Mexican • plenty veggie • $5-10

Woodward's Garden 1700 Mission St (at Duboce) **415/621-7122** • dinner seating at 6pm & 8pm, clsd Mon-Tue • wheelchair access

Retail Shops

A Taste of Leather 1339 Folsom (btwn 9th & 10th) **415/252-9166, 800/367-0786** • noon-8pm

Leather Etc 1201 Folsom St (at 8th St) **415/864-7558** • 10:30am-7pm, 11am-6pm Sat, noon-5pm Sun

Mr S Leather 310 7th St **415/863-7764** • 11am-7pm, noon-6pm Sun • erotic goods • custom leather • latex

Stompers 323 10th St (at Folsom) **415/255-6422** • noon-8pm, till 6pm Sun • boots • cigars • gloves

Stormy Leather 1158 Howard St (btwn 7th & 8th) **415/626-1672** • noon-7pm, 2pm-6pm Sun • leather • latex • toys • magazines • women-owned/run

Sex Clubs

Power Exchange Substation I 86 Otis St (btwn S Van Ness & Gough) **415/974-1460, 415/487-9944** • call for hours • playspace for female, transgendered, bi & straight couples

SF—Polk Street Area

Accommodations

Atherton Hotel 685 Ellis St (at Larkin) **415/474-5720, 800/474-5720** • gay-friendly • food served • full bar • IGLTA

▲ **Essex Hotel** 684 Ellis St **415/474-4664, 800/443-7739 (IN CA)** • gay-friendly • boutique hotel w/European-style hospitality • wheelchair access • IGLTA • $59-89

▲ **The Phoenix Hotel** 601 Eddy St (at Larkin) **415/776-1380, 800/248-9466** • gay-friendly • 1950s-style motor lodge • popular • swimming • kids ok • fabulous 'Back Flip' bar • IGLTA • $99-169

The Super 8 Lombard Hotel 1015 Geary St (at Polk) **415/673-5232, 800/777-3210** • gay-friendly • kids ok • non-smoking rms available • up to $100

Bars

Back Flip 601 Eddy St (at 'The Phoenix Hotel') **415/771-3547** • from 5pm • gay-friendly • cocktails w/ class • food served

The Cinch 1723 Polk St (at Clay) **415/776-4162** • 6am-2am • mostly gay men • neighborhood bar • patio • lots of pool tables & no attitude

Mother Lode/ Divas 1081 Post St (at Larkin) **415/928-6006, 415/474-DIVA** • 6am-2am • mostly gay men • neighborhood bar • dancing/DJ • multi-racial • transsexuals, transvestites & their admirers • live shows

Cafes

Quetzal 1234 Polk St (at Sutter) **415/673-4181** • 6am-11pm • food served • live shows • internet connections • beer/wine

Restaurants

Grubstake II 1525 Pine St (at Polk) **415/673-8268** • 5pm-4am, 10am-4am wknds • lesbians/gay men • beer/wine

Spuntino 524 Van Ness Ave **415/861-7772** • 7am-8pm, from 10am wknds, till 7pm Sun • Italian • also cafe & desserts

Bookstores

A Clean Well Lighted Place For Books 601 Van Ness Ave (at Turk) **415/441-6670** • 10am-11pm, till midnight Fri-Sat, till 9pm Sun • independent • lesbigay section • many readings

Retail Shops

Hog On Ice 1630 Polk St (at Sacramento) **415/771-7909** • 10am-10pm, till 6pm Sat • novelties • books • CDs

SF—Downtown & North Beach

Accommodations

▲ **The Abigail Hotel** 246 McAllister St (at Hyde) **415/861-9728, 800/243-6510** • gay-friendly • IGLTA • $85-125 • also 'Millennium' restaurant 415/487-9800 • gourmet vegetarian

Allison Hotel 417 Stockton St (at Sutter) **415/986-8737, 800/628-6456** • gay-friendly • some shared baths • IGLTA • $99-189

Amsterdam Hotel 749 Taylor St (at Sutter) **415/673-3277, 800/637-3444** • gay-friendly • charming European-style hotel • $69-89

Andrews 624 Post St **415/563-6877, 800/926-3739** • gay-friendly • Victorian hotel • also restaurant • Italian • $92-160

Canterbury Hotel 750 Sutter St (at Taylor) **415/474-6464, 800/528-1234** • gay-friendly • also 'Murray's Glasshouse' restaurant & bar • IGLTA • $125-250

Cartwright Hotel 524 Sutter St (at Powell) **415/421-2865, 800/227-3844** • gay-friendly • free gym passes • afternoon tea • wine hour • IGLTA • $129-230

▲ **The Commodore International Hotel** 825 Sutter St (at Jones) **415/923-6800, 800/338-6848** • gay-friendly • also popular 'Red Room' lounge • kids ok • $99-149

Dakota Hotel 606 Post St (at Taylor) **415/931-7475** • gay-friendly • near Union Square • $65-105

Grand Hyatt San Francisco 345 Stockton St (at Sutter) **415/398-1234, 800/233-1234** • gay-friendly • IGLTA

Harbor Court Hotel 165 Steuart St (btwn Howard & Mission) **415/537-7553, 800/346-0555** • gay-friendly • in the heart of the Financial District

Hotel Diva 440 Geary (at Mason) **415/202-8700, 800/553-1900** • gay-friendly • also Italian restaurant • IGLTA • $159-229

Hotel Griffon 155 Steuart St (at Mission) **415/495-2100, 800/321-2201** • gay-friendly • also restaurant • bistro/cont'l • wheelchair access • $145-199

Hotel Monaco 501 Geary St (at Taylor) **415/292-8132, 888/852-3551** • gay-friendly • full bar • IGLTA • $195-375

▲ **The Hotel Rex** 562 Sutter St (at Powell) **415/433-4434, 800/433-4434** • gay-friendly • full bar • wheelchair access • $129-165

Hotel Triton 342 Grant Ave (at Bush) **415/394-0500, 800/433-6611** • gay-friendly • wheelchair access • IGLTA • $135-185

Hotel Vintage Court 650 Bush St (at Powell) **415/392–4666, 800/654–1100** • gay-friendly • fireplaces • also world-famous 5-star 'Masa's' restaurant • French • $75 prix fixe • wheelchair access • IGLTA • $129-169

Hyatt Regency San Francisco 5 Embarcadero Center (at California) **415/788–1234, 800/233–1234** • gay-friendly • luxury waterfront hotel • IGLTA

Hyde Park Suites 415/771–0200, 800/227–3608 • gay-friendly • Mediterranean-inspired 1- & 2-bdrm suites • sundeck • kitchens • IGLTA • $165-220

Juliana Hotel 590 Bush St (at Stockton) **415/392–2540, 800/328–3880** • gay-friendly • recently featured on 'Lifestyles of the Rich & Famous' as one of SF's finest hotels

King George Hotel 334 Mason St (at O'Farrell) **415/781–5050, 800/288–6005** • gay-friendly • also 'The Bread & Honey Tearoom' • wheelchair access • $85-175

▲ **Maxwell Hotel** 386 Geary (at Mason) **415/986–2000, 888/734–6299** • gay-friendly • newly-restored 1908 art deco masterpiece • wheelchair access • $135-195

▲ **Nob Hill Lambourne** 725 Pine St (at Powell) **415/433–2287, 800/274–8466** • gay-friendly • luxurious 'business accommodation' • kitchens • kids ok • $200-325

Nob Hill Pensione 835 Hyde St (btwn Bush & Sutter) **415/885–2987** • gay-friendly • European-style hotel • shared/private baths • smokefree • kids ok • also restaurant • $89-129

Pensione International Hotel 875 Post St (at Hyde) **415/775–3344, 800/358–8123** • gay-friendly • Victorian-styled hotel built in early 1900s • shared/private baths • $65-90

Ramada Union Square 345 Taylor St (at Ellis) **415/673–2332, 800/228–2828** • gay-friendly • also restaurant & full bar • wheelchair access

Renoir Hotel 45 McAllister St (at Market St) **415/626–5200, 800/576–3388** • gay/straight • wheelchair access

Savoy Hotel 580 Geary St (at Jones) **415/441–2700, 800/227–4223** • gay-friendly • also popular restaurant & bar • IGLTA

▲ **Sutter Place 800/959–4991** • romantic 1-bdrm apt • perfect for couples • close to Union Square • 5-day minimum • $110

The York Hotel 940 Sutter St (at Leavenworth) **415/885–6800, 800/808–9675** • gay-friendly • boutique hotel • $129-210

Cafes

Cafe Claude 7 Claude (nr Bush & Kearny) **415/392–3505** • from 11:30am, clsd Sun • live jazz Th-Fri • as close to Paris as you can get in SF • beer/wine

Dottie's True Blue Cafe 522 Jones St (at Geary) **415/885–2767** • 7:30am-2pm, clsd Tue • plenty veggie • great brkfst • gay-owned/run

Restaurants

Cafe Akimbo 116 Maiden Ln (at Grant) **415/433–2288** • lunch & dinner, clsd Sun • lesbians/gay men • beer/wine • gay-owned/run

Campo Santo 240 Columbus Ave (at Broadway) **415/433–9623** • lunch & dinner, clsd Mon night • Mexican • some veggie • beer/wine • hip decor • $8-15

Mario's Bohemian Cigar Store Cafe 566 Columbus Ave (at Green) **415/362–0536** • great foccacia sandwiches • some veggie • beer/wine

Max's on the Square 398 Geary St (at Mason) **415/646–8600** • lunch & dinner • seafood • full bar

Millennium 246 McAllister St (at Hyde, at the Abigail Hotel) **415/487–9800** • lunch & dinner • Euro-Mediterranean • upscale vegetarian

Moose's 1652 Stockton (at Columbus & Union) **415/989–7800** • upscale bistro menu

Bookstores

City Lights Bookstore 261 Columbus Ave, North Beach (at Pacific) **415/362–8193** • 10am-midnight • historic beatnik bookstore • many progressive titles • whole flr for poetry

Retail Shops

Billy Blue 54 Geary (at Grant) **415/781–2111, 800/772–BLUE** • 10am-6pm, clsd Sun • men's clothing tailored for women

SF—Mission District

Accommodations

▲ **Andora Inn** 2434 Mission (btwn 20th & 21st) **415/282–0337, 800/967–9219** • lesbians/gay men • guesthouse • near Castro & public transportation • smokefree • also restaurant • full bar • IGLTA • $79-185

▲ **The Inn San Francisco** 943 S Van Ness Ave (btwn 20th & 21st) **415/641–0188, 800/359–0913** • gay-friendly • Victorian mansion • full brkfst • hot tub • shared/private baths • kitchens • fireplaces • patio • IGLTA • $85-225

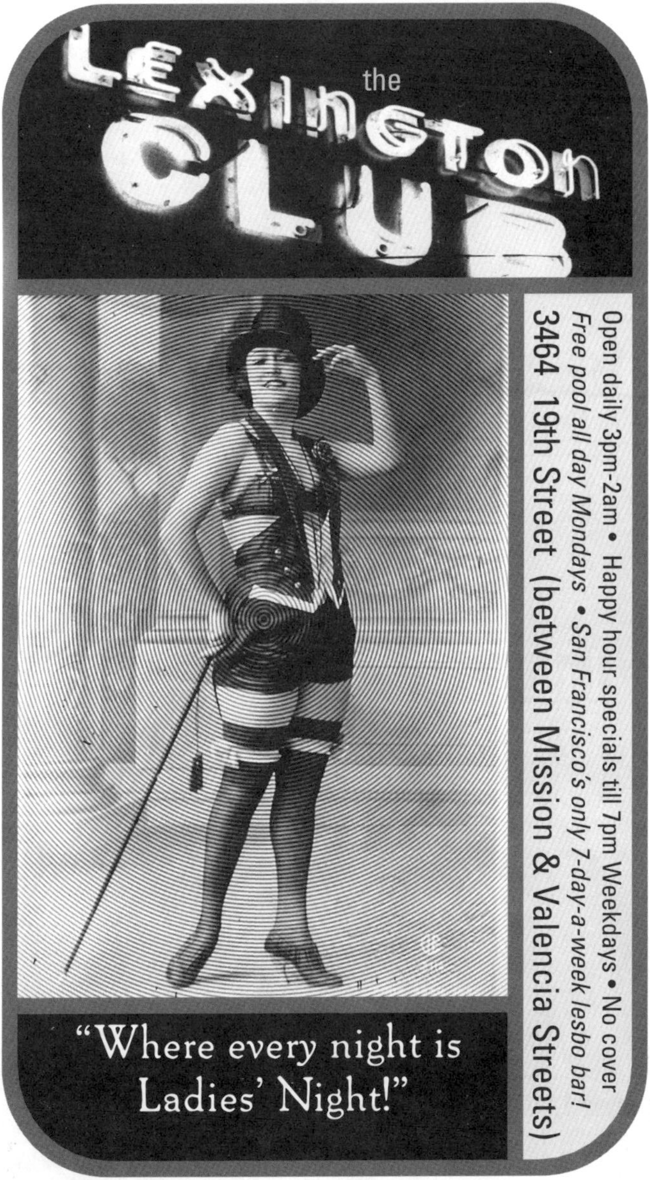

the
LEXINGTON
CLUB
Open daily 3pm-2am • Happy hour specials till 7pm Weekdays • No cover
Free pool all day Mondays • San Francisco's only 7-day-a-week lesbo bar!
3464 19th Street (between Mission & Valencia Streets)
"Where every night is Ladies' Night!"

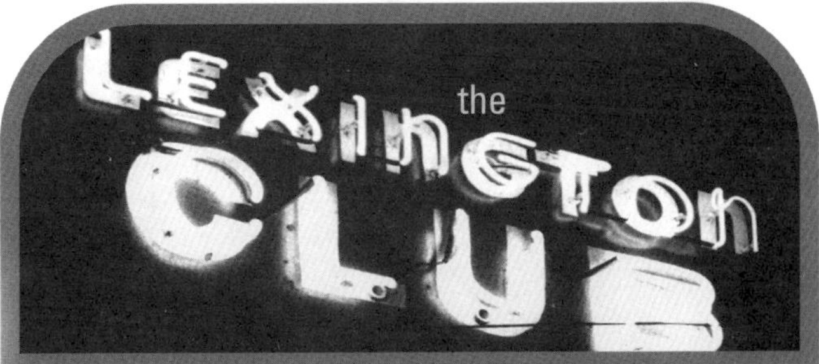

the BEST in the WEST!

backstreet
a funky fiesta mix for women
@ Club 550 • 10pm-3am
(2nd Saturday monthly)

MANGO
sweet sexy fun for women
@ EL RIO 9PM-2AM
(4th Saturday monthly)

clubred
sf's original hip-hop club for women
@ the stud • 10pm-3am
(3rd Friday monthly)

colors
100% Latina Soul
@ Jelly's 9pm-2am
(last Saturday monthly)

clubline: 415.339.8310
backstreetsf@hotmail.com

Bars

El Rio 3158–A Mission St (at Cesar Chavez) **415/282–3325** • 3pm-2am, till midnight Mon • gay/straight • neighborhood bar • multi-racial Latino/a clientele • live shows • patio • popular T-dance 'Mango' 4th Sat 3pm-7pm

▲ **Lexington Club** 3464 19th St (at Lexington) **415/863–2052** • 3pm-2am • popular • mostly women • neighborhood bar • hip younger crowd • lesbian-owned/run

Lot 99 811 Valencia (btwn 19th & 20th Sts) **415/285–5999** • noon-2am • lesbians/gay men • neighborhood bar • wheelchair access

Phone Booth 1398 S Van Ness Ave (at 25th) **415/648–4683** • 10am-2am • lesbians/gay men • neighborhood bar • piano bar wknds

Wild Side West 424 Cortland (at Bennington) **415/647–3099** • 1pm-2am • gay/straight • neighborhood bar • patio • magic garden

Nightclubs

▲ **Backstreet** 550 Barneveld (off Bayshore) **415/339–8310** • 10pm-3am 2nd Sat • women only • dancing/DJ

Chulo 2925 16th St (btwn Mission & S Van Ness, at 'Liquid') **415/248–1616** • from 9pm 4th Sun • mostly gay men • dancing/DJ • mostly Latino/a • go-go hombres • 'una fiesta para los nenes y nenas con sabor'

▲ **Colors** 295 China Basin Way (off 3rd & Pier 50, at 'Jelly's') **415/339–8310** • 9pm-2am last Sat • mostly women • dancing/DJ • multi-racial clientele • San Francisco's longest running Latina dance club

Esta Noche 3079 16th St (at Mission) **415/861–5757** • 1pm-2am • mostly gay men • dancing/DJ • mostly Latino/a • live shows • salsa & disco in a classic Tijuana dive

▲ **Mango** 3158 Mission St (at El Rio) **415/339–8310** • 3pm-7:30pm 4th Sat • women only • dancing/DJ • multi-racial clientele

Metronome Ballroom 1830 17th St (at De Haro) **415/252–9000** • 'same-sex' dance parties • call for times • swing 1st Fri • salsa 3rd Sun • ballroom tea dance 4th Sun • also lessons • cover charge

Stompy Hi-Fi 550 Barneveld (off Bayshore) **415/267–4807** • gay/straight • last Sat only • dancing/DJ • cover charge

Cafes

Cafe Commons 3161 Mission St (btwn Cesar Chavez & Valencia) **415/282-2928** • 7am-9pm, 8am-10pm wknds • sandwiches • plenty veggie • patio • wheelchair access • women-owned/run • $4-7

Farleys 1315 18th St (at Texas St, Potrero Hill) **415/648-1545** • 7am-10pm, from 8am wknds • coffeehouse

Radio Valencia 1199 Valencia St (at 23rd) **415/826-1199** • 5pm-midnight, noon till midnight Wed-Sun • sandwiches & dessert • artsy cafe • beer/wine

Red Dora's Bearded Lady Dyke Cafe & Gallery 485 14th St (at Guerrero) **415/626-2805** • 7am-7pm, from 9am wknds • mostly women • funky brunch & sandwiches • plenty veggie • wknd performances • patio • women-owned/run • $4-7

Restaurants

The Barking Basset Cafe 803 Cortland Ave (at Ellsworth) **415/648-2146** • 8am-3pm, clsd Tue, dinner 5pm-9pm Th-Sat only

Cafe Istanbul 525 Valencia St **415/863-8854** • noon-11pm, till midnight Fri-Sat, Mediterranean • some veggie • authentic Turkish coffee • bellydancers Sat

▲ **Charanga** 2351 Mission St (at 20th St) **415/282-1813** • popular • 5:30pm-10pm, till 11pm Th-Sat, clsd Sun-Mon • tapas • beer/wine/sangria • plenty veggie • wheelchair access • women-owned/run

Firecracker 1007 1/2 Valencia St (at 21st) **415/642-3470** • Chinese • some veggie

Just For You 1453 18th St, Potrero Hill (btwn Missouri & Connecticut) **415/647-3033** • hours vary • popular • lesbians/gay men • Southern brkfst • some veggie • women-owned/run • $4-7

Klein's Delicatessen 501 Connecticut St (at 20th St, Potrero Hill) **415/821-9149** • 7am-7pm, 8am-5:30pm Sun • patio • sandwiches & salads • some veggie • beer/wine • women-owned/run • $4-10

Pancho Villa 3071 16th St (btwn Mission & Valencia) **415/864-8840** • 10am-midnight • best 'Mission-style' burritos in city • also 'El Toro' at 18th & Valencia • some veggie • $4-8 • wheelchair access

Pauline's Pizza Pie 260 Valencia St (btwn 14th & Duboce) **415/552-2050** • 5pm-10pm, clsd Sun-Mon • popular • lesbians/gay men • gourmet pizza • beer/wine

Picaro 3120 16th St (at Valencia) **415/431-4089** • dinner only • Spanish tapas bar

The Slanted Door 584 Valencia St (at 17th) **415/861-8032** • popular • Vietnamese • reservations advised

Slow Club 2501 Mariposa (at Hampshire) **415/241-9390** • 11:30am-2:30 wkdys, dinner 6:30pm-10pm Tue-Sat, wknd brunch • full bar • wheelchair access

Ti-Couz 3108 16th St **415/252-7373** • 11am-11pm, from 10am wknds • Breton dinner & dessert crepes • plenty veggie • beer/wine • wheelchair access • $5-10

Entertainment & Recreation

Brendita's Latin Tour **415/921-0625** • walking tours of the Mission

Women's Building 3543 18th St (btwn Valencia & Guerrero) **415/431-1180** • check out some of the most beautiful murals in the Mission District

Bookstores

Bernal Books 401 Cortland Ave, Bernal Hts (at Bennington) **415/550-0293** • 10am-7pm, till 5pm Sat, till 4pm Sun, clsd Mon • community bookstore for Bernal Heights & beyond • lesbigay section

Dog Eared Books 900 Valencia St (at 20th) **415/282-1901** • 10am-10pm, till 8pm Sun • new & used • good lesbigay section

Modern Times Bookstore 888 Valencia St **415/282-9246** • 10am-9pm, till 10pm Fri-Sat, 11am-6pm Sun • alternative • lesbigay section • readings

Retail Shops

Body Manipulations 3234 16th St (btwn Guerrero & Dolores) **415/621-0408** • noon-7pm • piercing (walk-in basis) • jewelry

Leather Tongue Video 714 Valencia St (at 18th) **415/552-2900** • noon-11pm, till midnight Fri-Sat • great collection of camp, cult & obscure videos

Soho Gallery 1218 Valencia St (at 23rd) **800/742-8863** • cards • gifts

Spiritual Groups

The Episcopal Church of St John the Evangelist 1661 15th St (btwn Mission & Valencia, enter on Julian Ave) **415/861-1436** • 11am Sun & 6pm most Weds • Oasis congregation • wheelchair access

Gyms & Health Clubs

Osento 955 Valencia St **415/282-6333** • 1pm-midnight • women only • baths • hot tub • massage

Erotica

▲ **Good Vibrations** 1210 Valencia St (at 23rd) **415/550-7399** • 11am-7pm, till 8pm Fri-Sat • clean, well-lighted sex toy store • also mail order

SF—Haight, Fillmore, Hayes Valley

Accommodations

Alamo Square Inn 719 Scott St (at Grove) **415/922-2055, 800/345-9888** • gay-friendly • 1895 Queen Anne & 1896 Tudor Revival Victorian mansions • full brkfst • smokefree • kids ok • $85-295

▲ **The Archbishops Mansion** 1000 Fulton St (at Steiner) **415/563-7872, 800/543-5820** • gay-friendly • smokefree • one of SF's grandest homes • $129-385

Baby Bear's House 1424 Page St (btwn Central & Masonic) **415/255-9777, 888/9-BEAR-4-U** • gay-friendly • 1892 Victorian • close to the Castro • gay families especially welcome • $75-125

▲ **Bock's B&B** 1448 Willard St (at Parnassus) **415/664-6842** • gay-friendly • restored 1906 Edwardian residence • shared/private baths • smokefree • lesbian-owned/run • $45-80

Casa Loma Hotel 610 Fillmore St (at Fell) **415/552-7100** • gay-friendly • shared bath • kids ok • $35

The Chateau Tivoli 1057 Steiner St (at Golden Gate) **415/776-5462, 800/228-1647** • gay-friendly • historic San Francisco B&B • $80-200

Hayes Valley Inn 417 Gough St (at Hayes) **415/431-9131, 800/930-7999** • gay/straight • European-style pension • $70

Hotel Majestic 1500 Sutter St (at Gough) **415/441-1100, 800/869-8966** • gay-friendly • one of SF's earliest grand hotels • also restaurant • full bar • wheelchair access • $145-425

Inn 1890 1890 Page St (at Stanyan) **415/386-0486, 888/INN-1890** • gay/straight • Victorian near Golden Gate Park • kitchens • fireplaces • apt available • gay-owned/run

Inn at the Opera 333 Fulton St (at Franklin) **415/863-8400, 800/325-2708** • gay-friendly • also Mediterranean restaurant • $140-340

▲ **Jackson Court** 2198 Jackson St (at Buchanan) **415/929-7670** • gay-friendly • $150-205

Lombard Plaza Motel 2026 Lombard St (at Webster) **415/921-2444** • gay-friendly • $59-99

The Mansions 2220 Sacramento St (at Laguna) **415/929-9444, 800/826-9398** • gay-friendly • full brkfst • IGLTA • $187-368 (includes magic show)

Metro Hotel 319 Divisadero St (at Haight) **415/861-5364** • gay-friendly • food served • $55-104

The Queen Anne Hotel 1590 Sutter St (at Octavia) **415/441-2828, 800/227-3970** • gay-friendly • popular • 1890 landmark • fireplaces • IGLTA • $120-295

Radisson Miyako Hotel 1625 Post St (at Laguna) **415/922-3200, 800/533-4567** • gay-friendly • in the heart of Japantown • also 'Ristorante Yoyo' • wheelchair access • IGLTA • $179-299

Shannon-Kavanaugh Guest House 722 Steiner St **415/563-2727** • gay-friendly • 1-bdrm garden apt $125-175 • also 2-bdrm cottage $200-300

Stanyan Park Hotel 750 Stanyan St (at Waller) **415/751-1000** • gay-friendly • restored Victorian hotel listed on the Nat'l Register of Historic Places • fireplaces • kids ok • $110-300

Bars

Hayes & Vine 377 Hayes St (at Gough) **415/626-5301** • 5pm-midnight, till 1am wknds, 4pm-10pm Sun • gay/straight • wine bar

The Lion Pub 2062 Divisadero St (at Sacramento) **415/567-6565** • 3pm-2am • mostly gay men • professional • theme nights

Marlena's 488 Hayes St (at Octavia) **415/864-6672** • noon-2am, 10am-2am wknds • mostly gay men • neighborhood bar • drag shows wknds • wheelchair access

Noc Noc 557 Haight St (at Fillmore) **415/861-5811** • 5pm-2am • gay-friendly • beer/wine

Traxx 1437 Haight St (at Masonic) **415/864-4213** • noon-2am • mostly gay men • neighborhood bar • wheelchair access

Nightclubs

The Box (Version 2.0) 628 Divisadero (at 'The Justice League') • 9pm-2am Th only • popular • lesbians/gay men • dancing/DJ • multi-racial • cover charge

The Top 424 Haight St (at Webster) **415/864-7386** • gay-friendly • dancing/DJ • alternative • theme nights • call for events

Cafes

Fillmore Grind 711 Fillmore (at Hayes) **415/775-5680** • 6:30am-7pm

Mad Magda's Russian Tearoom & Cafe 579 Hayes St (at Octavia) **415/864-7654** • popular • lesbians/gay men • eclectic crowd • magic garden • tarot & palm readers daily

Restaurants

131 Supper Club 131 Gough St (at Page) **415/621-6766** • dinner Tue-Sat, Sun brunch, clsd Mon • some veggie • full bar • wheelchair access • $10-15

Alamo Square Seafood 803 Fillmore (at Grove) **415/440-2828** • dinner & Sun brunch

Blue Muse 409 Gough St (at Fell) **415/626-7505** • 8am-10pm, wknd brunch • some veggie • full bar • wheelchair access • $10-15

Cafe Delle Stelle 395 Hayes (at Gough) **415/252-1110** • popular • Italian • beer/wine

Cha Cha Cha's 1801 Haight St (at Shrader) **415/386-7670** • till 11pm • Cuban/Cajun • excellent sangria • worth the wait!

Doidge's 2217 Union St (at Fillmore) **415/921-2149** • great brkfst • wheelchair access

Garibaldi's 347 Presidio (at Sacramento) **415/563-8841** • lunch & dinner • Italian • full bar • wheelchair access • gay-owned/run

Greens Fort Mason, Bldg 'A' (nr Van Ness & Bay) **415/771-6222** • dinners, Sun brunch, clsd Mon • gourmet vegetarian • $20-40

Joubert's 4115 Judah St (at 46th Ave) **415/753-5448** • 6pm-10pm, 5pm-9pm Sun, clsd Mon-Tue (reservations a must Sat) • excellent South African vegeterian • beer/wine • gay-owned/run

Kan Zaman 1793 Haight (at Shrader) **415/751-9656** • noon-midnight, till 2am Fri-Sat, Mediterranean • some veggie • hookahs & tobacco available

Retail Shops

La Riga 1391 Haight St (at Masonic) **415/552-1525** • 11am-7pm • leather

Mainline Gifts 1928 Fillmore St (at Bush) **415/563-4438** • hours vary

Nomad 1808 McAllister St (at Baker) **415/563-7771** • noon-6pm, clsd Wed • piercing (walk-in) • jewelry

San Jose

Info Lines & Services

AA Gay/Lesbian 408/374-8511 • call for mtg schedule

Billy DeFrank Lesbian/Gay Community Center 938 The Alameda **408/293-2429, 408/293-4525** • noon-9pm, from noon Sat, 9am-6pm Sun • wheelchair access

Pro-Latino/Pro-Latina 938 The Alameda (at Billy DeFrank Ctr) **408/293-2429, 408/293-4525** • men's & women's support groups • meet 7pm alternate Mon • wheelchair access

Rainbow Gender Association **408/984-4044** • transgender group • recorded info

South Bay Queer & Asian 938 The Alameda (at Billy DeFrank Ctr) **408/345-1268 (VOICEMAIL)** • 7pm 2nd & 4th Tue • social/ support group for lesbigay Asians & Pacific Islanders • wheelchair access

Accommodations

▲ **Hensley House B&B** 456 N 3rd St **408/298-3537, 800/498-3537** • lesbians/gay men • located in a historic landmark • gay-owned/run • $135-255

Hotel De Anza 233 W Santa Clara **408/286-1000, 800/843-3700** • gay-friendly • art deco gem • Italian restaurant • $120-175

Bars

641 Club 641 Stockton (at Taylor) **408/998-1144** • 2pm-2am, from 11am Fri-Sun • lesbians/gay men • dancing/DJ • multi-racial clientele

The Foxtail 551 W Julian (at N Montgomery) **408/286-4388** • 3pm-2am, from noon wknds • lesbians/gay men • dancing/DJ • multi-racial clientele • transgender-friendly • live shows • patio

Entertainment & Recreation

Tech Museum of Innovation 201 S Market St (at Park Ave) **408/279-7150** • 10am-5pm, clsd Mon • a must-see for digital junkies • $8

Bookstores

Sisterspirit 175 Stockton Ave **408/293-9372** • 6:30pm-9pm, noon-6pm Sat, 1pm-4pm Sun • women's • periodic coffeehouse • IGLTA

Retail Shops

Out of the Closet 953 Park Ave **408/298-5833** • noon-10pm, till 6pm Sun

Publications

Entre Nous 408/281-4321 • lesbian newsmagazine & calendar for South Bay

Out Now! 1020 The Alameda **408/293-1598** • lesbigay newspaper

Spiritual Groups

MCC of San Jose 65 S 7th St **408/279-2711** • 10:30am Sun

Erotica

Leather Masters 969 Park Ave **408/293-7660** • leather & fetish • clothes • toys • publications

San Lorenzo

Spiritual Groups

MCC of Greater Hayward 100 Hacienda (at Christ Lutheran Church) **510/481-9720** • 12:30pm Sun

San Luis Obispo

Info Lines & Services

Central Coast Community Center 1306–B Higuera St (at Johnson) **805/541–4252** • call for hours, clsd Sun

Women's Resource Center 1009 Morro St #201 (at Monterey) **805/544–9313** • counseling • support • referrals

Accommodations

Adobe Inn 1473 Monterey St **805/549–0321, 800/676–1588** • gay-friendly • cozy, comfortable & congenial inn • full brkfst • kitchens • smokefree • kids ok • $55-110

Amber Hills B&B 805/239–2073 • gay-friendly • rural setting • kids/pets ok ($5 extra per) • women-owned/run • $65 ($5 /extra person)

Casa De Amigas B&B 1202 8th St, Los Osos **805/528–3701** • lesbians/gay men • suite • smokefree • women-owned/run • $75 (2-night minimum)

The J Patrick House B&B 2990 Burton Dr (at Hwy 1), Cambria **805/927–3812, 800/341–5258** • gay-friendly • full brkfst • authentic log cabin • fireplaces • smokefree • $125-180

The Madonna Inn 1000 Madonna Rd **805/543–3000, 800/543–9666** • gay-friendly • theme rooms • $117-225

Palomar Inn 1601 Shell Beach Rd, Shell Beach **805/773–4204** • lesbians/gay men • close to nude beach • gay-owned/run • $32-63

Cafes

Linnea's Cafe 1110 Garden (at Marsh) **805/541–5888** • 7am-midnight, till 2am wknds • plenty veggie • $5

Bookstores

Coalesce Bookstore & Garden Wedding Chapel 845 Main St, Morro Bay **805/772–2880** • 10am-5:30pm, 11am-4pm Sun • lesbigay section • women-owned/run

Volumes of Pleasure 1016 Los Osos Valley Rd, Los Osos **805/528–5565** • 10am-6pm, noon-5pm Sun • general • lesbigay section • wheelchair access • lesbian-owned/run

Retail Shops

Twisted Orbits 778 Marsh St **805/782–0278** • 11am-7pm, clsd Sun • cards • lesbigay gifts

Publications

GALA News & Reviews 805/541–4252 • news & events for Central California coast

Spiritual Groups

Integrity 805/467–3042, 805/534–0332 • 5:30pm 3rd Sun

San Rafael

see Marin County

Santa Ana

Spiritual Groups

Christ Chapel MCC 720 N Spurgeon **714/835–0722** • 10am Sun

Santa Barbara

Info Lines & Services

Pacific Pride Foundation 126 E Haley St #A–17 **805/963–3636, 805/965–2925 (CRISIS HOTLINE ONLY)** • 10am-5pm Mon-Fri • social/educational & support services • youth groups • newsletter

Accommodations

Glenborough Inn 1327 Bath St (at Sola) **805/966–0589, 800/962–0589** • lesbians/gay men • 3 different homes w/3 different personalities • full brkfst • private/shared baths • fireplaces • smokefree • kids ok • $100-360

Ivanhoe Inn 1406 Castillo St **805/963–8832** • gay-friendly • lovely old Victorian house • private/shared baths • kitchens • smokefree • kids/pets ok • $95-195

Old Yacht Club Inn 431 Corona Del Mar Dr **805/962–1277, 800/676–1676** • gay-friendly • only b&b on beach • $105-185

Bars

Chameleon Restaurant & Bar 421 E Cota (at Olive) **805/965–9536** • 4pm-2am • gay/straight • Californian • plenty veggie • patio • wheelchair access

Nightclubs

Gold Coast 30 W Cota (at State) **805/965–6701** • 4pm-2am • lesbians/gay men • neighborhood bar • dancing/DJ • wheelchair access

Cafes

Hot Spot Espresso Bar & Reservation Service 36 State St **805/564–1637** • 24hrs

Restaurants

Mousse Odile 18 E Cota St **805/962–5393** • clsd Sun • French • patio

Sojourner Cafe 134 E Canon Perdido (at Santa Barbara) **805/965–7922** • 11am-11pm • plenty veggie • beer/wine • wheelchair access

Zelo's 630 State (at Ortega) **805/966-5792** • 11am-2am, clsd Mon • full bar • also nightclub • from 9pm nightly • popular • dancing/DJ • Latin music

Bookstores

Chaucer's Books 3321 State St (at Las Positas) **805/682-6787** • 9am-9pm, till 10pm Fri-Sat • general • lesbigay section

Publications

We Are Visible PO Box 91304, 93190-1304

Erotica

The Riviera Adult Superstore 4135 State St **805/967-8282** • pride items

Santa Clara

Nightclubs

New Savoy 3546 Flora Vista **408/247-7109** • 3pm-2am, clsd Mon • popular • mostly women • dancing/DJ • country/western • live shows • karaoke • wheelchair access • women-owned/run

Tynker's Damn (TD's) 46 N Saratoga (at Stevens Creek) **408/243-4595** • 3pm-2am, 1pm-2am wknds • mostly gay men • dancing/DJ

Erotica

Borderline 36 N Saratoga Ave (at Stevens Creek) **408/241-2177** • toys • videos

Santa Cruz

Info Lines & Services

AA Gay/Lesbian **831/475-5782** • call for mtgs

Lesbian/Gay/Bisexual/Transgender Community Center 1328 Commerce Ln **831/425-5422** • 1pm-4pm Mon-Wed • call for events

Accommodations

Chateau Victorian B&B Inn 118 1st St **831/458-9458** • lesbians/gay men • 1885 Victorian inn w/warm friendly atmosphere • fireplaces • smokefree • women-owned/run • $115-145

Nightclubs

Blue Lagoon 923 Pacific Ave **831/423-7117** • 4pm-2am • lesbians/gay men • dancing/DJ • alternative • transgender-friendly • live shows • videos • wheelchair access

Dakota 1209 Pacific Ave (at Soquel) **831/454-9030** • noon-2am • lesbians/gay men • dancing/DJ • salsa Tue • women's night Wed • men's night Th

Cafes

Saturn Cafe 145 Laurel **831/429-8505** • noon-midnight • light fare • plenty veggie • lesbian-owned/run • $4-7

Restaurants

Costa Brava Taco Stand 505 Seabright **831/423-8190** • 11am-11:30pm • Mexican • some veggie • $4-8

Crêpe Place 1134 Soquel Ave **831/429-6994** • 11am-midnight, 10am-1am wknds • plenty veggie • full bar • garden patio • wheelchair access • $5-11

Bookstores

Book Loft 1207 Soquel Ave (at Seabright) **831/429-1812** • 10am-10pm, noon-6pm Sun, 10am-6pm Mon • mostly used books

Bookshop Santa Cruz 1520 Pacific Garden Mall **831/423-0900** • 9am-11pm • general • lesbigay section • cafe • wheelchair access

Herland Books 902 Center St **831/429-6636** • 10am-6pm, from noon wknds • wheelchair access

Publications

Manifesto **831/425-5422**

The Pride Press **831/425-5422**

Spiritual Groups

Lavender Road MCC Grace United Methodist Church, 1024 Soquel Ave **831/459-8442** • Sunday services at 5pm

Gyms & Health Clubs

Heartwood Spa Hot Tub & Sauna Garden 3150-A Mission Dr **831/462-2192** • noon-11pm • women only 6:30pm-11pm Sun

Kiva Retreat House Spa 702 Water St **831/429-1142** • noon-11pm, till midnight Fri-Sat • women-only 9am-noon Sun • 2 for 1 for women Mon-Wed

Santa Maria

Info Lines & Services

'Pacific Pride' Gay/Lesbian Resource Center 2255 S Broadway #4 (at Bettravia) **805/349-9947** • 9am-5pm Mon-Fri

Cafes

Cafe Monet 1555 S Broadway (at Battles) **805/928-1912** • 7am-7pm, till 10pm Wed & Fri, 9am-5pm Sun • wheelchair access

Erotica

Book Adventure 306 S Blosser Blvd (btwn Cook & Cypress) **805/928-7094**

Diamond Adult World 938 W Main St (at Western) **805/922-2828** • large lesbigay video section

Santa Rosa

Bars

Santa Rosa Inn 4302 Santa Rosa Ave **707/584-0345** • noon-2am • lesbians/gay men • dancing/DJ

Nightclubs

Club Diva 120 5th St (at Davis, Railroad Sq, in 'Rumors') **415/823-9751, 707/545-5483 (Rumors #)** • 9pm-4am Sun only • lesbians/gay men • dancing/DJ • live shows

Cafes

Aroma Roasters 95 5th St (Railroad Sq) **707/576-7765** • 7am-midnight, till 11pm wknds • lesbians/gay men • wheelchair access • lesbian-owned/run

Bookstores

North Light Books 550 E Cotati Rd, Cotati **707/792-4300** • 9am-9pm, till 10pm Fri-Sat, 10am-8pm Sun • anti-establishment • strong lesbigay emphasis • also coffeehouse • lesbian-owned/run

Sawyer's News 733 4th St (btwn 'D' & 'E') **707/542-1311** • 7am-9pm, till 10pm Fri-Sat • general news & bookstand

Publications

We the People 707/573-8896

Spiritual Groups

1st Congregational United Church of Christ 2000 Humboldt St (at Silva) **707/546-0998** • 10:30am Sun

New Hope MCC 855 7th St **707/526-4673** • 10am & 6pm Sun

Erotica

Santa Rosa Adult Books 3301 Santa Rosa Ave **707/542-8248**

Sausalito

see Marin County

Sebastopol

Retail Shops

Milk & Honey 137 N Main St **707/824-1155** • 10am-6pm, till 5pm Sun • goddess- & woman-oriented crafts

Sequoia Nat'l Park

Accommodations

Organic Gardens B&B 44095 Dinely Dr, Three Rivers **559/561-0916** • gay-friendly • 5 miles from entrance to Sequoia Nat'l Park • smokefree • lesbian-owned/run • $115

Stockton

see also Modesto

Nightclubs

Paradise 10100 N Lower Sacramento Rd **209/477-4724** • 6pm-2am, from 4pm wknds • lesbians/gay men • dancing/DJ • live shows • live bands • young crowd

Tiburon

see Marin County

Ukiah

Accommodations

Orr Hot Springs 13201 Orr Springs Rd **707/462-6277** • mineral hot springs • hostel-style cabins, private cottages & campsites • $39-160 per person

Bars

Perkins St Grill 228 E Perkins St **707/463-0740** • lunch & dinner, clsd Mon • gay-friendly • dancing/DJ • also restaurant • Californian • $10-15

Upland

Retail Shops

The Ninth Insight 231 E Ninth St (at Euclid) **909/946-2445** • 10am-5:30pm, 11am-4pm Sun • lesbigay books • jewelry • gifts

Erotica

The Toy Box 1999 W Arrow Rte (at Central) **909/920-1135** • 24hrs

Vacaville

Info Lines & Services

Solano County Gay/Lesbian Infoline 707/448-1010

Spiritual Groups

St Paul's United Methodist Church 101 West St (at Monte Vista) **707/448-5154** • 10:30am Sun

Vallejo

Accommodations

Captain Walsh House 235 E 'L' St, Benicia **707/747-5653** • gay-friendly • gracious gothic charm • full brkfst • smokefree • wheelchair access • $125-150

Nightclubs

Nobody's Place 437 Virginia St (at Sonoma Blvd) **707/645-7298** • noon-2am • mostly gay men • dancing/DJ • patio • wheelchair access

Bookstores

Booklovers Haven Bookstore & Cafe 725 Marin St (at Capitol) **707/557-4190** • 7:30am-6pm, 8am-4pm Sat, clsd Sun • cafe serves soups, salads, sandwiches

Van Nuys

Erotica

Diamond Adult World 6406 Van Nuys Blvd **818/997-3665** • 24hrs • books • toys • videos

Ventura

Info Lines & Services

AA Gay/Lesbian 739 E Main **805/389-1444** • women's mtg 7pm Wed at G/L Comm Center

Gay/Lesbian Community Center 1995 E Main **805/653-1979** • 9am-5pm, clsd wknds

Bars

Paddy McDermott's 2 W Main St (at Ventura) **805/652-1071** • 2pm-2am • lesbians/gay men • dancing/DJ • live shows

Erotica

Three Star Books 359 E Main St **805/653-9068** • 24hrs

Victorville

Bars

West Side 15 16868 Stoddard Wells Rd (off I-15) **760/243-9600** • 3pm-2am • lesbians/gay men • neighborhood bar

Walnut Creek

Info Lines & Services

AA Gay/Lesbian 193 Mayhew Wy (at St Paul's Church) **925/939-4155** • 8:30pm Fri • 5:30pm Sat at 193 Mayhew Wy

Bars

DJ's 1535 Olympic Blvd (at Main) **925/930-0300** • 4pm-2am • mostly gay men • dancing/DJ • strippers • wheelchair access

Nightclubs

JR's 2520 Camino Diablo **925/256-1200** • 7pm-2am, till 4am Fri-Sat • popular • mostly gay men • more women Sat • dancing/DJ • strippers/shows Sun • also 'Club X' from 8:30pm Fri-Sat, 18+ • wheelchair access

Twelve Twenty 1220 Pine St (at Civic Dr) **925/938-4550** • 4pm-2am • lesbians/gay men • women's night Fri • dancing/DJ • wheelchair access

Spiritual Groups

MCC of the New Vision 1543 Sunnyvale (at United Methodist Church) **925/283-2238** • noon Sun

Whittier

Info Lines & Services

Together in Pride AA 11931 Washington Blvd (at the church) **562/696-6213 (CHURCH #)** • 7:30pm Th

Accommodations

Whittier House 12133 S Colima Blvd **562/941-7222** • mostly women • full brkfst • hot tub • smokefree • kids/pets ok • IGLTA

Spiritual Groups

Good Samaritan MCC 11931 Washington Blvd **562/696-6213** • 10am Sun, 7:30pm Wed Bible study

Willits

Restaurants

Tsunami 50 S Main St **707/459-4750** • 11am-8pm • Japanese/int'l • $8-13

Entertainment & Recreation

Skunk Train California Western 299 E Commercial St **707/459-5248** • scenic train trips

Bookstores

Leaves of Grass 630 S Main St **707/459-3744** • 10am-5:30pm, noon-5pm Sun • alternative

Yosemite Nat'l Park

Accommodations

The Ahwahnee Hotel Yosemite Valley Floor **209/252-4848** • gay-friendly • incredibly dramatic & expensive grand fortress • swimming • also restaurant

▲ **The Homestead** 41110 Rd 600, Ahwahnee **559/683-0495** • gay-friendly • cottages • kitchens • fireplaces • smokefree • $125-225

THE HOMESTEAD... Near the southern entrance to **YOSEMITE NATIONAL PARK** lies 160 wooded acres that now embrace luxury cottages of adobe and stone. Experience a hideaway that flows in tune with nature's quiet rhythm.

Each cottage features romantic & comfortable:

- ✧ Country Kitchen
- ✧ Living Room
- ✧ Fireplace
- ✧ Bedroom
- ✧ Bathroom

The Homestead is a great place to be together alone or take advantage of nearby golfing, hiking, horseback riding, restaurants & shops.

CALL proprietors Cindy & Larry for assistance in planning your well deserved getaway.

(559) 683-0495

See us at http://www.homesteadcottages.com

Colorado

Statewide

Info Lines & Services

Colorado Travel and Tourism Authority 800/265-6723

Publications

▲ **Out Front Colorado 303/778-7900** • statewide lesbigay newspaper

Weird Sisters 970/482-4393 • statewide • calendar w/political, social & arts coverage

Alamosa

Accommodations

Cottonwood Inn 123 San Juan Ave **719/589-3882, 800/955-2623** • gay-friendly • smokefree • $64-85

Aspen

Info Lines & Services

Aspen Gay/Lesbian Community 970/925-9249 • 8pm-midnight (live) • recorded local info & events

Accommodations

Aspen B&B Lodge 311 W Main **970/925-7650, 800/362-7736** • gay-friendly • hot tub • swimming

Hotel Aspen 110 W Main St **970/925-3441, 800/527-7369** • gay-friendly • mountain brkfst • hot tub • swimming • $89-549

Hotel Lenado 200 S Aspen St **970/925-6246, 800/321-3457** • gay-friendly • full brkfst • hot tub • full bar

Sardy House 128 E Main St **970/920-2525, 800/321-3457** • gay-friendly • hot tub • swimming • also restaurant

Snow Queen Victorian B&B/Cooper St Lofts 124 E Cooper **970/925-8455** • gay-friendly • hot tub • $99-165

Bars

Double Diamond 450 S Galena **970/920-6905** • seasonal • gay-friendly • live shows

Howling Wolf 316 E Hopkins Ave **970/920-7771** • gay-friendly • live shows • also restaurant

Restaurants

Syzygy 520 E Hyman **970/925-3700** • seasonal • 5pm-10pm, bar till 2am • some veggie • live shows • wheelchair access

Bookstores

Explore Booksellers & Bistro 221 E Main **970/925-5336** • 10am-10pm • gourmet vegetarian • wheelchair access

Boulder

Info Lines & Services

LBGT Alliance 303/492-8567 • student group • events schedule & resource info

TLC (The Lesbian Connection) 2525 Arapahoe Ave **303/443-1105** • social/networking group • newsletter • info & referrals

Accommodations

Boulder Victorian Historic B&B 1305 Pine St (at 13th) **303/938-1300** • gay-friendly • patio • $109-189

The Briar Rose B&B 2151 Arapahoe Ave (at 22nd) **303/442-3007** • gay-friendly • $100-190

Bars

The Foundry 1109 Walnut **303/447-1803** • 11am-2am • gay-friendly • dancing/DJ • live shows • wheelchair access

Nightclubs

The Yard 2690 28th St #C (at Bluff) **303/443-1987** • 4pm-2am, from 2pm wknds • lesbians/gay men • dancing/DJ • wheelchair access • women-owned/run

Cafes

Walnut Cafe 3073 Walnut (at 30th) **303/447-2315** • 7am-4pm • popular • plenty veggie • patio • wheelchair access • women-owned/run • $5-9

Bookstores

Left Hand Books 1825 Pearl St, 2nd flr (btwn 18th & 19th) **303/443-8252** • noon-9pm, 11am-8pm Sat, 1pm-4pm Sun

Word Is Out 1731 15th St (btwn Canyon & Arapahoe) **303/449-1415** • 10am-6pm, noon-5pm Sun • women's • lesbigay section • wheelchair access

Retail Shops

Aria 2043 Broadway (at Spruce) **303/442-5694** • 10am-6pm, noon-5pm Sun • cards • T-shirts • gifts • wheelchair access

Publications

Rainbow List 303/443-7768 • extensive statewide resources

Erotica

The News Stand 1720 15th St (at Grove) **303/442-9515**

Breckenridge

Accommodations

Allaire Timbers Inn 9511 Hwy 9, S Main St **970/453-7530** • gay-friendly • full brkfst • hot tub • wheelchair access • $130-450

Mountain Lodge 970/453-6475 • rental home • sleeps 8 • sauna • gay-owned/run

Colorado Springs

Info Lines & Services

Pikes Peak Gay/Lesbian Community Center Helpline 719/471-4429 • 6pm-9pm Mon-Fri • call for events

Accommodations

Authentic Inns of the Pikes Peak Region 888/892-2237

Old Town Guest House B&B 115 S 26th St **719/632-9194, 888/375-4210** • gay-friendly • hot tub • $95-155

Pikes Peak Paradise Woodland Park **719/687-6335, 800/354-0989** • gay-friendly • mansion w/view of Pikes Peak • full brkfst • hot tub • fireplaces • smokefree • kids 12+ ok • $175-220

Quality Inn—Garden of the Gods 555 W Garden of the Gods **719/593-9119** • gay-friendly • IGLTA • $59-111

Rockledge Country Inn 328 El Paso Blvd, Manitou Springs **719/685-4515, 888/685-4515** • gay-friendly • Tudor country home on historic 35-acre estate

Bars

Hour Glass Lounge 2748 Airport Rd (at Circle) **719/471-2104** • 10am-2am • gay-friendly • neighborhood bar

Victor Victoria 2125 Fountain (at Circle) **719/328-1548** • 2pm-2am • lesbians/gay men • dancing/DJ • also a restaurant

Nightclubs

Hide & Seek Complex 512 W Colorado (at Walnut) **719/634-9303** • 10:30am-2am, till 5am Fri-Sat • popular • lesbians/gay men • dancing/DJ • country/western • live shows • also restaurant • some veggie • wheelchair access • $5-12

Restaurants

Dale Street Cafe 115 E Dale (at Nevada) **719/578-9898** • 11am-9pm, clsd Sun • vegetarian • full bar • $6-11

Spiritual Groups

Pikes Peak MCC 730 N Tejon (at Unitarian Church) **719/634-3771** • 5pm Sun

Erotica

First Amendment Adult Bookstore 220 E Fillmore (at Nevada) **719/630-7676**

Denver

Info Lines & Services

AA Gay/Lesbian 303/322-4440 • many mtgs

Gay/Lesbian/Bisexual Community Center 234 Broadway **303/733-7743, 303/837-1598 (TDD)** • 10am-6pm Mon-Fri • extensive resources & support groups • wheelchair access

Gender Identity Center of Colorado (GIC) 303/763-5097 • transgender resources & support

Accommodations

Elyria's Western Guest House 1655 E 47th Ave (btwn I-70 & Brighton) **303/291-0915** • lesbians/gay men • Western ambiance in historic Denver neighborhood • hot tub • shared baths • smokefree • $40-50

The Gregory Inn, LoDo 2500 Arapahoe St (at 25th St) **303/295-6570, 800/925-6570** • gay-friendly • jacuzzis • fireplaces • gay-owned/run • $99-169

Hotel Monaco 1717 Champa St (at 17th) **303/296-1717, 800/397-5380** • gay-friendly • gym • also restaurant • $155-345

The House at Peregrine's Perspective 303/697-0558 • mostly gay men • log lodge w/ great views of Kenosha Mtns • 20 minutes from Denver • hot tub • nudity • gay-owned/run • $75-125

L'Auberge 43774 Buckskin Rd (E Parker & Delbert) **303/805-8099** • gay/straight • 5,000 sq ft bio-dome home on 5 acres • jacuzzi • gay-owned/run

Lumber Baron Inn 2555 W 37th Ave (at Bryant) **303/477-8205, 800/697-6552** • gay-friendly • furnished w/antiques • full brkfst • hot tub • $125-210

Stapleton Plaza Hotel 3333 Quebec St (at 35th) **303/321-3500, 800/950-6070** • gay-friendly • swimming • also restaurant • wheelchair access • $50-125

Victoria Oaks Inn 1575 Race St (at 16th) **303/355-1818, 800/662-6257** • gay/straight • fireplaces • gay-owned/run • $50-95

Bars

BJ's Carousel 1380 S Broadway (at Arkansas) **303/777-9880** • noon-2am, from 10am wknds • popular • mostly gay men • neighborhood bar • live shows • volleyball court • patio • also restaurant • wheelchair access

Brick's 1600 E 17th Ave (at Franklin) **303/377-5400** • 11am-2am, from 10am wknds • lunch Mon-Fri, brunch wknds • mostly gay men • neighborhood bar • wheelchair access

C's 7900 E Colfax Ave (at Trenton) **303/322-4436** • 5pm-midnight, till 2am Fri-Sat • mostly women • dancing/DJ

Cafe Cero 1446 S Broadway (btwn Arkansas & Florida) **303/282-1446** • from 4pm • gay/straight • also restaurant

Centerfield 2936 Fox St (at 20th St) **303/298-7378** • open from 7pm Wed-Sat & 3hrs prior to all home games, clsd Mon-Tue • gay/straight • sports bar

The Compound 145 Broadway (at 2nd Ave) **303/722-7977** • 7am-2am, from 8am Sun • mostly gay men • neighborhood bar

Denver

Denver is a big city with a friendly small town feel. To get the most out of your stay, start with a visit to the women's **Book Garden,** and pick up a copy of **Weird Sisters,** the local lesbian paper. Next, drop by the **Gay/Lesbian/Bisexual Center** for the inside scoop on where to go and what to do in Denver.

Look for local lesbians in Capitol Hill, soaking up sun in Cheesman Park, or sipping coffee at **Java Creek** or with the boys on 9th Avenue between Ogden and Marion.

At night, taste the local cuisine at **Basil,** have a cocktail at the **Highland Bar,** check out the shows at the **Denver Detour,** or get down at **C's** dance bar.

Be sure to take advantage of the Rocky Mountain snows with a ski trip to one of the many nearby resorts: Aspen, Telluride, or Rocky Mountain National Park. And don't miss **Lesbian Pride Weekend** (303/778-7900) in March!

The Den 5110 W Colfax Ave (at Sheridan) **303/623-7998** • 10am-2am • lesbians/gay men • neighborhood bar • also restaurant • dinner nightly • brunch wknds • wheelchair access

Denver Detour 551 E Colfax Ave (at Pearl, use back entrance) **303/861-1497** • 11am-2am • popular • lesbians/gay men • live shows • lunch & dinner daily • some veggie • $5-9 • wheelchair access

The Grand 538 E 17th Ave (at Pearl) **303/839-5390** • 3pm-2am • mostly gay men • upscale piano bar • patio • wheelchair access

Highland Bar 2532 15th St (at Boulder) **303/455-9978** • 2pm-2am • mostly women • neighborhood bar • wheelchair access

R&R Denver 4958 E Colfax Ave (at Elm) **303/320-9337** • 11am-2am • lesbians/gay men • neighborhood bar

Safari Bar 500 Denargo Market (at 31st) **303/298-7959** • noon-2am • lesbians/gay men • neighborhood bar • dancing/DJ

The Triangle 2036 Broadway (at 20th Ave) **303/293-9009** • 3pm-2am, till 4am wknds, from 11am Sun • mostly gay men • leather

Zippz 3014 E Colfax Ave (at St Paul) **303/321-6627** • 10am-2am • lesbians/gay men • neighborhood bar • dancing/DJ • live shows • wheelchair access

The Zu 60 S Broadway (at Bayaud) **303/777-0193** • noon-2am • lesbians/gay men • dancing/DJ • wheelchair access • women-owned/run

Nightclubs

9th Avenue West 99 W 9th Ave (at Broadway) **303/572-8006** • 8pm-2am, from 9pm Mon-Tue, clsd Sun • swing dance club/lessons • live shows • food served

Amsterdam 2901 Walnut (at 29th) **303/405-4458** • gay/straight • afterhours • dancing/DJ

Club Synergy 3240 Larimer (at 33rd St) **303/296-9515** • 8pm-5am Fri, from 11pm Sat, 9pm-4am Sun • popular • lesbians/gay men • dancing/DJ • alternative • 18+

Maximillian's 2151 Lawrence St (at 21st St) **303/297-0015** • 9pm-2am Fri-Sat • gay-friendly • dancing/DJ • multi-racial

Rock Island 1614 15th St (at Wazee) **303/572-7625** • gay-friendly • dancing/DJ • alternative • young crowd • call for events • wheelchair access

Snake Pit 608 E 13th Ave (at Washington) **303/831-1234** • 4pm-2am • popular • gay/straight • dancing/DJ • alternative • also restaurant • home cookin' • wheelchair access

Tongues Untied 314 E 13th Ave (at Broadway) **303/837-8015** • 11am-2am • lesbians/gay men • dancing/DJ

Tracks 2000 2975 Fox St (btwn 20th & Chestnut) **303/292-6600** • 9pm-2am Wed-Sat, • mostly gay men • more women Fri • dancing/DJ • 18+ Th • wheelchair access

Cafes

Java Creek 287 Columbine St (at 3rd Ave) **303/377-8902** • 7am-6pm, 9am-4pm Sun

Restaurants

Basil Ristorante 846 S Broadway (at Bayaud) **303/832-8009** • dinner only • nouvelle Italian • plenty veggie • beer/wine • wheelchair access • women-owned/run • $6-16

Hugh's New American Bistro 1469 S Pearl (btwn Florida & Arkansas) **303/744-1940** • 5pm-10pm, clsd Sun-Mon • some veggie • full bar

Janleone 1509 Marion (at Colfax) **303/863-8433** • dinner, also Sun brunch, clsd Mon • live shows • patio • wheelchair access • $11-19

Las Margaritas 1066 Old S Gaylord St **303/777-0194** • from 11am, bar till 2am • Mexican • some veggie • wheelchair access

Racine's 850 Bannock St (btwn 8th & 9th) **303/595-0418** • brkfst, lunch, dinner & Sun brunch • plenty veggie • full bar

Sfuzzi 3000 E 1st Ave (in Cherry Creek Mall) **303/321-4700** • 11am-10pm • Italian • some veggie • full bar

Wazee Supper Club 1600 15th St (at Wazee) **303/623-9518** • 11am-2am • beer/wine

Denver

Where the Girls Are: Many lesbians reside in the Capitol Hill area, near the gay and mixed bars, but hang out in cafes and women's bars scattered around the city.

Entertainment: Denver Women's Chorus 303/274-4177.

Lesbigay Pride: June. 303/731-6268 ext. 15.

Annual Events: February - Mtn States Gay & Lesbian Film Festival. October - Annual Halloween Cheshire Ball.

City Info: 303/892-1112, web: www.denverco.org.

Attractions: 16th Street Mall.
Black American West Museum 303/292-2566.
Denver Art Museum 303/640-4433.
Elitch Gardens 303/595-4386.
LoDo (Lower Downtown).
Molly Brown House 303/832-4092.

Best View: Lookout Mountain (at night especially) or the top of the Capitol rotunda.

Weather: Summer temperatures average in the 90°s and winter ones in the 40°s. The sun shines an average of 300 days a year with humidity in the single digits.

Transit: Yellow Cab 303/777-7777.
Metro Taxi 303/333-3333.
Super Shuttle 303/342-5450.
RTD 303/628-9000 or 303/299-6000 (infoline).

Entertainment & Recreation

Denver Women's Chorus 303/274-4177

Q TV 303/433-8135 (Pink Pages #) • lesbigay cable TV program • call for times

Bookstores

The Book Garden 2625 E 12th Ave (at Elizabeth) **303/399-2004, 800/279-2426** • 10am-6pm, till 8pm Th • feminist

Isis Bookstore 5701 E Colfax Ave (at Ivanhoe) **303/321-0867** • 10am-7pm, till 6pm Fri-Sat, noon-5pm Sun • new age • metaphysical

Magazine City 200 E 13th Ave (at Sherman) **303/861-8249** • 10am-6pm, 11am-5pm wknds

Sinster's Newsstand 630 E 6th Ave (at Washington) **303/777-6060** • 7am-10pm, till 3pm Sun

Tattered Cover Book Store 2955 E 1st Ave (at Milwaukee) **303/322-7727, 800/833-9327** • 9am-11pm, 10am-6pm Sun • also 1536 Wynkoop St • 4 flrs

Retail Shops

Bound By Design 1336 E Colfax **303/830-7272, 303/832-TAT2** • 11am-11pm, noon-10pm Sun • piercing & tattoos • lesbian owned/run

Our Flower Shop 1510 E Colfax (at Humboldt) **303/864-9778** • 9am-6pm, clsd Sun

Unique of Denver 2626 E 12th (btwn Elizabeth & Clayton) **303/355-0689** • 10am-6pm, till 7pm summers • lesbigay gift shop

Publications

▲ **Out Front Colorado 303/778-7900** • statewide lesbigay newspaper

Spiritual Groups

Congregation Tikvat Shalom 303/331-2706 • lesbigay Jewish fellowship

Dignity Denver 1100 Fillmore (at Capitol Hts Presb Church) **303/322-8485** • 5pm Sun

MCC of the Rockies 980 Clarkson St (at 10th) **303/860-1819** • 9am, 11am & 6pm Sun • wheelchair access

St Paul's United Methodist Church 1615 Ogden (at 16th Ave) **303/832-4929** • 10:30am Sun • reconciling congregation • also Buddhist-Christian contemplative prayer • 5pm Sun

Gyms & Health Clubs

Broadway Bodyworks 160 S Broadway (at Maple) **303/722-4342** • lesbians/gay men • wheelchair access

Erotica

The Crypt 131 Broadway (btwn 1st & 2nd) **303/733-3112** • leather & more

Durango

Accommodations

Leland House 721 2nd Ave **970/385-1920, 800/664-1920** • popular • gay-friendly • full brkfst • $99-159

Florissant

Entertainment & Recreation

McNamara Ranch 4620 County Rd 100 **719/748-3466** • horseback tours for 2-3

Fort Collins

Accommodations

Never Summer Nordic 970/482-9411 • lesbians/gay men • camping in yurts (portable Mongolian round houses) in Colorado Rockies • sleep 8-12 • mountain-biking & skiing

Nightclubs

Tornado Club 1437 E Mulberry St **970/493-0251** • 4pm-2am, from 2pm Sun • lesbians/gay men • dancing/DJ • alternative Mon • country/western Th • hi-energy Fri-Sat • call for events • patio • wheelchair access

Grand Junction

Bars

Quincy's 609 Main St (btwn 7th & Main) **970/242-9633** • 7am-2am, gay after 8pm • gay-friendly • neighborhood bar • theater clientele • wheelchair access

Grand Lake

Accommodations

Grandview Lodge 12429 Hwy 34 **970/627-3914** • popular • gay-friendly • sundeck • women-owned/run

Greeley

Info Lines & Services

Greeley Gay/Lesbian/Bisexual/ Transgender Alliance U of Northern Colorado **970/351-1484** • hours vary • call for events • leave message for referrals

Bookstores

Wild Woman 915 13th St **970/356-7705**

Pueblo

Info Lines & Services

Pueblo After 2 **719/564-4004** • social/educational network • monthly mtgs • newsletter

Bars

Pirate's Cove 105 Central Plaza **719/542-9624** • 2pm-2am, from 4pm Sun, clsd Mon • lesbians/gay men • neighborhood bar • wheelchair access

Nightclubs

Aqua Splash 806 S Santa Fe Dr **719/543-3913** • hours vary • lesbians/gay men • dancing/DJ • live shows • wheelchair access

Spiritual Groups

MCC Pueblo 1003 Liberty Ln (at United Church of Christ), Belmont **719/543-6460** • 5pm Sun

Steamboat Springs

Accommodations

Elk River Estates **970/879-7556** • gay-friendly • suburban townhouse B&B near hiking, skiing & natural hot springs • full brkfst • $35-40

Vail

Accommodations

Antlers at Vail 680 W Lionshead Pl **970/476-2471** • gay-friendly • apts • hot tub • swimming • fireplace • balcony • kids ok • $205-755

Restaurants

Sweet Basil 193 E Gore Creek Dr **970/476-0125** • lunch & dinner • some veggie • full bar • wheelchair access

Winter Park

Accommodations

The Bear Paw Inn 871 Bear Paw Dr **970/887-1351** • gay-friendly • massive log lodge on top of mtn w/ spectacular views of Rocky Mtn Nat'l Park

Beau West B&B 148 Fir Dr **970/726-5145, 800/473-5145** • gay-friendly • full brkfst • gay-owned/run

Silverado II 490 Kings Crossing Rd **970/726-5753** • gay-friendly • condo ski resort

Connecticut

Statewide

Info Lines & Services

Gay/Lesbian Guide Line Hartford **203/366-3734** • 8pm-10pm Mon-Wed • statewide info

Bethel

Restaurants

Bethel Pizza House 206 Greenwood Ave **203/748-1427** • 11am-11pm

Emerald City Cafe 269 Greenwood Ave **203/778-4100** • dinner & Sun brunch, clsd Mon • cont'l • live shows

Bridgeport

Restaurants

Bloodroot Restaurant 85 Ferris St **203/576-9168** • 11:30am-2:30pm & 6pm-9pm Tue-Th, 7pm-9pm Wed, 6pm-10pm Fri-Sat, clsd Mon • women's night Wed • vegetarian • call for events • patio • wheelchair access • women-owned/run • $8-12

Bookstores

Bloodroot 85 Ferris St **203/576-9168** • clsd Mon, call for hrs • also vegetarian restaurant • wheelchair access

Collinsville

Bookstores

Gertrude & Alice's 2 Front St **860/693-3816** • 10am-10pm, till 6pm Tue, till 11pm Fri-Sat, till 5pm Sun, clsd Mon • live shows • cafe • patio • wheelchair access

Danbury

Bars

Triangles Cafe 66 Sugar Hollow Rd Rte 7 **203/798-6996** • 5pm-2am • popular • lesbians/gay men • dancing/DJ • live shows • patio

Restaurants

Goulash Place 42 Highland Ave **203/744-1971** • lunch & dinner, clsd Mon • Hungarian • beer/wine

Enfield

Erotica

Bookends 44 Enfield St / Rte 5 **860/745-3988**

Groton

Accommodations

Flagship Inn 470 Gold Star Hwy (Rte 184 off I-95) **860/445-7458, 888/800-0770** • gay-friendly • full brkfst • gym passes • in-room movies • wheelchair access • gay-owned/run

Bars

Sidecar Cafe 224 Poquonnock Rd **860/445-0444** • 3pm-1am, till 2am Fri-Sat • mostly women • neighborhood bar • live shows

Hartford

Info Lines & Services

Info Line for Southeastern Connecticut Rocky Hill **860/886-0516, 800/203-1234 (in CT)** • 8am-8pm Mon-Fri • info & referrals • crisis counseling

Lesbian Rap Group 135 Broad St (at YWCA) **860/525-1163** • 7:30pm Tue

Project 100/ The Community Center 1841 Broad St **860/724-5542, 860/683-8951** • hours vary • wheelchair access

Accommodations

The 1895 House B&B 97 Girard Ave (at Farmington) **860/232-0014** • gay-friendly • Victorian home designed by woman architect, Genevra Whittemore Buckland • $70-85

Butternut Farm 1654 Main St, Glastonbury **860/633-7197** • gay/straight • full brkfst • $79-99

Bars

A Bar With No Name 115 Asylum St (Trumbull) **860/522-4646** • gay-friendly • Sun gay night • dancing/DJ • wheelchair access

Chez Est 458 Wethersfield Ave (at Main St) **860/525-3243** • 3pm-1am, till 2am wknds • mostly gay men • dancing/DJ • patio

The Polo Club 678 Maple Ave (btwn Preston & Mapleton) **860/278-3333** • 3pm-1am, till 2am wknds • lesbians/gay men • live shows

Nightclubs

Nick's Cafe 1943 Broad St (at Mapleton) **860/956-1573** • 4pm-1am, till 2am wknds • lesbians/gay men • more women Fri • dancing/DJ • Latin & Bear night Sat

Velvet 50 Union Pl **860/278-6333** • clsd Mon-Wed • gay/straight • gay night Sun • dancing/DJ • live shows

Restaurants

The Union 2935 Main St, Glastonbury **860/633-0880** • 11:30am-1am • full bar • patio

Bookstores

Reader's Feast Bookstore Cafe 529 Farmington Ave (at Sisson Ave) **860/232-3710** • 11am-9pm, from 10am wknds, till 2:30pm Sun • feminist & progressive bookstore & cafe

Hartford

Lesbigay Pride: June. 860/524-8114, email: et_pride@hotmail.com.

Annual Events: June - Lesbian/Gay Film Festival.

City Info: Greater Hartford Tourism District 800/793-4480.

Attractions: Bushnell Park Carousel.
Harriet Beecher Stowe House.
Mark Twain House 860/247-0998.
Real Art Ways 860/232-1006.
Wadsworth Atheneum 860/278-2670.

Transit: Yellow Cab 860/666-6666.
Airport Connection 860/627-3400 (downtown hotels only).
Connecticut Transit 860/525-9181.

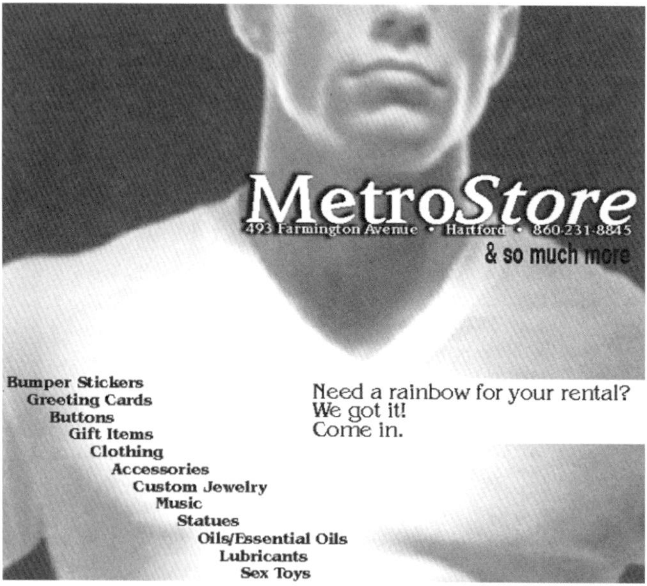

Retail Shops

▲ **MetroStore** 493 Farmington Ave (at Sisson Ave) **860/231-8845** • 8am-8pm, till 5:30pm Tue, Wed & Sat, clsd Sun • magazines • travel guides • leather & more

Publications

▲ **Metroline 860/233-8334** • regional newspaper & entertainment guide

Spiritual Groups

Congregation Am Segulah 860/674-5095, 800/734-8524 (in CT only) • call for service times & location

Dignity Hartford 144 S Quaker Ln (at Quaker Mtg House) **860/522-7334** • 6pm Sun

MCC 860/724-4605 • call for info

Erotica

Water Hole Custom Leather 982 Main St (at Governor), East Hartford **860/528-6195** • 9am-7pm, from noon wknds, clsd Mon, also by appt

Manchester

Info Lines & Services

Women's Center at Manchester Community College 60 Bidwell **860/647-6056** • hours vary

Meriden

Erotica

The D/S ToyChest 975 Broad St (at rear) **203/639-0622** • clsd Sun

Middletown

Info Lines & Services

Wesleyan Women's Resource Center 287 High St **860/347-9411 (Wesleyan switchboard #)** • library

New Haven

Info Lines & Services

New Haven Gay/Lesbian Community Center 50 Fitch St **203/387-2252** • call for hrs

Yale Women's Services 198 Elm St **203/432-0388** • 10am-10pm, till 5pm Fri, noon-5pm Sat, clsd Sun • resources • support groups • library • wheelchair access

Accommodations

The Inn at Oyster Point 194 Howard Ave (at 6th St) **203/773-3334** • gay-friendly

Bars

The Bar 254 Crown St **203/495-8924** • 4pm-1am • gay/straight • more gay Tue • dancing/DJ • wheelchair access

Gotham Citi Cafe 130 Crown St **203/498-2484** • lesbians/gay men • dancing/DJ from 10pm Tue & Th, Fri-Sun • live shows • happy hour Mon-Fri

Partners 365 Crown St (at Park St) **203/776-1014** • 5pm-1am, till 2am Fri-Sat • mostly gay men • neighborhood bar • dancing/DJ

Cafes

168 York St Cafe 168 York St **203/789-1915** • 3pm-1am • lesbians/gay men • some veggie • full bar • patio • gay-owned/run • $4-7

Restaurants

Claire's Corner 1000 Chapel St **203/562-3888** • 8am-10pm • vegetarian Mexican cafe • great soup • wheelchair access

Spiritual Groups

MCC 34 Harrison St (at United Church) **203/389-6750** • 9:30am & 4pm Sun

New London

Info Lines & Services

New London People's Forum Affirming Lesbian/Gay Identity 76 Federal (at St James Church) **860/443-8855** • 7:30pm Wed • educational/support group

Bars

Frank's Place 9 Tilley St **860/443-8883** • 4pm-1am, till 2am Fri-Sat • lesbians/gay men • dancing/DJ • live shows • patio • wheelchair access

Heroes 33 Golden St **860/442-4376** • 4pm-1am • lesbians/gay men • neighborhood bar • dancing/DJ

Bookstores

Greene's Books & Beans 140 Bank St (at Golden) **860/443-3312** • 8:30am-5pm, 9am-2pm Sat, clsd Sun • wheelchair access

Norfolk

Accommodations

Manor House B&B 69 Maple Ave **860/542-5690** • gay-friendly • elegant & romantic 1898 Victorian Tudor estate • full brkfst • fireplaces • hot tubs • smokefree • kids 12+ ok • $110-225

Norwalk

Info Lines & Services

Triangle Community Center 25 Van Zant St #7–C, East Norwalk **203/853–0600** • 7:30pm-9:30pm Mon-Fri • activities • newsletter

Accommodations

Silk Orchid 203/847–2561 • women only • 1 suite • full brkfst • swimming • $95

Norwich

Bookstores

Magazine's & More 77 Salem Tpke **860/886–1855** • 9am-9pm, till 8pm Sat, 10am-5pm Sun • lesbigay

Ridgefield

Restaurants

Gail's Station House 378 Main St **203/438–9775** • great cheddar corn pancakes

Sandy Hook

Accommodations

The Barrymore 11 Glen Rd **203/270–8688** • gay/straight • B&B in restored gristmill • gay-owned/run • $79-89

South Windsor

Accommodations

The Watson House 1876 Main St (at Sullivan Ave) **860/282–8888** • gay/straight • full brkfst • kids ok • gay-owned/run • $95-125

Stamford

Nightclubs

Art Bar 84 W Park Pl **203/973–0300** • 5pm-1am • gay-friendly • popular gay night Sun from 8pm • dancing/DJ • alternative

Stratford

Nightclubs

Stephanie's Living Room 203/377–2119 • popular • mostly women • 'quality social events for women' • dances • multi-racial • wheelchair access • discounts for physically challenged

Washington Depot

Restaurants

GW Tavern 200 Bee Brook Rd (Rte 47) **860/868–6633** • 11:30am-1am, more gay late & 3rd Tue 10pm • nouvelle Yankee food

Waterbury

Bars

The Brownstone 29 Leavenworth St **203/597–1838** • 5pm-1am, till 2am Fri-Sat • lesbians/gay men • women's night Th • live shows • also restaurant • wheelchair access

Spiritual Groups

Integrity/Waterbury Area 16 Church St (at St John's) **203/754–3116** • call for mtg times

Westport

Bars

Cedar Brook Cafe 919 Post Rd E **203/221–7429** • 5pm-1am, till 2am Fri-Sat, 4pm-11pm Sun • mostly gay men • dancing/DJ • live shows • patio • wheelchair access

Entertainment & Recreation

Sherwood Island State Park Beach left to gay area

Willimantic

Bars

Purple Monkey 103 Union St (btwn Jackson & Main) **860/456–7562** • 5pm-1am, 6pm-2am Fri-Sat, 4pm-1am Sun, clsd Mon • mostly gay men • neighborhood bar • gay-owned/run

Cafes

Cafe Earth 1244 Storrs **860/429–5304** • 8am-9pm

Paradise Eatery 713 Main St **860/423–7682** • 8am-8pm, clsd Sun-Mon • organic veggie • 'lesbian film fest' events 3rd Sat • wheelchair access • women-owned/run • $4-8

Delaware

Statewide

Info Lines & Services

Delaware Tourism Office 800/441-8846 (OUTSIDE DE), 800/282-8667 (IN-STATE ONLY)

Gay & Lesbian AA 302/856-6452

Claymont

Restaurants

Queen Bean Cafe 8 Commonwealth Ave (at Philadelphia Pike) **302/792-5995** • lunch & dinner • hours vary • veggie

Dover

Bars

Rumors 2206 N DuPont Hwy **302/678-8805** • 6pm-2am, only 18-21 Mon • popular • lesbians/ gay men • dancing/DJ • country/ western Th • live shows • also restaurant • wheelchair access • $10-15

Milton

Accommodations

▲ **Honeysuckle** 330 Union St **302/684-3284, 800/352-2489** • women only • full brkfst • swimming • nudity • women-owned/ run • $99-133 • rental houses $137-189

Rehoboth Beach

Info Lines & Services

Camp Rehoboth 39-B Baltimore Ave **302/227-5620** • 10am-5pm, clsd wknds • info service for lesbigay businesses • newsletter w/ extensive listings

Accommodations

At Melissa's B&B 36 Delaware Ave (btwn 1st & 2nd) **302/227-7504, 800/396-8090** • gay-friendly • women-owned/ run

Beach House B&B 15 Hickman St (at King Charles) **302/227-7074, 800/283-4667** • gay-friendly • swimming

Cabana Gardens B&B 20 Lake Ave (at Lake & 3rd) **302/227-5429** • lesbians/ gay men • lake & ocean views • deck • smokefree • $65-195

Chesapeake Landing B&B 101 Chesapeake St (at King Charles) **302/227-2973** • gay-friendly • full brkfst • swimming • smokefree • lakefront • near Poodle Beach • gay-owned/ run • $95-175

The Lighthouse Inn 20 Delaware Ave **302/226-0407, 800/600-9092** • lesbians/ gay men • B&B • also apt w/full kitchen & private deck (weekly rental) • seasonal • $65-150

The Pelican Loft 45 Baltimore Ave **302/226-5080, 800/550-9551** • mostly women • close to beach & boardwalk • private/ shared bath • lesbian-owned/ run • $40-150

Rehoboth Guest House 40 Maryland Ave (at King Charles) **302/227-4117, 800/261-2768** • lesbians/ gay men • Victorian beach house • near boardwalk & beach • seasonal • $55-125

Renegade Restaurant & Lounge/ Motel 4274 Hwy 1 (nr Rehoboth Ave) **302/227-4713** • lesbians/ gay men • 10-acre resort • swimming • full bar • dancing/DJ • also restaurant (dinner only) • some veggie • wheelchair access • $35-110

Sand in My Shoes Canal & 6th St **302/226-2006, 800/231-5856** • lesbians/ gay men • full brkfst • hot tub • sundeck • kitchens • pets ok • $75-200

Shore Inn at Rehoboth 703 Rehoboth Ave (nr Church) **302/227-8487, 800/597-8899** • mostly gay men • hot tub • swimming • $50-160

▲ **Silver Lake Guest House** 133 Silver Lake Dr **302/226-2115, 800/842-2115** • lesbians/ gay men • near Poodle Beach • IGLTA • pets ok • $60-190

Summer Place Hotel 30 Olive Ave (at 1st) **302/226-0766, 800/815-3925** • gay/ straight • also apts • $39-200

Bars

The Blue Moon 35 Baltimore Ave (btwn 1st & 2nd) **302/227-6515** • 4pm-2am, clsd Jan • gay-friendly • popular happy hour • T-dance • also restaurant • Sun brunch • plenty veggie • $12-26

Double L Bar 622 Rehoboth Ave **302/227-0818** • mostly gay men • leather

Nightclubs

The Beach House Restaurant & Bar 316 Rehoboth Ave **302/227-4227** • seasonal • dinner & dance club • wheelchair access

Purple Parrot Grill 247 Rehoboth Ave **302/226-1139, 302/226-1139** • 11am-1am • mostly gay men • dancing/DJ • T-dance Sun • videos • shows Mon-Wed • also restaurant • wheelchair access

Cafes

Java Beach 59 Baltimore Ave (at King Charles) **302/227-8418** • 7am-6pm, open later in summer • cafe • patio

Lori's 39 Baltimore Ave (at 1st Ave) **302/226-3066** • 8am-10pm, till midnight Fri-Sat

Restaurants

Back Porch Cafe 59 Rehoboth Ave **302/227-3674** • lunch & dinner • Sun brunch • some veggie • full bar • wheelchair access • $9-29

Celsius 50-C Wilmington Ave **302/227-5767** • dinner only • French-Mediterranean • some veggie • wheelchair access • $15-25

Rehoboth Beach

Annual Events: November - Rehoboth Beach Independent Film Festival 302/645-9095, web: www.rehobothfilm.com.
July - Fireworks 877/347-3999.

City Info: Rehoboth Beach-Dewey Beach Chamber of Commerce 302/227-2233 & 800/441-1329. Rehoboth Convention Center 800/282-8667(in-state) and 800/4418846(out-of-state).

Attractions: Poodle Beach. Main Street 302/227-2772.

Transit: Seaport Taxi 302/645-8100. Jolly Trolley 302/227-1197 (seasonal tour & shuttle).

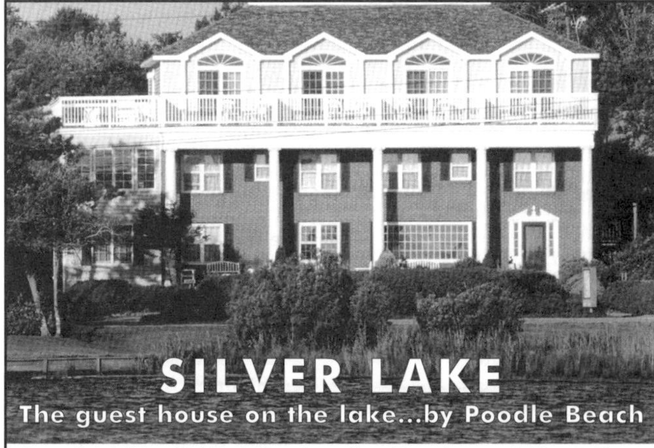

SILVER LAKE
The guest house on the lake...by Poodle Beach

CAMP
REHOBOTH
CREATING COMMUNITY
FOR MORE INFORMATION ABOUT REHOBOTH BEACH
VISIT US AT WWW.CAMPREHOBOTH.COM OR CALL 302-227-5620

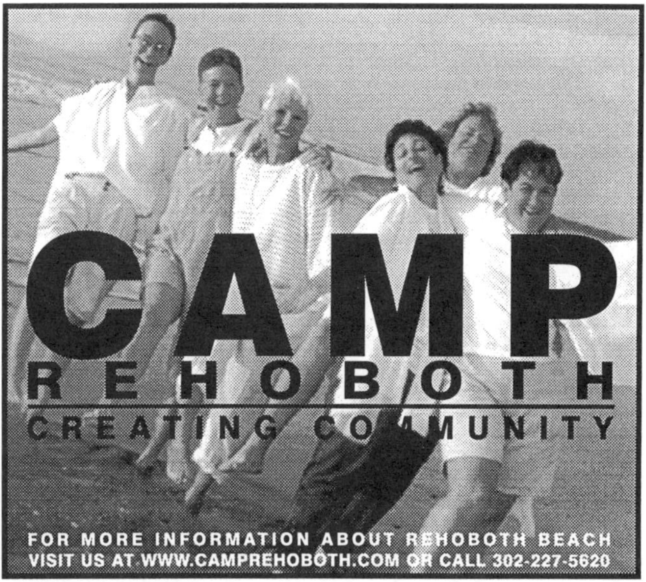

Cloud Nine 234 Rehoboth Ave (at 2nd) **302/226-1999** • 4pm-2am • bistro menu • full bar

The Cultured Pearl 19 Wilmington Ave (off 1st St) **302/227-8493** • 5pm-10pm Th-Sun • sushi bar • cocktail lounge • $16-24

Dream Cafe 26 Baltimore Ave **302/226-2233** • brkfst, lunch & dinner

Iguana Grill 52 Baltimore Ave **302/227-0948** • 11am-1am • Southwestern • full bar • patio • $7-12

La La Land 22 Wilmington Ave **302/227-3887** • 6pm-1am (seasonal) • full bar • patio • $19-33

Mano's Restaurant & Bar 10 Wilmington Ave (at 1st St) **302/227-6707** • dinner nightly, brkfst & lunch wknds • $9-14

Plumb Loco 10 N 1st St (btwn Baltimore & Rehoboth) **302/227-6870** • 5pm-1am, from noon wknds • popular • mostly women • American/ Southwestern • full bar

Sydney's Side Street Restaurant & Blues Place 25 Christian St (at 2nd St) **302/227-1339** • 4pm-1am (seasonal) • healthy entrees • full bar • live shows • patio • $12-20

Tijuana Taxi 207 Rehoboth Ave (at 2nd St) **302/227-1986** • 5pm-10pm, from noon wknds • full bar • wheelchair access • $6-13

Bookstores

Lambda Rising 39 Baltimore Ave (btwn 1st & 2nd) **302/227-6969** • 10am-midnight • call for winter hrs • lesbigay • wheelchair access

Publications

▲ **Letters from Camp Rehoboth** **302/227-5620** • newsmagazine w/ events & entertainment listings

Spiritual Groups

MCC of Rehoboth Beach Rte 271/ Glade Rd **302/226-0816** • 10am Sun

Gyms & Health Clubs

Body Shop 401 N Boardwalk (at Virginia) **302/226-0920** • lesbians/ gay men

The Firm 6 Camelot Shopping Ctr **302/227-8363** • 7am-9pm

Wilmington

Bars

814 Club 814 Shipley St **302/657-5730** • 5pm-1am • lesbians/ gay men • dancing/DJ • transgender-friendly • also restaurant • $5-15

Roam at 'The Shipley Grill' (upstairs) **302/658-7626** • 6pm-1am, from 5pm Fri • lesbians/ gay men • men's night Th • dancing/DJ • multi-racial

Restaurants

Mrs Robino's 520 N Union (at Pennsylvania) **302/652-9223** • family-style Italian

The Shipley Grill 913 Shipley St (at 10th) **302/652-7797** • lunch & dinner • fine dining • full bar • live shows upstairs • $17-24

Spiritual Groups

More Light Hanouver Presb Church (at 18th & Baynard) **302/764-1594** • 1st & 3rd Sun • dinner 5:30pm & worship 6:45pm

District of Columbia

Washington

Info Lines & Services

Asians & Friends **202/387-2742** • Tue happy hour 5:30pm-7:30pm at 'Club Chaos' (17th & 'Q') • call for more info

BiCentrist Alliance **202/828-3065** • nat'l bisexual organization • mtgs & newsletter • taped info

Black Lesbian Support Group 1734 14th St NW **202/797-3593** • 3pm 2nd & 4th Sat

Bon Vivant Foundation **202/234-2824, 800/864-6635** • professional women's networking group • sponsors dance parties 1st Sat • also publishes newsletter

Gay/ Lesbian Hotline (at Whitman-Walker Clinic) **202/833-3234** • 7pm-11pm • resources • crisis counseling

Hola Gay **202/332-2192** • 7pm-11pm Th • hotline en español

The HOPE Foundation **202/466-5783** • also monthly gathering for positive people • call for info

Lesbian/ Gay Youth Helpline at Sexual Minority Youth Assistance **202/546-5911** • 7pm-10pm Mon-Fri, drop-in 6pm-8pm Fri • for youth under 21

LLEGO (Latino/ a Lesbian/ Gay Organization) 1612 'K' St NW #500 **202/466-8240** • 9am-6pm Mon-Fri • also publishes newsletter 'Noticias de LLEGO'

Nat'l Black Gay/ Lesbian Leadership Forum **202/483-6786** • 10am-5pm Mon, Wed & Fri

OWLS (Older, Wiser Lesbians) **301/858-0554, 202/363-9647** • social club for women '39 & better'

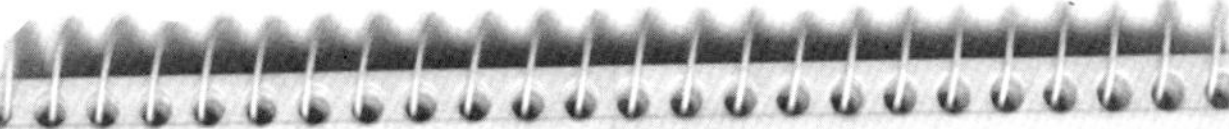

Washington

Even though Washington, DC is known worldwide as a showcase of American culture and a command center of global politics, many people overlook this international 'hot spot' when traveling in the United States. But DC is not all boring museums and stuffy bureaucrats.

For instance, begin your stay in DC at one of the gay-friendly hotels or guesthouses in and around the city. **Creekside B&B** in Maryland has a strong lesbian following.

Of course, you could tour the usual sites–starting with the heart of DC–the 'Mall'–a two-mile-long grass strip bordered by many museums and monuments: the Smithsonian, the National Air and Space Museum, the National Gallery of Art, the Museum of Natural History, the Museum of American History, the Washington Monument, the Lincoln Memorial, and the Vietnam Veterans Memorial.

For a truly interesting change of pace, check out these less touristy attractions: the outstanding National Museum of Women in the Arts, the hip shops and exotic eateries along Massachusetts Avenue, and of course, DuPont Circle, the pulsing heart of lesbigay DC. The Circle is also home to the oldest modern art museum in the country, the Phillips Collection, as well as the popular women's bookstore **Lammas**, the lesbigay bookstore **Lambda Rising**, and the kinky **Pleasure Place.**

For nightlife, don't miss the **Hung Jury**, DC's hippest dyke dance spot. **Phase One** is a more casual bar for lesbians, and there are several women's nights at the mixed bars. For the latest events for women in DC and its environs, pick up a copy of **Woman's Monthly** or **Women in the Life**.

Still can't find your crowd? Drop by **Sisterspace & Books**, specializing in books by and about African-American women; call **Hola Gay**, the lesbian/gay hotline in Spanish and English; call the **Black Lesbian Support Group**; or drop by the **Asians & Friends** happy hour at **Club Chaos**.

Transgender Education Association 301/949-3822 • social/ support group for crossdressers & transsexuals

Triangle Club 2030 'P' St NW **202/659-8641** • site for various 12-step groups • see listings in 'The Washington Blade'

Accommodations

1836 California 1836 California St NW (btwn 18th & 19th) **202/462-6502** • gay/ straight • 1900s house w/period furnishings & sundeck • $60-115

The Brenton B&B 1708 16th St NW (at 'R' St) **202/332-5550, 800/673-9042** • mostly gay men • IGLTA • $79

Capitol Hill Guest House 101 5th St NE (at 'A' St) **202/547-1050, 800/261-2768** • gay/ straight • Victorian rowhouse in historic Capitol Hill district • gay-owned/ run • $55-125

The Carlyle Suites 1731 New Hampshire Ave NW (btwn 'R' & 'S' Sts) **202/234-3200, 800/964-5377** • gay/ straight • art deco hotel • also 'The Wave Bar' • popular gay Sun brunch • wheelchair access

Creekside B&B 301/261-9438 • mostly women • private home south of Annapolis, MD • 45 minutes from DC • swimming

The Embassy Inn 1627 16th St NW **202/234-7800, 800/423-9111** • gay-friendly • small hotel w/ B&B atmosphere • $69-129

Embassy Suites—Chevy Chase Pavilion 4300 Military Rd NW **202/362-9300, 800/362-2779** • gay-friendly • wheelchair access

▲ **Kalorama Guest House at Kalorama Park** 1854 Mintwood Pl NW (at Columbia Rd) **202/667-6369** • gay/ straight • IGLTA • $50-110

▲ **Kalorama Guest House at Woodley Park** 2700 Cathedral Ave NW (off Connecticut Ave) **202/328-8730** • gay/ straight • IGLTA • $45-95

Maison Orleans 414 5th St SE (btwn 'D' & 'E' Sts) **202/544-3694** • gay-friendly • smokefree • $90-110

Morrison-Clark Historic Inn & Restaurant Massachusetts Ave (at 11th St NW) **202/289-1200** • gay-friendly • also a restaurant

Radisson Barcelo Hotel Washington 2121 'P' St NW (at 21st St) **202/293-3100, 800/333-3333** • gay-friendly • IGLTA • $145-285

The River Inn 924 25th St NW (at 'K' St) **202/337-7600, 800/424-2741** • gay-friendly • also 'Foggy Bottom Cafe' • wheelchair access

Savoy Suites Hotel 2505 Wisconsin Ave NW (at Calvert), Georgetown **202/337-9700, 800/944-5377** • gay-friendly • also restaurant • Italian • wheelchair access

Swann House Historic B&B 1808 New Hampshire Ave NW (at Swann St) **202/265-4414** • gay/ straight • 1883 Victorian mansion in Dupont Circle • swimming • hot tub & roof deck • $135-250

Washington Plaza 10 Thomas Cir NW (at 14th & Massachusetts) **202/842-1300, 800/424-1140** • full-service hotel • also restaurant • $79-165

The William Lewis House B&B 1309 'R' St NW (at 13th) **202/462-7574, 800/465-7574** • turn-of-the-century building • hot tub • $75-95

The Windsor Inn 1842 16th St NW **202/667-0300, 800/423-9111** • gay-friendly • small hotel w/ B&B atmosphere • $79-159

Bars

Club Chaos 1603 17th St NW (at 17th & 'Q') **202/232-4141** • 3pm-2am, brunch 11am Sun • lesbians/ gay men • ladies' night Wed • also restaurant • some veggie • live shows • wheelchair access

DC Eagle 639 New York Ave NW (btwn 6th & 7th) **202/347-6025** • 6pm-2am, from noon Fri-Sun, till 3am Fri-Sat • mostly gay men • leather • wheelchair access

The Fireplace 2161 'P' St NW (at 22nd St) **202/293-1293** • 1pm-2am • mostly gay men • neighborhood bar • videos • wheelchair access

JR's Bar 1519 17th St NW (at Church) **202/328-0090** • 11:30am-2am, till 3am Fri-Sat • mostly gay men • videos

Larry's Lounge 1836 18th St NW (at 'T' St) **202/483-1483** • 5pm-midnight, till 2am Fri-Sat • lesbians/ gay men • neighborhood bar • food served • wheelchair access

The Lillies 1731 New Hampshire (at 18th & 'R' St, in the 'Carlyle Suites') **202/518-5011** • 5pm-2am • mostly gay men • also restaurant • wheelchair access

Mr Henry's Capitol Hill 601 Pennsylvania Ave SE (at 6th St) **202/546-8412** • 11:30am-2am • popular • gay-friendly • multi-racial clientele • live jazz • also restaurant

Nob Hill 1101 Kenyon NW (at 11th St) **202/797-1101** • 6pm-2am • mostly gay men • neighborhood bar • dancing/DJ • mostly African-American • live shows

Phase One 525 8th St SE (btwn 'E' & 'G' Sts) **202/544-6831** • 7pm-2am, till 3am Fri-Sat (clsd Mon-Tue winter) • mostly women • neighborhood bar • dancing/DJ • wheelchair access

Remington's 639 Pennsylvania Ave SE (btwn 6th & 7th) **202/543-3113** • 4pm-2am, till 3am Fri-Sat • popular • mostly gay men • dancing/DJ • country/ western • dance lessons Mon, Wed-Th • karaoke Wed • videos

Nightclubs

Atlas PO Box 53025, 20009 **202/331-4422** • dance parties • mostly gay men • locations vary • call for info

Bachelors Mill downstairs at 'Back Door Pub' **202/544-1931** • opens 10pm, clsd Mon • lesbians/ gay men • more women Wed • dancing/DJ • multi-racial • live shows • wheelchair access

Chief Ike's Mambo Room 1725 Columbia Rd NW (at Ontario) **202/332-2211** • 4pm-2am • gay-friendly • dancing/DJ • also restaurant • Cajun • wheelchair access

Deco 2122 'P' St NW • hours vary • lesbians/ gay men • dancing/DJ • multi-racial • Latino/a • karaoke • live shows • Cuban food from 'Havana' next door • wheelchair access • cover charge

Washington

Where the Girls Are: Strolling around DuPont Circle or cruising a bar in the lesbigay bar ghetto southeast of The Mall.

Entertainment: Gay Men's Chorus 202/338-7464.

Lesbigay Pride: June. 202/986-1119.

Annual Events: October - Reel Affirmations Film Festival 202/986-1119.
March - Women's History Month at various Smithsonian Museums 202/357-2700.

City Info: DC Visitors Assoc. 202/789-7000, web: www.washington.org.

Attractions: Ford's Theatre 202/347-4833.
Jefferson Memorial.
JFK Center for the Performing Arts.
Lincoln Memorial.
National Gallery 202/737-4215.
National Museum of Women in the Arts 202/783-5000.
National Zoo 202/673-4717.
Smithsonian 202/357-1300.
Vietnam Veteran's Memorial.

Best View: From the top of the Washington Monument.

Weather: Summers are hot (90°s) and MUGGY (the city was built on marshes). In the winter, temperatures drop to the 30°s and 40°s with rain. Spring is the time of cherry blossoms.

Transit: Yellow Cab 202/544-1212.
Washington Flier 202/417-8400; 703/685-1400 (from Dulles or National).
Super Shuttle 800/809-7080.
Metro Transit Authority 202/637-7000.

The Edge 56 'L' St SE (at Half St) **202/488-1200** • from 10pm Mon-Th, 11pm-5am Fri-Sat, clsd Sun • mostly gay men • women's night Th • multi-racial clientele • women's party last Sat 3pm-7pm • dancing/DJ • wheelchair access

Élan 1129 Pennsylvania Ave SE (at 12th) **202/544-6406** • clsd Mon-Wed (some special events Wed) • mostly women • dancing/DJ • live shows • women-owned/ run

Escandalo! 2122 'P' St NW **202/822-8909** • lesbians/ gay men • dancing/DJ • mostly Latino/a • also 'Havana' Cuban restaurant

Hung Jury 1819 'H' St NW (at 18th St) **202/785-8181** • Fri-Sat only • mostly women • dancing/DJ • food served • call for events • wheelchair access • popular w/ French women

Lizard Lounge 1520 14th St NW (at the 'Eleventh Hour') **202/331-4422** • 8pm Sun • lesbians/ gay men • dance parties • locations vary • call for info • also restaurant

Moca Sundays @ Club Diversité 1526 14th St NW (btwn 'P' & 'Q' Sts) **202/234-5740** • 7pm-3am Sun • mostly gay men • dancing/DJ

Tracks 2000 1111 First St SE (at 'M' St) **202/488-3320** • 9pm-6am • popular • mostly gay men • dancing/DJ • alternative • young crowd • call for events • wheelchair access

Velvet Nation corner of S Capitol & 'K' St SE **202/554-1500** • 10pm Sat • mostly gay men • dancing/DJ • live shows • younger crowd • cover charge

Ziegfield's 1345 Half St SE **202/554-5141** • 8pm-3am Th-Sun • lesbians/ gay men • dancing/DJ • alternative • multi-racial clientele • live shows • wheelchair access

Cafes

Cafe Luna 1633 'P' St NW (at 17th & 'P') **202/387-4005** • 8am-11pm, from 11am wknds • popular • lesbians/ gay men • healthy • plenty veggie

Xando 697 20th St **202/332-6364** • make your own s'mores

Restaurants

Annie's Paramount Steak House 1609 17th St NW (at Corcoran) **202/232-0395** • opens 11am, 24hrs Fri-Sat • popular • full bar

Armand's Chicago Pizza 4231 Wisconsin Ave NW (at Veazey) **202/686-9450** • 11:30am-11pm • full bar • also 226 Massachusetts Ave NE, Capitol Hill, 202/547-6600

Banana Cafe & Piano Bar 500 8th St SE (at 'E' St) **202/543-5906** • lunch & dinner • Puerto Rican/ Cuban • some veggie

Cafe Berlin 322 Massachusetts Ave NE (btwn 3rd & 4th) **202/543-7656** • lunch & dinner, dinner only Sun • German • some veggie • wheelchair access • $7-20

Cafe Japoné 2032 'P' St NW (at 21st) **202/223-1573** • 6pm-2am • mostly Asian-American • Japanese food • full bar • live jazz Wed & Sat • karaoke • $10-15

Dupont Italian Kitchen & Bar 1637 17th St NW (at 'R' St) **202/328-3222, 202/328-0100** • 11am-2am, bar from 4pm • some veggie

Fio's 3636 16th St NW (at the 'Woodner') **202/667-3040** • dinner • Italian

Gabriel 2121 'P' St NW (at 21st) **202/956-6690** • 10:30am-midnight • Mediterranean/ Latin • some veggie • full bar • wheelchair access • $13-22

Guapo's 4515 Wisconsin Ave NW (at Albemale) **202/686-3588** • lunch & dinner • Mexican • some veggie • full bar • wheelchair access • $5-11

The Islander 1201 'U' St (at 12th) **202/234-4955** • lunch & dinner, clsd Mon • Caribbean • some veggie • full bar

Jaleo 480 7th St NW (at 'E' St) **202/628-7949** • lunch & dinner • tapas • full bar • wheelchair access

La Frontera Cantina 1633 17th St NW (btwn 'R' & 'Q') **202/232-0437** • 11:30am-11pm, till 1:30am Fri-Sat, clsd Sun • Tex-Mex

Lauriol Plaza 1801 18th St NW (at 'S') **202/387-0035** • lunch & dinner • Latin American

Mediterranean Blue 1910 18th St NW (at 'T') **202/483-2583** • dinner

Mr Henry's 601 Pennsylvania Ave SE (at Pennsylvania) **202/546-8412** • lunch & dinner • full bar

Occidental Grill 1475 Pennsylvania Ave NW (btwn 14th & 15th) **202/783-1475** • political player hangout

Pepper's 1527 17th St NW (btwn 'P' & 'Q') **202/328-8193** • global American • full bar • wheelchair access • $7-14

Perry's 1811 Columbia Rd NW (at 18th) **202/234-6218** • 5:30pm-11:30pm • full bar

Rocklands 2418 Wisconsin Ave NW (at Calvert) **202/333-2558** • bbq & take-out

Roxanne 2319 18th St NW (at Belmont) **202/462-8330** • dinner, bar till 2am wknds • Tex/ Mex • also 'Peyote Cafe'

Sala Thai 2016 'P' St NW (at 21st) **202/872-1144** • lunch & dinner • some veggie

Skewers 1633 'P' St NW (at 17th) **202/387-7400** • noon-11pm • Middle-Eastern • full bar • $6-13

Straits of Malaya (Larry's Lounge) 1836 18th St NW (at 'T' St) **202/483-1483** • lunch & dinner • Singaporean/ Malaysian • rooftop patio • gay-owned/ run

Trio 1537 17th St NW **202/232-6305** • 7:30am-midnight • some veggie • full bar • $6-16

Trocadero Cafe 1914 Connecticut Ave (in 'Hotel Sofitel') **202/797-2000** • French • intimate setting • wheelchair access • $25-35

Two Quail 320 Massachusetts Ave NE **202/543-8030** • lunch Mon-Fri & dinner nightly • popular • New American • some veggie • full bar • $10-18

Entertainment & Recreation

Anecdotal History Tours 301/294-9514 • variety of guided tours

Phillips Collection 1612 21st St NW (at 'Q' St) **202/387-0961** • clsd Mon • America's oldest museum of modern art • near Dupont Circle

Bookstores

ADC Map & Travel Center 1636 'I' St NW (at 17th St) **202/628-2608, 800/544-2659** • 9am-5:30pm, till 6:30pm Wed-Th, 10am-4pm Sat, clsd Sun • many maps & travel guides

Kramer Books & Afterwords 1517 Connecticut Ave NW (at 'Q') **202/387-1400** • 7:30am-1am, 24hrs wknds • general • also cafe • wheelchair access

Lambda Rising 1625 Connecticut Ave NW (btwn 'Q' & 'R' Sts) **202/462-6969** • 9am-midnight • lesbigay • wheelchair access

▲ **Lammas Women's Books & More** 1607 17th St NW (at 'Q' St) **202/775-8218, 800/955-2662** • 11am-9:30pm, till 10:30pm Fri-Sat, from noon wknds • lesbian/ feminist

Sisterspace & Books 1515 'U' St NW (at 15th St) **202/332-3433** • 10am-7pm, noon-5pm Sun • specialize in books by & about African-American women • women-owned/ run

Vertigo Books 1337 Connecticut Ave NW (at 'N' St) **202/429-9272** • 10am-7pm, noon-5pm Sun • African-American emphasis • wheelchair access

Retail Shops

Industrial Body Piercing 2147 'P' St NW (above 'Mr P's' bar) **202/822-3984** • 2pm-10pm Wed-Sun

Outlook 1706 Connecticut Ave NW (btwn 'R' & 'S' Sts) **202/745-1469** • 10am-10pm, till 11pm Fri-Sat • cards • gifts

Perforations 900 'M' St NW (at 9th) **202/289-8863** • 1pm-8pm, till 9pm Sat, till 6pm Sun, clsd Mon • piercing & tattooing

Universal Gear 1601 17th St NW **202/319-1157** • 11am-10pm, till midnight Fri-Sat, clsd Mon • casual, club, athletic & designer clothing

Publications

MW (Metro Arts & Entertainment) **202/638-6830** • extensive club listings

Washington Blade **202/797-7000** • huge lesbigay newspaper • extensive resource listings

Woman's Monthly 1612 'U' St NW #403 **202/234-2824** • covers DC & VA community events

Women in the Life 1611 Connecticut Ave NW **202/483-9818**

Spiritual Groups

Bet Mishpachah 5 Thomas Cir NW **202/833-1638** • lesbigay synagogue

Dignity Washington 1820 Connecticut Ave NW (at St Margaret's Church) **202/546-2235** • call for service times

Faith Temple (Evangelical) 1313 New York Ave NW **202/232-4911** • 1pm Sun

Friends (Quaker) 2111 Florida Ave NW (enter on Decatur Pl) **202/483-3310** • 9am, 10am, 11am Sun, 7pm Wed

MCC Washington 474 Ridge St NW (btwn M & N) **202/638-7373** • 9am, 11am & 7pm Sun, 6:30pm Wed

More Light Presbyterians 400 'I' St SW (at Westminister Church) **202/484-7700** • call for service times

Gyms & Health Clubs

Results—The Gym 1612 'U' St NW (at 17th St) **202/518-0001** • gay-friendly • also women-only fitness area • also 'Aurora Basics Health Cafe,' 202/234-6822

Washington Sports Club 1835 Connecticut Ave NW (at Columbia & Florida) **202/332-0100** • gay-friendly

Erotica

Leather Rack 1723 Connecticut Ave NW (btwn 'R' & 'S' Sts) **202/797-7401** • 10am-11pm

▲ **Pleasure Place** 1710 Connecticut Ave NW (btwn 'R' & 'S' Sts) **202/483-3297** • 10am-midnight, till 10pm Mon-Tue, noon-7pm Sun • leather • latex • shoes & more

▲ **Pleasure Place** 1063 Wisconsin Ave NW, Georgetown (at M) **202/333-8570** • 10am-midnight, till 10pm Mon-Tue, noon-7pm Sun • leather • latex • shoes & more

Florida

Alligator Point

Accommodations

Simple Addition **800/533-1973** • elegant & private waterfront vacation home on the Gulf of Mexico • $450-750 week

Amelia Island

Accommodations

The Amelia Island Williams House 103 S 9th St **904/277-2328, 800/414-9257** • gay-friendly • magnificent 1856 antebellum mansion • jacuzzi • fireplace • wheelchair access • gay-owned/ run • $135-200

Restaurants

Beech Street Grill 810 Beech St (at 8th St), Fernandina Beach **904/277-3662** • dinner only

Bretts 1 Front St **904/261-2660** • dinner only

Southern Tip 4802 First Coast Hwy **904/261-6184** • lunch & dinner • cont'l • full bar

Boyton Beach

Spiritual Groups

Church of Our Savior MCC 2011 S Federal Hwy, Boynton Beach **561/733-4000** • 9am & 11am Sun

Bradenton Beach

Accommodations

Bungalow Beach Resort 2000 Gulf Dr N **941/778-3600, 800/779-3601** • gay-friendly • swimming • hot tub • kitchens • non-smoking rms available • wheelchair access • gay-owned/ run • $90-290

Clearwater

see also St Petersburg

Accommodations

Americana Gulf Resort 325 S Gulfview Bvd **727/461-7695, 800/462-1213** • gay-friendly • rms, suites & efficiencies • on the beach • kids ok • $50-140

Bars

Lost & Found 5858 Roosevelt Blvd/ State Rd 686 **727/539-8903** • 4pm-2am • mostly gay men • live shows • karaoke • patio • wheelchair access

Pro Shop Pub 840 Cleveland St (at Prospect) **727/447-4259** • 11:30am-2am, from 1pm Sun • mostly gay men • neighborhood bar

Nightclubs

Club Mercedes 28780 US 19 North (N of Countryside) **727/791-8050** • 5pm-2am • mostly gay men • dancing/DJ

Turtle Club/ Condor Turtle Ln (off Roosevelt) **727/524-8777** • gay-friendly • dancing/DJ • gay night Sun • 18+ • wheelchair access

Cocoa Beach

Bars

Club Chances Cocoa 610 Forrest Ave (at US 1), Cocoa **407/639-0103** • 4pm-2am, from 2pm Sun • mostly gay men • dancing/DJ • patio • wheelchair access

Restaurants

Flaminias 3210 S Atlantic Ave **407/783-9908** • dinner only • Italian • beer/ wine

Lobster Shanty 2200 S Orlando Ave **407/783-1350** • lunch & dinner • full bar • wheelchair access

Mango Tree 118 N Atlantic Ave **407/799-0513** • opens 6pm, clsd Mon • fine dining • single malt Scotch bar • wheelchair access • $12-17

Spiritual Groups

Breaking the Silence MCC 1261 Range Rd (off 520), Cocoa **407/631-4524** • 6pm Sun

Crescent City

Accommodations

Crescent City Campground **904/698-2020, 800/634-3968** • gay-friendly • tenting sites • 85 RV hookups • swimming • laundry • showers • gay-owned • $18 day, $115 week

Daytona Beach

Info Lines & Services

Lambda Center 320 Harvey Ave (at Hollywood) **904/255–0280** • support groups • youth services • 12-step mtgs

Accommodations

Best Western Mayan Inn Beachfront 103 S Ocean Ave **904/252–2378, 800/237–8238** • gay-friendly • some rms w/ ocean views

Buccaneer Motel 2301 N Atlantic Ave **904/253–9678, 800/972–6056** • gay-friendly • swimming • $30-90

Coquina Inn 544 S Palmetto Ave **904/254–4969, 800/805–7533** • gay-friendly • full brkfst • fireplaces • hot tub • smokefree • IGLTA

The Villa B&B 801 N Peninsula Dr **904/248–2020** • gay-friendly • historic Spanish mansion • swimming • nudity • IGLTA • $100-185

Bars

The Barracks & Officers Club 952 Orange Ave (at Nova) **904/254–3464** • 5pm-3am • popular • mostly gay men • dancing/DJ • live shows • theme nights • wheelchair access

Beachside Club 415 Main St **904/253–3279** • noon-3am • popular • mostly gay men • dancing/DJ • live shows

Hollywood/ Barndoor Complex 615 Main St (off Wild Olive Ave) **904/252–3776** • 11am-3am • lesbians/ gay men • neighborhood bar • also restaurant ($3-7) • also 'Barndoor Complex' • mostly gay men • dancing/DJ

Restaurants

Anna's 304 Seabreeze Blvd **904/239–9624** • dinner only, clsd Sun • Italian • beer/ wine

Cafe Frappes 123 W Granada Blvd **904/615–4888** • lunch & dinner, clsd Sun • some veggie • patio

Sapporo 501 Seabreeze Ave **904/257–4477** • lunch Mon-Fri only, dinner 7 days • Japanese • full bar

Sweetwater's 3633 Halifax Dr, Port Orange **904/761–6724** • seafood & steaks • wheelchair access

Spiritual Groups

Hope MCC 500 S Ridgewood Ave **904/254–0993** • 10:45am Sun

Kingdom of God Worship Center **904/248–2163** • call for location & service time • lesbigay congregation

Delray Beach

Bars

Lulu's Place 640 E Atlantic Ave Bay 6 (at E Federal Hwy) **561/278–4004** • 4pm-2am • lesbians/ gay men • piano bar

Restaurants

Masquerade Cafe 640 E Atlantic Ave (at E Federal Hwy) **561/279–0229** • lunch & dinner • wheelchair access

Spiritual Groups

New Hope First Community Church 400 S Swinton Ave **561/540–8065** • 11am Sun

Dunedin

see also St Petersburg

Bars

1470 West 325 Main St (at Douglass) **727/736–5483** • 4pm-2am • lesbians/ gay men • dancing/DJ • live shows • patio • wheelchair access

Fort Lauderdale

Info Lines & Services

Gay/ Lesbian Community Center 1164 E Oakland Park Blvd (at Dixie Hwy) **954/563–9500** • 10am-10pm, from 1pm Sat, clsd Sun • wheelchair access

Lambda South 1231 E Las Olas Blvd **954/761–9072** • 12-step clubhouse • wheelchair access

Accommodations

Bahama Hotel 401 N Atlantic Blvd (at Bayshore) **954/467–7315, 800/622–9995** • full gym • also 'The Deck' restaurant & bar • IGLTA • $70-169

California Dream Inn 300–315 Walnut St, Hollywood **954/923–2100** • gay-friendly • located directly on oceanfront • very lesbian-friendly • gay-owned/ run • $49-99

Embassy Suites Hotel 1100 SE 17th St **954/527–2700, 800/362–2779** • gay-friendly • tropical outdoor pool

Flamingo Resort 2727 Terramar St (nr Birch) **954/561–4658, 800/283–4786** • mostly gay men • efficiencies • intimate art deco setting • IGLTA • gay-owned/ run • $83

Hidden Jungle Spa & Retreat 17210 SW 68 Ct (I 75 & Griffin Rd. W) **954/680–2032, 954/680–2206** • gay/ straight • 18+ • swimming pool • gay-owned/ run • full spa facilities 10am-7pm, clsd Sun

▲ **JP's Beach Villas** 4621 N Ocean Dr (btwn Commercial & A1A) **954/772-3672, 888/992-3224** • mostly gay men • all-suite hotel • full kitchen • swimming • 1/2 blk to ocean • $75-250

King Henry Arms Motel 543 Breakers Ave (nr Bayshore) **954/561-0039, 800/205-5464** • mostly gay men • small & friendly motel just steps from the ocean • swimming • IGLTA • gay-owned/ run • $64-119

Liberty Apartment Suites 1501 SW 2nd Ave (at Sheridan), Dania Beach **954/927-0090, 877/927-0090** • lesbians/ gay men • furnished apts • swimming • smokefree available • gay-owned/ run • $300-500/wk

Midnight Sea 3005 Alhambra St (at Birch) **954/463-4827, 800/910-2357** • mostly gay men • guesthouse on beach • hot tub • nudity • non-smoking available • IGLTA • gay-owned/ run • $59-159

Rainbow Ventures—The Inn 1520 NE 26th Ave (nr Sunrise & Bayview) **954/568-5770, 800/881-4814** • women only • commitment ceremonies • IGLTA • $50-150

Sea Grape House Inn 1109 NE 16th Pl (at Dixie Hwy) **954/525-6586, 800/447-3074 (CODE: 44)** • mostly gay men • complimentary cocktails • secluded • clothing-optional pool & gardens • gay-owned/ run • $79-189

Villa Torino 3017 Alhambra St (nr A1A) **954/527-5272** • lesbians/ gay men • motel & apts • 1/2 blk to beach • $65-120

Villa Venice Resort 2900 Terramar St **954/564-7855** • gay-friendly motel • 2 blks to beach • swimming • kitchens

BARS

The Bushes 3038 N Federal Hwy (at Oakland Park Blvd) **954/561-1724** • 9am-2am, till 3am Sat • mostly gay men • neighborhood bar • wheelchair access

Fort Lauderdale

Where the Girls Are: On the beach near the lesbigay accommodations, just south of Birch State Recreation Area. Or at one of the cafes or bars in Wilton Manors or Oakland Park.

Lesbigay Pride: June. 954/561-2020.

Annual Events: February - Winter Gayla circuit party.
June - Film Fest.
December- AIDS Walk 954/563-9500.

City Info: 954/765-4466 or 800/227-8669, web: www.sunny.org.

Attractions: Butterfly World 954/977-4400.
Broward Center for the Performing Arts 954/522-5334.
Everglades.
Flamingo Gardens 954/473-2955.
Museum of Art 954/525-5500.
Museum of Discovery & Science 954/467-6637.
Sawgrass Mills, world's largest outlet mall 954/846-2350.
Six Flags Atlantis:The Water Kingdom.

Weather: The average year-round temperature in this sub-tropical climate is 75-90°.

Transit: Yellow Cab 954/565-5400.
Super Shuttle 954/764-1700.
Broward County Transit 954/357-8400.

VINCE GABRIELLY
www.ravengallery.com
PHOTOGRAPHY

Chaps at the Corral 1727 N Andrews Wy (at 16th St) **954/767-0027** • 2pm-2am • mostly gay men • country/ western • leather

The Curve Club 1025 N Federal Hwy (at Sunrise) **954/523-5552** • 9am-2am, till 3am Fri-Sat, from 11am Sun • lesbians/ gay men • piano bar • drag shows • food served • wheelchair access

Eagle 1951 Powerline Rd/ NW 9th Ave (at NW 19th St) **954/462-7224** • 3pm-2am, till 3am wknds • mostly gay men • leather • wheelchair access

Everglades in Chainz 1931 S Federal Hwy (at 19th St) **954/462-9165** • 1pm-2am, till 3am wknds • mostly gay men • dancing/DJ • leather • wheelchair access

Georgie's Alibi 2266 Wilton Dr/ NE 4th Ave (at Sunrise) **954/565-2526** • 11am-2am, till 3am Sat • mostly gay men • food served • videos • wheelchair access

Mona's 502 E Sunrise Blvd (at 6th Ave) **954/525-6662** • noon-2am, from 7am Sat • lesbians/ gay men • neighborhood bar

Fort Lauderdale

Fort Lauderdale, one of Florida's most popular cities and resort areas, has everything that makes the whole state a natural paradise—sunny skies, balmy nights, hot sands, and a clear blue sea.

Honeycombed by the Intercoastal Waterway of rivers, bays, canals, and inlets, Fort Lauderdale is known as the American Venice. If you'd rather keep your feet on solid ground, you can tour the Seminole Indian Reservation, shop at Sawgrass Mills outlet mega-mall, or take in a jai alai game.

For more breathtaking attractions, however, check out Fort Lauderdale's growing lesbian community. You'll find a number of lesbian-friendly accommodations, including the women-only **Rainbow Ventures—The Inn**; ask about their chartered cruises, too.

Legends Cafe is a popular spot for dinner, and afterwards you can check out the **Whale & Porpoise** or **The Copa,** a complete bar complex, where women mix it up with the gay boys. Or you can head to nearby Hollywood (Florida, that is) and pay a visit to **Zachary's** women's bar. For retro fun, check out Fort Lauderdale's Gay Skate Night on Tuesdays at **Gold Coast Roller Rink.**

Nightclubs

Copa 2800 S Federal Hwy (N of airport) **954/463-1507** • 10pm-6am • popular • lesbians/ gay men • dancing/DJ • mostly Latino/a • live shows • food served • young crowd • inside & outside bars

The End Up 3521 W Broward Blvd (at 35th Ave) **954/584-9301** • 11pm-4am • mostly gay men • dancing/DJ • T-dance Sun

Jams 2232 Wilton Dr (in Wilton Plaza) • mostly gay men • dancing/DJ • opening soon • inquire locally

Omni 1421 E Oakland Park Blvd (east of Wilton Dr) **954/565-5151** • 4pm-2am, till 3am Sat , clsd Mon • lesbians/ gay men • more women Sat • dancing/DJ • Latin nights Fri & Sun

The Pier 3333 NE 32nd Ave (N of Oakland Park Blvd) **954/630-8990, 954/630-8130** • noon-2am, till 3am Fri-Sat • lesbians/ gay men • 4 bars • cabaret • restaurant • on the waterfront

The Saint 1000 State Rd 84 (at I-95) **954/525-7883** • 9pm-2am, till 3am wknds, clsd Mon & Th • mostly gay men • more women Fri • dancing/DJ

The Sea Monster 2 S New River Dr W (under the Andrews Drawbridge, across from Las Olas shopping ctr) **954/463-4641** • 8pm-2am, till 3am Fri-Sat, from 6pm Sun, clsd Mon • lesbians/ gay men • dancing/DJ • CW Tue • dancers Fri-Sun • Latin night Fri • T-dance Sun • wheelchair access

The Whale & Porpoise 2750 E Oakland Park Blvd (at Federal) **954/565-2750** • 5pm-2am, till 3am wknds • mostly women • dancing/DJ • food served • karaoke • live shows

Cafes

The Storks 2505 NE 15th Ave **954/567-3220** • 7am-midnight • patio • wheelchair access

Restaurants

Chardee's 2209 Wilton Dr (at NE 6th Ave) **954/563-1800** • dinner from 6pm, bar from 4:30pm-2am • lesbians/ gay men • some veggie • live shows • wheelchair access • $12-30

Costello's 2345 Winton Dr, Wilton Manors **954/563-7752** • lunch & dinner

The Deck 401 N Atlantic Blvd (at the 'Bahama Hotel') **954/467-7315** • also bar • wheelchair access

The East City Grill 505 N Atlantic **954/563-7752** • lunch & dinner • $20-25

Hi-Life Cafe 3000 N Federal Hwy (at Oakland Park Blvd, in the 'Plaza 3000') **954/563-1395** • dinner Tue-Sun • bistro • some veggie • $10-18

Legends Cafe 1560 NE 4th Ave/ Wilton Manors Dr **954/467-2233** • 6pm-10pm, clsd Mon • popular • lesbians/ gay men • multi-ethnic homecooking • some veggie • BYOB • wheelchair access • lesbian-owned/ run

Lester's Diner 250 State Rd 84 **954/525-5641** • 24hrs • popular • more gay late nights • $5-10

Mustards Bar & Grill 2256 Wilton Dr **954/564-5116** • 5pm-10pm, till 11pm Fri-Sat • Mediterranean/ California cuisine • wheelchair access • gay-owned/ run • $10-20

Sukothai 1930 E Sunrise Blvd **954/764-0148** • lunch Mon-Fri, dinner nightly • popular • Thai • some veggie

Tropics Cabaret & Restaurant 2004 Wilton Dr (at 20th) **954/537-6000** • dinner from 6pm • new American • also bar • 4pm-2am, till 3am Sat • lesbians/ gay men • live shows • wheelchair access

Victoria Park 900 NE 20th Ave **954/764-6868** • dinner only • clsd Sun • popular • beer/ wine • some veggie • call for reservations

The Zan(Z)Bar 602 E Las Olas **954/767-3377** • 10am-midnight • South African • plenty veggie

Entertainment & Recreation

Gold Coast Roller Rink 2604 S Federal Hwy **954/523-6783** • 8pm-midnight Tue • gay skate

John U Lloyd State Park-Dania Beach Dania • popular gay beach • first parking lot over the bridge, off Dania Beach Blvd • walk right

Bookstores

Pride Factory & CyberCafe 400 N Federal Hwy (at NE 4th St) **954/463-6600** • 10am-10pm, till 7pm Sun • books • pride gifts • coffee • also cybercafe

Retail Shops

Catalog X Retail & Clothing Outlet 850 NE 13th St **954/524-5050** • 9am-10pm, 10am-9pm Sat, 11am-7pm Sun

Underground Leather 3045 N Federal Hwy (at Oakland Park Blvd) **954/561-3977** • 10am-10pm, till 11pm wknds, 1-5pm Sun • leather • toys

Publications

Hot Spots 954/928-1862, 800/522-8775 • weekly bar guide

Scoop Magazine 954/561-9707 • gay magazine

Spiritual Groups

Congregation Etz Chaim 3970 NW 21st Ave (btwn Commercial & Oakland Park) **954/714-9232** • 8:30pm Fri • lesbigay synagogue

Dignity Fort Lauderdale 330 SW 27th St (upstairs at Sunshine Cathedral MCC) **954/463-4528** • 7pm Sun • Roman Catholic liturgy

Sunshine Cathedral MCC 330 SW 27th St **954/462-2004** • 9:15am, 11am & 7pm Sun • wheelchair access

Gyms & Health Clubs

Firm Fitness 928 N Federal Hwy (at Sunrise) **954/767-6277** • 5am-11pm, 8am-8pm wknds

Erotica

Fetish Factory 821 N Federal Hwy (at Sunrise) **954/462-0032**

Romantix 3520 N Federal Hwy (at Oakland) **954/568-1220**

Wicked Leather 2422 Wilton Dr **954/564-7529**

Fort Myers

Accommodations

Golf View Motel 3523 Cleveland Ave **941/936-1858** • gay-friendly • swimming • wheelchair access • $28+

▲ **The Resort on Carefree Blvd** 3000 Carefree Blvd (at Del Prado) **941/731-3000, 800/326-0364** • mostly lesbian • women's community for vacation rentals • swimming • nature trails

Bars

Fort Rowdy's 4226 Fowler St (btwn Winkler & Colonial) **941/275-9229** • noon-2am • mostly gay men • neighborhood bar

Office Pub 3704 Grove **941/936-3212** • noon-2am • mostly men • neighborhood bar • beer/ wine

Nightclubs

The Bottom Line (TBL) 3090 Evans Ave **941/337-7292** • 2pm-2am • lesbians/ gay men • dancing/DJ • live shows • wheelchair access

Restaurants

Oasis 2222 McGregor Blvd **941/334-1566** • brkfst & lunch only • beer/ wine • wheelchair access • women-owned/ run • $4-6

Spiritual Groups

St John the Apostle MCC 2209 Unity St (at Broadway) **941/278-5181** • 8:25am & 10am Sun & 7pm Wed • wheelchair access

Fort Walton Beach

Nightclubs

Frankly Scarlett 223 Hwy 98 E (at City Parking Lot) **850/664-2966** • 8pm-2am, till 4am wknds • lesbians/ gay men • dancing/DJ • live shows • patio • wheelchair access

Gainesville

Info Lines & Services

Gay Switchboard **352/332-0700** • live 6pm-11pm, 24hr touchtone service • extensive info on Gainesville area • AA info

Bars

Spikes 4130 NW 6th St **352/376-3772** • 4pm-2am • popular • lesbians/ gay men • country/ western

The University Club 18 E University Ave (enter rear) **352/378-6814** • 5pm-2am, till 4am Fri-Sat, till 11pm Sun • lesbians/ gay men • dancing/DJ • live shows • patio • wheelchair access

Bookstores

Wild Iris Books 802 W University Ave (at 8th St) **352/375-7477** • 10am-6pm, till 7pm Fri, 11am-5pm Sun • feminist bookstore • lesbigay • wheelchair access

Spiritual Groups

Trinity MCC 11604 SW Archer Rd **352/495-3378** • 10:15am Sun • wheelchair access

Hallandale Beach

Accommodations

Club Atlantic Beach Resort 2080 S Ocean Dr **954/458-6666, 888/258-6466** • gay-friendly • rooms & suites on the beach • swimming • also restaurant • wheelchair access

Holiday

Bars

Lovey's Pub 338 US 19 (at Moog Rd) **727/849-2960** • 10am-2am, from 1pm Sun • lesbians/ gay men • neighborhood bar • wheelchair access

Hollywood

see also Miami

Accommodations

Ocean Mist Motel 1500 N Ocean Dr **954/922-1744, 888/322-1744** • gay-friendly • deck • kids ok

Bars

Partners 625 Dania Beach Blvd (at Federal Hwy), Dania **954/921-9893** • noon-3am • mostly women • neighborhood bar • dancing/DJ • live shows

Zachary's 2217 N Federal Hwy **954/920-5479** • 4pm-2am, from 11am wknds • mostly women • neighborhood bar • beer/ wine • wheelchair access

Erotica

Hollywood Book & Video 1235 S State Rd 7 **954/981-2164** • 24hrs

Jacksonville

Bars

616 616 Park St (at I-95) **904/358-6969** • 4pm-2am, from 6pm wknds • mostly gay men • women's night Sat • neighborhood bar • patio • wheelchair access

Boot Rack Saloon 4751 Lenox Ave (at Cassat Ave) **904/384-7090** • 4pm-2am • mostly gay men • country/ western • patio • wheelchair access

Bourbon Street 10957 Atlantic Blvd (at St John's Bluff Rd) **904/642-7506** • noon-2am, from 4pm Sun • lesbians/ gay men • neighborhood bar • karaoke Fri • beer/ wine • wheelchair access

Eagle 1402-6 San Marco Blvd **904/396-8551** • 2pm-2am • mostly gay men • leather • patio • wheelchair access

HMS 1702 E 8th St (at Buckman) **904/353-9200** • 2pm-2am • mostly gay men • neighborhood bar • beer/ wine • patio

The Junction 1261 King St **904/388-3434** • 2pm-2am • lesbians/ gay men • neighborhood bar • live shows • beer/ wine • women-owned/ run

The Metro corner of College & Willow Branch **904/388-8719** • 4pm-2am • lesbians/ gay men • dancing/DJ • live shows • videos • patio

My Little Dude/ Jo's Place 2952 Roosevelt Blvd (at College) **904/388-9503** • 4pm-2am • mostly women • dancing/DJ • live shows • wheelchair access

Park Place Lounge 931 King St **904/389-6616** • noon-2am • mostly gay men • neighborhood bar • wheelchair access

Third Dimension 711 Edison Ave (btwn Riverside & Park) **904/353-6316** • 3pm-2am, from 6pm Sat, from 5pm Sun • mostly gay men • dancing/DJ • alternative • live shows • wheelchair access

Retail Shops

Rainbows & Stars 1046 Park St (in historic '5-Points') **904/356-7702** • 10am-6pm, till 9pm Fri-Sat, noon-5pm Sun • pride gift store • T-shirts • rainbow items • jewelry • also community bulletin board

Publications

The Last Word (TLW) 904/384-6514, 800/677-0772 • lesbigay newspaper

Spiritual Groups

St Luke's MCC 1140 S McDuff Ave (at Remington) **904/389-7726** • 8:30am & 10:15pm Sun

Jacksonville Beach

Bars

Bo's Coral Reef 201 5th Ave N **904/246-9874** • 2pm-2am • lesbians/ gay men • dancing/DJ • live shows

Key West

Info Lines & Services

Commitment Ceremonies by Capt Linda Schuh 305/294-4213 • on the sea or shore • certificate • woman-owned/ run

Gay/ Lesbian AA 305/296-8654

Accommodations

Alexander Palms Court 715 South St (at Vernon) **305/296-6413, 800/858-1943** • gay-friendly • swimming • hot tub • private patios • gay-owned/ run • $75-395

Alexander's Guest House 1118 Fleming St (at Frances) **305/294-9919, 800/654-9919** • lesbians/ gay men • swimming • nudity • sundeck • wheelchair access • gay-owned/ run • $80-300

Ambrosia House Tropical Lodging 615 Fleming St (at Simonton) **305/296-9838, 800/535-9838** • gay-friendly • swimming • hot tub • sea captain's house • $95-175

Andrew's Inn Zero Whalton Ln (at Duval) **305/294-7730, 888/263-7393** • gay-friendly • full brkfst • swimming • wheelchair access • $108-398

The Artist House 534 Eaton St (at Duval) **305/296-3977, 800/582-7882** • gay-friendly • Victorian guesthouse • jacuzzi • patio • smokefree • $119-249

Atlantic Shores Resort 510 South St (at Duval) **305/296-2491, 800/526-3559** • gay/ lesbian resort • swimming • nudity • sundeck • 2 bars • also restaurant ($3-8) • IGLTA • $125-240

Author's of Key West 725 White St (at Angela) **305/294-7381, 800/898-6909** • gay-friendly • swimming

Bananas Foster B&B 537 Caroline St (at Simonton St) **305/294-9061, 800/653-4888** • gay-friendly • hot tub • swimming • wheelchair access • gay-owned/ run • $109-300

Beach Bungalow & Beach Guest Suite Box 165, 33041 **305/294-1525** • gay/ straight • hot tub • gay-owned/ run • vacation rental • 3-day minimum stay • $89-169

Big Ruby's Guesthouse 409 Appelrouth Ln (at Duval & Whitehead) **305/296-2323, 800/477-7829** • mostly gay men • full brkfst • swimming • nudity • evening wine • sundeck • wheelchair access • IGLTA • gay-owned/ run • $100-320

Blue Parrot Inn 916 Elizabeth St (at Olivia) **305/296-0033, 800/231-2473** • gay-friendly • historic Bahamian home • swimming • nudity • sundeck • gay-owned/ run • $70-170

Key West

Where the Girls Are: You can't miss 'em during Women In Paradise in September, but other times they're just off Duval St., somewhere between Eaton and South Streets. Or on the beach. Or in the water.

Lesbigay Pride: June. 305/293-9348.

Annual Events: September - Women Fest 305/296-4238 or 800/535-7797, web: www.women-fest.com.
October - Fantasy Fest 800/535-779 or 305/296-5596. Week-long Halloween celebration with parties, masquerade balls & parades.
December - International Gay Arts Fest 800/535-7797. Cultural festival of film, theatre, art, concerts, seminars, parties & a parade.

City Info: Key West Chamber of Commerce 305/294-2587.

Attractions: Audubon House and Gardens 305/294-2116.
Dolphin Research Center.
Glass-bottom boats.
Mallory Market.
Red Barn Theatre 305/296-9911.
Southernmost Point U.S.A.
Hemingway House 305/294-1575.

Best View: Old Town Trolley Tour (1/2 hour).

Weather: The average temperature year-round is 78°, and the sun shines nearly every day. Any time is the right time for a visit.

Transit: Yellow Cab 305/294-2227. Key West Transit Authority 305/292-8161.

Key West

This tiny Caribbean island at the very tip of Florida, closer to Havana than to Miami, has had more crashing busts and facelifting booms than most Hollywood celebrities have had cosmetic surgeries. During its earliest boom days, it was home to pirates and those who salvaged the ships they and the reefs would wreck. Later came robber barons who made a killing in the cigar-rolling and sponge-harvesting businesses. With another boom came Harry Truman and his Little White House and Ernest Hemingway and his cats. And since the '80s, gays and lesbians have helped create the tropical boom town visited today by tourists from around the world.

The famous Old Town area is dotted with Victorian homes and mansions. Many of them are now fully renovated as accommodations, such as the women-only **Rainbow House.**

As soon as you arrive, you realize Key West is a way of life, not just an exotic resort. Locals have perfected a laissez-faire attitude and you'll quickly fall into the relaxed rhythm. You'll be thoroughly entertained spending your days lounging poolside with warm tropical breezes in your hair and a cool drink in your hand.

Or get out of that lounge chair and sail the emerald waters around Key West on the **Mangrove Mistress.** The ocean is home to the hemisphere's largest living coral reef, accessible by snorkeling and scuba vessels. For an inexpensive and fun way to get around the island, rent a bicycle or moped from one of the many bike rental shops.

Don't miss **Womenfest** in September, the annual women's week in Key West—the ideal time and place to experience women entertainers, sailing, boating, snorkeling, a street fair, dances, and more. **Fantasy Fest** in October is seven days of Halloween in a tropical heaven: costumes, contests, parades, and parties galore. For information on other fun events, pick up a **Southern Exposure** paper.

Brass Key Guesthouse 412 Frances St (at Eaton) **305/296-4719, 800/932-9119** • popular • mostly gay men • luxury guesthouse • full brkfst • swimming • nudity • hot tub • sundeck • IGLTA • wheelchair access • gay-owned/ run • $185-265

Chelsea House 707 Truman Ave (at Elizabeth) **305/296-2211, 800/845-8859** • gay-friendly • swimming • nudity • wheelchair access • gay-owned/ run • $79-305

The Courtyard of Key West 910 Simonton St (at Olivia) **305/296-1148** • gay-friendly • $59-299

Cuban Club Suites 1102-A Duval St (at Virginia) **305/296-0465, 800/432-4849** • gay-friendly • award-winning historic hotel • $200-300

Cypress House 601 Caroline (at Simonton) **305/294-6969, 800/525-2488** • gay-friendly • swimming • sundeck • guesthouse • $89-275

Deja Vu Resort 611 Truman Ave (at Simonton) **305/292-1424, 800/724-5351** • gay-friendly • hot tub • swimming • $59-195

Duval House 815 Duval St (at Petronia) **305/292-9491, 800/223-8825** • gay-friendly • swimming • sundeck • gay-owned/ run • $85-275

Eaton Lodge 511 Eaton St (at Duval) **305/292-2170, 800/294-2170** • gay-friendly • hot tub • swimming • $95-189

Heron House 512 Simonton St (at Fleming) **305/294-9227, 800/294-1644** • gay-friendly • swimming • hot tub • evening wine • wheelchair access • $99-269

Knowles House B&B 1004 Eaton St (at Grinnell) **305/296-8132, 800/352-4414** • lesbians/ gay men • restored 1880s conch house • swimming • nudity • gay-owned/ run • $69-165

La Casa de Luces 422 Amelia St (at Whitehead) **305/296-3993, 800/432-4849** • gay-friendly • early 1900s conch house • wheelchair access • $70-175

La Te Da 1125 Duval St (at Virginia) **305/296-6706** • popular • gay-friendly • tropical setting • swimming • nudity • restaurant & bar • Sun T-dance • wheelchair access • IGLTA • $75-155

Lavadia William St **305/294-3800, 888/294-3800** • gay-friendly • weekly rental - apts, cottages & houses • swimming • nudity • gay-owned/ run • $200-500

Lightbourne Inn 907 Truman Ave (at Packer) **305/296-5152, 800/352-6011** • gay-friendly • $98-218

Marquesa Hotel 600 Fleming St (at Simonton) **305/292-1919, 800/869-4631** • gay-friendly • swimming • also restaurant ($17-26) • some veggie • full bar • wheelchair access • $135-325

Merlinn Inn 811 Simonton St (at Petronia) **305/296-3336, 800/642-4753** • gay-friendly • full brkfst • swimming • wheelchair access • $79-189

The Mermaid and the Alligator 729 Truman Ave (at Elizabeth) **305/294-1894, 800/773-1894** • gay/ straight • full brkfst • swimming • smokefree • gay-owned/ run • $98-198

Nassau House 1016 Fleming St (at Grinnell) **305/296-8513, 800/296-8513** • gay-friendly • swimming • smokefree • sundeck • hot tub • wheelchair access • gay-owned/ run • $75-175

▲ **New Orleans House** 724 Duval St, 2nd flr (at Angela) **305/293-9800, 888/293-9893** • lesbians/ gay men • non-smoking available • hot tub • wheelchair access • IGLTA • gay-owned/ run • $75-250

Pegasus International 501 Southard (at Duval) **305/294-9323, 800/397-8148** • gay-friendly • swimming • also restaurant • $99-375

Pier House Resort & Caribbean Spa 1 Duval St (at Front) **305/296-4600, 800/327-8340** • gay-friendly • private beach • swimming • restaurants • bars • spa • fitness center • $195 & up

Pilot House Guest House 414 Simonton St (at Eaton) **305/293-6600, 800/648-3780** • gay-friendly • 19th century Victorian in Old Town • hot tub • swimming • nudity • non-smoking available • $100-300

▲ **The Rainbow House** 525 United St (at Duval) **305/292-1450, 800/749-6696** • popular • women only • hot tub • swimming • sundeck • nudity • smokefree • wheelchair access • IGLTA • lesbian-owned/ run • $69-189 • (see inside front cover)

Red Rooster Inn 709 Truman Ave (at Elizabeth) **305/296-6558, 800/845-0825** • gay-friendly • 19th century 3-story inn • swimming • nudity • smokefree • $59-189

Sea Isle Resort 915 Windsor Ln (at Olivia) **305/294-5188, 800/995-4786** • mostly gay men • hot tub • swimming • nudity • private courtyard • gym • sundeck • IGLTA • gay-owned/ run • $75-250

Seascape Guest House 420 Olivia St (at Whitehead) **305/296-7776, 800/765-6438** • gay-friendly • restored 1889 inn located in the heart of Old Town • swimming • sundeck • gay-owned/ run • $69-119

Sheraton Suites—Key West 2001 S Roosevelt Blvd **305/292-9800, 800/452-3224** • gay-friendly • swimming • hot tub • non-smoking available • IGLTA • $215-375

Simonton Court Historic Inn & Cottages 320 Simonton St (at Caroline) **305/294-6386, 800/944-2687** • popular • gay-friendly • 24-unit compound built in 1880s • hot tub • 4 pools • IGLTA • $125-300

Tropical Inn 812 Duval St (at Petronia) **305/294-9977** • gay-friendly • guesthouse • apts • $75-140

Watson House 525 Simonton St (btwn Fleming & Southard) **305/294-6712, 800/621-9405** • gay/ straight • swimming

White Street Inn 905-907 White St (at Truman) **305/295-9599, 800/207-9767** • gay-friendly • swimming • $75-220

William Anthony House 613 Caroline St (at Simonton) **305/294-2887, 800/613-2276** • gay-friendly • social hour • smokefree • wheelchair access • gay-owned/ run • $89-225

The William House 1317 Duval St (at United) **305/294-8233, 800/848-1317** • gay-friendly • sundeck • spa • gay-owned/ run • $86-180

Bars

801 801 Duval St (at Petronia) **305/294-4737** • 11am-4am • mostly gay men • neighborhood bar • live shows • also 'Red Light Bar' • mostly gay men • leather

Bourbon Street Pub 724 Duval St (at Angela) **305/296-1992** • noon-4am • lesbians/ gay men • live shows • wheelchair access

Diva's 711 Duval St (at Angela) **305/292-8500** • noon-4am • lesbians/ gay men • dancing/DJ • live shows • also 'Shag' next door from 4pm • more straight

Donnie's 900 Simonton St (at Olivia) **305/294-2655** • noon-4am • lesbians/ gay men • neighborhood bar

Epoch 623 Duval St (at Southard) **305/296-8522** • gay-friendly • dancing/DJ

La Te Da 1125 Duval St (at Virginia) **305/296-6706** • 5pm-9pm Sun T-dance • popular • mostly gay men • dancing/DJ

Discover A True Women's Paradise

The Rainbow House®

Key West's Only Exclusively Women's Guest House

Our Lovely Accommodations Include:

- *Bedroom with Queen or King Bed*
- *Private Bath* • *Color TV*
- *Air Conditioning & Bahama Fan*
- *Deluxe Continental Breakfast in our Air Conditioned Pavilion*

Other Amenities for your Vacationing Pleasure Include: *2 Swimming Pools • 2 Hot Tubs*

- *Massage Available* • *Extensive Decks for Sunbathing*
- *Shaded Tropical Pavilion for Lazy Day Lounging*
- *Restaurants & Nightlife within walking distance*
- *1/2 block to shopping district*
- *1 block to Atlantic Ocean & Southernmost Point in Continental United States*

Call for a free color brochure.

1-800-74-WOMYN • 1-800-749-6696
(305) 292-1450
www.rainbowhousekeywest.com
525 United Street, Key West, FL 33040 USA

Cafes

Croissants de France 816 Duval St (at Petronia) **305/294-2624** • 7:30am-6pm • lesbians/ gay men • French pastries • some veggie • beer/ wine • patio • $5-7

Restaurants

Antonia's 615 Duval St (at Southard) **305/294-6565** • 6pm-11pm • popular • northern Italian • full bar • some veggie • $16-22

BO's Fish Wagon corner of Duval & Fleming Sts **305/294-9272** • lunch, dinner in-season only, clsd Sun • 'seafood & eat it' • $4-12

Cafe des Artistes 1007 Simonton St (at Truman) **305/294-7100** • 6pm-11pm • tropical French • full bar • $22-30

Camille's 703 Duval St (at Angela) **305/296-4811** • 8am-3pm, 6pm-10pm, no dinner Sun-Mon • bistro • hearty brkfst

Dim Sum 613 Duval St (at Southard) **305/294-6230** • 5pm-11pm • Pan-Asian • plenty veggie • beer/ wine • sake cocktails • $13-17

Dynasty 918 Duval St (at Truman) **305/294-2943** • lunch & dinner • Chinese • beer/ wine • $7-16

Kelly's Caribbean Bar Grill & Brewery 301 Whitehead St (at Caroline) **305/293-8484** • lunch & dinner • owned by actress Kelly McGillis • $7-22

La Trattoria Venezia 524 Duval St (at Fleming) **305/296-1075** • 6pm-11pm • lesbians/ gay men • Italian • full bar • $10-22

Lobos 611 1/2 Duval St **305/296-5303** • 11am-6pm, clsd Mon • plenty veggie • $4-7

Louie's Backyard 700 Waddell Ave (at Vernon) **305/294-1061** • lunch & dinner, bar 11:30am-2am • popular • fine cont'l dining • $22-30

Mangia Mangia 900 Southard St **305/294-2469** • dinner only • fresh pasta • beer/ wine • patio • $9-16

Mangoes 700 Duval St (at Angela) **305/292-4606** • 11am-11pm • 'Floribbean' cuisine • plenty veggie • full bar • patio • wheelchair access • $6-23

The Quay 12 Duval St (at Front) **305/294-4446** • lunch & dinner • gourmet • some veggie • $6-30

Rooftop Cafe 310 Front St (at Duval) **305/294-2042** • best Key Lime pie • some veggie • $15 & up

Seven Fish 632 Olivia St (at Elizabeth) **305/296-2777** • 6pm-10pm, clsd Tue • $12-15

South Beach Seafood & Raw Bar 1405 Duval St (at South) **305/294-2830** • 7am-10pm • full bar • $15+ for dinner

Square One 1075 Duval St (at Truman) **305/296-4300** • 6pm-10:30pm • full bar • wheelchair access • $15-21

Yo Sake 722 Duval St (at Angela) **305/294-2288** • 6pm-11pm • Japanese entrees • sushi bar • beer/ wine • $10-18

Entertainment & Recreation

Bahia Honda State Park & Beach 35 miles N of Key West • Viking Beach is best

Brigadoon 201 William St, Dock E **305/923-7245** • all-gay sails • sunset & snorkel cruises • $35-60

Fort Zachary Taylor Beach • more gay to the right

▲ **Mangrove Mistress 305/745-8886** • nature exploring & snorkeling • woman-owned/ run

Moped Hospital 601 Truman **305/296-3344** • forget the car—mopeds are a must for touring the island

▲ **Venus Charters 305/292-9403, 305/744-8241** • snorkeling • light tackle fishing • dolphin watching • personalized excursions • woman-owned/ run

Water Sport People 511 Greene St **305/296-4546** • scuba-diving instruction & group charters

Bookstores

Blue Heron Books 1018 Truman Ave (at Grinnell) **305/296-3508** • 10am-7pm • general • lesbigay section

Flaming Maggie's 830 Fleming St (at Margaret) **305/294-3931** • 10am-6pm • lesbigay bookstore • also coffeehouse

Key West Island Books 513 Fleming St (at Duval) **305/294-2904** • 10am-9pm • new & used rare books • lesbigay section

Retail Shops

Fast Buck Freddie's 500 Duval St (at Fleming) **305/294-2007** • 10am-6pm, till 10pm Sat • clothing • gifts

In Touch 715 Duval St (at Angela) **305/292-7293** • 9:30am-11pm • gay gifts

Key West Aloe 524 Front St (at Duval) **305/294-5592, 800/445-2563 (MAIL ORDER)** • 8:30am-8pm • mail order available

Lido 532 Duval St (at Fleming) **305/294-5300** • 10am-10pm, 11am-7pm Sun • clothing • gifts • gay-owned/ run

Publications

Southern Exposure 305/294-6303

Spiritual Groups

MCC Key West 1215 Petronia St **305/294-8912** • 9:30am & 11am Sun • wheelchair access

St Paul's Episcopal Church 401 Duval **305/296-5142** • 7:30am, 9am & 11am Sun, 5:30pm Tue, 9am Wed

Gyms & Health Clubs

Club Body Tech 1075 Duval St (at Virginia) **305/292-9683** • lesbians/ gay men • full gym • steam room • massage therapy available

Pro Fitness 1111 12th St (at Flagler) **305/294-1865**

Erotica

Leather Master 418-A Appelrouth Ln (btwn Duval & Whitehead) **305/292-5051** • custom leather & more • also 'Annex' next door

Lake Worth

Bars

Inn Exile 6 S 'J' St **561/582-4144** • 3pm-2am, till midnight Sun • mostly gay men • karaoke • videos

K & E's 29 S Dixie Hwy **561/533-6020** • 4pm-2am, clsd Tue • lesbians/ gay men • food served

NuBar 502 Lucerne Ave **561/540-8881** • 4pm-2am, till midnight Sun, clsd Mon • lesbians/ gay men • more women Th • dancing/DJ • T-dance Sun • also restaurant • some veggie • wheelchair access

Lakeland

Info Lines & Services

PGLA (Polk Gay/ Lesbian Alliance) 941/299-8126

Accommodations

Sunset Motel & RV Resort 2301 New Tampa Hwy **941/683-6464** • gay-friendly • motels, apts & private home on 3 acres • swimming • wheelchair access • $30-90

Bars

Dockside 3770 Hwy 92 E **941/665-2590** • 4pm-2am • lesbians/ gay men • dancing/DJ • food served • live shows • patio • wheelchair access • gay-owned/ run • patio

Roy's Green Parrot 1030 E Main St **941/683-6021** • 4pm-2am, till midnight Sun • mostly gay men • dancing/DJ • live shows • beer/ wine

Largo

Bars

Sports Page Pub 13344 66th St N **727/538-2430** • 4pm-2am, from 1pm Sun • mostly women • food served • wheelchair access

Madeira Beach

see St Petersburg

Madison

Accommodations

The Mystic Lake Manor 850/973-8435 • lesbians/ gay men • full brkfst • hot tub • swimming • nudity

Melbourne

Info Lines & Services

Brevard Together 407/729-0669 x2082 • also a publication

Accommodations

Crane Creek Inn 907 E Melbourne Ave **407/768-6416** • gay/ straight • waterfront • wheelchair access • $90-120

Bars

Cold Keg 4060 W New Haven Ave **407/724-1510** • 2pm-2am • popular • lesbians/ gay men • dancing/DJ • live shows • wheelchair access

Miami

see also Miami Beach/ South Beach

Info Lines & Services

Cosmopolitan Community Center 6445 NE 7th Ave (at 64th St) **305/759-5210** • 10am-2pm, clsd Tue, Th & wknds

Lambda Dade AA 410 NE 22nd St **305/573-9608** • 8:30pm daily • call for other mtg times • wheelchair access

Switchboard of Miami 305/358-4357 • 24hrs • gay-friendly info & referrals for Dade County

Bars

Splash 5922 S Dixie Hwy (at US Hwy 1) **305/662-8779** • 4pm-2am, clsd Sun-Mon • mostly gay men • dancing/DJ • popular 'Bliss' women's night Fri

Sugar's 17060 W Dixie, North Miami Beach **305/940-9887** • 3pm-6am • mostly gay men • more women Fri • neighborhood bar • dancing/DJ • videos • wheelchair access

Nightclubs

Sabados Calientes! LeJeune & NW 19th (at 'Copacabana,' in the Howard Johnson's) **305/774-6969** • Sat only • gay/ straight • dancing/DJ • salsa & merengue & more • mostly Latino/a • live shows

Restaurants

Something Special 7762 NW 14th Ct (private home), Miami Beach/South Beach **305/696-8826** • noon-9pm, 2pm-7pm Sun • women only • vegetarian • also rental 1-bdrm apt on Miami beach • also tent space

Bookstores

Lambda Passages Bookstore 7545 Biscayne Blvd **305/754-6900** • 11am-9pm, noon-6pm Sun • lesbigay/ feminist bookstore

Spiritual Groups

Christ MCC 7701 SW 76th Ave **305/284-1040** • 9:30am, 2:30pm & 7pm Sun • wheelchair access

Grace MCC 10390 NE 2nd Ave (at 103rd St, Advent Lutheran Church), Miami Shores **305/758-6822** • 11:30am Sun

Miami Beach/South Beach

Accommodations

Abbey Hotel 300 21st St (at Collins) **305/531-0031, 888/612-2239** • gay/ straight • studios w/ kitchens • $95-265

The Astor 956 Washington Ave (at 10th St) **305/531-8081, 800/270-4981** • popular • gay-friendly • food served • swimming • wheelchair access

The Bayliss 504 14th St **888/305-4683** • lesbians/ gay men • art deco hotel

The Beachcomber 1340 Collins Ave (at 13th St) **305/531-3755, 888/305-4683** • gay-friendly • intimate hotel • bar & bistro • $60-135

The Blue Moon Hotel 944 Collins Ave **305/673-2262, 800/724-1623** • gay-friendly • swimming • 145+

Brigham Gardens 1411 Collins Ave (at 14th) **305/531-1331** • gay/ straight • kitchens • pets ok • women-owned/ run • $60-130

The Cardozo 1300 Ocean Dr **305/535-6500, 800/782-6500** • gay-friendly • food served (Chin Chin from LA) • Gloria Estefan's plush hotel • $100-400

Cavalier 1320 Ocean Dr **305/604-5000, 800/688-7678** • gay/ straight • oceanfront • wheelchair access

The Century 140 Ocean Dr **305/674-8855, 888/982-3688** • gay-friendly • $95-350

Chesterfield Hotel 855 Collins Ave **305/531-5831, 800/244-6023** • gay/ straight

Collins Plaza 318 20th St **305/532-0849** • gay-friendly • no frills • $39-55

The Colony Hotel 736 Ocean Dr (at 7th St) **305/673-0088, 800/226-5669** • gay-friendly • needs renovating • wheelchair access • $150-220

Colours Destinations International 255 W 24th St **305/532-9341, 800/277-4825** • lesbians/ gay men • hotel reservation service for several art deco hotels & apts • swimming • IGLTA • gay-owned/ run

Deco Walk Hotel 928 Ocean Dr **305/531-5511, 888/505-5027** • gay-straight • $95-150

Delano Hotel 1685 Collins Ave **305/534-6300, 800/555-5001** • gay-friendly • food served • great bar scene (see & be seen) • swimming

Fairfax Hotel 1776 Collins Ave **305/538-3837** • gay-friendly

Florida Hotel Network **305/538-3616, 800/538-3616** • gay-friendly • hotel reservations • vacation rentals • gay-owned/ run

Florida Sunbreak **305/532-1516, 800/786-2732** • reservation service

Fountainbleu Hilton Resort & Spa 4441 Collins Ave **305/538-2000, 800/445-8667** • gay-friendly • swimming • wheelchair access

The Governor Hotel 435 21st St **305/532-2100, 800/542-0444** • gay-friendly • swimming • $55-125

the hotel 801 Collins Ave **305/531-2222, 877/843-4683** • gay-friendly • interior design by Todd Oldham • swimming • gym • $155-375

Hotel Impala 1228 Collins Ave **305/673-2021, 800/646-7252** • gay-friendly • luxury hotel near beach • wheelchair access • IGLTA • $169-379

Hotel Leon 841 Collins Ave (at 8th St) **305/673-3767, 305/673-5866** • gay-friendly • stylish decor • $100-165

Hotel Shelley 844 Collins Ave **305/531-3341, 800/414-0612** • gay/ straight • 1930s art deco hotel • IGLTA

The Indian Creek Hotel 2727 Indian Creek Dr **305/531-2727, 800/491-2772** • gay-friendly • food served • swimming • simple & away from the action • IGLTA • gay-owned/ run

▲ **Jefferson House B&B** 1018 Jefferson **305/534-5247** • lesbians/ gay men • tropical garden • IGLTA • $99-170

Kenmore Hotel 1050 Washington Ave **305/674-1930** • gay/ straight • 4 small art deco hotels • swimming • IGLTA • $59-99

The Kent 1131 Collins Ave (at 11th St) **305/531-6771, 800/688-7678** • gay/ straight • good value on the beach • wheelchair access • $95-195

The Leslie 1244 Ocean Ave **305/531-8800, 800/688-7678** • gay/ straight • art deco gem featured in 'The Birdcage' • outdoor cafe • $120-350

Lily Guesthouse 835 Collins Ave **305/535-9900, 888/742-6600** • lesbians/ gay men • studios • suites • sundeck • IGLTA • $100-200

Lord Balfour 350 Ocean Dr **305/673-0401, 800/501-0401** • gay-friendly • tropical style • $65-155

Marlin Hotel 1200 Collins Ave **305/673-8770, 800/688-7678** • gay/ straight • fabulous studios • full kitchens • stereo & WebTV • wheelchair access • $250-400

The Nassau Suite Hotel 1414 Collins Ave **305/531-3755, 888/305-4683** • gay-friendly

The National 1677 Collins Ave **305/532-2311, 800/327-8370** • gay/ straight • food served • swimming • newly renovated • cigar bar • $215-775

Ocean Front Hotel 1230-38 Ocean Dr **305/672-2579, 800/783-1725** • popular • gay-friendly • great location • wheelchair access • $125-575

The Park Central 640 Ocean Dr **305/538-1611, 800/727-5236** • gay-friendly • food served • swimming • IGLTA

Park Washington 1020 Washington **305/532-1930, 888/424-1930** • gay/ straight • swimming • $49-129

The Pelican 826 Ocean Dr (at 8th St) **305/673-3373, 800/773-5422** • popular • gay/ straight • designer theme rms • $125-300

Penguin Hotel & Bar 1418 Ocean Dr **305/534-9334, 800/235-3296** • lesbians/ gay men • full restaurant • no frills rooms • IGLTA • $68-153

The Raleigh Hotel 1775 Collins Ave **305/534-6300, 800/848-1775** • gay/ straight • swimming • outdoor gym • IGLTA • $159-300

Miami/Miami Beach

As a key center of business and politics in the Americas, Miami has an incredibly multicultural look and feel. You'll discover a diversity of people, from a growing population of transplanted seniors to large communities of Cubans, Latin Americans, and African Americans.

Miami is also a tourist's winter wonderland of sun, sand, and sea. Make the most of it with trips to Seaquarium, Key Biscayne, or the nearby Everglades. For a relaxing evening with the girls, try the Women's Film Series on the fourth Friday at the New Alliance Theater (600 Lincoln Road #219 at Penn Avenue).

Or make reservations to dine at **Something Special,** a women-only restaurant in a private home. Get the latest on local nightlife from **Scoop** or **Wire**, available at **Lambda Passages,** the lesbigay bookstore.

But if you're really hungry for loads of lesbigay culture, head directly for South Beach (SoBe). This section of Miami Beach has been given an incredible makeover by gays and lesbians, and has fast become one of *the* hottest spots on the East Coast. Much of the SoBe scene is gay boys, drag queens, and straight couples in little more than sunscreen and a thong, but svelte, hot-blooded, women-loving-women can be found. During the day, start your search and deepen your tan at the 12th Street gay beach. Or, go window-shopping along Lincoln Road.

If you manage to look beyond the endless parade of body beautifuls, you'll discover South Beach's historic Art Deco architecture. To make the most of the Art Deco District, take the walking tour that leaves from the Miami Welcome Center at 1224 Ocean Drive (305/672-2014) for under $10.

Try the **Palace Grill** for a queer mid-afternoon munch and great people-watching. **News Cafe** on Ocean Drive (open 24 hrs) is always an option for late night snacks.

While there are no full-time women's bars in Miami or Miami Beach, there are several women's nights. **Laundry Bar** on Thursdays is all about the girls. On Friday you have two choices: "Bliss" at **Splash,** or **Sugar.** And on Saturday, dance into the wee hours with the gorgeous boys at **Salvation.**

There are also plenty of local lesbian promoters, so be sure to check out **She** magazine for roaming women's parties. Also check out **New Concept Video**, right off Lincoln Road, for upcoming party flyers.

–compiled with help from Marivi Iglesias

Miami

Where the Girls Are: In Miami proper, Coral Gables and the University district, as well as Biscayne Blvd. along the coast, are the lesbian hangouts of choice. You'll see women everywhere in South Beach, but especially along Ocean Dr., Washington, Collins and Lincoln Roads.

Entertainment: Bridge Theater Play Readings at the Community Center, Wednesdays.

Lesbigay Pride: October. 305/358-8245, email: pridemiami@aol.com.

Annual Events: March - Winter Party 305/460-3115. AIDS benefit dance on the beach. November - White Party Vizcaya 305/250-9133. AIDS benefit.

City Info: Greater Miami Convention and Visitors Bureau, 701 Brickell Ave. 305/539-3000 or 800/283-2707.

Attractions: Bass Museum of Art 305/673-7533.
Bayside Market Place 305/577-3344.
Art Deco Welcome Center 305/672-2014.
Miami Museum of Science & Space Transit Planetarium 305/854-4247.
Orchid Jungle.
Parrot Jungle and Gardens 305/666-7834.
Vizcaya Estate & Gardens 305/250-9130.
Sanford L. Ziff Jewish Museum of Florida 305/672-5044.

Best View: If you've got money to burn, a helicopter flight over Miami Beach is a great way to see the city. Otherwise, hit the beach.

Weather: Warm all year. Temperatures stay in the 90°s during the summer and drop into the mid-60°s in the winter. Be prepared for sunshine!

Transit: Yellow Cab 305/444-4444.
Metro Taxi 305/888-8888.
Super Shuttle 305/871-2000.
Metro Bus 305/638-6700.

The Regal Hotel 436 Ocean Dr (btwn 4th & 5th Sts) **305/532-7093, 888/531-8122** • gay-friendly • $95-195

Richmond Hotel 1757 Collins Ave **305/538-2331, 800/327-3163** • gay-friendly • swimming • food served • private beach access • robes & brkfst included • IGLTA • $170-400

The Shelborne Beach Resort 1801 Collins Ave **305/531-1271, 800/327-8757** • gay-friendly • swimming • IGLTA • $145-250

▲ **South Beach Villas** 1201 West Ave (at 12th St) **305/673-9600, 888/429-7623** • lesbians/ gay men • swimming • IGLTA • gay-owned/ run • $89-170

South Seas 1751 Collins Ave **305/538-1411, 800/345-2678** • gay-friendly • clean & basic • beach access • brkfst included • swimming • $75-165

The Tides 1220 Ocean Dr **305/604-5000, 800/688-7678** • gay/ straight • food served • swimming • showcase Island Outpost hotel • $150-275

Villa Paradiso Guesthouse 1415 Collins Ave **305/532-0616** • gay/ straight • studios w/ full kitchens • $69-145

The Winterhaven 1400 Ocean Dr **305/531-5571, 800/395-2322** • gay/ straight • no frills • also restaurant • IGLTA • $50-125

Nightclubs

Bar Room 320 Lincoln Rd • 10pm-5am, clsd Mon-Tue • gay/ straight • more gay Wed & Fri • dancing/DJ • dress code enforced nightly • cover charge

Bash 655 Washington Ave **305/538-2274** • 10pm-5am, clsd Mon-Tue • gay-friendly • dancing/DJ • patio

Groove Jet 323 23rd St **305/532-2002** • gay-friendly • dancing/DJ • live shows • call for events

Laundry Bar 721 Lincoln Ln **305/531-7700** • 7am-5am • more women Th • cafe • also laundromat • internet access

Liquid 1439 Washington Ave **305/532-9154** • 11pm-5am, clsd Tue-Wed • gay-friendly • more more gay at 'Comp' Fri & 'Liquid Sundays' Sun • dancing/DJ

Pump 841 Washington Ave (btwn 8th & 9th) **305/538-7867** • 4am-close Fri-Sun • mostly gay men • dancing • world-famous DJs • circuit crowd • wheelchair access

Salvation 1771 West Ave **305/673-6508** • Sat only • lesbians/ gay men • dancing/DJ • alternative • cover charge

Score 727 Lincoln Rd **305/535-1111** • lounge opens 1pm, dance club from 10pm-5am • popular • mostly gay men

Twist 1057 Washington Ave **305/538-9478** • 1pm-5am • popular • mostly gay men • neighborhood bar • dancing/DJ • wheelchair access

Cafes

News Cafe 800 Ocean Dr **305/538-6397** • 24hrs • popular • healthy sandwiches • some veggie • $4-6

Restaurants

11th Street Diner 11th & Washington **305/534-6373** • till midnight, 24hrs on wknds • also full bar

A Fish Called Avalon 700 Ocean Dr **305/532-1727** • 6pm-11pm • popular • some veggie • patio • full bar • wheelchair access • $12-22

Balans 1022 Lincoln Rd **305/534-9191** • 8am-2am

Bang 1516 Washington **305/531-2361** • popular • int'l • full bar • $17-28

El Rancho Grande 1626 Pennsylvania Ave **305/673-0480** • Mexican

The Front Porch 1420 Ocean Dr **305/531-8300** • 8am-midnight • healthy homecooking • some veggie • full bar • $6-10

Jams Tavern & Grill 1331 Washington **305/532-6700** • 11am-5am • full bar

Jeffrey's 1629 Michigan Ave (at Lincoln Rd) **305/673-0690** • 6pm-11pm, from 5pm Sun, clsd Mon • bistro

Joe's Stone Crab 227 Biscayne St **305/673-0365** • seasonal hours

Larios on the Beach 820 Ocean Dr **305/532-9577** • 11am-midnight, till 2am Fri-Sat • Cuban

The Living Room 671 Washington Ave **305/532-2340** • 8:30pm-2am • some veggie • full bar • wheelchair access • $7-12

Nemos 100 Collins Ave (at 1st St) **305/532-4550** • Pacifc Rim & South American cuisine • chic decor • $22

Norma's on the Beach 646 Lincoln Ave **305/532-2809** • opens 4pm, clsd Mon • popular • Caribbean • full bar • $11-19

Pacific Time 915 Lincoln Rd **305/534-5979** • lunch & dinner wkdys • Pan-Pacific • some veggie • beer/ wine • $10-30

Palace Bar & Grill 1200 Ocean Dr **305/531-9077** • 8am-2am • full bar • $10-15

Spiga 1228 Collins Ave (at 12th St) **305/534-0079** • tasty homemade pastas • $13

Sushi Rock Cafe 1351 Collins Ave **305/532-2133** • full bar

Wolfie's Jewish Deli 2038 Collins Ave (at 21st St) **305/538-6626** • 24hrs • $6-8

Yuca 501 Lincoln Rd (at Drexel Ave) **305/532-9822** • New Cuban cuisine • great afternoon tapas & cocktails • live shows Fri-Sat

Entertainment & Recreation

Cycles on the Beach 713 5th St **305/673-2055**

Lincoln Rd Lincoln Rd (btwn West & Collins Aves) • pedestrian mall that embodies the rebirth of South Beach—fabulous restaurants, stores, galleries, museums, theatres, people at every step

Scooters on the Beach 1131 5th St **305/531-7777**

Bookstores

The 9th Chakra 811 Lincoln Rd (at Meridian) **305/538-0671** • 2pm-8pm Sun-Mon, noon-9pm Tue-Th, noon-midnight Fri-Sat • metaphysical books • supplies • gifts

Retail Shops

Catalog X Retail & Clothing Outlet 1510 Alton Rd **305/534-1029** • 11am-midnight, till 8pm Sun

Gaymart 1200 Ocean Dr #2 **305/535-1545** • 10am-10pm

Whittal & Schön 1319 Washington **305/538-2606** • 11am-9pm, till midnight Fri-Sat • funky clothes & clubwear

Publications

She 954/561-9707

Wire 305/538-3111 • newspaper • also produces 'Live Wire' on cable channel 3 at 11pm

Gyms & Health Clubs

Crunch 1259 Washington Ave **305/674-8222** • gay-friendly • $18 day pass

David Barton Gym 1685 Collins Ave (in the 'Delano Hotel') **305/674-5757** • gay-friendly • $17 day pass

Erotica

Pleasure Emporium 1019 5th St **305/673-3311** • large section for women only

Naples

Info Lines & Services

Lesbian/ Gay AA **941/262-6535** • several mtgs

Bars

The Galley 509 3rd St S **941/262-2808** • 4pm-2am, 2pm-midnight Sun • lesbians/ gay men • more women Fri • neighborhood bar • karaoke • live shows

Cafes

Cafe Flamingo 536 9th St N **941/262-8181** • 7:30am-2:30pm • some veggie • women-owned/ run • $3-7

Bookstores

Book Nook 447 5th Ave S (at Lakewood) **941/262-4740** • 8am-7pm • general • wheelchair access

Ocala

Bars

Club Diversity 3750 S Pine Ave (US 441) **352/732-9992** • 2pm-2am • lesbians/ gay men • dancing/DJ • live shows • 18+ • wheelchair access

The Connection 3331 S Pine Ave/ US 441 **352/620-2511** • 2pm-2am • lesbians/ gay men • neighborhood bar • wheelchair access

Bookstores

Barnes & Noble 3500 SW College Rd (at Hwy 200) **352/854-3999** • 10am-10pm, from noon Sun • lesbigay section

Erotica

Secrets of Ocala 815 N Magnolia Ave **352/622-3858**

Orlando

Info Lines & Services

Free To Be AA 1815 E Robinson St (at Unitarian church) **407/898-3621** • 8pm daily

Gay/Lesbian/Bisexual Community Center 934 N Mills (at Virginia) **407/425-4527** • 11am-9pm, till 6pm Fri, noon-5pm Sat, clsd Sun, also 24hr hotline • also lesbigay library

Gay/ Lesbian Community Services of Central Florida **407/843-4297** • 24hr touchtone helpline • extensive referrals

LCN (Loving Committed Network) **407/332-2311** • lesbian community social/ support group • monthly events • 'LCN Express' newsletter

▲ **www.gaydays.com & www.gayorlandotravel.com** • your one-stop-shops for making your trip to Orlando magical

Accommodations

Leora's B&B **407/649-0009** • women only • $45-65

Parliament House Motor Inn 410 N Orange Blossom Tr **407/425-7571** • popular • mostly gay men • swimming • 5 bars on premises • full restaurant • wheelchair access • $44

Things Worth Remembering **407/291-2127, 800/484-3585 (CODE:6908)** • gay/ straight • owners are former Disney employees w/many behind-the-scenes stories • smokefree

The Veranda B&B 115 N Summerlin Ave **407/849-0321, 800/420-6822** • gay-friendly • hot tub • smokefree • wheelchair access • $99-189

Bars

The Cactus Club 1300 N Mills Ave **407/894-3041** • 3pm-2am • mostly gay men • professional • patio

Copper Rocket 106 Lake Ave (at 17-92), Maitland **407/645-0069** • 11:30am-2am, from 4pm wknds • gay-friendly • also restaurant • micro brews • wheelchair access

Faces 4910 Edgewater Dr **407/291-7571** • 4pm-2am • mostly women • dancing/DJ • live shows • wheelchair access

Full Moon Saloon 500 N Orange Blossom Tr **407/648-8725** • noon-2am, popular Sun afternoon • mostly gay men • leather • country/ western • patio

Hank's 5026 Edgewater Dr **407/291-2399** • noon-2am • mostly gay men • neighborhood bar • beer/ wine • patio • wheelchair access

Little Orphan Andy's 5700 N Orange Blossom Tr (in Rosemont Plaza) **407/299-7717** • 3pm-2am • lesbians/ gay men • neighborhood bar • wheelchair access

Sadie's Tavern 415 S Orlando Ave, Winter Park **407/628-4562** • 4pm-2am till midnight Sun • mostly women • neighborhood bar • wheelchair access

Stable 410 N Orange Blossom Tr (at 'Parliament House') **407/425-7571** • 8pm-2am • mostly gay men • country/ western

Will's Pub 1820-50 N Mills Ave **407/898-5070** • 4pm-2am • gay-friendly • many lesbians • neighborhood bar • food served • beer/ wine • wheelchair access • also 'Loch Haven Motor Inn' 407/896-3611

gayorlandotravel.com
Year-Round Travel
Accommodations
Attraction Tickets
Great Discounts
Secure Online Ordering
www.gayorlandotravel.com
gaydays.com
Parties
Theme Parks
Accommodations
Events
Great Prices
JUNE 1-4 2000
Secure Online Ordering
www.gaydays.com

Nightclubs

The Club 578 N Orange Ave **407/872-0066** • popular • lesbians/ gay men • dancing/DJ • 18+ • live shows • videos • call for events

Club Quest 745 Bennett Rd **407/228-8226** • 10pm-3am, clsd Sun-Wed • gay/ straight • dancing/DJ • live shows

House of Blues Downtown Disney West Side (at Disney World) **407/934-2583** • tourist spot except 6pm-10pm Th for 'Our House' gay night • dancing/DJ

Southern Nights 375 S Bumby Ave **407/898-0424** • 4pm-2am • popular • lesbians/ gay men • more women Sat • dancing/DJ • multi-racial clientele • live shows • wheelchair access

Cafes

Shaffer Coffeehouse 535 New England Ave, Winter Park **407/740-7782** • 8am-10pm, (clsd 5pm-7:30pm), 9am-4pm Sun • wheelchair access

White Wolf Cafe & Antique Shop 1829 N Orange Ave (at Princeton) **407/895-5590** • 10am-11pm, till midnight wknds, till 6pm Mon, clsd Sun • salads • sandwiches • beer/ wine • wheelchair access

Restaurants

Brian's 1409 N Orange Ave (at Virginia) **407/896-9912** • 6am-4pm, popular Sun

Captain Mary's 1881 Fairbanks Ave **407/599-9269** • lunch Mon-Fri, dinner Mon-Sat, clsd Sun • gay-owned/ run

Dug Out Diner at 'Parliament House' **407/425-7571x711** • 24hrs • lesbians/ gay men

Harvey's Bistro 390 N Orange Ave (in Nations Bank Tower) **407/246-6560** • popular cocktail hour

Hemingway's at the Hyatt 1 Grand Cypress Blvd, Lake Buena Vista **407/239-1234** • lunch & dinner, clsd Sun-Mon • popular • cont'l • $20-25

La Sontanella 900 E Washington **407/425-0033** • 11am-10:30pm • seafood/ Italian • some veggie • beer/ wine • patio • wheelchair access • $9-17

Le Provence 50 E Pine St **407/843-1320** • lunch & dinner, clsd Sun • French bistro • full bar • live jazz wknds

Nicole St Pierre 1300 S Orlando Ave, Maitland **407/647-7575** • lunch & dinner, clsd Sun • full bar • wheelchair access • $17-28

Orlando

Where the Girls Are: Women who live here hang out at Will's Pub or Faces bar. Tourists are—where else?—at the tourist attractions, including Disney World.

Entertainment: Orlando Gay Chorus 407/841-7464.

Lesbigay Pride: June.

Annual Events: June (1st Sat) - Gay Day at Disney World. 407/857-5444.

City Info: 407/363-5871. 8723 International Dr., 8am-8pm.

Attractions: Walt Disney World 407/824-4321.
Universal Studios 407/363-8000.
Wet & Wild Waterpark 407/351-3200.
Sea World 407/351-3600.

Weather: Mild winters, hot summers.

Transit: Yellow Cab 407/699-9999.
Gray Line 407/422-0744.
Lynx 407/841-8240.

Orlando

For most vacationers, Orlando means one thing: Disney World. Disney has been in the news of late as a supporter of gay civil rights. If you're a fan of the Mouse, show your appreciation during the first weekend of June at Disney's (unofficial) Gay Days. 'Family' traditionally wear red T-shirts, while protesters wear white. Queer Christians go for red-and-white stripes!

But save some time for the enormous Epcot Center and MGM Studios, too. You'll need at least three days to traverse the 27,000 acres of this entertainment mecca. And if you still crave infotainment, visit Universal Studios, Wet 'n' Wild, Sea World, the Tupperware Museum (yes, Tupperware), Busch Gardens, or Cypress Gardens—a natural wonderland of lagoons, moss-draped trees, and exotic plants from around the world.

Call the **GLCS** to find out when the next Gay Day in the Busch (Gardens, that is) will be. If you like fairs, be sure to stop by the Central Florida Fair in February for Gay/Lesbian day at the fair. After a long day of theme park-ing, settle in at one of the local lesbian-friendly B&Bs, like women-only **Leora's B&B.**

Faces is the neighborhood dyke bar, while **Southern Nights** and **The Club** (aka Firestone) are the places to dance. For education, stop by the local lesbigay store, **Out & About Books,** or the **Gay/Lesbian Community Center,** and pick up a copy of the **Watermark.**

And for fun, watch a lesbian/gay-themed movie at The Club on Monday nights. The lesbian social group **LCN** sponsors plenty of other events, including picnics at Wekiva Falls in the spring and around Halloween, and a dance in mid-January.

Taqueria Queztzalcoatl 350 W Fairbanks Ave, Winter Park **407/629-4123** • 11am-11pm, from noon Sun • some veggie • beer/wine

Entertainment & Recreation

The Enzian Theater 1300 S Orlando Ave (at Magnolia), Maitland **407/629-0054** • art house cinema cafe

Family Values WPRK 91.5 FM • 7pm Wed • lesbigay radio from Rollins College

Universal Studios Florida 1000 Universal Studios Pl **407/363-8000, 800/232-7827**

Walt Disney World Resort 407/824-4321 • don't even pretend you came to Orlando for any other reason

Bookstores

Out & About Books 930 N Mills Ave (at E Marks St) **407/896-0204** • 10am-8pm, till 9pm Fri-Sat, noon-7pm Sun • lesbigay

Retail Shops

Harmony Designs 496 N Orange Blossom Tr **407/481-9850** • 1:30pm-11pm • pride store • wheelchair access

Rainbow City 934 N Mills Ave **407/898-6096** • 10am-9pm, noon-6pm Sun • lesbigay giftshop • wheelchair access

Twisted Palms 942 N Mills Ave **407/894-1996** • 3:30pm-10pm, till midnight Fri-Sat, clsd Mon • new & gently worn clothing for men • also 'Twisted Palms Annex' 498 N Orange Blossom Tr • 407/999-0111 • clsd Mon

Publications

Watermark Tampa **407/481-2243** • bi-weekly lesbigay newspaper

Spiritual Groups

Joy MCC 2351 S Ferncreek Ave **407/894-1081** • 9:15am, 11am & 7:15pm Sun • wheelchair access

Erotica

Absolute Leather 942 N Mills Ave **407/896-8808, 800/447-4820** • noon-9pm, till midnight Th-Sat • wheelchair access

Fairvilla Video 1740 N Orange Blossom Tr **407/425-5352**

Palm Beach

Accommodations

Heart of Palm Beach 160 Royal Palm Wy **561/655-5600** • gay-friendly • charming European-style hotel • swimming • kids ok • also restaurant • full bar • $69-199

Restaurants

Ta-Boo 221 Worth Ave **561/835-3500** • 11:30am-10:30pm • cont'l • live shows • wheelchair access • $12-25

Panama City

Bars

La Royale Lounge & Liquor Store 100 Harrison **850/784-9311 (payphone)** • 3pm-3am • lesbians/ gay men • neighborhood bar • courtyard • wheelchair access

Nightclubs

Confetti's Bar & Grill 5101 W Hwy 98 **850/747-8455** • 6pm-3am, clsd Mon-Tue • gay-friendly • dancing/DJ • live shows

Fiesta Room 110 Harrison Ave **850/784-9285 (payphone)** • 8pm-3am, till 4am wknds • popular • lesbians/ gay men • dancing/DJ • live shows • wheelchair access

Pensacola

Info Lines & Services

AA Gay/ Lesbian 415 N Alcaniz **850/433-8528** • 7:30pm Mon & Fri

Accommodations

Mill House Inn 9603 Lillian Hwy **850/455-3400, 888/999-4575** • mostly men • B&B on Perdido Bay • hot springs spa • smokefree • gay-owned/ run • $65-89

Noble Manor B&B 110 W Strong St **850/434-9544** • gay-friendly • hot tub • gay-owned/ run

Bars

Red Carpet 937 Warrington Rd **850/453-9918** • 3pm-3am • mostly women • dancing/DJ • live shows • patio • wheelchair access

The Riviera 120 E Main St **850/432-1234** • noon-3am • lesbians/ gay men • more women Wed • live shows • patio • wheelchair access

Round-up 706 E Gregory (nr 9th Ave) **850/433-8482** • 2pm-3am • popular • mostly gay men • neighborhood bar • patio • wheelchair access

Nightclubs

Emerald City 406 E Wright St **850/433-9491** • 3pm-3am • mostly gay men • dancing/DJ • live shows • patio • wheelchair access

Bookstores

Silver Chord Bookstore 10901 Lillian Hwy **850/453-6652** • 10am-6pm, clsd Mon • metaphysical • lesbigay section • wheelchair access

Retail Shops

Gulf Coast Pride 675 W Garden **850/433-1443** • 11am-8pm, clsd Sun • gifts • toys • magazines • wheelchair access

Spiritual Groups

Holy Cross MCC 415 N Alcaniz **850/433-8528** • 11am Sun & 7pm Wed

Unitarian Universalist Fellowship 9888 Pensacola Blvd **850/475-9077**

Port Richey

Bars

BT's 7737 Grand Blvd **727/841-7900** • 6pm-2am • lesbians/ gay men • dancing/DJ • live shows • wheelchair access

Spiritual Groups

Spirit of Life MCC 4133 Thys Rd, New Port Richey **727/849-6962** • 10am Sun & 7:30pm Wed • wheelchair access

Port St Lucie

Nightclubs

Club Babylon 8283 S Federal Hwy (Fiesta Sq) **561/340-7777** • 3pm-2am, 1pm-midnight Sun • gay/ straight • dancing/DJ • drag shows • ladies' night Tue

Sarasota

Info Lines & Services

ALSO 941/252-2576 (pager) • lesbigay youth • confidential weekly mtgs

Friends Group (Gay AA) 2080 Ringling Blvd #302 **941/951-6810** • 8pm Mon, Wed & Fri

Gay Info Line 941/923-4636 • 24hrs • recorded info

Accommodations

The Cypress 621 Gulfstream Ave S **941/955-4683** • gay-friendly • B&B inn • overlooking Sarasota Bay • full gourmet brkfst

Normandy Inn 400 N Tamiami Tr **941/366-8979, 800/282-8050** • gay-friendly

Siesta Holidays 1017 Seaside Dr & 1011 Crescent St, Siesta Key **941/488-6809, 800/720-6885** • gay/ straight • smokefree • 2 locations • apts near Crescent Beach • gay-owned • $425-1095/wk

Bars

HG Rooster's 1256 Old Stickney Pt Rd **941/346-3000** • 3pm-2am • mostly gay men • neighborhood bar • live shows

Rowdy's 1330 Martin Luther King Jr Wy **941/953-5945** • noon-2am • popular • mostly gay men • dancing/DJ • live shows • patio • also a pride store from 5pm wknds • wheelchair access

Twisted Sisters 2941 N Tamiami Tr **941/355-7210** • 8pm-2am, from 3pm Sun, clsd Mon-Th • mostly women • neighborhood bar • live shows

Nightclubs

Club X 1927 Ringling Blvd **941/951-0335** • 9pm-2:30am • gay-friendly • more gay Th & Sat • dancing/DJ • live shows

Publications

MainStream 941/330-0888

Spiritual Groups

Church of the Trinity MCC 7225 N Lockwood Ridge Rd **941/355-0847** • 10am Sun • wheelchair access

Suncoast Cathedral MCC 3276 Venice Ave **941/484-7068** • 11am Sun

Seagrove Beach

Accommodations

▲ **For Your Pleasure Rental Properties 800/854-9266, 850/231-0254** • 2 cozy cottages

South Beach

see Miami Beach/ South Beach

St Augustine

Accommodations

The Azalea House 220 Madison St, Palatka **904/325-4547** • gay-friendly • fully restored Queen Anne Victorian on St Johns River

Pagoda 2854 Coastal Hwy **904/824-2970** • women only • guesthouse • near beach • swimming • kitchen privileges • wheelchair access • women-owned/ run • $20-35

St Petersburg

see also Tampa

Info Lines & Services

Gay Information Line (The Line) 727/586-4297 • volunteers 7pm-11pm • touchtone 24hrs

WEB (Women's Energy Bank) PO Box 15548 **727/823-5353** • many services & activities for lesbians

Accommodations

The Barge House St Pete Beach **727/360-0729 (Nancy Markoe Gallery)** • women only • historic beach cottage • full kitchen • parking • patio • women-owned/ run • $91

Bay Gables B&B and Garden 340 Rowland Ct **727/822-8855, 800/822-8803** • gay-friendly • 3-story Key West style inn • full brkfst • smokefree • kids ok

Boca Ciega 3526 Boca Ciega Dr N **727/381-2755** • women only • B&B in private home • swimming • lesbian-owned/ run • $40-50

Pass-A-Grille Beach Motel 709 Gulfway Blvd **727/367-4726** • gay-friendly • swimming

Sea Oats by the Gulf 12625 Sunshine Ln., Treasure Island **727/367-7568** • gay-friendly • motel & apts • on the Gulf of Mexico • $295-595/ week

Suncoast Resort 3000 34th St S/ Hwy 19 S (at 32nd Ave S) **727/867-1111** • lesbians/ gay men • swimming • 5 bars • 2 restaurants • outdoor recreation • also pride store • wheelchair access

Bars

The Back Room Bar @ Surf & Sand Bar 14601 Gulf Blvd, Madeira Beach **727/391-2680** • noon-2am • mostly gay men • neighborhood bar • beach access • wheelchair access

DT's 2612 Central Ave (at 34th) **727/327-8204** • 2pm-2am • mostly gay men • neighborhood bar • wheelchair access

The Hideaway 8302 4th St N (at 83rd) **727/570-9025** • 2pm-2am • mostly women • neighborhood bar • live shows • wheelchair access

The New Connection 3100 3rd Ave N (at 31st St N) **727/321-2112** • 1pm-2am • lesbians/ gay men • 3 bars • neighborhood bar • dancing/DJ • live shows

Sharp A's 4918 Gulfport Blvd S (at 49th), Gulfport **727/327-4897** • 4pm-2am • popular • lesbians/ gay men • dancing/DJ • wheelchair access

VIP Lounge & Mexican Food Grill 10625 Gulf Blvd **727/360-5062** • 9am-2am • food served 11am-10pm • gay-friendly • wheelchair access

West Side Lounge 4900 Central Ave (at 49th) **727/328-2636** • 1pm-2am • lesbians/ gay men • neighborhood bar • patio

Cafes

Beaux Arts 2635 Central Ave **727/328-0702** • noon-5pm • historic gallery w/ coffeehouse • sponsors events

The Purple Dolphin Coffee House 2908-1/2 Beach Blvd **727/328-9217** • 7:30am-10pm, clsd Sun-Mon • live shows

Restaurants

Anna's Ravioli & Pasta Company 5625 4th St N **727/522-6227**

The Pepper Tree Italian Garden Bistro 109 8th Ave, St Pete Beach **727/360-1367** • patio

Bookstores

Affinity Books 2435 9th St N (at 25th Ave) **727/823-3662, 800/355-3662** • 10am-6pm, till 8pm Wed-Fri, till 5pm Sat, noon-5pm Sun • lesbigay

Brigit Books 3434 4th St N #5 (at 34th Ave) **727/522-5775, 800/566-2333** • 10am-6pm, till 8pm Tue & Th, 1pm-5pm Sun • women's/ feminist

Retail Shops

The MC Film Festival Video & Music Store 3000 34th St S (in Suncoast Resort) **727/866-0904** • largest collection of nonerotic lesbigay videos

Millennium Gifts 6030 4th St N (at 60th) **727/520-1177** • 10am-6pm, till 8pm Fri, till 5pm Sat, 1pm-5pm Sun, clsd Mon • gay & new age gifts

PS 111 2nd Ave NE (at 1st St) **727/823-2937** • 10am-6pm, till 5pm Sat, clsd Sun • cards & gifts

Publications

The Gazette Tampa **813/689-7566**

MainStream 941/330-0888

Spiritual Groups

King of Peace MCC 3150 5th Ave N **727/323-5857** • 10am Sun & 6:30pm Th • wheelchair access

Tallahassee

Bars

Brothers 926 W Tharpe St **850/386-2399** • 4pm-2am, from 9pm Sat • lesbians/ gay men • dancing/DJ • live shows • videos • 18+ • wheelchair access

Restaurants

The Village Inn 2690 N Monroe St **850/385-2903** • dinner • 24hrs wknds • popular

St Petersburg

Lesbigay Pride: June. 727/586-4297.

Annual Events: October - Film Festival & Gay Men's Chorus 800/729-2787.

City Info: Chamber of Commerce 727/821-4715. 8am-5pm Mon-Fri.

Attractions: Salvador Dali Museum 727/823-3767. Great Explorations interactive kids museum 727/821-8885.

Best View: Pass-A-Grille Beach in Tampa.

Weather: Some say it's the Garden of Eden—winter temperatures occasionally dip into the 40°s but for the rest of the year temperatures stay in the 70°-80°s.

Transit: Yellow Cab 727/821-7777.

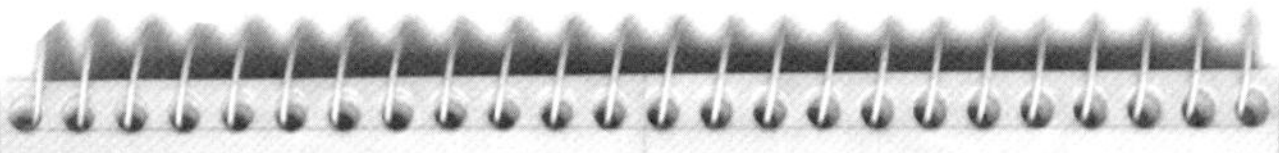

Tampa & St. Petersburg

The Sunshine State draws a fair number of lesbians to its shores, and the Tampa/St. Petersburg area seems to be particularly attractive. And no wonder—gorgeous Gulf-side beaches, sunny days, and a tolerant, laid-back attitude are certainly ideal qualities.

You'll find plenty of resources and activities here, and plenty of friendly women. When you arrive, call the **Women's Energy Bank (WEB)** or drop by the **Community Center** in Tampa to find out the latest.

Before you arrive, of course, you should reserve a place to stay. If you are interested in women-only accommodations, you have two choices: the **Barge House** or the **Boca Ciega** B&B, both of which are in St. Pete.

Despite the popular image of relaxed afternoons and sunset strolls on the beach, there is another side to Tampa and St. Pete: a great nightlife! There are not one, not two, but three (!) women's bars in the area: the **Hideaway** (in Tampa), **Kim's Club** (in Tampa), and the **Sahara** (in St. Pete). If you prefer a more mixed venue, head over to **Sharp A's** for drinks and dancing with the girls and boys there. If you're in town for the weekend, don't miss Tampa's own late-night lesbian nightclub: the **Cherokee Club.**

If partying is not your thang, don't fret! There are lots of other activities to keep you occupied while you're in town.... For some good old-fashioned/retro fun, don your pink satin jacket and knee-high socks and strut your stuff on the waxed floor of the **United Skates of America,** at Tuesday's lesbigay skate night.

Those in search of headier pursuits should pay a visit to **Affinity** lesbigay bookstore or **Brigit Books,** a women's bookstore. Look for a copy of the latest edition of **Watermark**—the local bi-weekly lesbigay paper—for other ideas.

Tampa

see also St Petersburg

Info Lines & Services

Gay Information Line (The Line) **727/586-4297** • volunteers 7pm-11pm • touchtone service 24hrs

Gay/ Lesbian Community Center of Tampa 4265 Henderson Blvd **813/287-2687** • 1pm-9pm, clsd Fri-Sat

Women's Center **813/677-8136** • women's helpline

Accommodations

Gram's Place B&B & Artist Retreat 3109 N Ola Ave **813/221-0596** • lesbians/ gay men • nudity • hot tub • BYOB • $50-100

Ruskin House B&B Ruskin **813/645-3842** • gay-friendly • 1910 Victorian home • 30 minutes south of Tampa & 30 minutes north of Sarasota • full brkfst • $75

Bars

2606 2606 N Armenia Ave (at St Conrad) **813/875-6993** • 8pm-3am • popular • mostly gay men • also leather shop from 9pm • wheelchair access

City Side 3810 Neptune St (at Dale Mabry) **813/254-6466** • noon-3am • mostly gay men • neighborhood bar • professional • patio

Jungle 3703 Henderson Blvd (at Dale Mabry) **813/877-3290** • 3pm-4am • mostly gay men • neighborhood bar • patio

Kim's Club 2408 W Kennedy Blvd (at Armenia) **813/254-4188** • 6pm-1am, till 3am Fri-Sat • mostly women • patio

Metropolis 3447 W Kennedy Blvd (at Himes) **813/871-2410** • noon-3am, 1pm-3am Sun • mostly gay men • neighborhood bar • live shows Fri • wheelchair access

Rascals 105 W Martin Luther King Blvd (at Tampa St) **813/237-8883** • 4pm-3am, from noon Sun • lesbians/ gay men • also restaurant • $4-13

The Sahara 4643 W Kennedy Blvd (at West Shore) **813/282-0183** • noon-3am • mostly women • neighborhood bar

The Tampa Brigg 9002 N Florida Ave (at Busch) **813/931-3396** • 3pm-3am • mostly gay men • neighborhood bar • gay-owned/ run

Nightclubs

Cherokee Club 1320 E 9th Ave, 2nd flr (at Republica de Cuba), Ybor City **813/247-9966** • 9pm-3am Fri-Sat only • mostly women • dancing/DJ • live shows • call for events

The Factory at the Garage 802 E Whiting (at Jefferson) **813/221-2582** • 9:30pm-3am Fri only • mostly gay men • dancing/DJ

Tampa

Entertainment: Tampa Bay Gay Men's Chorus.
Crescendo, Tampa Bay Womyn's Chorus.

Lesbigay Pride: July. 727/843-8160 or 800/825-1000.

City Info: Greater Tampa Chamber of Commerce 813/228-7777, web: www.tampachamber.com.
Tampa/Hillsborough Convention & Visitors Bureau 727/223-1111.

Attractions: Busch Gardens 813/987-5082.
Florida Aquarium 813/273-4000.
Harbour Island.
Museum of Science & Industry 800/283-6674.
Ybor Square.

Transit: The Limo 727/572-1111.
Yellow Cab 813/253-0121.
Hartline Transit (bus) 813/254-4278.

Pleasuredome 1430 E 7th Ave (at 15th) **813/247-2711** • 9pm-3am, clsd Sun-Mon & Wed • gay-friendly • more gay Tue • dancing/DJ • live shows • videos • wheelchair access

Cafes

Sacred Grounds 11118 N 30th St (btwn Fowler & Busch) **813/631-0035** • 5:30pm-1am, till 2am Fri-Sat, 6:30pm-midnight Sun • lesbians/ gay men • call for events

Restaurants

Boca 20th & 7th Ave, Ybor City **813/241-2622** • lunch & dinner • 'fusion' cuisine • 4-course Sun brunch • 2 full bars

Ho Ho Chinese 533 S Howard **813/254-9557** • 11:30am-10pm • full bar • wheelchair access • gay-owned/ run

La Teraseta 3248 W Tampa **813/879-4909** • lunch & dinner • Cuban/ Spanish • full bar

Taqueria 402 S Howard Ave **813/259-9982** • 11am-11pm, from noon Sun • Mexican • some veggie • beer/ wine

Entertainment & Recreation

United Skates of America 5121 N Armenia **813/879-1525** • lesbigay skate 9pm-11:30pm Tue

The Women's Show WMNF 88.5 FM **813/238-8001** • 10am-noon Sat

Bookstores

Tomes & Treasures 406-408 S Howard Ave (at Swann) **813/251-9368** • 11am-8pm, 1pm-6pm Sun • lesbigay • also coffeehouse

Retail Shops

The MC Film Festival Video & Music Store 3601 W Kennedy Blvd **813/870-6233** • largest collection of nonerotic lesbigay videos

Publications

Encounter 813/877-7913

The Gazette 813/689-7566

MainStream 941/330-0888

Watermark 407/481-2243 • bi-weekly lesbigay newspaper

Spiritual Groups

Dignity Tampa Bay 3010 Perry Ave (at Franciscan Center) **813/238-2868** • 7pm Sun

MCC 408 Cayuga St **813/239-1951** • 10:30am Sun & 7pm Wed

Gyms & Health Clubs

Metro Flex Fitness 2511 Swann Ave (at Armenia) **813/876-3539**

Venice

Restaurants

Maggie May's 1550 US 41 Bypass South **941/497-1077** • 10:30am-7:30pm, from 8am (winters) • homecooking • some veggie • beer/ wine • women-owned/ run • wheelchair access

West Palm Beach

Info Lines & Services

Compass Community Center 1700 N Dixie Hwy **561/833-3638** • 10am-8:30pm, 9am-5pm Fri, clsd wknds • wheelchair access

The Whimsey 561/686-1354 • resources & archives • political clearinghouse • also camping/ RV space & apt • wheelchair access

Accommodations

Hibiscus House B&B 501 30th St **561/863-5633, 800/203-4927** • lesbians/ gay men • full brkfst • swimming • smokefree • $75-160

Palmway Inn B&B 127 N Palmway, Lake Worth **561/588-2438** • gay-friendly • $65-105

Tropical Gardens B&B 419 32nd St, Old Northwood **561/848-4064, 800/736-4064** • mostly gay men • swimming • $65-125

Bars

5101 Bar 5101 S Dixie Hwy **561/585-2379** • 7am-3am, till 4am Fri-Sat, from noon Sun • mostly gay men • neighborhood bar • wheelchair access

HG Rooster's 823 Belvedere Rd **561/832-9119** • 3pm-3am, till 4am Fri-Sat • popular • mostly gay men • neighborhood bar • wheelchair access

Kozlow's 6205 Georgia Ave **561/533-5355** • noon-2am • popular • mostly gay men • neighborhood bar • country/ western • private club • patio • wheelchair access

Leather & Spurs WPB 5004 S Dixie Hwy **561/547-1020** • 7pm-3am, till 4am wknds • mostly gay men • leather • beer only • food served

Nightclubs

Krome 109 N Olive Ave (at Clematis) **561/832-5040** • 9pm-3am, clsd Mon-Wed • lesbians/ gay men • dancing/DJ • 2 stories • alternative • women's night Th

Respectable Street Cafe 518 Clematis St **561/832-9999** • 9pm-2am, clsd Mon-Tue • gay-friendly • dancing/DJ • retro & new wave nights • Goth night Fri • live shows Sat

Scandal 1900 Okeechobee Blvd (at I-95) **561/615-0332** • 10pm-5am, clsd Mon-Tue • lesbians/ gay men • dancing/DJ

Restaurants

Antonio's South 3001 S Congress Ave, Palm Springs **561/965-0707** • dinner only, clsd Sun • popular • southern Italian • beer/ wine • $9-18

Montana's Roadside Bar & Grill 122 N Dixie Hwy **561/366-1124**

Rhythm Cafe 3800 S Dixie Hwy **561/833-3406** • 7am-10pm, clsd Sun • some veggie • beer/ wine • $12-19

Bookstores

Changing Times Bookstore 911 Village Blvd #806 (at Palm Beach Lakes) **561/640-0496** • 10am-7pm, noon-5pm Sun • spiritual • lesbigay section • community bulletin board • wheelchair access

Retail Shops

Eurotique 3109 45th St #300 **561/684-2302** • 11am-7pm, noon-6pm Sat, clsd Sun • leather • books • videos

Studio 205 600 Lake Ave (at North 'L' St), Lake Worth **561/533-5272** • 10am-8pm Mon-Fri, from noon Sun • call for summer hrs • gay pride items • books & home accessories

Spiritual Groups

MCC 3500 W 45th St #2-A **561/687-3943** • 11am Sun

Georgia

Statewide

Publications

▲ **ETC Magazine** Atlanta **404/888-0063** • bar & restaurant guide for the Southeast

Southern Voice **404/876-1819** • newspaper w/ resource listings

Albany

Nightclubs

Juby's 323 W 7th Ave (at Jefferson) **912/446-9503** • from 7pm Mon-Th, from 8pm Fri-Sat, clsd Sun • lesbians/ gay men • neighborhood bar • multi-racial clientele • live shows Fri-Sat

Athens

Accommodations

The River's Edge 2311 Pulliam Mill Rd, Dewy Rose **706/213-8081** • mostly men • cabins • camping • RV • swimming • nudity • smokefree • wheelchair access • $12-14

Bars

Georgia Bar 159 W Clayton (at Lumpkin) **706/546-9884** • 3pm-2am, clsd Sun • gay-friendly • more gay wknights • neighborhood bar • wheelchair access

The Globe 199 N Lumpkin (at Clayton) **706/353-4721** • 4pm-2am, till 1am Mon-Tue, clsd Sun • gay-friendly • 55 single-malt scotches

Nightclubs

Boneshakers 433 E Hancock Ave **706/543-1555** • 8pm-3am, from 9:30pm Fri, till 4am Sat, clsd Sun • lesbians/ gay men • dancing/DJ • live shows • 18+ • wheelchair access

Forty Watt Club 285 W Washington St (at Pulaski) **706/549-7871** • 9pm-2am, clsd Sun • gay-friendly • alternative • live music • wheelchair access

Cafes

Espresso Royale Cafe 297 E Broad St (at Jackson) **706/613-7449** • 7am-midnight, from 8am wknds • best coffee in Athens • gallery • wheelchair access

Restaurants

The Bluebird 493 E Clayton **706/549-3663** • 8am-3pm • popular Sun brunch • plenty veggie • $5-10

The Grit 199 Prince Ave **706/543-6592** • 11am-10pm (clsd btwn 3pm-5pm Sat-Sun) • ethnic vegetarian • great wknd brunch • wheelchair access • $5-10

Bookstores

Barnett's Newsstand 147 College Ave (at Clayton) **706/353-0530** • 8am-10pm, till 11pm Fri-Sat

Atlanta

Info Lines & Services

Atlanta Gay/ Lesbian Center 71 12th St NE (at Crescent) **404/876-5372** • 1:30pm-5:30pm Mon-Fri • social services center • clinic

Galano Club 585 Dutch Valley Rd **404/881-9188** • lesbigay recovery club

Gay Helpline **404/892-0661** • 24hrs • live 6pm-11pm • info & counseling

Accommodations

▲ **Ansley Inn** 253 15th St **404/872-9000, 800/446-5416** • gay/ straight • 22-rm B&B • gay-owned/ run

Atlanta

Where the Girls Are: Many lesbians live in DeKalb county, in the northeast part of the city of Decatur. For fun, women head for Midtown or Buckhead if they're professionals, Virginia-Highlands if they're funky or 30ish, and Little Five Points if they're young and wild.

Entertainment: Atlanta Feminist Women's Chorus 770/438-5823. Lefont Screening Room 404/231-1924, gay film.

Lesbigay Pride: June. 404/876-3700.

Annual Events: May - Armory Sports Classic 404/872-9934 (Armory Bar). Softball & many other sports competitions.
July - International Ms. Leather contest 402/451-7987.
August - Hotlanta 404/874-3976. Weekend of river rafting, pageants & parties for boys.
December - Women's Christmas Ball/Good Friends for Good Causes 770/938-1194.

City Info: 404/521-6600 or 800/285-2682 (in GA), web: www.atlanta.com

Attractions: Atlanta Botanical Garden 404/876-5859.
CNN Center 404/827-1700.
Coca-Cola Museum.
Margaret Mitchell House 404/249-7015.
Martin Luther King Jr. Memorial Center.
Piedmont Park.
Underground Atlanta 404/523-2311.

Best View: 70th floor of the Peachtree Plaza, in the Sun Dial restaurant. Also from the top of Stone Mountain.

Weather: Summers are warm and humid (upper 80°s to low 90°s) with occasional thunderstorms. Winters are icy with occasional snow. Temperatures can drop into the low 30°s. Spring and fall are temperate – spring brings blossoming dogwoods and magnolias, while fall festoons the trees with Northeast Georgia's awesome fall foliage.

Transit: Yellow Cab 404/521-0200.
Atlanta Airport Shuttle 404/524-3400.
Marta 404/848-4711.

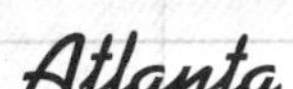

Atlanta

If you watched the 1996 Olympic Games, you saw how proud the residents of Atlanta are of their city. Today's Southerners have worked hard to move beyond stereotypes of the Old South. Of course, Atlanta's large population of lesbians and gay men is an integral part of that work.

The South's checkered past is a powerful agent for future understanding. Atlanta houses the must-see Martin Luther King, Jr. Center and the Carter Presidential Center—tributes to icons of peace and positive change—as well as the nationally known Black Arts Festival (404/730-7315).

Lesbian culture in Atlanta is spread out between **Charis** women's bookstore in L'il Five Points (cruise their readings), the **Atlanta Gay/Lesbian Center** in posh Midtown, and in between, along Piedmont and Cheshire Bridge roads. Midway between the gay Ansley Square area (Piedmont at Monroe) and downtown, stop by **Outwrite,** Atlanta's lesbian/gay bookstore. Pick up a copy of **Southern Voice** to scope out the political scene or **Etc.** to get the dish on the bar scene. For more shopping, **Brushstrokes** is Atlanta's lesbigay goodies store.

Unless you're a serious mall-crawler, skip the overly commercial (but much hyped) Underground Atlanta, and head for Lenox Mall instead, where you'll see more stylish queers. And, just a couple miles south on Highland, you'll run smack into funky shopping, dining, and live music in the alternative capital of Atlanta: **L'il Five Points** (not to be confused with 'Five Points' downtown).

The **Otherside of Atlanta,** the popular lesbigay bar that was the unfortunate site of a bombing a few years back, is going strong; you'll find more lesbians there on weekends. And don't miss nearby Decatur, home to two popular lesbian hangouts—**Eddie's Attic,** featuring live music (à la Indigo Girls), and **My Sister's Room** bar and restaurant, a recent immigrant from Atlanta.

If you're looking for women's accommodations, try the lesbian-owned **Bonaventure.** Or head an hour north to one of the women's guesthouses in lush, wooded Dahlonega.

If you're a fan of R.E.M., head northeast on Highway 306 or 78 about an hour-and-a-half to the university town of Athens, Georgia. Avoid visiting on weekends during football season, though, since traffic is hellish. Pick up a Flagpole magazine to find out what's going on, and stop by **Boneshakers,** Athens's lesbian/gay dance bar.

SENSORY TREATS
MUSIC
CDs
Including...
dance,
pop, country
...the full range
magazines
Including but
not limited to
CURVE
GIRLFRIENDS
ON OUR BACKS
BOOKS
pertinent
to our lives
Women's jewelry
Pride Items:
Flags, Windsocks, Door Mats
magnets
Stickers
T-shirts
...The best t-shirt collection in town
– Access Gay USA
Cards (for every family member)
SUNGLASSES
watches
and much more...
Brushstrokes©
ANSLEY SQUARE 1510 PIEDMONT AVENUE 404.876.6567 • SUNDAY-THURSDAY 10-10 • FRIDAY-SATURDAY 10-11
ACCEPTING CHECKS, ALL MAJOR CREDIT CARDS & TRAVELERS CHECKS

The Bonaventure 650 Bonaventure Ave (at Ponce de Leon) **404/817-7024** • gay/ straight • restored Victorian • committment ceremonies • French spoken • $85-140 • gay-owned/ run

Hello B&B 404/892-8111 • lesbians/ gay men • hot tub • $50-125

Midtown Manor 811 Piedmont Ave NE **404/872-5846, 800/724-4381 OR 800/680-9236** • gay/ straight • charming Victorian guesthouse • IGTLA • gay-owned/ run • $45-85

Quality Inn Midtown 870 Peachtree St (at 6th) **404/875-5511, 800/228-5151** • gay-friendly • IGLTA

Rendezvous for Two 770/933-8951 • provides romantic accommodations around Atlanta for $275+

Sheraton Colony Square Hotel 188 14th St (at Peachtree) **404/892-6000, 800/325-3535** • gay-friendly • gym • food served • full bar

Bars

Blake's (on the Park) 227 10th St (at Piedmont) **404/892-5786, 888/441-8984** • 3pm-2am • mostly men • neighborhood bar • food served • drag shows

Buddies 2345 Cheshire Bridge Rd (at La Vista) **404/634-5895** • 1pm-4am, till 3am Sat • mostly men • neighborhood bar

Buddies Midtown 239 Ponce de Leon (at Penn) **404/872-2655** • 4pm-4am, from 12:30pm wknds • lesbians/ gay men • wheelchair access

Burkhart's Pub 1492-F Piedmont Ave (at Monroe, in Ansley Mall) **404/872-4403** • 4pm-4am, 2pm-3am wknds • lesbians/ gay men • neighborhood bar • wheelchair access

Eddie's Attic 515-B N McDonough St (at Trinity Place), Decatur **404/377-4976** • 4pm-close • gay-friendly • rooftop deck • restaurant • live shows

Hoedowns 931 Monroe Dr (at 8th) **404/876-0001** • 3pm-3am • popular • mostly gay men • dancing/DJ • country/ western • live shows • wheelchair access

Kaya 1068 Peachtree St NE (at 12th) **404/874-4460** • noon-4am • lesbians/ gay men • dancing/DJ • mostly African-American • live shows • also restaurant • some veggie • $6-12

Le Buzz 585 Franklin Rd (at S Marietta Pkwy, in Longhorn Plaza), Marietta **770/424-1337** • 4pm-3am, from 6pm Sat • mostly gay men • neighborhood bar • karaoke Mon • drag Wed

Loretta's 708 Spring St NW (at 3rd) **404/874-8125** • 6pm-4am • gay-friendly • neighborhood bar • dancing/DJ • multi-racial clientele • live shows • wheelchair access

Midtown Saloon & Grill 736 Ponce de Leon Ave NE (at Ponce de Leon Plaza) **404/874-1655** • 2pm-4am • mostly gay men • neighborhood bar & grill

Miss Q's 560-B Amsterdam (at Monroe) **404/875-6255** • 4pm-close • gay/ straight • neighborhood bar • big screen TV

Model T 699 Ponce de Leon (at Barnett) **404/872-2209** • 9am-4am, from 12:30pm Sun • lesbians/ gay men • neighborhood bar • live shows • wheelchair access

The Moreland Tavern 1196 Moreland Ave SE (at Confederate) **404/622-4650** • noon-4am • lesbians/ gay men • neighborhood bar • food served • patio • wheelchair access

My Sister's Room 222 E Howard Ave (at E Trinity Pl), Decatur **404/370-1990** • 5pm-2am Tue-Th, till 3am Fri-Sat, 11am-midnight Sun, clsd Mon • mostly women • also restaurant

Opus I 1086 Alco St NE (at Cheshire Bridge) **404/634-6478** • 9pm-4am, from 12:30pm Sun • mostly gay men • neighborhood bar • wheelchair access

The Palace 91 Broad St **404/522-3000** • 5pm-close • mostly gay men • dancing/DJ • mostly African-American

Pin Up's 2788 E Ponce de Leon Ave, Decatur **404/373-9477** • 11am-3am, from 1pm Sat, from 6pm Sun • gay-friendly • strip club • food served • 18+ • wheelchair access

Scandals 1510-G Piedmont Ave NE (in Ansley Mall) **404/875-5957** • 11:30am-4am, till 3am Sat, from 12:30pm Sun • mostly gay men • neighborhood bar • wheelchair access

The Tower 2 735 Ralph McGill Blvd NE **404/523-1535** • 4pm-4am Fri, till 3am Sat, till 2am Sun • mostly women • neighborhood bar • DJ Fri • wheelchair access

The Upper Room 736 Ponce de Leon, NE (at Ponce de Leon Pl) **404/874-9934** • 11am-close, from 12:30pm Sun • piano bar • rooftop patio

Nightclubs

The Armory 836 Juniper St NE (at 7th) **404/881-9280** • 4pm-3am, till 4am Fri • mostly gay men • dancing/DJ • live shows • videos • young crowd • 4 bars • also restaurant • wheelchair access

Backstreet 845 Peachtree St NE (btwn 5th & 6th, enter rear) **404/873-1986** • 24hrs • popular • mostly gay men • dancing/DJ • 3 flrs • live shows • videos • young crowd • private club • cover charge

The Chamber 2115 Faulkner Dr (at Cheshire Bridge) **404/248-1612** • 10pm-4am Wed-Fri, till 3am Sat • gay-friendly • dancing/DJ • live shows • fetish crowd • 18+ Wed-Th

The Chili Pepper 208 Pharr Rd (btwn Piedmont & 'P', in Buckhead) **404/812-9266** • 9pm-4am, till 3am Sat, clsd Sun-Mon • gay-friendly • women's night Fri • dancing/DJ

Crystal Palace 502 Connell Ave SW (at Metropolitan) **404/762-7241** • midnight-8am Tue-Sat • gay-friendly • dancing/DJ • private club

ESSO 489 Courtland St (at Courtland & Pine) **404/872-3776** • 10pm-3am, clsd Sun-Wed • gay-friendly • dancing/DJ • 3 flrs • rooftop deck • wheelchair access

Masquerade 695 North Ave NE **404/577-8178, 404/577-2002** • gay-friendly • dancing/DJ • live shows • call for events • food served • 18+ • private club • cover charge

MJQ Concourse 736 Ponce de Leon Ave (at Ponce de Leon Pl) **404/870-0575** • 10pm-3am • gay-friendly • dancing/DJ • alternative • live shows • young crowd

The Otherside of Atlanta 1924 Piedmont Rd (at Cheshire Bridge Rd) **404/875-5238** • 6pm-4am, till 3am Sat • lesbians/ gay men • dancing/DJ • country/ western Mon • Latin music Th • food served • live shows • wheelchair access

Plush 3025 Peachtree Rd **404/266-1680** • gay/ straight • dancing/DJ • 2 flrs • T-dance Sun w/ more lesbians/ gay men

Cafes

Cafe Diem 640 N Highland Ave **404/607-7008** • 11:30pm-midnight, till 2am Fri-Sat, till midnight Mon-Wed • gay-friendly

Caribou Coffee 1551 Piedmont Ave (at Monroe) **404/733-5539** • 6am-11pm

Intermezzo 1845 Peachtree Rd NE **404/355-0411** • 8am-2am, 9am-3am Fri-Sat • classy cafe • plenty veggie • full bar • $7-20

Restaurants

Agnes & Muriel's 1514 Monroe Dr (at Piedmont) **404/885-1000** • 11am-11pm, till midnight Fri-Sat, from 10am Sat-Sun

The Big Red Tomato Bistro 980 Piedmont Rd **404/870-9881** • lunch, dinner & Sun brunch • Italian • full bar • patio • $8-18

Bridgetown Grill 689 Peachtree (across from Fox Theater) **404/873-5361** • noon-11pm • popular • funky Caribbean • some veggie • wheelchair access • $5-15

Camille's 1186 N Highland **404/872-7203** • dinner only • Italian • wheelchair access

Cowtippers 1600 Piedmont Ave NE (at Monroe) **404/874-3469** • 11:30am-11pm • transgender-friendly • wheelchair access

Dunk N' Dine 2277 Cheshire Bridge Rd (at Lenox) **404/636-0197** • 24hrs • popular • lesbians/ gay men • downscale diner • some veggie • $4-10

Einstein's 1077 Juniper (at 12th) **404/876-7925** • 11am-midnight Tue-Th, noon-1am Fri • some veggie • full bar • wheelchair access

Eureka! 242 Boulevard SE (at Memorial) **404/588-0006** • dinner from 5pm nightly, 9am-3pm wknd brunch • full bar • lesbian-owned/ run

The Flying Biscuit Cafe 1655 McLendon Ave (at Clifton) **404/687-8888** • 8:30am-10pm, clsd Mon • healthy brkfst all day • plenty veggie • beer/ wine • wheelchair access • lesbian-owned/ run • $6-12

Majestic Diner 1031 Ponce de Leon (at Clayton Terrace) **404/875-0276** • 24hrs • popular diner right from the '50s w/ cantankerous waitresses included • at your own risk • some veggie • $3-8

Murphy's 997 Virginia Ave **404/872-0904** • 7am-10pm, till midnight Fri-Sat • plenty veggie • best brunch in town

Pleasant Peasant 555 Peachtree St **404/874-3223** • lunch & dinner • full bar

R Thomas 1812 Peachtree Rd NE **404/872-2942** • 24hrs • popular • beer/ wine • healthy Californian/ juice bar • plenty veggie • $5-10

Swan Coach House 3130 Slaton Dr, Buckhead **404/261-0636** • lunch & dinner

Veni Vidi Vici 41 14th St **404/875-8424** • lunch & dinner • upscale Italian • some veggie • $14-25

Entertainment & Recreation

Alternative Talk WRFG 89.3FM **404/523-8989 (station #), 404/523-3471 (office #)** • 5-5:30pm Fri • radio program for Atlanta's African-American lesbigay community

Atlanta Feminist Women's Chorus 770/438-5823

Funny That Way Theatre Company 404/893-3344, 404/627-6672 • lesbigay theater company • seasonal musicals • call for schedule

Gay Graffiti WRFG 89.3 FM **404/523-8989** • 7pm Th • lesbigay radio program

Little 5 Points, Moreland & Euclid Ave S of Ponce de Leon Ave • hip & funky area w/ too many restaurants & shops to list

Martin Luther King, Jr. Center for Non-Violent Social Change Martin Luther King Jr. Historic District (at Auburn Ave) **404/524-1956** • includes King's birth home, the church where he preached in the 60s & his gravesite

Bookstores

▲ **Brushstrokes** 1510-J Piedmont Ave NE (nr Monroe) **404/876-6567** • 10am-10pm, till 11pm Fri-Sat • lesbigay variety store

Charis Books & More 1189 Euclid Ave NE (at Moreland) **404/524-0304** • 10:30am-6:30pm, till 8pm Wed-Sat, noon-6pm Sun • lesbigay

▲ **Outwrite Bookstore & Coffeehouse** 991 Piedmont Ave NE (at 10th) **404/607-0082** • 8am-11pm, till midnight Fri-Sat • lesbigay • wheelchair access

Retail Shops

The Boy Next Door 1447 Piedmont Ave NE (btwn 14th & Monroe) **404/873-2664** • 11am-7pm • clothing

The House of Warlords 2111 Faulkner Rd **404/314-9000** • 11am-7pm, til 9pm Sat, clsd Mon • custom leather

The Junkman's Daughter 464 Moreland Ave (at Euclid) **404/577-3188** • 11am-7pm • hip stuff

Metropolitan Deluxe 1034 N Highland (at Virginia) **404/892-9337** • 10am-10pm, till 11pm Fri-Sat, till 7pm Sun • flowers • gifts • wheelchair access

Piercing Experience 1654 McLendon Ave NE (at Clifton) **404/378-9100** • noon-9pm Tue-Sat, till 5pm Sun

Publications

Clikque Magazine 931 Monroe Dr, Ste 102-279, 30308 **404/486-9655** • glossy newsmagazine for lesbigay African-Americans • some nat'l club listings

Spiritual Groups

All Saints MCC 957 N Highland Ave **404/296-9822** • 11am Sun

Christ Covenant MCC 109 Hibernia Ave (off Adair), Decatur **404/373-2933** • call for schedule

Congregation Bet Haverim 701 W Howard Ave, Decatur **770/642-3467** • 8pm Fri • lesbigay synagogue

First MCC of Atlanta 1379 Tullie Rd NE (at I-85 & N Druid Hills Rd) **404/325-4143** • 11am & 7:30pm Sun, 7:30pm Wed • wheelchair access

Integrity Atlanta 2089 Ponce de Leon **770/642-3183** • call for schedule • lesbigay Episcopalians

Gyms & Health Clubs

Boot Camp 1544 Piedmont Ave NE #105 (in Ansley Mall) **404/876-8686** • gay-friendly • full gym

The Fitness Factory 500 Amsterdam (in 'Amsterdam Outlets') **404/815-7900** • popular • gay-friendly • full gym

Mid-City Fitness Center 2201 Faulkner Dr NE (at Cheshire Bridge) **404/321-6507** • lesbians/ gay men

Erotica

Heaven 2628 Piedmont (at Sidney Marcus Blvd) **404/262-9113**

Inserection 505 Peachtree St NE **404/888-0878** • call for other locations

The Poster Hut 2175 Cheshire Bridge Rd **404/633-7491** • clothing • toys

Southern Nights Videos 2205 Cheshire Br Rd (at Lenox Rd) **404/728-0701** • 24hrs

Starship 2275 Cheshire Bridge Rd **404/320-9101** • leather • novelties • 7 locations in Atlanta

Augusta

Nightclubs

B&D's Wet Spot 2623 Dean's Bridge Rd (Gordon Hwy) **706/793-5111** • 8pm-3am, clsd Sun-Mon • lesbians/ gay men • dancing/DJ • live shows • karaoke • women-owned/ run

The Coliseum 1632 Walton Wy **706/733-2603** • 8:30pm-3am, clsd Sun • lesbians/ gay men • dancing/DJ • live shows

Spiritual Groups

MCC 924 Green St **706/722-6454** • 11am & 7pm Sun

Columbus

Nightclubs

PTL Club 1207 1st Ave **706/322-8997** • 8pm-3am, clsd Mon • lesbians/ gay men • dancing/DJ • multi-racial • transgender-friendly • live shows

Spiritual Groups

Family of God MCC 1442 Double Churches Rd (at Unitarian Church) **706/321-9202** • 6:30pm Sun

Dahlonega

Accommodations

Above the Clouds 706/864-5211 • women only • mountainside B&B • full brkfst • wheelchair access • lesbian-owned/ run • $95

Black Mountain Lodge 330 Black Mountain Lodge Dr **706/864-5542, 800/923-5530** • gay/ straight • resort • nature trails • swimming • hot tub • smokefree

Swiftwaters Woman Space 706/864-3229, 888/808-5021 • women only • on scenic river • full brkfst • hot tub • seasonal • smokefree • deck • women-owned/ run • $69-95 (B&B)/ $40-50 (cabins)/ $10 (camping)

Restaurants

Renee's Cafe 135 N Chestatee (at Hawkins) **706/864-6829** • clsd Sun-Mon • gourmet • wine bar

Smith House 84 S Chestatee St **706/864-3566** • clsd Mon • family-style Southern

Dalton

Restaurants

Dalton Depot 110 Depot St **706/226-3160** • clsd Sun

Macon

Bars

Cherry St Pub 425 Cherry St **912/755-1400** • 7:30pm-2am, clsd Sun-Mon • lesbians/ gay men • dancing/DJ • live shows • 18+ Wed, Fri-Sat • young crowd • wheelchair access • cover charge

Mountain City

Accommodations

The York House York House Rd **706/746-2068** • gay-friendly • 1896 historic country inn • located btwn towns of Clayton & Dillard • full brkfst • smokefree • wheelchair access • $59-129

Savannah

Info Lines & Services

First City Network 335 Tatnall St **912/236-2489** • complete info & events line • social group • also newsletter

Accommodations

912 Barnard Victorian B&B 912 Barnard **912/234-9121** • lesbians/ gay men • shared baths • fireplaces • balcony • smokefree • $89

Paradise Inn 512 Tattnall St (at Gaston) **912/443-0200, 888/846-5093** • gay-friendly • newly renovated 1866 townhouse • afternoon cocktails • swimming • $95-135

Park Avenue Manor 107–109 W Park Ave **912/233-0352** • lesbians/ gay men • 1879 Victorian B&B • full brkfst • $89-110

Bars

Faces II 17 Lincoln St (at Bryan) **912/233-3520** • noon-3am • mostly gay men • neighborhood bar • also restaurant • patio • $8-10

Nightclubs

Club One 1 Jefferson St (at Bay) **912/232-0200** • 5pm-3am, till 2am Sun • lesbians/ gay men • dancing/DJ • food served • live shows Wed, Fri-Sun

Felicia's 416 W Liberty St **912/238-4788** • 4pm-3am • mostly gay men • dancing/DJ • live shows

Restaurants

Barbary Coast Burritos 103 W Congress St (at Whitaker St) **912/447-1099** • 11am-9pm, till midnight Th, till 2am Fri-Sat • gay-owned/ run • wheelchair access

Entertainment & Recreation

Savannah Walks, Inc 912/238-9255, 888/728-9255 • variety of walking tours of downtown Savannah, from 'Historic Homes' to an 'Evening Pub tour'

Hawaii

Please note that cities are grouped by islands:
Hawaii (Big Island)
Kauai
Maui
Molokai
Oahu (includes Honolulu)

Statewide

Accommodations

Bed & Breakfast Honolulu 3242 Kaohinani Dr (at Pelekane), Oahu **808/595-7533, 800/288-4666** • clientele & ownership vary • represents 414 locations on all islands • $55-200

Hawaii (Big Island)

Info Lines & Services

Big Island AIDS Project 808/981-2428

Lezbrunch Brunch 808/328-2441 • 2nd Sun

Publications

Island Lesbian Connection 808/575-2681 • newsletter • covers all islands

Outspoken 808/965-4004, 808/934-7178 • seasonal newsletter for east Hawaii

Captain Cook

Accommodations

Affordable Hawaii at Pomaika'i (Lucky) Farm B&B 83-5465 Mamalahoa Hwy **808/328-2112, 800/325-6427** • gay/ straight • working, century-old Kona farm • $50-60

Hale Aloha Guest Ranch 84-4780 Mamalahoa Hwy **808/328-8955, 800/897-3188** • lesbians/ gay men • full brkfst • jacuzzi in master suite • nudity • smokefree • kids ok • massage • gay-owned/ run • $70-140

Horizon Guesthouse 86-3992 Mamalahoa Hwy **808/328-2540, 888/328-8301** • gay/ straight • full brkfst • swimming • $250

Kealakekua Bay B&B 808/328-8150, 800/328-8150 • gay/ straight • Mediterranean-style villa • jacuzzi tub in master suite • smokefree • also 2-bdrm guesthouse w/ kitchen & laundry • gay-owned/ run • $95-225

Merryman's B&B 808/323-2276 • gay-friendly • full brkfst • smokefree • $75-125

Rainbow Plantation B&B 808/323-2393, 800/494-2829 • gay-friendly • on coffee & macadamia nut plantation • kayak rentals • smokefree • $65-95

Samurai House 808/328-9210 • popular • gay-friendly • traditional house brought from Japan • hot tub • wheelchair access

Hilo

Accommodations

The Butterfly Inn 808/966-7936, 800/546-2442 • women only • hot tub • kitchens • smokefree • women-owned/ run • $55-65

Oceanfront B&B 1923 Kalanianaole St (3 miles from intersection of Hwys 11 & 19) **808/934-9004** • 2 units • ocean views • $100-130

Our Place Papaikou's B&B 3 Mamalahoa Hwy, Papaikou **808/964-5250, 800/245-5250** • gay/ straight • 4-rm tropical healing retreat • 4 miles north of Hilo • organic meals available • lesbian-owned/ run • $55-110

Rainbow Dreams Cottage 13-6412 Kalapana Beach Rd **808/936-9883, 808/969-9268** • gay/ straight • oceanfront cottage • kitchen • smokefree • gay-owned/ run • $85

Entertainment & Recreation

Richardson's Beach at end of Kalanianaole Ave (Keaukaha)

Bookstores

Borders 301 Maka'ala St (at Kanoelehua Hwy) **808/933-1410** • 9am-10pm, till 11pm Fri-Sat • lesbigay section

Publications

Lesbian Brunch Bulletin 808/326-9549 • info on 2nd Sun brunch as well as calendar of events

Honaunau-Kona

Accommodations

Dragonfly Ranch 1 1/2 miles down City of Refuge Rd **808/328-2159, 800/487-2159** • gay/ straight • near ancient sanctuary w/ friendly dolphins • hot tub • $85-176

Honokaa

Accommodations

Paauhau Plantation Inn 808/775–7222, 800/789–7614 • gay-friendly • B&B • cottages built on ocean point

Kailua-Kona

Accommodations

1st Class B&B Kona Hawaii 77–6704 Kilohana (off Sunset Drive) **808/329–8778, 888/769–1110** • gay-friendly • ocean views • full gourmet brkfst • $95

▲ **The Hale Kipa 'O Pele** PO Box 5252 **808/329–8676, 800/528–2456** • lesbians/ gay men • plantation-style B&B • also bungalow w/kitchen • hot tub • IGLTA • $65-135

Pu'ukala Lodge 72-3998 E Mamalahoa Hwy (at Pu'ukala Rd) **808/325–1729, 888/325–1729** • lesbians/ gay men • on the slopes of Mt Hualalai • full brkfst • gay-owned/ run • $55-100

▲ **Royal Kona Resort** 75–5852 Ali'i Dr **808/329–3111, 800/222–5642** • gay-friendly • set atop dramatic lava outcroppings overlooking Kailua Bay • swimming • private beach • bar • live entertainment • $99-250 • see ad in front color section

Tropical Tune-ups 800/587–0405, 808/882–7355 • women only • week-long yoga retreats for women • all meals included • mostly veggie • lesbian-owned/ run • $1250-1750/week

Bars

Mask Bar & Grill 75–5660 Kopiko St (at Cathedral Plaza) **808/329–8558** • 6pm-2am • popular • lesbians/ gay men • neighborhood bar • dancing/DJ • live shows • karaoke • only lesbian/gay bar on the island

Restaurants

Edward's at Kanaloa 78–261 Manukai St (at Kamehameha III) **808/322–1434** • 8am-2pm & 5pm-9pm • Mediterranean • full bar from 8am-9pm

Huggo's 75-5828 Kahakai Rd (on Kailua Bay) **808/329–1493** • 11:30am-10pm, from 5:30pm wknds • seafood & steak • patio

Entertainment & Recreation

Eco-Adventures 75-5744 Ali'i Dr (in Kona Inn Shopping Village) **808/329-7116, 800/949-3483** • scuba diving • snorkeling

Publications

Lesbian Brunch Bulletin 808/326-9549 • info on 2nd Sun brunch as well as calendar of events

Kamuela

Accommodations

Ho'onanea PO Box 6450 **808/882-1177** • women only • hot tub • near beaches & outdoor recreation • kids ok • women-owned/ run • $40-75

Naalehu

Accommodations

Earthsong PO Box 916 **808/929-8043** • women only • retreat center w/cottages on 3 acres • Hawaiian massage • Goddess temple • substance-free • lesbian-owned/ run

Ocean View

Cafes

Cafe Ohia 525 Lotus Blossom Ln #3 (nr South Point, about 1 hr S of Kailua-Kona) **808/929-8086** • 7am-4pm Tue-Sat, till 2pm Sun, clsd Mon • lesbian-owned/ run

Pahoa

Accommodations

Huliaule'a B&B 808/965-9175 • lesbians/ gay men • shared baths • full brkfst • smokefree • gay-owned/ run • $45-80

Kalani Oceanside Eco-Resort 808/965-7828, 800/800-6886 • gay-friendly • coastal retreat • conference center & campground w/ in Hawaii's largest conservation area • full brkfst • swimming • food served • IGLTA • $20-25 camping • $65-130

Pamalu—Hawaiian Country House 808/965-0830 • gay/ straight • country retreat on 5 secluded acres • swimming • near hiking • snorkeling • warm ponds • kids ok • gay-owned/ run • $60-100

▲ **Rainbow's Inn 808/965-9011** • gay/ straight • B&B hideaway by the sea • see also 'Rainbow Adventures' • kids/ pets ok • offers activity desk to plan your Hawaii experience • lesbian-owned/ run • $65-85

Cafes

Mady's Cafe Makana 15923 Gov't Main Rd **808/965-0608** • 8am-3pm, clsd Sat • vegetarian cafe • also gift shop

Restaurants

The Godmother 15269 Gov't Main Rd **808/965-0055** • 7am-10pm • Italian • patio • full bar • lesbian-owned/ run

Entertainment & Recreation

Kehena Beach off Hwy 137 (trailhead at 19-mile marker phone booth) • lava rock trail to clothing-optional black sand beach

▲ **Rainbow Adventures** PO Box 983 **808/965-9011** • cutom-made remote land & sea excursions • lesbian-owned/ run

Bookstores

Huna Ohana Main St (in Akebono Theatre Bldg complex) **808/965-9661** • 8am-6pm, 9am-1pm Sun • metaphysical books • vegetarian cafe

Volcano Village

Accommodations

Chalet Kilauea Collection 808/967-7786, 800/937-7786 • gay-friendly • full brkfst • hot tub • smokefree • $45-395

Hale Ohia Cottages 808/967-7986, 800/455-3803 • gay/ straight • hot tub • wheelchair access • gay-owned/ run • $75-145

Kauai

Info Lines & Services

Black Bamboo Guest Services 808/328-9607, 800/527-7789 • free reservation service

Lambda Aloha 808/823-6248 • recording of events/ directory • also publishes newsletter

Lesbian Central 808/245-0505 • ask for Liz

Malama Pono 808/822-0878 • HIV service agency of Kauai

Anahola

Accommodations

Mahina Kai B&B 4933 Aliomanu Rd #699 **808/822-9451, 800/337-1134** • popular • gay/ straight • country villa rental overlooking Anahola Bay • swimming • hot tub • smokefree • women-owned/ run • $100-200

Hanalei

Nightclubs

Tahiti Nui 5-5134 Kuhio Hwy (nr Hanalei Ctr) **808/826-6277** • 9pm-2am • gay-friendly • live music most nights • also restaurant from 10am-9:30pm • Thai, Vietnamese & Chinese • luaus Wed & Sun • wheelchair access

Kapaa

Accommodations

Aloha Kauai B&B 156 Lihau St **808/822-6966, 800/262-4652** • lesbians/ gay men • full brkfst • swimming • smokefree • wheelchair access • IGLTA • gay-owned/ run • $60-95

Hale Kahawai 185 Kahawai Pl **808/822-1031** • lesbians/ gay men • hot tub • smokefree • mountain views • gay-owned/ run • $60-90

▲ **Kauai Coconut Beach Resort** **808/822-3455, 800/222-5642** • gay-friendly • newly redecorated oceanfront resort • swimming • tennis • nightly torchlighting ceremony & luau • kids ok • wheelchair access • $165-500 • see ad in front color section

Kauai Kualapa Cottage 1471 Kualapa Pl **808/822-1626** • gay-friendly • private cottage overlooking hidden valley • 10 minutes to beaches • kitchen • $75-85

Kauai Waterfall B&B 5783 Haaheo St **808/823-9533, 800/996-9533** • gay/ straight • swimming • hot tub • overlooking Wailua River State Park Waterfall • gay-owned/ run • $80 & up

Mahina's Guest House 4433 Panihi Rd **808/823-9364** • women-only beach house • hostel-style accommodations • lesbian-owned • $20-40

Mohala Ke Ola B&B Retreat 5663 Ohelo Rd (at Kuamoo Rd/ Hwy 580) **808/823-6398, 888/465-2824** • gay-friendly • swimming • jacuzzi • gay-owned/ run • $65-95

Villa Aloha 7160 Aina Pono St **808/823-9606, 800/830-3403 x39** • gay-friendly • modern 2-story house • lush tropical garden, waterfalls & water garden

Bars

Tropics 4-1330 Kuhio Hwy **808/822-0082** • noon-1:30am • gay/ straight • neighborhood bar • wheelchair access • gay-owned/ run

Restaurants

A Pacific Cafe 4831 Kuhio Hwy #200 **808/822-0013** • dinner only • gourmet • reservations req'd

Bull Shed 796 Kuhio Hwy **808/822-3791** • 5:30pm-10pm • steak & seafood • full bar

Eggbert's 4-484 Kuhio Hwy (in Coconut Plantation Marketplace) **808/822-3787** • 7am-3pm & 5pm-9pm • gay-owned/ run

Me Ma's Thai 4361 Kuhio Hwy (in shopping ctr) **808/823-0899** • lunch Mon-Fri, dinner nightly

Kilauea

Info Lines & Services

Women's Brkfst Club 4640 Hookui Rd (at Mango Mamas Fruitstand Cafe) **808/828-1020 (Mango Mama's #)** • Mango Mamas Fruitstand Cafe

Accommodations

Kai Mana 808/828-1280, 800/837-1782 • gay-friendly • Shakti Gawain's paradise home set on a cliff surrounded by ocean & mountains • cottages • hot tub • kitchens • smokefree • $75-150

Kalihiwai Jungle Home 808/828-1626 • gay/ straight • clifftop hideaway overlooking jungle & waterfalls • near beaches • snorkeling equipment & boogie boards • fireplace • nudity • smokefree • kids ok • gay-owned/ run • $100-135

▲ **Ku'oko'a at Plumeria Moon 808/828-0228, 888/8-KUOKOA** • lesbians/ gay men • swimming • smokefree • upscale 3-acre Hawaiian hideaway overlooking ocean • private path to secluded beach • jacuzzi • lesbian-owned/ run

▲ **Pali Kai 808/828-6691, 800/335-6968** • popular • lesbians/ gay men • hilltop B&B w/ocean view • cottages • hot tub • swimming • smokefree • IGLTA • lesbian-owned/ run • $70-100

Cafes

Mango Mamas Fruitstand Cafe 4640 Hookui Rd (at Kuhio Hwy) **808/828-1020** • 7:30am-6pm • natural foods, fruit smoothies & more • lesbian-owned

Lihue

Info Lines & Services

AA Alternative Lifestyles 4364 Hardy St (at Umi, in St Michael's Episcopal Church) **808/821-1911** • 7:30pm Sun

Bookstores

Borders Bookstore & Cafe 4303 Nawiliwili Rd **808/246-0862** • 8:30am-10pm, till 11pm Fri-Sat, till 8pm Sun • large lesbigay section

Puunene

Restaurants

Roy's Bar & Grill 2360 Kiahuna Plantation Dr **808/742-5000** • 5:30pm-9:30pm

Wailua

Accommodations

Royal Drive Cottages 147 Royal Dr **808/822-2321** • gay-friendly • private garden cottages w/kitchenettes • smokefree • wheelchair access • gay-owned/ run • $50-90

Cafes

Caffe Coco 4-369 Kuhio Hwy **808/822-7990** • 9am-9pm, clsd Mon • art gallery • live music wknds • patio

Maui

Info Lines & Services

Both Sides Now 808/244-4566 • recorded events info

▲ **Gay Hawaiian Excursions 808/891-8603, 800/311-4460** • extensive activities, tours & travel arrangements

Maui AIDS Foundation 808/242-4900

▲ **Maui Dreamtime Weddings 888/424-5550** • religious or non-religious commitment ceremonies in secluded Maui locations

Maui Honeymoon Getaways 808/290-9501 • romantic sunset ceremonies • lesbian-owned/ run • IGLTA

Personal Maui 808/572-1589, 800/258-8588 • guide & driver for tours of the hidden Maui

Royal Hawaiian Weddings 800/659-1866 • specializes in scenic gay weddings • IGLTA • women-owned/ run

Women's Information Line 808/573-3077 • covers entire island

Publications

Island Lesbian Connection 808/575-2681 • newsletter • covers all islands

Out In Maui 808/244-4566, 808/874-3950

Spiritual Groups

Dignity Maui 808/874-3950 • contact Ron

Haiku

Accommodations

Golden Bamboo Ranch 422 Kaupakalua Rd (at Holokai) **808/572-7824, 800/344-1238** • gay/ straight • 7-acre estate • panoramic ocean views • cottages & suites • wheelchair access • IGLTA • gay-owned/ run • $69-90

Hale Huelo B&B Door of Faith Church Rd, Huelo (at Hana Hwy) **808/572-8669** • gay/ straight • panoramic ocean views

Halfway to Hana House 100 Waipio Rd #675 **808/572-1176** • gay-friendly • private studio w/ ocean view • smokefree • women-owned/ run • $50-70

Kailua Maui Gardens 808/572-9726, 800/258-8588 • gay/ straight • also cottages • hot tub • swimming • nudity • kids ok • IGLTA • gay-owned/ run • $70-200

Nightclubs

Dance Club for Women 808/573-4035 • Sat only • call for more info

Hana

Accommodations

Hana Alii Holidays 808/248-7742, 800/548-0478 • reservations service

Hana Plantation Houses 2957 Kalakaua Ave **808/923-0772, 800/228-4262** • popular • mostly gay men • tropical cottage & house rentals • IGLTA • gay-owned/ run

Heavenly Flora 70 Maia Rd (Ulaino Rd) **808/248-8680** • gay-friendly • B&B on 5.5 acre tropical flower farm • panoramic ocean views • swimming • gay-owned/ run

Napualani O'Hana 808/248-8935, 800/628-7092 • gay/ straight • 2 full units • ocean & mtn views • non-smoking rms available • kids/ pets ok • lanai • wheelchair access • gay-owned/ run • $45-75

Huelo

Accommodations

Cliff's Edge 808/572-4530 • gay-friendly • seasonal • $100-115

Triple Lei B&B/ Huelo Point Lookout 808/573-0914 • gay-friendly • private cottages • full kitchens • swimming • hot tub

Kaanapali

Accommodations

▲ **The Royal Lahaina Resort** 2780 Kekaa Dr **808/661-3611, 800/222-5642** • gay-friendly • full service resort on 27 tropical acres of Ka'anapali • world-class tennis courts & golf courses • swimming • wheelchair access • $215-1,500 • see ad in front color section

Kahana

Accommodations

▲ **Kahana Beach Condominium Hotel** 4221 Lower Honoapiilani Rd **808/669-8611, 800/222-5642** • gay-friendly • oceanfront studios & 1-bdrm suites • swimming • kitchenettes • private lanai • wheelchair access • $120-225 • see ad in front color section

Kahului

Info Lines & Services

AA Gay & Lesbian 101 W Kam Ave (at Kahului Union Church) **808/874-3589** • 6:30pm Wed

Kihei

Info Lines & Services

AA Gay & Lesbian Kalama Park Gazebo **808/874-3589** • 7:30am Sun

Accommodations

Andrea's Maui Condos 800/289-1522 • gay/ straight • 1- & 2-bdrm oceanfront/ beachfront condos • swimming • near outdoor recreation • IGLTA • lesbian-owned/ run • $99-175

▲ **Anfora's Dreams 323/467-2991, 800/788-5046** • gay/ straight • rental condo near ocean • hot tub • swimming • gay-owned/ run • $79-135

Hale Makaleka Women's B&B 539 Kupulau Drive **808/879-2971** • women only • full brkfst • smokefree • lesbian-owned/ run • $60

Jack & Tom's Maui Condos **808/874-1048, 800/800-8608** • gay/ straight • fully equipped condos & apts • non-smoking rms available • gay-owned/ run • $45-175

Ko'a Kai Rentals **808/879-6058, 800/399-6058 x33** • gay/ straight • inexpensive rentals • swimming • gay-owned/ run • $49 day/$300 weekly

Koa Lagoon 800 S Kihei Rd **808/879-3002, 800/367-8030** • gay-friendly • oceanfront suites • 5-night minimum stay • swimming • wheelchair access • $80-130

Nightclubs

Lava Nites at Hapa's Brew Haus 41 E Lipoa St (in Lipoa Ctr) **808/879-9001** • 10:15pm-2am Sun only • lesbians/ gay men • dancing/DJ

Cafes

Stella Blues 1215 Kihei Rd **808/874-3779** • deli

Erotica

The Love Shack 1794 S Kihei Rd (across from Tony Roma's) **808/875-0303** • 9am-9pm • lingerie & gifts

Kula

Accommodations

Camp Kula—Maui B&B **808/876-0000** • popular • lesbians/ gay men • on the slopes of Mt Haleakala • HIV+ welcome • wheelchair access • IGLTA • $35-78

Lahaina

Restaurants

Lahaina Coolers 180 Dickenson St **808/661-7082** • international • patio • women-owned/ run

Entertainment & Recreation

Maui Surfing School **808/875-0625, 800/851-0543** • lessons for beginners, cowards & non-swimmers • 'surf-aris' for advanced • women-owned/ run

Retail Shops

Atomic Tattoo 193 Lahainaluna **808/667-2156** • body piercing

Skin Deep Tattoo 626 Front St (across from the Banyan Tree) **808/661-8531** • custom tattooing

Makawao

Accommodations

Hale Ho'okipa Inn B&B 32 Pakoni Pl **808/572-6698** • gay-friendly • restored Hawaiian plantation home • smokefree • women-owned • $60-130

Heavenly Gate Vacation Rental 276 Hiwalani Loop, Pukalani (at Iolani St) **808/572-0321** • cottage • smokefree • gay-owned/ run • $100

Maui Network **808/572-9555, 800/367-5221** • condo reservation service

Restaurants

Casanova's 1188 Makawao Ave **808/572-0220** • lunch & dinner • Italian • full bar till 2am • live shows & DJ Th

Paia

Accommodations

Huelo Point Flower Farm **808/572-1850** • gay/ straight • vacation rental • oceanfront estate & organic farm • swimming • kids 10+ ok • gay-owned/ run • $125-350 + 10.17% state tax

Waiehue

Accommodations

▲**Alohalani's Guesthouse** **808/249-0394, 800/511-3121** • women only • 180° ocean views • swimming • lanai • full kitchen • IGLTA member • $115-125

Molokai

Kaunakakai

Accommodations

Molokai Beachfront Escapes **808/923-0772, 800/228-4262** • gay-friendly • beachfront units on the exotic island of Molokai • IGLTA • gay-owned/ run • $89-109

Oahu

Info Lines & Services

Aloha Lambda Weddings **808/922-5176, 800/982-5176**

Life Foundation **808/521-2437** • AIDS services

Publications

Island Lesbian Connection **808/575-2681** • newsletter • covers all islands

Odyssey **808/955-5959** • all the dish on Honolulu's club scene

Pocket Guide to Hawaii **808/923-2400**

Aiea

Erotica

C 'n' N Liquor Aiea Shopping Ctr **808/487-2944**

Honolulu

Info Lines & Services

Always Yours by The Wedding Connection **808/537-9427, 800/388-6933** • lesbigay commitment ceremonies

Gay/ Lesbian AA 277 Ohua (at Waikiki Health Ctr) **808/946-1438** • 8pm daily

Gay/ Lesbian Community Center 1566 Wilder Ave (at Punahou, in YWCA) **808/951-7000** • 10am-1:30pm Mon-Tue & 5pm-9pm Mon-Fri • resource center • library

Hawaii Transgendered Outreach PO Box 4530 **808/923-4270** • social/ support mtgs every other Fri

Hawaii Visitors Bureau 2270 Kalakaua Ave #801 **808/923-1811**

Honolulu Gay & Lesbian Cultural Foundation 1877 Kalakaua Ave **808/941-0424 x18**

Leis of Hawaii **888/534-7644** • personalized Hawaiian greeting service complete w/ fresh flower leis

Accommodations

Bed & Breakfast in Manoa Valley 2651 Terrace Dr **808/988-6333** • gay-friendly • spectacular views • also apt available • $70-150

Breakers Hotel 250 Beachwalk **808/923-3181, 800/426-0494** • gay-friendly • swimming • also bar • $88-146

The Cabana at Waikiki 2551 Cartwright Rd (off Kapahulu Ave) **808/926-5555, 877/902-2121** • mostly gay men • 1-bdrm suites w/ kitchens & lanais • hot tub • IGLTA • gay-owned/ run • $99-175

Honolulu

Where the Girls Are: Where else? On the beach. Or cruising Kuhio Ave.

Lesbigay Pride: June. 808/951-7000 (GLCC).

Annual Events: April - Merrie Monarch Festival.
May - Golden Week, celebration of Japanese culture.
September - Aloha Week.

City Info: 808/923-1811, web: www.gohawaii.com.

Attractions: Bishop Museum 808/847-8205.
Foster Botanical Gardens.
Hanauma Bay.
Honolulu Academy of Arts 808/532-8700.
Polynesian Cultural Center.
Waimea Falls Park.

Best View: Helicopter tour.

Weather: Usually paradise perfect, but humid. It rarely gets hotter than the upper 80°s.

Transit: Charley's 808/955-2211.
The Bus 808/848-5555.

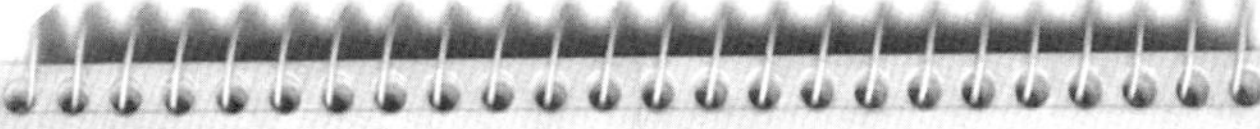

Honolulu

The city of Honolulu suffers from a bad case of mistaken identity. The highrise tourist hotels of Waikiki, six miles away, overshadow the downtown area of Honolulu, the center of the state government that teems with a vibrant culture all its own. Chinatown, a designated National Historic Landmark, offers a living history of Asian immigration to Hawaii, with street vendors, grocers, herbalists, and acupuncture clinics. Authentic Chinese, Vietnamese, and Filipino restaurants cram the area north of downtown, off of North King Street.

On the other side of downtown, on South King Street, sits 'Iolani Palace, the heart and soul of modern Hawaiian history. The graceful structure served as a prison for Queen Lili'uokalani, Hawaii's last reigning monarch, when she was placed under house arrest by armed US forces intent on her signing over the nation's sovereignty. Don't miss the Hawaii Maritime Center next door for a glance back at the history of the islands. If you're staying in Waikiki, you can catch a trolley downtown from any of the main streets, saving yourself a mountain of parking headaches.

Waikiki sits on the southwest corner of Oahu and offers a mind-boggling number of hotels, restaurants, and shops that are just waiting to consume your tourist dollars. Campy though it is, enjoy the postcard pleasure of a mai tai on the patio of the magnificently restored Sheraton Moana Surfrider while the sun sets over the Pacific. **Hula's,** a neighborhood bar with a homey feel, is the most welcoming of the local bars. If you want to shake it with the boys, you can dance the night away at **Fusion**.

Odyssey Magazine gives boys the dirt on the club scene. Occasionally, they have something for women. And **Island Lesbian Connection** lists events of interest to lesbians throughout the island chain.

The Coconut Plaza Hotel 450 Lewers St, Waikiki (at Ala Wai) **808/923-8828, 800/882-9696** • gay-friendly • swimming • kitchenettes • near beach • wheelchair access • $64-225

Hale Plumeria 3044 Hollinger St **808/732-7719** • 4 blks to Waikiki Beach • $45

Hawaiian Waikiki Beach Hotel 2570 Kalakaua Ave (at Paoakalani Ave) **808/922-2511, 800/877-7666** • gay-friendly • IGLTA

Jerry's Vacation Condo Waikiki, Hawaii (Big Island) **808/737-1281, 888/261-7092** • gay/ straight • 1/2 blk from gay beach • $500+/wk

Outrigger Hotels & Resorts 808/921-6820, 800/688-7444 • gay-friendly • IGLTA

Queen's Surf Vacation Rentals 134 Kapahulu St (at Lemon Rd) **808/732-4368, 888/336-4368** • gay -friendly • swimming • ocean views

Waikiki Joy Hotel 320 Lewers St **808/923-2300, 800/733-5569** • gay-friendly • boutique hotel • swimming • IGLTA • from $102

Waikiki Parkside Hotel 1850 Ala Moana Blvd (at Kalai/ Ena) **808/955-1567, 800/237-9666** • gay-friendly • IGLTA • $69-89

Waikiki Vacation Rentals 1580 Makaloa St #770 **808/946-9371, 800/543-5663** • furnished 1- & 2-bdrm units • smokefree • also reservation service • $55-175

Bars

Angles 2256 Kuhio Ave, 2nd flr, Waikiki (at Seaside) **808/926-9766, 808/923-1130 (INFOLINE)** • 10am-2am • lesbians/ gay men • neighborhood bar • dancing/DJ Wed-Sun • live shows • theme nights • free Internet access

Dis 'N Dat Lounge 1315 Kalakaua Ave **808/946-0000** • 4pm-2am • lesbians/ gay men • neighborhood bar • karaoke • live bands

Hula's Bar & Lei Stand 134 Kapahuluu Ave (2nd flr of Waikiki Grand Hotel) **808/923-0669** • 10am-2am • popular • lesbians/ gay men • dancing/DJ • transgender-friendly • live shows • theme nights • free Internet access

In Between 2155 Lau'ula St, Waikiki (off Lewers, across from 'Planet Hollywood') **808/926-7060** • 3pm-2am • gay/ straight • neighborhood bar • Sun brunch

Punani's 1041 Nu'uanu Ave (btwn Hotel & King) **808/526-9395** • gay/ straight • transgender-friendly • live Hawaiian music nightly • lunch Tue-Fri & dinner Wed-Sun

Nightclubs

Discotheque 478 Ena Rd (at Kalakaua Ave) **808/946-6499** • mostly gay men • dancing/DJ

Fusion Waikiki 2260 Kuhio Ave, upstairs (at Seaside) **808/924-2422** • 9pm-4am, from 8pm Fri-Sat, from 10pm Sun • popular • mostly gay men • dancing/DJ • transgender-friendly • live shows

Cafes

Caffe Giovannini 1888 Kalakaua Ave, Waikiki (across from the Wave), Honolulu **808/979-2299** • 7am-10pm, till 11pm Fri-Sat, till 8pm Sun • great coffee • sandwiches & desserts • patio

Mocha Java Cafe 1200 Ala Moana Blvd (in Ward Ctr) **808/591-9023** • 7am-9pm, till 4pm Sun • plenty veggie

Restaurants

A Pacific Cafe 1200 Ala Moana Blvd **808/593-0035** • dinner nightly • lunch weekdays • Pacific Rim & Mediterranean • reservations req'd • wheelchair access

The A1 Lounge 412 Lewers St (at the Marc Suites) **808/926-1881** • 5pm-10pm • steakhouse & oyster bar • wheelchair access

Cafe Sistina 1314 S King St **808/596-0061** • lunch Mon-Fri, dinner nightly • northern Italian • some veggie • full bar • wheelchair access • $9-16

Eggs n' Things 1911-B Kalakaua Ave **808/949-0820** • 11pm-2pm • diner • popular after-hours

Indigo 1121 Nu'uanu Ave **808/521-2900** • Eurasian • live jazz Fri-Sat 9pm-midnight

Keo's Thai 2040 Kuhio Ave **808/951-9355** • lunch & dinner • popular • reservations advised

Singha Thai 1910 Ala Moana **808/941-2898** • 4pm-11pm • live shows

Entertainment & Recreation

Taking the Plunge 808/922-2600, 808/941-5497 • various diving trips • hotel pickup

Retail Shops

Eighty Percent Straight 1917 Kalakaua Ave, Waikiki (at Ala Moana) **808/941-9996** • 9am-10pm, till 11pm Fri-Sat • lesbigay clothing • books • videos • cards

Publications

Odyssey 1750 Kalakaua Ave #3247 **808/955-5959** • all the dish on Honolulu's club scene

Pocket Guide to Hawaii 808/923-2400

Spiritual Groups

Dignity Honolulu 539 Kapahulu Ave (at St Mark's Church) **808/536–5536** • 7:30pm Sun

Ke Anuenue O Ke Aloha MCC 277 Ohua St (at Waikiki Community Ctr, in the chapel) **808/942–3060** • 7pm Sun

Our Family Christian Church 1666 Mott–Smith Dr (at Makiki, in RLDS Church) **808/926–3090** • 5:30pm Sun

Unitarian Universalists for Lesbian/ Gay Concerns (Interweave) 808/623–4726 • call for mtg times

Unity Church of Hawaii 3608 Diamond Head Cir (at Montserrat) **808/735–4436** • 7:30am, 9am & 11am Sun • wheelchair access

Erotica

Diamond Head Video 870 Kapahulu Ave (near Genki Sushi) **808/735–6066**

Kailua

Accommodations

Tropic Paradise 43 Laiki Place, Kailua **808/261–2299, 888/362–4488** • gay/ straight • serene & beautiful • swimming • kids ok • gay-owned/ run • $70

Windward Coast

Accommodations

Ali'i Bluffs Windward B&B 46–251 Ikiiki St, Kane'ohe **808/235–1124, 800/235–1151** • gay/ straight • swimming • gay-owned/ run • $55-65

Idaho

Statewide

Publications

▲ **Diversity 208/336–3870 #2** • statewide lesbigay newspaper • monthly

Boise

Info Lines & Services

AA Gay/ Lesbian 23rd & Woodlawn (at First Congregational Church) **208/344–6611** • 8pm Sun & Tue

The Community Center 919–A N 27th St (at Jordan) **208/336–3870, 208/939–1629** • 6pm-9pm Wed & 10am-2pm Sat • 24hr touchtone info line

Women's Night 208/344-4295, 208/336-8471 • events by women for women • dances • camp-outs • music • comedy • theatre

Bars

The Balcony 150 N 8th St (at Idaho) **208/336-1313** • 2pm-2am • gay/ straight • neighborhood bar • dancing/DJ • gay-owned/ run

Papa's Club 96 1108 Front St **208/333-0074** • 2pm-2am • mostly gay men • neighborhood bar • patio

Nightclubs

Emerald City Club 415 S 9th **208/342-5446** • 10am-2am • lesbians/ gay men • dancing/DJ from 10pm • live shows • women-owned/ run

Partners 2210 Main St **208/331-3551** • 2pm-2am • lesbians/ gay men • dancing/DJ • live shows • karaoke • wheelchair access

Cafes

Flying M Coffeehouse 500 W Idaho (at 5th St) **208/345-4320** • 6:30am-10pm, till 11pm Fri-Sat, 11:30am-6pm Sun • food served • some veggie & vegan • live shows Sat

Jumpin' Juice & Java 6748 Glenwood Ave (in Plantation Shopping Ctr), Garden City **208/853-6264** • 6:30am-8pm, till 9pm Fri-Sat, 8am-6pm Sun

Entertainment & Recreation

Flicks & Rick's Cafe American 646 Fulton St **208/342-4288** • 4:30pm-10pm, from noon wknds • 4 movie theaters • multi-racial • live shows • beer/ wine • patio

Triangle Connection 208/939-2338 • 24hr activities hotline

Bookstores

Crone's Cupboard 3013 Overland Rd **208/333-0831** • 11am-7pm, noon-5pm Sun • feminist/ lesbian books & art

Retail Shops

Auntie Em's Gifts & Coffee 2232 Main St (at 23rd St) **208/343-9984** • 7am-10pm, till midnight Fri-Sat, 11am-6pm Sun • lesbigay gifts • wheelchair access

The Edge 1101 W Idaho St (at 11th) **208/344-5383** • 6:30am-7pm, from 9am Sat, clsd Sun • gifts • lesbigay magazines • also cafe

Form 113 N 11th St (btwn W Idaho & Main) **208/336-5034** • 11am-7pm, till 6pm Sat, noon-5pm Sun • sassy stuff • pride gifts

Spiritual Groups

MCC 408 N Garden St **208/342-6764** • 5:45pm Sun

Coeur D'Alene

see also Spokane, Washington

Accommodations

The Clark House on Hayden Lake 4550 S Hayden Lake Rd, Hayden Lake **208/772-3470, 800/765-4593** • popular • gay-friendly • mansion on a wooded 12-acre estate • full brkfst • also fine dining • $85-225

Bars

Mik-N-Mak's 406 N 4th **208/667-4858** • noon-2am, till midnight Sun • lesbians/ gay men • neighborhood bar • DJ or live shows Fri-Sat

Ketchum

Retail Shops

Davis 320 Leadville Ave N (at 4th Ave) **208/725-0180** • 10am-6pm

Lava Hot Springs

see also Pocatello

Accommodations

Lava Hot Springs Inn 208/776-5830 • gay-friendly • full brkfst • mineral pools • wheelchair access • $59-185

Bookstores

Aura Soma Lava 97 N 2nd St East (at Portneuf River Rd) **208/776-5800, 800/757-1233** • seasonal • 11am-5pm • metaphysical & lesbigay books

Moscow

Info Lines & Services

University of Idaho Queer Students Association 208/885-2691 • seasonal • 6pm Mon at Women's Center

Women's Center (Univ of Idaho) corner of Idaho & Line Sts **208/885-6616** • library & resources • support • limited outreach • call first

Bookstores

Bookpeople 512 S Main **208/882-7957** • 9am-8pm • general

Pocatello

Nightclubs

Charleys 331 E Center **208/232-9606** • 2pm-2am, clsd Mon • lesbians/ gay men • dancing/DJ • live shows • wheelchair access

Cafes

Main St Coffee & News 234 N Main (btwn Lander & Clark) **208/234-9834** • 7am-9pm, till 6pm Sat, 9am-4pm Sun

Erotica

The Silver Fox 143 S 2nd St (at Center) **208/234-2477**

Stanley

Accommodations

Las Tejanas B&B Hwy 75, Lower Stanley **208 /376-6077, 208/774-3301** • May-Sept • gay-friendly • full brkfst • natural hot tub • btwn 2 wilderness areas in the Sawtooth Mtns • near outdoor recreation

Illinois

Statewide

Info Lines & Services

Illinois Bureau of Tourism 310 S Michigan #108, Chicago **800/822-0292**

Publications

▲ **Prairie Flame 217/753-2887** • lesbigay newspaper for central IL

Alton

Accommodations

MotherSource Travels 187 W 19th St **618/462-4051, 314/569-5795** • B&B network • St Louis & Alton locations

Nightclubs

Mabel's Budget Beauty Shop & Chainsaw Repair 602 Belle (at 6th) **618/465-8687** • 4pm-1:30am • mostly gay men • dancing/DJ • live shows • wheelchair access

Arlington Heights

see Chicago

Aurora

see also Chicago

Erotica

Denmark Book Store 1300 US Hwy 30 (2 miles S of Rte 34) **630/898-9838** • 24hrs

Bloomington

Info Lines & Services

Connections Community Center 313 N Main St (at Monroe St) **309/827-2437** • 24hr recorded info • staffed 7:30pm-10:30pm wkdys & 9am-noon Sat & special events

Bars

Bistro 316 N Main St (at Jefferson) **309/829-2278** • 4pm-1am, till 2am Fri-Sat, from 8pm Sat, from 6pm Sun • lesbians/ gay men • dancing/DJ Tue-Sat • wheelchair access

Erotica

Risque's 1506 N Main (at Division) **309/827-9279** • 24hrs

Calumet City

see also Chicago & Hammond, Indiana

Bars

Are You Crazy 48 154th Pl (at Forsythe) **708/862-4605** • 4pm-2am, till 3am Wed, Fri-Sat, clsd Sun • mostly gay men

The Patch 201 155th St (at Wentworth) **708/891-9854** • 4pm-2am, from noon Th, from 6pm Sun, clsd Mon • mostly women • neighborhood bar • dancing/DJ • live shows • women-owned/ run

Nightclubs

Pour House 103 155th Pl (at Forsythe) **708/891-3980** • 9:30pm-2am, till 3am Wed, Fri-Sat, clsd Th • mostly gay men • dancing/DJ

Carbondale

Info Lines & Services

AA Lesbian/ Gay 618/549-4633

The Saluki Rainbow Network (Southern Illinois University) **618/453-5151**

Women's Services 618/453-3655 • 8am-4:30pm

Accommodations

The Pit 618/542-9470 (summer), 618/549-6057 (Oct-April) • lesbians/ gay men • primitive camping from May 15-Oct 1 • 18+ • nudity permitted • swimming • wheelchair access

Nightclubs

Club Traz 213 E Main St **618/549-4270** • 8pm-2am, clsd Mon • lesbians/ gay men • dancing/DJ • alternative • live shows • wheelchair access

Champaign/Urbana

Info Lines & Services

OUTpost Community Center 123 W Church St, Champaign **217/239-4688** • 6pm-9pm, 1pm-4pm Sat, clsd Sun • lesbigaytrans events & groups • teen events Sun

People for LGBT Concerns of Illinois at University of Illinois, Urbana **217/333-1187** • 5:30pm Tue • student group

Transgender Outreach Project **217/367-1033**

Accommodations

The Little House on the Prairie RR 2, Patterson Rd (by Country Club Rd), Sullivan **217/728-4727** • gay-friendly • 'Home of the Stars' • Queen Anne Victorian • full brkfst • swimming • hot tub • $55-125

Nightclubs

Chester Street 63 Chester St (at Water St) **217/356-5607** • 5pm-1am • lesbians/ gay men • dancing/DJ • wheelchair access

Cafes

Espresso Royale 1117 W Oregon, Urbana **217/328-1112** • also 602 E Daniel in Champaign

Bookstores

Horizon Book Store 603 S Wright St (at Green), Champaign **217/356-9113** • 10am-6pm, till 5pm Sat, clsd Sun

Jane Addams Book Shop 208 N Neil (at University) **217/356-2555** • 10am-5pm, till 8pm Fri, 1pm-5pm Sun • full service antiquarian bookstore w/ children's room • lesbigay & women's sections

Chicago

Chicago is divided into 5 geographical areas:
Chicago—Overview
Chicago—North Side
Chicago—New Town
Chicago—Near North
Chicago—South Side

Chicago—Overview

Info Lines & Services

AA Gay/ Lesbian-Newtown Al-Anon Club 909 W Belmont St 2nd flr (btwn Clark & Sheffield) **773/529-0321** • 3pm-11pm, from 11am Fri, from 8am wknds • wheelchair access

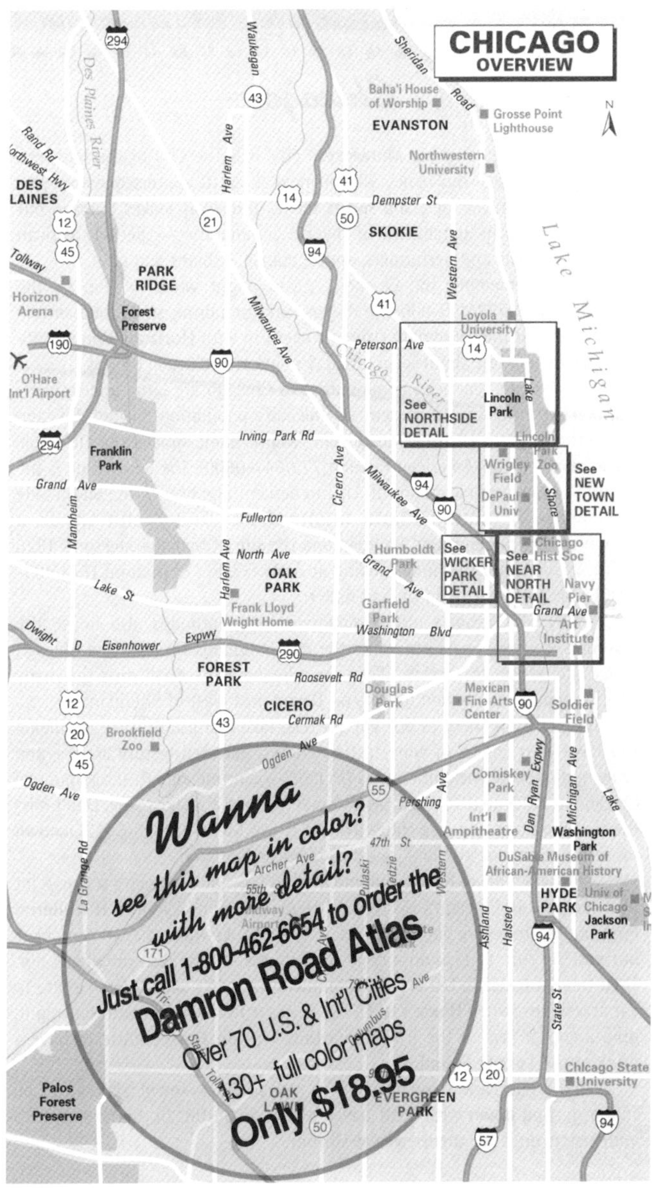
CHICAGO
OVERVIEW
Wanna
see this map in color?
with more detail?
Just call 1-800-462-6654 to order the
Damron Road Atlas
Over 70 U.S. & Int'l Cities
130+ full color maps
Only $18.95
EVANSTON
SKOKIE
PARK RIDGE
DES PLAINES
OAK PARK
FOREST PARK
CICERO
HYDE PARK
EVERGREEN PARK
OAK LAWN
Baha'i House of Worship
Grosse Point Lighthouse
Northwestern University
Loyola University
O'Hare Int'l Airport
Horizon Arena
Forest Preserve
Franklin Park
Lincoln Park
Lincoln Park Zoo
Wrigley Field
DePaul Univ
Chicago Hist Soc
Navy Pier
Art Institute
Humboldt Park
Garfield Park
Frank Lloyd Wright Home
Douglas Park
Mexican Fine Arts Center
Soldier Field
Comiskey Park
Int'l Ampitheatre
Washington Park
DuSable Museum of African-American History
Univ of Chicago
Jackson Park
Brookfield Zoo
Palos Forest Preserve
Chicago State University
See NORTHSIDE DETAIL
See NEW TOWN DETAIL
See WICKER PARK DETAIL
See NEAR NORTH DETAIL
Lake Michigan
Des Plaines River
Chicago River
Sheridan Road
Dempster St
Peterson Ave
Irving Park Rd
Fullerton
North Ave
Lake St
Grand Ave
Washington Blvd
Roosevelt Rd
Cermak Rd
Ogden Ave
Pershing
47th St
Eisenhower Expwy
Dan Ryan Expwy
Lake Shore
Michigan Ave
State St
Ashland
Halsted
Western Ave
Cicero Ave
Harlem Ave
Milwaukee Ave
Waukegan
Mannheim
La Grange Rd
Rand Rd
Northwest Hwy
Tollway
Dwight D Eisenhower Expwy

Not just another big Midwestern city, it is The City of the Midwest. Even those who've never been know about its winters, gansters, pizzas, museums, universities, and sports teams. But what makes Chicago our kind of town is its patchwork of diverse communities—especially African Americans, artists and performers, and of course, lesbians and gays.

If you remember the Chicago 7, you might want to stop by the Heartland Cafe (773/465-8005) in Rogers Park for a drink, some food, or a T-shirt from their radical variety store. Or check in with **Horizons Community Services** to find out about local lesbigay political and social groups.

The African-American communities in Chicago are large and influential, making up about 40 percent of Chicago's population. In fact, Chicago was settled by an African-French man, whose name graces the Du Sable Museum of African-American History (773/947-0600). The South Side is the cultural center for Chicagoans of African descent and houses the South Side Community Art Center (773/373-1026) and the Olivet Baptist Church, a station on the Underground Railroad and the site of Mahalia Jackson's 1928 debut. We've heard the homecooking at Army & Lou's Restaurant (773/483-3100) will make you stand up and holler.

Many of Chicago's other immigrant neighborhoods also house the museums, centers, and restaurants the city is famous for—call the Chicago Office of Tourism for details. If you love Indian food, don't miss the many delicious and cheap Indian buffets on Devon, just west of Sheridan.

What else is there to do? For starters, take a cruise on Lake Michigan. You have your choice of wine-tasting cruises, narrated history cruises, and brunch, dinner, or cocktail cruises. On land, you'll find superb shopping, real Chicago-style deep dish pizza, and a great arts and theater scene. Don't miss the thriving blues and jazz clubs, like the Green Mill (773/878-5552), known for originating 'poetry slams' and for its house big band.

And you'll never have a dull moment in Chicago's women's scene. A lot of it happens in Chicago's North Side. Here, you'll find **Women & Children First** bookstore where you can check out the books while the women check out you. Be sure to pick up a copy of **Outlines** for the dish on what's hot. Then treat yourself to the art at **Womanwild** women's gallery. Grab a bite to eat at lesbian-owned **Hoxie's BBQ**, and if you're in town on a Saturday night, grab a cup of java at the truly **Mountain Moving Coffeehouse** or have a drink at the **Lost & Found.**

And while New Town may be known as 'Boys' Town', sisters can be found getting down with their gay brothers at **Berlin**. Or, better yet, help your sisters do it for themselves at **Girlbar**.

Chicago

Where the Girls Are: In the Belmont area—on Halsted or Clark streets—with the boys, or hanging out elsewhere in New Town. Upwardly-mobile lesbians live in Lincoln Park or Wrigleyville, while their working-class sisters live in Andersonville (way north).

Lesbigay Pride: June. 773/348-8243, web: www.interpride.org.

Annual Events:
February - Hearts Party 773/404-8726.
March - Women's Film Festival 773/281-4988.
May - International Mr. Leather 800/545-6753. Weekend of events and contest on Sunday.
May - Bear Pride 312/509-5135.
June - Lambda Literary Awards 202/462-7924. The Oscars of lesbigay writing & publishing.
Chicago Blues Festival 312/744-3315.
August - Halsted Street Fair.
November - Chicago Gay/Lesbian Film Festival 773/384-5533.

City Info: Chicago Office of Tourism 312/744-2400 or 800/487-2446, web: www.chicago.il.org or www.ch.chi.il.us/tourism

Attractions: 900 North Michigan Shops.
Historic Water Tower.
Museum of Science and Industry 773/684-1414.
Sears Tower Skydeck Observatory 312/875-9696.
Second City & the Improv Comedy Clubs.
The Art Institute of Chicago 312/443-3530.

Best View: Skydeck of the 110-story Sears Tower.

Weather: 'The Windy City' earned its name. Winter temperatures have been known to be as low as -46°. Summers are humid, normally in the 80°s.

Transit: Yellow & Checker Cabs 312/ 829-4222.
Chicago Airport Shuttle Service 773/247-7678.
Chicago Transit Authority 312/836-7000.
Amtrak 312/655-2385.

Cafe Pride Lakeview Presbyterian, 716 W Addison (at Broadway) **773/784-2635** • 8pm-midnight Fri • lesbigay coffeehouse • for youth only

Chicago 35 929 Belmont (at Clark, at 'Ann Sather's' restaurant) **773/271-5909, 773/381-3853** • 3:30pm-6pm 3rd Sun • group for women over 35

The Chicago Area Gay/ Lesbian Chamber of Commerce **888/452-4262** • call for maps, member lists & more

Chicago Black Lesbians/ Gays **312/409-4917 (HOTLINE#)** • citywide group for lesbigaytrans activism & visibility • 24hr touchtone events line

Chicagoland Bisexual Network **312/458-0983** • variety of political, social & support resources

Gerber/ Hart Library & Archives 1127 W Granville Ave (at Broadway) **773/381-8030** • 6pm-9pm Wed-Th, noon-4pm Fri-Sun • lesbigay resource center

Horizons Community Services 961 W Montana (at Fullerton & Sheffield) **773/472-6469** • 9am-10pm Mon-Th, till 5pm Fri, 11am-3pm Sat

Khuli Zaban **312/409-2753** • organization for South Asian lesbians & bisexual women

Lesbian/ Gay Helpline **773/929-4357** • 6pm-10pm

SANGAT (Gay/ Lesbian South Asians) **773/506-8810**

Entertainment & Recreation

Artemis Singers **773/764-4465** • lesbian feminist chorus

Bailiwick Arts Center 1229 W Belmont **773/883-1090** • Bailiwick Repertory presents many lesbigay-themed productions w/ popular Pride Series

Chicago Neighborhood Tours **312/742-1190** • gay-friendly • the best way to make the Windy City your kind of town

The Hancock Observatory 875 N Michigan Ave (in John Hancock Center) **888/875-8439** • renovated 94th-flr observatory w/ outside 'Skywalk'

Sears Tower Skydeck 233 S Wacker Dr (enter at Jackson Blvd) **312/875-9696** • see the City from the world's tallest building

Bookstores

Barbara's Bookstore 1350 N Wells St (at Schiller, in Old Town) **312/642-5044** • 9am-10pm, 10am-9pm Sun • women's/lesbigay section • other locations: 700 E Grand Ave at Navy Pier, 312/222-0890 • Oak Park, 708/848-9140

Publications

The Alternative Phone Book **773/472-6319** • directory of local businesses

Gab **773/248-4542** • has got the dirt on Chicago's clubscene

Gay Chicago **773/327-7271** • weekly • extensive resource listings

▲ **Outlines/ Nightlines** **773/871-7610** • weekly lesbigay newspaper

Windy City Times **312/397-0020** • lesbigay newspaper

Spiritual Groups

Congregation Or Chadash 656 W Barry (at 2nd Unitarian Church) **773/248-9456** • call for Shabbat services & monthly activities

Dignity Chicago 3344 N Broadway (at Broadway United Methodist Church, in Lakeview) **773/296-0780** • mass & social hour 7pm Sun

Integrity/ Chicago **773/348-6362** • 7:30pm 1st & 3rd Fri • call for location

MCC Good Shepherd **773/262-0099** • 11am & 7pm Sun • call for location

Chicago—North Side

Accommodations

A Sister's Place **773/275-1319** • women only • guestrooms in artist's flat • women-owned/ run • $45-55

Bars

Augenblick 3907 N Damen (at Irving Park) **773/929-0994** • 7pm-2am, till 3am Sat • gay-friendly • live shows

Big Chicks 5024 N Sheridan (btwn Foster & Argyle) **773/728-5511** • 3pm-2am, from 1pm wknds • lesbians/ gay men • neighborhood bar • dancing/DJ • shows • wheelchair access

Chicago Eagle 5015 N Clark St (nr Argyle) **773/728-0050** • 8pm-4am, till 5am Sat • lesbians/ gay men • leather • wheelchair access

Clark's on Clark 5001 N Clark St (at Argyle) **773/728-2373** • 4pm-4am, till 5am Sat, 8pm-4am Sun • mostly gay men • neighborhood bar

Different Strokes 4923 N Clark St (btwn Argyle & Clark) **773/989–1958** • noon-2am, till 3am Sat • mostly gay men • neighborhood bar • shows

Lost & Found 3058 W Irving Park Rd (at Albany) **773/463–7599** • 7pm-2am, from 4pm wknds, clsd Mon • mostly women • neighborhood bar

Madrigal's 5316 N Clark St (at Balmoral) **773/334–3033** • 5pm-2am • lesbians/ gay men • live shows Th-Sun

Scot's 1829 W Montrose (at Damen) **773/528–3253** • 3pm-2am, from 11am wknds • lesbians/ gay men • neighborhood bar

Touché 6412 N Clark St (at Devon) **773/465–7400** • 5pm-4am, from 3pm wknds • mostly gay men • leather

Cafes

Mountain Moving Coffeehouse 1650 W Foster (at Ebenezer Lutheran Church) **773/477–8362** • Sat only, check gay paper for dates • women & girls only • non-alcoholic beverages • live shows • collectively run

Restaurants

Fireside 5739 N Ravenswood (at Rosehill) **773/878–5942** • 11am-3am, till 4am Sat • full bar • patio

Hoxie's BBQ 1801 W Lawrence (at Ravenswood) **773/989–4800** • 11am-1am, noon-11pm Sun • full bar • live shows • lesbian-owned/ run

Julie Mai's 5025 N Clark (at Winnemac) **773/784–6000** • 3pm-10pm • French/ Vietnamese • full bar

Lolita's Cafe 4400 N Clark St (at Montrose) **773/561–3356** • noon-11pm, till 2am Fri & 3am Sat • lesbians/ gay men • multi-racial (Latino/a) • transgender-friendly • authentic Mexican food • full bar • also club from 11pm Fri-Sat • dancing/DJ • live shows

Oo La La 3335 N Halsted (at Buckingham) **773/935–7708** • 5:30pm-11pm daily, 10am-3pm Sun brunch • patio

Tendino's 5335 N Sheridan (at Broadway) **773/275–8100** • 11am-11pm, till midnight wknds • pizzeria • full bar • wheelchair access

Tomboy 5402 N Clark (at Balmoral) **773/907–0636** • 5pm-10pm, till 11pm wknds, clsd Mon • popular • BYOB • wheelchair access • lesbian-owned

Entertainment & Recreation

Hollywood Beach at Hollywood & Sheridan Sts • popular • 'the' gay beach

Bookstores

KOPI: A Traveler's Cafe 5317 N Clark St (at Summerdale) **773/989–5674** • 8am-11pm, till midnight Fri, from 9am Sat, 10am-11pm Sun • live shows • also boutique & gallery • mostly veggie • soup, sandwiches, pastries

Women & Children First 5233 N Clark St (at Foster) **773/769–9299, 888/923–7323** • 11am-7pm, till 9pm Wed-Fri, 10am-7pm Sat, 11am-6pm Sun • women-owned/ run

Retail Shops

Specialty Video Films 5307 N Clark St (at Foster) **773/878–3434** • 10am-10pm, till 11pm Fri-Sat • foreign, cult, art house, lesbigay & erotic videos • gay-owned/ run

Chicago — New Town

Accommodations

Best Western Hawthorne Terrace 3434 N Broadway (at Hawthorne Pl) **773/244–3434, 888/675–2378** • gay-friendly • located in the heart of Chicago's gay community

City Suites Hotel 933 W Belmont (btwn Clark & Sheffield) **773/404–3400, 800/248–9108** • gay-friendly • accommodations w/ touch of European style • $99-159

Park Brompton Inn 528 W Brompton Pl (at Addison) **773/404–3499, 800/727–5108** • gay-friendly • romantic 19th century atmosphere • $109-139

Surf Hotel 555 W Surf St (at Broadway) **773/528–8400, 800/787–3108** • gay-friendly • 1920s hotel in Lincoln Park • $105-170

Villa Toscana B&B 3447 N Halsted St **773/404–2643, 800/684–5755** • lesbians/ gay men • gay-owned/ run • $79-129

Bars

Annex 3 3160 N Clark St (at Belmont) **773/327–5969** • noon-2am, till 3am Sat • lesbians/ gay men • videos • sports bar • wheelchair access

Beat Kitchen 2100 W Belmont (btwn Hoyne & Damen) **773/281–4444** • noon-2am • gay-friendly • live shows • also grill • some veggie • wheelchair access

Berlin 954 W Belmont (at Sheffield) **773/348–4975** • 5pm-4am, 8pm-5am Sat, from 9pm Mon • lesbians/ gay men • dancing/DJ • transgender-friendly • live shows • wheelchair access

Blues 2315 N Halsted **773/528–1012, 773/549–9436** • gay-friendly • classic Chicago blues spot • live shows

Buck's Saloon 3439 N Halsted St (btwn Cornelia & Newport) **773/525-1125** • 10am-2am • mostly gay men • patio

Buddies 3301 N Clark St (at Aldine) **773/477-4066** • 9am-2am, till 3am Sat • lesbians/ gay men • country/western • food

Cell Block 3702 N Halsted (at Waveland) **773/665-8064** • 4pm-2am,from 5pm Sat, from 2pm Sun • mostly gay men • leather • also 'Holding Cell' from 10pm Th-Sat • strict leather/latex/ uniform code • also 'Leather Cell' store

Charlie's Chicago 3726 N Broadway (btwn Waveland & Grace) **773/871-8887** • 3pm-4am, till 5am Sat • lesbians/ gay men

Circuit/ Rehab 3641 N Halsted St (at Addison) **773/325-2233** • 9pm-2am Tue-Th, till 4am Fri, till 5am Sat • gay-friendly • dancing/DJ • karaoke • live shows • also 'Club Rehab' from 4pm

The Closet 3325 N Broadway St (at Buckingham) **773/477-8533** • 2pm-4am, till 5am Sat, from noon wknds • lesbians/ gay men • videos

Cocktail 3359 Halsted St (at Roscoe) **773/477-1420** • 4pm-2am, from 2pm wknds, till 3am Sat • lesbians/ gay men • wheelchair access

Dandy's Piano Bar 3729 N Halsted St (at Waveland) **773/525-1200** • 3pm-2am, till 3am Sat • lesbians/ gay men • neighborhood bar • piano bar • wheelchair access

Gentry on Halsted 3320 N Halsted (at Aldine) **773/348-1053** • 4pm-2am, till 3am Sat, from 3pm Sun • lesbians/ gay men • live shows

Girlbar 2625 N Halsted St (btwn Fullerton & Diversey) **773/871-4210** • 7pm-2am, from 4pm Sun, till 3am Sat • mostly women • dancing/DJ • 'Boybar' Wed • patio

Little Jim's 3501 N Halsted St (at Cornelia) **773/871-6116** • 11am-4am, till 5am Sat • mostly gay men • neighborhood bar

Lucky Horseshoe 3169 N Halsted St (at Briar) **773/404-3169, 800/443-3169** • 5pm-2am, from noon wknds • patio • mostly gay men • neighborhood bar • live shows

The North End 3733 N Halsted St (at Grace) **773/477-7999** • 3pm-2am, till 3am Sat, from 2pm wknds • mostly gay men • neighborhood bar

Roscoe's 3354-56 N Halsted St (at W Roscoe) **773/281-3355** • 2pm-2am, till 3am Sat • lesbians/ gay men • neighborhood bar • dancing/DJ • videos • patio cafe in summer

Spin 3200 N Halsted (at Belmont) **773/327-7711** • 4pm-2am, till 3am Sat, from noon wknds • gay-friendly • dancing/DJ • live shows • videos • theme nights

Nightclubs

Clubhouse at Convent 1529 Armitage (at Elston) **773/395-8660** • 11pm-4am Mon & Wed • lesbians/ gay men • dancing/DJ • live shows • multi-racial

Fusion 3631 N Halsted (at Addison) **773/975-6622** • 10pm-4am Fri, till 5am Sat • popular • lesbians/ gay men • dancing/DJ • alternative • live shows • videos • wheelchair access

Manhole 3458 N Halsted St (at Cornelia) **773/975-9244** • 9pm-4am, till 5am Sat • mostly gay men • dancing/DJ • leather • videos

Smart Bar/ Metro 3730 N Clark St (at Irving Park Rd) **773/549-4140** • 9:30pm-4am, till 5pm Sat • gay-friendly • dancing/DJ • live shows

Cafes

Mike's Broadway Cafe 3805 N Broadway (btwn Grace & Halsted) **773/404-2205** • 7am-10pm, 24hrs summer wknds • lesbians/ gay men • some veggie • wheelchair access • $5-12

Restaurants

Angelina Ristorante 3561 Broadway (at Addison) **773/935-5933** • 5:30pm-11pm, Sun brunch • Italian • $10-20

Ann Sather's 929 W Belmont Ave (at Sheffield) **773/348-2378** • 7am-10pm, till 11pm Fri-Sat • Swedish diner & New Town fixture

Buddies Restaurant & Bar 3301 N Clark St (at Aldine) **773/477-4066** • 7am-2am, from 9am Sun • lesbians/ gay men • some veggie • $8-13 • wheelchair access

Cornelia's 750 W Cornelia Ave (at Halsted) **773/248-8333** • dinner, clsd Mon • some veggie • full bar • wheelchair access • $12-20

The Pepper Lounge 3441 N Sheffield (btwn Newport & Clark) **773/665-7377** • 6pm-1am, clsd Mon • lesbians/ gay men • supper club • gourmet Italian • plenty veggie • full bar • $12-20

The Raw Bar & Grill 3720 N Clark St (at Waveland) **773/348-7291** • 5pm-2am • seafood • $10-13

Bookstores

Unabridged Books 3251 N Broadway St (at Aldine) **773/883-9119** • 10am-10pm, till 8pm wknds

Retail Shops

Specialty Video Films 3221 N Broadway St (at Belmont) **773/248-3434** • 10am-10pm, till 11pm Fri-Sat • foreign, cult, art house, lesbigay & erotic videos • gay-owned/ run

Universal Gear 3153 N Broadway (at Belmont), Washington, DC **773/296-1090** • 11am-10pm, till 11pm Fri-Sat, clsd Mon • casual, club, athletic & designer clothing

We're Everywhere 3434 N Halsted St (at Newport) **773/404-0590, 800/772-6411** • noon-9pm, 11am-8pm wknds • also mail order catalog

Gyms & Health Clubs

Chicago Sweat Shop 3215 N Broadway (at Belmont) **773/871-2789** • gay-friendly

Erotica

Batteries Not Included 3420 N Halsted (btwn Roscoe & Addison) **773/935-9900** • 50% of all profits donated to charity

Male Hide Leathers 2816 N Lincoln Ave (at Diversey) **773/929-0069** • noon-8pm, 1pm-5pm Sun, clsd Mon

The Pleasure Chest 3155 N Broadway (at Belmont Ave) **773/525-7152**

Chicago—Near North

Accommodations

Allegro 161 W Randolph (at LaSalle) **312/236-0123** • gay-friendly • $165-295

Best Western Inn of Chicago 162 E Ohio St (at Michigan Ave) **312/787-3100, 800/557-2378** • gay-friendly • food service • wheelchair access • IGLTA • $109-189

Days Inn Gold Coast 1816 N Clark St (at Lincoln) **312/664-3040, 800/329-7466** • gay-friendly • also restaurant & lounge • wheelchair access • $109-189

Flemish House of Chicago 68 E Cedar St **312/664-9981** • gay/ straight • B&B, studios & apts in greystone rowhouse • gay-owned/ run • $125-150

Gold Coast Guesthouse 113 W Elm St (btwn Clark & LaSalle) **312/337-0361** • gay-friendly • full brkfst • women-owned/ run • $119-195 • also 2 studios available

Hotel Monaco 225 N Wabash (at S Water & Wacker Pl) **312/960-8500, 800/397-7661** • upscale • gay-friendly • gym • restaurant • $125+

Hyatt Regency Chicago 151 E Wacker Dr (at Michigan Ave) **312/565-1234, 800/233-1234** • gay-friendly

Old Town B&B **312/440-9268** • gay/ straight • roof deck • gym • $129-189

Bars

Artful Dodger 1734 W Wabansia (at Hermitage) **773/227-6859** • 5pm-2am, 8pm-3am Sat , till 2am Sun • gay-friendly • dancing/DJ

Boom Boom Room at Red Dog 1958 W North Ave (at Damen) **773/278-1009** • 10:30pm-4am Mon, also 'Resurrection' Sat • gay-friendly • dancing/DJ

Gentry on State 440 N State (at Illinois) **312/664-1033** • 4pm-2am, till 3am Sat • mostly gay men • live shows • videos

Nightclubs

Baton Show Lounge 436 N Clark St (btwn Illinois & Hubbard) **312/644-5269** • 8pm-4am Wed-Sun • lesbians/ gay men • live shows • wheelchair access

Club Intimus 312 W Randolph **312/901-1703** • 9pm-3am Sat only • mostly women • dancing/DJ • live shows • wheelchair access

The Crowbar 1543 N Kingsbury (at Sheffield) **312/243-4800** • 10pm-4am, clsd Mon-Tue • popular • gay-friendly • more gay Sun • dancing/DJ

Elixir 325 N Jefferson St **312/258-0523** • 10pm-4am till 5am Sat, clsd Sun-Wed • gay-friendly • hip fashion crowd

The Generator 306 N Halsted **312/243-8889** • 9pm-4am, till 5am Sat, clsd Mon-Tue • lesbians/ gay men • dancing/DJ • alternative • mostly African-American • wheelchair access

Second City 1616 N Wells St (at North) **312/337-3992** • legendary comedy club • call for reservations

Vinyl 1615 N Clybourn **312/587-8469** • 5:30pm-5am daily • gay-friendly • food served • live shows

Restaurants

The Berghoff 17 West Adams St (at State) **312/427-3170** • 11am-9pm, till 10pm Sat, clsd Sun • great mashed potatoes

Blue Mesa 1729 N Halsted St (at North Ave) **312/944-5990** • lunch & dinner • Southwestern • full bar

Fireplace Inn 1448 N Wells St (at North Ave) **312/664-5264** • 4:30pm-midnight ,till 1am Fri-Sat, from 11am wknds (summer) • lesbians/ gay men • BBQ/American • full bar • $13-25

Iggy's 700 N Milwaukee, River North (at Chicago) **312/829-4449** • dinner nightly, till 4am Th-Sat, till 2am Sun • int'l • full bar

Kiki's Bistro 900 N Franklin St (at Locust) **312/335-5454** • French • full bar

Manny's 1141 S Jefferson St (at Roosevelt) **312/939-2855** • 5am-4pm, clsd Sun • killer corned beef

The Mashed Potato Club 316 W Erie St (at Orleans) **312/255-8579** • dinner nightly, till 11:30pm wkdays, till 2am Fri-Sat • full bar

Shaw's Crab House 21 E Hubbard (at State St) **312/527-2722** • lunch & dinner • full bar • wheelchair access

Gyms & Health Clubs

Thousand Waves Spa 1212 W Belmont Ave (at Racine) **773/549-0700** • 1pm-9pm, 11am-7pm Sat-Sun, clsd Mon • women only • health spa only • women-owned/ run

Chicago—South Side

Bars

Club Escape 1530 E 75th St (at Stoney Island) **773/667-6454** • 3pm-2am, till 3am Sat • lesbians/ gay men • dancing/DJ • food served • mostly African-American

Inn Exile 5758 W 65th St (at Menard nr Midway Airport) **773/582-3510** • 8pm-2am, till 3am Sat • mostly gay men • dancing/DJ • videos • wheelchair access

Jeffery Pub 7041 S Jeffery (at 71st) **773/363-8555** • 11am-4am • popular • mostly gay men • dancing/DJ • mostly African-American • live shows • wheelchair access

Nightclubs

Escapades 6301 S Harlem **773/229-0886** • 10pm-4am, till 5am Sat • mostly gay men • dancing/DJ • videos

Bookstores

57th St Books 1301 E 57th St, Hyde Park (at Kimbark St) **773/684-1300** • 10am-10pm, till 8pm Sun • lesbigay section

Spiritual Groups

Resurrection MCC 5757 S University, Hyde Park (at Woodlawn) **773/288-1535** • 10:30am Sun

Decatur

Info Lines & Services

Gay/ Lesbian Assocation of Decatur (GLAD) 217/422-3277

Bars

The Flashback Lounge 2239 E Wood St (at 22nd) **217/422-3530** • 9am-2am • lesbians/ gay men • neighborhood bar • karaoke Fri • drag shows every other Sat

Effingham

Info Lines & Services

South Central Illinois Rainbow Society 217/536-5244

Bookstores

Langes News & Books 129 E Jefferson **217/342-6066** • 7am-8pm, till 6pm Sat, till 5pm Sun

Elgin

see also Chicago

Info Lines & Services

Fox Valley Gay Association 847/392-6882 • 7pm-10pm Mon-Fri

Elk Grove Village

see also Chicago

Nightclubs

Hunters 1932 E Higgins (at Busse) **847/439-8840** • 4pm-4am • popular • mostly gay men • dancing/DJ • videos • patio

Evanston

Info Lines & Services

Kinheart Women's Center 2214 Ridge Ave **847/604-0913** • call for events

Forest Park

see also Chicago

Nightclubs

Club 7301 7301 W Roosevelt Rd (at Marengo) **708/771-4459** • 3pm-2am, till 3am Fri-Sat • mostly gay men • dancing/DJ • live shows • videos • wheelchair access

Nut Bush 7201 Franklin (at Harlem) **708/366-5117** • 3pm-2am, till 3am Fri-Sat, from 1pm wknds • mostly gay men • dancing/DJ • live shows • videos

Franklin Park

Nightclubs

Temptations 10235 W Grand Ave (at Mannheim) **847/455-0008** • 6pm-4am, till 5am Fri-Sat • popular • mostly women • dancing/DJ • transgender-friendly • wheelchair access

Galesburg

Accommodations

The Fahnestock House 591 N Prairie St (at Losey) **309/344-0270** • gay/ straight • full brkfst • Queen Anne Victorian • gay-owned/ run • $125

Granite City

see also St Louis, Missouri

Nightclubs

Club Bridges 3145 W Chain of Rocks Rd **618/797-0700** • 7pm-2am, till 3am Sat, 5pm-12am Sun, clsd Mon-Tue • popular • lesbians/ gay men • food served • entertainment • live shows • videos • outdoor complex

Hinsdale

Spiritual Groups

MCC Holy Covenant Unitarian Church, 17 W Maple (at Washington) **630/325-8488** • 5:50pm Sun • wheelchair access

Joliet

Nightclubs

Maneuvers 118 E Jefferson **815/727-7069** • 8pm-2am, till 3am Fri-Sat • lesbians/ gay men • dancing/DJ • patio • unconfirmed '99

Minonk

Accommodations

Victorian Oaks B&B 435 Locust St (at 5th) **309/432-2771, 800/995-6085** • gay-friendly • private dinner with advanced reservation • $70-85

Mt Prospect

Bookstores

Prairie Moon 864 E Northwest Hwy (6 blks E of Rte 83) **847/342-9608** • 4pm-8pm, 10am-6pm Fri-Sat, noon-5pm Sun, clsd Mon • feminist • special events • wheelchair access • women-owned/ run

Oak Park

Spiritual Groups

MCC of the Incarnation 460 Lake St (at Ridgeland) **708/383-3033** • 11am Sun, 10am summers

Ozark

Accommodations

Coyote & Fox Rte 1 Box 218 (nr Solomon Ln) **618/695-2746** • gay/ straight • resort houses located on 40 acres • hot tub • $125-196

Peoria

Bars

David's 807 SW Adams (at Oak) **309/676-3987** • 1pm-2am, till 1am Sun-Wed • lesbians/ gay men

Quench Room 631 W Main (at Sheridan) **309/676-1079** • 5pm-1am, till 2am Th-Sat, from 1pm wknds • lesbians/ gay men • neighborhood bar • wheelchair access

Nightclubs

DJ's Timeout 703 SW Adams (at State) **309/674-5902** • 1pm-1am, till 2am Th-Sat • lesbians/ gay men • dancing/DJ • food served • live shows • wheelchair access

Red Fox Den 800 N Knoxville Ave (at Glendale) **309/674-8013** • 9pm-4am • lesbians/ gay men • dancing/DJ • live shows

Publications

The Alternative Times 309/688-1930

Erotica

Brown Bag Video 801 SW Adams (at Oak) **309/676-3003**

Quincy

Info Lines & Services

AA Gay/ Lesbian 124-1/2 N 5th **217/224-2800** • 7pm Th

Nightclubs

Irene's Cabaret 124 N 5th St **217/222-6292** • 9pm-2:30am, from 7pm Fri-Sat, clsd Mon • lesbians/ gay men • dancing/DJ • live shows • wheelchair access

Spiritual Groups

MCC 124-1/2 N 5th **217/224-2800** • 11am & 6pm Sun

Rock Island

see also Davenport, Iowa

Bars

Augie's 313 20th St (at 3rd) **309/788-7389** • 11am-3am, from 10am Sun • lesbians/ gay men • neighborhood bar

Nightclubs

JR's 325 20th St (at 4th Ave) **309/786-9411** • 3pm-3am, from noon Sun • lesbians/ gay men • dancing/DJ • live shows • also restaurant • under $10 • wheelchair access

Bookstores

All Kinds of People 1806 2nd Ave (at 18th St) **309/788-2567** • 10am-10pm, till midnight Fri-Sat • alternative • also cafe • plenty veggie • wheelchair access

Rockford

Bars

Oh Zone 1014 Charles St (at E State) **815/964-9663** • 5pm-2am, noon-midnight Sun • lesbians/ gay men • dancing /DJ • live entertainment • karaoke • shows

Nightclubs

Office 513 E State St (btwn 2nd & 3rd) **815/965-0344** • 5pm-2am, noon-midnight Sun • popular • lesbians/ gay men • dancing/DJ • food served • live shows • videos

Cafes

Cafe Esperanto 107 N Main (at W State) **815/968-0123** • 3pm-1am, till 2am Fri, noon-2am Sat, 7pm-midnight Sun • full bar • also gallery

Restaurants

Lucernes 845 N Church St (at Whitman) **815/968-2665** • 5pm-11pm, clsd Mon • fondue • full bar • wheelchair access

Maria's 828 Cunningham (at Corbin) **815/968-6781** • 4:30pm-9pm, clsd Sun-Mon • Italian • full bar • Denise's favorite • $7-20

Springfield

Info Lines & Services

Springfield Area Lesbian Outreach (SALO) 217/528-7256

Accommodations

The Inn on Edwards 810 E Edwards St (btwn 8th & 4th Sts) **217/528–0420** • gay-friendly • 19th-century inn • 1 blk south of Lincoln's home in historic Springfield • full brkfst • $65-75

Bars

The Station House 304–306 E Washington (btwn 3rd & 4th Sts) **217/525–0438** • 11am-1am, till 3am Fri-Sat, from noon Sun • gay-friendly • neighborhood bar • dancing/DJ Wed & Sat • country western • karaoke Tue • wheelchair access

Nightclubs

Smokey's Den 411 E Washington (btwn 4th & 5th) **217/522–0301** • 6pm-1am, till 3am Fri-Sat • lesbians/ gay men • dancing/DJ • wheelchair access

Zoo Babies 3036 Peoria Rd (nr State Fairgrounds) **217/528–0535, 217/787–0559** • 9pm-3am, from 8pm Fri-Sat, clsd Mon • lesbians/ gay men • dancing/DJ • food served • live shows • videos

Bookstores

Sundance 1428 E Sangamon Ave (at Peoria Rd) **217/788–5243** • 10am-6pm, clsd Sun-Mon • new age books & gifts • lesbigay titles

Publications

▲ **Prairie Flame 217/753–2887** • lesbigay newspaper for central IL

Erotica

Expo I Books 302 N 5th St (at Madison) **217/544–5145**

INDIANA

Bloomington

Info Lines & Services

Indiana University LGBT Student Services 705 E 7th St **812/855–4252** • hours vary • recorded info 24hrs at 812/855-5688

Indiana Youth Group 800/347–8336 (IN-STATE) • 7pm-midnight Th-Fri • lesbigay youth hotline

Office for Women's Affairs Memorial Hall East #123 **812/855–3849** • 8am-noon & 1pm-5pm, clsd wknds • support/ discussion groups • call for info

Accommodations

Enchanted Otter 812/323–9800 • women only • lake retreat for all seasons • full brkfst • hot tub • kitchen • smokefree • women-owned/ run • $60-85

Holiday Inn Bloomington 1710 Kinser Pike **812/334–3252, 800/465–4329** • gay-friendly

Bars

The Other Bar 414 S Walnut (btwn 2nd & 4th) **812/332–0033** • 5pm-3am, clsd Sun & Tue • lesbians/ gay men • neighborhood bar • patio • wheelchair access

Uncle Elizabeth's 502 N Morton (at 9th) **812/331–0060** • noon-3am, clsd Sun • lesbians/ gay men • neighborhood bar • food served • patio

Nightclubs

Bullwinkle's 201 S College St (at 4th St) **812/334–3232** • 8pm-3am, clsd Sun • lesbians/ gay men • more women Th • dancing/DJ • live shows

Restaurants

Village Deli 409 E Kirkwood **812/336–2303** • 8am-7pm, 7am-4pm wknds • some veggie

Retail Shops

Athena Gallery 108 E Kirkwood Ave (at Walnut) **812/339–0734** • 11am-6pm, till 8pm Fri-Sat, till 4pm Sun • wheelchair access

Spiritual Groups

Integrity Bloomington 400 E Kirkwood Ave (at Trinity Episcopal Church) **812/336–4466** • 7:30pm 2nd Wed • co-op dinner • wheelchair access

Unity of Bloomington 1101 N Dunn (at 14th) **812/333–2484** • 9am & 11am Sun • wheelchair access

Columbia City

Nightclubs

XTC 225 W VanBuren St (at Line St) **219/244–6907** • 11pm-4am, 4pm-1am Sun • gay-friendly • DJ Fri-Sat • karaoke • full menu served

Elkhart

see also South Bend

Info Lines & Services

Info Helpline 219/293–8671 • 24hrs

Spiritual Groups

Unitarian Universalist Fellowship 1732 Garden (at Johnson) **219/264–6525** • call for service times • wheelchair access

Evansville

Info Lines & Services

Tri-State Alliance 812/474–4853 • info • monthly social group • newsletter

Bars

Scottie's 2207 S Kentucky Ave (1/2 mile N of I–164) **812/425–3270** • Mon-Sat 4pm-3am • lesbians/ gay men • neighborhood bar • dancing/DJ • karaoke

Uptown Bar 201 W Illinois St (at Garfield) **812/423–4861** • 1pm-1am, till 3am Fri-Sat, clsd Sun • lesbians/ gay men • dancing/DJ Fri-Sat • videos • pizza served • patio • wheelchair access

Nightclubs

Someplace Else 930 Main St (at Sycamore) **812/424–3202** • 4pm-3am, clsd Sun • lesbians/ gay men • dancing/DJ Wed-Sat • live shows Fri-Sat • karaoke Wed • patio • also 'Down Under' pride gift shop from 10pm-3am Fri-Sat

Bookstores

AA Michael Books 1541 S Green River Rd (at Covert) **812/479–8979** • 10am-6pm, till 8pm Fri, 10am-5pm Sat, noon-5pm Sun • spiritual • wheelchair access

Fort Wayne

Info Lines & Services

Gay/ Lesbian AA at Up the Stairs Community Center **219/744–1199** • 7:30pm Tue & Sat, 4:30pm Sun

Up the Stairs Community Center 3426 Broadway **219/744–1199** • helpline 7pm-10pm, till midnight Fri-Sat, 8pm-9pm Sun • drop-in 8pm-midnight Fri • space for various groups

Bars

Hide-n-Seeks Pub & Eatery 1008 N Wells St **219/423–2202** • 5pm-3am, till midnight Sun • mostly gay men • neighborhood bar • dancing/DJ • food served

Out On Main 2809 W Main St (at W Jefferson Blvd) **219/436–4166** • 6pm-3am • mostly gay men • neighborhood bar • food served • wheelchair access

Up the Street 2322 S Calhoun (at Creighton) **219/456–7166** • 5pm-3:30am, clsd Sun • lesbians/ gay men • dancing/DJ Fri-Sat • food served • live shows Th-Fri • wheelchair access

Nightclubs

After Dark 231 Pearl St (at Maiden Ln) **219/424–6130** • noon-3am, clsd Sun • lesbians/ gay men • dancing/DJ • live shows • wheelchair access

Downtown On The Landing 110 W Columbia St **219/420–1615** • 7pm-3am, from 8pm Sat, clsd Sun-Tue • lesbians/ gay men • dancing/DJ Th-Sat • live shows

Retail Shops

Curt's Shirts & Gifts 1428 Main St (nr W Main & Osage) **219/424–1404** • 11am-7pm • lesbigay gifts

Subterranean 301 W Washington (at Webster) **219/424–8417** • 11am-9:30pm Mon-Th, till 10:30pm Fri-Sat, noon-6pm Sun • gifts • sex toys • leather

Spiritual Groups

Open Door Chapel at Up the Stairs Community Center **219/744–1199** • 7pm Sun

Hammond

Restaurants

Phil Smidt & Son 1205 N Calumet Ave (at Indianapolis Blvd) **219/659–0025** • lunch & dinner • seafood • full bar

Indianapolis

Info Lines & Services

AA Gay/ Lesbian 317/632–7864 • call for mtg times & locations • lesbian mtg 7pm Mon

Fellowship Indianapolis 317/328–8061, 317/921–9713 • social & support groups for lesbians/ gay men

The Switchboard 317/630–4297 • 7pm-11pm • resources • crisis counseling

Accommodations

Frederick Talbott Inn 13805 Allisonville Rd (116th), Fishers **317/257–2660** • gay-friendly • across from Conner Prairie Museum • full brkfst • smokefree • $99-179

Renaissance Tower Historic Inn 230 E 9th St (btwn Delaware & Alabama) **317/262–8648, 800/676–7786** • studio suites • full kitchens • downtown location • $32-85

Bars

501 Tavern 501 N College Ave (at Michigan) **317/632–2100** • 4:30pm-3:30am, clsd Sun • popular • mostly gay men • country/ western Tue • dancing/DJ Fri-Sat • also 'Options' safer-sex info center

Brothers Bar & Grill 822 N Illinois St (at St Clair) **317/636–1020** • 4pm-midnight • restaurant till 10pm • lesbians/ gay men • wheelchair access

Indianapolis

Indianapolis, the capital of the Hoosier state, may look like your typical Midwestern industrial city, but you'll find a few surprises under the surface.

You probably won't find lesbians dancing in the streets (unless it's Pride Day), but they're there. Check out some of the fun boutiques and restaurants in the Broad Ripple district. Later fuel up on caffeine at the **MT Cup** and dance with the girls at **Utopia** or **The Ten.**

If you're into women's music, plan to be in Indiana during the first weekend in June for the **National Women's Music Festival** in Bloomington. You can stay at the **Enchanted Otter,** a lakeside women's retreat and visit the **Athena Gallery** while you're in town.

If fast cars are more your style, be sure to be in Indianapolis for the Indy 500 on Memorial Day weekend.

Indianapolis

Entertainment: Women's Chorus 317/931-9464.
Men's Chorus at the Crossroads Performing Arts 317/931-9464.

Lesbigay Pride: June. 317/725-8840 (The Word).

Annual Events: Memorial Day Weekend - Indy 500 auto race.
June - National Women's Music Festival (in Muncie, IN) 927-9355.

City Info: Indianapolis Visitor's Bureau 317/639-4282, 800/323-4639, web: www.indianapolis.org or www.indy.org.

Attractions: Indianapolis Museum of Art 317/923-1331.
Speedway 500 317/484-6747.
Zoo 317/630-2001.

Weather: The spring weather is moderate (50°s-60°s) with occasional storms. The summers are typically midwestern: hot (mid-90°s) and humid. The autumns are mild and colorful in southeastern Indiana. As for winter, it's the wind chill that'll get to you.

Transit: Yellow Cab 317/487-7777.
Metro Transit 317/635-3344.

Illusions 1446 E Washington (at Arsenal) **317/266–0535** • 7am-3am, noon-12:30am Sun • lesbians/ gay men • dancing/DJ • karaoke • live shows

The Metro 707 Massachusetts Ave (at College) **317/639–6022** • 4pm-3am, noon-12:30am Sun • lesbians/ gay men • dancing/DJ • also restaurant • some veggie • patio • wheelchair access • $5-11 • also 'Colors' shop

Varsity Lounge 1517 N Pennsylvania St (at 16th) **317/635–9998** • 10am-3am, noon-midnight Sun • mostly gay men • neighborhood bar • food served • $4-10

Nightclubs

Club Cabaret 151 W 14th St (at Capitol) **317/767–1707** • call for hours & events • lesbians/ gay men • dancing/DJ • patio • wheelchair access

The Ten 1218 N Pennsylvania St (at 12th, enter rear) **317/638–5802** • 6pm-3am, clsd Sun • popular • mostly women • dancing/DJ • country/ western Mon • live shows • wheelchair access

Tropica Bay 2301 N Meridian (at 23rd St) **317/925–1710** • 4pm-midnight Mon, till 1am Tue-Wed, till 2am Th, till 3am Fri-Sat, from 3pm Sun • lesbians/ gay men • food served • dancing/DJ • karaoke • shows • wheelchair access

Utopia 924 N Pennsylvania St (at St Joseph's) **317/638–0215** • 6pm-1am Sun-Th, till 3am Fri-Sat • lesbians/ gay men • dancing/DJ • also restaurant

The Vogue 6259 N College Ave (at Broad Ripple) **317/259–7029** • 9pm-3am Sun, Wed, Fri-Sat • gay-friendly • gay night Sun w/ 'Boing' • dancing/DJ • alternative • live shows

Cafes

The MT Cup 314 Massachusetts Ave (at New Jersey) **317/639–1099** • 7am-11pm, till midnight wknds, 9:30am-9pm Sun • sandwiches • baked goods

Restaurants

Aesop's Tables 600 N Massachusetts Ave (at East) **317/631–0055** • 11am-9pm, till 10pm Fri-Sat • authentic Mediterranean • some veggie • beer/ wine • wheelchair access • $8-15

Peter's 8505 Keystone Crossing Blvd **317/465–1155, 800/479–0909** • dinner only, clsd Sun • upscale dining • full bar

Entertainment & Recreation

Women's Chorus 317/931–9464

Bookstores

Borders 5612 Castleton Corner Ln (at 86th St) **317/849–8660** • 9am-10pm, 11am-8pm Sun • some lesbigay titles

Out Word Bound 625 N East St (at Massachusetts Ave) **317/951–9100** • 11:30am-9pm, till 11pm Fri, 10am-11pm Sat, noon-6pm Sun • lesbigay books & gifts

Retail Shops

Colors Pride & Leather Shop 707 Massachusetts Ave (upstairs at 'Metro') **317/686–0984** • from 6pm Mon-Th, 4pm Fri-Sat, 2pm Sun

Contours/ Torso 719 Massachusetts **317/916–9054** • 2pm-11pm, till midnight Fri-Sat, 1pm-5pm Sun • clothing • gifts

Dawghouse Cards & Gifts 222E Market St (at Delaware) **317/822–1757** • 8am-6pm, from 10am Sat, clsd Sun • wheelchair access

Indy News 20 E Maryland (at Meridian) **317/632–7680** • 6am-7pm, till 6pm wknds

Southside News 8063 Madison Ave **317/887–1020** • 6am-9pm, till 7pm Sun

Publications

Outlines 317/923–8550 • lesbigay newsmagazine w/ extensive resources

The Word 317/725–8840 • lesbigay newspaper

Spiritual Groups

Jesus MCC Unitarian Church, 5805 E 56th (at Channing) **317/894–5110** • 6pm Sun & 7:30pm Wed

Lafayette

Bars

The Sportsman 644 Main St (at Columbia) **765/742–6321** • 1pm-3:30am, from 5pm Sat, clsd Sun • lesbians/ gay men • neighborhood bar • dancing/DJ Tue, Fri-Sat

Erotica

Fantasy East 2311 Concord Rd (at Teal) **765/474–2417** • books & videos

Lake Station

Nightclubs

Axcis Nightclub & Lounge 2415 Rush St (at Central Ave) **219/962–1017** • 7pm-3am • popular • lesbians/ gay men • dancing/DJ Tue & Th-Sat • live shows • ladies' night Tue • wheelchair access

Merrillville

see also Gary & Hammond

Michigan City

Nightclubs

Total Eclipse 4960 W US 20 **219/874-1100** • 7pm-2am, from 5pm Fri, 7pm-midnight Sun • lesbians/ gay men • dancing/DJ • transgender-friendly • live shows Th • patio in-season • food served • fish-fry Fri • wheelchair access

Mishawaka

see also South Bend

Muncie

Bars

Carriage House 1100 Kilgore (at Jackson) **765/282-7411** • 5pm-midnight • gay/ straight • neighborhood bar • also restaurant • steak/ seafood • wheelchair access • gay-owned/ run • $9-14

Mark III Tap Room 107 E Main St (at Walnut) **765/282-8273** • 11am-3am, 12:30pm-1am Sun • lesbians/ gay men • dancing/DJ • Italian food • shows

Richmond

Bars

Clarion Leland/ Legends Lounge 900 South 'A' St **765/966-5000** • 5pm-midnight • gay-friendly • more gay Sun • karaoke

Coachman 911 E Main St (at N 9th St) **765/966-2835** • 7pm-3am, clsd Sun • lesbians/ gay men • more women Sat • dancing/DJ Fri-Sat • wheelchair access

South Bend

Info Lines & Services

Community Resource Center Helpline 219/232-2522 • 9am-5pm Mon-Fri, limited lesbigay info • also 24hr crisis hotline 219/232-3344

Accommodations

The Gray Goose Inn B&B 350 Indian Boundary Rd (at I-95), Chesterton **219/926-5781, 800/521-5127** • gay/ straight • full brkfst

The Oliver Inn B&B 630 W Washington St **219/232-4545, 888/697-4466** • gay-friendly • restored 1886 mansion • carriage house & playhouse

Nightclubs

Sea Horse II Cabaret 1902 Western Ave **219/237-9139** • 8pm-3am, from 7pm Fri-Sat, clsd Sun • lesbians/ gay men • dancing/DJ • live shows Wed-Sat • wheelchair access

Truman's 100 N Center St, Mishawaka **219/259-2282** • 4pm-3am, till 12:30am Sun • popular • lesbians/ gay men • dancing/DJ • live shows • also 'John's Grille'

Terre Haute

Nightclubs

R-Place 684 Lafayette Ave **812/232-9119** • 8pm-3am, clsd Sun-Mon • lesbians/ gay men • dancing/DJ • drag shows Sat

Iowa

Statewide

Info Lines & Services

Iowa Division of Tourism 800/345-4692

Publications

Access Line 319/232-6805 • lesbigay newspaper

Ames

Info Lines & Services

Help Central 515/232-0000 • 8:30am-4:30pm • community info service • some lesbigay referrals

LGBT Alliance 515/294-2104 • 11am-5pm • LGBT Student Services at 515/294-5433

Margaret Sloss Women's Center Sloss House, ISU **515/294-4154** • 8am-5pm, clsd wknds • call for programs

Bars

Studio Cafe 604 E Lincoln Way **515/663-0929** • 5pm-1am, till 2am Fri-Sat, clsd Sun • food served • live shows • videos

Restaurants

Lucallen's 400 Main St (at Kellogg) **515/232-8484** • 11am-9pm, till 11pm Fri-Sat • Italian • some veggie • full bar • $6-12

Pizza Kitchen 120 Hayward (btwn Chamberlain & Lincoln) **515/292-1710** • 11am-9pm • beer/ wine

Burlington

Accommodations

Arrowhead Motel 2520 Mt Pleasant St **319/752-6353, 800/341-8000** • gay-friendly

Bars

Steve's Place 852 Washington (at Central Ave) **319/752-9109** • 9am-2am • gay-friendly • neighborhood bar • wheelchair access

Cedar Falls

see also Waterloo

Bookstores

Gateways 109 E 2nd St (at Main) **319/277-3973** • noon-5:30pm, 9:30am-4pm Sat, clsd Sun • gay section

Cedar Rapids

Info Lines & Services

Gay/ Lesbian Resource Center 1056 5th Ave SE (nr Mercy Hospital) **319/366-2055** • noon-3pm Mon, Wed & Fri • 24hr recorded info

Nightclubs

Club Basix 3916 1st Ave NE (btwn 39th & 40th) **319/363-3194** • 5pm-2am • lesbians/ gay men • dancing/DJ • live shows • gay-owned/ run

Spiritual Groups

Faith United Methodist Church 1000 30th St NE **319/363-8454, 319/895-6678** • 10:30am Sun

Council Bluffs

see Omaha, Nebraska

Davenport

see Rock Island, Illinois

Bars

Club Marquette 3923 Marquette St (at Kimberly) **319/386-0700** • 3pm-2am, from noon Fri & Sun • mostly gay men • dancing/DJ • food served • live shows • patio • wheelchair access

Spiritual Groups

MCC Quad Cities 3025 N Harrison **319/324-8281** • 11am Sun & 7pm Wed

Des Moines

Info Lines & Services

Central Iowa Gender Association **515/277-7754, 515/223-0069** • support group for transsexuals

GLRC (Gay/ Lesbian Resource Center) 414 E 5th St **515/281-0634** • live 7pm-10pm Mon-Sat • 24hr recorded info • youth groups • many other mtgs

Out-Reach **515/830-1777** • social/ support group

Young Women's Resource Center 1909 Ingersoll Ave (at 19th) **515/244-4901** • 8:30am-5pm, clsd wknds

Accommodations

Kingman House 2920 Kingman Blvd **515/279-7312** • lesbians/ gay men • turn-of-the-century B&B • full brkfst • wheelchair access • $40

Racoon River Resort 2920 Kingman Blvd **515/279-7312, 515/996-2829** • lesbians/ gay men • rustic • 20 minutes from Des Moines • full brkfst • food served • hot tub • nudity ok • available for groups • wheelchair access • $15-50

Bars

The Blazing Saddle 416 E 5th St (btwn Grand & Locust) **515/246-1299** • 2pm-2am, from noon wknds • mostly gay men • leather • shows • wheelchair access

Dally's Pub & Emporium 430 E Locust (1 blk S of Grand, btwn E 4th & 5th) **515/243-9760** • 2pm-2am, from noon wknds • popular • lesbians/ gay men • country western Th • karaoke Wed • live shows

Faces 416 E Walnut (at 4th) **515/280-5463** • 9am-2am • lesbians/ gay men • country/ western line dancing Tue • wheelchair access

Nightclubs

The Garden 112 SE 4th St **515/243-3965** • 8pm-2am, clsd Mon-Tue • lesbians/ gay men • dancing/DJ • live shows • karaoke • videos • young crowd • wheelchair access • patio

Cafes

Chat Noir Cafe 644 18th St (at Woodland) **515/244-1353** • 10am-11pm, till midnight Fri-Sat, clsd Sun-Mon • some veggie • beer/ wine • wheelchair access • $6-12

Java Joe's 214 4th St (at Court Ave) **515/288-5282** • 7:30am-11pm, till 1am Fri-Sat, 9am-11pm Sun • live shows • community artist gallery next door

Bookstores

Borders 4100 University (at 42nd), West Des Moines **515/223–1620** • 9am-11pm, till 9pm Sun • wheelchair access

Retail Shops

Axiom 412–1/2 E 5th St (btwn Grand & Locust) **515/246–0414** • piercings • fetishware

Publications

Outword 515/281–0634

Spiritual Groups

Church of the Holy Spirit MCC 909 E River Dr (at the Botanical Center) **515/287–9787** • 10am & 3pm Sun

Erotica

Gallery Book Store 1114 Walnut St (at 11th) **515/244–2916** • 24hrs

Dubuque

Info Lines & Services

Triangle Coalition of the Tri-State Area 319/583–1834 • lesbigay social/ support group • weekly meetings 7:30pm-9pm • call Kevin for info

Bars

One Flight Up 4448 Main St **319/582–8357** • 5pm-2am • lesbians/ gay men • food served • live shows

Fort Dodge

Erotica

Mini Cinema 15 N 5th St (on the square) **515/955–9756**

Grinnell

Info Lines & Services

Stonewall Resource Center Grinnell College 515/269–3327 • 4pm-11pm, till 6pm Fri, 1pm-4pm Sat • also quarterly newsletter

Iowa City

Info Lines & Services

AA Gay/ Lesbian 319/338–9111 (AA#)

Gayline 319/335–3251

LGBT People's Union 319/335–3251 • also publishes 'Iowa's Pride' newsletter

Women's Resource/ Action Center 130 N Madison (at Market) **319/335–1486** • 10am-5pm, clsd wknds • community center & lesbian support group • wheelchair access

Bookstores

Prairie Lights Bookstore 15 S Dubuque St (at Washington) **319/337–2681** • 9am-10pm, till 6pm Sun • also cafe • wheelchair access

Retail Shops

Alternatives 323 E Market St (at Gilbert) **319/337–4124** • 10am-6pm, noon-4pm Sun • pride gifts • wheelchair access

Lansing

Accommodations

Suzanne's B&B 120 N 3rd St (30 miles S of La Crosse, WI) **319/538–3040** • gay-friendly • clsd Jan • full brkfst • sauna

Newton

Accommodations

La Corsette Maison Inn 629 1st Ave E **515/792–6833** • gay-friendly • 3-course brkfst • antique jacuzzi • 4-star restaurant • $70-170

Sioux City

Bars

3 Cheers 414 20th St **712/255–8005** • Wed-Sat • lesbians/ gay men • neighborhood bar • dancing/DJ • live shows • wheelchair access

Waterloo

Info Lines & Services

Access 319/232–6805 • weekly info & support

Lesbian/ Bisexual Women Resources 319/233–7519 • 7pm 1st Fri • call evenings

Bars

The Bar 903 Sycamore (at E 7th) **319/232–0543** • 7pm-2am • lesbians/ gay men • dancing/DJ • live shows • wheelchair access

Kansas

Statewide

Info Lines & Services

Kansas Travel & Tourism Department Topeka **800/252-6727**

Publications

▲ **The Liberty Press 316/652-7737, 316/941-2882** • statewide lesbigay newspaper

Abilene

Retail Shops

Triangle Artworks 1605 NW 3rd St (at Buckeye) **785/263-7849** • clsd Sun • gallery & gifts • ask about gay discount

Kansas City

see also Kansas City, Missouri

Lawrence

Info Lines & Services

Decca Center AA Support & Counseling 714 Vermont (across from library) **785/841-4138** • lesbigay mtgs 7pm Tue & 11am Sun

KU Queers & Allies 785/864-3091 • student group

Bars

Teller's Restaurant & Bar 746 Massachusetts Ave **785/843-4111** • 11am-2am • gay-friendly • more gay Tue • also restaurant • southern Italian/ pizza • some veggie • $12-21 • wheelchair access

Nightclubs

Jazzhaus 926-1/2 Massachusetts **785/749-3320** • 4pm-2am • gay-friendly • live shows

Matfield Green

Accommodations

Homestead Ranch Guest Programs/ Prairie Women Adventures 316/753-3465 • bunkhouse for 4 • hot tub • also Youth Adventures for 10-14 yrs old • $150 for four ($15 each additional)

Topeka

Info Lines & Services

LIFT (Lesbians in Fellowship Together) 2425 SE Indiana (at MCC) **785/232-6196** • 6pm 3rd Th • call for details

Bars

Classics 601 SE 8th St **785/233-5153** • 4pm-2am, from noon Sun • lesbians/ gay men • neighborhood bar

Bookstores

Town Crier Books 1301 SW Gage Blvd #120 (at Huntoon) **785/272-5060** • 9am-8:30pm, till 5pm wknds, from 11:30am Sun

Spiritual Groups

MCC Topeka 2425 SE Indiana Ave **785/232-6196** • 10am & 6pm Sun

Wichita

Info Lines & Services

Land of Oz Info Line 316/269-0913 • touchtone info

Transitions 316/687-3524 • Sat mtgs for lesbigay youth 18-24 • also 'Project Acceptance' Tue • adult mtgs 7pm 1st Tue at 2930 E 1st St (College Hill Methodist)

Bars

America's Pub 900 E 1st St (at Mosely) **316/267-1782** • 8pm-2am • gay-friendly • gay Mon night only • dancing/DJ • live shows

Dreamers II 2835 S George Washington Blvd (at Oliver) **316/522-2028** • 4pm-2am, from 3pm wknds • mostly women • dancing/DJ • food served • women-owned/ run

'J' 513 E Central **316/262-1363** • 2pm-2am • gay/ straight • piano lounge • food served • wheelchair access

Kirby's Beer Store 3227 E 17th (at Holyoke) **316/685-7013** • 2pm-2am • lesbians/ gay men • live bands • food served • also 'Kirby's Too' at 1111 E Lincoln, 312/267-3331

Metro 458 N Waco (at Central) **316/262-8130** • 8pm-2am Th-Sun • mostly gay men • women's night Th • dancing/DJ • professional crowd • live shows • patio • also restaurant • kitchen open till 10pm

Ralph's 3210 E Osie (at George Washington Blvd) **316/682-4461** • 3pm-2am • lesbians/ gay men • neighborhood bar • karaoke

Sadie's 2835 S George Washington Blvd (at Oliver) **316/612-1020** • 3pm-2am • lesbians/ gay men • shows

Side Street Saloon 1106 S Pattie (nr Lincoln & Hydraulic) **316/267-0324** • 2pm-2am • mostly gay men • neighborhood bar • wheelchair access

The T-Room 1507 E Pawnee (at K-15) **316/262-9327** • 3pm-2am • lesbians/ gay men • leather

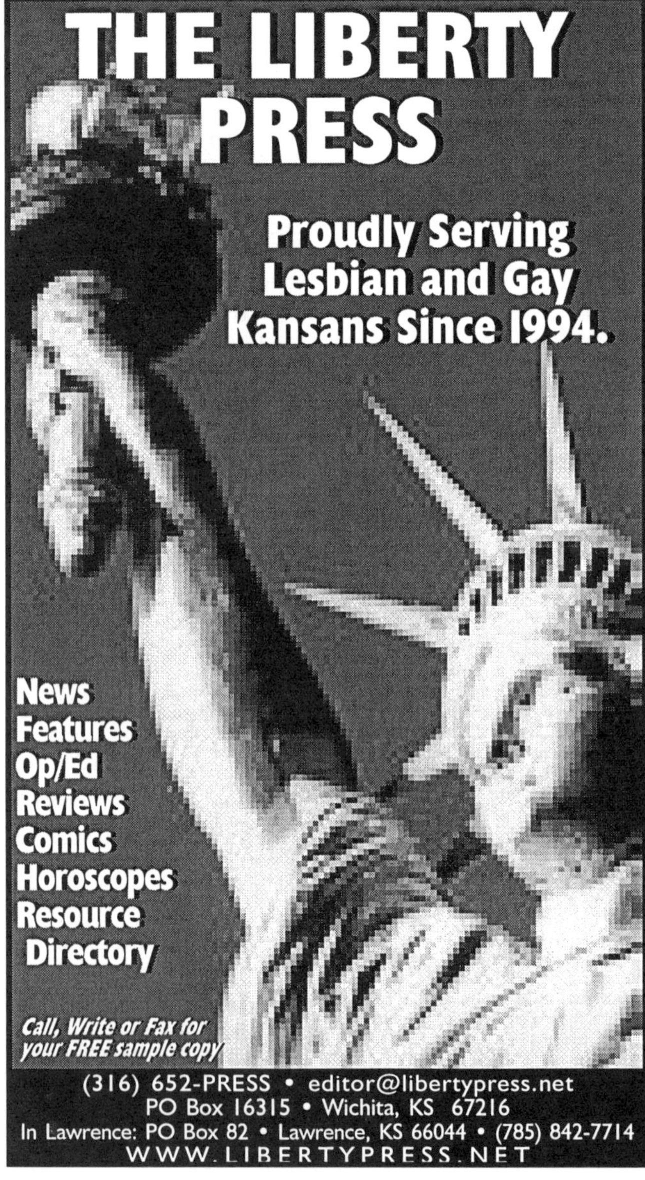
THE LIBERTY PRESS
Proudly Serving Lesbian and Gay Kansans Since 1994.
News
Features
Op/Ed
Reviews
Comics
Horoscopes
Resource Directory
Call, Write or Fax for your FREE sample copy
(316) 652-PRESS • editor@libertypress.net
PO Box 16315 • Wichita, KS 67216
In Lawrence: PO Box 82 • Lawrence, KS 66044 • (785) 842-7714
WWW.LIBERTYPRESS.NET

Nightclubs

The Edge 305 St Francis (btwn English & Water) **316/269-2626** • 8pm-2am Wed & Sun, from 7pm Th & Sat, from 4pm Fri • gay-friendly • dancing/DJ • food served • live shows

Our Fantasy Complex 3201 S Hillside (at 31st) **316/682-5494** • 8pm-2am, clsd Mon-Tue • also 'South Forty' (country/ western bar) open from 3pm • also 'Harbor Grill' restaurant

Cafes

Riverside Perk 1144 Bidding (at 11th) **316/264-6464** • 7am-10pm, till midnight Fri-Sat, 10am-10pm Sun

Velvet Rope 511 E Douglas (at St Francis) **316/263-2882** • lunch Mon-Wed & dinner nightly • $4-10

Restaurants

The Lassen 155 N Market St **316/263-2777** • lunch & dinner, clsd Sun • some veggie • full bar • $6-44

Moe's Sub Shop 2815 S Hydraulic (at Wassall) **316/524-5511** • 11am-8pm, clsd Sun

Old Mill Tasty Shop 604 E Douglas (at St Francis) **316/264-6500** • 11am-3pm, 8am-5pm Sat, clsd Sun • old-fashioned soda fountain • lunch menu • some veggie

The Upper Crust 7038 E Lincoln **316/683-8088** • lunch only, clsd wknds • homestyle • some veggie • $4-7

Retail Shops

Holier Than Thou Body Piercing 1111 E Douglas Ave (at Washington) **316/266-4100** • noon-8pm, clsd Sun-Mon

Mother's 3100 E 31st St S (at Hillside) **316/686-8116** • noon-9pm, till midnight Fri-Sat • lesbigay gifts

Spiritual Groups

College Hill United Methodist Church 2930 E 1st St **316/683-4643** • 8:30am & 11am Sun • also lesbigay group, 3rd Th

First Metropolitan Community Church 156 S Kansas Ave **316/267-1852** • 10:30am & 6:30pm Sun

First Unitarian Universalist Church 1501 Fairmount **316/684-3481** • 11am Sun

Erotica

Priscilla's 6143 W Kellogg (at Dugan) **316/942-1244**

Kentucky

Statewide

Publications

The Letter 502/772-7570 • statewide lesbigay newspaper

The Word 317/725-8840 • lesbigay newspaper for IN, KY, OH

Bowling Green

Accommodations

Maple Grove Farm 2841 Hwy 185 **502/843-7433** • gay/ straight • large 1916 bungalow on 8 acres • full brkfst • gay-owned/ run • $40-60

Covington

see also Cincinnati, Ohio

Bars

Rosie's Tavern 643 Bakewell St **606/291-9707** • 3pm-2:30am • gay/ straight • neighborhood bar • wheelchair access • lesbian-owned

Harned

Accommodations

Kentucky Holler House Rte 1 Box 51BB **502/547-4507** • B&B on 48 acres • lesbians/ gay men • private decks • smokefree • lesbian-owned/ run • $75-95

Lexington

Info Lines & Services

Gay/ Lesbian AA 606/224-4067 (PRIVATE HOME), 606/276-2917 (AA#) • 8pm Mon & Wed, 7:30pm Fri

Lexington Pride Center 387 Waller Ave

Bars

The Bar Complex 224 E Main St **606/255-1551** • 4pm-1am, till 3:30am Sat, clsd Sun • popular • lesbians/ gay men • dancing/DJ • live shows • wheelchair access

The Watering Hole 147 N Limestone St **606/223-0495** • 7pm-1am, clsd Sun • lesbians/ gay men • neighborhood bar

Nightclubs

Club 141 141 W Vine St (at Limestone) **606/233-4262** • 8:30pm-1am, till 3am Sat, clsd Sun-Mon • lesbians/ gay men • dancing/DJ • live shows • wheelchair access

Vertigo 123 W Main (btwn Limestone & Upper) **606/226-9904** • 9pm-1am Th-Sun • gay-friendly • dancing/DJ • theme nights • wheelchair access

Restaurants

Alfalfa 557 S Limestone **606/253-0014** • lunch & dinner • healthy multi-ethnic • plenty veggie • live folk music Fri-Sat • $6-12

Bookstores

Joseph-Beth 161 Lexington Green Circle **606/273-2911, 800/248-6849** • 9am-10pm, till 11pm Fri-Sat, 11am-8pm Sun • also cafe & travel agency • wheelchair access

Publications

GLSO (Gay/ Lesbian) News • calendar

The Letter 502/772-7570 • statewide lesbigay newspaper

Spiritual Groups

Lexington MCC 387 Waller Ave **606/255-4016** • 11:30am Sun • wheelchair access

Pagan Forum 606/268-1640 • call for info on 10+ area pagan groups

Louisville

Info Lines & Services

LGBT Hotline 502/454-7613 • 6pm-10pm • AA referrals

Louisville Gender Society 502/368-9918 • transgender group • contact Lori

Louisville Youth Group 502/894-9787, 800/347-8336 • bi-weekly mtgs • call for location

The Williams-Nichols Institute 502/636-0935 • 6pm-9pm • lesbigay archives • library • referrals

Accommodations

Holiday Inn Southwest 4110 Dixie Hwy (at I-264) **502/448-2020** • gay-friendly • food served • swimming • lounge

Bars

Magnolia Bar 1398 S 2nd St (at Magnolia) **502/637-9052** • noon-4am • gay-friendly • neighborhood bar • young crowd

Tryangles 209 S Preston St (at Market) **502/583-6395** • 4pm-4am • mostly gay men • live shows

Tynkers Too/ The Rage 319 E Market (at Floyd) **502/561-0752** • call for hrs & shows • lesbians/ gay men • food served • live shows • karaoke • wheelchair access • women-owned/ run

Nightclubs

The Connection Complex 120 S Floyd St (at Market) **502/585-5752** • 9pm-4am, from 6pm Fri-Sat, 7pm-1am Tue • popular • lesbians/ gay men • dancing/DJ • live shows • also restaurant • some veggie • $5-15

Sparks 104-108 W Main St (at 1st) **502/587-8566** • 10pm-4am • gay-friendly • mostly gay men Th-Fri • dancing/DJ • alternative • live shows Tue • wheelchair access

Cafes

Days Coffeehouse 1420 Bardstown Rd (at Edenside) **502/456-1170** • 8am-10pm, till 11pm wknds

Restaurants

Rudyard Kipling 422 W Oak St **502/636-1311** • lunch wkdys, dinner from 5:30pm Mon-Sat • also English pub & theater • live music

Entertainment & Recreation

Community Chorus 502/327-4099

Bookstores

Carmichael's 1295 Bardstown Rd (at Longest Ave) **502/456-6950** • 8am-10pm, till 11pm Fri-Sat, from 10am Sun

Hawley Cooke Books 3024 Bardstown Rd (in Gardiner Lane Shopping Ctr) **502/456-6660** • 9am-9pm, 10am-6pm Sun • also 27 Shelbyville Rd Plaza, 502/893-0133 • also 2400 Lime Kiln Ln, 502/425-9100

Retail Shops

MT Closets 120 S Floyd (in the Connection Complex) **502/587-1060, 800/606-4524** • 2pm-10pm Tue-Th, 6pm-midnight Fri-Sat, open later in summer • gay gifts • unique clothing

Publications

The Letter 502/772-7570 • statewide lesbigay newspaper

The Rainbow Pages 502/899-3551 • lesbigay resource guide

Louisville

Where the Girls Are: On Main or Market Streets near 1st, and generally in the north-central part of town, just west of I-65.

Entertainment: Community Chorus 502/327-4099.

Lesbigay Pride: June.

Annual Events: May - Kentucky Derby. June - Kentucky Shakespeare Festival 502/583-8738. October - Halloween Cruise on the Ohio River.

City Info: Louisville Tourist Commission 800/626-5646. Lousiville Visitor Center 800/792-5595.

Attractions: Kentucky Derby 502/584-6383. The Waterfront. Belle Of Louisville Steamboat 502/574-2355. Churchill Downs 502/636-4400. Farmington. Hadley Pottery 502/584-2171. Locust Grove. St. James Court. West Main Street Historic District.

Best View: The Spire Restaurant and Cocktail Lounge on the 19th floor of the Hyatt Regency Louisville.

Weather: Mild winters and long, hot summers!

Transit: Yellow Taxi 502/636-5511. TARC Bus System 502/585-1234. Toonerville II Trolley or Louisville Horse Trams 502/581-0100.

Louisville

Beautiful Louisville sits on the banks of the Ohio River and is home to the world-famous Kentucky Derby. This spectacular race occurs during the first week of May at Churchill Downs.

Louisville is also home to many whiskey distilleries. If neither watching horses run in circles, nor swilling homegrown booze excites you, check out the Louisville Slugger Museum (502/588-7228). Then there's the Belle of Louisville (502/574-2355), one of the last authentic sternwheelers in the country as well as the oldest operating steamboat on the Mississippi River.

Whatever you do, you're certain to enjoy this city's slower pace of life and Southern charm—Louisville is, after all, known as the 'northern border for southern hospitality.' The best way to get a feel for this Louisville is to walk among the elegant homes of St. James Court.

Before you leave, sample the whiskey and the hospitality at several of the city's lesbian and gay bars like **Tynkers** or the **Connection Complex**. And only a few hours to the east, make sure to rest a spell in the beautiful bluegrass country of Lexington, Kentucky. Then you can get up and dance at **The Bar Complex** or **Club 141**.

Spiritual Groups

B'nai Shalom **502/896-0475** • lesbigay Jewish group

Central Presbyterian Church **502/587-6935** • 11am Sun • 'More Light' congregation

Dignity 1432 Highland Ave (at Trinity Lutheran) **888/625-0005** • 7pm 2nd Sun

MCC Louisville 1432 Highland Ave **502/587-6225** • 11am Sun • wheelchair access

Somerset

Info Lines & Services

Lesbigay Info **606/678-5814** • call Linda for info

Accommodations

Hidden Mountain B&B Inn Burnside **606/561-5269** • gay/ straight • quiet location on banks of Lake Cumberland • also 4 campsites • wheelchair access • gay-owned/ run • $45-75

LOUISIANA

Statewide

INFO LINES & SERVICES

Louisiana Office of Tourism New Orleans **800/334-8626**

Alexandria

NIGHTCLUBS

Unique Bar & Lounge 1919 North MacArthur Dr **318/448-0555** • 9pm-2am, clsd Sun-Mon • popular • mostly gay men • dancing/DJ • live shows Fri • patio • wheelchair access

Baton Rouge

INFO LINES & SERVICES

AA Gay/ Lesbian 225/924-0030 (AA#) • call for mtg schedule

BARS

Baton Rouge Time Zone 668 Main St (at 7th) **225/344-9714** • 6pm-2am, clsd Sun • lesbians/ gay men • neighborhood bar

Bogart's Lounge 111 3rd St (at North Blvd) **225/387-6269** • 2pm-2am, clsd Sun • lesbians/ gay men • dancing/DJ • karaoke • wheelchair access

George's Place 860 St Louis **225/387-9798** • 3pm-2am, clsd Sun • popular • mostly gay men • neighborhood bar • wheelchair access

Hide-A-Way 7367 Exchange Pl **225/923-3632** • 8pm-2am, clsd Sun-Tue • mostly women • neighborhood bar • dancing/DJ • wheelchair access • women-owned/ run

NIGHTCLUBS

Traditions 2183 Highland Rd **225/344-9291** • 9:30pm-2am, clsd Sun-Tue • lesbians/ gay men • dancing/DJ • alternative • 18+ • wheelchair access

RESTAURANTS

Chalet Brant 7655 Old Hammond Hwy (nr Jefferson) **225/927-6040** • 5:30pm-10pm, lunch Wed-Fri only • cont'l • $15-30

Drusilla Seafood 3482 Drusilla Ln (at Jefferson Hwy) **225/923-0896** • dinner till 10pm • $15-20

Ralph & Kacoo's 6110 Bluebonnet (off I-10 & Perkins) **225/766-2113** • dinner till 10pm • Cajun • $8-20

BOOKSTORES

Hibiscus Bookstore 635 Main St (btwn 6th & 7th) **225/387-4264** • 11am-6pm, from 1pm Sun • lesbigay

SPIRITUAL GROUPS

Joie de Vivre MCC 333 E Chimes St **504/383-0450** • 11am Sun

Bossier City

INFO LINES & SERVICES

Homosexual Info Center 115 Monroe St (at Delhi) **318/742-4709** • 9am-5pm

Gretna

BARS

Cheers 1711 Hancock (at Kemper) **504/367-0149** • 11am-close • gay-friendly • neighborhood bar

Hammond

NIGHTCLUBS

Chances 42357 Veterans Ave (off I-12, exit 40) **504/542-9350** • 9pm-2am Th-Sat • lesbians/ gay men • dancing/DJ • karaoke • drag shows • wheelchair access

Houma

NIGHTCLUBS

Kixx 112 N Hollywood **504/876-9587** • 6pm-2am, clsd Sun-Mon • lesbians/ gay men • dancing/DJ • live shows • wheelchair access • unconfirmed '99

Lafayette

INFO LINES & SERVICES

AA Gay/ Lesbian 318/234-7814 (AA#) • call for mtg schedule

ACCOMMODATIONS

The Estorge House 417 N Market St (at Bloch), Opelousas **318/942-8151** • full brkfst • hot tub • smokefree • lesbian-owned • $95-125

NIGHTCLUBS

Sound Factory 209 Jefferson St (at Cypress) **318/269-6011** • 6pm-2am, noon-midnight Sun • mostly gay men • dancing/DJ • drag shows

Lake Charles

Accommodations

Aunt Ruby's 504 Pujo St (at Hodges) **318/430-0603** • gay-friendly • full brkfst • complimentary cocktails in evening • gay-owned/ run

Nightclubs

Crystal's 112 W Broad St **318/433-5457** • 8pm-2am, from 9pm Fri-Sat, till 4am Fri, clsd Sun • lesbians/ gay men • dancing/DJ • country/ western • live shows • food served • wheelchair access

Restaurants

Pujo St Café 901 Ryan St (at Pujo) **318/439-2054** • 11am-11pm

New Orleans

Info Lines & Services

AA Lambda Center 2106 Decatur St (at Frenchmen) **504/947-0548** • daily mtgs • call for schedule

Lesbian/ Gay Community Center 2114 Decatur St **504/945-1103** • hours vary • call first • wheelchair access

Accommodations

A Creole House Hotel 1013 St Ann (btwn Burgundy & Rampart) **504/524-8076, 800/535-7858** • gay/ straight • 1850s building furnished in period style • kids ok • $49-109

A Private Garden 1718 Philip St (at Jackson Ave) **504/523-1776** • lesbians/ gay men • 2 private apts • enclosed garden • hot tub • $65-85 • gay-owned/ run

▲ **Alternative Accommodations/ French Quarter Accommodation Service** 1001 Marigny St **504/949-5815, 800/209-9408**

Andrew Jackson Hotel 919 Royal St (btwn St Philip & Dumaine) **504/561-5881, 800/654-0224** • gay-friendly • historic inn

B&W Courtyards B&B 2425 Chartres St (btwn Mandeville & Spain) **504/945-9418, 800/585-5731** • gay/ straight • gay-owned/ run • $115-165

Big D's B&B 704 Franklin Ave (at Royal) **504/945-8049** • lesbians/ gay men • women-owned/ run • $65-95

Big Easy/ French Quarter Lodging 233 Cottonwood Dr, Gretna **504/433-2563, 800/368-4876** • lesbians/ gay men • reservation service • gay-owned/ run • $69-400

The Big Easy Guest House 2633 Dauphine St (at Franklin) **504/943-3717, 800/679-0640** • gay-friendly • 8 blks from French Quarter • $65

The Biscuit Palace 730 Dumaine (btwn Royal & Bourbon) **504/525-9949** • gay-friendly • B&B & apts • in the French Quarter • $85-125

Bon Maison Guest House 835 Bourbon St (btwn St Ann & Dumaine) **504/561-8498** • popular • gay-friendly • 3 studio apts • 2 suites • $75-145

Bourbon Orleans Hotel Bourbon & Orleans **504/523-2222, 800/521-5338** • popular • gay-friendly

Bourgoyne Guest House 839 Bourbon St **504/524-3621, 504/525-3983** • popular • lesbians/ gay men • 1830s Creole mansion • courtyard • $70-160

Bywater B&B 1026 Clouet St **504/944-8438** • gay-friendly • kitchen • fireplace • smokefree • kids/ pets ok • women-owned/ run • $60/shared bath • $75/private bath

Casa de Marigny Creole Guest Cottages 818 Frenchmen St (at Dauphine) **504/948-3875** • lesbians/ gay men • swimming • $125-450

The Chimes B&B Constantinople at Coliseum **504/488-4640, 800/729-4640** • gay-friendly • 5 guest suites & rms in an 1876 home • smokefree • kids/ pets ok • $83-107

Crescent City Guest House 612 Marigny (at Chartres) **504/944-8722** • gay-friendly • nudity • pets considered • $59-159

Dauzat House 337 Burgundy St (btwn Conti & Bienville) **504/524-2075** • gay-friendly • jacuzzis • fireplaces

Doubletree Hotel 300 Canal St (btwn S Peters & Tchoupitoulas) **504/581-1300** • gay-friendly • $109-215

Empress Hotel 1317 Ursulines Ave (btwn Treme & Marais) **504/529-4100, 888/524-9200** • gay-friendly • 2 blks to French Quarter • $25-50

Fourteen Twelve Thalia—A B&B 1412 Thalia (btwn Prytania & Coliseum) **504/522-0453** • gay/ straight • 1-bdrm apt in the Lower Garden District • pets ok • patio • gay-owned/ run • $75-200 (high season)

French Quarter B&B 1132 Ursulines (btwn N Rampart & St Claude Ave) **504/525-3390** • lesbians/ gay men • apt • swimming • pets ok on request • gay-owned/ run • $60-175

▲ **French Quarter Reservation Service** **504/523-1246, 800/523-9091** • IGLTA

New Orleans

If you haven't been to New Orleans for Mardi Gras, you've missed the party of the year. But there's still time to plan next year's visit to the French Quarter's blowout of a block party—complete with its elaborate balls, parades, and dancing in the streets.

Of course, there's more to 'The Big Easy' than Mardi Gras, especially if you like life hot, humid, and spiced with steamy jazz and hot pepper. Park your bags in one of the dozen lesbian/gay inns in the area. Then venture into the French Quarter, where you'll find the infamous Bourbon Street with people strolling—or occasionally staggering—from jazz club to jazz club, bar to bar, restaurants to shops, twenty-four hours a day. Kitsch-lovers won't want to miss Pat O'Brien's, home of the Hurricane and the #1 bar in the country for alcohol volume sold. Jazz lovers, make a pilgrimage to Preservation Hall.

If you love to shop, check out the French Market, the Jackson Brewery, and Riverwalk. Antique hunting is best on Rue Royal or Decatur Street. And you can't leave New Orleans without a trip through the Garden District to see the incredible antebellum and revival homes—a trip best made on the St. Charles Trolley.

Gourmands must try real Cajun & Creole food in its natural environment—though if you're vegetarian, the **Old Dog New Trick Cafe** is your best bet. For melt-in-your-mouth, hot, sugar-powdered beignets, run, don't walk to Café du Monde (504/525-4544).

For the morbidly inclined among us, you're bound to see shadows of vampires and other creatures of the night in this town of mysticism and the occult. With residents like Anne Rice, Poppy Z. Brite, and (the late) Marie LaVeau stirring up the spirits, perhaps a protective amulet from Marie LaVeau's House of Voodoo (504/581-3751; 739 Bourbon St.) would be a good idea. For a peek at traditional voodoo—the Afro-Caribbean religion, not the B-movie shlock—visit the Voodoo Museum (504/523-7685). Or sate that urge for blood with a body piercing at **Rings of Desire** or some fresh fetish wear from **Second Skin Leather.**

So, pick a realm of the senses and go wild. You'll be happy to know that the women-loving-women of New Orleans know how to do wild very well. Try **The Mint** for drinks and tall tales, or get crazy with the boys (try **Rubyfruit Jungle**) in the French Quarter—this Gay Central in New Orleans is also party central for everyone. And during **Southern Decadence,** the gay Mardi Gras on Labor Day weekend, the Quarter becomes a little queerer.

To find out the current women's nights at the guys' bars, stop by the lesbigay **Faubourg Marigny Bookstore** or **Alternatives** and pick up a copy of the Crescent City's lesbigay newspapers, **Impact** and **Ambush**. Or drop by the **Lesbian/Gay Community Center** on Decatur.

New Orleans

Where the Girls Are: Wandering the Quarter, or in the small artsy area known as Mid-City, north of the Quarter up Esplanade St.

Lesbigay Pride: September. 504/949-9555.

Annual Events: February - Mardi Gras 504/566-5011. North America's rowdiest block party.
April - Gulf Coast Womyn's Festival at Camp SisterSpirit (in Ovett, MS) 601/344-1411.
Labor Day - Southern Decadence 504/529-2860. Gay mini-Mardi Gras.

City Info: 504/566-5011, web: www.neworleanscvb.com. Louisiana Office of Tourism 800/334-8626.

Attractions: Bourbon St. in the French Quarter.
Cafe du Monde for beignets 504/581-2914.
Garden District.
Moon Walk.
Pat O'Brien's for a hurricane 504/525-4823.
Preservation Hall 504/522-2841.
Top of the Market.

Best View: Top of the Mart Lounge (504/522-9795) on the 33rd floor of the World Trade Center of New Orleans.

Weather: Summer temperatures hover in the 90°s with subtropical humidity. Winters can be rainy and chilly. The average temperature in February (Mardi Gras month) is 58° while the average precipitation is 5.23".

Transit: United Cab 504/522-9771.
Airport Shuttle 504/522-3500.
Regional Transit Authority 504/242-2600.

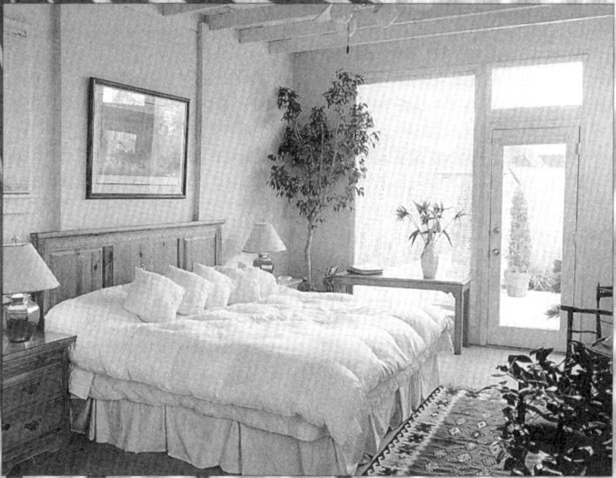

Go for a splash in our refreshing heated pool. Enjoy beautiful cottages and rooms with color cable TV, phone, private baths and continental breakfast. Great romantic getaway.

MACARTY
PARK
GUEST HOUSE

3820 Burgundy Street • New Orleans, LA 70117
(504) 943-4994 • (800) 521-2790
faxmehard@aol.com • www.macartypark.com

French Quarter Suites 1119 N Rampart (at Ursulines) **504/524–7725, 800/457–2253** • gay-friendly • apt & suites • hot tub • swimming • kitchens

The Frenchmen Hotel 417 Frenchmen St (where Esplanade, Decatur & Frenchmen intersect) **504/948–2166, 800/831–1781** • popular • gay/ straight • 1860s Creole townhouses • spa • swimming • kids ok • wheelchair access • $59-180

Glimmer House 1631 7th St (at St Charles) **504/897–1895** • gay-friendly • 1891 Victorian • women-owned/ run • $55-85

The Green House Inn 1212 Magazine St (at Erato) **504/525–1333, 800/966–1303** • lesbians/ gay men • 1840s home • hot tub • swimming • non-smoking rms available • IGLTA • gay-owned/ run • $68-128

Hotel de la Monnaie 405 Esplanade Ave (btwn Decatur & N Peters) **504/947–0009** • gay-friendly • all-suite hotel • wheelchair accesss • $140-190

House of David 735 Touro St (at Dauphine) **504/948–3438** • newly remodeled • jacuzzi • private courtyard • $79-99

Ingram House 1012 Elysian Fields Ave (btwn N Rampart & St Claude) **504/949–3110** • gay/ straight • gay-owned/ run

Inn The Quarter 888/523–5235 • gay-friendly • townhouse • private courtyard

La Dauphine, Residence des Artistes 2316 Dauphine St (btwn Elysian Fields & Marigny) **504/948–2217** • gay/ straight • smokefree • free airport pickup (call for details) • IGLTA • gay-owned/ run • $65-125

La Maison Marigny B&B on Bourbon 1421 Bourbon St **504/948–3638** • gay-friendly • on the quiet end of Bourbon St • gay-owned

La Residence Esplanade & Marais Sts **504/832–4131, 800/826–9718 x11** • lesbians/ gay men • 1- & 2-bdrm apts • kitchens • $75-175

Lafitte Guest House 1003 Bourbon St (at St Philip) **504/581–2678, 800/331–7971** • popular • gay/ straight • elegant French manor house • smokefree • kids ok • full bar • gay-owned/ run • $89-189

Lamothe House Hotel 621 Esplanade Ave (btwn Royal & Chartres) **504/947–1161, 800/367–5858** • gay-friendly • fine hotel • $60-250

Lanata House 1220 Chartres St, #5 (Governor Nicholls) **504/522–0374** • gay/ straight • furnished residential accomodations • gay-owned/ run • $130-300 (high season)

▲ **Macarty Park Guesthouse** 3820 Burgundy St (at Alvar) **504/943–4994, 800/521–2790** • lesbians/ gay men • swimming • hot tub • rooms & cottages • IGLTA • gay-owned/ run • $45-115

Maison Burgundy 1860 Burgundy St (on corner of Pauger, btwn Pauger & Burgundy) **504/948–2355, 800/863–8813** • gay-friendly • full brkfst • swimming • private entrances • off-street parking

Maison Dauphine 2460 Dauphine St (btwn Spain & St Roch) **504/943–0861** • mostly gay men • near French Quarter • gay-owned/ run • $69-125

Marigny Guest House 621 Esplanade (btwn Royal & Chartres) **504/944–9700, 800/367–5858** • gay-friendly • quaint Creole cottage • $60-175

Mazant Guest House 906 Mazant (at Burgundy) **504/944–2662** • gay-friendly

The McKendrick-Breaux House 1474 Magazine St (at Euterpe) **504/586–1700, 888/570–1700** • gay-friendly • 1860s restored Greek Revival • hot tub • $110-175

Mentone B&B 1437 Pauger St (at Kerlerec) **504/943–3019** • gay-friendly • suite in Victorian in the Faubourg Marigny district • smokefree • women-owned/ run • $100-150

New Orleans Guest House 1118 Ursulines Ave (at N Rampart) **504/566–1177, 800/562–1177** • gay-friendly • Creole cottage dated back to 1848 • courtyard • parking • $79-99

Olde Towne Inn 1001 Marigny St **504/949–5815, 800/209–9408** • gay/ straight • historic guesthouse • tropical courtyard • walk-ins welcome • $40-129

Parkview Marigny B&B 726 Frenchmen St (at Dauphine) **504/945–7875, 877/645–8617** • gay/ straight • Creole townhouse • smokefree • gay-owned/ run • $90-150

Pauger Guest Suites 1750 N Rampart St (at Pauger) **504/944–2601, 800/484–8334 x9834** • mostly gay men • near French Quarter • kids ok • gay-owned/ run • $50 & up

Radisson Hotel New Orleans 1500 Canal St (at LaSalle St) **504/522–4500** • gay-friendly

Reid House 3313 Prytania St (at Louisiana) **504/269–0692** • gay/ straight • Greek Revival mansion in uptown New Orleans • gay-owned/ run • $125-250

Rober House Condos 822 Ursulines Ave (at Dauphine) **504/527–5978** • gay/ straight • apt • swimming • non-smoking rm available • kids/ pets ok • courtyard • IGLTA • gay-owned/ run • $89-150

Royal Barracks Guest House 717 Barracks St (at Bourbon) **504/529-7269** • gay-friendly • hot tub • private patios • IGLTA • $85-270

Royal St Courtyard 2446 Royal St (at Spain) **504/943-6818, 888/846-4004** • lesbians/ gay men • suites • hot tub • kitchens • pets ok • gay-owned/ run • $55-85

Rue Royal Inn 1006 Royal St (at St Philip) **504/524-3900, 800/776-3901** • gay/ straight • historic 1830s Creole townhouse in the heart of the French Quarter • wheelchair access • IGLTA • gay-owned/ run • $85-165

Ruffino's Guest House 631 St Philip (at Chartres & Royal) **504/588-1483, 800/809-7815** • gay-friendly • small guest house in the French Quarter • kids ok • pets ok on request • $85-135

St Charles Guest House 1748 Prytania St (at Felicity) **504/523-6556** • gay-friendly • pensione-style guest house • swimming • patio • $35-85 (higher for special events)

St Peter Guest House 1005 St Peter St (at Burgundy) **504/524-9232, 800/535-7815** • gay-friendly • historic location • $60-250

Sun Oak Museum & Guesthouse 2020 Burgundy St **504/945-0322** • gay/ straight • Greek Revival Creole cottage circa 1836 • gardens • gay-owned • $75-150

Sweet Olive B&B 2460 N Rampart (at Spain) **504/947-4332, 877/470-5323** • gay-friendly • $99-125

Ursuline Guest House 708 Ursulines Ave (btwn Royal & Bourbon) **504/525-8509, 800/654-2351** • popular • gay/ straight • hot tub • evening socials • gay-owned/ run • $85-125

Vieux Carré Rentals 841 Bourbon St **504/525-3983** • gay-friendly • 1- & 2-bdrm apts • $95 & up

Bars

Angles 2301 N Causeway (at 34th), Metairie **504/834-7979** • 4pm-4am • lesbians/ gay men • neighborhood bar • dancing/DJ • karaoke Th • wheelchair access

Big Daddy's 2513 Royal (at Franklin) **504/948-6288** • 24hrs • lesbians/ gay men • neighborhood bar • wheelchair access

Cafe Lafitte in Exile/ The Corral 901 Bourbon St (at Dumaine) **504/522-8397** • 24hrs • popular • mostly gay men • videos

Country Club 634 Louisa St (at Chartres) **504/945-0742** • 10am-6pm • lesbians/ gay men • neighborhood bar • live shows • swimming

Double D's Half Moon Saloon 706 Franklin Ave (at Royal) **504/948-2300** • 24hrs • mostly gay men • neighborhood bar • dancing/DJ • wheelchair access

The Double Play 439 Dauphine (at St Louis) **504/523-4517** • 24hrs • mostly gay men • neighborhood bar

Footloose 700 N Rampart (at St Peter) **504/524-7654** • 24hrs • lesbians/ gay men • transgender-friendly • cabaret • shows on wknds

The Four Seasons 3229 N Causeway (at 18th), Metairie **504/832-0659** • 3pm-4am • lesbians/ gay men • neighborhood bar • live music • also the 'Outback Bar'

The Friendly Bar 2301 Chartres St (at Marigny) **504/943-8929** • 11am-3am • lesbians/ gay men • neighborhood bar • wheelchair access • women-owned/ run

Golden Lantern 1239 Royal St (at Barracks) **504/529-2860** • 24hrs • mostly gay men • neighborhood bar

Good Friends Bar 740 Dauphine (at St Ann) **504/566-7191** • 24hrs • mostly gay men • neighborhood bar • professional • wheelchair access • also 'Queens Head Pub' Th-Sun • piano singalong

The Mint 940 Elysian Fields Ave (at N Rampart) **504/944-4888** • 2pm-close • lesbians/ gay men • neighborhood bar • dancing/DJ • entertainment • live shows

Rawhide 2010 740 Burgundy (corner of Burgundy & St Ann) **504/525-8106** • 24hrs • popular • mostly gay men • neighborhood bar • alternative • leather/ fetish

Nightclubs

Onyx 2000 2441 Bayou Rd (at Esplanade Ave) **504/949-9939** • 9pm-close Th-Sun • lesbians/ gay men • women's night Th • dancing/DJ • mostly African-American • talent night Sun • live shows

Oz 800 Bourbon St (at St Ann) **504/593-9491** • 24hrs • lesbians/ gay men • dancing/DJ • wheelchair access

Rubyfruit Jungle 640 Frenchmen (at Royal) **504/947-4000** • 4pm-close, from 1pm wknds • popular • lesbians/ gay men • dancing/DJ • country/ western Tue & Fri • dance lessons 8pm • wheelchair access

Cafes

PJ's 634 Frenchmen St **504/949-2292** • 7am-11pm, till midnight Fri-Sat

Red Bike Bakery & Cafe 746 Tchoupitoulas (off Julia) **504/529-2453** • lunch & dinner

Restaurants

Cafe Sbisa 1011 Decatur **504/522-5565** • dinner & Sun brunch • French Creole • patio

Clover Grill 900 Bourbon St (at Dumaine) **504/523-0904** • 24hrs • popular • diner fare • $5-10

Commander's Palace 1403 Washington Ave (in Garden District) **504/899-8221** • lunch & dinner • upscale Creole • $30-50

Feelings Cafe 2600 Chartres St (at Franklin Ave) **504/945-2222** • dinner nightly, Fri lunch, Sun brunch • Creole • piano bar wknds • courtyard • $10-20

Fiorella's Cafe 45 French Market Pl (at Governor Nicholas & Ursulines) **504/528-9566** • 5am-5pm, clsd Sun • homecooking

La Peniche 1940 Dauphine St (at Touro St) **504/943-1460** • 24hrs • diner • some veggie • $5-20

Lucky Cheng's 720 St Louis (btwn Bourbon & Royal) **504/529-2045** • lunch & dinner, Sun brunch • Asian Creole • drag-queen waitresses • cabaret

Mama Rosa 616 N Rampart (at Toulouse & St Louis) **504/523-5546** • 11am-9pm • Italian • $6-11

Mona Lisa 1212 Royal St (at Barracks) **504/522-6746** • 11am-10:30pm • Italian • some veggie • beer/ wine • $10-15

Nola 534 St Louis St (btwn Chartres & Decatur) **504/522-6652** • lunch (except Sun) & dinner • Creole • wheelchair access

Old Dog New Trick Cafe 307 Exchange Alley (btwn Royal & Chartres off Conti) **504/522-4569** • 11:30am-9pm • vegetarian • wheelchair access • $5-10

Olivier's 911 Decatur St (at Iberville & Bienville) **504/525-7734** • lunch & dinner • Creole • wheelchair access • $10-15

Petunia's 817 St Louis (at Bourbon) **504/522-6440** • 8am-11pm • popular • Cajun/ Creole • crepes • full bar • $10-20

Pontchartrain Cafe 2031 St Charles Ave (in 'Grand Heritage Hotel') **504/524-0581** • 5:30pm-9pm • $8-15

Poppy's Grill 717 St Peter (at Royal & Bourbon) **504/524-3287** • 24hrs • diner • wheelchair access

Praline Connection 542 Frenchmen St (at Chartres) **504/943-3934** • till 10pm • soul food

Quarter Scene 900 Dumaine St (at Dauphine) **504/522-6533** • 8am-midnight, clsd Tue • homecooking • some veggie • $4-15

Sammy's Seafood 627 Bourbon St (across from Pat O' Brien's) **504/525-8442** • 11am-midnight • Creole/ Cajun • $9-28

Sebastian's 538 St Philip St (at Decatur) **504/524-2041** • 5:30pm-10pm, Sun brunch • Creole plus

Vaqueros 4938 Prytania (at Robert) **504/891-6441** • Southwestern-Mexican • good margaritas • $9-17

Vera Cruz 7537 Maple (at Hillary) **504/866-1736** • 5pm-11pm, clsd Sun • Mexican

Whole Foods Market 3135 Esplanade Ave **504/943-1626** • 8:30am-9:30pm • healthy deli • plenty veggie • $5-10

Entertainment & Recreation

Café du Monde 800 Decatur St (Old Jackson Square) **504/525-4544, 800/772-2927** • till you've a had a beignet—fried dough, powdered w/ sugar, that melts in your mouth—you haven't been to New Orleans & this is 'the' place to have them 24hrs a day

Gay Heritage Tour 907 Bourbon St **504/945-6789** • call for details • departs from 'Alternatives' bookstore

Haunted History Tour **888/644-6787** • guided 2-1/2 hr tours of New Orleans' most famous haunts, including Anne Rice's home

Pat O'Brien's 718 St Peter St (btwn Bourbon & Royal) **504/561-1200** • more than just a bar—come for the Hurricane, stay for the kitsch

St Charles Streetcar Canal St (btwn Bourbon & Royal Sts) **504/248-3900 (RTA #)** • it's not named Desire, but you should still ride it if you want to see the Garden District, Blanche

Bookstores

Alternatives 907 Bourbon St (at Dumaine) **504/524-5222** • 11am-7pm, till 9pm Fri-Sat, clsd Tue • lesbigay

Bookstar 414 N Peters (in Jax Brewery Complex) **504/523-6411** • 9am-midnight • wheelchair access

Faubourg Marigny Bookstore 600 Frenchmen St (at Chartres) **504/943-9875** • 10am-8pm, till 6pm wknds • lesbigay

Sidney's News Stand 917 Decatur St (btwn St Philip & Dumaine) **504/524-6872** • 8am-9pm, till 10pm Sat • some lesbigay titles

Retail Shops

Gay Mart 808 N Rampart St (btwn St Ann & Dumaine) **504/523-6005** • noon-7pm • gifts • T-shirts

Hit Parade 741 Bourbon St **504/524-7700** • 11am-midnight, till 2am Fri-Sat • popular • lesbigay books • designer circuit clothing & more

Out of Focus 1119-A St Mary (off Magazine) **504/586-1888** • 11am-6pm, clsd Sun-Tue, also by appt • art gallery

Postmark New Orleans 631 Toulouse St (btwn Chartres & Royal) **504/529-2052, 800/285-4247** • 10am-6pm, from noon Sun • gay gifts • furniture • art • postcards

Rings of Desire 1128 Decatur St, 2nd flr **504/524-6147** • piercing studio

Second Skin Leather 521 St Philip St (btwn Decatur & Chartres) **504/561-8167** • noon-10pm, till 6pm Sun

Something Different 5300 Tchoupitoulas (in Riverside Market) **504/891-9056** • 10am-9pm, till 7pm Sat, noon-6pm Sun • gay-owned/ run

Publications

Ambush 504/522-8049 • lesbigay newspaper

Impact 504/944-6722, 888/944-6722 (out-of-state) • lesbigay newspaper

Spiritual Groups

Vieux Carre MCC 1128 St Roch **504/945-5390** • 11am Sun

Erotica

Gargoyles 1205 Decatur St (at Gov Nicholls) **504/529-4387** • leather/ fetish store

Panda Bear 415 Bourbon St (at St Louis) **504/529-3593** • leather • toys • wheelchair access

Paradise 41 W 24th St (at Crestview), Kenner **504/461-0000** • wheelchair access

Shreveport

Bars

Korner Lounge 800 Louisiana (nr Cotton) **318/222-9796** • 5pm-close, sometimes clsd Sun • mostly gay men • neighborhood bar

Some Place Else 235 Wall St (btwn Stoner & Vine) **318/227-7615** • lesbians/ gay men • neighborhood bar • dancing/DJ • country/ western • karaoke • live shows • wheelchair access

Nightclubs

Central Station 1025 Marshall (btwn Fairfield & Creswell) **318/222-2216** • 3pm-6am • popular • lesbians/ gay men • dancing/DJ • country/ western • transgender-friendly • wheelchair access

Erotica

Fun Shop 1601 Marshall (at Creswell) **318/226-1308**

Slidell

Bars

Billy's 2600 Hwy 190 W **504/847-1921** • 6pm-2am, clsd Mon • lesbians/ gay men • neighborhood bar • karaoke • live shows

Maine

Statewide

Info Lines & Services

Maine Tourism Line Portland **800/533-9595** • vacation info

Augusta

Accommodations

Maple Hill Farm B&B Inn 207/622-2708, 800/622-2708 • gay/ straight • Victorian farmhouse on 130 acres • wheelchair access • gay-owned/ run • $55-145

Nightclubs

PJ's 80 Water St (btwn Laurel & Bridge) **207/623-4041** • 7pm-1am Wed-Sat • popular • lesbians/ gay men • dancing/DJ • piano bar • patio

Bangor

Accommodations

Maine Wilderness Lake Island Orono **207/990-5839** • lesbians/ gay men • clsd Sept-June • weekly rental cabins in the forest

Nightclubs

The Spectrum 190 Harlow St (next to Federal Bldg) **207/942-3000** • 8pm-1:30am, from 8pm Th-Sat, clsd Mon-Tue • lesbians/ gay men • dancing/DJ • karaoke Th

Bookstores

Pro Libris Bookshop 10 3rd St (at Union) **207/942-3019** • 10am-6pm, noon-4pm Sun • new & used

Retail Shops

Different Drum, Ltd 80 Columbia St **207/942-1716** • 10am-8pm, till 10pm Fri-Sat, noon-8pm Sun • pride gifts • novelties • local Native American crafts • gay-owned/ run

Bar Harbor

Accommodations

Devilstone Oceanfront Inn 207/288-2933, 760/321-1366 • located on the 'Bar Harbor Shorepath' • gay/ straight • seasonal • IGLTA • $125-345

Manor House Inn 106 West St (nr Bridge St) **207/288-3759** • open May-Nov • gay-friendly • full brkfst

Mountain View Southwest Harbor, Mt Desert Island **207/885-5026** • weekly home rental • seasonal • no pets

Bath

Accommodations

The Galen C Moses House 1009 Washington St **207/442-8771, 888/442-8771** • gay/ straight • 1874 Victorian • full brkfst • smokefree • gay-owned/ run • $79-119

Belfast

Accommodations

The Alden House 63 Church St **207/338-2151** • gay/ straight • full brkfst • lesbian-owned/ run • $75-110

Brunswick

Info Lines & Services

Bowdoin College Women's Resource Center 207/725-3620 • 7pm-11pm Sun-Th Sept-May

Bookstores

Gulf of Maine Books 134 Maine St (at Pleasant) **207/729-5083** • 9:30am-5:30pm, clsd Sun • alternative

Camden

Accommodations

The Old Massachusetts Homestead Campground Lincolnville Beach **207/789-5135, 800/213-8142** • open May-Nov • gay-friendly • cabins • tentsites • RV hookups • swimming • ocean view • nature trails • kids/ pets ok • $18-23

Caribou

Info Lines & Services

Gay/ Lesbian Phoneline 398 S Main St **207/498-2088, 800/468-2088 (ME only)** • 7pm-9pm Mon, Wed, Fri • social & networking group for northern ME & NW New Brunswick, Canada

Corea

Accommodations

The Black Duck Inn on Corea Harbor Crowley Island Rd (Rte 195), Corea Harbor **207/963-2689** • gay/ straight • restored farmhouse • also cottages • full brkfst • gay-owned/ run • $75-145

Restaurants

Fisherman's Inn 207/963-5585 • seasonal, 4:30pm-9pm, clsd Mon

Deer Isle

Restaurants

Fisherman's Friend School St, Stonington **207/367-2442** • open April-Oct, 11am-8pm

Dexter

Accommodations

Brewster Inn 37 Zions Hill **207/924-3130** • gay-friendly • historic mansion • $59-89

Freeport

Accommodations

The Bagley House 1290 Royalsborough Rd, Durham **207/865-6566, 800/765-1772** • gay/ straight • full brkfst • smokefree • kids ok • conference rm for 20 • lesbian-owned/ run • $65-135

Country at Heart B&B 37 Bow St **207/865-0512** • gay-friendly • full brkfst • located in Maine's outlet shopping mecca • $65-150

Restaurants

Harraseeket Lunch & Lobster Co 207/865-3535 • open May-Oct

Hancock

Restaurants

Le Domaine Restaurant & Inn 207/422-3395 • open June-Oct • 6pm-9pm, clsd Tue

Kennebunkport

Accommodations

Arundel Meadows Inn 1024 Portland Rd (at Walker Ln), Arundel **207/985-3770** • gay-friendly • full brkfst • $65-125

The Colony Hotel Ocean Ave & Kings Hwy **207/967-3331, 800/552-2363** • gay-friendly • 1914 grand oceanfront property • private beach • seasonal • wheelchair access • $140-299

White Barn Inn 37 Beach St **207/967-2321** • gay-friendly • $190-450 • dinner served

Restaurants

Bartley's Dockside by the bridge **207/967-5050** • lunch & dinner May-Dec, lunch only Jan-April • 11am-10pm • seafood • some veggie • full bar • wheelchair access

Retail Shops

All About Me 8 Spring St #3 **207/967-1001** • gallery & gift shop

Kittery

see also Portsmouth, New Hampshire

Restaurants

Chauncey Creek Lobster Pier Chauncey Creek Rd (off 103), Kittery Point **207/439-1030** • open May-Oct, 11am-8pm • BYOB

Lewiston

Info Lines & Services

Bates LGBT Alliance Hirasawa Lounge, Chase Hall, Bates College **207/786-6255** • 8:30pm Sun

Bars

The Sportsman's Club 2 Bates St (at Main) **207/784-2251** • 8pm-1am • popular • lesbians/ gay men • neighborhood bar • dancing/DJ • 'oldest gay bah in Maine'

Erotica

Paris Book Store 297 Lisbon St (at Chestnut) **207/783-6677** • 9am-9pm, noon-5pm Sun

Mt Desert Island

Accommodations

Duck Cove Retreat W Tremont **207/244-9079, 617/864-2372** • women only • swimming • seasonal • $25

Ogunquit

Accommodations

Admiral's Inn 70 S Main St (at Agamenticus) **207/646-7093** • lesbians/ gay men • swimming • $45-125

Beauport Inn & Suites 102 Shore Rd **207/646-8680, 800/646-8681** • gay/ straight • wheelchair access • $65-100

The Clipper Ship B&B 207/646-9735, 407/951-1977 • gay-friendly • smokefree • open May-Oct • $55-85 • also apts • $100-135

The Gazebo B&B Rte 1 (nr Capt Thomas Rd) **207/646-3733** • gay-friendly • 165-yr-old Greek Revival farmhouse • full brkfst • swimming • $95-105

▲ **The Heritage of Ogunquit** PO Box 1295, 03907 **207/646-7787** • mostly lesbian • hot tub • smokefree • lesbian-owned/ run • IGLTA • $55-110

The Inn at Tall Chimneys 94 Main St **207/646-8974** • lesbians/ gay men • open April-Nov • gay-owned/ run • $35-95

The Inn at Two Village Square 135 Main St **207/646-5779, 941/643-4874** • mostly gay men • oceanside Victorian • open May-Oct • smokefree • gay-owned/ run • $50-135

Leisure Inn 6 School St **207/646-2737** • gay/ straight • B&B & apts • seasonal • gay-owned/ run • $60-95

Moon Over Maine B&B Berwick Rd **207/646-6666, 800/851-6837** • gay/ straight • hot tub • gay-owned/ run • $49-105

Ogunquit Beach Inn 8 School St **207/646-1112, 888/976-2463** • lesbians/ gay men • cottage suites • some shared baths • gay-owned/ run • $59-110

The Ogunquit House 3 Glen Ave **207/646-2967** • clsd Jan-Feb • popular • lesbians/ gay men • Victorian B&B • also cottages • gay-owned/ run • $45-145

Ogunquit Weekly Rentals 207/646-0482 • cottage, apt & house rentals

Old Village Inn 30 Main St **207/646-7088** • gay-friendly • clsd Jan • $65-85 • dinner served

Rockmere Lodge B&B 40 Stearns Rd **207/646-2985** • gay/ straight • $100-175

The Seasons Hotel 207/646-6041, 800/639-8508 • gay-friendly • condo suites w/ kitchenettes • seasonal • $129-149

Shore House 7 Shore Rd **207/646-0627** • gay/ straight • seasonal guesthouse • also cottages w/ kitchenettes • gay-owned/ run • $80-120

Bars

Maxwell's Pub 27 Main St (at Berwick Rd) **207/646-2345** • noon-1am (seasonal) • gay-friendly • food served • patio

Nightclubs

The Club 13 Main St **207/646-6655** • seasonal, open Th-Sun • popular • mostly gay men • dancing/DJ • food served • videos

Cafes

Cafe Amoré 37 Shore Rd **207/646-6661** • open April-Sept, from 7:30am daily • wheelchair access

Restaurants

Arrows Berrick Rd (18 miles west of Center) **207/361-1100** • open April-Sept, 6pm-9pm, clsd Mon • popular • cont'l • some veggie • $20-27

The Cape Neddick Inn Bourne Ln **207/363-2899** • 5:30pm-9pm • also a brewery

Clay Hill Farm Agamenticus Rd (2 miles west of Rte 1) **207/646-2272** • clsd Mon-Wed • seafood • some veggie • also piano bar • $13-24

Grey Gull Inn 475 Webhannet Dr, Wells **207/646-7501** • dinner • New England fine dining • $13-22 • also oceanview rooms • $79-99

Johnathan's 2 Bourne Ln **207/646-4777** • 5pm-9pm • veggie/ seafood • full bar • wheelchair access • $13-25

Poor Richard's Tavern Perkins Cove (at Shore Rd & Pine Hill) **207/646-4722** • 5:30pm-9:30pm, clsd Sun • Sun brunch off-season • New England fare • some veggie • full bar • $11-22

Pembroke

Accommodations

Yellow Birch Farm **207/726-5807** • gay-friendly • B&B on working farm • daily & weekly rates • also cottage • kids ok • lesbian-owned/ run • $65 night/$300-400 wk

Portland

Info Lines & Services

Alliance for Sexual Diversity **207/874-6596**

Gays in Sobriety 32 Thomas St (at United Church of Christ) **207/774-4060** • 6:30pm Sun & 8pm Th

Outright 1 Pleasant St, 4th flr **207/828-6560, 888/567-7600** • 6pm Tue, Wed & 7:30pm Fri • youth organization

Accommodations

Andrews Lodging B&B 417 Auburn St **207/797–9157** • gay-friendly • full brkfst • kitchens • smokefree • pets ok • patio • $79-200

The Danforth 163 Danforth St **207/879–8755, 800/991–6557** • gay-friendly • 1821 mansion • conference/reception facilities • smokefree • kids/ pets ok • woman-owned • $125-225

▲ **The Inn at St John** 939 Congress St **207/773–6481, 800/636–9127** • gay/ straight • unique historic inn • gay-owned/ run • $35-145

The Inn By The Sea 40 Bowery Beach Rd, Cape Elizabeth **207/799–3134** • gay-friendly • condo-style suites w/ ocean views • women-owned • $129-449

The Parkside Parrot Inn 273 State St **207/775–0224** • gay/ straight • B&B • conveniently located in downtown Portland • hot tub • some shared baths • lesbian-owned/ run • $55-85

The Pomegranate Inn 49 Neal St **800/356–0408** • gay-friendly • upscale B&B • $95-175

Sea View Motel 65 W Grand Ave (at Atlantic Ave), Old Orchard Beach **207/934–4180, 800/541–8439** • gay-friendly • rooms & suites • on the beach • $70-170

West End Inn 146 Pine St **207/772–1377, 800/338–1377** • 1870 townhouse • $99-189

Bars

The Blackstones 6 Pine St (off Longfellow Sq) **207/775–2885** • 4pm-1am, from 3pm Sun • mostly gay men • neighborhood bar

Sisters 45 Danforth St (at Maple) **207/774–1505** • 5pm-1am, noon-8pm Sun, clsd Mon-Tue • mostly women • live shows

Somewhere 117 Spring St (at High) **207/871–9169** • 4pm-1am • lesbians/ gay men • neighborhood bar • piano bar

Nightclubs

The Underground 3 Spring St **207/773–3315** • 4pm-1am, from 8pm Mon-Tue • popular • lesbians/ gay men • dancing/DJ • live shows

Zootz 31 Forest Ave **207/773–8187** • 9pm-1am, till 3am Fri-Sat, clsd Tue • gay-friendly • dancing/DJ • alternative music • live shows • cover after 11pm wknds

Restaurants

Blue Mango Cafe 129 Spring St **207/772-1374** • 11:30am-10pm, 9am-2pm & 5pm-10pm wknds, clsd Mon • Maine coastal menu w/ Asian/Caribbean influences • full bar • wheelchair access • $7-15

Cafe UFFA 190 State St **207/775-3380** • 7am-11am & 5:30pm-10pm Wed-Fri, 9am-noon Sat, till 2pm Sun

Katahdin 106 High St (at Spring) **207/774-1740** • 5pm-10pm, clsd Sun-Mon • American menu • full bar

Street & Co 33 Wharf St (btwn Dana & Union) **207/775-0887** • 5:30pm-9:30pm, till 10pm Fri-Sat • seafood • Nancy's favorite • $12-18

Walter's Cafe 15 Exchange St **207/871-9258** • 11am-3pm & 5pm-9pm, dinner only Sun • some veggie • $11-16

Bookstores

Drop Me A Line 611 Congress St (at High) **207/773-5547** • 10am-6pm, till 8pm Fri, till 4pm Sun

Retail Shops

Communiques 3 Moulton St (at Commercial) **207/773-5181** • 9am-7pm, till 9pm summers • cards • gifts • clothing

Condom Sense 424 Fore St (at Union) **207/871-0356** • hours vary

Publications

▲ **Community Pride Reporter** **207/737-3498** • lesbigay newspaper

Spiritual Groups

Am Chofshi **207/833-6004** • lesbigay Jews

Congregation Bet Ha'am 81 Westbrook St, South Portland **207/879-0028** • 7:30pm Fri • gay-friendly synagogue

Dignity Maine 143 State St (at St Luke's, side chapel) **207/646-2820** • 6pm Sun

Feminist Spiritual Community **207/797-9217** • 7pm Mon • call for info

Erotica

Video Expo 666 Congress St (at State) **207/774-1377** • 9am-11pm, till midnight Th-Sat

Richmond

Entertainment & Recreation

Province Mountain Outfitters 13 Church St **207/737-4695** • April-Sept • women-owned/ run • fishing & ice-fishing & sightseeing day charters, biking & camping trips • mention 'Damron' for 10% discount

Rockport

Accommodations

The Old Granite Inn 546 Main St, Rockland **207/594-9036, 800/386-9036** • gay-friendly • wheelchair access • $75-130

White Cedar Accommodations 378 Commercial St **207/236-9069** • lesbians/ gay men • weekly apt rental • seasonal • lesbian-owned/ run • $300/wk

Restaurants

Chez Michel Rte 1, Lincolnville Beach **207/789-5600** • dinner, Sun brunch, clsd Mon • full bar

Lobster Pound Rte 1, Lincolnville Beach **207/789-5550** • 11:30am-8pm April-Sept • full bar

Sebago Lake

Accommodations

▲ **Lambs Mill Inn 207/693-6253** • mostly women • 1890s farmhouse on 20 acres • full brkfst • hot tub • IGLTA • lesbian-owned/ run • $75-105

Maine-ly For You 207/583-6980 (summer), 207/782-2275 (winter) • gay-friendly • cottages • $50+ • campsites • $10-25 • women's camping area

Restaurants

The Olde House Rte 85 off 302, Raymond **207/655-7841** • clsd Mon-Tue • cont'l

Sydney's Rte 302, Naples **207/693-3333** • open April-Jan • 4pm-9pm, till 10pm Sat • full bar

Tenants Harbor

Accommodations

Blueberry Cove Camp Harts Neck Road **207/372-6353, 617/876-2897** • gay-friendly • cabins • private camp sites • near Penobscot Bay

Eastwind Inn 207/372-6366 • clsd Dec-April • gay-friendly • rooms & apts • full brkfst • $90-275 • also restaurant • old fashioned New England fare • $14-18

Waterville

Erotica

Priscilla's Book Store 18 Water St **207/873-2774** • 10am-9pm, till 10pm Fri-Sat, clsd Sun

White Mtns

Accommodations

Speckled Mountain Ranch 207/836-2908 • gay/ straight • on a horse farm • full brkfst • kids ok • lesbian-owned/ run • $55-65

York Harbor

Accommodations

Canterbury House Box 881, 432 York St **207/363-3505, 888/385-3505** • gay-friendly • spacious Victorian home • gay-owned/ run • $70-120

Restaurants

York Harbor Inn Rte 1A **207/363-5119** • lunch Mon-Fri, dinner nightly • also the 'Cellar Pub' • also lodging

Maryland

Statewide

Info Lines & Services

Maryland Office of Tourism Baltimore **800/543-1036**

Accommodations

Bed & Breakfast of Maryland Annapolis **202/518-6066** • gay-friendly • accommodations service

Annapolis

Info Lines & Services

AA Gay/ Lesbian 199 Duke of Gloucester St (at St Anne's Parish) **410/268-5441** • 8pm Tue

Baltimore

Where the Girls Are: The women's bars are in southeast Baltimore, near the intersection of Haven and Lombard. Of course, the boy's playground, downtown around Chase St. and Park Ave., is also a popular hangout.

Lesbigay Pride: June. 410/837-5445 (GLCC).

City Info: Baltimore Tourism Office 410/659-7300 or 800/543-1036.

Attractions: Baltimore Museum of Art 410/396-7100.
Fort McHenry 410/962-4299.
Harborplace.
National Aquarium 410/576-3800.
Poe House & Museum 410/396-7932.

Best View: Top of the World Trade Center at the Inner Harbor.

Weather: Unpredictable rains and heavy winds. In summer, the weather can be hot (90°s) and sticky.

Transit: Yellow Cab 410/685-1212. MBA Transit 410/539-5000.

Accommodations

William Page Inn 8 Martin St **410/626-1506, 800/364-4160** • gay/ straight • elegantly renovated 1908 home • full brkfst • smokefree • older kids ok • gay-owned/ run • $105-200

Baltimore

Info Lines & Services

AA Gay/ Lesbian at 'G/L Community Center' **410/663-1922** • call for times and locations

Gay/ Lesbian Community Center 241 W Chase St (at Read) **410/837-5445** • 10am-4pm, clsd wknds • inquire about 'Womanspace'

Gay/ Lesbian Switchboard 410/837-8888, 410/837-8529 (TDD) • live 7pm-10pm

PACT (People of All Colors Together) 410/323-4720

Transgender Support Group at 'G/L Community Center' **410/837-5445** • 8pm 2nd Tue • also 'Tran-Quility' group • 8pm 4th Sat

Accommodations

Abacrombie Badger B&B 58 W Biddle St (at Cathedral) **410/244-7227** • gay/ straight • smokefree • also restaurant • gay-owned/ run • $79-145

Biltmore Suites 205 W Madison St (at Park) **410/728-6550, 800/868-5064** • gay-friendly • $109-149

Clarion Hotel—Mt Vernon Square 612 Cathedral St (at W Monument) **410/727-7101, 800/292-5500** • gay-friendly • jacuzzis • $109-199

Mr Mole B&B 1601 Bolton St (at McMechen) **410/728-1179** • popular • gay/ straight • splendid suites on historic Bolton Hill • gay-owned/ run • $105-165

Bars

The Allegro 1101 Cathedral St (at Chase) **410/837-3906** • 6pm-2am • mostly gay men • dancing/DJ • shows

Baltimore Eagle 2022 N Charles St (enter on 21st) **410/823-2453** • 6pm-2am • popular • mostly gay men • leather store • patio • wheelchair access

Central Station 1001 N Charles St (at Eager) **410/752-7133** • 3pm-2am • popular • lesbians/ gay men • neighborhood bar • videos • also restaurant • some veggie • $7-15

Club Bunns 608 W Lexington St (at Greene St) **410/234-2866** • 5pm-2am • Sat female strippers • lesbians/ gay men • dancing/DJ • mostly African-American

Coconuts Cafe 311 W Madison (at Eutaw) **410/383-6064** • 11am-2am, from 4pm wknds • call for summer hours • mostly women • dancing/DJ • food served • wheelchair access • $5-7

The Drinkery 203 W Read St (at Park) **410/669-9820** • 11am-2am, from 9:30am wknds • lesbians/ gay men • neighborhood bar

The Gallery Bar & Studio Restaurant 1735 Maryland Ave (at Lafayette) **410/539-6965** • 1pm-1:30am • lesbians/ gay men • dinner nightly • $10-15

Hippo 1 W Eager St (at Charles) **410/547-0069** • 4pm-2am • popular • lesbians/ gay men • more women Fri & at Sun T-dance • dancing/DJ • transgender-friendly • karaoke • videos • wheelchair access

Port in a Storm 4330 E Lombard St (at Kresson) **410/732-5608** • 10am-2am • mostly women • neighborhood bar • dancing/DJ • wheelchair access • women-owned/ run

Stagecoach 1003 N Charles St (at Eager) **410/547-0107** • 4pm-2am • lesbians/ gay men • dancing/DJ • country/ western • piano bar • free dance lessons • also restaurant • Tex/ Mex • some veggie • $5-18

Unicorn 2218 Boston St (at Patterson Park Ave) **410/342-8344** • 4pm-2am, from 2pm wknds • popular • mostly gay men • neighborhood bar

Nightclubs

Club 1722 1722 N Charles St (at Lafayette) **410/727-7431** • 1:45am-5am, clsd Mon-Wed • mostly gay men • dancing/DJ • BYOB

Club Midnite 2549 N Howard St (at 26th) **410/243-3535** • 10pm-2am, clsd Mon-Tue • gay-friendly • dancing/DJ • 'Revival' Fri • lesbians/ gay men

Orpheus 1001 E Pratt St (at Exeter) **410/276-5599** • gay-friendly • dancing/DJ • 18+ • call for events

The Paradox 1310 Russell St (at Ostead) **410/837-9110** • 10pm-4am, 11pm-5am Fri-Sat, more gay Sat • dancing/DJ • food served • entertainment • videos

Cafes

Donna's Coffee Bar 2 W Madison (at Charles) **410/385-0180** • 7:30am-11pm • beer/ wine

Louie's the Bookstore Cafe 518 N Charles (at Franklin) **410/962-1224** • live shows • plenty veggie • full bar • wheelchair access • $4-18

Restaurants

Cafe Hon 1002 W 36th St (at Roland) **410/243-1230** • 7am-9pm, from 9am wknds • some veggie • $6-11

Gampy's 904 N Charles St (at Read) **410/837-9797** • 11:30am-1am, till 2am Wed-Th, till 3am wknds • wheelchair access

Joy America 800 Key Hwy, Inner Harbor (at Covington) **410/244-6500** • 11:30am-10pm, clsd Mon

Loco Hombre 413 E Cold Spring Ln (at Roland) **410/889-2233** • till 10pm

The Millrace 5201 Franklintown Rd (at Security) **410/448-3663** • 10am-midnight, till 2am Th-Sat • seafood • $5-20

Mount Vernon Stable & Saloon 909 N Charles St (Between Eager & Read) **410/685-7427** • lunch & dinner • some veggie • bar 11:30am-2am • $8-12

Spike & Charlie's Restaurant/ Wine Bar 1225 Cathedral St (at Preston) **410/752-8144** • dinner only, clsd Mon • $9-23

Bookstores

Adrian's Book Cafe 714 S Broadway, Fells Point (at Aliceanna) **410/732-1048** • 10am-11pm, till midnight wknds, new & used • some gay titles

Lambda Rising 241 W Chase St (at Read) **410/234-0069** • 10am-10pm • lesbigay • wheelchair access

Publications

The Baltimore Alternative 410/235-3401 • lesbigay newspaper

Baltimore

Baltimore, one of the 'hub' cities of the Chesapeake Bay, is a quaint, working-class city by the sea, with a friendly and diverse population. It's not far from Washington, DC and, like the nation's capital, is packed with museums and history.

To many, Baltimore is best known as the nation's capital of kitsch, home and movie-set for the fabulously filthy queer filmmaker John Waters. You too can follow in the immortal footsteps of Divine, the biggest transvestite movie star we know of. Baltimore is also the site of Edgar Allen Poe's home and grave.

After visiting the Aquarium, dining on soft-shell crabs, and shopping, stop into **Lambda Rising**, Baltimore's lesbigay bookstore, and pick up a copy of the **Baltimore Alternative** or **Baltimore Gay Paper** to find out the latest goings on about town.

At night, visit one of Baltimore's two women's bars: **Coconuts**, and **Port in a Storm**. Women of color and their friends should check out Saturdays at **Club Bunns**, and **Hippo** is always a popular spot to mix it up with the boys, especially at the Sunday T-dance.

The Baltimore Gay Paper 410/837-7748 • lesbigay newspaper

Spiritual Groups

Beit Tikvah 5802 Roland Ave (at Lake in First Christian Church) **410/560-2062** • welcoming Jewish Reconstructionist congregation • call for services & times

Dignity Baltimore 740 N Calvert St (at Madison in St Ignatius Church) **410/325-1519** • 7:30pm 1st & 3rd Sat

Grace & St Peter's Episcopal Church 707 Park Ave **410/539-1395** • 7:45am & 10am Sun, 6pm daily

MCC 3401 Old York Rd (at 34th) **410/889-6363** • 10am Sun

St Mark's Lutheran Church 1900 St Paul St (at 20th) **410/752-5804** • 11am Sun & 6:30pm Th

Cumberland

Accommodations

Red Lamp Post B&B 849 Braddock Rd **301/777-3262** • lesbians/ gay men • full brkfst • dinner available • hot tub • smokefree • $65-75

Restaurants

Acropolis 25 E Main St (across from St Michael's Church), Frostburg **301/689-8277** • 4pm-10pm,clsd Sun-Mon • Greek & American • full bar

Au Petite Paris 86 E Main St **301/689-8946** • 6pm-9pm, clsd Sun-Mon • French • $12-20 • wheelchair access

Frederick

Cafes

The Frederick Coffee Co & Cafe 100 East St (at Church) **301/698-0039** • 7am-7pm, till 9pm Fri-Sat, 8am-6pm Sun • women-owned/ run • entertainment

Hagerstown

Bars

41 North 41 N Potomac St (at Franklin) **301/797-1553** • 4pm-2am, till midnight Sun • lesbians/ gay men • food served • dancing/DJ • live shows

Havre de Grace

Accommodations

La Clé D'Or 226 N Union Ave (at Chesapeake Bay) **410/939-6562, 888/HUG-GUEST (484-4837)** • gay/ straight • 1868 home of the Johns Hopkins family • full brkfst • teens ok • gay-owned/ run • $99-125

Rockville

Spiritual Groups

Open Door MCC 15817 Barnesville Rd **301/601-9112** • 9am & 10am Sun

Smith Island

Accommodations

Smith Island Get-A-Way 203/579-9400 • gay-friendly • apt • secluded community accessible only by ferry • $200 wknd/ $500 wk

MASSACHUSETTS

Statewide

Info Lines & Services

Massachusetts Office of Travel & Tourism 100 Cambridge St, 13th flr, Boston **800/447-6277**

Spiritual Groups

RI & SE Mass Gay Jewish Group Boston **508/992-7927 (PRIVATE HOME)**

Acton

Restaurants

Acton Jazz Cafe 452 Great Rd/ Rte 2A **978/263-6161** • 5:30pm-midnight, till 10:30pm Sun • full bar • live shows • women's performances Sun • smokefree

Amherst

Info Lines & Services

Everywoman's Center Wilder Hall, UMass **413/545-0883** • call for office hours

Accommodations

Ivy House B&B 1 Sunset Ct **413/549-7554** • gay-friendly • restored Colonial Cape • private/ shared baths • gay-owned/ run • $60-90

Bookstores

Food For Thought 106 N Pleasant St (at Main) **413/253-5432** • 9:30am-6pm, till 8pm Wed-Fri, noon-5pm Sun • progressive bookstore • wheelchair access • collectively run

Barre

Accommodations

Jenkins House Inn & Restaurant **978/355-6444, 800/378-7373** • gay-friendly • restaurant & full bar • English garden • $95-135

Winterwood 19 N Main St, Petersham **978/724-8885** • gay-friendly • Greek Revival mansion • fireplaces • $70-90

Restaurants

Barre Mill 90 Main St, South Barre **978/355-2987** • Italian • $9-12

Colonel Isaac 11 Exchange St **978/355-4629** • 5pm-8pm, till 9pm Fri-Sat, noon-3:30pm Sun, clsd Mon-Tue • full bar • $12-18

Bedford

Info Lines & Services

The Pinkham Center 227 The Great Rd **617/275-9071, 888/746-5426** • lgbt therapy & resource center

Berkshires

Info Lines & Services

GLBT Support Group **413/243-8484** • 6:30pm 1st Tue, call for location

Accommodations

The B&B at Howden Farm Rannapo Rd, Sheffield **413/229-8481** • gay/ straight • 50 acre working farm • full brkfst • smokefree • some shared baths • gay-owned/ run • $59-179

Summer Hill Farm 950 East St, Lenox **413/442-2057** • gay-friendly • colonial guesthouse & cottage • full brkfst • wheelchair access

Walker House 64 Walker St, Lenox **413/637-1271, 800/235-3098** • gay-friendly • smokefree • $70-190

Windflower Inn 684 S Egremont Rd, Great Barrington **413/528-2720, 800/992-1993** • gay-friendly • gracious country inn • full brkfst • smokefree • kids ok • $100-170

Restaurants

Cafe Lucia 80 Church St, Lenox **413/637-2640** • dinner only, clsd Mon • $13-22

Church Street Cafe 65 Church St, Lenox **413/637-2745** • 5:30pm-9pm • some veggie • $13-22

Gateways 51 Walker St, Lenox **413/637-2532** • till 9pm, clsd Mon • plenty veggie • wheelchair access • $13-30

Boston

Info Lines & Services

BAGLY (Boston Alliance of LGBT Youth) **617/227-4313** • youth talkline • ask about other services

Bisexual Resource Center 29 Stanhope St, 3rd flr **617/424-9595** • also Boston Bisexual Women's Network

Cambridge Women's Center 46 Pleasant St, Cambridge **617/354-8807**

Daughters of Bilitis 1151 Massachusetts Ave (in the Old Cambridge Baptist Church, in Harvard Sq), Cambridge **617/661-3633** • women's social & support networks • call for schedule

Entre Nous **617/282-0522** • men's & women's leather group • annual Provincetown wknd in Oct

Gay/ Lesbian Helpline **617/267-9001** • 6pm-11pm, 5pm-10pm wknds

International Foundation for Gender Education **781/899-2212** • transgender info & support

Lesbian Al-Anon at the Women's Center **617/354-8807** • 6:30pm Wed

Tiffany Club of New England **781/891-9325** • several open mtgs monthly

Accommodations

463 Beacon St Guest House 463 Beacon St **617/536-1302** • gay-friendly • minutes from Boston's heart • IGLTA • $65-99

't Amsterdammertje **617/471-8454** • lesbians/ gay men • Euro-American B&B • full brkfst • smokefree • $69-99

Carolyn's B&B 102 Holworthy St, Cambridge **617/864-7042** • gay-friendly • full brkfst • near Harvard Square • women-owned/ run • $80-95

▲ **Chandler Inn** 26 Chandler St **617/482-3450, 800/842-3450** • gay-friendly • centrally located • IGLTA • $89-129

Clarendon Square B&B 198 W Brookline St (at Tremont) **617/536-2229** • lesbians/ gay men • restored Victorian townhouse • fireplaces • $110-210

Just Right Reservations 18 Piedmont St, 2nd flr **617/247-6280** • covers Boston, NYC, Provincetown & Montreal

Oasis Guest House 22 Edgerly Rd **617/267–2262** • gay/ straight • Back Bay location • IGLTA • $69-109

Rutland Square House B&B 56 Rutland Sq **617/247–0018, 800/786–6567** • mostly gay men • Victorian townhouse • $85-150

Taylor House B&B 50 Burroughs St **617/983–9334, 888/228–2956** • gay-friendly • Italianate Victorian • smokefree • $79-155

Thoreau's Walden B&B 2 Concord Rd, Lincoln **781/259–1899** • gay-friendly • near historic Walden Pond • full brkfst • $75

Victorian B&B **617/536–3285** • women only • full brkfst • smokefree • lesbian-owned/ run • $60-95 (1-4 guests)

Bars

Chaps 100 Warrenton St (at Stuart) **617/695–9500** • noon-2am • popular • mostly gay men • more women Wed • dancing/DJ • videos • Latin night Wed • T-dance Sun

Club Cafe 209 Columbus (btwn Berkeley & Clarendon) **617/536–0966** • 2pm-2am, from 11:30am Sun • popular • lesbians/ gay men • more women Wed • 3 bars • piano bar • live shows • videos • also restaurant • some veggie • wheelchair access • $10-20

Lava Bar 575 Commonwealth, top flr **617/267–7707** • 10pm-close, clsd Sun-Wed • gay-friendly • more gay Sat • dancing/DJ

Luxor 69 Church St (btwn Stuart & Arlington, in Theater District) **617/423–6969** • 4pm-1am • mostly gay men • videos • also '69 Church St' lounge & 'Mario's' Italian restaurant downstairs • $9-13

Upstairs at the Hideaway 20 Concord Ln, Cambridge **617/661–8828** • Th & Sun only • mostly women • free pool bar for women

Nightclubs

Avalon 15 Lansdowne St **617/262–2424** • 9pm-2am Fri & Sun • popular • mostly gay men • dancing/DJ

Buzz 67 Stuart St **617/267–8969** • 10pm Th-Sat • popular • lesbians/ gay men • 'Le Femme' for women Th • gay Latino night Fri • dancing/DJ • cover charge

Joy Boston 533 Washington St (at West) **617/338–6999** • mostly gay men • dancing/DJ • alternative • dress code • 19+

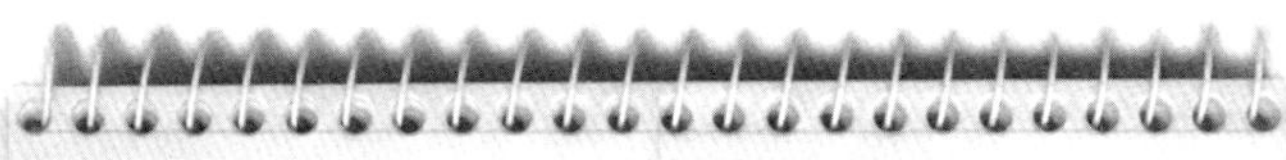

Boston

Home to 65 colleges and universities, Boston has been an intellectual center for the continent for three centuries. Since that famed tea party, it's also been home to some of New England's most rebellious radicals. The result is a city whose character is both traditional and free-thinking, high-brow and free-wheeling*, stuffy and energetic.

Not only is this city complex, it's cluttered...with plenty of historic and mind-sparking sites to visit. Check out the high/low culture in Harvard Square and the shopping along Newbury Street in the Back Bay, as well as the touristy vendors in Faneuil Hall. Don't miss the North End's fabulous Italian food.

Boston's women's community is, not surprisingly, strong and politically diverse. To find out what the latest hotspots are, pick up a copy of **Bay Windows** or **IN Newsweekly** at the well-stocked women's bookstore, **New Words Books.** While you're there, check out the many national lesbian magazines published in Boston, from feminist newsjournal **Sojourner** to **Bad Attitude,** an erotic 'zine for S/M dykes.

Tired of reading? Call **Hanarchy Now**'s info line (617/629-4727) to see what wild event this local promoter has on tap for alternadykes. Cruise by the **Hideaway** on Thursday or Sunday for a game of pool. If you like to dance the night away, try **Ryles** or **Man-Ray** on Sunday.

* About driving in Boston: its drivers are notoriously the most freeform in the country. The streets of Boston can be confusing—often streets of the same name intersect, and six-way intersections are the rule.

Boston

Where the Girls Are: Sipping coffee and reading somewhere in Cambridge or Harvard Square, strolling the South End near Columbus & Mass. Avenues, or hanging out in the Fenway or Jamaica Plain.

Entertainment: Gay Men's Chorus 617/424-8900.
The Theatre Offensive 617/542-4214.
Hanarchy Now Productions 617/629-4727.
Tool Box Productions 617/497-9215.

Lesbigay Pride: June. 617/522-7890.

Annual Events: February - Outwrite 617/262-6969. Annual national lesbian/gay writers & publishers conference.
May - Gay & Lesbian Film/Video Festival 617/369-3300 (MFA).
June - AIDS Walk 617/392-9255.

City Info: Boston Visitor's Bureau 800/447-6277.

Attractions: Beacon Hill.
Black Heritage Trail.
Boston Common.
Faneuil Hall.
Freedom Trail.
Harvard University.
Isabella Stewart Gardner Museum 617/566-1401.
Museum of Afro-American History 617/739-1200.
Museum of Fine Arts 617/369-9300.
Museum of Science 617/723-2500.
New England Aquarium 617/973-5281.
Old North Church 617/523-6676.
Walden Pond.

Weather: Extreme—from freezing winters to boiling summers with a beautiful spring and fall.

Transit: Boston Cab 617/536-5010.
MBTA (the 'T') 800/392-6100.

Manray 21 Brookline St (off Mass Ave, in Central Sq), Cambridge **617/864-0400** • 9pm-1am, clsd Mon-Tue • gay/ straight • more gay Th at 'Campus' (men) & Sat at 'Liquid' (disco, 19+) • more women Sun • dancing/DJ • alternative • creative dress encouraged

Upstairs at Ryles 212 Hampshire St (at Cambridge St), Cambridge **617/876-9330** • 5pm-2am • mostly women Sun • dancing/DJ

Cafes

CityGirl Caffe 204 Hampshire St (at Prospect), Cambridge **617/864-2809** • 11am-9pm Tue-Fri, from 10am wknds, clsd Mon • Italian • plenty veggie • wknd brunch

Francesca's 564 Tremont St (at Clarendon) **617/482-9026** • 8am-11pm, till midnight wknds • excellent pastries • wheelchair access

Geoffrey's Cafe 578 Tremont St (at Dartmouth) **617/266-1122** • 9am-10pm, till 11pm wknds • beer/ wine

Mildred's 552 Tremont St (at Clarendon) **617/426-0008** • 8am-11pm

Restaurants

Biba 272 Boylston St (at Arlington) **617/426-7878** • lunch & dinner • upscale dining • $30-45

Blue Diner 150 Kneeland St (at South St) **617/695-0087** • 11am-4pm, till 4am Th, 24hrs wknds • Southern BBQ • plenty veggie

Brandy Pete's 267 Franklin St (at Congress) **617/439-4165** • lunch & dinner Mon-Fri only

Casa Romero 30 Gloucester St **617/536-4341** • 5pm-10pm, till 11pm wknds • Mexican

Club Cafe 209 Columbus (btwn Berkeley & Clarendon) **617/536-0966** • 2pm-2am, from 11:30am Sun • popular • lesbians/ gay men • some veggie • also 3 bars • wheelchair access • $10-20

Icarus 3 Appleton St (off Tremont) **617/426-1790** • dinner only • $30-40

Laurel 142 Berkeley St (at Columbus) **617/424-6711, 617/424-6664** • lunch & dinner, Sun brunch

Rabia's 73 Salem St (at Cross St) **617/227-6637** • lunch & dinner • fine Italian • some veggie • wheelchair access • $10-25

Ristorante Lucia 415 Hanover St **617/367-2353** • great North End pasta • some veggie • $8-15

Trattoria Pulcinella 147 Huron Ave (at Concord), Cambridge **617/491-6336** • fine Italian • cash only

Entertainment & Recreation

Freedom Trail • start at the Visitor Information Center in Boston Common (at Tremont & West Sts), the most famous cow pasture & oldest public park in the US, & follow the red line to some of Boston's most famous sites

Hanarchy Now Productions Cambridge **617/629–4727** • queer & alternative events in & around Boston

Isabella Stewart Gardner Museum 280 The Fenway **617/566–1401** • Venetian palazzo filled w/ Old Masters to Impressionists • also cool courtyard • clsd Mon

John Hancock Observatory 200 Clarendon St, 60th flr (at St James St) **617/247–1977**

Museum of Afro-American History/ Black Heritage Trail 46 Joy St (at Smith Ct, on Beacon Hill) **617/739–1200** • exhibits in the African Meeting House, the oldest standing African-American church in the US

Theater Offensive 617/542–4214 • 'New England's foremost presenter of lesbian & gay theater'

Tool Box Productions Cambridge **617/497–9215** • multi-media cabaret & events • women of all colors

Bookstores

Glad Day Books 673 Boylston St (btwn Dartmouth & Exeter) **617/267–3010** • 9:30am-10pm, till 11pm Fri-Sat, noon-9pm Sun • lesbigay

▲ **New Words Bookstore** 186 Hampshire St (at Prospect), Cambridge **617/876–5310, 800/928–4788** • 10am-6pm, till 8pm Tue-Fri, from noon Sun • wheelchair access

Synchronicity Transgender Bookstore 14 Felton St (at Moody), Waltham **781/899–2212** • 9am-4pm, till 2pm every other Sat, clsd Sun • over 100 TG titles

Trident Booksellers & Cafe 338 Newbury St (off Mass Ave) **617/267–8688** • 9am-midnight • good magazine browsing • beer/ wine • wheelchair access

Unicorn Books 1210 Massachusetts Ave (at Appleton), Arlington Hts **781/646–3680** • 10am-9pm, till 5pm wknds, from noon Sun • spiritual titles

Waterstone's Booksellers 26 Exeter (at Newbury) **617/859–7300** • 9:30am-10pm, noon-8pm Sun • huge general bookstore • wheelchair access

We Think The World of You 540 Tremont St (btwn Berkeley & Clarendon) **617/423–1965** • open daily • popular • lesbigay

Wordsworth 30 Brattle St (at Mt Auburn), Cambridge **617/354–5201** • 9am-11pm, 10am-10pm Sun • general • lesbigay titles

Retail Shops

Body Xtremes 414 Hancock St, N Quincy **617/471–5836** • body piercing • jewelry

Designs for Living 52 Queensberry St **617/536–6150** • 7am-9pm, from 8am Sat, from 9am Sun • also cyber cafe

Publications

Bay Windows 617/266–6670 • lesbigay newspaper

In Newsweekly 617/426–8246, 800/426–8246 (in MA) • statewide lesbigay newspaper

Sojourner—The Women's Forum 617/524–0415

Spiritual Groups

Am Tikva 50 Sewall Ave (at Charles, in auditorium at Temple Sinai), Brookline **617/883–0893** • 8pm 1st & 3rd Fri • lesbigay Jewish services

Dignity 35 Bowdoin St (at St John the Evangelist Church, Beacon Hill) **617/421–1915** • 5:30pm Sun

MCC 131 Cambridge St (at Old West Church) **617/973–0404** • 6pm Sun

Gyms & Health Clubs

Metropolitan Fitness 209 Columbus **617/536–3006** • gay-friendly

Mike's Gym II 560 Harrison Ave (at Waltham St) **617/338–6210, 617/338–6677** • popular • gay-owned/ run

Erotica

Eros Boutique 581–A Tremont St, 2nd flr **617/425–0345** • fetishwear • toys

Grand Opening! 318 Harvard St, 2nd flr (at Beacon, in Arcade Bldg), Brookline **617/731–2626** • women's sex toy store

Hubba Hubba 534 Massachusetts Ave (at Brookline), Cambridge **617/492–9082** • noon-8pm, till 9pm Fri, till 7pm Sat, clsd Sun • fetish gear

Marquis de Sade 73 Berkeley St (at Chandler) **617/426–2120**

Brookline

see Boston

Cambridge

see Boston

Cape Cod

Info Lines & Services

Gay/ Lesbian AA Cape Cod Hospital, Bayview St, Hyannis **508/775-7060** • 5pm Sun

Accommodations

Blue Heron B&B 464 Pleasant Lake Ave, Harwich **508/430-0219** • mostly women • swimming • lesbian-owned/ run • $50-75

Gull Cottage 10 Old Church St, Yarmouth Port **508/362-8747** • mostly gay men • near beach • shared baths • wheelchair access • $50-70

Henry Crocker House 3026 Main St ((at Rendezvous Ln)), Barnstable **508/362-6348, 888/612-8820** • gay-friendly • 200-yr-old Georgian colonial • full brkfst • smokefree • $85-115

The Marlborough B&B Inn 320 Woods Hole Rd, Woods Hole **508/548-6218** • gay-friendly • full brkfst • smokefree • $85-155

Woods Hole Passage 186 Woods Hole Rd, Falmouth **508/548-9575, 800/790-8976** • gay-friendly • close to beaches • $95-145

Nightclubs

Club 477 477 Yarmouth Rd, Hyannis **508/775-9835** • 6pm-1am • popular • lesbians/ gay men • Cape Cod's largest gay complex • dancing/DJ • live shows • food served

Chelsea

see Boston

Gloucester

Bookstores

The Bookstore 61 Main St **978/281-1548** • 9am-9pm

Greenfield

Accommodations

Brandt House 29 Highland Ave **413/774-3329, 800/235-3329** • gay-friendly • full brkfst • kids ok • woman-owned/ run • $110-195

The Inn at Charlemont Rte 2, Mohawk Trail, Charlemont **413/339-5796** • gay-friendly • $35-125 • 2 restaurants • some veggie • full bar • $10-20 • women-owned/ run

Bookstores

World Eye Bookshop 156 Main St **413/772-2186** • 9am-7pm, till 8pm Fri, till 6pm Sat, noon-5pm Sun • community bulletin board • women-owned/run

Haverhill

Bars

Friend's Landing 85 Water St **978/374-9400** • 4pm-1am, till 2am Fri, from 11am Sun • mostly gay men • dancing/DJ • karaoke & line dancing Wed • Top 40 Th-Sat • wheelchair access

Lynn

Bars

Fran's Place 776 Washington (at Sagamore) **781/598-5618** • 1pm-2am • lesbians/ gay men • neighborhood bar • dancing/DJ • karaoke Tue • wheelchair access

Joseph's 191 Oxford St (off Market St) **781/599-9483** • 5pm-2am • lesbians/ gay men • dancing/DJ • videos • wheelchair access

The Pub at 47 Central 47 Central Ave **781/586-0551** • 2pm-2am • mostly gay men • neighborhood bar • dancing/DJ wknds • leather • gay-owned/ run

Marshfield

Bars

Spectra Room 260 Main St (Rte 3A & 139) **781/834-2176** • 7pm-2am, from 3pm Sun • lesbians/gay men • dancing/DJ • drag shows • wheelchair access

Martha's Vineyard

Accommodations

Captain Dexter House of Edgartown **508/627-7289** • gay-friendly • country inn circa 1840 • $165-225

Captain Dexter House of Vineyard Haven **508/693-6564** • gay-friendly • 1840s sea captain's home • $100-165

▲ **Martha's Place Inn** **508/693-0253** • lesbians/ gay men • harbor views • fireplaces • wheelchair access • gay-owned/ run • $125-395

Restaurants

The Black Dog Tavern Beach St Extension **508/693-9223** • wheelchair access • $13-25

Le Grenier 96 Main St, Vineyard Haven **508/693-4906** • French • $13-25

Louis' Cafe State Rd, Vineyard Haven **508/693-3255** • gay-owned/ run

Bookstores

Bunch of Grapes 44 Main St, Vineyard Haven **508/693-2291** • 9am-9:30pm • general • some lesbian/ gay titles & magazines

Nantucket

Accommodations

The Chestnut House 3 Chestnut St **508/228-0049, 508/228-9521** • gay-friendly • full brkfst • also cottage • $85-300

House of Orange 25 Orange St **508/228-9287** • gay/ straight • old captain's home • seasonal • teens ok • gay-owned/ run • $135-185

New Bedford

Bars

Le Place 20 Kenyon St **508/992-8156** • 2pm-2am • popular • lesbians/ gay men • karaoke Th • dancing/DJ Fri-Sun • women-owned/ run

Newburyport

Accommodations

46 High Road B&B 46 High Rd, Newbury **978/462-4664** • gay-friendly • full brkfst • $80-95

Restaurants

Glenns Restaurant 44 Merrimac St **978/465-3811** • 5:30pm-10pm, from 4pm Sun, clsd Mon, full bar till midnight • live music • wheelchair access • $17-22

Newton

see Boston

Northampton

With all the hype a while back about Northampton being the lesbian capital of the world, visitors are often surprised by the low-key atmosphere of this quaint and quiet New England town. It's the sort of place where the people are nice, the streets are safe, and most groups come in multiples of two.

Sure, you'll be free to smooch with your honey just about everywhere, but don't expect to see the throngs of Sapphic sisters you've heard about in the *National Enquirer* or on *20/20* milling around the streets. They're there all right, but they're probably home with the kids, cuddling with their other half, or studying for that big exam at one of the five colleges in the area.

Still, there's plenty for a visiting lesbian to enjoy in Northampton. For lesbian-friendly accommodations, check out the **Tin Roof** in Hadley. The **Green Street Cafe** is popular with local girls. For something different, make an appointment to view the **Sexual Minorities Archives,** or take a tour of Emily Dickinson's House in nearby Amherst.

With two women's colleges, Smith and Mount Holyoke, progressive Hampshire College, Amherst College, and the University of Massachusetts all in the area, there's something fun to do every night of the week, from readings to performance art. Check out the **Lesbian Calendar,** a comprehensive monthly listing of events. It's available at **Pride & Joy** lesbian/gay bookstore, the informal community center. While you're there, pick up a copy of the Lesbian/Gay Business Guild's listing of 'family' businesses in the area.

If you're in town around late July, look for the **Northampton Lesbian Festival,** which usually happens in Washington, Massachusetts, in the Berkshires—for lack of enough public space in the town of Northampton!

Northampton

Info Lines & Services

East Coast FTM Group 413/584-7616 • 3pm 2nd Sun • support group for FTM TG/TS, their partners & friends • call for mtg location

Sexual Minorities Archives 413/584-7616 • lgbt & SM collection • by appt

Accommodations

Clark Tavern Inn B&B 98 Bay Rd, Hadley **413/586-1900** • gay-friendly • full brkfst • smokefree • teens ok • $90-135

Corner Porches 82 Baptist Corner Rd, Ashfield **413/628-4592** • gay-friendly • 30 minutes from Northampton • full brkfst • kids ok • woman-owned/ run • $60-75

The Inn at Northampton 1 Atwood Dr **413/586-1211, 800/582-2929** • gay-friendly • swimming • wheelchair access • $109-149 • also restaurant & bar

The McKinley House 3 McKinley Ave (at Rte 10), Easthampton **413/527-7814** • gay-friendly • 4 miles S of Northampton • gay-owned/ run • $75-85

Old Red Schoolhouse 67 Park St **413/584-1228** • apts • studios • also 'Lesbian Towers' in East Hampton • gay-owned/ run • $75-200

Tin Roof B&B 413/586-8665 • mostly women • 1909 farmhouse w/spectacular view of the Berkshires • shared baths • kids ok • lesbian-owned/ run • $60-65

Bars

The Grotto 25 West St **413/586-6900** • 4pm-1am • lesbians/ gay men • dancing/DJ • food served • drag shows

The Iron Horse 20 Center St **413/584-0610** • 8:30pm-close • gay-friendly • live music • food served • some veggie • $5-15

Nightclubs

Club Metro 492 Pleasant St **413/582-9898** • clsd Mon • gay-friendly • gay night Wed • dancing/DJ • house Sat • Latin Sun • live shows

Pearl Street 10 Pearl St **413/584-0610** • call for events • lesbians/ gay men • dancing/DJ • live music • women-owned/ run

Northampton

Where the Girls Are: Just off Main St., browsing in the small shops, strolling down an avenue, or sipping a beverage at one of the cafés.

Annual Events: July - Northampton Lesbian Festival 413/586-8251. 2nd-largest women's music festival.
June - Golden Threads. Gathering for lesbians over 50 & their admirers, at the Provincetown Inn. PO Box 60475, Northampton, MA 01060-0475.
Fat Women's Gathering 212/721-8259.

Attractions: Academy of Music 413/584-8435.
Historic Northampton 413/584-6011.
Northampton Center for the Arts 413/584-7327.

Best View: At the top of Skinner Mountain, up Route 47 by bus, car or bike.

Weather: Late summer/early fall is the best season, with warm, sunny days. Mid-summer gets to the low 90°s, while winter brings snow from November to March, with temperatures in the 20°s and 30°s.

Transit: Florence/Paradise Taxi 413/584-0055.
Peter Pan Shuttle 413/586-1030.
Pioneer Valley Transit Authority (PVTA) 413/586-5806.

Cafes

Haymarket Cafe 15 Amber Ln **413/586-9969** • 10am-11pm • fresh pastries

Restaurants

Bela 68 Masonic St **413/586-8011** • noon-8pm, till 10pm Th-Sat, clsd Sun-Mon • vegetarian • wheelchair access • women-owned/ run • $5-10

Green Street Cafe 64 Green St **413/586-5650** • lunch & dinner • plenty veggie • beer/ wine • $11-17

Paul & Elizabeth's 150 Main St **413/584-4832** • lunch & dinner • seafood • plenty veggie • beer/ wine • wheelchair access • $7-12

Bookstores

Pride & Joy 20 Crafts Ave **413/585-0683** • 11am-6pm, till 8pm Th, from noon-6pm Sun • lesbigay books & gifts • wheelchair access

Third Wave Feminist Booksellers 42-A Green St **413/586-7851** • 11am-6pm, till 7pm Sat, call for Sun hrs • lesbian-owned/ run

Publications

Lesbian Calendar 413/586-5514

▲ **Metroline 860/233-8334** • regional newspaper & entertainment guide

Erotica

Intimacies 28 Center St **413/582-0709 (also TTY)** • lesbian-owned/ run

Provincetown

Info Lines & Services

In Town Reservations, Travel & Real Estate 4 Standish St **508/487-1883, 800/67P-TOWN (677-8696)**

Provincetown Business Guild 508/487-2313, 800/637-8696 • IGLTA

▲ **Provincetown Reservations System** 293-A Commercial St **508/487-2400, 800/648-0364** • IGLTA

Provincetown

Where the Girls Are: In this small resort town, you can't miss 'em!

Lesbigay Pride: June.

Annual Events: August - Provincetown Carnival 800/637-8696.
October - Women's Week 800/637-8696. It's very popular, so make your reservations early!
Fantasia Fair - for TS/TVs & their admirers.
December - Holly Folly.

City Info: Chamber of Commerce 508/487-3424.

Attractions: The beach.
Commercial St.
Heritage Museum 508/487-7098.
Herring Cove Beach.
Pilgrim Monument.
Provincetown Museum 508/487-1310.
Whale watching.

Best View: People-watching from an outdoor café or on the beach.

Weather: New England weather is unpredictable. Be prepared for rain, snow or extreme heat! Otherwise, the weather during the season consists of warm days and cooler nights.

Transit: Mercedes Cab 508/487-3333.
Provincetown Taxi 508/487-8294.
Ferry Bay State Spray & Provincetown Steamship Co. (from Commonwealth Pier in Boston, during summer) 617/723-7800.

Provincetown

Who would have thought that a little New England whaling village at the very tip of Cape Cod would be the country's largest gay and lesbian resort? But Provincetown is just that.

The season in Provincetown runs according to a time-honored schedule of who does what when where. According to one regular, the typical lesbian itinerary goes as follows:

Arrival: Rent a bike and explore the town's lesbigay shops and bookstores. (Nobody drives in Provincetown.) Pick up lunch at a deli on the way to Herring Cove. At the beach, head left to find the women.

At the beach: Take off your top, if you like. Just keep an eye out for the cops, who'll give you a ticket if they catch you bare-breasted. And a word to the wise: if you're heading toward the sand dunes for a tryst, don't forget your socks. The hot, white sand can burn your feet (Youch!).

3pm: Bike back to your room for a shower, then head to the afternoon T-dance at **Boatslip Beach Club** on Commercial Street. Drink and dance till dinnertime, then take a relaxing few hours for your meal.

After dinner: Check out the bars; **Vixen** is the pick for women. If you're not into the bar scene or all the sun and surf has tired you out, you can always go shopping. Most stores stay open till 11pm during the summer. When the bars close, grab a slice of pizza and an espresso milkshake at **Spiritus**, and cruise the streets until they're empty—sometimes not till 4 or 5am.

Before you leave, treat yourself to the excitement of a whale-watching cruise. There are several cruise lines, and **Portuguese Princess Whale Watch** is women-owned.

But if you really want a whale of a good time, pencil in **Provincetown's Women's Week** in October. The **Women's Innkeepers of Provincetown** will be sponsoring an opening party, a community dinner, a golf tournament and fun run, a prom, lots of entertainment...and more. Don't forget to call your favorite guest-house early—really early—to make your reservations!

Accommodations

155 Bradford St Guesthouse 155 Bradford St **617/524-4914** • gay-friendly • studios • wheelchair access • IGLTA

1807 House 54 Commercial St (btwn W Vine & Point St) **508/487-2173, 888/522-1807** • lesbians/ gay men • rooms, suites & apts • $75-125

Admiral's Landing Guest House 158 Bradford St (btwn Conwell & Pearl) **508/487-9665, 800/934-0925** • lesbians/ gay men • 1840s Greek Revival home & studio efficiencies • gay-owned/ run • $49-109

▲ **Anchor Inn Beach House** 175 Commercial St **508/487-0432, 800/858-2657** • popular • gay/ straight • central location • private beach • harbor view • gay-owned/ run • $75-325

Angel's Landing 353-355 Commercial St **508/487-1600** • lesbians/ gay men • efficiency units on waterfront • seasonal

Bayberry Accommodations 16 Winthrop St **508/487-4605, 800/422-4605** • gay/ straight • newly renovated award-winning home • smokefree

Bayshore 493 Commercial St (at Howland) **508/487-9133** • mostly women • apts • private beach • kitchens • lesbian-owned/ run • $75-195 ($795-2000/wk in summer)

Beachfront Realty 145 Commercial St **508/487-1397** • vacation rentals & housing/ condo sales

Beaconlight Guest House 12 Winthrop St **508/487-9603, 800/696-9603** • popular • mostly gay men • award-winning • hot tub • fireplaces • sundecks • smokefree • parking • IGLTA • gay-owned/ run • $45-250

▲ **Benchmark Inn & Annex** 6-8 Dyer St **508/487-7440, 888/487-7440** • lesbians/ gay men • hot tub • fireplace • harbor views • swimming • in heart of Provincetown • smokefree • IGLTA • gay-owned/ run • $115-325

Boatslip Beach Club 161 Commercial St (at Atlantic) **508/487-1669, 800/451-7547** • popular • lesbians/ gay men • resort • swimming • seasonal • also several bars • popular T-dance • IGLTA • gay-owned/ run • $65-169

▲ **The Bradford Carver House** 70 Bradford St **508/487-4966, 800/826-9083** • lesbians/ gay men • centrally located • gay-owned/ run • $39-110

▲ **Bradford Gardens Inn** 178 Bradford St **508/487-1616, 800/432-2334** • mostly women • 1820s Colonial & cottages • full brkfst • gardens • gay-owned/ run • $65-225

OPEN YEAR ROUND

Your home away from home, where there are no strangers—
only friends you haven't met!

Experience our warm hosipitality & cozy accommodations with
a convenient central location

"Highly Recommended" ***–Out & About Magazine***

Private Baths • King & Queen Beds • Color Cable TV/VCR • A/C
Refrigerators • Room Phones • Continental Breakfast • Parking
Large Videocassette Library • Patio • Common Room• Fireplaces

508 • 487-4966   800 • 826-9083
70 Bradford Street, Provincetown, MA 02657
www.capecod.net/bradfordcarver

DEXTER'S INN

A Traditional Cape Cod Guest House

Private Baths — Sundeck — Parking — TVs
In-Room Phones — Continental Breakfast
Central Location — Airport Pickup — A/C
OPEN YEAR ROUND

6 Conwell Street, Provincetown, MA 02657
508-487-1911 Toll-free 888-521-1999
e-mail — dextersinn@aol.com
www.provincetown.net/dextersinn

Bradford House & Motel 41 Bradford St **508/487-0173** • gay-friendly • $65-160

Brass Key Guesthouse 67 Bradford St (at Carver) **508/487-9005, 800/842-9858** • popular • lesbians/ gay men • hot tub • swimming • wheelchair access • IGLTA • gay-owned/ run • $75-295

Burch House 116 Bradford St **508/487-9170** • mostly gay men • studios • 302 • $79-179

The Captain & His Ship 164 Commercial St (btwn Winthrop & Central) **508/487-1850, 800/400-2278** • gay/ straight • 19th century sea captain's home • seasonal • sundeck • gay-owned/ run • $65-185

Captain Lysander's Inn 96 Commercial St (at Mechanic) **508/487-2253** • gay-friendly • $55-105

Captain's House B&B 350-A Commercial St (at Center) **508/487-9353, 800/457-8885** • lesbians/ gay men • smokefree • wheelchair access • gay-owned/ run • $40-95

Carpe Diem Guesthouse 12 Johnson St **508/487-4242, 800/487-0132** • lesbians/ gay men • hot tub • some shared baths • smokefree • $40-170

Chancellor Inn 17 Center St **508/487-9423** • mostly gay men • $55-65

Check'er Inn 25 Winthrop St (btwn Bradford & Brown) **508/487-9029, 800/894-9029** • women only • apts w/private entrances • hot tub • decks • IGLTA • lesbian-owned/ run • $125-200

Christopher's by the Bay 8 Johnson St (at Bradford) **508/487-9263, 877/487-9263** • lesbians/ gay men • full brkfst

The Clarendon House 118 Bradford St (btwn Ryder & Alden) **508/487-1645** • gay-friendly • also cottage • $60-135

The Commons Guesthouse & Bistro 386 Commercial St (at Pearl) **508/487-7800, 800/487-0784** • gay/ straight • deck w/ full bar • gay-owned/ run • $75-160

Crown & Anchor 247 Commercial St **508/487-1430** • mostly gay men • swimming • also bar • cabaret • $150-350

Crowne Pointe 80-82 Bradford St **508/487-3686, 877/276-9631** • gay/ straight • hot tub • wheelchair access • gay-owned/ run • $100-225

▲**Dexter's Inn** 6 Conwell St (at Railroad) **508/487-1911, 888/521-1999** • lesbians/ gay men • B&B • smokefree • sundeck • gay-owned/ run • $50-108

The Dunes Motel & Apartments **508/487-1956, 800/475-1833** • lesbians/ gay men • rooms & apts • seasonal • decks • $69-165

▲ **Elephant Walk Inn** 156 Bradford St (at Conwell) **508/487-2543 or 954/730-0664 (Nov-April), 800/889-9255** • popular • mostly gay men • sundeck • in the heart of Provincetown • parking • gay-owned/ run • $48-122

▲ **Fairbanks Inn** 90 Bradford St **508/487-0386, 800/324-7265** • popular • lesbians/ gay men • $46-225

▲ **Gabriel's Guestrooms & Apartments** 104 Bradford St **508/487-3232, 800/969-2643** • popular • mostly women • full brkfst • hot tub • nudity • smokefree • gym • sundecks • workshop center • gay-owned/ run • $65-185

Gifford House Inn & Dance Club 11 Carver St **508/487-0688, 800/434-0130** • lesbians/ gay men • seasonal • $43-139 • also '11 Carver' restaurant • dinner only • seafood • also 2 bars • 'The Union' dance club from 9pm-1am • 'Porchside Bar' from 5pm-1am • piano bar wknds • gay-owned/ run

Gracie House 152 Bradford St (at Conwell) **508/487-4808** • lesbians/ gay men • historic, restored Queen Anne • seasonal • smokefree • women-owned/ run • $75-95

Grand View Inn 4 Conant St **508/487-9193, 888/268-9169** • lesbians/ gay men • decks • gay-owned/ run • $45-125

The Gull Walk Inn 300-A Commercial St **508/487-9027** • women only • central location • shared baths • seasonal • sundeck • garden • women-owned/ run • $29-79

▲ **Halle's** 14 W Vine St (at Tremont) **508/487-6310** • mostly women • apt • women-owned/ run • $65-95

Harbor Lights 163 Bradford St (at Law St) **508/487-8246** • lesbians/ gay men • studio & 1-brm apt • smokefree • parking • gay-owned/ run • $800-1,000 (week in-season) & $75-95 (day off-season)

▲ **Heritage House** 7 Center St **508/487-3692** • popular • lesbians/ gay men • shared baths • lesbian-owned/ run • $55-90

Holiday Inn of Provincetown **508/487-1711, 800/422-4224** • gay-friendly • swimming • also restaurant • full bar • wheelchair access

The Inn at Cook Street 7 Cook St **508/487-3894, 888/266-5655** • gay-friendly • intimate & quiet • smokefree • gay-owned/ run • $50-125

Ireland House 18 Pearl St **508/487-7132** • lesbians/ gay men • gay-owned/ run • $45-85

John Randall House 140 Bradford St (at Standish) **508/487-3533, 800/573-6700** • lesbians/ gay men • year-round • gay-owned/ run • $50-135

▲ **Lady Jane's Inn** 7 Central St **508/487-3387, 800/523-9526** • mostly women • seasonal • lesbian-owned/ run • $70-90

Land's End Inn 22 Commercial St **508/487-0706, 800/276-7088** • gay-friendly • smokefree • $87-285

Lotus Guest House 296 Commercial St (at Ryder) **508/487-4644** • lesbians/ gay men • seasonal • decks • gardens • gay-owned/ run • $35-110

Mayflower Apartments & Cottages 6 Bangs St **508/487-1916** • gay-friendly • kitchens • $135 & up

Normandy House 184 Bradford St **508/487-1197, 800/487-1197** • gay/ straight • intimate guest house on the tip of Cape Cod • hot tub • sundeck • gay-owned/ run • $80-195

The Oxford 8 Cottage St **508/487-9103, 888/456-9103** • mostly gay men • smokefree • parking • gay-owned/ run

The Piaf 3 Prince St (at Bradford) **508/487-7458, 800/340-7423** • gay/ straight • restored 1790s fisherman's cottage • seasonal • gay-owned/ run

Pilgrim Colony Inn 670 Shore Rd Rte 6-A, North Truro **508/487-1100** • gay/ straight • private beach • seasonal • gay-owned/ run • $49-99

▲ **Pilgrim House Inn** 336 Commercial St **508/487-6424** • mostly women • seasonal • also restaurant • full bar • wheelchair access • $79-109

Prince Albert 166 Commercial St **508/487-0859, 800/992-0859** • lesbians/ gay men • Victorian • smokefree • $60-160

Provincetown Inn 1 Commercial St (at Rotary) **508/487-9500** • gay-friendly • swimming • private beach • poolside bar & grill • wheelchair access • $59-179

Ravenwood Guest House 462 Commercial St (at Cook) **508/487-3203** • mostly women • 1830 Greek Revival • also apts & cottage • $75-145

Red Inn 15 Commercial St (at Point) **508/487-0050** • lesbians/ gay men • elegant waterfront lodging & dining • $75-175

Revere Guesthouse 14 Court St (btwn Commercial & Bradford) **508/487-2292, 800/487-2292** • lesbians/ gay men • restored 1820s captain's home • also apt • smokefree • IGLTA • $35-145

Romeo's Holiday 97 Bradford St (btwn Gosnold & Masonic) **508/487-3082** • lesbians/ gay men • gay-owned/ run • $39-129

Roomers 8 Carver St **508/487-3532** • mostly gay men • seasonal • $95-165

▲ **Rose Acre** 5 Center St (at Commercial) **508/487-2347** • women only • decks • gardens • parking • always open • lesbian-owned/ run

Rose & Crown Guest House 158 Commercial St (btwn Central & Atlantic) **508/487-3332** • lesbians/ gay men • Victorian antiques • some shared baths • $50-110 • also cottage • $150-210

▲ **Sandbars Motel** 570 Shore Rd, Beach Pt, North Truro **508/487-1290** • gay/ straight • oceanfront rooms • kitchens • seasonal • private beach • woman-owned/ run

Sandpiper Beach House 165 Commercial St **508/487-1928, 800/354-8628** • gay/ straight • Victorian • swimming • sundeck • IGLTA • gay-owned/ run • $80-195

Shamrock Motel, Cottages & Apartments 49 Bradford St (at Central) **508/487-1133** • gay/ straight • hot tub • swimming • wheelchair access • IGLTA • gay-owned/ run • $65-140

Shiremax Inn 5 Tremont St (btwn Franklin & School) **508/487-1233, 888/744-7362** • lesbians/ gay men • seasonal • gay-owned/ run • $45-100 & $800 (apt)

▲ **Six Webster Place** 6 Webster Pl (at Bradford) **508/487-2266, 800/693-2783** • popular • lesbians/ gay men • 1750s B&B & apts • sundeck • IGLTA • gay-owned/ run • $65-195

Snug Cottage 342-B Commercial St **508/487-7435** • lesbians/ gay men • boutique B&B • gay-owned/ run

Somerset House 378 Commercial St (at Pearl) **508/487-0383, 800/575-1850** • popular • gay-friendly • Victorian mansion • gay-owned/ run • $60-135

Sunset Inn 142 Bradford St (at Center) **508/487-9810, 800/965-1801** • lesbians/ gay men • some shared baths • seasonal • clothing-optional sundeck • gay-owned/ run • $46-125

Three Peaks Guest House 210 Bradford St (at Howland) **508/487-1717, 800/286-1715** • lesbians/ gay men • 1870s Victorian • sundeck • gay-owned/ run • $60-125

Truro Vineyards Rte 6-A, North Truro **508/487-6200** • gay-friendly • seasonal • women-owned/ run • $79-129

▲ **The Tucker Inn** 12 Center St **508/487-0381, 800/477-1867** • lesbians/ gay men • also cottage (rented weekly) • smokefree • women-owned/ run • $85-145

Victoria House 5 Standish St **508/487-4455** • lesbians/ gay men • gay-owned/ run • $25-120

Watermark Inn Guest House 603 Commercial St **508/487-2506** • gay-friendly • kitchens • beachside • $945-2020/wk in summer

Watership Inn 7 Winthrop St **508/487-0094, 800/330-9413** • popular • mostly gay men • sundeck • gay-owned/ run • $36-200

Westwinds 28 Commercial St (at Point) **508/487-1841** • lesbians/ gay men • apts & cottages • seasonal • private beach • gay-owned/ run • weekly rates only in high season

▲ **White Wind Inn** 174 Commercial St (at Winthrop) **508/487-1526** • lesbians/ gay men • 1800s Victorian • gay-owned/ run • $75-180

Windamar House 568 Commercial St (at Conway) **508/487-0599** • mostly women • 1840s sea captain's home • also apts • IGLTA

Windsor Court 15 Cottage St **508/487-2620** • lesbians/ gay men • hot tub • swimming • kitchens • gay-owned/ run • $65-150 ($1000-1600/week in summer)

Bars

The Antro 258 Commercial **508/487-8800** • 8pm-1am (clsd Nov-April) • mostly gay men • dancing/DJ • cabaret • live shows • call for events • also restaurant

The Boatslip Beach Club in the 'Boatslip' accommodations **508/487-1669** • popular • lesbians/ gay men • resort • T-dance 3:30pm daily during season • swimming • seasonal • also restaurant • cont'l/seafood • some veggie • $10-25

Governor Bradford 312 Commercial St (at Standish) **508/487-2781** • 11am-1am • gay/ straight • food served • 'drag karaoke' • check schedule for performance times

Pied Piper 193-A Commercial St **508/487-1527** • noon-1am • popular • lesbians/ gay men • dancing/DJ • 'After Tea T-Dance' 6:30pm-9:30pm • more women later • women-owned/ run

Rooster Bar in the 'Crown & Anchor' accommodations **508/487-1430** • lesbians/ gay men • more women off-season • neighborhood bar • videos • food served

▲ **Vixen** 336 Commercial St **508/487-6424** • 4pm-1am, from 11am Fri-Sat, from noon Sun • mostly women • dancing/DJ 10pm-1am Fri-Sat • live shows

NIGHTCLUBS

Back Room in the 'Crown & Anchor' accommodations **508/487-1430** • 10:30pm-1am (seasonal) • popular • lesbians/ gay men • check locally for women's night • dancing/DJ

CAFES

Post Office Cafe Cabaret 303 Commercial St (upstairs) **508/487-3892** • 8am-midnight (brkfst till 3pm), call for off-season hours • lesbians/ gay men • some veggie

RESTAURANTS

Bubala's by the Bay 183-185 Commercial **508/487-0773** • 8am-11pm, bar till 1am • seasonal • patio

Chester 404 Commercial St **508/487-8200** • dinner from 6pm • popular

Clem & Ursie's 89 Shank Painter Rd **508/487-2333** • 11am-8:30pm • outdoor dining • cuisine theme nights • affordable • also fish market, deli & grocery

Front Street Restaurant 230 Commercial St **508/487-9715** • 6pm-10:30pm, bar till 1am • seasonal

Gallerani's 133 Commercial St **508/487-4433** • 8am-2pm, 6am-10:30pm Th-Mon • popular • lesbians/ gay men • Italian • pizza • some veggie • beer/ wine • $20-30

Grand Central 5 Masonic St **508/487-7599** • seasonal • popular • dinner • int'l/ seafood • full bar • $15-20

Lobster Pot 321 Commercial St (harborside) **508/487-0842** • noon-10pm • seafood • some veggie • wheelchair access • $15-20

Martin House 157 Commercial St **508/487-1327** • 6pm-close, clsd Tue-Wed • outdoor dining • $11-19

The Mews 429 Commercial St (btwn Lovett's & Kiley) **508/487-1500** • seasonal • lunch & dinner • popular • cont'l • some veggie • 'Cafe Mews' upstairs • live shows wknds • wheelchair access • $15-30

Napi's 7 Freeman St **508/487-1145** • lunch & dinner • int'l/ seafood • plenty veggie • wheelchair access • $15-25

Pucci's Harborside 539 Commercial St **508/487-1964** • seasonal • popular • some veggie • full bar • wheelchair access • $10-20

Sal's Place 99 Commercial St **508/487-1279** • popular • seasonal • publisher's choice: cheese & butter pasta

Spiritus 190 Commercial St **508/487-2808** • noon-2am • popular • great espresso shakes & late night hangout for a slice

Stormy Harbor 277 Commercial St **508/487-1680** • open Fri-Sun only • brkfst, lunch & dinner • American/ Italian, seafood • 'A Pair of Queens' drag cabaret from 9pm Fri-Sat

ENTERTAINMENT & RECREATION

▲ **Off the Coast Kayak** 3 Freeman St **508/487-2692, 877/785-2925** • rentals & guided tours for P-town, Truro & Wellfleet • gay-owned/run

Ptown Bikes 42 Bradford **508/487-8735** • 9am-7pm • rentals • also 306 Commercial location • gay-owned/ run

BOOKSTORES

Now, Voyager 357 Commercial St **508/487-0848** • 10am-11pm • 11am-5pm off-season • lesbigay

Provincetown Bookshop 246 Commercial St **508/487-0964** • 10am-11pm, till 5pm (off-season)

RETAIL SHOPS

Don't Panic 192 Commercial St **508/487-1280** • seasonal • 10am-11pm • lesbigay gifts • T-shirts

Pride's 182 Commercial St **508/487-1127** • 10am-11pm (in summer), call for off-season hrs • lesbigay gifts • T-shirts • books

Recovering Hearts 2-4 Standish St **508/487-4875** • 10am-11pm (in summer), call for off-season hrs • recovery • lesbigay & new age books • wheelchair access

▲ **Womencrafts** 376 Commercial St **508/487-2501** • 10am-11pm (in summer), call for off-season hrs

PUBLICATIONS

In Newsweekly 617/426-8246, 800/426-8246 • statewide lesbigay newspaper

Provincetown Banner 508/487-7400 • newspaper

Provincetown Magazine 508/487-1000 • seasonal • Provincetown's oldest weekly magazine

Spiritual Groups

Dignity 1 Commercial St (at Provincetown Inn) **508/487-9500** • 10:30am Sun (May-Oct)

Gyms & Health Clubs

Mussel Beach 35 Bradford St (btwn Montello & Conant) **508/487-0001** • 6am-9pm • lesbians/ gay men

Provincetown Gym 81 Shank Painter Rd (at Winthrop) **508/487-2776** • 6am-8pm • lesbians/ gay men • daily, weekly & monthly rates

Erotica

Wild Hearts 244 Commercial St **508/487-8933** • 11am-11pm (in summer) • noon-5pm, till 11pm wknds (off-season) • toys for women

Quincy

see Boston

Randolph

Bars

Randolph Country Club 44 Mazeo Dr/ Rte 139 **781/961-2414** • 2pm-2am, from 10am summer • popular • lesbians/ gay men • dancing/DJ • live shows • volleyball court • swimming • wheelchair access

Somerville

see Boston

Springfield

Info Lines & Services

Gay/ Lesbian Info Service 413/731-5403

Bars

David's 395-405 Dwight St **413/734-0566** • 9pm-2am Th-Sat • lesbians/ gay men • dancing/DJ • live shows • Latin night Th • wheelchair access • also 'Judge's Chambers' upstairs • open 3pm-2am daily

Friends/ Cellblock 23 Hampden St (at Main) **413/781-5878** • 11am-2am • lesbians/ gay men • dancing/DJ Th-Sun • videos • wheelchair access • also 'Cellblock' from 10pm

Pub/ Quarry 382 Dwight (at Taylor) **413/734-8123** • 11am-2am • mostly gay men • neighborhood bar • dancing/DJ • live shows • also restaurant • dinner Wed-Sun • wheelchair access

Restaurants

Silvio's Cafe 300 Worthington St **413/746-6999** • 5:30pm-11pm, clsd Mon-Tue

Erotica

Video Expo 486 Bridge St **413/747-9812**

Sturbridge

Restaurants

The Casual Cafe 538 Main St **508/347-2281** • 5pm-close, clsd Sun-Mon • Italian/ Japanese • plenty veggie • BYOB • wheelchair access • lesbian-owned/ run • $7-14

Ware

Accommodations

The Wildwood Inn 121 Church St **413/967-7798, 800/860-8098** • gay-friendly • full brkfst • smokefree • wheelchair access • $50-90

Watertown

see Boston

Williamstown

Accommodations

River Bend Farm B&B 643 Simonds Rd **413/458-3121** • gay-friendly • shared baths • seasonal • kids ok • $90

Restaurants

Mezze Bistro & Bar 84 Water St (Latham St) **413/458-0123** • 5:30pm-1am, Mediterranean • plenty veggie • full bar • summer theater crowd

Worcester

Info Lines & Services

AA Gay/ Lesbian 1 Freeland St **508/752-9000** • 7pm Sat

Floating Dance Floor 508/791-1327 • produces women's dances • call for info

WOBBLES (West of Boston Lesbians) 508/478-0242 • social group • covers eastern MA

Bars

MB Lounge 40 Grafton St (at Franklin) **508/799-4521** • 3pm-2am • mostly gay men • leather • wheelchair access

Nightclubs

A-MEN 21–23 Foster St **508/754–7742** • 9pm-2am, clsd Mon-Tue • mostly gay men • dancing/DJ • alternative • live shows • 18+ Th & Sun

Entertainment & Recreation

Face the Music WCUW 91.3 FM **508/753–2284 (REQUEST LINE)** • 8pm Th • women's radio show

Spiritual Groups

Morning Star MCC 231 Main St, Leicester **508/892–4320** • 11am Sun • wheelchair access

Gyms & Health Clubs

Midtown Athletic Club 22 Front St, 2nd flr **508/798–9703** • gay-friendly

Michigan

Statewide

Publications

Between the Lines 248/615–7003, 888/615–7003

Cruise Magazine 248/545–9040 • entertainment listings

Ann Arbor

Info Lines & Services

Lesbian/ Gay AA 734/482–5700

The Office of LGBT Affairs 3200 Michigan Union, 530 S State St **734/763–4186** • 9am-5pm, till 9pm Tue & Th • student services • events open to all

Bars

\aut\ Bar 315 Braun Ct (at Catherine) **734/994–3677** • 4pm-2am, from 10am Sun (brunch) • lesbians/ gay men • food served • American/ Mexican • some veggie • patio • wheelchair access • $5-8

Blind Pig 208 S 1st St (at Washington) **734/996–8555** • 3pm-2am • gay-friendly • neighborhood bar • live bands • wheelchair access

Nightclubs

Club Fabulous 734/763–4186 • lesbians/ gay men • occasional dances during school

The Nectarine 516 E Liberty **734/994–5436** • 9pm-2am Tue & Fri only • lesbians/ gay men • dancing/DJ • videos

Restaurants

Dominick's 812 Monroe St (at Tappan Ave) **734/662–5414** • 10am-10pm • Italian • full bar • wheelchair access

The Earle 121 W Washington **734/994–0211** • 6pm-10pm, till midnight Fri-Sat, clsd Sun (summer) • cont'l • some veggie • beer/ wine • wheelchair access • $15-25

Sweet Lorraines 303 Detroit St (at Catherine) **734/665–0700** • 11am-10pm, till midnight Fri-Sat • plenty veggie • full bar • patio • wheelchair access • $10-15

Entertainment & Recreation

The Ark 316 S Main St **734/761–1451** • gay-friendly • concert house • women's music shows

Bookstores

Common Language 215 S 4th Ave (at Liberty) **734/663–0036** • open daily • lesbigay • wheelchair access

Crazy Wisdom Books 206 N 4th Ave **734/665–2757** • 10am-7pm, till 8pm Wed-Fri, noon-7pm Sun • holistic & metaphysical

Webster's 2607 Plymouth Rd (at Nixon, in Traver Village Mall) **734/662–6150** • 8am-11pm • lesbigay section

Publications

Out Post 734/332–0066 • bi-weekly newspaper for metro Detroit

Atwood

Accommodations

Wunderschönes 12410 Antrim Dr, Ellsworth **616/599–2847** • lesbians/ gay men • red cedar log home • full brkfst • smokefree • gay-owned/ run • $60-90

Battle Creek

Nightclubs

Partners 910 North Ave (at Morgan) **616/964–7276** • 6pm-2am, from 5pm Sun • lesbians/ gay men • dancing/DJ • wheelchair access

Spiritual Groups

Sign of the Covenant MCC 35 S Cass St (at Jackson) **616/965–8004** • 4pm Sun

Bellaire

Accommodations

Bellaire B&B 212 Park St **616/533–6077, 800/545–0780** • gay/ straight • stately 1879 home • gay-owned/ run • $70-100

Big Bay

Accommodations

Big Bay Depot 906/345-9886 • gay-friendly • overlooking Lake Independence • smokefree rms available • $55

Detroit

Info Lines & Services

Affirmations Lesbian/ Gay Community Center 195 W 9-Mile Rd #106 (at Woodward), Ferndale **248/398-7105** • 10:30am-9pm, till 4pm Sat, 1pm-9pm Sun

Helpline 248/398-4297 • 4:30pm-9pm, clsd Sat

Bars

Club Gold Coast 2971 E 7-Mile Rd (at Conant) **313/366-6135** • 7pm-2am • popular • mostly gay men • dancing/DJ • live shows • wheelchair access

Gigi's 16920 W Warren (at Clayburn, enter rear) **313/584-6525** • noon-2am, from 2pm wknds • mostly gay men • dancing/DJ • transgender-friendly • live shows

Pronto 608 S Washington (at 6th St), Royal Oak **248/544-7900** • 11am-midnight, till 2am Fri-Sat, from 9am wknds • gay-friendly • food served • videos

Detroit

Known for its cars and stars, 'Motown' is the home of General Motors and was the starting point for many living legends, including Aretha Franklin, Diana Ross & the Supremes, the Temptations, Stevie Wonder, Anita Baker, and Madonna.

Detroit is also rich in African-American culture. Be sure to check out the Museum of African-American History, multicultural gallery Your Heritage House, the Motown Museum...and the lesbian/gay bar **Zippers.** And just across the river in Canada—via the underground Detroit/Windsor Tunnel—is the North American Black Historical Museum in Windsor, Ontario.

You might want to start your stay with a visit to the **Affirmations Lesbian/Gay Community Center** or **A Woman's Prerogative,** the women's bookstore, then check out **Sugarbakers,** a women's sports bar.

Downtown, discover the impressive Renaissance Center. This office and retail complex that dominates the city skyline houses shopping, restaurants, a 73-story hotel, even an indoor lake! Before moving on to explore the districts of Greektown, Bricktown, or Rivertown, take a spin around the Civic Center district on the Detroit People Mover, an elevated transit system that carries travelers in automated, weatherproof cars.

Stingers Lounge 19404 Sherwood (at 7-Mile) **313/892-1765** • 6pm-5am, from 8pm wknds • lesbians/ gay men • neighborhood bar • grill menu

Sugarbakers 3800 E 8-Mile Rd (at Ryan Ave) **313/892-5203** • 6pm-2am • mostly women • sports bar & grill

Nightclubs

Alvins 5756 Cass Ave (btwn Palmer St & I-94) **313/832-2355** • mostly gay men • 9pm-close Mon • dancing/DJ • mostly African-American

Backstreet 15606 Joy Rd (at Greenfield) **313/272-8959** • 9pm-2am Wed & Sat • popular • mostly gay men • dancing/DJ • wheelchair access

Off Broadway East 12215 Harper St **313/521-0920** • 9pm-2am • mostly gay men • more women Sat • dancing/DJ

The Rainbow Room 6640 E 8-Mile Rd (at Mound) **313/891-1020** • 7pm-2am Wed-Sun • lesbians/ gay men • dancing/DJ • live shows

Regine's 711 E McNichols Rd (at Oakland) **313/865-4747** • 10:30pm-2am Wed, Fri-Sat • mostly gay men • more women Sat • dancing/DJ • mostly African-American

Stiletto's 1641 Middlebelt Rd (at Michigan Ave), Inkster **734/729-8980** • 8pm-2am, clsd Mon • mostly women • dancing/DJ • live shows

Zippers 6221 E Davison **313/892-8120** • from 9pm, clsd Sun & Tue • popular • lesbians/ gay men • dancing/DJ • mostly African-American • live shows • wheelchair access

Cafes

Avalon Bakery 422 W Willis (at Cass) **313/832-0008** • 6am-6pm, clsd Sun-Mon • lesbian-owned/ run

Restaurants

Como's 22812 Woodward (at 9-Mile), Ferndale **248/548-5005** • 11am-2am, till 3:30am Fri-Sat, from 2pm wknds • Italian • full bar

Detroit

Where the Girls Are: At the bars on 8-Mile Road between I-75 and Van Dyke Ave., with the boys in Highland Park or Dearborn, or shopping in Royal Oak.

Lesbigay Pride: May/June. 248/547-5878 (Just for Us).

Annual Events: August - Michigan Womyn's Music Festival 616/757-4766 or 616/898-3707. One of the biggest annual gatherings of lesbians on the continent, in Walhalla.

City Info: 313/202-1800 or 800/338-7648, www.visitdetroit.com.

Attractions: Belle Isle Park.
Detroit Institute of Arts 313/833-7900.
Greektown.
Montreux Detroit Jazz Festival.
Motown Historical Museum 313/875-2264.
Museum of African-American History 313/494-5800.
Renaissance Center 313/568-5600.

Best View: From the top of the 73-story Westin Hotel at the Renaissance Center.

Weather: Be prepared for hot, humid summers and cold, dry winters.

Transit: Checker Cab 313/963-7000.
Shuttle 734/283-4800.
DOT bus service) 313/933-1300.
Detroit People Mover 313/962-7245.

La Dolce Vita 17546 Woodward Ave (at McNichols) **313/865-0331** • dinner Wed-Sun, Sun brunch, clsd Mon-Tue • lesbians/ gay men • Italian • plenty veggie • full bar • patio • wheelchair access • $7-16

Rhinoceros 265 Riopelle (at Franklin) **313/259-2208** • 5pm-2am • jazz club • full bar • $15-25

Sweet Lorraines 29101 Greenfield Rd (at 12-Mile), Southfield **248/559-5985** • 11am-10pm, till midnight Fri-Sat • modern American

Vivio's 2460 Market St (btwn Gratiot & Russell) **313/393-1711** • lunch & dinner, clsd Sun • Italian • full bar • $6-11

Entertainment & Recreation

Detroit Women's Coffeehouse 4605 Cass Ave (at 1st Unitarian Church) **313/832-5888** • 2nd Sat, except in August

Bookstores

A Woman's Prerogative Bookstore 175 W 9-Mile Rd (at Woodward), Ferndale **248/545-5703** • noon-7pm, till 9pm Th, till 5pm Sun • lesbian

Chosen Books 120 W 4th St (btwn Main St & Woodward), Royal Oak **248/543-5758** • noon-10pm • lesbigay • wheelchair access

Just 4 Us 211 W 9-Mile Rd (at Woodward), Ferndale **248/547-5878** • noon-8pm, clsd Sun

Retail Shops

The Dressing Room 42310 Hayes, Clinton Township **810/286-0412** • noon-9pm, till 5pm Sat, clsd Sun • cross-dressing boutique • larger sizes

Publications

Between the Lines 248/615-7003, 888/615-7003 • statewide

Cruise Magazine 248/545-9040 • statewide entertainment listings

Metra 248/543-3500 • covers IN, IL, MI, OH, PA, WI & Ontario, Canada

Out Post 734/332-0066 • bi-weekly newspaper for metro Detroit

Spiritual Groups

Dignity Detroit Marygrove College Campus, on W McNichols, east of Wyoming **313/278-4786** • 6pm Sun

Divine Peace MCC 23839 John R (at 9-Mile), Hazel Park **248/544-8335** • 10am Sun

MCC of Detroit 2411 Pinecrest (at Presbyterian Church), Ferndale **248/399-7741** • 9am, 11am & 7pm Sun

Erotica

Noir Leather 124 W 4th (at Main), Royal Oak **248/541-3979** • 11am-9pm, till 10pm Fri-Sat, noon-6pm Sun • toys • fetishwear

Escanaba

Nightclubs

Club Xpress 904 Ludington St (at 10th) **906/789-0140** • 8pm-2am, from 6pm Fri-Sat, clsd Sun-Tue • lesbians/ gay men • dancing/DJ • wheelchair access

Flint

Bars

Club MI 2402 N Franklin St (at Davison) **810/234-9481** • 1pm-2am • popular • lesbians/ gay men • neighborhood bar • multi-racial clientele • 18+

State Bar 2510 S Dort Hwy **810/767-7050** • 3pm-2am, from 1pm wknds • popular • lesbians/ gay men • dancing/DJ • karaoke • wheelchair access

Nightclubs

Club Triangle 2101 S Dort **810/767-7550** • 7pm-2am • popular • lesbians/ gay men • dancing/DJ • 18+

Spiritual Groups

Redeemer MCC of Flint 1665 N Chevrolet Ave (at Welch) **810/238-6700** • 11am Sun • wheelchair access

Glen Arbor

Accommodations

Duneswood at Sleeping Bear Dunes Nat'l Lakeshore **231/334-3346** • women only • also 'Marge & Joanne's B&B' • $45-85

Grand Rapids

Info Lines & Services

Lesbian/ Gay Network 909 Cherry SE (at Eastern) **616/458-3511** • 10am-10pm, from 6pm Tue & Th, till 2pm Sat • lounge • library

Bars

The Apartment 33 Sheldon NE (at Library) **616/451-0815** • 11am-2am, from 1pm Sun • mostly gay men • neighborhood bar • sandwiches served • wheelchair access

The Cell 76 S Division St (at Oake) **616/454-4499** • 2pm-2am • mostly gay men • dancing/DJ • leather • wheelchair access

The City Limits 67 S Division Ave (at Oake) **616/454-8003** • 11am-2:30am • popular • lesbians/ gay men • dancing/DJ • live shows • videos • wheelchair access

Diversions 10 Fountain St NW (at Division) **616/451-3800** • 11am-2am, from 8pm wknds • popular • lesbians/ gay men • dancing/DJ • live shows • food served • plenty veggie • wheelchair access • $5-10

Cafes

Discussions 6 Jefferson SE (at Fulton) **616/456-5060** • 10am-midnight, till 4am Fri-Sat, 11am-9pm Sun • live shows • karaoke • soup & sandwiches • gay-owned/ run

Restaurants

Brandywine 1345 Lake Drive SE

Cherie Inn 969 Cherry St (at Lake Dr) **616/458-0588** • 7am-3pm, clsd Mon • some veggie • wheelchair access • $4-6

Bookstores

Sons & Daughters 962 Cherry SE (at Diamond) **616/459-8877** • noon-midnight, from 10am wknds • lesbigay bookstore & coffeehouse

Spiritual Groups

Dignity 1100 Lake Dr (at Trinity Methodist Church) **616/454-9779** • 7:30pm 1st & 3rd Wed

Reconciliation MCC 300 Graceland NE (at Lafayette) **616/364-7633** • 10am Sun

Honor

Accommodations

Labrys Wilderness Resort **616/882-5994** • women only • cabins • lesbian-owned/ run • $40-65

Kalamazoo

Info Lines & Services

Kalamazoo Lesbian/ Gay Resource Line **616/345-7878** • 7pm-10pm, clsd Sat

Lavender Morning **616/388-5656** • sponsors women's dances • newsletter

Women's Resource Center **616/387-2995** • call for info

Bars

Tradewinds 562 Portage St **616/383-1814** • 2pm-2am • lesbians/ gay men • neighborhood bar • dancing/DJ • theme nights

Nightclubs

Brother's Bar 209 Stockbridge (btwn Portage & Burdick) **616/345-1960** • 2pm-2am • lesbians/ gay men • more women Sat • dancing/DJ • live shows • karaoke • private club • patio • wheelchair access

Bookstores

Pandora Books for Open Minds 226 W Lovell St **616/388-5656** • noon-7pm, till 6pm Fri-Sat, clsd Sun-Mon • feminist/ lesbigay

Spiritual Groups

Phoenix Community Church 394 S Drake (at Sky Ridge Church) **616/381-3222** • 6pm Sun • wheelchair access

Erotica

Triangle World 551 Portage Rd (at Walnut) **616/373-4005** • lesbigay books • leather • gifts • wheelchair access

Lansing

Info Lines & Services

AA Gay/ Lesbian East Lansing **517/321-8781** • call for mtg schedule

Lansing Lesbian/ Gay Hotline **517/332-3200** • 7pm-10pm, 2pm-5pm Sun, clsd Sat

Accommodations

Leaven Retreat Center & Guesthouse Lyons **517/855-2277** • women only • spiritual retreat center • also guesthouse available for individual use • $30-60

Bars

Club 505 505 E Shiawassee **517/374-6312** • 6pm-2am, clsd Mon • mostly women • neighborhood bar • dancing/DJ

Esquire 1250 Turner (at Clinton) **517/487-5338** • noon-2am, from 4pm Sun • lesbians/ gay men • neighborhood bar • karaoke • wheelchair access

Nightclubs

Paradise 224 S Washington Square **517/484-2399** • 9pm-2am • popular • mostly gay men • dancing/DJ • live shows

Bookstores

Community News Center 418 Frandor Shopping Center **517/351-7562** • 9am-9pm, till 7pm Sun • wheelchair access

Spiritual Groups

Dignity 327 MAC (at St John's Parish), East Lansing **517/351-7341** • 8pm 1st Tue

Marquette

Bookstores

Sweet Violets 413 N 3rd St (btwn Michigan & Arch) **906/228-3307** • 10am-6pm, clsd Sun • feminist

Midland

Accommodations

Jay's B&B 4429 Bay City Rd **517/496-2498** • gay-friendly • deck • shared baths • smokefree • $60

Mount Clemens

Nightclubs

JD's Macomb Theatre 31 N Walnut Ave (at Cass) **810/913-1921** • 4pm-2am • lesbians/ gay men • dancing/DJ • live shows • 8 bars on 4 levels

Owendale

Accommodations

Windover Resort 3596 Blakely Rd **517/375-2586** • women only • campsites • swimming • $25/yr membership fee • $18-20 camping fee

Pontiac

Nightclubs

Club Flamingo 352 Oakland Ave (at Montcalm) **248/253-0430** • 4pm-2am, from 2pm Sat • lesbians/ gay men • dancing/DJ • live shows • wheelchair access

Port Huron

Nightclubs

Seekers 3301 24th St (btwn Oak & Little) **810/985-9349** • 7pm-2am, from 4pm Fri-Sun • lesbians/ gay men • dancing/DJ

Saginaw

Nightclubs

Bambi's 1742 E Genesee **517/752-9179** • 7pm-2am • lesbians/ gay men • dancing/DJ • live shows

Saugatuck

Accommodations

Camp It II & Resort **616/543-4335** • lesbians/ gay men • campsites • RV hookups • seasonal • swimming • $12-17 • also B&B • $60+

Deerpath Lodge **888/DEER-PATH, 616/857-DEER** • women only • on 45 secluded acres • 2 night minimum • heated pool • kayaks • hot tub • $90-110

▲ **The Dunes Resort** 333 Blue Star Hwy, Douglas **616/857-1401** • lesbians/ gay men • swimming • food served • women's wknds: 1st week in April & Oct • $42-125

Grandma Arlene's House B&B 2135 Blue Star Hwy **616/543-4706** • lesbians/ gay men • Victorian country estate • full brkfst • hot tub • $70-80

Hillby Thatch Cottages 71st St, Glenn **847/864-3553** • gay-friendly • cottages • kitchens • fireplaces • women-owned/ run

Kirby House 294 W Center (at Blue Star Hwy) **616/857-2904** • gay-friendly • Queen Anne Victorian • full brkfst • swimming • smokefree • gay-owned/ run • $90-135

The Lighthouse Motel **616/857-2271** • gay-friendly • swimming • wheelchair access • $50-150

Moore's Creek Inn 820 Holland St (at Lucy) **616/857-2411, 800/838-5864** • gay-friendly • old-fashioned farmhouse • full brkfst • $65-95

The Newnham SunCatcher Inn 131 Griffith (at Mason) **616/857-4249** • gay-friendly • full brkfst • hot tub • swimming • women-owned/ run • $65-120

The Spruce Cutter's Cottage 6670 126th Ave, Fennville **616/543-4285, 800/493-5888** • gay/ straight • full brkfst • gay-owned/ run • $70-125

Tin Cricket Lodge 3291 Blue Star Hwy **616/857-5156** • gay-friendly • cabins • $55 • $500 weekly

Bars

Douglas Disco in the 'Dunes Resort' **616/857-1401** • 9am-2am, from noon Sun • mostly gay men • dancing/DJ • live shows

Cafes

Uncommon Grounds 123 Hoffman **616/857-3333** • 7:30am-9:30pm, open later on wknds • coffee & juice bar

Restaurants

Blue Frog Bar & Grille in the 'Dunes Resort' **616/857-1401** • 5pm-10pm, till 11pm Fri-Sat, Sun brunch, clsd Tue-Wed • cont'l

Loaf & Mug 236 Culver St (at Butler) **616/857-2974** • 8am-3pm • some veggie

Pumpernickel's 202 Butler St (at Mason) **616/857-1196** • seasonal • 8am-3pm (clsd Wed in winter) • sandwiches & fresh breads • some veggie • $5-10

Restaurant Toulouse 248 Culver St (at Griffith) **616/857-1561** • dinner only • country French • some veggie • full bar • wheelchair access • $10-20

RETAIL SHOPS

Hoopdee Scootee 133 Mason (at Butler) **616/857-4141** • 10am-9pm, till 6pm Sun (till 5pm in winter) • clothing • gifts

Sault Ste-Marie

BOOKSTORES

Open Mind Books 223 Ashmun St (at Ridge) **906/635-9008** • 11am-5pm (noon-6pm summer), clsd Sun-Mon • progressive

South Haven

ACCOMMODATIONS

Yelton Manor B&B 140 North Shore Dr **616/637-5220** • gay/ straight • jacuzzi • smoke-free • $95-235

St Clair

ACCOMMODATIONS

William Hopkins Manor 613 N Riverside Ave (at Clinton) **810/329-0188** • gay-friendly • full brkfst • $80-100

Traverse City

ACCOMMODATIONS

Neahtawanta Inn 1308 Neahtawanta Rd **616/223-7315** • gay-friendly • swimming • sauna • wheelchair access • $70-130

NIGHTCLUBS

Side Traxx Nite Club 520 Franklin **616/935-1666** • 6pm-2am, from 2pm wknds • lesbians/ gay men • dancing/DJ • live shows • wheelchair access

CAFES

Ray's Coffee House 129 E Front St **616/929-1006** • 7am-7pm, till 10pm Th-Sat (late hours in summer only) • wheelchair access

BOOKSTORES

The Bookie Joint 120 S Union St (btwn State & Front) **616/946-8862** • 10am-6pm, 1pm-4pm Sun • pride gifts • used books

Union Pier

ACCOMMODATIONS

Fire Fly Resort 15657 Lakeshore Rd **616/469-0245** • gay/ straight

Warren Woods Inn 15506 Lakeshore Rd **616/469-5880, 800/358-4754** • gay-friendly • full brkfst • jacuzzis • fireplaces • kids ok • gay-owned/ run • $95-160

Ypsilanti

SPIRITUAL GROUPS

Tree of Life MCC 218 N Adams St (at 1st Congregational Church) **734/485-3922** • 5:55pm Sun & 6pm Wed

EROTICA

The Magazine Rack 515 West Cross **734/482-6944**

MINNESOTA

Duluth

INFO LINES & SERVICES

Aurora: A Northern Lesbian Center 32 E 1st St #104 **218/722-4903** • discussion groups & socials

ACCOMMODATIONS

Stanford Inn B&B 1415 E Superior St **218/724-3044** • gay-friendly • full brkfst • $55-95

BOOKSTORES

At Sara's Table 728 E Superior St **218/723-8569** • 8am-6pm, clsd Tue • also cafe • wheelchair access • women-owned/ run

Ely

ACCOMMODATIONS

Log Cabin Hideaways 1321 N Hwy 21 **218/365-6045** • remote wilderness cabins • no running water/ electricity • smokefree

Hastings

ACCOMMODATIONS

Thorwood & Rosewood Inns 315 Pine St **612/437-3297, 888/846-7966** • gay-friendly • circa 1880 mansion • full brkfst

Hill City

ACCOMMODATIONS

Northwoods Retreat 33804 Mt Ash Dr **218/697-8119, 800/767-3020** • lesbians/ gay men • 2 cabins w/700 ft of lakeshore • all meals included • veggie cuisine • wheelchair access

Hinckley

Accommodations

Dakota Lodge B&B 320/384-6052 • gay/ straight • full brkfst • hot tub • wheelchair access • gay-owned/ run • $58-135

Kenyon

Accommodations

Dancing Winds Farm 6863 Country 12 Blvd **507/789-6606** • lesbians/ gay men • B&B on working dairy farm • tentsites • work exchange available

Mankato

Info Lines & Services

Mankato State U Lesbigay Center 507/389-5131

Cafes

The Coffee Hag 329 N Riverfront **507/387-5533** • 7:30am-11pm, 9am-midnight Sat, clsd Mon • veggie menu • live shows • wheelchair access • women-owned/ run • $3-7

Minneapolis/St Paul

Info Lines & Services

Chrysalis Women's Center 2650 Nicollett Ave, St Paul **612/871-0118** • 8:30am-8pm, till 5pm Fri, clsd wknds • many groups

District 202 1601 Nicollett Ave, St Paul **612/871-5559** • 3pm-11pm, till 1am Fri, noon-1am Sat, clsd Tue • resource center for lesbigay youth

Outfront MN 310 E 38th St, Minneapolis **612/822-0127, 800/800-0350** • info line

Quatrefoil Library 1619 Dayton Ave, St Paul **651/641-0969** • 7pm-9pm, noon-4pm Sat, 1pm-5pm Sun • lesbigay library & resource center

U of MN Queer Student Cultural Center 230-A Coffman Memorial Library, Minneapolis **612/626-2344** • call for info

Accommodations

Country Guest House 1673 38th St, Somerset, WI **715/247-3520** • lesbians/ gay men • rental home on 20 wooded acres in St Croix River Valley • women-owned/ run • $75

Cover Park Manor 15330 58th St N (at Peller), Stillwater **651/430-9292** • gay-friendly • full brkfst • in-room jacuzzi & fireplace • wheelchair access • $90-179

Garden Gate B&B 925 Goodrich Ave (at Milton), St Paul **612/227-8430, 800/967-2703** • gay-friendly • massage available

Nan's B&B 2304 Fremont Ave S (at 22nd), Minneapolis **612/377-5118** • gay-friendly • 1895 Victorian family home • full brkfst • shared bath • $50-60

Regal Minneapolis Hotel 1313 Nicollet Mall (btwn W Grant & 13th St), Minneapolis **612/332-6000, 800/222-8888** • gay-friendly • food served • swimming • wheelchair access • IGLTA • $109-250

Bars

19 Bar 19 W 15th St (at La Salle), Minneapolis **612/871-5553** • 3pm-1am, from 1pm Sat-Sun • mostly gay men • neighborhood bar • beer/ wine • wheelchair access

Bev's Wine Bar 250 3rd Ave N, Minneapolis **612/337-0102** • 4pm-1am Tue-Sat • gay-friendly • light food menu • patio

Brass Rail 422 Hennepin Ave (at 4th), Minneapolis **612/333-3016** • noon-1am • popular • mostly gay men • live shows • karaoke • videos • wheelchair access

Bryant Lake Bowl 1810 W Lake St (corner of Bryant & Lake), Minneapolis **612/825-3737** • 8am-1am • gay-friendly • also theater • restaurant ($5-9) • bowling alley • wheelchair access

Over the Rainbow 249 W 7th St (2 blks west of Civic Center), St Paul **651/228-7180** • 3pm-1am, from noon wknds • lesbians/ gay men • dancing/DJ • live shows • karaoke

Richie's 2211 Lowry Ave N, Minneapolis **612/588-8145** • 10am-1am, from 8am wknds • lesbians/ gay men • also restaurant

The Saloon 830 Hennepin Ave (at 9th), Minneapolis **612/332-0835** • 9am-1am, till 3am Fri-Sun • lesbians/ gay men • dancing/DJ • food served after 5pm • also 'The Tank' leather bar • wheelchair access

Town House 1415 University Ave (at Elbert), St Paul **651/646-7087** • 3pm-1am, from noon wknds • popular • lesbians/ gay men • dancing/DJ • theme nights • also 'Blanche's' piano bar from 9pm Th-Sat

Trikkx 490 N Robert St (at 9th St), St Paul **651/224-0703** • 4pm-1am, from noon wknds • mostly gay men • dancing/DJ • also restaurant • wheelchair access

Minneapolis/St. Paul

If you're searching for a liberal oasis in the heartland of America, if you love Siberian winters, and if you crave a diverse, intensely political lesbian community, you'll fit right into the Twin Cities of Minneapolis and St. Paul.

Located on the banks of the Mississippi River, these cities share the Minnesota Twins, 936 lakes, 513 parks, and a history of Native American and Northern European settlements. If you want more than glimpses into the various cultures of Minnesota, visit the Minneapolis American Indian Center or the American Swedish Institute.

Of course, you'll probably have more fun checking out the lesbian cultural scene. The place to go to find out about the latest poetry reading, play, or concert is **Amazon Bookstore** in Minneapolis. To find social groups for women of color, call **Outfront MN.**

Or stop by **Minnesota Women's Press** bookstore & library in St. Paul. Then go cafe-hopping in Minneapolis at the women-owned **Cafe Wyrd** or **Ruby's Cafe.** For a night on the town, you won't find any full-time women's bars, but there are women's nights: Friday is country-western dancing at the **Town House,** and the **Gay 90s** hosts 'Womyn 4 Womyn' on Sunday. **Club Metro** & **The Saloon** are also popular on weekends.

Whatever you do, don't stay indoors the whole time. In the summer, boating, fishing, sunbathing, water-skiing, walking, jogging, and bicycling are all popular. In winter, you can enjoy snowmobiling, ice hockey, cross-country skiing, or snuggling by a fire. For women's outdoor adventures, try **Adventures in Good Company** (877/439-4024).

Minneapolis/St Paul

Lesbigay Pride: July. 612/996-9250.

Annual Events: September - Gay Night at Knott's Camp Snoopy in Mall of America.

City Info: 800/445-7412, web: www.minneapolis.org.

Attractions: Frederick R. Weisman Art Museum 612/625-9494.
Mall of America (the largest mall in the US w/indoor theme park) 612/883-8800.
Minneapolis Institute of Arts 612/870-3131.
Museum of Questionable Medical Devices 612/379-4046.
Walker Art Center/Minneapolis Sculpture Garden 612/375-7622.

Best View: Observation deck of the 32nd story of Foshay Tower (closed in winter).

Weather: Winters are harsh. If driving, carry extra blankets and supplies. The average temperature is 19°, and it can easily drop well below 0°, and then there's the wind chill! Summer temperatures are usually in the upper-80°s to mid-90°s and HUMID.

Transit: Town Taxi (Minn) 612/331-8294.
Yellow Cab (St. Paul) 651/222-4433.
Airport Express 612/827-7777.
MTC 612/349-7000.

Nightclubs

Club Metro 733 Pierce Butler Rte (at Minnehaha), St Paul **651/489-0002** • 4pm-1am • popular • lesbians/ gay men • dancing/DJ • transgender-friendly • live shows • food served • $5-15

Gay 90s 408 Hennepin Ave (at 4th), Minneapolis **612/333-7755** • 8am-1am (dinner nightly 5pm-9pm) • mostly gay men • 8-bar complex • 'Womyn4Womyn' Sun 9pm-1am in upstairs retro bar • dancing/DJ • live shows • also erotica store • wheelchair access

Ground Zero/ The Front 15 NE 4th St (at Hennepin), Minneapolis **612/378-5115** • 9pm-1am, clsd Sun-Tue • more gay Th at 'Bondage-A-Go-Go' • 'The Front' from 8pm, clsd Sun • gay-friendly • dancing/DJ

Cafes

Cafe Wyrd 1600 W Lake St (at Irving), Minneapolis **612/827-5710** • 7am-1am • lesbians/ gay men • plenty veggie • women-owned/ run • $3-6

Cafe Zev 1362 La Salle Ave (at Grant), Minneapolis **612/874-8477** • 7am-1am • live shows

Cahoots 1562 Selby Ave (at Snelling), St Paul **651/644-6778** • 6:30am-9:30pm, 7:30am-11pm wknds • coffee bar

Camden Coffee Company 1500 N 44th Ave (at Humboldt Ave N), Minneapolis **612/529-6400** • 6:30am-10pm, till midnight Fri, 8am-midnight Sat, till 8pm Sun • patio • gay-owned/ run

Moose & Sadie's 212 3rd Ave N (at 2nd St), Minneapolis **612/371-0464** • 7:30am-11pm, till 1:30am wknds, 9am-10pm Sun • warehouse district cafe

Ruby's Cafe 1614 Harmon Pl, Minneapolis **612/338-2089** • 7am-2pm, from 8am Sun • popular • lesbians/ gay men • outdoor seating • women-owned/ run

Uncommon Grounds 2809 Hennepin Ave, Minneapolis **612/872-4811** • 10am-1am • outdoor seating

The Urban Bean 3255 Bryant Ave S (at 33rd), Minneapolis **612/824-6611** • also 2717 Hennepin Ave S location

Restaurants

A la Française 823 University Ave (at Avon), St Paul **651/291-2661** • 7am-8pm • Vietnamese • bakery

Al's Breakfast 413 14th Ave SE, Minneapolis **612/331-9991** • great hash

Anodyne at 43rd 4301 Nicollet Ave, Minneapolis **612/824-4300** • 6:30am-10pm, from 7am Sat, from 8am Sun, till midnight wknds • Egyptian

Bobino Cafe & Wine Bar 222 E Hennepin Ave, Minneapolis **612/623-3301** • classic bistro

Campiello 1320 W Lake St (at Hennepin), Minneapolis **612/825-2222** • dinner & Sun brunch

D'Amico Cucina 100 N 6th St (btwn 1st & 2nd Aves), Minneapolis **612/338-2401** • dinner nightly • à la carte • full bar • $60-70 per person

Goodfellows 800 Nicollet Mall, Minneapolis **612/332-4800** • lunch, dinner till 9pm, till 10pm wknds, clsd Sun

La Covina 1570 Selby Ave (at Snelling), St Paul **651/645-5288** • lunch & dinner • Mexican • wheelchair access • $6-10

Murray's 26 S 6th St (at Hennepin), Minneapolis **612/339-0909** • lunch Mon-Fri, dinner nightly • meat & potatoes

Rudolph's Bar-B-Que 1933 Lyndale (at Franklin), Minneapolis **612/871-8969** • 11am-midnight • wheelchair access

WA Frost & Co 374 Selby Ave (at Western), St Paul **612/224-5715** • 11am-11pm • patio • wheelchair access • $11-22

Entertainment & Recreation

32nd St Beach E side of Lake Calhoun (33rd & Calhoun Blvd), Minneapolis • gay beach

Fresh Fruit KFAI 90.3 FM, Minneapolis **612/341-0980** • 9pm-midnight Sun • gay radio program

Bookstores

A Brother's Touch 2327 Hennepin Ave (at 24th), Minneapolis **612/377-6279** • 11am-8pm, till 7pm Sat, noon-5pm Sun • lesbigay • wheelchair access

Amazon Bookstore 1612 Harmon Pl (at 16th/ Maple), Minneapolis **612/338-6560** • 10am-9pm, till 6pm Th, till 5pm Sun • feminist bookstore since 1970 • also gifts, music & art • women-owned/ run • no relation to Seattle's amazon.com

Borders Bookshop 3001 Hennepin S (at Lake, in Calhoun Sq), Minneapolis **612/825-0336** • 10am-10pm, till 11pm Fri-Sat, 11am-6pm Sun

Magus Books 1316 SE 4th St (at 13th/ 14th), Minneapolis **612/379-7669** • 10am-9pm, till 6pm wknds, from noon Sun • alternative spirituality books • also mail order

Retail Shops

The Rainbow Road 109 W Grant (at LaSalle), Minneapolis **612/872-8448** • 10am-10pm • lesbigay retail & video • wheelchair access

Publications

Focus Point **612/288-9008** • lesbigay newspaper

Inside Out 3010 Hennepin Avenue S #197, Minneapolis **612/362-3676, 612/822-8535** • events newsletter published by Twin Cities Quorum

Lavender Magazine **612/871-2237, 800/484-3901 x 9020** • lesbigay newsmagazine

Minnesota Women's Press 771 Raymond Ave, St Paul **651/646-3968** • 9am-6pm, till 3pm Sat, clsd Sun • bi-weekly newspaper • also bookshop & library

Woodswomen News 25 W Diamond Lake Rd, Minneapolis **612/822-3809**

Spiritual Groups

Dignity Twin Cities Prospect Park Unitarian Methodist (at Malcolm & Orwin), Minneapolis **612/827-3103** • 7:30pm 2nd & 4th Fri

Lutherans Concerned 100 N Oxford, Minneapolis **612/866-8941** • 7:30pm 3rd Fri • wheelchair access

MCC All God's Children 3100 Park Ave, Minneapolis **612/824-2673** • 10am Sun & 7pm Wed • wheelchair access

Shir Tikvah 5000 Girard Ave, Minneapolis **612/822-1440** • 10am 1st Sat, then 8pm every Fri • lesbigay Jewish congregation • wheelchair access

Gyms & Health Clubs

Body Quest 245 N Aldrich Ave N (at Glenwood), Minneapolis **612/377-7222** • lesbians/ gay men

Erotica

Back in Black Leather, Inc 733 Pierce Butler Route (in 'Club Metro'), St Paul **651/487-0513** • 8pm-11pm Th-Sat, 1:30pm-6pm Sun

Fantasy House 716 W Lake (at Lyndale), Minneapolis **612/824-2459** • adult gifts • wheelchair access

Lickety Split 901 Hennepin Ave (at 9th, across from the Orpheum Theatre), Minneapolis **612/338-7303** • 24hrs

SexWorld 241 2nd Ave N (at Washington), Minneapolis **612/672-0556** • 24hrs

Moorhead

see also Fargo, North Dakota

Nightclubs

The I-Beam 1021 Center Ave **218/233-7700** • 5pm-1am, clsd Sun • lesbians/ gay men • dancing/DJ • wheelchair access

Cafes

Atomic Coffee 15 4th St S (at Main) **218/299-6161** • 7am-11pm, from 9am Sat, from 10am Sun • also gallery • gay-owned/ run

Rochester

Info Lines & Services

Gay/ Lesbian Community Service **507/281-3265** • 5pm-7pm Mon & Wed

Rushford

Accommodations

Windswept Inn 2070 N Mill St **507/864-2545** • gay-friendly

Two Harbors

Accommodations

Grand Superior Lodge 1098 Hwy 61 E **218/834-3796, 800/642-6036** • gay-friendly • log cabins on the north shore of Lake Superior • wheelchair ramps available

Wolverton

Restaurants

District 31 Victoria's 101 First St **218/995-2000** • 5:30pm-9:30pm, clsd Sun • cont'l • beer/ wine • reservations required • $15-25

Mississippi

Biloxi

Accommodations

Lofty Oaks Inn 17288 Hwy 67 **228/392-6722, 800/280-4361** • full brkfst • hot tub • swimming • kids/ pets ok by arrangement • woman-owned/ run • $95-125

Bars

Joey's 1708 Beach Blvd/ Hwy 90 **228/435-5639** • 8pm-close, from 6pm Sun, clsd Mon-Tue • lesbians/ gay men • dancing/DJ • live shows

The Sanctuary 205 Veterans Ave **228/388-9998** • 3pm-7am, from 1pm wknds • lesbians/ gay men • dancing/DJ

Erotica

Satellite News 1632 Pass Rd **228/432-8229** • clsd Sun

Hattiesburg

Bars

The Courtyard 107 E Front St **601/545-2714** • hours vary • lesbians/ gay men • dancing/DJ • food served • live shows

Holly Springs

Accommodations

Somerset Cottage 135 Gholson Ave **601/252-4513** • gay-friendly • smokefree • hot tub • $65

Jackson

Info Lines & Services

Gay/ Lesbian Community Info Line **601/346-4379** • 6pm-11pm • switchboard for many organizations, including youth group

Lambda AA 4872 N State St (at Unitarian Church) **601/346-4379** • 6:30pm Mon & Wed, 8pm Sat

Bars

Jack's Construction Site (JC's) 425 N Mart Plaza **601/362-3108** • 5pm-close, from 2pm Sun • mostly gay men • more women Wed & Fri • neighborhood bar • beer/ wine • BYOB

Nightclubs

Club City Lights 200 N Mill St **601/353-0059** • 10pm-close, clsd Mon-Th • lesbians/ gay men • dancing/DJ • mostly African-American • live shows • beer/ wine • BYOB

Jack & Jill's 3911 Northview Dr (at Meadowbrook) **601/982-5225** • 10pm-close Th & 9pm-close Fri-Sat • lesbians/ gay men • dancing/DJ • live shows

Spiritual Groups

MCC of the Rainbow **601/981-4222** • 11:30am Sun • call for location

Natchez

Accommodations

Guest House Historic Inn 201 N Pearl St **601/442-1054** • gay/ straight • smokefree • wheelchair access • gay-owned/ run • $94-114

Cafes

Local Color Cafe at 'Guest House Historic Inn' **601/442-1054** • 7am-9pm • beer/ wine

Ovett

Accommodations

Camp Sister Spirit **601/344-2005** • mostly women • 120 acres of camping & RV sites • cabins • smokefree • lesbian-owned/ run • $10-20

Tupelo

Nightclubs

Rumors 637 Hwy 145 (10 miles S of Tupelo), Shannon **601/767-9500, 601/891-0761** • 8pm-midnight Th, till 1am Fri-Sat, from 7pm Sat • mostly gay men • dancing/DJ • live shows

Missouri

Cape Girardeau

Nightclubs

Independence Place 5 S Henderson St **573/334-2939** • 8:30pm-1:30am, from 7pm Fri-Sat, clsd Sun • lesbians/ gay men • dancing/DJ • transgender-friendly • live shows Sat

Columbia

Info Lines & Services

Gay/ Lesbian Helpline **573/449-4477**

Women's Center 229 Brady Commons UMC **573/882-6621**

Bars

Outrage Mexico Gravel Rd • clsd Sun-Wed

Styx 3111 Old 63 S **573/499-1828** • 5pm-1:30am, till 3:30am Fri-Sat, till midnight Sun • lesbians/ gay men • dancing/DJ • country/ western Tue • patio • wheelchair access

Cafes

Ernie's Cafe 1005 E Walnut (at 10th) **573/874-7804** • 6:30am-3pm

Spiritual Groups

Christ the King Agape Church 515 Hickman Ave **573/443-5316** • 10:45am Sun & 6:30pm Wed

United Covenant Church **573/449-7194** • 10am Sun • non-denominational • wheelchair access

Erotica

Eclectics 1122-A Wilkes Blvd **573/443-0873**

Jefferson City

Accommodations

Jefferson Inn B&B 801 W High St **573/635-7196** • gay-friendly • full brkfst • kids ok • $65-125

Joplin

Bars

Partners 720 Main St **417/781-6453** • 3pm-1:30am, clsd Sun • lesbians/ gay men • neighborhood bar • dancing/DJ • country/ western • wheelchair access

Ree's 716 Main St **417/627-9035** • 4pm-1:30am, clsd Sun • lesbians/ gay men • dancing/DJ

Kansas City

Info Lines & Services

Gay/ Lesbian Community Center **816/374-5945**

Gay/ Lesbian Hotline **816/753-0700**

Live & Let Live AA 4243 Walnut St **816/531-9668** • many mtgs

Accommodations

B&B in KC 9215 Slater, Overland Park, KS **913/648-5457** • mostly women • full brkfst • smokefree • lesbian-owned/ run • $30-55

Doanleigh Wallagh Inn 217 E 37th St **816/753-2667** • gay-friendly • full brkfst • smokefree • reservations required • lesbian-owned/ run • $95-150

Kansas City

Lesbigay Pride: June. 816/926-0400.

City Info: Convention & Visitors Bureau 816/691-3800, web: www.kansascity.com.

Attractions: Harry S. Truman Nat'l Historical Site (in Independence, MO) 816/254-2720.
Historic 18th & Vine District (includes Kansas City Jazz Museum & the Negro Leagues Baseball Museum).
Nelson-Atkins Museum of Art 816/561-4000.
Thomas Hart Benton Home & Studio 816/931-5722.

Transit: Yellow Cab 816/471-5000. KCI Shuttle 800/243-6383. Metro 816/221-0660.

Bars

AJ's on Grand 1809 Grand Blvd (at 18th) **816/283-0511** • 11am-1:30am, till 3am Fri-Sat • lesbians/ gay men • dancing/DJ • videos • wheelchair access

Balanca's 1107 Grand Ave (at 11th) **816/221-9220** • 4pm-1:30am, clsd Sun • lesbians/ gay men

Dixie Belle Complexx 1915 Main St (at 20th) **816/471-2424** • 11am-3am • 5 bars • mostly gay men • also leather shop & bar • wheelchair access

The Fox 7520 Shawnee Mission Pkwy (at Metcalf), Overland Park, KS **913/384-0369** • 2pm-2am, from 6pm Sat, clsd Sun • gay-friendly • neighborhood bar • more gay evenings

Missie B's 805 W 39th St (at Southwest Trafficway) **816/561-0625** • 6am-3am • mostly gay men • neighborhood bar • live shows

The Other Side 3611 Broadway (at 36th/ Valentine) **816/931-0501** • 4pm-1:30am, clsd Sun • mostly gay men • piano bar • videos

Pearls 1108 Grand Ave (at 11th) **816/421-1082** • 10am-1:30am, from 11am Sat, clsd Sun • mostly gay men • karaoke • live shows Fri-Sat

Sidekicks 3707 Main St (at 37th) **816/931-1430** • 2pm-3am, clsd Sun • mostly gay men • dancing/DJ • country/ western • wheelchair access

Soakie's 1308 Main St (at 13th) **816/221-6060** • 9am-1:30am, till 3am Fri-Sat, from 11am Sun • mostly gay men • dancing/DJ • mostly African-American • food served

Tootsie's 1818 Main (at 18th) **816/471-7704** • noon-3am, till midnight Tue, from 5pm Mon, clsd Sun • popular • mostly women • dancing/DJ • grill menu • some veggie • $3-6

UBU 1321 Grand (at 13th) **816/283-3828** • noon-1:30am, clsd Sun • lesbians/ gay men • neighborhood sports bar

Weatherbee's 2510 NE Vivian Rd (at Antioch) **816/454-2455** • 4pm-3am • mostly women • dancing/DJ • food served • wheelchair access

Nightclubs

The Cabaret 5024 Main St (at 51st) **816/753-6504** • 6pm-3am, from 3pm Sun, clsd Mon-Tue • popular • mostly gay men • dancing/DJ • food served • wheelchair access

The Hurricane 4048 Broadway (at Westport Rd) **816/753-0884** • 4pm-3am • gay-friendly • dancing/DJ • live bands

XO 3954 Central (btwn Westport & Broadway) **816/753-0112** • 9pm-3am, gay Th only • gay/ straight • dancing/DJ

Cafes

The Coffeehouse 1719 W 39th St (at Bell) **816/756-1997** • 7am-midnight, till 2am wknds

Planet Cafe 3535 Broadway Blvd (at 35th) **816/561-7287** • 8am-11pm, till midnight Fri-Sat, 10am-10pm Sun • gay-owned/ run

Restaurants

Classic Cup Cafe 301 W 47th St (at Central) **816/753-1840** • 7am-midnight, till 1am Fri-Sat

The Corner Restaurant 4059 Broadway (at Westport Rd) **816/931-6630** • 7am-3pm & 5pm-9pm Mon-Fri, 7am-2pm wknds • $6-9

Metropolis 303 Westport Rd (at Central) **816/753-1550** • dinner only, clsd Sun • popular • lesbians/ gay men • contemporary American • wheelchair access • $12-25

Otto's Malt Shop 3903 Wyoming (at 39th) **816/756-1010** • 11am-midnight • burgers • malts

Sharp's 63rd St Grill 128 W 63rd St **816/333-4355** • 7am-10pm, till 11pm Fri-Sat, from 8am Sat, from 9am Sun • beer/ wine • wheelchair access • women-owned/ run

Strouds 1014 E 85th St (btwn Troost & Holmes) **816/333-2132** • dinner • fried chicken • $9-20

Entertainment & Recreation

Unicorn Theatre 3820 Main **816/531-3033** • contemporary American theater

Retail Shops

Larry's Gifts & Cards 205 Westport Rd (btwn Main & Broadway) **816/753-4757** • 10am-7pm, till 6:30pm Sat, till 5pm Sun • lesbigay

Publications

The Alternative 3617 Broadway **816/471-2595**

Current News **816/561-2679**

News Telegraph **816/561-6266, 800/303-5468** • lesbigay newspaper

Spiritual Groups

MCC of Johnson County 87th & Lamar (at Overland Park Comm Ctr), Shawnee, KS **913/248-0390** • 10:30am Sun & 7:30pm Wed

Spirit of Hope MCC 3801 Wyandotte **816/931-0750** • 10:15am Sun & 7:15pm Wed

Erotica

Erotic City 8401 E Truman Rd (at I-435) **816/252-3370** • 24hrs • boutique • books • lounge

Hollywood at Home 9063 Metcalf (at 91st), Overland Park, KS **913/649-9666**

Noel

Accommodations

Sycamore Landing 417/475-6460 • open May-Sept • gay-friendly • campsites • canoe rental • wheelchair access

Overland

Erotica

Priscilla's 10210 Page Ave (E of Ashby) **314/423-8422**

Springfield

Info Lines & Services

AA Gay/ Lesbian SMS University at Ecumenical Ctr (at National off Cherry) **417/823-7125** • 6pm Sat

Gay & Lesbian Communtity Center of the Ozarks 518 E Commercial St **417/869-3978** • 6pm-midnight Fri-Sat, till 10pm Sun • youth group 3pm Tue • wheelchair access

Bars

The Edge 424 N Boonville **417/831-4700** • lesbians/ gay men

Martha's Vineyard 219 W Olive St **417/864-4572** • 4pm-1:30am • lesbians/ gay men • neighborhood bar • dancing/DJ • 18+ • also a quiet bar • patio • wheelchair access

Nightclubs

Xanadu 1107 W Commercial **417/866-8105** • 6pm-1:30am • lesbians/ gay men • dancing/DJ • live shows

Bookstores

Renaissance Books & Gifts 1337 E Montclair (at Fremont) **417/883-5161** • 10am-7pm, noon-5pm Sun • women's/ alternative • wheelchair access

Erotica

Priscilla's 1918 S Glenstone (at Sunshine) **417/881-8444**

St Louis

Info Lines & Services

Gay/ Lesbian Hotline 314/367-0084 • 6pm-10pm, clsd Sun

PACT (People of All Colors Together) 314/995-4683 • mtgs 7pm 2nd Wed

Steps Alano Club 1935-A Park Ave **314/436-1858** • call for mtg schedule

Accommodations

A St Louis Guesthouse 1032-38 Allen Ave (at Menard) **314/773-1016** • mostly gay men • located in historic Soulard district • nudity • hot tub • $65-100

Brewers House B&B 1829 Lami St (Lemp) **314/771-1542, 888/767-4665** • lesbians/ gay men • 1860s home • $70-75

Lafayette House B&B 2156 Lafayette Ave (at Jefferson) **314/772-4429, 800/641-8965** • gay-friendly • full brkfst • hot tub • kids/ pets ok • women-owned/ run • $85-135

MotherSource Travels 187 W 19th St, Alton, IL **314/973-1890, 618/462-4051** • women only • reservation service

Napoleon's Retreat B&B 1815 Lafayette Ave (at Mississippi) **314/772-6979, 800/700-9980** • gay/ straight • restored 1880s townhouse • full brkfst • gay-owned/ run • $80-125

The Waverly Place 2218 Waverly Place **314/776-8337** • gay-friendly B&B • jacuzzis • smokefree

Bars

Alibi's 3016 Arsenal (at Minnesota) **314/772-8989** • 11am-3am • lesbians/ gay men • live shows • wheelchair access

Clementine's 2001 Menard (at Allen) **314/664-7869** • 10am-1:30am, from 8:30am Sat, 11am-midnight Sun • mostly gay men • leather • food served • wheelchair access

Club Bridges 3145 W Chain of Rocks Rd, Granite City, IL **618/797-0700** • 11am-2am • lesbians/ gay men • outdoor complex • food served • live shows • videos

Club Escapades 113 W Main St, Belleville, IL **618/222-9597** • 5pm-2am • lesbians/ gay men • dancing/DJ • karaoke

The Drake Bar 3502 Papin St (at Theresa, 1 blk N & 1 blk E of Grand & Chouteau) **314/865-1400** • 5pm-1:30am, clsd Sun • lesbians/ gay men • live shows • patio • wheelchair access

Ernie's Class Act Restaurant & Lounge 3756 S Broadway (at Chippewa) **314/664-6221** • 3pm-1:30am, clsd Sun • mostly women • dancing/DJ • transgender-friendly • food served • $5-7

Loading Zone 16 S Euclid (at Forest Park Pkwy) **314/361-4119** • 2pm-1:30am, clsd Sun • popular • lesbians/ gay men • videos • wheelchair access

Magnolia's 5 S Vandeventer (at Forest Park Pkwy) **314/652-6500** • 6pm-3am, from 3pm Sun • dinner nightly • popular • mostly gay men • dancing/DJ • live shows • wheelchair access

Nero Bianco 6 S Sarah (btwn Laclede & Forest Park) **314/531-4123** • 4pm-1am • mostly gay men • dancing/DJ • mostly African-American

Novak's Bar & Grill 4146 Manchester **314/531-3699** • 4pm-close, from noon wknds • lesbians/ gay men • wheelchair access

Rainbow's End 4060 Chouteau **314/652-8790** • 9am-close • lesbians/ gay men • neighborhood bar • drag shows • patio

Tangerine 1405 Washington Ave (at 14th) **314/621-7335** • 11am-3pm Tue-Fri & 6pm-3am Tue-Sat • gay-friendly • lounge • also restaurant

St. Louis

Most visitors come to St. Louis see the famous Gateway Arch, the tallest monument in the U.S. at 630 feet, designed by renowned architect Eero Saarinen.

After you've ridden the elevator in the Arch and seen the view, come down to earth and take a trip to historic Soulard, the 'French Quarter of St. Louis.' Established in 1779 by Madame and Monsieur Soulard as an open-air market, it's now the place for great food and jazz. And the Market still attracts crowds—lesbigay and straight—on the weekends.

Laclede's Landing is also a popular attraction. While you're down by the Gateway Arch, treat yourself to riverfront dining aboard any of the several riverboat restaurants on the Mississippi. For accommodations, try **MotherSource Travels,** a women's B&B reservations service in nearby Alton, Illinois. Dining and shopping are most fun in the Central West End on Euclid Street between Delmar and Forest Park Boulevards, or in the University City Loop area near Washington University.

For nightlife, check out the two women's bars: **Attitudes** is a loud-and-rowdy dance bar, and **Ernie's Class Act** is a mellower neighborhood place, perfect for drinks and conversation.

St. Louis

Where the Girls Are: Spread out, but somewhat concentrated in the Central West End near Forest Park. Younger, funkier crowds hang out in the Delmar Loop, west of the city limits, packed with ethnic restaurants.

Lesbigay Pride: June. 314/772-8888, web: saintlouispride.com.

City Info: 421-1023 or 800/ 888-3861, web: www.explorestlouis.com.

Attractions: Anheuser-Busch Brewery.
Argosy Casino 800/336-7568.
Cathedral Basilica of St. Louis (world's largest collection of mosaic art).
Gateway Arch (duh).
Grant's Farm 314/843-1700.
St. Louis Art Museum 314/721-0072.
Stone Hill Winery (in Hermann) 800/909-9463.
The extremely quaint town of St. Charles.

Best View: Where else? Top of the Gateway Arch in the Observation Room.

Weather: 100% midwestern. Cold—little snow and the temperatures can drop below 0°. Hot, muggy summers raise temperatures back up into the 100°s. Spring and fall bring out the best in Mother Nature.

Transit: County Cab 314/991-5300.
Airport Express 314/429-4950.
The Bi-State Bus System 314/231-2345.

The Victorian 1449 Vandeventer (at Boyle) **314/535-6969** • 11am-1:30am • mostly gay men • food served • live shows • patio

Nightclubs

Attitudes 4100 Manchester **314/534-3858** • 6pm-3am, clsd Sun-Mon • popular • mostly women • dancing/DJ

The Complex/ Angles 3511 Chouteau (at Grand) **314/772-2645** • 4pm-3am • popular • lesbians/ gay men • multiple bars • live shows • patio • food served • wheelchair access

Faces Complex 130 4th St (at Missouri), East St Louis, IL **618/271-7410** • 3pm-6am • lesbians/ gay men • dancing/DJ • leather • live shows • 3 levels • patio

Mabel's Budget Beauty Shop & Chainsaw Repair 602 Belle St (at 6th St), Alton, IL **618/465-8687** • 4pm-1:30am • mostly gay men • dancing/DJ • wheelchair access

Velvet 1301 Washington Ave (at 13th Ave) **314/241-2997** • 9pm-3am Fri-Sat • gay-friendly • dancing/DJ • lounge & house music

Cafes

Einstein Bagels 2 N Euclid Ave (at Laclede) **314/367-7999** • 6am-6pm, from 7am wknds

Moka Be's 3606 Arsenal (at S Grand) **314/865-2009** • 11am-1am • occasional shows • wheelchair access

Restaurants

Busch's Grove 9160 Clayton Rd (at Price) **314/993-0011** • lunch & dinner, clsd Sun-Mon • $5-24

Cafe Balaban 405 N Euclid Ave (at McPherson) **314/361-8085** • popular • fine dining • some veggie • wonderful Sun brunch • full bar • wheelchair access • $6-24

Dressel's 419 N Euclid (at McPherson) **314/361-1060** • great Welsh pub food • full bar • $7-11

Duff's 392 N Euclid Ave (at McPherson) **314/361-0522** • clsd Mon • fine dining • some veggie • full bar • wheelchair access • $7-18

Kirk's Bistro & Bar 512 N Euclid **314/361-1456** • 11am-10pm, till 11pm Fri-Sat, clsd btwn lunch & dinner

Majestic Bar & Restaurant 4900 Laclede (at Euclid) **314/361-2011** • 6am-1:30am • diner fare • $4-7

On Broadway Bistro 5300 N Broadway (at Grand) **314/421-0087** • 11am-3am • full bar • wheelchair access • $4-12

Ted Drewes Frozen Custard 4224 S Grand Blvd (at Merrimack) **314/352-7376** • 11am-11pm • seasonal • a St Louis landmark

Tony's 410 Market St (at Broadway) **314/231-7007** • dinner only, clsd Sun • Italian fine dining • reservations advised

Zinnia 7491 Big Bend Blvd (at Shrewsbury) **314/962-0572** • lunch Tue-Fri & dinner Tue-Sun • bistro • $6-19

Entertainment & Recreation

Anheuser-Busch Brewery Tours/ Grant's Farm 314/577-2626, 314/843-1700 • all-American kitsch in-town & out: see the Clydesdales in their air-conditioned stables or visit the Busch family estate that was once the home of Ulysses S Grant

Int'l Bowling Museum & Hall of Fame 111 Stadium Plaza (across from Busch Stadium) **314/231-6340** • 5,000 yrs of bowling history (!) & 4 free frames

Wired Women Productions 314/352-9473 • concerts & events

Bookstores

Left Bank Books 399 N Euclid Ave (at McPherson) **314/367-6731** • 10am-10pm, 11am-6pm Sun • lesbian, feminist & gay titles

Retail Shops

Daily Planet News 243 N Euclid Ave (at Maryland) **314/367-1333** • 7am-8:30pm

Euclid News & Convenience 10 N Euclid Ave (at Forest Park Pkwy) **314/361-3420** • 9am-8pm, till 4pm Sun

Friends & Luvers 3550 Gravois (at Grand) **314/771-9405** • 10am-10pm, noon-7pm Sun • novelties • videos • dating service

Heffalump's 387 N Euclid Ave (at McPherson) **314/361-0544** • 11am-8pm, till 10pm Fri-Sat, noon-5pm Sun • gifts

Whiz Bam! 3206 S Grand Blvd, 1st flr **314/664-3663** • noon-9pm, till 10pm Fri-Sat, till 7pm Sun • non-erotic lesbigay videos • gifts

Publications

News Telegraph 314/664-6411, 800/301-5468 • lesbigay newspaper

SLAM! 314/481-2424 • alternative entertainment magazine

Women's Yellow Pages of Greater St Louis 314/567-0487

Spiritual Groups

Agape Church 2109 S Spring St **314/664-3588** • 2pm Sun

Dignity St Louis 6400 Minnesota Ave **314/997-9897 x63** • 7:30pm Sun

MCC Living Faith 6501 Wydown, Clayton **314/726-2855** • 5pm Sun

MCC of Greater St Louis 5000 Washington Pl **314/361-3221** • 9:30am & 11am Sun

St Louis Gay/ Lesbian Chavurah 77 Maryland Plaza (at Central Reform Cong) **314/771-8402**

Trinity Episcopal Church 600 N Euclid Ave **314/361-4655** • 8am & 10:30am Sun

Erotica

Cheap Trx 3211 S Grand **314/664-4011** • body piercing • sex supplies

Montana

Billings

Bars

The Loft 2910 2nd Ave N (at 29th) **406/259-9074** • 4:30pm-2am • lesbians/ gay men

Restaurants

Stella's Kitchen & Bakery 110 N 29th St (at 1st) **406/248-3060** • 6am-4pm, bakery till 6pm, clsd Sun • some veggie

Bookstores

Barjon's 2718 3rd Ave N **406/252-4398, 800/788-4318** • 9:30am-5:30pm, clsd Sun • metaphysical • women-owned/ run

Erotica

Big Sky Books 1203 1st Ave N **406/259-0051**

Boulder

Accommodations

Boulder Hot Springs Hotel & Retreat **406/225-4339** • gay-friendly • spirituality/ recovery retreat only • food served • swimming • smokefree • call for info

Bozeman

Info Lines & Services

Lambda Alliance of Gay Men/ Lesbians/ Bisexuals (QMSU) Strand Union Bldg Rm 273 (at MSU) **406/994-4551** • 7pm Tue

Women's Center 15 Hamilton Hall, MSU **406/994-3836** • some lesbian referrals

Accommodations

El Rancho Campobello 3111 Targhee Pass Hwy 20, West Yellowstone **406/646-7229, 800/244-7597** • gay/ straight • only luxury guest ranch open in winter • kids ok • $190-280

Gallatin Gateway Inn 76405 Gallatin Rd, Gallatin Gateway **406/763-4672, 800/676-3522** • gay-friendly • dinner nightly, Sun brunch • hot tub • swimming • smokefree rms available • wheelchair access • $60-135

Lehrkind Mansion B&B 719 N Wallace Ave **406/585-6932, 800/992-6932** • gay-friendly • full brkfst • hot tub • smokefree • $75-165

Cafes

The Leaf & Bean 35 W Main **406/587-1580** • 6:30am-10pm, till 11pm Fri-Sat • desserts • live shows • wheelchair access • women-owned/ run

Restaurants

Spanish Peaks Brewery 120 N 19th St **406/585-2296** • 11:30am-10:30pm, noon-10pm Sun • Italian • some veggie • $8-15

Erotica

Ms Kitty's Adult Store 12 N Wilson **406/586-6989**

Butte

Restaurants

Matt's Place 2339 Placer **406/782-8049** • 11:30am-7pm, clsd Sun-Mon • classic soda fountain diner

Peking Noodle Parlor 117 S Main, 2nd flr **406/782-2217** • 5pm-9pm, clsd Tue • Chinese • some veggie • $3-7

Pork Chop John's 8 W Mercury **406/782-0812** • 10:30am-7:30pm, clsd Sun • $3-5

Uptown Cafe 47 E Broadway **406/723-4735** • lunch & dinner • bistro • full bar • $15-20

Emigrant

Info Lines & Services

Yellowstone Riverview Lodge B&B 186 East River Rd **406/848-2156, 888/848-2550** • gay/ straight • B&B • also tipi • minutes from Yellowstone Nat'l Park • full brkfst • swimming • some shared baths • smokefree • gay-owned/ run • $80-110

Great Falls

Restaurants

Black Diamond Bar & Supper Club 64 Castner, Belt **406/277-4118** • 5pm-10pm, clsd Mon • steaks & seafood • 20 miles from Great Falls

Spiritual Groups

MCC Shepherd of the Plains 1501 & 1505 17th Ave SW **406/771-1070** • 11am Sun • call for social activities

Helena

Info Lines & Services

PRIDE 406/442-9322, 800/610-9322 (in MT) • info & newsletter

Livingston

Accommodations

The River Inn 4950 Hwy 89 S **406/222-2429** • gay-friendly • full brkfst • $40-90

Missoula

Info Lines & Services

AA Gay/ Lesbian 532 University Ave **406/523-7799** • 7pm Mon

Lambda Alliance Montana Rms, Univ Ctr, 3rd flr (at U of MT) **406/243-5922** • 8pm Mon

Western Montana Gay & Lesbian Community Center PO Box 7856, 59807-7856 **406/543-2224**

Women's Resource Center University Ctr #210, Campus Dr (at U of MT) **406/243-4153** • 10am-3pm, clsd wknds

Accommodations

Foxglove Cottage B&B 2331 Gilbert Ave **406/543-2927** • gay/ straight • swimming • gay-owned/ run • $65-95

Bars

Amvets Club 225 Ryman (at Broadway) **406/543-9174** • noon-2am (more gay after 8pm) • gay-friendly • dancing/DJ

Cafes

The Catalyst 111 N Higgins **406/542-1337** • 7am-6pm, 8am-5pm wknds

Restaurants

Montana Club/ Red Baron Casino 2620 Brooks **406/543-3200** • 6am-11pm, till midnight wknds, casino 24hrs • full bar • wheelchair access

New Black Dog Cafe 138 W Broadway **406/542-1138** • lunch & dinner, dinner only Sat, clsd Sun • vegetarian • wheelchair access

Entertainment & Recreation

Pangaea Expeditions 406/721-7719, 888/721-7719 • IGLTA

Bookstores

Second Thought 529 S Higgins (at 4th St) **406/549-2790** • 7am-10pm • also cafe & bakery • wheelchair access

University Center Bookstore Campus Dr (at U of MT) **406/243-4921** • 8am-6pm, from 10am Sat, clsd Sun • gender studies section

Publications

▲ **OutSpoken 406/549-8746, 406/542-6601**

Erotica

Fantasy for Adults Only 210 E Main St **406/543-7760** • also 2611 Brooks Ave, 406/543-7510

Ovando

Accommodations

Lake Upsata Guest Ranch 406/793-5890 • gay-friendly • cabins • hot tub • seasonal • wildlife programs & outings • outdoor recreation • meals provided • $150-220

Ronan

Accommodations

North Crow Vacation Ranch 2360 N Crow Rd **406/676-5169** • seasonal • lesbians/ gay men • cabin • tipis • camping • 80 miles south of Glacier Park • hot tub • nudity • seasonal • lesbian-owned/ run • $10-20

Three Forks

Accommodations

Sacajawea Inn 5 N Main St **406/285-6515, 800/821-7326** • gay-friendly • food served • wheelchair access • $75-105

NEBRASKA

Statewide

INFO LINES & SERVICES

Nebraska Travel & Tourism 800/228-4307

Grand Island

INFO LINES & SERVICES

Helpline 308/384-7474 • 24hrs • some gay referrals • crisis calls

ACCOMMODATIONS

Midtown Holiday Inn 2503 S Locust **308/384-1330** • gay-friendly • smokefree rms available • kids/ pets ok • hot tub • also 'Images Pink Cadillac Lounge' • wheelchair access • $59-75

Relax Inn 507 W 2nd St **308/384-1000** • gay-friendly • swimming • wheelchair access

BARS

Desert Rose Saloon 3235 S Locust (at 34th) **308/381-8919** • 6pm-2am Wed-Sat • gay-friendly • wheelchair access

NIGHTCLUBS

City Limits 123 East S Front **308/382-6259** • 7pm-1am, clsd Sun-Tue • gay/ straight • dancing/DJ • wheelchair access

RESTAURANTS

Tommy's 1325 S Locust **308/381-0440** • 24hrs

GYMS & HEALTH CLUBS

Health Plex Fitness Center 2909 W Hwy 30 **308/384-1110** • gay-friendly

EROTICA

Exclusively Yours Shop 214 N Locust **308/381-6984** • adult toys • lingerie

Sweet Dreams Shop 217 W 3rd St **308/381-6349** • lingerie • adult toys

Hastings

INFO LINES & SERVICES

GLB Alliance Health Center, Hastings College **402/461-7372**

Kearney

RETAIL SHOPS

Hastings Store 9 W 39th St **308/234-1130** • gay gifts & books

Lincoln

INFO LINES & SERVICES

AA Gay/ Lesbian 2748 'S' St (at 'The Meeting Place') **402/438-5214** • 7:30pm Mon

Crisis Center 402/476-2110, 402/475-7273 (24HRS)

Women's Resource Center Nebraska Union Rm 340, UNL **402/472-2597** • lesbian support services • wheelchair access

Youth Talkline 402/473-7932 • 7pm-midnight Fri-Sat • lesbigay info & referrals for ages 23 & under

BARS

Panic 200 S 18th St (at 'N') **402/435-8764** • 4pm-1am, from 1pm wknds • lesbians/ gay men • dancing/DJ • live shows • karaoke • videos • wheelchair access

NIGHTCLUBS

The Q 226 S 9th (btwn 'M' & 'N') **402/475-2269** • 8pm-1am, clsd Mon • lesbians/ gay men • dancing/DJ • 19+ Tue

ENTERTAINMENT & RECREATION

Wimmin's Radio Show KZUM 89.3 FM **402/474-5086** • 12:30pm-3pm Sun • also 'TGI-Femme' 10am-noon Fri

RETAIL SHOPS

Avant Card 1323 'O' St **402/476-1918** • hours vary

Omaha

INFO LINES & SERVICES

AA Gay/ Lesbian 402/345-9916 • call for mtg schedule

Rainbow Outreach & Resource Center 1719 Leavenworth St **402/341-0330** • 6pm-9pm, noon-6pm Sat, clsd Sun • 24hr info

BARS

Club 15 1421 Farnam (at 15th) **402/341-5705** • 10am-1am, from noon Sun • lesbians/ gay men • dancing/DJ • live shows • wheelchair access • also cafe

Connections 1901 Leavenworth St (at 19th) **402/933-3033** • 3pm-1am • lesbians/ gay men • dancing/DJ • live shows • karaoke • wheelchair access • gay-owned/ run

DC's Saloon 610 S 14th St (at Jackson) **402/344-3103** • 3pm-1am, from 2pm wknds • mostly gay men • neighborhood bar • country/ western • leather • live shows • wheelchair access

Diamond Bar 712 S 16th St **402/342-9595** • 9am-1am, from noon Sun • mostly gay men • neighborhood bar • wheelchair access

Gilligan's Pub 1407 Harney (at 14th St) **402/449-9147** • 2pm-1am, till 4am Fri-Sat • lesbians/ gay men • neighborhood bar • karaoke • also restaurant • burgers

The Junction 1507 Farnam (at 15th) **402/341-2500** • 4pm-1am • lesbians/ gay men • dancing/DJ • karaoke

Nightclubs

The Max 1417 Jackson (at 15th St) **402/346-4110** • 4pm-1am • popular • mostly gay men • 5 bars • dancing/DJ • live shows • videos • patio • wheelchair access

Cafes

Stage Right 401 S 16th (at Harney) **402/346-7675** • 7am-midnight, 10am-11pm wknds • live shows

Restaurants

Camille's 406 S 12th (at Harney) **402/346-1515**

Daisy May's 521 S 13th (at Jackson) **402/346-9342** • live shows

Dixie Quick's 105 S 15th (at Dodge) **402/346-3549** • Southern

French Cafe 1013 Howard St **402/341-3547** • lunch & dinner, Sun brunch • full bar • $11-22

Entertainment & Recreation

HGRA (Heartland Gay Rodeo Association) 800/561-6918

River City Mixed Chorus 402/341-7464

Bookstores

Heart & Soul 1117 Jackson St (btwn 10th & 13th) **402/342-1654** • 9am-10pm, till 11pm Fri-Sat, 10am-6pm Sun • also cafe

New Realities 1026 Howard St (in the Old Market) **402/342-1863** • 11am-10pm, till 6pm Sun • progressive • wheelchair access

Retail Shops

Bare Images 4332 Browne St **402/451-7987** • noon-7pm Th-Sat • piercing

Villain's 3629 'Q' St **402/731-0202** • noon-8pm, till 5pm Sun • tattooing • piercing • leather

Publications

River City Beat 402/341-2409

Spiritual Groups

MCC of Omaha 819 S 22nd St **402/345-2563** • 8:50am & 10:20am Sun • also support groups

Scotts Bluff

Info Lines & Services

Panhandle Gay/ Lesbian Support Service 308/632-3423 • social/ support

Restaurants

Pasta Villa 1520 10th St, Gering **308/436-5900** • 11am-8pm, clsd Sun-Mon • lesbian-owned/ run

Nevada

Carson City

Info Lines & Services

Nevada AIDS Hotline 505 E King St #304 **775/684-5941, 800/842-2437** • 8am-10pm • community info & resources • Spanish spoken

Lake Tahoe

see also Lake Tahoe, California

Accommodations

Haus Bavaria 702/831-6122, 800/731-6222 • gay-friendly • mountain views • full brkfst • smokefree • kids ok • gay-owned/ run • $110-145

Lakeside B&B 702/831-8281 • mostly gay men • full brkfst • near great skiing • hot tub • sauna • smokefree • kids/ pets ok • gay-owned/ run • $69-139

Nightclubs

Faces 270 Kingsbury Grade, Stateline **702/588-2333** • 5pm-close, from 3pm Sun, from 9pm Mon-Wed • lesbians/ gay men • dancing/DJ

Las Vegas

Info Lines & Services

Alcoholics Together 953 E Sahara #233 (in Commercial Arts Bldg) **702/737-0035** • 12:15pm & 8pm • lesbigay club for 12-step recovery programs • call for directions

Gay/ Lesbian Community Center 912 E Sahara Ln **702/733-9800** • 9am-noon & 1pm-8pm Mon-Fri

Bars

Backdoor Lounge 1415 E Charleston (nr Maryland Pkwy) **702/385-2018** • 24hrs • mostly gay men • neighborhood bar • dancing/DJ • comedy drag shows wknds • wheelchair access

Backstreet 5012 S Arville St (at Tropicana) **702/876-1844** • lesbians/ gay men • dancing/DJ Wed-Sun • country/ western • wheelchair access

Badlands Saloon 953 E Sahara #22–BH (at Maryland Pkwy) **702/792–9262** • 24hrs • mostly gay men • dancing/DJ • country/ western • wheelchair access

The Buffalo 4640 Paradise Rd (at Naples) **702/733–8355** • 24hrs • popular • mostly gay men • leather • videos • wheelchair access

Choices 1729 E Charleston (at Bruce) **702/382–4791** • 24hrs • mostly gay men • neighborhood bar • wheelchair access

Free Zone 610 E Naples **702/794–2300** • 24hrs • lesbians/ gay men • ladies' night Tue • neighborhood bar • dancing/DJ • live shows • food served

Goodtimes 1775 E Tropicana (at Spencer, in Liberace Plaza) **702/736–9494** • 24hrs • mostly gay men • more women Mon & Wed • neighborhood bar • dancing/DJ Fri, Sat & Mon 10pm-4am

Keys 1000 E Sahara Ave **702/731–2200** • 10am-4am • lesbians/ gay men • piano bar • dinner Wed-Sat • Sun brunch

The Las Vegas Eagle 3430 E Tropicana (at Pecos) **702/458–8662** • 24hrs • mostly gay men • leather • DJ Wed, Fri-Sat

Nightclubs

Frixion 3015 E Fremont St **702/384–3749** • from 10pm • gay/ straight • dancing/DJ • theme nights

The Gipsy 4605 Paradise Rd (at Naples) **702/731–1919** • 10pm-close • popular • mostly gay men • dancing/DJ • call for women's nights

Cafes

Mermaid Cafe 2910 Lake East Dr (off Canyon Gate) **702/240–6002** • open till 11pm, till midnight Fri-Sat • beer/ wine • food served

Las Vegas

Lesbigay Pride: April. 702/225-3389, web: www.biggestpride.com.

Annual Events: March - NGRA (Nat'l. Gay Rodeo Assn.) Bighorn Rodeo 888/643-6472, web: members.aol.com/ngra99.

City Info: Chamber of Commerce 702/457-4664.
Convention & Visitors Authority 702/892-0711.

Attractions: Bellagio Art Gallery 702/693-7111.
Guinness World Records Museum 702/792-3766.
Hoover Dam.
Imperial Palace Auto Collection 702/731-3311.
King Tut Museum (at the Luxor) 702/262-4000.
Las Vegas Art Museum 702/360-8000.
Liberace Museum 702/798-5595.
Museum of Natural History 702/384-3466.
StarTrek: The Experience.

Best View: Top of the Stratosphere. Or hurtling through the loops of the rollercoaster atop the New York New York Hotel. (Note: Do not ride immediately after the buffet.)

Transit: Western Cab 702/382-7100.
Yellow Cab 702/873-2000.
Various resorts have their own shuttle service.
CAT (Citizens Area Transit) 702/228-7433.

Restaurants

Coyote Cafe Las Vegas & Tropicana (in 'MGM Grand') **702/891-7349** • 8:30am-11pm • the original Santa Fe chef • $8-13

Pago Pago 6370 Windy St **702/896-1993** • 5pm-midnight, clsd Sun • lesbians/ gay men • live shows • some veggie • wheelchair access • $9-15

Entertainment & Recreation

Crystal Palace Skate Center 4680 Boulder Hwy **702/458-7107** • 8:30pm-11pm 3rd Mon • lesbigay skate

The Forum Shops at Caesars 3570 Las Vegas Blvd S (in 'Caesars Palace') • you saw it in 'Showgirls' & many other movies, now come shop in it for yourself

King Tutankhamun's Tomb & Museum 3900 Las Vegas Blvd S (in the 'Luxor Las Vegas') **702/262-4555** • exact replica of the tomb when Howard Carter opened it in1922

Las Vegas Gay & Lesbian Chorus **702/594-3393**

Liberace Museum 1775 E Tropicana Ave **702/798-5595** • this is one queen's closet you have to look into—especially if you love your pianos, clothes & cars covered w/ diamonds

The Volcano at The Mirage 3400 Las Vegas Blvd S • see the gimmick that inspired the rest of the showstoppers along The Strip—erupts every few minutes after dark

Bookstores

Borders 2323 S Decatur (at Sahara) **702/258-0999** • 9am-11pm, till 9pm Sun • lesbigay section • cafe • call for gay events • wheelchair access

Get Booked 4640 Paradise #15 (at Naples) **702/737-7780** • 10am-midnight, till 2am Fri-Sat • lesbigay

Retail Shops

Lock, Stock & Leather 4640 Paradise Rd #10 (at Naples) **702/796-9801** • 3pm-10pm, noon-2am Fri-Sat, from 4pm Sun • leather & more

Sin City 102 E Charleston (at Main) **702/387-6969** • piercing & tattoo studio

Publications

Las Vegas Bugle **702/369-6260** • lesbigay newspaper

Spiritual Groups

Christ Church Episcopal 2000 Maryland Pkwy (at E St Louis) **702/735-7655** • 8am, 10:30am & 5pm Sun, 10am & 6pm Wed

Dignity Las Vegas 1420 E Harmon Ave (in upstairs chapel at First Church) **702/593-5395** • 5:30pm Sat • call for location

MCC of Las Vegas 1208 E Charleston Blvd **702/369-4380** • 10am Sun

Valley Outreach Synagogue 2 S Pecos **702/436-4900** • 7:45pm 1st Fri

Erotica

Bare Essentials 4029 W Sahara Ave (nr Valley View Blvd) **702/247-4711** • exotic/ intimate apparel • toys • gay-owned/ run

Price Video 700 E Naples Dr #102 (at Swenson) **702/734-1342**

Rancho Adult Entertainment Center 4820 N Rancho #D (at Bone Mountain) **702/645-6104** • 24hrs

Video West 5785 W Tropicana (at Jones) **702/248-7055** • gay-owned/ run

Laughlin

see Bullhead City, Arizona

Reno

Info Lines & Services

Cornerstones Gay/ Lesbian AA 2850 Wrondel Way #J (at Gentry) **702/673-9633** • noon daily, 6:30pm Tue, 6pm Fri, 8pm Fri-Sat, 7:30pm Sun

Bars

1099 Club 1099 S Virginia (at Vassar) **702/329-1099** • 24hrs • popular • lesbians/ gay men • neighborhood bar • live shows • videos • wheelchair access

Bad Dolly's 535 E 4th (nr Valley) **702/348-1983** • 3pm-3am, from 1pm Sun • popular • mostly women • dancing/DJ • country/ western Th • wheelchair access

Carl's 3310 S Virginia St (at Moana) **702/829-8886** • 11am-2am, 24hrs wknds • lesbians/ gay men • neighborhood bar • dancing/DJ • patio

Five Star Saloon 132 West St (at 1st) **702/329-2878** • 24hrs • mostly gay men • neighborhood bar • dancing/DJ • wheelchair access

The Patio 600 W 5th St (btwn Washington & Ralston) **702/323-6565** • 11am-3am • lesbians/ gay men • neighborhood bar

The Quest 210 W Commercial Row (at West) **702/333-2808** • noon-5am, 24hrs wknds • mostly gay men • dancing/DJ • live shows

Visions 340 Kietzke Ln (btwn Glendale & Mill) **702/786-5455** • noon-4am, 24hrs wknds • popular • mostly gay men • dancing/DJ • theme nights • also 'Glitter Palace' gift shop Tue-Sat

Cafes

Sassy's Cafe & Deli 195 N Edison (at Mill) **702/856-3501** • 7:30am-4pm, clsd Sat, call for special coffee hour events Sun • women-owned/ run

Publications

Reno Informer 702/747-8833

Spiritual Groups

MCC of the Sierras 3405 Gulling Rd (at 'Temple Sinai') **702/829-8602** • 5pm Sun

Erotica

The Chocolate Walrus 2490 Wrondell (at Grove) **702/825-2267** • 10:30am-6:30pm Fri, till 5pm Sat, clsd Sun-Mon

Fantasy Faire 1298 S Virginia (at Arroyo) **702/323-6969** • leather • fetishwear

Suzie's 195 Kietzke Ln (at E 2nd St) **702/786-8557** • 24hrs

New Hampshire

Statewide

Info Lines & Services

Gay Info Line 603/224-1686 • active social & support groups • referrals • covers NH & VT • also some info for ME and northern MA

Travel & Tourism Office 603/271-2666, 800/386-4664

Ashland

Accommodations

▲ **Country Options** 27-29 N Main St **603/968-7958** • gay-friendly • full brkfst • smokefree • $45-55

Bath Village

Accommodations

Hibbard House 603/747-3947 • gay-friendly • hot tub • smokefree • camping available

Bridgewater

Accommodations

The Inn on Newfound Lake 1030 Mayhew Trpk Rte 3-A **603/744-9111, 800/745-7990** • gay/ straight • swimming • also restaurant • full bar • gay-owned/ run • $65-225

Center Harbor

Accommodations

Red Hill Inn 603/279-7001, 800/573-3445 • gay/ straight • overlooking Squam Lake & White Mtns • also restaurant • wheelchair access • IGLTA • gay-owned/ run • $105-175

Concord

Accommodations

The Englewood B&B 69 Cheney St (25 miles N of Concord), Franklin **603/934-1017, 888/207-2545** • gay/ straight • beautifully restored 1890 Queen Anne Victorian home • centrally located near White Mtns & coast • full brkfst • smokefree • $65-85

Spiritual Groups

Spirit of the Mountain 177 N Main (at 1st Cong Church) **603/225-5491** • 5pm 2nd & 4th Sun

Dover

Info Lines & Services

LGBT Helpline 141 Central St (at Quaker Mtg House) **603/743-4292 x3, 603/742-4470** • 7pm Sun, support group

Accommodations

Payne's Hill B&B 141 Henry Law Ave **603/742-4139** • gay/ straight • smokefree • lesbian-owned/ run • $60

Durham

Info Lines & Services

The UNH Alliance 603/862-4522 • 6:30pm Mon

Fitzwilliam

Accommodations

Hannah Davis House 603/585-3344 • gay-friendly • historic 1820 Federal bldg • full brkfst • smokefree • $60-115

Hillsboro

Accommodations

The Inn at Maplewood Farm 603/464-4242, 800/644-6695 • gay-friendly • full brkfst • $75-125

Keene

Accommodations

The Post and Beam B&B Centre St, Sullivan **603/847-3330, 888/376-6262** • gay/ straight • 1797 Colonial farmstead • full brkfst • wheelchair access • lesbian-owned/ run • $50-95

Manchester

Bars

313 313B Lincoln St (at Valley) **603/628-6813** • 2pm-1am, from noon wknds • lesbians/ gay men • dancing/DJ • food served • karaoke • wheelchair access

Club Merri-Mac 201 Merrimack (at Union) **603/623-9362** • 2pm-1:30am • popular • lesbians/ gay men • dancing/DJ • karaoke Fri & Sun • live shows • private club

Front Runner/ Manchester Civic Club 22 Fir St (at Elm St) **603/623-6477** • 5pm-1:30am, from 3pm Sun • popular • lesbians/ gay men • dancing/DJ Th-Fri • transgender-friendly • live shows • private club

Sporters 361 Pine St (at Hanover) **603/668-9014** • 5pm-1am • mostly gay men • neighborhood bar

Peterborough

Info Lines & Services

Gender Talk North 603/924-8828

Portsmouth

Nightclubs

Club 1 North 948 Rte 1 Bypass N **603/431-5400** • 8pm-1:30am, clsd Tue • mostly gay men • live shows • theme nights • men's night Wed • karaoke Th • gay-owned/ run

Bookstores

Artistic Amazon Bookstore 28 Chapel St (btwn Daniels & State) **603/422-0702** • call for hrs • feminist

Erotica

Spaulding Book & Video 80 Spaulding Tpke **603/430-9760** • gay-owned/ run

Suncook

Accommodations

White Rabbit Inn 62 Main St, Allenstown **603/485-9494** • lesbians/gay men • full brkfst • hot tub • swimming • personalized meals offered by chef/ host • also bar • $75-105

White Mtns

Accommodations

Bungay Jar B&B & Cottage 603/823-7775, 800/421-0701 • gay-friendly • full brkfst • saunas • smokefree • pets ok in cottage • wheelchair access • $100-225

Foxglove, A Country Inn 603/823-8840, 888/343-2220 • gay-friendly • food served • $85-165/ two people

▲ **Highlands Inn** Bethlehem **603/869-3978, 877/LES-B-INN (537-2466)** • a lesbian paradise • women only • ignore 'no vacancy' sign • hot tub • swimming • 100 mountain acres • special event wknds • wheelchair access • IGLTA • $55-110

The Horse & Hound Inn 205 Wells Rd, Franconia **603/823-5501** • clsd April & Nov • gay-friendly • full brkfst • kids/ pets ok • restaurant open for dinner except Mon-Tue • $13-18

The Inn at Bowman Rte 2, Randolph **603/466-5006, 888/919-8500** • gay/ straight • country inn gracing the White Mtns w/ charm & comfort • swimming • gay-owned/ run • $79-179

The Notchland Inn Rte 302, Hart's Location **603/374-6131, 800/866-6131** • gay/ straight • country inn on 400 acres • full brkfst • other meals available • gay-owned/ run • $140-280

Top Notch Vacation Rentals Rte 302, Glen **603/383-4133, 800/762-6636** • gay-friendly • 1- to 5-bdrm condos, cottages & chalets • private wooded areas • mtn views • $80-450

Wildcat Inn & Tavern Rte 16A, Jackson **603/383-4245** • gay-friendly • landscaped gardens • full brkfst • $30-50 • restaurant 6pm-9pm, till 10pm Fri-Sat • $14-23 • tavern 3pm-midnight, from noon wknds

Will's Inn Rte 302, Glen **603/383-6757, 800/233-6780** • gay-friendly • traditional New England motor inn • 2-bdrm cottages available • swimming

Restaurants

Polly's Pancake Parlor Rte 117 (exit 38 off 93 N), Sugar Hill **603/823-5575** • 7am-3pm, clsd winters

New Jersey

Statewide

Info Lines & Services

New Jersey Division of Travel & Tourism Atlantic City **800/537-7397**

Entertainment & Recreation

Out & About 201/843-1749, 201/801-0303 • lesbian hiking & outdoors adventures • call for events

Asbury Park

Info Lines & Services

Gay/ Lesbian Community Center 626 Bangs Ave **732/774-1809** • 7pm-10pm, 1pm-5pm Sat, clsd Sun (hotline)

Bars

Bond Street Bar 208 Bond St **732/776-9766** • 4pm-midnight, till close Fri-Sat • mostly women • neighborhood bar • unconfirmed '99

Down the Street 230 Cookman Ave (at Kingsley) **732/988-2163** • 2pm-2am (from 4pm in winter) • popular • mostly gay men • beach crowd • dancing/DJ Wed-Sat • live shows Sun • food served • videos • volleyball • wheelchair access

Nightclubs

The Box 911 Kingsley St **732/988-5799** • 9pm-5am, clsd Mon-Th • lesbians/ gay men • live shows • unconfirmed '99

LaMuray's 1213 Ocean Ave (at 5th) **732/776-9654 or 9655 (payphones)** • noon-midnight, till 2am Fri-Sun • lesbians/ gay men • dancing/DJ • Latin Th • T-dance Sun • leather last Sat

Paradise 101 Asbury Ave **732/988-6663** • 4pm-2am • lesbians/ gay men • dancing/DJ • 3 dance flrs • live shows • piano bar • tiki/ pool bar

Restaurants

Emeralds & Pearls 535 Bangs Ave **732/774-3522** • 11:30am-9pm, till 11pm Th-Sat, clsd Sun • also gift shop

Raspberry Cafe 16 Main Ave **732/988-0833** • brkfst & lunch

Spiritual Groups

Trinity Episcopal Church 503 Asbury Ave (at Grand Ave) **732/775-5084** • 8am & 10am Sun • call for Integrity mtg info

Atlantic City

Accommodations

The Rose Cottage 161 S Westminster Ave (btwn New York & Kentucky) **609/345-8196** • lesbians/ gay men • near bars & casinos

Bars

Brass Rail Bar & Grill 18 S Mt Vernon Ave (at Surfside Resort Hotel) **609/348-0192** • 24hrs • lesbians/ gay men • women's night Fri • neighborhood bar • live shows • food served

Reflections 181 South Carolina Ave (at Boardwalk) **609/348-1115** • 24hrs • lesbians/ gay men • neighborhood bar • videos • wheelchair access

Nightclubs

Ladies 2000 609/784-8341 • scheduled parties for women by women • call for times & locations

Studio Six Video Dance Club upstairs at 'Brass Rail' **609/348-3310** • 10pm-close • lesbians/gay men • dancing/DJ • live shows • videos

Restaurants

White House Sub Shop 2301 Arctic Ave (at Mississippi) **609/345-1564** • 10am-10pm, till 11pm Fri-Sat, from 11am Sun

Bloomingdale

Entertainment & Recreation

Gal-a-vanting 973/838-5318 • sponsors women's parties • call for details

Boonton

Nightclubs

Connexions 202 Myrtle Ave (off Washington) **973/263-4000** • 4pm-2am • lesbians/ gay men • dancing/DJ • country/ western Tue • food served • drag shows • karaoke Mon

Camden

see also Philadelphia, Pennsylvania

Info Lines & Services

Rainbow Place 1103 N Broad St, Woodbury **609/848-2455** • info line • community center

Cape May

Accommodations

The Virginia Hotel 25 Jackson St (btwn Beach Dr & Carpenter's Ln) **609/884-5700, 800/732-4236** • gay-friendly • also 'The Ebbitt Room' restaurant • seafood/ cont'l • IGLTA • $80-295

Cafes

Brad's Beachfront Cafe 314 Beach Ave **609/898-6050** • 7am-10pm in summer

Cherry Hill

Spiritual Groups

Unitarian Universalist Church 2916 Chapel Ave (at the school) **609/667-3618** • 10:15am Sun

Edison

Spiritual Groups

New Jersey's Lesbian & Gay Havurah 732/650-1010

Florence

Erotica

Florence Book Store Rte 130 S (4 miles S of Rte 206) **609/499-9853**

Hoboken

Nightclubs

Excalibur 2001 1000 Jefferson St (at 10th St) **201/795-1023** • 9pm-3am, clsd Mon-Wed • popular • lesbians/ gay men • dancing/DJ • live shows • Latin night Fri • wheelchair access

Maxwell's 1039 Washington St **201/656-9632** • gay-friendly • alternative • live music venue

Jersey City

Spiritual Groups

Christ United Methodist Church Tonnele Ave & JFK Blvd **201/332-8996** • also support groups

Lambertville

see also New Hope, Pennsylvania

Accommodations

York Street House B&B 42 York St **609/397-3007** • gay-friendly • smokefree • IGLTA • lesbian-owned/ run • $95-169

Erotica

Joy's Books 103 Springbrook Ave (nr Bridge St) **609/397-2907**

Madison

Bookstores

Pandora Book Peddlers 9 Waverly Pl (at Main) **973/822-8388** • 10am-6pm, till 7:30pm Th, clsd Sun-Mon • feminist bookstore & book club

Maplewood

Spiritual Groups

Dignity Metro New Jersey 550 Ridgewood Rd (at St George's Episcopal Church) **973/857-4040** • 4pm 3rd Sun

Marlton

Nightclubs

Gay Singles USA 841 Rte 73 S (at 'Cafe Society') **609/988-8305 x2** • 8pm-close Tue only • mostly gay men • dancing/DJ • live shows • patio

Montclair

Bookstores

Cohen's 635 Bloomfield Ave (at Valley) **973/744-2399** • 6am-8pm, clsd Sun • magazines • cafe

Erotica

Dressing for Pleasure 590 Valley Rd **973/746-5466** • 11am-9pm, 10am-6pm Sat, clsd Sun-Tue • lingerie • latex • leather

Morristown

Info Lines & Services

Gay Activist Alliance in Morris County **973/285-1595** • 7:30pm-10:30pm • mtgs/ activities 8:30pm Mon at 21 Normandy Hts Rd • also 'Women's Network

New Brunswick

Info Lines & Services

Bisexual Network of NJ at Pride Ctr **732/846-2232** • 7:30pm Tue • also BiNet couples group 7:30pm Sun

Pride Center of New Jersey 211 Livingston Ave (at Comstock) **732/846-2232** • info line • meeting space for various groups • call for info

Bars

The Den 700 Hamilton St (at Douglas), Somerset **732/545-7329** • 5pm-2am, from 8pm Fri-Sun, clsd Mon • popular • mostly gay men • dancing/DJ Fri-Sat • country/ western Fri • multi-racial clientele • live shows • wheelchair access

Restaurants

The Frog and the Peach 29 Dennis St (at Hiram) **732/846-3216** • lunch Mon-Fri, dinner nightly • full bar • wheelchair access • $40-60

Stage Left 5 Livingston Ave (at George) **732/828-4444** • popular • lesbians/ gay men • some veggie • full bar • patio • wheelchair access • $10-12

Spiritual Groups

Dignity New Brunswick 109 Nichol Ave (at Friends Mtg House) **732/254-7942** • 7:30pm 2nd Sat

MCC of Christ the Liberator 416 Victoria Ave (at Circle Playhouse), Piscataway **732/846-8227** • 10:45am Sun

Newark

Bars

Murphy's Tavern 59 Edison Pl (btwn Broad & Mulberry) **973/622-9176** • 8pm-2am • lesbians/ gay men • neighborhood bar • dancing/DJ Th-Sat • mostly African-American • wheelchair access

Spiritual Groups

Liberation in Truth Unity Fellowship Church 608 Broad St (at Rector, in Trinity & St Phillip's Cathedral) **212/228-3329** • 3:30pm Sun

Oasis **973/621-8151** • 1st Tue • lesbigay ministry of the Episcopal Church • call for info

Perth Amboy

Bars

The Other Half 3 Convery Blvd/ Rte 35 & Kennedy **732/826-8877** • 7am-2am, till 3am Th-Fri • popular • lesbians/ gay men • dancing/DJ • karaoke Wed • theme nights

Plainfield

Accommodations

▲ **The Pillars** 922 Central Ave (at 9th St) **908/753-0922, 888/PILLARS (745-5277)** • gay/ straight • Georgian/ Victorian mansion • full brkfst • smokefree • infants & kids over 12 ok • dogs ok (call first) • IGLTA • gay-owned/ run • $85-119

Bars

The Rusty Spigot 308 Watchung Ave (at E 4th) **908/755-4000** • noon-1am, till 2am Fri-Sat • gay-friendly • neighborhood bar

Red Bank

Info Lines & Services

Monmouth Ocean Transgender Infoline **732/219-9094** • mtgs • support

Bookstores

Earth Spirit 16 W Front St (at Broad) **732/842-3855** • 10am-6pm, till 8pm Fri, noon-5pm Sun • new age center & bookstore • lesbigay sections

River Edge

Nightclubs

Feathers 77 Kinder Kamack Rd **201/342-6410** • 9pm-2am, till 3am Sat • mostly gay men • dancing/DJ • Latin night Th • live shows • drag Tue & Sun

Rosemont

Restaurants

The Cafe 88 Kingwood-Stockton Rd **609/397-4097** • 8am-3pm, from 9am wknds, dinner 5pm-9pm Wed-Sun, clsd Mon • BYOB

Sayreville

Bars

Sauvage 1 Victory Bridge Plaza **732/727-6619** • 7pm-3am, from 4pm Sun • mostly women • neighborhood bar • live shows • food served

Nightclubs

Colosseum 7090 Rte 9 N (at Rte 35 N) **732/316-0670** • 9pm-3am, clsd Mon • lesbians/ gay men • women-only room Fri • dancing/DJ • salsa Sat • 18+ • live shows • drag Tue

Stockton

Accommodations

Woolverton Inn 6 Woolverton Rd **609/397-0802** • gay-friendly • full brkfst • jacuzzi • $100-200

Trenton

Bars

Buddies Pub 677 S Broad St **609/989-8566** • 5pm-2am, from 6pm wknds • lesbians/ gay men • dancing/DJ Th-Sat

Restaurants

Center House 499 Center St (at Cass) **609/599-9558** • 11am-midnight, till 11pm Fri-Sat, from 5pm Sat, 10am-9pm Sun • also bar • patio

New Mexico

Statewide

Publications

Out! Magazine 505/243-2540 • lesbigay newsmagazine

Alamogordo

Accommodations

Best Western Aire Motor Inn 1021 S White Sands Blvd **505/437-2110** • gay-friendly • swimming • wheelchair access • $52-109

Albuquerque

includes Bernalillo, Corrales, Placitas & Rio Rancho

Info Lines & Services

AA Gay/ Lesbian 505/266-1900 (AA#) • call for times/ locations • smokefree mtgs

Alternative Erotic Lifestyles 505/345-6484 • pansexual S/M group

Bi's R Us 505/836-5239, 505/836-0454 • men's & women's social networks

Albuquerque

Entertainment: New Mexico Gay Rodeo Association 505/255-5045.

Lesbigay Pride: June. 505/856-0871.

Annual Events: June - Albuquerque AIDS Walk 505/266-0552, email: aidswalk@aol.com.
October - Kodak Int'l Hot Air Balloon Fiesta 505/828-2887 or 888/422-7277, web: www.balloonfiesta.com.

City Info: 800/545-2040, web: www.nm.org.
Albuquerque Lesbian & Gay Chamber of Commerce 505/243-6767.

Attractions: Albuquerque Museum 505/243-7255.
Indian Pueblo Cultural Center 505/843-7270 or 800/766-4405 (outside NM).
New Mexico Museum of Natural History 505/841-2802.
Old Town.
Rattlesnake Museum 505/242-6569.
Wildlife West Nature Park & Chuckwagon 505/281-7655.

Best View: Sandia Peak Tram (505/856-7325) at sunset.

Weather: Sunny and temperate. Warm days and cool nights in summer, with average temperatures from 65° to 95°. Winter is cooler, from 28° to 57°.

Common Bond Info Line 505/891-3647 • 24hrs • covers lesbigay community

Hangers 4013 Silver Ave SE (at Morningside) **505/262-9696** • 10am-11pm, till 3am Fri-Sat • resource center for lesbigay community w/ coffeeshop & retail shop • wheelchair access

New Mexico Outdoors 505/822-1093 • active lesbigay outdoors group

Transgender Community Group **505/342-8077** • 7:30pm Fri mtg & social hr

UNM Women's Resource Center 1160 Mesa Vista Hall, NV **505/277-3716** • 8am-5pm, clsd wknds • resource library w/ computers for students & public • some lesbian outreach • wheelchair access

YIT (Youth In Transition) 3804 Central Ave SE (at Carlisle) **505/265-7690** • drop-in center for homeless youth 14-24 yrs • very gay-friendly

Accommodations

Brittania & WE Mauger Estate B&B 701 Roma Ave NW (at 7th) **505/242-8755, 800/719-9189** • gay-friendly • intimate 1897 Queen Anne residence • full brkfst • smokefree • IGLTA • $79-179

Casa de Alegria B&B 5 Alegria Ln (Old Church Rd), Corrales **505/890-0176** • gay/ straight • full brkfst • wheelchair access • lesbian-owned/ run • $80-95

▲ **Golden Guest Houses** 2645 Decker NW **503/344-9205, 888/513-GOLD** • lesbians/ gay men • individual & shared units

Hacienda Antigua Retreat 6708 Tierra Dr NW (close to corner of 2nd & Osuna) **505/345-5399, 800/201-2986** • gay/ straight • full brkfst • hot tub • swimming • smokefree • kids 3+ yrs ok • gay-owned/ run • $95-175

La Hacienda Grande 21 Baros Ln (off Camino del Pueblo), Bernalillo **505/867-1887, 800/353-1887** • gay-friendly • 250 year old historic adobe home btwn Santa Fe & Albuquerque • food served • $99-129

Mountain View **505/296-7277** • mostly women • full brkfst • hot tub • smokefree • kids ok • wheelchair access • lesbian-owned/ run • $40-65

Nuevo Dia 11110 San Rafael Ave NE (at Browning) **505/856-7910** • lesbians/ gay men • hot tub • kids ok • $55-130

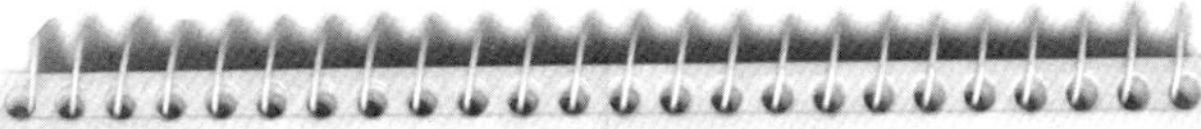

Albuquerque

We're going to let you in on a little secret: New Mexico is the overlooked gem of the Southwest. Arizona likes to take the lion's share of the credit for the Southwest style as it basks in its endless sun and endless supply of seniors and new agers. Nevada cashes in on the image too, but goes for the glitz with its desert filled with more casinos that cacti. Colorado likes to brag about how it's God's little green heaven when not under several feet of fresh powder. Even Texas likes to horn in with its vibrant Tejano music and arts. But it's New Mexico, with its fermentation of 300 years of Native American, Spanish, and Anglo cultures, that is the true heart and soul of the Southwest.

Sprawling in the shadow of Sandia Peak, New Mexico's largest city and cultural center is Albuquerque. The city's history can be glimpsed in its adobe constructions, cowboy decor, and proliferation of arts and crafts. And just outside of Albuquerque lies a more ancient piece of New Mexico's history: Petroglyph National Monument, covered with rock carvings created by the indigenous people of the area.

During the day, stop in at the lesbigay **Sisters & Brothers** bookstore and pick up a copy of New Mexico's own **OUT! Magazine** for the scoop on the latest activities around town. Or, give the **Common Bond Info Line** a call. At night, visit **Legends West,** Albuquerque's lesbian dance bar. Afterward, turn in for a good night's sleep at the lesbian-owned **Mountain View** inn.

For something a bit different to do, take to the air for a spectular view with woman-owned **Hugs 'n Hot Air Ballooning.** Albuquerque is a haven for those who enjoy the out-of-doors. Mountain bikers, especially, will love the scenery and endless terrain.

Rio Grande House 3100 Rio Grande Blvd NW (enter on Candeleria) **505/345-0120, 505/344-9463** • gay-friendly • adobe house near Old Town • full brkfst • swimming • hot tub

Taracotta 3118 Rio Grande Blvd NW (at Candelaria) **505/344-9443** • gay/ straight • hot tub • smokefree • small dogs ok • private patio • gay-owned/ run • $70-85

WJ Marsh House 301 Edith SE (nr Central & Broadway) **505/247-1001, 888/956-2774** • gay-friendly • full brkfst • shared bath • women-owned/ gay-run • $50-150

Wyndham Albuquerque Hotel 2910 Yale Blvd SE (at Gibson) **505/843-7000, 800/227-1117** • gay-friendly • 4-star hotel • swimming • also 'Rojo Bar & Grill' • rates depend on season & availability

Bars

Albuquerque Mining Co (AMC) 7209 Central Ave NE (at Louisiana) **505/255-4022** • 3pm-2am, till midnight Sun • mostly gay men • dancing/DJ • wheelchair access • also 'Pit Bar' • mostly gay men • leather

Albuquerque Social Club 4021 Central Ave NE (enter rear) **505/255-0887** • noon-2am, till midnight Sun • lesbians/ gay men • dancing/DJ • private club

Foxes Lounge 8521 Central Ave NE (btwn Wisconsin & Wyoming) **505/255-3060** • 10am-2am, noon-midnight Sun • mostly gay men • dancing/DJ • live shows • wheelchair access

The Ranch 8900 Central SE (at Wyoming) **505/275-1616** • 11am-2am, till midnight Sun • mostly gay men • dancing/DJ • country/ western • 'Cuffs' leather bar inside • wheelchair access

Nightclubs

Pulse 4100 Central Ave SE (at Montclaire, in Nob Hill) **505/255-3334** • 9pm-2am, till midnight Sun • mostly gay men • alternative • cover charge

Restaurants

Chef du Jour 119 San Pasquale SW (at Central) **505/247-8998** • 11am-2pm Mon-Fri, dinner Fri-Sat only • plenty veggie • wheelchair access • $4-9

Double Rainbow 3416 Central SE (2 blks W of Carlisle) **505/255-6633** • 6:30am-midnight • plenty veggie • wheelchair access • $4-8

Frontier 2400 Central SE (at Cornell) **505/266-0550** • 24hrs • good brkfst burritos

Entertainment & Recreation

Hugs 'N Hot Air Ballooning 12272 N Hwy 14, Cedar Crest **505/450-8692** • Albuquerque area scenic balloon rides • woman-owned/ run

Women in Movement 505/899-3627 • production company • Memorial Day festival

Bookstores

Newsland Books 2112 Central Ave SE (at Yale) **505/242-0694** • 8am-9pm

Page One 11018 Montgomery NE **505/294-2026, 800/521-4122** • 7am-11:30pm

Sisters & Brothers Bookstore 4011 Silver Ave SE (btwn Morningside & Montclair) **505/266-7317, 800/687-3480 (ORDERS ONLY)** • 10am-8pm, till 6pm Sun • lesbigay

Retail Shops

In Crowd 3106 Central SE (at Richmond) **505/268-3750** • 10am-6pm, noon-4pm Sun • local & folk art • clothing • accessories • wheelchair access • gay-owned/ run

Publications

Out! Magazine 505/243-2540 • lesbigay newsmagazine

Spiritual Groups

Dignity New Mexico 1815 Los Lomas (at University) **505/896-1095** • 7pm 1st Sun

Emmanuel MCC 341 Dallas NE (at Copper) **505/268-0599** • 10am Sun

First Unitarian Church 3701 Carlisle NE (at Comanche) **505/884-1801** • 9:30am & 11am Sun

Jewish Lesbian/ Gay Alliance 505/242-7508 • monthly Sabbath dinners • call for more info

MCC of Albuquerque 2404 San Mateo Pl NE **505/881-9088** • 10am Sun

Erotica

Castle Superstore 5110 Central Ave SE **505/262-2266**

The Leather Shoppe 4217 Central Ave NE (at Washington) **505/266-6690** • clsd Sun

Chimayo

Accommodations

Casa Escondida B&B 505/351-4805, 800/643-7201 • gay-friendly • hot tub • smokefree • wheelchair access • $80-150

Cloudcroft

Retail Shops

Off The Beaten Path 100 Glorieta Ave **505/682-7284** • 9am-6pm • eclectic gifts • original artwork • women-owned/ run • wheelchair access

Farmington

Accommodations

Microtel Inn & Suites 1901 E Broadway **505/325-3700, 800/823-4535** • gay-friendly • hotel w/ suites • 1 jacuzzi suite • wheelchair access • $39-99

Las Cruces

Info Lines & Services

Matrix PO Box 992, Mesilla, 88046 • local inquiries • newsletter

Retail Shops

Spirit Winds Gifts & Cafe 2260 Locust St **505/521-0222** • 7:30am-9pm, till 10pm Fri-Sat, 9:30am-7pm Sun

Spiritual Groups

Holy Family Parish 1701 E Missouri (at Lutheran Church) **505/522-7119** • 5:30pm Sun • inclusive Evangelical Anglican Church

Koinonia 505/521-1490 • 7:30pm Th • lesbigay group for people of all religious traditions

Madrid

Accommodations

Madrid Lodging 14 Opera House Rd **505/471-3450** • gay-friendly • suite • hot tub • smokefree • $75-85

Bars

Mineshaft Tavern 2846 State Hwy 14 **505/473-0743** • 11am-10pm, till 2am wknds • gay-friendly • live shows • also restaurant • some veggie

Cafes

Java Junction 2855 State Hwy 14 **505/438-2772** • 8am-7pm • also B&B • $55-65

Placitas

Accommodations

▲ **El Peñasco** 30 miles from Albuquerque **505/771-8909** • gay-friendly • historic adobe guesthouse • sleeps 1-4 • women-owned/ run • $75-95

Santa Fe

Info Lines & Services

AA Gay/ Lesbian 505/982-8932

Santa Fe Lesbian/ Gay Hotline 505/982-3301 • recorded info

Accommodations

Alexander's Inn 529 E Palace Ave **505/986-1431, 888/321-5123** • gay/ straight • wheelchair access • $75-160

▲ **Arius Compound** **505/982-2621, 800/735-8453** • gay-friendly • 4 adobe casitas • kitchens • hot tub • patio • $90-145

Casa Torreon 1613 Calle Torreon **505/982-6815, 505/982-2826** • gay-friendly • adobe guesthouse • kitchen • smokefree • kids ok • lesbian-owned/ run • $75-160

El Farolito B&B 514 Galisteo St **505/988-1631, 888/988-4589** • gay/ straight • adobe compound w/ romantic, private casitas • gay-owned/ run • $95-155

Four Kachinas Inn 512 Webber St **505/982-2550, 800/397-2564** • clsd Jan • gay-friendly • smokefree • kids 10+ ok • courtyard • wheelchair access • gay-owned/ run • $60-149

Heart Seed B&B Retreat & Spa **505/471-7026** • gay-friendly • located on Turquoise Trail (25 miles south of Santa Fe) • full brkfst • hot tub • smokefree • sundeck • also day spa

▲ **Inn of the Turquoise Bear** 342 E Buena Vista St **505/983-0798, 800/396-4104** • lesbians/ gay men • B&B in historic Witter Bynner estate • smokefree • some shared baths • gay-owned/ run • $90-275

La Tienda Inn 445-447 W San Francisco St **505/989-8259, 800/889-7611** • gay-friendly • smokefree • wheelchair access • $100-175

▲ **Madena's B&B** **505/989-1842** • Victorian B&B • just blks from the Plaza

Marriott Residence Inn 1698 Galisteo St **505/988-7300, 800/331-3131** • gay-friendly • swimming • smokefree rms available • wheelchair access

Open Sky B&B **505/471-3475, 800/244-3475** • gay-friendly • great views • smokefree • jacuzzi • kids & pets ok (call first) • wheelchair access • lesbian-owned/ run • $70-140

Saltamontes Retreat—Grasshopper Hill 1/2 hr NE of Santa Fe, in E Pecos **505/757-2528** • gay/ straight • 3 guestrooms in private home • communal kitchen • hot tub • smokefree • lesbian-owned/ run

▲ **Triangle Inn** Rte 11 (off Rte 285/84) **505/455-3375** • lesbians/ gay men • secluded rustic adobe compound • hot tub • smokefree casitas available • kids/ pets ok • wheelchair access • lesbian-owned/ run • $90-140

The Water Street Inn 427 W Water St **505/984-1193, 800/646-6752** • gay-friendly • historic adobe inn • jacuzzi • smokefree • kids/ pets ok • wheelchair access • $125-200

Nightclubs

Paramount 331 Sandoval (at Montezuma) **505/982-8999** • 5pm-close • popular • gay-friendly • dancing/DJ • theme nights (swing Tue, disco Wed, Latin Th, live music Fri & Sun, house Sat) • also 'Bar B' lounge

Restaurants

Anasazi Restaurant 113 Washington Ave **505/988-3236** • brkfst, lunch & dinner • wheelchair access

Cafe Pasqual's 121 Don Gaspar (at Water St) **505/983-9340** • 7am-10:30pm • popular • Southwestern • some veggie • beer/ wine • $7-27

Cowgirl Hall of Fame 319 S Guadalupe (btwn Aztec & Guadalupe) **505/982-2565** • lunch & dinner • Southwest cuisine • veggie

Dave's Not Here 1115 Hickock St (at Cortez) **505/983-7060** • 11am-10pm, clsd Sun • New Mexican • some veggie • beer/ wine • women-owned/ run

Geronimo's 724 Canyon Rd (at Camino del Monte Sol) **505/982-1500** • lunch Tue-Sun, dinner nightly • eclectic gourmet • full bar 11am-11pm

Jack's 135 W Palace Ave, Ste 300 (at Grant) **505/983-7220** • lunch Mon-Fri, dinner nightly • wheelchair access • $6-28

Paul's 72 Marcy St (at Lincoln & Washington) **505/982-8738** • dinner • modern int'l • some veggie • wheelchair access • $14-19

SantaCafe 231 Washington Ave **505/984-1788** • lunch & dinner • New American • some veggie • full bar • $17-28

Tecolote Cafe 1203 Cerrillos Rd (at Baca) **505/988-1362** • 7am-2pm, clsd Mon • popular • great brkfst • some veggie • wheelchair access • $5-8

Vanessie of Santa Fe 434 W San Francisco (at Guadalupe) **505/982-9966** • 5:30pm-10:30pm (bar till 1am) • popular • lesbians/ gay men • steak house • piano bar

Entertainment & Recreation

Ten Thousand Waves 3 miles out of town **505/992-5025** • Japanese health spa & lodging • sit under the stars & look out at the mtns • call for more info

Bookstores

Downtown Subscription 376 Garcia St (at Acequia Madre) **505/983-3085** • 7am-7pm • newsstand • coffee shop

Retail Shops

The Ark 133 Romero St (at Agua Fria) **505/988-3709** • 9:30m-7pm, 10am-6pm Sat, 11am-5pm Sun • spiritual

Silver City

Accommodations

The Jail House B&B 710 N Bayard (8th St) **505/388-3801** • gay/ straight • 1905 Carriage House in garden • jail theme • full brkfst • hot tub available

Taos

Accommodations

Brooks Street Inn 505/758-1489, 800/758-1489 • gay-friendly • full brkfst • smokefree • kids 10+ ok • $80-110

Dobson House El Prado **505/776-5738** • gay-friendly • luxury suites north of Taos • smokefree • $98-115

▲ **The Dreamcatcher B&B** 416 La Lomita (Valverde) **505/758-0613, 888/758-0613** • gay-friendly • near Taos Plaza • full brkfst • hot tub • smokefree • wheelchair access • $79-104

San Geronimo Lodge 1101 Witt Rd (at Kit Carson) **505/751-3776, 800/894-4119** • gay-friendly • popular • full brkfst • swimming • hot tub • massage available • $95-150

NEW YORK

Statewide

INFO LINES & SERVICES

New York State AIDS Hotline 800/541-2437

Adirondack Mtns

INFO LINES & SERVICES

Lesbigay Info 518/359-7358 • local contact

ACCOMMODATIONS

Amethyst B&B 315/848-3529, 410/252-5990 • summer only • women only • full brkfst • swimming • hot tub • smokefree • $80

Country Road Lodge B&B 115 Hickory Hill Rd, Warrensburg **518/623-2207** • gay-friendly • secluded riverside retreat at the end of a country road • full brkfst • smokefree • $46-135

The Doctor's Inn 518/891-3464, 888/518-3464 • gay-friendly • full brkfst • some shared baths • kids/ pets ok (call first) • IGLTA • $45-100

King Hendrick Motel 1602 State Rte 9, Lake George **518/792-0418** • gay-friendly • swimming • cabins available • wheelchair access • $50-105

RESTAURANTS

Artists' Cafe 1 Main St, Lake Placid **518/523-9493** • 11:30am-10pm, from 8am wknds • steak & seafood • full bar • $9-15

Albany

INFO LINES & SERVICES

Gay AA at Community Center • 7:30pm Sun • lesbian AA at 7:30pm Tue

Lesbian/ Gay Community Center 332 Hudson Ave **518/462-6138** • 7pm-10pm, till 11pm Fri-Sat, from 2pm wknds • 24hr directory • also cafe • women's night 7pm-11pm 1st & 3rd Fri

TGIC (Transgenderist Independence Club) 518/436-4513 • 8pm-10pm Th • call for location • also publish newsletter

Women's Building 79 Central Ave **518/465-1597** • community center

ACCOMMODATIONS

Auberge Stuyvesant 217 County Rte 26A (at Rte 9), Stuyvesant **518/758-1224, 800/758-3821** • gay/ straight • gay-owned/ run • $65-85

The State House 393 State St **518/465-8079** • gay/ straight • smokefree • gay-owned/ run • $135-165

BARS

Cafe Hollywood 275 Lark St (at Hamilton) **518/472-9043** • 3pm-4am • gay-friendly • neighborhood bar • videos

JD's Playhouse 519 Central Ave (at Manning Blvd) **518/446-1407** • 4pm-4am, till midnight Mon • lesbians/ gay men • neighborhood bar • dancing/DJ Fri-Sat • country/ western Wed • karaoke Sun

Longhorns 90 Central Ave (at Henry Johnson Blvd) **518/462-4862** • 4pm-4am • mostly gay men • country/ western • leather

Oh Bar 304 Lark St (at Madison) **518/463-9004** • 2pm-2am • mostly gay men • neighborhood bar • multi-racial • videos

Power Company 238 Washington Ave (btwn Henry Johnson & Lark) **518/465-2556** • 2pm-2am, till 4am wknds • mostly gay men • dancing/DJ Wed-Sat • wheelchair access

Waterworks Pub 76 Central Ave (btwn Lexington & Northern) **518/465-9079** • 3pm-4am • popular • mostly gay men • dancing/DJ wknds • garden bar

CAFES

C@fé Web 1040 Madison Ave (next to Madison Theater) **518/438-4826** • noon-10pm, till midnight Fri-Sat • Internet access

RESTAURANTS

Cafe Lulu 288 Lark St (at Madison) **518/436-5660** • 11am-midnight, till 1am Fri-Sat • Mediterranean • plenty veggie • beer/ wine • $5-9

Debbie's Kitchen 290 Lark St **518/463-3829** • 10am-9pm, 11am-6pm Sat, clsd Sun • sandwiches • salads • $3-5

El Loco Mexican Cafe 465 Madison Ave (btwn Lark & Willett) **518/436-1855** • clsd Mon • healthy Tex-Mex • some veggie • full bar

Mother Earth 217 Western Ave (at Quail) **518/434-0944** • 11am-11pm • vegetarian • BYOB • wheelchair access • $3-6

Planet Pizza & Grill 269 Lark St **518/432-9301, 518/432-9302**

The Unlimited Feast 340 Hamilton St (at Dove St) **518/463-6223** • lunch Mon-Fri • some veggie • full bar • patio • wheelchair access • $5-10

Yono's 289 Hamilton St (at S Swan) **518/436-7747** • 5:30pm-10pm, clsd Sun • Indonesian/ cont'l • some veggie • full bar • live jazz Fri

Entertainment & Recreation

Face the Music WRPI 91.5 FM **518/276-6248** • 4pm-6pm Sun • feminist radio

Homo Radio WRPI 91.5 FM **518/276-6248** • noon-2pm Sun

Two Rivers **518/449-0758** • lesbian & gay outdoor club

Retail Shops

Deja View Video 37 Central Ave (at Henry Johnson Blvd) **518/433-1607** • 10am-10pm, from 1pm Sun • lesbigay books • magazines

Romeo's Gifts 299 Lark St **518/434-4014** • 11am-9pm, noon-5pm Sun

Publications

Community **518/462-6138 x37**

Spiritual Groups

First United Presbyterian Church State & Willett Sts **518/449-7332** • 8:30am & 10:30am Sun • also 10am Sun in Troy • 1915 5th Ave • 518/272-2771

Grace & Holy Innocents Episcopal Church 498 Clinton Ave (at Robbins St) **518/465-1112** • 9am Th, Sat & Sun

MCC of the Hudson Valley 275 State St (btwn Dove & Swan, at Emmanuel Baptist Church) **518/785-7941** • 1pm Sun • wheelchair access

Gyms & Health Clubs

Fitness for Her 333 Delaware Ave, Delmar **518/478-0237** • 4:30am-9pm, 9am-5pm wknds • women-only • child care available • wheelchair access • lesbian-owned/ run

Erotica

Savage Gifts & Leather 88 Central Ave **518/434-2324** • clsd Sun

Annandale-on-Hudson

Info Lines & Services

Bard BiGALA (Bisexual/ Gay/ Lesbian Alliance) Bard College **914/758-6822 (general switchboard), 914/758-7454 (Dean of Students)** • active during school year

Binghamton

Info Lines & Services

AA Gay/ Lesbian 183 Riverside Dr (at Unitarian Church) **607/722-5983** • 7pm Wed & Sat

LGBT Resource Line **607/729-1921, 800/287-7557 (local only)** • 7:30pm-9:30pm Mon-Th

Rainbow Pride Union **607/777-2202** • call for info

Women's Center & Event Line **607/724-3462** • call for info

Bars

Squiggy's 34 Chenango St (at Court) **607/722-2299** • 5pm-1am, till 3am Fri-Sat, clsd Sun • gay/ straight • dancing/DJ Fri-Sat

Nightclubs

Risky Business 201 State St **607/723-1507** • 9pm-1am, from 5pm Th-Fri, till 3am Fri-Sat • popular • mostly gay men • dancing/DJ

Restaurants

The Whole in the Wall 43 S Washington St **607/722-5138** • 11:30am-9pm, clsd Sun-Mon

Publications

Amethyst **607/729-1921**

Lavender Life **607/771-1986**

Spiritual Groups

Affirmation (United Methodist) 83 Main St (enter in back through parking lot) **607/775-3986** • 7pm Sun

Buffalo

Info Lines & Services

Gay/ Lesbian Youth Services 190 Franklin St (across from the Convention Ctr) **716/855-0221** • 6pm-9pm, clsd Wed & wknds

LGBT Alliance 362 Student Union, SUNY-Buffalo, Amherst **716/645-3063**

Accommodations

Arlington Park Inn 168 College St **716/885-7585** • gay/ straight • gay-owned/ run • $70-90

Bars

Buddies 31 Johnson Park (at Elmwood) **716/855-1313** • 1pm-4am, from noon wknds • lesbians/ gay men • dancing/DJ Th-Sat • live shows • wheelchair access

Cathode Ray 26 Allen St (at N Pearl) **716/884-3615** • 1pm-4am • mostly gay men • neighborhood bar • videos • wheelchair access

Compton's After Dark 1239 Niagara St (btwn Ferry & Lafayette) **716/885-3275** • 4pm-4am, from 7pm Sat • mostly women • dancing/DJ • live music • in historic pre-1812 bldg

Lavender Door 32 Tonawanda St (at Dearborn) **716/874-1220** • 6pm-4am, from 4pm Fri, clsd Mon • mostly women • neighborhood bar • wheelchair access

Secrets 20 Allen St **716/886-9323** • noon-2am, till 4am Fri-Sat • lesbians/ gay men • neighborhood bar • karaoke • piano bar • patio

Nightclubs

Club Marcella 150 Theatre Pl (622 Main St) **716/847-6850** • 9pm-4am, from 4pm Fri, clsd Mon-Tue • lesbians/ gay men • dancing/DJ • drag shows Sun • wheelchair access

Metroplex 729 Main St **716/856-5630** • 10pm-4am, clsd Mon • lesbians/ gay men • dancing/DJ • alternative • 18+

Bookstores

Talking Leaves 3158 Main St (btwn Winspear & Hertel Aves) **716/837-8554** • 10am-6pm, till 8pm Wed-Th, clsd Sun

Spiritual Groups

Dignity 716/833-8995 • call for events

Erotica

Village Books & News 3104 Delaware Ave (at Hamilton), Kenmore **716/877-5027** • 24hrs

Canaseraga

Accommodations

Fairwise Llama Farm 1320 Rte 70 **607/545-6247** • lesbians/ gay men • full brkfst • located btwn Letchworth & Stony Brook Parks • $30-60

Canton

Info Lines & Services

PRISM 315/265-2422 • support group 1st & 3rd Fri

Catskill Mtns

Info Lines & Services

Ulster GALA 914/679-5039

Wise Woman Center 914/246-8081 • women only • workshops • correspondence courses • newsletter

Accommodations

Bradstan Country Hotel White Lake **914/583-4114** • gay-friendly • also piano bar & cabaret • 6pm-1am Fri-Sat

Inn at Stone Ridge Rte 209, Stone Ridge **914/687-0736** • gay-friendly • full brkfst • also fine dining • full bar • patio • $60-145

Palenville House B&B Junction Rtes 23-A & 32-A, Palenville **518/678-5649, 877/689-5101** • gay/ straight • Victorian guesthouse • full brkfst • hot tub • some shared baths • smokefree • gay-owned/ run • $60-125

Point Lookout Mountain Inn The Mohican Trail, Rte 23, East Windham **518/734-3381** • gay/ straight • hot tub • kids/ pets ok • wheelchair access • gay-owned/ run • $60-125 • also 'Bella Vista Restaurant' • $11-18 • also 'Rainbow Cafe & Cliffside Deck'

Red Bear Inn & Restaurant West Kill **518/989-6000, 888/232-7466** • gay-friendly • seasonal • also camping • leather-friendly • smokefree • full bar

River Run B&B Fleischmanns **914/254-4884** • gay/ straight • Queen Anne Victorian • full brkfst • IGLTA • gay-owned/ run • $65-110

Wild Rose Inn 66 Rock City Rd, Woodstock **914/679-8783** • gay-friendly • lesbian-owned/ run

Woodstock Inn 38 Tannery Brook Rd, Woodstock **914/679-8211** • gay-friendly • swimming hole • wheelchair access • $79-131

Restaurants

Catskill Rose Rte 212, Mt Tremper **914/688-7100** • 5pm-close Wed-Sun • some veggie • full bar • patio • $13-17

Entertainment & Recreation

Frog Hollow Farm Old Post Rd, Esopus **914/384-6424** • riding school & camp

Solstice Farm Stable Stanfordville **914/868-1413** • riding school & camp

Bookstores

Golden Notebook 29 Tinker St, Woodstock **914/679-8000** • 10:30am-7pm, till 6pm Sun (till 9pm summers) • lesbigay section • wheelchair access

Cooperstown

see also Sharon Springs

Restaurants

Tryon Inn 124 Main St, Cherry Valley **607/264-3790** • 5:30pm-10pm, from 3pm Sun • country French • some veggie • gay-owned/ run • $12-16

Cortland

Bookstores

Mandolin Winds Bookstore 33 Main St (at Central) **607/758–7460** • 10am-5pm, till 7pm Th, till 4pm Sat, clsd Sun • lesbigay section

Croton-on-Hudson

Accommodations

Alexander Hamilton House 49 Van Wyck St **914/271–6737** • gay-friendly • full brkfst • smokefree • pets ok • woman-owned/ run • $75-250

Elmira

Accommodations

Rufus Tanner House B&B 60 Sagetown Rd, Pine City **607/732–0213** • gay/ straight • full brkfst • jacuzzi • smokefree • gay-owned/ run • $55-95

Nightclubs

Angles 511–513 Railroad Ave (btwn Clinton & 3rd) **607/733–7676** • 4pm-1am, till 4am Fri-Sat • popular • lesbians/ gay men • dancing/DJ Wed-Sun • live shows • younger crowd • also restaurant • gay-owned/ run

Club TNT 425 Railroad Ave (at 2nd) **607/737–4610** • 5pm-1am • lesbians/ gay men • dancing/DJ • live shows • karaoke • women's night Tue • patio

Spiritual Groups

Ray of Hope Church 425 Railroad Ave (at 'Club TNT') **800/367–1463, 315/476–8544** • 10:30am Sat

Fire Island

see also Long Island

Info Lines & Services

AA Gay/ Lesbian 516/654–1150

Accommodations

Black Sheep in Exile B&B 71 Bay Walk E, Fire Island Pines **516/597–6565** • mostly gay men • full brkfst • pets ok • gourmet dinner available • $65-120

Boatel The Pines **516/597–6500** • lesbians/ gay men • swimming

Bob Howard Realtor The Pines **516/597–9400, 212/819–9400** • great source for rentals

Cherry Grove Beach Hotel Main & Ocean, Cherry Grove **516/597–6600** • mostly gay men • swimming • nudity • smokefree rm available • wheelchair access • IGLTA • $40-400

Dune Point Guesthouse 516/597–6261 • lesbians/ gay men • wheelchair access

Island Properties 37 Fire Island Blvd **516/597–6900** • weekly, monthly, & seasonal rentals

Pines Place 516/597–6162 • mostly gay men • guesthouse offers rooms in 2 locations • $150-325

Sea Crest Lewis Walk, Cherry Grove **516/597–6849** • lesbians/ gay men • seasonal

Bars

Cherry's 158 Bayview Walk, Cherry Grove **516/597–6820** • seasonal • noon-4am • lesbians/ gay men • piano bar • also restaurant

The Island Club & Bistro 36 Fire Island Blvd, The Pines **516/597–6001** • seasonal • 6pm-4am, from 4pm wknds • bistro open 6pm-11pm, clsd Wed • mostly gay men • dancing/DJ • $15-28 (bistro)

Nightclubs

Ice Palace at 'Cherry Grove Beach Hotel', Cherry Grove **516/597–6600** • hours vary • popular • lesbians/ gay men • dancing/DJ • live shows

The Pavilion Fire Island Blvd, The Pines **516/597–6131** • lesbians/ gay men • popular • dancing/DJ • also 'Yacht Club' restaurant • 10am-11pm

Restaurants

Cherry Grove Pizza Dock Walk (under the 'Ice Palace'), Cherry Grove **516/597–6766**

Michael's Dock Walk, Cherry Grove **516/597–6555** • seasonal • basic brkfst, lunch & late dinner

Top of the Bay Dock Walk at Bay Walk, Cherry Grove **516/597–6699** • seasonal • 7pm-midnight • popular • lesbians/ gay men • $18-23

Glens Falls

Bars

Club M 70 South St **518/798–9809** • noon-4am • lesbians/ gay men • dancing/DJ • wheelchair access

Highland

see also Poughkeepsie, New Paltz

Accommodations

Inn at Applewood 120 North Rd **914/691–2516** • full brkfst • $90 • also restaurant • plenty veggie

NIGHTCLUBS

Prime Time Rte 9 W **914/691-8550** • 9pm-4am Fri-Sun only • mostly gay men • dancing/DJ Fri-Sat • bingo for AIDS & karaoke Sun • male strippers • theme nights

RESTAURANTS

The Would Bar & Grill 120 North Rd (off Rte 9 W) **914/691-9883** • lunch Mon-Fri & dinner nightly, clsd Sun • some veggie • full bar • patio • $16-22

Hudson

ACCOMMODATIONS

Hudson City B&B 326 Allen St (at Rte 9-G/ 3rd St) **518/822-8044** • gay/ straight • 18th-century Victorian in antique district • some shared baths • full brkfst • gay-owned/ run

St Charles Hotel 16-18 Park Pl **518/822-9900** • gay-friendly • also 2 restaurants

Ithaca

INFO LINES & SERVICES

AA Gay/ Lesbian First Baptist Church (at Dewitt Park) **607/273-1541** • 6pm Sun

Ithaca Gay/ Lesbian Activities Board (IGLAB) 607/273-1505 (**COMMON GROUND BAR**) • 3rd Tue • sponsors events including 'Finger Lake Gay/ Lesbian Picnic'

Women's Community Building 100 W Seneca (at Cayuga) **607/272-1247** • 9am-5pm, evenings & wknds by appt

BARS

Common Ground 1230 Danby Rd/ Rte 96B (at Comfort) **607/273-1505** • 4pm-1:30am • popular • lesbians/ gay men • dancing/DJ • also restaurant Fri-Sun • some veggie • $5-8

CAFES

Harvest Deli 171 E State St (in Ithaca Commons), Center Ithaca **607/272-1961** • 9am-6pm, till 8pm Th-Fri, 11am-5pm Sun

RESTAURANTS

ABC Cafe 308 Stewart Ave (at Buffalo) **607/277-4770** • lunch & dinner, wknd brunch, clsd Mon • beer/ wine • vegetarian • $6-8

BOOKSTORES

Borealis Bookstore 111 N Aurora St (at State) **607/272-7752** • 10am-9pm, 11am-5pm Sun • independent alternative • lesbigay & transgendered sections • wheelchair access

Jamestown

BARS

Nite Spot 201 Windsor • 7pm-2am • lesbians/ gay men • dancing/DJ • live shows

Rascals 701 N Main St/ Rte 60 (at 7th) **716/484-3220** • 3pm-2am • lesbians/ gay men • dancing/DJ Fri-Sun • karaoke Wed • drag shows Sun

Sneakers 100 Harrison (at Institute) **716/484-8816** • 2pm-2am • lesbians/ gay men • dancing/DJ Fri-Sat • wheelchair access

Kingston

RESTAURANTS

Armadillo Bar & Grill 97 Abeel St **914/339-1550** • lunch & dinner • some veggie • full bar • patio

Crossroads Restaurant 38 Broadway **914/340-0151** • 11:30am-10pm, kitchen till 9pm, clsd Mon • piano bar • gay Wed eves in bar

LONG ISLAND

Long Island is divided into 2 geographical areas:
Long Island—Nassau County
Long Island—Suffolk County

see also Fire Island

Long Island - Nassau County

INFO LINES & SERVICES

Pride for Youth Coffeehouse 2050 Bellmore Ave, Bellmore **516/679-9000** • 7:30pm-11:30pm Fri

BARS

Auntie Em's 3547 Merrick Rd, Seaford **516/679-8820** • 5pm-4am • lesbians/ gay men • neighborhood bar • live shows wknds

Blanche 47-2 Boundary Ave, South Farmingdale **516/694-6906** • 7pm-4am, from 4pm Sun • mostly gay men • neighborhood bar • live shows • piano bar from 10pm Sat

SPIRITUAL GROUPS

Dignity at Church of the Advent, Westbury **516/781-6225** • 8pm 2nd & 4th Sat

Long Island - Suffolk County

INFO LINES & SERVICES

EEGO (East End Gay Organization) **516/324-3699** • social events

Accommodations

132 North Main 132 N Main, East Hampton **516/324-2246** • mostly gay men • seasonal mini-resort • swimming • smokefree • wheelchair access • $125-225

Centennial House 13 Woods Ln, East Hampton **516/324-9414** • gay/ straight • full brkfst • smokefree • swimming • gay-owned/ run • $225-395

Cozy Cabins Motel **516/537-1160** • lesbians/ gay men • seasonal • $79-125

EconoLodge—MacArthur Airport 3055 Rte 454, Ronkonkoma **516/588-6800, 800/553-2666** • gay-friendly • budget motel • smokefree rms available

EconoLodge—Smithtown/ Hauppauge 755 Rte 347, Smithtown **516/724-9000, 800/553-2666** • gay-friendly • $69-109

Gandalf House **516/298-4769** • gay-friendly

Summit Motor Inn 501 E Main St, Bay Shore **516/666-6000, 800/869-6363** • gay-friendly • $79-119

Sunset Beach 35 Shore Rd, Shelter Island **516/749-2001** • gay-friendly • seasonal • food served • $150-360

Bars

Forever Green 841 N Broome Ave, Lindenhurst **516/226-9357** • 8pm-4am, from 5pm Fri, from 7pm Sun • mostly women • neighborhood bar

Nightclubs

Bunkhouse 192 N Main St/ Montauk Hwy (at Foster Ave), Sayville **516/567-2865** • 7pm-4am • popular • mostly gay men • dancing/DJ • karaoke Mon

Shi 121 Woodfield Rd, West Hempstead **516/486-9516** • 8pm-4am • popular • mostly women • dancing/DJ Fri • live shows Sat

The Swamp 378 Montauk Hwy (at Eastgate Rd), Wainscott **516/537-3332** • 6pm-4am, clsd Tue • call for winter hours • mostly gay men • dancing/DJ • also 'Annex' restaurant • cont'l/ seafood • wheelchair access • $16-20

Restaurants

Babette's 66 Newtown Ln, East Hampton **516/329-5377** • breakfast, lunch & dinner • healthy • plenty veggie

Butchers Boy 220 Montauk Hwy, Sayville **516/563-6679** • 4pm-2am, clsd Tue • steakhouse • full bar • $9-17

Entertainment & Recreation

Fowler Beach Southampton

Spiritual Groups

Dignity **516/654-5367** • 7pm 2nd & last Sun

Unitarian Universalist Fellowship 109 Browns Rd, Huntington **516/427-9547** • 9:30am & 11:15am Sun

Mahopac

Info Lines & Services

Putnam/ N Westchester Women's Resource Ctr 2 Mahopac Plaza **914/628-9284** • drop-in hrs 9am-5pm wkdys

Bars

Rich Wood's Brewster Station Cafe 50 Main St (across from the train station), Brewster **914/279-7844** • 11:30am-3am, from 5pm wknds • mostly gay men • food served • live shows wknds

Mt Morris

Bars

Fred's Tavern 36 Main St (at State) **716/658-3267** • noon-2am • gay/ straight • neighborhood bar

New Paltz

Accommodations

Ujjala's B&B 2 Forest Glen **914/255-6360** • gay-friendly • full brkfst • body therapy • sweat lodges • kids/ pets ok • woman-owned/ run • $80-105

Restaurants

Locust Tree Inn 215 Hugenot St (behind conference ctr) **914/255-7888** • lunch & dinner, clsd Mon • cont'l • full bar • patio • $14-20

Northern Spy Cafe Rte 213, High Falls **914/687-7298** • dinner nightly & Sun brunch, clsd Wed • plenty veggie • full bar • wheelchair access • $11-18

Bookstores

The Painted Word 36 Main St (nr US 32 N) **914/256-0825** • 10am-6pm, till 8pm Fri-Sat • lesbigay • cafe • live music • poetry readings • wheelchair access

New York City

New York City is divided into 8 geographical areas:
NYC—Overview
NYC—Soho, Greenwich & Chelsea
NYC—Midtown
NYC—Uptown
NYC—Brooklyn
NYC—Queens
NYC—Bronx
NYC—Staten Island

NYC—Overview

Info Lines & Services

AA Gay/ Lesbian Intergroup at Lesbian/ Gay Community Ctr **212/647-1680** • call for mtg schedule

African Ancestral Lesbians United for Societal Change at Lesbian/ Gay Community Ctr **212/620-7310** • 8pm Th

Asians & Friends of NY at Lesbian/ Gay Community Ctr **718/488-0630** • 8pm 3rd Sat

Bisexual Gay/ Lesbian Transgender Youth of NY at Lesbian/ Gay Community Ctr **212/620-7310** • 3:30pm Sat

Bisexual Network 212/459-4784 • info on variety of social & political groups

Bisexual Women's Group at Lesbian/ Gay Community Ctr **212/620-7310** • 6:30pm Wed

Butch/ Femme Society at Lesbian/ Gay Community Ctr **212/388-2736** • 6:30pm 3rd Wed

Eulenspiegel Society 24 Bond St (btwn Lafayette & the Bowery) **212/388-7022** • 7:30pm Tue-Wed • $7 for non-members • pansexual S/M group • newsletter

FLAB (Fat is a Lesbian Issue) at Lesbian/ Gay Community Ctr **718/338-4530** • 5pm 2nd Sun • fat-positive discussion group & dinner • allies welcome

Gay/ Lesbian Switchboard of New York Project 212/989-0999 • 6pm-10pm Mon-Fri, noon-5pm Sat

Hetrick-Martin Institute 2 Astor Pl **212/674-2400, 212/674-8695 (TTY)** • extensive services for lesbigay youth • also publishes 'You Are Not Alone' resource directory

Identity House 39 W 14th St #205 (btwn 5th & 6th Aves) **212/243-8181** • walk-in 6pm-9pm Mon, Tue & Fri & 1pm-4pm wknds • peer-counseling • info & referrals

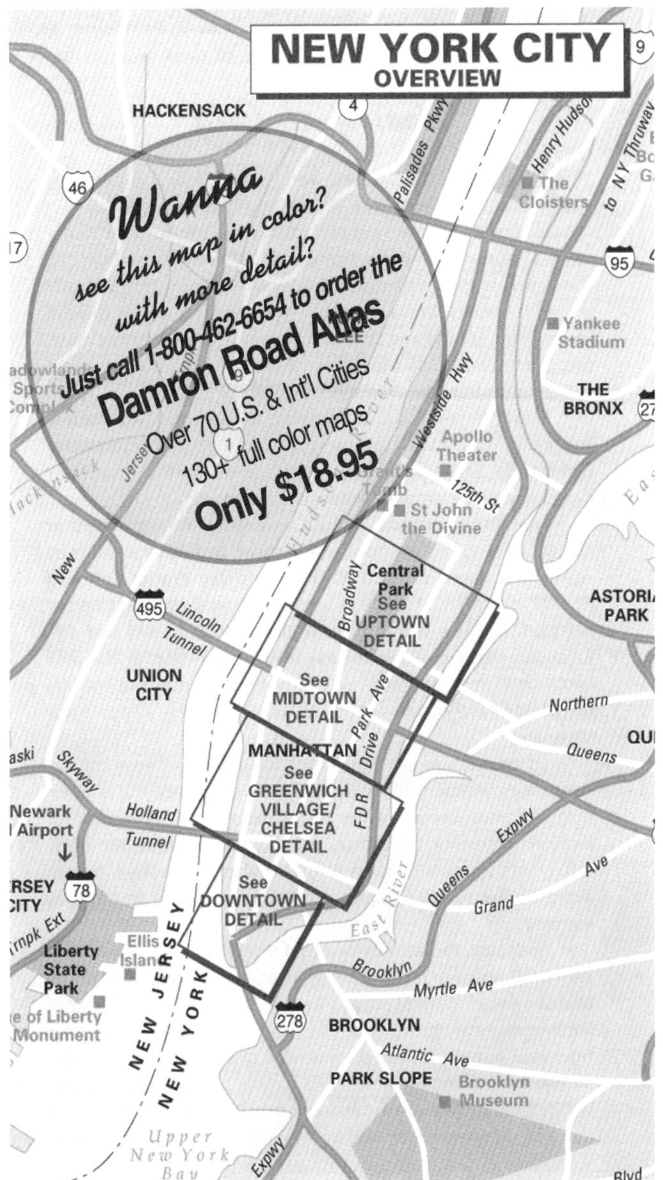
NEW YORK CITY
OVERVIEW
HACKENSACK
Wanna
see this map in color?
with more detail?
Just call 1-800-462-6654 to order the
Damron Road Atlas
Over 70 U.S. & Int'l Cities
130+ full color maps
Only $18.95
Palisades Pkwy
Henry Hudson
to NY Thruway
The Cloisters
Yankee Stadium
THE BRONX
Westside Hwy
Apollo Theater
125th St
St John the Divine
Central Park
See UPTOWN DETAIL
Broadway
ASTORIA PARK
Lincoln Tunnel
UNION CITY
See MIDTOWN DETAIL
Park Ave
Northern
MANHATTAN
Park Drive
Queens
Skyway
See GREENWICH VILLAGE/ CHELSEA DETAIL
FDR
Newark Airport
Holland Tunnel
Expwy
78
Queens
Ave
See DOWNTOWN DETAIL
East River
Grand
Ellis Island
Liberty State Park
Brooklyn
Myrtle Ave
NEW JERSEY
NEW YORK
278
BROOKLYN
Atlantic Ave
PARK SLOPE
Brooklyn Museum
Upper New York Bay
Expwy
Blvd

New York City

In the film *Mondo New York,* demi-monde denizen Joey Arias put it best: 'New York is the clit of the world!'

Get ready for the most stimulating trip of your life! You've come to *the* city of world-famous tourist attractions: from the skyscrapers to the subway, New York is like no other place. Whether you pride yourself on your cultural sophistication, or lack thereof, you're going to find endless entertainment. There are plays, musicals, operas, museums and gallery shows, performance art, street theater, and street life...and that's just for starters.

To get the most out of your visit, do your homework before you come. Call for a calendar of events at the **Lesbian/Gay Community Services Center,** which houses meeting spaces for every conceivable group of lesbigaytrans+ people.

New York's performance art is a must-see for any student of modern culture. The best bets for intelligent, cutting edge shows by women and queers are **W.O.W. (Women's One World) Café** and P.S. 122 on 1st Ave. at 9th St., where lesbian artist Holly Hughes got her start. For 'two-fers'—half-price tickets to Broadway and off-Broadway shows available the day of the show—stop by the TKTS booth on 47th St. at Broadway. For the latest reviews and hot off-off-Broadway theaters, check the queer-friendly *Village Voice* newspaper.

Of course, you can stimulate a lot more than your cultural sensibilities in New York. Gourmands cans experience oral orgasms ranging from a delicate quiver to a blinding throb every day. For instance, before that Broadway show, head to one of the many restaurants along 46th St. at 9th Ave. When in Brooklyn, brunch along 7th Ave.; you'll find plenty of lesbigay company on a Sunday morning.

Shopping, too, affords shivers of delight. Check out the fabulous thrift shops and the designer boutiques. Cruise Midtown on Madison Ave., E. 57th St., or 5th Ave. in the 50s, at Trump Tower or another major shopping mall, and touch clothing more expensive than your last car. Other recommended districts for blowing cash on hipster fashions and accessories include St. Mark's Place in the Village (8th St. between 1st and 2nd Aves.); Broadway from 8th to Canal St.; and any major intersection in Soho and the East Village.

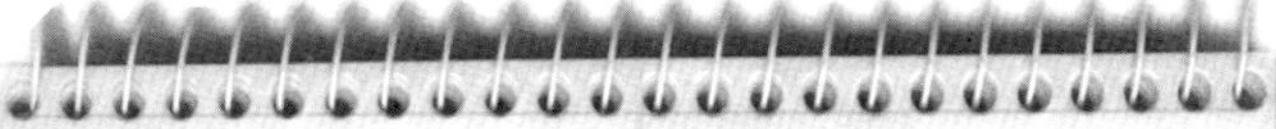

To titillate your mind, peruse the shelves at **A Different Light** or **Oscar Wilde Memorial Bookshop**, or make an appointment to stop by the **Lesbian Herstory Archives** in Brooklyn. If you're in the mood for love, visit **Eve's Garden,** New York's women's erotic boutique; men are only allowed in if accompanied by a woman.

You could spend days at the big art museums in Uptown near Central Park, but budget some time for the galleries in SoHo (south of Houston—pronounced How-ston, not like the city in Texas—between Broadway and 6th Ave.). You can pick up a gallery map in the area.

For musical entertainment, make your pilgrimage to The Kitchen, legendary site of experimental and freestyle jazz, or CBGB's, legendary home of noisy music (the Ramones started American punk here in 1974).

Nightlife...we know you've been holding your breath! Run, don't walk to the **Clit Club**; Friday nights on W. 14th St. are the sexiest, hottest dyke nights in town. **Crazy Nanny's** really happens seven days a week, and several other women's bars are nearby. **Shescape** produces women's club nights at various locations, so call for their latest events. (New York is also home to plenty of one-nighters, so be sure to pick up a copy of **HX** for up-to-the-minute club happenings.) Kinky dykes should get the latest schedule for the **Vault** party space in the Village. And no one should miss the Drag King scene in this gender-bending city.

If this isn't enough excitement, experience the City in June when New York hosts numerous Lesbian/Gay Pride-related cultural events, from their week-long Film Festival to the Pride March itself.

One last bit of advice: there's more to New York City than Manhattan. Brooklyn has long been home to lesbians escaping the extortionist rents of Manhattan. To taste dyke life in this borough, stop by **Rising Cafe**. If you'll be out on Long Island, stop by one of the two women's bars: **Forever Green** and **Shi**.

New York City

Where the Girls Are: Upwardly mobile literary types hang in the West Village, hipster dykes cruise the East Village, upper-crusty Lesbians have cocktails in Midtown, and working-class dykes live in Brooklyn.

Lesbigay Pride: Last Sunday in June. 212/807-7433.
Bronx Pride - June. 718/670-3396.
Brooklyn Pride - June. 718/670-3337.

Annual Events: February - Saint-at-Large White Party 212/674-8541.
March - Saint-at-Large Black Party.
Night of a Thousand Gowns 212/807-8767. Imperial Court benefit for AmFAR.
May - AIDS Walk-a-thon 212/807-9255.
June - New York Int'l Gay/Lesbian Film Festival 212/343-2707.
September - Wigstock 212/620-7310. Outrageous wig/drag/performance festival in Tompkins Square Park in the East Village.
October - All Saint's Party.
November - AIDS Walk New York 212/807-9255.
New York Lesbian/Gay Experimental Film/Video Fest 212/501-2309 or 212/571-4242. Film, videos, installations & media performances.
December 31 - Saint-at-Large New Year's Party.

City Info: 212/397-8222. nycvisit.com

Attractions: Broadway.
Carnegie Hall 212/903-9600.
Central Park.
Ellis Island.
Empire State Building 212/736-3100.
Greenwich Village.
Guggenheim Museum 212/423-3600.
Lincoln Center 212/546-2656.
Metropolitan Museum of Art.
Museum of Modern Art 212/708-9400.
Radio City Music Hall 212/247-4777.
Rockefeller Center.
Statue of Liberty.
Times Square.
United Nations.
Wall Street.
World Trade Center 212/435-4170.

Best View: Coming over any of the bridges into New York, the Empire State Building, or the World Trade Center.

Weather: A spectrum of extremes with pleasant moments thrown in. Spring and fall are the best times to visit.

Transit: Wave an arm on any streetcorner for a taxi.
Carey Airport Shuttle 718/706-9658.
Public transit MTA 718/330-1234.

Just Couples at Lesbian/ Gay Community Ctr **212/252-3154** • 3:30pm 1st Sun

Las Buenas Amigas at Lesbian/ Gay Community Ctr **212/614-2948** • 2pm 1st Sun • Latina lesbian group

▲ **Lesbian/ Gay Community Services Center** One Little West 12th St (at Hudson) **212/620-7310** • 9am-11pm • wheelchair access

Lesbian Herstory Archives 718/768-3953 • exists to gather & preserve records of lesbian lives & activities • located in Park Slope, Brooklyn • wheelchair access

NY CyberQueers at Lesbian/ Gay Community Ctr **212/620-7310** • 6pm 3rd Th (not in summer) • lesbigay & transgender 'computer pros'

SAGE: Senior Action in a Gay Environment at Lesbian/ Gay Community Ctr **212/741-2247** • call for events

SALGA (South Asian Lesbian/ Gay Association) at Lesbian/ Gay Community Ctr **212/358-5132** • 3:30pm 2nd Sat

Sirens Motorcycle Club at Lesbian/ Gay Community Ctr **212/749-6177** • 8pm 3rd Tue

Support Group for Single Lesbians at Lesbian/ Gay Community Ctr **212/620-7310** • 6:30pm Tue & Fri

Twenty Something at Lesbian/ Gay Community Ctr **212/439-8051** • 8pm 1st & 3rd Tue • social alternative to bars for lesbigays in late teens, 20s & early 30s • also 'Twenty Something–Lesbians' 9pm Fri • 212/283-3914

ENTERTAINMENT & RECREATION

Pro Musica Tours 800/916-0312 • performing arts itineraries

Think It's Not When It Is 718/949-5162 • theater company promoting positive lesbigay images

PUBLICATIONS

HX Magazine 212/352-3535 • complete weekly guide to gay New York at night

▲ **LGNY (Lesbian & Gay New York) 212/691-1100** • lesbigay newspaper

Manhattan Spirit 212/268-0454 • weekly community newspaper

New York Blade 242 W 30th St, 4th flr **212/268-2711** • lesbigay newspaper

Next 212/627-0165 • party paper

Spiritual Groups

Buddhist Lesbians/ Gays: Maitri Dorje at Lesbian/ Gay Community Ctr **212/620-7310** • 6pm 2nd Tue

Church of St Luke in the Fields (Episcopal) 487 Hudson St (at Christopher) **212/924-0562** • 8am, 9:15am, 11:15am Sun & 4:45pm Sat • call for summer mtg times

Congregation Beth Simchat Torah 28th St & 9th Ave **212/929-9498** • 8:30pm Fri • lesbigay synagogue • wheelchair access • also 57 Bethune St location • call for other mtg times

Dignity 218 W 11th St (at St John's) **212/627-6488** • 7:30pm Sun

Integrity NYC 212/691-7181

MCC of New York 446 W 36th St (btwn 9th & 10th) **212/629-7440** • 10am & 7pm Sun

Society of Friends (Quakers) Earl Hall (Columbia University, at 116th & Broadway) **212/777-8866** • 11am Sun

NYC—Soho, Greenwich & Chelsea

Accommodations

Abingdon Guesthouse 13 8th Ave (at W 12th St) **212/243-5384** • lesbians/ gay men • smokefree • wheelchair access • no party people welcome • $80-220

Chelsea Inn 46 W 17th St (btwn 5th & 6th Sts) **212/645-8989** • gay-friendly • $69-229

Chelsea Pines Inn 317 W 14th St (btwn 8th & 9th Aves) **212/929-1023** • lesbians/ gay men • IGLTA • $89-149

The Chelsea Savoy Hotel 204 W 23rd St (at 7th Ave) **212/929-9353** • gay/ straight • $99-175

Colonial House Inn 318 W 22nd St (btwn 8th & 9th Aves) **212/243-9669, 800/689-3779** • mostly gay men • IGLTA • $80-140

Commerce Court: Greenwich Village Lodging 36 Commerce St (btwn Bedford & Barrow) **212/741-0126** • gay/ straight • B&B in 1841 renovated brick row house • $135

East Village B&B 212/260-1865 • women only • apt rental • lesbian-owned • $60-85

The Gramercy Park Hotel 2 Lexington Ave (at E 21st St) **212/475-4320, 800/221-4083** • gay-friendly • aging hotel across from Gramercy Park • $135-180

Holiday Inn 138 Lafayette St (in Chinatown) **212/966-8898** • gay-friendly

Hotel Washington Square 103 Waverly Pl (at MacDougal St) **212/777-9515, 800/222-0418** • gay-friendly • renovated 100-yr-old hotel • 'C3' restaurant 7:30am-10:30pm, clsd Sun-Mon • $90-150

Incentra Village House 32 8th Ave (at W 12th St) **212/206-0007** • lesbians/ gay men • gay-owned/ run • $99-179

Soho Grand Hotel 310 W Broadway (at Canal St) **212/965-3000, 800/965-3000** • gay-friendly • big, glossy, over-the-top hotel • wheelchair access • $249-399

Bars

Androgyny 35 Crosby St (btwn Grand & Broome) **212/613-0977** • 8pm-2am, till 3am Fri-Sat, clsd Sun-Mon • lesbians/ gay men • transgender-friendly • beer/ wine only

The Bar 68 2nd Ave (at 4th St) **212/674-9714** • 3pm-4am • mostly gay men • neighborhood bar

Bar d'O 29 Bedford St (at Downing St) **212/627-1580** • 7:30pm-3am • gay-friendly • live shows • women's night Mon

Barracuda 275 W 22nd St (at 8th Ave) **212/645-8613** • 4pm-4am • popular • mostly gay men • live DJs

Blu 161 W 23rd St (at 7th Ave) **212/633-6113** • 4pm-4am • mostly gay men • DJ Tue-Sun • Internet access

BMW Bar 199 7th Ave (at 21st St) **212/229-1807** • 24hrs • gay-friendly • live music nightly • food served • beer/ wine only

The Boiler Room 86 E 4th St (at 2nd Ave) **212/254-7536** • 4pm-4am • popular • mostly gay men • neighborhood bar

Boots & Saddle 76 Christopher St (at 7th Ave S) **212/929-9684** • 8am-4am, noon-4pm Sun • mostly gay men • neighborhood bar

Bowery Bar 40 E 4th St (at Bowery) **212/475-2220** • gay-friendly • 11:30pm-2am, 10:30pm-4am Fri-Sat, more gay Tue • super-trendy models' bar • patio

The Break 232 8th Ave (at 22nd St) **212/627-0072** • 2pm-4am • mostly gay men

The Cock 188 Ave 'A' (at 12th St) **212/946-1871** • noon-4am • mostly gay men • a 'sleazy rock 'n roll bar' • live DJs

Crazy Nanny's 21 7th Ave S (at Leroy) **212/929-8356, 212/366-6312 (EVENT LINE)** • 4pm-4am • mostly women • dancing/DJ from 10pm Th-Sat • live shows • transgender-friendly • karaoke Th

Cubbyhole 281 W 12th St (at 4th St) **212/243-9041** • 3pm-3am • mostly women • neighborhood bar

The Dugout 185 Christopher St (at Washington St) **212/242-9113** • 4pm-2am, from noon Fri-Sun • mostly gay men • neighborhood bar • sports bar

Dusk 147 W 24th St **212/924-4490** • 6pm-close, clsd Sun • gay/ straight

g 223 W 19th St (at 7th Ave) **212/929-1085** • 4pm-4am • mostly gay men • lounge • live DJs • juice bar

hell 59 Gansevoort St (at Washington) **212/727-1666** • 7pm-4am, from 5pm Fri • lesbians/ gay men • swanky lounge • DJ Tue-Th & Sun

Henrietta Hudson 438 Hudson (at Morton) **212/924-3347** • 4pm-4am • mostly women • neighborhood bar • wheelchair access

Marie's Crisis 59 Grove St (at 7th Ave) **212/243-9323** • 5pm-3am • lesbians/ gay men • piano bar from 9:30pm, from 5:30pm Fri-Sun

Meow Mix 269 E Houston St (at Suffolk) **212/254-0688** • 8pm-4am, clsd Mon • popular • mostly women • dancing/DJ • live music/shows

The Monster 80 Grove St (at W 4th St, Sheridan Sq) **212/924-3558** • 4pm-4am, from 2pm Sun • mostly gay men • dancing/DJ • piano bar & cabaret • 'Sabor Latino' Mon • disco Tue

Phoenix 447 E 13th (at Ave A) **212/477-9979** • 3pm-4am • lesbians/ gay men • more women on occasional Th for 'Visionary' • neighborhood bar • patio

Rubyfruit Bar & Grill 531 Hudson St (at Charles St) **212/929-3343** • 3pm-2am, till 4am Fri-Sat • mostly women • full menu served 5pm-11pm, till midnight Fri-Sat • $20

Starlight Bar & Lounge 167 Ave 'A' (at 11th St) **212/475-2172** • 9pm-3am, clsd Mon-Wed • live DJs • live shows

Stonewall Inn 53 Christopher St (at 7th Ave) **212/463-0950** • 4pm-4am • mostly gay men • dancing/DJ

Wonder Bar 505 E 6th St (at Ave 'A') **212/777-9105** • 8pm-4am • lesbians/ gay men • cocktail lounge DJ • videos • trendy

Nightclubs

13 Bar & Lounge 35 E 13th St (at University Pl) **212/979-6677** • 10pm-4am • lounge from 4pm • gay-friendly • dancing/DJ • mostly gay men Sun

Aspara 221 2nd Ave (at 14th St, at 'Gemini Lounge'), New York City **212/330-8165** • 10pm-close every other Sun • women only • dancing/DJ • theme parties • performances

Big Apple Ranch 39 W 19th St, 5th flr (at 'Dance Manhattan') **212/358-5752** • 8pm-1am Sat only • lesbians/ gay men • two-step lessons • beer only • cover charge

Body & Soul at Vinyl 6 Hubert St (at Hudson) **212/343-1379, 212/330-9169** • 3pm Sun • gay/ straight • happy classic house dancing • multi-racial clientele • Latina/o • also 'Shelter' • 11pm Sat • alcohol-free dance party

Clit Club 432 W 14th St (at 'Mother') **212/366-5680** • 10pm-4am Fri only • popular • mostly women • dancing/DJ • multi-racial • live shows • wheelchair access

Coney Island High 15 St Marks Pl (at 3rd Ave) **212/674-7959** • gay/ straight • transgender-friendly • live shows

Dréd the Dragking Hotline 212/946-4475 • call for events

Flava Party 349 Broadway (enter on Leonard, at 'Club Fahrenheit') **212/340-1017** • 10pm Wed

Life 158 Bleecker St (at Thompson St) **212/420-1999** • 10pm Wed-Th • mostly gay men • dancing/DJ • live bands & drag shows Wed

Limelight 660 6th Ave (at W 20th St) **212/807-9109** • 10pm-4am Wed-Sun, afterhours Fri-Sat • cover charge • gay nights Wed & Sun (more men Sun at 'Drama!')

LoverGirl NYC 539 21st St (btwn 10th & 11th, at Opera) **212/631-1000, 212/726-8302** • 10pm-4:30am Sat • mostly women • dancing/DJ • multi-racial • live shows • cover charge

Mother 432 W 14th St (at Washington) **212/677-6060** • 10pm-4am, clsd Mon • lesbians/ gay men • dancing/DJ • queer performance & clubs • 'Clit Club' for women Fri • 'Click & Drag' Sat (cyberfetish)

Nowbar 22 7th Ave S (at Leroy St) **212/802-9502** • 10pm Th & Sat • mostly gay men • drag shows • cover charge

Opera 539 W 21st St (at 10th Ave) **212/229-1618** • gay-friendly • 10pm-5am • comfy, cozy decor • wheelchair access

Pyramid 101 Ave 'A' (at 7th St) **212/462-9077** • gay-friendly • 10pm-4am • more gay Fri at '1984', New Wave party • more women Wed at 'Cleopatra'

Queen of Hearts Pier 40 (3 blks S of Christopher) **212/631–1102** • 11:30pm-4:30am Tue • mostly women • party boat! • dancing/DJ • cover charge

Roxy 515 W 18th St (at 10th Ave) **212/645–5156** • 11pm-4am Fri-Sat, rollerdisco from 7pm Wed • gay/ straight • alternative • live shows • cover charge

Shescape 212/686–5665 • women only • dance parties held at various locations throughout NYC area

Squeeze Box 511 Greenwich St (at Spring St, at 'Don Hill's') **212/334–1390** • 10pm-close Fri only • gay/ straight • dancing/DJ • rock bands & punk drag queens • cover charge

Tomboy 208 W 23rd St (btwn 7th & 8th, at 'Twirl') **212/686–5665** • 9pm-4am Fri • mostly women • dancing/DJ • cover charge

Cafes

Big Cup 228 8th Ave (at 22nd St) **212/206–0059** • 7am-2am • mostly gay men

Caffe Raffaella 134 7th Ave S (at Charles St) **212/929–7247** • 10am-2am • armchair cafe

Restaurants

7A 109 Ave 'A' (at 7th St) **212/673–6583** • 24hrs • American • $9-15

Around the Clock 8 Stuyvesant St (at 9th St) **212/598–0402** • 24hrs

Benny's Burritos 93 Ave 'A' (at 6th St) **212/254–2054** • 11:30am-midnight • cheap & huge • also 113 Greenwich (at Jane) • 212/727-0584

Blue Ribbon 97 Sullivan St (at Spring St) **212/274–0404** • 4pm-4am, clsd Mon • chef hangout

Brunetta's 190 1st Ave (btwn 11th & 12th Sts) **212/228–4030** • popular • lesbians/ gay men • Italian • some veggie • patio • $8-10

Chelsea Bistro & Bar 358 W 23rd St (at 9th Ave) **212/727–2026** • 5:30pm-11pm • trendy French • full bar

Circa 103 2nd Ave (at 6th St) **212/777–4120** • lunch & dinner • Sun brunch • popular • full bar • wheelchair access • women-owned/ run

The Cloister Cafe 238 E 9th St (at 2nd Ave) **212/777–9128** • 11am-midnight • garden dining

Cola's 148 8th Ave (at 17th St) **212/633–8020** • 4:30pm-11pm • popular • Italian • some veggie • $8-12

Comfort Diner 214 E 4th St (at 3rd Ave) **212/867–4555** • 7am-10pm • reasonable '50s diner

Community Bar & Grill 216 7th Ave (at 22nd St) **212/242–7900** • lunch & dinner • gourmet • live shows • patio

CRATO 49 Grove St (at Bleecker) **212/367–9390** • 5pm-4am • also bar & lounge

East of Eighth 254 W 23rd St (at 8th) **212/352–0075** • lunch, dinner till midnight, till 2am wknds

Eighteenth & Eighth 159 8th Ave **212/242–5000** • boys, boys, boys

Empire Diner 210 10th Ave (at 22nd St) **212/243–2736** • 24hrs

First 87 1st Ave (at 6th St) **212/674–3823** • 5:30pm-2am, till 3am Fri-Sat, 11am-1am Sun • cont'l • hip crowd

Flamingo East 219 2nd Ave (at 13th St) **212/533–2860** • also bar • dancing Wed • 'offbeat rec room'

Florent 69 Gansevoort St (at Washington) **212/989–5779** • 9am-5am, 24hrs Fri-Sat • popular • French diner • $10-15

Food Bar 149 8th Ave (at 17th St) **212/243–2020** • Mediterranean • $4-15

Garage 99 7th Ave S (at Grove St) **212/645–0600** • plenty veggie • live jazz

Global 33 93 2nd Ave (at 5th St) **212/477–8427** • 5pm-midnight • int'l tapas • full bar • $8-15

JB Restaurant & Bar 202 9th Ave (btwn 22nd & 23rd) **212/989–2002**

La Nouvelle Justine 24 1st Ave (go thru 'Lucky Cheng's' to reach dungeon) **212/673–8908** • dominants & slaves serve it up in this SM-themed restaurant

Life Cafe 343 E 10th St (at Ave 'B') **212/477–8791** • 11am-1am, till 3am Fri-Sat • vegetarian artist hangout

Lips 2 Bank St (at Greenwich) **212/675–7710** • 6pm-midnight, till 3am Sat, 'Disco Fever Brunch' noon-6pm Sun • 'the Hard Rock cafe of drag' • Italian/ American served by queens

Lucky Cheng's 24 1st Ave (at 2nd St) **212/473–0516** • 6pm-midnight • popular • Asian/ fusion • full bar • drag shows • karaoke

Mary's Restaurant 42 Bedford St (at 7th Ave S) **212/741–3387** • 6pm-midnight, brunch Sun

Miracle Grill 113 1st Ave (at 6th St) **212/254–2353** • garden dining

Omjavi 112 Chambers St (nr the Brooklyn Bridge) **212/732–1949** • 9am-10pm, till 6pm Sat, clsd Sun • Caribbean cuisine

Restivo 209 7th Ave (at 22nd St) **212/366-4133** • noon-midnight • Italian • intimate ambiance • gay-owned/ run

Sacred Chow 522 Hudson St (at W 10th St) **212/337-0863** • 7:30am-11pm • gourmet vegan • wheelchair access

Sarong Sarong 343 Bleecker St (at 11th St) **212/989-0888** • noon-midnight • popular • Malaysian • some veggie • full bar

Sazerac House Bar & Grill 533 Hudson (at Charles) **212/989-0313** • noon-11pm • Cajun • full bar • $8-20

Stingy Lulu's 129 St Marks Pl (at Ave 'A') **212/674-3545** • 11am-5am • funky American diner • popular brunch • drag queen servers

Trattoria Pesce Pasta 262 Bleecker St **212/645-2993** • noon-midnight

The Viceroy 160 8th Ave (at 18th St) **212/633-8484** • noon-midnight • popular • fusion • full bar

Windows on India 344 E 6th St (at 1st Ave) **212/477-5956** • noon-midnight • best food in NYC's 'Little India'

Entertainment & Recreation

Leslie-Lohman Gay Art Foundation Gallery 127 Prince St, lower level **212/673-7007** • 1pm-6pm, clsd Mon-Tue

PS 122 150 1st Ave (at E 9th St) **212/477-5288, 212/477-5029** • it's rough, it's raw, it's real New York performance art

Wessel & O'Connor 242 W 26th St (btwn 7th & 8th Aves) **212/242-8811** • open Tue-Sun in winter, Mon-Fri in summer • gay art galllery • mainly photography

WOW Cafe Cabaret 59 E 4th St (btwn 2nd Ave & Bowery) **212/777-4280** • open Th-Sat • women's theater

Bookstores

A Different Light 151 W 19th St (at 7th Ave) **212/989-4850, 800/343-4002** • 10am-midnight • lesbigay • also cafe

Bleecker Street Books 350 Bleecker St (at W 10th St) **212/675-2084** • 10:30am-11:30pm

Bluestockings 172 Allen St (btwn Stanton & Rivington) **212/777-6042** • noon-8pm Tue-Sun • women's

Creative Visions Books 548 Hudson St (btwn Perry & Charles) **212/645-7573, 800/997-9899** • 11am-11pm • lesbigay

Oscar Wilde Memorial Bookshop 15 Christopher St (at 7th Ave) **212/255-8097** • 11:30am-8pm, till 7pm Sun • lesbigay

Soho Books 351 W Broadway (at Grant) **212/226-3395** • 10am-midnight

Retail Shops

Alternate Card & Gift Shop 85 Christopher St (at 7th Ave) **212/645-8966** • 11:30am-9:30pm

DeMask 135 W 22nd St (btwn 6th & 7th Aves) **212/352-2850** • 11am-7pm • European fetish fashion

Don't Panic 98 Christopher St (at Bleecker St) **212/989-7888** • 11am-10pm • lesbigay T-shirts & more

DV8 211 W 20th St (at 7th Ave) **212/337-9744** • noon-8pm, till 7pm Sat, till 5pm Sun, clsd Mon

Flight 001 96 Greenwich (btwn Jane & 12th) **212/691-1001** • noon-9pm, from 11am Sat, till 6pm Sun • travel gear

Rainbows & Triangles 192 8th Ave (at 19th St) **212/627-2166** • 11am-10pm • lesbigay

Gyms & Health Clubs

19th St Health & Fitness 22 W 19th St **212/929-6789** • lesbians/ gay men • day passes available

American Fitness Center 128 8th Ave **212/627-0065** • popular • mostly gay men • day passes available

David Barton Gym 552 6th Ave **212/727-0004** • lesbians/ gay men • day passes available

Sex Clubs

The Vault 565 W 23rd St (btwn 10th & 11th Aves) **212/255-6758** • 7pm-11pm 3rd Sun, doors close at 8:30pm • women only

Erotica

Pleasure Chest 156 7th Ave S (at Charles) **212/242-2158**

Toys in Babeland 94 Rivington (btwn Orchard & Ludlow) **212/375-1701** • noon-10pm, till 8pm Sun

NYC—Midtown

Accommodations

Gershwin Hotel 7 E 27th St (at 5th Ave) **212/545-8000** • gay-friendly • artsy, seedy hotel w/ model's floor dorms & rooms • $25-95 • also bar & cafe • jazz room • art gallery

The Hotel Metro 45 W 35th St (at 5th Ave) **212/947-2500, 800/356-3870** • gay-friendly • slick art deco hotel • 1 blk from Empire State Bldg • $145+

Park Central Hotel 870 7th Ave (at 56th St) **212/247-8000, 800/346-1359** • gay-friendly • also restaurant • wheelchair access

Travel Inn 515 W 42nd St (at 10th Ave) **212/695-7171, 800/869-4630** • gay-friendly • IGLTA

Bars

Cleo's Saloon 656 9th Ave (at 46th St) **212/307-1503** • 8am-4am, from noon Sun • mostly gay men • neighborhood bar

The Comfort Zone 405 3rd Ave (at 29th St) **212/684-8376** • 3pm-4am • mostly gay men • neighborhood bar • DJ Tue & Fri-Sun • live rock 'n roll Th

Danny's Skylight Room 346 W 46th St (at 9th Ave) **212/265-8133** • 4pm-midnight, brunch 11:30am-3pm Wed & wknds • gay-friendly • piano bar from 6pm • cabaret • cover + 2 drink minimum

Don't Tell Mama 343 W 46th St (at 9th Ave) **212/757-0788** • 4pm-4am • gay-friendly • young crowd • piano bar & cabaret • cover + 2 drink minimum • call for shows

Julie's 204 E 58th St, 3rd flr (at 2nd Ave) **212/688-1294** • 5pm-4am • mostly women • professional • DJ Wed-Sun • piano bar • 'Luscious Latinas' Wed • singles' night Th

Oscar Wilde 221 E 58th St (at 2nd Ave) **212/486-7309** • 4pm-4am • mostly gay men • professional

Regents 317 E 53rd St (at 2nd Ave) **212/593-3091** • noon-4am • mostly gay men • also restaurant • Italian • plenty veggie • $7-17

The Web 40 E 58th St (at Madison) **212/308-1546** • 4pm-3am • mostly gay men • dancing/DJ • Asian clientele • live shows • theme nights • karaoke Sun

Nightclubs

Clubhouse 215 W 28th St (at 7th Ave) **212/726-8820** • 10pm-4am Wed • lesbians/ gay men • dancing/DJ • mostly African-American

Edelweiss 578 11th Ave (at 43rd St) **212/629-1021** • 8:30pm-4am • gay-friendly • DJ Th-Sat • live shows • fun mix of drag, transgender & everything else • cover charge

Funhouse 251 W 30th St (btwn 7th & 8th, at 'Club Downtime') **212/591-1622** • Fri only

Her/ She Bar 227 W 27th St (btwn 11th & 12th Ave) **212/631-1093** • 10pm-4am Fri • mostly women • dancing/DJ • cover charge

Octagon 555 W 33rd St (at 11th Ave) **212/947-0400** • 10pm Fri only • mostly gay men • dancing/DJ • mostly African-American • cover charge

Twilo 530 W 27th St (at 10th Ave) **212/268-1600** • 11pm Fri-Sat • gay/ straight • more gay Sat at 'Juniorverse' • dancing/DJ • cover charge

Cafes

Cafe Un Deux Trois 123 W 44th St **212/354-4148** • noon-midnight • popular • bistro • $12-24

Restaurants

Bar Nine 807 9th Ave (at W 53rd St) **212/399-9336** • gay boy party Sun eves

Blue Plate Diner 554 11th Ave (at 42nd St) **212/714-0354** • 6am-midnight

Mangia e Bevi 800 9th Ave (at 53rd St) **212/956-3976** • noon-midnight • Italian

Martino's 230 E 58th St (at 2nd Ave) **212/751-0029, 212/753-2357** • dinner, Sun brunch • Italian • popular w/ local lesbians • close to 'Julie's' bar

Revolution 611 9th Ave (at 43rd St) **212/489-8451** • 5pm-midnight • trendy video dining

Rice & Beans 744 9th Ave (at 50th St) **212/265-4444** • 11am-10pm • Latin/ Brazilian • plenty veggie

Townhouse Restaurant 206 E 58th St (at 3rd Ave) **212/826-6241** • lunch & dinner, Sun brunch, open late wknds • lesbians/ gay men • live shows • $10-23

Erotica

Eve's Garden 119 W 57th St #420 **212/757-8651** • noon-7pm, clsd Sun • women's sexuality boutique

NYC—Uptown

Accommodations

333 West 88th Associates 333 West 88th St (at Riverside Dr) **212/724-9818, 800/724-9888** • gay-friendly • apts & B&B rooms • kitchens • fireplaces • gay-owned/ run • $494-1011 weekly

Bars

Brandy's Piano Bar 235 E 84th St (at 2nd Ave) **212/650-1944** • 4pm-4am • mostly gay men • wheelchair access

Bridge Bar 309 E 60th St (at 2nd Ave) **212/223-9104** • 4pm-4am • mostly gay men

Saints 992 Amsterdam (at 109th St) **212/222-2431** • lesbians/ gay men • neighborhood bar

Nightclubs

Columbia University Dance 116th St at Broadway (in Earl Hall) **212/854-1488** • 10pm-2am 1st Fri during school year • lesbians/ gay men • collegiate dance club

Restaurants

Carnegie Delicatessen 854 7th Ave (nr 55th St) **212/757-2245** • 7am-4am • one of NYC's most famous delis

Orinoco 1484 2nd Ave (btwn 77th & 78th Sts) **212/717-2204** • South American • Sun brunch

Republic 2290 Broadway (at 83rd St) **212/579-5959** • eclectic noodle dishes • $3-9

NYC—Brooklyn

Info Lines & Services

Brooklyn Pride 718/670-3337 • host events • also publish newsletter

Bars

Bar 4 444 7th Ave (at 15th St, in Park Slope) **718/832-9800** • noon-4am • lesbians/ gay men • neighborhood bar • DJ Sat • live music & performances

Carry Nation 363 5th Ave (btwn 5th & 6th Sts, in Park Slope) **718/788-0924** • 6pm-3am • lesbians/ gay men • neighborhood bar • DJ Sat

Celebrity's 8705 3rd Ave, Bay Ridge **718/745-9652** • 6pm-4am, from 4pm Sun, clsd Mon • lesbians/ gay men • ladies' night Tue

Rising Cafe 186 5th Ave (at Sackett) **718/789-6340** • 10am-midnight, till 2am wknds • live music • performances & poetry

The Roost 309 7th Ave (at 8th St, in Park Slope) **718/788-9793** • noon-2am • gay-friendly • neighborhood bar

Nightclubs

Spectrum 802 64th St (at 8th Ave) **718/238-8213** • 9pm-4am Wed-Sat • lesbians/ gay men • dancing/DJ • live shows

Restaurants

200 Fifth 200 5th Ave (btwn Union & Sackett) **718/638-0023, 718/638-2925** • 4pm-close • eclectic • full bar • live shows

Aunt Suzie 247 5th Ave (at Garfield Pl) **718/788-2868** • Italian

Healthy Henrietta's on the Slope 787 Union St (btwn 5th & 6th Aves) **718/622-2924** • cheap veggie & macrobiotic fare

Johnny Mack's 1114 8th Ave (btwn 11th & 12th) **718/832-7961** • 4pm-11pm, till 1am Fri-Sat, wknd brunch noon-3:30pm

Max & Moritz 426-A 7th Ave (btwn 14th & 15th) **718/499-5557** • 5:30pm-close • French/ American

Santa Fe Grill 62 7th Ave (at Lincoln) **718/636-0279** • 5:30pm-close

Entertainment & Recreation

Sing Out! Brooklyn 718/769-1421 • concerts & special events

Spiritual Groups

Brooklyn Heights Synagogue 131 Remsen St (btwn Henry & Clinton) **718/522-2070** • 6:30pm Fri

First Unitarian Church of Brooklyn 48 Monroe Pl (btwn Pierpont & Clark) **718/624-5466** • 11am Sun

NYC—Queens

Info Lines & Services

Q-GLU (Queens Gay/ Lesbians United) 718/205-6605 • 1st Tue

Bars

Amnesia 32-03 Broadway (at 32nd St), Astoria **718/204-7010** • noon-4am • popular • gay-friendly • dancing/DJ • more gay Tue at 'Insomnia'

Nightclubs

Atlantis 2010 76-19 Roosevelt Ave (at 77th St), Jackson Hts **718/457-3939** • 9pm-4am, clsd Mon-Tue • lesbians/ gay men • dancing/DJ • Latina/o clientele • live shows • more women at 'Her/ She Bar 2000' Th

Krash 34-48 Steinway St, Astoria **718/937-2400** • open Mon & Th-Sat • lesbians/ gay men • more women Sat • dancing/DJ Fri-Sat • multi-racial clientele

NYC—Bronx

Nightclubs

Up & Down Bar 1306 Union Port Rd (at Westchester Ave) **718/822-9585** • 9pm-4am Tue only

The Warehouse 141 E 140th St (btwn Grand Concourse & Walton) **718/992-5974** • 11pm Sat • mostly gay men • dancing/DJ • cover charge

NYC—Staten Island

Info Lines & Services

Lambda Associates of Staten Island 718/876-8786

Nightclubs

Visionz 492 Bay St **718/273-7354** • 9pm-4am Wed-Sat • lesbians/ gay men • women's night Wed • dancing/DJ • also outdoor cafe & jacuzzi

Niagara Falls

see also Buffalo, New York & Niagara Falls, Ontario, Canada

Accommodations

Danner House B&B 12549 Niagara River Pkwy, ON **905/295-5166** • lesbians/ gay men • full brkfst • jacuzzi • smokefree • 10 minutes from Buffalo • Can$95

Nyack

Bars

Coven Cafe 162 Main St **914/358-9829** • noon-midnight, till 3am Fri-Sat, clsd Mon • gay-friendly • women's night Tue • T-dance 4pm Sun in summer • also restaurant • cont'l w/ Southern accent • wheelchair access • $8-20

Nightclubs

Barz 327 Rte 9 W **914/353-4444** • 7pm-4am, from 8pm Sat, from 1pm Sun, clsd Mon • lesbians/ gay men • dancing/DJ • wheelchair access

Orange County

Info Lines & Services

Liaisons of Orange County 914/343-5721 • social & outdoor group for lesbians 30+

Orange County Gay/ Lesbian Alliance 914/782-1525 • 7:30pm Tue

Restaurants

Folderol II 795 Rte 284, Westtown **914/726-3822** • 5pm-close, clsd Mon-Tue • French/farmhouse • some veggie • piano Sat • wheelchair access • gay-owned/ run • $13-23

Ossining

Spiritual Groups

Trinity Episcopal Church 7 S Highland/ Rte 9 **914/941-0806** • 7:30am & 10am Sun

Oswego

Info Lines & Services

SUNY Oswego Women's Center 243 Hewitt Union, 2nd flr **315/341-2967**

Plattsburgh

Bars

Blair's Tavern 30 Marion St (btwn Clinton & Court) **518/561-9071** • 6pm-2am • lesbians/ gay men • dancing/DJ Fri-Sat

Port Chester

see also Greenwich & Stamford, Connecticut

Bars

Sandy's Old Homestead 325 N Main St (at Wilkins) **914/939-0758** • 8am-4am • gay-friendly • food served • wheelchair access

Poughkeepsie

Info Lines & Services

Poughkeepsie GALA (Gay/ Lesbian Association) 20 Carrol St (at Christ Episcopal Church) **914/431-6756** • 7:30pm Tue • call for events

Bars

Congress 411 Main St (off Academy) **914/486-9068** • 3pm-4am, from 8pm Sun • lesbians/ gay men • neighborhood bar • wheelchair access

Rochester

Info Lines & Services

AA Gay/ Lesbian 716/232-6720 (AA#) • call for mtg schedule

Coalition for Lesbian Visibility 315/539-6271 • 2nd Sat socials • call for details

Gay Alliance of the Genesee Valley (GAGV) 179 Atlantic Ave (at Elton) **716/244-8640** • community center hosting various groups • call for mtg times

Latino Mission 1350 University Ave (btwn Culver & Winton, at AIDS Rochester) • 7pm 2nd & 4th Th

Transgender Organization at GAGV Ctr **716/442-2425** • 2pm 2nd & 4th Sat

Bars

Anthony's 522 522 E Main St (at Scio) **716/325-2060** • noon-2am • lesbians/ gay men • neighborhood bar • karaoke Wed & Sat

Avenue Pub 522 Monroe Ave (at Goodman) **716/244-4960** • 4pm-2am • popular • mostly gay men • neighborhood bar • dancing/DJ Th

Enigma 113 State St (at Andrews) **716/262-2650** • 11am-2am • lesbians/ gay men • neighborhood bar

Muther's 40 S Union St **716/325-6216** • noon-2am, till 3am Fri-Sat • popular • lesbians/ gay men • women's night last Th • live shows Sun

Tara Lounge 153 Liberty Pole Wy (at Andrews) **716/232-4719** • noon-2am • popular • lesbians/ gay men • neighborhood bar • piano bar Fri-Sat

Nightclubs

Club Marcella 123 Liberty Pole Wy (off Franklin) **716/454-5963** • clsd Mon-Tue • lesbians/ gay men • dancing/DJ • live shows • 18+ • ladies' night Th

Freakazoid 169 N Chestnut St (off Main) **716/429-7777** • 9pm-3am Fri-Sat • gay-friendly • dancing/DJ • alternative • acoustic music Th • call for other events

Cafes

Little Theatre Cafe 240 East Ave **716/258-0412** • 5:30pm-10pm, from noon wknds, till midnight Fri-Sat • popular • beer/ wine • soups • salads • live jazz Fri-Sat • wheelchair access • $5-10

Restaurants

Slice of Life Cafe 742 South Ave (at Caroline) **716/271-8010** • 11:30am-8pm, 10am-2pm Sun, clsd Mon-Tue • vegetarian

Triphammer Grill 60 Browns Race (btwn Platt & Commercial) **716/262-2700** • lunch Mon-Fri, dinner nightly, clsd Sun • patio • full bar • $10-22

Bookstores

The Pride Connection 728 South Ave (1 blk from Gregory) **716/242-7840** • 10am-9pm, noon-6pm Sun • lesbigay

Silkwood Books 633 Monroe Ave (btwn Goodman & 490) **716/473-8110** • 11am-6pm, till 7pm Th-Fri, noon-5pm Sun, clsd Mon • women's/ new age • wheelchair access

Publications

Empty Closet **716/244-9030** • lesbigay newspaper • resource listings

Spiritual Groups

Calvary St Andrew's Parish (Presbyterian) 68 Ashland St (at Averill Ave) **716/325-4950** • 10am Sun & noon Tue • 'More Light' congregation

Dignity/ Integrity 17 S Fitzhugh St (at Broad, in Church of St Luke & St Simon Cyrene...look for the pink steeple) **716/262-2170** • 5pm Sun

Open Arms MCC 175 Norris Dr (off Culver Rd, nr Cobbs Hill Park) **716/271-8478** • 10:30am & 6:30pm Sun • wheelchair access

Saratoga Springs

Bookstores

Nahani 482 Broadway **518/587-4322** • 10am-6pm, noon-5pm Sun • wheelchair access

Schenectady

Bars

Blythewood 50 N Jay St (off Union) **518/382-9755** • 9pm-4am • mostly gay men • neighborhood bar • wheelchair access

Seneca Falls

Accommodations

Guion House 32 Cayuga St **315/568-8129, 800/631-8919** • gay-friendly • full brkfst • smokefree • $69-85

Sharon Springs

Accommodations

Brimstonia Cottage 149 Main St (on Rte 10) **518/284-2839** • gay friendly • suites w/ kitchens

Edgefield Washington St, PO Box 152 **518/284-3339** • gay/ straight • full brkfst • smokefree • well-appointed English Country house in quaint & quirky village • gay-owned/ run • $95-150

New Yorker Guest House Center St **518/284-2093** • gay-friendly • rms & suites • seasonal • $65-135

The Turnλround Spa 201 Washington St **518/284-2271** • lesbians/ gay men • small hotel & health spa • hot tub • smokefree • kids ok • clsd Nov-May • gay-owned/ run • $45-65

Restaurants

Rockville Cafe & Bakery 123 Main St (at Rtes 10 & 20) **518/284-2968** • 8am-3pm, clsd Mon

Retail Shops

Baby Jane's 123 Main St (btwn I-10 & I-20) **518/284-2070** • 10am-4pm, clsd Mon

The Finishing Touch 123 Main St (Rte 10) **518/284-2857** • 9am-4pm, clsd Mon • gallery & gift shop

Syracuse

Info Lines & Services

AA Gay/ Lesbian 315/463-5011 (AA#) • call for mtg schedule

Pride Community Center 745 N Salina St **315/426-1650** • 6pm-9pm Tue-Fri, noon-6pm Sat

SAGE Upstate 1st Presbyterian Church **315/478-1923** • mtg & potluck 4:30pm 2nd Sun for lgbt folks 40+ & friends

Women's Information Center 601 Allen St **315/478-4636** • 10am-4pm, clsd wknds • also Lesbian Social Group & Lesbian Discussion Group • wheelchair access

Accommodations

John Milton Inn 6578 Thompson Rd, Carrier Circle, Exit 35 **315/463-8555, 800/352-1061** • gay-friendly • wheelchair access • $35-70

Bars

The Armory Pub 400 S Clinton St **315/471-9059** • 8am-2am • mostly gay men • dancing/DJ Sun • wheelchair access

My Bar 205 N West St (at W Genessee) **315/471-9279** • 10am-2am, till 4am Fri-Sat • lesbians/ gay men • food served

Nightclubs

Sisters 1203 Milton Ave (at Erie Blvd) **315/468-9830** • 5pm-2am, 8pm-close Sat, clsd Sun-Tue • mostly women • dancing/DJ • food served • live shows

Trexx 319 N Clinton St (exit 18 off Rte 81) **315/474-6408** • 8pm-2am, till 4am Fri-Sat, T-dance from 4pm Sun, clsd Mon-Tue • mostly gay men • dancing/DJ • live shows • wheelchair access

Cafes

Happy Endings 317 S Clinton St (at W Fayette) **315/475-1853** • 10am-11pm, till 2am Fri-Sat, from 1pm wknds • lunch & coffee • live shows • wheelchair access

Restaurants

Tu Tu Venue 731 James St (enter on Willow St) **315/475-8888** • 4pm-1am, clsd Sun • popular • full bar • women-owned/ run • $12-15

Bookstores

My Sisters' Words 304 N McBride St (at James) **315/428-0227** • 10am-6pm, till 8pm Fri, call for Sun hours • women's • community bulletin board

Spiritual Groups

Ray of Hope Church 745 N Salina St (at Pride Comm Ctr) **315/471-6618** • 6pm Sun

Tivoli

Restaurants

Cafe Pongo 69 Broadway **914/757-4403** • 9am-3pm Fri-Sun & dinner from 5:30pm Tue-Sun • 'everything made from scratch' • full bar • live shows • call for details

Utica

Nightclubs

That Place 216 Bleecker St (at Genessee) **315/724-1446** • 8pm-2am, from 4pm Fri • popular • mostly gay men • dancing/DJ • leather • wheelchair access

White Plains

Info Lines & Services

Lesbian Line 914/949-3203 • 6pm-10pm

The Loft 180 E Post Rd (lower level) **914/948-4922** • lesbigay community center • annual local gay cruise • also newsletter • 914/948-2932

Nightclubs

Club 202 202 Westchester Ave (at S Lexington) **914/761-3100** • 5pm-4am, from 9pm wknds, clsd Mon • popular • mostly gay men • dancing/DJ Wed-Sun

Woodstock

see Catskill Mtns

NORTH CAROLINA

Statewide

PUBLICATIONS

Carolina Lesbian News PO Box 11776, Charlotte, 28220 **704/559-5991**

▲ **The Front Page 919/829-0181** • lesbigay newspaper for the Carolinas

Asheville

INFO LINES & SERVICES

CLOSER (Community Liaison for Support, Education & Reform) 828/277-7815 • also 'OutFit' youth group Sat

Lambda AA All Souls Church, Biltmore Village **828/254-8539 (AA#)** • 8pm Fri

ACCOMMODATIONS

27 Blake Street 27 Blake St **828/252-7390** • women only • romantic Victorian home • smokefree • $68

Acorn Cottage B&B 25 St Dunstans Cir **828/253-0609, 800/699-0609** • gay-friendly • full brkfst • smokefree • $75-100

The Bird's Nest B&B 41 Oak Park Rd **828/252-2381** • lesbians/ gay men • comfortable, secluded & quiet B&B • located on the 2nd flr of a turn-of-the-century home • lesbian-owned/ run • $85

▲ **Camp Pleiades 828/688-9201 (SUMMER) OR 904/241-3050 (WINTER), 888/324-3110** • open Memorial Day thru mid-October • mtn retreat • cabins, camping • all meals included • some shared baths • lesbian-owned/ run • $45-175

Cottage at Woodhaven 828/299-8757 • lesbians/ gay men • cottage rental • deck • fireplace • $85

Emy's Nook 828/281-4122 • women only • lesbian-owned/ run • $55-60

The Hawk & Ivy B&B 133 N Fork Rd, Barnardsville **828/626-3486, 888/395-7254** • gay/ straight • full brkfst • smokefree • kids ok • $70-115

The Inn on Montford 296 Montford Ave **828/254-9569, 800/254-9569** • gay-friendly • popular • English cottage • full brkfst • $145-195

Kindred Spirits B&B 395 Lakey Gap Acres, Black Mountain **828/669-3889** • lesbians/ gay men • experience free queer space in 'the stretch mark of the Bible Belt' • full brkfst • $60-75

Asheville

Magical. This word tends to appear in any discussion of Asheville. Maybe it's the ancient blue mountains on every horizon, or the alchemy of mixing artists, new agers, and an amazing lesbian population with mountain folk and Bible Belters, in one small Southern city. Whatever the reason, Asheville lives up to her magical reputation.

Downtown you will find a lively, walkable city center brimming with galleries, eclectic shops, and coffee houses. **Malaprop's Bookstore & Cafe** is a hub of womyn's community. Of particular note is 'Cafe of our Own,' a women's poetry reading held every third Saturday at Malaprop's and hosted by an inspiring lesbian poet. Malaprop's' bulletin boards and free alternative newspapers are invaluable in finding things to see and do. **Community Connections,** the LGBT monthly, contains a community calendar.

While you're downtown, catch a film at the 'Fine Arts Theater,' stop by **Rainbow's End** books & gifts for rainbow stickers and videos, and wander the galleries. At night, sample cool jazz at **Tressa's.** Weekends, dance late-nite at **Scandals.** You'll see us everywhere—after all, Asheville is rumored to have one of the largest per capita populations of lesbians in the country.

Downtown is just a part of what this area has to offer. Check out 'New Morning Gallery' and 'Blue' goldsmiths, both in Biltmore Village. Hop on the Blue Ridge Parkway and you'll find mountains, overlooks, and waterfalls, with great hiking and whitewater to tantalize outdoor types. Explore it all!

—Ottersen@yahoo.com

Mountain Laurel B&B 139 Lee Dotson Rd, Fairview **828/628-9903** • lesbians/ gay men • 25 miles from Asheville • full brkfst • lesbian-owned/ run • $80-100

Owl's Nest at Engadine 2630 Smokey Park Hwy (off I-40 at exit 37), Candler **828/665-8325, 800/665-8868** • gay/ straight • full brkfst • fireplace • women-owned/ run • $105-165

WhiteGate Inn & Cottage 173 E Chestnut St **828/253-2553, 800/485-3045** • gay/ straight • full-service B&B • 3-course brkfst • gay-owned/ run • $145-185

Bars

O'Henry's 59 Haywood St (nr Civic Center) **828/254-1891** • 1pm-2am, from noon wknds • lesbians/ gay men • neighborhood bar • dancing/DJ • private club

Nightclubs

The Metro/ Hairspray Cafe 38 N French Broad Ave (at Patton Ave) **828/258-2027** • 7pm-2am • lesbians/ gay men • dancing/DJ • live shows • private club

Scandals 11 Grove St (at Patton) **828/252-2838** • 10pm-3am Fri-Sat only • lesbians/ gay men • dancing/DJ • live shows • 18+ • wheelchair access • also 'Getaways' lounge • videos

Cafes

Laurey's 67 Biltmore Ave **828/252-1500** • 10am-6pm, till 4pm Sat, clsd Sun • popular • bright cafe w/ delicious salads & cookies • also dinners to-go • women-owned/ run • wheelchair access

Restaurants

Grove Street Cafe 11 Grove St **828/255-0010** • 6pm-1am Wed-Sat (T-dance & BBQ 2pm-8pm Sun in summer) • steaks/ seafood • some veggie • full bar • patio • $10-15

Laughing Seed Cafe 40 Wall St (at Haywood) **828/252-3445** • 11:30am-9pm, till 10pm Th-Sat, clsd Sun • vegetarian/ vegan • beer/ wine • patio • wheelchair access • $4-9

Entertainment & Recreation

Women Outdoors 828/254-7947 (Lee)

Bookstores

Downtown Books & News 67 N Lexington Ave (btwn Walnut & Hiawassee) **828/253-8654** • 8am-6pm • used books & new magazines

Malaprop's Bookstore & Cafe 55 Haywood St (at Walnut) **828/254-6734, 800/441-9829** • 9am-9pm, till 11pm Fri-Sat, till 6pm Sun • readings • performances • women's reading 8pm 3rd Sat

Rainbow's End 10 N Spruce St **828/285-0005** • 10am-6pm, till 7pm Fri-Sat, 1pm-5pm Sun • lesbigay • also gifts & video rentals

Retail Shops

The Goddess Store 382 Montford Ave **828/258-3102** • noon-6pm, clsd Sun-Mon • lesbian/ feminist gifts • divination tools • Wiccan items • call for class schedules • wheelchair access

Asheville

Annual Events: July - NC International Folk Festival (world cultural heritage celebration) 828/452-2997 or 877/365-5872, web: www.folkmoot.com.

City Info: 828/258-6100, web: www.ashevillechamber.org.

Attractions: Biltmore Estate 800/543-2961.
Blue Ridge Parkway.
North Carolina Arboretum 828/665-2492.

Weather: Gorgeous: temperate summers and mild winters, with a beautiful spring and fall.

Transit: Bluebird Taxi 828/258-8331.
Sky Shuttle 828/253-0006.
Asheville Transit Authority 828/253-5691.

Jewels That Dance: Jewelry Design 63 Haywood St **828/254-5088** • 10am-6pm, clsd Sun • gay-owned/ run

Spiritual Groups

The Cathedral of All Souls Biltmore Village **828/274-2681** • 8am, 9am & 11:15am Sun, noon & 5:45pm Wed • wheelchair access

MCC of Asheville 130 Shelburne Rd **828/232-0062** • 6:20pm Sun & 6:30pm Wed • wheelchair access

St Joan of Arc Catholic Church 919 Haywood Rd (at Mitchell Ave) **828/252-3151** • 5pm Sat, 8:30am & 11:30am Sun

Unitarian Universalist Church of Asheville 1 Edwin Pl (at Charlotte) **828/254-6001** • 9:30am & 11:30am Sun (10am Sun summers) • wheelchair access

Erotica

Bedtime Stories 2334 Hendersonville Rd, Arden **828/684-8250**

Blowing Rock

Accommodations

Stone Pillar B&B 144 Pine St **828/295-4141, 800/962-9955** • gay/ straight • historic 1920s house • full brkfst • wheelchair access • gay-owned/ run • $65-110

Boone

Accommodations

Grandma Jean's B&B 254 Meadowview Dr **704/262-3670** • Grandma Jean prides herself on her Southern hospitality • $65

Burnsville

Accommodations

Merry Macha 2650 Rock Creek Rd **828/675-9530** • women only • guesthouses • retreats • smokefree • lesbian-owned/ run • $55/night ($300/wk)

Cashiers

Accommodations

Jane's Aerie Cottage **828/743-9002** • mostly women • cottage in great mtn location • $95/ night ($450/ week)

Chapel Hill

see Raleigh/ Durham/ Chapel Hill

Charlotte

Info Lines & Services

AA Gay/ Lesbian 3200 Park Rd (at St Luke's Lutheran Church) **704/332-4387 (AA#)** • 8pm Fri

Gay/ Lesbian Switchboard **704/535-6277** • 6:30pm-10:30pm

Bars

Brass Rail 3707 Wilkinson Blvd (at Morehead) **704/399-8413** • 5pm-2am, from 3pm Sun • popular • mostly gay men • neighborhood bar • leather • private club • wheelchair access

Central Station 2131 Central Ave (at The Plaza) **704/377-0906** • 5pm-2am • lesbians/ gay men • neighborhood bar • multi-racial clientele

Charlotte

City Info: Convention & Visitors Bureau 704/334-2282 or 800/231-4636, web: charlottecvb.org.

Attractions: Discovery Place 704/372-0471 (for tickets). Mint Museum of Art 704/337-2000.

Transit: Yellow Cab 704/332-6161. K&K Airport Shuttle 704/394-6919. Charlotte Transit 704/336-7433.

Have a Nice Day Cafe 314 N College St (btwn 6th & 7th) **704/373-2233** • gay-friendly • dancing/DJ • women's night Th

Liaisons 316 Rensselaer Ave (at South Blvd) **704/376-1617** • 5pm-1am • popular • lesbians/ gay men • neighborhood bar • food served Wed-Sun • private club • women-owned/ run

Nightclubs

Chaser's 3217 The Plaza (at 36th) **704/339-0500** • 5pm-2am, till 10pm Sun • lesbians/ gay men • dancing/DJ • live shows • videos • private club • wheelchair access

Club Myxx 3110 S Tryon St **704/525-5001** • 11pm-4am Fri-Sat only • lesbians/ gay men • dancing/DJ • mostly African-American • call for events

The Crystal Room 431 E Trade St (at Caldwell) **704/334-3762** • 8:30pm-2am Fri-Sat only • mostly women • dancing/DJ

Mythos 300 N College St (at 6th) **704/375-8765, 704/559-5959 (INFO LINE)** • 10pm-3am, till 4am wknds, 11pm-4am Sun, clsd Mon • gay-friendly • more gay Wed-Th • dancing/DJ • alternative • live shows • private club • wheelchair access

Oleen's Lounge 1831 South Blvd (at East) **704/344-8382** • 8pm-2am, from 5pm Sun • popular • lesbians/ gay men • dancing/DJ • live shows • wheelchair access

Scorpio's Lounge 2301 Freedom Dr **704/373-9124** • 9pm-3:30am, clsd Mon & Th • lesbians/ gay men • dancing/DJ • country/ western Tue • live shows • karaoke • videos • private club • wheelchair access

Cafes

Cafe Dada 1220 Thomas St (Pecan) **704/373-0023** • 11am-midnight, till 2am Fri-Sat • Southwestern wraps • full bar • plenty veggie

Restaurants

300 East 300 East Blvd (at Cleveland) **704/332-6507** • 11:30am-10pm, till 11pm Tue-Th, till midnight Fri-Sat • New American • some veggie • full bar

Cosmos Cafe corner of 6th & College **704/372-3553** • 11am-2am • gay-friendly • new world cuisine • tapas • jazz brunch Sun 11am-3pm • $4-20 • also 'Thirsty Camel' cigar/ martini lounge • also 'Microcosm' art gallery

Fat City 3127 N Davidson St (at 35th) **704/343-0240** • noon-2am, from 2pm Sun

Hartigan's Pub 601 S Cedar St (at Moorehead) **704/347-1841** • 11am-10pm • Irish pub

Lupie's Cafe 2718 Monroe Rd (nr 5th St) **704/374-1232** • 11am-11pm, from noon Sat, clsd Sun • homestyle • some veggie • $5-10

Bookstores

Paper Skyscraper 330 East Blvd (at Euclid Ave) **704/333-7130** • 10am-7pm, till 6pm Sat, noon-5pm Sun • books • gifts • wheelchair access

White Rabbit Books 834 Central Ave (at 7th) **704/377-4067** • 10am-9pm, till 10pm Fri, noon-8pm Sun • lesbigay • also magazines, T-shirts & gifts

Retail Shops

Urban Evolution 1329 East Blvd (at Scott) **704/332-8644** • 10am-9pm, 1pm-6pm Sun • clothing & more

Publications

Carolina Lesbian News PO Box 11776, 28220 **704/559-5991**

The Front Page 919/829-0181 • lesbigay newspaper for the Carolinas

Q Notes 704/531-9988 • lesbigay newspaper

Spiritual Groups

Lutherans Concerned 1900 The Plaza (at Holy Trinity Church) **704/651-4328** • 5pm 1st Sun • dinner & program

MCC Charlotte 1825 Eastway Dr **704/563-5810** • 10:45am & 6:30pm Sun

Gyms & Health Clubs

Charlotte 24-Hour Fitness Center 3900 E Independence Blvd **704/537-9060**

Erotica

Carolina Video Source 8829 E Harris Blvd **704/566-9993**

Duck

Accommodations

Advice 5¢, a B&B 111 Scarborough Lane **919/255-1050, 800/238-4235** • gay-friendly • welcoming seaside cottage in village of Duck on North Carolina's outer banks • women-owned/ run • $95-175

Durham

see Raleigh/ Durham/ Chapel Hill

Fayetteville

Info Lines & Services

Lambda Association of Fayetteville PO Box 53281, 28305 **910/822-4802**

Nightclubs

Club Spektrum 107 Swain St (at Bragg Blvd) **910/868-4279** • 5pm-3am • lesbians/ gay men • dancing/DJ • live shows • multi-racial clientele • patio

Spiritual Groups

Emmaus MCC 1705 St Augustine Ave **910/678-8813** • 7pm Sun

Erotica

Fort Video & News 4431 Bragg Blvd (nr 401 overpass) **910/868-9905** • 24hrs

Priscilla's 3800 Sycamore Dairy Rd (at Bragg Blvd) **910/860-1776**

Franklin

Accommodations

Phoenix Nest 1905 Ambush Rd, Tallahassee, FL, 32311 **850/421-1984** • gay-friendly • mtn cabin • sleeps 4 • seasonal • smokefree • lesbian-owned • $350

Rainbow Acres 828/349-4663, 800/442-6400 (ask for Caren) • women only • rental home • smokefree • fireplace • great views • $575-675/week

Greensboro

Info Lines & Services

Gay/ Lesbian Hotline 336/855-8558 • 7pm-10pm

Live & Let Live AA 415 N Edgeworth **336/854-4278** • 8pm Tue

Nightclubs

Babylon 221 S Elm St **336/275-1006** • 8pm-close Wed, clsd Th, from 11pm Fri-Sat, from 10pm Sun, clsd Mon-Tue • popular • lesbians/ gay men • dancing/DJ • alternative • private club • call for events

The Palms 413 N Eugene St (at Smith) **336/272-6307** • 9pm-2:30am • mostly gay men • dancing/DJ • live shows • private club

Warehouse 29 1011 Arnold St **336/333-9333** • 9pm-3am, clsd Mon-Tue • mostly gay men • dancing/DJ • live shows • private club • patio

Bookstores

White Rabbit Books & Things 1833 Spring Garden St (at Chapman) **336/272-7604** • 10am-9pm, noon-8pm Sun • lesbigay

Publications

Shout! PO Box 21201, Roanoke, VA, 24018 **540/989-1579** • entertainment • personals

Spiritual Groups

St Mary's MCC 6720 W Friendly Ave **336/297-4054** • 10:30am & 7pm Sun

Erotica

Treasure Box Video & News 1203 E Bessemer **336/373-9849** • 24hrs

Greenville

Info Lines & Services

Down East GLBT Info Line 252/551-0316

Nightclubs

Paddock Club 1008-B Dickinson **252/758-0990** • 9pm-2:30am, clsd Mon-Tue • lesbians/ gay men • dancing/DJ • alternative • live shows • private club • wheelchair access

Spiritual Groups

Unitarian Universalist Congregation 131 Oakmont Dr **252/355-6658** • 10:30am Sun

Hickory

Nightclubs

Club Cabaret 101 N Center St (at 1st Ave) **828/322-8103** • 9pm-2am, clsd Sun • lesbians/ gay men • dancing/DJ • live shows • private club • wheelchair access

Spiritual Groups

MCC Hickory 109 11th Ave NW (at Unitarian Church) **828/324-1960** • 7pm Sun

Hot Springs

Accommodations

The Duckett House Inn 828/622-7621 • gay/ straight • Victorian farmhouse • full brkfst • shared baths • smokefree • creek swimming • also vegetarian restaurant (reservations required) • gay-owned/ run • $75-95

Jacksonville

Nightclubs

Asylum Hwy 258 • inquire locally

Erotica

Priscilla's 113-A Western Blvd **910/355-0765**

New Bern

Accommodations

Harmony House Inn 215 Pollock St **252/636-3810, 800/636-3113** • gay-friendly • full brkfst • kids ok • $89-140

Raleigh/Durham/Chapel Hill

Info Lines & Services

AA Gay/ Lesbian (Live & Let Live) 919/783-6144 • call for info

Duke Center for LGBT Life 919/684-6607 • 9am-5pm Mon-Fri

Gay/ Lesbian Helpline of Wake County 919/821-0055 • 7pm-10pm

Orange County Women's Center 210 Henderson, Chapel Hill **919/968-4610** • 9am-7:30pm, till 5pm Fri, clsd wknds • wheelchair access

Steps, Traditions & Promises AA 4907 Garrett Rd (at Christ Lutheran), Durham **919/286-9499 (AA#)** • 8pm Fri

Accommodations

Joan's Place 919/942-5621 • women only • shared baths • lesbian-owned/ run • $55-60

Mineral Springs Inn 718 S Mineral Springs Rd (nr Hwy 70), Durham **919/596-2162** • mostly gay men • full brkfst • jacuzzi • swimming • nudity • smokefree • $89-99

Morehead Manor B&B 914 Vickers Ave (at Morehead), Durham **919/687-4366, 888/437-6333** • gay/ straight • splendidly decorated colonial home • full brkfst • $100-450

The Oakwood Inn B&B 411 N Bloodworth St (at Oakwood), Raleigh **919/832-9712, 800/267-9712** • gay-friendly • Victorian in the heart of Raleigh • full brkfst • $85-140

Bars

Boxers 5504 Chapel Hill Blvd, Durham **919/489-7678** • 3:30pm-2am, from 5pm Sun, clsd Mon • mostly gay men • alternative • professional • videos

Nightclubs

All About Eve 711 Rigsbee Ave, Durham **919/688-3002** • 9pm-3am Fri-Sat, 6pm-10pm Sun • mostly women • dancing/DJ • live shows • deck • volleyball court • private club • wheelchair access

Raleigh/Durham/ Chapel Hill

City Info: 919/834-5900 or 800/849-8499, web: www.raleighcvb.org.

Attractions: Duke University, Durham.
Exploris (interactive global learning center), Raleigh 919/834-4040.
NC Museum of Art, Raleigh 919/839-6262.
NC Museum of Life & Science, Durham 919/220-5429.
Oakwood Historic District, Raleigh.
University of North Carolina, Chapel Hill.

Transit: Bus (Capital Area Transit) 919/828-7228.
Triangle Transit Authority 919/549-9999.

CC 313 W Hargett St (at Harrington), Raleigh **919/755-9599** • 8pm-close, from 4pm Sun • mostly gay men • dancing/DJ • live shows • piano bar • 18+ • private club • wheelchair access

Legends 330 W Hargett St (at Harrington), Raleigh **919/831-8888** • 9pm-close • mostly gay men • more women Th • mixed crowd wknds • dancing/DJ • private club • patio • wheelchair access

Restaurants

Crooks Corner 610 Franklin St (at Merritt Mill Rd), Chapel Hill **919/929-7643** • 6pm-10:30pm Mon-Sat, Sun brunch 10:30am-2pm • Southern • some veggie • full bar • wheelchair access • $6-17

Irregardless Cafe 901 W Morgan St (at Hillsborough), Raleigh **919/833-8898** • lunch Mon-Fri, dinner Mon-Sat, Sun brunch • plenty veggie • $9-15

Magnolia Grill 1002 9th St (at Knox), Durham **919/286-3609** • 6pm-9:30pm, clsd Sun • contemporary Southern • full bar • wheelchair access • $14-21

Rathskeller 2412 Hillsborough St (at Chamberlain), Raleigh **919/821-5342** • 11:30am-10pm, till 11pm Wed-Sat, from noon Sun • some veggie • also bar • wheelchair access • $4-16

Vertigo Diner 426 S McDowell St (at Cabarrus), Raleigh **919/832-4477** • lunch Mon-Fri, dinner Wed-Sat, Sun brunch • full bar

Weathervane Cafe Eastgate Shopping Ctr, Chapel Hill **919/929-9466** • lunch & dinner Mon-Sat, noon-6pm Sun • some veggie • full bar • patio • wheelchair access • $8-15

Bookstores

Internationalist Books 405 W Franklin St (at Columbia), Chapel Hill **919/942-1740** • 11am-8pm, noon-6pm Sun • progressive/ alternative • readings

Reader's Corner 3201 Hillsborough St (at Rosemary), Raleigh **919/828-7024** • 10am-8pm, till 6pm wknds, from noon Sun • used books

Regulator Bookshop 720 9th St (btwn Hillsborough & Perry), Durham **919/286-2700** • 9am-9pm, till 6pm Sun

White Rabbit Books 309 W Martin St (btwn Dawson & Harrington), Raleigh **919/856-1429** • 10am-9pm, noon-8pm Sun • lesbigay • gifts

Retail Shops

One-Hour Sin Shop/ Innovations 517 Hillsborough St (at Glenwood), Raleigh **919/833-4833** • 11am-7pm, from 1pm Sun, clsd Mon • leather • fetishwear • piercings

Publications

▲ **The Front Page** **919/829-0181** • lesbigay newspaper for the Carolinas

Spiritual Groups

Community Church (Unitarian Universalist) 106 Purefoy Rd (at Mason Farm Rd), Chapel Hill **919/942-2050** • 11am Sun

St John's MCC 805 Glenwood Ave, Raleigh **919/834-2611** • 11am & 7:15pm Sun

Unitarian Universalist Fellowship 3313 Wade Ave (at Dixie Tr), Raleigh **919/781-7635** • 9:30am & 11:15am Sun

Erotica

Castle Video & News 1210 Capitol Blvd, Raleigh **919/836-9189** • 24hrs

Salisbury

Accommodations

Renaissance Lodge **704/647-0919** • women only • outdoor recreation • kids ok • $170-600/week

Spruce Pine

Accommodations

The Lemon Tree Inn 912 Greenwood Rd **828/765-6161** • gay/ straight • also restaurant • gay-owned/ run

Spruce Ridge

Accommodations

Shepherd's Ridge **828/765-7809** • open March-Nov • mostly women • cottage in the woods • sleeps 2-4 • smokefree • $60 ($300/wk)

Wilmington

Info Lines & Services

GROW Switchboard 341-11 S College Rd #182 **910/762-0301** • info • counseling • AIDS resource

Accommodations

Blue Heaven B&B 517 Orange St **910/772-9929, 800/338-1748** • gay-friendly • smokefree • $60-125

Ocean Princess Inn 824 Ft Fischer Blvd S, South Kure Beach **910/458-6712, 800/762-4863** • gay/ straight • swimming • smokefree • wheelchair access • gay-owned/ run • $99-159

The Taylor House Inn 14 N 7th St **910/763-7581, 800/382-9982** • gay/ straight • romantic 1905 house • full brkfst • smokefree • $85-180

Bars

Mickey Ratz 115-117 S Front St (at Church Alley) **910/251-1289** • 5pm-2:30am, clsd Mon • lesbians/ gay men • dancing/DJ • live shows • private club

Nightclubs

Club Bizarre 121 Grace St **910/763-4900** • 9pm-2:30am, till 4am Fri-Sat, clsd Sun-Tue • gay/ straight • dancing/DJ

Spiritual Groups

St Jude's MCC 507 Castle St (at 5th) **910/762-5833, 252/939-1952** • 9am, 11am & 7pm Sun

Wilson

Spiritual Groups

GLAD (Gay & Lesbian Affirming Disciples) Alliance 252/291-7370

Winston-Salem

Info Lines & Services

Gay/ Lesbian Hotline 336/855-8558 • 7pm-10pm

Bars

Satellite 701 N Trade St (at 7th) **336/722-8877** • 5pm-close • lesbians/ gay men • more women Tue • dancing/DJ • live shows

Nightclubs

Club Odyssey/ Retro Bar 4019 Country Club Rd **336/774-7071** • 9pm-3am, clsd Mon • popular • lesbians/ gay men • dancing/DJ • live shows • 18+

Spiritual Groups

Holy Trinity Church 2873 Robinhood Rd **336/725-5355** • 10:30am & 6:30pm Sun, 7pm Wed

MCC of Winston-Salem 336/784-8009 • 6pm Sun • call for directions

North Dakota

Fargo

Info Lines & Services

Hotline 701/235-7335 • 24hrs • general info hotline • some lesbigay resources

Nightclubs

I-Beam 1021 Center Ave (at 11th), Moorhead, MN **218/233-7700** • 5pm-1am, clsd Sun • lesbians/ gay men • dancing/DJ

Restaurants

Fargo's Fryn Pan 302 Main St (at 4th) **701/293-9952** • 24hrs • popular • wheelchair access

Erotica

Adult Books & Cinema X 417 N Pacific Ave **701/232-9768** • 24hrs

Grand Forks

Info Lines & Services

The UGLC (University Gay/ Lesbian Community) 701/777-4321 • educational & social group

Erotica

Plain Brown Wrapper 102 S 3rd St (at Kittson) **701/772-9021** • 24hrs

Minot

Erotica

Risque's 1514 S Broadway **701/838-2837**

Ohio

Statewide

Info Lines & Services

Ohio Division of Travel & Tourism Columbus **800/282-5393**

Publications

Gay People's Chronicle 216/631-8646, 800/426-5947 • weekly lesbigay newspaper w/ extensive listings

Akron

Info Lines & Services

AA Intergroup 330/253-8181 (AA#) • call for times & locations

LGBT Community Center 71 N Adams St (off E Market St) **330/253-2220** • 2pm-6pm, till 8pm Tue & Th, from noon Sat, 1pm-5pm Sun

Bars

Adams Street Bar 77 N Adams St **330/434-9794** • 4:30pm-2:30am, from 3pm Sat, from 9pm Sun • popular • mostly gay men • dancing/DJ • live shows • also 'Barracks' 10pm Fri-Sat • mostly gay men • leather

Akron Underground 41 Stanton Ave (at Main) **330/434-7788** • 5pm-2am, from noon Sat • mostly gay men • dancing/DJ • male strippers

Lydia's 1348 S Arlington St (in Arlington Plaza) **330/773-3001** • 6pm-2:30am, clsd Sun • mostly women • neighborhood bar

The Roseto Club 627 S Arlington St **330/724-4228** • 6pm-1am, till 2:30am Th-Sun • mostly women • dancing/DJ • wheelchair access

Tear-Ez 360 S Main (nr Exchange St) **330/376-0011** • 11am-2:30am, from 2pm Sun • mostly gay men • neighborhood bar • live shows • wheelchair access

Nightclubs

Babylon 820 W Market St (btwn Portage Pass & Rhodes Ave) **330/252-9000** • 4pm-2:30am • mostly gay men • dancing/DJ • live shows • wheelchair access • gay-owned/ run

Interbelt 70 N Howard St (nr Perkins & Main) **330/253-5700** • 9:30pm-2:30am, from 2pm Sun, clsd Tue • lesbians/ gay men • dancing/DJ • live shows • patio

Cafes

Angel Falls Coffee Company 792 W Market St (btwn N Highland & Grand) **330/376-5282** • lunch & desserts • patio • wheelchair access • gay-owned/ run

Cheryl's Daily Grind 1662 Merriman Rd (nr Peninsula) **330/869-9980** • 7am-6pm, till 5pm Th, 8am-3pm Sun • lesbian-owned/ run

Restaurants

The Sandwich Board 1667 W Market St (at Hawkins) **330/867-5442** • 11am-8pm, clsd Sun • plenty veggie

Bookstores

Angie's Books Etc 816 1/2 W Market St (in Highland Sq) **330/374-0444** • 11am-8pm, from 9am Sat, clsd Sun-Mon • pride gifts & more • lesbian-owned/ run

Publications

Exposé Magazine 800/699-6131 • covers Cleveland, Akron, Canton, Warren, Youngstown & Lorain

Gay People's Chronicle 216/631-8646, 800/426-5947 • weekly lesbigay newspaper w/ extensive listings

Spiritual Groups

Cascade Community Church 1196 Inman St **330/773-5298** • 2pm Sun

Brunswick

Restaurants

Pizza Marcello 67-A Pearl Rd (nr Boston Rd) **330/225-1211** • 4pm-close, from 3pm wknds • Italian

Canton

Bars

La Casa Lounge 508 Cleveland Ave NW (btwn 5th & 6th Sts NW) **330/453-7432** • 1pm-2:30am • lesbians/ gay men • neighborhood bar • transgender-friendly • live shows • wheelchair access

Nightclubs

540 Club 540 Walnut Ave NE (at 6th) **330/456-8622** • 9pm-2:30am, 6pm-close Sun • mostly gay men • dancing/DJ • neighborhood bar • bears • leather

Boardwalk 1127 W Tuscarawas **330/453-8000** • 5pm-2:30am • mostly gay men • dancing/DJ • wheelchair access

Publications

Exposé Magazine 800/699-6131 • covers Cleveland, Akron, Canton, Warren, Youngstown & Lorain

Erotica

Tower Bookstore 219 12th St NE (nr Walnut) **330/455-1254**

Cincinnati

Info Lines & Services

AA Gay/ Lesbian 320 Resor Ave (in St John's Unitarian church), Clifton **513/351-0422 (AA#)** • 8pm Mon, Wed & Fri • call for locations of wknd mtgs

Cincinnati Youth Group 513/684-8405, 800/347-8336 (OH ONLY) • 24hr info

Gay/ Lesbian Community Center of Greater Cincinnati 4119 Hamilton Ave (nr Blue Rock) **513/591-0200** • 6pm-9pm, noon-4pm Sat, clsd Sun

Gay/ Lesbian Community Switchboard 513/591-0222 • 24hr touchtone directory

Ohio Lesbian Archives The Women's Building, 4039 Hamilton Ave, Room 304 (above 'Crazy Ladies Books') **513/541-1917** • call for appt

PACT (People of All Colors Together) **513/395-7228** • multiracial & multicultural social/ support group • call for events

Women Helping Women 216 E 9th St **513/872-9259, 513/977-5545 (TTY)** • 24hr hotline • crisis center • support groups • lesbian referrals

Accommodations

Prospect Hill B&B 408 Boal St (at Drake) **513/421-4408** • gay/ straight • 1867 Italianate townhouse • full brkfst • hot tub • smokefree • gay-owned/ run • $109-149

Bars

Bullfish's 4023 Hamilton Ave (at Blue Rock) **513/541-9220** • 7pm-close, clsd Mon • mostly women • neighborhood bar • dancing/DJ • karaoke • live entertainment

Colors 4042 Hamilton Ave (at Blue Rock) **513/681-6969** • 7pm-2:30am, from 5pm wknds • popular • lesbians/ gay men • neighborhood bar • videos • piano bar

Golden Lions 340 Ludlow (at Telford), Clifton **513/281-4179** • 4pm-2:30am • mostly gay men • neighborhood bar • live shows

Junkers Tavern 4158 Langland (at Pullan) **513/541-5470** • 7:30am-1am • gay-friendly • neighborhood bar

Milton's 301 Milton St (at Sycamore) **513/784-9938** • 4pm-2:30am • gay-friendly • neighborhood bar

Plum St Pipeline 241 W Court (at Plum) **513/241-5678** • 4pm-2:30am • popular • mostly gay men • neighborhood bar • dancing/DJ wknds on 4th flr • live shows • videos

Shirley's 2401 Vine St **513/721-8483** • 8pm-2:30am, from 4pm Sun, clsd Mon • mostly women • dancing/DJ • wheelchair access

Shooters 927 Race St (at Court) **513/381-9900** • 4pm-2:30am • mostly gay men • dancing/DJ • country/ western • dance lessons 8pm Th • karaoke Wed • live shows Fri-Sun

Simon Says 428 Walnut (at 5th) **513/381-7577** • 11am-2:30am, from 1pm Sun • popular • mostly gay men • neighborhood bar • wheelchair access

Spurs 326 E 8th St (at Broadway) **513/621-2668** • 4pm-2:30am • popular • mostly gay men • leather • wheelchair access

The Subway 609 Walnut St (at 6th) **513/421-1294** • 6am-2:30am, from noon Sun • mostly gay men • neighborhood bar • dancing/DJ • live shows • food served

Nightclubs

The Dock 603 W Pete Rose Wy (at Central) **513/241-5623** • 5pm-2:30am, till 4am wknds, from 8pm Mon (call for winter hours) • lesbians/ gay men • dancing/DJ • live shows • volleyball court • wheelchair access

Cincinnati

Lesbigay Pride: September. 513/591-0200 (GLCC).

City Info: 513/621-2142 or 800/344-3445 (in OH), web: www.cincyusa.com.

Attractions: The Beach waterpark (in Mason) 513/398-2040.
Carew Tower 513/241-3888.
Cincinnati Art Museum 513/721-5204.
Fountain Square.
Krohn Conservatory 513/421-4086.
Museum Center at Union Terminal 513/287-7000.
Paramount King's Island (24 miles N of Cincinnati) 513/754-5800.

Best View: Mt. Adams & Eden Park.

Transit: Yellow Cab 513/241-2100. Queen City Metro 513/621-4455.

Warehouse 1313 Vine St (2 blks north of Central Pkwy) **513/684-9313** • 10pm-1am, till 2:30am Wed-Th, till 4am Fri-Sat, clsd Sun & Tue • gay-friendly • dancing/DJ • food served • videos • 18+ • patio

Cafes

Kaldi's Cafe & Books 1204 Main St (at 12th) **513/241-3070** • 10am-1am • some veggie • full bar • live shows • wheelchair access

Restaurants

Boca 4034 Hamilton Ave (btwn Knowlton St & Broadway) **513/542-2022** • lunch & dinner, clsd Mon • nouvelle int'l • patio

Carol's Corner Cafe 825 Main St (btwn 8th & 9th) **513/651-2667** • 11am-1am • popular • wheelchair access

The Diner on Sycamore 1203 Sycamore (at 12th) **513/721-1212** • 11am-12:30am, till 2am Fri-Sat • full bar • wheelchair access

Mullane's 723 Race St (btwn 7th & Garfield) **513/381-1331** • 11:30am-11pm, from 5pm Sat, clsd Sun • plenty veggie • beer/ wine • wheelchair access • $5-12

Entertainment & Recreation

Alternating Currents WAIF FM 88.3 **513/333-9243, 513/961-8900** • 3pm Sat • lesbigay public affairs radio program • also 'Everywomon' 1pm Sat

Bookstores

Crazy Ladies Bookstore 4039 Hamilton Ave (at Blue Rock) **513/541-4198** • 11am-8pm, till 6pm Sat, noon-4pm Sun • women's

Pink Pyramid 907 Race St (btwn 9th & Court) **513/621-7465** • 11am-10:30pm, till midnight Fri-Sat, 1pm-8pm Sun • lesbigay

Retail Shops

Left-Handed Moon 48 E Court St (at Walnut) **513/784-1166** • 11:30am-6pm, till 7pm Fri, from noon Sat, clsd Sun-Mon • cards • gifts • wheelchair access

Publications

Dinah • local women's newsletter • unconfirmed

Spiritual Groups

Dignity 3960 Winding Wy (nr Xavier Univ, at Friends Mtg House) **513/557-2111** • 7:30pm 1st & 3rd Sat

New Spirit MCC 5501 Hamilton Ave (at Belmont, in Grace Episcopal Church) **513/681-9090** • 7pm Sun & Wed

Cleveland

Info Lines & Services

AA Gay/ Lesbian 7801 Detroit Ave **216/241-7387** • 8:30pm Fri

BlackOut 216/462-0257, 888/825-5226 • nonprofit org for 'Cleveland's African American Same Gender Loving (SGL) community' • sponsors popular 'BlackOut Weekend'

Cleveland Lesbian/ Gay Community Center 1418 W 29th St **216/522-1999** • noon-7pm, till 5pm Tue, clsd wknds • wheelchair access

Cleveland Lesbian/ Gay Hotline 216/781-6736 • extensive 24hr recorded info

GLOWS (Gay/ Lesbian Older Wiser Seniors) 440/331-6302 • 7:30pm 2nd Tue

Women's Center of Greater Cleveland 6209 Storer Ave **216/651-1450, 216/651-4357 (HELPLINE)** • 9am-5pm, clsd wknds

Accommodations

Bourbon House 6116 Franklin Blvd (at W 65th) **216/939-0535** • gay/ straight • full brkfst • smokefree • gay-owned/ run • $85

Clifford House 1810 W 28th St (at Jay) **216/589-9432** • gay/ straight • smokefree • close to downtown • fireplaces • IGLTA • gay-owned/ run

Greystone B&B 10405 Lake Ave (at W 104th St) **216/939-0405** • gay/ straight • smokefree • $85-95

Bars

The Eagle & The Falcon's Nest 8307 Madison **216/281-4064** • 3pm-2:30am • mostly gay men • dancing/DJ • leather • strict dress code Sat • strippers Tue, Th & Sun

Five Cent Decision (The Nickel) 4365 State Rd (Rte 94, at Montclair) **216/661-1314** • 6pm-2:30am • mostly women • neighborhood bar • all ages Sun

The Hawk 11217 Detroit Ave (at 112th St) **216/521-5443** • 10am-2:30am, from noon Sun • lesbians/ gay men • neighborhood bar • wheelchair access

Hi & Dry Inn 2207 W 11th St (at Fairfield) **216/621-6166** • 11:30am-2am, clsd Sun • gay-friendly • jazz club • also restaurant • plenty veggie • patio • $10-15

MJ's Place 11633 Lorain Ave (at W 117th St) **216/476-1970** • 4pm-2:30am, clsd Sun • mostly gay men • neighborhood bar • karaoke • live shows • women very welcome at 'the gay Cheers'

Ohio City Oasis 2909 Detroit Ave (at 29th St) **216/574-2203** • 7am-2:30am, from noon Sun • lesbians/ gay men • dancing/DJ wknds • country/ western Sun • patio

Paradise Inn 4488 State Rd (Rte 94 at Rte 480) **216/741-9819** • 11am-close, till 1am wknds • lesbians/ gay men • neighborhood bar

Rudy's Tavern 2032 W 25th St (at Lorain & 24), Cleveland Hts **216/621-1752** • 3pm-2:30am • mostly gay men • neighborhood bar

Scarlet Rose's Lounge 2071 Broadview Rd (at Roanoke) **216/351-7511** • 5pm-2am, noon-8pm Sun • gay-friendly • neighborhood bar

Twist 11633 Clifton (at 117th St.) **216/221-2333** • 9am-2:30am, from noon Sun • lesbians/ gay men • dancing/DJ • professional crowd

Victory's 13603 Madison Ave **216/228-5777** • 7pm-2:30am • mostly women • neighborhood bar • dancing/DJ Fri-Sat • karaoke Mon • wheelchair access

Nightclubs

Aunt Charley's The Cage 9506 Detroit Ave (at W 95th) **216/651-0727** • 8pm-2:30am • popular • mostly gay men • dancing/DJ • transgender-friendly • live shows • karaoke

Club Atlantis 620 Frankfort **216/621-6900** • 9pm-2:30am, 10pm-4am Sat, till 2:30am Sun, clsd Mon-Tue • gay/ straight • more gay Sat • dancing/DJ • multi-racial clientele • videos • wheelchair access

Code Blue 1946 St Clair Ave (at E 9th) **216/241-4663** • 6pm-midnight, till 2:30am Fri, 9pm-2:30am Sat, clsd Sun-Mon • lesbians/ gay men • dancing/DJ • live shows • wheelchair access

The Rec Room 15320 Brookpark Rd **216/433-1669** • 6pm-1am • mostly women • dancing/DJ • food served • wheelchair access • women-owned/ run

Cleveland

Where the Girls Are: Dancing downtown near Public Square, hanging out on State Rd. below the intersection of Pearl and Broadview/Memphis.

Lesbigay Pride: June. 216/371-0214.

City Info: 216/621-4110, web: www.travelcleveland.com.

Attractions: Cleveland Metroparks Zoo 216/661-6500.
Cleveland Museum of Art 216/421-7340.
Coventry Road district.
Cuyahoga Valley National Recreation Area.
The Flats.
Rock and Roll Hall of Fame 216/781-7625.

Transit: Yellow-Zone Cab 216/623-1500.
AmeriCab 216/881-1111.
Regional Transit Authority (RTA) 216/621-9500.
Lolly the Trolley 216/771-4484.

Cafes

Johnny Mango 3120 Bridge Ave (btwn Fulton & W 32nd) **216/575-1919** • 11am-10pm, full bar open till 1am Fri-Sat • healthy world food • juice bar

Lonesome Dove Cafe 3093 Mayfield Rd (at Lee) **216/397-9100** • 7am-6pm, till 5pm Sat, clsd Sun • some veggie • beer/ wine • $5-7

Red Star Cafe 11604 Detroit Ave (at 116th) **216/521-7827** • 7am-11pm, till 1am Fri-Sat • lesbians/ gay men • wheelchair access

Restaurants

Cafe Tandoor 2096 S Taylor Rd (at Cedar), Cleveland Hts **216/371-8500, 216/371-8569** • lunch & dinner • Indian • plenty veggie

Club Isabella 2025 University Hospital Rd (at Euclid Ave) **216/229-1177** • lunch Mon-Fri & dinner nightly, clsd Sun • Italian • full bar • live jazz nightly • $15-25

Harmony Bar & Grille 3359 Fulton **440/398-5052** • lunch Tue-Fri, dinner from 4pm Tue-Sat, 10:30am-8pm Sun • Eastern European & Italian • live shows

Hecks 2927 Bridge Ave (at W 30th) **216/861-5464** • dinner from 5pm • reservations advised • wheelchair access • $10-20

The Inn on Coventry 2785 Euclid Heights Blvd (at Coventry), Cleveland Hts **216/371-1811** • 7am-9pm, from 8:30am Sat, 9am-3pm Sun, 8am-3pm Mon • homestyle • some veggie • full bar • wheelchair access • women-owned/ run • $5-20

Snickers 1261 W 76th St (at Lake Ave) **216/631-7555** • 11:30am-10pm, 4pm-11pm Sat • some veggie • full bar • $10-18

The Tuna Club 522 Superior Ave **216/241-2582** • 11am-10pm, clsd Sat, Sun brunch • full bar • unconfirmed '99

Whistlestop 11100 Clifton Blvd (at 110th) **216/939-8006** • brkfst, lunch & dinner, wknd brunch, clsd Mon • some veggie

Cleveland

Cleveland is making a comeback, after the recession and several economic facelifts. Actually, only some districts, like the Flats, have had a beauty makeover. Other districts never lost the funky charm of this city that's home both to the Rock 'N Roll Hall of Fame and the Cleveland Symphony Orchestra.

Speaking of funky, flash back to the '60s with a trip down Coventry Road. University Circle is rumored to be another hangout of the avant garde, as is Murray Hill, known for its many galleries. While you're at it, make time for some serious art appreciation in the galleries of the world-famous Cleveland Museum of Art.

To touch base with the lesbian community, pick up a copy of the **Gay People's Chronicle** to find out more about the ever-changing bar/coffeehouse scene. For a wholesome meal, try the women-run **Inn on Coventry.** After dinner, head out to dance at the **Rec Room.** For a more laid-back atmosphere, check out **The Five Cent Decision** (known to locals as **The Nickel**).

Entertainment & Recreation

Rock and Roll Hall of Fame 1 Key Plaza **216/781-ROCK, 800/BUCKEYE** • even if you don't like rock, be sure to stop by & check out IM Pei's architectural gift to Cleveland

Bookstores

Bookstore on W 25th St 1921 W 25th St (at Lorain) **216/566-8897** • 10am-6pm, noon-5pm Sun • lesbigay section

Borders Bookshop & Espresso Bar 2101 Richmond Rd (at Cedar, in LaPlace Mall), Beachwood **216/292-2660** • 9am-11pm, till 9pm Sun

Retail Shops

Bank News 4025 Clark Ave (at W 41st St) **216/281-8777** • 10:30am-8:30pm, clsd Sun

Body Language 3291 W 115th St **216/251-3330, 888/429-7733** • 11am-10pm, till 6pm Sun • 'an educational store for adults in alternative lifestyles'

Body Work Productions 2710 Detroit Ave (at W 28th) **216/623-0744** • 1pm-8pm • piercing

The Clifton Web 11512 Clifton Blvd (at W 117th) **216/961-1120** • 11am-8pm, from 10am Sat, till 5pm Sun • cards & gifts

Publications

Exposé Magazine 800/699-6131 • covers Cleveland, Akron, Canton, Warren, Youngstown & Lorain

Gay People's Chronicle 216/631-8646, 800/426-5947 • lesbigay newspaper w/ extensive listings

Spiritual Groups

Chevrei Tikva 2728 Lankershire Rd (at the Unitarian Ctr), Cleveland Hts **216/932-5551** • 8pm 1st & 3rd Fri • lesbigay synagogue

Emmanuel Christian Fellowship Church 10034 Lorain Ave **216/651-0129** • 6:30pm Sun & 7pm Wed

Integrity NE Ohio 3445 Warrensville Center Rd (at Christ Episcopal Church), Shaker Hts **216/939-0405** • 5pm 3rd Sat

Presbyterians for Lesbian/ Gay Concerns 2780 Noble Rd, Cleveland Hts **216/932-1458** • 6pm 2nd Sat • potluck & mtg

Erotica

Laws Leather Shop 11516 Edgewater Dr (btwn W 111th & 112th Sts) **216/961-0544** • hours vary, clsd Mon-Tue

Columbus

Info Lines & Services

AA Gay/ Lesbian 614/253-8501 • call for mtg schedule

Dragon Leather Club 614/258-7100 • pansexual leather group

GLB Alliance 1739 N High St, rm 464 (on Ohio State U campus) **614/292-6200** • student group • call for info

Kaleidoscope Youth Coalition 203 King Ave **614/294-7886, 800/291-9109** • lgbt youth drop-in center • call for hours

Sisters of Lavender 93 W Weisheimer (at Unitarian Church) **614/575-9646** • 7:30pm Wed • lesbian support group

Stonewall Columbus—Hotline/ Community Ctr 1160 N High St **614/299-7764** • 10am-7pm, till 5pm Fri, clsd wknds • wheelchair access

WOW (Women's Outreach for Women) 1950-H N 4th St **614/291-3639** • 9am-5pm, mtgs 5pm-8pm • women's recovery center • wheelchair access

Accommodations

Columbus B&B 763 S 3rd St **614/444-8888** • gay-friendly • referral service for German Village district • $65

Courtyard by Marriott 35 W Spring St (at Front St) **614/228-3200, 800/321-2211** • gay-friendly • wknd discounts • wheelchair access • $69-150

The Gardener's House 556 Frebis Ave (at Ann St) **614/444-5445** • lesbians/ gay men • spa • smokefree • $38-48

Summit Lodge Resort & Guesthouse 740/385-3521 • popular • gay-friendly • clothing-optional resort • 45 miles to Columbus • camping available • hot tub • swimming • also restaurant • $50-110

Bars

Blazer's Pub 1205 N High St (at 5th) **614/299-1800** • 4pm-2:30am, 3pm-midnight Sun • mostly women • neighborhood bar

Club Diversity 124 E Main (btwn 3rd & 4th Sts) **614/224-4050** • 4pm-midnight, till 2:30am Fri-Sat, clsd Sun-Mon • lesbians/ gay men • piano bar • patio • also coffeehouse

Downtown Connection 1126 N High St (at 4th Ave) **614/299-4880** • 5pm-2am, from 3pm wknds • mostly gay men • sports bar

The Far Side 1662 W Mound St (at Reed) **614/276-5817** • 5pm-1am, till 2:30am Fri-Sat, from 2pm Sun • mostly women • neighborhood bar • food served • live bands wknds

Garrett's Saloon 1071 Parsons Ave (at Stewart) **614/449-2351** • 11am-2:30am • mostly gay men • neighborhood bar • country/western in the day • Top 40 at night • karaoke Mon

Grapevine Cafe 73 E Gay St (at 3rd St) **614/221-8463** • 5pm-1am, clsd Sun-Mon • lesbians rule the bar • occasional shows • also restaurant • lesbians/ gay men • Sun brunch • some veggie • wheelchair access • $7-15

Havana Video Lounge 862 N High (at 1st Ave) **614/421-9697** • 5pm-2:30am • popular • lesbians/ gay men • videos • male strippers Sun

Remo's 1409 S High St (at Jenkins) **614/443-4224** • 11am-2:30am, clsd Sun • lesbians/ gay men • neighborhood bar • food served • pizza & subs • live shows • karaoke

Slammers Pizza Pub 202 E Long St (at 5th St) **614/469-7526** • 11am-2:30am, from 2:30pm wknds • lesbians/ gay men • wheelchair access

Summit Station 2210 Summit St (btwn Alden & Oakland) **614/261-9634** • 4pm-2:30am • mostly women • neighborhood bar • dancing/DJ • live shows

Tabú 40 E Long St (at Pearl) **614/461-0076** • 5pm-2:30am • mostly gay men • neighborhood bar • food served • drag shows • patio

Union Station Video Cafe 630 N High St (at Goodale) **614/228-3740** • 11am-2am • lesbians/ gay men • video bar • food served • plenty veggie • Internet access • wheelchair access • $6-10

Columbus

Where the Girls Are: Downtown with the boys, north near the University area, or somewhere in-between.

Lesbigay Pride: June. 614/299-7764 (Stonewall).

Annual Events: June - Pagan Spirit Gathering in Athens campground, 1.5 hrs. south of Columbus 608/924-2216 (Wisconsin office).
September - Ohio Lesbian Festival 614/267-3953.

City Info: 614/221-2489, web: www.ohiotourism.com.

Attractions: Columbus Museum of Modern Art 614/221-6801.
Columbus Zoo 614/645-3550.
German Village district.
Wexner Center for the Arts 614/292-0330.

Weather: Truly midwestern. Winters are cold, summers are hot.

Transit: Yellow Cab 614/444-4444.
Northway Taxicab 614/299-4118, 614/299-1191.
Independent 614/235-5551.
Airport Express Shuttle 614/476-3004.
Central Ohio Transit Authority (COTA) 614/228-1776.

Nightclubs

Axis 775 N High St (at Hubbard) **614/291–4008** • 10pm-2:30am, clsd Mon-Wed • popular • mostly gay men • dancing/DJ • Varsity Night Th w/ dancers • wheelchair access • gay-owned/ run

The Garage 40 E Long St (at 'Tabú') **614/461–0076** • 9pm-2:30am • popular • mostly gay men • dancing/DJ • wheelchair access

Tradewinds II 117 E Chestnut (at 3rd St) **614/461–4110** • 4pm-2:30am, clsd Mon • mostly gay men • 3 bars • dancing/DJ • leather • videos • also restaurant • wheelchair access

Wall Street 144 N Wall St (at Long) **614/464–2800** • 6pm-2:30am, clsd Mon-Tue • popular • lesbians/ gay men • dancing/DJ • live shows • wheelchair access

Cafes

The Coffee Table 731 N High St (at Buttles) **614/297–1177** • 7:30am-midnight, till 1am wknds, 8am-10pm Sun • lesbians/ gay men

Cup-O-Joe Cafe 627 3rd St (at Sycamore) **614/221–1563** • 7am-11pm, till 1am Fri-Sat

Hollywood & High Coffeehouse 850 N High St (at 1st Ave) **614/294–2233** • 7am-10pm, till 1am Sat, from 9am Sun

Columbus

The center of lesbian life in Columbus is Clintonville (affectionately known as 'Clitville'), just north of the OSU campus. While you're in the neighborhood, stop by popular dyke hangout **Summit Station,** where you can also pick up copies of the **Gay People's Chronicle, Stonewall Union Journal, Outlook,** and the popular homegrown newsmagazine **The Word Is Out!,** for the latest news and events.

The Short North—the stretch of High Street just north of Downtown—is a funky, artsy neighborhood that hosts a Gallery Hop the first Saturday of every month. After the shops start closing around 10pm (or later), check out **Blazer's Pub,** or try the Short North Pole for fantastic ice cream concoctions. If you need to refuel, try the **Coffee Table;** we hear it's as popular with local dykes as with the cruisin' gay boys.

Sports dykes, check out Berliner Park, any season, to watch women's softball, volleyball, or basketball leagues. Even the non-athletic head to the **Far Side,** the **Grapevine,** or **Slammers** afterward to celebrate the thrill of victory.

The best time of all is the Gay Pride March that always falls the same weekend in June as ComFest. This is the community festival at Goodale Park in Victorian Village which hosts a wide variety of merchants, food, information, and music.

Restaurants

Chinese Village 2124 Lane St (at High) **614/297-7979** • 11am-10pm

Frank's Diner 59 Spruce St (at High) **614/621-2233** • 7am-7pm, 9am-5pm Sun, till 3pm Mon • full bar • wheelchair access

Fresno's 782 N High St (at Buttles Ave) **614/298-0031** • 11am-1am, from 4pm Sat, clsd Sun • popular • lesbian-owned/ run

King Ave 247 King Ave (at Neil Ave) **614/294-8287** • 11am-10pm, from 5pm Mon • popular • funky bohemian crowd • vegetarian/ vegan • $3-8

L'Antibes 772 N High St #106 (at Warren) **614/291-1666** • dinner from 5pm, clsd Sun-Mon • French (vegetarian on request) • full bar • wheelchair access • gay-owned/ run • $18-30

Lemon Grass 641 N High (N of Goodale St) **614/224-1414** • Pacific Rim Asian cuisine • reservations advised

Lost Planet Pizza & Pasta 680 N High St (at Russell) **614/228-6191** • 11am-10pm, till 11pm Fri-Sat, 3pm-9pm Sun • wheelchair access

Nacho Mama's 5277 US Hwy 23

No Attitude Bar & Grill 53 Parsons Ave (at Oak) **614/464-3663** • 11am-2:30am, from 10am-midnight Sun • some veggie • full bar • gay-owned/ run

Out on Main 122 E Main (btwn 3rd & 4th) **614/224-9510** • 5pm-9pm, till 11pm Fri-Sat, brunch 11am-2:30pm Sun • upscale casual dining • piano wknds • full bar till 2:30am • wheelchair access

Entertainment & Recreation

The Reality Theatre 736 N Pearl St (btwn Lincoln & Warren) **614/294-7541** • lesbigay plays & new releases • call for show dates

Bookstores

An Open Book 761 N High St (at Buttles) **614/291-0080** • 10am-10pm, till 8pm Sun • lesbigay • wheelchair access

The Book Loft of German Village 631 S 3rd St (at Sycamore) **614/464-1774** • 10am-11pm, till midnight Fri-Sat • lesbigay section

The Shadow Realm 3347 N High St (1 blk S of N Broadway) **614/262-1175** • metaphysical & occult bookstore • readings, workshops & classes • sponsors the annual 'Witch's Ball' in Oct • wheelchair access

Retail Shops

ACME Art Company 1129 N High St (at 4th Ave) **614/299-4003** • alternative art space • call for hours

Creative-A-Tee 874 N High St **614/297-8844** • noon-8pm, till 7pm Sat, clsd Sun-Mon • gay pride T-shirts & gifts • gallery

Hausfrau Haven 769 S 3rd St (at Columbus) **614/443-3680** • 10am-6:30pm, till 5pm Sun • greeting cards • wine • gifts

Kukala's Tanning & Tees 636 N High St (at Russell) **614/228-8337** • noon-8pm • lesbigay gifts • tanning salon

LJ Originals 745 N High St (btwn Buttles & Hubbard) **614/291-2787** • 11am-7pm, till 6pm Sat, clsd Sun • jewelry • gifts

Metro Video 848 N High St (at Hubbard) **614/291-7962** • 11am-midnight, from noon Sun • lesbigay videos • large selection

Pierceology 872 N High St (S of 1st) **614/297-4743** • noon-8pm, till 7pm Sat, 1pm-5pm Sun • body piercing studio

Rainbow Tribe 2997 Indianola Ave (at Weber Rd) **614/268-5424** • noon-8pm, till 6pm wknds • cards • gifts • pride items

Publications

Outlook 614/268-8525 • lesbigay newspaper • good resource pages

Spotlight Magazine 614/444-3255 • bi-weekly lesbigay paper for Central Ohio

The Stonewall Union Journal 614/299-7764

The Word Is OUT! 614/784-8146 • monthly publication for Columbus' lesbian community

Spiritual Groups

Dignity Columbus 444 E Broad St (at First Congregational Church UCC, side entrance) **614/451-6528** • 6pm 2nd & 4th Sun

Lutherans Concerned 1555 S James Rd **614/447-7018** • 1pm 1st Sun

New Creation MCC 787 E Broad St (at St Paul's Episcopal Church) **614/224-0314** • 10:30am Sun

Spirit of the Rivers 588 S 3rd St (at German Village Mtg House) **614/470-0816** • 10am Sun • ecumenical service

St Paul's Episcopal Church 787 E Broad St (at I-71 intersection) **614/221-1703** • 5pm Sun • wheelchair access

Gyms & Health Clubs

Body Life Fitness 384 Dublin Ave (at Neil Ave) **614/221-4766**

Erotica

Bexley Video 3839 April Ln (at Courtright) **614/235-2341**

Garden 1186 N High St (at 5th Ave) **614/294-2869** • adult toys

IMRU 235 N Lazelle (at Hickory, above the Eagle) **614/228-9660** • 11:30pm-2:30am Th-Sat, 10:30am-1:30am Sun • leather, pride & rave store

Conneaut

Accommodations

Josiah Manor 810 Main St, US Rte 20 **440/599-8010, 877/599-8010** • gay/ straight • private • close to beach • smokefree • gay-owned/ run • $65-100

Dayton

Info Lines & Services

AA Gay/ Lesbian 20 W 1st St (off Main, at Christ Episcopal Church) **937/222-2211** • 8pm Sat

Dayton Lesbian/ Gay Hotline **937/274-1776** • 24hr hotline, 7pm-11pm (volunteer staff)

Youth Quest **937/640-3333** • 7pm 1st & 3rd Wed • lesbigay youth group 22 & under

Bars

City Cafe 121 N Ludlow St (in Talbot Tower Bldg) **937/223-1417** • 5pm-2:30am • mostly gay men • karaoke • live shows • wheelchair access

Down Under 131 N Ludlow St (in Talbot Tower Bldg) **937/228-1050** • 11am-1:30pm for lunch Mon-Fri, bar from 8pm Fri-Sat only • mostly women • dancing/DJ • wheelchair access

Reflextions 629 S Main St (at Patterson) **937/223-1595** • 1pm-2:30am • mostly gay men • dancing/DJ • live shows

Right Corner 105 E 3rd St (at Jefferson) **937/228-1285** • noon-2:30am • mostly gay men • neighborhood bar • wheelchair access

Nightclubs

1470 West 34 N Jefferson St (btwn 2nd & 3rd) **937/461-1470** • 9pm-2:30am, till 4am Fri-Sat, clsd Mon-Wed • popular • lesbians/ gay men • dancing/DJ • live shows • videos • wheelchair access

The Asylum 605 S Patterson Blvd **937/228-8828** • 9pm-close, clsd Sun-Mon • gay-friendly • dancing/DJ • alternative • 18+

Jessie's Celebrity Showbar 850 N Main St (off I-75) **937/461-2582** • 9pm-2:30am, till 5am Fri-Sat • popular • mostly gay men • dancing/DJ • karaoke • live shows • wheelchair access

Cafes

Gloria Jean's Coffee Bean 2727 Fairfield Commons (in mall), Beavercreek **937/426-1672** • 9:30am-9pm, noon-6pm Sun • gay-owned/ run

Samuel Johnson Coffee House 39 N Main St (at 1st) **937/228-1948** • 9am-8pm, from noon Fri-Sat, till 7:30pm Sun, till 2:30pm Mon • wheelchair access

Restaurants

Cold Beer & Cheeseburgers 33 Jefferson St **937/222-2337** • 11am-11pm, noon-8pm Sun • grill • full bar • wheelchair access

The Spaghetti Warehouse 36 W 5th St (at Ludlow) **937/461-3913** • 11am-10pm, till 11pm Fri-Sat • more gay Mon w/ 'Friends of the Italian Opera'

Bookstores

Books & Co 350 E Stroop Rd (at Farhills) **937/298-6540** • 9am-11pm, till 8pm Sun

Retail Shops

Q Gift Shop 1904 N Main St (at Ridge St) **937/274-4400** • noon-7pm Mon & Fri-Sat, from 2pm Tue-Th, clsd Sun (winters) • lesbigay gifts

Spiritual Groups

Community Gospel Church 546 Xenia Ave (at Steele Ave) **937/252-8855** • Adult Sun School 10am Sun, worship service 11am • wheelchair access

MCC 1630 E 5th St (at McClure) **937/228-4031** • 10:30am & 6pm Sun

Findlay

Accommodations

Zelkova Country Manor 2348 S CR 19 (off 224), Tiffin **419/447-4043** • gay/ straight • full brkfst • smokefree • kids ok • $75-150

Glenford

Accommodations

Springhill Farm Resort 5704 Highpoint Rd, 43739-9727 • women only • cabins & restored barn on 30 acres • hot tub • swimming • smokefree rms available

Kent

Info Lines & Services

Kent LGB Union KSU **330/672-2068**

Cafes

The Zephyr Cafe 106 W Main St **330/678-4848** • 8am-9pm, from 9am Sat, till 7pm Sun, clsd Mon • live shows • vegetarian • wheelchair access • women-owned/ run • $3-7

Lima

Nightclubs

Somewhere 804 W North St **419/227-7288** • 4pm-2:30am, from 8pm wknds • lesbians/ gay men • dancing/DJ Fri-Sat • live shows

Logan

Accommodations

Glenlaurel—A Scottish Country Inn & Cottages 14940 Mt Olive Rd (off State Rte 180), Rockbridge **740/385-4070, 800/809-7378** • gay-friendly • full brkfst & dinner • smokefree • wheelchair access • $145-245

Spring Wood Hocking Hills Cabins 15 miles SE of Columbus **740/385-2042** • lesbians/ gay men • cabins • hot tub • smokefree • kids ok • wheelchair access • lesbian-owned/ run • $90-110

Lorain

Bars

The Serpent 2223 Broadway (btwn 22nd & 23rd) **440/246-9002** • 8pm-2:30am, from 4pm Sun, clsd Mon • lesbians/ gay men • neighborhood bar • dancing/DJ • live shows • patio • wheelchair access

Publications

Exposé Magazine 800/699-6131 • covers Cleveland, Akron, Canton, Warren, Youngstown & Lorain

Mentor

Info Lines & Services

Gay/ Lesbian Info Line 440/974-8909 • 7pm-9pm Wed, phone 24hrs • lesbigay info & referrals for Ashtabula, Geauga & Lake Counties

Newark

Bars

Bulldog Lounge 35 N 3rd St **740/345-9729** • 7pm-2:30am • lesbians/ gay men • neighborhood bar • unconfirmed '99

Oberlin

Info Lines & Services

Oberlin LGB Union 440/775-8179

Oxford

Info Lines & Services

Miami University GLB Alliance 513/529-3823 • meets 8pm Th • call for location

Sandusky

Accommodations

2-Twelve Guesthouse 212 Decatur St **419/625-8292** • lesbians/ gay men • 1890s house • kids/ pets ok

Nightclubs

Rainbow Bay 306 W Water St **419/624-8118** • 4pm-2:30am, from 1pm wknds • lesbians/ gay men • dancing/DJ • live shows

Bookstores

City News 139 Columbus Ave (btwn Market & Water) **419/626-1265** • 7am-5:30pm

Springfield

Nightclubs

Chances 1912 Edwards Ave **937/324-0383** • 8:30pm-2:30am, clsd Tue • gay-friendly • dancing/DJ • live shows • patio

Toledo

Info Lines & Services

AA Gay/ Lesbian 2272 Collingwood Blvd (at St Mark's Episcopal Church) **419/472-8242** • 8pm Wed & Sun

Pro Toledo Info Line 419/472-2364 • 7pm-11pm

Bars

Blu Jean Cafe 3606 Sylvania Ave (nr Monroe) **419/474-0690** • 4pm-2:30am, clsd Sun • popular • lesbians/ gay men • more women Th • live shows • karaoke • also restaurant • wheelchair access

Hooterville Station 119 N Erie St (btwn Jeff & Monroe) **419/241-9050** • 5:30pm-2:30am • mostly gay men • dancing/DJ • bears • leather • patio

Rip Cord 11 N Superior St (btwn Washington & Monroe) **419/243-3412** • 1pm-2:30am, from 5:30pm Sat • mostly gay men • leather • live shows • patio

Nightclubs

Bretz 2012 Adams St **419/243–1900** • 4pm-2:30am, till 4am Fri-Sat, clsd Mon-Tue • popular • mostly gay men • dancing/DJ • alternative • live shows • videos

Caesar's Show Bar 725 Jefferson **419/241–5140** • 8pm-2:30am, clsd Mon-Th • lesbians/ gay men • dancing/DJ • live shows • wheelchair access

Cafes

Sufficient Grounds 3160 Markway (at Cricket West Mall) **419/537–1988** • 7am-11pm, till midnight Fri-Sat, 8am-10pm Sun • live shows • wheelchair access • also 420 Madison, 419/243–5282

Bookstores

People Called Women 3153 W Central Ave **419/535–6455** • 11am-7pm, noon-5pm Sun, clsd Mon

Thackeray's 3301 W Central Ave (in Westgate Shopping Center) **419/537–9259** • 9am-9pm, 10am-6pm Sun • wheelchair access

Retail Shops

Rainy Day Creation 452 W Delaware Ave (at Collingwood Blvd) **419/242–4992** • 11am-6pm, till 8pm Fri-Sat, till 3pm Sun, clsd Mon • rainbow novelties • cards & gifts • lesbian-owned

Spiritual Groups

Eagle's Wing Christian Church 1483 W Sylvania (btwn Jackman Rd & Lewis Ave) **419/476–8197** • 10am & 6pm Sun, 7:30pm Wed

MCC Good Samaritan 720 W Delaware (in Old W End) **419/244–2124** • 9:30am & 11am Sun

Erotica

Adult Pleasures 4404 N Detroit (at US 24) **419/476–4587** • 24hrs

Warren

Bars

The Queen of Hearts 132–136 Pine St (btwn Market & Franklin) **330/395–1100** • 4pm-2:30am, from 2pm wknds • lesbians/ gay men • neighborhood bar • dancing/DJ • live shows • karaoke Wed • patio

Nightclubs

The Alley 441 E Market St (enter rear) **330/394–9483** • 2pm-2:30am • lesbians/ gay men • dancing/DJ • live shows • wheelchair access

The Crazy Duck 121 Pine St SE **330/394–3825** • 4pm-2:30am • popular • lesbians/ gay men • dancing/DJ • drag shows Sun • 18+ • wheelchair access

Publications

Exposé Magazine 800/699–6131 • covers Cleveland, Akron, Canton, Warren, Youngstown & Lorain

Wooster

Accommodations

Kimbilio Farm 6047 TR 501, Big Prairie **330/378–2481** • women only • log house & cabins • full brkfst • swimming • 45 minutes from Akron • shared baths • kids/ pets ok (cabin only) • wheelchair access (cabin only) • lesbian-owned/ run • $50

Yellow Springs

Info Lines & Services

Queer Center Antioch College **937/767–7331 x601**

Restaurants

Winds Cafe & Bakery 215 Xenia Ave **937/767–1144** • lunch & dinner, Sun brunch, clsd Mon • plenty veggie • full bar • wheelchair access • women-owned/ run • $15-20

Bookstores

Epic Bookshop 232 Xenia Ave **937/767–7997** • noon-6pm, from 10am Sat, clsd Mon

Youngstown

Info Lines & Services

Live & Let Live AA 26 Rayen Ave (at St Joseph Newman Ctr)

Bars

The Mixx 21 W Hilda (off Market) **330/782–6991** • 4pm-2:30am • lesbians/ gay men • neighborhood bar • dancing/DJ • karaoke • live shows • wheelchair access

Publications

Exposé Magazine 800/699–6131 • covers Cleveland, Akron, Canton, Warren, Youngstown & Lorain

OKLAHOMA

Statewide

INFO LINES & SERVICES

Oklahoma Traveler Information Oklahoma City **800/652-6552**

PUBLICATIONS

▲ **Gayly Oklahoman 405/528-0800** • lesbigay newspaper

El Reno

ACCOMMODATIONS

The Good Life RV Resort Exit 108 I-40 (1/4 mile S) **405/884-2994, 405/893-2345** • gay-friendly • 32 acres • 100 campsites & 100 RV hookups • swimming • kids ok • gay-owned/run • $10-15 (full hookup)

Enid

EROTICA

Priscilla's 4810-A W Garriott (at Garland) **580/233-5511** • toys • lingerie • books • videos

Lawton

BARS

Triangles 8-1/2 NW 2nd St (enter rear) **580/351-0620** • 9pm-2am, till 1am Sun, clsd Mon-Tue • lesbians/ gay men • neighborhood bar • dancing/DJ • live shows

BOOKSTORES

Ingrid's Books 1124 NW Cache Rd **580/353-1488** • 10am-10pm, 1pm-7pm Sun • new & used books • also adult novelties

SPIRITUAL GROUPS

Great Plains MCC 1415 SW Wisconsin **580/357-7899** • 5pm Sun

Norman

see also Oklahoma City

INFO LINES & SERVICES

OU GLB Alliance 405/325-4452

BOOKSTORES

Borders Books 300 Norman Ctr **405/573-4907** • lesbigay section

Retail Shops

Mystic Forest Treasures 323 White St (Campus Corner) **405/447-5111** • 11am-6pm, clsd Sun • pride gifts • music • metaphysical supplies • lesbian-owned

Oklahoma City

Info Lines & Services

AA Live & Let Live 3405 N Villa **405/524-1100 (AA#), 405/947-3834 (CLUB #)** • call for mtg schedule

The Center 2135 NW 39th St **405/524-6000, 405/525-2437** • hrs vary • pls call

Herland Sister Resources 2312 NW 39th St **405/521-9696** • 1pm-5pm Sat-Sun • women's resource center w/ books, crafts & lending library • also sponsors monthly events • wheelchair access

Young Gay/ Lesbian Alliance 4400 N Lincoln Blvd (Red Rock Mental Health Ctr) **405/425-0399 (OUTREACH HOTLINE #), 405/424-7711** • support group & more for lgbt youth • 6:30pm-8pm Tue • also 4pm Wed at 'The Center'

Accommodations

America's Crossroads B&B 405/495-1111 • reservation service for private homes • gay-owned/ run • $35-50

▲ **Habana Inn** 2200 NW 39th St (at Youngs) **405/528-2221, 800/988-2221 (RESERVATIONS ONLY)** • popular • lesbians/ gay men • swimming • also 2 clubs, piano bar & restaurant on premises • wheelchair access • $35-65

Bars

Coyote Club 2120 NW 39th St (at Youngs) **405/521-9533** • open Th-Sat • mostly women • dancing/DJ • live shows Fri

▲ **Finish Line** at 'Habana Inn' **405/525-0730** • noon-2am • lesbians/ gay men • dancing/DJ • country/ western • lessons 7pm Tue-Wed • wheelchair access

Hi-Lo Club 1221 NW 50th St (btwn Western & Classen) **405/843-1722** • noon-2am • lesbians/ gay men • neighborhood bar • live bands weekly

KA's 2024 NW 11th (at Pennsylvania) **405/525-3734** • 2pm-2am • mostly women • neighborhood bar • beer bar • live entertainment monthly

Oklahoma City

Lesbigay Pride: June. 405/525-2437 (Oasis).

Annual Events: May - Herland Spring Retreat 405/521-9696. Music, workshops.
September - Herland Fall Retreat.

City Info: 405/297-8912, web: www.okccvb.org.

Attractions: Historic Paseo Arts District.
Myriad Gardens' Crystal Bridge 405/297-3995.
National Cowboy Hall of Fame 405/478-2250.
National Softball Hall of Fame 405/424-5266.
Omniplex 405/602-6664.
Will Rogers Park.

Transit: Yellow Cab 405/232-6161.
Airport Express 405/681-3311.
Metro Transit 405/235-7433.

▲ **The Ledo** at 'Habana Inn' **405/525-0730** • 4pm-close • lesbians/ gay men • food served • karaoke Th • live shows Sat • wheelchair access

Partners 2805 NW 36th St (at May Ave) **405/942-2199** • 5pm-close, from 3pm Fri & Sun, clsd Mon-Tue • popular • mostly women • dancing/DJ • live shows

Tramps 2201 NW 39th St (at Barnes) **405/521-9888** • noon-2am, from 10am wknds • popular • mostly gay men • dancing/DJ • drag shows • wheelchair access

Nightclubs

Angles 2117 NW 39th St (at Pennsylvania) **405/524-3431** • 9pm-2am, clsd Mon-Wed • popular • lesbians/ gay men • dancing/DJ • live shows • wheelchair access

▲ **Copa** at 'Habana Inn' **405/525-0730** • 9pm-2am, clsd Mon • lesbians/ gay men • dancing/DJ • live shows • wheelchair access • cover charge Sun

The Park 2125 NW 39th St (at Barnes/ Pennsylvania) **405/528-4690** • 5pm-2am, from 3pm Sun • mostly gay men • dancing/DJ • patio • wheelchair access

Wreck Room 2127 NW 39th St (at Pennsylvania) **405/525-7610** • 10pm-close Th-Sat • popular • lesbians/ gay men • dancing/DJ • live shows • 18+ after 1am • juice bar • Goth Night Th

Cafes

Diversity Coffee Shop 1739 NW 16th St (at Indiana) **405/524-7375** • 4pm-midnight, from 10am Wed-Sat, till 2am Fri-Sat • lesbians/ gay men • live shows w/open mic & poetry readings • Internet access

Grateful Bean Cafe & Soda Fountain 1039 Walker **405/236-3503** • 11am-5pm, clsd wknds • plenty veggie • 'Seattle-style' espresso

Restaurants

Bricktown Brewery Restaurant 1 N Oklahoma **405/232-2739** • 10am-10pm, till 2am Fri-Sat • live bands Fri-Sat

▲ **Gusher's Bar & Grill** at 'Habana Inn' **405/528-2221 x411** • 11am-10:30pm, from 7am wknds, till 3:30am Fri-Sat for after-hours brkfst • wheelchair access

Hunkie's 2124 NW 39th St (at Pennsylvania) **405/521-9545** • 5pm-11pm, till 4am Th-Sat, clsd Mon • classic burgers

The Patio Cafe 5100 N Classen **405/842-7273** • 7am-2pm, from 9am Sun, also 9pm-3am Fri-Sat (summers)

Retail Shops

Ziggyz 4005 N Pennsylvania (at I-240) **405/521-9999** • novelty gifts • smokeshop • also 1500 SW 74, 405/682-2299

Publications

▲ **Gayly Oklahoman 405/528-0800** • lesbigay newspaper

The Herland Voice 405/521-9696 • newsletter

Spiritual Groups

Oklahoma City Religious Society of Friends (Quakers) 312 SE 25th St **405/631-4174, 405/632-7574** • 10am Sun ('Forum') • 11am Sun (worship)

Erotica

Christie's Toy Box 3126 N May Ave (at 30th) **405/946-4438** • also 1039 S Meridian, 405/948-3333

▲ **Jungle Red** at 'Habana Inn' **405/524-5733** • 1pm-close, from noon wknds • novelties • leather • gifts • wheelchair access

Randi's Playthings 4711 S Pennsylvania (at 44th) **405/681-0308** • adult toys • lingerie • plus sizes

Sulphur

Accommodations

The Artesian B&B 1022 W 12th St **580/622-5254, 888/557-5254** • gay-friendly • Victorian close to Arbuckle Wilderness • full brkfst • $65-80

Tulsa

Info Lines & Services

BLGTA at TU 2839 E 8th St (Canterbury Center, U of Tulsa) **918/583-9780 (United Ministries Ctr #)** • 6:30pm Sun

The Pride Center 1307 E 38th St (at Peoria) **918/743-4297** • touchtone info • center open 6pm-10pm, noon-9pm Sat • wheelchair access

TULSA (Tulsa Uniform/ Leather Seekers Assoc) 918/298-4895

Bars

Bamboo Lounge 7204 E Pine **918/832-1269** • 11am-2am • mostly gay men • neighborhood bar • wheelchair access

The Mix 2630 E 15th **918/749-1563** • 2pm-2am • lesbians/ gay men • neighborhood bar • live shows

New Age Renegades/ The Rainbow Room 1649 S Main St (at 17th) **918/585–3405** • 2pm-2am • popular • lesbians/ gay men • neighborhood bar • live shows • patio

TNT 2114 S Memorial (at 21st) **918/660–0856** • 4pm-2am • popular • mostly women • dancing/DJ

Nightclubs

Silver Star Saloon 1565 S Sheridan **918/834–4234** • 9pm-2am, from 8pm Fri-Sat • mostly gay men • more women Sat • dancing/DJ • country/ western • wheelchair access

The Storm 2182 S Sheridan (at 23rd) **918/835–2376** • 9pm-2am, clsd Mon • DJ Th-Sun • mostly gay men • more mixed wknds • wheelchair access

Cafes

Java Dave's 1326 E 15th St (at Lincoln Plaza) **918/592–3317** • 7am-11pm

Restaurants

Burger Sisters Cafe (2 doors down from 'Silver Star Saloon') **918/835–1207** • lunch & dinner, 24hrs Fri-Sat

St Michael's Alley 3324 E 31st (in Ranch Acres) **918/745–9998**

Wild Fork 1820 Utica Square **918/742–0712** • 7am-10pm, clsd Sun • full bar • wheelchair access • women-owned/ run • $10-20

Entertainment & Recreation

Gilcrease Museum 1400 Gilcrease Museum Rd **918/596–2787** • one of the best collections of Native American & cowboy art in the US

Philbrook Museum of Art 2727 S Rockford Rd (1 blk E of Peoria, at end of 27th St) **918/749–7941** • Italian villa built in the '20s oil boom complete w/ kitschy lighted dance flr, now museum • the gardens are a must in spring & summer

Retail Shops

Body Piercing by Nicole 2727 E 15th St (btwn Harvard & Lewis) **918/712–1122**

The Pride Store 1307 E 38th St, 2nd flr (at the Pride Center) **918/743–4297** • 6pm-9pm, from noon Sat • lesbigay cards • gifts • shirts • some books • wheelchair access

Publications

Queer Times **918/749–3857, 800/598–7533**

Tulsa Family News **918/583–1248**

Spiritual Groups

MCC United of Tulsa 1623 N Maplewood **918/838–1715** • 11am Sun

Erotica

Priscilla's 11344 E 11th (at Garnett) **918/438–4224** • toys • lingerie • books • videos • 3 other locations: 5634 W Skelly Rd at 56th, 918/446-6336 • 2333 E 71St, 918/499-1661 • 7925 E 41st at Memorial, 918/627-4884

Oregon

Statewide

Info Lines & Services

Gay Resource Connection/ Oregon AIDS Hotline Portland **503/223–2437, 800/777–2437 (Pacific NW only)** • 10am-9pm, noon-6pm wknds

Oregon Tourism Commission Portland **800/547–7842** • call for a free catalog

Ashland

Info Lines & Services

Lambda Community Center 56 3rd St **541/488–6990** • volunteer hours vary

Womansource **541/482–7416, 541/482–2026** • feminist group • sponsors cultural activities like '1st Fri Coffeehouse' & annual Fall Gathering (wheelchair access) • also publishes 'Community News'

Women's Resource Center 1077 Ashland St **541/552–6216** • hours vary • library • mtg space • gallery

Accommodations

The Arden Forest Inn 261 W Hersey St **541/488–1496, 800/460–3912** • gay/ straight • full brkfst • smokefree • kids ok • wheelchair access • gay-owned/ run • $90-115

Country Willows B&B Inn 1313 Clay St **541/488–1590, 800/945–5697** • gay-friendly • full brkfst • swimming • jacuzzi • smokefree • teens ok • wheelchair access • IGLTA • gay-owned/ run • $76-195

Dandelion Garden Cottage **541/488–4463** • women-only retreat

Lithia Springs Inn 2165 W Jackson Rd **541/482–7128, 800/482–7128** • gay/ straight • full brkfst • natural hot-springs-fed whirlpools • smokefree • teens ok • $95-195

Neil Creek House B&B 341 Mowetza Dr **541/482–6443, 800/460–7860** • gay-friendly • full brkfst • swimming • smokefree • teens ok • $100-175

Pedigrift House B&B 407 Scenic Dr **541/482–1888, 800/262–4073** • gay-friendly • restored 1888 Queen Anne Victorian • full brkfst • $125

Rogues Inn Apartments 541/488-5162, 800/276-4837 • gay-friendly • apts • smokefree • kids ok • pets ok w/ deposit • $95-110

Cafes

Ashland Bakery/ Cafe 38 E Main **541/482-2117** • 7am-8:30pm • plenty veggie • wheelchair access • $5-8

Renaissance Chocolates 240 E Hersey #12 **541/488-8344** • 7am-5pm

Restaurants

Geppetto's 345 E Main **541/482-1138** • 8am-midnight • Italian • full bar • wheelchair access • $8-13

Greenleaf Restaurant 49 N Main St (on The Plaza) **541/482-2808** • 8am-8pm • Mediterranean/ Italian • creekside dining • beer/ wine

Bookstores

Bloomsbury Books 290 E Main St (btwn 1st & 2nd) **541/488-0029** • 8am-10pm, from 9am Sat, 10am-9pm Sun

Retail Shops

Travel Essentials 264-A E Main St **541/482-7383** • 10am-5:30pm, clsd Sun • luggage • guidebooks • maps • travel accessories

Astoria

Info Lines & Services

North Coast Pride Network Gay/ Lesbian Resource Center 10 6th St #209 **503/338-0161** • 3pm-5:30pm Tue & Th

Accommodations

Rosebriar Hotel 636 14th St **503/325-7427, 800/487-0224** • gay-friendly • upscale classic hotel • full brkfst • wheelchair access

Beaverton

Accommodations

The Yankee Tinker B&B 5480 SW 183rd Ave **503/649-0932, 800/846-5372** • gay-friendly • in suburban neighborhood • full brkfst

Restaurants

Swagat Indian Cuisine 4325 SW 109th Ave **503/626-3000** • lunch & dinner • beer/ wine

Bend

Info Lines & Services

Beyond the Closet 541/317-8966 • social/ support • newsletter

Gay/ Lesbian Information 541/388-2395 • sponsors socials & potlucks

Accommodations

Diamond Stone Guest Lodge & Gallery 16693 Sprague Loop, La Pine **541/536-6263, 800/600-6263** • gay-friendly • Western hotel-style B&B • full brkfst • kids ok • $80-120

Cafes

Cafe Paradiso 945 NW Bond St **541/385-5931** • 8am-11pm, till midnight wknds

Royal Blend 1075 NW Newport **541/383-0873** • 7am-6pm

Blue River

Accommodations

River's Edge Inn 91241 Blue River Rd **541/822-3258, 800/250-1812** • gay-friendly • 40 miles east of Eugene • full brkfst • gay-owned/ run • $85-125

Burns

Accommodations

Bontemps Motel 74 W Monroe **541/573-2037, 877/229-1394** • gay/ straight • smokefree rms available • gay-owned/ run

Corvallis

Info Lines & Services

After 8 Club 101 NW 23rd **541/752-8157** • 7pm 2nd Tue • lgbt educational & support group

LGBT Student Alliance 541/737-6360 • 7pm Mon at Women's Center

Bookstores

Book Bin 228 SW 3rd (btwn Madison & Jefferson) **541/752-0040** • 9am-9pm, from 10am Sat, noon-6pm Sun • also 'Monroe Ave Book Bin' • 2305 NW Monroe, 541/753-8398 • more text books

Grass Roots Bookstore 227 SW 2nd St (btwn Jefferson & Madison) **541/754-7668** • 9am-7pm, till 9pm Fri, till 5:30pm Sat, 11am-5pm Sun • music section • espresso bar • wheelchair access

Days Creek

Accommodations

Owl Farm 541/679-4655 (info line only) • women only • women's land open to visitors • camping sites available

Eugene

Info Lines & Services

Gay/ Lesbian AA 541/342-4113 • call for mtg schedule

LGBT Alliance 541/346-3360 • 9am-5pm (office) • various drop-in groups • social 4pm-6pm Th • wheelchair access

TLC (The Lesbian Connection) 2360 Fillmore **541/683-2793** • active lesbian social group

Women's Center University of Oregon **541/346-4095, 541/346-3327** • 8am-5pm wkdys (office) • some lesbian outreach

Bars

Neighbor's 1417 Villard St (at Franklin) **541/338-0334** • 11am-2:30am, from 2pm Sun • lesbians/ gay men • neighborhood bar • dancing/DJ • also restaurant

Restaurants

Keystone Cafe 395 W 5th (at Lawrence) **541/342-2075** • 7am-5pm • popular brkfst • plenty veggie

Entertainment & Recreation

Soromundi 541/688-6646 • lesbian chorus of Eugene

Bookstores

Hungry Head Bookstore 1212 Willamette (at 13th) **541/485-0888** • 10:30am-6pm, noon-5pm Sun • progressive/ alternative titles • some lesbigay titles

▲ **Mother Kali's Bookstore** 720 E 13th Ave (at Hilyard) **541/343-4864** • 10am-6pm, clsd Sun • lesbigay/ feminist & multi-racial sections • wheelchair access

Retail Shops

High Priestess Piercing 675 Lincoln St **541/342-6585** • piercing studio

Ruby Chasm 152 W 5th Ave #4 (btwn Olive & Charnelton) **541/344-4074** • 10am-6pm, noon-5pm Sun • goddess gifts • books • wheelchair access

Spiritual Groups

MCC 23rd & Harris (at 1st Congregational Church) **541/345-5963** • 4pm Sun

Erotica

Exclusively Adult 1166 S 'A' St, Springfield **541/726-6969** • 24hrs

Gaston

Accommodations

Art Springs 40789 SW Hummingbird Ln **503/985-9549** • women only • B&B, cabin & camping on 12 acres of women's land • hot tub • smokefree • chem-free • also retreats

Grants Pass

Accommodations

Womanshare 541/862-2807 • women only • cabin • campground • hot tub • $10-30 (sliding scale)

Lincoln City

Accommodations

Ocean Gardens Inn 2735 NW Inlet **541/994-5007, 800/866-9925** • gay-friendly • spectacular views of the ocean • hot tub • smokefree • teens ok • lesbian-owned/ run • $65-150

Restaurants

Over the Waves 2945 NW Jetty Ave **541/994-3877** • 8am-10pm, lounge open later wknds • $12-18

Road's End Dory Cove Logan Rd **541/994-5180** • 11:30am-8pm, till 9pm Fri-Sat • steak & seafood

Medford

Restaurants

Cadillac Cafe 207 W 8th St **541/857-9411** • 11am-3pm only

Retail Shops

McGee on Main 406 E Main St (at Riverside) **541/770-5591** • 10am-5:30pm, clsd Sun • women's clothing

Publications

Prizm 541/482-7989

Erotica

Castle Superstore 1113 Progress Wy (at Bittle) **541/608-9540** • 9am-1am

Newport

Accommodations

Cliff House B&B 541/563-2506 • gay-friendly • oceanfront • full brkfst • hot tub • smokefree • women-owned/ run • $120-245

Green Gables B&B 156 SW Coast St (at SW 2nd St) **541/265-9141, 800/515-9065** • gay-friendly • full brkfst • ocean view • jacuzzi • smokefree • kids 11+ ok • lesbian-owned/ run • $85-95

Restaurants

Mo's Annex 657 SW Bay Blvd **541/265-7512** • great chowder

Bookstores

Green Gables Bookstore 156 SW Coast St **541/265-9141** • 10am-5pm, clsd Tue-Wed • women's • also used/ children's books & women's music

Portland

see also Vancouver, Washington

Info Lines & Services

50+ Portland 503/281-4424, 503/331-0415 • 3rd Sat • social group for lesbians 50+

Asian/ Pacific Islander LGBT Info Hotline 503/232-6408 • educational/ social/ support group

Bisexual Community Forum 503/285-4848 • 7:30pm 2nd & 4th Wed • Utopia Coffeehouse at 3320 SE Belmont St

Cascade AIDS Project 620 SW 5th Ave #300 **503/223-5907, 800/777-2437 (Pacific NW only)** • provides a variety of non-medical services

Lesbian Community Project 1001 E Burnside **503/233-3913** • multicultural political & social events

Live & Let Live Club 2940-A SE Belmont St **503/238-6091** • call for mtg schedule

Love Makes a Family 503/228-3892 • many groups • call for locations

Northwest Gender Alliance 503/646-2802 • 3rd Tue & 2nd Sat • transgender support group • newsletter

Accommodations

Holladay House B&B 1735 NE Wasco St (btwn 7th & 9th) **503/282-3172** • gay-friendly • full brkfst • $45

Hotel Vintage Plaza 422 SW Broadway **503/228-1212, 800/243-0555** • popular • gay-friendly • wheelchair access • $150-250

MacMaster House 1041 SW Vista Ave (at Park Pl) **503/223-7362, 800/774-9523** • gay-friendly • historic mansion near the Rose Gardens • full brkfst • smokefree • $80-130

The Mark Spencer Hotel 409 SW Eleventh Ave (nr Stark) **503/224-3293, 800/548-3934** • gay-friendly • kitchens • kids ok • $79-129

Portland

Where the Girls Are: Snacking on granola while cycling (that's motorcycling) in the mountains, wearing boots and flannel. (Aw, hell, we don't know!) Lesbian Community Project tip: Try along SE Hawthorne Blvd. where some of the women's businesses are, or the NW section, 21st & 23rd Ave., for the more upscale lesbians.

Lesbigay Pride: June. 503/295-9788.

Annual Events: August - Annual Women's Softball 503/233-3913 (LCP).
June - The Gathering. Annual pagan camp in the Oregon Woods.
September - Northwest Women's Music Celebration.
October - Living in Leather 614/899-4406. National conference for the leather, SM & fetish communities.

City Info: 503/244-5794 ext. 5051.
Oregon Tourism Commission 800/547-7842, web: www.pova.com.

Attractions:
Microbreweries.
Mt. Hood Festival of Jazz.
Old Town.
Pioneer Courthouse Square.
Rose Festival.
Washington Park.

Best View: International Rose Test Gardens at Washington Park.

Weather: The wet and sometimes chilly winter rains give Portland its lush landscape that bursts into beautiful colors in the spring and fall. Summer brings sunnier days. (Temperatures can be in the 50°s one day and the 90°s the next.)

Transit: Radio Cab 503/227-1212.
Raz 503/684-3322.
Tri-Met System 503/233-3511.

Sullivan's Gulch B&B 1744 NE Clackamas St (at 17th) **503/331–1104** • lesbians/ gay men • decks • IGLTA • gay-owned/ run • $60-85

Bars

Bar of the Gods 4801 SE Hawthorne (at 48th Ave) **503/232–2037** • 5pm-2:30am • gay-friendly • neighborhood bar • beer/ wine • wheelchair access

Boxx's 1035 SW Stark (at SW 11th Ave) **503/226–4171** • 11:30am-2:30am, from 3pm wknds • mostly gay men • videos • wheelchair access • also 'Brig' from 9pm • dancing/DJ • also 'Red Cap Garage' restaurant • noon-2:30am

Candlelight Room 2032 SW 5th (at Lincoln) **503/222–3378** • 10am-2:30am, from 11am wknds • gay-friendly • live shows • food served

CC Slaughter's 219 NW Davis (at 3rd) **503/248–9135** • 11am-2:30am • popular • mostly gay men • dancing/DJ • country/ western Wed & Sun • videos • food served

Darcelle XV 208 NW 3rd Ave (at NW Davis St) **503/222–5338** • 5pm-11pm, till 2:30am Fri-Sat, clsd Sun-Tue • gay-friendly • live shows • food served • wheelchair access

Eagle PDX 1300 W Burnside (at 13th Ave) **503/241–0105** • 4pm-2:30am • mostly gay men • leather • videos

Egyptian Club 3701 SE Division (at SE 37th Ave) **503/236–8689** • 11:30am-2:30am, Sun brunch • popular • mostly women • dancing/DJ Fri-Sat • strippers Tue • food served • $5-12 • wheelchair access

Fox & Hound 217 NW 2nd Ave (btwn Everett & Davis) **503/243–5530** • 9:30am-2am, from 8am wknds • mostly gay men • also restaurant • brunch wknds • wheelchair access

Gail's Dirty Duck Tavern 439 NW 3rd (at Glisan) **503/224–8446** • 3pm-1:30am, from noon wknds • mostly gay men • neighborhood bar • leather • wheelchair access

Hideaway Pub 4229 SE 82nd Ave (at Holgate) **503/788–2213** • 11am-2:30am, till midnight Sun • gay-friendly • neighborhood bar • food served

Hobo's 120 NW 3rd Ave (btwn Davis & Couch) **503/224–3285** • 4pm-2am • gay-friendly • live shows • also restaurant • some veggie • wheelchair access • $5-20

Kokopeli's Choice 2845 SE Stark St (at SE 29th Ave) **503/236–4321** • 4pm-1am, 2pm-2:30am Fri-Sat • mostly women • dancing/DJ Fri-Sat • wheelchair access

Shanghai Tunnel 211 SW Ankeny St (at 2nd) **503/220–4001** • 4pm-2:30am, clsd Mon • gay-friendly • neighborhood bar • also restaurant

Silverado 1217 SW Stark St (btwn SW 11th & 12th Aves) **503/224–4493** • 9am-2:30am • popular • mostly gay men • dancing/DJ • live shows • also restaurant • wheelchair access

Starky's 2913 SE Stark St (at SE 29th Ave) **503/230–7980** • 11am-2am • popular • lesbians/ gay men • neighborhood bar • also restaurant • some veggie • patio • $10-20

Tiger Bar 317 NW Broadway (btwn Everett & Flanders) **503/222–7297** • 5pm-2:30am • gay-friendly • also Asian restaurant • wheelchair access

Nightclubs

Embers 110 NW Broadway (at NW Couch St) **503/222–3082** • 11am-2:30am • popular • mostly gay men • dancing/DJ • live shows • wheelchair access

La Luna 215 SE 9th Ave **503/241–5862** • 9pm-2am • gay-friendly • queer Mon • dancing/DJ • live shows • 18+

The Misfits 333 SW Park (btwn Oak & Stark) **503/242–2899, 503/286–1764 (EVENTS HOTLINE)** • 10pm-4am, till 2am Wed-Th, clsd Sun-Tue • popular • lesbians/ gay men • dancing/DJ • alcohol-free • drag Sat • 15+ (18+ Wed)

Panorama 341 SW 10th Ave (at Stark) **503/221–7262** • 9pm-4am Fri-Sat only • popular • gay-friendly • dancing/DJ • beer/ wine • wheelchair access

Cafes

Bread & Ink Cafe 3610 SE Hawthorne Blvd (at 36th) **503/239–4756** • 7am-9pm, till 10pm Fri-Sat, from 9am Sun (clsd btwn lunch & dinner) • popular • beer/ wine • wheelchair access

Cafe Lena 2239 SE Hawthorne Blvd (at SE 23rd) **503/238–7087** • 8am-midnight, clsd Mon • popular • live shows • wheelchair access

Coffee People 533 NW 23rd St (at Hoyt) **503/221–0235** • 6am-10pm, from 7am Sun • popular

Cup & Saucer Cafe 3566 SE Hawthorne Blvd (btwn 34th & 36th) **503/236–6001** • 7am-9pm • popular • full menu • smokefree

Portland

Sprawling along the Columbia River at the foot of Mount Hood, you'll find this city that's home to rainy days, roses, and the punk activist Riot Grrrls of 'zine & grunge fame. If you're searching for the proof that Portland is a lesbian-friendly city, look no further than the Portland Building. Atop the roof you'll find a statue of Portlandia, a city landmark and an amazon icon.

Nearby you can explore the Mount St. Helens National Volcanic Monument or the 5,000 acres of Macleay Park. And if you love jazz, head for the hills: the Mount Hood Festival of Jazz brings the best of the jazz world to town every August.

Lesbian life here focuses on the outdoors and cocooning at home with small groups of friends. To get in touch, pick up a recent copy of the statewide newspaper **Just Out,** call the **Lesbian Community Project,** or contact **Sisterspirit,** a women's spirituality resource.

Portland's bar scene for women has exploded in recent years: For a night of dancing, don't miss **Kokopeli's Choice.** For a nourishing meal, visit **Old Wives Tales** or the popular **Egyptian Club**, or enjoy the java and art at the smokefree **Cup & Saucer Cafe.**

Culturally minded visitors won't want to miss **In Other Words,** the only women's bookstore in town. They carry music along with a large selection of women's literature. **Powell's** is a new/used bookstore that's both legendary and huge, and we've heard that its lesbian/gay section is a good meeting place on weekend nights—there's even a little cafe. **It's My Pleasure** serves up erotica for women, and **In Her Image Gallery** shows women's art.

Marco's Cafe & Espresso Bar 7910 SW 35th (at Multnomah Blvd), Multnomah **503/245-0199** • 7am-9:30pm, from 8am wknds, till 2pm Sun

Sacred Grounds Coffee House 3106 NE 64th St (at Sandy Blvd) **503/493-4374** • 11am-7pm, till 9pm Fri-Sat, till 6pm Sun, from 10am wknds

Saucebox 214 SW Broadway (at Stark) **503/241-3393** • 11:30am-1:30pm & 6pm-10pm, clsd Sun-Mon • lesbians/ gay men • multi-ethnic cafe • plenty veggie • full bar • wheelchair access

Restaurants

The Adobe Rose 1634 SE Bybee Blvd (at Milwaukee) **503/235-9114** • 5pm-9pm, till 10pm Fri-Sat, clsd Sun-Mon • New Mexican • some veggie • beer/ wine • $5-7

Assaggio 7742 SE 13th (at Lambert) **503/232-6151** • 5pm-9:30pm, clsd Sun-Mon • Italian • plenty veggie • wine bar

Bastas Trattoria 410 NW 21st (at Flanders) **503/274-1572** • lunch Mon-Fri & dinner nightly • northern Italian • some veggie • full bar • $7-12

Bijou Cafe 132 SW 3rd Ave (at Pine St) **503/222-3187** • 7am-2pm, from 8am wknds, also 6pm-10pm Tue-Sat • popular • plenty veggie • $4-7

Brasserie Montmartre 626 SW Park (at Alder) **503/224-5552** • lunch & dinner, Sun brunch • bistro • live jazz • full bar

Cafe des Amis 1987 NW Kearney (at 20th) **503/295-6487** • 5:30pm-10pm, clsd Sun • French • full bar • wheelchair access • $12-24

Caffe Fresco 2387 NW Thurman (at 24th) **503/243-3247** • 7am-3pm, till 2pm Sun • Italian

Caribou Cafe & Bar 503 W Burnside (at 5th) **503/227-0245** • noon-1am, from 5pm Sat • diner • some veggie • full bar • wheelchair access • $4-9

Daydream Cafe 1740 SE Hawthorne (at 17th) **503/233-4244** • 7am-5pm • popular • gay-owned/ run

Esparza's Tex-Mex Cafe 2725 SE Ankeny St (at 28th) **503/234-7909** • 11:30am-10pm, clsd Sun-Mon • popular

Fish Grotto 1035 SW Stark (at SW 11th Ave, at 'Boxx's') **503/226-4171** • 5pm-close, clsd Mon • popular • some veggie • full bar • $8-24

Genoa 2832 SE Belmont (at 29th) **503/238-1464** • by reservation only • clsd Sun • Italian • beer/ wine • 7-course prix-fixe • $55

Gypsy Cafe 625 NW 21st (btwn Hoyt & Irving) **503/796-1859** • 11:30am-midnight, from 9am wknds • some veggie • full bar

Hamburger Mary's 239 SW Broadway Dr (at Oak St) **503/223-0900** • 7am-2:30am • popular • full bar • $7-11

Hobo's 120 NW 3rd Ave (btwn Davis & Couch) **503/224-3285** • 4pm-2am • popular • live shows • wheelchair access

Indigine 3725 SE Division St **503/238-1470** • dinner Tue-Sun, brunch 9am-2pm Sun, clsd Mon • à la carte Tue-Th • 3-course dinner Fri • East Indian feast Sat

L'Auberge 2601 NW Vaughn St **503/223-3302** • 5:30pm-9pm, till 10pm Fri-Sat, clsd Sun • French • full bar • also bistro • 5pm-midnight, till 1am Fri-Sat, till 10pm Sun

Majas Taqueria 1000 SW Morrison **503/226-1946** • 10am-10pm, clsd Sun

Old Wives Tales 1300 E Burnside St (at 13th) **503/238-0470** • 8am-9pm, till 10pm Fri-Sat • multi-ethnic vegetarian

The Original Pancake House 8600 SW Barbur Blvd **503/246-9007** • great brkfst

Papa Haydn 701 NW 23rd Ave (at Irving) **503/228-7317** • lunch & dinner • bistro • some veggie • full bar

Pizzacato 505 NW 23rd (at Glisan) **503/242-0023** • 11:30am-9pm, till 10pm Fri-Sat • plenty veggie

Santa Fe Taqueria 831 NW 23rd (at Kearney) **503/220-0406** • 11am-10pm, till 11pm Fri-Sat • patio • full bar (open later)

Starky's 2913 SE Stark St **503/230-7980** • 11am-2pm & 5:30pm-9:30pm, from 9:30am Sun • also full bar till 2:30am • lesbians/ gay men

Vista Spring Cafe 2440 SW Vista (at Spring) **503/222-2811** • 11am-10pm, from noon wknds, till 9pm Sun • pasta & pizza • beer/ wine

Wildwood 1221 NW 21st Ave (at Overton) **503/248-9663** • 11am-9pm (reservations advised) • popular • full bar

Zefiro 500 NW 21st (at Glisan) **503/226-3394** • lunch & dinner, clsd Sun • Mediterranean/ Southeast Asian • some veggie • full bar

Bookstores

Countermedia 927 SW Oak (btwn 9th & 10th) **503/226-8141** • 11am-7pm, noon-6pm Sun • alternative comics • vintage gay books/ periodicals

In Other Words 3734 SE Hawthorne Blvd (at 37th) **503/232-6003** • 10am-9pm, 11am-6pm Sun • women's books • music • resource center • wheelchair access

Laughing Horse Bookstore 3652 SE Division (at 37th) **503/236-2893** • 11am-7pm, clsd Sun • alternative/ progressive • wheelchair access

Looking Glass Bookstore 318 SW Taylor (btwn 3rd & 4th) **503/227-4760** • 9am-6pm, from 10am Sat, clsd Sun • general • some lesbigay titles

Powell's Books 1005 W Burnside St (at 10th) **503/228-4651, 800/878-7323** • 9am-11pm • new & used books • cafe • wheelchair access

Twenty-Third Ave Books 1015 NW 23rd Ave (at Lovejoy) **503/224-5097** • 9:30am-9pm, from 10am Sat, 11am-7pm Sun • general • lesbigay section • wheelchair access

Retail Shops

In Her Image Gallery 3208 SE Hawthorne (at 32nd) **503/231-3726** • 10am-6pm, till 5pm wknds, clsd Mon-Tue

It's My Pleasure 3106 NE 64th Ave (at Sandy Blvd) **503/280-8080** • 11am-7pm, till 9pm Fri-Sat, noon-6pm Sun

The Jellybean 721 SW 10th Ave (at Morrison) **503/222-5888** • 10am-6pm, noon-5pm Sun • cards • T-shirts • gifts • wheelchair access

Presents of Mind 3633 SE Hawthorne (at 37th Ave) **503/230-7740** • 10am-7pm, 11am-5:30pm Sun • jewelry • cards • unique toys • wheelchair access

Publications

Just Out 503/236-1252 • lesbigay newspaper w/ extensive resource directory

Qink Northwest Magazine 206/419-7009 • news & entertainment magazine for Seattle, Portland & Vancouver

Spiritual Groups

Congregation Neve Shalom 503/246-8831 • 8:15pm Fri & 9am Sat • conservative synagogue w/ lesbigay outreach • call for directions

MCC Portland 2400 NE Broadway (at 24th Ave) **503/281-8868** • 9am & 11am Sun • wheelchair access

Pagan Info Line 503/650-7045 • also publishes 'Open Ways' newsletter

Sisterspirit 503/736-3297 • celebration of women sharing spirituality • wheelchair access

St Stephen's Episcopal Church 1432 SW 13th Ave (at Clay) **503/223-6424** • 7:45am & 10am Sun, 12:10pm Wed

Gyms & Health Clubs

Inner City Hot Tubs 2927 NE Everett St (btwn 29th & 30th) **503/238-1065** • 10am-11pm, 1pm-10pm Sun • gay-friendly • wellness center • reservations required

Princeton Athletic Club 614 SW 11th Ave (at Alder) **503/222-2639** • gay-friendly

Erotica

The Crimson Phoenix 1876 SW 5th Ave (btwn Harrison & Hall) **503/228-0129** • 11am-9pm, till 11pm Fri-Sat • 'sexuality bookstore for lovers' • wheelchair access

Fantasy for Adults 3137 NE Sandy Blvd (nr NE 39th) **503/239-6969** • 24hrs

Spartacus Leathers 302 SW 12th Ave (at Burnside) **503/224-2604**

Richland

Restaurants

Longbranch Grille 112 Main St **541/893-6126, 888/265-0015** • 4pm-10pm, clsd Sun-Mon • steak & seafood

Rogue River

Accommodations

Whispering Pines B&B/ Retreat 9188 W Evans Creek Rd **541/582-1757, 800/788-1757** • popular • lesbians/ gay men • full brkfst • hot tub • swimming • shared baths • smokefree • $60-75

Roseburg

Info Lines & Services

Gay/ Lesbian Switchboard 541/672-4126 • 24hrs • publishes newsletter

Salem

Accommodations

Brightridge Farm B&B 18575 SW Brightridge Rd, Sheridan **503/843-5230** • gay-friendly • in the rural heart of Oregon wine country • full brkfst

Bars

The Right Side Showbar 300 Liberty St SE **503/365-9722** • 11am-2am • lesbians/ gay men • more men Tue • live shows • wheelchair access

Nightclubs

300 Club 300 Liberty St SE **503/365-9721** • 11am-2am • gay/ straight • dancing/DJ • live shows • young crowd • wheelchair access

Restaurants

Off Center Cafe 1741 Center St NE (at 17th) **503/363-9245** • 7am-2:30pm, from 8am wknds, 6pm-9pm Th-Sat • popular brkfst • some veggie • wheelchair access • $7-12

Bookstores

Rosebud & Fish 524 State St (at High) **503/399-9960** • 10am-7pm, noon-5pm Sun • alternative bookstore

Spiritual Groups

Sweet Spirit MCC 3322 Lancaster Dr NE (at Silverton Rd in back room of Beauty College) **503/363-6618** • 11am Sun

Unitarian Universalist Congregation of Salem 5090 Center St NE **503/364-0932** • 10:30am Sun

Sheridan

Accommodations

Middle Creek Run 25400 Harmony Rd **503/843-7606, 800/843-7606** • gay-friendly • full brkfst • hot tub • swimming • some shared baths • gay-owned/ run • $75-125

Tiller

Accommodations

Kalles Family RV Ranch 233 Jackson Creek Rd **541/825-3271** • lesbians/ gay men • camping sites • RV hookups • btwn Medford & Roseburg • kids/ pets ok • lesbian-owned/ run • $10 (incl electric)

Yachats

Accommodations

Morningstar Gallery & B&B 95668 Hwy 101 S **541/547-4412** • mostly women • oceanfront • full brkfst • hot tub • smokefree • women-owned/ run • $85-150

Ocean Odyssey 541/547-3637, 800/800-1915 • gay-friendly • vacation rental homes in Yachats & Waldport • women-owned/ run • $75-125

The Oregon House 94288 Hwy 101 **541/547-3329** • gay-friendly • smokefree • wheelchair access • $55-135

See Vue Motel 95590 Hwy 101 S **541/547-3227** • gay-friendly • kids/ pets ok • wheelchair access • lesbian-owned • $35-65

PENNSYLVANIA

Statewide

Publications

SPOTS 570/698-7725 • monthly newspaper for northeastern PA & southern NY

Allentown

see also Bethlehem

Bars

Candida's 247 N 12th St **610/434-3071** • 2am-2pm • lesbians/ gay men • neighborhood bar • food served • karaoke

Moose Lounge/ Stonewall 28-30 N 10th St (at Hamilton) **610/432-0706** • 4pm-2am • popular • lesbians/ gay men • dancing/DJ • live shows • videos • food served • karaoke

Erotica

Adult World 80 S West End Blvd/ Rte 309, Quakerstown **215/538-1522**

Altoona

Nightclubs

Escapade 2523 Union Ave, Rte 36 **814/946-8195** • 8pm-2am • lesbians/ gay men • dancing/DJ • also restaurant • gay-owned/ run

Bethlehem

Info Lines & Services

Lehigh Valley Lesbians 424 Center St (at Unitarian Church) **610/954-7775** • 7pm 3rd Th

Nightclubs

Diamonz 1913 W Broad St (at Pennsylvania Ave) **610/865-1028** • 4pm-2am, from 3pm wknds • mostly women • dancing/DJ • live shows • also restaurant (clsd Tue) • fine dining • some veggie • wheelchair access • $7-15

Spiritual Groups

MCC of the Lehigh Valley 424 Center St (at Unitarian Church) **610/954-7775** • 6pm Sun

Bridgeport

Nightclubs

The Lark 302 Dekalb St/ Rte 202 N **610/275-8136** • 8pm-2am, from 4pm Sun (dinner served) • mostly gay men • dancing/DJ • live shows

Bristol

Erotica

Bristol News World 576 Bristol Pike/ Rte 13 N **215/785-4770** • 24hrs

Conshohoken

Nightclubs

Rio 225 Washington St (at Ash) **610/941-9911** • 5pm-2am Wed-Sat • gay-friendly • dancing/DJ • patio

East Stroudsburg

Accommodations

Rainbow Mtn Resort & Restaurant **570/223-8484** • popular • lesbians/ gay men • B&B w/ deluxe suites • cabins (seasonal) • swimming • IGLTA • $217-400 • also restaurant • full bar • dancing/DJ Fri-Sat • piano bar • transgender-friendly

Easton

Bars

Millennium Club 411 Northampton St (at 4th) **610/252-4918, 610/250-8646** • gay/ straight • neighborhood bar • dancing/DJ • also restaurant

Edinboro

Info Lines & Services

Identity 814/732-2000 • student group

Erie

Info Lines & Services

Erie Gay News 814/456-9833 • excellent resource • newsletter

Trigon: LGBT Coalition 814/898-6164 • student group

Womynspace 7180 New Perry Hwy (at Unitarian Universalist Church) **814/454-2713** • 7:30pm 1st Sat • alcohol- & smokefree women's coffeehouse

Accommodations

The Castle Guest House 231 W 21st St **814/454-6465** • lesbians/ gay men • smokefree • $50-75

Nightclubs

The Village 133 W 18th St (at Peach) **814/452-0125** • 8pm-2am • lesbians/ gay men • dancing/DJ • live shows • karaoke • wheelchair access

The Zone 1711 State St **814/459-1711** • 4pm-2am, clsd Sun • mostly gay men • dancing/DJ • piano bar • food served

Cafes

Aroma's Coffeehouse 2164 W 8th St **814/456-5282** • 7am-11pm, 9am-1am Sat, till 4pm Sun • light fare • smokefree

Cup-A-Ccinos Coffeehouse 18 N Park Row (nr Erie County Courthouse) **814/456-1151** • 7:30am-10pm, till midnight Th-Sat, from 9am Sat, till 8pm Sun • live shows • wheelchair access

Restaurants

Pie in the Sky Cafe 463 W 8th St (at Walnut) **814/459-8638** • 7:30am-2pm, dinner from 5pm Fri-Sat, clsd Sun • BYOB • wheelchair access

Tapas 17 W 9th St **814/454-8797** • 4pm-9pm, till 11pm Th-Sat, clsd Sun

Publications

Gay People's Chronicle 216/631-8646, 800/426-5947 • Cleveland lesbigay newspaper w/ extensive listings

Spiritual Groups

Temple Anshe Hesed 930 Liberty St **814/454-2426** • 8pm Fri

Unitarian Universalist Congregation of Erie 7180 New Perry Hwy **814/864-9300** • 10:30am Sun

Gettysburg

Accommodations

Maplecrest Farm 749 Dicks Dam Rd **717/624-3339** • gay/ straight • swimming • gay-owned/ run • $95-325

Greensburg

Nightclubs

RK's Safari Lounge 108 W Pittsburgh St (at Pennsylvania Ave) **724/837-6614** • 9pm-2am, clsd Sun • popular • mostly gay men • dancing/DJ • patio • wheelchair access

Harrisburg

Info Lines & Services

Gay/ Lesbian Switchboard 717/234-0328 • 6pm-10pm Mon-Fri

Bars

704 Strawberry 704 N 3rd St **717/234-4228** • 2pm-2am • mostly gay men • neighborhood bar • videos • wheelchair access

B-tls 891 Eisenhower Blvd **717/939-1123** • 8pm-2am, clsd Sun-Wed • mostly women • dancing/DJ • food served • videos • pool table • women-owned/ run

Mary's Brownstone Cafe 412 Forster St **717/234-7009** • 4pm-2am, clsd Sun • lesbians/ gay men • dancing/DJ • country/ western • wheelchair access

Neptune's Lounge/ Paper Moon 268 North St (at 3rd) **717/233-3078, 717/233-0581** • 4pm-2am, from 2pm Sun • popular • mostly gay men • neighborhood bar • dinner 6pm-10pm, Sun brunch

Nightclubs

Stallions 706 N 3rd St (enter rear) **717/233-4681** • 4pm-2am • popular • mostly gay men • separate women's bar from 9pm Fri-Sat • dancing/DJ • karaoke • wheelchair access

Restaurants

Colonnade 300 N 2nd St (at Pine) **717/234-8740** • 7am-8:30pm, clsd Sun • seafood • full bar • wheelchair access • $8-15

Spiritual Groups

MCC of the Spirit 2973 Jefferson St (nr Uptown Shopping Plaza) **717/236-7387** • 10:30am & 7pm Sun

Johnstown

Nightclubs

Casanova 5977 Somerset Pike/ Rte 985, Boswell **814/629-9911** • 6pm-2am • lesbians/ gay men • dancing/DJ • food served

Lucille's 520 Washington St (nr Central Park) **814/539-4448** • 6pm-2am, clsd Sun-Mon • lesbians/ gay men • dancing/DJ • live shows

Kutztown

Accommodations

Grim's Manor B&B 10 Kern Rd **610/683-7089** • lesbians/ gay men • 200 yr old stone farmhouse on 5 acres • full brkfst • older kids ok • gay-owned/ run • $65-70

Lancaster

Accommodations

The Noble House B&B 113 W Market St, Marietta **717/426-4389, 888/277-6426** • gay/ straight • full brkfst • smokefree • $90-115

Bars

Tally Ho 201 W Orange (at Water) **717/299-0661** • 6pm-2am, from 8pm Sun • popular • lesbians/ gay men • dancing/DJ • younger crowd

Nightclubs

Sundown Lounge 429 N Mulberry St (at James) **717/392-2737** • 8pm-2am, from 3pm Fri-Sat, clsd Sun • mostly women • dancing/DJ

Restaurants

Loft above 'Tally Ho' bar **717/299-0661** • lunch Mon-Fri, dinner Mon-Sat • French • $15-25

Bookstores

Borders Bookshop 940 Plaza Blvd (at Harrisburg Pike) **717/293-8022** • 9am-11pm, till 9pm Sun • lesbigay section

Spiritual Groups

MCC Vision of Hope 130 E Main St, Mountville **717/285-9070** • 10:30am & 7pm Sun

Malvern

Accommodations

Pickering Bend B&B 656 Church Rd **610/933-0183** • gay/ straight • built in 1790 • private suite • kitchen • fireplaces • kids/ pets ok • gay-owned/ run • $90-115

Manheim

Bars

Cellar Bar 168 S Main St (below 'The Attic') **717/665-1960** • 6pm-2am • lesbians/ gay men • restaurant upstairs

Monroeville

Erotica

Monroeville News 2735 Stroschein Rd (off Rte 22) **412/372-5477** • 24hrs

Montgomeryville

Erotica

Adult World Book Store Rtes 202 & 309 **215/362-9560**

Mt Pleasant

Bars

Yuppie's 241 E Main St **724/547-0430** • 9pm-2am, from 8pm Fri-Sat, clsd Sun • lesbians/ gay men • neighborhood bar • food served

New Hope

see also Lambertville, New Jersey

INFO LINES & SERVICES

AA Gay/ Lesbian 215/574-6900 (AA#)

ACCOMMODATIONS

The Fox & Hound B&B 246 West Bridge St **215/862-5082, 800/862-5082** • gay-friendly • 1850s stone manor • gay-owned/ run • $65+

The Lexington House 6171 Upper York Rd **215/794-0811** • lesbians/ gay men • 1749 country home • full brkfst • swimming • gay-owned/ run • $100-175

The Raven 385 West Bridge St **215/862-2081** • mostly gay men • motel • swimming • $81-106 • also restaurant

▲ **The Victorian Peacock B&B** 309 E Dark Hollow Rd, Pipersville **215/766-1356** • gay/ straight • swimming • spa • smokefree • women-owned/ run • $65-145

York Street House B&B 42 York St, Lambertville, NJ **609/397-3007** • gay-friendly • 1909 Manor house • smokefree • IGLTA • lesbian-owned/ run • $95-169

BARS

The Raven Bar & Restaurant at 'The Raven' accommodations **215/862-2081** • 11am-2am • lesbians/ gay men

NIGHTCLUBS

The Cartwheel 437 Old York Rd/ US 202 **215/862-0880** • 5pm-2am • popular • lesbians/ gay men • dancing/DJ • live shows • piano bar • also restaurant • wheelchair access • $6-18

Ladies 2000 609/784-8341 • scheduled parties for women by women • call for times & locations

RESTAURANTS

Country Host 463 Old York Rd/ Rte 202 **215/862-5575** • 7am-10pm • full bar • wheelchair access • $7-12

Havana 105 S Main St **215/862-9897** • 11am-midnight, bar till 2am • some veggie • live shows • $9-16

Karla's 5 W Mechanic St **215/862-2612** • lunch & dinner, late night brkfst Fri-Sat • Mediterranean • some veggie • full bar • $15-25

Mother's 34 N Main St **215/862-5270** • 9am-10pm • some veggie • $10-20

Odette's South River Rd **215/862-3000** • 11am-10pm, piano bar & cabaret till 1am • some veggie • wheelchair access • $15-25

Wildflowers 8 W Mechanic St **215/862-2241** • (seasonal) noon-10pm, till 11pm Fri-Sat • some veggie • BYOB • outdoor dining • $8-15

Bookstores

Book Gallery 19 W Mechanic St **215/862-5110** • 11am-7pm (call for Feb-May hours) • feminist/ lesbian

Retail Shops

Bucks County Video & CD Exchange 415-C York Rd **215/862-0919** • 10am-10pm • gay-themed & adult videos • gay-owned/ run

Erotica

Grownups 2 E Mechanic St (at Main) **215/862-9304** • 11am-7pm, till 11pm Fri-Sat

Le Chateau Exotique 31-A W Mechanic St **215/862-3810** • fetishwear

New Kensington

Bars

Zebra Lounge 910 Constitution Blvd (at 9th) **724/339-0298** • 4pm-2am, from 1pm Sat, clsd Sun • lesbians/ gay men • dancing/DJ

New Milford

Accommodations

Oneida Camp & Lodge **570/465-7011** • mostly gay men • oldest gay-owned/ operated campground dedicated to the lesbigay community • swimming • nudity • seasonal

Philadelphia

Info Lines & Services

AA Gay/ Lesbian **215/574-6900** • call for mtg schedule

Penn Women's Center 3643 Locust Walk **215/898-8611**

Philadelphia Convention & Visitors Bureau 16th St & JFK Blvd **215/636-4400, 800/225-5745** • publishes 'Philadelphia Gay & Lesbian Travel News' • IGLTA

Sisterspace of the Delaware Valley **215/546-4890** • sponsors 'Sisterspace Pocono Weekend' & other events • newsletter

Unity 1207 Chestnut St **215/851-1912** • 9am-5:30pm Mon-Fri, clsd wknds • lgbt support/ social services

William Way GLBT Commmunity Center 1315 Spruce St **215/732-2220** • noon-9pm Mon-Th, special events Fri, clsd wknds

Women in Transition Hotline **215/751-1111** • 4:30pm-8pm Tue

Accommodations

▲ **The Alexander Inn** 301 S 12th St (at Spruce) **215/923-3535, 877/253-9466** • gay/ straight • gym • wheelchair access • gay-owned/ run • $89-149

Antique Row B&B 341 S 12th St (at Pine) **215/592-7802** • gay-friendly • 1820s townhouse in heart of gay community • full brkfst • $65-100

Doubletree Hotel 237 S Broad St (at Locust) **215/893-1659, 800/222-8733** • gay-friendly

Embassy Suites Center City 1776 Ben Franklin Pkwy (at 18th) **215/561-1776, 800/362-2779** • gay-friendly • IGLTA

Gaskill House 312 Gaskill St (btwn 3rd & 4th) **215/413-0669** • gay/ straight • on Society Hill • full brkfst • smokefree • $125+

Glen Isle Farm 30 miles out of town, in Downingtown **610/269-9100, 800/269-1730** • gay-friendly • full brfkst • smokefree • older kids ok (call first)

Latham Hotel 135 S 17th St (at Walnut) **215/563-7474, 800/528-4261** • gay-friendly

Rittenhouse Hotel 210 W Rittenhouse Sq (at 19th) **215/546-9000, 800/635-1042** • gay-friendly • food served • from $195

Spring Garden Manor 2025 Spring Garden St (at 20th) **215/567-2484** • gay/ straight • located in city center near museums • gay-owned/ run • $119-139

Ten Eleven Clinton B&B 1011 Clinton St (at 10th) **215/923-8144** • gay-friendly • suites • quiet retreat in the heart of the city • $125-200

Walnut Street Inn 1208 Walnut St (btwn 12th & 13th) **215/546-7000, 800/887-1776** • gay-friendly • kids ok • IGLTA • $95-145

Bars

247 Bar 247 S 17th St (at Academy) **215/545-9779** • noon-2am • popular • mostly gay men • live shows • videos • also restaurant

Bonaparte 260 S Broad St (at Spruce) **215/735-2800** • 5pm-2am, clsd Mon • fine dining & cabaret

CR Bar 6405 Market St (at Park Ave), Upper Darby **610/734-1130, 610/352-9840** • 8pm-2am, clsd Sun • mostly gay men • neighborhood bar

Where the Girls Are: Partying downtown near 12th St., south of Market.

Lesbigay Pride: June. 215/875-9288.

Annual Events: April/May - PrideFest America Philadelphia 215/732-3378. Weekend of gay/lesbian film, performances, literature, sports, seminars, parties & more.
June - Womon-gathering 609/694-2037. Women's spirituality fest.

City Info: 215/636-1666.

Attractions: Academy of Natural Sciences 215/299-1000.
African American Museum 215/574-0380.
Betsy Ross House 215/627-5343.
Independence Hall.
Liberty Bell Pavilion.
National Museum Of American Jewish History 215/923-3811.
Norman Rockwell Museum 215/922-4345.
Philadelphia Museum of Art 215/763-8100.
Rodin Museum 215/763-8100.

Best View: Top of Center Square, 16th & Market.

Weather: Winter temperatures hover in the 20°s. Summers are humid with temperatures in the 80°s and 90°s.

Transit: Quaker City Cab 215/728-8000.
Transit Authority (SEPTA) 215/580-7800.

Philadelphia

Key West 207–209 S Juniper (btwn Walnut & Locust) **215/545-1578** • 4pm-2am, from 2pm Sun • lesbians/ gay men • dancing/DJ • live shows • piano bar • wheelchair access

The Khyber 56 S 2nd St (at Market & Chestnut) **215/238-5888** • gay-friendly • live shows • also restaurant (lunch only)

Love Lounge 232 South St (btwn 2nd & 3rd) **215/922-0499** • 10pm-close Fri-Sat only • gay/ straight

Port Blue 2552 E Allegheny Ave (at Belgrade), Port Richmond **215/425-4699** • 5pm-2am, clsd Sun-Mon • gay-friendly • neighborhood bar

Tavern on Camac 243 S Camac St (at Spruce) **215/545-0900** • noon-2am • lesbians/ gay men • dancing/DJ wknds • piano bar • food served

The Westbury 261 S 13th (at Spruce) **215/546-5170** • 10am-2am, dinner till 10pm, till 11pm wknds • mostly gay men • neighborhood bar • wheelchair access

Wilhelmina's 305 S 11th St (btwn Spruce & Pine) **215/829-9151** • open Wed-Sun • gay-friendly • dancing/DJ • drag & cabaret shows

Woody's 202 S 13th St (at Walnut) **215/545-1893** • 11am-2am • popular • mostly gay men • dancing/DJ • country/ western • dance lessons • 18+ Wed • videos Mon • cover charge some nights • food served • wheelchair access

Nightclubs

2-4 Club 1221 St James St (off 13th & Locust) **215/735-5772** • midnight-close Mon-Th, call for wknd hours • mostly gay men • dancing/DJ • private club • cover charge

Philadelphia

Though it's packed with sites of rich historical value, don't miss out on Philadelphia's multicultural present. To get a feel for this city, browse the Reading Terminal Market, a quaint old farmer's market preserved within the new Convention Center. Here, smalltime grocers and farmers of many cultures sell their fresh food.

A vital element in many of these cultures is the growing lesbian community. To connect with the scene, call the **William Way GLBT Community Center**; check out **Sisters**, a women's dance bar; or call **Ladies 2000** to find out about their next women's party.

And don't even think of leaving town before you visit **Giovanni's Room,** Philadelphia's legendary lesbian/gay bookstore. Here you can pick up the latest lesbian bestseller, the love of your life, or copies of the **Philadelphia Gay News, Labyrinth** women's paper, and **Au Courant**.

Bike Stop 204–206 S Quince St (at St James) **215/627–1662** • 4pm-2am, from 2pm wknds • popular • mostly gay men • 4 flrs • dancing/DJ • leather (very leather-women-friendly) • live bands Sun

Fluid 613 S 4th St (at South) **215/629–3686** • 9pm-2am • gay-friendly • more gay Sun • dancing/DJ • drag shows • cover charge

Ian Productions 215/732–6047 • weekly entertainment • mostly gay men • dancing/DJ • mostly African-American • call for info

Ladies 2000 609/784–8341 • scheduled parties for women by women • call for times & locations

Milborn Social Club upstairs at 'CR Bar' **610/734–1130** • midnight-close Fri-Sat, 4pm-2am Sun • mostly gay men • dancing/DJ • private club

Palmer Social Club 601 Spring Garden St (at 6th) **215/925–5000** • 11pm-3am, from midnight Wed & Sun, clsd Mon-Tue • gay-friendly • dancing/DJ • 3 flrs • private club

Shampoo 417 N 8th St (at Willow) **215/922–7500** • 9pm-2am, clsd Tue-Wed • gay-friendly • more gay Fri • dancing/DJ • alternative

▲ **Sisters** 1320 Chancellor St (at Juniper) **215/735–0735** • 5pm-2am • mostly women • dancing/DJ • live shows • karaoke • also restaurant • dinner Wed-Sun • $9 & less • wheelchair access

Upstairs at Frangelica 200 S 12th St (at Walnut) **215/731–9930** • gay/ straight • cabaret theater & restaurant • shows Fri-Mon

Cafes

10th Street Pour House 262 S 10th St (at Spruce) **215/922–5626** • 7:30am-3pm, from 8:30am wknds

Cheap Art Cafe 260 S 12th St (btwn Locust & Spruce) **215/735–6650** • 24hrs

Millennium Coffee 212 S 12th St (btwn Locust & Spruce) **215/731–9798** • open till midnight

Rhino Coffee Roastery & Cafe 212 South St (at 2nd) **215/923–2630** • 7am-midnight, from 8:30am wknds

Restaurants

The Adobe Cafe 4550 Mitchell St (at Greenleaf), Roxborough **215/483–3947** • lunch & dinner, till 11pm Fri-Sat

Astral Plane 1708 Lombard St (btwn 17th & 18th) **215/546-6230** • lunch & dinner • some veggie • full bar • $10-20

Backstage Bar & Restaurant 614 S 4th St (at South) **215/627-9887** • 4pm-2am, dinner 6pm-10pm, Sun brunch • $10-20

Fifth Street Cafe 517 S 5th St (at Gaskill) **215/925-3500** • 4pm-11pm, 11am-midnight wknds • BYOB

Harmony Vegetarian 135 N 9th St (at Cherry) **215/627-4520** • 11am-10pm, till midnight Fri-Sat

The Inn Philadelphia 251 S Camac St (btwn Locust & Spruce) **215/732-2339** • 4:30pm-10pm, till 9pm Sun, clsd Mon • some veggie • full bar

Judy's Cafe 627 S 3rd St (at Bainbridge) **215/928-1968** • 5:30pm-midnight, Sun brunch from 10:30am • full bar • women-owned/ run • $9-17

Latimer's Deli 255 S 1st St **215/545-9244** • 9am-9pm, till 11pm Fri • Jewish deli

Liberties 705 N 2nd St (at Fairmount) **215/238-0660** • lunch & dinner, Sun brunch • full bar • live jazz wknds • $10-16

Mont Serrat 623 South St (at 6th) **215/627-4224** • noon-midnight • healthy American • some veggie • full bar • $6-15

My Thai 2200 South St (at 22nd) **215/985-1878** • 5pm-10pm, till 11pm Fri-Sat

Palladium/ Gold Standard 3601 Locust Walk (at 36th) **215/387-3463** • lunch & dinner, bar till 12:30am

Roosevelt's Pub 2222 Walnut (at 23rd) **215/636-9722** • lunch & dinner • some veggie • full bar • $5-12

Savoy Restaurant 232 S 11th St (at Locust) **215/923-2348** • 24hrs • popular after-hours • $5-7

Shing Kee 52 N 9th St **215/829-8983** • lunch & dinner • BYOB • gay-owned/ run

Striped Bass 1500 Walnut St (at 15th) **215/732-4444** • lunch, dinner & Sun brunch • upscale dining

Waldorf Cafe 20th & Lombard Sts **215/985-1836** • dinner, clsd Mon • some veggie • full bar • wheelchair access • $12-18

White Dog Cafe 3420 Sansom St (at Walnut) **215/386-9224** • lunch & dinner • full bar • $7-18

Entertainment & Recreation

'Q Zine' WXPN–FM 88.5 **215/898–6677** • 10pm Sun • lesbigay radio

The Walt Whitman House 328 Mickle Blvd (btwn S 3rd & S 4th Sts), Camden, NJ **609/964–5383** • the last home of America's great & controversial poet, just across the Delaware River

Bookstores

Afterwords 218 S 12th St (btwn Locust & Walnut) **215/735–2393** • 11am-10pm, till midnight Fri-Sat

Giovanni's Room 345 S 12th St (at Pine) **215/923–2960** • call for hours, open daily • popular • lesbigay/ feminist bookstore

Retail Shops

Infinite Body Piercing 626 S 4th St (at South) **215/923–7335**

Thrift for AIDS 633 South St (at 6th) **215/592–9014** • noon-9pm, till 7pm Sun

Travelers Emporium 210 S 17th St (at Walnut) **215/546–2021** • 10am-6pm, clsd Sun

Publications

▲ **Au Courant 215/790–1179** • lesbigay newspaper

Greater Philadelphia Women's Yellow Pages 610/446–4747

▲ **Labyrinth 215/546–6686** • women's newspaper

PGN (Philadelphia Gay News) 215/625–8501 • lesbigay newspaper

Spiritual Groups

Beth Ahavah 8 Letitia St (btwn Market & Chestnut) **215/923–2003** • 8pm 1st, 3rd & 5th Fri

Christ Episcopal Church 2nd above Market (at Church) **215/922–1695** • 9am & 11am Sun

Dignity 330 S 13th St (btwn Spruce & Pine) **215/546–2093** • 7pm Sun

Integrity 1904 Walnut St (at the church) **215/382–0794** • 7pm 1st & 3rd Wed • pastoral counseling available

MCC 1315 Spruce St, 3rd flr (at William Way GLBT Center) **215/735–6223** • 11am & 7pm Sun

Old First Reformed Church (United Church of Christ) 4th & Race Sts **215/922–4566** • 11am

Gyms & Health Clubs

12th St Gym 204 S 12th St (btwn Locust & Walnut) **215/985–4092** • 5:30am-11pm • gay-friendly

Erotica

Condom Kingdom 441 South St (at 5th) **215/829–1668** • safer sex materials • toys

Fetishes Boutique 704 S 5th St (at Bainbridge) **215/829–4986, 877/2–CORSET** • noon-close

The Pleasure Chest 2039 Walnut (btwn 20th & 21st) **215/561–7480** • clsd Sun-Mon

Pitman

Accommodations

The Hermitage at Mahantongo Spirit Garden RD 1, Box 149, Grove Rd (at Mill Hill Rd) **570/425–2548** • mostly men • queer spiritual retreat center (Pantheist) • working farm & historic site • $20-25

Pittsburgh

Info Lines & Services

AA Gay/ Lesbian 412/471–7472

FACT (Friends of all Colors Together) 412/441–4441

Gay/ Lesbian Community Center Phoneline 412/422–0114 • 6:30pm-9:30pm, 3pm-6pm Sat, clsd Sun

ISMIR (International Sexual Minorities Information Resource) 412/422–3060 • monthly calendar of regional, national, int'l lesbigay events

Accommodations

The Inn on the Mexican War Streets 1606 Buena Vista St **412/231–6544** • lesbians/ gay men • located on the historic & gay-friendly North Side • gay-owned/ run • $65-85

The Priory 614 Pressley (nr Cedar Ave) **412/231–3338** • gay-friendly • 24-rm Victorian • kids ok • wheelchair access • $68-175

Three Rivers Hospitality House 922 N St Clair St **412/441–4441** • lesbians/ gay men • full brkfst

Bars

Brewery Tavern 3315 Liberty Ave (at Herron Ave) **412/681–7991** • 10am-2am, from noon Sun • gay-friendly

Images 965 Liberty Ave (at 10th St) **412/391–9990** • 5pm-2am, from 7pm wknds • mostly gay men • karaoke Mon, Wed-Th • videos

Liberty Avenue Saloon 941 Liberty Ave (at Smithfield) **412/338–1533** • 11am-2am, from 5pm Sat • lesbians/ gay men • neighborhood bar • drag shows • also restaurant

New York, New York 5801 Ellsworth Ave (at Maryland) **412/661-5600** • 4pm-2am, from 11am Sun • popular • mostly gay men • also restaurant • some veggie • $9-15

Pittsburgh Eagle 1740 Eckert St (nr Beaver) **412/766-7222** • 9pm-2am, clsd Sun-Mon • popular • mostly gay men • dancing/DJ • leather • wheelchair access

Real Luck Cafe 1519 Penn Ave (at 16th) **412/566-8988** • 3pm-2am • lesbians/ gay men • neighborhood bar • food served • cafe menu • some veggie • wheelchair access • $5

Sidekicks 931 Liberty Ave (at Smithfield) **412/642-4435** • 5pm-close, clsd Sun • mostly gay men • piano bar • also restaurant

Nightclubs

Donny's Place 1226 Herron Ave (at Liberty) **412/682-9869** • 4pm-2am, from 3pm Sun • popular • lesbians/ gay men • dancing/DJ • live shows • food served

House of Tilden 941 Liberty Ave, 2nd flr (at Smithfield) **412/391-0804** • 10pm-3am • lesbians/ gay men • dancing/DJ • private club

Metropol 1600 Smallman St **412/261-4512** • 8pm-2am Th-Sun • popular • gay-friendly • dancing/DJ • alternative • fetish crowd Fri • live shows • food served • wheelchair access

Pegasus Lounge 818 Liberty Ave (at 9th) **412/281-2131** • 9pm-2am, from 8pm Sat, clsd Sun • popular • mostly gay men • dancing/DJ • drag shows • younger crowd

Cafes

Tuscany Cafe 1501 E Carson St (15th) **412/488-4475** • 7am-2am, from 8am wknds • full bar

Restaurants

Rosebud 1650 Smallman St **412/261-2221** • dinner nightly, lunch summer only, clsd Mon • live music • wheelchair access • $8-15

Entertainment & Recreation

Andy Warhol Museum 117 Sandusky St (at General Robinson) **412/237-8300** • clsd Mon-Tue • is it soup or is it art—this museum tells all

Bookstores

The Bookstall 3604 5th Ave (at Meyran) **412/683-2644** • 9:30am-5:30pm, till 4:30pm Sat, clsd Sun

St Elmo's Books & Music 2208 E Carson St (at 22nd St) **412/431-9100** • 10am-9pm • progressive

Retail Shops

A Pleasant Present 2301 Murray Ave (at Nicholson) **412/421-7104** • 11am-7pm, till 8:30pm Th, clsd Sun

Iron City Ink Tattoo/ Hellion House Body Piercing 314 N Craig (at Center) **412/683-9888** • noon-8pm, clsd Sun

The Outer Skin 415 E 8th Ave, Munhall **412/461-5975** • noon-9pm, clsd Sun • clubwear • fetish • leather • gifts

Slacker 1321 E Carson St (btwn 13th & 14th) **412/381-3911** • 11am-9pm, till 11pm Fri-Sat, till 6pm Sun • magazines • clothing • leather • piercing

Publications

Out 412/243-3350 • lesbigay newspaper

Spiritual Groups

First Unitarian Church 605 Moorewood Ave (at Ellsworth) **412/621-8008** • 11am Sun (10am summers) • also 'Three Rivers Unitarian Universalists for Lesbigay Concerns,' 412/343-2523

MCC of Pittsburgh 4836 Ellsworth Ave (at Devonshire) **412/683-2994** • 7pm Sun

Erotica

Boulevard Videos & Magazines 346 Blvd of the Allies (at Smithfield) **412/261-9119** • 24hrs • leather • toys

Golden Triangle News 816 Liberty Ave (at 9th) **412/765-3790** • 24hrs

Poconos

Accommodations

▲ **Blueberry Ridge 570/629-5036** • women only • full brkfst • hot tub • smokefree • kids ok • holiday packages • $55-80

Rainbow Mtn Resort 570/223-8484 • popular • lesbians/ gay men • atop Pocono Mtn on 85 acres (see listing under East Stroudsburg)

▲ **Stoney Ridge 570/629-5036** • lesbians/ gay men • secluded log home • kitchen • kids/ pets ok • $250/ wknd, $550/ week

Quakertown

Restaurants

The Brick Tavern Inn 2460 Old Bethlehem Pike (at Brick Tavern Rd) **215/538-0865** • live shows • full bar

Reading

Accommodations

The Barnyard Inn 2145 Old Lancaster Pike, Reinholds **717/484-1111, 888/738-6624** • gay-friendly • full brkfst • 150 yr old restored German school house • petting zoo • $75-125

Bars

Nostalgia 1101 N 9th St (at Robinson) **610/372-5557** • 9am-11pm, till 2am Fri-Sat • mostly women • neighborhood bar

Red Star 11 S 10th St (at Penn) **610/375-4116** • 6pm-2am, clsd Mon-Tue • mostly gay men • dancing/DJ • leather • live shows

Nightclubs

Club Millennium 124 N 4th St (at Washington) **610/376-7233** • lesbians/ gay men • dancing/DJ • karaoke • drag shows • videos • also restaurant

Scarab 724 Franklin (at Lemon) **610/375-7878** • 9pm-2am, clsd Sun • popular • lesbians/ gay men • dancing/DJ

Scranton

Nightclubs

The Buzz 131 N Washington Ave (at Spruce) **570/969-2899** • 9pm-2am, from 8pm Fri-Sat, from 7pm Mon • lesbians/ gay men • women's night Fri • dancing/DJ • live shows • 18+ Mon • wheelchair access

Spring Grove

Nightclubs

Atlands Ranch 6543 Orchard Rd **717/225-4479** • 8pm-2am Fri-Sat only • mostly gay men • dancing/DJ • country/ western Fri

State College

Info Lines & Services

GLBT Switchboard 814/237-1950 • 6pm-9pm • info • peer counseling

Women's Resource Center 140 W Nittany Ave (at Frasier) **814/234-5050 (24hr hotline), 814/234-5222** • 9am-7pm, clsd wknds

Bars

Chumley's 108 W College **814/238-4446** • 5pm-2am, from 6pm Sun • lesbians/ gay men • wheelchair access

Nightclubs

Players 112 W College Ave **814/234-1031** • 8pm-2am, clsd Mon & Wed • gay/ straight • more gay Sun • dancing/DJ • videos

Wilkes-Barre

Info Lines & Services

Coming Home (AA) 97 S Franklin Blvd (at Presbyterian Church) • noon Th

Nightclubs

Rumors Lounge 315 Fox Ridge Plaza **570/825-7300** • 6pm-2am, from 9pm Mon-Tue • popular • lesbians/ gay men • dancing/DJ • also restaurant • wheelchair access

Selections 45 Public Sq, Wilkes-Barre Ctr **570/829-4444** • 8pm-2am, from 4pm Fri-Sun • popular • lesbians/ gay men • dancing/DJ • also restaurant • wheelchair access • $5-15

Williamsport

Bars

Peachie's 144 E 4th St **570/326-3611** • 3pm-2am, from 1pm Sun • lesbians/ gay men • dancing/DJ Fri-Sun • karaoke Wed • food served • wheelchair access

Nightclubs

The Rainbow Room 761 W 4th St **570/320-0230** • 8pm-2am, clsd Sun • popular • lesbians/ gay men • dancing/DJ • live shows • videos

York

Info Lines & Services

York Area Lambda 717/846-6618, 717/846-2560 • lesbigay social/ educational group • newsletter

York Lesbian Alliance 717/848-9142

Bars

14 Karat 600 block of W Market • lesbians/ gay men

Bookstores

Her Story Women's Bookstore 2 W Market St, Hallam **717/757-4270** • noon-8pm, till 5pm Sun • women's books • music • videos • gifts • gourmet coffee • lesbian-owned/ run • wheelchair access

Erotica

Cupid's Connection Adult Boutique 244 N George St (at North) **717/846-5029** • 9pm-2am, noon-midnight Sun

Rhode Island

Statewide

Publications

In Newsweekly 617/426-8246, 800/426-8246 • New England lesbigay newspaper w/ some RI listings

Options 401/831-4519 • extensive resource listings

Spiritual Groups

RI & SE Mass Gay Jewish Group Boston, MA **508/992-7927**

Little Compton

Restaurants

Common's Lunch Town Center **401/635-4388** • brkfst & lunch • great lace-thin johnnycakes

Newport

Info Lines & Services

Sobriety First 135 Pelham St (at Channing Memorial Church) **401/438-8860** • 8pm Fri

Accommodations

Brinley Victorian Inn 23 Brinley St **401/849-7645** • gay-friendly • smokefree • $89-199

Captain James Preston House 378 Spring St (at Pope) **401/847-4386** • gay-friendly • elegant Victorian B&B • smokefree • $70-150

Hydrangea House Inn 16 Bellevue Ave **401/846-4435, 800/945-4667** • popular • gay/ straight • full brkfst • near beach • gay-owned/ run • $100-280

The Melville House Inn 39 Clarke St **401/847-0640, 800/711-7184** • lesbians/ gay men • full brkfst • $65-145

The Prospect Hill Guest House 32 Prospect Hill St **401/847-7405** • gay/ straight • smokefree • gay-owned/ run • $75-145

Restaurants

Restaurant Bouchard 505 Thames St **401/846-0123** • dinner, clsd Tue • $16-26

Whitehorse Tavern 26 Marlborough (at Farewell) **401/849-3600** • upscale dining • $22-36

Pawtucket

Info Lines & Services

Gay & Lesbian AA 71 Park Place (at Congregational church) **401/438-8860** • 7:30pm Tue

Providence

Info Lines & Services

Enforcers RI 401/737-5113 • leather/ SM/ fetish group for men & women

Gay/ Lesbian Helpline of Rhode Island 401/751-3322 • 7pm-10pm Mon & Fri

GLBT Alliance 401/863-3062 • student group

Sarah Doyle Women's Center 185 Meeting St (Brown University) **401/863-2189** • referrals • also lesbian collective group

Sisters in Sobriety 25 Pomona (at Pemberton, at St Peter & Andrew Church) **401/438-8860** • 7pm Sat

Bars

Club In Town 95 Eddy St (at Westminster) **401/751-0020** • noon-1am, till 2am Fri-Sat • mostly gay men • piano bar • videos

Devilles 1 Allens Ave (at Eddy) **401/751-7166** • 6pm-1am, till 2am Fri-Sat, clsd Mon • mostly women • neighborhood bar • dancing/DJ Th-Sat • also restaurant • wheelchair access

The Providence Eagle 200 Union St (at Weybosset) **401/421-1447** • 6pm-1am, till 2am Fri-Sat • mostly gay men • leather • wheelchair access

Union Street Station 69 Union St (at Washington) **401/331-2291** • noon-1am, till 2am Fri-Sat • mostly gay men • dancing/DJ • live shows • wheelchair access

Wheels 125 Washington (at Mathewson) **401/272-6950** • noon-1am, till 2am Fri-Sat • lesbians/ gay men • dancing/DJ wknds • karaoke • videos • wheelchair access

Nightclubs

Bar One 1 Throop Alley (off S Main St) **401/621-7112** • 9pm-close, clsd Mon • dancing/DJ • 18+

Gerardo's 1 Franklin Sq (btwn Allens & Eddy) **401/274-5560** • 4pm-1am, till 2am Fri-Sat • lesbians/ gay men • dancing/DJ • live shows • karaoke • theme parties • wheelchair access

Mirabar 35 Richmond St (at Weybosset) **401/331-6761** • 3pm-1am, till 2am Fri-Sat • mostly gay men • dancing/DJ • karaoke Mon • wheelchair access

Pulse 86 Crary St (at Plain) **401/272-2133** • 9pm-close, clsd Sun-Mon • lesbians/ gay men • dancing/DJ • live shows • karaoke Sun • 18+ Wed-Th • cover charge

Cafes

The Castro 77 Ives (at Wickenden) **401/421-1144** • 7am-10pm, till midnight Fri-Sat • pizza, salads, sandwiches

Coffee Cafe 257 S Main St (at Power) **401/421-0787** • 7am-5pm, 8am-4pm Sat, clsd Sun • patio • gay-owned/ run

Restaurants

Al Forno 577 South Main St **401/273-9760** • dinner only, clsd Sun-Mon • popular • Little Rhody's best dining experience • $13-24

Camille's 71 Bradford St (at Atwell's Ave) **401/751-4812** • lunch & dinner • full bar

Down City Diner 151 Weybosset St **401/331-9217** • lunch & dinner • popular Sun brunch (very gay) • full bar • wheelchair access

Julian's 318 Broadway (at Vinton) **401/861-1770** • 9am-3pm & 6pm-9pm, clsd Sun-Mon

Lucy's 441 Atwells Ave (at Knight) **401/273-1189** • lunch & dinner, Sun brunch, clsd Mon • full bar • patio • wheelchair access • lesbian-owned/ run • $6-17

Rue de l'Espoir 99 Hope St (at John) **401/751-8890** • lunch & dinner, clsd Mon • full bar • women-owned/ run • $12-20

Bookstores

Books on the Square 471 Angell St (at Wayland) **401/331-9097** • 9am-9pm, till 10pm Fri-Sat, noon-6pm Sun • some lesbigay

Retail Shops

Esta's on Thayer St 257 Thayer St (across from Avon cinema) **401/831-2651** • videos • pride items • Tarot readings

Flux Gallery 260 Weybosset St **401/274-9120**

Headlines 265 Wickenden St (at Brook) **401/274-6397** • 8am-11pm, till midnight Fri-Sat, till 9pm Sun • videos • newsstand • smokeshop

Publications

In Newsweekly 617/426-8246, 800/426-8246 • New England lesbigay newspaper w/ some RI listings

Options 401/831-4519 • extensive resource listings

Spiritual Groups

Bell St Chapel (Unitarian) 5 Bell St **401/273-5678** • 10am Sun

Integrity 474 Fruit Hill Ave (at St James Church) **401/274-4109** • 4:30pm 2nd Sun

Morning Star MCC 231 Main St, Cherry Valley, MA **508/892-4320** • 11am Sun

St Peter's & Andrew's Episcopal Church 25 Pomona Ave **401/272-9649** • 8am & 10am Sun, 7pm Wed (healing service)

Smithfield

Bars

The Loft 325 Farnum Pike **401/231-3320** • 4pm-1am, till 2am wknds, from 10am summers • lesbians/ gay men • dancing/DJ • swimming • food served • wheelchair access

Warwick

Bookstores

Barnes & Noble 1441 Bald Hill Rd/ Rte 2 **401/828-7900** • 9am-11pm, 11am-7pm Sun • lesbigay section

Westerly

Accommodations

The Villa 190 Shore Rd **401/596-1054, 800/722-9240** • gay-friendly • near beach • swimming • smokefree • $85-245

Restaurants

Mary's Rte 1 & Post Rd (off 1A) **401/322-0444** • 5pm-close, clsd Mon-Tue • Italian

Woonsocket

Bars

Kings & Queens 285 Front St (at Vernon) **401/762-9538** • 7pm-1am, till 2am wknds • lesbians/ gay men • neighborhood bar • dancing/DJ Fri-Sat • karaoke

South Carolina

Statewide

Publications

The Front Page 919/829-0181 • lesbigay newspaper for the Carolinas

Charleston

Info Lines & Services

Acceptance Group (Gay AA) St Stephen's Episcopal on Anson St (btwn Society & George) **843/762-2433, 843/723-9633 (AA#)** • 8pm Tue & 6:30pm Sat

LGLA (Lowcountry Gay/ Lesbian Alliance) Infoline 843/720-8088

Accommodations

1854 B&B 34 Montagu St **803/723-4789** • lesbians/ gay men • private home in historic district • gay-owned/ run • $95-115

65 Radcliff Street 65 Radcliff St **843/577-6183** • lesbians/ gay men • private home • smokefree • $70

A B&B @ 4 Unity Alley 4 Unity Alley **843/577-6660** • gay/ straight • full brkfst • parking inside • $95-175

▲ **Calhoun House** 273 Calhoun St (Ashley Ave) **843/722-7341** • lesbians/ gay men • comfortable lodging in historic district • gay-owned/ run • $80-135

Charleston Beach B&B 843/588-9443 • lesbians/ gay men • unobstructed views of the Atlantic Ocean • full brkfst • swimming • nudity • 8-person spa • $45-100

Bars

Patrick's Pub & Grill 1377 Ashley River Rd (Hwy 61) **843/571-3435** • lesbians/ gay men • neighborhood bar • transgender-friendly • DJ Fri-Sat • country/ western alternate Fri • karaoke Th • live shows • full restaurant • $4-8 • wheelchair access

Nightclubs

The Arcade 5 Liberty St **843/722-5656** • 9:30pm-close, clsd Mon-Wed • popular • mostly gay men • dancing/DJ • alternative • live shows • karaoke • wheelchair access

Deja Vu II 445 Savannah Hwy **843/556-5588** • 5pm-3am, clsd Mon-Tue • mostly women • dancing/DJ • country/ western Sun • live shows • food served • private club • wheelchair access

Cafes

Bear E Patch 801 Folly Rd **843/762-6555** • 7am-6pm • patio • wheelchair access

Restaurants

Blossom Cafe 171 E Bay St **843/722-9200** • 11:30am-midnight, till 1am wknds • walled courtyard

Cafe Suzanne 4 Center St **843/588-2101** • 5:30pm-9:30pm, Sun brunch, clsd Mon-Tue • live jazz • $10-15

Mickey's 137 Market St **843/723-7121** • 24hrs • popular

St Johns Island Cafe 3406 Maybank Hwy, St Johns Island **843/559-9090** • brkfst & lunch Mon-Sat, dinner Wed-Sat • popular • Southern homecooking • beer/ wine • $6-15

Vickery's of Beaufain Street 15 Beaufain St (at St Philip) **843/577-5300** • 11am-3am • popular • Cuban influence • some veggie • full bar • $6-15

Entertainment & Recreation

Historic Charleston Foundation 108 Meeting St **843/723-1623** • call for info on architectural walking tours

Spoleto Festival 843/723-0402 (**ASK FOR BROCHURE**) • 2-week avant-garde art festival in late May-early June

Bookstores

Healing Rays—A Woman's Place in the Sun 57 Broad St **843/853-4499** • 12:30pm-6pm, clsd Sun-Mon • holistic • many lesbian titles • also workshops & art gallery

Publications

The Front Page 919/829-0181 • lesbigay newspaper for the Carolinas

Q Notes 704/531-9988

Spiritual Groups

MCC Charleston 7860 Dorchester Rd, North Charleston **843/760-6114** • 11:15am Sun • wheelchair access

Columbia

Info Lines & Services

AA Gay/ Lesbian 803/254-5301(AA#) • call for mtg schedule

South Carolina Pride Center 1108 Woodrow St **803/771-7713** • 24hr message, live 2pm-10pm Sat

Accommodations

Lord Camden Inn 1502 Broad, Camden **803/713-9050, 800/737-9971** • gay/ straight • 35 min east of Columbia • swimming • $75-110

Bars

Affairs 2 1919 Airport Blvd (exit 113 off I-26), Cayce **803/936-0690** • 5pm-2am, till midnight Sat, clsd Sun • lesbians/ gay men • neighborhood bar • dancing/DJ • food served

Capital Club 1002 Gervais St **803/256-6464** • 5pm-2am • mostly gay men • neighborhood bar • professional • private club • wheelchair access

The Downtown Club 1109 Assembly **803/799-6031** • 5pm-4am, till 2am Sat, clsd Sun • mostly gay men • neighborhood bar • live shows • private club

Traxx 416 Lincoln St (at Blossom) **803/256-1084** • 4pm-2am, 6pm-close Sat, 2pm-close Sun • mostly women • dancing/DJ • live bands • outdoor volleyball court • private club • wheelchair access

Nightclubs

Candy Shop 1903 Two Notch Rd • mostly gay men • dancing/DJ • mostly African-American • private club

Metropolis 1800 Blanding St (at Barnwell) **803/799-8727** • 10pm-close, clsd Mon-Tue • lesbians/ gay men • dancing/DJ • live shows • private club

Restaurants

Alley Cafe 911 Lady St **803/771-2778** • lunch Tue-Fri, dinner Tue-Sat • full bar • $4-9

Bookstores

Intermezzo 2015 Devine St **803/799-2276** • 10am-midnight • lesbigay section • wheelchair access

Stardust Books 2000 Blossom St **803/771-0633** • 10:30am-6pm, clsd Sun-Mon • spiritual • psychic readings • wheelchair access

Retail Shops

Moxie 631-C Harden St **803/929-0644** • 10am-6pm, clsd Sun-Mon • lesbigay gifts • cards • books

Spiritual Groups

MCC Columbia 1111 Belleview (at Main St) **803/256-2154** • 11am & 6pm Sun

Florence

Bars

Rascal's Deli & Lounge 526 S Irby St **843/665-2555** • 5pm-2am, from 7pm Sat, from 3pm Sun • lesbians/ gay men • live shows • private club

Greenville

Info Lines & Services

Greenville L/ G Switchboard 864/422-1645

Nightclubs

The Castle 8 Le Grand Blvd **864/235-9949** • 9:30pm-4am, clsd Mon-Wed • popular • lesbians/ gay men • dancing/DJ • drag shows • videos • private club • wheelchair access

New Attitude 706 W Washington St **864/233-1387** • 10pm-close wknds • lesbians/ gay men • dancing/DJ • mostly African-American • unconfirmed

Bookstores

Out of Bounds 219-E W Antrim Dr **864/239-0106** • noon-midnight, clsd Sun-Mon • cards • gifts • magazines

Spiritual Groups

MCC 314 Lloyd St (at Duncan) **864/233-0919** • 11am Sun & 7pm Wed

Hilton Head

Bars

MJ's (Moon Jammers) 11 Heritage Plaza, Pope Ave **843/842-9195** • 8pm-2am • lesbians/ gay men • neighborhood bar • dancing/DJ • alternative • live shows • private club • wheelchair access

Myrtle Beach

Bars

The Back Door & The Swing'n Door 2891 Tourism Dr (17 Business), Garden City **843/357-6941** • 7pm-close • lesbians/ gay men • dancing/DJ • live shows • 18+ • wheelchair access

Time Out 520 8th Ave N (at Oak) **843/448-1180** • 5pm-close, till 2am Sat • popular • mostly gay men • neighborhood bar • dancing/DJ • karaoke Tue & Sun • patio • private club • wheelchair access

Restaurants

Rainbow House Bistro 1004 N Chester St (at 11th Ave) **843/626-7298** • 3pm-5am, till 2am wknds • lesbians/ gay men • patio • wheelchair access

Rock Hill

Bars

Hideaway 405 Baskins Rd **803/328-6630** • 8pm-close, clsd Mon-Wed • lesbians/ gay men • neighborhood bar • private club

Spartanburg

Nightclubs

Cheyenne Cattlemen's Club 995 Asheville Hwy **864/573-7304** • 8pm-2am, till 4am Fri, from 3pm Sun • mostly gay men • dancing/DJ • live bands • private club

Cove Lounge & Club 9112 Greenville Hwy **864/576-2683** • 8pm-close, from 6pm Sun • lesbians/ gay men • dancing/DJ • live shows • private club • patio • wheelchair access

South Dakota

Statewide

Info Lines & Services

South Dakota Dept of Tourism 800/952-3625 (IN-STATE ONLY), 800/732-5682 (OUT-OF-STATE ONLY)

Publications

Faces of South Dakota 605/343-5577

Aberdeen

Bars

Wagon Wheel 208 S Main St **605/226-2140** • 11am-2am, clsd Sun • gay/ straight but this fact is unknown to the owners • more gay late

Batesland

Accommodations

Wakpamni B&B HC64 Box 43 (on the Pine Ridge Indian Reservation) **605/288-1800** • gay-friendly • full brkfst • dinner available • $60-100

Rapid City

Info Lines & Services

FACES 2218 Jackson Blvd, Ste 8 **605/343-5577** • drop-in 7pm-10pm Tue, 2pm-5pm Wed, 1pm-5pm wknds • AA mtg 8pm Th

Gay/ Lesbian Talk Line 605/394-8080 • 6pm-10pm, clsd Sun

Publications

Faces of South Dakota 605/343-5577

Spiritual Groups

MCC Hotel Alex Johnson, 3rd flr (Rushmore room) **605/399-3932** • 10am Sun

Erotica

Heritage Bookstore 912 Main St **605/394-9877**

Sioux Falls

Info Lines & Services

The Sioux Empire Gay & Lesbian Coalition 401 E 8th St #217 (at Webber) **605/333-0603, 605/978-1512** • 6pm-9pm Mon & Wed, 1pm-4pm Sat • 24hr info

Accommodations

Camp America 605/425-9085 • gay-friendly • 35 miles west of Sioux Falls • camping • RV hookups • women-owned/ run • $10-16

Nightclubs

Touchez 323 S Phillips Ave (enter rear) **605/335-9874** • 8pm-2am • popular • lesbians/ gay men • dancing/DJ • food served

Spiritual Groups

St Francis & St Clair MCC 1129 E 9th St **605/332-3966** • 5:30pm Sun, 7pm summers

Erotica

Studio One Book Store 311 N Dakota Ave (btwn 6th & 7th) **605/332-9316** • 24hrs

Spearfish

Cafes

The Bay Leaf Cafe 126 1/2 W Hudson St **605/642-5462** • lunch & dinner • some veggie • espresso bar

Tennessee

Bristol

Accommodations

Penshurst Cottage 529 Sharp's Creek Rd **423/878-3242** • women only • newly renovated cabin/cottage located in the Cherokee Nat'l Forest • full brkfst • creek, paths & birds • kids/ pets ok • wheelchair access • lesbian-owned/ run • $50-150

Chattanooga

Bars

Chuck's II 27-1/2 W Main (at Market) **423/265-5405** • 6pm-1am, till 3am Fri-Sat • lesbians/ gay men • neighborhood bar • dancing/DJ • country/ western • patio

Nightclubs

Alan Gold's 1100 McCallie Ave (at Central) **423/629-8080** • 4:30pm-3am • popular • lesbians/ gay men • dancing/DJ • drag shows Wed-Sun • food served • wheelchair access

Mirage 115-B Honest St (at Lee Hwy) **423/855-8210** • 4pm-3am • lesbians/ gay men • dancing/DJ • drag shows • wheelchair access

Tool Box 1401 E 23rd St **423/697-9400** • 3pm-3am • popular • mostly gay men • dancing/DJ • live shows Wed-Sun • full restaurant

Erotica

Condoms & Etc 27 W Main St (at Market) **423/266-3668**

Cleveland

Bars

Shooters 1685 Clingin Ridge Dr **423/614–4185** • 2pm-midnight, clsd Sun • lesbians/ gay men • neighborhood bar • dancing/DJ • patio w/ volleyball • 18+ • wheelchair access

Gatlinburg

Accommodations

Stone Creek Cabins 423/429–0400 • gay/ straight • 14-acre paradise • women-owned/ run • $125-150

Haley

Restaurants

Our House 1059 Haley Rd **615/389–6616, 800/876–6616** • clsd Mon • popular • fine dining • some veggie • by reservation only • BYOB • wheelchair access • $10-20

Jackson

Bars

The Other Side 3883 Hwy 45 N (at Ashport) **901/668–3749** • 5pm-close, till 3am Fri-Sat, from 7pm Sat • lesbians/ gay men • karaoke • live shows

Johnson City

Accommodations

Safehaven Farm 336 Stanley Hollow Rd, Roan Mountain **423/725–4262** • gay-friendly • creekside privacy • fireplace & wraparound porch • kids ok • $80-90

Bars

Try-Angles 123 E Springbrook Dr **423/915–0015** • 5pm-2am, till 3am Th-Sat, till 1am Sun, clsd Mon • lesbians/ gay men • neighborhood bar • dancing/DJ • drag shows Fri-Sat

Nightclubs

New Beginnings 2910 N Bristol Hwy **423/282–4446** • 9pm-2am, 8pm-3am Fri-Sat, clsd Mon • popular • mostly gay men • dancing/DJ • live shows • also restaurant • wheelchair access

Retail Shops

Spikes Gift Shop 2910 N Bristol Hwy (inside 'New Beginnings') **423/753–0072** • 9pm-3am Wed, Fri-Sat only • pride gifts

Spiritual Groups

MCC of the Tri-Cities Coast Valley Unitarian Church **423/283–7554** • 7pm Sun

Knoxville

Info Lines & Services

AA Gay/ Lesbian 3219 Kingston Pike (at Tenn Valley Unitarian Church) **423/522–9667** • 7pm Mon & Fri

Gay/ Lesbian Helpline 423/531–2539 (MCC#) • 7am-11pm

Lesbian Social Group 423/693–1587

Nightclubs

Carousel II 1501 White Ave (on U Tenn campus, behind the law library) **423/522–6966** • 9pm-3am • popular • lesbians/ gay men • dancing/DJ • live shows • also 24hr restaurant

Electric Ballroom 1213 Western Ave **423/525–6724** • 9pm-3am, from 6pm Fri-Sat, clsd Mon • mostly gay men • dancing/DJ • live shows • food served • wheelchair access

Bookstores

Davis Kidd Bookstore The Commons, 113 N Peters Rd **423/690–0136** • 9:30am-10pm, 10am-6pm Sun • general • wheelchair access

Spiritual Groups

MCC Knoxville 1059 Tranquilo (off Nubbins Ridge, look for unmarked driveway to church) **423/531–2539** • 11am & 6pm Sun

Memphis

Info Lines & Services

Gay/ Lesbian Switchboard 901/324–4297 • live 7:30pm-11pm, 24hr info

Memphis Lambda Center (AA) 1488 Madison **901/276–7379** • meeting place for 12-Step groups • call for times

Accommodations

Talbot Heirs Guesthouse 99 S 2nd St (btwn Union & Peabody Place) **901/527–9772, 800/955–3956** • gay-friendly • funky decor • smokefree • kids ok • $150-250

Bars

501 Club 111 N Claybrook (at Jefferson) **901/274–8655** • noon-3am • mostly gay men • dancing/DJ • country/ western • drag shows Fri-Sun • food served • wheelchair access

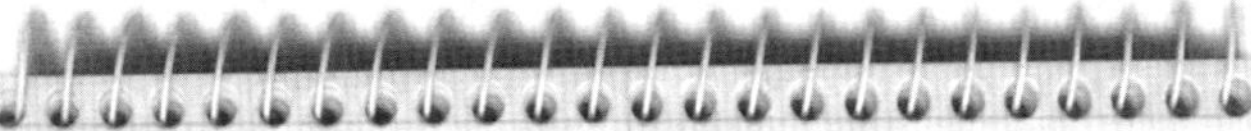

Memphis

Many people around the world know Memphis as the city of two musical phenomena—the blues and the King. The blues were born when W.C. Handy immortalized 'Beale Street,' and, as for the King, Elvis lived and died here. From everywhere on earth, people come to visit his home and pay their respects at Graceland (800/238-2000).

There are a number of mixed bars & clubs, like the popular **Amnesia** and **Backstreet.** For the complete rundown of local groups and events, check out the latest editions of **Family & Friends** and **Triangle Journal News** or call the **Gay/Lesbian Switchboard.**

Memphis

Where the Girls Are: On Madison Ave., of course, just east of US-240.

City Info: 901/543-5333, web: www.memphistravel.com.

Attractions: Beale Street.
Graceland 800/238-2000.
Mud Island.
Nat'l Civil Rights Museum 901/521-9699.
Overton Square.
Sun Studio 901/521-0664.

Best View: A cruise on any of the boats that ply the river.

Weather: Suth'n. H-O-T and humid in the summer, cold (30°s-40°s) in the winter, and a relatively nice (but still humid) spring and fall.

Transit: Yellow Cab 901/526-2121. MATA 901/274-6282.

Autumn Street Pub 1349 Autumn St (at Cleveland) **901/274-8010** • 1pm-3am, clsd Mon-Tue • lesbians/ gay men • neighborhood bar • dancing/DJ • drag shows Fri-Sat • food served • patio • wheelchair access

Crossroads 1278 Jefferson (at Claybrook) **901/276-8078** • noon-3am • lesbians/ gay men • neighborhood bar • drag shows Th-Sat • beer & set-ups only • country/ western Wed

The Jungle 1474 Madison (at McNeil) **901/278-4313** • 3pm-3am, from noon Sat • mostly gay men • neighborhood bar • leather • food served • beer & set-ups only

Lorenz 1528 Madison Ave (at Avalon) **901/274-8272** • 11am-3am, 24hrs wknds • lesbians/ gay men • dancing/DJ • live shows • patio

Madison Flame 1588 Madison (at Avalon) **901/278-9839** • 5pm-3am • lesbians/ gay men • neighborhood bar • dancing/DJ

Nightclubs

Amnesia 2866 Poplar (nr Walnut Grove) **901/454-1366** • 8pm-3am, clsd Mon-Wed • popular • lesbians/ gay men • dancing/DJ • alternative • cover charge • younger crowd • swimming • patio • dinner nightly • wheelchair access

Backstreet 2018 Court Ave (at Morrison) **901/276-5522** • 8pm-3am, till 6am wknds • lesbians/ gay men • dancing/DJ • wheelchair access • beer & set-ups only

Chaos 60 S Front St (at Union) **901/578-8432** • 11pm-6am Sat, till 2am Sun-Mon • mostly women • dancing/DJ

Cafes

Java Cabana 2170 Young Ave (at Cooper) **901/272-7210** • 8am-10pm, till midnight Fri-Sat, 1pm-6pm Sun • also art gallery

P&H Cafe 1532 Madison (at Adeline) **901/726-0906** • 11am-3am, from 5pm Sat, clsd Sun • beer/ wine • wheelchair access

Restaurants

Automatic Slim's Tonga Club 83 S 2nd St (at Union) **901/525-7948** • lunch & dinner Mon-Fri, dinner till 11pm Fri-Sat, clsd Sun • Caribbean & Southwestern • plenty veggie • full bar

Cafe Society 212 N Evergreen Ave (btwn McLean & Belvedere) **901/722-2177** • lunch & dinner, till 11pm Fri-Sat • full bar

Saigon Le 51 N Cleveland **901/276-5326** • 11am-9pm, clsd Sun • Chinese/ Vietnamese/ Thai

Entertainment & Recreation

Graceland PO Box 16508, 38186 **901/332-3322, 800/238-2000** • no visit to Memphis would be complete without a trip to see The King

Bookstores

Davis Kidd Booksellers 397 Perkins Rd Ext (at Poplar & Walnut Grove) **901/683-9801** • 9am-10pm, 10am-6pm Sun • general • lesbigay titles • also cafe

Publications

▲ **Family & Friends 901/682-2669** • lgbt newsmagazine

Triangle Journal News 901/454-1411 • lgbt newspaper • extensive resource listings

Spiritual Groups

First Congregational Church 246 S Watkins **901/278-6786** • 9am & 10:30am Sun, 6pm Wed

Holy Trinity Community Church 3430 Summer Ave **901/320-9376** • 11am & 7pm Sun

Integrity 102 N Second St (at Calvary Episcopal Church) **901/525-6602** • 6pm 3rd Tue

Safe Harbor MCC 2117 Union Ave (at Union Ave UMC—Union & Cooper—in the Chapel of the Good Shepherd) **901/458-0501** • 11am

Erotica

Cherokee Video & Adult Book Store 2947 Lamar **901/744-7494** • 24hrs

Nashville

Info Lines & Services

AA Gay/ Lesbian 615/831-1050 • call for mtg schedule

Center for Lesbian/ Gay Community Services 703 Berry Rd **615/297-0008** • 6pm-9pm

Nashville Women's Alliance • call 'Center' for times & locations

Accommodations

IDA 904 Vikkers Hollow Rd, Dowelltown **615/597-4409** • lesbians/ gay men • private 'commune' in the hills • 1 hr SE of Nashville • camping available May-Sept (no RV hookup) • from $7

Savage House 165 8th Ave N (btwn Church & Commerce) **615/244-2229** • gay-friendly • 1840s Victorian townhouse • full brkfst • $75-95

Nashville

Where the Girls Are: Just north of I-65/40 along 2nd Ave. S. or Hermitage Ave.

Lesbigay Pride: September.

City Info: 615/259-4730, web: www.nashvillecvb.com.

Attractions: Country Music Hall of Fame 615/256-1639.
Grand Ole Opry & Opryland USA 615/889-6611.
Jack Daniel Distillery 615/327-1551.
The Parthenon 615/862-8431.
Ryman Auditorium 615/254-1445.
Tennessee Antebellum Trail 931/486-9055.

Best View: Try a walking tour of the city.

Weather: See Memphis.

Transit: Yellow Cab 615/256-0101.
Music City Taxi 615/889-0038.
Gray Line Airport Shuttle 615/275-1180.
MTA 615/862-5950.

Nashville

There's only one 'Country Music Capital of the World,' and that's Nashville. And there's no better place on earth to enjoy country and western music than at the Grand Ole Opry (615/889-6611). Be sure to plan ahead and get a performance schedule.

Many of the greats of country music have homes in Nashville, and there are plenty of bus tours to show you exactly where your favorite stars live. The Country Music Hall of Fame and Museum (615/256-1639) is also a favorite stop for diehard fans.

After you've sat still listening to great music so long you can't stand it, get up and dance. Nashville has two women's bars–**Chez Collette** and the **Your Way Cafe/ Women's Choice Bar.** Keep your star-gazing eyes open while you're cloggin' away on the floor; you never know who you might see! For more sedate activities, pick up a copy of **Query** or **Xenogeny** at the **Center for Lesbian/ Gay Community Services.**

If you're driving east, you'll pass through Knoxville–a small city with a quaint old town section and the main University of Tennessee. Call the **Gay/ Lesbian Helpline** about local events.

Bars

Chez Collette 300 Hermitage Ave (at Lea) **615/256-9134** • 4pm-3am • mostly women • neighborhood bar • women-owned/ run

The Gas Lite Lounge 167-1/2 8th Ave N (btwn Church & Commerce) **615/254-1278** • 4:30pm-1am, till 3am Fri-Sat, from 3pm wknds • lesbians/ gay men • piano bar • also restaurant

TC's Triangle 1401 4th Ave S (btwn Lafayette & Chestnut) **615/242-8131** • 11am-midnight, till 3am Fri-Sat, from noon Sun • lesbians/ gay men • neighborhood bar • also restaurant • wheelchair access

Your Way Cafe/ Women's Choice Bar 515 2nd Ave S (btwn Lea & Peabody) **615/256-9682** • 11am-3am, brunch noon-5pm Sun • mostly women • movies Mon • poetry Tue • dancing/DJ Th • live shows wknds • wheelchair access • women-owned/ run

Nightclubs

The Chute Complex 2535 Franklin Rd (at Wedgewood) **615/297-4571** • 5pm-3am • 5 bars • popular • mostly gay men • dancing/DJ • country/ western • leather • karaoke • live shows • also 'Silver Stirrup' restaurant/piano bar • wheelchair access

Connection Complex 901 Cowan St (at Jefferson) **615/742-1166** • 8pm-3am, clsd Mon • popular • lesbians/ gay men • dancing/DJ • country/ western • live shows • gift shop • also restaurant from 8pm Wed-Sun • some veggie • $5-15

Restaurants

The Mad Platter 1239 6th Ave N (at Monroe) **615/242-2563** • lunch, dinner by reservation only, clsd Sun • Californian • some veggie • wheelchair access • $20-30

Towne House Tea Room 165 8th Ave N (btwn Church & Commerce) **615/254-1277** • brkfst & lunch wkdays, clsd wknds • buffet • $5-7

World's End 1713 Church St (at 17th & 18th) **615/329-3480** • 4pm-1am, clsd Mon • American • full bar • $8-15

Entertainment & Recreation

Gay Cable Network Channel 19 • 9pm Tue & 10pm Sat

Bookstores

Davis-Kidd Booksellers 4007 Hillsboro Rd (at Abbot-Martin) **615/385-2645** • 9am-10pm • lesbigay section

Outloud Books & Gifts 1709 Church St (at 18th Ave) **615/340-0034** • 10am-10pm, till midnight Fri-Sat, from noon Sun • lesbigay

Tower Books 2404 West End Ave (at 22nd Ave) **615/327-8085** • 9am-midnight • large lesbigay section

Publications

Query 615/259-4135 • lesbigay newspaper

Xenogeny 615/831-1806 • lesbigay newspaper

Spiritual Groups

MCC 4425 Ashland City Hwy (at Briley Pkwy) **615/259-9636** • 10am & 7pm Sun

Newport

Accommodations

Christopher Place, An Intimate Resort 1500 Pinnacles Wy **423/623-6555, 800/595-9441** • gay/ straight • full brkfst • swimming • smokefree • wheelchair access • IGLTA • gay-owned/ run • $150-300

Texas

Statewide

Info Lines & Services

Texas Tourist Division 512/462-9191, 800/888-8TEX

Publications

Texas Triangle 512/476-0576 • lesbigay newspaper w/ arts calendar & resource list

TWT (This Week in Texas) 713/527-9111 • great resource listings

Abilene

Spiritual Groups

Exodus MCC 904 Walnut **915/672-7922** • 10:45am Sun

Amarillo

Bars

Atomic Lounge 3806 W 6th (btwn Prospect & Bellview) **806/351-0084** • 5pm-2am, from 8pm Sat, clsd Sun-Mon • gay/ straight • martini bar • wheelchair access

The Ritz 323 W 10th Ave (at Van Buren) **806/372-9382** • 2pm-2am • lesbians/ gay men • dancing/DJ wknds • country/ western • live shows

Sassy's 309 W 6th St **806/374-3029** • 4pm-2am • lesbians/ gay men • dancing/DJ Th-Sat • alternative

Nightclubs

Classifieds 519 E 10th St (at Buchanan) **806/374-2435** • 4pm-2am, from 8pm Sun-Tue • gay/ straight • dancing/DJ • live shows • wheelchair access

Restaurants

Italian Delight 2710 W 10th Ave (at Georgia) **806/372-5444** • lunch & dinner, clsd Sun • some veggie • beer/ wine • wheelchair access • $5-10

Spiritual Groups

Amarillo Unitarian Universalist Fellowship 4901 Cornell (at 49th) **806/355-9351** • 10am Sun, 11am in winter

MCC of Amarillo 2123 S Polk St (at 22nd St) **806/372-4557** • 10:30am Sun & 7pm Wed

Erotica

Boulevard Book Store & Video 601 N Eastern (at Eastern) **806/379-9002** • 24hrs

Studio One 9000 Triangle Dr **806/372-0648** • 24hrs

Arlington

see also Fort Worth

Info Lines & Services

Tarrant County Lesbian/ Gay Alliance 1219 6th Ave, Fort Worth **817/877-5544** • info line • newsletter

Women's Fellowship 609 Truman (at Trinity MCC) **817/265-5454** • monthly social/ support group • call for info

Nightclubs

Arlington 651 1851 W Division (at Fielder) **817/275-9651** • 2pm-2am • popular • mostly gay men • dancing/DJ • live shows • karaoke • wheelchair access

Spiritual Groups

Trinity MCC 609 Truman St (at Sandford) **817/265-5454** • 10:45am Sun • call for other events

Austin

Info Lines & Services

ALLGO (Austin Latino/ a Lesbian/ Gay Organization) 1715 E 6th St #112 **512/472-2001**

Lambda AA (Live and Let Live) 2700 W Anderson Ln #412 (in the Village Shopping Ctr) **512/453-1441** • 8pm nightly

Accommodations

Belle Springs PO Box 90623, 78709 • women only • camping • events • women's land • lesbian-owned/ run

Carrington's Bluff 1900 David St (at W 22nd St) **512/479-0638, 800/871-8908** • gay-friendly • full brkfst • wheelchair access • $79-109

Driskill Hotel 604 Brazos St (at 6th) **512/474-5911, 800/252-9367** • gay-friendly • food served • wheelchair access • $175-275 (even if you don't stay in this landmark hotel, be sure to check out the lobby)

Austin

Where the Girls Are: Downtown along Red River St., or 4th/5th St. near Lavaca, or at the music clubs and cafes downtown and around the University.

Annual Events: August/Sept - Austin G/L Int'l Film Festival 512/302-9889.
May & Labor Day - Splash Days. Weekend of parties in clothing-optional Hippie Hollow.

City Info: Texas Tourist Division 800/888-8839.
Greater Austin Chamber of Commerce 478-9383.

Attractions: Aqua Festival.
Elisabet Ney Museum 512/458-2255.
George Washington Carver Museum 512/472-4809.
Hamilton Pool.
Laguna Gloria Art Museum.
McKinney Falls State Park.
Mount Bonnell.
Museo del Barrio de Austin.
Zilker Park/Barton Springs.

Best View: State Capitol.

Weather: Summers are real scorchers (high 90's—low 100's) and last forever. Spring, fall and winter are welcome reliefs.

Transit: Yellow-Checker 512/472-1111.
Various hotels have their own shuttles.
Austin Transit 512/474-1200.

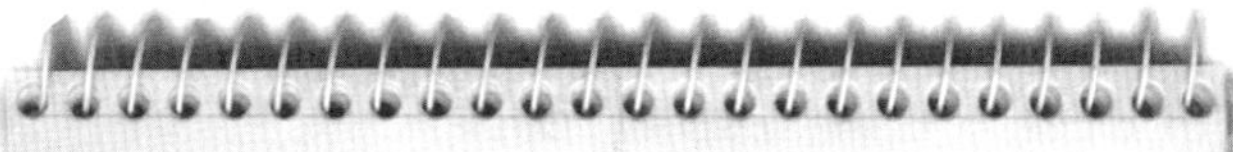

Austin

Austin is a cultural oasis in the heart of Texas. A refreshing bastion of left-wing, non-confrontational radicalism and the home of the South By Southwest (SXSW) music festival, this most collegiate of cities seems to belong anywhere but the Lone Star State. But it does. In fact, Austin is actually the state capital and the seat of the Texas legislature.

When harried urbanites in Dallas and Houston want a quick getaway, many head to the natural beauty of the Texas Hill Country. Just outside of the capital city, local boys and girls entertain themselves in the naturally cool (68° year-round) waters of Barton Springs. And Hippie Hollow, site of the lesbigay First and Last Splash Festivals, has long been a favorite of the clothing-optional crowd.

In town, entertainment centers around the Mardi Gras atmosphere of 6th Street downtown, where live and recorded music offerings run the gamut from hard-core punk to tear-jerkin' country & western. Most of the bars are mixed, female and male, straight and gay. But if you're in for a rousin' good time at a women's bar, then check out **Gaby & Mo's.**

The popular bookstore, **Book Woman,** is a great resource for connecting with like-minded women of every hue. The store regularly schedules seminars, book signings, and discussion groups; check in for details on all the women's events around town. Austin Women's Rugby Club matches are also popular, as are spring and summer softball and volleyball leagues. Try Fans of Women's Sports for the latest schedules and contacts.

Austin's lesbigay newsweekly, the **Texas Triangle,** is the best source for checking out all the current goings-on.

Governor's Inn 611 W 22nd St (at Rio Grande) **512/477-0711, 800/871-8908** • gay-friendly • neo-classical Victorian • full brkfst • $59-109

Lazy Oak Inn 211 W Live Oak (btwn S 1st & Congress) **512/447-8873** • gay-friendly • 1911 plantation-style farmhouse • full brkfst • $80-150

Omni Hotel 700 San Jacinto (at 8th) **512/476-3700, 800/843-6664** • gay-friendly • rooftop pool • health club • wheelchair access

Park Lane Guest House 221 Park Ln (at Drake) **512/447-7460, 800/492-8827** • lesbians/ gay men • kids ok • also cottage • wheelchair access • lesbian-owned/ run • $79-129

Summit House B&B 1204 Summit St (at Lupine) **512/445-5304** • lesbians/ gay men • reservation required • full brkfst • smokefree • pets ok • gay-owned/ run • $69-99 (barter for gardeners)

Bars

'Bout Time 9601 N IH-35 (at Rundberg) **512/832-5339** • 2pm-2am • popular • lesbians/ gay men • neighborhood bar • transgender-friendly • drag shows • volleyball court • wheelchair access

Casino El Camino 517 E 6th St (at Red River) **512/469-9330** • 4pm-2am • gay-friendly • neighborhood bar • psychedelic punk jazz lounge • great burgers

The Edge 213 W 4th (at Colorado) **512/480-8686** • 6pm-2am • lesbians/ gay men • neighborhood bar • dancing/DJ • wheelchair access

The Forum 408 Congress Ave (at 4th) **512/476-2900** • 2pm-2am, afterhours Fri-Sat • popular • mostly gay men • dancing/DJ • live shows • patio • Sun BBQ (seasonal)

Gaby & Mo's 1809 Manor Rd (at Chicon) **512/457-9027** • 7am-midnight, 9am-1am Sat, 9am-10pm Sun • mostly women • also cafe • food served • plenty veggie • live shows

Rainbow Cattle Company 305 W 5th St (btwn Guadalupe & Lavaca) **512/472-5288** • 2pm-2am • mostly gay men • dancing/DJ • country/ western

Nightclubs

1920's Club 918 Congress Ave (at E 11th St) **512/479-7979** • jazz club • food served

Dick's Dejà Disco 113 San Jacinto Blvd (btwn 1st & 2nd) **512/457-8010** • 2pm-2am, from noon wknds • mostly gay men • dancing/DJ • patio

Cafes

High Life Cafe 407 E 7th St (btwn Trinity & Neches) **512/474-5338** • 9am-midnight, till 1am Fri-Sat • bistro fare

Joe's Bakery & Coffeeshop 2305 E 7th St **512/472-0017** • 7am-3pm, clsd Mon • Tex-Mex

Restaurants

Castle Hill Cafe 1101 W 5th St (at Baylor) **512/476-0728** • lunch & dinner, clsd Sun • $11-16

Eastside Cafe 2113 Manor Rd (at Coleto, by bright yellow gas station) **512/476-5858** • lunch & dinner • some veggie • beer/ wine • wheelchair access • $8-15

Katz's 618 W 6th St (at Rio Grande) **512/472-2037** • 24hrs • NY-style deli • full bar • wheelchair access • $8-15

Romeo's 1500 Barton Springs Rd (nr Lamar) **512/476-1090** • 11am-10pm, till 11pm Fri-Sat • Italian • some veggie • beer/ wine • wheelchair access • $10-14

Suzi's Chinese Kitchen 1152 S Lamar (at Treadwell) **512/441-8400** • lunch & dinner

Threadgill's 6416 N Lamar (at Koenig) **512/451-5440** • 11am-10pm • great chicken-fried steak

West Lynn Cafe 1110 W Lynn (at W 12th St) **512/482-0950** • vegetarian • beer/ wine • $5-10

Entertainment & Recreation

Barton Springs Barton Springs Rd • natural swimming hole

Bat Colony Congress Ave Bridge (at Barton Springs Dr) • everything's bigger in Texas—especially the colony of bats that flies out from under this bridge every evening March-Oct

Historic Austin Tours 201 E 2nd St (in the Visitor Information Center) **512/478-0098, 800/926-2282 x4577** • free guided & self-guided tours of the Capitol, Congress Ave & 6th St, Texas State Cemetery, Hyde Park

Bookstores

Book Woman 918 W 12th St (at Lamar) **512/472-2785** • 10am-9pm, noon-6pm Sun • cards • jewelry • music • wheelchair access • women-owned/ run

Congress Avenue Booksellers 716 Congress Ave (at 8th) **512/478-1157** • 8am-6pm (till 8pm summers), 9am-4pm Sat, 10am-4pm Sun • lesbigay section

Lobo 3204-A Guadalupe (btwn 32nd & 33rd) **512/454-5406** • 9am-10pm, till 11pm Fri-Sat • lesbigay

Retail Shops

Celebration! 108 W 43rd (at Speedway) **512/453-6207** • 10am-6:30pm, clsd Sun • eclectic gift shop • women-owned/ run

Publications

Texas Triangle 512/476-0576 • lesbigay newspaper w/ arts calendar & statewide resource list

Spiritual Groups

First Unitarian Universalist Church 4700 Grover Ave (at 49th) **512/452-6168** • 9:30am & 11:15am Sun • wheelchair access

MCC Austin 4700 Grover Ave **512/708-8002** • 7pm Sat

Mishpachat Am Echad 512/451-7018 • lesbigay Jewish social group & info line

Erotica

Forbidden Fruit 512 Neches (btwn 5th & 6th) **512/478-8358**

Beaumont

Info Lines & Services

Lambda AA 6300 College (at Langham) **409/835-1508** • 8pm Mon, Tue, Th & Sat

Nightclubs

Copa 304 Orleans St (at Liberty) **409/832-4206** • 9pm-2am, till 3am Fri-Sat • popular • lesbians/ gay men • dancing/DJ • live shows • wheelchair access

Crockett Street Station 497 Crockett St (at Park) **409/833-3989** • 5pm-2am, from 4pm Sun • lesbians/ gay men • dancing/DJ Sat • live shows

Restaurants

Carlo's 2570 Calder (at 10th) **409/833-0108** • 11am-10:30pm, till 11pm Fri-Sat, clsd Sun • Italian/ Greek • live shows

Spiritual Groups

Spindletop Unitarian Church 1575 Spindletop Rd (off Martin Luther King Pkwy) **409/833-6883** • 10:25am Sun

College Station

Info Lines & Services

Gayline Texas A&M GLB Student Services **409/847-0321**

Lambda AA Bryan **409/361-7976 (AA#)** • call for mtg schedule

Bars

Dudley's Draw 311 University (on north side of campus) **409/846-3030** • 11am-1am • gay-friendly • neighborhood bar • wheelchair access

Nightclubs

The Club 308 N Bryan Ave (btwn 23rd & 24th Sts), Bryan **409/823-6767** • 9pm-2am, clsd Sun-Mon • popular • lesbians/ gay men • dancing/DJ • drag shows • 18+

Corpus Christi

Info Lines & Services

Lambda AA 1315 Craig (at MCC Corpus Christi) **512/882-8255** • 7pm Th & 8pm Fri

Accommodations

Anthony's By The Sea 732 S Pearl St, Rockport **512/729-6100, 800/460-2557** • gay/ straight • quiet retreat • full brkfst • swimming • hot tub • gay-owned/ run • $65-90

The Belles by the Sea 512/749-5221 • gay/ straight • Euro-style inn on dunes of Mustang Island & Port Aransas • swimming • $75-125

Christy Estates Suites 3942 Holly St **512/854-1091** • gay-friendly • 1- & 2-bdrm suites • hot tubs & spas • swimming • smokefree rms available • wheelchair access

Bars

The Hidden Door 802 S Staples St (at Coleman) **512/882-5002** • 3pm-2am, from noon wknds • lesbians/ gay men • neighborhood bar • wheelchair access

Mingles 512 S Staples (at Mary) **512/884-8022** • 9pm-2am, from 6:30pm Sun, clsd Mon-Tue • mostly women • dancing/DJ

Spiritual Groups

MCC of Corpus Christi 1315 Craig St (btwn 11th St nr Morgan & Staples intersection) **512/882-8255** • 11am Sun • wheelchair access

Dallas

see also Fort Worth

Info Lines & Services

Crossdressers/ TV Helpline 972/264-7103

Gay/ Lesbian Information Line 214/520-8781 • 24hr recorded info

John Thomas Gay/ Lesbian Community Center 2701 Reagan St (at Brown) **214/528-9254** • hours vary • call first • wheelchair access

Lambda AA 2438 Butler #106 **214/267-0222** • call for mtg schedule

Accommodations

The Courtyard on the Trail 8045 Forest Trail (at White Rock Trail) **214/553-9700, 800/484-6260 x0465** • gay/ straight • full brkfst • swimming • smokefree • gay-owned/ run • $105-150

Dallas Grand Hotel 1914 Commerce St (btwn St Paul & Harwood) **214/747-7000, 800/421-0011** • gay-friendly • rooftop spa • bar onsite • wheelchair access • $129+

Holiday Inn Dallas 1955 N Market Center Blvd **214/747-9551**

▲ **The Inn on Fairmount** 3701 Fairmount (nr Oak Lawn) **214/522-2800** • lesbians/ gay men • hot tub • gay-owned/ run • $95-135

Melrose Hotel 3015 Oak Lawn Ave (at Cedar Springs) **214/521-5151, 800/635-7673** • gay-friendly • full brfkst • swimming • smokefree rms available • also piano bar & lounge • also 4-star restaurant • wheelchair access • $129-275

Symphony House Rental Home 6327 Symphony Ln (nr Thornton Fwy & Jim Miller Rd) **214/388-9134** • gay/ straight • fully furnished house • IGLTA

Bars

Anchor Inn 4024 Cedar Springs (at Throckmorton) **214/526-4098** • 4pm-2am • mostly gay men • live shows • also 'Numbers,' 214/521-7861 • open 7am

Buddies II 4025 Maple Ave (at Throckmorton) **214/526-0887** • 11am-2am, from noon Sun, clsd Mon • mostly women • country/ western wknds • live shows • volleyball court

The Fraternity House 2525 Wycliff (at Dallas Tollway) **214/520-3728** • noon-2am • mostly gay men • show bar • male dancers Fri-Sat • karaoke Sun • also game room • wheelchair access

Hideaway Club 4144 Buena Vista (at Fitzhugh) **214/559-2966** • 8am-2am, from noon Sun • mostly gay men • professional • piano bar • patio

JR's Bar & Grill 3923 Cedar Springs Rd (at Throckmorton) **214/528-1004** • 11am-2am • popular • mostly gay men • grill till 4pm • wheelchair access

Jugs 4117 Maple Ave (at North Dallas Toll Rd) **214/521-3474** • noon-2am • mostly women • dancing/DJ • multi-racial clientele • live shows • wheelchair access • women-owned/ run

Moby Dick 4011 Cedar Springs Rd (btwn Douglas & Throckmorton) **214/520-6629** • noon-2am • lesbians/ gay men • videos • wheelchair access

Santa Fe 3851 Cedar Springs Rd (at Reagan) **214/521-7079** • noon-2am • lesbians/ gay men • neighborhood bar

Side 2 Bar 2615 Oak Lawn Ave (btwn Fairmount & Brown) **214/528-2026** • 10am-2am, from noon Sun • mostly gay men • neighborhood bar • wheelchair access

Sue Ellen's 3903 Cedar Springs Rd (at Reagan) **214/559-0707** • 3pm-2am, from noon wknds • popular • mostly women • dancing/DJ • live shows/ bands • 'Sue Ellen's Variety Show' Th • BBQ/ volleyball Sun • patio • wheelchair access

Z Bar 4100 Maple Ave **214/521-2311** • 7pm-2am, clsd Tue • mostly gay men • dancing/DJ • drag shows at midnight • wheelchair access

Nightclubs

Bamboleo's 5027 Lemmon Ave **214/520-1124** • 9pm-2am, clsd Mon-Th • lesbians/ gay men • dancing/DJ • Latino/a clientele • wheelchair access • unconfirmed

Club NV 216 N Crowdus (in Deep Ellum) **214/742-2708** • 9pm-2am, from 6pm Sun • mostly women • dancing/DJ • professional • mostly African-American • food served • live jazz Fri • Sun BBQ (BYOBBQ-ables) • 23+

Round-Up Saloon 3912-14 Cedar Springs Rd (at Throckmorton) **214/522-9611** • 3pm-2am, clsd Sun • mostly gay men • dancing/DJ • country/ western • lessons Tue & Th • wheelchair access

Village Station 3911 Cedar Springs Rd **214/559-0650** • 9pm-3am, from 5pm Sun • popular • mostly gay men • dancing/DJ • videos • T-dance Sun • also 'Rose Room' cabaret

Cafes

Dream Cafe 2800 Routh St (in the 'Quadrangle') **214/954-0486** • 7am-10pm, till 11pm Fri-Sat • plenty veggie

Restaurants

Ali Baba Cafe 1905 Greenville Ave (nr Ross) **214/823-8235** • lunch & dinner, clsd Sun-Mon • Middle Eastern

Black-Eyed Pea 3857 Cedar Springs Rd (at Reagan) **214/521-4580** • 11am-10:30pm • Southern homecooking • some veggie • wheelchair access • $5-10

Blue Mesa Grill 5100 Beltline Rd (at Tollway), Addison **972/934-0165** • 11am-10pm, from 10am Sun • great fajitas • full bar

Bombay Cricket Club 2508 Maple Ave (at Cedar Springs) **214/871-1333** • lunch & dinner • Indian

The Bronx Restaurant & Bar 3835 Cedar Springs Rd (at Oak Lawn) **214/521-5821** • lunch & dinner, Sun brunch, clsd Mon • some veggie • wheelchair access • gay-owned/ run • $8-15

Cremona Bistro & Cafe 3136 Routh St (at Cedar Springs) **214/871-1115** • 11am-10:30pm • Italian • full bar

Fresh Start Market & Deli 4108 Oak Lawn (nr Avondale) **214/528-5535** • 7am-7pm, 8am-6pm Sat, noon-6pm Sun • organic • plenty veggie • wheelchair access • gay-owned/ run

Hunky's 4000 Cedar Springs Rd (at Throckmorton) **214/522-1212** • 11am-10pm, till 11pm Th, till midnight Fri-Sat, noon-11pm Sun • beer/ wine • patio • wheelchair access • gay-owned/ run

Mansion on Turtle Creek 2821 Turtle Creek Blvd (at Gillespie) **214/526-2121** • lunch, dinner, Sun brunch • Southwestern • $26-48

Monica Aca Y Alla 2914 Main St (at Malcolm X) **214/748-7140** • popular • clsd Mon • Tex-Mex • full bar • live shows Fri-Sat • transgender-friendly • wheelchair access

Sushi on McKinney 4500 McKinney Ave (at Armstrong) **214/521-0969** • lunch & dinner, till 11pm Fri-Sat • full bar

Thai Soon 2018 Greenville Ave (at Prospect) **214/821-7666** • lunch & dinner, till midnight Fri-Sat

Vitto's 316 W 7th St (at Bishop) **214/946-1212** • lunch & dinner, till 11pm Fri-Sat • Italian • beer/ wine • wheelchair access • gay-owned/ run

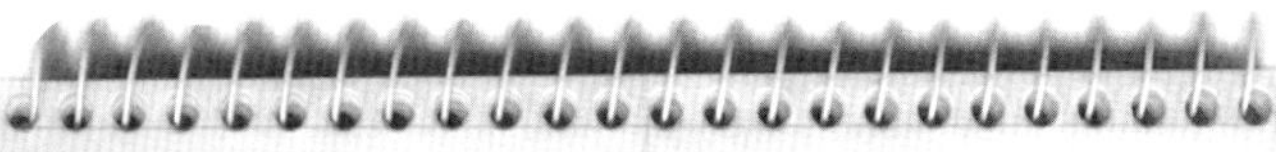

Dallas

Despite Dallas's conservative reputation as the buckle of the Bible Belt, this city has mellowed a great deal since the economic meltdown of the late 1980s. Two openly gay men have been elected to the City Council and sexual orientation is included in the city's anti-discrimination policy.

Dallas is a relatively young city, but wealthy residents have created a legacy of art museums, historical sites, and entertainment districts that will keep you busy. The Arts District in downtown is home to the Dallas Museum of Art (DMA) and a fabulous collection of modern masters, pre-Columbian artifacts, and the Reeves Collection of Impressionist art and decorative pieces. The 6th Floor Museum, on the site where Oswald allegedly perched while assassinating JFK, is a fascinating exploration of the facts and conspiracy theories. Old City Park recreates a pioneer village with original dwellings, period re-enactments, and exhibits. The West End, home of Planet Hollywood, the West End Marketplace, and the Dallas World Aquarium, offers a concentration of shops, restaurants, and diversions in one spot.

East of downtown is Deep Ellum, one of Dallas's earliest African-American communities ('ellum' is the way early residents pronounced Elm). Today it's live music central, with a variety of clubs offering a host of local and national bands, seven nights a week. Just about anything goes here, as long as it's left of center. Every segment of the population is represented in an ever-growing collection of offbeat bars, restaurants, shops, and tattoo parlors.

Further east is Fair Park, site of the State Fair of Texas every fall. Any time of the year you can enjoy a wonderful day here touring the African-American Museum, the Science Place and its IMAX theater, and the Dallas Aquarium and Horticulture Center. The surrounding neighborhood is the current habitué of choice for artists, with studios, showrooms, and gathering places along State and Parry Streets.

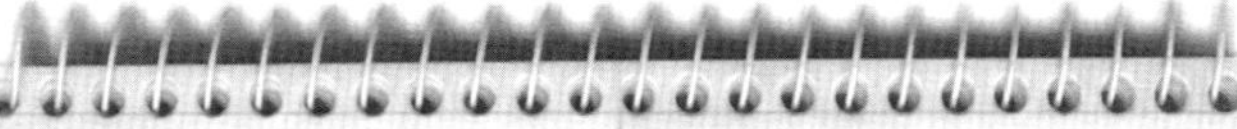

The lesbian and gay community of Dallas is thriving, concentrated in Oak Lawn, just north of downtown. Most of the businesses along the Cedar Springs Strip (Cedar Springs Road between Douglas and Oak Lawn Avenue) are gay-owned, and all are lesbigay-friendly. Same-sex couples populate the sidewalks and restaurant tables day and night. Parking can be next to impossible on weekend nights, though, and take care if you decide to park on darkened side streets.

The local women's community is less visible than the gay men's, but you will find three full time women's bars—**Buddies II, Jugs,** and **Sue Ellen's**—and several active women's organizations. The community's churches and sports groups are also popular meeting places for singles. Lesbian couples are concentrated in the suburb of Oak Cliff or in Casa Linda, near White Rock Lake.

Dallas

Where the Girls Are: Oak Lawn in central Dallas is the gay and lesbian stomping grounds, mostly on Cedar Springs Ave.

Lesbigay Pride: September. 214/521-0638.

Annual Events: February - Black Gay/Lesbian Conference.

City Info: 800/752-9222.

Attractions: Dallas Arboretum & Botanical Garden 214/327-8263.
Dallas Museum of Art 214/922-1200.
Dallas Theatre Center/ Frank Lloyd Wright.
Texas State Fair & State Fair Park 214/565-9931.

Best View: Hyatt Regency Tower.

Weather: Can be unpredictable. Hot summers (90°s—100°s) with possible severe rain storms. Winter temperatures hover in the 20°s through 40°s range.

Transit: Yellow Cab 214/426-6262. Dallas Area Rapid Transit (DART) 214/979-1111.

Ziziki's 4514 Travis St, #122 (in Travis Walk) **214/521-2233** • 11am-11pm, till midnight Fri-Sat, Sun brunch • Greek • full bar • wheelchair access

Entertainment & Recreation

Conspiracy Museum 110 S Market (in the Katy Bldg) **214/741-3040** • 9am-5pm, 10am-7pm wknds • dedicated to infamous US assassinations since 1835 & their cover-ups

Bookstores

Crossroads Market Bookstore/ Cafe 3930 Cedar Springs Rd (at Throckmorton) **214/521-8919** • 7am-midnight • lesbigay • wheelchair access

Retail Shops

Off the Street 4001-B Cedar Springs (at Throckmorton) **214/521-9051** • 10am-9pm, noon-6pm Sun • lesbigay gifts

Tapelenders 3946 Cedar Springs Rd (at Throckmorton) **214/528-6344** • 9am-midnight, from 11am Sun • lesbigay gifts • video rental • gay-owned/ run

Publications

Dallas Lesbian News 214/520-8108 • free quarterly newsletter

Dallas Voice 214/754-8710 • lesbigay newspaper

TWT (This Week in Texas) 214/521-0622 • great statewide resource listings

Spiritual Groups

Cathedral of Hope MCC 5910 Cedar Springs Rd (at Inwood) **214/351-1901** • 9am & 11am Sun, 6pm Sat • wheelchair access

Dignity Dallas 6525 Inwood Rd (at St Thomas the Apostle Episcopal Church) **214/521-5342 x835** • 6pm Sun • wheelchair access

First Unitarian Church of Dallas 4015 Normandy (at Preston) **214/528-3990** • 9am & 11am Sun (10am Sun summers)

Holy Trinity Community Church 4402 Roseland (btwn Peak & Carrol) **214/827-5088** • 11am Sun

Honesty Texas (Baptist) 5910 Cedar Springs (Cathedral of Hope MCC) **214/521-5342 x233** • 7:30pm 1st Tue

St Thomas the Apostle Episcopal Church 6525 Inwood Rd (at Mockingbird Ln) **214/352-0410** • 8am & 10am Sun

White Rock Community Church 9353 Garland Rd **214/320-0043** • 9:30am & 10:45am Sun

Gyms & Health Clubs

Centrum Sports Club 3102 Oak Lawn (at Cedar Springs) **214/522-4100** • gay-friendly • swimming • day pass $15

Erotica

Alternatives 1720 W Mockingbird Ln (at Hawes) **214/630-7071** • 8am-6am

Leather by Boots 2525 Wycliff #124 (at Maple) **214/528-3865** • 10am-6pm, till 8pm Th-Sat, clsd Sun

Shades of Grey Leather 3928 Cedar Springs Rd (at Throckmorton) **214/521-4739** • 11am-8pm, till 10pm Fri-Sat, till 6pm Sun

Denison

Bars

Goodtime Lounge 2520 N Hwy 91 N **903/463-9944** • 7pm-2am, from 6pm Fri-Sun • lesbians/ gay men • private club

Denton

Nightclubs

Bedo's 1215 E University Dr **940/566-9910** • 8pm-midnight, from 6pm Fri, till 1am Sat, from 5pm Sun • lesbians/ gay men • dancing/DJ • live shows • private club • wheelchair access • women-owned/ run • unconfirmed

Cafes

Cupboard Natural Foods 200 W Congress St (at Elm) **940/387-5386** • 9am-9pm, 11am-6pm Sun • health food store & cafe

Spiritual Groups

Harvest MCC 2011 Carpenter Ln (in Corinth) **940/321-2332** • 9am & 11am Sun

El Paso

Info Lines & Services

GLBT Community Center 910 N Mesa (btwn Montana & Rio Grande, enter rear) **915/562-4297** • also 'Generation Q' pride store

Lambda Line/ Lambda Services **915/562-4297** • 24hr info

Youth OUTreach (contact Lambda Line) **915/562-4297**

Bars

Briar Patch 508 N Stanton (at Missouri) **915/577-9555** • noon-2am • lesbians/ gay men • neighborhood bar • patio

The Whatever Lounge 701 E Paisano St (at Ochoa) **915/533-0215** • 2pm-2am • mostly gay men • dancing/DJ • Latino/a clientele • wheelchair access

Nightclubs

The New Old Plantation 301 S Ochoa St (at Paisano) **915/533-6055** • 9pm-2am, till 4am Fri-Sat, clsd Mon-Wed • popular • lesbians/ gay men • dancing/DJ • live shows Sun • videos • wheelchair access • also 'Generation Q II' pride store upstairs

San Antonio Mining Co 800 E San Antonio Ave (at Ochoa) **915/533-9516** • 3pm-2am • popular • lesbians/ gay men • dancing/DJ • live shows • videos • wheelchair access

Restaurants

The Little Diner 7209 7th St, Canutillo **915/877-2176** • true Texas fare

Spiritual Groups

MCC of El Paso 9828 Montana, Ste R (in Plaza del Sol) **915/591-4155** • 10:30am Sun

Fort Worth

see also Dallas

Info Lines & Services

Lambda AA **817/332-3533** • call for mtg schedule

Tarrant County Lesbian/ Gay Alliance 1219 6th Ave **817/877-5544** • info line • newsletter

Accommodations

Two Pearls B&B 804 S Alamo St (at Akard), Weatherford **817/596-9316** • gay/ straight • modernized 1898 home • full brkfst • women-owned/ run • $70-125

Bars

The Corral Club & Patio Bar 621 Hemphill St (at Pennsylvania) **817/335-0196** • 11am-2am, from noon Sun • mostly gay men • live shows wknds • videos • patio • wheelchair access

Lancaster Beach Club 2620 E Lancaster (at Beach) **817/535-4363** • 2pm-2am • lesbians/ gay men • dancing/DJ Th-Sun • karaoke Wed • live shows wknds

Nightclubs

651 Club Fort Worth 651 S Jennings Ave (at Pennsylvania) **817/332-0745** • noon-2am • mostly gay men • more women Fri-Sat • dancing/DJ • country/ western • wheelchair access

DJ's 1308 St Louis Ave (at Magnolia) **817/927-7321** • 7pm-2am, till 3am Fri-Sat, clsd Mon-Tue • popular • lesbians/ gay men • dancing/DJ • live shows Fri-Sat • also restaurant

Cafes

Paris Coffee Shop 704 W Magnolia (at Hemphill) **817/335-2041** • 6am-2:30pm, till 11am Sat, clsd Sun

Publications

Alliance News **817/877-5544**

Spiritual Groups

Agape MCC 4615 California Pkwy (take the Anglin exit off I-20) **817/535-5002** • 8:45am & 10:30am Sun, 7pm Wed • wheelchair access

First Jefferson Unitarian Universalist 1959 Sandy Ln (at Meadowbrook Dr) **817/451-1505** • 11am Sun • lesbigay group 7pm 1st Th • wheelchair access

Fredericksburg

Accommodations

Town Creek B&B 304 N Edison (at W Travis) **830/997-6848** • gay/ straight • full brkfst • $110-160

Galveston

Accommodations

Galveston Island Women's Guesthouse **409/763-2450** • women only • smokefree • near beach • sundeck • lesbian-owned/ run • $50

Bars

Robert's Lafitte 2501 'Q' Ave (at 25th St) **409/765-9092** • 10am-2am, from noon Sun • mostly gay men • drag shows wknds • wheelchair access

Nightclubs

Evolution 2214 Ships Mechanic Rd (at 23rd) **409/763-4212** • 8pm-2am, till 4am Fri-Sat • popular • lesbians/ gay men • dancing/DJ Th-Sun • videos

Kon Tiki Club 315 23rd St (btwn Market & Mechanic) **409/763-6264** • 4pm-2am, from 2pm Sun • popular • lesbians/ gay men • dancing/DJ & live shows Fri-Sun

Granbury

Accommodations

Pearl Street Inn B&B 319 W Pearl St **817/579-7465, 888/732-7578** • gay-friendly • full brkfst • hot tub • $79-108

Groesbeck

Accommodations

Rainbow Ranch Campground Rte 2, Box 165 **254/729-5847, 888/875-7596** • lesbians/ gay men • open all year • located on Lake Limestone on 100+ acres • 40 campsites & 36 RV hookups • women-owned/ run • $10/person

Gun Barrel City

Accommodations

Triple 'B' Cottages 903/451-5105 • gay/ straight • 78 miles from Dallas on Cedar Creek Lake • camping available • motor homes & travel trailers welcome • kids/ pets ok • gay-owned/ run • $75-125

Bars

Friends 602 S Gun Barrel/ Hwy 198 **903/887-2061** • 4pm-midnight, till 1am Sat, from 3pm wknds • lesbians/ gay men • neighborhood bar • food served • patio • wheelchair access

Houston

Info Lines & Services

Gay/ Lesbian Switchboard 713/529-3211 • 7pm-10pm, clsd wknds

Houston Area Women's Center/ Hotline 1010 Waugh Dr (at W Dallas) **713/528-2121** • 9am-9pm, till noon Sat, clsd Sun • wheelchair access

Lambda AA Center 1201 W Clay (btwn Montrose & Waugh) **713/521-1243** • noon-midnight, from 8pm Sat • wheelchair access

LOAFF (Lesbians Over Age Fifty) 1505 Nevada (at Houston Mission Church) • 2pm 3rd Sun

Accommodations

Angel Arbor B&B Inn 848 Heights Blvd (at 9th) **713/868-4654, 800/722-8788** • gay-friendly • full brkfst • smokefree • close to downtown • $95-125

Houston

Where the Girls Are: Strolling the Montrose district near the intersection of Montrose and Westheimer or out on Buffalo Speedway at the Plaza.

Lesbigay Pride: June. 713/529-6979.

City Info: 800/231-7799.

Attractions: Astroworld 713/799-1234.
Contemporary Arts Museum 713/284-8250.
The Galleria.
Menil Museum 713/525-9400.
Museum of Fine Arts 713/639-7300.
Rothko Chapel 713/524-9839.

Best View: Spindletop, the revolving cocktail lounge on top of the Hyatt Regency.

Weather: Humid all year round—you're not that far from the Gulf. Mild winters, although there are a few days when the temperatures drop into the 30°s. Winter also brings occasional rainy days. Summers are very hot.

Transit: Yellow Cab 713/236-1111. Metropolitan Transit Authority 713/635-4000.

Houston

With mild winters and blazing summers, Houston is the hottest lesbian spot in the Southwest. From the Astrodome to San Jacinto, Houston welcomes sports fans, historians, and shoppers. This thriving urban center even has bars bigger than your hometown where you can dance the night away.

Shop the emporiums devoted to women, from **Lobo** and **Crossroads Market** with their hip coffee bar and periodicals, to **Lucia's Garden**. Fine and casual dining among beautiful women takes place all over the cruisy Montrose (where lesbians are said to shop and party) and Heights neighborhoods. Try elegant **Baba Yega's** and **Java Java**. Take some time to admire the mansions of the Montrose and the elegant Victorian homes of the Heights.

For a change of scenery, check out the babes on Galveston Island Beach, about a one-hour drive south. While you're there, refresh yourself and dance at **Evolution,** a popular lesbigay bar.

After you've seen and done all that Houston has to offer, collapse in your jacuzzi suite at the historic **Lovett Inn** and kick back with a copy of the **Houston Voice.**

Galveston Island Guest House 1426 Ave N 1/2, Galveston **409/763-2450** • women only • 1/2 blk from beach & many restaurants • friendly home atmosphere • lesbian-owned/ run • $45-55

Gar-Den Suites 2702 Crocker St (at W Dallas) **713/528-2302, 800/484-1036 x2669** • gay/ straight • nudity ok at hot tub • smokefree • gay-owned/ run • $60-90

The Lovett Inn 501 Lovett Blvd, Montrose (at Whitney) **713/522-5224, 800/779-5224** • gay/ straight • historic home of former Houston mayor & Federal Court judge • hot tub • swimming • IGLTA • gay-owned/ run • $75-175

Patrician B&B Inn 1200 Southmore Blvd (at San Jacinto) **713/523-1114, 800/553-5797** • gay-friendly • 1919 three-story mansion • full brkfst • $90-125

Bars

Chances 1100 Westheimer (at Waugh) **713/523-7217** • 10am-2am, from noon Sun • lesbians/ gay men • dancing/DJ • live shows • wheelchair access

Club Rainbow 1417-B Westheimer **713/522-5166** • 5pm-close, after-hours Fri-Sat • mostly women • dancing/DJ • professional crowd • dress code • cover charge wknds

Cousins 817 Fairview (at Converse) **713/528-9204** • 11am-2am, from noon Sun • lesbians/ gay men • neighborhood bar • live shows

Decades 1205 Richmond (btwn Mandel & Montrose) **713/521-2224** • 11am-2am, from noon Sun • mostly gay men • neighborhood bar • women-owned/ run

Guava Lamp 2159 Portsmouth (btwn Shepherd & Greenbriar, in Shepherd Plaza) **713/524-3359** • 4pm-2am • mostly gay men • swanky lounge w/ martinis & more • karaoke Wed & Sun • drag shows Sat • wheelchair access

JR's 808 Pacific (at Grant) **713/521-2519** • noon-2am • popular • mostly gay men • more women Sun • live shows • videos • patio • wheelchair access

Michael's Outpost 1419 Richmond (at Mandell) **713/520-8446** • 11am-2am, from noon Sun • mostly gay men • neighborhood bar

The New Barn 1100 Westheimer (at Waugh) **713/521-9533** • 3pm-2am, from noon Sat, clsd Sun-Mon • lesbians/ gay men • dancing/DJ • country/ western

Zimm's Bar 4321 Montrose (at Richmond) **713/521-2002** • 4pm-midnight • gay/ straight • wine & martini bar

Nightclubs

Club Nsomnia 202 Tuam Ave (at Helena St) **713/522-6100** • midnight-5am Fri-Sun • mostly gay men • dancing/DJ • 18+

Club Picasso 2151 Richmond Ave (btwn Shepherd & Greenbriar, in Shepherd Plaza) **713/520-8636** • 8pm-2am, clsd Mon • popular • mostly gay men • dancing/DJ • live shows • videos • wheelchair access

Incognito 2524 McKinney (at Live Oak) **713/237-9431** • 9pm-2am, from 6pm Sun, clsd Tue-Th • lesbians/ gay men • mostly African-American • live shows

Inergy 5750 Chimney Rock (at Glemon) **713/666-7310** • 8pm-2am, clsd Tue • popular • lesbians/ gay men • dancing/DJ • Latina/o clientele • dancers Fri-Sat

Numbers 300 Westheimer (at Taft) **713/526-6551** • gay-friendly • dancing/DJ • younger crowd • live music venue

Pacific Street 710 Pacific St (at Crocker) **713/523-0213** • 9pm-2am, from 7pm Fri & Sun • popular • mostly gay men • dancing/DJ • leather • live shows • videos • patio • wheelchair access

Rascals 1318 Westheimer (at Commonwealth) **713/942-2582** • 9pm-2am, from 7pm Fri, clsd Mon-Wed • lesbians/ gay men • dancing/DJ • mostly African-American • live shows • videos • 18+

Rich's 2401 San Jacinto (at McIlhenny) **713/759-9606** • 9pm-2am, from 7pm Sun, clsd Mon-Wed • popular • mostly gay men • dancing/DJ • alternative • 18+ • live shows • videos

South Beach 810 Pacific (at Grant) **713/521-9123** • 9pm-2am, from 7pm Sun, clsd Mon-Tue • popular • mostly gay men • dancing/DJ • 18+ Wed & Sat • live shows Th • videos

Venus 2151 Richmond Ave (at 'Club Picasso') **713/520-8636** • 8pm-2am Wed only • popular • mostly women • dancing/DJ • videos • wheelchair access

Cafes

Diedrich Coffee 4005 Montrose (btwn Richmond & W Alabama) **713/526-1319** • 6am-midnight

Java Java Cafe 911 W 11th (at Shepherd) **713/880-5282** • open till midnight Fri-Sat • popular

Toopees Coffee Company 1830 W Alabama (at Woodhead) **713/522-7662** • 6am-11pm, till 12:30am Fri-Sat • beer/ wine • patio • wheelchair access

Restaurants

A Moveable Feast 2202 W Alabama (at Greenbriar) **713/528-3585** • 9am-10pm, 11am-7pm Sun • plenty veggie • also health food store • wheelchair access • $7-12

Baba Yega's 2607 Grant (at Pacific) **713/522-0042** • 11am-10pm, till 11pm Fri-Sat • popular • full bar • patio • wheelchair access

Barnaby's Cafe 604 Fairview (at Stanford) **713/522-0106** • 11am-10pm, till 11pm Fri-Sat, clsd Mon • popular • beer/ wine • wheelchair access

Black-Eyed Pea 2048 W Grey (at Shepherd) **713/523-0200** • 11am-10pm • popular • Southern • wheelchair access • $5-10

Brasil 2604 Dunlavy (at Westheimer) **713/528-1993** • 9am-2am • bistro • plenty veggie • beer/ wine

Cafe Annie 1728 Post Oak Blvd (at San Felipe) **713/840-1111** • lunch Mon-Fri, dinner nightly, clsd Sun

Captain Benny's Half Shell 8506 S Main **713/666-5469** • lunch & dinner, clsd Sun • beer/ wine

Chapultepec 813 Richmond (btwn Montrose & Main) **713/522-2365** • 24hrs • Mexican • some veggie • beer/ wine • $8-15

Charlie's 1100 Westheimer (at Montrose) **713/522-3332** • 24hrs, clsd Mon • lesbians/ gay men • full bar • wheelchair access • $5-10

Fox Diner 905 Taft **713/523-5369** • lunch & dinner Mon-Fri, dinner Sat, brunch Sun • gourmet salads, steak & fish • beer/ wine • smokefree • gay-owned/ run

House of Pies 3112 Kirby (at Richmond/ Alabama) **713/528-3816** • 24hrs • popular • wheelchair access • $5-10

Magnolia Bar & Grill 6000 Richmond Ave (at Fountain) **713/781-6207** • Cajun • full bar • wheelchair access

Ming's Cafe 2703 Montrose (at Westheimer) **713/529-7888**

Mo Mong 1201 Westheimer #B (at Montrose) **713/524-5664** • 11am-11pm, till midnight Fri-Sat • Vietnamese • full bar

Ninfa's 2704 Navigation **713/228-1175** • 11am-10pm • popular • Mexican • some veggie • full bar • $7-12

Ninos 2817 W Dallas (btwn Montrose & Waugh) **713/522-5120** • lunch & dinner, dinner only Sat, clsd Sun • Italian • some veggie • full bar • $10-20

Pot Pie Pizzeria 1525 Westheimer (at Mandell) **713/528-4350** • 11am-11pm, till 10pm Sun • some veggie • beer/ wine

Spanish Flower 4701 N Main (at Airline) **713/869-1706** • 24hrs, till 10pm Tue • beer/ wine

Entertainment & Recreation

'After Hours' KPFT-FM 90.1 **713/526-4000** • midnight-3am Sat • lesbigay radio • also 'Lesbian/ Gay Voices' 6pm Fri

Bookstores

Crossroads Market Bookstore/ Cafe 1111 Westheimer (at Yoakum) **713/942-0147** • 7am-midnight • lesbigay

Lobo—Houston 3939 Montrose Blvd (at Alabama) **713/522-5156** • 9am-midnight, from 7am wknds • lesbigay books • videos • also coffeeshop • wheelchair access

Retail Shops

Basic Brothers 1232 Westheimer (at Commonwealth) **713/522-1626** • 10am-9pm, noon-6pm Sun • lesbigay gifts • wheelchair access

Hyde Park Gallery 711 Hyde Park (at Montrose) **713/526-2744** • noon-6pm, clsd Tue-Wed • lesbigay art gallery

Lucia's Garden 2942 Virginia (at W Alabama) **713/523-6494** • 10am-6pm, till 7pm Tue & Th, clsd Sun • spiritual herb center

Publications

Houston Voice 713/529-8490, 800/729-8490 • lesbigay newspaper

▲ **OutSmart 713/520-7237** • free monthly lesbigay newsmagazine

TWT (This Week in Texas) 713/527-9111 • great statewide resource listings

Spiritual Groups

Dignity Houston 1307 Yale #H **713/880-2872** • 7:30pm Sat & 5:30pm Sun

MCC of the Resurrection 1919 Decatur St (at White) **713/861-9149** • 9am & 11am Sun, 7pm Wed

Mishpachat Alizim 713/748-7079 • Jewish worship & social/ support group

Gyms & Health Clubs

Fitness Exchange 4040 Milan **713/524-9932** • gay-friendly

YMCA Downtown 1600 Louisiana St (at Pease) **713/659-8501** • gay-friendly • swimming

Erotica

Diners News 240 Westheimer (at Mason) **713/522-9679** • 24hrs

Leather by Boots 807 Fairview (at Crocker) **713/526-2668** • noon-8pm

Leather Forever 711 Fairview (at Crocker) **713/526-6940** • noon-8pm

Killeen

Nightclubs

Krosover 1509 W Veterans Memorial Blvd E (Business Rte 190), Harker Heights **254/680-5239** • 9pm-2am Th-Sun • lesbians/ gay men • dancing/DJ • talent night Th • drag shows Sat • strict dress code

Laredo

Nightclubs

Discovery 2019 Farragut **956/722-9032** • 7pm-2am, clsd Mon-Tue • lesbians/ gay men • dancing/DJ • Latina/o clientele • live shows • beer/ wine

Longview

Info Lines & Services

Lambda AA 906 Padon **903/236-3974** • call for mtg times

Bars

Decisions 2103 E Marshall (2 blks E of Eastman Rd) **903/757-4884** • 5pm-2am • lesbians/ gay men • dancing/DJ Fri-Sun • live shows Sun • wheelchair access

Lifestyles 916 S Eastman Rd **903/758-8082** • noon-2am • lesbians/ gay men • dancing/DJ Sat

Spiritual Groups

MCC Longview (Church With A Vision) 420 E Cotton St **903/753-1501** • 11am Sun • wheelchair access

Lubbock

Info Lines & Services

AA Lambda 4501 University Ave (at MCC) **806/828-3316** • 8pm Tue & Fri

Bars

The Luxor 2211 4th St (at 'W') **806/744-3744** • 9pm-close Th-Sat • gay/ straight • dancing/DJ

Nightclubs

The Loft 2401 Main St (at Ave X) **806/744-4222** • 8pm-2am • lesbians/ gay men • dancing/DJ • country/ western • live shows • wheelchair access • cover charge

Spiritual Groups

MCC 4501 University Ave (at 45th) **806/792-5562** • 11am & 6pm Sun, 7:30pm Wed • wheelchair access

Odessa/Midland

Nightclubs

Fictxions 409 N Hancock **915/580-5449** • 9:30pm-2am, clsd Mon • lesbians/ gay men • dancing/DJ • live shows • wheelchair access • unconfirmed

Miss Lillie's Nitespot 8401 Andrews Hwy **915/366-6799** • 8pm-2am, clsd Mon • lesbians/ gay men • dancing/DJ • live shows • videos • wheelchair access • unconfirmed

Spiritual Groups

Holy Trinity Community Church 412 E Gist (at Fort Worth), Midland **915/570-4822** • 11am Sun

Erotica

B&L Adult Bookstore 5890 W Univ Blvd (at Mercury) **915/381-6855** • clsd Sun

Rio Grande Valley

Accommodations

La Mirada Country Estates 8901 W Business Hwy 83 (at Tamm Ln), Harlingen **956/428-1966** • gay-friendly • swimming • hot tub • club house • also camping & RV hookups • gay-owned/ run

San Antonio

Info Lines & Services

Gay/ Lesbian Community Center 3126 N St Mary's (at 281) **210/732-4300** • 1pm-8pm, till 6pm Sun • movie night Fri • wheelchair access

The Happy Foundation 411 Bonham (next to the Alamo) **210/227-6451** • lesbigay archives

Lambda Club AA 923 E Mistletoe **210/732-4300** • call for times

LISA Line (Lesbian Information San Antonio) 210/828-5472

Accommodations

Adams House B&B 231 Adams St (at S Alamo) **210/224-4791, 800/666-4810** • gay-friendly • full brkfst • also carriage house • $89-159

Arbor House at La Villita 540 S St Mary's St (btwn S Alamo & S St Mary's) **210/472-2005, 888/272-6700** • gay/ straight • kids/ pets ok • IGLTA • gay-owned/ run • $95-195

Bella Vista 2121 Hilltop, Wimberley **512/847-6425** • lesbians/ gay men • swimming • smokefree • wheelchair access • $95-125

The Garden Cottage 800/235-7215 • gay-friendly • private cottage • $50/ night (ask about weekly rates)

▲ **The Painted Lady Inn on Broadway** 620 Broadway (at 6th) **210/220-1092** • popular • lesbians/ gay men • private art deco suites • kids ok • rooftop deck & spa • $79-189

San Antonio B&B in King William Historic District **210/222-1828** • lesbians/ gay men • full brkfst • hot tub • $89 & up

Villager Lodge 1126 E Elmira (at Wilmington) **210/222-9463, 800/584-0800** • gay-friendly • $34

Bars

2015 Place 2015 San Pedro (at Woodlawn) **210/733-3365** • 4pm-2am, from 2pm wknds • mostly gay men • neighborhood bar • patio

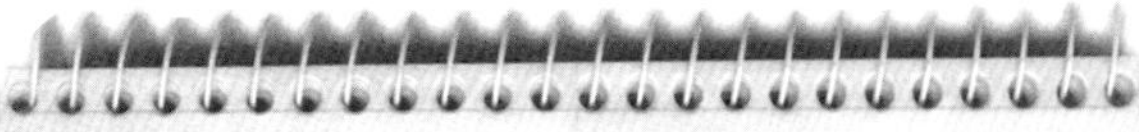

San Antonio

Although its moment of glory was more than 150 years ago, the Alamo has become a mythological symbol that still greatly influences San Antonians of today. The Alamo was a mission in which a handful of Texans—including Davy Crockett and Jim Bowie—kept a Mexican army of thousands at bay for almost two weeks.

San Antonians are fiercely proud of this heritage, and maintain a rough-n-ready attitude to prove it. This is just as true of the dykes in San Antonio as anyone else.

You'll find most of them at **Chances, Petticoat Junction,** or at **Textures**, the feminist bookstore, and the lesbigay **Q Bookstore** catching up on the latest good reading.

Though there's no gay ghetto in this spread-out city, there are some lesbian-friendly businesses clustered along various streets, including the 5000 blocks of S. Flores and McCullough, the 1400–1900 blocks of N. Main, and scattered along Broadway and San Pedro. But get the real 411 by calling **LISA**, the **Lesbian Information Line**, at 210/828-5472.

For more traditional sightseeing, there's always the Alamo or the River Walk. The architecture in old San Antonio is quaint and beautiful—stop by the **Bonham Exchange** for a taste. Better yet is the view from the deck of the **Painted Lady Inn on Broadway** bed & breakfast.

The Annex 330 San Pedro Ave (at Euclid) **210/223-6957** • 4pm-2am • mostly gay men • neighborhood bar • patio • wheelchair access

Around the Corner 2323 Quintana Rd (at Bynum) **210/923-9032** • 1pm-2am • mostly women • dancing/DJ • Latina/o clientele • menudo Tue • BBQ 5pm Sun

Chances 115 General Krueger (at Blanco) **210/377-1022** • 2pm-2am, clsd Sun-Mon • lesbians/ gay men

Myth 1902 McCullough Ave (at Dewey) **210/733-1516** • 4pm-2am • mostly gay men • dancing/DJ • wheelchair access

Petticoat Junction 1818 N Main (at Dewey) **210/737-2344** • 6pm-2am, from 2pm Sun • mostly women • patio & volleyball court • wheelchair access

Silver Dollar Saloon 1418 N Main Ave (at Laurel) **210/227-2623** • 2pm-2am, from 5pm Fri-Sat • mostly gay men • dancing/DJ • country/ western • live shows • theme nights • 'Trash Disco' Sun • videos • 2-story patio bar • wheelchair access

Nightclubs

The Bonham Exchange 411 Bonham St (at 3rd/ Houston) **210/271-3811** • 4pm-2am, from 8pm wknds, till 4am Fri-Sat • lesbians/ gay men • dancing/DJ • videos • 18+ • gay-owned/ run

Cameo 1123 E Commerce (nr I-37) **210/226-7055** • gay-friendly • gay 1st Wed only • dancing/DJ • beer/ wine • underground mini-rave

Copa SA 119 El Mio (at San Pedro) **210/342-2276** • 4pm-2am • mostly gay men • dancing/DJ • also large game room • wheelchair access

The Saint 1430 N Main (at Evergreen) **210/225-7330** • 9pm-2am Fri, till 4am Sat • lesbians/ gay men • dancing/DJ • alternative • live shows • 18+

The Vance Jackson 2405 Vance Jackson **210/524-9324** • 8pm-2am, from 9pm Fri-Sat, 6pm-midnight Sun, clsd Mon & Wed • lesbians/ gay men • dancing/DJ Fri-Sat • BYOB

Woody's/ Rebar 826 San Pedro (at Laurel) **210/226-2620** • 9pm-2am, till 4am Fri-Sat, clsd Sun-Wed • lesbians/ gay men • dancing/DJ • 18+

Cafes

Candlelight Coffeehouse 3011 N St Mary's (at Rte 281) **210/738-0099** • 4pm-midnight, clsd Mon

Restaurants

Giovanni's Pizza & Italian Restaurant 913 S Brazos (at Guadalupe) **210/212-6626** • 10am-8pm, clsd Sun • some veggie • $7-12

San Antonio

Where the Girls Are: Coupled up in the suburbs or carousing downtown.

Lesbigay Pride: June. 210/333-1635.

Annual Events: Late April - Fiesta San Antonio.

City Info: 210/270-8748, 800/447-3372, web: www.sanantoniocvb.com.

Attractions: The Alamo 210/225-1391.
Hemisfair Park.
El Mercado.
Plaza de Armas.
River Walk.
San Antonio Museum of Art 210/978-8100.

Best View: From the deck of The Inn on Broadway.

Weather: 60°s-90°s in the summer, 40°s-60°s in the winter.

Transit: Yellow Cab 210/226-4242.
Via Info 210/362-2020.

Madhatter's Tea 3606 Ave 'B' (at Mulberry) **210/821-6555** • 10am-9pm, till 10pm Fri-Sat, brunch 9am-5pm Sun • BYOB • patio • wheelchair access

North St Mary's Brewing Co Pub & Deli 2734 N St Mary's **210/737-6255** • lunch Mon-Fri, dinner nightly, clsd Sun • live shows

Bookstores

Q Bookstore 2803 N St Mary's (at French) **210/734-4299** • noon-8pm, till 7pm Sat, clsd Sun • lesbigay • wheelchair access

Textures Books & Gifts 5309 McCullough (at Hildebrand) **210/805-8398** • 10am-6pm • feminist

Retail Shops

Backbone Body Mods 4741 Fredericksburg Rd **210/349-6637** • 1pm-8pm, till 10pm Fri-Sat • piercing

FleshWorks/ Skins & Needles 110 Jefferson (at Houston) **210/472-0313** • 3pm-8pm, from noon wknds, till 6pm Sun, clsd Mon

Minx 1621 N Main Ave #2 **210/225-2639** • 1pm-8pm, till 5pm Mon • piercing studio

On Main 2514 N Main (btwn Woodlawn & Mistletoe) **210/737-2323** • 10am-6pm, clsd Sun • gifts • cards • T-shirts

Zebra'z 1216 E Euclid Ave (at E Locust) **210/472-2800** • 11am-9pm • lesbigay

Publications

Bar Talk 210/732-4433

The Marquise 210/493-9049

WomanSpace 210/828-5472 • monthly newsletter

Spiritual Groups

Dignity St Anne's St & Ashby Pl (at St Anne's Convent) **210/558-3287** • 5pm Sun

MCC of San Antonio 611 E Myrtle (btwn McCullough & N St Mary's) **210/472-3597** • 10:30am & 6pm Sun, 7pm Wed

River City Living MCC 202 Holland St (nr McCullough & Hildebrand) **210/822-1121** • 11am Sun

Erotica

Apollo News 2376 Austin Hwy (at Walzem) **210/653-3538** • 24hrs

South Padre Island

Accommodations

Upper Deck—A Guesthouse 120 E Atol (at Padre Blvd) **956/761-5953** • mostly gay men • swimming • nudity • $60-80

Temple

Bars

The Triangle 414 S 1st St (at 3rd) **254/778-9604** • 8pm-2am, clsd Tue • lesbians/ gay men • military clientele • dancing/DJ Fri-Sun • shows Sun • karaoke • private club

Tyler

Nightclubs

Outlaws Hwy 110 (4 miles S of Loop 323) **903/509-2248** • gay-friendly • more gay Wed • dancing/DJ • 18+

Spiritual Groups

St Gabriel's Community Church 13904 Country Rd 193 **903/581-6923** • 10:30am Sun • newsletter • wheelchair access

Waco

Info Lines & Services

Gay/ Lesbian Alliance of Central Texas 254/715-6501 • info • newsletter • events

Nightclubs

David's Place 507 Jefferson (at N 5th) **254/753-9189** • 9pm-2am • lesbians/ gay men • dancing/DJ • live shows • wheelchair access

Retail Shops

'O' 1703 Austin **254/753-7583** • call for hours • 'funky stuff' • retro clothing • costumes • gifts

Spiritual Groups

Central Texas MCC From the Heart 1601 Clay Ave **254/752-5331** • 11am Sun

Unitarian Universalist Fellowship of Waco 4209 N 27th St **254/754-0599** • 10:45am Sun

Unity Church of the Living Christ 400 S 1st, Hewitt **254/666-9102** • 11am Sun

Wichita Falls

Nightclubs

Rascals 408 N Scott (at Lincoln) **940/723-1629** • 3pm-2am • lesbians/ gay men • dancing/DJ • drag shows • BYOB

Utah

Capitol Reef

Accommodations

Capitol Reef Inn & Cafe 360 W Main St, Torrey **435/425-3271** • gay-friendly • seasonal • $48+ • also restaurant • great vegetarian menu • beer/ wine

Sky Ridge B&B Inn 435/425-3222 • gay-friendly • full brkfst • hot tubs • near Capitol Reef Nat'l Park • smokefree • woman-owned/ run • $82-120

Escalante

Accommodations

Eagle Star Ranch 330 E Boulder Pines Rd, Boulder **435/335-7438** • gay-friendly • $65-100

Rainbow Country B&B & Tours 801/826-4567, 800/252-8824 • gay/ straight • full brkfst • hot tub • smokefree • kids ok • gay-owned/ run • $39-65

Logan

Info Lines & Services

Utah State University Pride Alliance Taggart Student Center, Rm 335 **435/755-3943** • 7pm Mon

Spiritual Groups

MCC Bridgerland 1315 E 700 N (at Faith & Fellowship Center) **435/750-5026** • 4pm Sun

Moab

Accommodations

Mt Peale Resort B&B Hwy 46, milepost 14, La Sal **435/686-2284, 888/687-3253** • gay-friendly • hot tub • gay-owned/ run • $70-115

Monument Valley

Accommodations

Pioneer House PO Box 219, Bluff, 84512 **435/672-2446, 888/637-2582** • gay-friendly • full brkfst • also guided tours • $49-65

Ogden

Bars

Brass Rail 103 27th St (at Wall) **801/399-1543** • 3pm-1am • lesbians/ gay men • women's night Fri • dancing/DJ Th-Sat • line dancing Th • appetizers served • private club

Spiritual Groups

MCC Ogden 210 W 22nd St **801/394-0204** • 11am Sun

Unitarian Universalist Society of Ogden 2261 Adams Ave (YCC) **801/394-3338** • 10:30am Sun

Park City

Accommodations

The 1904 Imperial Hotel 221 Main St **435/649-1904, 800/669-8824** • gay-friendly • full brkfst • hot tub • kids ok • $150-220

The Old Miners Lodge—A B&B Inn 801/645-8068, 800/648-8068 • gay-friendly • full brkfst • hot tub • smokefree • kids ok • $70-275

Resort Property Management 800/243-2932 • IGLTA

Salt Lake City

Info Lines & Services

AA Gay/ Lesbian 801/322-5869 • 8pm Tue & Fri, call for location

Aardvark Lesbigay Helpline 801/533-0928 • info • support

Gay/ Lesbian Community Center 770 S 300 W **801/539-8800** • info • referrals • mtgs include youth, bisexual & S/M social & support

U of U Women's Resource Center 801/581-8030 • info • lesbian support group

Accommodations

Aardvarks' City Creek Park B&B 128 E 2nd Ave **801/915-3893** • mostly gay men • hot tub • gym • some shared baths • run by nonprofit Gay Helpline of Utah

Anton Boxrud B&B 57 S 600 E (at S Temple) **801/363-8035, 800/524-5511** • gay-friendly • full brkfst • $78-140

Maple Grove B&B 539 E 3rd Ave **801/322-5372** • gay-friendly • hot tub • $50-100

Peery Hotel 110 W Broadway **801/521-4300, 800/331-0073** • popular • gay-friendly • kids ok • also restaurant • full bar • wheelchair access • $79-149

Saltair B&B/ Alpine Cottages 164 S 900 E (at State) **801/533-8184, 800/733-8184** • popular • gay-friendly • full brkfst • hot tub • also cottages from 1870s • smokefree • $55-229

Bars

Paper Moon 3424 S State St **801/466-8517** • 3pm-1am, 1pm-midnight Sun • mostly women • dancing/DJ • karaoke Tue • country/ western Th • live shows • private club • food served • wheelchair access

Radio City 147 S State St (btwn 1st & 2nd) **801/532-9327** • 11am-1am • mostly gay men • beer only • wheelchair access

The Trapp 102 S 600 W (at 1st St S) **801/531-8727** • 11am-1am • lesbians/ gay men • dancing/DJ • country/ western • private club • wheelchair access

Nightclubs

Bricks Tavern 579 W 200 S (at 600 W) **801/328-0255** • 9:30pm-2am, clsd Sun-Mon • popular • gay/ straight • more gay Th-Fri • dancing/DJ • 18+ • private club

Club Fusion 740 S 300 W (at 8th St S) **801/328-3661** • 9pm-2am, clsd Sun-Tue, from 7pm nightly in summer • gay/ straight • dancing/DJ

Cafes

Bill & Nadas Cafe 479 S 600 E **801/359-6984** • 24hrs

Coffee Garden 898 E 900 S **801/355-3425** • 7am-10pm • wheelchair access

Cup of Joe 353 W 200 S (btwn 300 & 400 W) **801/363-8322** • Internet access

Tea & Trumpets 1515 S 1500 E **801/487-0717** • 8am-7pm Tue-Sat • pastries, sandwiches, salads & tea, of course

Restaurants

Baci Trattoria 134 W Pierport Ave **801/328-1333** • lunch & dinner, clsd Sun • some veggie • full bar • wheelchair access • $6-25

Capitol Cafe 54 W 200 S **801/532-7000** • 11am-10pm, till 11pm Fri-Sat, from 4pm Sun • full bar

Lambs Restaurant 169 S Main St **801/364-7166** • 7am-9pm

Market St Grill 50 Market St **801/322-4668** • lunch & dinner, Sun brunch • seafood & steak • full bar • wheelchair access • $15-30

Rio Grande Cafe 270 S Rio Grande **801/364-3302** • lunch & dinner • popular • Mexican • some veggie • full bar • $4-8

Santa Fe 2100 Emigration Canyon **801/582-5888** • lunch & dinner, Sun brunch • some veggie • $10-12

Entertainment & Recreation

Concerning Gays & Lesbians KRCL 91 FM **801/363-1818** • 12:30pm-1pm Wed

Bookstores

Golden Braid Books 151 S 500 E **801/322-1162, 801/322-0404 (CAFE)** • 10am-9pm, till 6pm Sun • also 'Oasis Cafe', 7am-10pm Mon-Fri

Inklings 245 E 900 S **801/355-4991, 800/931-3369 (MAIL ORDER)** • 10am-9pm, noon-5pm Sun • lesbigay • also gifts & videos

Retail Shops

Cahoots 878 E 900 S (at 900 E) **801/538-0606** • 10am-8pm, noon-5pm Sun • wheelchair access

Gypsy Moon Emporium 1011 E 900 S **801/521-9100** • hours vary, clsd Sun • metaphysical

Publications

The Pillar 801/265-0066 • lesbigay newspaper

Spiritual Groups

Restoration Church (Mormon) 2900 S State #205 **800/677-7252** • 11:30am Sun

Sacred Light of Christ MCC 823 S 600 E **801/595-0052** • 11am Sun

South Valley Unitarian Universalist Society 6876 S Highland Dr **801/944-9723** • 10:30am Sun

Erotica

All For Love 3072 South Main St (at 33rd St S) **801/487-8358** • 10am-6:30pm, till 7pm Fri-Sat, clsd Sun • leather/SM boutique

Blue Boutique 2106 S 1100 E (at 2100 S) **801/485-2072** • 10am-9pm, 1pm-6pm Sun

Mischievous 559 S 300 W (at 6th St S) **801/530-3100** • clsd Sun

Video One 484 S 900 W **801/524-9883** • also cult & art films

Zion Nat'l Park

Accommodations

Red Rock Inn 998 Zion Park Blvd, Springdale **435/772-3139** • gay/ straight • cottages w/ canyon views • full brkfst • 1 mile to Zion Nat'l Park • smokefree • wheelchair access • lesbian-owned/ run • $65-135

Vermont

Statewide

Info Lines & Services

Gay Info Line 603/224-1686 • active social & support groups • referrals • covers VT & NH • also some info for ME and northern MA

Publications

Out in the Mountains PO Box 1078, Richmond, 05477 **802/434-6486**

Andover

Accommodations

The Inn At High View 753 East Hill Rd **802/875-2724** • gay/ straight • full brkfst • swimming • smokefree • IGLTA • gay-owned/ run • $90-145

Arlington

Accommodations

Candlelight Motel 802/375-6647, 800/348-5294 • gay/ straight • swimming • IGLTA • gay-owned/ run • $48-80

Hill Farm Inn 802/375-2269, 800/882-2545 • gay-friendly • full brkfst • kids ok • $70-125

Restaurants

Arlington Inn Rte 7A **802/375-6532, 800/443-9442** • clsd Sun-Mon • cont'l

Belmont

Accommodations

Alice's Place 802/259-2596 • gay-friendly • full brkfst • women-owned/ run

Bennington

Accommodations

Country Cousin B&B 802/375-6985, 800/479-6985 • lesbians/ gay men • full brkfst • hot tub • smokefree • IGLTA • gay-owned/ run • $80-90

Brattleboro

Info Lines & Services

Brattleboro Area Dykes (BAD Grrrls) 802/254-7345

Bars

Rainbow Cattle Company Rte 5 (btwn exits 3 & 4 off I-91), Dummerston **802/254-9830** • 8pm-2am, clsd Mon-Tue • lesbians/ gay men • dancing/DJ • drag shows

Restaurants

Common Ground 25 Elliott St (at Main) **802/257-0855** • lunch & dinner, clsd Mon-Wed • vegetarian • local seafood • beer/ wine • $6-13

Peter Haven's 32 Elliott St (at Main) **802/257-3333** • 6pm-10pm, clsd Sun-Mon • cont'l

Bookstores

Everyone's Books 23 Elliott St **802/254-8160** • 9:30am-5:30pm, till 6pm Fri, 10am-6pm Sat, 11am-5pm Sun • wheelchair access

Bridgewater Corners

Restaurants

Blanche & Bill's Pancake House US Rte 4 **802/422-3816** • 7am-2pm Wed-Sun • great flapjacks & maple syrup

Burlington

Info Lines & Services

AA Gay/ Lesbian 2 Cherry St (at St Paul's Church) **802/658-4221** • 7pm Th

Outright Vermont 802/865-9677, 800/452-2428 (in VT) • support/ education for lgbt youth • also hotline

Univ of VT GLBT Alliance 802/656-0699 • 7pm Mon

Vermont Gay Social Alternatives • social events • newsletter

Accommodations

Allyn House B&B 57 Main St, Essex Junction **802/878-9408** • gay/ straight • full brkfst • gay-owned/ run • $65-75

The Black Bear Inn Bolton Valley **802/434-2126, 800/395-6335** • gay/ straight • full brkfst • hot tub • swimming • smokefree • wheelchair access • gay-owned/ run • $69-139

Hartwell House B&B 170 Ferguson Ave **802/658-9242, 888/658-9242** • gay-friendly • swimming • shared bath • woman-owned/ run • $45-65

Bars

135 Pearl 135 Pearl St **802/863-2343** • 7:30pm-2am, from 5pm Fri-Sun • lesbians/ gay men • dancing/DJ Th-Sat • 18+ • smokefree dance flr Fri-Sat • karaoke Wed

Restaurants

Daily Planet 15 Center St (at College) **802/862-9647** • 11:30am-10:30pm • plenty veggie • full bar till 1am • $6-15

Loretta's 44 Park St (nr 5 Corners), Essex Junction **802/879-7777** • lunch Tue-Fri, dinner Tue-Sat • Italian • plenty veggie

Silver Palace 1216 Williston Rd **802/864-0125** • 11:30am-9:30pm • Chinese • some veggie • full bar • $10-15

Retail Shops

Peace & Justice Store 21 Church St (at Pearl) **802/863-8326** • 10am-6pm Mon-Sat, noon-5pm Sun

Spiritual Groups

Dignity Vermont **802/655-6706**

First Unitarian Universalist Society 152 Pearl St (at top of Church St) **802/862-5630** • 'Interweave' (LGBT Group) • 12:30pm 2nd Sun

Ludlow

Restaurants

Michael's Seafood & Steak Rte 103 **802/228-5622** • 5pm-9:30pm • full bar

Lyndonville

Restaurants

Miss Lyndonville Diner Rte 5 **802/626-9890** • 6am-8pm

Manchester

Cafes

The Black Swan Rte 7A S **802/362-3807** • dinner from 5:30pm, clsd Tue-Wed • cont'l/ game

Little Rooster Cafe Rte 7A, Manchester Center **802/362-3496** • 7am-2pm, clsd Wed (winters)

Restaurants

Bistro Henry Rtes 11 & 30, Manchester Village **802/362-4982** • dinner only, clsd Mon • also bar

Chanticleer Rte 7A N, Manchester Center **802/362-1616** • clsd Mon-Tue

Bookstores

Northshire Bookstore Main St, Manchester Center **802/362-2200** • 10am-9pm, till 7pm Sun-Mon

Marlboro

Restaurants

Skyline Restaurant Rte 9, Hogback Mountain **802/464-5535** • 7:30am-9pm, clsd Tue-Th (winters) • wheelchair access

Montgomery Center

Accommodations

Phineas Swann B&B **802/326-4306** • gay/ straight • full brkfst • dinner available • some shared baths • smokefree • gay-owned/ run

Montpelier

Info Lines & Services

Vermont Bisexual Network (BiNet) **802/229-0112** • meets 3rd Fri • call for location

Women of the Woods **802/229-0109** • lesbian social group

Restaurants

Julio's 44 Main St **802/229-9348** • lunch & dinner, from 4pm wknds • Mexican

Sarducci's 3 Main St **802/223-0229** • 11:30am-10pm • Italian • some veggie • full bar • wheelchair access • $8-15

Wayside Restaurant Rte 302 **802/223-6611** • 6:30am-9:30pm • wheelchair access

Retail Shops

Phoenix Rising 104 Main St, 2nd flr **802/229-0522** • 10am-5pm, till 6pm Fri, from 11am Sat, clsd Sun • jewelry • gifts • lesbian-owned/ run

Richmond

Accommodations

The Spa 961 Hinesburg-Richmond Rd (at Huntington Rd) **802/434-2037** • overnight women-only health spa • swimming • exercise room

Rutland

Accommodations

Cortina Inn & Resort Rte 4, Killington **802/773-3333, 800/451-6108** • gay-friendly • hot tub • also tavern • food served • wheelchair access

Lilac Inn 53 Park St, Brandon **802/247-5463, 800/221-0720** • full brkfst • $115-180

Maplewood Inn Rte 22A South, Fair Haven **802/265-8039, 800/253-7729** • gay-friendly • romantic, historic-register 1843 Greek revival • beautiful antiques • centrally located • $75-135

Springfield

Accommodations

Chester House Inn 266 Main St, Chester **802/875-2205, 888/875-2205** • gay/ straight • smokefree • gay-owned/ run • $89-169 • also restaurant • beer/ wine

St Johnsbury

Info Lines & Services

Umbrella Women's Center 1 Prospect Ave **802/748-8645** • 8am-4:30pm Mon-Fri • lesbian support & resources

Accommodations

▲ **Greenhope Farm B&B 802/533-7772** • mostly women • full brkfst (vegetarian) • horseback-riding, camping, skiing & hiking on 140 private acres • smokefree • kids ok • call for free brochure • lesbian-owned/ run • $65-125

▲ **Highlands Inn** Bethlehem, NH **603/869-3978** • a lesbian paradise • women only • ignore 'no vacancy' sign • hot tub • swimming • 100 mountain acres • wheelchair access • IGLTA • $55-110 • special event wknds

Stowe

Accommodations

Buccaneer Country Lodge 3214 Mountain Rd **802/253-4772, 800/543-1293** • gay-friendly • full kitchen suites • full brkfst • hot tub • swimming • smokefree • $55-225

Fitch Hill Inn 802/888-3834, 800/639-2903 • gay/ straight • full brkfst • dinner by arrangement • swimming • hot tub • older kids ok • gay-owned/ run • $89-189

Waterbury

Accommodations

Grünberg Haus B&B and Cabins 802/244-7726, 800/800-7760 • gay-friendly • full brkfst • jacuzzi • sauna • fireplace • smokefree • kids ok • $59-145

Moose Meadow Lodge 607 Crossett Hill Rd **802/244-5378** • gay-friendly • log home on 86-acre wooded estate • hot tub • gay-owned • $95

Erotica

Video Exchange 21 Stowe St **802/244-7004** • clsd Sun

Woodstock

Accommodations

The Ardmore Inn 23 Pleasant St **802/457-9652, 800/497-9652** • gay-friendly • full brkfst • jacuzzi • IGLTA • $85-150

Country Garden Inn B&B 37 Main St, Quechee **802/295-3023** • gay-friendly • full brkfst • swimming • $110-180

Rosewood Inn 802/457-4485, 203/829-1499 • gay-friendly • full brkfst • smokefree • kids ok • $70-125

Twin Gables 802/436-3070 • gay/ straight • near outdoor recreation • shared baths • smokefree • kids ok • gay-owned/ run • $60-75

Virginia

Statewide

Info Lines & Services

Virginia Division of Tourism 800/847-4882

Virginians for Justice 804/643-4816 • lesbigay organization

Publications

Shout! 540/989-1579 • entertainment & personals for the Virginias & Carolinas

Alexandria

see also Washington, District of Columbia

Spiritual Groups

Church of the Resurrection (Episcopal) 2280 N Beauregard St **703/998-0888** • 8am & 10am Sun, 10am Wed

Mt Vernon Unitarian Church 1909 Windmill Ln (off Fort Hunt Rd) **703/765-5950** • 9am & 11am Sun, 10am Sun (summer)

Arlington

see also Washington, District of Columbia

Info Lines & Services

Arlington Gay/ Lesbian Alliance 703/522-7660 • monthly mtgs • call for schedule

Accommodations

Best Western Arlington Hotel 2480 S Glebe Rd (at 24th St) **703/979-4400, 800/486-6228** • gay-friendly • IGLTA

Cafes

Java Shack 2507 N Franklin Rd (at Wilson Blvd & N Barton) **703/527-9556** • 7am-10pm, till 11pm Fri-Sat, from 8am wknds • lesbians/ gay men

Publications

Woman's Monthly 1612 'U' St NW #403, Washington, DC **202/234-2824** • covers DC & VA community events

Spiritual Groups

Clarendon Presbyterian Church 1305 N Jackson St **703/527-9513** • 10am Sun

Cape Charles

see also Norfolk & Virginia Beach

Accommodations

Cape Charles House B&B 645 Tazewell Ave (at Fig) **757/331-4960** • gay-friendly • 1912 colonial revival home filled w/ antiques • smokefree • $85-120

Pelican Watch Cottage 116 Tazewell Ave **757/331-2709** • gay/ straight • charming effeciency • 2 blks to bay • women-owned/ run • $55/night, $275/week

Sea Gate B&B 9 Tazewell Ave **757/331-2206** • gay-friendly • full brkfst • afternoon tea • near beach on quiet, tree-lined street • gay-owned/ run • $80-90

Wilson-Lee House 403 Tazewell Ave **757/331-1954** • gay/ straight • full brkfst • smokefree • IGLTA • gay-owned/ run • $65-120

Charlottesville

Info Lines & Services

Gay AA at Church House, Thomas Jefferson Unitarian Church, Rugby Rd **804/293-8227** • 7pm Mon

Women's Center 14th & University, UVA **804/982-2361** • 8:30am-5pm, clsd wknds

Accommodations

▲ **1817 Historic B&B** 1211 W Main St (at 12 1/2 St) **804/979-7353, 800/730-7443** • gay-friendly • also antique shop & cafe • 5 miles to Monticello • smokefree • $89-199

Intouch Women's Center 804/589-6542 • women only • campground • recreational area • wheelchair access • $5-15

The Mark Addy 56 Rodes Farm Dr, Nellysford **804/361-1101, 800/278-2154** • gay/ straight • full brkfst • dinner available • smokefree • wheelchair access • gay-owned/ run

Nightclubs

Club 216 216 W Water St (enter rear, near South St) **804/296-8783** • 6pm-2am, 9pm-4:30am Fri-Sat • lesbians/ gay men • dancing/DJ • live shows • private club • wheelchair access

Restaurants

Bistro 151 Valley Green Center, Nellysford **804/361-1463** • lunch & dinner, clsd Mon • full bar till midnight, till 2am wknds

Eastern Standard/ Escafe in West End downtown mall (next to the Omni Hotel) **804/295-8668** • 5:30pm-10pm Wed-Sat • lesbians/ gay men • Asian/ American fusion • some veggie • also 'Escafe' downstairs • 5:30pm-midnight, till 2am Th-Sat, from 4:30pm Sun, clsd Mon • bistro • full bar • music Th & Sun • gay-owned/ run

Spiritual Groups

Lesbian & Gay Chavurah 804/982-2774 • lesbigay Jewish study group

MCC 717 Rugby Rd (at Thomas Jefferson Memorial Church) **804/979-5206** • 6pm Sun

Falls Church

Spiritual Groups

MCC of Northern VA 2709 Hunter Mill Rd (at Fairfax Unitarian Church), Oakton **703/532-0992** • 6pm Sun

Fredericksburg

Restaurants

Merrimans 715 Caroline St (btwn Charlotte & Hanover) **540/371-7723** • lunch & dinner, lounge till 2am • popular • lesbians/ gay men • fresh natural homemade cuisine • plenty veggie • full bar • dancing/DJ • $7-22

Hampton

see Newport News

Lexington

Accommodations

Longdale Inn 6209 Longdale Furnace Rd, Clifton Forge **540/862-0892, 800/862-0386** • gay-friendly • full brkfst • smokefree • $80-130

Lynchburg

Info Lines & Services

Gay/ Lesbian Helpline 804/847-5242 • live 7pm-10pm Mon, Tue & Fri

Newport News

see also Norfolk & Virginia Beach

Erotica

Mr D's Leather & Novelties 9902-A Warwick Blvd (at Randolph Rd) **757/599-4070**

Norfolk

see also Virginia Beach

Info Lines & Services

AA Gay/ Lesbian 757/495-3113

Transgender Support Group 757/625-2992 • meets 2nd Tue, call for info

Bars

The Garage 731 Granby St (at Brambleton) **757/623-0303** • 8am-2am, from 10am Sun • popular • mostly gay men • neighborhood bar • food served • wheelchair access • $3-9

Hershee Bar 6117 Sewells Pt Rd (at Norview) **757/853-9842** • 4pm-2am, from noon wknds • mostly women • dancing/DJ • live shows Fri • karaoke Sun • food served • some veggie • Sun buffet • $2-7

Nutty Buddy's 143 E Little Creek Rd **757/588-6474** • 4pm-2am, Sun brunch • popular • lesbians/ gay men • dancing/DJ • karaoke • live shows • also restaurant • some veggie • wheelchair access • $10-15

P Eyes/ White House Cafe 249 W York St (at Boush) **757/533-9290** • 11am-2am • lesbians/ gay men • dancing/DJ • live shows • grand buffet Sun • some veggie • wheelchair access • $5-15

The Wave 4107 Colley Ave (at 41st St) **757/440-5911** • 11am-2am, till 3am wknds • mostly gay men • dancing/DJ • country/ western Mon • also restaurant • $3-12

Nightclubs

Charlotte's Web 6425 Tidewater Dr (btwn Little Creek & Norview, in Roland Park Shopping Ctr) **757/853-5021** • 8am-2am • mostly women • dancing/DJ • theme nights • Sun dinner buffet • wheelchair access

Restaurants

Charlie's Cafe 1800 Granby St (at 18th) **757/625-0824** • 7am-3pm • some veggie • beer/ wine • $3-7

Uncle Louie's 132 E Little Creek Rd (at Granby) **757/480-1225** • 8am-11pm, till midnight Fri-Sat, till 10pm Sun • Jewish fine dining • also bar & deli

Bookstores

Lambda Rising 9229 Granby St (at Tidewater) **757/480-6969** • 10am-10pm • lesbigay • wheelchair access

Phoenix Rising East 619 Colonial Ave, 2nd flr (at Olney) **757/622-3701** • 11am-9pm, till 10pm Fri-Sat, till 7pm Sun • lesbigay

Publications

Shout! 540/989-1579 • entertainment & personals for the Virginias & Carolinas

Spiritual Groups

All God's Children Community Church 9229 Granby St (at Tidewater Dr) **757/480-0911** • 10:30am Sun & 7:30 pm Wed

Dignity 600 Tabbot Hall Rd **757/625-5337** • 6:30pm Sun

New Life MCC 4035 E Ocean Ave **757/362-3056** • 10:30am Sun, 7:30pm Th

Erotica

Leather & Lace 149 E Little Creek Rd (at Granby) **757/583-4334** • 11am-9pm, clsd Sun

Richmond

Info Lines & Services

AA Gay/ Lesbian 804/355-1212 • call for mtg schedule

Richmond Lesbian Feminist 804/796-9988 • community entertainment & educational group

Richmond Organization for Sexual Minority Youth 804/353-2077 • 3pm-8pm Mon & Wed

Accommodations

Bellmont Manor B&B Inn 6600 Belmont Rd, Chesterfield **804/745-0106, 800/809-9041 x69** • gay/ straight • full brkfst • other meals available • smokefree • wheelchair access • gay-owned/ run

The High Street Inn 405 High St (at Cross St), Petersburg **804/733-0505, 888/733-0505** • gay-friendly • full brkfst • $75-110

Bars

Babe's of Carytown 3166 W Cary St (at Auburn) **804/355-9330** • 11am-1am, till 2am Fri-Sat, from 8pm Sat, 9am-5pm Sun • mostly women • dancing/DJ • food served • homecooking • some veggie • wheelchair access • women-owned/ run • $4-7

Broadway Cafe & Bar 1624 W Broad St (at Lombardi) **804/355-9931** • 5pm-2am, from 6pm Sat, from 7pm Sun • wheelchair access • $7-10

Cafine's Cafe/ Boom 401 E Grace St (at 4th) **804/775-2233** • lunch Mon-Fri, dinner Wed-Fri, open till 3am Fri-Sat, clsd Sun • gay/ straight • dancing/DJ Fri-Sat • more gay Sat • swing dancing Wed & Fri • gay-owned/ run

Casablanca Lounge & Restaurant 6 E Grace St (btwn 1st & Foushee Sts) **804/648-2040** • 11am-2am, from 3pm Sat • mostly gay men • karaoke • videos • lunch served • some veggie • wheelchair access • $5-8

NIGHTCLUBS

Club Colors 536 N Harrison St (at Broad) **804/353-9776** • 9pm-4am Sat • more women until 11:30 pm • dancing/DJ • multi-racial • food served • wheelchair access

Fielden's 2033 W Broad St **804/359-1963** • midnight-close, clsd Mon-Wed • popular • mostly gay men • dancing/DJ • BYOB • private club • wheelchair access

BOOKSTORES

Carytown Books 2930 W Cary St (at Sheppard) **804/359-4831** • 9am-7pm, till 5pm Sun • lesbigay section • wheelchair access

Phoenix Rising 19 N Belmont Ave **804/355-7939, 800/719-1690** • 11am-7pm • lesbigay • wheelchair access

PUBLICATIONS

Shout! **540/989-1579** • entertainment & personals for the Virginias & Carolinas

SPIRITUAL GROUPS

MCC Richmond 2501 Park Ave (at Davis) **804/353-9477** • 10:45am & 6:30pm Sun

Roanoke

BARS

Backstreet Cafe 356 Salem Ave (off Jefferson) **540/345-1542** • 7pm-2am, till midnight Sun • lesbians/ gay men • neighborhood bar • food served

NIGHTCLUBS

Fusion 2923 Franklin Rd SW **540/342-8257** • 4pm-2am, 9pm-3am Fri-Sat, clsd Sun-Tue • mostly gay men • dancing/DJ • transgender-friendly

The Park 615 Salem Ave **540/342-0946** • 9pm-2am, clsd Mon-Tue & Th • popular • lesbians/ gay men • dancing/DJ • live shows Sun • videos • private club • wheelchair access

Bookstores

Out Word Connections 114 Kirk Ave SW (btwn 1st & 2nd) **540/985-6886** • noon-8pm, from 2pm Sun • lesbigay

Publications

Blue Ridge Lambda Press 540/890-6612 • covers western VA

Shout! 540/989-1579 • entertainment & personals for the Virginias & Carolinas

Spiritual Groups

MCC of the Blue Ridge 2015 Grandin Rd SW (at Unitarian Church) **540/344-4444** • 3pm Sun

Unitarian Universalist Church 2015 Grandin Rd SW **540/342-8888** • 11am Sun (10am summers)

Shenandoah Valley

Info Lines & Services

SVGLA (Shenandoah Valley Gay/ Lesbian Assoc) 540/574-4636 • 24hr touchtone info • weekly mtgs • also dances & potlucks

Accommodations

▲ **The Ruby Rose Inn** Stanley **540/778-4680** • mostly women • full brkfst • jacuzzi • smokefree • lesbian-owned/ run • $115-145

Ruffner House Ruffner House Ln (at Hwy 340 & 211), Luray **540/743-7855** • gay/ straight • full brkfst • smokefree • $88-135

Virginia Beach

see also Norfolk

Bars

Ambush 475 S Lynnhaven Rd (behind Lynnhaven Mall) **757/498-4301** • 3pm-2am • mostly gay men • food served • shows • neighborhood bar

Rainbow Cactus 3472 Holland Rd (at Diana Lee) **757/368-0441** • 5:30pm-2am, clsd Mon • lesbians/ gay men • dancing/DJ • country/ western • food served • karaoke Tue

Publications

Lambda Directory 757/486-3546

Washington

Bellevue

see also Seattle

Spiritual Groups

East Shore Unitarian Church 12700 SE 32nd St (1 1/2 blks from Richards Rd) **425/747-3780** • 9am & 11am Sun (10am summers) • wheelchair access

Bellingham

Info Lines & Services

LGBT Alliance Western Washington University **360/650-6120** • social/ political group

Bars

Rumors 1119 Railroad Ave (at Chestnut) **360/671-1849** • 4pm-2am • lesbians/ gay men • dancing/DJ Wed-Sun • multi-racial clientele

Cafes

Tony's Coffee 1101 Harris Ave (at 11th), Fairhaven **360/738-4710** • 7am-9pm • plenty veggie • patio • wheelchair access

Bookstores

Rainbow Bridge 304 W Champion St **360/715-3684** • noon-8pm, clsd Sun • call for winter hours • lesbigay • gifts • women-owned/ run

Village Books 1210 11th St (at Harris) **360/671-2626** • 9am-10pm, 10am-8pm Sun

Retail Shops

Kalamalka Studio 2518 Meridian **360/733-3832** • noon-8pm, clsd Sun-Mon • tattoos • piercings

Erotica

Great Northern Bookstore 1308 Railroad Ave (at Holly) **360/733-1650**

Bremerton

Info Lines & Services

West Sound Family 360/792-3960 • lesbigay social/ support group

Bars

Brewski's 2810 Kitsap Wy (enter off Wycuff St) **360/479-9100** • 11am-2am • gay-friendly • neighborhood bar • food served • wheelchair access

Nightclubs

Ultravox Nite Club 113 Pacific Ave (at 1st) **360/475-0808** • 9pm-4am Fri-Sat • more gay Sat • also tavern from 4pm-9pm daily

Chelan

Accommodations

Whaley Mansion 415 3rd St **509/682-5735, 800/729-2408** • gay-friendly • full brkfst • smokefree • woman-owned/ run • $85-135

Everett

Nightclubs

Everett Underground 1212 California St (at Grand Ave) **425/339-0807** • 4pm-2am, from 3pm Fri-Sun • lesbians/ gay men • dancing/DJ • multi-racial clientele • live shows Th • karaoke Wed • food served • wheelchair access

Gig Harbor

Entertainment & Recreation

Blue Heron Sailing 253/756-9194 • women-owned/ run

Kent

Bars

Sappho's 226 1st Ave S **253/813-2776** • 3pm-2am, till 11pm Mon, from noon Fri, from 11am Sat, clsd Tue • lesbians/ gay men • neighborhood bar • dancing/DJ Fri-Sat • karaoke Th & Sun • also restaurant

Bookstores

New Woman Books 315 W Meeker (btwn 2nd & 4th) **253/854-3487** • 10am-5:30pm, clsd Sun • also 'Tea Room & Cafe'

Lynnwood

Retail Shops

Lynnwood Tattoo 15315 Hwy 99, #7 (at 153rd) **425/742-8467** • noon-10pm, till midnight Fri-Sat

Mt Vernon

Accommodations

The Heron/ Wild Iris 117 Maple Ave, La Conner **360/466-4626** • gay-friendly • full brkfst • hot tub • smokefree • wheelchair access

The White Swan Guesthouse 15872 Moore Rd **360/445-6805** • gay-friendly • farmhouse B&B • also cottage • smokefree • $75-150

Restaurants

Deli Next Door 210 S 1st St (at Memorial Hwy) **360/336-3886** • 9am-8pm, till 6pm Sun • healthy American • plenty veggie • wheelchair access • $4-7

Bookstores

Scott's Bookstore 121 Freeway Dr **360/336-6181** • 9am-close

North Beach Peninsula

Accommodations

Shakti Cove 360/665-4000 • lesbians/ gay men • cottages on the peninsula • pets ok • lesbian-owned/ run • $65-100

Sou'wester Lodge Beach Access Rd/ 38th Place, Seaview **360/642-2542** • gay-friendly • inexpensive suites • cabins w/ kitchens • vintage trailers • smokefree • $39-119

Olympia

Info Lines & Services

Free at Last AA 11th & Washington (at United Church) **360/352-7344** • 7pm Th

Queer Alliance Evergreen State College **360/866-6000 x6544** • social/ support group • call for mtg times

Accommodations

Oyster Bay 2830 Bloomfield Rd, Shelton **360/427-7643** • lesbians & gay men • hot tub • private decks • smokefree • $85-140

Nightclubs

Liquid 311 E 4th Ave **360/956-0825** • gay-friendly • dancing/DJ • 16+ • smoke/ alcohol-free club • cover charge

Thekla 116 E 5th Ave (at Capitol Way, enter alley) **360/352-1855** • 8pm-2am • popular • gay-friendly • dancing/DJ • karaoke Mon • wheelchair access

Restaurants

Urban Onion 116 Legion Way SE (at Capitol) **360/943-9242** • 7am-10pm, from 8pm wknds • plenty veggie • wheelchair access

Orcas Island

Accommodations

Spring Bay Inn on Orcas Island PO Box 97, Olga, 98279 **360/376-5531** • gay/ straight • full brkfst • kayak tours available • $195-235

Pasco

Nightclubs

Out and About 327 W Lewis **509/543-3796** • 6pm-midnight, 4pm-2am Fri-Sat, clsd Mon-Tue • gay-friendly • dancing/DJ Fri-Sat • karaoke Th • wheelchair access

Port Angeles

Accommodations

Maple Rose Inn 112 Reservoir Rd **360/457-7673, 800/570-2007** • gay/ straight • full brkfst • hot tub • smokefree • decks • gay-owned/ run • $79+

Port Townsend

Accommodations

Get-Away at Discovery Bay 360/797-7239 • women only • RV resort on private women's land • 15 miles from Port Townsend

The James House 1238 Washington St **360/385-1238** • gay-friendly • smokefree • near tennis, golf & kayaking • $65-175

Ravenscroft Inn 533 Quincy St (at Clay St) **360/385-2784, 800/782-2691** • gay-friendly • seaport inn w/ views of Puget Sound • gourmet brkfst • smokefree • $65-175

Pullman

Info Lines & Services

Washington State U GLBA Program 509/335-6388

San Juan Islands

Accommodations

Blue Rose B&B 1811 9th St, Anacortes **360/293-5175, 877/293-3285** • gay-friendly • full brkfst • $80-95

The Gallery Suite B&B 302 1st St, Langley **360/221-2978** • gay/ straight • condo rental on the water • art gallery/B&B • smokefree • wheelchair access • gay-owned/ run • $90-110

The Inn at Swifts Bay 360/468-3636 • popular • gay/ straight • full brkfst • Tudor-style B&B on San Juan Islands • hot tub • fireplace • smokefree • IGLTA • gay-owned/ run • $100-185

Lopez Farm Cottages 555 Fisherman Bay Rd, Lopez Island **360/468-3555, 800/440-3556** • gay/ straight • on 30-acre farm • hot tub • $99-150

The Whidbey Inn 106 1st St, Langley **360/221-7115, 888/313-2070** • gay-friendly • full brkfst • located on bluff over Saratoga Passage Waterway & Mtns • smokefree • $85-160

WindSong B&B Inn 360/376-2500, 800/669-3948 • gay-friendly • full brkfst • hot tub • smokefree • $100-150 for 2

Seattle

Info Lines & Services

Capitol Hill Alano 1222 E Pine St, 2nd flr (at 13th) **206/587-2838 (AA#), 206/322-9590 (club)** • noon, 5:30pm & 8pm

Counseling Service for Sexual Minorities 1820 E Pine **206/323-0220** • 3pm-9pm Mon-Fri

FTM Outreach Phoneline 1812 E Madison St #106 (Ingersoll Gender Center) **206/329-6651** • live one-on-one info/ support for FTMs, by FTMs

Lambert House 1818 15th Ave (at Denny) **206/322-2735** • 4pm-10pm, till midnight Fri-Sat, from noon Sat • drop-in center for sexual minority youth

Lesbian Resource Center 2214 S Jackson St (at 23rd St) **206/322-DYKE (3953)** • drop-in noon-7pm Tue-Fri & noon-5pm Sat

Partners Task Force for Gay/ Lesbian Couples 206/935-1206

Seattle Bisexual Women's Network 206/517-7767 • active social/ support organization

STEP 206/329-4857 • AIDS talkline • also offer free classes

TEN (The Eastside Network) 425/450-4890 • lgbt social/ support group for Seattle's East Side

Accommodations

Bacon Mansion/ Broadway Guesthouse 959 Broadway E (at E Prospect) **206/329-1864, 800/240-1864** • gay/ straight • Edwardian-style Tudor • IGLTA • $74-144

Bed & Breakfast on Broadway 722 Broadway Ave E (at Aloha) **206/329-8933, 888/329-8933** • gay/ straight • full brkfst • $85-125

Capitol Hill Inn 1713 Belmont Ave (2 blks north of Pine) **206/323-1955** • gay-friendly • full brkfst • women-owned/ run • $85-165

Chambered Nautilus B&B 5005 22nd Ave NE (at N 50th St) **206/522-2536, 800/545-8459** • gay-friendly • full brkfst • sundecks • $79-124

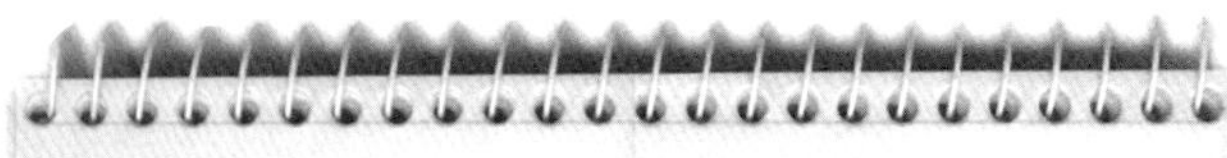

Seattle

Seattle's lush natural beauty—breathtaking views of Puget Sound and the Cascade Mountains—is actually more incredible than most let on.

You can see for yourself from the deck of The Space Needle. This Seattle landmark is located in the Seattle Center, a complex that includes an opera house, the Arena Coliseum, and the Pacific Science Center. If the line isn't too long, take the Monorail from downtown. (Be sure to sit on the right-hand side and keep your face pressed to the window. This scenic ride is almost over before it begins.) Another landmark is the quaint/touristy Pike Place Market (where all those commercials that feature mounds of fish are filmed).

For the perfect day trip, ferry over to the Olympic Peninsula and enjoy the fresh wilderness, or cruise by 'Dykiki,' a waterfront park on Lake Washington. Or sign up for an outdoors trip with one of the women-owned tour operators: **Adventure Associates** has trips listed in our *Tour Operators* section in the back of this book.

If you enjoy island life, ferry over to the San Juan Islands for a relaxing stay at one of the lesbian-friendly guesthouses. Or head up north to Vancouver, British Columbia, Seattle's beautiful Canadian cousin.

But Seattle is more than just another pretty place. It has a small-town friendliness that you won't always find in a big West Coast city, as well as an international reputation for sophisticated cafe culture and cyber-cool.

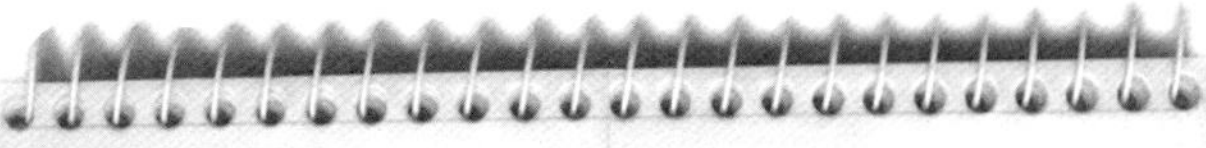

Speaking of coffee, be careful to order your java correctly, or ask questions if you're unsure. The natives respect frank ignorance more than confused pretense. Lattes—one-third espresso, two-thirds hot foamy milk—are the standard, and come iced or hot. Don't do dairy? Order a soy latte instead.

Of course, where to drink in Seattle is just as important as what to drink. For strong coffee served by strong women, stop in at **Cafe Vivace** on Denny. If, however, you want a hip cafe with comfy chairs, then muse away those hours in a wingback at **Cafe Vita.**

For shopping, the Broadway Market in queer Capitol Hill is a multicultural shopping center. The **Pink Zone** lesbian-owned body art shop is here, and we're told the girl-watching is best from the Market's espresso bar. If you're not a caffeine junkie, check out the **Gravity Bar** at the Market, where you can get almost any fruit or vegetable in liquid, shake, or sandwich form.

Beyond the Closet is the local lesbigay bookstore where you can get a copy of the **Seattle Gay News**. Seattle's main women's bar is the **Wildrose Tavern**. For dancing, head to the alterna-queer **Re-bar** on Thursdays. Country gals line-dance at **Timberline**.

For sex toys, check out **Toys in Babeland** women's erotica. Pick up your safer sex supplies at the nonprofit **Rubber Tree**.

Seattle

Where the Girls Are: Living in the Capitol Hill District, south of Lake Union, and working in the Broadway Market, Pike Place Market, or somewhere in between.

Entertainment: Chicken Soup Brigade 206/328-8979, monthly gay bingo.
Harvard Exit 206/323-8986, repertory film theater.
Seattle's Gay Men's Chorus 206/323-0750.
Tacky Tourists 206/233-8842, annual Queen City Cruise, The Bump and other fabulous social events/fundraisers.
Team Seattle 206/322-7769, a 35-team gay network.

Lesbigay Pride: Last Sunday in June. 206/292-1035.

Annual Events: September - AIDSwalk, 4th Sunday, 206/329-6923.

City Info: 206/461-5800, web: www.seattle.org.

Attractions: International District.
Pike Place Market.
Pioneer Square.
Seattle Art Museum 206/654-3100.
Space Needle 206/443-9800.
Woodland Park Zoo 206/684-4800.

Best View: Top of the Space Needle, but check out the World's Fair Monorail too.

Weather: Winter's average temperature is 50° while summer temperatures can climb up into the 90°s. Be prepared for rain at any time during the year.

Transit: Farwest 206/622-1717.
Gray Top Cab 206/622-4800.
Airport Shuttle Express 206/622-1424.
Metropolitan Transit 206/553-3000.

Gaslight Inn 1727 15th Ave (at E Olive St) **206/325-3654** • popular • gay/ straight • swimming • smokefree • IGLTA • also 'Howell St Suites' next door • gay-owned/ run • $78-178

Hill House B&B 1113 E John St (at 12th Ave) **206/720-7161, 800/720-7161** • gay-friendly • full brkfst • smokefree • $75-155

▲ **Landes House B&B** 712 11th Ave E (at Roy) **206/329-8781, 888/329-8781** • gay/ straight • two 1906 houses joined by deck • hot tub • gay-owned/ run • $55-95

Pioneer Square Hotel 77 Yesler Wy (at 1st St) **206/340-1234, 800/800-5514** • gay-friendly • $129-159

The Shafer-Baillie Mansion 907 14th Ave E (at Aloha) **206/322-4654** • gay-friendly • $95-145

Wild Lily Ranch B&B **360/793-2103** • lesbians/ gay men • on Skykomish River • 1 hr from Seattle • hot tub • swimming • camping available • smokefree • gay-owned/ run • $65-85

Bars

21st Century Foxes 1501 E Olive Wy (at Bellevue) **206/720-9963** • 6am-2am • mostly gay men • drag shows • also restaurant

The Baltic Room 1207 Pine St (at Melrose) **206/625-4444** • 6pm-2am, clsd Mon • gay/ straight • piano bar

CC Attle's 1501 E Madison (at 15th Ave) **206/726-0565** • 6am-2am • popular • mostly gay men • neighborhood bar • videos • also 'Cadillac Grill Diner' • 206/323-4017 • 7am-4am, 24hrs wknds • some veggie • wheelchair access

Changes 2103 N 45th St (at Meridian) **206/545-8363** • noon-2am • mostly gay men • neighborhood bar • karaoke Mon & Wed • videos • beer/ wine only • wheelchair access

The Cuff 1533 13th Ave (at Pine) **206/323-1525** • 11am-2am • popular • mostly gay men • dancing/DJ • leather • uniform bar • popular party Sun • also restaurant • wheelchair access

Double Header 407 2nd Ave (at Washington) **206/624-8439** • 10am-1am • mostly gay men • neighborhood bar • 'one of the oldest gay bars in the US'

Elite Tavern 622 Broadway Ave E (at Roy) **206/324-4470** • 10am-2am • lesbians/ gay men • neighborhood bar • beer/ wine only • wheelchair access

Elite Two 1658 E Olive Wy (at Belmont) **206/322-7334** • noon-2am • lesbians/ gay men • neighborhood bar • beer/ wine only

Hana Restaurant & Lounge 1914 8th Ave (at Stewart) **206/340-1536** • noon-2am • mostly gay men • Japanese food 10am-6pm • wheelchair access

HopScotch 332 15th Ave E (at John St) **206/322-4191** • 3pm-2am, from 2pm Fri-Sat, clsd Sun-Mon • gay-friendly • 100+ single-malt scotches • food served till 11pm

R Place 619 E Pine (at Boylston) **206/322-8828** • 2pm-2am • mostly gay men • neighborhood bar • videos • 3 stories • wheelchair access

Rendezvous 2320 2nd Ave (at Battery) **206/441-5823** • 6am-2am • gay-friendly • neighborhood bar • live bands Th-Sat

Romper Room 106 1st Ave N (at Denny) **206/284-5003** • 4pm-2am, till 3am wknds • dancing/DJ Th-Sat

The Seattle Eagle 314 E Pike St (at Bellevue) **206/621-7591** • 2pm-2am • mostly gay men • leather • rock 'n' roll • patio • wheelchair access

Thumpers 1500 E Madison St (at 15th) **206/328-3800** • 11am-2am • popular • mostly gay men • videos • full restaurant • more women in dining room • $7-15 • wheelchair access • gay-owned/ run

Timberline Tavern 2015 Boren Ave (nr Fairview & Denny) **206/622-6220** • 6pm-2am, from 4pm Sun, clsd Mon • lesbians/ gay men • dancing/DJ • country/ western • dance lessons Tue-Wed • swing Th • disco T-dance Sun • beer/ wine only

Wildrose Tavern & Restaurant 1021 E Pike St (at 11th) **206/324-9210** • 11am-midnight, till 1am Tue-Th, till 2am Fri-Sat • mostly women • neighborhood bar • wheelchair access

NIGHTCLUBS

ARO.space 925 E Pike St (at 10th Ave) **206/320-0424** • open till 2am, clsd Tue • popular • lesbians/ gay men • dancing/DJ • alternative music • transgender-friendly • live shows

Jazz Alley 2033 6th Ave (at Lenora) **206/441-9729** • gay-friendly • call for events & reservations • live music • cover charge • also restaurant

Neighbours Restaurant & Lounge 1509 Broadway (at E Pike, enter on alley) **206/324-5358** • 3pm-2am, till 4am Fri-Sat • mostly gay men • dancing/DJ • 2 flrs • live shows • young crowd • wheelchair access

Re-bar 1114 Howell (at Boren Ave) **206/233-9873** • open till 2am • gay/ straight • dancing/DJ • cabaret/ theater • 'Queer Disco' Th • young crowd • call for events

Showbox 1426 1st Ave (at Pike) **206/628-3151** • gay-friendly • dancing/DJ • live music • 'Zoot Suit Sundays' w/ swing lessons • cover charge

Spintron 916 E Pike **206/568-6190** • 5pm-2am, till 4am Fri-Sat • mostly gay men • dancing/DJ • also restaurant & lounge upstairs • wheelchair access

The Vogue 2018 1st Ave (at Virginia) **206/443-0673** • 9pm-2am • gay-friendly • dancing/DJ • alternative • live shows • goth Wed • new wave Sat • fetish Sun

Cafes

Addis Cafe 61224 E Jefferson (at 12th) **206/325-7805** • 8am-midnight • popular • Ethiopian • $3-7

Cafe Septieme 214 Broadway Ave E (at Thomas & John) **206/860-8858** • 9am-midnight • popular • lesbians/ gay men

Cafe Vita 1005 E Pike (at 10th) **206/325-2647** • 6am-midnight

Espresso Vivace 901 E Denny Wy #100 **206/860-5869** • 6:30am-11pm • popular • very cute girls

Restaurants

Al Boccalino 1 Yesler Wy (at Alaskan) **206/622-7688** • lunch Mon-Fri, dinner nightly • classy southern Italian

Broadway New American Grill 314 Broadway E (at E Harrison) **206/328-7000** • 9am-2am, from 8am wknds • popular • full bar

Campagne 86 Pine St (at 1st) **206/728-2800** • 5:30pm-10pm • French • reservations advised • also 'Cafe Campagne' • brkfst, lunch & dinner

Dahlia Lounge 1904 4th Ave (at Stewart) **206/682-4142** • lunch & dinner • some veggie • full bar • $9-20

Frontier Restaurant & Bar 2203 1st Ave (at Blanchard) **206/441-3377** • 10am-2am • best cheap food in town • full bar • wheelchair access

Giorgina's Pizza 131 15th Ave E (at John) **206/329-8118** • 11am-10pm, from 5pm wknds

Gravity Bar 415 Broadway E (at Harrison) **206/325-7186** • 10am-10pm, till 11pm Fri-Sat • vegetarian/ juice bar • also downtown location, 206/448-8826 • wheelchair access

Hamburger Mary's 1525 E Olive Wy (at Denny) **206/324-8112** • 11am-11pm, bar till 2am

Jack's Bistro 405 15th Ave E (at Harrison) **206/324-9625** • lunch & dinner • some veggie • full bar • wheelchair access • $10-12

Kokeb 9261 12th Ave **206/322-0485** • 5pm-10pm • Ethiopian • some veggie • beer/ wine • $5-10

Mae's Phinney Ridge Cafe 6410 Phinney Ridge N (at 65th) **206/782-1222** • 7am-3pm • brkfst menu • some veggie • wheelchair access

Queen City Grill 2201 1st Ave (at Blanchard) **206/443-0975** • noon-11pm, from 5pm wknds • popular • fresh seafood • some veggie • wheelchair access

Rosebud Restaurant & Bar 719 E Pike St (at Harvard Ave) **206/323-6636** • 10am-2am

Sunlight Cafe 6403 Roosevelt Wy NE (at 64th) **206/522-9060** • 7am-9pm • vegetarian • beer/ wine • wheelchair access • $3-9

Szmania's 3321 W McGraw St (in Magnolia Bluff) **206/284-7305** • lunch Tue-Fri, dinner nightly, clsd Mon

Wild Ginger Asian Restaurant & Satay Bar 1400 Western Ave (at Union) **206/623-4450** • lunch Mon-Sat, dinner nightly • bar till 1am

Entertainment & Recreation

Gay Bingo **206/328-8979** • monthly, run by the Chicken Soup Brigade

Harvard Exit 807 E Roy St **206/323-8986** • rep film theater

Lesbian/ Gay History Walking Tours 1122 E Pike St #797 **206/233-8955** • seasonal • call for info & reservations

Skydive Snohomish **800/338-5867 (JUMP)** • train & jump the same day

The Space Needle 219 4th Ave N (in the Seattle Center) **206/443-2111, 800/937-9582** • where else can you get a latte & a view like this

Tacky Tourists **206/233-8842** • fabulous social events

Team Seattle **206/322-7769** • gay athletic network

Bookstores

Bailey/ Coy Books 414 Broadway Ave E (at Harrison) **206/323-8842** • 10am-10pm, till 11pm Fri-Sat

Beyond the Closet Bookstore 518 E Pike (at Belmont) **206/322-4609** • 10am-11pm, till midnight Fri-Sat • lesbigay

Edge of the Circle 701 E Pike (at Boylston) **206/726-1999** • noon-9pm, till 11pm Fri-Sat • alternative spirituality store

Fremont Place Book Company 621 N 35th (at Fremont Ave N) **206/547-5970** • 10am-8pm, till 9pm Wed-Th, till 10pm Fri-Sat, till 6:30pm Sun

Left Bank Books 92 Pike St (at 1st Ave) **206/622-0195** • 10am-7pm, noon-6pm Sun • worker-owned collective • new & used books • some lesbigay titles

Pistil Books & News 1013 E Pike St (at 11th) **206/325-5401** • 10am-10pm, till 8pm Sun

Retail Shops

Broadway Market 401 E Broadway (at Harrison & Republican) • popular mall full of funky, queer & hip stores

Green Light Tattoo & Body Piercing 7615 Aurora Ave N **206/706-0333**

Metropolis 7220 Greenwood Ave N (at 73rd) **206/782-7002** • 10am-8pm • cards & gifts • also Wallingford Center location, 206/547-2789

The Pink Zone 211 Broadway (at John) **206/325-0050** • 10am-10pm • tattoos & piercings

Sunshine Thrift Shops 1718 12th Ave (at Pike/ Broadway) **206/324-9774** • 11am-7pm • nonprofit for AIDS organizations • call for details • wheelchair access

Venus 1017 E Pike St, downstairs (btwn 12th & Broadway) **206/322-5539** • noon-7pm, clsd Sun-Mon • plus-size consignment clothing, leather & corsets • lesbian-owned/ run

Publications

Qink Northwest Magazine 206/419-7009 • news & entertainment magazine for Seattle, Portland & Vancouver

Seattle In Your Pocket! 206/242-5240 • alternative paper w/ gay section

SGN (Seattle Gay News) 1605 12th Ave #31 **206/324-4297, 206/322-7188** • lesbigay newspaper • weekly

The Stranger 206/323-7101 • queer-positive alternative weekly

Women's Resource & Business Directory 206/726-9687

Spiritual Groups

Affirmation (Mormon) 206/215-4522 • monthly potluck • also newsletter

Congregation Tikvah Chadashah 20th Ave E & E Prospect (at Prospect Cong Church) **206/329-2590** • 8:15pm 2nd & 4th Fri • lesbigay Shabbat services

Dignity Seattle 723 18th Ave E (at St Joseph's Church on Capitol Hill) **206/325-7314** • 7:30pm Sun • Catholic

Grace Gospel Chapel 2052 64th St NW (at 22nd Ave N), Ballard **206/784-8495** • 10am & 7pm Sun

Integrity Puget Sound 1245 10th Ave E (at Chapel of St Mark's) **206/525-4668** • 7pm Sun • Episcopal

MCC 704 19th Ave E (at Roy, in Russian Ctr) **206/325-2421** • 9am & 11am Sun

Gyms & Health Clubs

World Gym 825 Pike St (at 8th Ave) **206/583-0640**

Erotica

The Crypt 1310 E Union St (at 14th) **206/325-3882** • 10am-midnight, till 1am Fri-Sat

Fantasy Unlimited 2027 Westlake Ave (at 7th) **206/682-0167** • 24hrs

Onyx Leather 206/328-1965 • by appt only

The Rubber Tree 4426 Burke Ave N (at 45th) **206/633-4750** • 11am-7pm, 10am-6pm Sat, clsd Sun • nonprofit • safer sex supplies • referrals

Toys in Babeland 707 E Pike (btwn Harvard & Boylston) **206/328-2914** • 11am-10pm, noon-8pm Sun

Spokane

Info Lines & Services

AA Gay/ Lesbian 224 S Howard (upstairs) **509/624-1442** • 6:30pm Mon

Lesbian/ Gay Community Services Hotline 509/489-2266 • 24hrs

Rainbow Regional Community Center 315 W Mission #2 **509/458-2741**

Accommodations

Sun Flower Cottage 4114 N Wall St **509/326-7707** • lesbians/ gay men • full brkfst • smokefree • $45-55

Bars

Hour Place 415 W Sprague (at Washington) **509/838-6947** • noon-2am • lesbians/ gay men • dancing/DJ • also restaurant • some veggie • wheelchair access • $5-8

Pumps II W 4 Main St (at Division) **509/747-8940** • 3pm-2am, from noon wknds • lesbians/ gay men • dancing/DJ Fri-Sat • live shows Wed • karaoke Tue-Th • food served

Nightclubs

Dempsey's Brass Rail 909 W 1st St (btwn Lincoln & Monroe) **509/747-5362** • 3pm-2am, till 4am Fri-Sat • popular • lesbians/ gay men • dancing/DJ Wed-Sat • drag shows Fri-Sat • piano bar downstairs • also restaurant • wheelchair access • $5-12

Bookstores

Auntie's Bookstore & Cafe W 402 Main St (at Washington) **509/838-0206** • 9am-9pm, till 10pm Fri, 11am-6pm Sun • wheelchair access

Retail Shops

Boo Radley's 232 N Howard (at Spokane Falls Blvd) **509/456-7479** • 10am-7pm, 11am-5pm Sun • gift shop

Rings & Things 714 W Main St (at Wall) **509/624-8949** • 9:30am-8pm, till 7pm Sat, 11am-5pm Sun • gay gifts

Publications

Stonewall News Northwest 509/456-8011

Spiritual Groups

Emmanuel MCC 307 W 4th Ave (btwn Washington & Bernard) **509/838-0085** • 10:15am Sun

Erotica

Castle Superstore 11324 E Sprague (btwn Gillis & Bowdish) **509/893-1180** • 9am-1am

Tacoma

Info Lines & Services

AA Gay/ Lesbian 209 S 'J' St (at the church, enter on alley) **253/474-8897** • 7:30pm Fri • also 6:30pm Tue (at 301 N 'K' St)

Oasis 253/798-2860 • lesbigay youth group run by Health Dept

Tacoma Lesbian Concern 253/752-6724 • social events • resource list

Accommodations

Chinaberry Hill—An 1889 Grand Victorian Inn 302 Tacoma Ave N **253/272-1282** • gay-friendly • very romantic • full brkfst • jacuzzis • kids ok • smokefree • $95-195

Commencement Bay B&B 3312 N Union Ave **253/752-8175, 800/406-4088** • gay-friendly (mostly women) • full brkfst • hot tub • $80-120

Bars

Spout & Toad 1111 Center St (at 'M') **253/272-1412** • 6am-10pm, 24hrs wknds, till 2am Sun • gay/ straight • karaoke Wed-Th • live shows Fri-Sun • also restaurant • gay-owned/ run

Nightclubs

24th Street Tavern 2409 Pacific Ave (at 25th) **253/572-3748** • 2pm-2am, from noon Fri-Sun • lesbians/ gay men • dancing/DJ • transgender-friendly • live shows • beer/ wine only • wheelchair access

Publications

South End News 206/324-4297 (SGN#)

Spiritual Groups

New Heart MCC 2150 S Cushman **253/272-2382** • 11am Sun & 7pm Wed

Erotica

Castle Superstore 6015 Tacoma Mall Blvd **253/471-0391** • 24hrs

Vancouver

see also Portland, Oregon

Bars

North Bank Tavern 106 W 6th St/ Main **360/695-3862** • noon-1am, till 2am Fri-Sat, 1pm-midnight Sun • lesbians/ gay men • beer/ wine only • food served • wheelchair access

Spiritual Groups

MCC of the Gentle Shepherd 913 W 13th St (at Kauffmann) **360/695-1480** • 10:30am Sun • wheelchair access

Wenatchee

Cafes

The Cellar Café 249 N Mission St (at 5th) **509/662-1722** • 9am-5pm, 10am-4pm Sat, clsd Sun • some veggie • beer/ wine • patio • lesbian-owned/ run • $5-$9

WEST VIRGINIA

Statewide

INFO LINES & SERVICES

West Virginia Tourism Division 800/225-5982

Beckley

EROTICA

Blue Moon Video 3427 Robert C Byrd Dr (at New River Dr) **304/255-1200**

Bluefield

BARS

The Shamrock 326 Princeton Ave **304/327-9570** • Fri-Sat only • lesbians/ gay men • dancing/DJ

Charleston

INFO LINES & SERVICES

AA Gay/ Lesbian Asbury United Methodist Church, 501 Elizabeth St **304/343-5330** • 8pm Th

COGLES (Community Oriented Gay/ Lesbian Events/ Services) 304/345-0491 • call for events

West Virginia Lesbian/ Gay Coalition 304/343-7305

BARS

Lee Street Deli 1109 Lee St E (at Washington) **304/343-3354** • 3pm-1am • gay-friendly

The Tap Room 1022 Quarrier St (enter rear) **304/342-9563** • 5pm-close • mostly gay men • neighborhood bar • country/ western Sun • private club

NIGHTCLUBS

Broadway 210 Broad St (at Lee) **304/343-2162** • 4pm-3am, from 1pm wknds • mostly gay men • dancing/DJ • private club

Grand Palace 617 Brooks St (nr Lee; take Broad St exit off I-64) **304/342-9532** • noon-3:30am, till 2:30am Sun • mostly gay men • dancing/DJ • drag shows • videos • private club

Trax 504 W Washington (at Maryland) **304/345-8931** • 4pm-3am, till 2:30am Sat • lesbians/ gay men • dancing/DJ Wed-Sun • live shows

PUBLICATIONS

Across the Threshold 1420-B Quarrier St **304/342-2512, 800/319-6275**

Graffiti 1425 Lee St **304/342-4412** • alternative entertainment guide • mostly non-gay

Shout! 540/989-1579 • entertainment & personals for the Virginias & Carolinas

SPIRITUAL GROUPS

Appalachian MCC 520 Kanawha Blvd W (in Unitarian Bldg) **304/343-5330** • 6pm Sun

Huntington

BARS

Driftwood Lounge 1121 7th Ave **304/696-9858** • 5pm-3am • lesbians/ gay men • videos • wheelchair access • also 'Beehive' upstairs • open wknds • lesbians/ gay men • dancing/DJ • live shows

Polo Club 733 7th Ave (enter rear) **304/522-3146** • 3pm-3:30am, from 1pm wknds • lesbians/ gay men • more women Tue • dancing/DJ Th-Sun • live shows • private club • wheelchair access

The Stonewall 820 7th Ave (enter rear) **304/523-1069** • 8pm-3:30am • popular • lesbians/ gay men • more women Wed-Th • dancing/DJ • live shows

RESTAURANTS

Calamity Cafe 1555 3rd Ave **304/525-4171** • 11am-10pm, till 3am wknds • live shows • Southern/ Western • plenty veggie • full bar • wheelchair access • $10-15

EROTICA

Bookmark Video 1119 4th Ave (btwn 11th & 12th) **304/525-6861**

House of Video 1109 4th Ave (at 11th) **304/525-2194**

Lost River

ACCOMMODATIONS

The Guesthouse Settlers Valley Wy **304/897-5707** • lesbians/ gay men • full brkfst • swimming • steam & spa • smokefree • $108-116

Martinsburg

BARS

Ghost Lady Pub 127 E King St **304/267-0635** • gay/ lesbian party Tue

EROTICA

Variety Books & Video 244 N Queen St (at Race) **304/263-4334** • 24hrs

Morgantown

INFO LINES & SERVICES

Gay/ Lesbian Switchboard 304/292-4292

NIGHTCLUBS

Class Act 335 High St (enter rear) **304/292-2010** • 8pm-3am, clsd Mon • lesbians/ gay men • dancing/DJ • live shows • private club

Parkersburg

BARS

Genders 316 5th St **304/485-2929** • clsd Mon • lesbians/ gay men • more women Wed • dancing/DJ • karaoke

Stonewall Jackson Lake

ACCOMMODATIONS

▲ **FriendSheep Farm** 304/462-7075 • mostly women • secluded farm retreat • cottage • B&B • $10 campsites • smokefree

Upper Tract

ACCOMMODATIONS

Wildernest Inn 304/257-9076 • gay-friendly • full brkfst • smokefree • $75-105

Vienna

BARS

True Colors 102 12th St (at Grand Central) **304/295-8783** • 7pm-close, clsd Mon • lesbians/ gay men • dancing/DJ • live shows • 18+

Wheeling

BARS

KC Dream Harbor • clsd Mon-Tue • mostly women • neighborhood bar • dancing/DJ

NIGHTCLUBS

Tricks 1429 Market St (behind 'Market St News') **304/232-1267** • 9pm-2am, till 3am Fri, clsd Mon-Tue • lesbians/ gay men • dancing/DJ • live shows

EROTICA

Market St News 1437 Market St (at 14th St) **304/232-2414** • 24hrs

WISCONSIN

Statewide

INFO LINES & SERVICES

Wisconsin Division of Tourism Madison **800/432-8747**

Appleton

BARS

Rascals Bar & Grill 702 E Wisconsin Ave (at Meade) **920/954-9262** • 5pm-2am, from noon Sun • lesbians/ gay men • more women Fri • food served • patio

EROTICA

Eldorado's 2545 S Memorial Dr (at Hwys 47 & 441) **920/830-0042**

Beloit

BARS

Kloset 232 Shirland Ave **608/363-8764** • lesbians/ gay men • dancing/DJ

Eagle River

ACCOMMODATIONS

Edgewater Inn 5054 Hwy 70 W **715/479-4011** • gay-friendly • smokefree rms available • $40-77

Eau Claire

ACCOMMODATIONS

Back of the Moon S3625 County Rd N, Augusta **715/286-2409** • women only • B&B retreat • smokefree • $35-40

BARS

Wolf's Den 302 E Madison **715/832-9237** • 6pm-2:30am • mostly gay men • neighborhood bar

NIGHTCLUBS

Scooters 411 Galloway (at Farwell) **715/835-9959** • 5pm-2am, from 3pm wknds • lesbians/ gay men • dancing/DJ • live shows • wheelchair access

Gays Mills

ACCOMMODATIONS

Chela's B&B and Forest Camping Retreat Gays Mills, La Crosse **608/735-4829** • women only • $15-65

Geneva Lakes

ACCOMMODATIONS

Allyn Mansion Inn 511 East Walworth Ave (btwn 5th & 6th), Delavan **414/728-9090** • gay/ straight • full brkfst • smokefree • gay-owned/ run • $75-125

Eleven Gables Inn on the Lake 493 Wrigley Dr, Lake Geneva **414/248-8393, 800/362-0395** • gay-friendly • full brkfst wknds • smokefree • wheelchair access • $89-250

Green Bay

INFO LINES & SERVICES

Gay AA 920/494-9904 • call for mtg schedule

BARS

Brandy's II 1126 Main St (nr Webster Ave) **920/437-3917** • 1pm-2am • mostly gay men • neighborhood bar • wheelchair access

Napalese Lounge 515 S Broadway (at Clinton) **920/432-9646** • 3pm-2am • mostly gay men • wheelchair access

Sass 840 S Broadway **920/437-7277** • 6pm-2am, from noon Sun (winters) • mostly women • dancing/DJ

NIGHTCLUBS

Java's/ Za's 1106 Main St (at Clay) **920/435-5476** • 8pm-2:30am • lesbians/ gay men • dancing/DJ • videos • 16+ Sun

PUBLICATIONS

Quest 920/433-0611, 800/578-3785

SPIRITUAL GROUPS

Angel of Hope MCC 3607 Libal St **920/432-0830** • 11am Sun

Hayward

ACCOMMODATIONS

The Lake House 5793 Division, Stone Lake **715/865-6803** • gay-friendly • full brkfst • swimming • smokefree • kids ok by arrangement • wheelchair access • lesbian-owned/ run •$55-75

Hazel Green

ACCOMMODATIONS

Percival's Country Inn 1030 S Percival St/ Hwy 80 **608/854-2881, 800/484-5306 CODE 3344** • gay/ straight • queen suites • full brkfst • jacuzzi • smokefree • wheelchair access • $75-95

Hazelhurst

Bars

Willow Haven Resort/ Supper Club 4877 Haven Dr (at Willow Dam Rd) **715/453-3807** • gay-friendly • also cabin rentals

Hixton

Accommodations

Inn at Pine Ridge 715/984-2272 • women only • full vegetarian brunch • seasonal hot tub • sauna • lesbian-owned/ run • $40-80

Kenosha

see also Racine

Bars

Capers Illusions 6305 120th Ave (on east frontage road of 94) **414/857-3813** • 8pm-2am • lesbians/ gay men • dancing/DJ • live shows

Clubhouse Filling Station 6325 120th Ave (on east frontage road of 94) **414/857-3744** • 7pm-2am, from noon Sun • lesbians/ gay men • dancing/DJ • live shows • food served

Nightclubs

Club 94 9001 120th Ave (off I-94) **414/857-9958** • 7pm-2am, from 3pm Sun, clsd Mon • popular • lesbians/ gay men • dancing/DJ • live shows • videos

La Crosse

Info Lines & Services

Gay/ Lesbian Support Group 126 N 17th St **608/784-7600** • 7:30pm Sun

Accommodations

Rainbow Ridge Farms B&B N 5732 Hauser Rd (at County S), Onalaska **608/783-8181, 888/336-9295** • gay-friendly • near outdoor recreation • restored farmhouse on 35 acres • lesbian-owned/ run • $60-95

Trillium B&B 608/625-4492 • gay-friendly • cottage (sleeps 5) • 35 miles from La Crosse • full brkfst • $55-85

Bars

My Place 3201 South St (at East Ave) **608/788-9073** • 3pm-close • lesbians/ gay men • friendly neighborhood bar • karaoke • games • gay-owned/ run

Our Cavalier Lounge 144 5th Ave N (at Main) **608/798-1056** • 4pm-close • mostly gay men • dancing/DJ

Players 214 Main **608/782-9279** • 4pm-2am • lesbians/ gay men • dancing/DJ • live shows • wheelchair access

Rainbow's End 417 Jay St (at 4th) **608/782-9802** • 2pm-2am, from 6pm Sat, clsd Sun • lesbians/ gay men • neighborhood bar

Bookstores

Red Oaks Books 323 Pearl St **608/782-3424** • 9am-8pm, till 9pm Fri, from noon Sun • lesbigay section

Retail Shops

Rainbow Revolution 122 5th Ave S (at Jay) **608/796-0383** • 10am-5:30pm, till 5pm Sat, clsd Sun • wheelchair access

Publications

Leaping La Crosse • newsletter

Laona

Accommodations

Laona Hostel 5397 Beech St **715/674-2615** • gay-friendly • dorm-style/ youth hostel rms • $12-15

Madison

Info Lines & Services

Apple Island 2718 Longview Ln, 53713 **608/256-8883** • women's space • sponsors social events

Campus Women's Center 800 Langdon, 4th flr Memorial Union, UW **608/262-8093** • support programs

LesBiGay Campus Center 800 Langdon, 2nd flr Memorial Union, UW **608/265-3344** • drop-in 10am-5pm • social events • general info

OutReach 600 Williamson St **608/255-4297, 608/255-8582** • 9am-9pm, clsd wknds • drop-in center • library • newsletter • AA group meets 6pm Sat

Accommodations

Wild Rose Guest House 1437 CTH W (off I-90), Stoughton **608/877-9942** • gay/ straight • full brkfst • 5 acres of nature located between Madison & Janesville • gay-owned/ run • $57-62

Bars

CE's 2415 Winnebago St (at Florence) **608/241-5042** • 4pm-close Wed-Sun • mostly women • women-owned/ run

Club 5 (formerly Manoeuvres) 5 Applegate Ct (btwn Fish Hatchery Rd & W Beltline Hwy) **608/277-9700, 608/277-8700** • 11am-2am Th-Fri, 4pm-2am Sat-Mon • mostly gay men • dancing/DJ • karaoke • live shows • food served

Green Bush 914 Regent St (at Park) **608/257-2874** • 4pm-midnight • gay-friendly • food served

Kirby Klub 121 W Main (at Fairchild) **608/251-5838** • 4pm-2am • mostly gay men • dancing/DJ

Ray's Bar & Grill 3054 E Washington Ave (at Milwaukee) **608/241-9335** • 4pm-2am, from 2pm Sun • lesbians/ gay men • dancing/DJ • food served • patio • wheelchair access

Shamrock 117 W Main St (at Fairchild) **608/255-5029** • 2pm-2am, Sun brunch from 10am • lesbians/ gay men • dancing/DJ • also grill

Nightclubs

Cardinal 418 E Wilson St (at S Franklin) **608/251-0080** • 8pm-2am, clsd Mon • gay-friendly • more gay Tue & early Fri • dancing/DJ

Restaurants

Fyfe's 1344 E Washington (at Dickinson) **608/251-8700** • lunch Mon-Fri, dinner nightly • popular • full bar

Monty's Blue Plate Diner 2089 Atwood Ave (at Winnebago) **608/244-8505** • 7am-10pm, till 9pm Sun-Tue, from 7:30am wknds • some veggie • beer/ wine • wheelchair access • $5

Sunporch Cafe 2701 University Ave (at University Bay Dr) **608/231-1111** • 7am-10pm, till 11pm Fri-Sat, from 8am Sun • homecooking • plenty veggie • live music Sun

Wild Iris 1225 Regent St (at Mills) **608/257-4747** • 11:45am-10pm, from 9am wknds • Italian/ Cajun • some veggie • beer/ wine • $8-12

Entertainment & Recreation

Nothing to Hide cable Ch 4 **608/241-2500** • 4pm-5pm Tue, 9pm-11pm Wed • lesbigay TV show

Bookstores

A Room of One's Own Feminist Bookstore & Coffeehouse 307 W Johnson St **608/257-7888** • 8am-8pm, till 10pm Fri-Sat, 10am-6pm Sun • wheelchair access

Borders Book Shop 3416 University Ave **608/232-2600** • 9am-11pm, till 8pm Sun • lesbigay section • also espresso bar

The Complete Traveler 2860 University Ave **608/233-7222** • travel-oriented books

Mimosa 210 N Henry **608/256-5432** • 10am-6pm, noon-5pm Sun • self-help books

Retail Shops

By the Light of the Moon 427 State St (at Broom) **608/250-9810** • 10am-6pm, noon-5pm Sun • women's music & books • gifts

Piercing Lounge 461 W Gilman (at University) **608/284-0870** • 11am-9pm, noon-6pm Sun

Publications

Of a Like Mind **608/257-5858** • women's newsletter of goddess spirituality

Spiritual Groups

Integrity/ Dignity 1001 University Ave (at St Francis Episcopal) **608/836-8886** • 6pm 2nd & 4th Sat

James Reeb Unitarian Universalist Church 2146 E Johnson St (at 4th St) **608/242-8887** • 10am Sun (summers) • call for winter hours

Erotica

A Woman's Touch 600 Williamson (at Gateway Mall) **608/250-1928** • 11am-6pm, till 8pm Tue & Th, noon-5pm wknds • wheelchair access

Red Letter News 2528 E Washington (at North) **608/241-9958** • 24hrs

Maiden Rock

Accommodations

Eagle Cove B&B **715/448-4302, 800/467-0279** • gay/ straight • hot tub • smokefree • wheelchair access • gay-owned/ run • $40-100

Mauston

Accommodations

CK's Outback W 5627 Clark Rd **608/847-5247** • women only • cabin & tipi • camping • $10-13

Milton

Accommodations

Chase on the Hill B&B 11624 State Rd 26 **608/868-6646** • gay/ straight • full brkfst • gay-owned/ run • $50-75

Milwaukee

Info Lines & Services

AA Galano Club 2408 N Farwell Ave (at North) **414/276-6936** • call after 5pm for mtg schedule

Gay Information & Services PO Box 510406 **414/444-7331** • 24hr referral service

Gay People's Union Hotline 414/562-7010

Gay Youth Milwaukee 414/272-8336, 888/429-8336 (outside Milwaukee)

Gemini Gender Group 414/297-9328 • 2nd Sat • transgender support • call for location

Lesbian Alliance 414/272-9442

Milwaukee LGBT Community Center 170 S 2nd St (at Pittsburgh) **414/271-2656** • drop-in Th-Fri eves

SAGE Milwaukee 414/271-0378 • for older lesbigays • call after 4pm

Accommodations

The Milwaukee Hilton 509 W Wisconsin Ave (at 5th St) **414/271-7250, 800/445-8667** • gay-friendly • food service • swimming

Park East Hotel 916 E State St (at Marshall) **414/276-8800, 800/328-7275** • gay-friendly • smokefree • also restaurant • some veggie • wheelchair access

Bars

1100 Club 1100 S 1st St (at E Washington) **414/647-9950** • 7am-2am • mostly gay men • food served

Barbie Doll's Playhouse 700 E Meineke (at Pierce) **414/374-7441** • 3pm-2am • gay-friendly • neighborhood bar

Milwaukee

Milwaukee holds a place of honor in the collective dyke cultural memory as the home of TV's *Laverne & Shirley,* a cute couple if we ever saw one. (You didn't really think that big 'L' on Laverne's chest was a monogram, did you?)

You'll find plenty of breweries in this historically German-American city...and plenty of lesbians, too. The bars here are relaxed: **Dish** is a dance bar while **Kathy's Nut Hut** and **Station 2** are more intimate bars. **Club 219** is a mixed lesbian/gay bar with dancing, shows, and a multiracial clientele. **AfterWords** is the lesbigay bookstore, and it's got an espresso bar to boot!

Just an hour and a half west of Milwaukee is Madison—home of the University of Wisconsin, and, from what we hear, a hotbed of academic and cultural feminism. That includes dyke separatism and feminist spirituality, as well as anti-violence and anti-pornography activism. If that branch of feminism interests you, call the **Campus Women's Center,** the **LesBiGay Campus Center,** or **Apple Island** for current events. Stop by **A Room of One's Own** for java and a copy of the local publication **Of A Like Mind**, an excellent resource for pagan women's networking.

Club 219 219 S 2nd St (btwn Florida & Pittsburgh) **414/271-3732** • 5pm-2am • lesbians/ gay men • dancing/DJ • multi-racial clientele • live shows

▲ **Dish** 235 S 2nd St (at Oregon) **414/273-3474** • 6:30pm-2am, clsd Mon-Tue • popular • mostly women • dancing/DJ • wheelchair access

Emeralds 801 E Hadley (at Humboldt) **414/265-7325** • 3pm-2am • lesbians/ gay men

Henry's Pub & Grill 2523 E Belleview Pl (at Downer) **414/332-9690** • 3pm-2am • gay/ straight • full menu • wheelchair access

In Between 625 S 2nd St (at Bruce) **414/273-2693** • 5pm-2am, from 3pm wknds • lesbians/ gay men • neighborhood bar • wheelchair access

Kathy's Nut Hut 1500 W Scott (at 15th St) **414/647-2673** • 2pm-2am, from noon wknds • mostly women • neighborhood bar

M&M Club 124 N Water St (at Erie) **414/347-1962** • 11am-2am • mostly gay men • more women wknds • live shows • food served • some veggie • wheelchair access • $5-10

The Nomad 1401 E Brady St (at Warren) **414/224-8111** • noon-2am • gay-friendly

South Water Street Dock 354 E National (at Water St) **414/225-9676** • 3pm-2am • mostly gay men • wheelchair access

Station 2 1534 W Grant (at 15th Pl) **414/383-5755** • 6pm-2am, from 3pm Sun, clsd Mon-Tue • mostly women • neighborhood bar

Taylor's Bar 795 N Jefferson St (at Wells) **414/271-2855** • 4pm-2am, from 5pm wknds • gay/ straight • patio • wheelchair access • gay-owned/ run

Woody's 1579 S 2nd St (at Lapham St) **414/672-0806** • 4pm-2am • lesbians/ gay men • neighborhood bar

Nightclubs

Fluid Lounge 819 S 2nd St (at National) **414/645-8330** • 5pm-2am • lesbians/ gay men • mostly African American • live jazz/ DJ

La Cage (Dance, Dance, Dance) 801 S 2nd St (at National) **414/383-8330** • 8pm-2am • popular • mostly gay men • more women wknds • dancing/DJ • live shows • videos • food served • wheelchair access

Cafes

Alterra Coffee Roasters 2211 N Prospect Ave (at North) **414/273-3753** • 7am-11pm, till 8pm Sun

Annex Cafe 1106 S 1st St **414/649-8232** • 8pm-4am

Wild Thyme Cafe 231 E Buffalo (btwn Water & Broadway) **414/276-3144** • lunch & brunch

Restaurants

Cafe Vecchio Mondo 1137 N Old World Third St (at Juneau) **414/273-5700** • lunch & dinner • full bar • coffee & wine

Coquette Cafe 316 N Milwaukee St (btwn Buffalo & St Paul) **414/291-2655** • lunch Mon-Fri, dinner nightly, clsd Sun

The Knick 1030 E Juneau Ave **414/272-0011** • 6:30am-10pm, till 11pm wknds • some veggie • full bar

La Perla 734 S 5th St (at National) **414/645-9888** • 10:30am-10pm, till 11:30pm Fri-Sat • Mexican

Sanford Restaurant 1547 N Jackson St **414/276-9608** • dinner only, clsd Sun • Milwaukee elegant Euro-style • $20-25

Entertainment & Recreation

Boerner Botanical Gardens 5879 S 92nd St (in Whitnall Park), Hales Corners **414/529-1870** • 8am-dusk • 40-acre garden & arboretum

Mitchell Park Domes 524 S Layton Blvd (at Pierce) **414/649-9830** • 9am-5pm • botanical gardens

▲ **Pridefest Milwaukee 414/272-FEST**

Bookstores

AfterWords Bookstore & Espresso Bar 2710 N Murray (at Park) **414/963-9089** • 11am-10pm, till 11pm Fri-Sat, noon-6pm Sun • lesbigay

Peoples' Books 2122 E Locust St (at Maryland) **414/962-0575** • 10am-7pm, till 6pm Sat, clsd Sun

Schwartz Bookstore 2559 N Downer Ave **414/332-1181** • 9am-10pm, till 9pm Sun

Retail Shops

Adambomb Gallery 524 S 2nd St (at Bruce) **414/276-2662** • 11am-9pm, noon-10pm Fri, till 7pm wknds, from 1pm Sun, clsd Mon • tattoo studio

Milwaukee

Where the Girls Are: In East Milwaukee south of downtown, spread out from Lake Michigan to S. Layton Blvd.

Lesbigay Pride: June. 414/272-3378.

Annual Events: August - PrideFest Milwaukee 414/272-3378.
September - AIDS Walk.

City Info: 414/273-7222 or 800/231-0903.

Attractions: Annunciation Greek Orthodox Church.
Breweries.
Grand Avenue.
Mitchell Park Horticultural Conservatory.
Pabst Theatre 414/286-3665.
Summerfest.

Best View: 41st story of First Wisconsin Center. Call 414/765-5733 to arrange a visit to the top floor observatory.

Weather: Summer temperatures can get up into 90°s. Spring and fall are pleasantly moderate but too short. Winter brings snow, cold temperatures and even colder wind chills.

Transit: Yellow Cab 414/271-6630. Milwaukee Transit 414/344-6711.

Designing Men 1200 S 1st St (at Scott) **414/389-1200** • noon-7pm, till 9pm Fri-Sat, till 6pm Sun

Yellow Jacket 2225 N Humboldt Ave (at North Ave) **414/372-4744** • noon-7pm, till 5pm Sun, clsd Mon in summer • vintage clothes

Publications

In Step 414/278-7840 • lesbigay newspaper

Q Voice 414/278-7524 • lesbigay newspaper

Wisconsin Light 414/372-2773 • lesbigay newspaper

Spiritual Groups

Dignity 76th & Wright St (at St Pius X Church) **414/444-7177** • 6pm Sun

First Unitarian Society 1342 N Astor (at Ogden) **414/273-5257** • 9:15am Sun

Lutherans Concerned 414/372-9663 • call for info

Milwaukee MCC 924 E Juneau (at the Astor Hotel) **414/332-9995** • 11am & 7pm Sun

St James Episcopal Church 833 W Wisconsin Ave **414/271-1340** • 10:30am Sun

Erotica

Booked Solid 7035 W Greenfield Ave (at 70th), West Allis **414/774-7210**

Popular News 225 N Water St (at Buffalo) **414/278-0636** • toys • videos

Mineral Point

Accommodations

The Cothren House 320 Tower St (nr Cothren) **608/987-2612** • gay/ straight • full brkfst • gay-owned/ run • $65-125

Restaurants

Chesterfield Inn 20 Commerce St **608/987-3682** • seasonal • Cornish/ American • some veggie • full bar • $10-16

Norwalk

Accommodations

Daughters of the Earth 18134 Index Ave **608/269-5301** • women only • women's land • camping • retreat space

Oshkosh

see also Appleton

Erotica

Pure Pleasure 1212 Oshkosh Ave (off Hwy 21) **920/235-9727**

Portage

Erotica

Naughty But Nice Hwy 33 at exit 106 (off I-90) **608/742-8060** • 24hrs

Racine

Bars

What About Me? 600 6th St (at Villa) **414/632-0171** • 7pm-2am, from 3pm Tue & Fri, clsd Mon • lesbians/ gay men • neighborhood bar

Nightclubs

JoDee's International 2139 Racine St/ S Hwy 32 (at 22nd) **414/634-9804** • 7pm-close • lesbians/ gay men • dancing/DJ • live shows • courtyard • park in rear

Erotica

Racine News & Video 316 Main St (at State) **414/634-9827**

Rhinelander

Accommodations

The Edgewater Hotel & Resort 5054 Hwy 70 W, Eagle River **715/479-4011, 888/334-3987** • gay/ straight • hotel rms & waterfront cottages • gay-owned/ run • $39-59 room • $270-868 cottage

Sheboygan

Bars

The Blue Lite 1029 N 8th St (off Rte 143) **920/457-1636** • 7pm-2am, till 2:30am Fri-Sat • mostly gay men • neighborhood bar

Stevens Point

Info Lines & Services

Women's Resource Center 1209 Fremont (University of Wisconsin Nelson Hall) **715/346-4242 x4851** • 10am-4pm, clsd wknds • some lesbian outreach

Nightclubs

Platwood Club 701 Hwy 10 W **715/341-8862** • 8pm-close Fri-Sat only • lesbians/ gay men • dancing/DJ • wheelchair access

Erotica

Eldorado's 3219 Church St (at Business 51 S) **715/343-9877** • clsd Sun-Wed

Sturgeon Bay

Accommodations

Blacksmith Inn B&B 8152 Hwy 57, Baileys Harbor **920/839-9222, 800/769-8619** • gay-friendly • smokefree • $145-175

Chadwick Inn 25 North 8th Ave **920/743-2771** • gay/ straight • gay-owned/ run • $105-120

The Chanticleer B&B 4072 Cherry Rd **920/746-0334** • gay-friendly • on 30 acres • swimming • hot tub • smokefree • kids ok • wheelchair access • gay-owned/ run • $120-190

Superior

Bars

Jook Joint 820 Tower Ave (at Winter) **715/392-5373** • 1pm-2am • lesbians/ gay men • neighborhood bar • food served • wheelchair access

JT's Bar & Grill 1506 N 3rd St (at Blaknik Bridge) **715/394-2580** • 3pm-2am, from 1pm wknds • popular • lesbians/ gay men • dancing/DJ • patio • wheelchair access

The Main Club 1217 Tower Ave (at 12th) **715/392-1756** • 3pm-2am, till 2:30am Fri-Sat • mostly gay men • dancing/DJ • country/ western • leather • Internet access • wheelchair access

Molly & Oscar's 405 Tower Ave **715/394-7423** • 3pm-2am, till 2:30am Fri-Sat • gay-friendly • neighborhood bar

Wascott

Accommodations

Wilderness Way 715/466-2635 • women only • resort property • cabins • camping • RV sites • swimming • camping $14 • cottages $53-72

Wausau

Nightclubs

Oz 320 Washington **715/842-3225** • 7pm-2am, from 5pm Sun • mostly gay men • dancing/DJ • wheelchair access

WYOMING

Cheyenne

Info Lines & Services

United Gay/ Lesbians of Wyoming 307/778-7645 • info • referrals • also newsletter

Entertainment & Recreation

Hart Center Coffeehouse 307/635-5262 • Th eve only

Erotica

Cupid's 511 W 17th (at Thomes) **307/635-3837**

Etna

Retail Shops

Blue Fox Studio & Gallery 107452 Hwy 89 **307/883-3310** • open 7 days • hours vary • pottery & jewelry studio • local travel info

Jackson

Accommodations

Bar H Ranch 208/354-2906, 888/216-6025 • lesbians/ gay men • seasonal • also women-only horseback-riding trips in Grand Tetons (see 'Bar H Ranch' under Tour Operators section) • lesbian-owned/ run • $50-90/night, $580/week

Fish Creek Lodging 208/652-7566 • lesbians/ gay men • rental log cabin near Yellowstone Nat'l Park & Jackson Hole • women-owned/ run • $80-95/night, $400/wk

Nowlin Creek Inn 307/733-0882 • gay-friendly • B&B • log cabin • full brkfst • hot tub • $105-350

Redmond Guest House 110 Redmond St, Jackson Hole **307/733-4003** • lesbians/ gay men • apt rental • seasonal • smokefree • kids/ pets ok • lesbian-owned/ run • $110

Spring Creek Resort 1800 Spirit Dance Rd **307/733-8833, 800/443-6139** • popular • gay-friendly • food served • swimming • smokefree rms available • wheelchair access • $140-250

Three Peaks Inn 53 S Hwy 33, Driggs, ID **208/354-8912** • gay-friendly • full brkfst • kids ok • women-owned/ run • $50-75

Bookstores

Valley Books 125 N Cache **307/733-4533** • 9am-9:30pm, 10am-9pm Sun

Riverton

Restaurants

Country Cove 301 E Main (at First) **307/856-9813** • 7am-3pm, clsd Sun • plenty veggie • wheelchair access • women-owned/ run • $3-7

Canada 483
Caribbean 514
Mexico 522
Costa Rica 534
Europe 536

Note: *In most countries other than the USA and Canada,* ***listings are alphabetical by city*** *rather than by state, province or region.*

ALBERTA

Calgary

INFO LINES & SERVICES

Front Runners AA 1315 7th St SW (at Wesley United Church, enter on 14th Ave) **403/777-1212** • 8:30pm Tue, Th & Sat

Gay/ Lesbian Centre & Info Line 223 12th Ave SW #206 **403/234-8973** • 7pm-10pm • women's drop-in 7pm Sun • many groups

Illusions Transgender Club of Alberta 403/265-7789

Xtensions 403/777-9499, 877/882-2011 (IN CANADA ONLY) • province-wide lesbigay info line

ACCOMMODATIONS

11th Street Lodging 403/209-0111 • lesbians/ gay men • rms & suites • $35-100

Black Orchid Manor B&B 1401 2nd St NW **403/276-2471** • lesbians/ gay men • leather-friendly • private/ shared baths • $50-120

Calgary Westways Guest House 216 25th Ave SW **403/229-1758** • gay/ straight • full brkfst • hot tub • smokefree • gay-owned/ run • Can$55-89

The Foxwood B&B 1725 12th St SW **403/244-6693** • lesbians/ gay men • smokefree • gay-owned/ run • Can$65-145

BARS

The Backlot 209 10th Ave SW (at 1st St SW) **403/265-5211** • 2pm-2am, from 4pm winters • lesbians/ gay men • martini lounge • patio • wheelchair access

Detour 318 17th Ave SW **403/244-8537** • 3pm-3am • mostly gay men • neighborhood bar • dancing/DJ

Midnight Cafe/ Bar 840 14th Ave SW (at 'Best Western Hotel') **403/229-9322** • 7am-2am, from 9am Sat, 11am-midnight Sun • gay-friendly • food served

Money Pennies 1742 10th Ave SW (nr 14th St) **403/263-7411** • 11am-2am • lesbians/ gay men • neighborhood bar • food served • patio • wheelchair access

Rooks Bar & Beanery 112 16th Ave NW (at Center St) **403/277-1922** • 11am-2am • mostly women • dancing/DJ • karaoke • food served • brunch 11am-3pm Sun

NIGHTCLUBS

The Warehouse 731 10th Ave SW (alley entrance) **403/264-0535** • 9pm-3am, clsd Sun-Mon • gay-friendly • dancing/DJ • private club

CAFES

Cafe Beano 1613 9th St SW (at 17th Ave) **403/229-1232** • 7am-midnight • some veggie • wheelchair access

Grabbajabba 1610 10th St SW (btwn 16th & 17th Ave) **403/244-7750** • 7am-midnight • lesbians/ gay men • some veggie • patio • wheelchair access • $2-7

RESTAURANTS

Chicken Hawks Bistro 550 11th Ave SW **403/263-7177** • 11am-10pm, till 11pm Fri • patio

Entre Nous 1800 4th St SW **403/228-5525** • 11am-11pm, till 9pm Sun-Mon • French • patio

Melrose Cafe 730 17th Ave SW (at 7th St) **403/228-3566** • 11am-midnight • patio

Thai Sa-On 351 10th Ave SW **403/264-3526** • lunch & dinner • Thai

Victoria's 306 17th Ave SW **403/244-9991** • lunch, dinner, wknd brunch • homecooking • some veggie • full bar • wheelchair access • $6-10

Wicked Wedge Pizza 618 17th Ave SW (at 6th St) **403/228-1024** • 11am-2am

BOOKSTORES

A Woman's Place 1412 Centre St S **403/263-5256** • 10am-6pm, clsd Sun • women's bookstore • large lesbigay section • wheelchair access

Books 'n Books 738-A 17th Ave SW (at 7th St) **403/228-3337** • 10am-6pm wkdays & Sat, till 8pm Wed, till 10pm Th-Fri • wheelchair access

Daily Globe News Shop 1004 17th Ave SW **403/244-2060** • 9am-11pm • periodicals

With the Times 2212-A 4th St SW (at 22nd Ave) **403/244-8020** • 8:30am-11pm, from 9am wknds

PUBLICATIONS

Outlooks #200, Box 439, Suite 100, T2T 0B2 **403/228-1157, 888/228-1157**

Perceptions 306/244-1930 • covers the Canadian prairies

SPIRITUAL GROUPS

Integrity Calgary 1121 14th Ave SW (at St Stephen's Church) **403/234-8973** • 7:30pm 2nd & 4th Sun

EROTICA

After Dark 1314 1st St SW **403/264-7399** • clsd Sun

B&B Leatherworks 426 8th Ave SE **403/265-7789** • 10:30am-6pm, clsd Sun • drag/ fetish items

Tad's Bookstore 1421 9th Ave SE **403/237-8237** • wheelchair access

Edmonton

Info Lines & Services

AA Gay/ Lesbian 780/424-5900

Gay/ Lesbian Community Centre 10612 124th St #103 **780/488-3234** • 7pm-10pm, clsd wknds • also youth group

Gay/ Lesbian Info Line 780/482-2855 • 24hr recorded info & event listing

Womonspace 780/482-1794 • dances & other events

Xtensions 877/882-2011 (in Canada only) • province-wide lesbigay info line

Accommodations

Labyrinth Lake Lodge 780/878-3301 • women only • retreat space • swimming • hot tub

Northern Lights B&B 8216 151st St **780/483-1572** • lesbians/ gay men • full brkfst • swimming • gay-owned/ run • Can$50-60

Bars

Boots 'N Saddle/ Garage Burger Bar 10242 106th St (at 104th Ave) **780/423-5014** • 3pm-2am, cafe from 11am-8pm • mostly gay men • private club • wheelchair access

Buddy's 10112 124th St (upstairs) **780/488-6636** • 3pm-2am • lesbians/ gay men • neighborhood bar

The Roost 10345 104th St **780/426-3150** • 4pm-3am • mostly gay men • dancing/DJ

Secrets Bar & Grill 10249 107th St **780/990-1818** • 11am-2am • lesbians/ gay men • neighborhood bar • also restaurant

Nightclubs

Rebar 10551 Whyte Ave **780/433-3600** • 8pm-3am • gay-friendly • dancing/DJ • live shows • wheelchair access

Restaurants

Cafe de Ville 10112 124th St (side entrance) **780/488-6636** • lunch, dinner & Sun brunch • cont'l

Jazzberry's II 10116 124th St **780/488-6636**

Vi's by the River 9712 111th St **780/482-6402** • 11am-1am • full bar

Bookstores

Audrey's Books 10702 Jasper Ave (at 107th) **780/423-3487** • 9am-9pm, 9:30am-5:30pm Sat, noon-5pm Sun

The Front Page 10356 Jasper Ave (at 104th St) **780/426-1206** • 9am-8pm, clsd Sun • periodicals

Greenwood's Bookshoppe 10355 82nd Ave (at 104th St) **780/439-2005** • 9:30am-9pm, till 5:30pm Sat, noon-5pm Sun

Orlando Books 10123 Whyte Ave **780/432-7633** • 10am-6pm, till 9pm Fri, noon-5pm Sun • women's • lesbigay section • wheelchair access

Retail Shops

Divine Decadence 10441 82nd Ave (at 105th) **780/439-2977** • 10am-8pm • hip fashions • accessories

Spiritual Groups

Lambda Christian Church 8303 112th St, Rm 247 **780/474-0753** • 7pm Sun

MCC Edmonton 10086 MacDonald Dr **780/429-2321** • 7:15pm Sun

Lethbridge

Info Lines & Services

GALA (Gay/ Lesbian Association of Lethbridge) 403/329-4666 • 7pm-10pm Wed • peer support line 7pm-9pm Mon

Red Deer

Bars

The Other Place Bay #4, 5579 47th St **403/342-6440** • 4pm-3am, till 11pm Sun • lesbians/ gay men • dancing/DJ • wheelchair access

Cafes

49th Street Cafe 4917 49th St **403/342-4227** • 8am-8pm

Rocky Mtn House

Accommodations

Country Cabin B&B 403/845-4834 • gay-friendly • cabin • hot tub • swimming • kids/ pets ok • $65

British Columbia

Birken

Accommodations

Birkenhead Resort Pemberton **604/452-3255** • gay-friendly • cabins • campsites • hot tub • swimming • pets ok • Can$55-80

Courtenay

Info Lines & Services

Women's Resource Centre 780 Grant, unit 103 (btwn 6th & Cumberland) **250/338-1133, 250/334-9251** • 10am-4pm, clsd Fri-Sun

Cranbrook

Info Lines & Services

Cranbrook Women's Resource Centre 20-A 12th Ave N (at 2nd St) **250/426-2912** • 9am-4pm Mon-Th, clsd wknds

Fernie

Accommodations

Fernie Westways Guest House 202 4A Ave, Box 658 **250/423-3058** • lesbians/ gay men • full brkfst • smokefree • pets ok • gay-owned/ run • Can$45-70

Fort Nelson

Info Lines & Services

Women's Resource Centre 5004 52nd Ave W **250/774-3069** • noon-5pm Mon & Wed, 10am-noon Tue & Th, 1pm-4pm Fri, clsd wknds • call for appts

Golden

Info Lines & Services

Golden Women's Resource Centre 419C N 9th Ave **250/344-5317** • 9am-4pm, 11am-3pm Fri, clsd wknds

Gulf Islands

Info Lines & Services

Gays & Lesbians of Salt Spring Island (GLOSSI) 250/537-2227, 250/537-8797 • social events, support & info line

Accommodations

The Blue Ewe 1207 Beddis Rd, Salt Spring Island **250/537-9344** • lesbians/ gay men • full brkfst • hot tub w/ ocean view • nudity ok • Can$69-150

Eden Guesthouse 127 Orchard Rd, Salt Spring Island **250/653-9962** • lesbians/ gay men • gay-owned/ run • $95-119

Green Rose by the Sea 388 Scott Point Dr, Salt Spring Island **250/537-9927** • gay-friendly • apt rental • waterfront suite • Can$125/ night (2 night minimum)

The Rex Galiano Island **250/539-2365** • mostly gay men • designer log home on 5 acres • full brkfst • deck w/ hot tub • nudity permitted

Saltspring Driftwood Bed & Brunch 1982 N End Rd, Salt Spring Island **250/537-4137** • gay-friendly • miniature farm for art & animal lovers • kids/ dogs ok • sauna • Can$70-85

Summerhill Guesthouse 209 Chu-An Dr, Salt Spring Island **250/537-2727** • lesbians/ gay men • on the water • full brkfst • gay-owned/ run • Can$100-125

Sunnyside Up B&B 120 Andrew Pl, Salt Spring Island **250/653-4889** • lesbians/ gay men • panoramic views • full brkfst • hot tub • deck • shared baths • Can$65-110

Tutu's B&B 3198 Jemima Rd, Denman Island **250/335-0546, 877/560-8888** • gay-friendly • lakefront • private dock • swimming • Can$40-60

The Wheatley's Country Home 2154 Sturdies Bay Rd, Galiano Island **250/539-5980, 888/539-5980** • gay/ straight • also 4-bdrm cottage available in summer • Can$65-185

Bars

Moby's Pub 124 Upper Ganges, Salt Spring Island **250/537-5559** • 10am-midnight Mon-Th, 11am-1am Fri-Sun • gay-friendly • neighborhood bar

Kelowna

Info Lines & Services

Kelowna Women's Resource Centre 347 Leon #107 **250/762-2355** • 9am-4pm Mon-Th, clsd Fri-Sun

Okanagan Rainbow Coalition 436 Bernard Ave, 2nd flr **250/860-8555** • 7pm-10pm, clsd Sun • sponsors dances & coffeehouse • women's group Wed

Accommodations

The Flags B&B 2295 McKinley Rd **250/868-2416** • mostly gay men • mini-resort • full brkfst • hot tub • swimming • nudity • some shared baths • seasonal • gay-owned/ run • Can$40-65

Cafes

Bean Scene 274 Bernard Ave **250/763-1814** • 7am-10pm, from 8am Sat, 9am-9pm Sun • patio • wheelchair access

Restaurants

Greek House 3159 Woodsdale Rd **250/766-0090** • 11am-10pm, from 4pm wknds • cont'l • $7-17

Nanaimo

Accommodations

Dorchester Hotel 70 Church St **250/754-6835, 800/661-2449** • gay-friendly • $90-160

Bars

Neighbours 70 Church St (in hotel) **250/716-0505** • 7:30pm-1am Mon-Wed, till 2am Th, from 4pm Fri-Sat, till midnight Sun • lesbians/ gay men • neighborhood bar •

Restaurants

Flo's Diner 187 Commercial St **250/753-2148** • 7am-5pm • gay-owned/ run

Retail Shops

A Different Drummer 189 Church St (at Bastion) **250/753-0030** • 9:30am-5:30pm • cards • gifts • wheelchair access

Nelson

Info Lines & Services

Nelson Women's Centre 420 Mill St (at Ward) **250/352-9916** • noon-4pm Tue-Fri • occasional wknd events

West Kootaney Gay/ Lesbian Line **250/354-4297** • social group

Accommodations

Dragonfly Inn 1016 Hall Mines Rd **250/354-1128** • gay/ straight • full brkfst • gay-owned/ run • $55-85

Penticton

Accommodations

Bear's Den B&B **250/497-6721** • gay/ straight • full brkfst • hot tub • smokefree • gay-owned/ run • Can$85-100

Port Renfrew

Accommodations

Wild Women Retreat **250/388-0754, 250/748-1579** • 3-bdrm rental home • steps from the ocean on the west coast of Vancouver Island • kids ok • dogs ok • lesbian-owned/ run • Can$50-70

Prince George

Info Lines & Services

GALA North **250/562-6253** • 24hr recorded info • social group • call for drop-in hours & location

Teen Crisis Line **250/564-8336** • 4pm-11pm

Accommodations

Hawthorne B&B 829 PG Pulp Mill Rd **250/563-8299** • gay-friendly • full brkfst • hot tub • smokefree • gay-owned/ run • Can$60-70

Cafes

The Isle Pierre Pie Co 409 George St **250/564-1300** • 9am-5:30pm Mon-Wed, till 10pm Th-Sat

Prince Rupert

Info Lines & Services

Prince Rupert Gay Info Line **250/627-8900**

Qualicum Beach

Accommodations

Bahari B&B 5101 Island Hwy W **250/752-9278, 877/752-9278** • gay-friendly • full brkfst • hot tub • apt rental • smokefree • kids ok • $60-150

Quesnel

Info Lines & Services

Women's Resource Centre 690 Mclean St **250/992-8472** • 9am-4pm, clsd wknds

Tofino

Accommodations

Alderview Suite/ B&B 1108 Abraham Dr **250/725-4427** • gay-friendly • some shared baths • gay-owned/ run • Can$60-120

Beachwood 1368 Chesterman Beach Rd **250/725-4250** • private suite • steps to the beach • gay-friendly • gay-owned/ run

Bri Mar B&B 1375 Thornberg Crescent **250/725–3410, 800/714–9373** • gay/ straight • full brkfst • teens ok • Can$110-160

Lone Cone Guest Suites 170 2nd St **250/725–3394** • gay-friendly

West Wind 1321 Pacific Rim Hwy **250/725–2224** • lesbians/ gay men • 5 minutes from beach • hot tub • smokefree • gay-owned/ run • Can$75-175

Restaurants

Blue Heron 634 Campbell St **250/725–4266** • 7am-10pm • full bar • wheelchair access

Vancouver

Info Lines & Services

AA Gay/ Lesbian **604/434–3933, 604/434–2553 (TDD)**

Vancouver Gay/ Lesbian Centre 1170 Bute St **604/684–6869** • 7pm-10pm • also 'Out on the Shelves' lesbigay lending library

Accommodations

The Albion Guest House 592 W 19th Ave (at Ash) **604/873–2287** • lesbians/ gay men • full brkfst • hot tub • Can$110-155

Apricot Cat Guest House 628 Union St (4 blks east of Main) **604/215–9898** • gay-friendly • restored 1898 character home • full brkfst • women-owned/ run • Can$75-105

Brighton House B&B 2826 Trinity St (at Renfrew) **604/253–7175** • gay-friendly • 1906 character home w/ views • full brkfst • kids 12+ ok • Can$125-139

The Buchan Hotel 1906 Haro St (btwn Denman & Gilford) **604/685–5354, 800/668–6654** • gay-friendly • some shared baths • Can$45-135

The Chelsea Cottage B&B 2143 W 46th Ave (at West Blvd) **604/266–2681** • gay-friendly • full brkfst • hot tub • Can$65-120

Colibri B&B 1101 Thurlow St (at Pendrell) **604/689–5100** • lesbians/ gay men • full brkfst • deck • gay-owned/ run • Can$55-160

Columbia Cottage 205 W 14th Ave (at Manitoba) **604/874–5327** • gay-friendly • 1920s Tudor • full brkfst • smokefree • kids ok • IGLTA • $65-120

Dufferin Hotel 900 Seymour St (at Smithe) **604/683–4251** • gay-friendly • food served • also 3 bars

Vancouver

Where the Girls Are: In the West End, between Stanley Park and Gastown, or exploring the beautiful scenery elsewhere.

Entertainment: Wreck Beach (great gay beach).

Lesbigay Pride: August. 604/687-0955.

Annual Events: January - New Year's Day Polar Bear Swim.
May - Vancouver International Marathon 604/872-2928.
June - Dragon Boat Festival 604/688-2382.
Du Maurier Jazz Festival Vancouver 604/872-5200.
Stonewall Festival in the Park 604/684-6869.
July - Folk Music Festival 604/602-9798.
September/October - International Film Festival 604/685-0260, web: www.viff.org.

City Info: web: www.tourism-vancouver.org.
Vancouver Travel Info Center 604/683-2000.

Attractions: Capilano Suspension Bridge.
Chinatown.
Gastown.
Science World 604/443-7440.
Stanley Park.
Van Dusen Botanical Gardens 604/878-9274.

Best View: Biking in Stanley Park, or on a ferry between peninsulas and islands. Atop one of the surrounding mountains.

Weather: It's cold and wet in the winter (32-45°F), but it's absolutely gorgeous in the summer (52-75°F)!

Transit: Yellow Cab 604/681-1111.
Vancouver Airporter 604/946-8866.
BC Transit 604/521-0400.
A Visitors' Map of all bus lines is available through the tourist office listed below.

Vancouver

Just three hours north of Seattle is Vancouver, one of the most beautiful cities in the world. Much of its charm and attraction lie in natural scenery and outdoor activities. Great skiing is close by, and snow bunnies might want to schedule their trip to Vancouver around Altitude, Whistler's annual lesbigay ski week.

Be sure to visit Stanley Park, the largest city park in North America. There you can see the Aquarium, the Zoo, and famous Native American totem poles. Also worth a visit is the historic Gastown district: a lively area of boutiques, antique shops, and a vast array of restaurants. Once you've seen these sites, it's time to appreciate the beauty of the women of Vancouver. And, like everything in Vancouver, they *are* beautiful.

Dyke dancing machines should check out the women's nights at the city's many mixed bars—start out Friday at the **Lotus Club** women's night. There are also plenty of one-nighters at the mixed clubs: call the **Fly Girl** hotline to find out what's on while you're in town. (If you happen to be here over a long weekend, don't miss **Her/She** women's night at the popular dance club **Celebrities.**)

For a more laid-back evening out, shoot the breeze and some pool at **Homer's;** Tuesdays are women's nights.

For bookstores, try **Women in Print** or the famous lesbigay bookstore, **Little Sister's**. At either one, you can pick up a copy of **Kinesis,** the women's newsmagazine; **Xtra! West,** British Columbia's splashy lesbigay paper; **Qink,** the lesbigay entertainment mag; or the aptly named **Lezzie Smut.** Speaking of smut, check out **Womyn's Ware** for all your erotica needs.

Vegetarians will fare well at **La Quena, Naam,** or **Dish,** the only vegetarian fast-food place we know of. Vancouver has tons of lesbian-friendly services, so inquire at the **Vancouver Gay/Lesbian Centre** to find the perfect activity. And ask about their annual Lesbian Pride Week!

▲ **Hawks Ave B&B** 734 Hawks Ave **604/253-0989** • women only • smokefree • no credit cards

Heather Cottage 5425 Trafalgar St (btwn 38th & 39th) **604/261-1442** • lesbians/ gay men • full brkfst • hot tub • $60-95

Hotel Dakota 654 Nelson St **604/605-4333, 888/605-5333** • gay-friendly • Can$99-169

The Johnson Heritage House B&B 2278 W 34th Ave (at Vine) **604/266-4175** • gay-friendly • full brkfst • smokefree • Can$70-155

Les n' Bo's Bed & Brunch Escape **604/886-4227** • women only • cottage rental • 40 minute ferry from Vancouver • steps to beach

The Manor Guest House 345 W 13th Ave (at Alberta) **604/876-8494** • gay-friendly • full brkfst • hot tub • also apt available • $55-110

Mountain B&B 258 E Balmoral Rd (at Lonsdale) **604/987-2725** • gay-friendly • full brkfst • $65-85

Nelson House B&B 977 Broughton St (btwn Nelson & Barclay) **604/684-9793** • lesbians/ gay men • full brkfst • jacuzzi in suite • sundeck • gay-owned/ run • Can$58-168

'O' Canada House 1114 Barclay St (at Thurlow) **604/688-0555, 877/688-1114** • gay-friendly • restored 1897 Victorian home • full brkfst • gay-owned/ run • $125-215

Penny Farthing Inn 2855 W 6th Ave (at MacDonald) **604/739-9002** • gay-friendly • 1912 heritage house in Kitsilano • full brkfst • Can$85-165

Pillow 'n Porridge Guest Suites 2859 Manitoba St (btwn 12th & 13th) **604/879-8977** • gay-friendly • apts w/ private entrances • kitchenettes • fireplaces • kids ok • wheelchair access • women-owned/ run • $65-135

River Run Cottages 4551 River Rd W, Ladner **604/946-7778** • gay-friendly • on the Fraser River • wheelchair access • Can$160-220

Royal Hotel 1025 Granville St **604/685-5335, 877/685-5337** • gay/ straight • also Royal Pub bar • IGLTA • gay-owned/ run

Rural Roots B&B 4939 Ross Rd, Mt Lehman **604/856-2380** • lesbians/ gay men • 1 hr from Vancouver • full brkfst • nudity ok at hot tub • smokefree • wheelchair access • gay-owned/ run • $55-75

Stonewall Guest House 4171 Stonewall Dr, RR 3, Ladysmith, Vancouver Island **250/245-3346** • gay-friendly • hot tub • full brkfst • lesbian-owned/ run

Sunshine Hills B&B 11200 Bond Blvd, North Delta **604/596-6496** • gay-friendly • full brkfst • shared bath • Can$60-70

Treehouse B&B 2490 W 49th Ave (btwn Larch & Balsam) **604/266-2962** • gay-friendly • full brkfst • Can$90-155

Walnut House B&B 1350 Walnut St (btwn Whyte & Cornwall) **604/739-6941** • gay-friendly • full brkfst • Can$90-140

The West End Guest House 1362 Haro St (at Broughton) **604/681-2889** • gay-friendly • 1906 historic Victorian • full brkfst • $95-210

Bars

Lotus Club 455 Abbott St (at 'Heritage House Hotel') **604/685-7777** • 9pm-2am, 11am-1am Sun-Mon • lesbians/ gay men • women-only Fri • dancing/DJ • drag king shows

The Pub 455 Abbott St (at 'Heritage House Hotel') **604/685-7777** • 11am-midnight, till 1am Sun • lesbians/ gay men • dancing/DJ • live shows • leather events Sat • also 'Charlie's Lounge'

The Royal Pub 1025 Granville St (at 'Royal Hotel') **604/685-5335** • 11am-midnight • mostly gay men • neighborhood bar • live shows

Nightclubs

23 West 23 W Cordova (at Carrall) **604/688-5351** • 9pm-2am, 7pm-midnight Sun, clsd Mon-Wed • mostly gay men • dancing/DJ

Celebrities 1022 Davie St (at Burrard) **604/689-3180** • 9pm-2am • mostly gay men • dancing/DJ • theme nights • also 'Her/ She' women's bar Sun (during long wknds)

Denman Station 860 Denman (btwn Haro & Robson) **604/669-3448** • 9pm-2am, till midnight Sun • mostly gay men • neighborhood bar • dancing/DJ • karaoke • live shows • videos

Fly Girl/ Jet Boy **604/688-9378, EXT 2154, 604/875-9907** • circuit party event line • usually held at 'Celebrities'

Ms T's Cabaret 339 W Pender St **604/682-8096** • 8pm-2am • lesbians/ gay men • dancing/DJ • transgender-friendly • karaoke

The Odyssey 1251 Howe St (at Davie) **604/689-5256** • 9pm-2am • popular • mostly gay men • dancing/DJ • drag Wed

Cafes

The Edge 1148 Davie St (btwn Bute & Thurlow) **604/688-3395** • 7am-4am, till 3am Sun • popular after-hours spot

Harry's 1716 Charles St (at Commercial) **604/253-1789** • 9am-11pm, 10am-5pm wknds • deli • wheelchair access

Homer's 1249 Howe St (at Davie) **604/689-2444** • 6pm-2am • coffee & billards • beer/ wine • 'Girl to Girl' Tue

The Second Cup 1184 Denman (at Davie) **604/669-2068** • 7am-11pm • pastries • wheelchair access

Restaurants

Cafe S'il Vous Plaît 500 Robson St (at Richards) **604/688-7216** • lunch & dinner till 9pm, till 11pm Sat, clsd Sun

Canton Village 1043 Davie St **604/669-2638** • lunch & dinner • free delivery after 5pm

Chianti's 1850 W 4th St (at Burrard) **604/738-8411** • lunch & dinner

Cincin 1154 Robson (off Bute) **604/688-7338** • lunch & dinner only wknds • Italian/ Mediterranean • full bar

Delilah's 1739 Comox St (at Denman) **604/687-3424** • 5:30pm-11pm • some veggie • full bar • wheelchair access • $21-33

The Dish 1068 Davie St **604/689-0208** • 7am-midnight • lowfat vegetarian fast food

Doll & Penny's Cafe 1167 Davie St (off Bute) **604/685-3417** • 7am-3am, till 4am Fri-Sat, till 2am Sun • dinner shows Fri

Elbow Room Café 560 Davie St (at Seymour) **604/685-3628** • 7:30am-3:30pm, 2pm-4pm wknds • great brkfst

Hamburger Mary's 1202 Davie St (at Bute) **604/687-1293** • 8am-3am, till 4am Fri-Sat • some veggie • full bar

Henry's Landing 2607 Ware St (at S Fraser Way) **604/854-3679** • lunch & dinner • full bar

India Gate 616 Robson St (at Granville) **604/684-4617** • lunch & dinner

La Quena 1111 Commercial Dr (at William) **604/251-6626** • 11am-11pm • vegan • $3-10

Luxy Bistro 1235 Davie St (btwn Bute & Jervis) **604/681-9976** • 11am-11pm • some veggie • full bar • wheelchair access • $9-17

Mario's 33555 S Fraser Wy (at Kent Ave) **604/852-6919** • lunch & dinner • Italian

Martini's 151 W Broadway (btwn Cambie & Main) **604/873-0021** • 11am-2am, 3pm-3am Fri-Sun • great pizza • full bar • $7-14

Milestone's 1145 Robson St (at Thurlow) **604/682-4477** • lunch & dinner • full bar • $4-12

Naam 2724 W 4th St (at MacDonald) **604/738-7151** • 24hrs • vegetarian • wheelchair access • $3-10

Riley Cafe 1661 Granville St (at Beech) **604/684-3666** • 11:30am-10pm • BBQ • some veggie • full bar • wheelchair access • $5-12

Entertainment & Recreation

Lotus Land Tours 1251 Cardero St, Ste 2005 **604/684-4922, 800/528-3531** • day paddle trips • no experience necessary (price includes pick-up & meal)

Rockwood Adventures 1330 Fulton Ave, West Vancouver **604/926-7705** • rain forest walks for all levels w/ free hotel pick-up

Sunset Beach right in the West End

Wreck Beach below UBC

Bookstores

Little Sister's 1238 Davie St (btwn Bute & Jervis) **604/669-1753, 800/567-1662 (IN CANADA ONLY)** • 10am-11pm • lesbigay

Spartacus Books 311 W Hastings (at Hamilton) **604/688-6138** • 10am-8:30pm, 10am-6pm Fri-Sat, 11:30am-5:30pm Sun • progressive

Women in Print 3566 W 4th Ave (at Dunbar/ Collingwood) **604/732-4128** • 10am-6pm, noon-5pm Sun • women's • wheelchair access • women-owned/ run

Retail Shops

Mack's Leathers 1043 Granville (at Nelson) **604/688-6225** • 11am-7pm, till 8pm Th-Fri • also body piercing

Next Body Piercing 1068 Granville St (at Nelson) **604/684-6398** • call for hours • also tattooing

State of Mind 1100 Davie St (at Thurlow) **604/682-7116** • 9am-8pm • designer queer clothes

Publications

Kinesis 604/255-5499 • women's newsmagazine

Qink Northwest Magazine 206/419-7009 • news & entertainment magazine for Seattle, Portland & Vancouver

▲ **Rainbow Choices Directory 416/762-1320, 888/241-3569 (CANADA ONLY)** • lesbigay entertainment & business directory for Canada

Xtra! West 604/684-9696 • lesbigay newspaper

Spiritual Groups

Dignity/ Integrity 604/432-1230

MCC 1155 Thurlow **604/739-7959** • 7:15pm Sun

Erotica

Love's Touch 1069 Davie St **604/681-7024** • 10am-8pm, till 9pm Fri-Sat, noon-6pm Sun

Womyn's Ware 896 Commercial Dr (at Denables, in East End) **604/254-2543, 888/WYM-WARE (orders only)** • toys • fetishwear • lesbian-owned/ run

Vernon

Info Lines & Services

NOGO (North Okanagan Gay Org) 250/558-6198, 250/542-4842 • social/ support group

Accommodations

Rainbow's End 8282 Jackpine Rd **250/542-4842** • lesbians/ gay men • full brkfst • hot tub • some shared baths • gay-owned/ run

Victoria

Info Lines & Services

Gay/ Lesbian AA 250/383-7744

LGB Alliance 250/472-4393 • student group

Women's Creative Network 1910 Store St **250/382-7768** • women's private social club • mtgs • dances • events • visitors most welcome

Accommodations

The Back Hills 4470 Leefield Rd **250/478-9648** • women only • 30 minutes from Victoria in the Metchosin Hills • full brkfst • near outdoor recreation • smokefree • girls 10+ ok • lesbian-owned/ run • Can$50-60

Oak Bay Guest House 1052 Newport Ave **250/598-3812, 800/575-3812** • gay-friendly • 1912 Tudor-style house in quiet garden setting • near beaches • kids 10+ ok • $120-165

The Weekender B&B 10 Eberts St **250/389-1688** • April-Oct (wknds only Nov-March) • lesbians/ gay men • seaside • smokefree • gay-owned/ run • Can$75-110

Bars

BJ's Lounge 642 Johnson (enter on Broad) **250/388-0505** • noon-2am • lesbians/ gay men • shows • karaoke • food served

Cafes

Fiddleheads 1284 Gladstone Ave, Fernwood Village **250/386-1199** • 9am-8pm

Bookstores

Bolen Books 1644 Hillside Ave #111 (in shopping ctr) **250/595-4232** • 8:30am-10pm

Publications

Lavender Rhinoceros 250/598-6490

Whistler

Accommodations

Coast Whistler Hotel 4005 Whistler Wy **604/932-2522, 800/663-5644** • gay-friendly • full-service resort hotel • full bar & restaurant • swimming • wheelchair access • $105-199

The Whistler Retreat B&B 8561 Drifter Wy **604/938-9245** • lesbians/ gay men • outdoor hot tub • sauna • gay-owned/ run • $65-125

Cafes

Death By Chocolate at base of the Gondola

Restaurants

Boston Pizza 2011 Innsbruck Dr **604/932-7070** • 11am-11pm • full bar

La Rua 4557 Blackcomb Blvd **604/932-5011** • 5:30pm-close • Italian/ cont'l

Monks Grill base of Blackcomb **604/932-9677** • lunch & dinner • grill menu • full bar

Zueski's 4314 Main St **604/932-3888** • 11am-11pm • full bar • wheelchair access

Manitoba

Brandon

Info Lines & Services

Gays/ Lesbians of Western Manitoba 204/727-4297 • 7pm-9pm Fri • socials & coffeehouses

LGBT Youth Group 731B Princess Ave **204/727-0417** • 7pm-9pm Wed • for youth under 25

Winnipeg

Info Lines & Services

Gay/ Lesbian Info Line 1-222 Osborne St S **204/284-5208** • 7:30pm-10pm, clsd Sun • info in French Wed • sponsors lesbian, youth & TG groups

New Freedom AA Group at Gay/ Lesbian Resource Center **204/284-5208** • call for info

Women's Centre at U of Winnipeg **204/786-9788** • drop-in resource center during school year

Women's Resource Centre 1088 Pembina Hwy **204/477-1123** • 9am-noon, 1pm-4pm Mon-Th, clsd wknds

Accommodations

Masson's B&B 181 Masson St **204/237-9230** • gay/ straight • full brkfst • hot tub • shared baths • gay-owned/ run • $40-50

Winged Ox Guest House 82 Spence St **204/783-7408** • lesbians/ gay men • full brkfst • smokefree • shared baths • gay-owned/ run • $35-50

Bars

Club 200 190 Garry St (at Mary Ave) **204/943-6045** • 4pm-2am, till 10pm Sun • lesbians/ gay men • dancing/DJ • live shows • wheelchair access • dinner served • some veggie • $7-11

Nightclubs

Gio's 272 Sherbrooke St (at Portage) **204/786-1236** • 8pm-2am, clsd Sun • lesbians/ gay men • dancing/DJ • live shows • private club

Happenings 274 Sherbrooke St (upstairs) **204/774-3576** • 9pm-2am, till 3am Sat, clsd Sun • lesbians/ gay men • dancing/DJ • live shows • private club

Ms Purdy's Women's Club 226 Main St **204/989-2344** • 8pm-2am, clsd Sun-Mon • women only • men welcome Fri • dancing/DJ • live shows • private club • women-owned/ run

Restaurants

Step'N Out 283 Bannatyne Ave (at King St) **204/956-7837** • lunch & dinner, clsd Sun • fresh dynamic entrees • wheelchair access

Times Change Blues Cafe 234 Main **204/957-0982** • 8pm-2am, clsd Mon-Wed • some veggie • live shows • under $6

Bookstores

Dominion News 263 Portage Ave **204/942-6563** • 8am-9pm, noon-6pm Sun • some gay periodicals

McNally Robinson 1120 Grant Ave #4000 (in the mall) **204/453-2644** • 9am-10pm, till 11pm Fri, non-6pm Sun • some gay titles • wheelchair access

Mondragon Bookstore & Cafe 91 Albert St (at McDermott) **204/946-5241** • 10am-midnight, clsd Sun-Mon • veggie/ vegan • smokefree

Publications

Perceptions **306/244-1930** • covers the Canadian prairies

Swerve **204/942-4599** • lesbigay newspaper

Spiritual Groups

Dignity **204/287-8583** • 7:30pm 1st Fri • call for location

MCC 396 Broadway (at Kennedy, at Broadway United Church) **204/774-5354** • 3pm Sun

Erotica

Discreet Boutique 340 Donald (at Ellice) **204/947-1307** • 10am-10pm, till 6pm wknds, from noon Sun • also 'Discreet Video' next door

New Brunswick

Fredericton

Info Lines & Services

Fredericton Gay Line **506/457-2156** • recorded info, live 6:30pm-8:30pm Th

Nightclubs

G Spot 377 King St, 3rd flr (above 'Corleone Pizza') **506/455-7768** • 8pm-2am, clsd Mon • lesbians/ gay men • dancing/DJ • wheelchair access

Moncton

Nightclubs

Triangles 234 St George St (at Archibald) **506/857-8779** • 7pm-2am, from 8pm wknds, clsd Mon • lesbians/ gay men • dancing/DJ • karaoke Th

Sackville

Accommodations

Georgian House 114 Mt Whatley Loop Rd, Aulac **506/536-1481** • gay-friendly • 1840 home in quiet country setting • full brkfst • shared baths • seasonal • gay-owned/ run • $45-60

St John

Accommodations

Mahogany Manor 220 Germain St **506/636-8000, 800/796-7755** • gay-friendly • full brkfst • smokefree • kids ok • wheelchair access • Can$55-75

Nightclubs

Bogarts 9 Sydney St (off King Sq) **506/652-2004** • 8pm-2am, clsd Mon-Tue • lesbians/ gay men • dancing/DJ • also 'Mars Bar' lounge upstairs Fri-Sat • jazz, blues, martinis

St Leonard

Accommodations

L'Auberge du Haut St-Jean 760 Rue Principale **506/423-9229, 888/423-9229** • gay/ straight • large 1904 home in Acadian community • full brkfst • shared baths • gay-owned/ run • Can$45

Newfoundland

Corner Brook

Info Lines & Services

Women's Corner Brook Resource Centre 709/639-8522

St John's

Info Lines & Services

Gay/ Lesbian Info Line 709/753-4297 • 7pm-10pm Tue & Th

Women's Centre 83 Military Rd **709/753-0220** • 9am-5pm, clsd wknds

Accommodations

Banberry House 116 Military Rd (at Rawlins Cross) **709/579-8006, 877/579-8226** • gay/ straight • full brkfst • kids/ small pets ok • gay-owned/ run • $69-99

Bars

Schroders Piano Bar 10 Bates Hill (off Queens Rd) **709/753-0807** • 4pm-1am, 10pm-close Fri-Sat, till midnight Sun • gay-friendly • also 'Zapata's' restaurant downstairs • Mexican • some veggie

Nightclubs

Zone 216 216 Water St **709/754-2492** • 9pm-2am, till 4:30am Fri, clsd Sun-Wed • lesbians/ gay men • dancing/DJ

Bookstores

Bennington Gate Bookstore 8-10 Rowan St, Churchill Sq (lower level, Terrace on the Square) **709/576-6600** • lesbigay section

Stevenville

Info Lines & Services

Bay St George Women's Centre 54 St Clare Ave **709/643-4444**

Nova Scotia

Annapolis Royal

Accommodations

King George Inn 902/532-5286, 888/799-5464 • lesbians/ gay men • smokefree • seasonal • Can$59-145

Bear River

Accommodations

Lovett Lodge Inn 1820 Main St **902/467-3917, 800/565-0000 (Canada only)** • full brkfst • seasonal • smokefree • kids ok • gay-owned/ run • $40-44

Bridgetown

Accommodations

Pumpkin Ecological Wimmin's Farm RR 5 **902/665-5041** • catalog available • women-owned/ run

Chéticamp

Accommodations

Seashell Cabins 125 Chéticamp Island Rd **902/224-3569, 902/224-3569 (summer)** • gay-friendly • housekeeping units on the ocean • seasonal • kids ok • lesbian-owned/ run • Can$40-90

Halifax

Info Lines & Services

Lesbigay Youth Project 800/566-2437 (Canada only) • 5:30pm-9:30pm Sat

Accommodations

Bob's B&B 2715 Windsor St (btwn North & Almond) **902/454-4374** • lesbians/ gay men • full brkfst • hot tub • Can$65-95

Centre Town Guest House 2016 Oxford St (at Quinpool Rd) **902/422-2380** • lesbians/ gay men • hot tub • smokefree/ scentfree • some shared baths • French spoken • Can$79-85

Forevergreen House B&B 18 Garden Rd (at Hwy 214), Elmsdale **902/883-4445** • gay-friendly • full brkfst • smokefree • women-owned/ run • $45-85

Fresh Start B&B 2720 Gottingen St (at Black) **902/453-6616, 888/453-6616** • gay-friendly • full brkfst • some shared baths • kids/ pets ok • women-owned/ run • $57-77

The Old Fisher House B&B 204 Paddys Head Rd, RR 1, Indian Harbour **902/823-2228** • gay/ straight • full brkfst • shared baths • kids ok • lesbian-owned/ run • Can$75-90

Bars

The Eagle 2104 Gottingen St (upstairs at 'Chris's Cuisine') **902/423-2956** • 11:30am-2am • mostly gay men • neighborhood bar • full menu till 5pm

Reflections Cabaret 5184 Sackville St (at Barrington) **902/422-2957** • 4pm-3:30am • lesbians/ gay men • dancing/DJ • live shows • wheelchair access

Cafes

The Daily Grind 5686 Spring Garden Rd (nr South Park) **902/429-6397** • 7am-10pm, from 8am wknds • also newsstand

Restaurants

Le Bistro 1333 South Park (nr Spring Garden Rd) **902/423-8428** • lunch & dinner • some veggie • full bar • wheelchair access • $7-16

Satisfaction Feast 1581 Grafton St (off Blower St) **902/422-3540** • 11am-10:30pm, from 4pm Sun • vegetarian • patio • $5-12

Soho 1582 Granville St (at Sackville) **902/423-3049** • lunch & dinner • cont'l • $6-14

Sweet Basil 1866 Upper Water St (nr Duke) **902/425-2133** • lunch & dinner • full bar • $7-18

Entertainment & Recreation

Queer News CKDU 97.5FM **902/494-6479** • 12:05pm Fri

Bookstores

Atlantic News 5560 Morris St (at Queen) **902/429-5468** • 9am-10pm, clsd Sun • periodicals

Entitlement Book Sellers Lord Nelson Arcade (on Spring Garden Rd) **902/420-0565** • 9:30am-9pm, till 6pm Sat & Mon, from noon Sun

Frog Hollow Books 5640 Spring Garden Rd, 2nd flr (at Dresden Row) **902/429-3318** • 9:30am-6pm Mon-Wed, till 9pm Th-Fri, noon-5pm Sun

Inside Out Books 1574 Argyle St #2 **902/425-1538** • noon-6pm, till 7pm Fri, from 10am Sat, 1pm-5pm Sun • lesbigay

Schooner Used Books 5378 Inglis St **902/423-8419** • 9:30pm-6pm, till 9pm Fri, till 5:30pm Sat, clsd Sun • large selection of women's titles

Smithbooks 5201 Duke St (in Scotia Sq) **902/423-6438** • 9:30am-6pm, till 9pm Th-Fri

Trident Booksellers & Cafe 1570 Argyle St (at Blowers St) **902/423-7100** • 8am-9pm, 9am-6pm Sun

Retail Shops

Venus Envy 5365 Inglis St **902/422-0004** • 11am-6pm, till 8pm Fri, clsd Sun • women's books, health & sexuality store

Publications

Wayves 902/429-2661

Spiritual Groups

Safe Harbour MCC 5500 Inglis St (church) **902/453-9249** • 7:30pm Sun

Lunenburg

Accommodations

Brook House 3 Old Blue Rocks Rd **902/634-3826** • gay-friendly • seasonal • gay-owned/ run • $45-60

Sydney

Info Lines & Services

Women's Unlimited Feminist Association 902/564-5926

Yarmouth

Accommodations

Murray Manor B&B 225 Main St (at Forest) **902/742-9625, 877/742-9629** • gay-friendly • heritage home w/ lovely gardens & greenhouse • full brkfst • shared baths • kids ok • one all-natural-fiber, environmentally friendly room available • $55-70

Ontario

Bancroft

Accommodations

Pineview Guesthouse for Women RR 5 **613/332-5454** • women only • country setting • meals included • jacuzzi • sauna • lesbian-owned/ run • $135-170

Belleville

Accommodations

Nightingale's Therapeutic Spa & Rehabilitation 305 Main St, Box 352, Bloomfield **613/393-5335** • mostly women • full brkfst • shared baths • lesbian-owned/ run • $60-180

Brighton

Accommodations

Apple Manor 96 Main St Box 11 **613/475-0351** • gay-friendly • 150-year-old Victorian • full brkfst • swimming • shared baths • $55-65

Butler Creek B&B 613/475-1248 • gay-friendly • full brkfst • Can$55-85

Bookstores

Lighthouse Books 17 Prince Edward St **613/475-1269** • 9:30am-5:30pm, till 7pm Fri, clsd Sun-Mon (winters), open Mon (summers)

Cambridge

Entertainment & Recreation

Out & About CKWR 98.7 FM **519/895-2949** • 9:30pm Fri

Dutton

Accommodations

Victorian Court B&B 235 Main St **519/762-2244** • lesbians/ gay men • restored Victorian • smokefree • wheelchair access • $55-85

Gananoque

Accommodations

Boathouse Country Inn & Heritage Boat Tours 17-19 Front St, 1000 Islands, Rockport **613/659-2348, 800/584-2592** • gay/ straight • full brkfst • $75-150

Trinity House Inn 90 Stone St South, 1000 Islands **613/382-8383, 800/265-4871 (ON ONLY)** • gay-friendly • historic country inn • fine dining restaurant • smokefree • kids ok in suites • sailing charters • gay-owned/ run • $75-190

Guelph

Info Lines & Services

Out Line 519/836-4550 • volunteer hours vary

Bookstores

Bookshelf Cafe 41 Quebec St **519/821-3311** • 9am-10pm, 10:30am-9pm Sun (bar noon-1am) • also cinema & restaurant • some veggie • $5-10

Hamilton

Accommodations

The Cedars Tent & Trailer Park 1039 5th Concession Rd RR2, Waterdown **905/659-3655** • lesbians/ gay men • private campground • swimming • also social club • dancing/DJ • karaoke • wknd restaurant • some veggie

Bars

The Embassy Club 54 King St E (at Houston) **905/522-7783** • 2pm-2am • mostly gay men • neighborhood bar • dancing/DJ

Windsor Bar & Grill 31 John St N (at King William) **905/308-9939** • 11am-2am • lesbians/ gay men • dancing/DJ

Bookstores

The Women's Bookstop 333 Main St W (at Locke) **905/525-2970, 888/339-6626 (CANADA ONLY)** • 10:30am-7pm, till 5pm Sat, clsd Sun • call for summer hours • wheelchair access

Retail Shops

Gomorrah's 158 James St S, lower level (btwn Duke & Bold) **905/526-1074, 888/338-8278** • 11am-6pm, till 8pm Fri, from 10am Sat, noon-4pm Sun • pride gifts & jewelry • books

Kingston

Info Lines & Services

LGBT Phoneline & Directory 613/531-8981 • 7pm-9pm, clsd Fri-Sun

Nightclubs

Club 477 477 Princess St (at University) **613/547-2923** • 6pm-3am, from 4pm Fri-Sun • popular • lesbians/ gay men • dancing/DJ • alternative

Kitchener

Nightclubs

Club Renaissance 24 Charles St W **519/570-2406** • 9pm-3am, clsd Mon-Tue • lesbians/ gay men • dancing/DJ • food served • live shows

London

Info Lines & Services

AA Gay/ Lesbian 649 Colborne (at 'Halo Club') **519/433-3762** • 7pm Mon & Wed • Al-Anon 7pm Th

Bars

The Complex 722 722 York St **519/438–2625** • 24hrs • mostly gay men • food served • wheelchair access

Partners 186 Dundas St (at Clarence) **519/679–1255** • 2pm-2am • lesbians/ gay men • dancing/DJ • food served • patio • wheelchair access

Sinnz 347 Clarence St **519/432–0622** • 8pm-close, from 2pm wknds, clsd Mon-Tue • lesbians/ gay men • dancing/DJ • patio • wheelchair access

Nightclubs

Diversity 355 Talbot St **519/432–8181** • lesbians/ gay men • more women Sat • dancing/DJ

Halo Club (Gay/ Lesbian Community Centre) 649 Colborne St **519/433–3762** • 7pm-midnight, 9pm-2am wknds • lesbians/ gay men • women only last Fri • dancing/DJ • live shows • private club • wheelchair access • also monthly newsletter

Restaurants

Blackfriars Cafe 48 Blackfriars (2 blks S of Oxford) **519/667–4930** • lunch & dinner • popular • lesbians/ gay men • plenty veggie • full bar • $4-10

The Green Tomato 172 King St (at Richmond) **519/660–1170** • 11am-11pm, till 10pm Sun

Marla Jane's 460 King St (at Maitland) **519/858–8669** • lunch & dinner • French/ Cajun cuisine • gay-owned/ run

Murano 394 Waterloo St (at Dundas) **519/434–7565** • lunch & dinner, clsd Sun • northern Italian • gay-owned/ run

Veranda 546 Dundas St **519/434-6790** • lunch & dinner, clsd Sun-Mon • gay-owned/ run

Bookstores

Mystic Book Shop 616 Dundas St (at Adelaide) **519/673–5440** • 11am-6pm, clsd Sun • spiritual

Publications

Girl Cult 519/434–0961 • literary porn zine

Spiritual Groups

Holy Fellowship MCC 649 Colborne St, 2nd flr (at 'Halo Club') **519/645–0744** • 11:30am Sun

Maynooth

Accommodations

Wildewood Guesthouse 613/338–3134 • mostly women • all meals included • hot tub • swimming • smokefree • wheelchair access • gay-owned/ run • Can$130-150

Meaford

Accommodations

The Cedars RR 2 **519/538–3974** • women only • full brkfst • hot tub • near skiing & beaches • lesbian-owned/ run • Can$65

Niagara Falls

see also Niagara Falls & Buffalo, New York

Accommodations

Amelia E's 722 Rye St, Niagara-on-the-Lake **905/468–5550** • gay/ straight • B&B-private home • full brkfst • gay-owned • $60-80

Danner House B&B 12549 Niagara River Pkwy **905/295–5166** • lesbians/ gay men • full brkfst • jacuzzi • smokefree • gay-owned/ run • Can$95

Fairbanks House 4965 River Rd **905/371–3716** • lesbians/ gay men • 1877 restored Victorian • full brkfst • fireplaces • kids ok • lesbian-owned/ run • $75-150

The Pride of Niagara B&B 279 Nassau St (at Johnson), Niagara-on-the-Lake **905/468–8181, 877/586–1212** • gay/ straight • swimming • smokefree • gay-owned • from Can$125

The Saltbox 223 Gate St (at Queen St), Niagara-on-the-Lake **905/468–5423** • gay-friendly • full brkfst • charming 1820s downtown home • smokefree • shared baths • teens ok • $58

North Bay

Info Lines & Services

LGBT North Bay Area 705/495–4545 • 7pm-9pm Mon • social & support group • newsletter

Oshawa

Info Lines & Services

Proud & Out Durham 905/571–7263

Nightclubs

Club 717 717 Wilson Rd S #7 **905/434–4297** • 9pm-3am, clsd Mon-Wed • mostly gay men • also referral service

Ottawa

see also Hull, Province of Québec

Info Lines & Services

237-XTRA 613/237-9872 • touch-tone lesbigay info

Gayline/ Télégai 613/238-1717 • 7pm-10pm • bilingual helpline

Pink Triangle Services 71 Bank St (above McD's) **613/563-4818** • many groups & services

Women's Place 755 Somerset St W **613/231-5144** • 9am-4pm, clsd wknds • drop-in center

Accommodations

Ambiance B&B 330 Nepean St **613/563-0421** • gay-friendly

Rainbow B&B 203 York St **613/789-3286** • gay/ straight • 4-course brkfst • in Byward Market • minutes to everything

Rideau View Inn 177 Frank St (at Elgin) **613/236-9309, 800/658-3564** • gay-friendly • 3-story Victorian • full brkfst • smokefree • some shared baths • kids ok • Can$63-68

Bars

Centretown Pub 340 Somerset St W (at Bank) **613/594-0233** • 1pm-2am • lesbians/ gay men • dancing/DJ • videos • leather bar upstairs • 'Silhouette Lounge' piano bar downstairs Th-Sat

Club Polo Pub 65 Bank St (2nd floor, at Sparks) **613/235-5995** • 11am-2am • mostly gay men • neighborhood bar • dancing/DJ • food served • Internet access

The Lookout 41 York, 2nd flr **613/789-1624** • noon-2am • lesbians/ gay men • food served • balcony • wheelchair access

Market Station Bar & Bistro 15 George St (downstairs) **613/562-3540** • 2pm-2am • gay-friendly • dancing/DJ • patio

Nightclubs

Coral Reef Club 30 Nicholas **613/234-5118** • 8pm-close Fri-Sat only • lesbians/ gay men • more women Fri • dancing/DJ

Icon 366 Lisgar St **613/235-4005** • 8pm-3am, clsd Sun-Wed • lesbians/ gay men • martini lounge 1st flr • karaoke Wed • dancing/DJ 2nd flr from 10pm Fri-Sat

Cafes

The L-bow Room 214 Nepean St (at Bank) **613/563-7754** • 10am-10pm, till 8pm Sat, clsd Sun • homemade desserts • also lesbigay gift boutique

Restaurants

Alfonsetti's 5830 Hazeldern, Stittsville **613/831-3008** • noon-11pm, from 5pm Sat, clsd Sun • Italian • plenty veggie • $12-22

Fairouz 343 Somerset St W (at Bank) **613/233-1536** • lunch & dinner, dinner only Sat, clsd Sun • Lebanese

Manfred's 2280 Carling Ave **613/829-5715** • lunch & dinner • cont'l • some veggie • full bar • $10-16

Bookstores

After Stonewall 370 Bank St (nr Gilmour) **613/567-2221** • 10am-6pm Mon-Th,till 9pm Fri, till 5:30pm Sat, noon-5pm Sun • lesbigay

Mags & Fags 254 Elgin St (btwn Somerset & Cooper) **613/233-9651** • till 10pm • gay magazines

mother tongue books/ femmes de parole 1067 Bank St (at Sunnyside Ave) **613/730-2346, 800/366-0514 (Canada only)** • 10am-6pm, till 9pm Fri, clsd Sun

Octopus Books 116 3rd Ave (at Bank) **613/233-2589** • 10am-6pm clsd Sun • progressive

Wilde's 367 Bank St **613/234-5512** • 11am-9pm, till 6pm Sun • lesbigay • wheelchair access

Retail Shops

One in Ten 216 Bank St (at Nepean) **613/563-0110, 888/563-0110** • 11am-9pm, noon-6pm Sun • pride gifts • T-shirts • videos • toys

Publications

Capital Xtra! 613/237-7133 • lesbigay newspaper

▲ **Rainbow Choices Directory** 416/762-1320, 888/241-3569 • lesbigay entertainment & business directory for Canada

Spiritual Groups

Dignity Ottawa Dignité 386 Bank St **613/746-7279**

Perth

Accommodations

Bed, Breakfast, Etc RR 4 **613/267-5918** • women only • guest house • retreat center • workshops • 3 organic meals/ day • lesbian-owned/ run • $60

Peterborough

Info Lines & Services

Rainbow PO Box 1742, K9J 7X6 **705/876-1845, 877/554-4210 (Canada only)** • phoneline from 5:30pm • many social events

Erotica

Forbidden Pleasures 91 George St N **705/742-3800**

Picton

Accommodations

Hadden-Holme B&B 79 W Mary St **613/476-7555** • gay-friendly • Can$45-70

Port Sydney

Accommodations

Divine Lake Resort & Cottages **705/385-1212, 800/263-6600** • gay-friendly • resort • brkfst & dinner included • some veggie • swimming • nudity • spa pkgs available • wheelchair access • $110-180

Stratford

Accommodations

A Hundred Church Street 100 Church St **519/272-8845** • gay/ straight • full brkfst • some shared baths • kids 10+ ok • gay-owned/ run • Can$70-98

Burnside Guest Home 139 William St **519/271-7076** • gay-friendly • on Lake Victoria • full brkfst • hot tub • smokefree • gay-owned/ run • $50-80

The Maples of Stratford 220 Church St **519/273-0810** • gay-friendly • smokefree • some shared baths • $53-95

Bars

Old English Parlour 101 Wellington St (at St Patrick) **519/271-2772** • 11:30am-1am, brunch from 10am Sun • gay-friendly • some veggie • wheelchair access • $10-16

Restaurants

Down the Street 30 Ontario St **519/273-5886** • noon-11pm • int'l • full bar • $10-12

Sudbury

Accommodations

Rainbow Guest House 43 Lorne St **705/688-0561** • gay-friendly • some shared baths • gay-owned/ run • $30-40

Bookstores

Elm Tree Books & Things 61 Elm St (at Durham) **705/675-2670** • call for hours

Thunder Bay

Info Lines & Services

Northern Women's Centre 184 Camelot St (at Water) **807/345-7802** • 9:30am-5pm, clsd wknds

Accommodations

Pine Brook Lodge B&B **807/683-6114** • gay-friendly • full brkfst • full dinners • plenty veggie • shared baths • jacuzzi • sauna • kids/ pets ok • $35-55

Bars

Backstreet 24 S Cumberland St (at Red River Rd) **807/344-5737** • 4pm-2am, clsd Sun-Mon • lesbians/ gay men

Bookstores

Northern Women's Bookstore 65 Court St S (at Wilson) **807/344-7979** • 11am-6pm, clsd Sun-Mon • wheelchair access

Rainbow Books 264 Bay St (at Court St) **807/345-6272** • 11am-10pm, noon-6pm Sun

Toronto

Info Lines & Services

519 Church St Community Centre 519 Church St **416/392-6874** • 9am-10pm, noon-5pm wknds • location for numerous events • wheelchair access

925-XTRA **416/925-9872** • touch-tone lesbigay visitors' info

AA Gay/ Lesbian 234 Edmonton Ave E #202 **416/487-5591** • call for mtg schedule

Canadian Lesbian/ Gay Archives 86 Temperance St **416/777-2755** • 7:30pm-10pm Tue-Th & by appt

Lesbigay Youth Line **416/962-9688, 800/268-9688 (Canada only)** • 7pm-10pm, clsd Sun

Toronto Convention & Visitors Association **800/363-1990**

Transsexual Transition Support Group at 519 Center **416/925-9872 x2121** • 7pm-10pm 2nd & 4th Fri • for all members of the gender community & their significant others

Two-Spirited People of the First Nations 14 College St, 4th flr **416/944-9300** • lesbigay Native group

Women's Centre 563 Spadina Ave **416/978-8201** • pro-lesbian center • call for times

ACCOMMODATIONS

Allenby B&B 223 Strathmore Blvd (nr Danforth & Greenwood) **416/461-7095** • gay-friendly • smokefree • shared bath • Can$45-55

Amazing Space B&B 246 Sherbourne St (at Dundas) **416/968-2323, 800/205-3694** • lesbians/ gay men • also 'Immaculate Reception' on Cawthra Park • Can$75-110

Amblecote B&B 109 Walmer Rd (at Bernard) **416/927-1713** • gay-friendly • smokefree • Can$60-95

Banting House B&B 73 Homewood Ave (at Wellesley) **416/924-1458** • lesbians/ gay men • Edwardian home • $60-100

Cawthra Square—Great Inns of Toronto 10 Cawthra Sq (at Jarvis) **416/966-3074, 800/259-5474** • lesbians/ gay men • fireplaces • smokefree • IGLTA • Can$79-248

▲ **Dundonald House** 35 Dundonald St (at Church) **416/961-9888, 800/260-7227** • lesbians/ gay men • full brkfst • hot tub • Can$65-135

Hotel Selby 592 Sherbourne St (at Selby) **416/921-3142, 800/387-4788** • lesbians/ gay men • swimming • IGLTA • $50+

House on McGill 110 McGill St (at Church & Carlton) **416/351-1503** • gay/ straight • Victorian townhouse • shared baths • garden w/ deck • Can$50-85

Huntley House 65 Huntley St (at Bloor) **416/923-6950** • gay-friendly • full brkfst • $75-115

The Mansion 46 Dundonald St **416/963-8385** • gay/ straight • elegant Victorian

Toronto B&B **416/588-8800, 416/927-0354** • gay-friendly • reservation service • Can$65-120

The Toronto Towne House **416/469-8230, 416/469-1016** • gay/ straight • upscale townhouse • $69+

Victoria's Mansion 68 Gloucester St **416/921-4625** • gay-friendly • converted mansion • Can$85-125

Toronto

Where the Girls Are: On Parliament St. or elsewhere in 'The Ghetto'—south of Bloor St. W., between University Ave. and Parliament St.

Lesbigay Pride: June/July. 416/927-7433, web: www.toronto-pride.com.

Annual Events: June - duMaurier Downtown Jazz Festival 416/363-8717, web: www.tojazz.com. International Dragon Boat Race Festival 416/364-0046. July - Caribana Caribbean festival 416/969-3110 or 416/465-4884. September - International Film Festival 416/967-7371, web: www.bell.ca/filmfest.

City Info: 800/363-1990, web: www.tourism-toronto.com.

Attractions: Art Gallery of Ontario 416/979-6648. CN Tower 416/868-6937. Dr. Flea's International Flea Market 416/745-3532. Hockey Hall of Fame 416/360-7735. Ontario Science Centre 416/696-1000. Power Plant Gallery 416/973-4949. Royal Ontario Museum 416/586-5549. SkyDome 416/341-2300. Underground City.

Best View: The top of the one of the world's tallest buildings, of course: the CN Tower. Or try a sight-seeing air tour or a three-masted sailing ship tour.

Weather: Summers are hot (upper 80°s–90°s) and humid. Spring is gorgeous. Fall brings cool, crisp days. Winters are cold and snowy, just as you'd imagined they would be in Canada!

Transit: Co-op Taxi 416/504-2667. Grey Coach 416/393-7911. Transit Information 416/393-4636.

Toronto

Toronto is more than just the capital city of Ontario, eh! It's the cultural and financial center of English-speaking Canada. And though it's not far from Buffalo, New York, and Niagara Falls, Toronto has a European ambiance, fostered by its eclectic architecture and peaceful diversity of cultures, that makes it a great vacation getaway.

Restaurants and shops from Asia, India, Europe, and many other points on the globe attract natives and tourists alike to the exotic Kensington Market (buy your fresh groceries here), the malls of Eaton Centre, and the crafts and antiques available at the Harbourfront. Toronto's Chinatown is just north of funky shops and artsy cafes on Queen Street West.

For intrepid shoppers, Toronto has a lot to offer. **Out in the Street** carries lesbigay accessories. Big, beautiful femmes can check out **Take a Walk on the Wide Side** for larger-size finery. **Good For Her** is a women's erotica shop. And the **Omega Centre** is the place for metaphysical literature and supplies.

Toronto is also well-known for its repertory film scene, so try not to miss the two-week Lesbian Gay Film Fest in the spring, or the Film Festival of Festivals in September. In April, Toronto has *two* weeks of leather pride events, topped by the Ms. & Mr. Leather Toronto contests.

Any other time of year, you'll find the women hanging out at **Tango**, **Pope Joan,** or **52 Inc**—unless it's Saturday night, when they might be hanging at **Ciao Edie.** To find out about the latest women's nights, check out the weekly **Xtra!,** available at the **Toronto Women's Bookstore** and other queer-friendly establishments like the lesbigay **Glad Day Bookshop**.

'With Friends' B&B 12 Monteith St (at Church & Wellesley) **416/925-2798** • gay/ straight • restored 1877 terrace house • overlooks Cawthra Square Park • deck • Can$70-125

Bars

52 Inc 394 College St (east of Bathurst) **416/960-0334** • open from 5pm Tue-Fri • mostly women • also a restaurant • wknd brunch

Bar 501 501 Church (at Wellesley) **416/944-3163** • 11am-2am • lesbians/ gay men • neighborhood bar • live shows • infamous 'Window Show' Sun

The Black Eagle 457 Church St (at Alexander) **416/413-1219** • 2pm-2am, brunch from noon Sun • mostly gay men • leather • theme nights • patio

Carrington's 618 Yonge (at St Joseph) **416/944-0559** • 11am-2am • mostly gay men • sports bar & dance club

Ciao Edie 489 College St (at Bathurst) **416/927-7774** • 8pm-2am • gay/ straight • women's night Sat • oh-so-nice lounge

Crews/ Tango 508 Church (at Alexander) **416/972-1662** • noon-3am • mostly gay men • deck overlooking Church St • also 'Tango' from 8pm Tue-Sat • mostly women • dancing/DJ • live shows

Pegasus Billiard Lounge 489 Church St, 2nd flr (at Wellesley) **416/927-8832** • 11am-1am, till 2am Fri-Sat • lesbians/ gay men • neighborhood bar

Queen's Head Pub 263 Gerrard St E (btwn Seaton & Parliament) **416/929-9525** • 4pm-2am • gay-friendly • neighborhood bar • food served 5:30pm-11pm • patio • wheelchair access

Red Spot Lounge & Bar 459 Church St (at Carlton) **416/967-7768** • 4pm-2am • lesbians/ gay men • lounge • food served • live shows • comedy to drag

Trax V 529 Yonge St (at Maitland) **416/963-5196** • 11am-2am • popular • mostly gay men • dancing/DJ • piano bar • live shows • wheelchair access

The Web 619 Yonge St, 2nd flr (enter on Gloucester Ln) **416/922-3068** • noon-2am • popular • mostly gay men • dancing/DJ • hip urban feel • young crowd

Woody's/ Sailor 465-467 Church (at Maitland) **416/972-0887** • noon-2am • popular • mostly gay men • neighborhood bar • wheelchair access

Zipperz 72 Carlton St (at Church) **416/921-0066** • noon-3am • mostly gay men • dancing/DJ • drag shows • patio • piano bar

Nightclubs

Barn 418 Church (at Granby) **416/977-4684** • 9pm-3am, till 4am Fri-Sat, from 4pm Sun • mostly gay men • dancing/DJ • leather • also 'Stables' • 416/977-4702

El Convento Rico 750 College St (at Ossington) **416/588-7800** • 8pm-4am, clsd Mon-Wed • mostly gay men • dancing/DJ • Latin/ salsa music • Latino/a clientele • live shows

Fluid 217 Richmond St W **416/593-6116** • 10pm-4am, clsd Mon-Tue • gay/ straight • more gay wknds • dancing/DJ • dress code • cover charge

Pope Joan 547 Parliament (at Winchester) **416/925-6662, 416/925-9990** • 8pm-3:30am, clsd Sun-Tue • mostly women • more men Sun • dancing/DJ • live shows Th • African-American clientele • seasonal beach, pool & patio • food served • some veggie • brunch from noon summer wknds • women-owned/ run

Slam @ Industry 901 King St W (2 blks west of Bathurst) **416/260-2660** • 10pm-8am Sat only • gay-friendly • dancing/DJ • patio • wheelchair access • cover charge

Tallulah's Cabaret 12 Alexander St (at Wellesley) **416/975-8555** • cabaret from 10:30pm Fri-Sat only • lesbians/ gay men

Whiskey Saigon 250 Richmond (at Duncan) **416/593-4646** • 10pm-2am, clsd Mon-Wed • gay-friendly • dancing/DJ • live shows • '80s Sun • rooftop patio

Cafes

Cafe Diplomatico 594 College (at Clinton, in Little Italy) **416/534-4637** • 8am-1am • popular • patio

The Joy of Java 884 Queen St E **416/465-8855** • 7:30am-11pm • live jazz Sun • patio

The Second Cup 548 Church St (at Wellesley) **416/964-2457** • 24hrs except Mon-Wed • popular • coffee & desserts

Sweet City Bakery 24 Wellesley St W (at Yonge) **416/962-0358** • 6:30am-5:30pm, 8am-4pm wknds

Restaurants

Allen's Restaurant 143 Danforth Ave (at Broadview) **416/463-3086** • lunch & dinner • great scotch selection • patio

Avalon 270 Adelaide St W (at John) **416/979-9918** • dinner nightly, lunch Wed-Fri only, clsd Sun • intimate dining

The Babylon 553 Church St **416/923-2626** • noon-3am • also martini bar

Bistro 422 422 College St **416/963-9416** • 4pm-midnight

Byzantium 499 Church St (south of Wellesley) **416/922-3859** • 5:30pm-11pm • eastern Mediterranean • martini bar open till 2am • patio

Cafe Jambalaya 501 Yonge St (at Alexander, in Little Italy) **416/922-5262** • 8am-1am • Cajun, Caribbean & vegetarian • patio

Cafe Volo 587 Yonge St (at Dundonald) **416/928-0008** • 11am-10pm, bar till 1am • some veggie

The Courtyard at 'Hotel Selby' **416/921-0665** • open May-Sept • clsd Mon-Tue • BBQ • full bar • patio

The Gypsy Co-op 815 Queen St W (west of Bathurst) **416/703-5069** • noon-3am, 5pm-2am Mon, clsd Sun • also bar • kitschy

Hughie's Burgers Fries & Pies 777 Bay St (at College) **416/977-2242** • 11am-10pm • full bar • patio

Il Fornello 1560 Yonge St (1 blk north of St Clair) **416/920-8291** • Italian • plenty veggie • also 214 King, 416/977-2855 • also 576 Danforth Ave, 416/466-2931

La Hacienda 640 Queen W (nr Bathurst) **416/703-3377** • lunch & dinner • Mexican • sleazy, loud & fun

Living Well 692 Yonge St (at Isabella) **416/922-6770** • noon-1am, till 3am Fri-Sat • plenty veggie • full bar • $8-12

The Mango 580 Church St (at Dundonald) **416/922-6525** • 11am-1am • popular • lesbians/ gay men • full bar • patio

Oasis 294 College St (at Spadina) **416/975-0845** • 11am-1am, till 2am Fri-Sat, till 11pm Sun, from 3pm wknds • eclectic tapas • also bar • live shows

PJ Mellon's 489 Church St (at Wellesley) **416/966-3241** • 11am-11pm • some veggie • wheelchair access • $7-12

Rivoli Cafe 332 Queen St W (at Spadina) **416/597-0794** • 11:30am-11pm • bar till 1am • some veggie

Slack Alice 562 Church St (at Wellesley) **416/969-8742** • noon-2am • also bar

Splendido 88 Harbord St **416/929-7788** • 5pm-11pm, clsd Sun • great decor & gnocchi

Superior Restaurant 253 Yonge St **416/214-0416** • 11:30am-midnight • full bar • wheelchair access

Trattoria Al Forno 459 Church St (at Carlton) **416/944-8852** • 11am-10pm, from 5pm wknds

Village Rainbow 477 Church St **416/961-0616** • 7am-midnight, till 1am Th-Sat • full bar • big patio

Wilde Oscars 518 Church St **416/921-8142** • 11am-3am • Mediterranean • huge patio • also lounge (clsd summer) upstairs

Zelda's Living Well 76 Wellesley St E **416/922-2526** • 11am-2am • full drag service Sat • all-you-can-eat Sun brunch

ZiZi Trattoria 456 Bloor St W (at Bathurst) **416/533-5117** • 5pm-close

Entertainment & Recreation

Gay/ Lesbian History Walking Tour **416/463-8274** • 2 hour tour • meets at 519 Church St Community Centre

Bookstores

A Different Booklist 746 Bathurst St (at Bloor) **416/538-0889** • 10am-7pm, till 6pm Sat, clsd Sun • multicultural titles & authors

Glad Day Bookshop 598-A Yonge St (at Wellesley) **416/961-4161** • 10am-7pm, till 9pm Th-Fri, from noon Sun • lesbigay

The Omega Centre 29 Yorkville Ave (btwn Yonge & Bay) **416/975-9086, 888/663-6377 (IN CANADA)** • 10am-9pm, till 6pm Sat, 11am-5pm Sun • metaphysical

This Ain't The Rosedale Library 483 Church St (at Wellesley) **416/929-9912** • 10am-10pm, clsd Sun

Toronto Women's Bookstore 73 Harbord St (at Spadina) **416/922-8744, 800/861-8233** • 10:30am-6pm Mon-Wed & Sat, till 8pm Th-Fri, noon-5pm Sun

Wonderworks 79-A Harbord St (at Spadina) **416/323-3131** • 10:30am-6pm • books & gifts

Retail Shops

Out in the Street 551 Church St **416/967-2759, 800/263-5747** • hours vary • lesbigay accessories

Passage Body Piercing 473 Church St **416/929-7330** • noon-7pm, clsd Sun-Mon • also tattoos & scarification

Studio Auroboros 580 Yonge St (at Wellesley) **416/962-7499** • noon-8pm, clsd Sun-Mon • body ornaments & piercing

Take a Walk on the Wide Side 161 Gerrard St E (at Jarvis) **416/921-6112** • 10am-7pm, till 11pm Sat, noon-4pm Sun • drag emporium

Publications

▲ **Rainbow Choices Directory 416/762-1320, 888/241-3569** • lesbigay entertainment & business directory for Canada

Siren 416/778-9027

Xtra! 416/925-6665 • lesbigay newspaper

Spiritual Groups

Christos MCC 427 Bloor St W (at Spadina in Trinity & St Paul's Church) **416/925-7924** • 7pm Sun

Congregation Keshet Shalom 416/925-9872 x2073, 416/925-1408

Dignity Toronto Dignité 11 Earl St **416/925-9872 x2011** • 6:30pm 2nd & 4th Sat

Integrity Toronto 416/925-9872 x2050, 905/273-9860 • 7:30pm 3rd Wed

MCC Toronto 115 Simpson Ave **416/406-6228** • 9am, 11am & 7pm Sun

Gyms & Health Clubs

The Bloor Valley Club 555 Sherbourne St (at Bloor) **416/961-4695** • gay-friendly • swimming

Erotica

Allure 357-1/2 Yonge St (at Gould) **416/597-3953**

Come As You Are 701 Queen St W (at Bathurst) **416/504-7934** • 11am-7pm, till 9pm Th-Fri, till 6pm Sat, noon-5pm Sun • co-op owned sex store

Good For Her 175 Harbord St (nr Bloor) **416/588-0900, 877/588-0900** • 11am-7pm, till 6pm Sat, women only till 2pm Th & noon-5pm Sun • women's sexuality products • wheelchair access

Northbound Leather 586 Yonge **416/972-1037** • toys & clothing • wheelchair access

Priape 465 Church St (at Wellesley) **416/586-9914, 800/461-6969** • clubwear • leather • books • toys & more

Windsor

see also Detroit, Michigan

Info Lines & Services

Gay/ Lesbian AA 1440 Windsor Ave **519/973-4951** • 7:30pm Tue

LGBT Phone Line 519/973-4951, 519/973-7671 (24HR INFO) • 8pm-10pm Th-Fri

Bars

Club Happy Tap Tavern 1056 Wyandotte St E **519/256-8998** • 2pm-1am, from 8pm Sun • mostly gay men • more women Sun • dancing/DJ

Nightclubs

Frankie's 634 Chilver Rd (at Wyandotte East) **519/254-4449, 519/254-3792** • 3pm-2am, from noon wknds • lesbians/ gay men • dancing/DJ • live shows • karaoke • food served • also 'Plum Cooley's' on 2nd flr 10pm-2am Fri-Sat only • dancing/DJ • theme nights

Spiritual Groups

MCC Windsor 897 Windemere Rd (at Niagara in Chilvers United Church) **519/977-6897** • 1pm Sun

PRINCE EDWARD ISLAND

Charlottetown

Info Lines & Services

Women's Network 902/368-5040

Accommodations

Charlottetown Hotel 75 Kent St (at Pownall) **902/894-7371** • gay-friendly • swimming • also restaurant • cont'l/ seafood • lounge clsd Sun • wheelchair access • $10-25

Rainbow Lodge Station Main, Vernon Bridge **902/651-2202, 800/268-7005** • gay-friendly • full brkfst • 15 minutes outside of town • gay-owned/ run • $80

Bars

Baba's Lounge 81 University Ave **902/892-7377** • noon-2am, from 5pm Sun • gay-friendly • live bands • also 'Caesar's Eatery' restaurant • Canadian/ Lebanese • some veggie

Bookstores

Book Mark 172 Queen St (in mall) **902/566-4888** • 8:30am-9pm, 9am-5:30pm wknds • will order lesbian titles

Publications

Gynergy Books/ Ragweed Press 902/566-5750 • feminist press • lesbian-owned/ run

Summerside

Info Lines & Services

East Prince Women's Info Centre 75 Central St **902/436-9856** • 9am-4pm, clsd wknds

PROVINCE OF QUÉBEC

Chicoutimi

BARS

Bistro des Anges 332 rue de Havre **418/698-4829** • 11am-3am • lesbians/ gay men • neighborhood bar

Drummondville

ACCOMMODATIONS

Motel Alouette 1975 Boul Mercure **819/478-4166** • gay-friendly • $45-80

BARS

Nuance 336 rue Lindsay, 2nd flr **819/471-4252** • 4pm-close, clsd Mon-Tue • lesbians/ gay men • neighborhood bar

Granby

ACCOMMODATIONS

Le Campagnard B&B 146 Denison ouest **450/770-1424** • gay-friendly • in a quiet village • bikes available • also camping • Can$40-45

Hull

see also Ottawa, Ontario

BARS

Le Pub de Promenade 175 Promenade de Portage **819/771-8810** • 11am-3am • popular • lesbians/ gay men • neighborhood bar • dancing/DJ

Joliette

ACCOMMODATIONS

L'Oasis des Pins 381 boul Brassard, St-Paul-de-Joliette **450/754-3819** • lesbians/ gay men • swimming • camping April-Sept • restaurant open year-round

BARS

Le Flirt 343 Beaudry Sud (at Lepine) **450/753-7225, 450/759-1297** • 8pm-3:30am • mostly gay men • dancing/DJ • drag shows

Jonquière

see Chicoutimi

Laurentides (Laurentian Mtns)

ACCOMMODATIONS

B&B du Mont Sauvage 2340 chemin du Mont Sauvage, Ste-Adèle **450/229-7821** • gay-friendly • swimming

Sainte-Adèle 1694 chemin Pierre-Peladeau, Ste-Adèle **450/228-3140, 888/825-4273** • lesbians/ gay men • superb ancestral home • close to slopes • Can$60-65

Le Septentrion B&B St-Sauveur-des-Monts **450/226-2665** • gay/ straight • swimming • jacuzzi • smokefree • gay-owned/ run

NIGHTCLUBS

Différent 257 St-Georges (Autoroute 15, take exit 'sortie 43'), St-Jérôme **450/569-8769** • 9pm-close, from 3pm Sat, clsd Sun-Tue • lesbians/ gay men • dancing/DJ

Magog

see also Sherbrooke

ACCOMMODATIONS

Au Gîte du Cerf Argenté 2984 chemin Georgeville **819/847-4264, 514/521-2712 (MONTRÉAL)** • lesbians/ gay men • B&B in century-old farmhouse • 4 beaches nearby • Can$28-72

Mont Tremblant

ACCOMMODATIONS

Versant Ouest B&B 110 chemin Labelle **819/425-6615, 800/425-6615** • lesbians/ gay men • full brkfst • gay-owned/ run • $60-95

Montréal

INFO LINES & SERVICES

AA Gay/ Lesbian 4024 Hingston Ave (at the church) **514/376-9230** • call for mtg times in French or English

Gay/ Lesbian Community Centre of Montréal 2075 rue Plessys (at Ontario) **514/528-8424** • 9am-noon & 1pm-4pm, clsd wknds

Gay Line/ Gai Ecoute 514/866-5090, 888/505-1010 (CANADA ONLY) • 7pm-11pm

Women's Centre of Montréal 3585 St-Urbain **514/842-4780** • 9am-5pm, till 9pm Tue, clsd wknds • wheelchair access

ACCOMMODATIONS

Angelica B&B 1213 Ste-Elisabeth (at Ste-Catherine) **514/844-5048** • gay-friendly • full brkfst • $55-120

Au Stade B&B Box 42 Stn 'M', H1V 3L6 **514/254-1250 x1** • lesbians/ gay men

Auberge & Atelier la Chaumiere B&B 1071 Rang des Ecossais (off Rte 203), Howick **450/825-0702** • gay-friendly • farmhouse & cottage • lesbian-owned/ run • Can$50-100 (for 2)

Montréal

Where the Girls Are: In the popular Plateau Mont-Royal neighborhood or in the bohemian area on Ste-Catherine est.

Entertainment: Info Gay Events Hotline 514/252-4429.

Lesbigay Pride: July/August. 514/285-4011.

Annual Events: June - Festival International de Jazz de Montréal 514/871-1881.
August - Montréal World Film Festival 514/848-9933.
October - Black & Blue Party 514/875-7026. AIDS benefit dance & circuit party.

City Info: 514/844-5400, web: www.tourism-montreal.org.

Attractions: Bonsecours Market 514/872-7730.
Latin Quarter.
Montréal Botanical Garden & Insectarium 514/872-1400.
Montréal Museum of Fine Arts 514/285-2000.
Old Montréal & Old Port.
Olympic Park.
Underground City.

Best View: From a caleche ride (horse-drawn carriage), from the top of the Montréal Tower, or from the patio of the old hunting lodge atop Mont Royal.

Weather: It's north of New England so winters are for real. Beautiful spring and fall colors. Summers get hot and humid.

Transit: Diamond Cab 514/273-6331.
Montréal Urban Transit 514/280-5100.

Auberge de la Fontaine 1301 Rachel St est (at Chambord) **514/597-0166, 800/597-0597** • gay-friendly • kids ok • wheelchair access • $115-175

Le Chasseur B&B 1567 rue St-André (at Maisonneuve) **514/521-2238, 800/451-2238** • mostly gay men • 1920s European townhouse • summer terrace • $49-99

Chateau Cherrier 550 Cherrier St (at St-Hubert) **514/844-0055, 800/816-0055** • lesbians/ gay men • May-Nov • full gourmet brkfst • $50-80

Chez Roger Bontemps 1447 Wolfe (at Ste-Catherine) **514/598-9587, 888/634-9090** • gay/ straight • B&B in two 1873 homes • also furnished apts • $55-240

Crowne Plaza Metro Centre 505 rue Sherbrooke est (at Berri) **514/842-8581** • gay-friendly • breathtaking view of Montréal • swimming • hot tub • also restaurant • full bar • $159-270

Les Dauphins 1281 Beaudry St (at Ste-Catherine est) **514/525-1459** • lesbians/ gay men • brkfst included • $50-70

La Douillette 7235 de Lorimier St (at Jean Talon) **514/376-2183** • women only • full brkfst • homey & cozy • $40-60

Ginger Bread House 1628 St-Christophe (at Maisonneuve) **514/597-2804** • mostly gay men

Hébergement Touristique du Plateau Mont-Royal 1301 rue Rachel est **514/597-0166, 800/597-0597** • gay-friendly • B&B network/ reservation service

Home Suite Hom 514/523-4642, 800/429-4983 • home exchange

Hotel de la Couronne 1029 St-Denis (at Viger) **514/845-0901** • gay-friendly • $50-75

Hotel du Parc 3625 Parc Ave (at Prince Arthur) **514/288-6666** • gay-friendly • $125-199

Hotel Kent 1216 rue St-Hubert (at Ste-Catherine) **514/845-9835** • gay-friendly • $30-65

Hotel Le St-Andre 1285 rue St-André (at Ste-Catherine) **514/849-7070** • gay-friendly • $65+

Hotel Lord Berri 1199 rue Berri (at Réné Lévesque) **514/845-9236** • gay-friendly • also restaurant • Italian/ cont'l • $99-159

Hotel Manoir des Alpes 1245 rue St-André (at Ste-Catherine) **514/845-9803** • gay-friendly • $55-65

Hotel Pierre 169 Sherbrooke est (btwn St-Denis & St-Laurent) **514/288-8519, 877/288-8577** • gay-friendly • kitchen • $55-85

Hotel Visitel Network 1617 Rue St-Hubert (at Maisonneuve) **514/529-0990** • hotel & reservation service

Hotel Vogue 1425 rue de la Montagne (nr Ste-Catherine) **514/285-5555, 800/465-6654** • popular • gay-friendly • full service upscale hotel • also restaurant

King's Guesthouse (Roy d'Carreau Guest House) 1637 Amherst (at Maisonneuve) **888/309-2493** • lesbians/ gay men • smokefree • gay-owned/ run • $75-150

Lindsey's B&B 3974 Laval Ave (nr Duluth) **514/843-4869** • women only • charming townhouse close to Square St-Louis & rue Prince Arthur • full brfkst

Le Pension Vallieres 6562 de Lorimier St (at Beaubien) **514/729-9552** • women only • full brkfst • $62-75

Ruta Baggage 1345 Ste-Rose (at Panêt) **514/598-1586** • gay-friendly • full brkfst • $60-70

Turquoise B&B 1576 rue Alexandre de Sève (at Maisonneuve) **514/523-9943** • mostly gay men • shared baths • gay-owned/ run • $50-70

Bars

Le Ballroom 1003 rue Ste-Catherine est **514/287-1360** • 8pm-3am, from 7pm Sun • lesbians/ gay men • dancing/DJ • theme nights (swing to disco) • also piano bar Th-Sat

Cabaret L'Entre Peau 1115 Ste-Catherine est (below 'Le Campus' at Amherst) **514/525-7566** • 3pm-3am • lesbians/ gay men • drag shows • wheelchair access

Café Fetiche 1426 Beaudry (at Ste-Catherine est) **514/523-3013** • 10am-3am, clsd Sun-Wed • mostly gay men • fetish night Fri • ladies' night Sat • shows

Le Campus 1111 Ste-Catherine est, 2nd flr (at Amherst) **514/526-9867** • 3pm-3am • mostly gay men • nude dancers • couples shows Th-Sun • ladies night some Sat nights 9pm-3am (call first)

Citibar 1603 Ontario est (at Champlain) **514/525-4251** • 11am-3am • lesbians/ gay men • neighborhood bar

Club Bolo 960 rue Amherst (at Viger) **514/849-4777** • 8pm-1am Fri, 9pm-2am Sat • mostly gay men • dancing/DJ • country/ western • T-dance 4pm-2am Sun

Montréal

Montréal is the world's second-largest French-speaking city. As you take in the architecture and arts, the fashion and the food, the style and sophistication of Canada's most cosmopolitan city, you will catch glimpses of the world's largest French-speaking city, Paris.

But, make no mistake; while it does have strong historical and cultural ties to Paris (it too has a Latin Quarter), Montréal is no 'Paris-lite.'

Montréal is home to many museums, like the Musée d'art contemporain de Montréal and the Montréal Museum of Fine Arts. Theater, dance, and music companies as well as a celebrated symphony orchestra thrive in this historic city. There is also a wealth of Old World architecture in the streets of Old Montréal and around Mont Royal.

Then there are the various symbols and events that mark Montréal as its own force in the comtemporary world, like the World Film Festival (every August) and the Palais des Congrès and Montreal World Trade Center.

But, clichéd as it may sound, what makes Montréal such a beautiful city to visit is its people. And they are beautiful.

Just take a walk through the Plateau Mont-Royal neighborhood and stroll through St-Louis Square to the rue Prince-Arthur. You'll not only see an interesting mix of tourists and Quebeçois but you'll also pass several of the women's guesthouses, including **Lindsey's.** Then wander up along the boul St-Laurent and into the excellent lesbigay bookstore **L'Androgyne.**

Or, better yet, head over to The Village, Montréal's gay community. Though, at first glance, it's a thriving Boy's Town, you'll see plenty of sisters in the bars and shops and stores along Ste-Catherine. When you tire of the testosterone, take off for one of Montréal's women's bars: **Sisters** or the women-only **Le Dietrich.** We also hear there are plenty of women to be found on the second floor of **Le Drugstore.**

Just remember that the people of Montréal are proud of their French heritage and language. Most signs will be in French—sometimes with an English translation, sometimes not. So brush up on your French, or at least learn some of the polite basics: *s'il vous plaît* (please), *merci* (thank you), *pardon* (excuse me), and the all-important question, *Parlez-vous anglais?* (Do you speak English?).

Club Date 1218 Ste-Catherine est (at Beaudry) **514/521-1242** • 8am-3am • lesbians/ gay men • neighborhood bar • karaoke • singers wknds

Le Dietrich Pub 4282 St-Denis (nr Rachel) **514/499-9342** • 2pm-2am • women only • neighborhood bar w/ great terrace • beer only

Le Drugstore 1360 Ste-Catherine est (at Panêt) **514/524-1960** • 9am-3am • popular • lesbians/ gay men • 8 bar complex • 3 flrs • food served

Foufounes Electriques 87 Ste-Catherine est (at St-Laurent) **514/844-5539** • 3pm-3am • gay-friendly • dancing/DJ • live bands • patio

Fun Spot 1151 Ontario (at Wolfe) **514/522-0416** • 11am-3am • mostly gay men • dancing/DJ • transgender-friendly • karaoke • drag shows

Météor 1661 Ste-Catherine est (at Champlain) **514/523-1481** • 11am-3am • lesbians/ gay men • dancing/DJ • '60s themed bar • food served • 40+ crowd

La Relaxe 1309 Ste-Catherine Est, 2nd flr • mostly gay men • neighborhood bar • very laid-back

Le St-Sulpice 1680 St-Denis (at Ontario) **514/844-9458** • 11:30am-3am • gay-friendly • dancing/DJ

West Side 1071 Beaver Hall (at Belmont) **514/866-4963** • 3pm-3am, from 7pm wknds • mostly gay men • nude dancers • ladies night Wed

Nightclubs

Blade 1296 Amherst (below Ste-Catherine est) • popular • lesbians/ gay men • after-hours bar in the Village

Chez Cleopatra 1230 St-Laurent, 2nd flr **514/871-8065** • 8pm-3am • mostly gay men • transgender-friendly • drag shows

Club Mississippi 1584 rue Ste-Catherine est (at 'Hotel Bourbon') **514/521-1419** • lesbians/ gay men • dancing/DJ • transgender-friendly • live shows

Disco Cleo 1230 blvd St-Laurent (at Ste-Catherine) **514/871-8066** • 8pm-3am • mostly gay men • dancing/DJ • transgender-friendly • live shows

Groove Society 1288 Amherst (at Ste-Catherine) **514/284-1999** • 9pm-3pm, clsd Mon-Tue • gay-friendly • dancing/DJ • live bands • open bar for women before midnight

Red Light 1955 rue Notre-Dame de Fatima, Duvernay-Laval **450/967-3057** • popular • gay-friendly • after-hours club in Laval

Sisters 1333 rue Ste-Catherine est, 2nd flr (at Panêt) **514/522-4717** • 6pm-3am Th-Sat only • popular • mostly women • dancing/DJ • live shows • upstairs from 'Le Saloon Café'

Sky 1474 Ste-Catherine est **514/529-6969** • 10pm-3am • popular • lesbians/ gay men • more women Th • pub on 1st flr w/ discos on 2nd & 3rd • T-dance from 4pm Sun

Sona 1439 Bleury (at Place des Arts) **514/282-1000** • gay/ straight • after-hours club

Stereo 858 Ste-Catherine est • after-hours • lesbians/ gay men • young crowd • inquire locally

Unity 1400 rue Montcalm **514/523-4429** • lesbians/ gay men • dancing/DJ • 4 flrs & great rooftoop terrace • women's night Fri

Cafes

Café Lafayette corner of Ste-Catherine est & Alexandre de Sève • outdoor cafe w/ several terraces

Café Titanic 445 St-Pierre **514/849-0894** • 7am-5pm, clsd wknds • popular • salad & soup

Restaurants

L' Ambiance (Salon de thé) 1874 Notre-Dame ouest (at des Seigneurs) **514/939-2609** • lunch daily, dinner Wed-Sat only, clsd Sun

L' Anecdote I 801 Rachel est (at St-Hubert) **514/526-7967** • 8am-10pm • burgers • some veggie

Après le Jour 901 Rachel est (at St-Andre) **514/527-4141** • 11:30am-11pm, from 4pm Sun • Italian/ French • seafood

L' Armoricain 1550 Fullum (at Maisonneuve) **514/523-2551** • lunch & dinner

Bacci 4205 St-Denis (at Rachel) **514/844-3929** • 11am-3am • full bar

Bazou 2004 Hôtel de Ville (at Ontario) **514/982-0853** • 5pm-11pm

La Campagnola 1229 rue de la Montagne (at Ste-Catherine) **514/866-3234** • 11am-1am • popular • Italian • great eggplant! • some veggie • beer/ wine • $12-20

Cantarelli 2181 Ste-Catherine est **514/521-1817** • 11am-10pm, clsd Sun • Italian

Chablis 1639 St-Hubert (at Maisonneuve) **514/523-0053** • dinner nightly, lunch wkdys only • Spanish/ French • some veggie • full bar • patio

Commensal 1720 St-Denis (at St-Denis) **514/845-2627** • till 10pm • vegetarian

Da Salossi 3441 St-Denis (at Sherbrooke) **514/843-8995** • lunch & dinner • clsd Sun-Mon • Italian • some veggie • beer/ wine • wheelchair access

L' Exception 1200 St-Hubert (at Réné-Lévesque) **514/282-1282** • burgers & sandwiches

L' Express 3927 St-Denis (at Duluth) **514/845-5333** • 8am-2am, 1pm-10pm Sun • popular • French bistro • full bar • great pâté

La Paryse 302 Ontario est (nr Sanguinet) **514/842-2040** • 11am-11pm, from 2pm (July only) • lesbians/ gay men • burgers • sandwiches

Piccolo Diavolo 1336 Ste-Catherine est (at Panêt) **514/526-1336** • 5pm-2am, lunch Tue & Fri • Italian • charming waiters

Pizzédélic 1329 Ste-Catherine est (at Panêt) **514/526-6011** • noon-midnight • pizzeria • some veggie • also 3509 boul St-Laurent, 514/282-6784 • also 370 Laurier ouest, 514/948-6290

Le Saloon Café 1333 Ste-Catherine est (at Panêt) **514/522-1333** • 11am-midnight, till 2am Fri-Sat • big dishes & even bigger drinks • 'Sisters' upstairs

Thai Grill 5101 boul St-Laurent **514/270-5566**

L' Un & L'Autre 1641 rue Amherst **514/597-0878** • 7am-10pm, from 5pm wknds • bistro • full bar

Entertainment & Recreation

Ça Roule 27 rue De la Commune est **514/866-0633** • in case you want to join all the other beautiful & buffed ones inline skating up & down Ste-Catherine

Cinéma du Parc 3575 Parc (btwn Milton & Prince Arthur) **514/281-1900** • repertory film theatre

Prince Arthur est at blvd St-Laurent, not far from Sherbrooke Métro station • closed-off street w/ many outdoor restaurants & cafés • touristy but oh-so-European

Bookstores

L' Androgyne 3636 blvd St-Laurent (at Prince Arthur) **514/842-4765** • 9am-6pm, till 9pm Th-Fri, 10am-5pm Sun • lesbigay bookstore w/ English & French titles

Publications

Fugues 514/848-1854 • glossy lesbigay bar/ entertainment guide

Le Guide Gai du Québec/ Insiders Guide to Gay Québec 514/523-9463 • bi-annual guide book

▲ **Rainbow Choices Directory 416/762-1320, 888/241-3569 (Canada only)** • lesbigay entertainment & business directory for Canada

Gyms & Health Clubs

Body Tech 1010 Ste-Catherine est (at Amherst) **514/849-7000**

Physotech 1657 Amherst (nr Maisonneuve) **514/527-7587** • lesbians/ gay men

Sex Clubs

Colonial Bath 3963 Colonial **514/285-0132** • women only 1pm-10pm Tue (men only rest of week)

Erotica

Il Bolero 6842-46 St-Hubert (enter at St-Zotique & Bélanger) **514/270-6065** • 9am-6pm, till 9pm Th-Fri, till 5pm wknds • fetish clothing • ask about monthly fetish party

Priape 1311 Ste-Catherine est (at Visitation) **514 /521-8451** • clubwear • leather • books • toys & more

Québec

Accommodations

727 Guest House 727 rue d'Aiguillon (btwn St-Augustin & Côte Ste-Geneviève) **418/648-6766, 800/652-6766** • lesbians/ gay men

Apartments St-Angelè 30 St-Angelè (at Ste-Jean) **418/655-7685** • gay-friendly • full brkfst

L' Auberge Du Quartier 170 Grande Allée ouest (at Av Cartier) **418/525-9726** • gay-friendly • buffet brkfst • Can$85-90

Auberge Montmorency Inn 6810 blvd Ste-Anne (at Gilles La Pointe), L'Ange-Gardien **418/822-0568** • gay-friendly • 15 minutes outside Québec • $55-100

Le Coureur des Bois Guest House 15 rue Ste-Ursule (at St-Jean) **418/692-1117, 800/269-6414** • lesbians/ gay men • also apts • Can$45-100

Le Gîte 772 Côte Ste-Geneviève (nr St-Jean) **418/648-9497** • gay-friendly • Can$25-45

Gîte le Piano 1064 chemin Royal, St-Jean **418/829-3930** • lesbians/ gay men • 4-sun (star) B&B along St-Laurent River • 20 minutes from Québec City • swimming • Can$70-100

Lucarne Enchantée 225 chemin Royal, St-Jean **418/829-3792** • gay-friendly • 20 minutes from Québec City • swiming • animals on premises • near beach • gay-owned/ run • Can$60

Bars

L' Amour Sorcier 789 Côte Ste-Geneviève (at St-Jean) **418/523-3395** • 2pm-3am • popular • lesbians/ gay men • neighborhood bar • videos • terrace

Bar 889 889 Côte Ste-Geneviève **418/524-5000** • 8am-3am • lesbians/ gay men • neighborhood bar • live shows • patio

Bar L' Eveil 670 rue Bouvier #118 **418/628-0610** • 3pm-close, from 8pm Sat, clsd Mon-Wed • mostly women • neighborhood bar • patio

Paradisio Café-Bar 161 rue St-Jean (at Turnbull) **418/522-6014** • 2pm-midnight, clsd Mon • lesbians/ gay men • neighborhood bar

Taverne Le Drague 815 rue St-Augustin (at St-Joachim) **418/649-7212** • 8am-3am • popular • mostly gay men • neighborhood bar • dancing/DJ Fri-Sun • food served • live shows • beer/ wine • wheelchair access

Nightclubs

Le Ballon Rouge 811 rue St-Jean (at St-Augustin) **418/647-9227** • 9pm-3am • popular • mostly gay men • dancing/DJ • videos • young crowd • patio

Restaurants

Le Commensal 860 rue St-Jean **418/647-3733** • 11am-10pm • vegetarian

Le Hobbit 700 rue St-Jean (at Ste-Geneviève) **418/647-2677** • from 8am • some veggie

La Playa 780 rue St-Jean (at St-Augustin) **418/522-3989** • lunch & dinner • 'West Coast cuisine' • martini bar • heated terrace • gay-owned/ run

Poisson d'Avril 115 St-André (at St-Paul) **418/692-1010** • lunch & dinner • French for 'April Fools'

Restaurant Diana 849 rue St-Jean (at St-Augustine) **418/524-5794** • 8am-1am, till 5am Fri-Sat • popular

Zorba Grec 854 St-Jean (near Dufferin) **418/525-5509** • 24hrs • Greek • wheelchair access

Publications

Le Magaizine de Québec 707, boul Charest ouest **418/529-5892**

Erotica

Importation André Dubois 46 Côte de la Montagne (at Frontenac Castle) **418/692-0264** • 9am-7pm, till 9pm Fri-Sat, 10am-7pm Sun

Rimouski

Info Lines & Services

Maison des Femmes de Rimouski 16 Evèche (at rue Cathédral) **418/723-0333** • 9am-noon & 1:30pm-4:3pm, clsd wknds • women's resource center

Accommodations

Gîte aux Trois Pains 3 rue des Pins, Baie-des-Sables **418/772-6047** • gay-friendly • 1880 renovated home • shared baths • dinner on request • gay-owned/ run • Can$50

Rouyn-Noranda

Bars

Station D 82 Perreault ouest **819/797-8696** • 9pm-3am Th-Sat • lesbians/ gay men • dancing/DJ • drag shows • karaoke

Sherbrooke

Accommodations

Abenaki Lodge 4030 Chemin Magog, CP628, North Hatley **819/842-4455** • gay/ straight • full brkfst • on the lake and nearby skiing • Can$130-145

Nightclubs

Complex 13-17 13-15-17 Bowen sud (at King St) **819/569-5580** • 11am-3am • lesbians/ gay men • dancing/DJ • pub & dance club • strippers Fri-Sun • lesbian bar downstairs • also sauna

Restaurants

Café Bla-Bla rue King est **819/565-1366** • 11am-9pm • full bar

St-Didace

Accommodations

La Barcarolle 480 Principale **450/835-3154** • gay-friendly • 100-yr-old home in quaint village • nr lakes & rivers • swimming • bikes available • gay-owned/ run • Can$40-50

St-Donat

Accommodations

Havre du Parc Auberge 2788 Rte 125 N **819/424-7686** • gay-friendly • quiet lakeside inn • food served • $145-450

St-Hyacinthe

Bars

Bistrot Mondor 1400 Cascades ouest **450/773-1695** • 8am-3am • mostly women • neighborhood bar

La Main Gauche 470 rue Mondor **450/774-5556** • 3pm-3am • lesbians/ gay men • dancing/DJ • live shows

Trois Rivières

Info Lines & Services

Gay Ami 819/373-0771, 819/693-1884 (for women) • lesbigay social contacts

Accommodations

Le Gîte du Huard 42 rue St-Louis **819/375-8771** • gay-friendly • $45-55

Verdun

Info Lines & Services

Centre des Femmes de Verdun 4255 rue Wellington **514/767-0384** • clsd wknds • general women's center • limited lesbian info

Saskatchewan

Ravenscrag

Accommodations

Spring Valley Guest Ranch 306/295-4124 • popular • gay-friendly • 1913 character home • cabin • kids/ pets ok • also restaurant • country-style • gay-owned/ run • Can$40-60

Regina

Info Lines & Services

Pink Triangle Community Services 24031 Broad St **306/525-6046** • 8:30pm-11pm, 10pm-1am Sat, clsd Sun-Mon & Wed

Regina Women's Community Centre 1907 11th Ave #250 (at Rose St) **306/522-2777** • 9am-4:30pm, clsd wknds

Nightclubs

Oscar's/ Brixx 1422 Scarth St **306/522-7343** • 8:30pm-2am • lesbians/ gay men • dancing/DJ • live shows

Entertainment & Recreation

Oscar Wilde & Company 2232 Retallack St **306/352-2919** • gay theatre troupe

Saskatoon

Info Lines & Services

Circle of Choice Gay/ Lesbian AA 10th St & Broadway (at Grace Westminster United Church) **306/665-5626** • 8pm Wed

Gay/ Lesbian Line 203-220 3rd Ave S (Gay/ Lesbian Health Services of Saskatoon) **306/665-1224, 800/358-1833 (in SK only)** • noon-4:30pm & 7:30pm-10:30pm, till 5:30pm Sat

Accommodations

Brighton House 1308 5th Ave N **306/664-3278** • gay-friendly • hot tub • smokefree • kids ok (family rate available) • wheelchair access • lesbian-owned/ run • $60

Nightclubs

Diva's 220 3rd Ave S #110 (alley entrance) **306/665-0100** • 8pm-2am, clsd Mon • lesbians/ gay men • dancing/DJ • private club

Bookstores

Spiritworks 1814 Lorne Ave (at Taylor) **306/653-7966** • women's

Retail Shops

Out of the Closet 203-220 3rd Ave S, 3rd flr **306/665-1224** • boutique run by the 'Gay/ Lesbian Line' • lesbigay gifts

Publications

Perceptions 306/244-1930 • covers the Canadian prairies

Yukon

Whitehorse

Info Lines & Services

Gay/ Lesbian Alliance of the Yukon Territory PO Box 5604, Y1A 5H4 **867/667-7857**

Victoria Faulkner Women's Centre 503 Hanson **867/667-2693** • 11am-2pm, clsd wknds

Accommodations

Inn on the Lake Lot 12/13 McClintock Pl, Marsh Lake **867/393-1932** • gay-friendly • luxury lakefront log inn • $98-125

Dominican Republic

Santo Domingo

Accommodations

Aida Hotel Calle El Conde 464 **809/657-2880** • gay-friendly • close to gay bars

Bars

Le Pousse Café Calle 19 de Marzo 107 (nr harbor) • 10pm-2am, clsd Mon-Wed • popular • lesbians/ gay men • dancing/DJ

Nightclubs

The Penthouse Calle Seybo (at Calle 20, difficult to find) • 11pm-5am, clsd Sun-Wed • popular • lesbians/ gay men • dancing/DJ

Cafes

Industrias Taveras Bonao **809/682-2735** • cheese market on the way to the beaches of Puerto Plata • 40 miles north of Santo Domingo on west side of Autopista Duarte

Restaurants

Café Coco Calle Sanchez 153 **809/687-9624** • noon-10pm • English • full bar • live shows

Dutch West Indies/Aruba

Oranjestad

Bars

Café the Paddock 94 LG Smith Blvd **297/83-23-34** • gay-friendly • neighborhood bar

The Cellar 2 Klipstraat **297/82-64-90** • 3pm-5am • popular • gay-friendly • neighborhood bar • also 'The Penthouse' from 11pm • lesbians/ gay men • dancing/DJ • alternative

Jewel Box Revue La Cabana Resort & Casino **297/87-90-00** • gay-friendly • live shows

Jimmy's Waterweg & Middenweg **297/82-25-50** • after-hours • popular • gay-friendly • neighborhood bar • food served

Cafes

Grand Café Cobra 60 LG Smith Blvd (in Marisol Bldg) **297/83-31-03**

Entertainment & Recreation

Sonesta Island European (topless) side

French West Indies

St Barthelemy

Accommodations

Hostellerie des 3 Forces Vitet **596/27-61-25, 800/932-3222** • gay-friendly • mountaintop new age retreat/ inn • swimming • food served • IGLTA • US$120-170

Hotel Normandie **596/27-62-37** • gay-friendly

Hotel Saint-Barth Isle De France **596/27-61-81** • gay-friendly • ultra-luxe hotel includes French cuisine • US$300-800

St Bart's Beach Hotel Grand Cul de Sac **596/27-60-70** • gay-friendly

Village St-Jean **596/ 27-61-39, 800/633-7411** • gay-friendly

Bars

American Bar Gustavia • gay-friendly • food served

Nightclubs

Le Sélect Gustavia **596/ 27-86-87** • gay-friendly • more gay after 11pm

Restaurants

Eddie's Ghetto Gustavia • Creole

Newborn Restaurant Anse de Caye **596/ 27-67-07** • French Creole

Entertainment & Recreation

Anse Gouverneur St Jean Beach • nudity

Anse Grande Saline Beach • nudity • gay section on the right side of Saline

L'Orient Beach • gay beach

St Martin

Accommodations

Holland House Philipsburg **590/52-25-72** • gay-friendly • on the beach • US$79-195

Meridien L'Habitation Anse Marcel **590/87-67-00, 800/543-4300** • gay-friendly • great beach • US$160-450

Orient Bay Mont Vernon **590/873-1110, 800/223-5695** • gay-friendly • studio & apt units • US$105-185

Nightclubs

Pink Mango at 'Laguna Beach Hotel', Nettle Bay **590/87-59-99** • 6pm-3am • popular • lesbians/ gay men • dancing/DJ

Restaurants

Le Pressoir **590/87-76-62** • US$18-20

Rainbow Grand Case Beach **590/87-55-80** • lunch & dinner • US$23-27

Jamaica

Montego Bay

Accommodations

Half Moon Golf, Tennis & Beach Club 809/954-2211, 800/237-3237 • gay-friendly • US$145-500

Moun Tambrin Retreat set in the mountains (28 miles from Montego Bay) 876/918-4487, 876/955-2852 • gay/ straight • run by gay men • food service • swimming • art deco house • US$210

Puerto Rico

Note: For those w/ rusty or no Spanish, 'carretera' means 'highway.' 'Calle' means 'street.'

Statewide

Publications

Puerto Rico Breeze 787/282-7184 • lesbigay newspaper

Aguada

Accommodations

San Max 787/868-2931 • 3 day minimum stay • lesbians/ gay men • guesthouse/ studio apt on the beach • US$30/ day • weekly rentals

Bars

Johnny's Bar Carretera 115 • gay-friendly • inquire at 'San Max' accommodations for directions

Aguadilla

Bars

The Factory Club C Belt 703 Punto Borinquen Shopping Ctr (at Base Ramey) 787/890-1530 • 9pm-close Th-Sun • dancing/DJ • live shows

Bayamón

Bars

Gilligan's Ave Betances D-18, Hans Davila (nr Pepin Ct) 787/786-5065 • 8:30am-4am Fri-Sat, till 1:30am Th • lesbians/ gay men • live shows • private club

Caguas

Bars

Kenny's Caguas Hwy km 232 • wknds only • popular • lesbians/ gay men • dancing/DJ • food served • swimming • inquire locally

Coamo

Accommodations

Parador Baños de Coamo end of Rte 546 787/825-2186, 787/825-2239 • gay-friendly • resort • mineral baths • also restaurant • full bar • kids ok • public baths • US$65-97

Isabela

Nightclubs

Keops Club Bario Jobas, Carretera 459, Sector La Sierra (entrance in front of Brendy Pizza) • 10pm-close Fri-Sat, from 8:30pm Sun • lesbians/ gay men • dancing/DJ • live shows • performance art

Lajas

Bars

Milagro's Place Carretera 116, on way from Lajas to La Parguera, at km 3.4 • 10am-midnight • gay-friendly

Ponce

Bars

Michelangelos on Carretera 10 from Ponce to Adjuntas (at km 13.7) • mostly gay men • dancing/DJ • live shows

San German

Bars

Norman's Bar Carretera 318, Barrio Maresúa • 6pm-1am • lesbians/ gay men • dancing/DJ • salsa & merengue

San Juan

Info Lines & Services

GEMA Hotline 787/723-4538 • lesbian alternative to the bar scene • en español

Madres Lesbianas 787/764-9639 • lesbian mothers group

Telefino Gay (CPLH) 787/722-4838, 800/981-9179

Accommodations

Atlantic Beach Hotel Calle Vendig 1, Condado (off Ave Ashford) 787/721-6900, 888/611-6900 • popular • lesbians/ gay men • swimming • also 'Indiana John's' restaurant • rooftop deck w/ hot tub • IGLTA • US$70-115

Casa del Caribe Guest House Calle Caribe 57, Condado 787/722-7139 • gay-friendly • US$35-50

Condado Inn Ave Condado 6 (at Ave Ashford) 787/724-7145 • lesbians/ gay men • near beach • also bar

El Canario Inn Ave Ashford 1317, Condado (at Cervantes) **787/722-3861, 800/533-2649** • gay-friendly • US$75-109

El San Juan Hotel & Casino Ave Isla Verde 6063 (at Baldorioty de Castro), Carolina **787/791-1000, 800/468-2818** • gay-friendly • great Asian restaurant & cigar bar • swimming

Embassy Guest House Calle Seaview 1126, Condado (off Calle Vendig) **787/725-8284, 787/724-7440** • gay/ straight • across the street from beach • also bar & grill • US$45-145

Glorimar Guesthouse Ave University 111, Rio Piedras **787/759-7304, 787/724-7440** • lesbians/ gay men • rms & apts • gay-owned • US$35-65

Gran Hotel El Convento Calle Cristo 100, Old San Juan (btwn Caleta de las Monjas & Calle Sol) **787/723-9020, 800/468-2779** • popular • gay-friendly • 17th-century former Carmelite convent • swimming • 'plunge' jacuzzi • US$190-300

Hotel Iberia Ave Wilson 1464, Condado (btwn Aves de Diego & Washington) **787/722-5380, 787/723-0200** • gay/ straight • European-style hotel • also restaurant & bar 'La Fonda de Cervantes' • lunch & dinner daily, Spanish/ int'l cuisine • gay-owned/ run • US$88-132

L' Habitation Beach Guesthouse Calle Italia 1957, Ocean Park (nr Santa Ana) **787/727-2499** • lesbians/ gay men • on the beach • also restaurant & bar • IGLTA • gay-owned/ run • US$51-73

Marriott Resort & Casino Ave Ashford 1309 (at Ave Cervantes) **787/722-7200, 800/223-6388** • gay-friendly • food served • swimming • US$190-280

Numero Uno on the Beach Calle Santa Ana 1, Ocean Park (nr Calle Italia) **787/726-5010, 787/727-9687** • gay/ straight • swimming • also 'Pamela's,' full bar & grill • Caribbean • brkfst, lunch & dinner • wheelchair access • US$65-185

San Juan

Lesbigay Pride: June. 787/261-2590.

Annual Events: February - Ponce Carnival.
June - Casals Festival 809/721-7727 or 809/728-5744.
October - Bomba y Plena (African-Caribbean music festival).

City Info: 800/223-6530.

Attractions: Casa Blanca Museum 787/724-4102.
Condado Beach.
La Fortaleza.
Historic Old San Juan.
El Morro Fortress & Fort San Cristobal 787/729-6960.
Pablo Casals Museum 787/723-9185.
Quincentennial Plaza.
San José Church.
San Juan Museum of Art & History 787/724-1875.
El Yunque rain forest 787/887-2875.

Best View: From El Morro or alternatively, one of the harbor cruises that depart from Pier 2 in Old San Juan.

Weather: Tropical sunshine year-round, with temperatures that average in the mid-80°s from November to May. Expect more rain on the northern coast.

Transit: Metro Bus 787/763-4141.

▲ **Ocean Walk Guest House** 1 Atlantic Pl, Ocean Park (off Ave MacLeary) **787/728-0855, 800/468-0615** • gay-friendly • swimming • IGLTA

Bars

Atlantic Beach Bar Calle Vendig 1 (at 'Atlantic Beach Hotel') **787/721-6900** • 11am-1am • popular • lesbians/ gay men • live shows • T-dance Sun w/ strippers & show

Baccheus Del Parke 609, Santurce Stop 23 (next to Domino's Pizza), Santurce • Th-Sun • mostly women

Bebo's Playa Piñones, Isla Verde • noon-close Wed-Sat • lesbians/ gay men • beachfront neighborhood bar • dancing/DJ • live shows • fun crowd

Café Bohemio Calle Cristo 100, Old San Juan (in 'Gran Hotel El Convento') **787/723-9020** • 11am-2am • gay-friendly • professional crowd • popular Tue • also restaurant

Café Violeta Calle Fortaleza 56, Old San Juan (btwn Calle del Cristo & Recinto Oeste) **787/723-6804** • noon-2am • intimate piano bar • courtyard • gay-owned/ run

Cups Calle San Mateo 1708, Santurce (btwn Calles Barbe & San Jorge) **787/268-3570, 787/268-5640** • 7pm-close, clsd Mon-Tue

Junior's Calle Condado 602, Santurce (btwn Calle Benito Alonso & Ave Ponce de León) • 5:30pm-6:30am • lesbians/ gay men • neighborhood bar • drag & strip shows • local crowd

Rivera Hermanos Calle San Sebastián 157, Old San Juan **787/724-5828** • 10am-7pm • gay-friendly • liquor shop & bar

Tia Maria's Ave Jose de Diego 326, Stop 22, Santurce (at Ponce de León) **787/724-4011** • 10am-midnight, till 1am Th-Sun • popular • lesbians/ gay men • liquor shop & bar

Nightclubs

Abbey Disco Calle Cruz 251 (Lazer Bar) **787/725-7581** • 9:30pm-close • gay-friendly • gay Th • dancing/DJ

Bachelor Ave Condado 112, Santurce (behind Egypto) **787/725-2734** • 10pm till close, clsd Mon-Tue • lesbians/ gay men • dancing/DJ • drag & strip shows • rooftop garden

Colors Ave Roosevelt (next to the 'Spy Shop'), Hato Rey • wknds • lesbians/ gay men • professional crowd • live music

Concepts (The Downtown Club) Ave Chardón 9 (in 'Le Chateau'), Hato Rey **787/763-7432** • Sun only • lesbians/ gay men • dancing/DJ • popular drag shows

Eros Ave Ponce de León 1257, Santurce (btwn Calles Villamil & Labra) **787/722-1131** • 10pm-5am, from 9pm Sun, clsd Mon-Tue • popular • lesbians/ gay men • dancing/DJ • live shows • videos • theme nights • gay-owned/ run

La Laguna Calle Barranquitas 53, Condado (btwn Calle Mayagüez & Ave Ashford) • 11pm-close • popular • mostly gay men • dancing/DJ • live shows • private club

Cafes

Café Berlin Calle San Francisco 407, Plaza Colón, Old San Juan (btwn Calles Norzagary & O'Donnel) **787/722-5205** • 9am-11pm • popular • espresso bar • plenty veggie

Restaurants

Al Dente Calle Recinto Sur, Old San Juan **787/723-7303** • lunch & dinner • Italian • US$10-16

Bistro Gambaro Calle Fortaleza 320, Old San Juan **787/724-4592** • dinner from 7pm, clsd Sun • Italian/ Mediterranean • full bar • US$4-18

Café Amadeus Calle San Sebastián 106, Old San Juan (btwn Calles San José & del Cristo) **787/722-8635** • lunch & dinner • popular • nouvelle Puerto Rican/ cont'l • also bar • noon-midnight Tue-Sat • gay-owned/ run

Café Matisse Ave Ashford 1351, Condado (at Calle Cervantes) **787/723-7910** • 5pm-2am, till 4am Fri-Sat, 7:30pm-midnight Mon, clsd Sun • more gay Tue • also bar

Fussion Calle Fortaleza 317, Old San Juan **787/721-7997** • lunch & dinner, Sun brunch • French/ Latin • also bar

The Gallery Cafe Calle Fortaleza 305, Old San Juan **787/725-8676** • lunch & dinner, clsd Sun • also swanky & hip 'Gallery Lounge' upstairs

Golden Unicorn Calle Laurel 2415 **787/728-4066** • 11am-11pm • Chinese • US$6-26

La Bella Piazza Calle San Francisco 355, Old San Juan **787/721-0936** • lunch & dinner • Italian

La Bombonera Calle San Francisco 259, Old San Juan **787/722-0658** • 7:30am-8pm • popular • come for the strong coffee & pastries • since 1903!

The Parrot Club Calle Fortaleza 363, Old San Juan (btwn Plaza Colón & Callejón de la Capilla) **787/725-7370** • lunch & dinner, clsd Mon • chic Nuevo Latino bistro & bar • bar open daily • US$20+

Sam's Patio Calle San Sebastián 102, Old San Juan **787/723-1149** • lunch & dinner • US$9-22

Transylvania Restaurant Ave Isla Verde 5890 (next to Condom World Isla Verde) **787/726-4363** • lunch Tue-Sat & dinner nightly • Romanian/ Greek/ Italian

Villa Appia Ave Ashford 1350, Condado **787/725-8711** • 11am-11pm • Italian • US$8-15

Entertainment & Recreation

Animation Cruises 787/725-3500 • gay cruises Th eves • lesbians/ gay men • dancing/DJ • full bar • call for reservations

Bookstores

The Book Store Calle San José 255, Old San Juan (btwn Calles Tetuán & Fortaleza) **787/724-1815** • Spanish & English titles • lesbigay section • also cafe

Scriptum Ave Ashford 1129-B (at Calle Vendig) **787/724-1123** • Spanish & English titles • lesbigay section • also newspapers & magazines • cafe

Retail Shops

Subnation Ave Ashford 1129, Condado (at Calle Vendig) **787/723-4750** • noon-10pm, till midnight Fri-Sat, clsd Sun • locally designed clubwear

Publications

Puerto Rico Breeze 787/282-7184 • lesbigay newspaper

Spiritual Groups

Iglesia Comunitaria Metropolitana Cristo Sanador (MCC) Ave Ponce de León 1416, 3rd flr (in front of Escuela Superior Central) **787/721-6358** • 11am Sun

Vieques Island

Accommodations

Rainbow Realty HC-01 Box 6307, Esperanza **787/741-4312** • 20 fully-equipped properties available • most w/ views • some on the water • lesbian-owned • US$450-2400

Villas of Vieques Island 787/741-0023, 800/772-3050 • gay-friendly • villa rentals • easy access to San Juan

Entertainment & Recreation

Camp Garcia South Shore, Vieques • best beach • must have ID to enter

Tobago

Scarborough

Accommodations

Grafton Beach Resort 868/639-0191 • gay-friendly • food served • swimming • US$160-250

Kariwak Village Crown Point **868/639-8442** • gay-friendly • 1-room cabañas • no kitchen • swimming • US$80-125

Restaurants

Rouselles Bacolet St **868/639-4738** • West Indian • US$12-15

Store Bay Beach

Restaurants

Miss Jeans E side of the island at Crown Pt (nr the airport) **868/639-0211** • great crab legs

Virgin Islands

St Croix

Accommodations

▲ **Cormorant Beach Club & Hotel** 4126 La Grande Princesse, Christiansted **340/778-8920, 800/548-4460** • gay-friendly • beachfront resort • food served • swimming • kids ok • gay-owned/ run • US$180-210

King Christian Hotel 59 Kings Wharf, Christiansted **340/773-6330, 800/524-2012** • gay-friendly • swimming • also restaurant • US$85-150

Pink Fancy Hotel 27 Prince St, Christiansted **340/773-8460, 800/524-2045** • gay-friendly • swimming • cont'l brkfst • full bar • US$50-120

Richards & Ayre Associates Frederiksted **340/772-0420** • gay-friendly • upscale vacation rentals

Sand Castle On the Beach 127 Smithfield, Frederiksted **340/772-1205, 800/524-2018** • gay-friendly • hotel • swimming • kitchens • wheelchair access • US$65-305

Seaview Farm Inn 180 Two Brothers, Frederiksted **340/772-5367, 800/792-5060** • gay-friendly • suites w/ kitchenettes • also restaurant • US$65-160

Restaurants

Café du Soleil 625 Strand St (upstairs), Frederiksted • deli open daily

Café Madeleine Teague Bay **340/778-7377, 340/773-8141** • Italian/ cont'l • US$20-25

Le St-Tropez 67 King St, Frederiksted • French cuisine • full bar

St John

Accommodations

Gallows Point Suite Resort Cruz Bay **340/776-6434, 800/323-7229** • gay-friendly • beachfront resort • all suites • swimming • kitchens • also restaurant • full bar • US$145-365

Maho Bay & Harmony VI National Park **340/776-6240, 800/392-9004** • gay-friendly • rustic cottages & studios • environmentally aware resort • US$70-195

Sago Palms Estate 2B, Denis Bay **340/776-6384, 340/776-6876** • gay-friendly • private homes • US$980-$1680 (weekly for two)

St John Inn PO Box 37, 00831 **340/693-8688, 800/666-7688** • gay-friendly • kids ok • swimming • US$70-200

Sunset Pointe 340/773-8100 • rental residences

Restaurants

Asolare Rte 20, Cruz Bay **340/779-4747** • Asian & French fusion • US$22-32

Le Château de Borbeaux Junction 10, Centerline Rd **340/779-4078** • great view • US$20-25

St Thomas

Accommodations

Danish Chalet Guest House **340/774-5764, 800/635-1531** • gay-friendly • overlooking harbor • spa • deck • limited wheelchair access • US$65-100

Hotel 1829 Government Hill **340/776-1829, 800/524-2002** • gay-friendly • swimming • also full bar & restaurant • US$75-275

Pavilions & Pools Hotel 6400 Estate Smith Bay **340/775-6110** • gay-friendly • 1-bdrm villas each w/ own private swimming pool • wheelchair access • US$195-275

Restaurants

Fiddle Leaf Restaurant Government Hill • dinner only, clsd Sun • popular

Lulu's • also full bar

Entertainment & Recreation

Morning Star Beach • popular gay beach

Tortola

Accommodations

▲ **Fort Recovery Seaside Resort** **284/495-4354, 800/367-8455** • gay-friendly • grand home on beach & private beachfront villas • swimming • kids ok • US$145-260 or house US$480-710

Mexico

Note: Mexican cities are often divided into districts or Colonias which we abbreviate as Col. Please use these when giving addresses for directions.

Acapulco

Accommodations

Casa Condesa 125 Bella Vista **52-74/84.16.16** • mostly gay men • full brkfst • close to beach • US$50-100

Casa Le Mar Calle Lomas del Mar 32-B **52-74/84.10.22** • lesbians/ gay men • full brkfst • swimming • maid & cook available

Castilla Vista del Mar #29 Fracc Las Playas (in Caleta) **708/862-0490 (US#)** • lesbians/ gay men • food served • full brkfst • swimming • nudity

Fiesta Americana Condesa Costera Miguel Aleman **52-74/84.23.55, 800/223-2332 (US#)** • gay-friendly • deluxe hotel above the gay beach • 2 swimming pools • 4 star dining • US$135-155

Hotel Acapulco Tortuga 132 Costera Miguel Aleman **52-74/84.88.89** • gay-friendly • across from the gay beach

Las Brisas **52-74/84.15.80, 800/223-6800 (US#)** • popular • gay-friendly • luxury resort • rms w/ private pools

Quinta Encantada Privada Roca Sola 108, Col Club Deportivo **52-74/84.65.08, 310/657-1945 (US#)** • small house rental

Royale De Acapulco & Beach Club Calle Caracol 70, Fracc Amiento Farallón **52-74/84.37.07** • gay-friendly • swimming • food served

Villa Costa Azul Calle Fernando Magallanes 555, Fracc Costa Azul **52-74/84.54.62** • lesbians/ gay men • swimming • IGLTA

Nightclubs

Demas Privada Piedra Picuda 17 (behind 'Carlos & Charlie's') **52-74/84.13.70** • 9pm-3am • popular • mostly gay men • dancing/DJ • live shows • cover charge

Princes Disco Calle Juan de la Cosa 12 (across from the Hotel Continental) **52–74/84.76.01** • after-hours • gay-friendly • popular • dancing/DJ

Relax Calle Lomas de Mar 4 **52–74/84.04.21** • 9pm-3am, clsd Mon-Wed • mostly gay men • dancing/DJ • live shows

Tequila's Le Club Calzada A, Urdaneta 29 **52–74/85.86.23** • 10:30pm-close • popular • gay-friendly • drag shows

Restaurants

Beto's Beach Restaurant Ave Costera Miguel Alemán 99 (at Condesa Beach) **52–74/84.04.73** • lesbians/ gay men • full bar • palapas • also 'Beto's Safari' next door, 52-74/84.47.62 • upscale

Café Tres Amigos Calle La Paz 10 (behind the Hotel Alameda) • cheap, local hangout

Jovitos Costera (across from the 'Fiesta Americana Condesa') • traditional fare • plenty veggie

Kookaburra Carretera Escénica (at Marina Las Brisas) **52–74/884.14.48** • popular • int'l • US$20-25

La Guera de Condesa Condesa Beach

La Tortuga Calle Lomas del Mar 5–A **52–74/84.69.85** • 10am-2am • full bar • good Mexican seafood

Le Bistroquet Calle Andrea Doria 5, Fracc Costa Azul (nr the convention ctr, turn off the costera at the Oceanic Park) **52–74/84.68.60** • popular • lesbians/ gay men • outdoor dining • int'l • gay-owned/ run

Su Casa/ La Margarita Ave Anahuac 110 **52–74/84.43.50** • traditional cuisine • great views

Retail Shops

Benny's Ave Costera Miguel Alemán 98 **52–74/84.15.47** • gay boutique

Aguascalientes

Bars

Merendero Kikos Calle Arturo J Pani 132 • open till 11pm • gay-friendly • food served

Nightclubs

Mandiles Blvd Lopez Mateos 730 (btwn Agucate & Chabacano) **52–49/15.32.81** • lesbians/ gay men • dancing/DJ

Restaurants

Restaurant Mitla Calle Madero 220

Restaurant San Francisco Plaza Principal

Cabo San Lucas

Accommodations

Chile Pepper Inn 16 de Septiembre y Abasolo **52–114/3.47.80** • gay/ straight • smokefree • kids/ pets ok • wheelchair access • US$52.50-105/ night • also weekly rates

Hotel Hacienda Beach Resort Playa el Medano **52–114/3.01.22, 800/733–2226 (US#)** • gay-friendly • upscale • US$145-350

Bars

The Rainbow Bar & Grill Blvd Marina 30 (in the Marina Cabo Plaza) **52–114/3.14.55** • popular • lesbians/ gay men • dancing/DJ • patio

Restaurants

Casa Rafael's Playa el Medano **52–114/3.07.39** • elegant • US$19-42

Da Giorgio on the corridor **52–114/3.29.88** • romantic Italian • US$7-20

Damiana Blvd Mijares 8, San Jose del Cabo **52–114/3.04.99** • seafood • US$11-26

Mi Casa Ave Cabo San Lucas **52–114/3.19.33** • great chicken mole • US$8-16

Cancún

see also Cozumel & Playa del Carmen

Accommodations

Aventura Mexicana Resort Avenida 10 (at Calle 22) **52–98/76.26.69, 954/462–6035 (US#)** • lesbians/ gay men • 45 minutes south of Cancún • 1 blk to beach

Camino Real Paseo Kukulcán **52–98/85.23.00, 800/722–6466 (US#)** • gay-friendly • swimming • 2 beaches • 3 restaurants

Caribbean Reef Club Puerto Morelos **800/322–6286 (US#)** • popular • gay-friendly • swimming • food served

Casa Cancún 212/598–0469 (US#) • mostly women • rental home on the beach • 20 minutes south of Cancún • lesbian-owned/ run • US$60-80

Playa Del Sol Ave Yaxchilan 31 **52–98/84.36.90** • gay-friendly • US$60-95

Villa Catarina Calle Privada, Playa del Carmen **52–98/73.09.70** • gay-friendly • US$35-65

Zona Hotelera (The Hotel Zone) Blvd Kukulcán • Cancún's answer to the Las Vegas Strip: resorts ranging from the Sheraton Cancún's Mayan pyramids to small boutique hotels

Bars

Picante Bar SM 2, Ave Tulum 20 (E of Ave Uxmal, next to Galerias Mall) **52-98/84.09.57** • 9:30pm-3am, till 4am Fri, till dawn Sat-Sun, clsd Mon • popular • mostly gay men

Nightclubs

Backstage Tulipanes Ave (nr Ave Tulum) • mostly gay men • dancing/DJ • shows

Karamba SM 22, Ave Tulum 87 (at Calle Azucenas, above 'Bananas' restaurant) **52-98/84.00.32** • 10pm-4am, clsd Sun-Mon • mostly gay men • dancing/DJ • drag shows

Restaurants

Avenida Tulum • take a stroll & take your pick

Entertainment & Recreation

Caesar Park Beach in the Hotel Zone • gay beach

Chichén Itza • the must-see Mayan ruin 125 miles from Cancun

Gyms & Health Clubs

Shape Calle Conoco (1 blk from San Yaxchen) • gay-friendly

Celaya

Bars

Los Caballos Hidalgo 220 (Centro) **52-461/3.31.08** • Fri-Sat only • mostly gay men • dancing/DJ • live shows

Ciudad Juárez

Accommodations

Hotel de Luxe Ave S Lerdo de Tejada 300 S (Col Monumental) **52-16/15.02.02** • gay-friendly • restaurant & bar • inexpensive

Plaza Continental Ave S Lerdo de Tejada 112 **52-16/12.26.10** • gay-friendly • also restaurant • close to bars

Bars

Club La Escondida Calle Ignacio de la Peña 366 Oriente **52-16/12.78.68** • gay/ straight • neighborhood bar

Club La Luz Calle I Mariscal N • lesbians/ gay men • dancing/DJ • live shows

Club La Madelon Calle Santos Degollado 771 N • lesbians/ gay men • popular wknds • dancing/DJ • drag shows

Club Padrino Calle Santos Degollado N • lesbians/ gay men • popular • dancing/DJ • live shows

Nebraska Calle Mariscal 251 N • open till midnight • popular dive • lesbians/ gay men • rough neighborhood

Ritz Calle Ignacio de la Peña Oriente (1/2 block N & 1/2 block E of Hotel de Luxe) **52-16/14.22.91** • open till 2am • popular after midnight wknds • mostly gay men • neighborhood bar • dancing/DJ • professional • young crowd

Restaurants

El Coyote Invalido Ave Lerdo Sur (next to the 'Plaza Continental') • 24hrs

Taco Cabaña Ave Lerdo Sur (next to the 'Plaza Continental') • cheap, popular late-night

Cozumel

see also Cancún & Playa del Carmen

Accommodations

Sol Cabañas del Caribe beachfront **52-98/72.00.17 or 72.00.72, 800/336-3542 (US#)** • gay-friendly • food served

Restaurants

5th Ave Pizza 5a Avenida Sur #543 (btwn 7th & 9th) **52-987/2.62.00** • 6pm-midnight, clsd Mon • natural gourmet pizzas • full bar • patio

La Casa Nostra 15 Ave Sur 548 (btwn Calles 5 & 7) **52-987/2.12.75** • Italian • also room rental available

Cuernavaca

Accommodations

Casa Aurora B&B Calle Arista 12 (btwn Calles Guerrero & No Reelección) **52-73/18.63.94** • gay/ straight • Spanish classes can be arranged • US$18-24

Hotel Marjaba Ave Sonora 1000, Col Vista Hermosa **52-73/15.33.32** • gay-friendly • swimming • also restaurant & bar

Nido de Amor **52-73/18.06.31** • gay-friendly • suites in private home

Nightclubs

Scala Ave Plan de Ayala 100 (at Ave Lopéz Mateos) • 9pm-2am • mostly gay men • dancing/DJ

Shadee Ave Adolfo Lopez Mateos **52-73/12.43.67** • 9pm-4am, clsd Mon • popular • mostly gay men • food served • drag shows Sat • cover charge

Restaurants

La India Bonita Calle Dwight Morrow **52-73/18.69.67** • clsd Mon • in historic home of former US ambassador & father-in-law of Charles Lindbergh

Entertainment & Recreation

Diego Rivera Murals Plaza de Museo (in Cuauhnáhuac Regional Museum)

Durango

Bars

Bar Country Constitución N 122 • lesbians/ gay men • food served

Buhós Restaurant & Bar 5 de Febrero 615 **52-16/12.58.11** • gay-friendly

Eduardos 20 de Noviembre Pte 805 • lesbians/ gay men

Ensenada

Bars

La Ola Verde Calle 2 #459-A, Centro (btwn Ave Gastelum & Calle Miramar) • 9pm-2am Th-Sun only • popular late • lesbians/ gay men • food served

Nightclubs

Club Ibis at Blvd Costero & Ave Sangines • 9pm-2am Th-Sun • mostly gay men • dancing/DJ • drag shows • cover charge

Coyote Club 1000 Blvd Costero 4 & 5 (nr the Hotel Corona) **52-68/77.36.91** • 9pm-2am, clsd Mon-Tue • popular • lesbians/ gay men • dancing/DJ • 2 flrs • patio • cover charge

Restaurants

Casamar Blvd Lázaro Cárdenas 987, Centro (at Blvd Costero) **52-68/74.04.17** • popular

Mariscos California at Calle 2 & Calle Ruiz • 9am-8pm, clsd Sun • seafood

Guadalajara

Accommodations

Guadalajara B&B Galaxia 4063, Col Lomas Altas **52-3/813.08.42** • gay/ straight • full brkfst in garden • some shared baths • maid service • 20 minute taxi ride to bars

Hotel Calinda Roma Ave Juárez 170 (Sector Juárez) **800/228-5151 (US#), 52-3/614.86.50** • gay-friendly • also rooftop restaurant

Travel Recreation International 1875 Ave Libertad, Local-C (Sector Juárez) **52-3/626.33.98** • gay-friendly • IGLTA

Bars

Gerardo Ave de la Paz 2529 (Sector Juárez) **52-3/616.12.07** • 9pm-2am, till 4am wknds • popular • upscale • mostly gay men • food served • live music Th & Sun • patio

Maskara's Calle Maestranza 238 **52-3/614.81.03** • 8am-2am • lesbians/ gay men • neighborhood bar • food served

Nightclubs

Candilejas Ave Niños Héroes 961 (next to the Hotel Carlton) **52-3/614.55.12** • 8pm-4am, clsd Mon • gay/ straight • dancing/DJ • lavish drag shows • cover charge

La Malinche Ave Álvaro Obregón 1230 (btwn Calles 48 & 50, Sector Libertad; look for the large black canopy) **52-3/643.65.62** • 9pm-2am, clsd Mon-Tue • popular late night • mostly gay men • dancing/DJ • drag/ strip shows wknds • food served

Monica's Disco Bar Ave Álvaro Obregón 1713 (btwn Calles 68 & 70, Sector Libertad; no sign, look for canopy under a big palm tree) **52-3/43.95.44** • 9pm-2am, clsd Mon-Tue • popular after midnight • mostly gay men • dancing/DJ • drag/ strip shows wknds • best to cab to & from

SOS Club Ave La Paz 1413 (Sector Juárez) **52-3/826.41.79** • 9pm-3am, clsd Mon • lesbians/ gay men • popular lesbian hangout • dancing/DJ • drag shows Fri & Sun • patio • cover charge

Restaurants

Brasserie 1171 Prisciliano Sanchez St, downtown Juárez District

El Paraíso at 'Angel's' club **52-3/615.25.25** • clsd Sun-Mon

Sanborn's Ave Juárez 305 (at Ave 16 de Septiembre)

Sanborn's Vallarta 1600 Vallarta Ave, downtown Juárez District

Guanajuato

Accommodations

Castillo Santa Cecilia Camino a La Valenciana **52-47/32.04.77** • excellent food

Hotel Museo Posada Sante Fe downtown **52-47/32.00.84** • gay-friendly

Bars

El Incendio Calle Cantarranas 15 **52-47/32.13.72** • gay-friendly

La Lola Ancha de San Antonio #31, San Miguel de Allende **52-415/2.40.50** • 1pm-2am, clsd Mon • gay/ straight • also restaurant • gay-owned/ run

Irapuato

Bars

Blanco y Negro Ave Ejército National 890 **52-462/4.23.81** • Th-Sun only • gay-friendly • dancing/DJ

Ixtapa-Zihuatanejo

Bars

Chido's One Carretera Playa La Ropa (next to Hotel Irma) • Wed-Sun only • gay-friendly • dancing/DJ • live shows • cover charge

Jalapa

Nightclubs

DKché at Calles Zaragoza & Prolongación (take road to Banderilla, 2 blks S of the hwy, on a rough dirt road) • 10pm-close Fri-Sat • popular • lesbians/ gay men • dancing/DJ • drag shows

La Mansion take a cab toward Banderilla (20 minutes NW of town, turn right at sign for El Paraíso Campestre & go past RR tracks) • 9pm-4am Fri-Sat only • lesbians/ gay men • live shows

La Paz

Accommodations

Casa La Paceña Inn Calle Bravo 106 (btwn Madero & Mutualismo) **52-112/5.27.48, 707/869-2374 (US#)** • open Nov-June • gay-friendly • smokefree • woman-owned

Gran Baja • gay-friendly • near harbor Mariano Abasolo

Hotel Mediterrane Allende 36 (at malecón) **52-112/5.11.95** • lesbians/ gay men • food served 7am-11pm • sun terrace • gay-owned/ run • US$50-75

Hotel Perla 1570 Ave, Alvaro Obregón **52-68/22.07.77 x131** • gay-friendly

Bars

Bar Intimo Calle 16 de Septiembre • lesbians/ gay men

Manzanillo

Accommodations

Las Hadas Santiago Peninsula **52-33/34.19.50, 800/722-6466 (US#)** • gay-friendly • great resort & location • US$180-400

La Leyanda Villas Club de Yates 12 **52-33/33.02.81, 800/232-8482 (US#)** • gay-friendly • private tropical setting

Bars

OK Independencia 42 (Centro) • Th-Sun only • mostly gay men • dancing/DJ • live shows

Matamoros

Bars

Montezuma Lounge Calle Gonzalez #6 • gay-friendly

Nightclubs

Mr Lee Disco Ave de las Rosas, Col Jardin • gay-friendly • dancing/DJ

Mazatlán

Accommodations

Hotel Los Sábalos Rodolfo T Loaiza #190 (Zona Dorada) **52-69/83.53.33, 800/528-8760 (US#)** • gay-friendly • upscale resort w/ 2 pools, beach, health club • also popular 'Joe's Oyster Bar'

Bars

Pepe Toro Ave de las Garzas 18, Zona Dorado (1 blk W of Ave Camarón Sábalo) **52-69/14.41.76** • 9pm-4am, clsd Mon-Wed • mostly gay men • dancing/DJ • drag/ strip shows

Nightclubs

Valentino's Ave Camarón Sábalo • till 4am • straight • dancing/DJ • rumors of gays frequenting its 'Bora Bora' bar

Cafes

Panama Restaurant Pasteleria at Aves de las Garzas & Camarón Sábalo • lesbians/ gay men

Restaurants

Roca Mar Ave del Mar (at Calle Isla de Lobos, Zona Costera) **52-69/81.60.08** • till 2am • popular • seafood • full bar

Señor Frogs Ave del Mar, Zona Costera **52-69/82.19.25** • dancing/DJ • upscale • seafood • full bar

Mérida

Accommodations

Gran Hotel Calle 60 #496 **52-99/24.77.30** • gay-friendly • historic turn-of-the-century hotel • courtyard w/ balconies • also restaurant

Bars

Bar Rincon Maya at Calles 61 & 66 • gay/ straight • neighborhood bar

Romanticos Piano Bar Calle 60 #461 • 9pm-3am • gay-friendly • live shows

Nightclubs

Kabuki's Ave Jacinto Canek #381 (ext of Calle 59-A, west of Calle 124, along the Corralón) • 10pm-3am Th-Sat • lesbians/ gay men • dancing/DJ • drag/ strip shows • cover charge • many bars come & go in the area—follow the crowd

Cafes

Café Express Calle 60 #502 (across from Hidalgo Park)

Restaurants

La Bella Época Calle 60 #447 (upstairs in the Hotel del Parque) **52-99/28.19.28** • 6pm-1am • Yucatécan cuisine • try to get one of the balcony tables

Mexicali

Bars

Cantine Tare at Calle Uxmal & Ave Jalisco (across the Rio Nuevo from downtown) • till 2am • mostly gay men • neighborhood bar • drag shows wknds

Cinco Estrellas corner of Calle Jalisco & Calle 3 (next door to 'Cantine Tare') • 7pm-2am, clsd Mon-Tue • mostly women • neighborhood bar

El Taurino Ave Juan de Zuazua 480 (at Ave José Maria) • open late • popular • lesbians/ gay men • dancing/DJ

Rey de Copas Ave Tuxtla Gutierrez & Baja California St • lesbians/ gay men • neighborhood bar

Shafarelos Ave de la Reforma 604 (at Calle Mexico) • till 2am wkdys, till 5am wknds • gay-friendly • transgender-friendly • drag shows wknds

Mexico City

Note: Mexico City is divided into 'Zonas' (ie, Zona Rosa) & 'Colonias' (abbreviated here as Col). Remember to use these when giving addresses to taxi drivers.

Info Lines & Services

Canal Amigo Ave Lázaro Cárdenas 228, #102 (Col Obrera) **52-5/588.19.93** • social club for lesbians & gay men • women only Tue • call for events

Gay/ Lesbian AA Ave Chapultepec 465-202 (Col Juárez, Metro Sevilla) • 8pm Mon-Fri, 7pm Sat

Voz Humana AC 52-5/530.28.73, 52-5/530.25.92

Accommodations

Aristos Paseo de la Reforma 276 **52-5/211.01.12, 800/527-4786 (US#)** • gay-friendly • swimming • gym • 2 restaurants

Hotel Casa Blanca Lafragua 7 **52-5/566.32.11, 800/448-8355 (US#)** • gay-friendly • swimming • food served

Hotel Del Ángel Calle Río Lerma 154 (at Calle Río Tiber, Col Cuauhtémoc) **52-5/533.10.32** • gay-friendly • swimming • rooftop restaurant & bar • inexpensive

Hotel Geneve (Quality Inn) Londres 130 (Zona Rosa) **52-5/211.00.71, 800/228-5151 (US#)** • gay-friendly • 3-story colonial style hotel • no AC • moderately priced • also restaurant

Hotel Krystal Rosa Liverpool 155 **52-5/221.34.60, 800/231-9860 (US#)** • gay-friendly • upscale • 2 restaurants & nightclub • swimming

Hotel Michelangelo Calle Rio Amazonas 78 **52-5/566.98.77** • gay-friendly • kitchen • US$40

Marco Polo 27 Amberes (Zona Rosa) **52-5/207.18.93, 800/223-0888 (US#)** • gay-friendly • upscale hotel

Westin Galeria Plaza Hamburgo 195 (Col Juárez, Zona Rosa) **52-5/211.00.14, 800/228-3000 (US#)** • gay-friendly • swimming • 2 restaurants & disco

Bars

Bar Milan Calle Milán 18 (Col Juárez, enter east side of brick townhouse) **52-5/592.00.31** • 9pm-1am, clsd Sun • gay/ straight • upscale & intimate • lesbigay night Wed

Dolce Vita Orizaba 146 (Col Roma) **52-5/585.74.06** • gay-friendly • popular • dancing/DJ

Enigma Calle Morelia 111 (4 blks from Metro Niño Héroes, Zona Rosa) **52-5/207.73.67** • 9pm-3:30am, 6pm-2am Sun, clsd Mon • lesbians/ gay men • shows for women Th • drag shows • cover charge

Nightclubs

Alquimia Calle Ponciano Arriaga 31 (at the Angel monument, Zona Rosa) **52-5/566.43.01** • 9pm-6am Th-Sat • mostly gay men • dancing/DJ • salsa • drag & strip shows • cover charge

Anyway/ Exacto Calle Monterrey 47 (Zona Rosa) **52-5/533.16.91** • 9pm-4am • lesbians/ gay men • dancing/DJ • drag/ strip shows • food served • 3 flrs • 'Exacto' is a women's bar on 2nd flr • cover charge

Butterflies Calle Izazaga 9 (at Ave Lazaro Cárdenas S, Centro Historico) **52-5/761.13.51** • 9pm-3am, till 4:30am Fri-Sat, clsd Mon • popular • lesbians/ gay men • dancing/DJ • 2 flrs • lavish drag shows Fri-Sat • cover charge

Caztzi Calle Carlos Arellano 4, Ciudad Satélite (east of Periférico, on south side of Plaza Satélite) **52-5/393.66.91** • 10pm-6am Fri-Sat • lesbians/ gay men • dancing/DJ • drag/ strip shows • cover charge

Dreams Paseo de la Reforma Norte 76 • 10pm-5am Fri-Sat • gay/ straight • dancing/DJ

El Ansia Calle Algéciras 26 (in Centro Armand) **52-5/611.61.18** • 9:30pm-3am Th-Sat • mostly gay men • dancing/DJ • live shows

El Don Calle Tonolá 79 (at Alvaro Obregón, Zona Rosa) **52-5/207.08.72** • 9pm-4am Wed-Sat • lesbians/ gay men • dancing/DJ • transgender-friendly • 'show for real women' Th • drag shows Fri-Sat

GAB Ave Oaxaca 85-B (at Durango, Zona Rosa) **52-5/514.55.63, 52-5/514.13.72** • 6pm-close, clsd Mon • women only • dancing/DJ • live music

Kao's Calle Querétaro 217 (btwn Calles Monterrey & Medellín) **52-5/264.25.67** • 9pm-4am Wed-Sat, 8pm-3am Sun • mostly gay men • dancing/DJ • drag & strip shows • cover charge

L'Baron Avenida Alvarado Obregón 85-B (Col Roma) **52-5/208.63.85** • 9pm-4am, till 8am Fri-Sat • mostly gay men • dancing/DJ • live shows • young crowd

Privata Ave Universidad 1909 (btwn Ave Copilco & Calle Miguel Ángel de Quevada, Col Copilco) **52-5/661.59.39** • 9pm-3am Wed-Sat • mostly gay men • dancing/DJ • live shows • videos • cover charge

Restaurants

The Doors Calle Monterrey 47 (downstairs from 'Anyway' & 'Exacto') • 1pm-3am • also bar

El Hábito 13 Madrid St (Coyoacan District) • avante-garde theater

Fonda San Ángel Plaza San Jacinto 3 (Col San Ángel, across from Bazar San Ángel) • popular after 7pm Fri-Sat • classic Mexican dishes

La Opera Calle 5 de Mayo 10 (Centro Historico) **52-5/512.89.59** • noon-midnight, clsd Sun • upscale

La Taberna Griega Ave Insurgentes Sur 1381 (at Calle Algéciras) **52-5/611.69.58** • 1:30pm-midnight, till 6pm Sun-Mon • Greek & int'l • 'gay day' Wed • live music wknds

Meson d'Miss Calle Tlacotalpan 18 **52-5/564.53.28** • 1pm-11pm, till 6pm Sun, clsd Mon • Mexican & int'l

Tonin' Tony's Calle Ameyalco 3 (btwn Calle Eugenia & Ave Insurgentes Sur) **52-5/536.23.99** • Italian • homemade pasta • reservations required

Vips Hamburgo 126 Calle Hamburgo (Zona Rosa) • American-style • also at Paseo de la Reforma & Florencia, nr Independence Angel Statue • popular after-hours

Bookstores

Las Sirenas Ave de la Paz 57 (San Angel) **52-5/500.93.86** • women's

Retail Shops

El Angel Azul 64 Londres A & B • periodicals • clothing

Sueños Salvajes 177 E Zapata, Col Portales

Publications

Ser Gay **52-5/534.38.04** • covers all Mexico nightlife, limited resources

Spiritual Groups

MCC Ave de las Granjas (N off Glorieta de Camarones traffic circle) **52-5/396.77.68** • 12:30pm & 7pm Sun • look for the blue cross painted above the entrance

Monterrey

Accommodations

Hotel Rio Calle Padre Mier 194 Poniente (at Garibaldi, Centro) **52-8/345.15.16, 800/432-2520 (US#)** • gay-friendly • close to Zona Rosa • swimming • also restaurant

Bars

Charao's at Calles Isaac Garza Oriente & Zaragoza N (Centro) • 10pm-6am, clsd Sun • lesbians/ gay men • dancing/DJ • strippers • popular after-hours • cover charge

Nightclubs

Arcanos Calle Ruperto Martínez 845 (close to Calle Cuauhtémoc) • open Wed-Sun • lesbians/ gay men • dancing/DJ • drag shows Sat • video bar downstairs • cover charge

Vongolé Ave Constitución (at Santa Bárbara) **52-8/336.03.35** • 10pm-4am Wed, Fri-Sat • lesbians/ gay men • dancing/DJ • drag & strip shows Sat • cover charge

RESTAURANTS

Vips Calle Emilio Carranza 999 Sur (at Hildago, Zona Rosa) • popular w/ gay men evenings & late night

Morelia

ACCOMMODATIONS

Casa Camelinas B&B 52-43/14.09.63, 415/661-5745 (US#) • mostly women • 3 1/2 hours from Mexico City

NIGHTCLUBS

Con la Rojas Aldama 343 (Centro) **52-43/12.15.78** • 11pm-2am, clsd Sun-Wed • mostly gay men • upscale • dancing/DJ • cover charge

Los Eloines Ave Francisco I Madero Poniente 5039 (nr the Libramiento Poniente) **52-43/14.28.18** • 9pm-3am, clsd Sun • lesbians/ gay men • dancing/DJ • drag/ strip shows Th-Sat • cover charge

¡No Que No! Periférico República 7551 (Col Sindurio) **52-43/11.14.25** • 10pm-3am, clsd Mon • mostly gay men • dancing/DJ • live shows

CAFES

Café Catedral Portal Hidalgo 23 (N side of Plaza de Armas, at the Hotel Catedral)

RESTAURANTS

Café Bizare 90 Ignacio Zaragoza (at Posada de la Soledad Hotel) **52-43/12.18.18** • in charming old hotel in converted convent

Fonda de las Mercedes Calle Leon Guzmán 47 **52-43/12.61.13** • inside beautiful colonial home

Oaxaca

ACCOMMODATIONS

El Camino Real Oaxaca Calle 5 de Mayo 300 **52-951/6.06.11, 800/722-6466 (US RESERVATIONS)** • gay-friendly • 5-star hotel in restored 16th century convent • frescoes & courtyards abound • restaurant • swimming

Mission de los Angeles Hotel Calzada Porfirio Díaz 102 **52-951/5.15.00 OR 5.10.00, 800/221-6509 (US#)** • gay-friendly • resort w/ bungalows • restaurant & dance clubs • swimming • tennis courts

BARS

Bar Jardin Portal de Flores 10 (on the zócalo) **52-951/6.20.92** • 7:30am-1am • gay-friendly • sidewalk cafe • more gay as day goes by • also restaurant

NIGHTCLUBS

Snob Calzada Niños Héroes de Chupultepec (1 blk W of bus station) • gay from 10pm Wed only • dancing/DJ

RESTAURANTS

El Asador Vasco Portal de Flores 11 (above 'Bar Jardin') **52-951/6.97.19** • popular • great views • authentic Oaxacan cuisine (can you say ¡mole!)

Orizaba

NIGHTCLUBS

Sky Drink Madero Norte 1280 • clsd Sun-Tue, drag/ strip shows Sat

Pátzcuaro

ACCOMMODATIONS

Hotel Posada San Rafael Plaza Vasco de Quiroga **52-45/42.07.70** • gay-friendly • food served

RESTAURANTS

Doña Pala Calle Quiroga

Playa Del Carmen

see also Cancún & Cozumel

ACCOMMODATIONS

Aventura Mexicana Resort Ave 10 (at Calle 22) **954/462-6035 (US#), 52-987/6.26.69** • gay-friendly • swimming • jacuzzi • nudity permitted • 15 minutes to gay nude beach • also restaurant & bar

Pension San Juan 5th Ave 165 (btwn 6th & 8th Sts) **52-987/3.06.47** • gay-friendly motel

Puebla

BARS

La Cigarra Calle 5 Poniente 538 (at Calle 7 Sur) • 6pm-3am • popular • mostly gay men • beer bar

NIGHTCLUBS

Cherri's Prolongacíon 11 (at Zapotecas, Col Mayorazgo) **52-22/28.89.37** • Fri-Sat only • gay-friendly • dancing/DJ • drag shows

Garrotos Ave 22 Oriente 602 (close to Blvd 5 de Mayo, Barrio de Xenenetla) **52-22/42.42.32** • Fri-Sat only • gay-friendly • dancing/DJ

Keops Disco Calle 14 Poniente 101, Cholula (at Calle 5 de Mayo) **52–22/47.03.68** • 10pm-3am Th-Sun • popular • lesbians/ gay men • dancing/DJ • drag/ strip shows Fri-Sat • videos

La Fuente Blvd Hermanos Serdán 343 (at Calle Francisco I Madera) • from 7pm Fri-Sat • gay-friendly • dancing/DJ • drag shows • cover charge

Puerto Vallarta

Accommodations

Bugambilia Blanca Off Hwy 200 **800/936–3646 (Doin' It Right #)** • lesbians/ gay men • 4 levels • full brkfst • gay-owned/ run • US$50-105

Casa Boana Torre Malibu Calle Amapas 325 (Col El Cerro) **52–322/2.66.95** • gay-friendly • condo-hotel • bay views • food served • swimming • poolside bar

Casa de los Arcos 52–322/2.59.90, 800/424–3434 x277 (US#) • lesbians/ gay men • private villa • sleeps 8 • swimming • terrace w/ amazing view

Casa dos Comales Calle Aldama 274 **52–322/3.20.42, 888/881–1822 (US#)** • gay-friendly • guesthouse & apts nr Old Town • swimming • US$75-125

▲ **Casa Fantasía** Francisco Madero 203 (Col Emiliano Zapata, at Pino Sueno) **503/233–8118 (US#), 800/232–5944 (Hawthorne Travel #)** • mostly gay men • B&B made up of 3 traditional haciendas • full brkfst • terrace • swimming • IGLTA • gay-owned/ run • US$40-125

Casa Panoramica B&B Apartado Postal #114, CP 48300 **52–322/2.36.56** • gay-friendly • overlooking Bandares Bay & old downtown Puerto Vallarta • full brkfst • terrace pool • IGLTA

Discovery Vallarta 52–322/2.69.18 • gay accommodations reservation service • IGLTA

Doin' It Right Travel 619/297–3642 (US#), 800/936–3646 (US#) • Puerto Vallarta gay travel specialist • also publishes newsletter 'PV-PS' ('Puerto Vallarta Purple Sheets') • IGLTA

Las Pilitas Antiguas Conchas Chinas **800/936–3646 (Doin' It Right #)** • lesbians/ gay men • villa on Los Muertos beach • dipping pool • also day spa w/ massage, body work, aromatherapy & more • US$80-115

Mision Recuerdo 800/936–3646 (Doin' It Right #) • lesbians/ gay men • resort on banks of Rio Cuale • swimming • US$60-115

Paco Paco Descanso del Sol Hotel 583 Pino Suárez (Col Emiliano Zapata) **52–322/3.02.77, 800/936–3646 (Doin' It Right #)** • lesbians/ gay men • apts, casitas & tents • swimming • rooftop bar w/ incredible sunset views • also 'Paco's Hidden Paradise' (20-acre resort w/ restaurant & bar accesible only by boat) • gay-owned/ run • US$45-125

Paco's Olas Altas B&B 465 Olas Altas **52–322/2.56.32** • lesbians/ gay men • bar open from 11am • food served from 7am

Quinta Maria Cortez 132 Calle Sagitario, Playa Conchas Chinas **801/531–8100 (US#), 888/640–8100 (US#)** • gay/ straight • 'Mexaterranian Villa' w/ sunny terraces & spectacular ocean views

Villa Felíz 52–322/2.07.98, 800/424–3434 x277 (US#) • lesbians/ gay men • in Old Town • full brkfst • great views

Villas David B&B Calle Galeana 348 (at Calle Miramar) **724/573–4693 (US#), 52–322/3.03.13** • mostly gay men • swimming • rooftop jacuzzi & pool • balconies • gay-owned/ run • US$53-140

Bars

Apache Club Olas Atlas 439 (at Francisco Rodriguez) **52–322/2.52.35** • 5pm-2am, till 1am Sun-Mon • lesbians/ gay men • classy martini bar • food served • lesbian-owned/ run

Aria Pino Suárez 210 (at Francisco Madero) **52–322/2.57.32** • 9pm-2am • popular • gay/ straight • piano bar • also downstairs bar from 4pm

Blue Chairs (Tito's) southern Los Muertos Beach • mostly gay men • food served

Boana's Bar Calle Amapas 325 (Col El Cerro) **52–322/2.66.95** • gay-friendly • T-dance noon-9pm Sun

Green Chairs (Looney Tunes) southern Los Muertos Beach (at 'Looney Tunes' restaurant) • mostly gay men • food served

Kit Kat Bar Pulpito 120 (next door to 'Chiles' restaurant) **52–322/3.00.93** • 5pm-1:30am • lesbians/ gay men • swanky New York-style cocktail lounge • drag shows 11:30pm some nights • also restaurant (pricey but fun) • gay-owned/ run

La Katrina Olas Altas 508 (at Rodolfo Gomez) **52–322/2.19.04** • 6pm-3am • lesbians/ gay men • dancing/DJ • drag shows nightly • strippers Th-Sun

Los Balcones Calle Juárez 182, 2nd flr (at Calle Libertad) **52–322/2.46.71** • 9pm-3am, till 4am wknds • mostly gay men • dancing/DJ • popular male strippers late night • T-dance 6pm-11pm Sun

Paco's Olas Altas 465 Olas Altas (at Emiliano Zapata) **52–322/2.56.32** • 7am-2am • lesbians/ gay men • women's night Sat & Wed • theme nights

Paco's Sunset Bar Calle Pino Suárez 583 (on rooftop of 'Paco Paco Descanso del Sol') **52–322/3.20.77** • noon-10pm • popular • lesbians/ gay men • the spot to watch the sun set • swimming • also restaurant

Nightclubs

Club Paco Paco Ignacio L Vallarta 278 **52–322/2.18.99** • 3pm-6am • popular • lesbians/ gay men • cantina on 2nd flr • disco downstairs from 10pm • also rooftop terrace w/ live piano • cover charge

Paco's Ranch Calle Venustiano Carranza 239 (walk thru 'Club Paco Paco' to back of dance flr) • 8pm-6am • popular • mostly gay men • dancing/DJ • leather • country/ western • packed for 3 nightly strip shows • videos • cover charge

Por Que No? (Why Not?) Calle Morelos 101, Plaza Río (at Rodriguez/ Encino) **52–322/3.03.03, 52–322/2.63.92** • noon-4am • lesbians/ gay men • 3 levels: intimate rooftop bar, game bar, basement disco • drag & strip shows Fri-Sun • young crowd

Cafes

A Page in the Sun Olas Altas 299 • 7:30am-11:30pm • popular • coffeehouse & English bookstore

Este Cafe Libertad 336, Centro (around corner from flea market) **52–322/2.42.61** • 8am-10pm, clsd Sun • espresso & juice bar • desserts • ice cream

The Net House Ignacio Vallarta 232 **52–322/2.69.53** • 24hrs • cybercafe • organic coffee, sandwiches, ice cream • gay-owned

Señor Book Cafe Olas Altas 490 **52–322/2.03.24** • 8am-11:30pm • cafe & new/ used English bookstore

Restaurants

Adobe Café Calle Basilio Badillo 252 **52–322/2.67.20** • 6pm-11pm, clsd Tue • popular • Southwestern flair • also bar • gay-owned/ run

Andreas y Gato Calle Ignacio Vallarta 230 **52–322/3.27.80** • 6pm-11pm, till midnight Th-Sat, clsd Sun • popular • Mediterranean • also bar • gay-owned/ run

¡Chiles! Pulpito 122 **52-322/3.03.73** • 10am-3pm, clsd July-Sept • popular • roasted chicken • sandwiches • hamburgers • large patio • gay-owned/ run

Cuiza Isla Rio Cuale 3, West Bridge **52-322/2.56.46** • 9am-midnight, clsd Tue • lesbians/ gay men • near Rio Cuale • New World • martinis • live jazz

Le Bistro Jazz Café Isla Río Cuale 16-A **52-322/2.02.83** • 9am-midnight, clsd Sun • popular • PV's classiest

Memo's Casa de los Hotcakes Calle Basilio Badillo 289 **52-322/2.62.72** • 8am-2pm • popular • long lines for cheap & good brkfsts • indoor patio

Pancho's Pizza Amapas 325 (at 'Casa Boana Torre Malibu') **52-322/2.66.95** • noon-9pm • gourmet pizza • delivers

Porphyria Olas Altas 443 (above 'Apache' bar) **52-322/2.20.74** • 6pm-1am, clsd Sun-Mon • int'l • also lounge

Red Cabbage Calle Rio Ribera 206-A **52-322/3.04.11** • Mexican • on Rio Cuale w/ great kitschy decor • lesbian-owned/ run

Rosie's 31 de Octubre 149 (nr McDonalds, 2 blks from malecón) **52-322/2.44.77** • good home-cooked American for the homesick

Trio's Guerrero 264 **52-322/2.21.96** • 6pm-midnight • Mediterranean/ Mexican • patio • live music • reservations advised

Entertainment & Recreation

Boana Tours Calle Amapas 325 (Col El Cerro, at Casa Boana Torre Malibu) **52-322/2.66.95** • boat cruises (Mon, Wed & Sat) • horseback tours (Wed) • BBQ & tour of traditional hat factory

Playa Los Muertos S of Rio Cuale (southern end by green chairs at 'Looney Tunes') • the gay beach

Retail Shops

Azul Siempre Azul Ignacio Vallarta 228 **52-322/3.00.60** • 10am-2pm & 5pm-10pm • beautiful Mexican art & handicrafts • gay-owned/ run

La Rosa de Cristal Insurgentes 272 **52-322/2.56.98** • 10am-8pm • local handicrafts & beautiful blown-glass items • gay-owned/ run

La Tienda Rodolfo Gomez 122 **52-322/2.15.35** • 10am-2pm & 4pm-8pm • popular • furniture & home accessories • also Basilio Badillo 276 location, 52-322/3.06.92 • gay-owned/ run

Safari Accents Olas Altas 224 **52-322/3.26.60** • 10am-11pm • pricey but beautiful home furnishings • gay-owned/ run

Gyms & Health Clubs

Tito's Gym Calle Encino 287-1 (W of flea market) **52-322/2.22.77** • 6am-10pm, 8am-6pm Sat, 10am-2pm Sun • aerobics, free weights, juice bar

Querétaro

Bars

Villa Jardín/ Bar Oz Blvd Bernardo Quintana 556 (Col Arboledas, across from Cinemark) **52-42/24.13.96** • Sat only • mostly gay men • dancing/DJ • cover charge

Nightclubs

La Creación Monte Sinai 113 (Col Vista Hermosa, before 'Disco Qui') **52-42/13.51.90** • Fri-Sat • gay-friendly • dancing/DJ • cover charge

La Iguana Ave Universidad 308 (at Hotel Maria Teresa) • till 2am wknds only • gay-friendly • dancing/DJ

San Jose del Cabo

Accommodations

Palmilla Apartado Postal 52, 23400 **714/833-3025 (US#), 800/637-2226 (US#)** • gay-friendly • beachfront suites

San Miguel De Allende

Accommodations

Aristos San Miguel De Allende 30 Calle Ancha de Santonio **52-415/2.01.49, 800/223-0880 (US#)** • gay-friendly • full-service hotel

Casa de Sierra Nevada 35 Calle Hospicio **52-415/2.04.15, 800/223-6510 (US#)** • gay-friendly

Bars

La Lola Calle Ancha de San Antonio 31 (across from the Instituto Allende) **52-415/2.40.50** • gay/ straight • also restaurant

Nightclubs

Cien (100) Ángeles Tinajitas 24 (Col San Antonio, across from Hotel Real de Minas) • 9pm-3am Fri-Sat • mostly gay men • dancing/DJ • live shows • cover charge

El Ring Calle Hidalgo 25 (1 1/2 blks N of el jardín) • 10pm-4am Wed, Fri-Sat • gay-friendly • dancing/DJ • cover charge

Tampico

Bars

Bilbao W of Calle Francisco I Madero Oriente & A Serdan Sur • lesbians/ gay men

Tropicana Bar Calle de General López de Lara Sur • lesbians/ gay men

Tepic

Cafes

Café La Parroquia Calle Amado Nerro 18 (upstairs) **52-32/12.67.72**

Restaurants

Wendy's Ave México, Norte 178 • not burgers

Tijuana

Info Lines & Services

Gay/ Lesbian Community Center Calle 1 #7648 (Zona Centro) **52-66/80.99.63**

Gay/ Lesbian Info Line 52-66/88.02.67

Accommodations

La Villa De Zaragoza Ave Madero 1120, Centro **52-66/85.18.32** • gay-friendly motel • close to downtown bars

Plaza De Oro Hotel Calle 2 & Ave 'D' **52-66/85.14.37** • gay-friendly

Bars

Emilio's Cafeteria Musical Calle 3 #1810, Ste 11 (in entry to 'Parking América' garage) **52-66/88.02.67** • 8pm-3pm • lesbians/ gay men • food served • live music • beer/ wine

Noa Noa Ave Miguel F Martínez 678 (at Calle 1) **52-66/81.79.01** • 5pm-3am, till 5am Sat • popular • lesbians/ gay men • dancing/DJ • drag shows • young crowd

Nightclubs

Exstasis Larroque 213 (in Viva Tijuana shopping ctr, next to International Line) **52-66/82.83.39** • 10pm-4am Th-Sun • popular • lesbians/ gay men • dancing/DJ • strip shows

Los Equipales Calle 7 #8236 (at Calle Revolución, opposite Jai Alai Palace) **52-66/88.30.06** • 10pm-2am, clsd Mon-Tue • popular • lesbians/ gay men • dancing/DJ • live shows

Mike's Ave Revolución 1220 (at Calle 6) **52-66/85.35.34** • 3pm-6am • popular • mostly gay men • dancing/DJ • drag/ strip shows

Terraza 9 Calle 6 #8150 (at Ave Revolución) **52-66/85.35.34** • 8pm-5am Th-Sun • lesbians/ gay men • dancing/DJ • drag/ strip shows • cover charge

Restaurants

The Boy'z Plaza Santa Cecilia (Zona Centro) • 7am-11pm

Vittorio's Ave Revolución (at Novena) **52-66/85.17.29** • pizza & pasta

Publications

Bandera Gay 52-66/80.99.63

Frontera Gay 52-66/88.02.67

Toluca

Bars

Bar El Conde 201-E Passaje Curi Norte • gay-friendly • food served

Bar El Jardín 100-D Ave Hildalgo Oeste • gay-friendly

Café del Rey Portal 20 de Noviembre • gay-friendly • food served

Vip's Toluca Paseo Tollocán & Blvd Isidoro Fabela • lesbians/ gay men

Tuxtla Gutierrez

Bars

Sandy's Bar Calle 9 Sur & 8 Poniente (inquire in 'Via Fontana') • gay-friendly • transgender-friendly

Veracruz

Accommodations

Hotel Imperial Portales de Miguel Lerdo de Tejada 153 (N side of the Plaza de Armas) **52-29/32.87.88** • gay-friendly • food served • expensive

Hotel Villa del Mar Blvd Miguel Ávila Camacho 2707 (Col Zaragoza, across street from Playa del Mar beach) **52-29/31.33.66** • gay-friendly • hotel w/ separate motel & bungalows • moderate price

Bars

La Esfinge Calle 3 #1221 (Col 21 de Abril, behind Bodega Comercial Mexicana) **52-29/34.49.78** • 11pm-close Th-Sat • mostly gay men • dancing/DJ • drag shows

Stonewall Ave Pino Suárez 2191 (at Arista) • clsd Sun-Mon • mostly gay men • dancing/DJ • drag shows

Nightclubs

Deeper Calle Icaza 1005 (btwn Aves G Victoria N & Revillagigedo N) **52-29/35.02.65** • 9pm-4am Th-Sun • mostly gay men • dancing/DJ

El Cid Americo Vespucio 178 (opposite the stadium) **52-29/37.77.14** • gay/ straight • popular drag shows • cover charge

Hip Pop Potamus Calle 11, Col Costa Verde (1 blk W of Blvd Miguel Ávila Camacho, at Calles 20 & 12) • 9pm-6am, clsd Mon-Wed • gay/ straight • dancing/DJ • drag shows

Vieu Carre Ave Independencia Norte 19-A (at Calle Padilla) **52-29/30.60.60** • 9pm-4am Th-Sat • mostly gay men • dancing/DJ • drag shows & go-go boys

Villahermosa

Accommodations

Hotel Don Carlos Ave Madero 418, Centro **52-93/12.24.99** • gay-friendly • food served

Hyatt Villahermosa 106 Juarez Ave **52-93/13.44.44, 800/233-1234 (US#)** • gay-friendly

Bars

Yardas 1318 Ave 27 de Febrero **52-93/13.43.62** • lesbians/ gay men

Zacatecas

Info Lines & Services

Closet Sor Juana **52-492/3.76.78** • women's group • call for info

Accommodations

Quinta Real Zacatecas Ave Rayon 434 **52-492/2.91.04, 800/878-4484 (US#)** • gay-friendly • 5-star hotel

Nightclubs

Escándalo Esplanada La Feria **52-492/4.14.76** • 9pm-3am Fri-Sat • lesbians/ gay men • dancing/DJ • live shows

La Toma Calle Juárez 116 • clsd Sun-Tue • gay-friendly • dancing/DJ

Cafes

Café Acropolis Ave Hidalgo

Zihuatanejo

Bars

La Cambina del Capitan Calle Vincente Guerrero & Nicolas Bravo, 2nd flr • gay-friendly

La Casita Camino Escénico a Playa La Ropa (across from 'Kontiki' restaurant) **52-753/4.45.10** • mostly gay men

Nightclubs

Roca Rock at Calles 5 de Mayo & Nicolás Bravo • gay/ straight • dancing/DJ • drag shows

Restaurants

Splash at Calles Ejido & Vincente Guerrero **52-753/4.08.80** • noon-midnight • popular • lesbians/ gay men • also bar

Costa Rica

Alajuela

see also San José

Bars

Marguiss (250 meters S of Almacénes Llobet) 2nd flr **506/443-5310** • 6pm-close • lesbians/ gay men • neighborhood bar • live shows last Sun

Arenal

Accommodations

Arenal Lodge **506/228-3189** • gay-friendly • volcano views • US$95

Entertainment & Recreation

The Arenal Volcano • hourly eruptions

Tabacon Hot Springs La Fortuna **506/222-1072** • 10am-10pm • US$13

Manuel Antonio, Quepos

Accommodations

El Parador **506/777-1437, 800/451-4398 (US#)** • gay-friendly • large resort w/ mini golf course & health club • swimming • also gourmet restaurant

El Parque **506/777-0096** • gay-friendly • hillside condos w/ ocean views • waterfall swimming pool • restaurant • US$55-75

Hotel Casa Blanca **506/777-0253** • lesbians/ gay men • short hike to gay beach • swimming • IGLTA • gay-owned/ run • US$50-80

Hotel Villa Roca **506/777-1349** • mostly gay men • great ocean views • near beaches • US$40-90

La Plantacion Big Ruby's apdo 94-6350 **506/777-1332, 800/477-7829** • mostly gay men • women welcome • infinity pool • shuttle service to gay beach • full brkfst • also Madres restaurant • US$90-320

Makanda by the Sea 506/777-0442 • gay-friendly • private oasis • swimming • US$110-250

Si Como No 506/777-0777, 800/237-8207 (US#) • popular • gay-friendly • swimming • US$85-210

Villas Nicolas 506/777-0481 • gay-friendly • oceanview rental suites • US$39-155

Bars

Cockatoo Bar above Jardin Gourmet Restaurant (in Hotel Eclipse) **506/777-1728** • 5pm-close

Kamuk Pub at Katuk Hotel (downtown) • till 4am • gay-friendly • live shows

Mar y Sombra on Playa Espadilla beach • gay-friendly • local flavor • dancing/DJ (Nov-April) • also full restaurant

Vela Bar 1st Beach (at Vela Bar Hotel) **506/777-0413** • gay-friendly • also restaurant

Nightclubs

Arco Iris behind iron bridge at the waterfront **506/777-0449** • 7pm-close • gay-friendly • more gay late night & wknds • dancing/DJ • live shows wknds

Restaurants

Dulú 506/777-1297 • full bar

El Barba Roja Quepos • popular • great sunset location

El Gran Escape Quepos • clsd Tue • Tex-Mex

Karola's Quepos • clsd Wed • lunch & dinner w/ a view • full bar • gay-owned/ run

Madres at 'La Plantacion Big Ruby's' **506/777-1332** • 8am-9pm

The Plinio at the 'Hotel Plinio' **506/777-0055** • Italian

Tico Rico paved road to national park, Quepos (in 'Hotel Si Como No') • lunch & dinner • includes use of pool bar

Playa Jaco

Accommodations

Hotel Poseidon Calle del Bohio (30 meters W of Jaco Centro) **506/643-1642** • gay-friendly • 50 meters to beach • also bar & restaurant

Puntarenas

Accommodations

Casa Yemaya 506/661-0956 • women-only guesthouse

Bars

Capitan Moreno Paseo de Los Turistas **506/661-0810** • gay-friendly

San José

Info Lines & Services

Uno @ Diez Central St (btwn Aves 7 & 9) **506/254-4561** • 9am-8pm, clsd Sun • lesbigay tourist info center w/ Internet service • also outdoor terrace for coffee

Accommodations

Amstel Amón 800/575-1253 • gay-friendly • modern hotel • quiet location • food served

Cariari Hotel & Country Club **800/227-4274** • gay-friendly • luxury resort w/ great golfing • swimming

Colours—The Guest Residence El Triangulo NE, Blvd Rohrmoser **506/296-1880 & 506/232-3504, 800/277-4825 & 305/532-9341 (US#)** • lesbians/ gay men • premier full-service accommodations w/ tours & reservation services throughout Costa Rica • swimming • also bar & restaurant • shows • IGLTA

Don Carlos B&B 506/221-6707 • popular • gay-friendly • US$50-60

Hotel Kekoldi Ave 9 (Calle 3 Bis, Barrio Amón) **506/223-3244**

Joluva Guesthouse Calle 3 B (Aves 9 & 11 #936) **506/223-7961, 800/298-2418 (US#)** • lesbians/ gay men

Las Banderas B&B (200 meters W of Parque La Amistad, Rohrmoser) **506/381-5768** • mostly gay men • intimate & homey • US$40-70

Bars

Bar Los Bigotitos next to Banco Popular, San Pedro **506/383-1815, 506/382-9259** • 6:30pm-2am • mostly gay men • neighborhood bar • live shows

Buenas Vibraciones Ave 14th (btwn Calles 7 & 9, in front of parking for 'Más x Menos,' Paseo de los Estudiantes) **506/223-4573** • 6pm-close • mostly women • neighborhood bar

Cantábrico Ave 6 (btwn Calle Central & 2nd) • lesbians/ gay men

Highlander Ave 6 (200 meters S & 50 meters W of SW corner of Parque Central) **506/223-5344** • 4pm-2:30am • mostly gay men • neighborhood bar • drag/ strip shows Fri-Sat

Kashbah Calle Central (btwn Avenidas 7 & 9, 150 meters N of 'Hotel Europa') **506/258-0774** • 5pm-close • mostly gay men • dancing/DJ Wed, Fri-Sat • also restaurant • hamburgers & sandwiches

La Calle Ave 8 (btwn Calles 3 & 5, 200 meters W of 'La Casa del Tornillo') **506/221-5552** • 4pm-2:30am • mostly gay men • neighborhood bar • live shows

La Tertulia 100 meters E & 150 meters N of Iglesia de San Pedro, San Pedro **506/225-0250** • open daily • mostly women • neighborhood bar

Puchos Calle 11 (btwn Aves 8 & 10, knock to enter) **506/256-1147** • 6pm-2:30am • lesbians/ gay men • strippers Mon, Wed & Fri • also restaurant

Nightclubs

Dejá Vú Calle 2 (btwn Aves 14 & 16) **506/223-3758** • 8pm-close, from 9pm Fri-Sat, clsd Mon-Th • popular • lesbians/ gay men • dancing/DJ • 2 dance flrs • live shows • also 'Sinners' lounge Fri-Sat only • take taxi to avoid bad area

La Avispa Calle 1 #834 (pink house btwn Aves 8 & 10) **506/223-5354** • clsd Mon & Th • mostly women last Wed • popular T-dance Sun • dancing/DJ

Los Cucharones Ave 6 (btwn Calles Central & 1st, 75 meters E of Farmacia Jara—no sign; look for big, black wooden doors & enter) **506/233-5797** • 7pm-close • mostly gay men • dancing/DJ

Cafes

Café de Teatro National National Theatre **506/223-4488** • lunch

Restaurants

Anochecer 2 km from Centro Aserri on Carretera A Tarbaca (nr 'Colours') **506/230-5152** • 11am-midnight • full bar

Café Mundo Ave 9 & Calle 15 (200 meters E of parking lot for INS, Barrio Amón) **506/222-6190** • Italian • garden seating • also cafe/ bar

El Bochinche Calle 11 (btwn Aves 10 & 12, Paseo de los Etudiantes), San Pedro **506/221-0500** • 7pm-2am Wed-Sun • Mexican • also video bar

La Cocina de Leña in El Pueblo complex **506/255-1360** • 5 minutes from downtown • Costa Rican • US$12

La Esquina El triangulo noreste Boulevard Rohrmoser (inside 'Colours') **506/232-3504, 506/296-1880** • poolside dining • full bar

La Perla Calle Central Ave 2 (on corner)

La Piazetta Paseo Colón • Italian • US$18

Machu Pichu off Paseo Colón • just outside downtown area • Peruvian • seafood • US$18

Nimbe in Escazu (San José suburb) **506/281-1739**

Vishnu Vegetarian Restaurant Ave 1 (btwn Calles 3 & 1) • popular

Publications

Gayness Apartado Postal 1581-1002, Paseo Estudiantes **506/258-0230** • monthly lesbigay newsmagazine • also map w/ listings (en español w/ some English)

Gente 10 Apartado Postal 1910-2100, Sector Guadalupe • bimonthly lesbigay magazine • also map w/ listings (en español w/ some English)

Erotica

Tabú 75 meters W of 'Banco Popular', San Pedro **506/283-7320** • 10am-8pm, till 7pm Sun • also locations in Escazú & Real Cariari

Austria

Vienna

Info Lines & Services

AIDS-Help Vienna Mariahilfergürtel 4 **43-1/599.37**

Rosa-Lila-Tip Linke Wienzeile 102 (nr Hofmühlgasse, U4-Pilgramgasse) **43-1/586.81.50** • Austrian lesbigay switchboard • mtg place for various groups • also cafe-bar

Accommodations

Arcotel Hotel Wimberger at Europaplatz, Neubaugürtel 34-36 (at Goldschlagstr) **43-1/521.65-0, 43-660/84.06** • gay-friendly • centrally located 4-star hotel • restaurant & bar on premises • also fitness club • AS2,000-2,600

Hotel Urania Obere Weißgerberstr 7 (U-Schwedenplatz) **43-1/713.17.11** • gay-friendly • centrally located • pizzeria & bar on premises • wheelchair access • AS430-890

Pension Wild Lange Gasse 10 (off Lerchenfelder Str) **43-1/406.51.74** • mostly gay men • rooms & apts • AS450+

Bars

Café Berg Berggasse 8 (at Wasagasse, U2-Schottentor) **43-1/319.57.20** • 10am-1am • popular • lesbians/ gay men • cafe-bar • young crowd

Vienna

Lesbigay Pride: Vienna will host EuroPride 2001.

Annual Events:
Rainbow Parade.
Life Ball (AIDS benefit).

City Info: 43-1/211.14.0, web: www.vienna-tourism.at. In US, call 212/944-6880 or 310/477-3332.

Attractions: Schönbrunn Palace 43-1/811.13.
Imperial Palace.
State Opera House 43-1/514.44.2613.
Vienna Boys' Choir 43-1/533.99.27.75.
Museum of Fine Arts 43-1/525.24.0.
Belvedere Palace/Austrian Gallery 43-1/795.57.0.
Art Nouveau buildings.
Jewish Museum 43-1/535.0431.
Sigmund Freud Museum 43-1/319.1596.

Weather: Mild, rainy summers and chilly winters. September is a good time to visit.

Transit: Vienna Airport Lines. Vienna has an excellent public transit system. Consider purchasing a Vienna Card for 72 hours of unlimited travel by subway, bus, and tram, plus discounts on airport shuttle, at museums, and at many shops and restaurants. 43-1/211.14.0.

Café Savoy Linke Wienzeile 36 (at Köstlergasse) **43-1/586.73.48** • 5pm-2am, 9am-6pm & 9pm-2am Sat, clsd Sun • popular • lesbians/ gay men • upscale cafe-bar

Café Stein Währinger Str 6-8 (nr U-Schottentor) **43-1/319.72.41** • 7am-1am, from 9am Sun • gay-friendly cafe-bar • Internet access • terrace

Peter's Operncafé Hartauer Riemergasse 9 (at Singer) **43-1/512.89.81** • 8am-2am, from 5pm Sat, clsd Sun • gay/ straight • food served • terrace

Das Versteck Grünangergasse 10, downstairs (at Singer, U1-Stephansplatz) **43-1/513.40.53** • 6pm-midnight, from 7pm Sat, clsd Sun • gay/ straight • young crowd

Nightclubs

Heaven Gay Night at U4 Schönbrunnerstr 222 (at Meidlinger, U4-Meidlinger Haupstr) • 11pm-5am Th only • popular • mostly gay men • dancing/DJ • transgender-friendly • live shows • wheelchair access

Why Not? Tiefer Graben 22 (at Wipplinger, U-Schottentor) **43-1/535.11.58** • 10pm-close Fri-Sat, 9pm-2am Sun, clsd Mon-Th • mostly gay men • dancing/DJ • live shows • videos

Cafes

Santo Spirito Kumpfgasse 7 (U-Stefans-platz) **43-1/512.99.98** • 11am-2am, till 3am Fri-Sat • Mediterranean/ vegetarian • also bar • terrace • wheelchair access

Restaurants

Café-Restaurant Kunsthaus Weißgerberlände 14 (btwn Kollergasse & Custozzagasse, U-Schnellbahn Landstr) **43-1/712.04.97** • 10am-midnight • full bar • terrace

Café-Restaurant Willendorf Linke Wienzeile 102 (nr Hofmuhlgasse, U4-Pilgramgasse) **43-1/587.17.89** • 7pm-2am, food served till midnight • lesbians/ gay men • plenty veggie • full bar • terrace

Kantine Porzellangasse 19 (btwn Grünentorgasse & Müllnergasse, Bauernfeldplatz tram) **43-1/319.59.18** • 6pm-3am, food served till 1am • full bar • terrace • wheelchair access

The Living Room Franzensgasse 18 (at Grüngasse, U4-Kettenbrückengasse) **43-1/585.37.07** • 6pm-2am, from 11:30am wknds • mostly gay men • Viennese • also bar

Margaritaville Bartensteingasse 3 (U-Lerchenfelder Str) **43-1/405.47.86** • 6pm-2am, till midnight Sun • Tex-Mex • full bar • terrace

Motto Schönbrunnerstr 30 **43-1/587.06.72** • 6pm-4am • trendy • gay/ straight • also bar • terrace

Orlando Mollardgasse 3 (U-Pilgramgasse) **43-1/586.23.27** • 5pm-2am (food served 6pm-1am), brunch from 10am Sun • popular • mostly women • also bar • terrace

Bookstores

American Discount Rechte Wienzeile 5 (at Paniglgasse) **43-1/587.57.72** • 9:30am-6:30pm, 9am-1pm Sat, clsd Sun • magazines & books • also Neubaugasse 39 location, 43-1/523.37.07 • also Donaustadt Str 1 location, 43-1/203.95.18

Löwenherz Berggasse 8 (next to 'Cafe Berg', enter on Wasagasse, U2-Schottentor) **43-1/317.29.82** • 10am-7pm, till 5pm Sat, clsd Sun • lesbigay • large selection of English titles

Publications

Bussi **43-1/505.07.42** • free city mag w/ event & club listings

Vienna Gay Guide **43-1/789.97.37** • city-map & guide

Erotica

Art-X Percostr 3 **43-1/258.04.44** • 10am-8pm, till 5pm Sat, clsd Sun • leather, latex, rubber • toys • music • videos • magazines

Tiberius Lindengasse 2-A (at Stiftgasse, U3-Neubaugasse) **43-1/522.04.74** • 3pm-6:30pm, 11am-3pm Sat, clsd Sun, also by appt • leather, latex, tools & toys • wheelchair access

England

London

London is divided into 6 regions:

London—Overview
London—Central
London—West
London—North
London—East
London—South

Note: London area codes will change in early 2000: 171 becomes 207, and 181 becomes 208.

London — Overview

Info Lines & Services

Audre Lorde Clinic 44–171/377–7312, 44–181/846–1576/7 • Wed & Fri • lesbian health clinic • call for appt & location

Black Lesbian/ Gay Centre 5/5A Westminster Bridge Rd, Rm 113 (SE1) **44–171/620–3885** • 11:30am-5:30pm Tue & Th

Freedom Cab Company 44–171/734–1313

London Holiday Accommodation Bureau 44–181/809–1899

London Lesbian/ Gay Switchboard 44–171/837–7324 • 24hrs

London Lesbian Line 44–171/251–6911 • 2pm-10pm Mon & Fri, 7pm-10pm Tue-Th

The London Women's Centre The Wheel, Wild Court (Holborn) **44–171/831–6946** • also cafe, theatre & gym • call for events

Outlinks LGBT Youth Project 44–171/378–8732 • drop-in 4pm-7pm Tue • call for more info

Entertainment & Recreation

Gay Sweatshop 44–171/242–1168 • gay theater troupe

Publications

Attitude 44–171/308–5090

▲ **Diva 44–171/482–2576** • glorious glossy lesbian magazine

Gay Times 44–171/482–2576, 44–171/267–0021 • gay glossy

The Pink Paper 44–171/296–6000 • free lesbigay newspaper

Time Out 44–171/813–3000 • weekly city scene guide w/ gay section

Spiritual Groups

Jewish Gay/ Lesbian Group 44–181/381–1235

MCC London Camden Trinity URC, Buck St, Kentish Town Rd (NW1) **44–181/304–2374** • 7pm Sun • also MCC Brixton, 44-181/678-0200 • also MCC Mile End, 44-171/538-8376

London — Central

London—Central includes Soho, Covent Garden, Bloomsbury, Mayfair, Westminster, Pimlico & Belgravia

Accommodations

14 Thornhill Bridge Wharf Guest House 14 Thornhill Bridge Wharf **44–171/713–5287** • lesbians/ gay men • gay-owned/ run

Noel Coward Hotel 111 Ebury St (off Eccleston St, SW1, Belgravia) **44–171/730–2094, 44–171/730–9005** • gay-friendly • swimming • some shared baths • US$103-120

Number Two Dorset Street Number Two Dorset Street (at Baker, W1, St Marylebone) **44–171/224–7172** • gay/ straight • 5-star hotel

Soho Guestrooms 44–973/167–103, 44–171/497–7000 • lesbians/ gay men • guesthouse & apartment • smokefree • 3-night minimum stay • gay-owned/ run • £100–225

Bars

Note: 'Pub hours' usually means 11am-11pm Mon-Sat & noon-3pm and 7pm-10:30pm Sun

The Admiral Duncan 54 Old Compton St (W1) **44–171/437–5300** • pub hours • lesbians/ gay men • this landmark pub reopened summer '99 after a tragic bombing in April

The Bar 36 Hanway St (btwn Oxford St & Tottenham Court Rd, W1) **44–171/580–9811** • lesbians/ gay men • live DJ Wed, Th & Sat

Bar Aquda 13–14 Maiden Lane (btwn Bedford & Southampton, WC2, Covent Garden) **44–171/577–9891** • popular • lesbians/ gay men • cafe-bar

The Box 32–34 Monmouth St, Seven Dials (nr Shaftesbury Ave, WC2, Covent Garden) **44–171/240–5828** • pub hours • popular • lesbians/ gay men • dancing/DJ • cafe-bar • videos • wheelchair access

The Candy Bar 4 Carlisle St (nr Soho Sq, off Dean St, WC1) **44–171/494–4041** • 5pm-11pm, pub hours Sat, till 10:30pm Sun • popular • mostly women • males welcome as guests • 3 flrs • dancing/DJ • live shows • theme nights • 'Tease' Wed w/ dancers • call for events • organic food & wines served

London

London is an amalgam of the most staid and traditional elements of English society and the most innovative in youth culture. Visitors can easily spend several weeks on only the best known tourist attractions and still miss the spirit of London. Like New York, London is really a collection of smaller towns and neighborhoods, each with a distinct feel.

Like London itself, the women's scene is varied and vast. While you're out taking in the sights, stop by **Silver Moon Women's Bookstore,** or the aptly named bookstore **Gay's the Word,** and pick up a copy of **Diva**—London's slick lesbian magazine. To check in on what's happening and meet some like-minded women, visit the **London Women's Centre**—which also houses a gym, theater, and cafe! For more suggestions on how to experience it all, call the **Lesbian Line.** And if you happen to be in London in April, don't miss the week-long **Lesbian Film Festival.**

In the evening, start out at one of London's trendy cafe-bars, like the **Angel, Freedom, First Out,** or the **Box.** For a meal without the bar atmosphere, try the **Kulcha Kafe,** popular with local women.

London has two full-time women's bars—**Candy Bar** and **Sister George**—and a vast array of women's nights at various mixed bars and clubs. Check **Diva's** listings for the latest.

If you like dancing well into the morning hours, and mixing it up with the boys, visit one of the popular mixed clubs like **Popstarz, Duckie,** or the **Fridge Bar.** For a comprehensive listing of mixed clubs in and around London, pick up a copy of the glossy mag **Gay Times.**

For something a bit different, check out the **Drill Hall Theatre & Bar**: an alternative theater, bar, and vegetarian restaurant; Mondays are women-only, and Thursdays are smokefree.

London

Lesbigay Pride: July. 44-171/738.76.44.

Annual Events: March - Lesbian & Gay Film Festival 44-171/928.32.32.
May - Soho Pink Weekend.
Mr. Gay UK Contest.
August - Summer Rites 44-171/737.26.29.
October - Stonewall Equality Show 44-171/336.88.60. Huge charity concert.

City Info: 44-171/824.88.44.

Attractions: British Museum 44-171/636.15.55.
Buckingham Palace 44-171/799.23.31.
Kensington Palace 44-171/937.95.61.
Madame Tussaud's 44-171/935.68.61.
National Gallery 44-171/839.33.21.
Oscar Wilde's house (34 Tite Street).
St. Paul's Cathedral 44-171/236.41.28.
Tate Gallery 44-171/887.80.00.
Tower of London 44-171/709.07.65.
Westminster Abbey 44-171/222.51.52.

Best View: From Tower Bridge (Tower Hill Tube).

Weather: London is warmer and less rainy than you may have heard. Summer temperatures reach the 70°s and the average annual rainfall is about half of that of Atlanta, GA or Hartford, CT.

Transit: Freedom Cars 44-171/734.13.13.
Ladycabs 44-171/272.30.19.
Q Cars 44-181/671.00.11.
London Travel Information (Tube & buses) 44-171/222.12.34, 24hr info.

Compton's of Soho 53 Old Compton St (W1) **44–171/437–4445** • pub hours • popular • mostly gay men • leather • food served • wheelchair access

Drill Hall Theater & Bar 16 Chenies St (btwn Alfred Pl & Ridgmount, WC1, Bloomsbury) **44–171/637–8270, 44–171/631–5107** • 5pm-11pm • gay/ straight • women-only Mon • 200-seat theater • workshops • also bar • 6pm-11pm, clsd Sun • smokefree Th • also 'Greenhouse' vegetarian restaurant • 10:30am-8:30pm, noon-4:30pm Sun • wheelchair access

The Escape 10 Brewer St (nr Regent St, W1) **44–171/734–2626** • noon-11pm • popular • mostly gay men • dancing/DJ • 'bar with a nightclub feel in the evenings'

King's Arms 23 Poland St (W1) **44–171/734–5907** • pub hours • lesbians/ gay men • neighborhood bar • food served • videos

Ku Bar 75 Charing Cross Rd (W1) **44–171/437–4303** • pub hours • lesbians/ gay men • cafe-bar

Kudos 10 Adelade St (btwn William IV St & the Strand, WC2) **44–171/379–4573** • pub hours • lesbians/ gay men • professional • cafe-bar • videos • wheelchair access

Madame JoJo's 8–10 Brewer St (W1, Soho) **44–171/734–2473** • 10pm-4am • gay/ straight • campy drag cabaret • cover charge

The Nile 152 Ebury St (SW1, Belgravia) **44–171/824–8432** • pub hours • gay-friendly • neighborhood cafe-bar

The Retro Bar 2 George Ct (WC1, off Strand) **44–171/839–4012** • pub hours • lesbians/ gay men • neighborhood bar

Rupert Street Cafe-Bar 50 Rupert St (off Brewer, W1) **44–171/734–5614** • pub hours • lesbians/ gay men • wheelchair access

Sister George Hugh St (Victoria, SW1) **44–171/592–9911** • Th-Sun only • mostly women

The Village Soho 81 Wardour St (at Old Compton, W1) **44–171/434–2124** • noon-11pm, from 4pm Sun • mostly gay men • trendy • cafe menu till 5pm • wheelchair access

West Central 29–30 Lisle St (WC2, behind Leicester Sq cinemas) **44–171/479–7981** • noon-11pm, till 10:30pm Sun • lesbians/ gay men • dancing/DJ • transgender-friendly • drag shows • also 'Theatre Bar' upstairs • 5pm-close, from 3pm wknds • also 'Club Bar' downstairs • 10:30am-2am, till 3am Fri-Sat, clsd Sun-Tue

Wow Bar at the 'Global Bar,' 15 Golden Sq (off Brewer St, W1) • 8pm-midnight Sat • women only • Internet access

The Yard Bar 57 Rupert St (off Brewer, W1) **44–171/437–2652** • noon-11pm • lesbians/ gay men • women-only upstairs at 'Her/ She Bar' 8pm-11pm Fri • queer comedy night Wed upstairs at 'Screamers' • food served till 5pm • US$5-10 • wheelchair access

Nightclubs

Ace of Clubs 52 Piccadilly (W1) **44–171/408–4457** • 9:30pm-4am Sat • women only • dancing/DJ

Diva Dive 64 Wilton Rd (SW1) **44–956/477–724** • 9pm-2am Fri • women only • dancing/DJ • popular w/ lesbians 30+

DTPM at 'The End,' 16–A West Central St (WC1, Bloomsbury) **44–171/609–9699** • 8pm-3:30am Sun • popular • lesbians/ gay men • dancing/DJ • stylish techno club

G.A.Y. 157 Charing Cross Rd (at Oxford St, in London Astoria theatre complex, WC2) **44–171/434–9592, 44–171/734–6963** • 10:30pm-5am Mon & Th-Sat • popular • mostly gay men • dancing/DJ • live shows • young crowd • retro Mon

The Gardening Club 4 The Piazza (WC2, Covent Garden) **44–171/836–4052** • 9pm-3am Th only • lesbians/ gay men • dancing/DJ • int'l crowd

Heaven The Arches (off Villiers St, WC2) **44–171/930–2020** • the mother of all London gay clubs • call for hours/ events • mostly gay men • dancing/DJ

Kitty Lips 4 Gray's Inn Rd (at Gray's Inn Nightclub, WC1) • 11pm-5am Fri • women-only • dancing/DJ • trendy

The Limelight 136 Shaftesbury Ave (at Charing Cross, W1) **44–171/437–4303, 44–171/434–0572** • 6pm-11pm Sun only • popular T-dance • lesbians/ gay men • dancing/DJ

Renegade Ranch at 'Central Club Hotel' on Great Russell St (W1) **44–181/765–0049** • 8pm-midnight Fri • lesbians/ gay men • dancing/DJ • country/ western

Ruby's Tea Dance 49 Carnaby St (W1) **44–181/302–6651** • 5:30pm Sun • lesbians/ gay men • ballroom/ Latin dancing

SubStation 1A Dean St (at Oxford St, W1) **44–171/287–9608** • 9pm-3:30am, till 5am Fri-Sat, 6pm-11pm Sun • mostly gay men • popular • dancing/DJ • cruising clubsters • theme nights • men only Sun

DIVA
EUROPE'S LEADING LESBIAN MAGAZINE IS NOW OUT MONTHLY.
THE ONLY ONE OF ITS KIND IN EUROPE DIVA OFFERS THE BEST LESBIAN READ AROUND, IN A QUALITY GLOSSY FORMAT.
SUBSCRIBE TO THE BEST LESBIAN MAGAZINE, WITH THIS ADVERTISEMENT AND SAVE ON THE STANDARD PRICE.
OR SUBSCRIBE VIA OUR WEBSITE HTTP://WWW.GAYTIMES.CO.UK
DIVA IS ALSO AVAILABLE IN MOST GOOD BOOK STORES AND NEWSAGENTS.
Complete the order form below & send with your payment to Dept: DDAM, Millivres Ltd., Worldwide House, 116-134 Bayham Street, London, NW1 0BA.
Please send me a 1 year subscription to Diva:-
1 year (12 issues) Outside Europe £60 ❒
1 year (12 issues) Europe £50 ❒
1 year (12 issues) UK residents £24 ❒
(DDAM)
I enclose cheque postal order for £.................... payable to Millivres Ltd.
Name..
Address..
....
Please debit my credit card no:
Expiry Date

The Tube Falconberg Court (off Charing Cross, next to the 'Astoria,' W1) **44-171/738-2336** • 10:30pm-3:30am • mostly gay men • dancing/DJ • theme nights

Waltzing with Hilda at 'Central Club Hotel' on Great Russell St (W1) **44-850/318-720** • 8:30pm Fri • ballroom dancing

Cafes

Blue Room 3 Bateman St (W1) **44-171/437-4827** • 8am-midnight, noon-11pm Sun • coffee, smoothies & sandwiches • US$4-6

Cafe Joy 69 Endell St (btwn High Holborn & Long Acre, WC2) **44-171/419-1295** • Caribbean

First Out 52 St Giles High St (btwn Charing Cross & Shaftesbury, WC2) **44-171/240-8042** • 10am-11pm, from noon Sun • lesbians/ gay men • cont'l • full bar • smokefree upstairs • women-only Fri at 'Girl Friday'

Freedom Cafe-Bar 60-66 Wardour St (off Old Compton St, W1) **44-171/734-0071** • 9am-11pm • trendy scene cafe • US$6-11 • also downstairs bar • open 9:30pm-3am Wed-Sat • live shows

Old Compton Cafe 34 Old Compton St (W1) **44-171/439-3309** • 24hrs • popular • sandwiches & salads • US$3-7

Restaurants

Balans 60 Old Compton St (W1) **44-171/437-5212** • 8am-4am, till 6am Fri-Sat • all-day/ night brunch • cafe-bar • transgender-friendly • live shows • wheelchair access • US$10-22

Creole Garden 85 Battersea Rise (SW11) **44-171/924-4454** • 8am-11pm, from noon Sun • full bar • Cajun/ Creole

Food for Thought 31 Neal St, downstairs (WC2) **44-171/836-0239** • noon-3:30pm & 5:30pm-8:15pm, noon-4pm Sun • vegetarian • US$5-10

The Gay Hussar 2 Greek St (on Soho Sq, W1) **44-171/437-0973** • lunch & dinner, clsd Sun • Hungarian • US$28-41

Mildred's 58 Greek St (off Shaftesbury, W1) **44-171/494-1634** • noon-11pm, clsd Sun • plenty veggie

Nusa Dua 11-12 Dean St (W1) **44-171/437-3559** • Indonesian • US$15

Rossana's 17 Strutton Ground (btwn Victoria St & Horseferry Rd, SW1, Westminster) **44-171/233-1701** • cont'l/ English

Steph's 39 Dean St (W1) **44-171/734-5976** • noon-3pm Mon-Fri & 5:30pm-11:30pm nightly, clsd Sun • English • US$12-26

The Stockpot 18 Old Compton St (W1) **44-171/287-1066** • 11:30am-11:30pm • cheap!

Wagamamma Noodle Bar 10A Lexington St (W1) **44-171/292-0990** • noon-11pm, 12:30pm-10pm Sun • Japanese • smokefree • US$6-13

Entertainment & Recreation

Gay Film Night at Prince Charles Cinema (Leicester Pl, WC2) **44-171/437-8181** • every Mon • discount tickets available at 'Ku Bar'

Walking Tours of Gay & Lesbian SOHO 56 Old Compton St **44-171/437-6063**

Bookstores

Gay's the Word 66 Marchmont St (nr Russell Sq, WC1) **44-171/278-7654** • 10am-6:30pm, 2pm-6pm Sun • lesbigay • new & used books • magazines

Silver Moon Women's Bookshop 64-68 Charing Cross Rd (WC2) **44-171/836-7906** • lesbian/ feminist

Retail Shops

American Retro 35 Old Compton St (W1) **44-171/734-3477** • 10:15am-7pm, clsd Sun • clothing & gifts

Metal Morphosis 10-11 Moor St (at Old Compton St, W1) **44-171/434-4554** • piercing studio

Prowler 3-7 Brewer St (behind 'Village Soho' bar, W1) • large gay department store • also coffeeshop & travel agency

Gyms & Health Clubs

Soho Athletic Club 10-14 Macklin St (at Drury Ln, WC2) **44-171/242-1290** • gay-friendly

Erotica

Paradiso Bodyworks 41 Old Compton St (W1) **44-171/287-2487** • fetishwear • transgender-friendly • wheelchair access

RoB London 24-25 Wells St (nr Berwick St, W1) **44-171/735-7893** • leather/ fetish shop • wheelchair access

London—West

London—West includes Earl's Court, Kensington, Chelsea & Bayswater

Info Lines & Services

Webshack 58 Kenway Rd **44–171/835–0203** • 10am-9pm, till 6pm Fri-Sat, clsd Sun • email/ Internet access & other computer services • also Camden Town location (206 Chalk Farm Rd, 44-207/482-0102)

Accommodations

Bailey's Hotel 140 Gloucester Rd (at Old Brompton Rd, SW7, Kensington) **44–171/373–6000** • gay-friendly 4-star hotel • located in the heart of Kensington • £120-250 • also 'Olives' restaurant & bar • Mediterranean

Comfort Hotel 22–32 West Cromwell Rd (SW5) **44–171/373–3300** • gay-friendly • food served • also bar • £75-90

George Hotel Templeton Pl (btwn W Cromwell & Trebovir Rds, SW5) **44–171/370–2285** • gay-friendly • full brkfst • some shared baths • £45-95

Holland Park Hotel 6 Ladbroke Ter (W11, Kensington) **44–171/792–0216** • gay-friendly

The New York Hotel 32 Philbeach Gardens (SW5) **44–171/244–6884** • lesbians/ gay men • some shared baths • jacuzzi & sauna • non-smoking rms available • wheelchair access • US$120-154

The Philbeach Hotel 30–31 Philbeach Gardens (SW5, Earl's Court) **44–171/373–1244** • lesbians/ gay men • some shared baths • also restaurant & bar from 7pm • US$95-120

Redcliffe Hotel 268 Fulham Rd (SW10, Chelsea) **44–171/823–3494** • lesbians/ gay men • also restaurant & bar • US$103-120

Bars

Cafe Au-Reole 233 Earls Court Rd (SW5) **44–171/912–1409** • 5pm-midnight, from noon wknds • lesbians/ gay men • cafe-bar

The Penny Farthing 135 King St (W6, Hammersmith) **44–181/600–0941, 44–208/748–7045** • noon-midnight, till 2am Th-Sat, till 10:30pm Sun • lesbians/ gay men • neighborhood bar • food served • cabaret • wheelchair access

The Rocket 10–13 Churchfield Rd (Acton, W3) **44–181/992–1545** • 11am-11pm, till 10:30pm Sun • lesbians/ gay men • dancing/DJ • cabaret

Ted's Place 305–A North End Rd (W14) **44–171/385–9359** • 6pm-11:30pm, from 5pm Wed, Th & Sat, clsd Sun • lesbians/ gay men • dancing/DJ • transgender-friendly • drag shows • videos • private club

Restaurants

Amazonas 75 Westbourne Grove (behind Whiteley's Shopping Ctr, W2, Bayswater) **44–171/243–0090** • 7pm-11pm nightly, lunch noon-3pm wknds only • Brazilian/ South American • full bar • terrace

Balans West 239 Old Brompton Rd **44–171/244–8838** • 8am-1am • lesbians/ gay men • English • US$10-20

Goolie's 21 Abingdon Rd **44–171/938–1122** • contemporary • £10-15

Le Gourmet 312 King's Rd (SW3, Chelsea) **44–171/352–4483** • 6:30pm-11:30pm nightly, lunch 1pm-3:30pm Sun • int'l • transgender-friendly

Phoenicia 11–13 Abingdon Rd **44–171/937–0120** • Lebanese/ Mediterranean • £7-15

Roy's 234 Old Brompton Rd (SW5) **44–171/373–9995** • 6:30pm-11:30pm • mostly gay men • full bar • wheelchair access

Wilde About Oscar at the 'Philbeach Hotel' **44–171/835–1858, 44–171/373–1244** • 7pm-11pm • lesbians/ gay men • eclectic/ French • reservations required • wheelchair access • US$15-22

London—North

London—North includes Paddington, Regents Park, Camden, St Pancras & Islington

Accommodations

160 Regents Park Road 160 Regents Park Rd (NW1, Primrose Hill) **44–171/586–5266** • lesbians/ gay men • full brkfst • some shared baths

Bars

The Angel 65 Graham St (N1, Islington) **44–171/608–2656** • noon-midnight, pub hours Sun • lesbians/ gay men • cafe-bar • women only 7:30pm-midnight Tue

Bar Fusion 45 Essex Rd (at Queen's Head St, N1, Angel) **44–171/686–1857** • 11:30am-11pm • neighborhood cafe-bar

Due South 35 Stoke Newington High St (at Arcola St, N16, Stoke Newington) **44–171/249–7543** • 4pm-close, from 1pm wknds • mostly gay men • women only Th

Duke of Wellington 119 Balls Pond Rd (N1, Islington) **44–171/249–3729** • 11:30am-1am, till 11pm Sun • lesbians/ gay men • neighborhood bar

George 114 Twickenham Rd (at South St, N1, Isleworth) **44–181/560–1456** • 5pm-11pm, from noon Sun • lesbians/ gay men • neighborhood bar • also restaurant • live shows

King William IV 77 Hampstead High St (NW3, Hampstead) **44–171/435–5747** • noon-11pm • lesbians/ gay men • neighborhood bar • transgender-friendly • drag shows • food served • wheelchair access

Lower Ground 269 West End Ln (NW6, West Hampstead) **44–171/431–2211** • noon-close • lesbians/ gay men • dancing/DJ • terrace

The Oak 79 Green Lanes (N16) **44–171/354–2791** • 1pm-midnight, till 2am Fri-Sat, from 2pm Sun • lesbians/ gay men • women only 9pm-2am Fri at 'Kiss' • dancing/DJ • live shows • cafe-bar • 'Club Ha'de' for Cypriots, Greeks, Turks & friends last Sat

Scott's 230 Woodhouse Rd (N12, Finchley) **44–181/361–0499** • 5pm-close • lesbians/ gay men • live shows

The White Hart 51 Station Rd (N15) **44–181/808–5049** • 7pm-midnight, noon-11:30pm Sun • gay/ straight • live shows • wheelchair access

Nightclubs

The Garage 20–22 Highbury Corner (N1, Islington) **44–171/607–1818** • gay-friendly • more gay at 'Club V' 2nd Sat • dancing/DJ • live music

Popstarz at 'The Complex', 1–5 Parkfield St (in Islington) **44–171/738–2336** • popular • 10pm-5am Fri • lesbians/ gay men • dancing/DJ • Britpop & indie music • cover charge

Restaurants

Eden du Carib 74 Kingsgate Rd (at Kilburn High Rd, NW6, Kilburn) **44–171/624–0024** • Caribbean

Bookstores

Compendium 234 Camden High St (NW1, Camden Town) **44–171/485–8944** • lesbigay

Erotica

Sh! Women's Erotic Emporium 43 Coronet St (off Old St & Pitfield St, N1, Shoreditch) **44–171/613–5458** • 11:30am-6:30pm, till 8pm Th, clsd Sun • also mail order

Zipper Store 283 Camden High St (NW1, Camden Town) **44–171/284–0537, 44–171/267–0021 (MAIL ORDER)** • 10:30am-6:30pm, noon-5pm Sun • fetishwear • books • videos • sex toys • also mail order

London—East

London—East includes City, Tower, Clerkenwell & Shoreditch

Bars

The Coronet 119 The Grove (E15, Stratford) **44–181/522–0811** • lesbians/ gay men • neighborhood bar • karaoke

The Joiner's Arms 116–118 Hackney Rd (nr Shoreditch, E2) **44–171/739–9654** • lesbians/ gay men • neighborhood bar • live shows

The Old Ship 17 Barnes St (in Stepney, E14) **44–171/790–4082** • 6pm-11pm, from 7:30pm Sat, 1:30pm-10:30pm Sun • lesbians/ gay men • neighborhood bar • drag shows • wheelchair access

Raw The Pigeons, 120 Romford Rd (E15) **44–181/534–1955** • 9pm-2am Sat only • lesbians/ gay men • dancing/DJ • food served • live shows

Royal George 7 Selby St, Valance Rd (E1) **44–171/247–4150** • pub hours • gay/ straight • neighborhood bar • transgender-friendly • cabaret • wheelchair access

Royal Oak 73 Columbia Rd (E2, Bethnal Green) **44–171/739–8204** • 4pm-midnight, 1pm-2am Sat, from noon Sun • lesbians/ gay men • neighborhood bar • transgender-friendly • food served

The Spiral 138 Shoreditch High St (E1, across from Shoreditch Church) **44–171/613–1351** • lesbians/ gay men • neighborhood bar • dancing/DJ • 60s/70s/80s Th • karaoke Fri • disco Sat • piano bar Sun • private club • cheap non-member entry fee

The Tap 2 Markhouse Rd (E17, Walthamstow) **44–171/223–0767** • 5pm-11pm, from noon wknds • lesbians/ gay men • neighborhood bar • dancing/DJ • karaoke • cabaret

Woolwich Infant 9 Plumstead Rd (SE18) **44–181/854–3712** • pub hours • lesbians/ gay men • women only Mon • neighborhood bar • dancing/DJ • live shows

Nightclubs

Benjy's 562–A Mile End Rd (E3) **44–171/980–6427** • 9pm-1am Sun only • popular • gay/ straight • dancing/DJ

Club Travestie Extraordinaire at 'Stepneys,' 373 Commercial Rd (enter on Aylward St, off Jubilee St, E1, Stepney) **44–181/788–4154** • TV/TS night 8:30pm-close 2nd & 4th Sat • lesbians/ gay men • dancing/DJ • drag shows

Reflections 8 Bridge Rd (Stratford, E15) **44–181/519–1296** • open late • lesbians/ gay men • dancing/DJ • cabaret

Turnmills 63B Clerkenwell Rd (EC1, Clerkenwell) **44–171/250–3409** • after hours • popular • mostly gay men • dancing/DJ • private club • cover charge • call for events

Way Out Club 28 Minories (at 'Tiffanies', nr the Tower of London, EC3) **44–181/363–0948** • 9pm-4am Sat only • transsexuals & their friends • dancing/DJ • live shows • cover charge

The Woodman 119–121 High St (E15, Stratford) **44–181/519–8765** • pub hours • lesbians/ gay men • dancing/DJ • live shows

Erotica

Expectations 75 Great Eastern St (EC2, Shoreditch) **44–171/739–0292** • 11am-7pm, till 8pm Sat, noon-5pm Sun • leather/ rubber store • also mail order

London—South

London—South includes Southwark, Lambeth, Lewisham & Greenwich

Accommodations

Guy's 38 Baldry Gardens (SW16, Streatham) **44–181/679–7269** • gay-friendly

Manor House Hotel 53 Manor Park (SE13, Lewisham) **44–181/318–5590** • gay/ straight • rooms & apts • £28-80

Bars

Clock House 156 Clapham Park Rd (SW4, Clapham) **44–171/498–4651** • lesbians/ gay men • women only Sat at 'Snog' • neighborhood bar • gay-owned/ run

The Gloucester 1 King William Walk (btwn Greenwich Pk & Footway Tunnel, SE10, Greenwich) **44–181/293–6131** • pub hours • mostly gay men • neighborhood bar • food served • live shows • wheelchair access

Kazbar 50 Clapham High St (SW4, Clapham) **44–171/622–0070** • open till midnight • mostly gay men • transgender friendly • cafe-bar

The Little Apple 98 Kennington Ln (SE11) **44–171/735–2039** • noon-midnight, till 10:30pm Sun • lesbians/ gay men • dancing/DJ • transgender-friendly • food served • terrace • wheelchair access

The Queen's Arms 63 Courthill Rd (SE13, Lewisham) **44–181/318–7305** • noon-11pm • lesbians/ gay men • neighborhood bar • dancing/DJ Fri • upscale cabaret bar • beer garden • wheelchair access

Red Stiletto 108 Wandsworth Rd (SW8) **44–171/207–4944** • 7am-11pm, from 8am Sun • lesbians/ gay men • neighborhood bar • dancing/DJ • food served • male strippers • drag shows • terrace

The Roebuck 25 Rennell St (off Lewisham High St, SE13) **44–181/852–1705** • pub hours • lesbians/ gay men • neighborhood bar • also 'Voltz' downstairs till 2am • dancing/DJ • disco • karaoke • live shows • also restaurant

The Two Brewers 114 Clapham High St (SW4, Clapham) **44–171/622–3621, 44–171/498–4971** • lesbians/ gay men • dancing/DJ • cabaret

Nightclubs

Crash Arch 66 Goding St (SE11) **44–171/278–0995** • monthly dance party • mostly women • call for details

Diamonds at 'Jacque of Clubs,' 47 Ossory Rd (off Old Kent Rd, SE1) **44–171/252–0009** • 9pm-4am Sat only • women only • dancing/DJ

The Fridge 1 Town Hall Parade (SW2, Brixton Hill) **44–171/326–5100** • lesbians/ gay men • dancing/DJ • women only 9pm-3am Th at 'Clitorati' • cover charge

Royal Vauxhall Tavern 372 Kennington Ln (SE11, Vauxhall) **44–171/582–0833** • 9pm-1am, till 2am Fri-Sat, noon-10pm Sun • mostly gay men • women only Fri at 'Vixens' • neighborhood bar • dancing/DJ • drag shows • wheelchair access

Cafes

Surf.Net Cafe 13 Deptford Church St (at Deptford Broadway, SE8) **44–181/488–1200** • 11am-9pm, till 7pm Sat, noon-4pm Sun • cybercafe

Restaurants

Fileric 12 Queenstown Rd (SW8) **44–171/720–4844** • French

The Green Room 62 Lavender Hill (SW11, Battersea) **44-171/223-4618** • 7pm-midnight daily, lunch noon-4pm Sat only • vegetarian/ vegan • full bar • live jazz Fri

Il Pinguino 62 Brixton Rd (SW9) **44-171/735-3822** • Italian

Retail Shops

London Piercing Clinic 55 Portland Rd (SE25) **44-171/278-7654**

Gyms & Health Clubs

Paris Gymnasium Arch 73, Goding St (behind 'Vauxhall Tavern,' SE11, Vauxhall) **44-171/735-8989** • mostly gay men • daypass £6.50

Erotica

Invincible Rubber 19e Riley Rd, 2nd flr (in Tower Workshops, Southwark, SE1) **44-171/237-4017** • all rubber, all the time

PARIS

Note: M°=Métro station

Paris is divided by arrondissements (city districts); 01=1st arrondissement, 02=2nd arrondissement, etc

Paris—Overview

Note: When phoning Paris from the US, dial the country code + the city code + the local phone number

Info Lines & Services

Centre Gai et Lesbien 3 rue Keller (M°Bastille) **33-1/43.57.21.47** • drop-in 2pm-8pm, till 7pm Sun • women 8pm Fri • call for other events/ groups • also wine bar

Ecoute Gaie 33-1/44.93.01.02 • helpline staffed 7pm-11pm Mon & 6pm-10pm Tue-Fri

FACTS-line 33-1/44.93.16.69 • AIDS information in English 6pm-10pm Mon, Wed & Fri

Gay AA 33-1/43.25.75.00 (24HR INFO), 33-1/48.06.43.68 • 8:30pm Fri

Paris

Lesbigay Pride: June. 33-1/47.70.01.50 or 33-1/43.57.21.47.

Annual Events: July 13 - Bastille Ball.
December - Paris Gay & Lesbian Film Festival.

City Info: 33-1/49.52.53.54, 127 Ave. des Champs-Elysées (8e).

Attractions: Arc de Triomphe 33-1/55.37.73.77.
Cathédrale Notre Dame 33-1/42.34.56.10.
Eiffel Tower 33-1/44.11.23.23.
Louvre 33-1/40.20.53.17.
Picasso Museum 33-1/42.71.25.21.
Rodin Musuem 33-1/44.18.61.10.
Sacre-Coeur 33-1/53.41.89.00.
Sainte-Chapelle 33-1/53.73.78.50.

Best View: Eiffel Tower (of course!) and Sacre Coeur.

Weather: Paris really is beautiful in the springtime. Chilly in the winter, the temperatures reach the 70°s during the summer.

Transit: Alpha Taxis 33-/45.85.85.85.
Taxis Bleues 33-1/49.36.10.10.
Taxis-Radio Etoile 33-1/41.27.27.27.
RATP (bus and Métro) 33-1/43.46.14.14 (in French), 33-1/40.46.42.12 (in English).

La Maison des Femmes 163 rue de Charenton **33-1/43.43.42.13** • lesbian archives & library • open to public 7pm-10pm Fri • also hosts mtg of women's network 1st Tue (33-1/69.57.07.13)

Les Maudites Femelles ('Damned Females') 33-6/62.05.93.96 • SM/ fetish events for women

Accommodations

Insightful Travelers 617/859-0720 (US#) • gay-friendly • short-term apt rentals • 5-day minimum stay • daily & monthly rates

Publications

3 Keller 33-1/43.57.21.47, 33-1/43.57.75.95 • magazine of the Paris Gay/ Lesbian Center

Housewife 33-1/40.26.60.31 • monthly satirical club scene 'zine for lesbians • published by 'Pulp' nightclub • free at venues around Paris • also sell such can't-live-without items as 'Lesbian Powder' ('great for office parties!')

Têtu 33-1/43.14.71.60 • stylish & intelligent lesbigay monthly

Spiritual Groups

Beit Haverim 33-1/44.84.08.54, 33-1/40.40.00.71 • 8pm-10pm 1st & 3rd Wed • lesbigay Jewish social group

Paris—01

Accommodations

Agora 7 rue de la Cossonnerie (at rue St-Denis, M°Châtelet) **33-1/42.33.80.99** • gay-friendly hotel • 345-690FF

Castille 33 rue Cambon (at rue de Rivoli) **33-1/44.58.44.58, 800/448-8355 (US#)** • gay-friendly • ultra-luxe hotel • US$385-470

The Ritz 15 Place Vendôme (M°Tuileries) **33-1/42.60.30.30, 800/223-6800 (US#)** • gay-friendly • ultra-luxe hotel • 2,450-4,150FF

Bars

A La Datcha des Voisins 49 rue Berger (M°Châtelet) **33-1/40.28.00.00** • 5pm-5am, clsd Sun-Mon

Le Banana Café 13-15 rue de la Ferronnerie (nr rue St-Denis, in Les Halles, M°Châtelet) **33-1/42.33.35.31** • 4:30pm-5am • dancing/DJ • theme nights • Latina/o night Sun • terrace

Le Cap Horn 37 rue des Lombards (M°Châtelet) **33-1/40.28.03.08** • noon-2am • lesbians/ gay men • cafe-bar • dancing/DJ • navy decor

Le Tropic Café 66 rue des Lombards (at rue St-Martin, M°Châtelet) **33-1/40.13.92.62** • 4pm-5am • lesbians/ gay men • transgender-friendly • terrace • wheelchair access

Nightclubs

L' Espace Madeleine 11 rue Duphot **33-1/40.20.43.31** • mostly women • dancing/DJ • cover charge

Restaurants

L' Amazonial 3 rue Ste-Opportune (at rue Ferronnerie, M°Châtelet) **33-1/42.33.53.13** • noon-3pm & 7pm-1am • brunch wknds • lesbians/ gay men • Brazilian/ int'l • cabaret Th • terrace • wheelchair access • US$12-23

Au Diable des Lombards 64 rue des Lombards (at rue St-Denis, M°Châtelet) **33-1/42.33.81.84** • 8am-1am • brunch daily • American • full bar • 60-120FF

Au Petit Bonheur 9 rue St-Germain-d'Auxerrois (M°Châtelet) **33-1/42.21.17.12** • noon-2pm Tue-Fri & 7pm-1am Tue-Sun, clsd Mon • lesbians/ gay men • traditional French • 65-115FF

Au Rendez-Vous des Camionneurs 72 Quai des Orfèvres (M°Pont Neuf) **33-1/43.54.88.74** • noon-2:30pm & 7pm-11:30pm, noon-11:30pm Sun • lesbians/ gay men • traditional French bistro • 88-200FF

Chez Max 47 rue St-Honoré (M°Châtelet) **33-1/45.08.80.13** • noon-2pm & 7:30pm-midnight, dinner only Sat, clsd Sun • clsd Aug • 65-150FF

Dave 39 rue St-Roch **33-1/42.61.49.48** • 7:30pm-11pm • popular • Chinese • gay-owned

Le Gut 64 rue J-J-Rousseau (M°Châtelet) **33-1/42.36.14.90** • 8am-7pm, from noon Sat, clsd Sun • French bistro • full bar

Le Petit Goulot 20 rue de la Roule (M°Châtelet) **33-1/42.33.05.18** • 7:30pm-10:30pm

La Poule au Pot 9 rue Vauvilliers (M°Les Halles) **33-1/42.36.32.96** • 7pm-5am, clsd Mon • clsd Aug • bistro • traditional French • 160-250FF

Yvan sur Seine 26 quai du Louvre (M°Pont-Neuf) **33-1/42.36.49.52** • noon-2pm Mon-Fri & 8pm-midnight nightly, till 2am Sat • 130-170FF

Entertainment & Recreation

Les Halles • underground sports/ entertainment complex w/ museums, theatres, shops, clubs, cafes & more

Paris

It's hard not to wax poetic about Paris. The most romantic city in the world, Paris has all the characteristics of a capricious lover. Beautiful and witty, dignified and grand, flirtatious and coy—Paris's admirers will tell you she's worthy of lifelong devotion. It's not surprising, then, that so many artists and thinkers have made Paris their home. Whether it's the museums, the couture, the cafes, the history, the churches, or the people...Paris seduces at every turn.*

During the day, enjoy the incredible sights of Paris. After you've had your fill of famed landmarks, artworks, and boulevards, drop out of the tourist circuit and find out for yourself why they call it *'Gay Paree.'* Of course, for Parisians, nowhere is as *très gai* as the **Marais** district (most of the Marais's listings can be found with those in the 4th arrondissement).

To get the latest editions of Paris lesbigay magazines and to scope out the latest in one-off parties and hot club nights of the moment, drop in at the lesbigay bookstore **Les Mots à la Bouche** or **Le Kiosque des Amis.** Or pay a visit to the **Centre Gai et Lesbien** on rue Keller.

At night, Paris truly is 'The City of Lights.' Don't even dare turn in for bed until you've made the most of this city's incredible nightlife.

There is a dizzying array of women's bars and clubs in Paris. For pre-dinner cocktails, stop by **L'Unity Bar** in Les Halles; **Le Barbar** (near Place de la République); **La Champmeslé** (a 'lesbian landmark' located near the Palais Royal and the Bibliothéque Nationale); **L'Utopia** (near the Centre Pompidou); or **Les Scandaleuses,** located in the heart of the Marais. You'll also find plenty of hip urban dykes at one of the trendy, mixed cafe-bars like **L'Open Café.**

Then head for a lesbian-friendly restaurant; once again, there are choices! There are several lesbo-popular eateries in the Montparnasse/Grenelle area, including **L'Accent, Au Feu Follet,** and **L'Imprevu** (whose clientele is said to be 'exclusively *lesbienne*'). The relatively new **L'Ange Heurtebize** is the first women's restaurant in the Marais.

After dinner, groove till dawn at one of the (you guessed it!–there are several) women's nightclubs.... **Pulp** is popular and open late. If your *français* is halfway decent, pick up a copy of the club 'zine **Housewife** to find out what theme nights are coming up. (Look in cafes, bars, and clubs for the latest issue. Even if you don't speak a word of French, you'll get a kick out of the clever collages and retro ads.) **Le Magic** (near the Moulin Rouge) and **La Rive-Gauche** are open on Friday and Saturday nights only. Closer to the Louvre, you'll find *les femmes* at **L'Espace Madeleine.** Of course, there are also various one-nighters (see above) and plenty of mixed clubs (like the aptly named **Queen**).

*(Paris's streets, however, confuse if you don't understand there's a method to her madness. The city spirals out from the Louvre and Jardin des Tuileries in a string of districts called arrondissements. We've divided our listings according to arrondissements, using the following notation: 01=1st, 02=2nd, 03=3rd, etc. So, before you go, you might want to look over your maps and get a general idea of what falls in which district. Once you're there, you can get around using a combination of Métro stops and district names and numbers. *Bonne chance*–good luck!)

Gyms & Health Clubs

Gymnase Club 147b rue St-Honoré (M°Louvre) **33-1/40.20.03.03** • gay-friendly • day passes available • many locations throughout the city

Paris—02

Bars

La Champmeslé 4 rue Chabanais (at rue des Petits Champs, M°Pyramides) **33-1/42.96.85.20** • 5pm-2am, till 6am Th-Sat, clsd Sun • mostly women • live shows • theme nights

Nightclubs

Pulp 25 bd Poissonnière (M°Grands-Blvds) **33-1/40.26.01.93** • midnight-dawn, clsd Mon-Wed • popular • mostly women • dancing/DJ • theme nights • cover charge

Le Scorp 25 bd Poissonnière (M°Grands-Blvds) **33-1/40.26.01.50, 33-1/40.26.28.30** • midnight-7am • mostly gay men • dancing/DJ • shows Sun-Tue • disco Wed • cover charge Fri-Sat

Cafes

Lezard Café 32 rue Etienne-Marcel (at rue Tiquetonne, M°Etienne-Marcel) **33-1/42.33.22.73** • noon-4pm & 7pm-midnight • tarts (no, not that sort!) • 60-100FF • also bar • open 9am-2am • terrace

Restaurants

Aux Trois Petits Cochons 31 rue Tiquetonne (at rue St-Denis, M°Etienne-Marcel) **33-1/42.33.39.69** • 8:30pm-1am, clsd Mon • traditional French made w/ fresh seasonal produce • menu changes daily • 125-149FF

Le Loup Blanc 42 rue Tiquetonne (M°Etienne-Marcel) **33-1/40.13.08.35** • 7:30pm-midnight, brunch 11am-4:30pm wknds • popular • lesbians/ gay men • French • 49-116FF

Matinée-Soirée 5 rue Marie Stuart (M°Etienne-Marcel) **33-1/42.21.18.00** • noon-2:30pm & 7pm-10:30pm, clsd Sun

Le Monde à l'envers 35 rue Tiquetonne (M°Etienne-Marcel) **33-1/40.26.13.91** • noon-2pm Tue-Fri & 8:30pm-11:30pm nightly, clsd Mon • traditional French • 78-128FF

Bookstores

Le Kiosque des Amis 29 bd des Italiens (M°Opéra) **33-1/42.65.00.94** • 10am-10pm • lesbigay • French & int'l magazines

Paris—03

Accommodations

Hôtel de Saintonge 16 rue de Saintonge (off rue du Perche btwn rue Charlot & rue Vieille du Temple, M°Rambuteau) **33-1/42.77.91.13** • gay-friendly • 490-560FF

Bars

Le Duplex 25 rue Michel-le-Comte (at rue Beaubourg, M°Rambuteau) **33-1/42.72.80.86** • 8pm-2am • lesbians/ gay men • neighborhood bar • 'cyber-bar' • artist types

L' Unity Bar 176-178 rue St-Martin (nr rue Réaumur, M°Rambuteau) **33-1/42.72.70.59** • 4pm-2am • mostly women • neighborhood bar

L' Utopia 15 rue Michel-le-Comte (M°Rambuteau) **33-1/42.71.63.43** • 5pm-2am, clsd wknds • clsd 8/1-8/15 • mostly women • live shows • theme nights • piano bar Mon • men welcome when accompanied by women

Nightclubs

Les Bains 7 rue du Bourg-l'Abbé (M°Etienne-Marcel) **33-1/48.87.01.80** • 11:30pm-close, from 5pm Sun • gay-friendly • gay Sun & Mon • dancing/DJ • cover charge

La Boîte à Frisson au Tango 13 rue au Maire (M°Arts-et-Métier) **33-1/40.40.96.56** • 10:30pm-5am, from 5pm Sun • clsd Aug • lesbians/ gay men • dancing/DJ • waltz, tango • T-dance Sun

Restaurants

Les Epicuriens du Marais 19 rue Commines (M°Filles-du-Calvaire) **33-1/40.27.00.83** • noon-3pm & 7pm-midnight, till 1:30am wknds • traditional French • 69-149FF

La Madame sans gène 19 rue de Picardie (M°Filles-du-Calvaire) **33-1/42.71.31.71** • noon-2:30pm daily & 7:30pm-11:30pm Mon-Fri • clsd Aug • inexpensive traditional French • live shows • 59-115FF

Le Petit Cabanon 7 rue Ste-Apolline (M°Strasbourg) **33-1/48.87.66.53** • noon-3pm daily & 7pm-midnight Th-Sat, clsd Sun • clsd Aug • lesbians/ gay men • gourmet French • reservations suggested • 130-150FF

Le Valet de Carreau 2 rue du Petit Thouars (M°Temple) **33-1/42.72.72.60** • clsd Sun

Entertainment & Recreation

Musée Picasso 5 rue de Thorigny (in the Hôtel Salé, M°St-Paul) **33-1/42.71.25.21** • 9:30am-6pm, clsd Tue

Erotica

Rexx 42 rue de Poitou (at rue Charlot, M°St-Sébastien-Froissard) **33–1/42.77.58.57** • clsd Sun • new, custom & secondhand leather & S/M accessories

Paris—04

Accommodations

Hôtel Beaubourg 11 rue Simon Lefranc (btwn rue Beaubourg & rue du Temple, M°Hôtel-de-Ville) **33–1/42.74.34.24** • gay-friendly • 630-860FF

Hôtel de la Bretonnerie 22 rue Ste-Croix-de-la-Bretonnerie (M°Hôtel-de-Ville) **33–1/48.87.77.63** • gay-friendly • clsd Aug • 17th-century hotel w/ Louis XIII decor • US$125-155

Hôtel Place des Vosges 12 rue de Birague (nr Place des Vosges) **33–1/42.72.60.46** • gay-friendly • small historic hotel • some shared baths • US$60-98

Hôtel Saint-Louis Marais 1 rue Charles V (at rue du Petit Musc) **33–1/48.87.87.04** • gay-friendly • small hotel • US$120-140

Libertel Grand Turenne 6 rue de Turenne (at rue St-Antoine, M°St-Paul) **33–1/42.78.43.25, 800/949–7562 (US#)** • gay-friendly • 872-938FF

Bars

AccesSoir Café 41 rue des Blancs-Manteaux (M°Rambuteau) **33–1/42.72.12.89** • 6pm-2am • lesbians/ gay men • theme nights • food served • 59FF

Le Bar du Palmier 16 rue des Lombards (at bd de Sébastopol, M°Châtelet) **33–1/42.78.53.53** • 5pm-5am • lesbians/ gay men • food served • terrace

Le Mixer Bar 23 rue Ste-Croix-de-la-Bretonnerie (at rue des Archives, M°Hôtel-de-Ville) **33–1/48.87.55.44** • 4pm-2am • lesbians/ gay men • dancing/DJ • techno/ house • younger crowd

Monkey's Cafe 30 rue du Roi-de-Sicile (M°St-Paul) **33–1/42.74.45.00** • noon-2am • lesbians/ gay men • food served • Italian

Okawa 40 rue Vieille du Temple (at rue Ste-Croix-de-la-Bretonnerie, M°Hôtel-de-Ville) **33–1/48.04.30.69** • 9am-2am • gay/ straight • in 12th/ 13th century caves • theme nights • cabaret Sun, Tue & Th • piano bar Wed • food served from 7pm • 55-130FF

L' Open Café 17 rue des Archives (at rue Ste-Croix-de-la-Bretonnerie, M°Hôtel-de-Ville) **33–1/42.72.26.18** • 11am-2am, Sun brunch • popular • lesbians/ gay men • food served • sidewalk cafe • 40FF

Le Piano Zinc 49 rue des Blancs Manteaux (at rue du Temple, M°Hôtel-de-Ville) **33–1/40.27.97.42** • 6pm-2am, clsd Mon • popular • lesbians/ gay men • cabaret & piano bar • smokefree

Les Scandaleuses 8 rue des Ecouffes (btwn rue de Rivoli & rue des Rosiers, M°St-Paul) **33–1/48.87.39.26** • 6pm-2am • mostly women • live shows • videos

Le Skeud Bar 35 rue Ste-Croix-de-la-Bretonnerie (at rue du Temple, M°Hôtel-de-Ville) **33–1/40.29.44.40** • 12:30pm-2am • popular • gay/ straight • neighborhood bar • live DJ

Cafes

Amnesia Café 42 rue Vieille du Temple (at rue des Blancs-Manteaux, M°Hôtel-de-Ville) **33–1/42.72.02.59** • 10am-2am • popular • gay/ straight • also bar

Café Beaubourg 100 rue St-Martin (M°Rambuteau) **33–1/48.87.63.96** • next to Centre Pompidou • also bar

Le Coffe-Shop 3 rue Ste-Croix-de-la-Bretonnerie (at rue Vieille du Temple, M°Hôtel-de-Ville) **33–1/42.74.24.21** • noon-2am • lesbians/ gay men • full bar

Restaurants

L' Ange Heurtebize **33–1/42.72.40.10** • 7pm-close • mostly women

L' Auberge de la Reine Blanche 30 rue St-Louis-en-l'Ile (nr Rue des 2 Ponts, M°Pont-Marie) **33–1/46.33.07.87** • noon-midnight, from 6pm Th, clsd Wed • lesbians/ gay men • homestyle French • 89-250FF

Le Bucheron 9 rue du Roi-de-Sicile (M°St-Paul) **33–1/48.87.71.31** • noon-3:30pm daily & 6:30pm-11pm Mon-Sat • gay/ straight • Italian • also bar • 7:30am-1am, till 8pm Sun

La Canaille 4 rue Crillon (M°Quai-de-la-Rapée) **33–1/42.78.09.71** • 11:45am-2:15pm Mon-Fri & 7:30pm-midnight nightly • French • full bar • 61-150FF

Le Chant des Voyelles 4 rue des Lombards (M°Châtelet) **33–1/42.77.77.07** • 11:30am-3pm & 6:30pm-midnight • traditional French • terrace • 68-120FF

Chez Tsou 16 rue des Archives (at rue de la Verrerie) **33–1/42.78.11.47** • Chinese

Le Croc' Man 6 rue Geoffroy l'Angevin (M°Rambuteau) **33–1/42.77.60.02** • noon-11pm, from 7pm wknds, clsd Tue • 69-120FF

Le Divin 41 rue Ste-Croix-de-la-Bretonnerie (at rue du Temple, M°Hôtel-de-Ville) **33–1/42.77.10.20** • noon-2pm Tue-Fri & 7:30pm-11:30pm nightly, clsd Mon • clsd 8/1-8/15 • lesbians/ gay men • traditional & Provençal cuisine • wheelchair access • 89-170FF

L' Eglantine 9 rue de la Verrerie (M°Hôtel-de-Ville) **33–1/48.04.75.58** • 11:30am-2pm Mon-Sat & 7:30pm-11pm nightly, clsd Mon • French • 73-200FF

Equinox 33–35 rue des Rosiers (M°St-Paul) **33–1/42.71.92.41** • 11:30am-3:30pm & 7pm-midnight, clsd Mon • Québeçois/ French • full bar • 69-170FF

Le Flyer 94 rue St-Martin (M°Hôtel-de-Ville) **33–1/48.04.78.75** • lunch Mon-Fri & dinner nightly

Fond de Cour 3 rue Ste-Croix-de-la-Bretonnerie (at rue Vieille du Temple, M°Hôtel-de-Ville) **33–1/42.74.71.52** • 12:30pm-2:30pm Tue-Fri & 7:30pm-11:30pm nightly, brunch 12:30pm-4:30pm Sun • gourmet French • terrace • wheelchair access • 160-210FF

Le Gai Moulin 4 rue St-Merri (at rue du Temple, M°Hôtel-de-Ville) **33–1/48.87.47.59** • noon-midnight • lesbians/ gay men • French/ int'l • 59-100FF

Le Krokodil 20 rue La Reynie (at bd Sébastopol, M°Châtelet) **33–1/48.87.55.67** • 7pm-2am • popular • mostly gay men • traditional French • live shows Mon-Wed • male strippers Fri-Sat • 85-200FF

O'2F 4 rue du Roi-de-Sicile (M°St-Paul) **33–1/42.72.75.75** • 7:30pm-12:30am, clsd Mon • gay/ straight • homestyle French • live entertainment • 78-128FF

Le Pavé 7 rue des Lombards (at rue St-Martin) **33–1/44.54.07.20** • mostly gay men • seasonal specials • outdoor dining • prix-fixe menu

Le Petit Picard 42 rue Ste-Croix-de-la-Bretonnerie (M°Hôtel-de-Ville) **33–1/42.78.54.03** • noon-1:45pm Tue-Fri & 7:30pm-11pm nightly, clsd Mon • lesbians/ gay men • 64-200FF

Piano dans la Cuisine 20 rue de la Verrerie (M°Hôtel-de-Ville) **33–1/42.72.23.81** • 8pm-midnight, clsd Mon

Les Piétons 8 rue des Lombards (M°Châtelet) **33–1/48.87.82.87** • 11am-2am, brunch noon-6pm Sun • gay/ straight • tapas • 45-100FF • also bar • dancing/DJ from 8pm Wed

Plateau 26 26 rue des Lombards (M°Châtelet) **33–1/48.87.10.75** • 7pm-2am • karaoke from 11:30pm Sat

Le Rude 23 rue du Temple (at rue Ste-Croix-de-la-Bretonnerie) **33–1/42.74.05.15** • noon-12:30am • mostly gay men • French/ American • 79-160FF

Bookstores

Les Mots à la Bouche 6 rue Ste-Croix-de-la-Bretonnerie (nr rue du Vieille du Temple, M°Hôtel-de-Ville) **33–1/42.78.88.30** • 11am-11pm, 2pm-8pm Sun • lesbigay • English titles

Gyms & Health Clubs

Les Bains du Marais 31–33 rue des Blancs Manteaux **33–1/44.61.02.02** • day spa • call for women's days

Erotica

Phylea 61 rue Quincampoix (M°Rambuteau) **33–1/42.76.01.80** • 11am-8pm, clsd Sun • vinyl, rubber, corsets, S/M accessories • original creations

Paris—05

Accommodations

Hotel des Nations 54 rue Monge (at rue des Écoles, M°Pl-Monge) **33–1/43.26.45.24** • gay-friendly • small independent hotel in the Latin Quarter • pets ok • 490-650FF (US$79-104) • ask about discounts for Damron readers

La Vie en Rose Bateau Jolia, Face Au 11 Quai St-Bernard (nr Pont de la Tournelle) **33–1/43.54.03.46, 888/866–4730 (US#)** • gay-friendly • luxury vessel on the Seine • full brkfst • deck w/ garden

Restaurants

Restaurant le Petit Prince de Paris 12 rue de Lanneau (M°Maubert-Mutualité) **33–1/43.54.77.26** • 7:30pm-midnight • popular • French • 82-118FF

Entertainment & Recreation

Open-Air Sculpture Museum **33–1/42.71.25.21** • along the Seine btwn the Jardin des Plantes & the Institut du Monde Arabe

Bookstores

Les Amazones 4 rue des Grands Degrés **33–1/46.34.25.67** • specializes in antique, lesbian & feminist books

Paris—06

Accommodations

Du Vieux Paris 9 rue Gîte-le-Coeur **33-1/44.32.15.90** • gay friendly • historic bldg • in-room minibar

L' Hôtel 13 rue des Beaux-Arts (btwn rue Bonaparte & rue de Seine, M°St-Germain-des-Près) **33-1/44.41.99.00** • gay-friendly • eccentric hotel where Oscar Wilde died • US$190-560

Nightclubs

La Rive-Gauche 9 rue du Sabot (M°St-Sulpice) **33-1/42.22.51.70** • 11:30pm-close Fri-Sat only • mostly women • dancing/DJ

Bookstores

La Librairie des Femmes 74 rue de Seine **33-1/43.29.50.75** • 11am-7pm, clsd Sun • women's

The Village Voice 6 rue Princesse (M°Mabillon) **33-1/46.33.36.47** • 10am-8pm, from 2pm Sun-Mon, till 7pm Sun • English-language bookshop

Paris—07

Accommodations

Hôtel Muguet 11 rue Chevert (at av de Tourville, nr the Eiffel Tower) **33-1/47.05.05.93** • gay-friendly • recently renovated • US$92-102

Paris—08

Accommodations

Crillon 10 place de la Concorde **33-1/44.71.15.00, 800/888-4747 (US#)** • gay-friendly • ultra-luxe hotel • restaurant • US$510-820

Bars

Le Day Off 10 rue de l'Isly (M°Gare-St-Lazare) **33-1/45.22.87.90** • 4pm-4am • gay/ straight • neighborhood bar • food served noon-3pm Mon-Fri • 74-128FF

Nightclubs

Queen 102 av des Champs-Élysées (btwn rue Washington & rue de Berri, M°Georges-V) **33-1/43.43.28.48, 33-1/42.89.31.32** • popular • midnight-7am, till 8am wknds • mostly gay men • dancing/DJ • live shows • theme nights • disco Mon • '80s Sun

Restaurants

Le Petit Yvan 1 bis, rue Jean-Mermoz (M°F-D-Roosevelt) **33-1/42.89.49.65** • noon-2pm Mon-Fri & 8pm-midnight Mon-Sat, clsd Sun • traditional French • 148-200FF

Le Singe d'eau 28 rue de Moscou (M°Rome) **33-1/43.87.72.73** • lunch & dinner, clsd Sun • clsd Aug • Tibetan • 65-100FF

Xavier 89 bd de Courcelles **33-1/43.80.78.22** • lesbians/ gay men • light fare

Paris—09

Accommodations

The Grand 2 rue Scribe **33-1/40.07.32.32, 800/327-0200 (US#)** • gay-friendly • ultra-luxe Art Deco hotel • restaurant • US$340-500

Nightclubs

Folies Pigalle 11 pl Pigalle (M°Pigalle) **33-1/42.80.12.03 (INFO LINE), 33-1/48.78.25.56** • after-hours party 6am-noon Sat • 'Black, Blanc, Beur' T-dance 5:30pm-11:30pm Sun • gay/ straight • dancing/DJ • multi-racial clientele • cover charge

Le Magic 98 blvd de Clichy **33-1/40.26.01.93** • Fri-Sat only • mostly women • dancing/DJ • cover charge

Restaurants

Les Colonnes de Madeleine 6 rue de Sèze (M°Madeleine) **33-1/47.42.60.55** • noon-3pm & 7pm-midnight, clsd Sun • French bistro • also bar • 7pm-4am

Gilles et Gabriel 24 rue Rodier (M°Cadet) **33-1/45.26.86.26** • 11:30am-2:30pm & 7pm-10:30pm, clsd Sun

Paris—10

Accommodations

Hôtel Moderne du Temple 3 rue d'Aix **33-1/42.08.09.04** • gay/ straight • economy-class hotel in the middle of Paris • gay-owned/ run • 90-270FF

Louxor 4 rue Taylor (at bd St-Martin, M°République) **33-1/42.08.23.91** • gay-friendly • clsd Feb

Bars

Le Coming-Out 20 rue Beaurepaire (M°République) **33-1/42.01.01.77** • 5pm-2am • lesbians/ gay men • neighborhood bar • terrace

Restaurants

Le Châlet Maya 5 rue des Petits Hôtels (M°Gare de l'Est) **33-1/47.70.52.78** • noon-2pm & 7pm-midnight, clsd Sun

L' Insensé 10 rue Marie-et-Louise (M°Goncourt) **33-1/42.01.25.26** • noon-2:30pm & 8pm-11pm, till midnight Fri-Sat, clsd Sun • homestyle French • 59-95FF

Paris—11

Accommodations

Hôtel Beaumarchais 3 rue Oberkampf (btwn bd Beaumarchais & bd Voltaire, M°Filles-du-Calvaire) **33-1/53.36.86.86** • gay-friendly • beautiful hotel • 350-700FF

Hôtel Les Iris 80 rue de la Folie Regnault **33-1/43.57.73.30** • gay-friendly

Libertel Croix-de-Malté 5 rue de Malté (M°Oberkampf) **33-1/48.05.09.36, 800/949-7562 (US#)** • gay-friendly • 544-610FF

Bars

L' Arambar 7 rue de la Folie-Méricourt (M°St-Ambroise) **33-1/48.05.57.79** • noon-2am • lesbians/ gay men • neighborhood bar • art exhibits • theme nights

Le Barbar 9 rue de Crussol **33-6/60.96.80.23 (INFOLINE)** • 4pm-2am Sun only • women only

Interface 34 rue Keller (M°Bastille) **33-1/47.00.67.15** • 3pm-2am • lesbians/ gay men

Le K 20 rue Keller (M°Bastille) **33-1/53.36.03.96** • 5pm-2am, clsd Mon • lesbians/ gay men • also restaurant • Provençal • 100FF

Nightclubs

Le Gibus Club 18 rue du Faubourg-du-Temple (M°République) **33-1/47.00.78.88** • midnight-close, clsd Mon-Tue • gay-friendly • gay Th & Sat • dancing/DJ • cover charge

Restaurants

Terranova 45 rue de Montreuil (M°Faidherbe-Chaligny) **33-1/43.67.82.83** • noon-2:30pm Mon-Fri & 7pm-11pm nightly, clsd Sun • clsd Aug • Italian • pizza • 92-120FF

Bookstores

Le Funambule 48 rue Jean-Pierre Timbaud (M°Parmentier) **33-1/48.06.74.94** • 4pm-8pm Wed-Sat & by appt • fine art/ photography books • lesbigay section

Livralire 145 rue de Charonne **33-1/43.73.33.22** • 11am-8pm, clsd Sun-Mon • lesbigay section

Retail Shops

Tribal Act 161 rue Amelot (M°République) **33-1/43.38.85.11** • 2pm-8pm, clsd Sun • piercing • tattoos • branding • scarification

Erotica

Démonia 10 cité Joly (M°Pere-Lachaise) **33-1/43.57.09.93** • 11am-7pm • BDSM shop

Paris—12

Accommodations

Le Saint-Hubert 27 rue Traversière (M°Gare de Lyon) **33-1/43.43.39.16** • gay-friendly • 290-335FF

Restaurants

Bella Tavola 161 ave Daumesnil (M°Daumesnil) **33-1/44.74.07.06** • 11:30am-11:30pm

Caviar & Co 5 rue de Reuilly (M°Faidherbe-Chaligny) **33-1/43.56.13.98** • noon-2pm Tue-Fri & 7:30pm-midnight nightly, clsd Sun-Mon • clsd Aug • lesbians/ gay men • foies gras & caviar • 79-129FF

Spiritual Groups

David & Jonathan 92 bis, rue de Picpus **33-1/43.42.09.49** • 6:30pm-8:30pm Fri • interdenominational lesbigay Christian group

Paris—13

Entertainment & Recreation

Bibliotheque Marguerite Durand 79 rue Nationale **33-1/45.70.80.30** • 2pm-6pm, clsd Sun-Mon • unique collection of books by & about women

Paris—14

Accommodations

Le 55 Guest House 55 av Reille (M°Porte d'Orléans) **33-1/45.89.91.82** • gay/ straight • gay-owned/ run • 900-1200FF

Restaurants

Au Feu Follet 5 rue Raymond Losserand (M°Gaîté) **33-1/43.22.65.72** • 7:30pm-11:30pm, clsd Sun • mostly women • 95-150FF

La Roue du Château 36 rue Raymond Losserand (M°Gaîté) **33-1/43.20.09.59** • noon-2pm Tue-Sat & 7:30pm-10pm nightly, clsd Sun • lesbians/ gay men • French • 86-200FF

La Route du Château 36 rue Raymond Losserand (M°Gaîté) **33-1/43.20.09.59** • noon-2pm & 7pm-11pm, clsd Sun

Entertainment & Recreation

Catacombes 1 Pl Denfert Rochereau **33-1/43.22.47.63** • a ghoulish yet intriguing tourist destination, these burial tunnels were the headquarters of the Résistance during World War II

Paris—15

Bars

L' Hémis 21 rue Mademoiselle (M°Commerce) **33-1/48.56.80.32** • 9am-3pm & 6pm-midnight, clsd Sun-Mon

Restaurants

L' Accent 93 rue de Javel (M°Charles-Michel) **33-1/45.79.20.26** • 8pm-12:30am, clsd Sun • mostly women • pizzeria • 60-130FF

Le Boudoir 22 rue Frémicourt (M°La-Motte-Piquet) **33-1/40.59.82.28** • noon-2:30pm Tue-Fri & 5:30pm-1am, clsd Mon • lesbians/ gay men • French • 70-120FF • also bar • 5:30pm-1am

L' Imprevu 7 rue de Cadix **33-1/40.45.09.81** • 11:30am-3pm & 6pm-2am • lesbians • good fondue • also bar • woman-owned/ run

Paris—18

Bars

Michou 80 rue des Martyrs **33-1/46.06.16.04** • gay-friendly • drag shows • comedy

Restaurants

Le Poulailler de la Butte 18 rue Bachelet **33-1/46.06.01.99** • mostly women • egg & chicken specialties

Paris—20

Entertainment & Recreation

Père Lachaise Cemetery bd de Ménilmontant • perhaps the world's most famous resting place, where lie such notables as Chopin, Gertrude Stein, Oscar Wilde, Sarah Bernhardt, Isadora Duncan & Jim Morrison

Germany

Berlin

Berlin is divided into 5 regions:
Berlin—Overview
Berlin—Kreuzberg
Berlin—Prenzlauer Berg-Mitte
Berlin—Schöneberg-Tiergarten
Berlin—Outer

Berlin—Overview

Info Lines & Services

AHA Lesbian/ Gay Center Mehringdamm 61 (in Kreuzberg, U-Mehringdamm) **49-30/692.36.48, 49-30/692.36.00** • community center, houses the Gay & Lesbian Archives

Club Rosa **49-30/693.66.66** • call girl service for lesbians

Compania Anklamer Str 18 (in Mitte) **49-30/44.35.87.04** • services & tours for lesbians • no sex

Enjoy B&B Motzstr 5 (at M-O-M) **49-30/215.16.66** • accommodation referral service • DM30-70

Gay AA for English Speakers at M-O-M **49-30/216.80.08**

Mann-O-Meter Motzstr 5 (at Nollendorfplatz) **49-30/216.80.08** • open 5pm-10pm, from 4pm wknds • community center hosting a variety of groups & events • also cafe • also B&B referral service

Movin' Queer Berlin Liegnitzer Str 5 (U-Görlitzen Bahnhof) **49-30/618.69.55** • information & concierge services for lesbigay visitors

Nightclubs

MegaDyke Productions • popular parties & events for lesbians, including monthly 'Ms TitaniCa' party, monthly 'Chit Chat Club' party & twice-yearly 'MegaLesben Party' • check out website or local publications for more details

Entertainment & Recreation

English Movie Night at Kurbel Theater, Giesebrechstr 4 (in Charlottenberg, U-Adenauer Platz) **49-30/883.53.25 (THEATER #)** • that's (mainstream) movies in English, not British cinema...meet 7pm 1st Tue at 'Juleps' cafe next door to the theater; films begin around 8pm

Gay Movie Night Babylon Theater, Rosa-Luxemburg-Str 30 (in Mitte) • 9pm last Fri • gay-themed films • call Mann-O-Meter for more info

Schwules (Gay) Museum Mehringdamm 61 (at Gneisenaustr, U-Mehringdamm) **49-30/693.11.72** • 2pm-6pm, clsd Mon-Tue • exhibits, archives & library

Publications

BlattGold **49-30/215.66.28, 49-30/786.85.47** • monthly entertainment guide for women (in German)

Siegessäule **49-30/23.55.39.32, 49-30/23.55.39.31** • free monthly lesbigay city magazine (in German)

Spiritual Groups

Yachad—Lesbigay Jewish Association **49-30/216.80.08** • contact Mann-O-Meter for more info

Berlin

In the past century, Berlin has seen just about everything: the outrageous art and cabaret of the Weimar era; the ravages of world war; ideological standoffs that physically divided families, lovers, and the city itself; and a largely peaceful revolution that brought Germany and the world together. Through it all, the Berliners have retained their own brand of cheeky humor—*Berliner Schnauze*, it's called—and a fierce loyalty to their city. While Berlin's museums and monuments are world-class, the city's real charm is in its cafes and counter-cultural milieu.

You may find the women's scene in Berlin more political than in other places, but as a result you'll find a lot of support for women's culture and arts here, too. Berlin has two major women's community/social centers: The **Schoko-Cafe** in Kreuzberg is a community center with a bar, cafe, and steam bath! And **Begine,** located in Schöneberg, is a women's cafe, bar, and cultural center.

After stopping in at one of the women's centers, grab a bite to eat at **Café Berio** or **Futuro.** If you're a girl who just wants to have fun, visit **Fishbelly** for women's erotic toys and fashions.

Later, check out one of the women's bars—**Pour Elle** or **Whistle Stop**—or shake your booty at women-only **K.O.B. SO 36** is a popular mixed club that hosts a monthly 'Jane Bond' party. There are also a number of women's nights at the boy's bars. Pick up a copy of the local newsmagazine **Siegessäule** or the women's entertainment mag **BlattGold** (both in German) for the latest hot spots. Or give **MegaDyke Productions** a call—these women organize not-to-be-missed monthly parties and other events.

After your night of dancing, wind down in Kreuzberg at **Roses,** a popular late-night spot.

If the club scene is not your scene, you might enjoy spending some time at **Cafe Seidenfaden** (in Mitte)—a chem- and alcohol-free women's cafe.

Berlin—Kreuzberg

Accommodations

Transit Hagelberger Str 53–54 (U-Mehringdamm) **49–30/789.04.70** • gay-friendly • also bar • DM35-105

Bars

Bierhimmel Oranienstr 183 (U-Kottbusser Tor) **49–30/615.31.22** • 2pm-3am • gay/ straight

Café Anal Muskauer Str 15 (at Mannteufel Str, U-Görlitzer Bahnhof) **49–30/618.70.64** • 8pm-close, from 6pm summer • popular wknds • lesbians/ gay men • women only Mon • leather • transgender-friendly • live shows • terrace • wheelchair access

Excel Warschauer Platz 18 (in Friedrichshain, S/U-Warschauer Str) **49–30/29.49.18.15** • 3pm-3am, from 10am Sun • lesbians/ gay men • cafe-bar • dancing/DJ from 9:30pm Wed & Fri-Sun • live shows • Internet access

O-Bar Oranienstr 168 (at Kottbusser Tor) **49–30/615.28.09** • 8pm-3am • lesbians/ gay men • dancing/DJ • live music

Roses Oranienstr 187 (at Kottbusser Tor) **49–30/615.65.70** • 9:30pm-5am • popular • lesbians/ gay men • transgender-friendly

Nightclubs

BKA Cabaret Mehringdamm 32–34 (at Gneisenaustr, U-Mehringdamm) **49–30/251.01.12** • gay/ straight • shows 8pm Wed-Sun • dancing/DJ from 11pm Fri-Sat • wheelchair access • cover charge

Berlin

Entertainment: Schwules Museum (Gay Museum), 49-30/881-1590, at AHA Center.

Lesbigay Pride: Last Sunday in June. 49-30/21.68.08 (M-O-M).

Annual Events: January - Tuntenball. Drag ball.
June - Leather Party Barbecue.
July - Love Parade. Berlin's queer Mardi Gras.
October - Lesbian Week.
November - Berlin Gay & Lesbian Film Festival.

City Info: Europa Center 49-30/626.031, Budapester Str 2.
Berlin Hotline 49-30/250.025.

Attractions: Bauhaus Design Museum 49-30/254.00.20.
Brandenburg Gate.
Charlottenburg Palace 49-30/32.09.11.
Egyptian Museum 49-30/20.90.55.55.
Homo Memorial (at Nollendorfplatz station).
Kaiser Wilhelm Memorial Church.
Museuminsel (Museum Island).
New National Gallery 49-30/20.90.55.55.
Reichstag.

Weather: Berlin is on the same parallel as Newfoundland, so if you're visiting in the winter, prepare for snow and bitter cold. Summer is balmy while spring and fall are beautiful, if sometimes rainy.

Transit: Würfelfunk Berlin 49-30/21.01.01.
Express-Bus X9 from Tegel Airport to central Berlin.
U-Bahn (subway) 49-30/194.49.
S-Bahn (elevated train).
Bus 49-30/301.80.28.

SO 36 Oranienstr 190 (at Kottbusser Tor) **49-30/61.40.13.06** • popular • lesbians/ gay men • dancing/DJ • transgender-friendly • live shows • videos • wheelchair access • 'Café Fatal' 7pm-1am Sun • 'Electric Ballroom' 11pm-close Mon • 'Hungrige Herzen' 10pm-close Wed • 'Jane Bond' party ("for women, lesbians & drag queens") 10pm 3rd Fri • 'Gayhane' 11pm 4th Sat

Terminal Columbiadamm 6 (in Tempelhof Airport, U-Platz der Luftbrücke) **49-30/69.04.13.67, 49-30/69.04.13.29** • 10:30pm-close, clsd Mon, Tue & Th • lesbians/ gay men • dancing/DJ • cafe-bar

Cafes

Café Sundström Mehringdamm 61 (at Gneisenaustr, U-Mehringdamm) **49-30/692.44.14** • noon-midnight, 24hrs wknds • lesbians/ gay men • terrace • wheelchair access • also lesbigay bookstore

Futuro Adalbertstr 79 (U-Köttbusser Tor) **49-30/615.28.23** • 6pm-1am • mostly women • woman-owned/ run

Schoko-Café Mariannenstr 6 (at Kottbusser Tor) **49-30/615.15.61, 49-30/694.10.77** • 1pm-midnight, clsd Mon • women only • community center • also cafe & bar • dancing/DJ • live music • also 'Hamam' steam bath

Restaurants

Abendmahl Muskauer Str 9 (U-Görlitzer Bahnhof) **49-30/612.51.70** • 6pm-11:30pm • vegetarian & seafood • also bar (open till 1am) • terrace • wheelchair access

Bookstores

Chronika Buchhandlung Kreuzberg Bergmannstr 26 (at Marheinekeplatz) **49-30/693.42.69** • many lesbian titles

Berlin—Prenzlauer Berg-Mitte

Info Lines & Services

Spinnboden Lesbian Archive Anklamer Str 18 (in Mitte) **49-30/448.58.48**

Accommodations

Schall & Rauch Pension Gleimstr 23 (at Schönhauser Allee) **49-30/443.39.70** • lesbians/ gay men • also bar & restaurant

Bars

Amsterdam Gleimstr 24 (at Schönhauser Allee) **49-30/448.07.92, 49-30/231.67.96** • 5pm-close, from 3pm Sun • gay/ straight • transgender-friendly • also restaurant • terrace • wheelchair access

Café Senefelder Schönhauser Allee 173 (at Senefelder Platz) **49-30/449.66.05** • 7pm-3am, 8pm-5am Fri-Sat • lesbians/ gay men • dancing/DJ Fri-Sat • food served

Flax Chodwieckistr 41 (off Greifswalder Str) **49-30/44.04.69.88** • 5pm-3am, from 3pm Sat, from 10am Sun • lesbians/ gay men • also restaurant • Sun brunch

Image Jägerstr 67 (U-Französische Str) **49-30/20.45.25.80** • 9am-close, from 2pm Sat, from 11am Sun • lesbians/ gay men • cafe-bar • all-you-can-eat brunch buffet till 4:30pm Sun • terrace • wheelchair access

Na Und Prenzlauer Allee 193 (at Dimitroffstr, S-Prenzlauer Allee) **49-30/442.89.48** • 24hrs • gay/ straight • neighborhood bar • food served • terrace

Oh-Ase Rathausstr 5 (at Alexanderplatz) **49-30/242.30.30** • 10am-2am, from 2pm Sun • mostly gay men • food served • terrace • tropical theme

Romeo Greifenhagener Str 16 (S/U-Schönhauser Allee) **49-30/447.67.89** • 11pm-8am • gay-friendly • cafe-bar

Shambala Greifenhagener Str 12 (S/U-Schönhauser Allee) **49-30/447.62.26** • 6pm-3am • gay/ straight • neighborhood cafe-bar • women only from 9pm Mon

Sonderbar Käthe-Niederkirchner-Str 34 (nr "Märchenbrunnen") **49-30/425.84.94** • 8pm-8am • lesbians/ gay men • food served • terrace • also art gallery

Stiller Don Erich-Weinert-Str 67 (at Schönhauser Allee) **49-30/445.59.57** • 7pm-close • popular • lesbians/ gay men • neighborhood bar • leather • food served

Whistle Stop Knaackstr 94 (at Uhlandstr, U-Eberswalder Str) **49-30/442.78.47** • 6pm-close, clsd Sun-Mon • mostly women • food served • live music • terrace

Nightclubs

Ackerkeller Ackerstr 12 (Hinterhaus, enter at Ackerstr 13, U-Rosenthaler Platz) **49-30/280.72.16** • 9pm-2am Tue & 10pm-4am Fri, also 3rd Sat party • popular • mostly gay men • dancing/DJ

GMF Johannistr 19-21 (opposite Kalkscheune, S/U-Friedrichstr) **49-30/215.23.83, 49-30/21.47.41.00** • 9pm-3am Sun • popular • mostly gay men • dancing/DJ • transgender-friendly • live shows • terrace • gay-owned/ run • cover charge

Cafes

Cafe Seidenfaden Dircksenstr 47 (U-Alexanderplatz) **49-30/283.27.83** • 11am-11pm, noon-7pm Sat, 10am-9pm Sun, clsd Mon • women only • drug- and alcohol-free cafe

Kapelle Zionskirchplatz 22-24 (U-Rosenthaler Platz) **49-30/449.22.62** • 9am-3am, open later wknds • also cocktail bar from 8pm • gay/ straight

Restaurants

Schall & Rauch Wirtshaus Gleimstr 23 (at Schönhauser Allee) **49-30/443.39.70, 49-30/448.07.70** • 10am-close • lesbians/ gay men

Thüringer Stuben Stargarder Str 28 (at Dunckerstr, S/U-Schönhauser Allee) **49-30/446.33.39** • 4pm-1am, from noon wknds • full bar

Erotica

Black Style Seelower Str 5 (S/U-Schönhauser Allee) **49-30/44.68.85.95** • 1pm-6:30pm, till 8pm Th, 10am-2pm Sat, clsd Sun • latex & rubber wear • also mail order

Berlin—Schöneberg-Tiergarten

Accommodations

Arco Hotel Geisbergstr 30 (at Ansbacherstr, U-Wittenbergplatz) **49-30/235.14.80** • gay-friendly • centrally located • wheelchair access • gay-owned/ run • US$67-94

Connection Cityhotel Berlin Fuggerstr 33 (nr Welser Str, U-Wittenbergplatz) **49-30/217.70.28, 49-30/217.70.29** • mostly gay men • leather • wheelchair access • US$61-100 • special 'fantasy' apt for kink/SM types • US$444/ night

Hotel California Kurfürstendamm 35 (at Knesebeckstr, U-Uhlandstr) **49-30/88.01.20, 49-30/88.01.21.11** • gay-friendly • non-smoking floor • DM155-235

Hotel Sachsenhof Motzstr 7 (at Nollendorfplatz) **49-30/216.20.74** • gay/ straight • centrally located • DM57-156

Hotel-Pension Zum Schild Lietzenburger Str 62 (at Marheinekestr, S/U-Zoologischer Garten) **49-30/885.92.50** • gay/ straight • centrally located • some shared baths • DM59-98

Pension Niebuhr Niebuhrstr 74 (at Savignyplatz) **49-30/324.95.95, 49-30/324.95.96** • gay/ straight • some shared baths • US$67-94

Bars

Club Banana Fasanenstr 81-A (next to the 'Arc' restaurant) **49-30/313.37.73** • 6pm-2am • lesbians/ gay men • trendy cocktail bar

Die Espresso Bar Joachimstaler Str 24 (nr Kurfürstendamm) **49-30/881.94.88** • 24hrs • lesbians/ gay men • centrally located

Fledermaus Joachimsthaler Str 14-19 (U-Kurfürstendamm) **49-30/292.11.36** • noon-4am, till 6am Fri-Sat

Movie Kleiststr 7 (at Courbièrestr, U-Nollendorfplatz) **49-30/211.77.02** • 4pm-2am, from 2pm wknds • lesbians/ gay men • food served • wheelchair access

Pour Elle Kalckreuthstr 10 (at Nollendorfplatz) **49-30/218.75.33** • 7pm-2am, from 9pm Fri-Sat • women only • dancing/DJ • terrace • Berlin's oldest lesbian bar • men welcome as guests Mon & Wed

Pussy-Cat Kalckreuthstr 7 (at Nollendorfplatz) **49-30/213.35.86** • 6pm-6am, clsd Tue • lesbians/ gay men • dancing/DJ • transgender-friendly • live shows • food served • terrace

Vagabund Knesebeckstr 77 (at Uhlandstr) **49-30/881.15.06** • 5pm-late • mostly gay men • some dancing • professional clientele • terrace

Nightclubs

90 Grad Dennewitzstr 37 (at Kurfürstenstr) **49-30/21.47.41.00, 49-30/262.89.84** • 11pm-close Th-Sat • popular • gay-friendly • more gay Th at 'Soap' • dancing/DJ • transgender-friendly • live shows • terrace

Chez Nous Marburger Str 14 (at Tauentzienstr, U-Wittenbergplatz) **49-30/213.18.10** • gay/ straight • famous drag revue • shows 8:30pm & 11pm nightly • pricey 1-drink minimum

KOB Potsdamer Str 157 (at Wittenbergplatz) **49-30/215.20.60** • 10pm-close • women only • dancing/DJ

Kumpelnest 3000 Lützowstr 23 (at Potsdamer Str, U-Kurfürstenstr) **49-30/261.69.18** • 5pm-5am, till 8am Fri-Sat • popular wknds • dancing/DJ

Cafes

Anderes Ufer Hauptstr 157 (at Kleistpark) **49-30/78.70.38.00** • 11am-2am • popular cafe-bar • lesbians/ gay men • late-night brkfst • terrace • wheelchair access • 'oldest openly gay café in Europe'

Begine Potsdamer Str 139 (at Bülowstr) **49-30/215.43.25** • 5pm-1am, noon-midnight Sun • women only • full bar • also cultural center

The Berlin Connection Cafe & Bistro Martin-Luther-Str 19 (at Motzstr, U-Nollendorfplatz) **49-30/213.11.16** • 2pm-2am • popular • lesbians/ gay men • also bar • terrace

Café Berio Maaßenstr 7 (at Winterfeldtstr, U-Nollendorfplatz) **49-30/216.19.46** • 8am-1am • popular • serve brkfst all day • terrace • wheelchair access

Café Savigny Grolmannstr 53-54 (at Savignyplatz) **49-30/312.81.95** • 9am-1am • artsy crowd • full bar • terrace

Da Neben Motzstr 5 (next to M-O-M) **49-30/217.06.33** • 10am-1am, from noon Sat, 3pm-midnight Sun • full bar

Windows Martin-Luther-Str 22 (at Motzstr, U-Nollendorfplatz) **49-30/214.23.94** • 2pm-4am, from 11am Sun • full bar • terrace

Restaurants

Arc Fasanenstr 81-A (in S-Bahn arches, S/U-Zoologischer Garten) **49-30/313.26.25** • 11am-2am • lesbians/ gay men • int'l cuisine • wheelchair access • US$11-18 • also bar

La Kantina Kantstr 146 (at Savignyplatz) **49-30/312.31.35** • full bar

Rheingold Bistro Rheinstr 66 (at Eisenacherstr/ Nollendorfplatz) **49-30/859.23.00** • 7am-6pm, 8am-1pm Sat, clsd Sun

Erotica

Fishbelly Grunewaldstr 71-A (at Eisenacherstr, U-Bayerischer Platz) **49-30/788.30.15** • fetish fashions & toys for women

Hautnah Uhlandstr 170 (U-Spichernstr) **49-30/882.34.34** • noon-8:30pm, 10am-4:30pm Sat, clsd Sun • leather & fetish wear

Berlin—Outer

Accommodations

Albatros Hotel Rudolstädter Str 42 (in Wilmersdorf, U-Heidelberger Platz) **49-30/89.78.30** • gay-friendly • some shared baths • also apts • bar & restaurant (5:30pm-midnight) • DM99-190

Artemisia Women's Hotel Brandenburgischestr 18 (at Konstanzerstr) **49-30/873.89.05, 49-30/873.63.73** • the only hotel for women in Berlin • a real bargain • quiet rooms • bar • sundeck w/ an impressive view • some shared baths • US$94-122

Charlottenburger Hof Stuttgarter Platz 14 (at Wilmersdorfer Str) **49-30/32.90.70** • gay-friendly • centrally located • also 'Cafe Voltaire' • open 24hrs • also bar • US$67-100

Hotel Kronprinz Berlin Kronprinzendamm 1 (at Kurfürstendamm, in Halensee) **49-30/89.60.30** • gay-friendly • kids ok • DM195-380

Bars

Albrecht-Klause Albrechtstr 125 (at Rathaus Steglitz, in Steglitz) **49-30/791.56.21** • 2pm-2am, from 6pm wknds • gay/ straight

Nightclubs

Die Busche Mühlenstr 11-12 (at Kurfürstenstr, in Friedrichshain, S/U-Warschauer Str) **49-30/296.08.00** • 9:30pm-5am Wed & Sun, 10pm-6am Fri-Sat • popular • lesbians/ gay men • dancing/DJ • terrace

Lützower Lampe Witzlebenstr 38 (U-Kaiserdamm) **49-30/321.20.97** • gay/ straight • some dancing • cabaret & piano bar • drag shows • wheelchair access

Cafes

Virtuality Cafe Lewishamstr 1 (S5-Charlottenberg) **49-30/327.51.43** • cybercafe

Restaurants

Guf Nordufer 4 (at Volkspark Rehberge) **49-30/453.27.32** • 6pm-3am, food served till 12:30am, clsd Mon

Jim's Eberswalder Str 32 (at Fr-Ludwig-Jahn-Sportpark) **49-30/440.63.79** • 10am-3am, from 2pm Fri-Sun • lesbians/ gay men • also bar

Storch Wartburgstr 54 **49-30/784.20.59**

Gyms & Health Clubs

Apollo Fitness Haupstr 150 (U-Kleistpark) **49-30/784.82.03** • 10am-10pm, 1pm-6pm wknds • mostly gay men • also Borodinstr 16 location, 49-30/927.42.31 • gay-friendly

Swiss Training Alboinstr 36-42 (nr Tempelhof Airport) **49-30/754.15.91** • also Immanuelkirchstr 14 location, 44.35.83.44 • gay-friendly

Italy

Rome

Info Lines & Services

Circolo Mario Mieli Via Corinto 5 (Metro San Paolo) **39-06/541.39.85** • switchboard, mtgs & discussion groups

Coordinamento Lesbiche Italiano Via San Francesco di Sales 1/a **39-06/686.42.01** • lesbian cultural center & archives • also publish newsletter

Accommodations

Campo dei Fiore Via del Biscione 6 **39-06/6880.6865, 39-06/687.48.86** • gay-friendly • some shared baths • US$78-156

Center Hotel Via Achille Grandi 7 (Metro Manzoni) **39-06/7030.0058, 39-06/7030.0059**

Hotel Eden Via Ludovisi 49 **39-06/478.121, 800/225-5843 (US#)** • gay-friendly • restaurant & rooftop bar • US$290+

Locanda Cairoli Club House Hotel Piazza Benedetto Cairoli 2 **39-06/6880.9278** • gay-friendly • charming hotel in center of Rome

Scalinata di Spagna Piazza Trinità dei Monti 17 (Metro Piazza di Spagna) **39-06/6994.0896, 39-06/679.30.06** • gay-friendly • roof garden • US$111-250

Bars

L' Angelo Azzuro Via Cardinal Merry del Val 13 (in Trastevere, Tram 8) **39-06/580.04.72** • 11pm-late Fri-Sun only • lesbians/ gay men • women only Fri • dancing/DJ • transgender-friendly • cover charge

Frutta e Verdura Via Principe Umberto 36 (Metro Vittorio) **39-06/446.48.62** • 10pm-3am, clsd Tue • lesbians/ gay men • dancing/DJ • live shows • videos

Garbo Vicolo di Santa Margherita 1a (in Trastevere, Tram 8) **39-06/581.67.00** • 10pm-3am • gay/ straight • cocktail bar • food served

Shelter Via dei Vascellari 35 (in Trastevere, Tram 8) **39-06/588.0862** • 8pm-4am • cocktail bar • food served

Skyline Via degli Aurunci 26-28 (in San Lorenzo district, Metro Policlinico) **39-06/444.08.17** • 10pm-2am, clsd Tue • American bar • lesbians/ gay men • live shows • videos

Nightclubs

L' Alibi Via di Monte Testaccio 39-44 (Metro Piramide) **39-06/574.34.48** • 11pm-4am, clsd Mon-Tue • popular • lesbians/ gay men • dancing/DJ • roof patio in summer

Jolie Couer Via Sirte 5 **39-06/8621.5827** • 11pm-close Wed & Sat only • lesbians/ gay men • women only Sat • dancing/DJ • karaoke • videos • cover charge

Max's Bar Via Achille Grandi 7a (nr Porta Maggiore, below Hotel Grandi, Metro Manzoni) **39-06/7030.1599** • 10:30pm-late, clsd Mon • popular • mostly gay men • dancing/DJ • cover charge

Muccassassina Via del Commercio 36 (at 'Alpheus', Metro Piramide) **39-06/541.39.85** • 10:30pm-5am Fri only • popular • lesbians/ gay men • dancing/DJ • live shows • cover charge

New Superstars Vicolo de Modelli 51 (nr Trevi Fountain, Metro Barberini) **39-06/679.19.09** • 10:30pm-4am, clsd Mon • lesbians/ gay men • men only Wed • dancing/DJ • piano bar • private club w/ free membership

Restaurants

Da Nerone Via delle Terme di Tito 96 **39-06/474.52.07** • clsd Sun • full bar • US$15

Isola del Sole Lungotevere A da Brescia **39-06/320.14.00** • lunch & dinner, clsd Mon

Ristorante Asinocotto Via dei Vascellari 48 (in Travestere, Tram 8) **39-06/589.89.85** • lunch & dinner • creative Mediterranean • gay-owned

Bookstores

La Libreria Babele Via dei Banchi Vecchi 116 **39-06/687.66.28** • 10am-7:30pm, clsd Sun • lesbigay

Rinascita Via delle Botteghe Oscure 1 **39-06/679.71.36** • large lesbigay section

Erotica

La Bancarella Piazza Alessandria 2 (nr Porta Pia, Metro Repubblica) **39-06/8530.3071** • erotic comics & lesbigay magazines

Europa 92 Via Vitelleschi 38-40 (nr Piazza Risorgimento) **39-06/687.12.10** • clsd Sun • clothing • magazines • books • videos

Rome

Where the Girls Are: Discussing politics at a cafe, or dancing at one of the one-nighters that make up lesbian nightlife in Rome. Visit the Coordinamento Lesbiche Italiano center, the bulletin board at the Libreria Babele, or the Circolo Mario Mieli center for the latest events.

Lesbigay Pride: June/July. Rome hosts the first ever World Pride in 2000, web: www.europride.se.

City Info: Commune di Roma 39-6/4890.6300. Enjoy Rome 39-6/445.18.43, web: www.enjoyrome.com.

Attractions: Capitoline Museums 39-6/6710.2071. Colosseum 39-6/700.42.61. Galleria Borghese 39-6/32.81.01. National Etruscan Museum 39-6/322.65.71. Pantheon 39-6/6830.0230. Roman Forum 39-6/699.01.10. Sistine Chapel. Spanish Steps. St. Peter's. Trevi Fountain. The Vatican 39-6/6988.3333.

Weather: Late summer is hot & humid. Winter is mild but rainy. The best times to visit Rome are late spring and early fall.

Transit: Taxi stands are located in several popular piazzas. You can also call 3570 for pick-up service. ATAC 39-6/4695.4444.

NETHERLANDS

AMSTERDAM

Amsterdam is divided into 5 regions:
Amsterdam—Overview
Amsterdam—Centre
Amsterdam—Jordaan
Amsterdam—Rembrandtplein
Amsterdam—Outer

Amsterdam—Overview

INFO LINES & SERVICES

COC Amsterdam Rozenstr 14 (in the Jordaan) **31–20/626.30.87** • 1pm-6pm, clsd Sun-Tue • queer center • also cafe, theater & disco

Gay/ Lesbian Switchboard **31–20/623.65.65, 31–20/422.65.65 (TTY)** • 10am-10pm • English spoken

Homodok Nieuwportkade 2A **31–20/606.07.12** • lesbigay info center & archives • open 10am-4pm

Wild Side **31–71/512.86.32** • S/M women's group • mtgs, events & play parties

ENTERTAINMENT & RECREATION

The Anne Frank House Prinsengracht 263 (in the Jordaan) **31–20/556.71.00, 31–20/626.45.33** • the final hiding place of Amsterdam's most famous resident

Homomonument Westermarkt (in the Jordaan) • moving sculptural tribute to lesbians & gays killed by Nazis

The van Gogh Museum Paulus Potterstr 7 **31–20/570.52.00** • a must-see museum dedicated to this Dutch master painter

PUBLICATIONS

Gay News Amsterdam **31–20/679.15.56**

Gay & Night **31–20/420.42.04** • free monthly bilingual entertainment paper w/ club listings

Shark **31–20/420.6775** • bi-weekly queer-oriented alternative culture guide & calendar (in English)

SPIRITUAL GROUPS

Stichtig Dignity Nederland **31–20/679.82.07**

Amsterdam—Centre

ACCOMMODATIONS

Grand Hotel Krasnapolsky Dam 9 **31–20/554.91.11** • gay-friendly • full-service hotel • located in the city center opposite Royal Palace • business center • 5 restaurants, including 'Edo' (good Japanese)

Holiday Inn Crowne Plaza Amsterdam City Centre NZ Voorburgwal 5 **31–20/620.05.00, 800/465–4329 (US#)** • gay-friendly • swimming

Hotel Brian Singel 69 **31–20/624.46.61** • gay-friendly • bargain rooms

Hotel New York Herengracht 13 (at Brouwersgracht) **31–20/624.30.66** • lesbians/ gay men • also bar & coffeeshop • US$105-132

Tulip Inn Spuistr 288–292 **31–20/420.45.45, 800/344–1212 (US#)** • gay-friendly • US$153+

BARS

Getto Warmoesstr 51 **31–20/421.51.51** • 4pm-1am, from 7pm Tue, 1pm-midnight Sun, clsd Mon • popular • lesbians/ gay men • women only Tue • cocktail lounge • live DJs • drag-queen bingo Th • also restaurant • food served till 11pm • Sun brunch • eclectic cuisine • US$10-14

Mix Cafe Amstel 50 **31–20/622.52.02** • popular • 8pm-3am, till 4am Fri-Sat • lesbians/ gay men

Vrankrijk Spuistr 216 • gay-friendly • rowdy squat bar • alternative

RESTAURANTS

Camp Cafe Kerkstr 45 (at Leidsestr) **31–20/622.15.06** • 3pm-1am, till 3am Fri-Sat • lesbians/ gay men • cont'l • kitchen open till 11:30pm • full bar • terrace • gay-owned/ run • US$10-14

Gerard Geldersekade 23 **31–20/638.43.38** • 5:30pm-11pm, clsd Tue • French

Greenwoods Singel 103 (nr Dam Square) **31–20/623.70.71** • English-style brkfst & tea snacks

Hemelse Modder Oude Waal 9 **31–20/624.32.03** • 6pm-10pm, clsd Mon • French/ Italian • wheelchair access • US$24-30

Klaverkoning Koningsstr 29 **31–20/626.10.85** • 5:30pm-11pm, clsd Sun-Mon • organic meat & fish dishes • plenty veggie

La Strada NZ Voorburgwal 93 **31–20/625.02.76** • 4pm-1am, till 2am wknds • Mediterranean • plenty veggie • full bar • terrace • lesbian-owned/ run • US$14-17

Amsterdam

The day that Amsterdam is known as the *Lesbian* and Gay Capital of Europe, there will be a lot of 'loud and proud' women-loving-women walking around. Until then, you're really going to have to search hard to find them.

For the sad truth is that most Dutch dykes hold back more than just water. Still, we encourage you to keep the faith—not all Dutch girls are as straightlaced as they seem.

In fact, just looking back over three centuries of dyke drama, there's reason to believe it's only a matter of time before the riot grrrls take Amsterdam. Way back in 1792, the jealous, murderous Bartha Schuurman was hung from the gallows back for knifing her girlfriend's lover to death. In the 1970s, lesbian activists—in between scrawling pro-dyke graffiti—did manage to squat a few places and start some women's collectives. In fact, many of the women's establishments enjoyed today—ranging from bars to bookshops—emerged directly as a result of that era when Dutch dykes did indeed get mad and get rad.

Until the spirit of those good ol' days returns, lesbian visitors can enjoy a pleasant time—if you can stand the ubiquitous cloud of smoke—at most of the gay establishments. And one thing they definitely can share with those naughty Dutch boys is Amsterdam's largely tolerant atmosphere that allows same-sex couples to walk the quaint canals and winding streets hand-in-hand.

While you're out and about, experience a little of Amsterdam's touted counter-culture' for yourself...stop in at one of the famous brown cafes. Or take a tour of the Heineken brewery.

To find out what queer events are going on about town, or just to take a break from sight-seeing, stop by the **COC** center/cafe. Or head over to the women's bookstore **Xantippe,** the lesbigay bookstore **Vrolijk,** or the **American Book Center,** to pick up some flyers, the local newspaper **Gay News,** and a copy of the bi-weekly entertainment guide **Shark.**

Have a meal at one of the lesbian-friendly restaurants in town. Try **La Strada, Sarah's Grannies, Walem,** or **'t Sluisje** (if you like your steak served by drag queens).

At night, hang out with the lipstick femmes and cute baby dykes at 'Amsterdam's only lesbian bar,' **Vive-la-Vie.** Later, hit the dancefloor. There is supposedly a new women's nightclub in Rembrandtplein called **You II.** It's located next door to 'Sinners in Heaven,' an otherwise straight club that hosts **Lip Lickers Club** for lesbians on the first Sunday of the month. The **RoXY** used to host a popular monthly women's party called 'Pussy Lounge.' Unfortunately, the building burned down in summer 1999, but they do plan to reopen. Don't miss the weekly women-only party at the **COC** nightclub on Saturdays.

If you're looking for a different kind of 'culture,' don't miss the incredible masterworks this city's museums have to offer. (There is even an entire museum dedicated to van Gogh.) One very Amsterdam-esque way to see them is to take the 'Museum Boat' along the canal from museum to museum. The fare entitles you to discounted admissions.

Maoz Reguliersbreestr 45 **31–20/624.92.90** • 6pm-2am • falafel

No 7 & 9 Warmoesstr 7 **31–20/624.51.73** • 8am-11pm • full bar • gay-owned

Oibibio Prins Hendrikkade 20–21 **31–20/553.93.28** • 10:30am-10pm • vegetarian • wheelchair access

Pygmalion Nieuwe Spiegelstr 5a (in Spiegelhof Arcade) **31–20/420.70.22** • 11am-10pm, till 3pm Mon, clsd Sun • South African • gay-owned/ run • US$13-19

't Sluisje Torensteeg 1 **31–20/624.08.13** • 6pm-1am, till 3am Fri-Sat, clsd Mon-Tue • popular steakhouse • lesbians/ gay men • full bar • drag shows nightly • US$13-20

Song Kwae Kloveniersburgwal 14a (nr Nieuwmarkt & Chinatown) **31–20/624.25.68** • 1pm-10:30pm • Thai • Dfl25-35

Tom Yam Staalstr 22 **31–20/622.95.33** • 6pm-10:30pm, clsd Mon • eclectic/ Thai • terrace • wheelchair access • gay-owned

Vegetarisch Eethuis Sisters Nes 12 **31–20/626.39.70** • 5pm-11:30pm • int'l vegetarian & vegan

Walem Keizersgracht 449 **31–20/625.35.44** • 10am-4:30pm & 6pm-10:30pm • int'l • inexpensive • local crowd • patio • wheelchair access • lesbian-owned

BOOKSTORES

The American Book Center Kalverstr 185, downstairs (at Heiligeweg) **31–20/625.55.37** • 10am-8pm, till 10pm Th, 11am-6pm Sun • books & magazines in English imported from US & UK • large lesbigay section • wheelchair access

Boekhandel Vrolijk Paleisstr 135 (nr Dam Sq) **31–20/623.51.42** • 10am-6pm, from 1pm Mon, till 9pm Th, till 5pm Sat, clsd Sun • lesbigay • also mail order

Amsterdam

Entertainment: MacBike (31–20/620.09.85) rents bikes & has created a self-guided tour-by-map of Amsterdam's gay points of interest.

Lesbigay Pride: August. 31–20/623.65.65.

Annual Events: April 30 - Queen's Birthday.
May 4-5 - Memorial Day & Liberation Day.
June - Holland Festival.
July - Zomerfestijn. International performing arts festival.
August - Heart's Day. Drag festival.
October - Leather Pride 31–20/422.37.37, web: www.gayplanet.nl/lpn.

City Info: VVV 900/400.40.40 or 31–6/34.03.40.66, web: www.visitholland.com. Visit their office directly opposite Centraal Station.

Attractions: Anne Frank House 31–20/556.71.00.
Homomonument.
Jewish Historical Museum 31–20/626.99.45.
Rembrandt House 31–20/624.94.86.
Rijksmuseum 31–20/673.21.21.
Royal Palace 31–20/620.40.60.
Vincent van Gogh Museum 31–20/570.52.00.

Weather: Temperatures hover around freezing in the winter and rise to the mid-60°s in the summer. Rain is possible year-round.

Transit: 31–20/677.77.77.
Can also be found at taxi stands on the main squares.
KLM Bus.
GVB 33–6/92.92 or visit their office across from the Centraal Station. Trams, buses, and subway.

Retail Shops

Conscious Dreams Warmoesstr 12 **31–20/421.78.98** • 11am-10pm • 'psychedelicatessen': smart drinks & such

Doctor Who Kerkstr 93 **31–20/427.28.29** • 11am-7pm, till 8pm Fri-Sat • 'smartshop': magic mushrooms & more

Gay Rental Videos NZ Voorburgwal 51 **31–20/622.52.20** • 1pm-1am

Magic Mushroom Spuistr 249 **31–20/427.57.65** • 11am-7pm, till 8pm Fri-Sat • 'smartshop': magic mushrooms & more

Gyms & Health Clubs

Garden Gym Jodenbreestr 158 **31–20/626.87.72** • women's health club

Erotica

DeMask Zeedijk 64 **31–20/620.56.03** • noon-6pm, clsd Sun • fetish fashion

Female & Partners Spuistr 100 **31–20/620.91.52** • fashions & toys for women

Amsterdam—Jordaan

Accommodations

Freeland Hotel Marnixstr 386 **31–20/622.75.11, 31–20/627.75.78** • gay-friendly • full brkfst

Hotel Pulitzer Prinsengracht 315–331 **31–20/523.52.35, 800/325–3535 (US#)** • gay-friendly • occupies 24 17th-century buildings on 2 of Amsterdam's most picturesque canals

Maes B&B Herenstr 26 **31–20/427.51.65** • lesbians/ gay men • smokefree • Dfl110-175

Rembrandt Residence Hotel Herengracht 255 **31–20/622.17.27** • gay/ straight • non-smoking rms available • Dfl285+

Bars

Doll's Place Vinkenstr 57 **31–20/627.07.90** • 9pm-3am, till 4am wknds • gay-friendly neighborhood bar

Saarein Elandsstr 119 **31–20/623.49.01** • 3pm-1am, till 2am Fri-Sat, clsd Mon • lesbians/ gay men • cafe-bar

Nightclubs

COC Rozenstr 14 **31–20/623.40.79, 31–20/626.30.87** • 10pm-4am Fri • lesbians/ gay men • dancing/DJ • women only 10pm-4am Sat • Arabian disco 8pm-12:30am Sun • HIV+ 8pm-12:30am Th • call for other parties/ events • cover charge

Mazzo Rozengracht 114 (nr Westermarkt) **31–20/626.75.00** • midnight-4am, clsd Mon-Tue • gay-friendly • dancing/DJ • young, raver crowd • cover charge

de Trut **31–20/612.35.24** • 11pm-3:30am Sun only • lesbians/ gay men • hip underground dance party • alternative

Cafes

Café 't Smalle Egelantiersgracht 12 **31–20/623.96.17** • 10am-1pm • brown cafe • full bar • outdoor seating

Tops Prinsengracht 480 • smoking Internet cafe

't Wonder Huidenstr 13 (at Bijbelsmuseum) **31–20/639.10.32** • 2pm-midnight, clsd Mon • smoking coffeeshop

Restaurants

Bojo Lange Leidsedwarsstr 49–51 (nr Leidseplein) **31–20/622.74.34** • noon-late, clsd Mon-Wed • popular • Indonesian

De Bolhoed Prinsengracht 60–62 (at Tuinstr) **31–20/626.18.03** • noon-10pm, from 11am Sat • vegetarian/ vegan • US$8-13

Burger's Patio 2e Tuindwarsstr 12 **31–20/623.68.54** • Italian • plenty veggie

Granada Leidsekruisstr 13 **31–20/625.10.73** • 5pm-close, clsd Sun • Spanish • tapas • also bar

't Swarte Schaep Korte Leidsedwarsstr 24 (nr Leidseplein) **31–20/622.30.21** • noon-11pm • French • US$22-31

De Vliegende Schotel Nieuwe Leliestr 162 **31–20/625.20.41** • 5pm-11pm • vegetarian

Entertainment & Recreation

De Looier Antiques Market Elandsgracht 109 **31–20/624.90.38**

Bookstores

Vrouwenindruk Westermarkt 5 **31–20/624.50.03** • rare, out-of-print & secondhand books by, for, and about women

Xantippe Prinsengracht 290 **31–20/623.58.54, 31–20/679.96.09** • women's bookstore • lesbian section • English titles • lesbian-owned

Retail Shops

Clubwear House Herengracht 265 (nr Dam Sq) **31–20/622.87.66** • noon-6pm, clsd Sun • clothing • club tickets & flyers

Erotica

Black Body Lijnbaansgracht 292 (across from Rijksmuseum) **31–20/626.25.53** • 10am-6:30pm, 11am-6pm Sat, clsd Sun • rubberwear • leather • toys • wheelchair access

Mail & Female Prinsengracht 489 **31–20/623.39.16** • erotic fashions & toys for women

Amsterdam—Rembrandtplein

Accommodations

Hotel Monopole Amstel 60 **31–20/624.62.71** • gay-friendly • also 'Monopole Taveerne', 31-20/624.64.51 • open 4pm-1am, till 3am Fri-Sat • mostly gay men

Hotel Orlando Prinsengracht 1099 (at Amstel River) **31–20/638.69.15** • gay-friendly • beautifully restored 17th-c canalhouse • US$76-118

ITC Hotel Prinsengracht 1051 (at Utrechtsestr) **31–20/623.02.30** • gay-friendly • some shared baths • US$74-89

Jolly Hotel Carlton Vijzelstr 4 **31–20/622.22.66** • gay-friendly • overlooking the famous flower market & Munt Tower • Dfl330-460

Schiller Hotel Rembrandtplein 26–36 **31–20/554.07.00, 31–20/554.07.77** • gay-friendly • art deco style • recently renovated • US$221-395

Waterfront Hotel Singel 458 **31–20/421.66.21, 31–20/623.97.75** • gay-friendly • Dfl145+

Bars

April Reguliersdwarsstr 37 (at Rembrandtplein) **31–20/625.95.72** • 2pm-1am, till 3am Fri-Sat • mostly gay men • cafe-bar

Entre-Nous Halvemaansteeg 14 (at Rembrandtplein) **31–20/623.17.00** • 8pm-3am, till 4am Fri-Sat • lesbians/ gay men • neighborhood bar

Havana Reguliersdwarsstr 17–19 **31–20/620.67.88** • 4pm-1am, till 3am Fri-Sat, from 2pm wknds • mostly gay men • cafe-bar • dancing/DJ wknds

Vive-la-Vie Amstelstr 7 (at Rembrandtplein) **31–20/624.01.14** • 3pm-1am, till 3am Fri-Sat • mostly women

Nightclubs

Exit Reguliersdwarsstr 42 **31–20/625.87.88** • 11pm-4am, till 5am Fri-Sat • mostly gay men • dancing/DJ • 3 bars on 4 flrs

It Amstelstr 24 **31–20/421.69.24** • temporarily clsd at publication time, but worth checking into if it reopens in the future

Lip Lickers Club Wagenstr 3–7 (at Amstel, at 'Sinners in Heaven') **31–20/620.13.75** • 8pm-2am 1st Sun

RoXY Singel 465 **31–20/620.03.54** • popular nightclub burned down June 1999 but plans to reopen

You II Amstel 178 (at Wagenstraat) • 10pm-4am, till 5am Fri-Sat, 4pm-1am Sun, clsd Mon-Wed • mostly women • dancing/DJ

Cafes

Downtown Reguliersdwarsstr 31 **31–20/622.99.58** • 10am-7pm • popular • mostly gay men • terrace open in summer

Global Chillage Kerkstr 51 • smoking coffeeshop • publisher's choice • across from wasserette

The Other Side Reguliersdwarsstr 6 **31–20/421.10.14** • 10am-1am • mostly gay men • smoking coffeeshop

Restaurants

Dia de Sol Reguliersdwarsstr 23 **31–20/623.42.59** • open till midnight • tapas/ Mediterranean

Garlic Queen Reguliersdwarsstr 27 **31–20/422.64.26** • 6pm-close, clsd Tue • even the desserts are made with garlic!

Gary's Late Nite Reguliersdwarsstr 53 (across from 'Exit') **31–20/420.24.06** • 10am-3am, till 4am Fri-Sat • fresh muffins, cookies & bagels

Golden Temple Utrechtsestr 126 **31–20/626.85.60** • 5pm-10pm, noon-3pm Tue & Sat • Indian-influenced vegetarian & vegan • smokefree • Dfl21.50+

Kort Amstelveld 12 **31–20/626.11.99** • 11:30am-10pm, till 11pm Fri-Sat, clsd Tue • French/ Italian • terrace • US$9-19

Malvesijn Prinsengracht 598 **31–20/638.08.99** • 10am-midnight • food served till 10pm • lesbians/ gay men • Dutch • also bar • terrace overlooking the canal • US$10-17

Le Monde Rembrandtplein 6 **31–20/626.99.22** • 8am-11pm, brkfst till 4pm (open 4pm-10pm Mon-Fri in winter) • lesbians/ gay men • Dutch • plenty veggie • terrace dining • gay-owned/ run

Rose's Cantina Reguliersdwarsstr 38–40 (nr Rembrandtplein) **31–20/625.97.97** • 5pm-10:30pm, till 11:30pm Fri-Sat • popular • Tex-Mex • US$13-22

Sarah's Grannies Kerkstr 176 **31–20/624.01.45** • 10am-5pm, clsd Sun-Mon • mostly women • terrace

Saturnino Reguliersdwarsstr 5H **31–20/639.01.02** • noon-midnight • Italian • full bar

't Schooiertje Lijnbaansgracht 190 (at Looier Antiques Market) **31–20/638.40.35** • 9am-11pm, clsd Fri • full bar

Shizen Kerkstr 108 **31–20/622.86.27** • lunch & dinner, clsd Mon • macrobiotic Japanese

Entertainment & Recreation

Bridge-Societeit de Looier Lijnbaansgracht 185 **31–20/627.93.80** • gay prize bridge 7:30pm Wed

Retail Shops

Conscious Dreams Kerkstr 117 **31–20/626.69.07** • 11am-7pm, till 8pm Th-Sat, 2pm-6pm Sun • 'psychedelicatessen': smart drinks & such

Amsterdam—Outer

Accommodations

Aadam Wilhelmina Hotel Koninginneweg 169 **31–20/662.54.67** • gay-friendly • charming • recently renovated • Dfl65-335

Chico's Guesthouse St Willibrordusstr 77 **31–20/675.42.41** • gay-friendly • Dfl40-140

Hotel Sander Jacob Obrechtstr 69 **31–20/662.75.74** • gay-friendly • also 24hr bar & coffee lounge • Dfl185+

Johanna's B&B Van Hogendorpplein 62 **31–20/684.85.96** • women only

Liliane's Home Sarphatistr 119 **31–20/627.40.06** • women only • full brkfst • shared bath • smokefree • also apt • US$68-137

Prinsen Hotel Vondelstr 36-38 (nr Leidseplein) **31–20/616.23.23** • gay-friendly • Dfl130-235

Quentin Hotel Leidsekade 89 (at Lijnbaansgracht) **31–20/626.21.87** • gay-friendly • some shared baths • US$58-97

Toro Hotel Koningslaan 64 (next to Vondelpark) **31–20/673.72.23** • gay-friendly • refurbished mansion

Nightclubs

De Brug NZ Kolk 25 (at 'Akhnaton') • 9pm-2am 1st Sat • for lesbians & bisexual women 35 & older • ballroom dancing till 11pm • disco from 11pm

Restaurants

De Vrolijke Abrikoos Weteringschans 76 **31–20/624.46.72** • 5pm-11:30pm • eclectic organic cuisine • plenty veggie • patio

De Waaghals Frans Halsstr 29 **31–20/679.96.09** • 5pm-11pm • healthy int'l • plenty veggie

Warung Swietie 1e Sweelinckstr 1 (at Albert Cuyp Straat) • popular • Surinamese/Javanese

Gyms & Health Clubs

Eastern Bath House Zaanstr 88 **31–20/681.48.18** • women-only Turkish sauna

Spain

Barcelona

Info Lines & Services

Casal Lambda Ample 5 **34–93/412.72.72** • 5pm-9pm, till 11pm Sat, clsd Sun • also publish magazine

Colectivo Gay de Barcelona (CGB) **34–93/318.16.65** • also publish 'Info Gai'

Telefono Rosa **34–900/601.601 (in Spain)** • 6pm-10pm wkdys

Accommodations

Barcelona Plaza Hotel Plaza d'Espanya 6–8 (across from Montjuïc Castle) **34–93/426.26.00** • gay-friendly • swimming • jacuzzi • also restaurant & piano bar • 15.700ptas+

California Hotel Rauric 14 **34–93/317.77.66** • gay-friendly

Gran Hotel Catalonia Balmes 142–146 **34–93/415.90.90** • gay-friendly • food served • wheelchair access • 15.700ptas+

Hotel Albeniz Aragó 591–593 **34–93/265.26.26** • gay-friendly • food served • wheelchair access • 9.900ptas+

Hotel Duques de Bergara Bergara 11 **34–93/301.51.51** • gay-friendly • 4-star hotel in the heart of old Barcelona • food served • 13.975ptas+

Hotel Mikado Paseo de Bonanova 58 **34–93/211.41.66** • gay-friendly • 3-star hotel in a beautiful residential area • food served • 9.900ptas+

Hotel Roma Avda de Romo 31 **34–93/410.66.33** • gay-friendly • 4-star hotel next to the Sants train station • food served • 8.500ptas+

Regencia Colon Hotel Sagristans 13–17 **34–93/318.98.58** • gay-friendly • some shared baths

Bars

Aire Enrique Granados 48 **34–93/451.84.62** • 10pm-3am, clsd Mon • lesbians/ gay men • cafe-bar

Bahía Séneca 12 (Metro Diagonal) • 7pm-3am • lesbians/ gay men

Cafe de la Calle Vic 11 (Metro Gracia) **34–93/218.38.63** • 6pm-3am • lesbians/ gay men • food served

Cafe de Lola Paris 173 • 6:30pm-3am • lesbians/ gay men

El Coño Tu Prima Consell de Cent 294 (in midtown) • mostly women • unconfirmed '99

Daniel's Plaza Cardona 7–8 **34–93/209.99.78** • mostly women • neighborhood bar

Dietrich Consell de Cent 255 (in midtown, enter at Muntaner & Aribau) **34–93/451.77.07** • 6pm-3am • popular • lesbians/ gay men • upscale • drag shows

Este Bar Consell de Cent 257 (in midtown) **34–93/323.64.06** • 5pm-3am • popular • lesbians/ gay men

Free Girl Mariano Cubí 4 • mostly women • dancing/DJ

La Illa Reig I Benet 3 • mostly women

Medusa Casanova 75 • 10pm-close • lesbians/ gay men • food served

Members Séneca 3 **34–93/237.12.04** • 8pm-3am • lesbians/ gay men

Monaco Cafe Diputació 210 (btwn Muntaner & Aribau) • 6pm-3am, from 8pm wknds • lesbians/ gay men • dancing/DJ • food served

Padam Padam Rauric 9 **34–93/302.50.62** • 7pm-3am, clsd Sun • lesbians/ gay men • also cafe

Punto BCN Muntaner 63–65 (enter on Consejo de Ciento Yragón) **34–93/453.61.23** • 6pm-2am, till 3am wknds • mostly gay men • upscale cafe-bar • wheelchair access

Queen Francolí 68 (at Balmes) **34–909/80.57.49** • lesbians/ gay men

La Rosa Brusi 39 (Pasaje) **34–93/414.61.66** • 8pm-3am Th-Sun • mostly women • dancing/DJ • live shows

Satanassa Aribau 27 (Metro Universitat) • 10pm-2:30am • gay/ straight • dancing/DJ • private club

Theseo Comte Borrell 119 (Metro Urgell) **34–93/453.87.96** • 8:30am-2:30am, clsd Sun • gay/ straight • also restaurant • wheelchair access:

Barcelona

Lesbigay Pride: June.

Annual Events: February - Carnival. October/November - Gay/Lesbian Film Festival.

City Info: Oficina de Informació Turistica 34–93/301.74.43.

Attractions: Barri Gotic.
Catedral de Barcelona 34–93/315.15.54.
Fundació Joan Miró 34–93/329.19.08.
Modern Art Museum of Barcelona 34–93/412.08.10.
Museu Picasso 34–93/319.63.10.
National Museum of Catalan Art 34–93/423.71.99.
Parc Guëll.
La Sagrada Familia 34–93/455.02.47.

Weather: Barcelona boasts a mild Mediterranean climate, with summer temperatures in the 70°s-80°s, and 40°s-50°s in winter. Rain is possible year-round, with July being the driest month.

Transit: Taxis: 34–93/433.10.20 or 34–93/357.77.55.
Public Transit: 34–93/412.00.00.

Barcelona

An enormous open-air museum to its patron artist Gaudí, Barcelona is by turns handsome, quaint, sleek, wry, and hip. Gaudí's Dr. Seuss-like art nouveau apartment buildings are scattered throughout the city, and you can't miss his massive still-under-construction cathedral—La Sagrada Familia—or the amusing Park Guëll overlooking the city.

As all the guidebooks will tell you, the Barri Gotic is both the tourists' quarter and a crowded maze of ancient Gothic towers, narrow alleys, plazas, and cathedrals bisected by a wide pedestrian mall known as Las Ramblas.

The Ramblas is the main artery of the quarter, and most days you can't walk more than a few feet without bumping into street hawkers, cartoonists, jugglers, clowns, live statues, and buskers of all sorts—in between the omnipresent bright red *¡Hola!* bookstands, knots of tourists, and sidewalk cafes. Unlike many tourist areas, the Ramblas is also frequented by locals strolling for evening and weekend entertainment.

A few blocks away, Raurich Street (*carrer* in Catalan, the local tongue of Barcelona; or *calle* in Spanish, pronounced 'kí-yay') meanders past most of the gay bars and bookstores in the Barri Gotic. But the heart of gay Barcelona is in L'Eixample, the most recently redeveloped part of town, with wide streets and sidewalks and plush middle-class businesses. You'll find well-dressed lesbians here among the chic gay boys at expensive dance clubs like **Satanassa,** whose life-size mirror-encrusted statue of a fat-and-happy goddess deserves some adoration.

Urban dykes may feel more at home in the less glossy Gracia (remember to pronounce all c's appearing in the middle of a word like a short 'th') neighborhood, home to a mix of queers, families of color, punks, and other misfits—most of whom still go to the Barri Gotic for excitement.

For casual hanging out, there's **La Illa**, a tiny, friendly dyke bar that's open late on weekends, or the **Café de la Calle,** which is actually a bar-cum-community center that opens at 6pm but doesn't start filling up till 10pm. If you wander around its mazes, you'll find a narrow hallway in the back crammed with gay papers, flyers, free disco tickets, and all the current information you need.

Of course, the most exciting women's nights happen monthly or so. Look for flyers advertising events for *dones* ('women' in Catalan), or ask the friendly bartenders, many of whom will answer you in English if your accent gives you away.

Nightclubs

Arena Balmes 32 (at Diputació) • midnight-5am • popular • mostly gay men • dancing/DJ • food served • live shows Wed • videos • cover charge

Arena Classic Diputació 233 (at Balmes) **34-93/487.83.42** • midnight-5am Th-Sat only • popular • mostly gay men • dancing/DJ • live shows • cover charge

Arena VIP Gran Via 593 • midnight-6am Fri-Sat only • popular • mostly gay men • dancing/DJ • live shows • videos • cover charge

Glamour Moià 1 • midnight-5am • lesbians/ gay men • dancing/DJ • live shows

Heyday Bruniquer 59-61 (Metro Plaza Joanich) **34-93/450.36.75** • midnight-5am, 10pm-3am Sun, clsd Mon-Wed • lesbians/ gay men • dancing/DJ • live shows • videos

Martin's Passeig de Gràcia 130, lower level **34-93/218.71.67** • midnight-5am • popular • mostly gay men • dancing/DJ • live shows • videos

Metro Sepúlveda 185 (Metro Universitat) **34-93/323.52.27** • midnight-5am • popular • mostly gay men • dancing/DJ • live shows • videos • also cafe • cover charge

Salvation Ronda San Pere 19-21 (at Plaza Urquinaona) • midnight-close Fri-Sat only • mostly gay men • dancing/DJ • live shows • food served • cover charge

Tatu Cai Celi 7 (Metro Plaza d'Espanya) **34-93/425.33.50** • 6pm-5am • mostly gay men • dancing/DJ • live shows • patio • cover charge

Topxi València 358 **34-93/425.33.50** • 10pm-5am • mostly gay men • dancing/DJ • drag shows

Cafes

Cafe de la Opera Las Ramblas 74 **34-93/317.75.85** • outdoor cafe • light fare • US$5

Il Cafe di Francesco Passeig de Gràcia 66 **34-93/488.25.90**

G Cafe Muntaner 24 • 8:30am-10pm, 10am-2am Fri-Sat, clsd Sun • lesbians/ gay men • also bar

Restaurants

Botafumeiro Mayor de Gràcia 81 **34-93/218.42.30** • Galician seafood specialities • US$55

Cafe Miranda Casanova 30 (btwn Gran Via & Sepúlveda) **34-93/453.52.49** • 9pm-1am • mostly gay men • int'l • live shows • US$20

Los Caracoles Escudellers 14 **34-93/302.31.85** • seafood • US$20

Castro Casanova 85 **34-93/323.67.84** • 1pm-6pm & 9pm-midnight • mostly gay men • 1.200ptas

La Diva Diputació172 **34-93/454.63.98** • lunch & dinner • lesbians/ gay men

Egipte Jerusalem 3 **34-93/317.74.80** • Catalonian • popular • US$10

L' Elx al Moll Moll d'Espanya (Maremagnum) **34-93/25.81.17** • seafood • US$30

Eternal Casanova 42 **34-93/453.17.86** • lesbians/ gay men

La Mossegada Diputació 214 **34-93/454.72.75** • 8pm-1am • lesbians/ gay men • live shows

La Nostra Illa Reig I Bonet 3 • mostly women • sandwiches • US$5

Tragaluz Passeig de la Concepció 5 **34-93/487.06.21** • dinner • int'l gourmet • US$30

Bookstores

Antinous Josep Anselm Clavé 6 (btwn Las Ramblas & Ample) **34-93/301.90.70** • 10:30am-2pm & 4:30pm-9pm • books • gifts • also cafe • wheelchair access

Cómplices Cervantes 2 (at Avinyó) **34-93/412.72.83** • 10:30am-8:30pm, from noon Sat, clsd Sun • lesbigay • Spanish & English titles

Publications

Info Gai **34-93/318.16.65** • free bi-monthly newspaper in Catalan

Spiritual Groups

EXODE **34-93/301.31.37** • Christian lesbian & gay men's group

Erotica

Condonería Piuo 7 **34-93/301.57.45** • clsd Sun

Erotic Museum of Barcelona Ramblas 3 **34-93/318.98.65**

Madrid

Info Lines & Services

COGAM (Colectivo de Gays y Lesbianas de Madrid) Calle Fuencarral 37 **34-91/522.45.17** • lesbigay center • groups • library

Gai Inform **34-91/523.00.70** • 5pm-9pm • helpline

Info Lesbi **34-91/319.16.90** • clsd Aug

Accommodations

Gay Hostal Puerta del Sol Plaza Puerta del Sol 14, 4° (at Calle de Alcalá) **34-91/522.98.15** • mostly gay men • centrally located • gay-owned/ run • 4.000-6.000ptas

Hostal Hispano Hortaleza 38, 2° A (at Perez Galdos) **34-91/531.48.71** • mostly gay men • 3.500-4.500ptas

Hostal Sonsoles Fuencarral 18, 2°D **34-91/532.75.23, 34-91/532.75.22**

Hotel A Gaudí Gran Via 9 **34-91/531.22.22** • 4-star hotel • 15.700ptas+

Mónaco Hotel Residencia Barbieri 5 **34-91/522.46.30** • gay-friendly

Palace Hotel Plaza de Las Cortes, 7 **34-91/360.77.70** • gay-friendly • 35.000ptas+

Suecia Hotel Marqués de Casa Riera 4 **34-91/531.69.00** • gay-friendly • jacuzzis

Bars

A Diario Zurita 39, 2° (Metro Lavapies) **34-91/530.27.80** • lesbians/ gay men • DJ wknds

Ambient San Mateo 21 • 9pm-3am, clsd Mon • mostly women • food served

La Bohemia Plaza de Chueca 10 • mostly women • neighborhood bar

Chueca's Friends Plaza de Chueca 9 • mostly women

The Fame Pérez Galdós 1 (at Fuencarral) **34-91/532.12.86** • 8:30pm-3:30am • lesbians/ gay men • live shows

Lucas San Lucas 11 • lesbians/ gay men • neighborhood bar • drag shows

La Lupe Torrecilla del Leal 12 (Metro Antón Martín) **34-91/527.50.19** • 9pm-2:30am (from 10pm summers) • popular • lesbians/ gay men • neighborhood bar

Medea Cabeza 33 • women only • dancing/DJ • popular Th

Mito Plaza de Chueca 1 • 11pm-close • lesbians/ gay men • neighborhood bar • live shows

El Mojito Olmo 6 (Metro Antón Martin) • 9pm-2:30am, till 3:30am Fri-Sat • gay/ straight • more gay Sun afternoon • neighborhood bar

El Mosquito Torrecilla del Leal 13 • gay/ straight

Olivia 51 San Bartolomé 16 (btwn Figueroa & San Marcos) • 8:30pm-close, clsd Mon • lesbians/ gay men • live shows • food served

Papillón Augusto Figueroa 20 • 10am-3am

Ras Barbieri 7 (btwn San Marcos & Infantas) **34-91/522.43.17** • 9:30pm-4am, till 4:30am Fri-Sat, clsd Sun • popular • mostly gay men

Regine's Terraza Paseo de la Castellana 56 • lesbians/ gay men • terrace bar

Rick's Clavel 8 (at Infantas, Metro Gran Vía) **34-91/531.91.86** • 10pm-5am • popular • mostly gay men

Madrid

Lesbigay Pride: June.

City Info: 34-91/541.23.25.

Attractions: Museo del Prado 34-91/420.28.36.
Museo Thyssen-Bornemisza 34-91/369.01.51.
Queen Sofía Nat'l Art Center (home of Picasso's 'Guernica') 34-91/467.50.62.
Royal Palace 34-91/542.00.59.

Best View: From the funicular in the Parque des Atracciones.

Weather: Winter temps average in the 40°s (and maybe even a little snow!). Summer days in Madrid are hot, with highs well into the 80°s.

Transit: 34-91/580.19.80

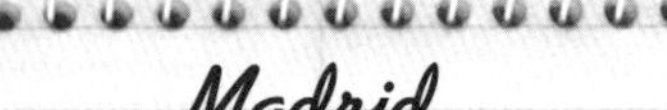

Madrid

The sprawling capital of Spain, Madrid is both grandiose and intimate, more gifted in spirit and bustling street life than in tourist spots. Of course, even if museums aren't your thing, you shouldn't miss Picasso's *Guernica* in the Sophia Reina Museum, or Hieronymus Bosch's quirky paintings crawling with mutated fairytale monsters in the Prado museum. And definitely poke your head into one of the 'Museo del Jamon' sandwich shops festooned with hanging hamhocks—it's a truly Madrileño experience.

But the quintessential Madrileño activity—some would argue the quintessential Spanish activity—is *la marcha*, the full night of barhopping that most Spaniards apparently engage in many nights a week. What is not clear, is which—*la marcha* or the three-hour lunchtime siesta—came first, but now they are inextricably intertwined.

After a modest dinner around 10pm—or perhaps just some *cañas* (half-bottles of beer) and *tapas* (hearty snackfood you're guaranteed with almost any alcohol purchase after 6pm)—it's off to another bar several blocks away for another single drink...then a 10 to 15-minute brisk walk to yet another bar for another single drink.

The combination of friendly company, mild alcohol, plentiful snacks, and exercise is what keeps the evening going until at least 2 or 3am. Don't be surprised to find yourself in the middle of a crowded street or plaza at 4 or 5am!

Generally the bar/cafeterias serving snacks close around midnight, and then it's on to a bar—which won't have wine, but may have *calamocho*, a *marcha*-fueling drink of wine mixed with cola. After 3am you'll have to find a nightclub, which may charge a cover, at least on Fridays and Saturdays, but the cover usually includes a drink ticket.

The lesbo stronghold of the city is Embajadores, southeast of the Center, bounded by the metro stations Lavapiés, Anton Martin, and Embajadores. Here you'll find the gay-friendly film repertory house and the mixed artsy gay bar **La Lupe** (in honor of the performer-icon of the same name, sort of a Latina version of Judy Garland). Not far is the lesbian dance club **Medea,** which packs 'em in on Thursdays with free entrance.

You'll also find plenty of sisters in the gay barrio of Chueca. After browsing the shelves at the lesbigay **Berkana Bookstore,** visit the girls at **La Bohemia.** Or get funky at the small-but-hip dance club **Mito.** And right around the corner is the aptly named bar **Smoke.** For more nightlife ideas, pick up a copy of the free paper **Shangay Express.** Whatever you do, don't forget to take your siesta!

Smoke San Bartolomé 11 (at Plaza de Chueca) • mostly women • neighborhood bar

Truco Gravina 10 (at Plaza de Chueca) **34-91/532.89.21** • 8pm-close Th & 9pm-close Fri-Sat • mostly women • neighborhood bar • great parties • seasonal terrace

Undata Clavel 5 (at Reina) **34-91/523.33.63** • 10am-late • lesbians/ gay men • dancing/DJ from midnight • live shows • also cafe

Nightclubs

Angels of Xenon Atocha 38 • midnight-7am Fri-Sat • gay/ straight • more gay Sat • also cafe

Escape Gravina 13 (at Plaza de Chueca) • midnight-close Th-Fri & 1am-close Sat • lesbians/ gay men • dancing/DJ • drag shows

Goa After Club Mesoneros Romanos 13 (at 'Flamingo Club,' Metro Callaos **34-91/531.48.27** • 6am-close wknds • lesbians/ gay men • dancing/DJ • cover charge

Griffin's Villalar 8 (Metro Banco de España) • lesbians/ gay men • dancing/DJ

Heaven Veneras 2 (at Plaza Santo Domingo) **34-91/548.20.22** • 1:30am-8am, 2am-10am Fri-Sat • mostly gay men • dancing/DJ • live shows • videos

Ohm Plaza del Callao 4 (at 'Bash') • midnight-5am Fri-Sat • mostly gay men • dancing/DJ

Refugio Dr Cortezo 1 (below Teatro Calderón, Metro Tirso de Molina) **34-91/369.40.38** • midnight-6am, till 8am Fri-Sat, clsd Mon • popular • mostly gay men • dancing/DJ • leather • videos

La Rosa Tetuán 27 **34-91/531.01.85** • 10pm-close, clsd Mon • lesbians/ gay men • dancing/DJ • also 'Stop' after-hours club wknds

Sachas Plaza de Chueca 8 • lesbians/ gay men • dancing/DJ • drag shows

Shangay Tea Dance Mesoneros Romanos 13 (at 'Flamingo Club,' Metro Callao) **34-91/531.48.27** • 9pm-2am Sun • popular • lesbians/ gay men • dancing/DJ • live shows • cover charge

Tábata Vergara 12 (next to Teatro Royal) **34-91/547.97.35** • 11pm-close • lesbians/ gay men • dancing/DJ • cover charge

Cafes

Argensola Argensola 17 **34-91/319.75.84** • 10am-3am, 9pm-close Sat • also cocktail bar • art exhibits

Cafe Acuarela Gravina 10 **34-91/532.87.35** • 3:30pm-2:30am • lesbians/ gay men

Cafe la Troje Pelayo 26 (at Figueroa) • 3pm-3am • lesbians/ gay men • full bar

Ciber Espacio Cafe Pelayo 42 • Internet cafe • also bar

La Sastrería Hortaleza 74 (at Gravina) **34-91/532.07.71**

Star's Marqués de Valdeiglesias 5 (at Infantas) **34-91/522.27.12**

Restaurants

A Brasileira Pelayo 49 **34-91/308.36.25** • Brazilian • US$15

El Armario San Bartolomé 7 (btwn Figueroa & San Marcos) **34-91/532.83.77** • lesbians/ gay men • drag shows • 1.100-2.500ptas

Artemisa Ventura de la Vega 4 (at Zorrilla) **34-91/429.50.92** • lesbians/ gay men • vegetarian • also Tres Cruces 4 location, 34-91/521.87.21

Cafe Miranda Barquillo 29 **34-91/521.29.46** • lesbians/ gay men

Cañeiro Fernán González 4 **34-91/575.51.87** • lesbians/ gay men • Galician

Casa Vallejo San Lorenzo 9 **34-91/308.61.58** • creative homestyle • US$20

Chez Pomme Pelayo 4 **34-91/532.16.46** • lunch & dinner • vegetarian

Cornucopia Flora 1 (at Plaza Descalzas Reales) **34-91/547.64.65** • 1:30pm-4pm & 8:30pm-11:30pm, clsd Mon • lesbians/ gay men • European/ American • knock to enter

La Dolce Vita Cardenal Cisneros 58 **34-91/445.04.36** • lunch & dinner • Italian

Gula Gula Infante 5 **34-91/420.29.19** • lunch & dinner, clsd Mon • salad bar • also Gran Vía 1 location, 34-91/522.87.64

Momo Augusto Figueroa 41 **34-91/532.71.62** • US$12

Qoricancha Augusto Figueroa 32 **34-91/531.35.66** • clsd Sun • Peruvian/ vegetarian • 1.500ptas

Restaurante Rochi Pelayo 19 **34-91/521.83.10** • lunch & dinner • Spanish

El Restaurante Vegetariano Marqués de Santa Ana 34 **34-91/532.09.27** • lunch & dinner, clsd Mon • vegetarian

El Rincón de Pelayo Pelayo 19 **34-91/521.84.07** • lunch & dinner • lesbians/ gay men • 1.100-1.600ptas

Bookstores

Berkana Bookstore Gravina 10 (in Chueca) **34-91/532.13.93** • 10am-9pm • lesbigay • Spanish & English titles • wheelchair access

Publications

Shangay Express **34-91/308.11.03, 34-91/308.66.23** • free gay paper

Erotica

California Valverde 20

Condoms & Co Colón 3

XXX San Marcos 8 **34-91/522.17.70**

Sitges

Accommodations

Apartments Bonaventura San Buenaventura 7 **34-93/894.97.62** • gay-friendly • studio apts

Hostal Madison Sant Bartomeu 9 **34-93/894.61.47** • popular • gay-friendly • 5.000-6.000ptas

Hotel Calípolis Paseo Maritimo **34-93/894.15.00** • gay-friendly • upscale hotel

Hotel Montserrat Espalter 27 **34-93/894.03.00** • popular • gay-friendly

Hotel Renaixença Isla de Cuba 7 **34-93/894.83.75** • gay-friendly • full brkfst • some shared baths

Hotel Romàntic Sant Isidre 33 **34-93/894.83.75** • popular • gay-friendly • full brkfst • some shared baths • seasonal • kids/pets ok • also full bar

Madison Bahía Hotel Parellades 31–33 **34-93/894.00.12** • popular • gay-friendly • 5.500-8.750ptas

Mirador Apartments San Gaudencio 32–34 **34-93/894.24.12** • gay-friendly • studio apts

Pensión Espalter Espalter 11 **34-93/894.03.00** • popular • gay-friendly • balconies

La Roca Cami cal Antoniet **34-93/894.00.43** • popular • gay-friendly • camping sites

San Sebastian Playa Port Alegre 53 **34-93/894.86.76** • gay-friendly • swimming

El Xalet Isla de Cuba 35 **34-93/894.55.79** • gay-friendly • food served

Bars

Alfred Santa Bárbara 10 (at Plaza España) • 9am-3:30am • lesbians/ gay men • cafe-bar

Bourbon's Sant Bonaventura 13 **34-93/894.33.47** • 10:30pm-3am, till 3:30am • mostly gay men • dancing/DJ

El Candil Carreta 9 **34-93/894.73.86** • seasonal • 10pm-3am, till 3:30am Fri-Sat • lesbians/ gay men • dancing/DJ • food served from 7pm

The Edge Isla de Cuba 9 **34-93/811.02.57** • 6pm-3am • lesbians/ gay men • dancing/DJ • live shows

Mitja Lluna Santa Tecla 8 **34-93/894.51.57** • 6pm-3am • gay-friendly

Parrot's Plaza Industria 2 (at Primero de Mayo) • 5pm-3am • lesbians/ gay men • seasonal • patio

Pym's Sant Bonaventura 37 **34-929/71.06.24** • 7:30pm-3am • lesbians/ gay men • dancing/DJ

Nightclubs

New Discotheque Bonaire 15 **34-93/894.22.30** • midnight-6am • mostly gay men • dancing/DJ

Trailer Angel Vidal 36 • midnight-5am • popular • mostly gay men • dancing/DJ • young crowd

Cafes

Cafe Goya San Francisco 42 • 9am-1am, clsd Wed off-season • full bar • terrace

Eddie's Café San Pablo 34 **34-93/894.95.01**

Picnic Passeig del Mar (at Av Fernández) **34-93/811.00.40** • 9:30am-3am • call for winter hours • terrace

Restaurants

Can Pagès Sant Pere 24–26 **34-93/894.11.95** • 1pm-4pm & 8pm-midnight, clsd Mon • lesbians/ gay men

Casa Hidalgo San Pablo 12 **34-93/894.38.95** • seafood • wheelchair access

Ma Maison Bonaire 28 **34-93/894.60.54** • lesbians/ gay men • full bar • patio

Oliver's Isla de Cuba 39 **34-93/894.35.16** • Spanish

Sucré-Salé Sant Pau 39 **34-93/894.23.02** • lesbians/ gay men • creperie

El Trull Mossèn Felix Clará 3 **34-93/894.47.05** • lesbians/ gay men • French

Camping & RV Spots 580

2000 Tours & Tour Operators

Cruises 585
Luxury Tours 588
The Great Outdoors 588
Spiritual/Health Vacations 595
Thematic Tours 595
Custom Tours 599
Various Tour Operators 599

2000 Calendar

Lesbian/Gay Events 601
Women's Festivals/Gatherings 612
Film Festivals 615
Leather & Fetish Events 618
Conferences & Retreats 620
Spiritual Gatherings 621
Breast Cancer Benefits 623
Kids' Stuff 625

Mail Order 627

Updates 631

USA

Alabama

Geneva

Spring Creek Campground 163 Campground Rd (at Hwy 52 & Country Rd 4) **334/684-3891** • gay-friendly • cabins • also tent & RV sites • swimming • some theme wknds w/ DJ • $15-40

Alaska

Fairbanks

Billie's Backpackers Hostel 2895 Mack Rd **907/457-2034** • gay-friendly • hostel & campsites • kids ok • food served • women-owned/ run • $18

Arizona

Apache Junction

RVing Women Inc PO Box 1940, 85217 **888/557-8464 (55R- VING), 480/983-4678** • RV club for women only

Sedona

Mustang B&B 4257 Mustang Dr, Cottonwood **520/646-5929** • lesbians/ gay men • full brkfst • 25 minutes from Sedona • smokefree • 1 RV hookup • movie theater • $35-65

Tucson

Adobeland Campground 12150 W Calle Seneca **520/883-6471** • women only • $3/night

Arkansas

Eureka Springs

Greenwood Hollow Ridge B&B 501/253-5283 • exclusively lesbigay • on 5 quiet acres • full brkfst • near outdoor recreation • some shared baths • kitchens • pets ok • RV hookups • wheelchair access • gay-owned • $45-65

California

Clearlake

Edgewater Resort 6420 Soda Bay Rd (at Hohape Rd), Kelseyville **707/279-0208, 800/396-6224** • 'gay-owned, straight-friendly' • cabin • camping & RV hookups • lake access & pool • theme wknds • boat facilities • smoking outside • pets ok • $25-250

Garberville

Giant Redwoods RV & Camp 707/943-3198 • gay-friendly • campsites • RV • located off the Avenue of the Giants on the Eel River • shared baths • kids/ pets ok • $19(tent)-27

Placerville

Rancho Cicada Retreat 209/245-4841 • mostly gay men • secluded riverside retreat in the Sierra foothills w/two-person tents & cabin • swimming • nudity • gay-owned/ run • $100-200 (lower during wk)

Russian River

Faerie Ring Campground 16747 Armstrong Woods Rd, Guerneville **707/869-2746** • gay-friendly • on 14 acres • RV spaces • near outdoor recreation • pets ok • $20-25

▲**Fife's Resort** 16467 River Rd (at Brookside Lane), Guerneville **707/869-0656, 800/734-3371** • lesbians/ gay men • cabins • campsites • also restaurant • some veggie • full bar • gym • $50-215

Schoolhouse Canyon Park 12600 River Rd (at Oddfellows Park Rd) **707/869-2311** • gay-friendly • campsites • RV • private beach • kids/ pets ok • $20

The Willows 15905 River Rd (at Hwy 116), Guerneville **707/869-2824, 800/953-2828** • lesbians/ gay men • old-fashioned country lodge & campground • smokefree • $69-139

Sacramento

Verona Village River Resort 6985 Garden Hwy, Nicolaus **530/656-1320** • lesbians/ gay men • RV space $15 • full bar • restaurant • store • marina

Ukiah

Orr Hot Springs 13201 Orr Springs Rd **707/462-6277** • mineral hot springs • hostel-style cabins, private cottages & campsites • $39-160 per person

COLORADO

Fort Collins

Never Summer Nordic 970/482-9411 • lesbians/ gay men • camping in yurts (portable Mongolian round houses) in Colorado Rockies • sleep 8-12 • mountain-biking & skiing

FLORIDA

Crescent City

Crescent City Campground 904/698-2020, 800/634-3968 • gay-friendly • tenting sites • 85 RV hookups • swimming • laundry • showers • gay-owned • $18 day, $115 week

Miami

Something Special 7762 NW 14th Ct (private home), Miami Beach/South Beach **305/696-8826** • noon-9pm, 2pm-7pm Sun • women only • vegetarian • also rental 1-bdrm apt on Miami beach • also tent space

West Palm Beach

The Whimsey 561/686-1354 • resources & archives • political clearing-house • also camping/ RV space & apt • wheelchair access

GEORGIA

Athens

The River's Edge 2311 Pulliam Mill Rd, Dewy Rose **706/213-8081** • mostly men • cabins • camping • RV • swimming • nudity • smokefree • wheelchair access • $12-14

Dahlonega

Swiftwaters Woman Space 706/864-3229, 888/808-5021 • women only • on scenic river • full brkfst • hot tub • seasonal • smokefree • deck • women-owned/ run • $69-95 (B&B)/ $40-50 (cabins)/ $10 (camping)

HAWAII

Hawaii (Big Island)

Kalani Oceanside Eco-Resort 808/965-7828, 800/800-6886 • gay-friendly • coastal retreat • conference center & campground w/ in Hawaii's largest conservation area • full brkfst • swimming • food served • IGLTA • $20-25 camping • $65-130

ILLINOIS

Carbondale

The Pit 618/542-9470 (SUMMER), 618/549-6057 (OCT-APRIL) • lesbians/ gay men • primitive camping from May 15-Oct 1 • 18+ • nudity permitted • swimming • wheelchair access

KENTUCKY

Somerset

Hidden Mountain B&B Inn Burnside **606/561-5269** • gay/ straight • quiet location on banks of Lake Cumberland • also 4 campsites • wheelchair access • gay-owned/ run • $45-75

MAINE

Camden

The Old Massachusetts Homestead Campground Lincolnville Beach **207/789-5135, 800/213-8142** • open May-Nov • gay-friendly • cabins • tentsites • RV hookups • swimming • ocean view • nature trails • kids/ pets ok • $18-23

Sebago Lake

Maine-ly For You 207/583-6980 (SUMMER), 207/782-2275 (WINTER) • gay-friendly • cottages • $50+ • campsites • $10-25 • women's camping area

Tenants Harbor

Blueberry Cove Camp Harts Neck Road **207/372-6353, 617/876-2897** • gay-friendly • cabins • private camp sites • near Penobscot Bay

Michigan

Owendale

Windover Resort 3596 Blakely Rd **517/375-2586** • women only • campsites • swimming • $25/yr membership fee • $18-20 camping fee

Saugatuck

Camp It II & Resort 616/543-4335 • lesbians/ gay men • campsites • RV hookups • seasonal • swimming • $12-17 • also B&B • $60+

Minnesota

Kenyon

Dancing Winds Farm 6863 Country 12 Blvd **507/789-6606** • lesbians/ gay men • B&B on working dairy farm • tentsites • work exchange available

Mississippi

Ovett

Camp Sister Spirit 601/344-2005 • mostly women • 120 acres of camping & RV sites • cabins • smokefree • lesbian-owned/ run • $10-20

Missouri

Noel

Sycamore Landing 417/475-6460 • open May-Sept • gay-friendly • campsites • canoe rental • wheelchair access

Montana

Boulder

Boulder Hot Springs Hotel & Retreat 406/225-4339 • gay-friendly • spirituality/ recovery retreat only • food served • swimming • smokefree • call for info

Ronan

North Crow Vacation Ranch 2360 N Crow Rd **406/676-5169** • seasonal • lesbians/ gay men • cabin • tipis • camping • 80 miles south of Glacier Park • hot tub • nudity • seasonal • lesbian-owned/ run • $10-20

New York

Catskill Mtns

Red Bear Inn & Restaurant West Kill **518/989-6000, 888/232-7466** • gay-friendly • seasonal • also camping • leather-friendly • smokefree • full bar

North Carolina

Asheville

▲ **Camp Pleiades 828/688-9201 (summer) or 904/241-3050 (winter), 888/324-3110** • open Memorial Day thru mid-October • mtn retreat • cabins, camping • all meals included • some shared baths • lesbian-owned/ run • $45-175

Ohio

Columbus

Summit Lodge Resort & Guesthouse 740/385-3521 • popular • gay-friendly • clothing-optional resort • 45 miles to Columbus • camping available • hot tub • swimming • also restaurant • $50-110

Oklahoma

El Reno

The Good Life RV Resort Exit 108 I-40 (1/4 mile S) **405/884-2994, 405/893-2345** • gay-friendly • 32 acres • 100 campsites & 100 RV hookups • swimming • kids ok • gay-owned/ run • $10-15 (full hookup)

Oregon

Days Creek

Owl Farm 541/679-4655 (info line only) • women only • women's land open to visitors • camping sites available

Gaston

Art Springs 40789 SW Hummingbird Ln **503/985-9549** • women only • B&B, cabin & camping on 12 acres of women's land • hot tub • smokefree • chem-free • also retreats

Grants Pass

Womanshare 541/862-2807 • women only • cabin • campground • hot tub • $10-30 (sliding scale)

Tiller

Kalles Family RV Ranch 233 Jackson Creek Rd **541/825-3271** • lesbians/ gay men • camping sites • RV hookups • btwn Medford & Roseburg • kids/ pets ok • lesbian-owned/ run • $10 (incl electric)

Pennsylvania

New Milford

Oneida Camp & Lodge 570/465-7011 • mostly gay men • oldest gay-owned/ operated campground dedicated to the lesbigay community • swimming • nudity • seasonal

South Dakota

Sioux Falls

Camp America 605/425-9085 • gay-friendly • 35 miles west of Sioux Falls • camping • RV hookups • women-owned/ run • $10-16

Tennessee

Nashville

IDA 904 Vikkers Hollow Rd, Dowelltown **615/597-4409** • lesbians/ gay men • private 'commune' in the hills • 1 hr SE of Nashville • camping available May-Sept (no RV hookup) • from $7

Texas

Austin

Belle Springs PO Box 90623, 78709 • women only • camping • events • women's land • lesbian-owned/ run

Groesbeck

Rainbow Ranch Campground Rte 2, Box 165 **254/729-5847, 888/875-7596** • lesbians/ gay men • open all year • located on Lake Limestone on 100+ acres • 40 campsites & 36 RV hookups • women-owned/ run • $10/person

Gun Barrel City

Triple 'B' Cottages 903/451-5105 • gay/ straight • 78 miles from Dallas on Cedar Creek Lake • camping available • motor homes & travel trailers welcome • kids/ pets ok • gay-owned/ run • $75-125

Rio Grande Valley

La Mirada Country Estates 8901 W Business Hwy 83 (at Tamm Ln), Harlingen **956/428-1966** • gay-friendly • swimming • hot tub • club house • also camping & RV hookups • gay-owned/ run

Vermont

St Johnsbury

▲ **Greenhope Farm B&B 802/533-7772** • mostly women • full brkfst (vegetarian) • horseback-riding, camping, skiing & hiking on 140 private acres • smokefree • kids ok • call for free brochure • lesbian-owned/ run • $65-125

Virginia

Charlottesville

Intouch Women's Center 804/589-6542 • women only • campground • recreational area • wheelchair access • $5-15

Washington

Port Townsend

Get-Away at Discovery Bay 360/797-7239 • women only • RV resort on private women's land • 15 miles from Port Townsend

Seattle

Wild Lily Ranch B&B 360/793-2103 • lesbians/ gay men • on Skykomish River • 1 hr from Seattle • hot tub • swimming • camping available • smokefree • gay-owned/ run • $65-85

West Virginia

Stonewall Jackson Lake

▲ **FriendSheep Farm 304/462-7075** • mostly women • secluded farm retreat • cottage • B&B • $10 campsites • smokefree

Wisconsin

Gays Mills

Chela's B&B and Forest Camping Retreat Gays Mills, La Crosse **608/735-4829** • women only • $15-65

Mauston

CK's Outback W 5627 Clark Rd **608/847-5247** • women only • cabin & tipi • camping • $10-13

Norwalk

Daughters of the Earth 18134 Index Ave **608/269-5301** • women only • women's land • camping • retreat space

Wascott

Wilderness Way 715/466-2635 • women only • resort property • cabins • camping • RV sites • swimming • camping $14 • cottages $53-72

Canada

British Columbia

Birken

Birkenhead Resort Pemberton **604/452-3255** • gay-friendly • cabins • campsites • hot tub • swimming • pets ok • Can$55-80

Nova Scotia

Bridgetown

Pumpkin Ecological Wimmin's Farm RR 5 **902/665-5041** • catalog available • women-owned/ run

Ontario

Hamilton

The Cedars Tent & Trailer Park 1039 5th Concession Rd RR2, Waterdown **905/659-3655** • lesbians/ gay men • private campground • swimming • also social club • dancing/DJ • karaoke • wknd restaurant • some veggie

Province of Québec

Granby

Le Campagnard B&B 146 Denison ouest **450/770-1424** • gay-friendly • in a quiet village • bikes available • also camping • Can$40-45

Joliette

L'Oasis des Pins 381 boul Brassard, St-Paul-de-Joliette **450/754-3819** • lesbians/ gay men • swimming • camping April-Sept • restaurant open year-round

Saskatchewan

Ravenscrag

Spring Valley Guest Ranch 306/295-4124 • popular • gay-friendly • 1913 character home • cabin • kids/ pets ok • also restaurant • country-style • gay-owned/ run • Can$40-60

Caribbean

Virgin Islands

St John

Maho Bay & Harmony VI National Park **340/776-6240, 800/392-9004** • gay-friendly • rustic cottages & studios • environmentally aware resort • $70-195

Mexico

Puerto Vallarta

Paco Paco Descanso del Sol Hotel 583 Pino Suárez (Col Emiliano Zapata) **52-322/3.02.77, 800/936-3646 (Doin' It Right #)** • lesbians/ gay men • apts, casitas & tents • swimming • rooftop bar w/ incredible sunset views • also 'Paco's Hidden Paradise' (20-acre resort w/ restaurant & bar accesible only by boat) • gay-owned/ run • US$45-125

Europe

Spain

Sitges

La Roca Cami cal Antoniet **34-93/894.00.43** • popular • gay-friendly • camping sites

Cruises

Women Only

▲ **Olivia Cruises 510/655-0364, 800/631-6277** 4400 Market St, Oakland, CA 94608 • huge resorts & cruises to Alaska, Caribbean, Mediterranean, Club Med Ixtapa • see ad in front section • **IGLTA** member

March—13—Australia & New Zealand Land Package
April—29-May 6—Mexican Caribbean Cruise
June—3-10—Cruise Rome to Venice
July—8-15—Cruise Greece, Egypt & Israel
October—7-14—Mexico Resort in Sonora Bay

Pacific Yachting & Sailing 831/462-6835 or 423-7245 790 Mariner Park Way, Santa Cruz, CA 95062 • international yachting vacations for lesbians

Professional Marine Services 906/847-6580 or 517/733-8569 (winter), 888/847-6580 16293 Orchard Creek Hwy, Ocqueoc, MI 49757 • sightseeing & commitment ceremonies off the shore of Mackinac Island

Whelk Women 941/964-2027 PO Box 1006-D, Boca Grande, FL 33921 • custom boat tours for women • outfitted camping • accommodations

Gay/Lesbian

Castlemain Yacht Charters 954/760-4730, 888/760-4730 757 SE 17th St #780, Fort Lauderdale, FL 33316 • gay & lesbian yacht charter company • charters worldwide

Holidays at Sea 707/573-8300, 800/444-8300 1208 4th St, Santa Rosa, CA 95404 • **IGLTA** member

Journeys By Sea 954/522-5865, 800/825-3632 1402 E Las Olas Blvd, Suite 122, Fort Lauderdale, FL 33301 • yacht vacations

Ocean Voyager 305/379-5722, 800/435-2531 1717 N Bayshore Dr #4041, Miami, FL 33132 • hosted gay groups on mainstream upscale cruise ships • **IGLTA** member

December—28, 1999—11 day Millennium Caribbean Cruise
February—12-19—Belize/Mexico Valentine's Day Cruise
March—11-18—Eastern Caribbean Cruise
April—22-29—Southern Caribbean Easter Cruise
May—22-June 1—Greek Islands & Turkey Cruise
July—1-8—Eastern Caribbean Cruise

Port Yacht Charters 516/883-0998, 800/213-0465 9 Belleview Ave, Port Washington, NY 11050 • custom charters world-wide • commitment ceremonies • gourmet cuisine

Rainbow Charters 808/595-6682 2087 Iholena St, Honolulu, HI 96817 • gay & lesbian weddings • sunset cruises • whale watching

Sailing Affairs 212/228-5755 404 E 11th St, New York, NY 10009 • group & individual charters on the East Coast & in the Caribbean • **IGLTA** member

Straight/Gay

Amazon Tours & Cruises 305/227-2266, 800/423-2791 8700 W Flagler #190, Miami, FL 33174 • weekly cruises, including upper Amazon • **IGLTA** member

Sea Safaris Sailing 941/619-7183, 800/497-2508 3630 County Line Rd, Lakeland, FL 33811 • sailing from St Petersburg • some women-only charter sail trips & cruises to the Keys

Whitney Yacht Charters 941/966-9767, 800/223-1426 3214 Casey Key Rd, Nokomis, FL 34275 • yacht charters in the Caribbean, Mediterranean & New England states • **IGLTA** member

Luxury Tours

Gay/Lesbian

David's Trips & Tours 949/723-0699, 888/723-0699 310 Dahlia Pl Ste A, Corona del Mar, CA 92625-2821 • luxury tours to Eastern Europe, South Africa, Turkey, India & more • **IGLTA** member

December—25, 1999-January 2—Morocco
December—26, 1999-January 9—South Africa Ultra Luxurious New Year's Fantasy Tour
December—28, 1999-January 4—Morocco
December—28, 1999-January 3—Millennium New Orleans French Quarter Weekend
December—29, 1999-January 3—Millennium Vienna Adventure
February—26-March 12—South Africa & Botswana
March—4-12—Morocco
April—1-16—Budapest, Vienna, Marienbad, Prague
July—15-30—South Africa & Botswana
July—15-23—Morocco
August—5-20—Budapest, Vienna, Marienbad, Prague
September—Southern Decadence
September—7-11—Laguna Beach SPLASH
October—Halloween
November—4-19—South Africa & Botswana
November—4-12—Morocco
November—9-26—India
December—23-January 7, 2001—South Africa & Botswana
December—28-January 7, 2001—Morocco

Great Outdoor Adventures

Women Only

Adventures for Women 201/930-0557 PO Box 515, Montvale, NJ 07645 • hiking, canoeing & cross-country skiing in NJ, the Adirondacks & beyond

Adventures in Good Company 651/998-0120, 877/439-4042 5506 Trading Post Tr, Afton, MN 55001 • outdoor & adventure travel for women of all ages & abilities

January—14-22—Sea kayaking in Baja
February—5-12—Whitewater rafting in Mexico
April—Rock climbing in Joshua Tree
June—Cycling in Provence, France
July—Hut to hut in the Austrian Alps
August & September—Canoeing Boundary Waters
October—Backpacking in the Grand Canyon

Alaska Women of the Wilderness Foundation 907/688-2226, 800/770-2226 (Alaska only) PO Box 773556, Eagle River, AK 99577 • year-round wilderness & spiritual empowerment programs for women & girls

December—31, 1999-January 2—Dream Drum 2000

Arctic Ladies 907/783-1954 PO Box 308, Girdwood, AK 99587 • adventure packages in Alaska & Canada

Atlantis Yacht Charters 415/332-0800 Schoonmaker Pt Marina, 85 Liberty Ship Way #110-A, Sausalito, CA 94965 • sailing classes for all levels • weekend & mid-week packages available

Bushwise Women 64-3/332-4952 PO Box 28010, Christchurch 2, New Zealand • wilderness trips in Fiji, Tonga & New Zealand • also a B&B

Call of the Wild Wilderness Trips 510/849–9292, 888/378–1978 (outside CA) 2519 Cedar St, Berkeley, CA 94708 • hiking & wilderness trips for all levels in Western US • in business for over 20 years

February—12-19—Midwinter Escape to Hawaii's Big Island
May—7-12—Havasu in the Grand Canyon
July—10-18—Alaska: Denali National Park, Friends in Fairbanks
August—7-13—John Muir Trail: Ansel Adams Wilderness to Yosemite
August—15-21—Backpacking Mt Whitney: Highest Peak in the Lower 48
September—25-October 2—Anasazi Odyssey: Rafting the San Juan, Ancient Ruins, Canyonlands Nat'l Park, Utah
October—TBA—Trekking in Nepal
October—28-November 13—Mt Kilamanjaro Climb & Serengeti Safari
November—13-19—Africa Optional Add-On: Zanzibar

Cloud Canyon Backpacking 805/692–9615 PO Box 41359, Santa Barbara, CA 93140-1359 • seasonal wilderness backpacking in Utah & the Sierra Nevadas

Dandelion Adventures 303/415–3751 PO Box 483, Boulder, CO 80306 • wilderness trips for women with a spiritual focus • herbal medicine workshops & retreats

Equinox Wilderness Expeditions 907/274–9087 618 W 14th Ave, Anchorage, AK 99501 • rafting, canoeing, sea-kayaking & backpacking in Alaska's best wilderness

Gaia Adventures 604/875–0066 875 E 31st Ave, Vancouver, BC V5V 2X2, Canada • outdoor adventures for women • hiking, rock climbing & more • ecotourism

Grand Canyon Field Institute PO Box 399, Grand Canyon, AZ 86023 • women's backpacking classes in the Grand Canyon • also co-ed trips

Herizen Sailing for Women, Inc 250/741–1753 36 Cutlass Lookout, Nanaimo, BC V9R 6R1, Canada • women-only sailing retreats

It's Our Nature 727/441-2599, 888/535-7448 929 Bay Esplanade, Clearwater, FL 33767 • kayak & hike the Tampa Bay area of Florida • co-ed trips available

Mangrove Mistress 305/745-8886 Murray Marine, 5710 US 1, Key West, FL 33040 • snorkeling • nature exploring • sunset cruises • ceremonies

Mariah Wilderness Expeditions 510/233-2303, 800/462-7424 PO Box 70248, Point Richmond, CA 94807 • woman-owned • whitewater rafting in California & Central America • call for catalogs

April—12-25—Machu Picchu in Peru
April—22-29—Cruise Belize & Guatamala

Mountain Mama 505/351-4312 General Delivery, Tesukue, NM 87574 • horseback riding & camping in New Mexico

National Women's Sailing Association 800/566-6972 16731 McGregor Blvd, Fort Myers, FL 33908

Nature Through Nurture 207/787-2379 RR2 Box 550-F, Naples, ME 04055 • holistic outdoor adventure retreats for women & girls

OceanWomyn Kayaking 206/325-3970 620 11th Ave E, Seattle, WA 98102 • guided sea kayaking adventures

Octopus Reef Dive Training & Tours 808/875-0183 Maui, HI • experienced guides teaching SCUBA diving in Maui • all levels

Pangaea Expeditions 406/721-7719, 888/721-7719 PO Box 5753, Missoula, MT 59806 • river rafting in Montana • co-ed trips also available • call for complete calendar

Prairie Women Adventures & Retreat 316/753-3465 RR 1 Box 24, Matfield Green, KS 66862 • working ranch where guests help out • specialty weekends • call or write for details

Raven Retreat 207/546-2456, 800/841-4586 PO Box 12, Millbridge, ME 04658 • hiking, biking, kayaking & snowshoeing in Maine's coastal mountain wilderness

Sea Sense 860/444-1404, 800/332-1404 25 Thames St, St Petersburg, FL 33731 • Women's Sailing & Powerboating School • world-wide custom sailing courses

Segue 209/753-2267 PO Box 5195, Bear Valley, CA 95223 • writing, art & yoga retreats • learn outdoor skills & nature crafts

Sheri Griffith River Expeditions 435/259-8229, 800/332-2439 PO Box 1324, Moab, UT 84532 • women-only river journeys

Silver Waters Sailing 315/594-1906 PO Box 202, Wolcott, NY 14590 • sailing instruction on Lake Ontario • also day trips

September—30-October 1—The Sacred Lake

South American Expeditions 818/352-8289, 800/884-7474 9921 Cabanas Ave, Tujunga, CA 91042 • hiking, fishing, camping & more in Peru & South American • co-ed trips available

Spirited Women, Inc: Women's Wilderness Ways 501/677-2235 PO Box 112, St Paul, AR 72760 • ancient life skills • nature-awareness school

Tethys Offshore Sailing for Women 360/379-3873, 877/379-3880 PO Box 1665, Pt Townsend, WA 98368 • join Capt Nancy Erley for a segment in her circumnavigation of the world

WanderWomen 64 9/360 7330 PO Box 68, Newton, Auckland 058, New Zealand • alpine retreats, adventure treks & more

Wild Women Expeditions 705/866-1260, 888/993-1222 PO Box 145, Stn B, Sudbury, ON P3E 4N5, Canada • Canada's outdoor adventure company for women • wilderness canoe trips in Ontario's near-North • x-country skiing & dogsledding in winter • get-aways at 200-acre waterfront property

Wild Women Snowboard Camps 307/734-5154, 877/SHE-RIPS 3341 Love Cir, Nashville, TN 37212 • 3-day instructional vacation for women of all levels

Wilderness of Women 250/725-3240 PO Box 548, Tofino, BC V0R 2Z0, Canada • backpack on the West Coast of Canada • theme weekends • spiritual getaways

Winter Moon Summer Sun 218/848-2442 3388 Petrell, Brimson, MN 55602 • dogsledding trips in winter • kayaking Lake Superior in summer • rustic accommodations with meals provided

Woman Tours 208/354-8804, 800/247-1444 PO Box 68, Coleman Falls, VA 24536 • bicycle tours for women • call for complete calendar

January—Tucson
March—New Zealand
April—TransAmerica 2000
May—Blue Ridge Rambler
June—Yellowstone
July—Tour de Tetons
August—Alaska
August—Vermont
September—Utah
September—Kentucky Bluegrass
October—California Vineyards
November—Hawaii

Womanship 410/267-6661, 800/342-9295 137 Conduit St, Annapolis, MD 21401 • a sailing school for women, by women, where nobody yells! • sail & 'see' adventures offered in 15 locations around the world

Women Backcountry Guided Adventures 207/846-3036 26 Bates St, Yarmouth, ME 04096 • taking women to wild places • canoeing, backpacking & more

Women in Motion 760/754-6747, 888/469-6636 PO Box 4533, Oceanside, CA 92052 • active vacations for women, with women, by women

December—26, 1999-January 2—Hawaii New Years
December—30, 1999-January 2—San Francisco New Years
February—TBA—Women's Ski Week, Lake Tahoe
March—12-19—Costa Rica Cycling
March—24-26—Dinah Shore Weekend
April—14-16—Canoe Imperial Wildlife Refuge on CA/AZ border
April—21-25—New Orleans Jazz Festival
April—22-29—Eco-Adventure Cruise: Belize/Guatemala
May—7-9—Las Vegas
June—24-26—San Francisco Pride
July—27-August 6—Colorado Outward Bound
August—11-13—Women's Sacred Circle, Northern Sierras
April—21-27, 2001—Tour Paris, France

Women in the Wilderness 651/227-2284 566 Ottawa Ave, St Paul, MN 55107 • adventure travel, outdoor skills & nature study

Women on a Roll 310/578-8888 PO Box 5112, Santa Monica, CA 90409-5112 • travel, sporting, cultural & social club for women • wide range of events & trips

Women's Flyfishing 907/274-7113 PO Box 243963, Anchorage, AK 99524 • women-only flyfishing courses in different locations around Alaska

Women's Outdoor Challenges 603/763-5400 40 Winn Hill Rd, Sunapee, NH 03782 • outdoor adventure programs for women & girls of all ages

Mostly Women

Adventure Associates 206/932-8352, 888/532-8352 PO Box 16304, Seattle, WA 98116 • co-ed & women-only outdoor adventures • call for complete schedule • **IGLTA** member
- **December—27, 1999-January 11—Kauai New Years Celebration**
- **December—27, 1999-January 11—Tanzania/Kenya New Years Celebration**
- **February—19-March 3—Copper Canyon Mule Trek**
- **February—26-March 12—Nepal Royal Village Trek**
- **March—11-20—Costa Rica Adventure**
- **March—11-20—Kayak Sea of Cortez, Baja California, Mexico**
- **March—31-April 21—Nepal Manasulu Trek**
- **June—Climb Kilimanjaro**
- **September—16-29—Turkey**
- **October—Nepal Everest Trek**

Bar H Ranch 208/354-2906, 888/216-6025 PO Box 297, Driggs, ID 83422 • guesthouse & summer horseback trips in Wyoming's Tetons • near Jackson Hole, WY
- **August—Trail Riding, North Leigh Base Camp**
- **August—Trail Riding, Green Lakes High Altitude Camp**
- **August—Horsepacking, Teton Crest**
- **September—Traverse the Tetons, Millennium Horseback Trail Ride**

Earthwise Journeys 503/736-3364 PO Box 16177, Portland, OR 97292 • research & promote responsible travel companies

Mountain Trek Fitness Retreat & Health Spa 250/229-5636, 800/661-5161 Box 1352, Ainsworth Hot Springs, BC V0G 1A0, Canada • a vacation for the mind & body • comprehensive health programs

Province Mountain Outfitters 207/737-4695 13 Church St, Richmond, ME 04357 • guided fishing, camping & biking trips for women

Venus Charters 305/292-9403 PO Box 4394, Key West, FL 33041 • snorkeling • light tackle fishing • dolphin watching

Women Sail Alaska 907/463-3372, 888/272-4525 PO Box 20348, Juneau, AK 99802 • experience the pristine beauty of southeast AK with lesbian guides

Gay/Lesbian

Alaska Fantastic Fishing Charters 800/478-7777 PO Box 2807, Homer, AK 99603 • deluxe cabin cruiser for big-game fishing (halibut)

Alyson Adventures 617/542-1177, 800/825-9766 PO Box 180179, Boston, MA 02118 • active vacations • **IGLTA** member
- **January—19-26—An Octopus's Garden**
- **February—24-March 10—Boomerang, Australia**
- **March—10-27—Wild Kiwi, New Zealand**
- **May—6-13—Provencal, France**
- **May—24-June 1—Golden Hillsides, France**
- **June—9-16—Valley of the Kings, France**
- **June—24-July 1—Edelweiss, Switzerland**
- **June—26-July 3—The Mistral, France**

Dextours 64-3/337-1438 9 The Crescent, St Martins, Christchurch 8002, New Zealand • gay adventure tours in New Zealand

Great Expeditions Travel 828/281-3994, 888/887-2668 PO Box 8091, Asheville, NC 28814 • events & packages, from mountain biking on the East Coast to European travel

Maui Surfing School 808/875-0625 PO Box 424, Puunene, HI 96784 • **IGLTA** member

▲ **Off The Coast Kayaking508/487-2692, 877/785-2925** Provincetown • rentals & guided tours for P-town, Truro & Wellfleet

Outside Sports 415/864-7205, 888/813-8747 584 Castro #338, San Francisco, CA 94114 • active travel for lesbians & gay men • sea kayaking, mountain biking, rock climbing, snowboarding & skiing

OutWest Adventures 406/446-1533, 800/743-0458 PO Box 2050, Red Lodge, MT 59068 • specializing in active outdoor vacations worldwide • **IGLTA** member

- **January—Aspen Gay Ski Week**
- **February—Big Sky Gay Ski Tour**
- **March—Canadian Rockies Gay Ski Tour**
- **March—Zermatt Gay Ski Tour**
- **April—Baja, Mexico Adventure**
- **May—Grand Canyon Explorer**
- **May—Backpacking in the Southwest**
- **June—White Water Rafting on the Colorado River**
- **June—Yellowstone/Grand Teton Adventure**
- **July—Alaska Adventure**
- **July—Montana Backpacking**
- **August—Gay & Lesbian Ranch Weeks**
- **August—Biking in Banff, Canada**
- **September—Grand Canyon Adventure**
- **September—Hiking in the Swiss Alps**
- **October—Trekking in the Himalayas**
- **October—Costa Rica Adventure**
- **November—Sea Kayaking in Baja, Mexico**

Rainbow Kayak Adventures 808/965-9011 PO Box 983, Pahoa, HI 96778 • hiking, camping, kayaking, scuba & more • also B&B

Rainbow Tours 808/328-8406 87-3202 Guava Road, Kona Paradise, Captain Cook, HI 96704 • kayaking & snorkeling off black sand beaches of Kona Coast

Undersea Expeditions 858/270-2900, 800/669-0310 PO Box 9455, Pacific Beach, CA 92169 • warm water diving & scuba trips worldwide • **IGLTA** member

- **December—25, 1999-January 1—Millennium Charter**
- **December—30, 1999-January 6—Galapagos Islands**
- **March—19-26—Truk Aboard the Truk Aggressor**
- **March—29-April 9—Palau Aboard the Sun Dancer II**
- **April—1-8—Los Roques, Venezuela**
- **August—20-28—FeBrina, Papua New Guinea**

Straight/Gay

10,000 Waves 406/549-6670, 800/537-8315 PO Box 7924, Missoula, MT 59807 • whitewater rafting & kayaking

Adventure Photo Tours 702/889-8687 311 S Valley View Blvd #X-106, Las Vegas, NV 89102 • off-road sight seeing tours

Ahwahnee Whitewater Expeditions 209/533-1401, 800/359-9790 PO Box 1161, Columbia, CA 95310 • women-only, co-ed & charter rafting • **IGLTA** member

Alpenglow Adventure Tours 702/588-0044, 888/325-7456 PO Box 6961, Stateline, NV 89449 • outdoor adventure at Lake Tahoe & the Sierra • small groups

Amphibious Horizons 410/267-8742, 888/458-8786 600 Quiet Waters Park Rd, Annapolis, MD 21403 • lesbian-owned sea kayaking & adventure travel in Chesapeake Bay, Louisiana & Baja Mexico • all levels

Blue Moon Explorations 360/856-5622, 800/966-8806 4658 Blank Rd, Sedro-Woolley, WA 98284 • sea kayaking & ski trips in Pacific Northwest & Hawaii • women-only & co-ed trips

Bluff Expeditions 435/672-2446, 888/637-2582 PO Box 219, Bluff, UT 84512 • wilderness experience with an archaeological emphasis • hiking, biking & van tours

Cow Pie Adventures 801/250–8266, 888/4–COWPIE PO BOX 6, Magna, UT 84044 • back-country adventures in southern Utah • Dutch-oven cooking, hiking, biking & fishing

Great Canadian Ecoventures 868/920–7110, 800/667–9453 PO Box 2481, Yellowknife, NT X1A 2P8, Canada • wildlife photography tours

Greentracks 970/884–6107, 800/9–MONKEY 10 Town Plaza, Suite 231, Durango, CO 81301 • Amazon expeditions

Keane Bush Tours 61 2/9545 4955 PO Box 823, Sutherland, NSW 1499, Australia • retrace the voyage of the First Fleet • guided tours of Sydney Cove

Lodestar Llama Trekking Adventures 250/229–5354 Box 84, Procter, BC V0G 1V0, Canada • wilderness treks • some women-only trips

Lotus Land Tours 604/684–4922, 800/528–3531 1251 Cardero St, Ste 2005, Vancouver, BC V6G 2H9, Canada • day paddle trips, no experience necessary (price includes pick-up & meal)

McKinley Air Service 907/733–1765, 800/564–1765 PO Box 544, Talkeetna, AK 99676 • '2 babes & a bird' • women-owned flight-seeing company at Mt McKinley, AK

McNamara Ranch 719/748–3466 4620 County Rd 100, Florissant, CO 80816 • horseback tours & vacations for up to 4 people

Mountain Madness 206/937–8389, 800/328–5925 4218 SW Alaska, Ste 206, Seattle, WA 98116 • climbs in US & abroad • several women-only trips

Natural Habitat Adventures 303/449–3711, 800/543–8917 2945 Center Green Ct, Ste H, Boulder, CO 80301 • up-close encounters world-wide with wildlife in their natural habitats

Outland Adventures 206/932–7012 PO Box 16343, Seattle, WA 98116 • ecologically sensitive cultural tours with snorkeling & biking in Central America, Canada, Alaska & Washington State

Paddling South & Saddling South 707/942–4550, 800/398–6200 PO Box 827, Calistoga, CA 94515 • horseback, mountain biking, & sea kayak trips in Baja • call for complete calendar

Passage to Utah 801/519–2400, 800/677–0553 113 South 900 East, Salt Lake City, UT 84102 • custom trips in the West including hiking, horseback riding & river riding

Planet Explorer 250/656–5181, 877/SEAL–ADV PO Box 8659, Victoria, BC V8W 3S2, Canada • worldwide adventure travel

Puffin Family Charters 907/278–3346, 800/978–3346 PO Box 90743, Anchorage, AK 99509

Rainbow Country Tours/B&B 801/826–4567, 800/252–8824 PO Box 333, Escalante, UT 84726 • gay-friendly hiking in Utah with custom tours available

Rockwood Adventures 604/926–7705, 888/236–6606 1330 Fulton Ave, West Vancouver, BC V7T 1N8, Canada • rain forest walks for all levels with free hotel pick up

Sila Sojourns 867/633-8453 Box 5095, Whitehorse, YK Y1A 4Z2, Canada • wilderness & creative journeys • women's writing retreat

Snow Lion Expeditions 801/355–6555, 800/525–8735 350 South 400 East #G-2, Salt Lake City, UT 84111 • treks through the Himalayas

SNV International 604/683–5101 Ste 402, 1045 Howe St, Vancouver, BC V6Z 2A9, Canada • hiking & helicopter-hiking trips in Northern & Western Canada

Voyager North Outfitters 218/365–3251, 800/848–5530 1829 E Sheridan, Ely, MN 55731 • canoe outfitting & trips

Water Sport People 305/296–4546 1430 Thompson, Key West, FL 33040 • scuba-diving instruction & group charters

Wildlife Safari 925/376–5595, 800/221–8118 346 Rheem Blvd #107, Moraga, CA 94556 • photographic safaris • Eastern & Southern Africa, Egypt & Saychelles Islands • **IGLTA** member

Spiritual/Health Vacations

Women Only

Earthing Spirit 860/930-8761 18 Summerwood Rd, W. Simsbury, CT 06092 • vision quests for women in transition

Her Wild Song 207/721-9005 PO Box 515, Brunswick, ME 04011 • contemplative wilderness journeys for women

Sacred Journeys for Womyn 707/874-9040, 888/779-6696 PO Box 893, Occidental, CA 95465 • mystical adventures in England & Ireland
March—16-24—Spring Retreat in Hawaii
June—16-28—Sheela-na-Gig journey to Ireland
August—1-13—Mists of Avalon Journey to England
September—10-22—Pilgrimage to the Awakening Mother in Israel

Venus Adventures 207/773-9235 PO Box 7616, Portland, ME 04112 • goddess-oriented tours for women to sacred sites in England & Ireland

Wilderness Rites 415/457-3691 20 Spring Grove Ave, San Rafael, CA 94901 • vision quests for women

Women's Mysteries Tours 303/399-1646 1544 York St, Denver, CO 80206 • sacred adventures • healing journeys

Ya-ya Journeys/ Goddess Tours 970/352-1643 2101 24th St, Greeley, CO 80631 • pilgrimages for women to sacred places of the world
December—7-14, 1999—Goddesses of Maya Land
February—28-March 12—Goddesses of Central Mexico

Mostly Women

Hawk, I'm Your Sister 505/984-2268 PO Box 9109-WT, Santa Fe, NM 87504 • women's wilderness canoe trips & writing retreats in the Americas, Norway & New Zealand

Gay/Lesbian

Spirit Journeys 828/258-8880, 800/490-3684 PO Box 3046, Asheville, NC 28802 • spiritual retreats, workshops, & adventure trips

Thematic Tours

Mostly Men

Connections Tours 305/673-3153, 800/688-8463 (OUT-TIME) 169 Lincoln Rd, Ste 302, Miami Beach, FL 33139 • local arrangements in Florida • also Moscow, UK, Rio & more • **IGLTA** member

Women Only

Canyon Calling 520/282-0916, 800/664-8922 215 Disney Ln, Sedona, AZ 86336 • 7-day tours of the Southwest, Canada & New Zealand & Fiji • May-October each year

Club Skirts 888/443-4624 Club Skirts/Girl BarDinah Shore Women's Weekend parties • Dinah Shore hotline: 888-44-DINAH • also Club Skirts Labor Day in Monterey • Monterey hotline: 888-5-SKIRTS

In the Company of Women 407/331-3466 PO Box 522344, Longwood, FL 32752 • various packages & adventures for women

International Women's Studies Institute 650/323-2013 PO Box 1067, Palo Alto, CA 94302 • travel-study programs • cross-cultural • school credit available

Joani Weir Productions & Klub Banshee 310/289-9430 all-inclusive hotel & entertainment package for women during Dinah Shore Weekend • special events throughout the year

Robin Tyler Tours 818/893-4075 15842 Chase St, North Hills, CA 91343
August—28-September 8, 2002—Women's Tour to Sydney Gay Games

RVing Women 480/983-4678, 888/557-8464 PO Box 1940, Apache Jct., AZ 85217 • RV club for women • call for events

Tours of Exploration 604/886-7300, 800/690-7887 PO Box 48225, Vancouver, BC V7X 1N8, Canada • eco-cultural journeys for women
August—4-19—Ecuador

Tropical Tune-ups 808/882-7355, 800/587-0405 PO Box 4488, Waikoloa, HI 96738 • customized all-inclusive retreats for 2 or more women • beachfront locations

Wild Women Adventures 707/829-3670, 800/992-1322 152 Bloomfield, Sebastopol, CA 95472 • 'insanity with dignity' • absolutely fabulous travel for small groups & individuals • call for complete schedule
January—8-15—The Vacation That Never Ends, Costa Azul, Mexico
February—26-March 4—What's Mayan is Yours, Yucatan Peninsula, Mexico
March—14-27—The Queens of Sheba, Tanzania, Africa
April—21-May 1—It's Good To Be the Queen, London, England
May—5-17—Les Femmes Sauvages, Paris and the Loire Valley, France
June—4-14—Enchanted Italy, Florence, Italy
July—8-15—Red Hot Mamas, San Miguel de Allende, Mexico
August—26-September 5—Erin Go Braghless, Dublin, Ireland
September—30-October 7—Get to Know Taro, Rio Calente, Mexico
October—27-November 12—Thaim of Your Life, Thailand
November—16-20—Wild Women Take Manhattan
December—17-27—Yes, Virginia, There is a Santa Claus, Windstar off Costa Rica & Panama Coast

Mostly Women

Lost Coast Llama Caravans 77321 Usal Rd, Whitehorn, CA 95489 • women-led pack trips

Gay/Lesbian

Adventure Tours 207/885-9889, 888/206-6523 PO Box 6538, Scarborough, ME 04070-6538 • custom & group packages to Costa Rica, Montreal & Quebec City • **IGLTA** member

African Outing 27 21/61 4028 5 Alcyone Rd, Claremont, Capetown 7700, South Africa • gay/lesbian safaris & more • **IGLTA** member

Aloha Lambda Weddings 808/922-5176, 800/982-5176 PO Box 159005, Honolulu, HI 96830 • all-inclusive wedding ceremonies in Hawaii

Arco Iris Services 619/297-0897, 800/765-4370 1286 University Ave, #154, San Diego, CA 92103 • gay Mexico experts
December—28, 1999-January 4—Puerto Vallarta New Year's
March—4-9—Veracruz
May—4-8—Puerto Vallarta
June—22-26—Mexico City
October—5-9—Cancun
October—26-30—Guadalajara

Cruisin' the Castro 415/550-8110 375 Lexington St, San Francisco, CA 94110 • guided walking tour of the Castro, includes brunch • **IGLTA** member

Doin' It Right In Puerto Vallarta 619/297–3642, 800/936–3646 1010 University Ave #C113-741, San Diego, CA 92103 • your gay Puerto Vallarta specialist • **IGLTA** member

Eat Quiche Tour & Travel 514/279–0698, 800/575–6955 5143 St-Laurent, Montreal, PQ H2T 1R9, Canada • packages to Montreal, Quebec City, Toronto & other major Canadian destinations • **IGLTA** member

Fiesta Tours 415/986–1134, 888/229–8687 323 Geary St #619, San Francisco, CA 94102 • tours to Latin America for New Year's & Carnival in Rio • **IGLTA** member

Gay Hawaiian Excursions 808/891–8603, 800/311–4460 PO Box 1067, Kihei, HI 96753 • inbound travel arrangements • also weddings • **IGLTA** member

Going Your Way Tours 860/447–1845 or 447–9180, 800/283–8408 109 Dayton Rd #A, Waterford, CT 06385 • escorted tours to London, Paris & more

December—23, 1999-January 3—A Dickens Christmas in London & Gay Millennium New Years in Paris
May—Italy by Rail: Rome, Florence, Venice & Milan
October—Athens & Isles of Greece

Good Time Gay Productions 305/864–9431, 888/429–3527 485 South Shore Dr, Miami Beach, FL 33141 • specializing in gay Florida • custom packages • **IGLTA** member

Mistral Tours 33 490/438 690 4 Rue Pissantour, 13150 Boulbon, France • sightseeing, hiking, biking in Provence, France • also French language courses

National Gay Pilots Association 703/660–3852 PO Box 27542, Washington, DC 20038-7542 • several annual gatherings • call for more info

P.A.T.H. Adventure Tours of Australia 011/61–8–8271 4068 17 Rose Terrace, Wayville, SA 5034, Australia

Pacific Ocean Holidays 808/923–2400, 800/735–6600 Honolulu, HI • Hawaii vacation packages • **IGLTA** member

Pro Musica Tours 800/916–0312 48 Eighth Ave #127, New York, NY 10014 • gay-only or mixed • performing arts/cultural tours • gay-owned/run

VentureOut 415/626–5678, 888/431–6789 575 Pierce St #604, San Francisco, CA 94117 • cultural & soft adventure travel in 7 different countries

December—20, 1999-January 2—Discovering South Africa
March—5-18—Thailand
April—10-15—Caribbean
May—Italy
June—France
July—Costa Rica
July-August—Holland
September—France
October—Northern California
November—Thailand

Victorian Home Walks 415/252–9485 2226 15th St, San Francisco, CA 94114 • historical walking tour of San Francisco's Victorian homes • **IGLTA** member

Way To Go Costa Rica 919/782–1900, 800/835–1223 2801 Blue Ridge Rd, Raleigh, NC 27607 • personalized itineraries • **IGLTA** member

Straight/Gay

Alaska Railroad Scenic Tours 907/265–2494, 800/544–0552 PO Box 107500, Anchorage, AK 99510-750

Asian Pacific Adventures 818/886–5190, 800/825–1680 9010 Reseda Blvd #227, Northridge, CA 91324-5872 • custom tours to Asia, India, Nepal & more • call for complete schedule

December—16, 1999-January 2—Millennium Extravaganza at Angkor Wat
December—16, 1999-January 1—Rainforests of Northern Vietnam
December—17, 1999-January 1—Tribal Burma
December—18, 1999-January 2—Millennium Special Vietnam Bike
December—19, 1999-January 5—Millennium a la Rudyard Kipling: on the Banks of the Irrawaddy
December—20, 1999-January 11—Ancient Cultures of a Young Nation: Pakistan
December—25, 1999-January 11—Authentic Vietnam

Carol Nashe Group 617/437–9757 566 Commonwealth Ave #601, Boston, MA 02215 • golf trips to Ireland • some women-only trips

Earth Walks 505/988–4157 PO Box 8534, Santa Fe, NM 87504 • guided tour of American Southwest & Mexico

Ecotour Expeditions, Inc 401/423–3377, 800/688–1822 PO Box 128, Jamestown, RI 02835-1822 • small group boat tours of the Amazon & more • call for color catalog

Escape Cruises 305/296–4608 Key West Bight Marina, Key West, FL • 3-hr reef trip & sunset cruise on 'SS Sunshine'

Heritage Tours 212/206–8400, 800/378–4555 216 W 18th St #1001, New York, NY 10011 • custom trips to Turkey, Spain, South Africa & Morocco

December 25, 1999—January 6—New Millennium in Morocco

Holbrook Travel 352/377–7111, 800/451–7111 3540 NW 13th St, Gainesville, FL 32609 • natural history tours in Central America • small groups

Kenny Tours, Ltd. 410/643–9200, 800/648–1492 106 Market Ct, Stevensville, MD 21666-2162 • trips to Ireland & Britain • **IGLTA** member

New England Vacation Tours 802/464-2076, 800/742-7669 PO Box 560, West Dover, VT 05356 • gay/lesbian tours (including fall foliage) conducted by a mainstream tour operator

Pacha Tours 408/777-9310 1447 Johnson Ave, San Jose, CA 95129 • trips to Turkey • **IGLTA** member

Provence in Three Dimensions 503/233-1934 222 SE 18th Ave, Portland, OR 97214 • cooking tours in Provence, France

Ski Connections/Passport to Europe 310/752-9151, 800/754-1888 11601 Wilshire Blvd #101, Los Angeles, CA 90025 • **IGLTA** member

March—Ski Safari, Salzburg, Austria

Skunk Train California Western 707/459-5248 299 E Commercial St, Willits, CA • scenic train trips in Northern California

Stockler Expeditions 954/472-7163, 800/591-2955 10266 NW 4th Ct, Plantation, FL 33324 • trips to Bolivia, Brazil, Costa Rica & more

Tall Ship Adventures 303/755-7983, 800/662-0090 1389 S Havana St, Aurora, CO 80012 • Caribbean tours & cruises • **IGLTA** member

Custom Tours

Gay/Lesbian

L'Arc en Ciel Voyages 610/964-7888, 800/965-LARC (5272) PO Box 234, Wayne, PA 19087-0254 • custom-designed tour programs for the gay/lesbian community • groups or individuals • **IGLTA** member

June—Eurogames VII, Zurich, Switzerland

Various Tours

Women Only

International Association for Women's Accommodation 011-031/331-5497 Polygonstr 5, CH-3014 Bern, Switzerland • organization arranging overnight accommodations for travelling women on the basis of reciprocity • $25 membership

Silke's Travel for Women 02/9380 6244 263 Oxford St, Darlinghurst, NSW 2010, Australia

Gay/Lesbian

All About Destinations 602/277-2703, 800/375-2703 Gallery 3 Plaza, 3819 N 3rd St, Phoenix, AZ 85012-2074 • **IGLTA** member

Allegro Travel 212/666-6700 900 West End Ave #12C, New York, NY 10025 • 22 departures yearly to Russia, Italy, Egypt & Scandinavia

Family Abroad 212/459-1800, 800/999-5500 40 W 57th St, New York, NY 10019 • all-inclusive package & guided motorcoach tours in Europe, Asia, Africa & South America • **IGLTA** member

Friends of Dorothy Cruises 415/864-1600, 415/865-0100 1177 California St #B, San Francisco, CA 94108 • cruises, tours & adventures • **IGLTA** member

Sundance Travel 949/453-8687, 800/424-3434 x277 8687 Research Dr, Irvine, CA 92618-4204 • group tours to Rio de Janeiro • **IGLTA** member

Urban Travel 401/751-5624 161 Federal Street, Providence, RI 02903 • tours, cruises, commitment ceremonies & more

Straight/Gay

Beechman Agencies 808/923-2433, 888/233-2462 408 Lewers St, Oahu, HI 96815 • discount tickets & tours

altitude 2000

above it all

FEBRUARY 6-13, 2000

Out On The Slopes Productions presents the 8th annual gay & lesbian ski week at Whistler Resort

1-888-ALTITUDE **www.outontheslopes.com**

COMPLETE PACKAGES Bliss Tours - Official Tour Operator of Altitude 1-800-636-0810

ACCOMMODATION ONLY Powder Resort Properties - mention Altitude for reduced rates 1-800-777-0185

Coast Mountain Photography

Events

December 1999

New Year's: **Millennium Party** *Egypt*
10 days in Cairo & more • sail the Nile • gay/lesbian ☎415/**931-1026**, 888/**922-2916** Web: www.songmaster1.com

January 2000

22-29: **Aspen Gay Ski Week** *Aspen, CO*
gay/lesbian • 2000+ attendees ☎970/**925-9249** ✉ c/o **Aspen Gay/Lesbian Community Fund**, PO Box 3143, Aspen, CO 81612 Web: www.gayskiweek.com

27-30: **Women's Ski & Snowboard Camp** *Jackson Hole, WY*
4 days of skiing & parties on the slopes • women only ☎307/**739-2686** ✉ c/o **Women's Ski Camp**, PO Box 290, Teton Village, WY 83025 Email: lessons@jacksonhole.com Web: www.jacksonhole.com

February 2000

3-6: **Girlz 'n the Snow** *Copper Mountain, CO*
benefit for National Center for Lesbian Rights • women only ☎303/**433-9234** Email: girlznthesnow.com Web: www.girlznthesnow.com

6-13: **Whistler Gay Ski Week: Altitude 2000** *Whistler, Canada*
6th Annual Gay/Lesbian Ski Week • popular destination 75 miles N of Vancouver • gay/lesbian ☎604/**688-5079**, 888/**258-4883** ✉ c/o **Out On The Slopes Productions**, 101-1184 Denman St #190, Vancouver, BC, Canada V6G 2M9 Email: altitude@outontheslopes.com Web: www.outontheslopes.com

13: **Desert AIDS Walk** *Palm Springs, CA*
gay/lesbian ☎760/**325-9255** ✉ c/o **Desert AIDS Project**, 750 S Vella Rd, Palm Springs, CA 92264

19-26: **Annual Women's Get-Away Week** *Banff, Canada*
skiing, theme parties, wine tasting & more • 1% of proceeds go to American Society Breast Cancer Program • women only • 200 attendees ☎800/**875-6408** ✉ c/o **Alpine Ski & Sun Holidays**, 651 Topeka Way #720, Castle Rock, CO 80104 Email: pinholst@slash.net Web: www.assh.com/snow

TBA: **Oregon Gay/ Lesbian Ski Week & Winter Carnival** *Bend, OR*
a week of fun on Mt Bachelor • gay/lesbian ☎800/**660-2754**, 818/**553-3333** Email: reservations@sportours.com Web: sportours.com

March 2000

7: **Mardi Gras** *New Orleans, LA*
North America's rowdiest block party • mixed gay/straight ☎504/**566-5011** ✉ c/o **New Orleans Convention & Visitors Bureau**, 1520 Sugarbowl Dr, New Orleans, LA 70112 Web: www.neworleanscvb.com

20-26: **Nabisco Dinah Shore Golf Tournament** *Palm Springs, CA*
see Club Skirts under Tour Operators for party & accomodation info • mostly women ☎760/**324-4546** ✉ c/o **Nabisco Dinah Shore**, 2 Racquet Club Dr, Rancho Mirage, CA 92270 Email: info@nabisco.com Web: www.nabiscodinahshore.com

23-26: **Dinah Shore Women's Weekend** *Palm Springs, CA*
huge gathering of lesbians for mega dance parties, huge pool parties, comedy, national recording artists & yes, some golf watching • women only ☎888/**44-DINAH** ✉ c/o **Club Skirts & Girl Bar**, 584 Castro St, San Francisco, CA 94114 Email: info@clubskirts.com Web: www.girlspot.com/dinah.htm

TBA: **Fest'iver de Quebec** *Quebec City, Canada*
Quebec's annual gay/lesbian festival of skiing & winter activities • gay/lesbian ☎877/**686-9243** ✉ c/o **Benoit Morency**, 1122 Boul de Maisonneuve Est, Montreal, QC, Canada H2L 1Z5 EMAIL: terdezom@laval.com

TBA: **SWING (Skiing With International Gays)** *Lenzerheide, Switzerland*
skiing, ice skating & moonlit tours • special dinners • disco at night • movies, cabaret & more • 90 min from Zurich • mostly men ☎011-41-81/**384-0111** ✉ c/o **Hotel Schweizerhof**, Hotel Schweizerhof, 7078 Lenzerheide, Switzerland EMAIL: mail@gayski.ch WEB: www.gayski.ch

TBA: **Women on Top Theatre Festival** *Boston, MA*
ground-breaking theater from local female artists • takes place during Women's History Month • mostly women • $16-35 ☎617/**426-0320** ✉ c/o **Boston Center for the Arts, Black Box Theatre**, 539 Tremont St, Boston, MA 02116

April 2000

1-4: **Rainbow Ski Weekend** *Mammoth Mountain, CA*
3 days of fun on the slopes in Northern California • complete packages available • book early • gay/lesbian ☎619/**435-0996** ✉ c/o **Rainbow Ski Weekend**, PO Box 182170, Coronado, CA 92178-2170 EMAIL: Leftie69@aol.com WEB: www.rainbowski.com

28-30: **PFLAG Convention** *Washington, DC*
annual convention of Parents, Friends & Family of Lesbians & Gays • 1000+ attendees ☎202/**638-4200** ✉ c/o **PFLAG**, 1101 14th St NW, Ste 1030, Washington, DC 20005 EMAIL: bmckew@pflag.org WEB: www.pflag.org

30: **Millennium March on Washington** *Washington, DC*
show your support for the lesbigaytrans+ community in Washington DC • gay/lesbian ☎818/**893-4075**, 800/**936-8514** ✉ c/o **Robin Tyler Events**, 15842 Chast St, North Hills, CA 91343

30: **Queensday** *Amsterdam, Netherlands*
huge street festival to celebrate what was originally the birthday of the Queen Mother • gay/lesbian

TBA: **AIDS Dance-a-thon LA** *Los Angeles, CA*
AIDS benefit at Universal Studios • mixed gay/straight • $75+ pledges EMAIL: aidswalkLA@aol.com

TBA: **AIDS Dance-a-thon San Francisco** *San Francisco, CA*
mixed gay/straight ☎415/**282-2072** ✉ c/o **Dance-a-thon**, 584-B Castro St, San Francisco, CA 94114

TBA: **Russian River Women's Wknd** *Guerneville, CA*
this tiny town is packed with dykes for a fun weekend of parties • 2 hrs north of San Francisco • mostly women ☎707/**869-3533**, 800/**253-8800**

May 2000

1-7: **Pridefest America** *Philadelphia, PA*
national conference on lesbian & gay culture • film, performances, literature, sports, seminars, parties & more • gay/lesbian ☎215/**732-3378**, 800/**990-3378** ✉ c/o **Pridefest Philadelphia**, 200 S Broad St #200, Philadelphia, PA 19102 EMAIL: info@pridefest.org WEB: www.pridefest.org

16: **Minnesota AIDS Walk** *Minneapolis, MN*
enjoy a walk through Minnehaha Park & raise money for local AIDS organizations • mixed gay/straight • 15,000 attendees ☎612/**373-2437** ✉ c/o **Minnesota AIDS Project**, 1400 Park Ave, Minneapolis, MN 55404 WEB: www.mnaidsproject.org

Memorial Day Wknd: **Black Lesbian/Gay Pride Weekend** *Washington, DC*
gay/lesbian ☎202/**667-8188** ✉ c/o **BLGPD**, PO Box 77071, Washington, DC 20013 EMAIL: dcblackpride@hotmail.com WEB: www.dcblackpride.org

May 1-7, 2000

Celebrate gay and lesbian culture in Philadelphia for 7 days at the nation's largest gay and lesbian symposium and festival. The celebration commences the day after the Millennium March on Washington.

www.pridefest.org
1-800-990-FEST
info@pridefest.org

San Francisco Lesbian, Gay, Bisexual, Transgender Pride Parade & Festival

JUNE 24th & 25th, 2000

Visit our website:
www.sfpride.org

26-29: **Club Curve Women's Weekend** *Pensacola, FL*
☎800/**998-5565**

26: **Gay/ Lesbian Day at Great America** *Santa Clara, CA*
join 7000 men & women for a special night at California's favorite amusement park • gay/lesbian ☎415/**646-0890** ✉ c/o **Gus Presents**, 1459 18th St #141, San Francisco, CA 94107 **Email:** gus@guspresents.com **Web:** www.guspresents.com

26-29: **Pensacola Memorial Day Weekend** *Pensacola, FL*
many parties on beaches & in bars • gay/lesbian • 35,000+ attendees ☎850/**438-0333** **Email:** DeltaDyke1@aol.com

26-June 11: **Spoleto Festival** *Charleston, SC*
one of the continent's premier avant-garde cultural festivals • mixed gay/straight ☎803/**722-2764** ✉ c/o **Spoleto Festival USA**, PO Box 157, Charleston, SC 29402-0157 **Web:** www.spoletousa.org

TBA: **St Martin Vacation for Women** *St Martin, Virgin Islands*
week-long vacation at a beautiful, private resort • entertainment, optional excursions, all food & drink included • women only ☎888/**443-4624** ✉ c/o **Club Skirts & Girl Bar**, 584 Castro St, San Francisco, CA 94114 **Email:** info@clubskirts.com **Web:** www.girlspot.com

TBA: **20th Annual Tournament of the Int'l Gay Bowling Organization**
☎703/**820-8313** ✉ c/o **IGBO**, PO Box 1692, Arlington, VA 22206 **Email:** IGBO99DC@aol.com

TBA: **AIDS Walk-a-thon** *New York City, NY*
AIDS benefit • mixed gay/straight ☎212/**807-9255** ✉ c/o **Gay Men's Health Crisis**, PO Box 10, Old Chelsea Stn, New York, NY 10113-0010

TBA: **Art for AIDS** *Pittsburgh, PA*
huge party benefitting AIDS charities • gay/lesbian ☎412/**441-9786** ✉ c/o **Persad Center**, 5150 Penn Ave, Pittsburgh, PA 15224

TBA: **Splash: Houston Black Gay Pride** *Houston, TX*
gay/lesbian ✉ c/o **Houston Splash**, PO Box 35431, Houston, TX **Email:** info@houstonsplash.com **Web:** www.houstonsplash.com

TBA: **We're Funny That Way** *Toronto, Canada*
comedians from around the world perform at Canada's International Gay/Lesbian Comedy Festival • gay/lesbian ☎416/**699-1974** ✉ c/o **WFTW Productions**, 50 Alexander St, Ste 201, Toronto, ON, Canada M4Y 1B6 **Email:** funnythat@aol.com **Web:** www.members.aol.com\werefunny

TBA: **Wigswood** *Atlanta, GA*
annual festival of peace, love & wigs • street party fundraiser • wig watchers welcome • 1000+ attendees ☎404/**874-6782** ✉ c/o **Act Up Atlanta**, 828 W Peachtree St NW, Ste 206-A, Atlanta, GA 30308-1146

TBA: **Wild Women's Weekend** *Clearlake, CA*
parties • BBQ • tournaments • not for the mild mannered! • women only • $25+camping/RV ☎707/**279-0208**, 800/**396-6224** ✉ c/o **Edgewater Resort**, 6420 Soda Bay Rd, Kelseyville, CA 95451 **Web:** www.edgewaterresort.net

June 2000

on-going: **Lesbigaytrans Pride** *Everywhere, USA*
celebrate yourself & attend one – or many – of the hundreds of Gay Pride parades & festivities happening in cities around the continent **Web:** www.interpride.org/igc99/index.htm

on-going: **Music in the Mountains** *Nevada City, CA*
summer music festival • mixed gay/straight ☎530/**265-6124**, 800/**218-2188** ✉ c/o **Music in the Mountains**, PO Box 1451, Nevada City, CA 95959 **Email:** mim@nccn.net **Web:** www.ncgold.com/MIM

June thru July: **National Queer Arts Festival** *San Francisco, CA*
series of cultural events, performances & exhibitions highlighting artists in the San Francisco Bay Area • gay/lesbian ☎415/**552-7709**, 415/**552-7200** ✉ c/o **National Queer Arts Festival**, PMB 451, 584 Castro St , San Francisco, CA 94114 **EMAIL:** qcc99@aol.com **WEB:** www.queerculturalcenter.org

1-4: **Gay Day at Disneyworld** *Orlando, FL*
☎888/**429-3527** ✉ c/o **Good Time Gay Productions**, 450 W 62nd St, Miami Beach, FL 33140 **EMAIL:** gayfla@aol.com **WEB:** goodtimegaytravel.com

4-10: **California AIDS Ride** *San Francisco, CA*
AIDS benefit bike ride from San Francisco to LA • mixed gay/straight ☎800/**825-1000**, 415/**908-0400** ✉ c/o **Pallotta TeamWorks**, 1525 Crossroads of the World, Los Angeles, CA 90028 **WEB:** www.aidsride.org

6: **PrideFest** *Milwaukee, WI*
celebrate lesbigay pride at Henry W Maier Festival Park • gay/lesbian ☎414/**272-3378** ✉ c/o **PrideFest**, PO Box 511763, Milwaukee, WI 53203-0301 **EMAIL:** pridemilw@aol.com **WEB:** www.pridefest.com

18: **Unofficial Gay Day at Cedar Point** *Sandusky, OH*
wear red to show your support on the unofficial Gay Day at this popular amusement park • mixed gay/straight

21: **Pearl Day at Six Flags** *Atlanta, GA*
unofficial gay celebration at Six Flags amusement park • show your support with a string of Commemorative Pearls • proceeds go to local charities • gay/lesbian ☎404/**885-6800 EXT 232**, 404/**872-3975** **EMAIL:** info@pearlday.com **WEB:** www.pearlday.com

22-25: **Washington DC AIDS Ride** *Washington, DC*
AIDS benefit bike ride from North Carolina to Washington DC • gay/lesbian ☎800/**825-1000**, 202/**293-7433** ✉ c/o **Pallotta TeamWorks**, 1525 Crossroads of the World, Los Angeles, CA 90028 **WEB:** www.aidsride.org

24: **San Francisco Dyke March** *San Francisco, CA*
join thousands of dykes of all shapes, colors & sizes for music, marching & more through the streets of the Mission & the Castro ☎415/**241-8882** **WEB:** www.fireworx.org/dykemarch.html

24-25: **San Francisco LGBT Pride Parade/ Celebration** *San Francisco, CA*
gay/lesbian ☎415/**864-3733** ✉ c/o **SFLGBTPCC**, 1390 Market St #1225, San Francisco, CA 94102 **EMAIL:** sfpride@aol.com **WEB:** www.sf-pride.org

TBA: **AIDS Walk Boston** *Boston, MA*
mixed gay/straight • 7000+ attendees ☎415/**392-9255** ✉ c/o **Miller Zeichik & Assoc**, PO Box 193920, San Francisco, CA 94119-3920 **EMAIL:** awsf@earthlink.net **WEB:** www.aidswalk.net

TBA: **Annual Black Lesbian/ Gay Cruise** *Baja, Mexico*
cruise from LA to Baja Mexico • gay/lesbian ☎415/**931-1026**, 888/**922-2916** **EMAIL:** bgc@songmaster1.com **WEB:** www.songmaster1.com

TBA: **Baltimore Black Gay Pride** *Baltimore, MD*
gay/lesbian

TBA: **Black Gay Pride** *Memphis, TN*
gay/lesbian **WEB:** www.chocolatecityusa.com/hotspots/events.htm

TBA: **Black Lesbian/ Gay Pride** *Oakland, CA*
celebrate with a weekend of conferences, awards ceremonies & parties • gay/lesbian ☎510/**268-0646** ✉ c/o **OBGLTP**, 484 Lakepark Ave #1, Oakland, CA 94610 **EMAIL:** peopleinpride@hotmail.com

TBA: **Gay Day at Six Flags** *Jackson, NJ*
unofficial Gay Day at this popular amusement park • wear red to show your support • gay/lesbian

July 2000

1-2: **At the Beach Weekend** *Los Angeles, CA*
celebrate a weekend of Black gay pride in Malibu • gay/lesbian ☎213/**969–1919** ✉ c/o ATB, PO Box 480439, Los Angeles, CA 90048

1-9: **World Pride Roma 2000** *Rome,Italy*
celebrate GLBT pride in this beautiful city • gay/lesbian ☎0039/**06.54.13.985** ✉ c/o Mario Mieli, via Corinto 5, 00146 Rome, Italy EMAIL: info@mariomieli.it WEB: www.mariomieli.it

3: **Independence 2000: Celebrate the African-American Lesbigaytrans Community** *Chicago, IL*
a weekend of parties, seminars & more • gay/lesbian ☎773/**731–8665** ✉ c/o Chicago Black Pride, Inc, 7836 S Kingston Ave, Chicago, IL 60649 EMAIL: chicagoblackpride@yahoo.com WEB: www.geocities.com/WestHollywood/Cafe/2381/

10-15: **Twin Cities-Wisconsin-Chicago AIDS Ride** *Minneapolis, MN*
bike from Minneapolis to Chicago • proceeds donated to AIDS charities • gay/lesbian ☎800/**825–1000,** 612/**871–0002** ✉ c/o Pallotta TeamWorks, 1525 Crossroads of the World, Los Angeles, CA 90028 WEB: www.aidsride.org

16: **AIDS Walk San Francisco** *San Francisco, CA*
mixed gay/straight • 7000+ attendees ☎415/**392–9255** ✉ c/o Miller Zeichik & Assoc, PO Box 193920, San Francisco, CA 94119–3920 EMAIL: awsf@earthlink.net WEB: www.aidswalk.net

TBA: **Black Out 2000** *Cleveland, OH*
Ohio's oldest & largest event celebrating African American gay/lesbian culture • gay/lesbian ☎216/**462–0257,** 888/**825–5226** ✉ c/o Black Out, PO Box 14553, Cleveland, OH 44114

TBA: **CAP the Rockies: Ride for AIDS** *Denver, CO*
a five day ride • 300 miles at elevations up to 12,000 feet • gay/lesbian ☎888/**572–4537,** 303/**837–0166** ✉ c/o Colorado AIDS Project, PO Box 18529, Denver, CO 80218–0529 EMAIL: cap@coloaids.org WEB: www.capride.org

TBA: **Crape Myrtle Festival** *Raleigh-Durham, Chapel Hill, NC*
week-long festival to raise money for AIDS & lesbigay concerns • movies • tournaments • raffle • gala Saturday • mixed gay/straight • 1500 attendees ☎919/**967–3606,** 800/**494–8497** ✉ c/o Crape Myrtle Festival, Inc, PO Box 9054, Chapel Hill, NC 27515 WEB: www.datalounge.com\cmf

TBA: **Hotter Than July Weekend** *Detroit, MI*
gay/lesbian ☎313/**438–2613** ✉ c/o Hotter Than July, PO Box 3025, Detroit, MI 48231

TBA: **Northwest Gay/ Lesbian Summer Sports Festival** *Seattle, WA*
gay/lesbian ☎206/**322–7769** ✉ c/o Team Seattle, 1122 East Pike #515, Seattle, WA 98122 EMAIL: info@teamseattle.org WEB: www.teamseattle.org

TBA: **SNAP! Fest** *Omaha, NE*
local theater festival • mixed gay/straight ☎402/**342–9053** ✉ c/o SNAP! Productions, 900 Farnum St #708, Omaha, NE 68102 EMAIL: info@snapproductions.com WEB: www.snapproductions.com

August 2000

3-6: **Black Gay Pride** *New York City, NY*
gay/lesbian ☎212/**613–0097** ✉ c/o Black Pride NYC Inc, PO BOX 20399, London Terrace Station, New York City, NY 10011–0004 EMAIL: blackpridenyc@hotmail.com WEB: www.blackpridenyc.com

8-13: **Michigan Womyn's Music Festival** *Walhalla, MI*
40 theater, music & dance performances • workshops, film festival & craft fair • ASL interpreting & differently-abled resources • child care • camping • women only • 5-8000 attendees ☎616/**757–4766,** 616/**898–3707** ✉ c/o WWTMC, PO Box 22, Walhalla, MI 49458 WEB: www.michfest.com

21-27: **Camp Camp** *Kezar Falls, ME*
summer camp for gay/lesbian adults • sports, pottery, theater, yoga & more • gay/lesbian • $725 ☎888/**924-8380** ✉ c/o **Camp Camp**, 91 Jamaica St, Boston, MA 02130
EMAIL: info@campcamp.com **WEB:** www.campcamp.com

TBA: **Aspen Summerfest** *Aspen, CO*
comedy • BBQ • music • hiking, softball & more • gay/lesbian • 350+ attendees
☎970/**925-9249** ✉ c/o **Aspen Gay/Lesbian Community Fund**, PO Box 3143, Aspen, CO 81612

TBA: **Beachfest** *Daytona Beach, FL*
T-dances, beach games, sand sculpture contest, entertainment • gay/lesbian
☎904/**760-9075**, 800/**854-1234 (CONVENTION & VISITORS BUREAU)** ✉ c/o **Greater Daytona Beach Business Guild**, PO Box 3148, Daytona Beach, FL 32126
EMAIL: gordon@bigbeach.net **WEB:** www.daytonabeachfest.com

TBA: **Black Gay Pride** *Cleveland, OH*
gay/lesbian **WEB:** www.chocolatecityusa.com/hotspots/events.htm

TBA: **Black Gay Pride** *Minneapolis/St Paul, MN*
gay/lesbian **WEB:** www.chocolatecityusa.com/hotspots/events.htm

TBA: **Gay Fest** *Toronto, Canada*
celebrate gay pride at Wonderland • fundraiser for various AIDS/Lesbigay organizations of Toronto • gay/lesbian

TBA: **Halsted Street Fair** *Chicago, IL*
a good ol' summer block party on Main St of Boys' Town, USA • gay/lesbian
☎773/**883-0500**

TBA: **National Gay Softball World Series** *Toronto, Canada*
gay/lesbian ☎412/**362-1247** ✉ c/o NAGAAA, 1014 King Ave, Pittsburgh, PA 15206
EMAIL: ndyke@juno.com **WEB:** www.nagaaa.com

September 2000

1-3: **Club Skirts Monterey Bay Women's Wknd** *Monterey, CA*
3 huge dance parties • golf & volleyball tournament • live comedy night • book early! • mostly women ☎888/**5-SKIRTS** ✉ c/o **MT Productions**, 584 Castro St, San Francisco, CA 94114 **EMAIL:** info@clubskirts.com **WEB:** www.girlspot.com/mont.html

1-4: **Great Alberta Campout** *Red Deer, Canada*
3 days of friendly camping fun • meet & greet Friday • pancake breakfast Saturday • games, dances, more • presented by Gay & Lesbian Assoc of Central Alberta • gay/lesbian ☎403/**309-7733**, 403/**340-2198** ✉ c/o **GALACA**, Box 1078, Red Deer, AB, Canada T4N 6S5

1-3: **In the Life Weekend** *Atlanta, GA*
celebrate Black Pride over Labor Day weekend in Atlanta • gay/lesbian ☎404/**872-6410** **EMAIL:** malik64@juno.com **WEB:** www.inthelifeatl.com

2-3: **Festival of Babes** *San Francisco, CA*
annual women's soccer tournament & celebration • mostly women ☎510/**428-1489**, 510/**848-4684** ✉ c/o **GirlJock**, PO Box 882723, San Francisco, CA 94188

4: **Wigstock** *New York City, NY*
outrageous wig/drag/performance festival in Tompkins Square Park in the East Village • gay/lesbian ☎212/**774-7470**

10: **AIDS Walk Denver** *Denver, CO*
☎303/**837-0166** ✉ c/o **Colorado AIDS Project**, PO Box 18529, Denver, CO 80218-0529 **EMAIL:** cap@coloaids.org **WEB:** www.capwalk.org

15-17: **Boston/New York AIDS Ride 4** *Boston, MA*
☎800/**825-1000**, 212/**242-7433** ✉ c/o **Pallotta TeamWorks**, 1525 Crossroads of the World, Los Angeles, CA 90028 **WEB:** www.aidsride.org

17: **Gay Day at Waterworld** *Concord, CA*
20 acres of wet'n'wild waterslide fun • all-park exclusive • plus Dance Island dance party • gay/lesbian ☎415/**646-0890** ✉ c/o **Gus Presents**, 1459 18th St #141, San Francisco, CA 94107 **EMAIL:** gus@guspresents.com **WEB:** www.guspresents.com

24: **AIDS Walk Toronto** *Toronto, Canada*
walk in Toronto & cities across Canada to raise money to fight AIDS • gay/lesbian ☎416/**340-2437** ✉ c/o **AIDS Committee of Toronto**, 399 Church St, Toronto, ON, Canada M5B 2J6

TBA: **AIDS Walk LA** *Los Angeles, CA*
mixed gay/straight ☎323/**466-9255** ✉ c/o **AIDS Walk LA**, PO Box 933005, Los Angeles, CA 90093 **EMAIL:** aidswalkLA@aol.com

TBA: **AIDS Walk Seattle** *Seattle, WA*
mixed gay/straight • 7000+ attendees ☎415/**392-9255** ✉ c/o **Miller Zeichik & Assoc**, PO Box 193920, San Francisco, CA 94119-3920 **EMAIL:** awsf@earthlink.net **WEB:** www.aidswalk.net

TBA: **Catalina Day Cruise from Long Beach** *Catalina, CA*
snacks • entertainment • dancing/DJ • T-Dance at Casino Ballroom in Avalon, Catalina • gay/lesbian • $60 ☎805/**222-7788** ✉ c/o **Odyssey Adventures**, PO Box 221477, Newhall, CA 91322 **WEB:** www.odysseyadventures.com

TBA: **Divafest** *Russian River, CA*
presented by Fife's & the Institute for the Musical Arts • mostly women ☎800/**734-3371** **WEB:** www.ima.org or www.fifes.com

TBA: **Gay Day at Paramount Kings Island** *Cincinnati, OH*
gay/lesbian ☎513/**591-0200** ✉ c/o **Gay & Lesbian Community Center**, 214 E 9th St, 5th flr, Cincinnati, OH 45202 **WEB:** www.gaycincinnati.com

TBA: **Gay Night at Knott's Berry Farm** *Orange County, CA*
amusement park rides, dancing & gay comedy ☎805/**222-7788** ✉ c/o **Odyssey Adventures**, PO Box 221477, Newhall, CA 91322 **WEB:** www.odysseyadventures.com

TBA: **Houston Women's Festival** *Houston, TX*
women from Houston & across Texas gather to enjoy music, art & culture • produced by the Athena Art Project • mostly women ☎713/**861-3316** ✉ c/o **Houston Women's Festival**, PO Box 66604, Houston, TX 77266 EMAIL: hwfestival@earthlink.com WEB: www.hwfestival.org

TBA: **Russian River Women's Wknd** *Guerneville, CA*
this tiny town is packed with dykes for a fun weekend of parties • 2 hrs north of San Francisco • mostly women ☎707/**869-3533**, 800/**253-8800**

TBA: **Wild Western Women's Weekend** *Kent's Store, VA*
live country/western music & dancing • women only • 200 attendees • $85 ☎804/**589-6542** ✉ c/o **Intouch**, Rte 2, Box 1096, Kent's Store, VA 23084 EMAIL: intouchjg@aol.com WEB: www.intouchva.com

TBA: **Wild Women's Weekend** *Clearlake, CA*
parties • BBQ • tournaments • not for the mild mannered! • women only • $25+camping/RV ☎707/**279-0208**, 800/**396-6224** ✉ c/o **Edgewater Resort**, 6420 Soda Bay Rd, Kelseyville, CA 95451 WEB: www.edgewaterresort.net

October 2000

on-going: **October is Breast Cancer Awareness Month** *Cross-country, USA*
check local listings for fund-raising events in your area to fight breast cancer

1: **AIDS Walk** *Islip, NY*
gay/lesbian ☎516/**385-2451** ✉ c/o **Long Island Association for AIDS Care**, PO Box 2859, Huntington Stn, NY 11746 EMAIL: infoLIAAC@aol.com WEB: www.liaac.org

1: **Castro Street Fair** *San Francisco, CA*
arts & community groups street fair • co-founded by Harvey Milk ☎415/**467-3354**

8-14: **Provincetown Women's Week** *Provincetown, MA*
very popular – make your reservations early! • mostly women ☎800/**637-8696**, 508/**487-2313** ✉ c/o **Women Innkeepers of Provincetown**, PO Box 573, Provincetown, MA 02657

11: **National Coming Out Day** *Everytown, USA*
check local listings for events in your area • gay/lesbian ☎800/**866-6263** ✉ c/o **National Coming Out Day**, PO Box 34640, Washington, DC 20043-4640 WEB: http://www.hrc.org

12-15: **Texas AIDS Ride** *Austin, TX*
ride from Houston to Dallas • gay/lesbian ☎800/**825-1000**, 888/**780-7433** ✉ c/o **Pallotta TeamWorks**, 1525 Crossroads of the World, Los Angeles, CA 90028 WEB: www.aidsride.org

15: **Philadelphia AIDS Walk** *Philadelphia, PA*
gay/lesbian ☎215/**731-9255** ✉ c/o **AIDSFUND**, 1227 Locust St, Philadelphia, PA

TBA: **AIDS Walk Atlanta** *Atlanta, GA*
mixed gay/straight • 7000+ attendees ☎415/**392-9255** ✉ c/o **Miller Zeichik & Assoc**, PO Box 193920, San Francisco, CA 94119-3920 EMAIL: awsf@earthlink.net WEB: www.aidswalk.net

TBA: **Black Gay Pride** *Dallas, TX*
gay/lesbian ☎972/**283-1047** ✉ c/o **Underground Station**, PO Box 224571, Dallas, TX 75222 EMAIL: undrgrdsta@aol.com WEB: www.chocolatecityusa.com/hotspots/events.htm

TBA: **Pink Ball Classic** *Dallas, TX*
fund raising golf tournament • mostly women ☎214/**521-5342 x 886 x 4** ✉ c/o **DSGA**, PO Box 190869, Dallas, TX 75219 EMAIL: dsgassn@aol.com

November 2000

TBA: **AIDS Dance-a-thon** *New York City, NY*
AIDS benefit • mixed gay/straight • 6000+ attendees • $75+ pledges ☎212/**807-9255** ✉ c/o **Gay Men's Health Crisis**, PO Box 10, Old Chelsea Stn, New York, NY 10113-0010

TBA: **Divas in the Desert: Black Gay Pride Weekend** *Phoenix, AZ*
mostly men ✉ c/o FinWill Productions, 5713 W Zoe Ella Wy, Glendale, AZ 85306 EMAIL: wfinch@dancris.com

TBA: **Puerto Vallarta Vacation for Women** *Puerto Vallarta, Mexico*
week-long vacation at a beautiful, private resort • entertainment, optional excursions, all food & drink included • women only ☎888/**443-4624** ✉ c/o Club Skirts & Girl Bar, 584 Castro St, San Francisco, CA 94114 EMAIL: info@clubskirts.com WEB: www.girlspot.com/Mexico/mexico.html

December 2000

1-3: **Holly Folly** *Provincetown, MA*
gay & lesbian weekend holiday festival • parties • holiday concert • open houses • proceeds to Provincetown AIDS Support Group & Helping Our Women ☎800/**533-1983** ✉ PO Box 573, Provincetown, MA 02657 EMAIL: hollyfolly@provincetown.com

31: **Mummer's Strut** *Philadelphia, PA*
New Year's Eve party benefitting Pridefest • mixed gay/straight • $40-50 ☎215/**732-3378** ✉ c/o Pridefest, 200 S Broad St, Philadelphia, PA 19102

August 2002

TBA: **Gay Games 2002** *Sydney, Australia*
support lesbian & gay athletes as they compete in Sydney • gay/lesbian WEB: http:/www.dds.nl/~gaygames

WOMEN'S FESTIVALS & GATHERINGS

February 2000

4-6: **South Coast Women's Music & Arts Festival** *Thirroul, Australia*
3 hours south of Sydney • cabins & camping • women only • 200+ attendees ☎61-2/**242-683393** ✉ c/o Waves Music, PO Box 336, 2515 Thirroul, NSW, Australia EMAIL: migwaves@illawarra.starway.net.au

March 2000

31-April 2: **Friends Fest Music Festival** *Dripping Springs, TX*
women only • also Oct 6-8, 2000, open to all ☎512/**894-0567** ✉ c/o Recreation Plantation Campground, 3650 Pursley Rd, Dripping Springs, TX 78620 EMAIL: treeo1@flash.net

TBA: **Gulf Coast Womyn's Festival at Camp SisterSpirit** *New Orleans, LA*
a celebration of womyn's land in the South! • 2 1/2 hours from New Orleans, LA • entertainment & politics • camping available • mostly women ☎601/**344-1411** ✉ c/o Camp SisterSpirit, PO Box 12, Ovett, MS 39464 EMAIL: sisterspir@aol.com

TBA: **Lesbian Pride Weekend** *Denver, CO*
a weekend of parties, events & street festivals in Denver • mostly women ☎303/**778-7900** ✉ c/o Out Front Colorado, 244 Washington St, Denver, CO 80203 EMAIL: outfrontc@aol.com WEB: www.denver.sidewalk.com/outfront

April 2000

TBA: **Women's Week St Croix** *St Croix, Virgin Islands*
relax at the beautiful Cormorant Beach Club • women only ☎800/**998-5565**, 415/**863-1609**

May 2000

26-28: **Wiminfest** *Albuquerque, NM*
music, comedy, art, recreation & dances • mostly women ☎800/**499–5688**, 505/**899–3627** ✉ c/o Women in Movement in New Mexico (WIMINM), PO Box 80204, Albuquerque, NM 87198

29-31: **Campfest Memorial Day Wknd** *Oxford, PA*
'The Comfortable Womyn's Festival' • women only • 1400+ attendees • $200 ☎609/**694–2037** ✉ c/o Womongathering, PO Box 559, Franklinville, NJ 08322 **EMAIL:** camfest@aol.com **WEB:** http//members.aol.com/Campfest

TBA: **Herland Spring Retreat** *Oklahoma City, OK*
music, workshops, campfire events & potluck • boys under 10 only • $15-60 sliding scale registration • mostly women ☎405/**521–9696** ✉ c/o Herland, 2312 NW 39th, Oklahoma City, OK 73112

TBA: **Texas Lesbian Conference** *Houston, TX*
workshops, lectures, films & more • host city rotates between Dallas, Austin, Houston & San Antonio • women only ☎214/**521–5342 x468** ✉ c/o TLC, PO Box191482, Dallas, TX 85219 **EMAIL:** tlcinc@cyberramp.net

Memorial Weekend: **Women Outdoors National Gathering** *Peterborough, NH*
camping • hiking • workshops • women only • 140+ attendees • $120-175 ☎860/**688–7637** ✉ c/o Women Outdoors, Inc, 55 Talbot Ave, Medford, MA 02155 **EMAIL:** info@women-outdoors.org **WEB:** www.women-outdoors.org

June 2000

2-4: **Virginia Women's Music Festival** *Kent's Store, VA*
women only • 600 attendees • $85 ☎804/**589–6542** ✉ c/o Intouch, Rte 2, Box 1096, Kent's Store, VA 23084 **EMAIL:** intouchjg@aol.com **WEB:** www.intouchva.com

8-11: **Womongathering** *Pocono Mtns, PA*
women's spirituality fest • women only • 300+ attendees • $200 ☎609/**694–2037**, 301/**598–9035 (TTY)** ✉ c/o Womongathering, PO Box 559, Franklinville, NJ 08322 **EMAIL:** womongathr@aol.com

24: **Golden Threads Celebration** *Provincetown, MA*
annual gathering of older lesbians • women only ☎802/**848–7037** ✉ c/o Golden Threads, PO Box 65, Richford, VT 05476 **EMAIL:** goldentred@aol.com **WEB:** members.aol.com/goldenthread/index.htm

TBA: **From Gaia's Heart: Maryland Womyn's Gathering** *Maryland Line, MD*
crafts • music • camping • women only ☎410/**435–3111**, 888/**740–GAIA** ✉ c/o From Gaia's Heart, PO Box 65237, Baltimore, MD 21209 **WEB:** www.fromgaiasheart.org

TBA: **Hopland Women's Festival** *Hopland, CA*
women only ☎707/**523–9593 VOICE MAIL** ✉ c/o HWF, 4381 25th St, San Francisco, CA 94114

TBA: **National Women's Music Festival** *Muncie, IN*
mostly women ☎317/**927–9355** ✉ c/o NWMF, PO Box 1427-WT, Indianapolis, IN 46206 **EMAIL:** wia@indy.net or marybyrne9@aol.com **WEB:** www.a1.com/wia (#1, not letter L)

July 2000

14-16: **LandFest** *Holmes County, OH*
camping • workshops • music & more • women only • 100+ attendees ☎216/**371–2434** ✉ c/o Egg Moon Farm & Kimbilio Farm, 1340 Orchard Hts Dr, Mayfield, OH 44124 **EMAIL:** plmichalski@hotmail.com

27-30: **Women's Motorcycle Festival** *Catskill Mtns, NY*
mixed gay/straight ☎914/**657–6227** ✉ c/o Women for Safe Riding, PO Box 146, West Shokan, NY 12494 **EMAIL:** womenride@aol.com

TBA: **National Conference for Lesbians of Size** *Kingston, NY*
women only ☎201/**843–4629** ✉ c/o NOLOSE, 245 8th Ave, New York, NY 10011 EMAIL: nolosee@aol.com WEB: www.breakinc.com

August 2000

first week: **Dyke Art Camp** *Gaston, OR*
45 mi SW of Portland • daily life drawing plus many workshops • vegetarian meals & espresso bar • on 12 secluded acres of women's land • women only ☎503/**985–9549** ✉ c/o Art Springs, 40789 SW Hummingbird Ln, Gaston, OR 97119 EMAIL: artsprng@transport.com

8-13: **Michigan Womyn's Music Festival** *Walhalla, MI*
40 theater, music & dance performances • workshops, film festival & craft fair • ASL interpreting & differently-abled resources • child care • camping • women only • 5-8000 attendees ☎616/**757–4766**, 616/**898–3707** ✉ c/o WWTMC, PO Box 22, Walhalla, MI 49458 WEB: www.michfest.com

26-27: **Women Celebrating Our Diversity** *Luisa, VA*
usually last wknd in Aug • camping, music & more • mostly women ☎540/**894–5126** ✉ c/o Twin Oaks Community, 138 Twin Oaks Rd, Luisa, VA 23093 EMAIL: gathering@twinoaks.org WEB: www.twinoaks.org

TBA: **Sister Subverter** *Minneapolis, MN*
radical women's gathering • trans-women-friendly • women only ☎612/**822–2951** ✉ c/o Sister Subverter, 3926 Stevens Ave, Minneapolis, MN 55409

TBA: **West Kootenay Women's Festival** *Nelson, Canada*
music • art • entertainment • Canada's oldest women's festival • women only • 200-300 attendees • $45-65 ☎250/**352–9916** ✉ c/o West Kootenay Women's Assoc, 420 Mill St, Nelson, BC, Canada V1L 4B8 EMAIL: wkwomyn@netidea.com

September 2000

1-4: **Northeast Women's Musical Retreat** *Branford, CT*
mostly women ☎860/**293–8026** ✉ c/o NEWMR, PO Box 57, Hartford, CT 06141 EMAIL: newmr99@aol.com

3: **Midwest Womyn's Autumnfest** *Dekalb, IL*
one-day outdoor festival the Sunday of Labor Day Weekend • music, crafts, workshops & more • women only ☎815/**748–5359** ✉ c/o Athena Productions, 217 S 2nd St #193, Dekalb, IL 60115 EMAIL: mwautumn@aol.com WEB: www.mwautumnfest.com

8-10: **Sisterspace Wknd** *MD*
women only ☎215/**546–4890**, 215/**546–4202 TDD** ✉ c/o Sisterspace of the Delaware Valley, 1315 Spruce St, Philadelphia, PA 19107 EMAIL: sodvnew@aol.com

9: **Ohio Lesbian Festival** *Colombus, OH*
women only • 3000 attendees ☎614/**877–4367 EXT 571** ✉ c/o Lesbian Business Assoc, PO Box 82086, Colombus, OH 43202

TBA: **Dyketopia** *Ottawa, Canada*
10 day dyke celebration in Ottawa • women only ☎613/**237–9872** WEB: www.gayottawa.com/oilw

TBA: **The Fall Gathering** *Ashland, OR*
annual women's camp near Oregon mountain lake • vegetarian & vegan meals provided • workshops • crafts • entertainment • women only • 150+ attendees • $65-95 ☎541/**482–7416**, 541/**488–1907** ✉ c/o Womansource, PO Box 335, Ashland, OR 97520

TBA: **Iowa Women's Music Festival** *Iowa City, IA*
mostly women ☎319/**335–1486** ✉ c/o Prairie Voices Productions, PO Box 3411, Iowa City, IA 52244

TBA: **Northern Lights Womyn's Music Festival** *McGregor, MN*
day-long festival in Minnesota wilderness • women only • 600-1000 attendees ☎218/**722–4903** ✉ c/o Aurora Northland Lesbian Center, 32 E 1st St, Ste 104, Duluth, MN 55802 EMAIL: lesbian@computerpro.com WEB: www.geocities.com/westhollywood/8331

TBA: **Northwest Women's Music Celebration** *Portland, OR*
participatory event for musicians, songwriters & singers, NOT performance-oriented • mostly women ✉ PO Box 66842, Portland, OR 97290

TBA: **WomenFest** *Key West, FL*
concerts, dances, theater, fair, film festival, seminars & more • mostly women ☎305/**296-4238** ✉ 201 Coppitt Rd #106A, Key West, FL 33040 **EMAIL:** women1fest@aol.com **WEB:** www.womenfest.com

TBA: **Womyn's Musical & Spiritual Awareness Festival** *Lava Hot Springs, ID*
camping on the Portneuf River • workshops • entertainment • women only ☎208/**776-5800** ✉ c/o **Aura Soma Lava**, PO Box 129, Lava Hot Springs, ID 83246

October 2000

26-29: **Radical Lesbian Feminist Uprising!** *near Kansas City, MO*
a weekend of workshops, discussions & more • women only ☎501/**677-2235** ✉ c/o **RLF**, PO Box 32983, Kansas City, MO 64171 **EMAIL:** susan@wiseheart.com

TBA: **Herland Fall Retreat** *Oklahoma City, OK*
music, workshops, campfire events & potluck • boys under 10 only • $15-60 sliding scale registration • mostly women ☎405/**521-9696** ✉ c/o **Herland**, 2312 NW 39th, Oklahoma City, OK 73112

TBA: **SistahFest** *Malibu, CA*
join other women of color for a weekend of concerts, sports, arts, dance, games & more • women only ☎213/**960-5051** ✉ c/o **ULOAH**, 1626 N Wilcox Ave #190, Los Angeles, CA 90028 **EMAIL:** uloah@aol.com **WEB:** www.uloah.com

November 2000

TBA: **Fall Fatwomen's Gathering** *West Coast, CA*
fat women & their female allies • contact Judy Freespirit for exact date • women only ☎510/**836-1153** ✉ c/o **NAAFA Feminist Caucus**, PO Box 29614, Oakland, CA 94614 **EMAIL:** fatmaven@aol.com

FILM FESTIVALS

February 2000

3-6: **Seeing Queerly** *Denver, CO*
Mountain States annual lesbian/gay film festival ☎303/**733-7743 EXT 15** ✉ c/o **The Center**, PO Drawer 18E, Denver, CO 80218 **EMAIL:** cntrevents@aol.com

March 2000

17-26: **Women in the Director's Chair Int'l Film Festival** *Chicago, IL*
largest & longest-running women's film festival • get your tickets early for 'dyke night'! • mostly women ☎773/**907-0610** ✉ c/o **WIDC**, 941 W Lawrence #500, Chicago, IL 60640 **EMAIL:** widc@widc.org **WEB:** www.widc.org

April 2000

TBA: **London Lesbian Film Festival** *London, Canada*
mostly women ☎519/**680-1631** ✉ c/o **London Lesbian Film Fest**, PO Box 46014, 956 Dundas St E, London, ON, Canada N5W 3A1

May 2000

25-June 3: **Honolulu Gay/ Lesbian Film Festival** *Honolulu, HI*
☎808/**941–0424** ✉ c/o Honolulu Gay & Lesbian Cultural Foundation, 1877 Kalakaua Ave, Honolulu, HI 96815 EMAIL: hglcf@aloha.net WEB: hawaiiscene.com/HGLCF

TBA: **Boston Gay/ Lesbian Film/ Video Festival** *Boston, MA*
☎617/**369–3300** ✉ c/o Museum of Fine Arts, 465 Huntington Ave, Boston, MA 02115

TBA: **Inside Out** *Toronto, Canada*
annual lesbian & gay fim fest ☎416/**925–XTRA EXT 2229** WEB: www.insideout.on.ca

June 2000

15-25: **San Francisco Int'l Lesbian/Gay Film Festival** *San Francisco, CA*
get your tickets early for a slew of films about us • 53,000+ attendees ☎415/**703–8650** ✉ c/o Frameline, 346 9th St, San Francisco, CA 94103

TBA: **Connecticut Gay/ Lesbian Film Festival** *Hartford, CT*
gay/lesbian ☎860/**586–1136,** 860/**232–3402** ✉ c/o Alternatives, Inc, PO Box 231192, Hartford, CT 06123 EMAIL: glff@yahoo.com WEB: www.eng2.uconn.edu/~garrick/glff.htm

TBA: **New York Int'l Gay/Lesbian Film Festival** *New York City, NY*
week-long fest in early June ☎212/**254–7228** ✉ c/o The New Festival, 47 Great Jones St, 6th flr, New York, NY 10012 EMAIL: newfest@idt.net WEB: www.newfestival.org

July 2000

6-16: **Outfest** *Los Angeles, CA*
Los Angeles' lesbian/gay film & video festival in mid-July ☎323/**960–9200** ✉ c/o Outfest, 1125 N McCadden Pl #235, Los Angeles, CA 90038 EMAIL: outfest@outfest.org

13-24: **Philadelphia Gay/Lesbian Film Festival** *Philadelphia, PA*
☎215/**733–0608,** 800/**333–8521 EXT 33** ✉ c/o TLA Video, 234 Market St, Philadelphia, PA 19106 EMAIL: rmurray@tlavideo.com WEB: www.tlavideo.com/piflff

August 2000

25-Sept 7: **Austin Gay/Lesbian International Film Festival** *Austin, TX*
☎512/**476–2454** ✉ c/o AGLIFF, PO Box 'L', Austin, TX 78713 EMAIL: kino@agliff.org WEB: www.agliff.org

TBA: **North Carolina Gay/ Lesbian Film Festival** *Durham, NC*
☎919/**560–3040 EXT 115** ✉ c/o Carolina Theatre, 309 W Morgan St, Durham, NC 27701 EMAIL: steve@carolinatheatre.org WEB: www.carolinatheatre.org

September 2000

29-Oct 8: **Tampa Int'l Gay/ Lesbian Film Festival** *Tampa Bay, FL*
☎727/**865–9004** ✉ c/o Tampa Bay Arts, 3000 34th St S #C-206, St Petersburg, FL 33711 EMAIL: pridefilm@aol.com WEB: www.tampabayarts.com

TBA: **Making Scenes** *Ottawa, Canada*
Ottawa's lesbian/gay film festival • also production workshops ☎613/**566–2113** ✉ c/o Making Scenes c/o Arts Court, 2 Daly Ave, Ottawa, ON, Canada K1N 6E2 EMAIL: scenes@fox.nstn.ca WEB: http://fox.nstn.ca/~scenes

TBA: **St Louis Int'l Lesbian/ Gay Film Festival** *St Louis, MO*
☎314/**997–9846** ✉ c/o SLILAG, PMB 388, 6614 Clayton Rd , St Louis, MO 63117 EMAIL: slilagff@aol.com WEB: www.slilagfilmfestival.org

October 2000

12-15: **Out on Film** *Atlanta, GA*
Atlanta's lesbian/gay film festival ☎404/**352-4225** ✉ c/o IMAGE Film & Video Center, 75 Bennett St NW, Ste N-1, Atlanta, GA 30309 EMAIL: imageinfo@imagefv.org WEB: www.imagefv.org

TBA: **Reel Affirmations Film Festival DC** *Washington, DC*
lesbian/gay films ☎202/**986-1119**

November 2000

2-5: **Santa Barbara Lesbian/Gay Film Festival** *Santa Barbara, CA*
☎805/**963-3636** ✉ c/o Gay/Lesbian Resource Center, 126 E Haley, Ste A-17, Santa Barbara, CA 93101 EMAIL: pride@silcom.com

TBA: **Blowing Bubbles** *Europe*
international film & video contest promoting AIDS prevention & education • sponsored by the Italy National Lesbian/Gay Assoc • gay/lesbian ☎39-051/**644-6824** ✉ c/o Circolo Arcigay Il Cassero, PO Box 691, 40100 Bologna, Italy EMAIL: dor5142@iperbole.bologna.it

TBA: **Fresno Reel Pride** *Fresno, CA*
annual lesbian & gay film festival in central California ☎209/**266-2716** ✉ c/o FIGLEAF Educational Festivals, PO Box 4647, Fresno, CA 93744 EMAIL: fresnoreelpride@hotmail.com

TBA: **Mix 2000: New York Lesbian/Gay Experimental Film/Video Fest** *New York City, NY*
film, videos, installations & media performances • write for info ☎212/**571–4242** ✉ 11 John St #406, New York, NY 10038 **EMAIL:** mix@echonyc.com **WEB:** echonyc.com

TBA: **Out on Film** *Palm Springs, CA*
come out for a weekend of gay films, film makers & parties ☎760/**770–2042**

TBA: **Reeling 2000: Chicago Lesbian/ Gay Int'l Film Fest** *Chicago, IL*
☎773/**384–5533** ✉ c/o Chicago Filmmakers, 5243 N Clark St , 2nd flr, Chicago, IL 60640 **EMAIL:** reeling@chicagofilmmakers.org **WEB:** www.chicagofilmmakers.org/reeling

LEATHER

January 2000

14-17: **Mid-Atlantic Leather Weekend** *Washington, DC*
gay/lesbian ☎202/**347–6025** ✉ c/o Centaurs MC c/o DC Eagle, 639 New York Ave NW, Washington, DC 20001

TBA: **Portland Uniform Weekend 8** *Portland, OR*
gay/lesbian ☎503/**228–6935** ✉ c/o In Uniform Magazine, PO Box 3226, Portland, OR 97208 **EMAIL:** uniformmag@aol.com

TBA: **Santa Clara County Leather Weekend** *San Jose, CA*
3 days of leather celebration in the South Bay • gay/lesbian ☎408/**934–9137** ✉ c/o Billy DeFrank L/G Community Ctr, 175 Stockton Ave, San Jose, CA 95126 **EMAIL:** sccleather@aol.com **WEB:** http://members.aol.com/SCCLeather/

February 2000

25-27: **Pantheon of Leather** *New Orleans, LA*
annual SM community service awards • mixed gay/straight ☎323/**656–5073** ✉ c/o The Leather Journal, 7985 Santa Monica Blvd #109-368, West Hollywood, CA 90046 **EMAIL:** pljandcuir@aol.com

March 2000

23-26: **International Master/ slave Weekend & Contest** *Atlanta, GA*
two-day series of workshops & seminars on lifestyle-related issues • the only couples title in the world • a pansexual event • mixed gay/straight ☎404/**874–4838** OR **770–638–7984,** 888/**638–8111** ✉ c/o IMsWC, Inc, 1417 Dutch Valley Place NE, Atlanta, GA 30324 **EMAIL:** info@thesanctuary.net **WEB:** http://www.mast.net/

31-April 2: **Leather Leadership Conference** *Washington, DC*
join us to develop & strengthen problem-solving & camaraderie in the leather community • gay/lesbian ☎415/**289–7982** ✉ c/o LLC, PO Box 4494, Woodbridge, VA 22194–4494 **EMAIL:** RoseBrebm@aol.com **WEB:** www.leatherweb.com/LLCIII/

31-April 2: **Rubbout 9** *Vancouver, Canada*
annual pansexual rubber weekend • mostly men • 60-100 attendees ☎604/**253–1258** ✉ PO Box 2253, Vancouver, BC, Canada V6B 3W2 **EMAIL:** nrthwnd@rocketmail.com

April 2000

TBA: **American Leather Woman Contest** *Washington, DC*
contest to be held during American Brotherhood Weekend • women only ☎773/**561–9678** ✉ c/o ONYX, 1340 W Irving Park Rd #188, Chicago, IL 60613 **EMAIL:** ONYXmail@aol.com **WEB:** www.onyxmen.com

June 2000

TBA: **Folsom Street East** *New York City, NY*
New York City's answer to the famous San Francisco fetish street fair • gay/lesbian ☎212/**727-9878** ✉ c/o GMSMA, 332 Bleecker St #D-23, New York City, NY 10014 **Email:** info@gmsma.org **Web:** www.gmsma.org/gmsma.html

TBA: **Southeast Leatherfest** *Atlanta, GA*
gay/lesbian ✉ c/o Southeast Leatherfest, PO Box 78974, Atlanta, GA 30357

July 2000

20-22: **International Ms Leather Contest** *Toronto, Canada*
contest • workshops • parties • mostly women ☎402/**451-7987** ✉ c/o Bare Images, 4332 Browne St, Omaha, NE 68111 **Email:** imsl@synergy.net **Web:** www.IMsL.org

28-30: **Thunder in the Mountains** *Denver, CO*
weekend of pansexual leather events & seminars in the Rocky Mountains • Mr & Ms Rocky Mountain Leather contest • gay/lesbian • 600+ attendees ☎303/**698-1207** ✉ c/o Thunder Mountain Leather, 258 Acoma St, Denver 80223-1339 **Email:** MrLthrCO@aol.com **Web:** http://www.thunderinthemountains.com

TBA: **International Ms Bootblack Contest**
contest takes place the weekend of International Ms Leather weekend • mostly women ☎402/**451-7987** ✉ c/o Bare Images, 4332 Browne St, Omaha, NE 68111 **Email:** imsl@synergy.net **Web:** www.leatherspace.com

September 2000

1-4: **Love & Leather** *Atlanta, GA*
pansexual event celebrating the BDSM lifestyle • mixed gay/straight ✉ c/o Love & Leather, PO Box 78551, Atlanta, GA 30357 **Email:** 1199@boyinchains.com **Web:** loveandleather.mybdsm.com

1-4: **Power Surge** *Seattle, WA*
biannual leatherwomen's SM conference • women only ☎206/**233-8429** ✉ c/o Seattle Madness, Broadway Stn, PO Box 23352, Seattle, WA 98102

24: **Folsom Street Fair** *San Francisco, CA*
huge SM/leather street fair, topping a week of kinky events • gay/lesbian • thousands of local & visiting kinky men & women attendees ☎415/**861-3247** ✉ c/o SMMILE, 1072 Folsom St #272, San Francisco, CA 94103

October 2000

5-8: **Living in Leather** *TBA, USA*
national conference for the leather, SM & fetish communities • gay/lesbian • 600 attendees • $115-175 ☎614/**470-2093**, 614/**899-4406** ✉ c/o National Leather Association, PMB 155, 3439 NE Sandy Blvd, Portland, OR 97232 **Email:** LIL2000@aol.com **Web:** www.nla-i.com

TBA: **Central Valley Leatherfest** *Fresno, CA*
gay/lesbian ☎559/**252-7583** ✉ c/o Knights of Malta, Yosemite Chapter, PO Box 4162, Fresno, CA 93744

TBA: **Leather Pride Amsterdam** *Amsterdam, Netherlands*
3 days of hot leather events • gay/lesbian ☎31-020/**422-3737** ✉ c/o Leather Pride Nederland, PO Box 2674, 1000 CR Amsterdam, Netherlands **Email:** info@leatherpride.nl **Web:** www.leatherpride.nl

CONFERENCES & RETREATS

February 2000

12-13: **Black Gay/Lesbian Conference** *TBA, USA*
gay/lesbian ☎202/**483-6786** ✉ c/o **Nat'l Black Gay/Lesbian Leadership Forum**, 1612 'K' St NW #500, Washington, DC 20006 EMAIL: ForumConf@aol.com

25-27: **Outwrite** *Boston, MA*
annual national lesbian/gay writers & publishers conference • gay/lesbian • 1500+ attendees • $55-65 ☎617/**262-6969** ✉ c/o **Bromfield St Educational Foundation**, 29 Stanhope St, Boston, MA 02116

April 2000

28: **Lambda Literary Awards** *Chicago, IL*
the 'Lammies' are the Oscars of lesbigay writing & publishing • gay/lesbian ☎202/**462-7924** ✉ c/o **Lambda Literary Foundation**, PO Box 73910, Washington, DC 20056 EMAIL: LLF@lambdalit.org WEB: www.lambdalit.org

TBA: **Readers/Writers Conference** *San Francisco, CA*
annual weekend of workshops & roundtables with queer writers & readers, at the Women's Building ☎415/**431-0891**

July 2000

2-9: **Dyke Art Retreat Encampment (DARE)** *Roseburg, OR*
exciting week of group & individual art projects • vegetarian meals provided • send SASE for info • women only ☎541/**679-4655** ✉ c/o DARE, 6018 Coos Bay Wagon Rd, Roseburg, OR 97470

13-16: **Women's Motorcycling Conference** *TBA*
mostly women ☎614/**891-2429**, 800/**262-5646**

TBA: **Lesbian/Gay Health Conference** *Dallas, TX*
health & AIDS/HIV issues facing our communities ☎202/**939-7880** ✉ c/o **Nat'l L/G Health Assoc**, 1407 'S' St NW, Washington, DC 20009 EMAIL: nlgha@aol.com

September 2000

7-10: **National Lesbian/ Gay Journalists Association Convention** *San Francisco, CA*
workshops • keynote speakers • entertainment • gay/lesbian ☎202/**588-9888** ✉ c/o **NLGJA**, 2120 'L' St NW #840, Washington, DC 20037 EMAIL: nlgja@aol.com WEB: www.nlgja.org

October 2000

5-9: **National Latino/a Lesbian/Gay Conference** *New York City, NY*
come together to strengthen, empower & mobilize the Latina/o LGBT community • gay/lesbian ☎202/**466-8240** ✉ c/o **LLEGO**, 1612 'K' St NW #500, Washington, DC 20006 EMAIL: aquilgbt@llego.org WEB: www.llego.org

28-29: **Mid-Atlantic LGBT Writers' Conference** *Washington, DC*
gay/lesbian ☎202/**462-7924** ✉ c/o **Lambda Literary Foundation**, PO Box 73910, Washington, DC 20056 EMAIL: lbradvert@aol.com WEB: www.lambdalit.org

November 2000

TBA: **Creating Change Conference** *TBA, USA*
for lesbians, gays, bisexuals, transgendered people & queers into social activism • gay/lesbian • 1500+ attendees ☎202/**332-6483 x3329** ✉ c/o National Gay/Lesbian Task Force, 2320 17th St NW, Washington, DC 20009 **EMAIL:** delliot@ngltf.org **WEB:** www.ngltf.org

SPIRITUAL

February 2000

18-21: **Pantheocon** *San Francisco, CA*
pagan convention • mixed gay/straight ☎510/**653-3244** ✉ c/o Ancient Ways, 4075 Telegraph Ave, Oakland, CA 94609 **WEB:** www.ancientways.com

April 2000

7-9: **Moonsisters Drum Camp** *Sausalito, CA*
women only • 150 attendees • $215 ☎510/**547-8386** ✉ c/o Moonsisters Drum Camp, PO Box 20918, Oakland, CA 94620 **EMAIL:** moonsistah@aol.com

TBA: **Int'l Conference on Spirituality for Gays/Lesbians** *San Francisco, CA*
gay/lesbian • 500+ attendees ☎415/**281-9377** ✉ c/o Q Spirit, 3739 Balboa St #211, San Francisco, CA 94121 **EMAIL:** QSpirit1@aol.com **WEB:** www.qspirit.org

May 2000

19-21: **A Gathering of Priestesses** *Southwestern WI*
women's spirituality conference • mostly women ☎608/**257-5858** ✉ c/o Reformed Congregation of the Goddess, PO Box 6677, Madison, WI 53716 **EMAIL:** rcgi@itis.com

June 2000

8-11: **International Goddess Festival** *La Honda, CA*
celebration of goddess culture & Beltane • workshops, rituals, dances, music • mostly women ☎510/**444-7724** ✉ c/o Women's Spirituality Forum, PO Box 11363, Oakland, CA 94611 **EMAIL:** Silverzb@aol.com **WEB:** www.netwiz.net/ZBudapest/

18-25: **Pagan Spirit Gathering** *near Athens, OH*
summer solstice celebration in Ohio • primitive camping • workshops • rituals • advance registration required • mixed gay/straight ☎608/**924-2216** ✉ c/o Circle Sanctuary, PO Box 219, Mt Horeb, WI 53572 **EMAIL:** circle@mhtc.net **WEB:** www.circlesanctuary.org/psg

TBA: **Ancient Ways Festival** *Harbin Hot Springs, CA*
annual 4-day mixed gender/orientation spring festival in May or June • pan-pagan rituals, workshops & music w/ lesbian/gay campsite • mixed gay/straight ☎510/**653-3244** ✉ c/o Ancient Ways, 4075 Telegraph Ave, Oakland, CA 94609 **WEB:** www.ancientways.com

TBA: **Annual LGBT Spiritual Gathering** *Albuquerque, NM*
gay/lesbian ☎505/**247-8296** ✉ PO Box 25582, Albuquerque, NM 87125 **EMAIL:** QGathering@aol.com **WEB:** members.aol.com/QGathering/Spirit.htm.

July 2000

14-16: **Northern California Women's Goddess Festival** *Occidental, CA*
workshops • music • camping • swimming • hiking • solstice ritual • at Ocean Song, a private nature reserve • women only • $150 ☎707/**824-0737** ✉ c/o Black Kat Productions, 8031 Mill Station Rd, Sebastopol, CA 95472 **EMAIL:** kat@monitor.net **WEB:** www.monitor.net/~ross/blackkat/default.html

TBA: **BC Witchcamp** *Vancouver, Canada*
week-long Wiccan intensive • mixed gay/straight • 100+ attendees • $550 ☎604/**253-7195**, 604/**253-7189** ✉ c/o **Sounds & Furies**, PO Box 21510, 1850 Commercial Dr, Vancouver, BC, Canada V5N 4A0 EMAIL: path@lynx.bc.ca

TBA: **Sappho's Sisters** *Saco Bay, ME*
lesbian & bi-sexual women can focus on their own growth in a safe, nurturing community • workshops • group activities • Unitarian Universalist • women only ☎207/**284-8612** EMAIL: ferrybeach@ferrybeach.org WEB: www.ferrybeach.org

August 2000

4-6: **Greenspirit Festival** *Mt Horeb, WI*
summer solstice celebration in Ohio • primitive camping • workshops • rituals • advance registration required • mixed gay/straight ☎608/**924-2216** ✉ c/o **Circle Sanctuary**, PO Box 219, Mt Horeb, WI 53572 EMAIL: circle@mhtc.net WEB: www.circlesanctuary.org/greenspirit

18-20: **Sisters in a Strange Land** *Michigan City, MI*
explore ways in which lesbians are challenging & reshaping Christian spirituality • women only ☎517/**855-2277** ✉ c/o **Leaven**, PO Box 23233, Lansing, MI 48909 EMAIL: leaven@ecunet.org WEB: www.leaven.org

TBA: **Elderflower Womenspirit Festival** *Mendocino, CA*
in the Mendocino Woodlands • earth-centered spirituality retreat • reasonably priced, volunteer-run • women only ☎415/**263-5719**, 916/**658-0697** ✉ PO Box 7153, Redwood City, CA 94063

September 2000

TBA: **Sappho Lesbian Witchcamp** *Vancouver, Canada*
week-long gathering • women only • 35-40 attendees • $425 ☎604/**253-7189**, 604/**253-7189** ✉ c/o **Sounds & Furies**, PO Box 21510, 1850 Commercial Dr, Vancouver, BC, Canada V5N 4A0 EMAIL: path@lynx.bc.ca

October 2000

13-15: **Moonsisters Drum Camp** *Sausalito, CA*
women only • 150 attendees • $215 ☎510/**547-8386** ✉ c/o **Moonsisters Drum Camp**, PO Box 20918, Oakland, CA 94620 EMAIL: moonsistah@aol.com

31: **Halloween Spiral Dance** *Oakland, CA*
annual ritual to celebrate turning of seasons & the crone • mostly women ☎510/**444-7724** ✉ c/o **Women's Spirituality Forum**, PO Box 11363, Oakland, CA 94611

TBA: **Real Witches Ball** *Columbus, OH*
weekend pagan celebration of Samhain • mixed gay/straight ☎614/**421-7557** ✉ c/o **Salem West**, 1209 N High St, Columbus, OH 43201 EMAIL: ajdrew@neopagan.com WEB: www.neopagan.com

BREAST CANCER BENEFITS

January 2000

on-going throughout the year: **Race for the Cure** *Cross-country, USA*
5K & 1-mile run/fitness walks in cities around the country to fight breast cancer • call for local city dates • organized & funded by Susan G Komen Breast Cancer Foundation volunteers • mostly women ☎888/**603-7223** ✉ c/o **Susan G Komen Breast Cancer Foundation: Race for the Cure**, 5005 LBJ Fwy #370, Dallas, TX 75244

February 2000

19-26: **Annual Women's Get-Away Week** *Banff, Canada*
skiing, theme parties, wine tasting & more • 1% of proceeds go to American Society Breast Cancer Program • women only • 200 attendees ☎800/**875-6408** ✉ c/o **Alpine Ski & Sun Holidays**, 651 Topeka Way #720, Castle Rock, CO 80104 **EMAIL:** pinholst@slash.net **WEB:** www.assh.com/snow

June 2000

18-20: **Avon's Breast Cancer 3-Day Walk** *Chicago, IL*
walk from Kenosha, WI to Chicago to raise money to fight breast cancer • mostly women ☎877/**286-6324**, 773/**525-2960** ✉ c/o **AVON Breast Cancer 3-Day Chicago**, 1350 West Belmont, Chicago, IL 60657 **WEB:** www.avoncrusade.com

TBA: **Tour for the Cure** *Jackson, NJ*
amateur golfers & LPGA members take part in charity golf tournament benefitting the National Breast Cancer Coalition Fund • mostly women ☎609/**392-8383** ✉ c/o **Gluck/Shaw Group**, 428 Riverview Plaza, Trenton, NJ 08611 **WEB:** www.natlbcc.org/tour_cure.htm

July 2000

9-12: **Pony Express Tour 2000** *Heartland, USA*
women motorcyclists ride from 6 locations to St Joseph, MO • proceeds to Susan G Komen Breast Cancer Research Center • women only ☎716/**768-6054** ✉ c/o **Women's Motorcyclist Foundation**, 7 Lent Ave, LeRoy, NY 14482 **EMAIL:** WMFGINSUE@aol.com

August 2000

TBA: **Avon's Breast Cancer 3-Day Walk** *New York City, NY*
walk from West Point to Manhattan to raise money to fight breast cancer • mostly women ☎877/**286-6369** ✉ c/o **AVON Breast Cancer 3-Day New York**, 16 W 36th St, 10th flr, New York, NY 10018 **WEB:** www.avoncrusade.com

September 2000

21-Nov 2: **America's Breast Cancer Ride** *San Diego, CA to Jacksonville, FL*
42-day bicycle ride across the southern USA • San Diego, CA to Jacksonville, FL • proceeds go to Susan G Komen Breast Cancer Foundation • mostly women ☎888/**469-6636**, 760/**754-6747** ✉ c/o **Women in Motion**, PO Box 4533, Oceanside, CA 92052-4533 **EMAIL:** eventsrus@aol.com **WEB:** www.gowomen.org

TBA: **'Fore Women & A Few Good Men' Golf Tournament** *Boston, MA*
tournament to raise money for Breast Cancer research • terrific prizes! • mixed gay/straight • 100+ attendees ☎617/**437-9757**, 888/**562-2874** ✉ c/o **Carol Nashe Group**, 566 Commonwealth Ave, Boston, MA 02215 **EMAIL:** nashe@priority1.net **WEB:** www.golfonthego.com

TBA: **Mt Tamalpais Peak Hike** *Marin County, CA*
for breast cancer survivors & those who support them • sensitivity, support & skill-building are provided for those new to hiking • proceeds from this 10 mile hike benefit The Breast Cancer Fund • mixed gay/straight • 700+ attendees ☎415/**543-2979** ✉ c/o **The Breast Cancer Fund**, 282 Second St, San Francisco, CA 94105 **EMAIL:** TBCFund@aol.com **WEB:** www.breastcancerfund.com

TBA: **Wigging Out** *San Francisco, CA*
annual wig drive to benefit the American Cancer Society's wig bank • mixed gay/straight ☎415/**552-0220** ✉ c/o **Sisters of Perpetual Indulgence**, 584 Castro St #392, San Francisco, CA 94114 **WEB:** www.sisters.org

October 2000

on-going: **October is Breast Cancer Awareness Month** *Cross-country, USA*
check local listings for fund-raising events in your area to fight breast cancer

on-going throughout the year: **Race for the Cure** *Cross-country, USA*
5K & 1-mile run/fitness walks in cities around the country to fight breast cancer • call for local city dates • organized & funded by Susan G Komen Breast Cancer Foundation volunteers • mostly women ☎888/**603-7223** ✉ c/o **Susan G Komen Breast Cancer Foundation: Race for the Cure**, 5005 LBJ Fwy #370, Dallas, TX 75244

27-29: **Avon's Breast Cancer 3-Day Walk** *Los Angeles, CA*
walk from Santa Barbara to Malibu to raise money to fight breast cancer • mostly women ☎888/**332-9286** ✉ c/o **AVON Breast Cancer 3-Day Los Angeles**, 3435 Ocean Park Blvd, Santa Monica, CA 90405 **WEB:** www.avoncrusade.com

TBA: **Avon's Breast Cancer 3-Day Walk** *Atlanta, GA*
walk from Lake Lanier to Atlanta to raise money to fight breast cancer • mostly women ☎404/**257-5553**, 877/**257-5553** ✉ c/o **AVON Breast Cancer 3-Day Atlanta**, 290 Carpenter Drive, Bldg 200, Ste A, Atlanta, GA 30328 **WEB:** www.avoncrusade.com

TBA: **Walk for Hope Against Breast Cancer** *Cross-country, USA*
walk to raise money to fight breast cancer • proceeds benefit City of Hope National Medical Center & Beckman Research Institute • events in cities across the country • call for dates in your city • mostly women ☎800/**266-7920** ✉ c/o **City of Hope**, 208 W 8th St, Los Angeles, CA 90014 **WEB:** http://walk.coh.org

KIDS' STUFF

June 2000

on-going thru the summer: **Prairie Youth Adventures** *Matfield Green, KS*
week-long summer sessions focusing on horseback skills & historic prairie activities • camp takes place on the women-run Homestead Ranch • separate camps for boys & girls • youth age 10-14 ☎316/**753-3465** ✉ c/o **Homestead Ranch**, RR 1 Box 24, Matfield Green, KS 66862

July 2000

TBA: **Greenhope Equestrian Summer Camp** *East Hardwick, VT*
horse-back riding programs offered in July & August • lots of other activities • courses for adults, too • kids 8-18 ☎802/**533-7772** ✉ c/o **Greenhope Farm**, 5177 Noyestar Rd, East Hardwick, VT 05836 **EMAIL:** greenhopefarm@kingcon.com **WEB:** www.angelfire.com/VT/greenhope

August 2000

13-26: **Mountain Meadow Summer Camp** *South Jersey, NJ*
camp for kids with lesbigaytrans parents & their allies • girls & boys age 9-16 • $200-1000 ☎215/**848-7566** ✉ c/o Mountain Meadow, 7042 Greene St, Philadelphia, PA 19119 EMAIL: mountainmeadow@yahoo.com

TBA: **Camp Lavender Hill** *Sierra Nevadas, CA*
one-week summer camp for kids with lesbigay parents • swimming • hiking • theater & more • kids 7-17 • 30+ attendees • $400 ☎707/**544-8150** ✉ c/o Camp Lavender Hill, PO Box 11335, Santa Rosa, CA 95406

TBA: **Family Week** *Provincetown, MA*
join hundreds of GLBT parents & their children for a week of clam bakes, BBQs, boat rides, campfires, sandcastle competitions & more • gay/lesbian • $25 per family (meals and housing not included) ☎619/**296-0199** ✉ c/o Family Pride Coalition, PO Box 34337, San Diego, CA 92163 EMAIL: pride@familypride.org WEB: www.familypride.org

September 2000

22-24: **Keshet Camp: Jewish Family Camp** *Yosemite, CA*
a rainbow camp for lesbigay families & their friends • sports, music, arts & crafts & more • gay/lesbian ☎415/**543-2267** ✉ c/o Camp Tawonga, 121 Steuart St, San Francisco, CA 94105 EMAIL: www.tawonga.org WEB: tawonga@aol.com

Books & Magazines

A Different Light Bookstores ☎**800/343-4002** books • cards • calendars • videos Email: adl@adlbooks.com Web: www.adlbooks.com

Brigit Books ☎**727/522-5775** lesbian & feminist titles Email: brigit@earthlink.net Web: www.brigitbooks.com

Dykes to Watch Out For send a stamp for catalog ✉ c/o Alison Bechdel, PO box 215, Dept. LC, Jonesville, VT 05466

Lammas ☎**800/955-2662** women's books • music • jewelry • much more Email: drblammas@aol.com

▲ **Lesbian Health News, Inc** ☎**614/481-7656** see ad in mail order section ✉ PO Box 12121, Columbus, OH 43212 Email: lhnews@aol.com

Magus Books ☎**612/379-7669** 10am-9pm, til 6pm wknds • alternative spirituality books • also mail order ✉ 1316 SE 4th St., Minneapolis, MN 55414 Email: store@magusbooks.com Web: www.magusbooks.com

Naiad Press, Inc. ☎**850/539-5965, 800/533-1973** lesbian books & videos ✉ PO Box 10543, Tallahassee, FL 32302 Web: www.naiadpress.com

Spinsters Ink ☎**218/727-3222, 800/301-6860 (orders only)** feminist fiction & non-fiction publishers • mail order ✉ 32 E. 1st St. #330, Duluth, MN 55802 Web: www.spinster-ink.com

Thunder Road Books ☎**201/863-3931, 888/846-3773** lesbian mail order • discounted books • CDs • videos • call for free flyer • send $2 for catalog ✉ PO Box 1203, Secaucus, NJ 07096 Email: ThundrRdBk@aol.com Web: www.thunder-roadbooks.com

Woman in the Moon ☎**408/279-6626** ✉ PO Box 2087, Cupertino, CA 95015-2087 Email: womaninmoon@earthlink.net Web: www.womaninthemoon.com

Womankind Books ☎**520/795-2444, 800/675-0415** large selection of lesbian books & videos ✉ 1740 E Water, Tucson, AZ 85719

Womansline Books ☎**519/457-9595** ✉ Box 24092, London, ON N6H 5C4 Email: contact@womansline.com Web: www.womansline.com

Women in the Wilderness ☎651/227-2284 books for outdoorswomen & armchair adventurers ✉ 566 Ottawa Ave., St. Paul, MN 55107

Women's Press ☎416/921-2425 lesbian/feminist book publisher • catalog available

CLOTHING

Banshee Designs 'garments for goddesses of every size' • adult sizes to 8X • send SASE with 55¢ postage for catalog ✉ 923 SE 37th Ave, Portland, OR 97214

Girl World Sports ☎713/290-9969 T-shirts ✉ 1022 Wirt Rd #312, Houston, TX 77055

GLADrags ☎888/452-3748 tasteful casualwear for the community • catalog

Lavender Ink, LLC ☎203/787-0817, 800/621-2725 pride apparel & gifts • catalog ✉ PO Box 9235, New Haven, CT 06530 EMAIL: lavink@aol.com WEB: www.lavenderink.com

Strip T's ☎603/755-2926 feminist T-shirts • catalog ✉ PO Box 605, Farmington, NH 03835 WEB: www.stephaniepiro.com

JEWELRY

Bande Designs womyn's jewelry • send $1 for catalog ✉ 7102 Castor Ave, Philadelphia, PA 19149

▲ **Jewelry by Poncé** ☎949/494-1399, 800/969-7464 specializing in commitment rings • free brochure ✉ 219 N Broadway, PMB 331, Laguna Beach, CA 92651

Lizzie Brown/Pleiades ☎413/245-9484 woman-identified jewelry ✉ PO Box 389, Brimfield, MA 01010

Sappho Studios jewelry • gifts • cards • free catalog • ✉ PO Box 48365, Watauga, TX 76148

VARIETY

Avalon Herbaly handmade herbal soaps & natural bath products ✉ PO Box 69, Euless, TX 76039

Avena Botanicals organically grown herbal products for women • catalog ✉ 219 Mill St, Rockport, ME 04856

Family Celebrations ☎888/335-5998 lesbigay wedding & special occasion catalog • lesbian-owned/run ✉ PO Box 3700, San Dimas, CA 91773 **EMAIL:** famcplz@aol.com **WEB:** www.familycelebrations.com

Femail Creations ☎800/969-2760 catalog for, by & about womyn **WEB:** www.femailcreations.com

Goddess Stamps send $1 for brochure ✉ PO Box 103, Gratan, CA 95444 **WEB:** www.nbn.com/~katecart

Key West Aloe ☎800/445-2563 mail order available ✉ 524 Front St, Key West, FL 33040 **WEB:** www.keywestaloe.com

Lady Slipper, Inc. ☎800/634-6044 women's music • videos ✉ 3205 Hillsboro Rd, Durham, NC 27705

Music for the Masses T-shirts • photos • posters • videos • songbooks • all of your favorite women recording artists • send two 32-cent stamps for catalog ✉ PO Box 90272, San Jose, CA 95109

Snake & Snake Productions goddess • crone • astrology items ✉ 511 Scott King Rd., Durham, NC 27713

We're Everywhere ☎773/404-0590, 800/772-6411 noon-9pm, 11am-8pm wknds • also catalog ✉ 3434 N Halsted St, Chicago, IL 60657 **WEB:** www.wereeverywhere.com

Wildfire Glass ☎419/836-2294 womyn-owned glass studio • catalog ✉ PO Box 12, Millbury, OH 43447 **EMAIL:** wildfirestudio@glasscity.net

Wing of the Heron Drums ☎303/499-0840 lesbian-owned/run ✉ PO Box 18171, Boulder, CO 80308

Women Fly ☎800/304-9342 t-shirts • caps • coffee mugs • free catalog ✉ 100 S Baldwin #206, Madison, WI 53703 **WEB:** www.womenfly.com

EROTICA

After Midnight Collection sexual supplies for women • send $5 for catalog ✉ PO Box 13176, Scottsdale, AZ 85267

Batteries Not Included ☎954/467-7025 adult products ✉ 1007 N Federal Hwy #262, Fort Lauderdale, FL 33304 **WEB:** www.batteriesnotincluded.com

Eve's Garden ☎212/757-8651 sex toys • books • videos • all from the first sexuality boutique created by women for women • send $3 for catalog ✉ 119 W. 57th St. # 420, New York, NY 10019

Good Vibrations ☎415/974-8990, 800/289-8423 lesbian-made erotica • sex toys • books • videos • send $2 for catalog ✉ 1210 Valencia St, San Francisco, CA 94110 **EMAIL:** goodvibe@well.com **WEB:** www.goodvibes.com

Greedy Dyke Productions ☎505/890-1376 women-crafted sex toys ✉ 2400 Rio Grande NW #1-110, Albuquerque, NM 87104 **EMAIL:** misskell@nmia.com **WEB:** ww.nmia.com/~misskell/gdprod.html

Lashes by Sarah ☎510/638-3564 high quality hand-crafted leather floggers ✉ PO Box 5245, Oakland, CA 94605 **EMAIL:** topgrrl@sirius.com **WEB:** www.sirius.com/~topgrrl/sarah.htm

Pitiful Boot Licker hand-crafted leather goods ✉ PO Box 822, Terre Haute, IN 47808

Pleasure Chest ☎800/753-4536 for all your erotic needs • catalog **WEB:** www.thepleasurechest.com

Pleasure Place ☎800/386-2386 erotic gifts • toys • catalog

Socket Science ☎415/587-7459 sex toys designed by & for women ✉ 4014 24th St #187-1194, San Francisco, CA 94114

Hey! Don't Forget...

Do you know of a new business we should list? Or a business that's closed since publication? Found out some new information about a listing we already have? We reward the best letters (those packed with new info we haven't already found) with a ***FREE COPY*** of next year's edition—***Please let us know!***

Business Name ____________________________________

Type of Business __________________________________

Street Address ____________________________________

City/State/Zip ____________________________________

★Phone/Fax _____________________________________

Clientele _______________________________________

Description ______________________________________

Please suggest a **lesbian/gay-oriented activity or attraction** we should list under **ENTERTAINMENT & RECREATION** in your favorite city (for example, theater, music, skate/bowl, or tourist attraction):

City/State ______________________________________

Attraction ______________________________________

★Phone/Fax _____________________________________

Description ______________________________________

____

To be added to our mailing list, and entered in the sweepstakes, please fill in:

My Name ____

Address ____

City/State/Zip ____________________________________

Daytime Phone/Email _______________________________

(We will only contact you discreetly — to verify information or to notify sweepstakes winners!)

Please Mail to: **Damron Updates — Attn. Editor**
PO Box 422458
San Francisco, CA 94142-2458 USA

or e-mail: **Updates@Damron.com**

or fax: **(415) 703-9049**